Ireland Since the Famine

Ireland Since the Famine is a full-scale study of the political and social history of Ireland from 1850 to the present day. The political evolution of the Irish nation forms the basis of the book: the state of the Union, the demands for Home Rule, the violence and the compromises ending in a divided Ireland, and the separate evolutions of Eire and Ulster.

But Professor Lyon's study of Irish society also examines the conflicting forces of social change: the deep roots of religious division and its tragic consequences; the cultural climate that produced the nationalism of Pearse and the bitterness of Joyce; and the all-important economic factors, often overlooked by the more traditional Irish historians.

F. S. L. Lyons is Provost of Trinity College, Dublin. His works include *The Irish Parliamentary Party*, *The Fall of Parnell*, *Internationalism in Europe, 1815-1914*, *John Dillon: A Biography*.

IRELAND SINCE THE FAMINE

F. S. L. Lyons
Provost of Trinity College, Dublin

We had fed the heart on fantasies,
The hearts grown brutal from the fare;
More substance in our enmities
Than in our love . . .
> W. B. YEATS, 'The Stare's Nest by
> My Window', from *The Tower*, 1928

FONTANA/COLLINS

First published by Weidenfeld and Nicolson 1971
First issued in Fontana 1973
Third Impression October 1975

Printed in Great Britain by
William Collins Sons & Co. Ltd Glasgow

FOR JOHN AND NICHOLAS

The author and publishers wish to express their thanks
to M. B. Yeats and Macmillan and Company Limited for
permission to quote from the poems of William Butler
Yeats on the title page and on pages 241 and 368.

Contents

PART IV: THE PARTITIONED ISLAND

A. From Free State to Republic

B. Northern Ireland under Home Rule   695

Preface

No ancient Israelite condemned to make bricks without straw can have been more embarrassed than the modern Irish historian who, in an unwary moment, agrees to write a general history of his country, even for so short and well documented a period as the last hundred and twenty years. For although a work of synthesis is long overdue, it is not until one settles in earnest to the job of trying to provide it that one realises how much specialist study still needs to be undertaken. That there has been an historiographical revolution in the last forty years nobody would deny, least of all myself, who have benefited from it more than most. Yet, by a paradox which is more apparent than real, although this revolution has to a large extent taken politics out of history, it has only been able to do so by concerning itself mainly with political history. Much of the most important research done on the nineteenth century during the past generation has revolved round the making and the breaking of the Union with Britain. Obviously this is a major theme, but the fact that students have allowed themselves to become obsessed with it has meant that other themes – economic, social, administrative, constitutional, cultural – have been seriously neglected.

In the fields of economic and social history there have, indeed, always been a few distinguished exceptions to this generalisation – and it is pleasant to record that their number is growing – but so many gaps in our knowledge remain to be filled that the general historian has either to admit ignorance and pass by on the other side, or else do some of the spade-work himself. I have adopted both procedures in this book, but where monographic studies have been conspicuously lacking, I have tried to supply at least a little of what we miss through their absence by providing rather more detail than is usually to be found in books of this kind. Some readers may find it excessive, in which case it is their privilege to skip to the political narrative, but for my part I am unrepentant and only wish space had allowed more intensive analysis than I have been able to afford.

If the writing of the economic and social history of Ireland may be compared to a series of holes held together by a few tenuous threads, what are we to say about the writing of contemporary Irish history? Here apart from one or two brave ventures, a few volumes of Thomas Davis lectures, and a handful of scattered articles, there is almost nothing to go upon. Nor is this surprising, for in Ireland the ordinary hazards of contemporary history are powerfully reinforced by others, such as the persistence of tension in Northern Ireland or the legacy of the Civil War in the south, to say nothing of the longevity of many of the chief actors in the drama. This last, though no one would wish it otherwise, does have a peculiarly inhibiting effect on the historian, virtually excluding, as it does, many fascinating subjects from investigation and discussion. Yet the degree of inhibition should not be overstated, for if the *minutiae* of politics must remain hidden from us for some time yet, and if even the main developments can only be very tentatively sketched, there is a great deal else that can be done, especially if we turn away from the strife of parties and try to gain an impression of how Irish society, in both parts of the island, has evolved during the last half-century. An impression is perhaps the most one can expect to gain until much more specialist research has been directed towards our recent past and I shall be content if Part IV of this book is regarded as a pioneering enterprise which will have fulfilled its main purpose should it stimulate others to dig more deeply.

In writing a book of this nature one inevitably gives numerous hostages to fortune, but for me this has been more than counterbalanced by the many kindnesses I have received from friends. I have benefited, either in conversation or by the study of their writings, from nearly all the historians who in the last forty years have transformed their discipline and our knowledge of modern Ireland. I give below a selection of the names of those from whom I have learned most, but a few names I must mention separately. First, my venture into economic history, amateurish as it may seem to many of my colleagues, would have been quite disastrous without the detailed and expert criticism a part of my manuscript received from Professor Kenneth Connell, a task discharged amid many other pressures with a meticulous scholarship for which I am deeply indebted. I am thankful, secondly, to Mrs Miriam Daly and to Dr M. O'Donoghue who, to my great advantage, dealt similarly with a later section of this work. Next, I should like to acknowledge the immense and unwearying helpfulness of the Reverend Professor F. X. Martin, OSA, who not only read through a considerable part of the book and made many valuable suggestions, but did not hesitate to levy aid from others on my behalf. I am most grateful, also, to Professor B. Chubb and Mr J. H. Whyte for reading and commenting upon certain other chapters. None of these scholars, of course, must be held responsible for any errors of fact or obstinacies of misinterpretation which may still persist. Finally, I would pay tribute to Professor T. W. Moody; his connection with this book has been less intimate than with any of my others, but since it embodies the results of some twenty-five years spent learning about Irish history, and since most of that learning has been from or through him, he will not, I hope, object to his name being once more invoked by an affectionate and devoted pupil.

To all other historians and friends whose work has helped to make this book possible I should like to record my thanks and especially to the following: D. H. Akenson, J. C. Beckett, R. D. C. Black, P. M. A.

8

Bourke, John Boyle, Colonel D. Bryan, T. P. Coogan, Monsignor P. Corish, R. D. Crotty, L. M. Cullen, L. P. Curtis, James and Myles Dillon, Michael Drake, R. Dudley Edwards and Owen Dudley Edwards, Richard Ellmann, E. Estyn Evans, Brian Farrell, E. R. R. Green, D. W. Harkness, Richard Hawkins, G. A. Hayes-McCoy, C. H. D. Howard, Michael Hurst, A. N. Jeffares, Emmet Larkin, R. J. Lawrence, Joseph Lee, Patrick Lynch, L. J. McCaffrey, B. MacGiolla Choilley, J. L. McCracken, Oliver MacDonagh, R. B. McDowell, T. J. McElligott, N. S. Mansergh, James Meenan, Kenneth Milne, E. R. Norman, K. B. Nowlan, Conor Cruise O'Brien, Maurice O'Connell, T. P. O'Neill, Donal O'Sullivan, W. J. L. Ryan, A. T. Q. Stewart, Father C. J. Travers, Maureen Wall, Terence de Vere White, T. Desmond Williams.

I should like also to acknowledge my gratitude to the staffs of the various libraries where I have worked during the preparation of this book, and especially to the libraries of the University of Kent, the British Museum, Trinity College, Dublin, the National Library of Ireland and the Royal Irish Academy.

I have great pleasure in acknowledging the generosity of the University of Kent, and of my colleagues in the Faculty of Humanities in particular, for affording me the leave of absence without which this book could not have been written.

I wish further to express my warmest thanks to Miss Mary O'Connell for the care and patience with which she saw this book through the press.

I have on this occasion been even luckier than usual with secretarial assistance. I wish to thank first Mrs Jeannette Timms for typing most of the manuscript and for producing with great speed a marvellously clear copy from the chaotic material with which she had often to work. And secondly, it gives me much pleasure to record my very special debt to Miss Margaret Hawkins who not only saw the typescript safely through its last contortions, but by her calm and unflagging efficiency in the discharge of all sorts of collegiate duties allowed me to go on thinking about Ireland even in the midst of quite other preoccupations.

Finally, as always and most of all, I must thank my wife and my two sons for their forbearance in putting up with yet another period of disruption in the life of the family.

Eliot College, University of Kent   F. S. L. LYONS
Canterbury

Preface to the Second Edition

In preparing this new edition I have tried to do three things. First, I have naturally wanted to correct any errors and misprints which I have noticed myself or which have been pointed out by others. Second, I have sought to profit from the extraordinarily large volume of specialised work in various relevant fields which has been published even in the two years since my own book appeared. These fresh publications have been listed at the appropriate places in my Select Bibliography, but the reader who may be curious to know in what respects this edition differs most from the original will find his answer in the chapters which deal with the economic environment, with the struggle for independence and its aftermath, and the history of the south since the Civil War. To the Civil War itself, in response to several requests, I have given more space than formerly, although I remain unrepentantly of the opinion that it will not be possible to deal with that subject with full understanding until the archives of the Bureau of Military History are opened – if then.

Finally, in this revised version I have set myself the aim of providing a somewhat more coherent account of the last few years in Northern Ireland than the hurried Postscript which was all I was able to include in the first edition. That Postscript has now vanished (save for two paragraphs) and its place has been taken by a chapter called 'The continuing crisis'. The title is intended to suggest what is, alas, no more than the stark truth – that no end was anywhere in sight while I was writing. With a continuously evolving situation it is obviously impossible to be completely up to date, or, indeed, to do much more than provide a brief narrative of events. I have therefore chosen to end my account with the imposition of direct rule in March 1972, since the disappearance of Stormont – at any rate in the form in which it had existed for the previous half-century – seems to me to mark the end of a definable historical epoch.

I hope it does not need to be stressed that I am fully aware of the hazards that await anyone foolish enough to sail into the eye of the hurricane. Of course we are all too near to know the truth, of course we are all too emotionally involved, of course any interpretation is at the mercy of events which have still to happen. Nevertheless, while giving due weight to these formidable objections, I have still felt that a book purporting to describe the development of Ireland in the last hundred and twenty years ought not simply to ignore an episode which has not only been of profound importance in itself, but has also been so deeply rooted in the past of the whole island. In the circumstances, any account of the northern crisis must be studiously unambitious, confining itself to outlining, as clearly and fairly as possible, what has taken place. To attempt more, at this present time, would be foolish; but to attempt less would in my view be a kind of intellectual treason.

I should like to thank Miss Paula Shea for her help in seeing this new edition through the press and not least for keeping me at least within hailing distance of our original timetable. The fact that I have previously expressed my indebtedness to Miss Margaret Hawkins does not deter me from doing so again, the more so as the manuscript of this revision confronted her with a number of complex typing problems, all of which she solved with her usual imperturbable and good-humoured efficiency.

Eliot College, University of Kent   F. S. L. LYONS
Canterbury
October, 1972

Abbreviations

DNB	*Dictionary of National Biography*
EHR	*English Historical Review*
Econ. Hist. Rev.	*Economic History Review*
FJ	*Freeman's Journal*
IHS	*Irish Historical Studies*
JSSISI	*Journal of the Statistical and Social Inquiry Society of Ireland*
PRO	Public Record Office
SPO	State Paper Office

NOTE ON TERMINOLOGY

In the course of this book I have spelt the words 'nationalist' and 'nationalism' with a small 'n' when referring to general matters connected with the needs and demands of Irish nationality. But I have used Nationalist with a capital 'N' whenever it seemed necessary to identify a specific party and its supporters – as, for example, in Northern Ireland after 1921. This is not to suggest that any such party had a monopoly of Irish nationalism, which it obviously had not; the term is simply used as an aid to quick and easy identification.

F.S.L.L.

PART I

Reorientations

1. Changing the Question?

The tired old witticism that every time the English came within sight of solving the Irish question the Irish changed the question, contains, like most jokes about Ireland, a small grain of truth submerged in a vast sea of misconception. The Irish did not change the question between the Famine and the war of independence any more than they had changed it between the Union and the Famine. The 'national demand', as it used to be called, remained in essence what Wolfe Tone had declared it to be as long ago as 1791, 'to break the connection with England, the never-failing source of all our political evils'. It is true, of course, that men differed in the nineteenth century, as they have continued to differ in the twentieth, about how complete the break should be, or more precisely, perhaps, about how far the full separatist ideal was practicable. But whether they took their stand on the rock of the republic, or were prepared to settle for repeal of the Union and some form of Home Rule based upon a reanimated Irish parliament, they were emphatic that the first step towards real independence was to recover for Irishmen the right to control their own affairs.

Yet, if the Irish question did not change in its essentials, it is clear that the context within which it was debated and fought out was very different in, say, 1914 from what it had been in 1800, or even in 1850. Many agencies, as we shall see, were at work to alter that context, but of them all the Famine itself was without doubt the most fundamental. To contemporaries, stunned by the magnitude and visibility of a disaster which, with its attendant consequences of disease and massive emigration, reduced the population by some two million inside a single decade, the Famine signalled the total collapse of their society. Historians, conscious of a rural crisis in Ireland which went back far beyond the immediate event and continued long after it, have tended to see the tragedy, in the words of the editors of the most authoritative work on the subject, 'as but a period of greater misery in a prolonged age of suffering'.[1] For in purely economic terms it could be argued that what the Famine mainly did was to accentuate the existing tensions in Irish rural society and to hasten the transformation of which the faint beginnings could be discerned even before the catastrophe had struck.* This, of course, is not to deny either the exceptional severity of that catastrophe or its symbolic significance. However much refined and analysed, it still remains an appalling phenomenon, etching itself ineradicably on

* This point is considered in greater detail in the next chapter.

the hearts and minds not only of those who experienced it, but of all the generations that have lived in Ireland since those terrible years.

Yet while the immediate effect of the 'great hunger' was to impose an overwhelming burden of suffering upon an impoverished and defenceless people, it may well be that its most profound impact on Irish history lay in its ultimate psychological legacy. Expressed in its simplest terms, this legacy was that the long-standing and deep-rooted hatred of the English connection was given not only a new intensity, but also a new dimension. It was not just that within the shores of Ireland the old bitterness of a depressed peasantry against an alien and often ruthless landlord class was reinforced by resentment towards a government which (though it had made more effort than a starving people was likely to give it credit for) had shown itself manifestly inadequate, at the levels both of administration and of policy, to contain the crisis unrolling before the eyes of its horrified and harassed officials. It was rather that this hatred, this bitterness, this resentment were carried overseas, and especially to America, by nearly four million Irish men, women and children who left their homeland, decade by decade and year by year in the half-century after the Famine.[2] The political consequences of this unending exodus of a permanently antagonised population were literally incalculable, but the most fundamental effect is plain to be seen. With the establishment of strong Irish settlements in the United States, Canada, Australia and New Zealand, as well as in Britain herself, the Irish question became and remained an international question. However much successive British governments affected to regard the condition of Ireland as essentially a domestic issue, the great migration ensured that a domestic issue was precisely what it would never be again. As a complicating factor in foreign relations, and particularly Anglo-American relations, Ireland continued to plague her masters until the Union was ended in 1921; indeed even after that, when effective self-government had at length been conceded, she was still to baffle English statesmen for a generation longer by playing, with evident zest and success, the role of 'restless dominion' in Commonwealth affairs.[3] Nor was it only in the international sphere that the Irish overseas made their anti-British sentiment explicit. On the contrary, their involvement with what happened to their motherland remained deep and continuous, leading them both to give the large-scale financial support without which the development of vigorous Irish nationalism would have been impossible in the seventy years after the Famine, and also, at certain crucial moments, to affect directly and decisively the maintenance and development of the revolutionary movement which worked secretly but tirelessly for the violent overthrow of British rule in Ireland and its replacement by a republic.

The Famine, however, though clearly of fundamental importance in determining the political and psychological climate of Ireland, and deeply significant also for its subsequent economic and social configuration, was by no means the only element of change of which we have to take account in the decades after 1850. The problem of governing the country, and the balance of power within it, were alike influenced by four other factors, each of which loomed large in the second half of the nineteenth century. These were the growing tendency of long-standing religious differences to act as a divisive force in Irish society; the intensification of political conflict by the infusion into it of economic elements, and especially of a desperate, almost elemental, struggle for possession of the land; the emergence of – and eventually conflict between – newer and more articulate forms of nationalism; and finally, but by no means least, a slow but steady movement towards greater prosperity and better government which raised equally in the minds of anxious patriots and hopeful administrators the question whether not merely Home Rule, but all forms of Irish separatism, might not in the end be killed by kindness. The action and interaction of these major themes will form the greater part of the story that follows in these pages. First, however, it may be helpful to preface them with some general and introductory remarks.

(ii)

We may most appropriately begin with religion because for most Irishmen throughout the period this not only remained at the centre of their personal lives, but stood out as one of the most formidable, if not the most formidable, of the barriers separating them from each other. Religious rivalries – unhappily complicated by the fact that they coincided closely (though not completely) with the division between native and settler, conquered and conqueror – had been part of the very fabric of Irish history since the Reformation. But it is important to realise that these rivalries changed their character very markedly during the nineteenth century. Traditionally, and leaving aside the smaller denominations, three principal interests had been engaged – Catholic, Presbyterian and Anglican. Of these, the first had always been, and still remained, the faith of the great mass of the people, but although the other two were both settler religions the outcome of the wars of the seventeenth century had been such that the Anglican established church, the Church of Ireland, had achieved a virtual monopoly of power, enabling it to impose indignities and deprivations upon Presbyterians as well as upon Catholics. True, by 1800 this discrimination had been considerably lessened by the steady relaxation of the penal laws during the preceding twenty years, but after the passing of the Act of Union in that year, and with the development thereafter of a more concerted drive for full Catholic emancipation, the divisions between Protestants within or without the establishment came to seem less important than the gulf which yawned between all of them and the

Roman Catholic majority.* The size of that majority, and its relation to the other denominations, was not reliably calculated until the Census of 1861 demonstrated with precision what had long been known to be broadly true, that Catholics accounted for just over three-quarters (77·7 per cent) of a total population of 5,800,000. Fifty years later, in a population which had shrunk to 4,400,000, their proportion was 73·9 per cent. Of the other denominations, the Anglicans remained the most numerous throughout that half-century. Comprising slightly over 693,000 in 1861 and about 577,000 in 1911, their share of the total percentage had actually risen from just under twelve to just over thirteen. The only other Protestant church to rival them in numbers was the Presbyterian, for which the Census recorded 523,000 in 1861 and a little over 440,500 in 1911, giving it rather more than nine per cent of the total in 1861 and just over ten per cent in 1911; to these figures should perhaps be added for each year various Presbyterian splinter-groups accounting for about 9,000 people. Among the remaining denominations the largest was that of the Methodists, but although rising from 45,000 at the earlier date to 62,000 at the later, they never amounted to as much as 1·5 per cent of the total and did not therefore seriously affect what might be called the triangular balance of religious power in Ireland.[4]

What made this triangular balance so precarious from the viewpoint of Anglicans and Presbyterians was not so much the sheer numerical bulk of the Catholic component, but rather that that component had been steadily growing in organisation and influence since the achievement of Catholic emancipation in 1829. Emancipation itself, indeed, had been Daniel O'Connell's triumphant demonstration that, if the organisation was good enough, then the influence of the Catholic masses could rapidly be made formidable. Yet although it may be true, as has been said, that O'Connell used the movement for emancipation to give, for the first time since the Union, 'a national character' to Irish politics, his subsequent and abortive campaign for the repeal of the

* In Ireland religious terminology has always been, and still is, full of pitfalls. It has long been customary, for example, to confine the word 'Protestant' to the Church of Ireland and to call the various dissenting or free churches by their individual names. To me, as a member of the Church of Ireland, this exclusiveness is almost as objectionable as the comprehensiveness of the label 'non-Catholics' frequently bestowed by Roman Catholics upon all who are not of their persuasion. For that matter, the term 'Roman Catholic' itself, though regularly and elaborately applied by Irish Protestants of all affiliations to the church of the great majority of their fellow-countrymen, gives rise to a certain restiveness among some at least of that majority. In this book, for the sake of clarity and simplicity (though at the risk of alienating some of my co-religionists), I shall describe Roman Catholics as 'Catholics' and will use the generic term 'Protestant' to designate the Anglican and dissenting or free churches alike, while distinguishing these by name whenever necessary.

Union revealed the limits both of his own personality and of the power of mass-agitations to affect British policy.[5] In the short run at least, the true beneficiary of Catholic emancipation was not the peasantry hovering perpetually on the brink of starvation, nor even O'Connell's own followers, manoeuvring anxiously and amateurishly between English parties at Westminster, but the Catholic Church itself. The outward and visible signs of emancipation were already apparent long before the Famine. They took the form of churches, schools, seminaries, monasteries and convents, provided for the most part by legacies from the more prosperous sons and daughters of the Church, and by subscriptions and dues from all classes of the community. Estimates of the expenditure under these heads are difficult to come by, but it is possible that the total cost of building, combined with the cost of maintaining the clergy, between 1817 and 1847 may have amounted to as much as thirty million pounds, of which capital outlay accounted for at least five million pounds.[6]

In this development, as in so much else, the Famine marked a turning-point. Although during the crisis itself subscriptions, and consequently expenditure, naturally fell off, the economic improvement of the succeeding twenty years, and particularly the possibilities increasingly open to Catholics to make money out of cattle-farming, could only redound to the advantage of the Church. The building of schools, colleges, hospitals, churches and cathedrals went ahead faster than ever and it is no accident that most of the main examples of Catholic ecclesiastical architecture in Ireland belong to the period between 1850 and 1880. Thereafter, the deepening agricultural depression halted a process which in any event had been reaching saturation point. It was noteworthy, however, that the numbers of religious continued to increase. Where in 1850 there were about 5,000 priests, monks and nuns for a Catholic population of five million, in 1900 there were over 14,000 priests, monks and nuns to minister to approximately $3\frac{1}{3}$ million Catholics, and this vastly increased figure takes no account of the steady flow of Irish missionaries overseas.[7]

All this is evidence of impressive growth which will constantly have to be borne in mind when we come to assess the rôle of the Church not only in matters with obvious religious implications – such as education – but also in the more purely political sphere. It would be very wrong, however, to think of the Church, as its opponents tended all too easily to do, in monolithic terms, or to seek to apply to it any of the fashionable nineteenth century adjectives such as nationalist, ultramontane, liberal, or conservative. Not only could the Church be all of these things in turn, and some of them simultaneously, but its inner history was a history of division almost as much as of unity – of division among bishops, and frequently also of division between bishops and clergy. Outwardly, it is true, the Church generally contrived to present an imposing front to the world and when, as happened for most of the period between the Famine and the Anglo-Irish Treaty of 1921, it was dominated by strong personalities – in fact, by two Archbishops of Dublin, Paul Cullen from 1852 to 1878 and William Walsh from 1885 to 1921 – it seemed indeed one and indivisible. Yet this appearance was to some extent misleading. Not only did both men encounter considerable opposition (and in Cullen's case real personal animosity) from among their fellow-prelates, but both were condemned to grapple with the same intractable problem. Essentially it was the problem of how to reconcile Catholicism and nationalism. Broadly speaking, the leaders of the Church succeeded in making this reconciliation, but only at the price of severe internal tensions and even, occasionally, of actual conflict between the hierarchy and individual clergy, especially the younger and fiercer country curates.

The dilemma of the bishops was that they were often pulled in several different directions. As princes of the Church their first loyalty was, or seemed to be, to Rome. During the Cullen era this loyalty had become so deeply ingrained as to give rise then and subsequently to charges of ultramontanism to which, however, the Archbishop, or Cardinal as he became in 1866, gave his own interpretation. 'If I were asked', he observed on one occasion, 'am I an Ultramontane, I would say I am in this sense – that I respect the decision of the Head of the Church, and that I am always an obedient subject in religious matters to the Pope.'[8] The implication of this statement, that ultramontanism was a question of discipline rather than of politics, was scarcely true for Cullen himself and was certainly not true of the hierarchy as a whole. Irish Catholicism, though without doubt distinguished by a real devotion to the Papacy, had enough Gallicanism about it for the British government to discover in due course that whenever they sought to use the Vatican as a means of influencing ecclesiastical attitudes in Ireland it turned out, unlike Lord Randolph Churchill's famous Orange card, to be the two of trumps and not the ace.

In the last resort, after all, Irish bishops were Irish men and a host of influences combined to draw them onto a course that was sometimes tangential to the line laid down in Rome. Springing for the most part, like the parish clergy, from the farming and trading community, it would have been unnatural if they had not identified closely with many of the national aspirations of their fellow-countrymen, or if they had failed to resent both the privileged position of the Anglo-Irish minority and the unpalatable fact that no decision affecting the deepest interests either of their Church or of their country could be taken except by leave of the British authorities.* They could therefore scarcely avoid becoming involved in politics even though that involvement was sometimes to

* The social origins of the Catholic bishops and priests still await statistical analysis, but it is unlikely that if such an analysis were made it would seriously disturb the conclusion reached by Professor K. H. Connell – that the clergy and their flocks came from essentially the same background. Professor Connell concedes the difficulty of obtaining reliable figures, but has adduced some formidable literary evidence in support

lead them to keep strange company in deep waters. Cardinal Cullen himself, though of all men the most intent on uniting his Church in willing obedience to Rome, was driven by two of his guiding ambitions – to achieve the disestablishment of the Church of Ireland and to secure for his people a thoroughly denominational system of education – into an alliance with English liberalism which ran counter to almost every rule of politics acceptable to the Papacy at that time. And later in the century, when confronted with the moral and political problems raised by the passion of the peasants to become the owners of their farms, the bishops were to display considerable ingenuity in reconciling obedience to the dictates of the Pope with obedience to the dictates of their own consciences.

Involvement in politics did not, however, extend to involvement in revolutionary politics. On the contrary, most bishops, through the whole period between the Famine and the Treaty, were almost by definition opposed to violent and radical change with all that this implied for the stability of society in general, as well as for the safety and moral well-being of individual Catholics caught up in secret, oath-bound societies and committed to acts of outrage or even of open, armed rebellion. But the reasons, both pastoral and political, which led members of the hierarchy to condemn, say, Fenianism in the 1860s or the worst excesses of the Land War twenty years later, were not always convincing to the rank and file. At the parish level, indeed, identification with an oppressed people goaded into acts of violence might lead a priest not merely to condone such acts, but himself to become so deeply committed as to land unrepentantly in jail. And although most clergy did no doubt conform to the cautious instructions of their bishops, it was perhaps well for the future of Catholicism in Ireland that in each generation enough of the younger men were found to justify the right of revolution and so to prevent that total cleavage between Church and laity which might otherwise have come about. Even bishops could learn from experience and whereas in Fenian times the hierarchy had been loud in its denunciations of political extremism, the rebellion of 1916 which probably took them, like many other people, by surprise, did not elicit from them any corporate condemnation. True, they did not as a group follow the example of the intrepid Dr Edward O'Dwyer, Bishop of Limerick, in violently condemning the repressive measures of the military authorities, but the very fact that, to a large extent, they withheld criticism suggests that for them, again as for many other people, the shock of the Rising was cancelled out by the greater shock of the executions. Lower down the scale there were, naturally, fewer inhibitions, and there is evidence to indicate that by 1916 numbers of the younger clergy, especially the country curates, were already extreme in their political opinions.[9]

of his contention. See the essay 'Catholicism and Marriage in the Century after the Famine', in his *Irish Peasant Society* (Oxford, 1968), especially pp. 123-6 and 148-9.

Nevertheless, despite external pressures and internal hesitations, the connection between the Roman Catholic clergy and their flocks remained intimate and intense. The existence of this connection, and the inevitable embroilment in politics of bishops and priests alike which it entailed, was to provoke in due course the accusation that Home Rule would mean Rome rule. The extravagance of this accusation when seen in the light of the subsequent history of most of the country, should not blind us, however, to its contemporary importance. An essential element in the case for retaining the Union unchanged was that it offered the only effective guarantee for the security of the various Protestant groups. All these groups professed to be alarmed to a greater or lesser degree at the threat to their religious liberty which the coming to power of a native government might involve, but the two chief denominations – Anglicans and Presbyterians – upon whom fell the main burden of resisting the onset of what was seen as a clerical regime were very differently placed for fighting the battle. The Church of Ireland, though ostensibly in a stronger position, had actually been on the defensive ever since the relaxation of the penal laws in the latter half of the eighteenth century. With the coming of Catholic emancipation its authority was further eroded, while the long and bloody war waged by Catholics in the 1830s against paying tithes to Anglican clergy was yet another blow against the established church. And apart altogether from such agrarian convulsions, the new self-confidence of Irish Catholicism – especially, as we shall see, in matters of education – threw into sharp relief the limitations and inadequacies of a Protestant regime which in the last resort depended on the good-will of the British government. As early as 1833 there were ominous indications that this good-will could not be relied upon indefinitely, for in that year parliament, in response to radical as well as Catholic pressures, passed the Irish Church Temporalities Act which suppressed ten sees altogether, reduced the revenues of the remaining twelve, and entrusted the surplus to a body of commissioners to be applied to ecclesiastical purposes. The logical corollary of this onslaught – complete disestablishment – had to wait for another thirty-six years, but the intellectual case for disestablishment had in effect been conceded, both in England and in Ireland (except, obviously, by devoted Anglicans), many years before the political situation afforded an opportunity to drive the policy home.*

In a sense, of course, disestablishment, when it came at last, was to be something of an anti-climax. The Church of Ireland, though shorn of its special status, emerged from its ordeal with much of its wealth intact, with its entrenched position in the educational life of the country heavily guarded, and its social prestige almost undimmed. Its traumatic descent to the level of a poor relation, existing on the sufferance of a Catholic majority magnanimous enough to overlook past injuries, while a legacy of the changes of the nineteenth century, was in fact to be a twentieth century phenomenon. Yet although this descent was long in

* For the political background to disestablishment, see Part II, chap. 1.

coming it was easily predictable, if only because the geographical distribution of Anglicanism in Ireland made it conspicuously vulnerable. Thus in 1861, out of a total of 693,357 'Episcopalian Protestants' (as the Census called them) nearly two-thirds (417,011) were concentrated in the province of Ulster. The great majority of the remainder were in Leinster, especially in and around Dublin; in Munster they numbered 81,000 and in all Connaught only about 40,000. Fifty years later 'Episcopalian Protestants' totalled 576,611, of whom nearly 367,000 were in Ulster and 140,000 in Leinster; the figure for Munster had by then dwindled to approximately 51,000, and in Connaught to a mere 19,000.[10]

The picture that here emerges is the familiar one of a small minority very thin on the ground over much of the country (the practice of uniting parishes and dioceses had already begun in the nineteenth century) and relatively populous only in the neighbourhood of the capital and in the northern province. But even in Ulster, though this was where the Church of Ireland was strongest, it was less strong than either Catholicism or Presbyterianism, both of which had suffered in the past from Anglican intolerance and neither of which would be likely to waste much sympathy on the downfall of an ancient tyrant. And indeed, in Ulster as elsewhere in Ireland, there were deeply marked social differences, apart altogether from doctrinal differences, separating Anglicans from Presbyterians as well as from Catholics. The landed gentry and the professions tended to be the preserve of the Church of Ireland, whereas Presbyterianism dominated the world of business and was also well represented among the more prosperous farmers. Catholics, by contrast, gravitated in industry towards the lower-paid jobs and in the countryside took the poorer farms and supplied much of the labouring population. To some extent the social distinctions between Anglicans and Presbyterians were reflected in politics, the former supplying the backbone of Ulster conservatism for much of the nineteenth century, the latter carrying forward into liberalism a tradition of Presbyterian radicalism that dated from the eighteenth century. But neither the social distinctions nor the political differences between these two main Protestant groups should be pressed too far. Both were to sink quickly into insignificance the moment the supposed threat from Roman Catholicism took visible shape with the development of a dynamic Home Rule movement in the 1880s. Thereafter, the tendency of most Northern Protestants was to close ranks against the common enemy; since Catholics reacted in the same way, the sectarianism which has bedevilled politics in the province from that day to this became inevitable.*

* It is only fair to add that there were some Protestants in Ulster – the famous Presbyterian minister J. B. Armour of Ballymoney is a notable example – who took the Home Rule side and continued to work for reconciliation with their Catholic neighbours through all the political storms of that tempestuous period. But although an articulate minority

This new-found cohesion between Anglicans and Presbyterians was helped, no doubt, by the fact that both denominations were deeply marked by evangelicalism during the nineteenth century. The initiative in stating the Protestant case in Ulster, however, came mainly from the Presbyterians, perhaps because, while the Church of Ireland was flinching under first the threat and then the actuality of disestablishment, Presbyterianism seemed to go from strength to strength. The sources of that strength were both organisational and emotional. Although the habit of Protestant dissent in the north of Ireland was to splinter into smaller and smaller groups (no fewer than six of those listed in the Census of 1911 numbered less than ten people each), that fissiparous tendency had been counteracted in the first half of the nineteenth century by one very important development. This was the success of the evangelical (or 'orthodox') party in enforcing after 1836 the rule requiring of all candidates for the ministry unqualified subscription to the Westminster Confession of Faith. That decision, though obnoxious to a wide range of non-subscribers, opened the way for union with the other main Presbyterian group in the province – the 'seceders' – and by 1840 this union had been consolidated in the General Assembly of the Presbyterian Church of Ireland, the body which soon became, and long remained, the driving force behind orthodox Presbyterianism. Within twenty years this significant move towards organisational unity was given a further impulse by the great wave of religious emotion known as the 'Ulster revival', which in 1859 affected Protestant denominations of every variety, but especially Presbyterianism in all its moods and tenses. No doubt, like other such phenomena, some of its most striking effects were also its most transient, but it did apparently lead to a rise in the number of candidates for the ministry, and it did reinforce that taste for high-powered evangelical preaching which, together with a conservative, not to say fundamentalist, approach to the Bible were to be the hall-marks of Ulster Presbyterianism until well into the twentieth century.[11]

This heightening of religious fervour contributed inevitably to the intensification of sectarian rivalry within the province which in time overflowed into politics, especially after Home Rule had emerged as a real challenge to the status quo. From this followed two consequences, each of them profoundly influencing not just Ulster but all Ireland. First, because Protestantism was increasingly identified with the maintenance of the Union, the old liberal tradition was fatally undermined and between 1885 and 1914 parliamentary contests with few exceptions tended to be straight fights between the highly organised Nationalist and Unionist parties, the former strongest in the west and south, the

they remained, nevertheless, a minority. It should also be noted that, for reasons connected with immigration from rural Ulster into Belfast in the early stages of the industrial revolution, many Protestant working-men were Anglican, not Presbyterian.

latter predominant in the north and east. But the second consequence of the increasing identification of Protestantism with Unionism was even more important. The Orange Order, which had come into being at the end of the eighteenth century as an instrument of defence (or of aggression, according to the point of view) against Catholics, had languished for some seventy years after the Union. With the rise of the Home Rule movement it rapidly revived, evoking from the Catholic side a similar enthusiasm for a counter-organisation, the Ancient Order of Hibernians. Orangeism, in its new incarnation, had both a social and a psychological value for its devotees. On the one hand it provided a rallying-point for Protestant Unionists regardless of denominational, social or economic differences.* And on the other, with its parades, its banners and its pounding drums, it injected into Ulster life (as also did the Hibernians in their own fashion) an element of political hysteria not essentially different from, though unhappily more permanent than, the religious hysteria to which the province had already shown itself so prone.

(iii)

The tensions in Irish life were not, of course, solely racial and religious. Parallel with the clash between Irish and Anglo-Irish, between Catholic and Protestant, went also an economic rivalry which was itself deeply intertwined with the ethnic and denominational divisions in Irish society. From the time of the Norman conquest in the twelfth century – or, more recently, at least from the Cromwellian and Williamite confiscations of the seventeenth – there had been an economic aspect to the Irish question. Expressed in the crudest terms it was an elemental conflict between the former owners of the land and those who had dispossessed them and reduced them to the status of tenants or labourers. That elemental conflict was left unchanged by the Union, and the story of its final resolution must be one of the central themes in any history of Ireland since the Famine. The changes in the economic environment which occurred in the second half of the nineteenth century, partly as a result of the struggle for the land, partly for other reasons, are described in the next chapter of this book – here it is only necessary to point to some of the ways in which these economic changes aggravated the social and political problems by which the country was confronted.

Between the Famine and the First World War three developments in particular helped to complicate an already complex situation. The first was that under the impact of the Famine itself the idea was firmly grasped and clearly enunciated (chiefly by James Fintan Lalor†) that

* Even here, however, the inevitable schism occurred when, early in the twentieth century an Independent Orange Order was launched to secure working-class support. For this development, see Part II, chap. 9.

† For Lalor's brief but important career, see chap. 4, section 1 below.

the key not merely to the betterment of the peasant, but to the regeneration of society as a whole, might lie in the abolition of the existing landlord-tenant relationship.* That the land question was the engine which would draw the national question in its train was partially glimpsed by the tenant-right agitation of the 1850s and then brilliantly vindicated in the Land War which, between 1879 and 1882, laid the foundations for the ultimate revolution in land tenure whereby over the next thirty years the tenant was enabled to become the owner of the farm he worked. But this was much more than a purely agrarian triumph. It demonstrated not merely the force of organised opinion in the Irish countryside, but also something that had been forgotten since O'Connell's time and was to be of fundamental importance in the development of Irish nationalism – the tremendous political leverage and power which an Irish political party operating at Westminster could derive from the simultaneous conduct of a successful mass-agitation at home.

It would, however, be a naïve over-simplification to view the struggle for the land only in terms of the ancient quarrel between native and settler, even though contemporaries were still obsessed by that familiar and dramatic aspect of the question. For the Famine had brought with it a second kind of change. Under the shock of that disaster many of the old landlords had broken, succumbing to the crushing burden of paying vast sums in poor relief at a time when rents drastically diminished. Post-famine legislation, notably the Encumbered Estates Act of 1849, enabled numbers of them to dispose of their estates to a new type of owner who knew the value of money and knew also how to take advantage of a changing economic situation which gave more importance to the cow than to the plough. From this fresh breed of hard-fisted graziers, the bulk of them Irish and not a few springing from Catholic and Gaelic families, tenants and labourers alike could hope for little mercy, perhaps even for less mercy than from the older aristocracy, for if that class as a whole had deserved its generally odious reputation, some members of it at least had practised a benevolent, if erratic, paternalism.† But the friction between the poor man and the man of substance in the Irish countryside was not just a friction between the tenant and his landlord (new or old), as the abolition of landlordism itself was soon to demonstrate. On the contrary, once Irish agriculture settled into the pattern of the small farm, run by a single family, with the succession and the revenue alike jealously guarded, the gulf between

* Whether this really was the key or not has begun to be queried by economists. But that contemporaries believed it to be so is itself a fact with which historians have to reckon. For further consideration of this point, see below.

† It has been argued recently that many of the old landlords were in fact too indulgent, at least in terms of maximising the returns from agriculture. See B. Solow, *The Land Question and the Irish Economy, 1870-1903* (London and Yale, 1972), chaps. 3 and 4, and below.

the farmer and the landless man came to mirror all too faithfully the gulf that had formerly existed between landlord and tenant. The problem which this posed was to some extent evaded by the steady emigration both of labourers and of younger sons, but, as will later appear, antagonism between the owner of the soil and the wage-earner working at his behest did not vanish from Irish rural society. It merely moved further down the scale and grew no less bitter in the process.

These agrarian changes, though fundamental, were at least predictable, since they developed logically enough from the long history of Ireland. But the advent of large-scale industrialisation to the northeast corner of the island was a change of a totally different kind. The causes and character of that change will be examined in due course; meanwhile, it is only necessary to suggest at this stage some of the ways in which this important shift in the economic balance of the country affected other areas of Irish life. First of all, the very fact that the main industries which developed in Ulster (linen, shipbuilding and engineering) were export industries, depending both on free access to external markets and on the cheap and easy import of fuel and raw material for their survival, meant that for the Unionists of Ulster industrial well-being, no less than religious liberty or political security, depended upon the maintenance of the British connection. In social terms, also, this rapid industrialisation reinforced some of the existing tensions in Ulster society. The ownership of big business and the most profitable employment tended alike to be in Protestant hands, and Catholics for the most part found themselves either excluded or condemned to the lowlier and worse paid jobs. Inevitably, there was resentment which sometimes boiled over, or was provoked into, violence, too often leading in its turn to counter-violence by way of reprisal. Thus, and as if by some perverse stroke of genius, the creation of this great industrial complex in the Lagan valley, which by any reckoning was one of the major achievements of Irishmen in the nineteenth century, added its share of discord to all the other factors that kept the different communities of Ulster aloof and angry generation after generation.

Industrialism, if it brought a hectic though ultimately precarious prosperity to Belfast, brought also its own familiar evils of sweated labour, bad housing, malnutrition and disease, though it needs to be said that these were also shared by the urban populations of other parts of Ireland, and nowhere more than in the decaying tenements of Dublin. To combat these evils, to transcend the differences of creed and origin, to build a workers' movement out of this depressed proletariat, were the aims of a few bold spirits in the opening years of the twentieth century. The careers of two of them, James Larkin and James Connolly, will come before us at a later stage of this book, for between them they added a new dimension to the Irish question – Larkin by his insistence that the workers must organise themselves in trade unions before they could hope to rise from their knees, Connolly because he was to provide the first thorough and effective analysis of Irish history in socialist terms.

Analysis for Connolly was only the first stage towards a refashioning of society, but although time was to deal harshly with his dream, the dream itself and the fate that overtook it are not the least of the transformations with which the historian of Ireland in these years has to reckon.

Economic stresses and religious rivalries, although an essential part of the developing pattern in post-Famine Ireland, remained nevertheless a subordinate part, affecting, but themselves even more affected by, the unremitting struggle to maintain the Union on the one side, and on the other side to destroy it. The struggle was the same old struggle that had been waged intermittently since the days of O'Connell, but it too underwent its own transformations, not the least interesting of which were the internal frictions that beset both those who were for the status quo and those who were against it.

Amongst the opponents of the British connection, especially, there was almost incessant change and regrouping, in which three main elements can be discerned. The oldest, and outwardly the least amenable to new departures of any kind, was the underground, revolutionary movement that looked back to the republicanism of Wolfe Tone. It was to re-emerge fleetingly into the light of day in 1848, but its more enduring influence was to date from the rise of Fenianism, itself to some extent a product of that abortive year of revolution. Yet the influence of the Fenians was only partially derived from their own protest in arms of 1867 which, militarily speaking, was hardly more impressive than the Young Ireland promenade nearly twenty years earlier. The rising of 1867 *was* important, admittedly, in the sense that it kept alive the tradition of armed revolt and also because, as we shall see presently, it restated the fundamentals of militant nationalism. But in the long run Fenianism was probably most significant, neither for the mingled gallantry and bathos of its failure in 1867, nor even for the overhaul of its organisation, the Irish Republican Brotherhood, which followed as a necessary consequence a few years later, but simply for its refusal to die. For forty years after its brief moment of rebellion it languished, indeed, but it never disappeared. On the contrary, it found new sources of strength and ruthlessness in the Irish of the dispersion, and when the moment for the next rising duly arrived Irish-American republicanism was, directly and indirectly, to have a profound effect upon the course of the revolutionary movement in Ireland itself.

The real change among the militants, therefore, was a change neither of attitudes nor of objectives, but rather that their resources were in the end (and it was a gradual process) so greatly enlarged by assistance from America, in terms both of money and of conspiratorial enthusiasm, that for the first time a successful rising came to seem something more than the fantasy it had always been in the past. And although the crushing of the Easter Rising in 1916 might have appeared to belie that hope, the history of the next five years was to show that the revolutionary movement had changed so vastly in resilience, tenacity and stamina as to transmute all too predictable defeat into unimagined victory.

The Irish-American factor, which was to be so important for the militants, was no less so for the constitutionalists, since many Irishmen in America, like most Irishmen at home, pinned their hopes, not on the violent quest for a seemingly unattainable republic, but on persistent and peaceful pressure for the restoration of an Irish parliament, endowed with powers of self-government, but operating still within the framework of the British Empire. In retrospect, this demand for limited Home Rule may seem almost pathetically inadequate, but to those who spent their lives pursuing that phantom, Home Rule represented the only practicable policy on which Irish and British could reach agreement. Certainly, no one who studies the painful odyssey of the nationalist representatives in the House of Commons will be under any illusions either about the difficulties they encountered in converting just one English party, the Liberals, to Home Rule, or about the evanescent nature of that conversion. Nor could even this triumph, such as it was, be achieved until changes in the franchise and the coming of the secret ballot had cleared the way for the creation of a compact, disciplined and dedicated Irish parliamentary party, able both to hold the balance of political power at Westminster and also, through sheer persistence and sincerity, to bring home to British audiences on British platforms the nature and extent of their country's grievances and the most acceptable means of removing them.

The growth of the Irish party as a major factor in Anglo-Irish relations, far more permanent and pervasive in its influence than anything O'Connell had been able to achieve, was to be the most striking change in constitutional politics in the two generations after the Famine. But that party, as time was to prove, could only command respect so long as it was successful. And success in turn depended on three things – outstanding leadership, Irish-American support expressed in terms of the dollars without which the elaborate machinery for winning elections and controlling constituencies could not be maintained, and, above all, what might be called the visibility of progress. This was to be progress, preferably towards Home Rule, but progress also in other directions – in the solution of the land question, in education, in housing and in the promotion of Irish interests in a multitude of different ways.

As we shall see, of progress measured in these terms – progress, that is, short of Home Rule – the Irish party contributed a great deal. Such progress, however, was itself subject to two serious reservations. One was the danger that the end might be lost sight of in the means. There can be little doubt that for some of the abler politicians of the period –

Isaac Butt and John Redmond were, in their different ways, conspicuous examples – the House of Commons had an almost irresistible attraction and the pleading of Ireland's case there became less an unavoidable necessity than a pleasurable duty. But the strength of the Irish at Westminster depended in the last resort not upon careful manipulation of the power-balance in the House of Commons, but upon mass-support at home, and whenever that support was not forthcoming their parliamentary effectiveness dwindled. It was no accident that the heyday of the party under Parnell coincided with his leadership of a formidable popular movement in Ireland, and it was no accident either that the divisions within the party after his downfall and death both contributed to, and were accentuated by, the disenchantment with constitutional politics that spread like a blight over the country in the decade of the 'nineties.

Herein precisely lay the second danger that threatened the Home Rule movement. It was, to put it bluntly, the danger that politicians mesmerised by the legislative process would tend to soften, or even to forget, the differences that divided Irishmen from Englishmen. To the dedicated nationalist benevolent reforms conceded by a British parliament were ultimately no substitute for the reassertion of a separate national identity. And in that same decade of disenchantment with constitutionalism there began to appear the faint but unmistakable signs of such a reassertion – a reassertion not through heroic and hopeless violence, but through a steady and relentless emphasis on the need to resurrect the idea of 'Irish Ireland'. As it developed, this new nationalism was to take a variety of forms – part political, part economic, part cultural – but however diverse the manifestations bodied forth in Sinn Féin, the Gaelic League, or the industrial movement, the underlying aims were the same: to reawaken in Irishmen a sense of pride in their past, to recover in the present their self-respect, and to work for a future which would not be contained within the parochial boundaries of Home Rule. The burgeoning of this new nationalism, its grafting onto the old republican stock, and the subsequent withering of constitutionalism – these were to be the major transformations within the anti-Unionist camp in the thirty years between the death of Parnell in 1891 and the great compromise of 1921.

(v)

In the unending struggle between those who upheld the Union and those who opposed it, the initiative had habitually rested with the latter. The business of a conservative, after all, is to conserve, and to Irish and British conservatives alike a stern, unyielding resistance to change had seemed for most of the nineteenth century the only course open for those who wished to maintain intact the connection between the two countries. And, certainly, it cannot be denied that simple repression remained a standard instrument of British rule in Ireland throughout the whole period of the Union. Even as late as 1887 Lord Salisbury's administration could pass a 'permanent' coercion act intended to build irrevocably into the law of the land restrictions upon agitation which had hitherto been regarded as exceptional responses to exceptional situations. Nor did repression stop short at the legal form of coercion, whether temporary or permanent. Whenever agitation passed into actual rebellion the government in power, regardless of its political complexion, reacted instinctively in the traditional manner by calling in the military arm. In 1848 and 1867, it is true, this was little more than a precautionary measure, but the full import of what it could mean was to be felt by Dublin in 1916 and by the whole country between 1919 and 1921.

Yet, although these collisions between insurgent nationalism and repressive authority continued until British rule disappeared from most of the country, and served to fix in the minds of many Irishmen a bitterness towards England which remained long after the events that had inspired it had passed into history, here, too, there was change. Unionists, who for nearly a century had been doing their best to disprove Napoleon's maxim that you can do anything with bayonets except sit on them, did in fact begin from the 1880s onward to edge their way slowly towards a more constructive policy. Initially, no doubt, they were pushed in this direction, partly through the power exerted by the Irish party in the House of Commons, and partly because of the electoral necessity to have something to offer as an alternative once Gladstone had committed the Liberal party to Home Rule. The alternative they produced, 'killing Home Rule with kindness', may have begun as the expedient of hard-pressed politicians, but it was not long before it was elevated into a philosophy of government. And out of it were to come very substantial concessions – the settlement of the land question, the reform of local administration, the creation of a Department of Agriculture and Technical Instruction, a sustained attempt to rescue the impoverished 'congested districts' of the west of Ireland from decay, improvements in health and housing, and repeated efforts to meet the Irish demand for a Catholic university.

Not the least significant of these developments was the emergence, outside the circle of government, of a group of Irish Unionists (never very large, but influential far beyond their numbers) who sought, as private individuals, and by willing co-operation with their moderate nationalist counterparts, to prepare the way for these and other social reforms. Their efforts, unhappily, were doomed to disaster. Disowned by the reactionary majority of their own caste, and distrusted by many on the other side – including parliamentarians like John Dillon as well as critics from the more extreme left – as a kind of Trojan horse, they were unable to move beyond their initial triumph in laying down the lines along which the land problem was at last solved (a solution highly favourable, incidentally, to their own landlord colleagues), and although some of them, notably the Earl of Dunraven and Sir Horace Plunkett, did not easily abandon their efforts to build bridges between Irishmen of different classes, creeds and origins, their enterprise came to nothing. It failed for several reasons. First, it coincided with the rise of that new nationalism already mentioned, which created a climate almost totally inimical to the sort of joint activities constructive Unionists had in mind. Second, it coincided also with the return of Home Rule to the centre of the stage as a political possibility from 1906, or more accurately 1910, onwards, provoking in Ireland (especially in Ulster), and in Britain too, a hardening of Unionist attitudes that left no room for collaboration with 'the enemy'. But finally, and most important, constructive Unionism, whether of governments or of individuals, failed because it was founded on the false assumption that the spectre of Irish nationalism would be banished if only the wand of some magician, or conference of magicians, could cause the desert of Anglo-Irish relations to blossom like the rose.

It is only fair to add, however, that the falsity of the assumption only became apparent after the event. The fear that benevolent legislation might indeed lessen the impetus of the Irish drive for independence was present in the minds of many nationalists from the moment such legislation first made its appearance. And there can be little doubt that on the Unionist side the whole policy of social amelioration was adopted in the hope that it would prove a viable alternative to self-government. Both the fear and the hope were not without foundation. Between about 1890 and 1910 Ireland appeared, outwardly at least, to have become a more prosperous, more contented, more somnolent country. For ordinary men and women the prospect of earning a slightly better, slightly less laborious, living than their forbears seemed horizon enough. It is common knowledge, after all, that when the renewed political tension after the introduction of the third Home Rule Bill in 1912 ushered in the critical phase of the Irish revolution, that revolution was the work of a small, though devoted and highly articulate, minority. For the minority to be transformed into a majority, as happened in Ireland between 1916 and 1918, many strange things, and some things that are inexplicable even yet, would have to happen. Yet although, as we shall later see, the British government by its own infirmities and errors of policy contributed much to the transformation, it did not contribute everything. The key to change was to be sought, as always, in Ireland itself. That men were found in sufficient numbers to fight a long war of independence between 1919 and 1921, that the population as a whole was prepared to endure stoically, if passively, the reprisals which the war brought in its train, suggests that more than the pursuit of economic well-being, more than the love of a quiet life uncomplicated by any emotion more profound than the itch to add field to field, was involved in the last act of the drama. The impulse to fight, to hold on, to contend

32

with almost insuperable difficulties and almost impossible odds, had its roots in a tradition of insurrection and a spirit of resistance which, however irrational, were too strong and too deeply implicit in the history of the country to be ignored. The embers of Irish identity had been subdued, they had not been extinguished; and out of them, as dedicated and desperate men blew on the glowing coals, rose once more the phoenix of independent nationality.

2. The Economic Environment

Although, as we have already seen, the Famine was in many ways a profoundly significant event in modern Irish history, its traditional place as a watershed in the economic and social development of the country has lately begun to be questioned. That it accelerated certain trends and intensified certain problems nobody would deny. The trends and the problems, however, may have gone further back into the past than many historians have been prepared to recognise, and although the historians themselves are still so deeply divided on a number of important issues as to make generalisations of any kind exceedingly difficult, an effort towards some sort of synthesis may yet prove worthwhile.

We may start from what would still seem to be a point of general agreement, that nineteenth century Ireland underwent a 'rural crisis' of which the Famine was the supreme manifestation. But it is when we try to discern the origins of this crisis that difficulties begin to thicken. The easiest way into the minefield of controversy which surrounds the subject is to summarise very briefly the most recent twist in the argument. This is the contention that the critical situation which developed in Ireland during the first half of the nineteenth century was in part a legacy from the previous century and in part the outcome of a radical change in market conditions in the years after Waterloo. During the reign of George III, it is suggested, the increasing demand for food in Britain had an effect upon Irish agriculture which was, in the long run, revolutionary. From being a heavy corn-importer in the middle of the eighteenth century Ireland became a substantial net exporter of both grain and livestock. Since she did so at a time of relative prosperity at home, this implied a striking expansion of production, characterised chiefly by an increasing emphasis on tillage and also, within the still important sector of pasture farming, by a movement away from dry cattle towards dairying.[1] That was in itself remarkable, for the Irish climate normally favours pasture rather than tillage. For tillage to be predominant for any length of time two things were needed – a continuing demand at stimulating prices, and the reasonable prospect of a high yield per acre. The former was supplied partly, perhaps mainly, by the British market (though the needs of brewing, distilling and the provision trade inside Ireland were also a contributory factor), the latter by skilful use of such fertilizers as were available – for example, seaweed – and by the lavish employment of root crops, more specifically

34

by the prevalence of the potato.

The economic role of the potato in Irish history has been a subject of dispute as prolific as the crop itself, but here it is only necessary to point to its more obvious virtues in the context of an expanding economy in the late eighteenth century.[2] It was useful in cleaning, restoring and reclaiming the soil, it could be used for fattening pigs (for which there was a growing demand) and, above all, it could form the basis of the dietary of the people. Provided Irishmen were willing to accept the potato as their staple food – and it has been suggested that roughly between 1740 and 1780 more of them were moving towards this position – then not only would landlords be assured of a cheap supply of labour for the cultivation of their crops, but it might actually pay them to permit, or even encourage, the multiplication of small holdings (either by the reclamation of new land or by the subdivision of existing farms) on which the life-sustaining potato could be grown.* It might pay them because the potato, being economical as well as nutritious, would not only support a tenantry numerous enough to provide an adequate labour-force, but would release for profitable cash-crops land that might otherwise have been needed for subsistence.[3]

Perhaps the most striking result of the increasing reliance of the cottiers and labourers upon the potato was that it removed, or at any rate diminished, the ordinary prudential considerations affecting marriage. Traditionally, rural communities have been able to prevent a too rapid growth of population through the tight control exercised by fathers or by village elders upon the sources of wealth, whether land or cattle. Because children had to wait for their inheritance – and often to wait long years – marriage tended to be late; because marriage tended to be late, it tended also to be less prolific of children. In the latter part of the eighteenth century, however, it would seem that the young man content to exist upon potatoes, and confronted with an economic situation which, for the time being at least, gave him sufficient return for his labour to enable him to pay rent for his small holding, began to be

* The date of the transition is still a matter of debate. It has recently been argued by an authority whose views command respect that we should look to the last two decades of the eighteenth century for the emergence of the potato as a major dietetic influence, and that even then we should find it most closely associated with the very poor cottier class. As this became a larger section of society, so a potato diet became more characteristic of that society as a whole. 'As we move backwards into Irish history from the outset of the nineteenth century, and forwards from 1845, the identification of Irish diet and agriculture with the potato increasingly loses force' (L. M. Cullen, 'Irish History without the Potato', in *Past and Present* (July 1968), No. 40, pp. 72-83). It is proper to add that Professor Connell, the doyen of Irish demographic historians, is sceptical both about the time-scale and about the class-identification used by Dr Cullen. Professor Connell still holds to the view that the main dietetic influence of the potato was exerted when it was supplementing, and had not yet displaced, other foods.

liberated from the restraints habitually imposed by society and free to follow his own biological urge to marry. It used to be argued, indeed, that the early and fruitful marriages which resulted from this state of affairs were in reality the characteristic response of a rural population which, assured of cheap food, and ambitious for little else, took its pleasure without counting the cost from a pattern of marriage that in less happily constituted communities would have been regarded as heedlessly improvident.[4] But although an element of social recklessness may sometimes have been present, historians have come latterly to lay more stress on the operation of three other explanations for this shift towards earlier marriage. One – though in the nature of things unlikely to have been effective before the early years of the nineteenth century – was that in the absence of adequate institutional provision for old age, sickness or widowhood, a large family could serve as a shield against disaster, and the earlier the marriage the more effective the shield. A second is that if there were improvidence, then it was improvidence for which the way had been prepared by the destruction of the old familial landholding by the Cromwellian and Williamite conquests and settlements which made possible a more individualist use of the land 'determined', as has been said, 'solely by the principle of maximising the incomes of those who had acquired ownership of it through the violence of the seventeenth century'.[5] And the third factor, linked closely with the second, is that the means adopted to maximise incomes in the late eighteenth century – the increasing emphasis on tillage – were those best suited to allow young couples to disregard the traditional checks and to embark upon marriage in the realisation that they could live – and breed – independently of parental land or cattle and therefore independently of parental control.

The absence of reliable statistics makes it well-nigh impossible to measure these changes in any truly satisfactory way. The first figures to achieve a reputation for reliability were those of the census of 1841 and even these have been subject to frequent criticism and reinterpretation. Nevertheless, and despite the generally discordant voices of the experts, there seems to be a fairly wide measure of agreement that before about 1740, growth, whether of prosperity or of population, had not been exceptional, but that after that approximate date both prosperity and population showed a marked and prolonged increase. How marked and how prolonged is still the subject of close argument, but it has recently been suggested that prosperity at least had begun to falter around 1820 in response to a change in market conditions. Once the demand for the produce of Irish tillage faltered the tillage system itself – inherently vulnerable because of persistent subdivision, overcropping and undermanuring – was doomed. And this clearly had begun to happen within a decade of Waterloo. As government spending was reduced and deflationary policies were pursued, the high prices which had persisted since the latter half of the eighteenth century began at last to break. Between 1816 and the mid-1830s there was, despite some fluctuations, a steep decline in the return from each of the major Irish agricultural products – wheat, oats, barley, butter, bacon, beef and mutton – and although considerable recovery was apparent by 1840 the prices then prevailing were still below those ruling when the French wars had ended.[6]

From this drastic change in the price structure there followed a consequence which, though slow to emerge, was in the end to be of the utmost importance to Irish society. In a time of falling prices it would have been natural for landlords to revise their estimates of the kind of farming likely to bring them the best return. But in the generation following Waterloo the best was not easy to detect, since all prices were falling and it only gradually became apparent that those of livestock products fell less drastically and were stabilised sooner than the price of what had been produced by the plough. We can see now that the writing was on the wall – that improved transport, combined with a rising standard of living in the British urban centres, would accentuate the demand for Irish meat while at the same time the growing accessibility of the same market to European corn producers would lessen demand for Irish grain. At the time, however, this future was so far shrouded in uncertainty that Irish exports of both grain and livestock continued at a high level for nearly two decades after 1815.

If the future was shrouded from landlords it was still more obscure for tenants. Yet hindsight again suggests that for them it would be bleaker than for their masters. The latter might in due course adjust to changed circumstances – presently we shall see them struggling to do so – but for the peasantry the effects of that upsurge of population which was a legacy of the good times had now to work themselves out in the bad times. And slow though they might be in coming, bad times there would inevitably be as the decades of subdivision and overcropping came to impose their cumulative and in the end intolerable strain upon the soil; still more so when this process began to coincide with the landlords' realisation that for them the path to prosperity would in future lie through the consolidation of holdings and the clearance of now unwanted tenants from the land.

Unhappily, the situation was made yet more complicated by the fact that the unwanted tenants were not only numerous but still increasing. True, it has been suggested (though on scanty evidence which has probably induced an error of exaggeration) that whereas the decadal increase between 1780 and 1821 may have been about seventeen per cent for each ten-year period within that span, this declined between 1821 and 1831 to just under fifteen per cent and in the decade 1831 to 1841 fell dramatically to 5.25 per cent.[7] Yet even if a fall of this order be admitted, the tragic paradox remains. Although the *rate* of increase may have been diminishing, the former prodigious advance still made its impact felt in an absolute rise in the number of people in the country. So great was the biological momentum that the population moved relentlessly upwards from perhaps 6.8 million in 1821 to just over eight million in 1841. What made the situation so serious was not just that these pressures were felt mainly by those sections of the rural population least able to help themselves – the landless labourers and the cottiers with holdings of less than five acres – but also in the western counties where the scarcity of good farming-land intensified the drive towards subdivision and so also towards intolerable overcrowding.*

Why this avalanche of people did not overwhelm Irish society sooner than it did is a question that is still argued by scholars and, in the absence of decisive statistics, will no doubt continue to be argued for a long time to come. Broadly speaking, three restraining factors have been put forward by way of explanation. One – and probably the most important – was emigration, which between 1780 and 1845 may have taken as many as one and three-quarter million out of the country. Some of this was already directed towards Canada and the USA – as many as 33,000 a year on average may have gone there between 1815 and 1845 – but most followed the easier route to Britain.[8] A second restraining factor may have been high mortality. There are no satisfactory figures to support this thesis, but when it is remembered that the poorer part of the population depended on potatoes and that the potato crop is estimated to have failed, partially or totally, fourteen times between 1816 and 1842, it will be obvious that hunger was a frequent visitor; a hungry people was also a people peculiarly vulnerable to the deadly fever which from time to time swept through their cabins and cottages during those years.[9]

More dubious than emigration or mortality – yet central to any discussion of Irish demographic history – is the third explanation, which is based upon an apparent fall in the birth rate. As it is generally presented, this is not an argument connected with a decline in fertility; on the contrary, most students of the subject seem to accept that fertility remained high. But if fertility remained high, and if there was no widespread and deliberate control of births (this latter point has begun to be questioned, though not yet conclusively), then those who argue for a fall in the birth rate have been tempted to do so on the ground that marriages were becoming later and fewer. The statistical evidence relat-

* Since the woes of the cottiers and labourers were repeatedly investigated by commissions of inquiry in the pre-Famine decades, historians have tended to generalise from the findings of these commissions and to apply to the farming community as a whole what properly relates only to the lowest strata. Recent research indicates that even among smallholders there were some – chiefly those with farms of between about eight and fifteen acres – whose condition on the eve of the Famine was by no means unsatisfactory. On the other hand, it is true that the 1841 census indicates that about seventy per cent of the rural population was either landless or dependent on inadequate holdings of less than five acres, and that while the percentage was much below this figure in some of the eastern counties it was as high as eighty-five in Mayo. For this whole question, see especially L. M. Cullen. *An Economic History of Ireland since 1660* (London, 1972), pp. 109-13.

ing to this first occurs in the census of 1841 and then only in relation to the decade 1830-40. It would seem to indicate that in that ten-year period the proportion of girls in rural districts marrying at the age of twenty years or under fell from 36·72 to 22·55 per cent and that the parallel decrease for men below the age of twenty was from 11·01 to 5 per cent. One would expect to find from this that there would be a marked decline in the number of rural marriages during the decade, but although there was a fall in the number of first marriages in the country districts from 32,650 in 1830 to 28,662 in 1840, the progression was not consistent and in some years, for example 1838 and 1839, the number was actually higher than it had been in 1830.* It is true that modern criticism has cast some doubt on the census figures which form the basis of these calculations and it is possible that they over-emphasise the differences existing between the terminal dates. The subject is a complex one and still requires further investigation, but even if it be correct, as a modern authority has recently contended, that the decade of the thirties was less exceptional than has hitherto been supposed, two comments have yet to be made. One is that the relatively low number of marriages in 1840 has to be seen against the background of a population which itself had risen to just over seven million in that year from its 1830 total of a little more than 6½ million.[10] And the other is that the Census Commissioners themselves reached the conclusion that in 1836 (a year in which men apparently married earlier than in any other between 1831 and 1840) the median age of bridegrooms in marriages where neither partner had been married before was about twenty-five years, and that 'the greatest proportion of men marry between twenty-six and thirty-five'. If they were correct in this supposition then the Irish farmer soberly marrying in his middle or late 'twenties can by no stretch of the imagination be depicted as a headstrong, feckless youth hurrying into early and excessively fruitful marriage regardless of the cost.†

* These are the figures given in R. D. Crotty, *Irish Agricultural Production*, pp. 40-1. For a criticism of them see the review article by Joseph Lee in *Agricultural History Review* (1969), xvii, part 1, pp. 64-76. Dr Lee shares Mr Crotty's view that the rate of natural increase was slowing down in the 1830s but believes that he has exaggerated this deceleration.

† For a searching analysis of the figures see Professor Drake's article, 'Marriage and Population Growth in Ireland, 1750-1845', in *Economic History Review*, 2nd series, xvi (1963), 301-13. He would maintain that demographically the 1830s may not have been very different from the rest of the two generations before the Famine, but we still await the reinterpretation of Irish population history which this would imply. Some steps towards this reinterpretation are suggested by J. Lee, 'Marriage and Population in pre-Famine Ireland' in *Economic History Review*, xxi (1968), 283-95. He not only draws attention to neglected sources (e.g. parish registers) but somewhat redresses the balance between Connell and Drake by pointing out that closer study is needed of differences in marriage patterns between regions and between classes. More specifically, he

Yet whether there was a dramatic change in the marriage pattern or not, the continuing growth in the absolute number of people on the land made it very difficult for Irish agriculture to adjust to the changing character of the British market. In other words, the very fact that the population was still increasing may have tended to hold the farmer in his labour-intensive tillage phase longer than was economically desirable. The area of tillage continued to expand at least up to the 1830s, possibly up to the Famine itself, while exports of grain and flour to Britain remained high (apart from a falling-off between 1838 and 1842 which was probably due to bad harvests) until 1846. Indeed, it has been demonstrated that even after the population had been drastically reduced the turn away from tillage was more gradual than was once supposed, for although the immediate effect of the Famine may have been to reduce the acreage of grain crops from perhaps 3·8 million acres in 1845 to about 3·1 million acres in 1851 and that under root crops from about 2·8 million acres in 1845 to approximately 1·5 million in 1851, the total acreage of tillage declined only by a further four per cent between 1851 and 1859, compared with a much more dramatic decrease of fourteen per cent in the succeeding nine years, by which time the post-Famine adjustments had been virtually completed. The tenacity with which tillage held its place in the scheme of things is most probably to be explained less in terms of the reclamation of waste land, which up to 1840 – and possibly even up to 1851 – does not seem to have been extensive, than by the simple reluctance of farmers to move out of a form of cultivation which, in the short view that was the easiest and most human for them to take, still seemed to be profitable, even if by the 1850s the stimulus may have been coming increasingly from home-consumption rather than from exports.

Nevertheless, the importance of tillage farming up to and after the Famine should not be overstressed, for the future, after all, lay with the cattle industry, and there is reason to believe that farmers – large farmers, at any rate – had begun to read the signs of the times correctly as early as the 1830s, with results that were to be seen in the mounting exports of livestock. Thus, whereas in the period 1821–5 cattle exports had averaged 47,000 a year, by 1835 these had gone up to 98,000 and in the years 1846 to 1849 were to rise still further to an annual average of 202,000.[11] The cattle population as a whole, which had grown at a rate of perhaps two per cent per annum between 1841 and 1847, doubled that rate between 1847 and 1851 and continued to grow very

---

contends that because labourers do appear to have married early, this does not necessarily mean that other sections of the community did the same. 'Connell reached his conclusions concerning male age at marriage in the 1830s by generalizing for the whole rural population from evidence relating mainly to labourers; Drake, on the other hand, simply reverses the process, assuming that the median age at marriage for the whole rural community should also apply to all classes within that community' (p. 285). Clearly, we are still far from finality on this matter!

rapidly up to 1859; thereafter, though growth persisted, the process was more sedate and by 1914 the increase in absolute numbers between that date and 1859 just about equalled the increase in absolute numbers between 1847 and 1859.*

This changing pattern would in itself have dictated a policy of consolidation of holdings and of widespread clearance; a numerous tenantry, once an economic advantage, had now become an economic liability. But to recognise this was one thing, to act on it another. And while it was true that some landlords in the generation before the Famine took advantage of long leases falling in to replace them by much shorter lettings, and no less true that they could call upon the assistance of authority in evicting tenants from their holdings, nothing characterised the Irish peasantry in that twilight of the old economy more than the desperate and often violent tenacity with which they clung to their small farms. And just how small these were may be judged from the fact that twenty-four per cent of all the holdings in the country in 1845 were between one and five acres in size and approximately another forty per cent were between five and fifteen acres; beyond that precision seems impossible to achieve, though it is likely that the number of farms exceeding thirty acres was not very large. In addition, it has to be remembered that there were 135,314 holders of plots of land of less than one acre each.† Some idea of the gravity of the problem presented by this distribution of holdings may be gathered from the further fact that on the eve of the Famine roughly two-thirds of the entire population of about eight million was dependent for its existence upon agriculture.¹²

It was an agriculture that was still somewhat conservative in technique and to which the landlords, with some honourable exceptions, made little positive contribution. They were, no doubt, concerned to maximise their profits, but they pursued this aim less single-mindedly, and certainly less efficiently, than traditional interpretations would lead us to believe. The classical picture of a tyrannical gentry imposing high

* For the working out of these tendencies in the latter part of the nineteenth century, see pp. 48-9

† These figures are markedly different from the ones traditionally given and I derive them from two important essays in revision by P. M. A. Bourke: 'Uncertainties in the Statistics of Farm Size in Ireland, 1841-1851', in *JSSISI*, (1959-60), xx, 20-6; 'The Agricultural Statistics of the 1841 Census of Ireland: A Critical Review', in *Econ. Hist. Rev.*, 2nd series (1965) xviii, 376-92. The figures hitherto accepted give a more dramatic picture of the situation on the eve of the Famine composed of the following elements: forty-four per cent of all holdings between one and five acres, thirty-seven per cent between five and fifteen acres and only seven per cent over thirty acres. These figures are used in the main secondary works on this topic (see *n* 12 above), but they portray a maldistribution so extreme as to be inherently suspect; it has remained for Mr Bourke to expose the defects of measurement and assessment embodied in the 1841 Census on which these estimates were based.

rents upon a hapless tenantry, and enforcing payment by the threat or actuality of eviction, has been painted in colours too lurid to be wholly credible. In practice rents do not seem to have risen outrageously in the half-century before the Famine, and the obstacles – legal, prudential, even moral – in the way of eviction were such as to make all but the most ruthless landlords falter. No-one would deny, certainly, that many Irish countrypeople lived in dire poverty, but it is arguable that their unhappy plight was due much more to the pressure of population on inadequate land, combined with a market-situation which was turning men's minds increasingly towards an extensive rather than an intensive agriculture. Viewed from this standpoint landlords appear as victims of circumstance hardly less than their tenants.[13] But there is, of course, another sense in which the tenure-system, though it was not the root of the problem, may have helped to produce the catastrophe of the Famine. That system, as it had operated since the upheavals of the seventeenth century, had substituted a rent economy for the old familial economy and had thus opened the way for an individualistic scramble for land which, in the relatively favourable circumstances of the late eighteenth and early nineteenth centuries, had made possible the upsurge of population. But the greatly swollen agricultural proletariat resulting from that upsurge was from first to last terribly vulnerable – a vulnerability of which much contemporary opinion was fully conscious. The fashionable remedy – clearance of surplus population and consolidation of uneconomic small holdings – seemed impossible, for obvious human reasons, to impose. Yet it was precisely this remedy which the Famine, through the ravages it wrought upon the poorest sections of the population, seemed suddenly in the mid-forties to have brought within the bounds of possibility.

(ii)

This was in fact the most important and most immediate consequence of the starving years through which Ireland passed between 1845 and 1850. The partial failure of the potato crop in the earlier of these years was followed by total failure in 1846 and that in turn by a harsh winter and an epidemic of 'famine fever', which was actually two separate diseases – typhus and relapsing fever – soon to be joined by dysentery and scurvy. In the autumn of 1847 the potato blight, though still in evidence, was less virulent than before, but in 1848 it returned in full fury and the tale of death and disease and flight entered yet another grim cycle. The response of the government to this *débâcle*, though prompt and relatively successful while Sir Robert Peel was prime minister, became increasingly inadequate when in 1846, at the height of the crisis, he gave place to Lord John Russell, whose Whig administration was dominated by the prevailing laissez-faire doctrines of the age. When the main crop failure came in that year the official policy was to limit assistance to the provision of employment through public works, the cost of which was to fall entirely on the rates. This produced within four months a fantastic rise in the numbers dependent on this casual labour – from 30,000 in September 1846 to half a million in December. Not surprisingly, the machinery of administration cracked under the strain and in the New Year the crucial decision was taken to close the public works and rely instead upon direct relief, partly through the medium of soup-kitchens, partly by concentrating the destitute so far as possible in the work-houses set up under the poor law which had been extended to Ireland only a decade earlier. In these bleak and disease-ridden surroundings hundreds of thousands of starving people received relief of a kind. Even so, despite the strenuousness with which the 'indoor' solution was applied – nearly a million spent some part of 1849 in these institutions – it proved impossible to impose the work-house test on all who needed succour, and the longer the crisis lasted the more 'outdoor relief' had to be granted.

To utilise the ramshackle apparatus of the poor law was still, of course, to place the burden of cost upon the rates, in effect upon the landlords who, in the eyes of many contemporaries, were the principal villains in a tragedy which nowadays we might prefer to regard as the product, not of individual or class wickedness, but of a century or more of Irish history. Many of them sank under the mounting pressure of their poor rates with important economic and social consequences to which we must presently return. On the short term, they sought to minimise their payments and stave off disaster by clearing as many tenants as possible off the land, since landlords were liable for all rates on holdings and cottages or cabins of less than four pounds' valuation. It seems likely also that eviction was stimulated by an amendment of the poor law itself – the so-called 'Gregory clause' – which excluded from relief all those holding more than a quarter of an acre of land. Whenever hunger bit deeply enough the temptation to the tenant to abandon his farm for a mess of workhouse pottage might well prove irresistible, and in fact the displacement of small farmers – especially the cottiers, the smallest of all – went ahead rapidly during the Famine. In 1849, for example, nearly 17,000 families, or 90,000 people, were driven from their homes and the following year the respective totals increased to 20,000 families and 104,000 people. It is true that between a quarter and a third of these were subsequently readmitted (on an unsatisfactory basis as 'caretakers'), but nevertheless the social upheaval and human suffering that lay behind these statistics were on an unprecedented scale.[14]

The calamitous years burnt themselves deep into the imagination of the people and have haunted their descendants ever since. Yet the Famine did not change the central problem confronting Irish rural society. That problem remained what it had been for a generation or more – to alter the structure of Irish agriculture in response to the changing pattern of British demand. What the Famine did do – and do most traumatically – was to transform the terms in which the problem would have to be solved. In the first instance and most obviously it did this by reducing the pressure of population upon the land. Had there been no catastrophe and had the population continued its pre-Famine curve the likelihood is that in 1851 it would have reached nine million. But when that date arrived the actual total was $6\frac{1}{2}$ million, roughly two million less than the estimated total for 1845, on the eve of disaster. Of that missing two million, about half had perished from hunger and disease, but the remainder had vanished in the headlong exodus from the country which was the instinctive reaction of a panic-stricken people to the spectacle of their traditional way of life breaking into pieces before their very eyes. 'All we want', as one group put it, 'is to get out of Ireland . . . we must be better anywhere else than here.'[15] The initial hysteria, as it revealed itself in the autumn of 1846, had been confined mainly to the smaller farmers, but by the next year the larger tenants, and even townspeople too, were caught up in what had already become a flood of emigration. Thus the formidable figure for 1846, some 116,000, was easily surpassed the following year when 230,000 left for North America and Australia, apart altogether from the uncounted thousands who crossed the Irish Sea to Britain. The false dawn of the better season of 1847 reduced the flow considerably, but the renewed crop failure of 1848 at once swelled it again to a torrent and in a few short months in the latter part of the year more than 200,000 left the country – a haemorrhage which was to become an annual *average* for the years 1849 to 1852 and to produce a total emigration of some two million for the decade 1845 to 1855.[16]

Yet, although the immediate demographic effect of this mass-flight was very great, its psychological legacy may have been even more profound. The traditional resistance to emigration already, as we have seen, weakening before the Famine, had been still further broken down and leaving the old country now came to be regarded as the most practical, if still unpalatable, alternative to dumb acquiescence in extreme poverty and insecurity at home. It is true that once the worst intensity of the crisis was over the desire to remain in one's own familiar countryside reasserted itself, and true also that the social pattern of emigration began to reflect this reversion to an earlier attitude. It was noticeable, for example, that whereas in the Famine years even the more substantial families had yielded to the prevailing panic, in the early 'fifties it was the landless man (and woman) who predominated. No doubt this was partly the 'attraction' of remittances from those who had already gone to assist the passages of those who remained behind – receipts from this source went up from £460,000 in 1848 to £1·4 million in 1852 – but partly also it was the 'repulsion' due to the difficulty of obtaining economically viable farms at a time when, as we shall see presently, landlords were bent upon a policy of clearance and consolidation. Thus, although there were some parts of Ireland – most notoriously, Mayo – where there was enough inferior land available for the population actually to increase after the Famine, in the more fertile areas often the only alternative to pauperism for the landless man was emigration.[17]

Emigration, therefore, there had to be, emigration which in one form or another was to form part of the very fabric of Irish society during the succeeding hundred years. Naturally it varied according to the economic climate, but although this was relatively benign in the twenty years after the Famine the bad times that came again in the 'seventies raised the outflow immediately to half a million in that decade and 600,000 in the next. Thereafter there was a sharp decline, but never anything approaching a complete cessation. Moreover, the movement outwards continued to be largely an irrevocable movement towards the countries from which there was little prospect of return. It is unfortunately not possible to be very precise about the short-haul traffic to Britain, as much because of the difficulty of distinguishing permanent from tempo-rary emigration as because of the fact that the figures date only from 1852 and only became really reliable from the mid-seventies onwards. But there is no doubt about the strength of the current that flowed to the far corners of the earth, and it is beyond dispute that between 1841 and 1925 gross 'overseas' emigration included 4¾ million going to the USA, 70,000 to Canada and over 370,000 to Australia.[18]

But if emigration was the most obvious demographic factor influenc-ing Irish society in the post-Famine years, it was not the only one. Parallel with the exodus of population went an intensification of that marriage pattern which, as we have already seen, may have begun to reveal itself even before the catastrophe. Significantly, it was a pattern which, from having been originally confined mainly to the poorer classes and regions, now spread to all sections and areas of rural society. Marriage statistics in any true sense date only from 1864, but even by then it was evident that the Irish marriage-rate was one of the lowest in the world. During 1864–70 the crude marriage-rate (marriages per thousand of the population) was 5·10, falling as low as four on average for the decade 1881-90 and hovering about five in the years immediately before the First World War. The annual average number of marriages per thousand of the unmarried population between the ages of fifteen and forty-nine fell from 36·7 for men in the early 1870s to 24·1 twenty years later and for women at the same two periods from 38·8 to 26·9.[19] Not only were marriages relatively fewer than before, they also tended to be later – a tendency which from the Famine onwards produced in almost every age-group an increasing proportion of single men and women. By 1951, after a century of this kind of progression, a situation had been reached where in the countryside nearly ninety-seven per cent of young men and eighty-one per cent of young women between the ages of twenty and twenty-four were unmarried; between the ages of twenty-five and twenty-nine, the respective percentages were eighty-

45

four and fifty-four; and between thirty and thirty-four they were sixty-eight and thirty-six per cent.[20] Or to put the matter another way, just after the Second World War farmers did not on average marry until their thirty-ninth year or women until they were thirty, while of farmers between sixty-five and seventy-four one in four was a bachelor.[21]

It is true that the fertility of Irish marriages, although possibly less intense than before the Famine, remained high in comparison with that of other non-Asiatic countries, and in 1911 the average number of children per marriage in all marriages taken together was four (6¾ in marriages of 'completed fertility', i.e. of thirty to thirty-four years' duration, when no more children could be expected).[22] Against this has to be set a death-rate which, while remaining fairly steady at between sixteen and eighteen per thousand in the period 1864–1911, revealed a heavy and continuing mortality in children of under one year. In the late 1860s the annual average was as high as ninety-six per thousand live births, rising to ninety-nine in the last decade of the century and only then beginning to decline.[23] Exceptional fertility operated, despite later and fewer marriages and high infant mortality, to produce a continuing, if diminished, natural increase of births over deaths, but since this increase was regularly wiped out by emigration the net result was an inexorable fall of the total population to 4⅓ million in 1911, at which point the situation at last began to stabilise itself.

Perhaps the most striking feature of this loss of numbers was that it hit the rural areas far more heavily than the towns. Whereas in Ireland as a whole the town population (a town being defined as containing not less than 1,500 people) rose steadily, apart from a temporary setback in the 'fifties, from 1,215,000 in 1841 to 1½ million in 1911, the agrarian population went down from almost seven million at the earlier date to just under three million at the later. This pressure was felt in both parts of the country but it was more marked in the future republic than in the future Northern Ireland. In the latter, town-dwellers rose from 213,000 before the Famine to 603,000 on the eve of the First World War, while the non-urban community shrank from 1½ million at the earlier date to about 650,000 at the later. In the rest of the country, however, the non-urban element dwindled from 5½ million in 1841 to 2¼ million in 1911, while the town population of 920,000 in the latter year, though higher than at any time since 1881, still lagged behind the million listed for 1841.[24]

(iii)

Rural depopulation was in effect an integral part of an economic structure which had begun to take its characteristic and familiar shape in the very shadow of the Famine itself. The outward and visible sign of this transformation was the rapidity and completeness with which the very small farm of earlier years disappeared. Holdings of from one

46

to five acres, for example, declined from nearly 182,000 in 1845 to 88,000 in 1851 and this decline continued steadily thereafter, until by 1910 there were only 62,000 of them. Farms of from five to fifteen acres underwent a similar, though less extreme, reduction from 311,000 in 1845 to 154,000 in 1910. Comparisons between 1845 and later periods are difficult to make in respect of the larger farms, but it would appear that the number of holdings between fifteen and thirty acres declined from what was possibly a high peak of 146,000 in 1847 (the year of the first detailed return of agricultural produce in Ireland) to nearly 137,000 in 1910, while those above thirty acres rose in the same two years from 157,000 to 167,000.[25] Initially, at least, this movement towards consolidation was made possible both by the clearances of the Famine and post-Famine years and by the fact that many of the old landlords, long burdened by debts, had themselves gone under in the crisis, to be replaced by a new generation, and in some cases a new kind of owner, less impoverished and bringing a more constructive approach to the intractable problems of Irish farming. The way was prepared for this phenomenon by the Encumbered Estates Act of 1849 under which, during the succeeding years, some five million acres, about a quarter of the whole of Ireland, passed into the hands of landlords, some of whom no doubt were speculators, but others of whom belonged to the existing landed families. It rapidly became a part of Irish historical mythology that these post-Famine landlords, whether 'new' or 'old', were a flinty-hearted, rack-renting crew who dealt the death-blow to the surviving elements of the old cottier-based economy. In fact, recent research suggests that the purchasers of land under the Encumbered Estates Act did not in general charge excessive rents – with some notorious and well-publicised exceptions – and were even remarkable for their tendency to put capital into their property rather than to extract revenue from it. Indeed, so far were they from obliterating the pre-Famine economy that in some parts of the west it continued to persist for several decades with all the familiar evils attendant upon over-crowding and subdivision.[26] On the other hand, it cannot be denied that the impact of the Famine itself, allied to the continuing drain of subsequent emigration, did cumulatively have a significant effect upon the size, and therefore upon the character, of Irish farms. Provided the economic environment remained even relatively favourable, those who stayed at home, at least in the more prosperous parts of the country, would have every incentive to go on adding field to field.

The economic environment, in its turn, dictated the way in which the land was utilised. Here the most striking indication of a new balance was the falling away of the area under wheat which in 1847 had reached almost three-quarters of a million acres. Four years later that figure had already dropped to half a million and thereafter it went into a galloping decline, totalling slightly less than 48,000 acres by 1910. The reduction of other corn crops was not so extreme (oats and barley had important other outlets for animal feed and for distilling respectively), but even so

47

the entire area under corn crops fell in that sixty years from about $3\frac{1}{3}$ million acres to about $1\frac{1}{3}$ million. There was, it is true, a brief expansion of the total area of tillage in the years immediately after the Famine, but this seems mainly to have been due to increased planting of root and green crops and of flax. Whereas the whole area of tillage (including grain with root and green crops and flax) reached its post-Famine peak around 1851, the non-grain crop area continued to grow until about 1861; after that it declined from its maximum of almost $1\frac{3}{4}$ million acres in 1861 to just over a million in 1910. Hay or meadow by contrast went up steadily from just over a million acres in 1847 to nearly $2\frac{1}{2}$ million in 1910, while the area under pasture increased from $8\frac{3}{4}$ million acres in 1851 to over $10\frac{1}{2}$ million in 1901, levelling out at about 10 million in 1910.

The key to this transformation is to be found in the price structure. Broadly speaking, while the market was generally buoyant between 1851 and the early 1870s it was more favourable to animals and animal products than it was to products of the plough. Taking 1851 as base= 100, it appears that whereas general wholesale prices rose by fifty per cent between then and 1873, wheat, oats, barley, potatoes and flax, while they did rise, did not rise to the same extent (though wheat came very close to it); and they certainly did not achieve the increases registered by hay (two-hundred per cent), beef (one-hundred per cent), butter (seventy-seven per cent), wool (eighty-one per cent), eggs (seventy-one per cent) and store cattle under two years old (one-hundred and twenty-nine per cent).[27]

Thereafter, with the intensification of foreign competition, bad times ensued for almost everyone and lasted for the next twenty years. Taking 1873 as base = 100, only barley and eggs ended in 1896 with a higher index, though since general prices fell slightly more than agricultural prices the effect upon the farmer, while severe enough, was not quite so bad as might have been expected. Moreover, within this framework of widely diffused depression, and despite the special threat posed to the Irish livestock producer by refrigerated meat from across the world, animal and animal produce prices, even if undeniably in decline, were still for the most part more resilient than those of tillage produce. From 1896 to the First World War agricultural prices began to rise again and every department showed an increase. This was, however, to a certain extent offset by the fact that for the first time for many years general prices had begun to move markedly ahead of food prices, thus confronting the farmer with a potentially dangerous threat, anticipating, indeed, that failure to achieve parity with industry which was to dog the farming community far into the twentieth century.

It has to be remembered that while this change was proceeding, Irish agriculture remained technically backward and in some of its aspects did not rise much above subsistence level. As late as 1908, for example, out of the six leading crops the proportion of the produce sold for cash exceeded thirty per cent in only three instances – wheat, barley and flax – and each of these was to some degree in decline. In the case of the other crops grown the traditional practice was to consume on the farm the greater part of what had been produced. Consequently, to the extent that Irish agriculture was an export industry, it was an industry based upon dairy-farming and upon the breeding of cattle to be sold overseas, the tendency being increasingly to sell the latter alive. In fact, in the Irish livestock industry perhaps the most outstanding feature of the half century after 1850 was the way in which the price of store cattle rose and the way in which the farmer responded to this stimulus, by far the most favourable to which he was being subjected with the single exception of the demand for eggs, and egg production, after all, remained essentially a domestic activity. Exports of live cattle to Great Britain rose from about 195,000 a year in the early 1850s to half a million in the early 1870s. Thereafter, despite competition from chilled meat from abroad (and of live animals from North America) the numbers continued to climb even during the years of bad prices to three-quarters of a million in the late 1890s, reaching a peak of some 835,000 a year just before the First World War.* Two consequences of this export trade were particularly significant. One was that the shift of demand in England led to a change of emphasis in Ireland away from fat cattle and towards store cattle which could be easily and quickly exported once the railways had linked the production areas to the ports; fat cattle did not cease to be important, but they undoubtedly bulked less large than formerly.[28] The other consequence of the influence exerted by the market was that while the total number of cattle in Ireland obviously increased very greatly between the Famine and the First World War, the most striking aspect of this increase was in the number of cattle under one year old. This went up from half a million in 1850 to more than twice that figure in 1910, the implication being that the tendency was to rear calves rather than slaughter them. Since the number of milch-cows remained fairly constant during that period not fluctuating very much above or below 1½ million at any given time) it seems clear that the effect was to stabilise the dairy industry while the total number of dry cattle very nearly doubled – it rose from just under two million in 1861 to 3½ million in 1914. Given also that dairy produce by the latter date was beginning to meet heavy competition from far afield (as it already had done from European competitors, especially Denmark, from the 1860s onward) it is easy to see that the continuing demand for store-cattle would be a dominant factor influencing the Irish farmer in his choice of economic goals.

* Exports of sheep and pigs, though more subject to fluctuations caused by disease or by competition, also showed a heavy overall increase. Sheep and lambs together went up from an average 214,000 in 1850-4 to 869,000 in the early 1900s and pigs from 134,000 in 1850-4 to a high point of 626,000 in the last years of the nineteenth century.

B

The impact of this choice upon Irish society was profound and made itself felt in three principal ways. The most obvious, and one whose political implications we shall presently be examining, was a revolution in land-tenure. The old order before the Famine had rested upon a powerful, still-confident aristocracy on the one hand and upon an impoverished and insecure peasantry on the other. But whereas economic circumstances before 1850 had conspired to produce a rural proletariat, improved conditions in the second half of the nineteenth century, combined with the rudiments of education and the ability to accumulate a little capital, had begun to transform that proletariat into a bourgeoisie. Indeed, it is even possible that the very effectiveness of the Land War of the 1870s and 1880s, and the tenacity with which the tenants sustained it, may have been as much a reflection of their improved status as of their desperation. There was a solid property interest behind the land agitation and as that agitation bore fruit – first in improved conditions of tenancy, later in actual ownership – the position of this property interest was strengthened.

It remained, however, the property interest of a small farmer, for although the consolidation of holdings had gone steadily forward in the half-century after the Famine, the effect of that consolidation had not in general been to create numerous large farms. On the contrary, its achievement had been simply to substitute a tolerable competence for an intolerable deficiency. It is certainly true that the number of holdings above thirty acres stood at just under 150,000 in 1851 and that, having increased only slightly more in the next thirty years, these holdings accounted for about three-quarters of the agricultural land of the country by 1881. But in terms of numbers, farms of more than thirty acres were still in 1851 only about twenty-six per cent of the entire total of holdings of more than one acre, whereas farms of between five and thirty acres amounted to some fifty-eight per cent of the whole; these proportions were little changed at the turn of the century.[29] We have, therefore, a situation where relatively few large farms occupied a wide area – most of them, no doubt, for grazing – and where a much greater number of small farms took up much less actual space. And if we think of a typical farm as being the kind of farm on which most of the agricultural population were dependent we shall probably not be far wrong in thinking of it as being a farm of from fifteen to thirty acres, though even then it is necessary to remember that something like thirty per cent of all holdings in Ireland were still, up to 1900 at least, between five and fifteen acres in extent.* These, we may say, were small mixed farms

* The meaning of the word 'typical' tends to vary, of course, with the viewpoint of the beholder and it is perfectly possible to view Irish

on which the owners consumed a high proportion of what they grew, relying mainly upon cattle-raising or dairying for such cash profits as they might hope to make.

It was against this background that the second major consequence of economic change worked its way through Irish society. We have seen already that the pattern of population decline was linked with the tendency, especially in rural areas, towards fewer and later marriages. There is good reason to believe that this in its turn was related to the growing security and acquisitiveness of the Irish farmer. So long as his rights against his landlord were negligible or unregarded, the tenant had no incentive either to improve the land or himself to aspire to a higher standard of living, since any betterment in his condition was liable to lead to an increase in the rent asked of him. But once his legal position was protected – and effectively it was so from the Land Act of 1881 onwards – then he could begin to raise his sights socially and economically. Since cattle represented wealth, his instinct was to extend his holding, for a pastoral economy obviously required extensive rather than intensive farming; indeed, even where intensive farming was practised for the growing of crops, the very fact that the potato was losing its primary place in the countryman's diet and was being used merely as one of several staples, meant that for this purpose also more land was needed. This land seems to have been acquired partly from colonisation of waste and partly, perhaps more significantly, from the fields left vacant by continuing emigration.* But because the demand for land never lost its sharpness in an era of extensive farming the reduction of the total population did not have the effect on distribution that might have been expected. On the contrary, the farmer, with his eyes fixed on profit and in his memory the recollection of the terrible nemesis that had overtaken the pre-Famine fragmentation of holdings, had a powerful motive not only to add field to field but to bequeath the end result to his heir. To his heir – not necessarily to his family. If fragmentation was to be avoided there must be no division of the painfully acquired fields

---

agriculture as divided into small and large farms, but sociologically as well as economically there is something to be said for laying particular emphasis on the small farm which bounded the horizon of so many country folk. (See, for a view of this problem based on field-work of the 1920s, C. M. Arensberg and S. T. Kimball, *Family and Community in Ireland* (2nd ed., Cambridge, Mass. 1968), chaps. i and ii.)

* The problem of calculating reclamation is bedevilled by periodic re-classifications in the latter part of the nineteenth century of what constituted 'waste'; increasingly rigorous definition contributed, especially in 1876-8 and 1906-8, to sharp apparent declines in the total area of tillage and pasture combined. But reclamation statistics are notoriously unreliable and there had in fact been an almost unbroken decline in the decadal combined totals of tillage and pasture between 1871 and 1910 apart from a marginal improvement at the turn of the century.

among all the children. Instead, one son (not necessarily the eldest) must be selected to succeed, and one daughter (perhaps) equipped with the dowry that would enable her to make a suitable dynastic alliance with a neighbour whose affairs were in a satisfactory condition. Upon the rest of the family this unifying, centralising tendency had of course the effect of presenting them with two bleak alternatives – either to emigrate or to remain at home as relatives assisting on the farm, with little hope of ever breaking out of the pattern of perpetual bachelordom or spinsterhood that had been devised for them. Even the son destined to marry was unlikely to marry young, for his father would seldom hand on the farm until obliged to do so by old age or infirmity, and sometimes not even then. Equally, the chosen daughter must remain single until her dowry had been painfully accumulated and her marriage elaborately negotiated, frequently by a professional match-maker.

It will be clear from all this that rural society in the period between the Famine and the First World War was dominated (and is still dominated today) by the pursuit of profit interpreted in a very special and precise fashion. It is true, of course, that while some rural tyrannies may have been the product of simple avarice, the emphasis on money was also partly dictated by the steadily increasing number of things it could buy. By the end of the century country families, already long habituated to the postal order as a means of receiving remittances from their emigrant members, were becoming frequent users of the parcel post and the mail-order catalogue, while increasing ease of transport – to which the bicycle contributed vastly – brought more and more of them into contact with the country towns where general stores offered a new and exciting range of consumer goods to those who had cash to pay for them.[30] Yet it is doubtful if grown men and women endured lifelong chastity simply because of the economic benefit that would accrue to the family as a unit. Loyalty to father and mother, brother or sister, there certainly was, but it has been argued that this loyalty was powerfully reinforced by the precept and example of a Church many of whose clergy came themselves from peasant backgrounds and who, pledged to celibacy, urged upon their flocks the chastity which had become their own obsession.*

The third social consequence of the economic transformation of which we have to take account is closely linked with the second. Just as the 'typical' farm of the late nineteenth century or early twentieth century was a close-knit family unit, largely worked by the family and dedicated to the well-being of the family, so too did the character of the labour-force change. With the consolidation of holdings and the grow-

* The case for this is made by K. H. Connell in the essay 'Catholicism and Marriage in the Century after the Famine', included in his book *Irish Peasant Society* (London, 1968), pp. 113-61. It is fair to say that his thesis, which draws heavily upon literary material, is still the subject of controversy.

ing dominance of pasture-farming went a decline in the demand for agricultural labour over and above that which could be supplied by the family unit. It is difficult to generalise with confidence about the fate of the agricultural labourer since the method of identification used to describe this class at different times is by no means clear, but it does seem beyond dispute that the number employed as labourers on Irish farms underwent a very considerable reduction between the Famine and the First World War. In 1841 their total was reckoned to be 1,326,000. By 1881 this had fallen to 329,000. And in 1911, the last Census before the war, their numbers (even if we include *all* the general labourers 'the majority of whom', the Census vaguely says, 'may be assumed to be agricultural labourers') could not have amounted to more than 277,000.[31]

A reduction in numbers need not inevitably have involved a reduction in the quality of life. Indeed, given the conditions prevailing in pre-Famine Ireland, it was much more likely to result in an improvement. And in one sense, at least, there *was* an improvement. Wages certainly rose fairly steadily and where the labourer had sometimes earned as little as three shillings a week in the 1840s he could earn from twice to three times that amount thirty years later, while in the early years of the new century he might expect about eleven shillings a week over most of the country and upwards of thirteen shillings in the neighbourhood of Dublin or Belfast. Against this had to be set the fact that although he might seem to gain from being more closely attached to a wage economy, he had also to suffer its uncertainties. Employment was often seasonal and irregular and to get it at all frequently involved long journeys in every kind of weather. Moreover, the trend towards consolidation meant that farmer-employers were reluctant to set aside small plots in which the labourer could anchor himself firmly to the potato. In times past conacre had been his salvation but conacre, though it did not completely die out, became peripheral where it had been central and the labourer suffered accordingly. Unable now to be sure of growing his own food he had perforce to buy it, and when money was scarce he soon felt the pinch. Nor could he count on adequate protection against the elements. Compared with the kind of housing he had to put up with before the Famine, no doubt there was some amelioration. We know that in country districts the proportion of one-roomed cabins made of mud or some other perishable material (Class IV houses in the Census classification) declined from about forty per cent of the total in 1841 to about 1.5 per cent in 1901 and we know also that from the time the first Labourers' Acts were passed in 1883 and 1885 a sustained attempt was made to raise the standard of the rural worker's housing. Between then and 1901, 15,000 cottages had been built and another 20,000 authorised, while a further 6,000 had been supplied by Poor Law Unions. Yet, although these cottages were of good quality, and were let at a blatantly uneconomic rent (sometimes as little as sixpence or eightpence a week) there were not nearly enough of them.* Most labourers, if they no longer lived in mud cabins, still lived in dilapidated cottages, many of which were by any normal reckoning unfit for human habitation.[32]

The existence of this depressed class reminds us that if the general effect of the economic changes of the second half of the nineteenth century was to substitute a rural bourgeoisie for a rural proletariat, proletarian elements nevertheless remained. These elements, it is true, were for the most part submerged and the annals of the rural poor still await their historian. Yet, even though contemporaries also ignored the problems of the landless man, there are indications that real and potentially dangerous tensions existed in the Irish countryside, tensions which were if anything sharpened by the emergence of the family farm as the social and economic unit dominating the lives of the agricultural population. It was no accident, for example, that agricultural labourers and the smaller farmers were powerfully attracted by Fenianism; no accident that in the midst of the very Land War which gave the tenants their long looked-for security, there was resentment amongst the wage-earners that their interests were being overlooked; and no accident, finally, that reformers, from Michael Davitt and William O'Brien at the turn of the century to the framers of the Democratic Programme of the first Dáil in 1919, turned their attention increasingly to what Wolfe Tone had long ago called 'that large and respectable class – the men of no property'.† Yet if that large and respectable class signally failed, as it did, to become also a revolutionary class, this was not only because it shared to the full the deep and instinctive conservatism of the countryman, but also because it was, as a class, steadily becoming less large and therefore less formidable. Of all sections of the rural population the landless man – the man, that is, without even any expectations that he would ever own land – was the least rooted in the soil, the least likely to resist the pressures and temptations that would drive or attract him to Dublin, Birmingham or Boston. For this class, therefore, even more than for the nation as a whole, emigration, while remaining a human tragedy, had become an economic and social necessity.

(v)

Throughout the entire history of the Union, Irishmen analysing the economic condition of their country, however much they might argue about the state of agriculture, were agreed in deploring both the lack of industrial development and the fact that this, with some significant

* Particularly if one adds to the labourers the very poor tenants who occupied holdings of less than four pounds' annual valuation and who in many cases sought to augment their meagre income by casual labour. As late as 1911 there were still 161,000 such holdings.

† These developments are treated pp. 216-17, 402-3

54

exceptions, was concentrated in the northeastern corner of the island. The exceptions were probably more important than contemporaries were able to realise, and some of them – for example, textiles, distilling and shipbuilding – had a history of considerable growth even in the first half of the nineteenth century. Nevertheless, it remains true that over most of Ireland the conditions for speedy, extensive and successful industrialisation simply did not exist. The rapid decline of the population in the decades after the Famine; the poverty of the people and the retarding effect of the land system upon their ability to accumulate substantial savings and thus to provide either the nucleus for industrial development or a market for its products; the frequently disturbed state of the country; the scarcity of coal and of raw materials; the cost and difficulty of transporting Irish goods to centres of trade other than Britain, or for that matter to Britain itself; the impossibility of building up manufactures in a backward country under a free trade regime which exposed it to the formidable rivalry of far more highly developed competitors – all these things together combined to make Ireland a place where, with a few important exceptions, businessmen preferred not to risk capital in the hazardous enterprise of creating new industry in so unpromising an economy. And in the last resort it was unwillingness to take certain minimal risks that lay at the heart of the problem. For although it is probably true to say that large concentrations of capital were rare in Ireland before the Famine (and none too frequent outside the northeast even after that date) there were quantities of uninvested, or under-invested, money which were gradually attracted into substantial enterprises such as railway building. On the other hand, it has to be admitted that a good deal of such capital as existed was either invested out of Ireland altogether or, as frequently happened, was diverted from business use by the Irishman's obsessive pursuit of status, measured either by the acquisition of land or by the education of his children to seek their fulfilment in a profession rather than in trade.*

But perhaps it is an over-simplification to speak of 'an economy'. Historians have lately begun to suggest that there were really two economies – a maritime and a subsistence economy, increasingly differentiated since the eighteenth century. The former, it is argued, existed mainly along the eastern coastal fringe from Belfast to Cork (with offshoots in Limerick and Galway) and in this there had developed a cash economy tied to that of England by trade, traffic of people and growth of credit – in short, an outward-looking community which was a part, even if a peripheral part, of a wider world. At its back, and supplying it with its cheap labour and some of its essential foodstuffs, was the rural, subsistence economy on which – by the time of the Famine – depended about three-quarters of the population, if we in-

* On this general theme, see J. Lee, 'Capital in the Irish Economy', in L. M. Cullen (ed.), *The Formation of the Irish Economy* (Cork, 1969), pp. 53-63.

clude the inhabitants of small towns and villages as well as the actual workers on the land. This was a population with so little cash to dispose of, and therefore so little sense of what could be done with it, that cases were known, in the early nineteenth century, of money being pawned rather than put to commercial use. But, indeed, there was little commercial use to which it could be put, for there was no retail trade to speak of and over wide areas a barter system still prevailed.[33]

This concept of two economies is useful provided it is not pushed too far, or the lines of division between them too precisely demarcated. Where it has been too heavily stressed the concept has come under severe criticism from scholars who point out both that some of the conditions regarded as typical of the nineteenth century were already present in the eighteenth, and that the contrast between 'maritime' and 'subsistence' was less a contrast between economic health and economic sickness than between varying degrees of the same fragility.* The geographical distinction between east and west was by no means absolute, for behind every maritime 'pocket' there was a subsistence hinterland which, as the population grew in the decades before the Famine, pressed ever more insistently upon the scattered outposts of economic civilisation. Moreover, although the maritime economy may have appeared buoyant by the side of its subsistence neighbour, its very sensitivity to external factors made it in some ways more vulnerable than the somnolent countryside. Thus, whereas the maritime centres prospered in the late eighteenth century and in the early years of the nineteenth (a prosperity shared as we saw earlier, by the agricultural sector), they were particularly exposed to the effects of the rapid inflation which set in with the French wars and was intensified by the suspension of cash payments enforced, in Ireland as in England, from 1797 until 1821. On the short term, this inflation and the consequent price-rise helped to produce boom conditions which lasted so long as the wartime demand for Irish produce (mainly foodstuffs) continued. Once that demand had ceased, however, depression swiftly followed with its inevitable concomitant of high unemployment, creating internal tensions which were aggravated by serious crop failures, especially of potatoes, in 1817, 1819 and 1822.

The fact that the depression dragged on so long after Waterloo led many contemporaries – and has since led a number of historians – to look behind the immediate crisis to the passing of the Act of Union as

* Two revisionist essays by L. M. Cullen should be noted: 'Problems in the interpretation and revision of eighteenth century Irish economic history', in *Transactions of the Royal Historical Society*, 5th series, xvii (1967); 'The hidden Ireland: re-assessment of a concept', in *Studia Hibernica*, No. 9 (1969). The most forthright statement of the concept of the dual economy is in P. Lynch and J. Vaizey, *Guinness's Brewery in the Irish Economy, 1759-1876* (Cambridge, 1960). For an important criticism of the point of view embodied in that book, see J. Lee, 'The dual economy in Ireland, 1800-50', in T. Desmond Williams (ed.), *Historical Studies*, vii (1971).

the ultimate source of Ireland's economic woes. It was true, of course, that the Union did have the effect of binding the country closer to Britain economically as well as politically, and true also that the links were perceptibly tightened by the coming into force of full free trade within the British Isles in 1825 and by the assimilation of the British and Irish currencies in the following year.[34] Nor can it be denied that those Irish industries – notably wool and cotton – which still depended on obsolete methods of production were soon overwhelmed by the competition from the more cheaply manufactured English goods which began to come on the market in increasing quantities after cross-channel transport costs had been reduced by the introduction of steamships in and after 1824.* To this, however, it is necessary to add two comments. One is that not all industry in Ireland was similarly distressed. On the contrary, not only was there the growth as already mentioned in certain key sectors – we shall see presently how pronounced this was in shipbuilding, brewing and distilling, and linen – but there were also numerous widely dispersed local industries, mainly craft in character and reflecting both the skills and the needs of an agrarian society. It is true that some of these later became vulnerable to competition from their more highly organised rivals in Britain, but up to the Famine they at least held their own. And the other is that such stringency as did exist in the decade after 1815 may have owed something to the 'sound money' policies of the day which, in an attempt to counteract the wartime inflation, may have promoted, almost inadvertently, an excessive degree of deflation. Not too much, however, should be made of this argument. It is unwise to impute too much conscious determination to the fairly amateurish manoeuvres of the British Treasury and the Bank of Ireland. And although there was indeed a depreciation of the Irish pound just after Waterloo, the weight of opinion nowadays inclines to the view that the post-war depression was part of a wider and more complex situation in which monetary devaluation counted for very little.†

* It is, however, unlikely that steam transport, though more reliable and regular than sail, substantially reduced costs until the 1850s, when technological advance at last enabled the steamship to compete with the sailing-ship which up to that time had continued to hold a commanding position in the cross-channel trade. For information on this subject, I am indebted to Mr G. Bowie, of University College, Dublin.

† A traditional nationalist argument has always been that the monetary difficulties Ireland experienced were accentuated – or even caused – by the export of capital from the country in the form of rents paid to absentee landlords. Some movement of this kind did undoubtedly take place – which absence of statistics makes it impossible to measure though it may have been as much as £2 million a year for most of the nineteenth century – but there seems to be growing support for the view that it could not have been very large, given that the estates of most absentee landlords lay within the subsistence area. If the argument were extended to include all rents and not just absentee rents it might have greater

57

It is usually assumed that this chronic shortage of money only began to be rectified after the Famine had drastically established a less extreme ratio between the size of the population and the amount of the circulating medium. This is broadly true, but, like the distinction between the two economies, it must not be pressed too far. Not only are there indications that the use of cash was becoming slowly more widespread in some parts of the country in the decade or so before the Famine, but the always somewhat artificial barrier between the maritime and the subsistence sectors had begun to be diminished by two major developments. The first of these was the coming of the railways. With the opening of six miles of track between Dublin and Kingstown in 1834 there began a transformation of Irish transport which, despite early setbacks and later criticisms, was to have far-reaching effects upon the economic situation. Within fifteen years the mileage had increased to 361, and although the major expansion was to come in the second half of the nineteenth century – by 1912 the total was 3,403 miles – the foundation was laid during the Famine years.

But if the railways were one of the most striking achievements of nineteenth century technology in Ireland, their contribution to the economy was somewhat ambiguous. On the one hand, it could fairly be claimed for them that they greatly reduced transport costs, thus opening up remote parts of the country to a range of consumer goods wider and cheaper than ever before, while at the same time facilitating the growth of Irish exports, especially cattle, at competitive prices. On the other hand, the process of opening up the country could also lead to emptying it, and it is undeniable that the same network which brought commodities to rural outposts so swiftly also took emigrants away from them with equal ease. In addition – and this was an ever-recurring contemporary complaint – the railway companies, by reason of the cheap carriage they provided, exposed local industries such as

---

validity, for there seems little doubt that a large part of the rental of Irish land went either to pay the annual debt on mortgages held by English or Dublin insurance companies, or was spent on imported goods, or else was lodged in Irish banks whose gaze was firmly fixed on the London money-market. It even seems that the outflow from the provinces may from time to time have been balanced by an inflow of capital into the eastern towns, largely as a result of increasing government expenditure. For the present state of the controversy see P. Lynch and J. Vaizey, *Guinness's Brewery in the Irish Economy, 1759-1876* (Cambridge, 1960), pp. 27-8 and sources there listed; also R. D. C. Black, *Economic Thought and the Irish Question* (Cambridge, 1960), chap. iii, especially pp. 79-81; J. Lee, 'Capital in the Irish Economy' in L. M. Cullen, op. cit., pp. 53-63; L. M. Cullen, 'The Re-interpretation of Irish Economic History', *Topic*, no. 13 (1967), Pennsylvania. For the question of inflation and deflation in the early years of the nineteenth century, see J. Lee, 'The dual economy in Ireland, 1800-50', op. cit., pp. 198-201, and F. W. Fetter (ed.), *The Irish Pound* (London, 1955), pp. 52-5.

brewing and milling to outside competition (from Dublin as much as from England) which too often overwhelmed them. No doubt this tendency was helped by the policy, followed in Ireland as elsewhere, of giving preferential rates to through traffic at the expense of local traffic. But to this accusation – as also to the parallel accusation that Irish railways had been expensive to build and maintain from the beginning – geography and demography combined to give a crushing answer. A largely rural economy catering for a falling population, with its chief towns on the coast, lacking minerals and debarred by nature from enjoying a lucrative international through-traffic, was bound to find its railways as costly as they were necessary. And neither private enterprise nor the much touted alternative of nationalisation was likely to resolve the paradox which haunted Ireland in the nineteenth century and still does so to-day. It is the paradox that, as a modern authority has well put it, 'before 1850 economic development had been hindered by an underdeveloped transport network. Since 1850 Ireland has been an underdeveloped economy with a highly developed transport system.'*

No less catalytic was the second agency of change – the growth of joint-stock banking. During the inflationary period of the French wars the scene had been dominated by the firmly-based Bank of Ireland (founded in 1783), though its function of note-issue was shared by a number of much less firmly-based private banks, several of which came to grief during the post-1815 depression. Partly to replace these unstable concerns by more dependable banks, and partly also to counteract the Bank of Ireland's tendency towards monopoly, the British parliament legislated in 1820, and again in 1824 and 1825, to enable what were in effect joint-stock banks to be established outside a radius of fifty Irish miles from Dublin. The first to take advantage of this facility was the Northern Bank, founded in Belfast in 1824. It was followed in rapid succession by the Hibernian and Provincial Banks (both set up in 1825), by the Belfast Bank (1827), the National Bank (Daniel O'Connell's creation of 1835), the Ulster and Royal Banks (1836), and the Munster Bank (1862) transformed in 1885 into the Munster and Leinster Bank. Most of these institutions, and also the Bank of Ireland itself from 1825 on, were active in establishing branch-offices and by the time of the Famine few Irish towns of any size were without a joint-stock branch of some sort. In 1850 the total number of banks doing business in the whole of Ireland was 165; by 1870 the total was 304 (including sub-offices) and by 1910 this had gone up to 809, and whereas in 1840 the banks together held deposits and cash balances amounting only to about five-and-a-half million pounds, by 1910 this figure had been multiplied almost ten times.[35] It is true that the banks were criticised for not using these deposits to stimulate productive enterprise inside Ireland and the criticism was probably just. But in their defence it may

* This is the conclusion reached by J. Lee in his illuminating essay, 'The Railways in the Irish Economy', in L. M. Cullen (ed.), *The Formation of the Irish Economy*, pp. 77-87.

be said that they would have found it difficult to establish a policy markedly different from that followed by their powerful opposite numbers in England and that in any event their conservatism mirrored rather than influenced the habits of their own best customers. Their real achievement was rather to familiarise a backward country with the use of money and gradually to place the whole mechanism of credit on a more stable and less extortionate basis than before.

Yet if the 'subsistence' economy was steadily being linked more closely with the 'maritime' economy by the development of transport, and if the use of money was becoming gradually more pervasive, this did not disturb the economic supremacy of the maritime sector, a supremacy which rested securely upon a near monopoly of commerce and manufactures. In the achievement of this supremacy both Dublin and Belfast played major roles, but whereas the capital remained primarily a financial centre and an essential link in the import and export trade of the country, it was of course the northern city – more precisely the Lagan valley which it dominated – that provided Ireland's one example of large-scale industrialisation. Initially, it was an industrialisation based not upon the traditional northern industry of linen, but upon new-fangled cotton. In the course of the eighteenth century Belfast had become a thriving port which had developed a considerable foreign trade, much of it with the West Indies and the American colonies, sending out linen and foodstuffs, importing sugar, timber, coal, flax-seed, bleaching materials and wines and spirits. Linen at that time was still very much a domestic industry carried on in farm-houses and cottages all over the north and several towns besides Belfast had markets where the brown or unbleached linen could be bought and sold. By the 1780s, however, a considerable trade in white (bleached) linen had begun to grow up round Belfast and the exports resulting therefrom were increasingly sold through that port rather than through Dublin.

This flourishing domestic industry was undoubtedly one source of the capital which would be needed if the city were ever to make the great leap forward to a factory system. A second source was the external trade of the port in which considerable fortunes could be made even in the eighteenth century. A third source, often suggested as the key to industrial advance in Ulster, was the alleged prosperity of the farming community, itself said to be the product of the Ulster custom, that gave the tenant reasonable security in his holding and allowed him to sell his interest in his farm, thus making possible modest savings which were then available for investment. It is in fact doubtful if this had as much influence as is commonly believed, for in the early decades of important textile development Ulster farming, as no less an authority than Arthur Young testified, was in a very backward condition. The weaver-farmer managed to support life by combining his meagre agricultural and industrial earnings, but it is unlikely that he had much spare cash for investment. We shall probably be safer if we look for our key factor to the capital, skill and marketing experience of the

Huguenots who came to the north of Ireland at the beginning of the eighteenth century. It was their presence which made the crucial difference when the right moment for the technological breakthrough arrived.* At first, it seemed as if the introduction of cotton-spinning into Belfast in 1777 had provided precisely this right moment. Once established, the new industry grew quickly from 8,000 spindles in or around the city in 1790 to at least three times that number by 1811. Simultaneous with this growth was the introduction of steam power, with its inevitable concomitant of an increasing concentration of labour into mills and factories. By 1810 cotton manufacture engaged 2,000 people in Belfast alone, and by 1813 there was at least one factory which employed 300 people.

Yet cotton, though it continued to expand into the post-1815 years, was always something of an exotic growth. Its raw material and its technical expertise alike came from outside and its development had initially depended upon the protection granted to it by the old Irish parliament before the Union. But behind its tariff wall the industry had enjoyed a pampered existence, producing inferior goods at high cost for a too limited market. When the disappearance of that protection coincided with the rapid advance of cotton-spinning in Lancashire the fate of the Ulster industry was sealed. Fortunately, there was an alternative road to salvation, though it was only chance that pointed it out. In 1828 one of the leading cotton-mills in Belfast (that belonging to the firm of Mulholland) was burnt down. After much anxious consideration it was decided (so the managing director's son later recorded) 'that as the English and Scottish competition in the cotton-spinning business was so great, and as the linen trade was the natural business of Ireland, it would be advisable in rebuilding the mill to adapt it for the spinning of flax by machinery, which was accordingly done'.[36] Momentous consequences followed from this decision. The reconstructed mill was such a resounding success that other firms soon followed Mulholland's example. Within ten years the pendulum had swung from cotton to linen and the Lagan valley was launched on a new and prosperous course. Nor was it only linen that profited from this development. Machinery needed to be maintained, improved and eventually replaced. To supply these needs there grew up an engineering industry at first ancillary but then so important in its own right that it acquired an international reputation and a flourishing export market.[37]

Already by the eve of the Famine this industrial renaissance was making its impact on the demographic pattern of the province. Movement from the countryside into the towns, and especially of course into Belfast, was facilitated first by the expansion of the road system from the end of the eighteenth century onwards, and then by the coming of the railways in and after 1839. Thus the city which in 1800 had

* For a radical reassessment of tenant right in Ulster, and elsewhere in Ireland, see Barbara Solow, *The Land Question and the Irish Economy, 1870-1903* (Harvard and London, 1972), chap. 2.

numbered probably no more than 20,000 people, had risen to 75,000 (including nearly 5,000 just outside the municipal boundary) in 1841. It was still much smaller than Dublin (which in 1841 had a population of about a quarter of a million) and slightly smaller than Cork, but as early as 1835 it had emerged – in terms of the value of its trade – as the premier port of the whole country, exporting in that year nearly eight million pounds' worth of goods, about half of which consisted of linen. But so far as textiles were concerned, this was only the beginning. It was in the twenty years after the Famine that the most rapid and massive expansion took place, marked, as was to be expected, by ever increasing mechanisation and centralisation. Even so early as 1850 over three-quarters of the flax spindles in Ireland were in Antrim and Down, and whereas in 1852 there was only a single power-loom in the Belfast linen industry, ten years later there were 6,000. The increased output resulting from all this new machinery found its markets mainly in Britain and the United States, and although the latter was temporarily barred by the American Civil War, this loss was more than compensated by the accompanying cotton famine which in its turn led to an unprecedented demand for Irish linen. The response to this demand enabled the industry to transform itself from its former part-handicraft part-machine basis to a virtually complete system of factory organisation; by the end of the nineteenth century there were no less than 828,000 spindles and 31,000 power-looms in full-time operation.

Yet if this was a success story, it was not a story only of success. As the industry grew larger and more heavily dependent on world markets it became more sensitive to world conditions and especially to the competition of its old enemy, cotton. Here it was at a serious disadvantage. Cotton was cheaper to make than linen, could be finished in a greater variety of ways and could easily be developed as a mass product. Linen, by contrast, paid a high price for one of its own chief virtues, its durability. Not only that, the very fact of its expansion meant that it far out-stripped its original domestic source of raw material, drawing decade by decade more and more freely upon the cheaper flax grown on the continent, especially in Belgium, Holland and Germany. Where in 1853 175,000 acres had been devoted to growing flax in Ireland, in 1914 the acreagre was just under 50,000. On the eve of the First World War the amount of Irish flax available for the industry was only 8,000 tons, compared with nearly 37,000 tons imported from abroad. The very existence of foreign flax implied also the threat of competition from foreign linen, and in spinning especially continental manufacturers, with their lower wages and longer hours, were able to produce certain types of yarn more cheaply than their Irish counterparts. Weavers, in Ireland as elsewhere, no doubt benefited from this development, but the growth of tariff barriers in the last quarter of the nineteenth century set a limit to the extent to which the market could be widened. Thus, although the labour force in the Irish industry (employed in linen mills and factories of all kinds) went up from 21,000 in 1850 to 60,000 in 1875, it hovered about that mark for the next quarter of a century and even by 1914 had risen no higher than 73,000. In terms of exports the peak was reached between 1910 and 1912; in the first of those years linen yarn exported from Ireland was almost 24¾ million pounds, and on the latter date the quantity of linen goods produced amounted to just over 1¼ million hundredweight.[38] What this amounted to in terms of value is more difficult to calculate, but an attempt was made in the Census of Industrial Production of 1907 to arrive at the value of output after deducting the cost of materials and certain other expenses. For linen and hemp together this amounted in that year to £4·4 million of which slightly more than half was accounted for by linen yarn, cordage, rope and twine.[39]

By whatever tests one cares to apply this was clearly a major industry, at least by the modest standards to which Ireland was accustomed. Even though the later years of the nineteenth century had not been free of crisis, the linen trade was still well placed to profit from the boom times of the First World War. Thereafter, as we shall see presently, it entered on hard times, made harder still by its vulnerability to competition from other fabrics, especially the man-made fabrics which were then beginning to come into fashion.* If this was true of linen, the keystone of the Irish cloth industry, it was even more true of less well-established textiles. Most of these textiles – for example, lace-work or the manufacture of poplin – continued into the twentieth century on a minor scale, carried on mainly by out-workers in their own homes or in small and compact factories. To this, however, there were two significant exceptions, one recent and one much older. The new arrival was the shirt and collar industry which began to be concentrated into one principal centre – the city of Londonderry – in the second half of the nineteenth century. The technical innovation that made this possible, the sewing-machine, was introduced into Londonderry in 1856. After half a century of growth the town contained thirty-eight firms employing about 18,000 people and giving work to perhaps another 80,000 in the countryside who were employed in the making-up side of the business. It was a high-productivity industry, exporting just before the First World War about twenty million collars a year, valued at upwards of one million pounds.[40] It too was to benefit from wartime contracts, but, like linen, was to be exposed to mounting competition in the years after 1918. It resembled the linen industry in another sense also, both being largely dependent on female labour. In Londonderry, indeed, opportunities for men were almost non-existent and the socially degrading pattern of the present-day town, with large numbers of men out of work and living on the wages of their wives and daughters, was on the way to being established even before 1914. In the linen industry reliance on young and female labour was also heavy. In the last quarter of the nineteenth century about twenty-five

* For these developments see Part IV B, chap. 2.

per cent of the work force consisted of juveniles under eighteen years of age and about seventy per cent of the whole total were women. But Belfast had the advantage that was denied to Londonderry of being able to redress the imbalance of the sexes by the employment of male labour, not only on the heavier tasks in the linen industry, but also in shipbuilding, engineering, ropemaking and allied trades.

The other industry, wool and woollen goods, was much less centralised, and much less sophisticated, than linen. Spread up and down the country, in the first half of the nineteenth century it was relatively prosperous, but in the second half, under the stress of competition, it shrank in upon itself. In 1856, it has been estimated, there were only thirty-three woollen mills in the whole of Ireland and though this situation steadily improved it was not until the early years of the new century that the total exceeded one hundred. By then there had been some mechanisation, but even so the labour force disclosed by the Census of Production in 1907 was just under 4,500, divided almost equally between men and women.[41] Within the industry there was a good deal of diversification and the range was considerable, varying from friezes, homespuns and blankets to flannels, cheviots, dress-cloths and suitings. Some of the finer products were made from yarn, or even raw wool, specially imported for the purpose, and, as the domestic market was small and poor, and therefore unable to absorb the home-grown wool, large quantities of the latter were exported. By 1913, for example, Ireland was importing not only about a quarter of a million pounds' worth of yarn, but also raw wool to the value of £185,000; her own exports of raw wool at the same date were worth about half a million pounds and in previous years had sometimes gone above this total. In 1907 the net value of the industry's output of finished woollen goods was £248,000 and there are indications of a steady increase on this figure between then and the outbreak of the war, reaching ultimately about £678,000 in 1914.[42] In an underdeveloped economy like that of Ireland this was a not insignificant achievement, but its magnitude should not be overestimated. No amount of contemporary emphasis on the industry's potentialities could disguise the fact that its entire labour force was about a fifth of the numbers employed in a single Belfast shipyard or that its total wage-bill was less even than a fifth of the wage-bill of that one yard.

To contrast the wool trade with shipbuilding is, of course, to attempt to compare incompatibles, or rather to confront the old industrialism with the new. For among textiles only linen had really taken the imprint of the technological revolution, and even linen, as we have seen, was rooted in an ancient tradition. Shipbuilding, on the other hand, was an artificial creation. More truly, perhaps, than anything else it represented the triumph of human ingenuity over the many obstacles Ireland presented to the growth of heavy industry in an environment where coal supplies were inadequate and iron and steel virtually non-existent. Ships, indeed, had been built in Irish ports, and particularly in Belfast, for generations, but it was not until the second quarter of the nineteenth century, and then only very gradually, that the possibility of a major transformation, both of scale and of technique, began to emerge. The foundation for this development was laid when in 1792 two brothers, William and John Ritchie, arrived from Scotland to set up as ship-builders. They prospered greatly during the Napoleonic wars – William was later to earn the title of 'father of Belfast shipbuilding' – and it was his firm (more precisely Ritchie and McLaine) which in 1820 built the first steamboat in Ireland.

This early venture was, however, premature, and although Belfast was linked with Britain by a more or less regular steamship service only four years later, the vessels employed were not built in Ireland. The reason for the hiatus may partly have been the lack of local capital and initiative, but it may also have had something to do with the fact that although Belfast had begun to emerge as a centre for building wooden ships of fairly moderate size, it would never be able to tackle anything more ambitious until the facilities of the port itself had been im-proved. What was needed was more quays and deeper water in the river channel at the head of the lough. These works were begun in 1837 and in little more than four years the first bend of the old twisting channel of the Lagan had been eliminated by the deep cut on which, as has been said, 'the whole future prosperity of Belfast was built'. In 1847 the existing port authorities were replaced by a more dynamic body, the Harbour Commissioners, and under their impulse another deep water cut was made and the quays were further extended. In the last quarter of the nineteenth century alone nearly 10,000 linear feet of quay space was added to the port's resources.

One of the most crucial decisions of the Harbour Commissioners was to separate trading from shipbuilding, and from this flowed a second decision, to allocate part of the land reclaimed in the course of their improvements – the Queen's Island – to the latter function. This oppor-tunity to build ships in an exceptionally favourable site was seized initially (in 1853) not by a recognised ship-builder, but by Robert Hickson, the owner of the newly established Belfast Iron Works. Pri-marily concerned to seek an outlet for the iron plates manufactured in his foundry, he nevertheless revolutionised the industry by appointing as his manager one of the great creative geniuses in the history of ship-building, Edward Harland. When he arrived in Belfast in 1854, Harland, a doctor's son from Scarborough, was still only twenty-three and had little but an engineering apprenticeship at Newcastle to recommend him. Within a few years he had proved himself to such a degree that Hickson sold him his interest and Harland took full control, assisted, and then partnered, by the brilliant marine draughtsman, G. W. Wolff. Har-land recruited him in 1858, probably as part of a bargain with Wolff's uncle, G. C. Schwabe, the man responsible for putting the partners in touch with the great Liverpool firm of Bibby's, whose orders laid the real basis for the prosperity of Harland and Wolff.

The partners were fortunate in that they came together at a time of economic expansion, when the demand for larger ships was steadily growing, but they also reaped a just reward for their readiness to innovate and to take risks. Harland himself, for example, was the pioneer of the idea that if an iron ship were increased in length without a corresponding increase of beam its carrying capacity for both cargo and passengers would be greater. Older hands warned him that his ships would break their backs, but he solved this problem by making the upper deck entirely of iron, and in the event Belfast rapidly became famous for its big ships. In other respects – the construction of vessels with flatter bottoms, experimentation with marine engines, the development of large passenger liners – Harland and Wolff towered over their rivals. The liner trade effectively began when the first White Star Line contract was signed in 1869. From this derived not only a whole series of ocean-going passenger steamers, from the *Oceanic* in 1870 to the *Titanic* in 1912, but also the recruitment of another great innovator, W. J. Pirrie. Unlike the two original partners, Pirrie was of Ulster origin (though born in Quebec) and after a childhood spent in county Down he entered the firm as an apprentice. Rapidly establishing himself as a draughtsman of outstanding ability, he became a partner in 1874 when he was only twenty-seven. Thirty years later he took over sole control and retained it until his death in 1924. Like his precursors Pirrie was remarkable for his ability to think ahead of other competitors. It was during his ascendancy, for instance, that Harland and Wolff began to build the engines for their own ships. And it was Pirrie himself who recognised very early that oil was to be the fuel of the future and who in 1912 concluded an agreement with the Danish holders of the patent for the Diesel engine allowing him to manufacture such engines near Glasgow (in the works specially bought for the purpose), where they could be fitted into the firm's ships. Even more striking was the expansion of Harland and Wolff's business from building ships to sailing them. Here again Pirrie was the prime mover. He became a director of the White Star Line and of many other shipping companies, especially those concerned with passenger traffic, for the hard-headed Presbyterian shipbuilder was possessed by his conception (in due course fully realised, like most of his conceptions) of a liner as a floating hotel, an idea he pursued with a passion and success which might have moved even Arnold Bennett to envy.

Harland and Wolff were the giants of the Irish shipbuilding industry, though they did not quite monopolise it. Outside Belfast, indeed, it was a negligible quantity – except for small works carried on in Dublin, Larne, Londonderry, Queenstown and Warrenpoint – but on the further side of the Lagan, opposite the Queen's Island, a second important firm began business in 1879, though it did not have the stamina or resources of Harland and Wolff and closed down in 1934. This was Workman and Clark, which specialised in rather smaller ships, but also gained an international reputation, chiefly from its readiness to transfer from iron to steel and to pioneer the use of steam-turbine engines.

What did all this ingenuity and hard work amount to in practical terms? The statistics are not unimpressive. In 1842 the total tonnage of ships built in Ireland was 1,042. The figure did not exceed 1,000 tons again until 1850 and only began to mount steadily in the 'sixties and 'seventies after Harland and Wolff had begun their main expansion. By 1891 the total had risen to 103,466 tons for that year alone and, although fluctuations continued, that decade and the next were marked by intense activity, the annual figure seldom falling below 100,000 tons and in 1914 reaching 256,547. This, it should be noted, represented commercial tonnage only and took no account of considerable Admiralty contracts. In most of these years Harland and Wolff had the lion's share. By the outbreak of the First World War they were employing over 12,000 men, with Workman and Clark not far behind at 10,000.[43] It is more difficult to assess accurately the value of the product since large ships took a long time to complete and the graph of profits zigzagged accordingly, but the Census of Industrial Production in 1907 estimated that the combined gross output of iron, steel, engineering and shipbuilding taken together was just under six million pounds.[44]

It was perhaps symptomatic of the lack of a broad industrial base in Ireland that this group – corresponding to what elsewhere would have been regarded as one of the largest and most important in the economy – should have actually ranked only third, being subordinate to textiles, which in 1907 had a gross output valued at nearly sixteen million pounds, and to the food and drink trades which dominated the list of manufactures with an estimated gross output of £27⅓ million. The supremacy of this last group reflected the overwhelming importance of agriculture, but it owed at least some of its commanding position to two industries which, in addition to supplying the home demand, had gained a footing in international markets during the nineteenth century. The smaller of these was the manufacture of biscuits. Biscuits were produced in Belfast, Londonderry and Dublin, but it was in Dublin, and especially in the firm of W. and R. Jacob, that the trade was most highly developed. In 1907 the industry as a whole employed nearly 10,000 people and, if all the products of the bakeries are included, its output had a net value of almost a million pounds. It was and remained essentially an export industry, sending out each year vastly greater quantities of biscuits than were imported even from the very competitive English firms in Reading and elsewhere. On the eve of the First World War imports amounted to just under 90,000 hundredweight, whereas exports totalled 332,000 hundredweight, and this pattern was characteristic of the whole decade before 1914. During the fifteen years 1904–18 the value of imports was £1¾ million as against an export trade worth £8⅔ million.[45]

This was naturally a highly specialised and ultimately a strictly limited business, but the liquor industry was quite a different matter.

In both its main branches – brewing and distilling – Ireland had a world-wide fame and large export surpluses. Each branch had an ancient history, but the modern expansion in the manufacture of beer and porter was closely identified with the fortunes of a single firm – Arthur Guinness and Sons. Founded in Dublin in 1759 the firm grew steadily, and then more rapidly, until by 1800 its production of thirty-six-gallon barrels had reached the 10,000 mark. Progress in succeeding years was more chequered but the figure of 100,000 barrels in one year was reached in 1846, during the worst part of the Famine. Thirty years later the annual total exceeded three-quarters of a million barrels and by the turn of the century it is probable that Guinness's accounted for about two-thirds of all the beer and porter produced in Ireland. By 1914 this global total had reached the imposing figure of $3\frac{1}{2}$ million barrels.[46] A few years earlier, when the Census of Industrial Production attempted to estimate the value of the gross output – which was even then only just short of $3\frac{1}{2}$ million barrels – the figure given was almost £6 million, though the net total of £$3\frac{1}{2}$ million was perhaps more realistic.[47]

Breweries throughout the nineteenth century and up to the First World War were widely scattered through the country, many of them of long-standing and of considerable prosperity. The distilling of spirits by pot-stills, though also much dispersed, showed as time went on a greater tendency towards concentration. Whereas at the end of the nineteenth century there were twenty-nine distilleries in operation, by 1914 this had been reduced to twenty-two and was soon to be diminished still further. In 1907 the industry employed some 2,400 people (as against 6,600 occupied in brewing), but its productivity was higher than this might suggest. In that year the Irish industry distilled twelve million proof gallons and exported about two-thirds of this total. The net value of this output was about half a million pounds but when sold in the export market its price was of course much greater, and the 1907 exports were actually worth about £$2\frac{1}{3}$ million; thereafter, steeply mounting duties, added to a general price-rise, made it increasingly difficult to relate the income from sales to the cost of production and in 1918 a much reduced export of three million proof-gallons brought in no less than £$3\frac{3}{4}$ million.[48]

If we ask how far this industrial growth was reflected in higher pay for the workers we shall find evidence of some advance, though, in certain areas, of curiously uneven and unsustained advance. Geographical differences and varieties of employment make it almost impossible to generalise about industrial wages, but a few examples may serve to illustrate the trend. On the eve of the Famine a bricklayer (i.e. a tradesman) could get as much as twenty-five shillings a week, whereas a labourer might earn only nine shillings. In the generation after the Famine Guinness's (who even then had a reputation as benevolent employers) were paying their labourers twelve to thirteen shillings a week; in Dublin as a whole the average earnings of the head of a family just before the First World War was just under sixteen shillings, though the average per entire family (based on a 1910 survey of 1,254 families) was 22/6, with the majority earning less than a pound a week. At that time it was probably the case that the wages of unskilled men in Dublin were from a quarter to a third less than those of their counterparts in Britain; skilled men came off rather better, but even they may have earned from ten to twenty per cent less than if they had crossed the Irish Sea.

In the north things seem to have been a little easier. There, in the early 1900s, a builder's labourer could earn about one pound a week, though in bad times and in depressed areas like Londonderry, this could drop to eighteen, or even twelve, shillings. Craftsmen, on the other hand, could get from thirty-six shillings in the building trade to two pounds or more in engineering or shipbuilding. In the linen industry, with its predominance of female and child labour, wage-rates were generally low. As late as 1906 the average was twelve shillings (men, however, could earn twice that), but this, little though it seems, was more than double the average paid in 1850. It has been reckoned, indeed, that in terms of real wages the rise between 1850 and 1906 was more like two hundred per cent. Against this has to be set the fact that in all these industries, in the north as well as in the south, there was constant and considerable underemployment, especially among the general labourers.[49]

It is clear enough from this brief survey that some improvements in the wage-structure did occur between the Famine and the First World War, yet it cannot be too heavily stressed that they were insufficient to conceal the existence of deep abysses of poverty. Much the same may be said about industrial development as a whole. It had occurred, beyond doubt, but it had been too limited really to have altered the essentials of the picture.* Ireland remained at bottom an agricultural country with one industrial region and a handful of trading centres. That was the lesson driven home over and over again by the 1907 Census of Production. This established that the value of the gross output of all Irish industries at that time was £66,777,000, and even this figure has to be reduced by almost two-thirds, to £22,777,000, to arrive at a true estimate of the value of the net output.[50] By any standards this was a modest level of performance.

It was in fact so modest as to leave the economy in a permanently subservient position, overshadowed by the wealth and sophistication of its formidable neighbour. Just how marked this subservience had become can be deduced from the trade figures of the decade before the First World War. Between 1825 and 1904 no systematic separate record was kept of the total import and export trade of Ireland and even after the latter date estimates continued to be approximate, almost experimental. Of the ten years before the First World War for which we do

* The limitations were clearly exposed in the *Report of the Select Committee on Industries* (Ireland), H. C. 1884-5, ix.

have records 1906 may serve as a not untypical example. The total trade of Ireland was then £112 million, almost evenly divided between imports and exports, with the former (as they usually were) slightly ahead of the latter. About four-fifths of Irish exports went to Britain and about two-thirds of imports came from Britain.[51] This was a situation that cut two ways. On the one hand, it presented British manufacturers and importers with a strong argument for maintaining the Union. On the other hand, it seemed to present Irish nationalists with an even stronger argument for becoming the masters of their own economic destiny. Moreover, the position was disquieting from another point of view. Although the total of foreign trade was not large in itself, it *was* large in relation to the population, actually larger per head than the external trade of the United Kingdom. This meant that Ireland was extremely dependent on outside – in effect, British – markets for the sale of her commodities and that, as the first government after independence was to find out, protective tariffs would be likely to have a double-edged effect. Even in 1904, for example, the first year for which calculations were possible, the distribution of imports and exports was ominous enough. Imports of food and farm produce accounted for £20·7 million; of raw materials, for £8·8 million; of manufactured goods, for £23·8 million. Against this, agricultural exports were £30·4 million, raw materials £3·4 million and manufactures £15·3 million. The implications of this pattern were unmistakable. 'To sum up', as an acute contemporary observer remarked, 'the one broad feature of Ireland's economy is that what we produce we do not consume, and what we consume we do not produce.'[52] And although the pattern might be justified by the then prevailing free trade doctrines regarding the international division of labour – the country, it could be said, was selling in the dearest market and buying in the cheapest – nothing could disguise the prime fact of her dependence, itself a melancholy epitaph on the economic history of Ireland under the Union.

3. Government and Society

In a poor and backward country, with virtually no tradition of entre-preneurial enterprise and lacking even the leadership of an effective ruling class, the impact of government upon society must always be direct and powerful. Nineteenth century Ireland was no exception to this rule. Indeed, so far was she from being an exception that no descrip-tion of the changes which altered the context of the Irish question between the Famine and the First World War can be regarded as com-plete if it does not include some account of the tangled, tragi-comic relationship between Dublin Castle and the unruly nation over which that nerve-centre of the British administration in Ireland was intended to maintain control.

On the surface, admittedly, the situation in the second half of the nineteenth century seemed little different from the situation in the first half. The shock of the Union had long since been absorbed and the pattern of government which had begun to operate in 1801, however unacceptable politically, had rapidly acquired a degree of permanence and familiarity that made it appear almost ineradicable. The most dramatic consequence of the Union had of course been the suppression of the Irish parliament, to which distance came eventually to lend a growing but mostly undeserved enchantment. In place of that vanished legislature Ireland received a substantial representation in the two houses of the Imperial Parliament – four bishops and twenty-eight peers in the Lords, one hundred members in the Commons. The figure of one hundred was intended to be related to population, but in later years was to fluctuate between 103 and 105 even after the population had been drastically reduced. In the early years of the Union, it must be confessed, this considerable Irish influx into Westminster made little difference either to the fate of Ireland or to the British party system. The Irish members, whether they had been opposed to the Union before 1800 or not, adjusted themselves readily enough to their changed cir-cumstances and for a brief space there was, as has been well said, 'a kind of vacuum in Irish politics'.* This was presently to be filled by the

* The phrase is used by Professor J. C. Beckett in *The Making of Modern Ireland*, 1603-1923 (London, 1965), p. 285. In chap. xv of his valuable survey Professor Beckett rightly stresses what he calls the 'inner contradiction' of a Union which by perpetuating a separate administration for Ireland advertised from the very beginning the imperfections of the integration for which the younger Pitt and his advisers had hoped. Another modern

struggle for Catholic emancipation, but although Daniel O'Connell, in leading that fight, certainly galvanised the Irish question into new life, his subsequent failure to achieve the repeal of the Union, and the still more striking failure of any independent Irish parliamentary party to emerge for thirty years after his death (apart from one brief but ultimately abortive experiment in the early 1850s), seemed to indicate that although Ireland never ceased to present her masters with fearsome problems of government, at the parliamentary level at least assimilation was proceeding more or less as had been anticipated.

Time was to show that even this assumption was misguided, but circumstances would have to alter greatly before the fallacy became plain. In the meantime, and in the absence of any successful challenge to the constitutional arrangements which bound Ireland so closely to her dominant neighbour, the character of British rule after 1850 remained substantially what it had been since the Union. Responsibility for the administration of the country rested nominally in the hands of the Viceroy or Lord Lieutenant, though increasingly, as the nineteenth century wore on, real power had come to rest with the Chief Secretary, that is to say with the minister answerable to parliament for Irish affairs. Very soon after the Union this essentially political figure had begun to outshine the formal head of the government, whose functions consequently became mainly decorative and so very costly that only noblemen of vast wealth could afford to take the post. It was, however, in the fifty years after the Famine that the Chief Secretaryship really came into its own, frequently carrying with it a seat in the cabinet and also attracting some of the ablest men in British politics, for although it was notorious as a graveyard of reputations it could on occasion – as in the pre-eminent case of Arthur Balfour – lead on to higher things.

The tendency to entrust matters of policy to the Chief Secretary meant that the holders of the office habitually spent much more time in London than they did in Ireland, with the result that the day-to-day running of the country devolved more and more upon the Under-Secretary who, in the later stages of the nineteenth century, was always a permanent official and very much a civil servant of the type then becoming familiar in Whitehall. The incumbents, indeed, came from widely differing backgrounds (four of them in the fifty years after 1870 had been soldiers and others had served in the police, the post office and the Indian Civil Service), but their function remained always the same. It was primarily to oversee the ramshackle collection of boards and councils that did duty for an Irish administration, and also to provide the Chief Secretary with the information, and sometimes the advice, he needed if he was to keep his end up in the cabinet and in the House

authority, Professor Oliver MacDonagh, has described the Union as 'an act of miscalculations' for much the same reasons. The first chapter of his brilliant essay, *Ireland* (Englewood Cliffs, N.J., 1968) is the best analysis known to me of the defects inherent in the Union, defects which contained the seeds of its ultimate destruction.

of Commons. Sir Henry Robinson, though in fact not an Under-Secretary but the head of a senior department, might have spoken for Under-Secretaries as a class in the reply he gave to a characteristic question from Beatrice Webb about what kind of society he would like to see in Ireland if he had power to bring it about. 'Well, Mrs Webb', he said candidly, 'I have lived all my life at concert pitch and I really never thought of all those questions in which you are interested. What has concerned me is keeping my successive Chief Secretaries out of trouble.'[1]

As a civil servant the Under-Secretary was normally subservient to his political master, the Chief Secretary, and to the ostensible head of affairs, the Lord Lieutenant, but as the difficulties and complexities of ruling Ireland increased in the later nineteenth century so too did the potential, and sometimes the actual, power of the Under-Secretary. On at least two crucial occasions between 1900 and 1916, as we shall see presently, holders of the office played a far from subordinate role in the formulation as well as the execution of policy. Generally, however, they had their hands full with the routine business of exacting an acceptable minimum of efficiency from the creaking machinery of Irish government. By 1914 more than a hundred years of ill-regulated growth had produced some forty departments; of these, eleven were branches of departments functioning for the United Kingdom as a whole, but the remainder were solely devoted to Irish affairs. The most important matters – for example, fiscal and defence questions – were of course controlled from London and virtually all the Irish departments came in one way or another under the scrutiny of the Treasury in Whitehall. It is perhaps indicative of the extent to which the Irish civil service was dominated by its formidable neighbour that of the 26,000 officials who staffed the forty departments in 1914, only about 2,500 were employed in the twenty-nine specifically Irish departments (and eight departments absorbed eighty-three per cent of this total), whereas nearly 24,000 belonged to the United Kingdom departments operating in Ireland. It should be said in mitigation, however, that about 20,000 of these were connected with the post office and that the *corps d'élite* of the Irish administration – the forty-eight departmental heads and other senior officials – was overwhelmingly Irish in composition, though critics were quick to point out that of this higher directorate, Protestants accounted for a disproportionate twenty-eight. Nevertheless, although the amount of initiative open to these administrators was obviously limited by the amount of money allotted to the Irish departments in a budget drawn up in England and requiring the approval of the British parliament, the growing emphasis upon more and better government in the later years of the nineteenth century was to lead to a steady extension of functions and accretion of powers by the various agencies.[2]

Because Dublin Castle was, so to speak, British rule in Ireland made manifest, it was, naturally, the target for incessant nationalist attack. But although the rigidity, and sometimes the sheer incompetence, of

Irish departments certainly offered a wide target for criticism, it would be easy to take too jaundiced a view of their workings. They were not altogether as 'chaotic and effete' as one disgruntled Under-Secretary described them.[3] On the contrary, Ireland after the Union formed, as has been aptly said, 'a social laboratory' in which Englishmen were prepared to conduct experiments in government which contemporary opinion at home was not prepared to tolerate, or at least not until their success had been proven across the Irish Sea.[4] No doubt this readiness to dip a toe in the deep waters of *étatisme* was less a conscious heresy against the prevailing orthodoxies of *laissez-faire* than an almost instinctive response to the realities of life in a small and underdeveloped country, too poor to support an administrative structure based, like the English one, upon the parish, too disturbed in its history to have achieved any effective continuity in local government, and lacking above all a ruling élite numerous and selfless enough to spend time and energy on the multifarious tasks performed in England by the unpaid Justices of the Peace. Even so, and when the worst has been said that can be said of the Protestant Ascendancy class, it has to be acknowledged that the vast majority of such justices as did function, belonged to that class. As late as 1886, out of 5,000 only 1,200 were Catholics and more than half the total were landlords. Later governments attempted to redress the balance, but in 1912 the Catholic element still accounted for no more than 2,400 out of 6,000.

So inadequate was the existing machinery that it was felt necessary to supplement the unpaid amateur with the paid professional. Precedents for doing so had been established just before the Union and from these sprang two of the most characteristic Irish legal institutions of the nineteenth century.* One was the appointment of 'Assistant Barristers'

* This may be the most appropriate place to mention that the structure of higher courts existing at the time of the Union was carried over intact into the nineteenth century. It continued to administer justice, with only minor additions and amendments, until the whole system was radically overhauled by the Supreme Court of Judicature Act of 1877. This provided that the principal courts already in existence – Chancery, Queen's Bench, Common Pleas, Exchequer, Probate, Matrimonial Causes and Matters, Admiralty, and the Landed Estates Court – should be fused into one court, 'the Supreme Court of Judicature in Ireland', which was to administer law and equity concurrently. It was to have two permanent divisions, the High Court of Justice, with original jurisdiction and power to hear appeals from local courts, and the Court of Appeal, exercising appellate jurisdiction. The High Court was initially divided into five divisions but these were reduced by fusions during the next twenty years to a Chancery division of four judges and a King's Bench division of eight judges, supplemented by two judicial Commissioners concerned with land law and appointed under the Land Acts of 1881 and 1903. It should be noted, however, that these reforms, though certainly far-reaching, were not specifically Irish innovations but were rather modelled on the parallel British legislation of 1873.

to aid the Justices of the Peace at Quarter Sessions by sitting as sole and exclusive judges in cases involving civil bills. Dating initially from 1796 the powers of this office were steadily enlarged until in 1851 the Assistant Barristers became Chairmen of Quarter Sessions and in 1877 blossomed out under the new and more resplendent title of County Court Judges. The other eighteenth century precedent adapted to the needs of the nineteenth century was the 'stipendiary magistrate'. First appointed in Dublin in 1795 with special responsibility for police matters, these salaried officials were extended to the country at large in 1822 and in 1836, when the police forces were being reorganised, were divorced from their constabulary duties and transformed into magistrates resident in the various districts into which the country was divided – by 1912 there were sixty-four 'resident magistrates' functioning in every part of Ireland except Dublin. Well-paid, sometimes with previous legal experience, sometimes coming to the bench from the police or the army, they were considerable figures in their localities. No doubt their existence was often as agreeable as Somerville and Ross have described it, but it was not all hunting and shooting, and apart altogether from their judicial functions, in their regular reports to the Chief Secretary they played a role not unlike that of the inspectors of the Royal Irish Constabulary in keeping the central government informed about developments in the provinces.[5]

This trend towards closer government control over the magistracy represented not merely a drive for greater efficiency but also, of course, a form of security both for the Ascendancy class and for the Union itself. If the administration of justice in the local courts could be kept under surveillance by Dublin Castle this would in itself be a valuable safeguard against, or at least forewarning of, disaffection. And what applies to the administration of justice applies *a fortiori* to administration in general. It was noteworthy, for example, that in Ireland, even before the Famine, the tendency was for reform of local government to mean centralisation. Urban government was perhaps the most striking illustration of this point. When after long debate a Municipal Corporations Act for Ireland was passed in 1840 the cleansing of the Augean stables did not result in a process of democratisation. On the contrary, apart from the fact that fifty-eight corporations were dissolved and the administration of their boroughs entrusted either to the counties or to special commissioners in the ten that survived, the franchise was strictly limited to ten-pound householders, while the powers entrusted to these reconstructed councils were considerably less than those vested in their English counterparts. And since Dublin Castle could appoint some of their officers directly and veto any of their bylaws, it was clear that not even at the humblest level was self-rule going to mean very much.

If the watchwords of the British authorities in all that pertained to local affairs were caution, conservatism and centralisation, this was even more true of the preservation of law and order on which, after all, the entire connection with Britain in the last resort depended. Even in the earliest years of the nineteenth century Ireland had the rudiments of a police force organised by counties, and in the mid-1830s a centrally controlled national force, the Irish Constabulary, was already taking shape. Gradually this force extended its ramifications over the entire country (though the capital retained its own Dublin Metropolitan Police dating effectively from 1836) and as the Royal Irish Constabulary – which title it adopted in 1867 – assumed the primary responsibility for keeping the peace. This was never an easy task, involving as it so frequently did the quelling of outbreaks of agrarian violence or of actual revolution. The RIC was, therefore, almost of necessity an armed police operating from formidable posts scattered at strategic points through the countryside. It is revealing of the difference between the two countries that whereas in England the police were housed in a 'station', in Ireland the approved term was a 'barrack'. Inevitably, the RIC incurred a good deal of odium, especially when they were called upon to assist at evictions, and there can be no doubt that a policeman's lot in rural Ireland was often not a happy one. On the other hand, the rank-and-file were recruited from the people among whom they lived (officers were specially commissioned, the inspectorate having considerable social cachet), and the steady stream of reports going from them to their superiors, and thence to the Chief Secretary's office, revealed a remarkable range of knowledge about what went on in their districts. Gradually, they were to be drawn into all sorts of governmental duties – collecting agricultural statistics, acting as census enumerators, enforcing the fishery laws, the food and drug regulations and a host of other enactments. The numbers at their disposal were far from excessive for the work they had to do, though they fluctuated with the temper of the times. Initially composed of about 8,400 officers and men, the strength of the force went up to over 14,000 in the troubled years of the early 'eighties. On the eve of the First World War the total stood at about 12,000 to which should be added the 1,200 unarmed Dublin Metropolitan Police.[6] The RIC declined somewhat in numbers during the war (to between 9 and 10,000) and events were soon to show that this, especially when scattered among 1,400 separate establishments, was insufficient to enable it to surmount the gravest threat, the Anglo-Irish war, it had had to meet since its foundation.*

(ii)

Government intrusion into the ordinary life of the citizen was, however, by no means limited to the basic necessities of maintaining law and order. On the contrary, the 'social laboratory' of Ireland was being used, well before the Famine, for other more constructive purposes, in some respects more advanced than anything then known in England. In the

* For the ultimate fate of the RIC, see Part III, chap. 5.

field of health, for example, dispensaries, of which half the cost was met by the state, were being set up as early as 1805 and by 1840 more than six hundred were in operation. No doubt the services they rendered were minimal, but had they not existed during the Famine years an already dire situation might have been even worse. It would certainly have been worse had not each county by that time also possessed one fever hospital and one infirmary. These were partially maintained by public money, and although appointments to them were initially made by *ad hoc* local committees, here too the government, spurred on, no doubt, by the impact of the Famine, stepped in to set up a central and permanent board of health in 1850. In the overlapping field of mental health the Lord Lieutenant was empowered as early as 1817 to establish district asylums for the insane to be built and maintained at the expense of the area served, the local authorities (at that time the grand juries*) voting the necessary sums. By 1835 ten of these district asylums had been built in various parts of the country and between 1852 and 1869 another twelve were added. In 1898, after the great local government reforms of that year, the management of the asylums was transferred to the newly established county councils, but even so a measure of central control was retained both by the provision that the asylums should be subject to government inspection and by the necessity to obtain the Lord Lieutenant's approval for alterations to buildings, for revisions of the rules governing administration, and for appointments and dismissals of medical officers.[7] All these initiatives, it may be said, were not much more than gestures towards a health service which would not seriously begin to take shape for another hundred years, but in terms of unification and of centralisation, they represented a new departure that was truly radical in the nineteenth century context. 'If one takes policy and structure as the criteria', it has even been claimed, 'Ireland had one of the most advanced health services in Europe in the first half of the nineteenth century.'[8] The standards of the age, admittedly, were not exacting, and it is reasonably certain that here, as in other aspects of Irish government, performance fell far short of design; nevertheless, in this important area of public administration the evidence of originality and of willingness to experiment is undeniably striking.

Concern for health was naturally in large measure concern for the

* The grand juries were a survival from the eighteenth century and though their administrative powers diminished during the nineteenth, these did not disappear completely until the Irish Local Government Act of 1898 transferred them to elected county councils. Traditionally the grand juries were groups of property-owners in the different counties nominated by the high sheriff who was in his turn appointed by the crown. Grand juries were empowered to fix local revenues (the county cess) but in doing so were controlled partly by the fact that their 'presentments' (or appropriations) had to be approved by the judges of assize, and still more by a lively realisation that whatever money they voted would have to be met largely out of their own pockets and those of their fellow landlords.

health of the poor, and it was a similar preoccupation with the problems of poverty that led in 1838 to the extension of the English Poor Law of 1834 to Ireland. The essence of this new development was that the country was to be divided into 'unions' in each of which a workhouse was to be established. To superintend the workhouses and the general operation of poor relief boards of guardians were to be set up composed of members elected by the ratepayers and of Justices of the Peace resident in the unions. The intention behind the law was to get rid of outdoor relief and to administer assistance only within the workhouses, which, under the notorious principle of 'less eligibility', were to be so bleak that only those driven by absolute destitution would darken their doors. The system, as contemporaries pointed out even before it began to operate, was highly unsuitable to Ireland where extreme poverty was often rural and where recourse to a workhouse could only be at the expense of surrendering the plot of land on which the peasant normally depended for his subsistence. The law was rigorously applied notwithstanding, and the country was soon covered with a network of institutions just in time to receive the full shock of the Famine. Such machinery proved quite inadequate to absorb that shock and willy-nilly the poor law authorities were gradually forced into allowing a measure of outdoor relief to those who were too ill and too weak to reach a workhouse, or for whom there was often no room if they succeeded in reaching one. The precedent of outdoor relief, once accepted, proved impossible to abandon and in the latter half of the nineteenth century the principle that relief should be given only inside a workhouse was steadily eroded both by legislation and by force of circumstances. The system probably worked best between about 1851 and 1871 when the numbers receiving outdoor relief were small compared with those provided for in the workhouses, but it only needed the economy to take another lurch towards collapse for the weakness of the whole concept of the workhouse test to be once more exposed. In 1881, for example, when the country was in the midst of agricultural depression, those in workhouses numbered 364,000, but those relieved in their own homes were no fewer than 226,000.[9] This was admittedly an exceptionally bad year, and the workhouse population, or for that matter the total population on relief, soon shrank in better times. Thus in 1901 the more or less able-bodied poor in workhouses totalled only 43,000 and by 1911 this figure was down to 38,000; in both years the numbers receiving relief in their own homes (58,400 and 39,000 respectively) were actually greater than those incarcerated in 'the house'.[10]

It seems, therefore, that although, as has rightly been pointed out, the application of the New Poor Law to Ireland was an exception to the general rule that Irish administrative experiments were made independently of, and frequently in advance of, what was happening in Britain, even the exception seems in practice to have been distorted, as English legislation so often tended to be, by Irish conditions. Furthermore, pressure of necessity soon harnessed the poor law imposed from without to the fumbling native improvisations in the spheres of medicine and public health. The Famine itself had demonstrated with appalling clarity the intimate connection between destitution and sickness, and it was no accident that the first formal, institutional link between them should have followed hard on the heels of that disaster. It was in 1851 that the Poor Relief (Ireland) Act – sometimes called the Medical Charities Act – laid upon the Boards of Guardians the duty of dividing their unions into dispensary districts in each of which a local committee would maintain a dispensary and appoint and pay a medical officer. This was to rationalise the somewhat haphazard system of dispensaries that had grown up in the first half of the nineteenth century, and although a later age was to see in the free medical treatment meted out at the dispensaries, on presentation of the 'red ticket', a humiliating badge of poverty, it established at the time of its creation, and for nearly a century thereafter, the essential framework for adequate general medical care of the poor.

Partly as a consequence of this increased burden of work, partly because of the growing acceptance in official circles of the need for centralised oversight of a multiplicity of services that had previously been left to the casual mercies of local authorities, the Poor Law Commission (the government appointed board set up in 1847 at the height of the Famine to take over responsibility for Ireland from the English Poor Law Commissioners) was transmuted in 1872 into the Local Government Board which thenceforward became one of the most important departments of the Irish administration with an area of responsibility that continued steadily to expand. To its original functions of supervising the Poor Law and the dispensary system it added many others, of which the following are merely a selection : the organisation of relief in distressed areas at times of famine or near-famine; the business of arbitrating and adjudicating between rival local authorities, and especially of arranging for the transfer of power to the county councils and rural district councils created by the Local Government Act of 1898; the supervision of the Housing Acts and of the Public Health Act of 1878, which for the first time gave Ireland a code governing not only water supply and sewage disposal, but also public hygiene, especially in prohibiting the sale of diseased or contaminated food; the supervision of the hospitals set up under the Tuberculosis Prevention (Ireland) Act of 1908 and also of the distress committees established by the Unemployed Workmen's Act of 1905; and, if all this were not enough, it fell also to the Board to become the central pension authority under the Old Age Pensions Act of 1908, a task of fearsome complexity since the statutory registration of births had only begun in Ireland in 1864 and the Board had therefore to grapple with the inexhaustible fertility shown by a wide variety of Irishmen of indeterminate age in inventing what they hoped would be valid claims to a pension.[11]

It has been necessary to insist on these somewhat technical details at the outset of our survey in order to make the point which is so often overlooked in histories of Ireland – that, apart altogether from the benefits accruing from the general, if modest, economic advance registered in the fifty years after the Famine, the government itself was consciously and continuously seeking means to improve the conditions under which most Irishmen passed their daily lives. Nor is the list of improvements exhausted by reference to the poor law, public health or local government. No less important were the agencies for economic development and for the creation of a national system of education. The latter, which was always a controversial subject and not one of the happier examples of government activity, will be dealt with separately below, but first we may consider briefly the economic agencies. Four of these were of pre-eminent importance, and of the four three were mainly concerned with the Irish countryside. Historically, the earliest to emerge was the Land Commission, set up by Gladstone's Land Act of 1881. Its primary purpose was to fix 'fair' rents where disputes existed between landlords and tenants and in this purpose it succeeded to a remarkable extent over the next thirty years. Rack-renting, it is true, could not be legislated out of existence – agrarian agitation as well as acts of parliament would contribute to its demise – but if the bulk of Irish farmers over the years came to enjoy tolerable conditions of tenure a good part of the credit belonged to the Land Commission. Right from the beginning, however, the Commission, in addition to acting as a court of arbitration, had entrusted to it the further duty of making loans from public funds to tenants who wished to become the owners of their farms. As the trend of government policy moved inexorably towards the ending of landlordism, this latter function grew increasingly significant and when the Commission was remodelled by the Wyndham Act of 1903 it became clear that its main emphasis in the future would be upon land purchase. By 1914, in fact, of the seventeen administrative sections into which the Commission was divided, no less than twelve were exclusively concerned with that subject. So central had the Commission become to the process of creating a class of farmer-owners in Ireland that it was destined to survive the ending of the Union itself and, albeit greatly changed in structure, still continues in being to the present day in the Republic of Ireland.

If the impact of the Land Commission sprang initially from the fact that it marked a successful attempt to import an element of judicial calm into what was at bottom an explosively political question, the success of the remaining three agencies was due rather to their preoccupation with the practical problems involved in developing both industry and agriculture in a country too poor to be able to help itself. Two of these – the Congested Districts Board, dealing with the most impoverished areas of the west of Ireland, and the Department of Agriculture and Technical Instruction, charged with improving the economy as a whole by inculcating improved techniques and developing new industries – were both products of the 'constructive Unionism' of the 1890s and are dealt with later in the political context which gave them birth.* But the fourth – the Board of Works – needs to be mentioned here, partly because it eventually became the largest of all the Irish departments, and partly because the mere recital of its functions helps to underline the extent to which Ireland was dependent upon official initiatives. In the early years of the nineteenth century sporadic attempts had been made, with the aid of public money and under the general supervision of the Lord Lieutenant, to improve inland navigation, to encourage coastal fisheries and to explore the economic potentialities of the vast bogs which covered so much of the country. In addition, the government had found itself from time to time obliged to grapple with periodic unemployment by making grants or loans for public works, notably the building of roads and bridges. To deal with these diverse problems an old eighteenth century institution – known as the Barrack Board or Board of Works – was reconstituted in 1831. It speedily began to gather other matters besides relief works into its hands and to assume responsibility for, among other things, the upkeep of public buildings, drainage, canals and waterways, and fisheries. The last-named was later removed from its control (not surprisingly, since the officials in charge had been instructed 'never to recommend any course calculated to produce expenditure'), but in one of its original functions – the organisation of public works as a means of relieving the very poor – it performed vigorously and on the whole competently during the Famine period, or at least for so long as relief-works remained the principal official panacea for the crisis. In the second half of the nineteenth century it had become so indispensable as to attract yet more duties, many of them arising out of the trend towards 'constructive' legislation. Thus, it was empowered to lend money for land improvement, for farm buildings, for labourers' cottages and for working-class dwellings in the towns; it arbitrated between railway companies and landowners over the acquisition of land needed for track; it investigated promotional schemes for railroads and tramways; it cared (though not, to the eye of a later generation, very understandingly) for national monuments; it constructed piers and harbours all round the coast, and in general it watched over the whole public building programme of the government, itself becoming in the process an essential part of the fabric of the Irish administration.[12]

(iii)

Social improvement in nineteenth century Ireland needs, however, to be measured not just by an increase in material well-being, but also in terms of the growth of an educated and literate opinion. The difficulties of creating such an opinion were enormously complicated by the religious and political problems inherent in any attempt to frame a comprehensive educational policy. The Catholic fear – a legacy from

* See below, Part II, chap. 4.

the old penal laws – that education would be used by a Protestant government as a means of proselytisation may have been exaggerated, but was certainly not without foundation, at least up to Famine times. Yet this should not blind us to the fact that even by then considerable progress had already been made in teaching a backward population the basic elements of reading and writing, if in a narrow and unimaginative way. The essence of this progress, and what distinguished it so sharply from the chaotic condition of primary education in the England of that day, was that it was made at the national rather than at the local level.

The crucial decision in determining that the system should be national was taken in 1831, when the sum of £30,000 (later much increased) was voted by parliament 'to enable the Lord Lieutenant of Ireland to assist with the education of the people'. This assistance was in practice rendered by a National Board of Education which sought to substitute what was in effect a state-controlled grant for the haphazard allocation of funds hitherto prevailing. Up to 1831 such public money as was allotted to education had been distributed mainly in the form of grants to various Protestant societies. Two of these – the Incorporated Society in Dublin for Promoting English Protestant Schools in Ireland (founded in 1733) and the Association for Discountenancing Vice and Promoting the Knowledge and Practice of the Christian Religion (dating from 1792, but incorporated in 1800) – were avowedly proselytising agencies. A third, the Society for Promoting the Education of the Poor in Ireland (better known as the Kildare Place Society), though established in 1811 to set up and support schools in which the Bible should be read without note or comment, and for a time giving promise of forming the basis of a truly non-denominational system of education, became too biased towards Protestantism to be in the long run satisfactory to Catholics. The latter, despite the obstacles put in their way during penal times, had by the early nineteenth century evolved their own institutions. These fell broadly into two categories. The first included day schools run for the most part by parish priests and supported by parish contributions, girls' schools attached to convents, and boys' schools started by the Christian Brothers. In this category the day schools accounted for about 350 schools and contained just over 33,000 pupils, while forty-six convent schools looked after 7,000 girls. The Christian Brothers' schools, which before long were to play such an important role in Irish education, were still in their infancy. Founded by Edmund Rice of Waterford in the early years of the century, the Christian Brothers had received papal approval only in 1820 and at the time of the 1824 inquiry their twenty-four schools accounted for about 5,500 pupils. The bulk of Catholic children, however, were still educated not in these, on the whole well-organised institutions, but in the second category of schools – the so-called 'pay schools', deriving for the most part from the hedge schools of the eighteenth century, or in other schools of a similar kind started and maintained by private individuals. All told, taking Protestant and Catholic schools together, it would seem that in 1824 there were approximately 10,400 day schools containing upwards of half a million children, of whom between 350,000 and 400,000 were Catholic.* This was still far less than was needed. The commission of inquiry reckoned in fact that only about two-fifths of the population of school age was then receiving instruction, and much even of this instruction, it may be presumed, was of inferior quality, carried on with the minimum of equipment and often in highly unsuitable surroundings.[13]

The launching of a national system of education was intended to correct these deficiencies and, despite the criticisms levelled against it then and since, it did so to a considerable degree. The intention was to provide for 'combined moral and literary and separate religious education', thus enabling Protestant and Catholic children to come together in the same schools. But however admirable the ideal of integrated or 'mixed' education may have been in prospect, in actuality it could scarcely avoid running immediately onto the rocks of denominational controversy. Anglicans objected to it because of the government's refusal to allow Bible teaching except from a book of agreed (i.e. denominationally non-controversial) extracts, and, more fundamentally, because the whole concept of mixed education was *de facto* a stroke at the ascendancy of the Established Church. In an attempt to opt out, they created a new body, the Church Education Society, with the object of founding, or taking over, schools in which the Bible would be the basic medium of religious instruction. The new Society in time absorbed the Kildare Place Society's Schools and by 1859 it had 1,700 establishments and 80,000 children on its register. But efforts to secure backing from the National Board were vain and the Church Education Society struggled along on voluntary contributions until in 1860 the Anglican Archbishop of Dublin advised it to come to terms with the Board, which, gradually, it did. The Presbyterians were no less emphatic about preserving denominational distinctions and at one time withdrew many of their schools from the purview of the Board; having secured a compromise agreement in 1838, which in effect underpinned their denominationalism, they then came back into the system.

The Catholics, by contrast, tended at first to look favourably on the

* Irish education statistics for the early nineteenth century are notoriously unreliable. The figures given above are rounded out from those recently published in D. H. Akenson, *The Irish Education Experiment* (London, 1970). He points out that the source of these figures (*First Report of the Commissioners of Irish Education Inquiry*, published in 1825) lists two sets of figures, one based on Protestant returns, the latter on Catholic returns. The former listed 10,387 day schools, containing 498,641 pupils, of whom 357,249 were Catholics; the latter recorded 10,453 schools, with a total of 522,016 pupils, 397,212 of these being Catholic. The second report, however, cited in G. Balfour, *The Educational Systems of Great Britain and Ireland* (London, 1898), p. 82, gives a total for 1824 of 11,823 schools catering for 560,549 pupils (Protestant figure) or 568,964 (Catholic figure).

experiment of mixed education and the Catholic Archbishop of Dublin actually joined the National Board.[14] However, the system soon aroused the suspicions of the formidable John MacHale, created Archbishop of Tuam in 1834, who saw in it an invitation to proselytism and demanded instead a thorough-going Catholic education for Catholic children. There followed a serious split inside the hierarchy, resulting in an appeal to Rome and a somewhat evasive papal judgment which did not condemn the system outright, but placed on individual bishops the onus of safeguarding the faith of such Catholic children as came within the system. The Christian Brothers, on the other hand, found the Board's regulations inconsistent with their conception of a Catholic education and, except for a few schools, withdrew from the system in 1836, thereafter carrying through their massive mid-century expansion outside the range of public assistance. Such exclusiveness, though, was rare, for the National Board offered too many inducements to be easily ignored. Not only did it make grants towards the payment of teachers' salaries and the provision of cheap textbooks, but in addition it helped with the expense of building new schools wherever a local committee or an individual manager undertook to provide a part of the building cost and also to maintain the school and contribute to the teacher's salary. It was, however, a condition of a building grant, though a condition by no means always enforced, not merely that a proportion of the total cost (usually one-third) should be locally contributed, but that any building to which the state contributed a quarter of the outlay should be 'vested' in trustees chosen by the applicants but acceptable to the public authority – that is, the National Board or, to give it its full title, the Board of Commissioners of National Education in Ireland. Predictably, the Board, having once got its foot in the door, tried in 1845 to open that door completely by insisting that all schools receiving building grants should be vested, not in trustees, but in the Board itself. This aroused intense suspicion on all sides, but especially among Catholics, about the overweening pretensions of the state and in the end a compromise was reached whereby the school authorities had a choice of three courses of action. They could vest their school in the Board, which would then pay all building and maintenance costs; or they could vest it in their own trustees, in which case the latter would have to contribute towards these costs; or, finally, they could refuse to vest the school at all and retain responsibility for maintenance and building. Significantly, the total number of non-vested schools remained constantly higher than those vested. In 1850 there were just over 3,000 non-vested schools as against 1,500 vested; in 1910 the respective figures were 5,000 and 3,400. Moreover, within the vested schools those vested in trustees outnumbered those vested in the Board by approximately two to one.[15]

If this pattern reflects, as it certainly does, the triumph of denominationalism, that triumph was apparent in other aspects of the national system also. It was evident, for example, in the composition of the Board itself. Originally heavily weighted in favour of Protestants, it gradually changed its character until by 1860 Catholics and Protestants exactly balanced each other with ten members each. These Commissioners were with one exception unpaid – the exception was the Resident Commissioner who was the effective head of the whole department – and consisted for the most part of eminent churchmen, lawyers and university dons. They were appointed by the Lord Lieutenant and removable by him (though in practice they never were removed) and their principal function was, with the assistance of a small professional staff including a corps of inspectors, to administer the funds annually voted to them by parliament.

The prime charge upon these funds was the payment of teachers' salaries. But, despite the high hopes of 'mixed' education, by the turn of the century almost all the national schools in Ireland were under denominational control, being managed, in the great majority of cases, by clergymen of the various churches. This had important consequences both for religious instruction and for the training of the teachers. As for the former, the Board, after many controversies and vicissitudes, arrived in 1866 at a compromise which, as has been well said, was 'denominational in practice with a conscience clause'. The formula ran as follows:

> Religious instruction must be so arranged that each school shall be open to children of all communions; that due regard be had to parental right and authority; that accordingly no child shall receive, or be present at, any religious instruction of which his parents or guardians disapprove; and that the time for giving it be so fixed that no child shall thereby in effect be excluded directly or indirectly, from the other advantages which the school affords.[16]

Perhaps the best commentary on this well-meaning regulation is the fact that by 1900 no less than sixty-five per cent of all primary school children were at schools attended by adherents of a single denomination.

The training of teachers, given the influence they might be supposed to have over the minds of the young, was, from a denominational point of view, almost as critical a matter as religious instruction itself. Initially, the Board had provided the barest rudiments of training at a Model School (later increased to three) in Dublin. From this base it was hoped to spread out over the whole of Ireland, with one such training establishment in each county – the training to be 'mixed' and equally available to Catholics and Protestants. Once again, good intentions were not proof against denominational suspicions and the scheme was widely opposed, especially by the Catholic hierarchy, on the grounds that such schools tended 'to throw into the hands of the State, acting through a body of Commissioners, the education of the country and the formation of masters and mistresses of the rising generation'.[17] From 1850 onwards Catholic clerical managers were in general forbidden to appoint teachers trained in such Model Schools as then existed, and some of the Protestant denominations took a similar line. The results were, educationally speaking, not far short of disastrous, for in the early 'eighties, when the Board at last decided to recognise denominational training colleges, only twenty-seven per cent of Catholic teachers and fifty-two per cent of Protestant teachers had had any formal training at all. Since the Board at that point agreed to make grants to denominational colleges the situation then slowly began to improve. The two most important Catholic colleges (St Patrick's, Drumcondra, and Our Lady of Mercy) were opened in 1883, to be followed the next year by the affiliation of the Church of Ireland Training College to the Board. Others were added during the next twenty years, but even so the proportion of all teachers (Catholic and Protestant combined) who had received one or two years' training was still, at the turn of the century, only just over fifty per cent.[18]

It was hardly surprising, therefore, that the education the children received was fairly rudimentary, or that methods of instruction tended to be mechanical, a tendency enforced by the introduction in the 1870s of paying teachers' salaries, at least partially, by the results of highly stereotyped examinations. The system was discontinued after 1900, but it was not until 1917 that a properly graduated salary scale was introduced. Reading, spelling, writing and arithmetic, with a little geography, remained the staple on which most boys and girls were reared, though in the senior classes grammar, more advanced geography, and, where appropriate, needlework or agriculture, could be added. Other subjects, including Irish from 1879 onwards, could be taught on a voluntary basis and out of regular school hours. A few gestures were made in the latter part of the nineteenth century to introduce more practical elements into this programme, but they were generally quite inadequate. Agriculture, for example, was taught almost exclusively from textbooks, an absurdity which attracted even contemporary derision. One report of 1870 declared bluntly that 'there clearly could be no more useless expenditure of the public funds than to teach Irish farmers to lose money', and a second, nearly thirty years later, was still describing this branch of instruction as 'wholly useless, if not worse'. Some schools, it is true, did have farms attached, but the number was never large; in 1875 there were 228, but by the end of the century the total had fallen to 38. By that time agricultural training was being vested increasingly in the newly created Department of Agriculture and Technical Instruction. Right up to the First World War elementary science teaching was virtually non-existent, and although some technical training was given in a handful of Mechanics' Institutes and the like in Dublin, Belfast, Cork and one or two other places, it was not until after the passing of the Technical Education Act of 1889, and more specifically the setting up of the Board of Technical Instruction under the Act of 1899 which had created the Department of Agriculture and Technical Instruction, that real progress began to be made. This, however, was at the secondary rather than the primary level, and even so, although twenty-five years of experience had produced sixty-five technical schools in the area of what was later to be the Irish Free State, it was notable that only eighteen per cent of the total of nearly 22,000 students had opted for science, and only five per cent for handicrafts. Commerce and languages (forty per cent) and domestic economy (twenty-four per cent) accounted for the great bulk of those subscribing for the various courses. Nor was physical training any better provided for. At the primary or pre-primary level it was confined almost entirely to kindergarten classes, and in fact figured only in 385 out of over 8,600 National Schools in 1897.[19]

Yet it would be wrong to condemn the whole for the inadequacy of some of the parts. When all has been said that has to be said about defects of method and of curriculum, the main achievement of the National Schools remains unchallenged. Not only did the number of schools in operation rise from 4,500 in 1850 to nearly 9,000 in 1900, but there is fairly reliable evidence to show that the number of children making at least one attendance in the year had grown from about 800,000 in 1860 to around a million thirty years later. Thereafter, the absolute number seems to have fallen away – in 1900 it was about three-quarters of a million – but the increase in the number of schools in proportion to the number of children was in itself a precondition for an improvement in quality. Moreover, these numbers were the product of what was to all intents and purposes a voluntary system. True, the Irish Education Act of 1892 was intended to impose a measure of compulsion, combined with the abolition (total or partial) of fees for all children between the ages of three and fifteen who attended state-aided elementary schools. Such compulsion, however, was initially aimed only at the larger centres of population and although School Attendance Committees had been established within two years of the Act in eighty-eight out of the hundred and eighteen places where it was to have been applied, it is probable that they functioned efficiently in only about half of these; how little effective the legislation was may be judged from the fact that Dublin, Cork, Waterford and Limerick had done virtually nothing to implement it. As a result of the Local Government Act of 1898 the system was extended to the countryside, but by the turn of the century it was operating in only forty-three rural districts. The great obstacle to compulsory attendance, and one that was not really overcome until after British rule had ended, was that many local authorities simply refused to use the Act so long as denominational, non-vested schools were excluded from its scope. Nevertheless, compulsion or no compulsion, regular school attendance improved fairly steadily over the years until by the 1890s it had passed the sixty per cent mark, rising to just above seventy-five per cent in 1908. And on this basis was built the virtual elimination of illiteracy. The figures may be left to speak for themselves. In 1851 the proportion of persons five years old and upwards who could neither read nor write was forty-seven per cent (to the nearest round number); in 1911 this had dropped to twelve per cent.* Correspondingly, the proportion of those who could read only had fallen from twenty to four per cent, and the proportion of those who could both read and write had risen from thirty-three to eighty-four per cent. Without this revolution, the foundations of a modern Irish state could not have been laid.

The real criticism to be made of the system is a criticism of the narrowness of its curriculum and the meagreness of its content. It was not just that the teaching was mechanical or that the texts used were dull and unimaginative. It was rather – and this was the main burden of contemporary nationalist complaints – that there was nothing in the system to differentiate it from the system applied in England, nothing to indicate that these were Irish schools catering for Irish children. It is important, however, not to exaggerate the charges made against the National Schools and in particular not to saddle them with the sole responsibility for the dramatic decline in Irish as a language of everyday use in the second half of the nineteenth century.† No doubt the heavily anglicised bias of the system did contribute to that result, but so also did the fact that economic betterment and social advancement of all kinds depended upon mastering the tongue of the foreigner. There was not, in fact, as is often supposed, a planned, coherent policy for the extermination of Irish ready formed in the minds of the Commissioners. On the contrary, not only did Irish become an optional subject before the Gaelic League had begun its campaign for the revival of the language, but in 1904, when 'Irish-Ireland' pressures were much more insistent, the Board made an important concession in deciding to allow the teaching in Irish-speaking and bilingual districts of both Irish and English to all classes, and the teaching of other subjects through the medium of either language. This opened the way for a forward policy and in Donegal, Mayo, Galway, Kerry and Cork, some twenty-seven schools took advantage of the opportunity, a figure which had in-

* The 1911 Census, though continuing to use five years of age as the point of departure for measuring illiteracy for purposes of comparison with earlier Censuses, accepted the contention of educationists that nine years was a more realistic age. The effect, of course, was to lower the illiteracy rate still further. In 1911, by that measurement, 87·6 per cent of the population of nine years and over could read and write, 3·2 per cent could read only, and 9·2 per cent were completely illiterate.

† Accurate statistics are unobtainable before 1851, but at that date about 1½ million people, or just over twenty-three per cent of the population, had some knowledge of Irish, though all but 320,000 of these spoke English as well. This suggests that the decline in the language had begun before the introduction of the national school system. In the second half of the century the decline was greatly accelerated and by 1901 the total of those with some knowledge of Irish had fallen to 641,000 (14·4 per cent of the population; Irish speakers only numbered no more than 21,000 (*Census of Ireland*, 1901, part ii; *General Report, etc.*, pp. 170, 575).

creased to 240 before the work of the Board came to an end in 1922; if the schools where some Irish was optionally taught are added to this number then the whole total was 1,900 by the time the old regime staggered to a halt.[20]

Nevertheless, this encouragement of the language, though it deserves to be recorded, did not remotely penetrate to the heart of a problem which the National Board, indeed, had scarcely begun to recognise as a problem. The original aim of the schools, as one of the earliest Commissioners, the Protestant Archbishop Whateley, had expressed it in an unfortunate phrase that has never been allowed to die, was to make of every pupil 'a happy English child'. To this end Irish history was virtually ignored and Irish music and poetry might never have existed. This constituted an important difference between the National Schools and the Christian Brothers schools. In the latter attention was paid to such matters, especially history, and this partly explains why the latter were so often nurseries of the new nationalism. Even the strictly vicarious revolutionary ardours of the English poets were suspect and inflammatory lines like 'Breathes there a man with soul so dead', or 'Freedom shrieked as Kosciusko fell', were banished from the National Schools. Small wonder that Patrick Pearse, a real revolutionary whose revolution began in his own small but immensely influential school, St Enda's, should have condemned the whole system as a 'murder machine', lacking the two essentials he found necessary to true education – freedom and inspiration. 'Without these two things', he wrote in 1912, 'you cannot have education, no matter how you may multiply educational programmes. And because those two things are pre-eminently lacking in what passes for education in Ireland, we have in Ireland strictly no education system at all. . . .'

What he contended for was not simply 'freedom for the individual to grow in his own natural way', but also that Irish schools should nurture 'the heroic spirit' in their children. For him this meant the deliberate cultivation and rehabilitation of a nationalist tradition looking back equally to myth and legend and to Wolfe Tone and the Fenians:

The value of the national factor in education [he wrote] would appear to rest chiefly in this, that it addresses itself to the most generous side of the child's nature, urging him to live up to his finest self. If the true works of the teacher be, as I have said, to help the child to realise himself at his best and worthiest, the factor of nationality is of prime importance. . . .

It is because the English education system in Ireland has deliberately eliminated the national factor that it has so terrifically succeeded. For it has succeeded – succeeded in making slaves of us. And it has succeeded so well that we no longer realise we are slaves. . . . It remains the crowning achievement of the 'National' and Intermediate systems that they have wrought such a change in this people that once loved freedom so passionately.[21]

Although Pearse in his denunciations struck equally at primary and at secondary schools, the situation was in fact far worse at the higher than at the lower level. Up to the end of the eighteenth century almost all the schooling that was provided beyond the elementary grade (though at that date distinctions between elementary and other education were exceedingly blurred) had been at foundations intended exclusively for Protestant children, or else to convert Catholic children into Protestants. Not that these Protestant schools were either numerous or wealthy. 'The history of Irish secondary education', it has been well said, 'is a record of poverty, of abused endowments and of numerous inquiries preceding tardy reforms.'[22] The burden of this secondary education, such as it was, was carried partly by a handful of diocesan schools (provided for by an act of parliament of 1570), partly by the Royal Free Schools (founded mainly under James I in Ulster), and partly by private benefactions of which that of the Cromwellian, Erasmus Smith, was, and has remained, the best known. Yet, in 1791, after more than two centuries of endeavour, the number of pupils taught by these and other institutions (forty-six in all) aiming vaguely at grammar-school status was no more than 1,200, and it was evident that the surface of the problem had barely been scratched.[23]

So far as Catholics were concerned not even the surface had been scratched. It was only after the relaxation of the penal laws at the end of the eighteenth century, and in the more favourable climate of the early years of the Union, that priests and teachers were able to emerge completely from underground and to organise a form of higher education for their people. This was all the more necessary since the French wars had denied them access to the seminaries on the continent where many had been trained during the penal period, but although the new Catholic schools that began to spring up were certainly intended to supply candidates for the priesthood that was never their exclusive function. This was true, for example, of the Kilkenny and Carlow colleges, founded immediately after the Catholic Relief Act of 1793, and it was true also of St Patrick's College, Maynooth, if not at its foundation in 1795, at least from 1801 until its lay department was closed down in 1817. Once the way was open for the religious orders, and for private individuals, to establish secondary schools – or 'classical' schools as they were sometimes called – for Catholic children, the number began to grow rapidly. Ten were set up before Catholic emancipation in 1829, ten more between then and 1850, and a further twenty-seven between 1850 and 1867.[24]

The rise of these Catholic schools, and indeed of Presbyterian ones also in the north of Ireland, alongside the Anglican foundations, emphasised, if the fact needed emphasising, the inexorably denominational character of Irish education. This in itself may have been part of the reason for the failure of the state to brace itself to the task of organising secondary schooling on a national basis as it had done at the primary level. For most of the nineteenth century it was deemed sufficient to appoint a Commission to oversee the endowments of a number of Anglican schools, but this carried with it no obligation to frame an educational policy, or even to inspect the schools for which the Commission had some responsibility. It was a body of amateurs whose members were busy men in their own professions (predominantly they were members of the Protestant Ascendancy) and since some of the more important schools were outside the Commission's purview altogether, it is not surprising that it performed its duties half-heartedly and ineffectively. For the first glimmerings of reform the Irish endowed schools had to wait for the report of a Vice-regal Commission of Inquiry under the Earl of Rosse (1878–80) and for the passing of the Educational Endowments Act of 1885. As a result of this flurry of interest in 'superior' education, the permanent Commission was reconstituted on a basis of religious equality, and a number of endowments were redistributed to Catholic and Protestant boards of education in different parts of the country. Certain schools (for example, those on the Erasmus Smith foundation, or those exclusive to particular denominations) were still outside the scope of the Commission's authority, but within its admittedly limited sphere it was much more active than formerly and reasonably successful in making money available over a wider area than had previously been the case.

But redistributing endowments was one thing, reconstructing education quite another. And to this latter aim the government never really succeeded in addressing itself during the whole period of the Union. The nearest it came to doing so was to create, by the Intermediate Act of 1878, an unpaid Board of seven members whose function was to promote 'intermediate education' (defined by the act as that stage of education which intervened between primary instruction and professional or higher studies) by holding examinations, granting prizes and certificates to successful candidates, and paying fees based on the examination results to the managers of schools which complied with certain conditions. The funds at the Board's disposal consisted originally of the interest on one million pounds deriving from the surplus revenues of the disestablished Church of Ireland, supplemented from 1890 onwards by an annual grant from the Customs and Excise and after 1914 by a further annual grant under the Intermediate Education Act of that year. The intention, as already indicated, was merely to organise examinations and reward proficiency, not to frame policy. Yet examinations, especially when money was attached to passing them, could not but influence policy, and in fact did so in two principal ways. First, and most obviously, they influenced the curriculum. Since prizes were offered in Latin, Greek, modern languages, Irish, English (including some geography and an outline of English and Irish history), mathematics, science, drawing and commerce, these were the subjects that formed the basis of Irish secondary education. This was natural enough and there was nothing discreditable about it. But the second consequence of the examination system was more serious. Even though the Board, to its credit, did obtain acceptance at the turn of the century for the principle that in the award of fees to schools other factors reflecting a school's efficiency besides examination successes should be taken into account, and even though it went on from that ten years later to win a long battle for the establishment of an inspectorate, the fact remains that just at the time payment by results was being discredited elsewhere it was being embalmed in the Irish secondary schools. The fact that money and prestige could best be earned by gearing the whole effort of the school to the rules and regulations of the Board made for a degree of uniformity which was perhaps an advance on the chaos of earlier years. On the other hand, the underlying assumption that to pass certain stereotyped written tests was the main goal of a child's career had a stultifying effect upon good, if individualistic, teaching, and also put a premium on those schools (notably the establishments run by the Christian Brothers) which had brought examination technique to a fine art that had little to do with education.*

Perhaps on balance the gain exceeded the loss. Yet the gain was not overwhelmingly large. True, in 1911 the last Census before the war revealed that in the previous thirty years, while the number of 'superior schools' had hardly changed (488 in 1881, 489 in 1911), the number of pupils attending them had almost exactly doubled, from 20,405 at the earlier date to 40,840 at the later, and this despite a continuing decline in the population. True also, the Catholic share in this secondary school population had greatly improved during that period. In 1881, with 10,145 pupils, they accounted for about fifty per cent, whereas by 1911, with nearly 30,000, they represented about three-quarters of the total.[25]

* Those who recollect the prowess of James Joyce as an examinee (he won Intermediate Exhibitions in 1894, 1895 and 1897) will appreciate something of the tensions, as well as the rewards, that accompanied the system. Joyce, of course, was educated by the Jesuits, and the two schools he attended – Clongowes Wood College and Belvedere College – were, together with a few other schools run by other religious orders, the best (they were certainly the most fashionable) available to the Catholic middle-class, or to those, like Joyce's father, who were clinging desperately to the coat-tails of that class. There were interesting social distinctions between these schools and those of the Christian Brothers, but not even the Jesuits, though possessing their own revised *Ratio Studiorum*, could ignore the magnet of the Intermediate examinations. The Christian Brothers, incidentally, besides being very good at drilling their pupils for these examinations, also passed an exceptionally large proportion of the future leaders of the Irish revolution through their hands. It should be remembered, of course, that *primary* education remained the principal preoccupation of the Brothers.

However, this picture of general growth is subject to two reservations. One is that the quality of much of the teaching was highly suspect. At the turn of the century only 11·5 of the Catholic male teachers in secondary schools, and 8 per cent of the women teachers, were university graduates, and most of these, probably, were concentrated in the Diocesan Colleges or in the schools run by the Jesuits and a few other orders which demanded high intellectual calibre from their members. Protestant schools were notably better served in this respect – nearly fifty-six per cent of the men and thirty per cent of the women were graduates – and in this they undoubtedly reflected the better facilities available to them for higher education.[26] The other reservation is more serious. It is simply this – that when one considers the school-going population as a whole, the proportion that reached a secondary level was pitifully small. Again the 1911 Census tells its own tale. In that year the total school-going population was just short of 705,000, yet the total number who went on to intermediate standard was, as we have seen, actually no more than 40,840. A system which allows only one in seventeen of its children to proceed beyond the primary stage provides its own most effective condemnation.[27]

This stunted growth of secondary education helps to explain the slow development of university institutions in the country. But that slow development was also a product of the all-prevailing denominationalism that blighted every kind of educational experiment. Until the closing years of the eighteenth century Trinity College, Dublin (founded in 1591 as a constituent college of the University of Dublin, but to this day its sole college) was the only institution of higher learning in the whole of Ireland. Protestant, indeed Puritan, by origin and for much of its history intensely conscious of its position as a bastion of the Ascendancy in general and of Anglicanism in particular, it began in 1793–4 to edge its way towards a somewhat more liberal policy by admitting students to degree courses without religious tests. Far beyond that, however, it did not venture for another eighty years, for it was not until 1873 that Fellowships and Scholarships were opened to non-Anglicans. Inevitably, therefore, those who were not Anglicans – in effect, the Catholics and Presbyterians – sought satisfaction elsewhere and in other ways. It was to meet the needs of the former that Maynooth was founded in 1795 – primarily, though not, as we saw earlier, exclusively in its earlier years – as a seminary for the training of priests. The other neglected denomination, the Presbyterians, had traditionally looked to Scotland for their higher education, but in 1810 set up their own establishment, the Belfast Academical Institution. Initially half-school, half-college (though nowadays entirely a school) it was free from tests and ostensibly non-theological. In practice, however, it was bedevilled by staff disputes between orthodox and non-subscribing Presbyterians and never showed much promise of graduating to full university status.

From a political, as well as an educational, standpoint it was unsatisfactory, if not actually dangerous, to have one institution virtually monopolising higher education for the benefit of a small and privileged minority. Official opinion, which from the 1830s onwards had begun to harden into a firm belief in the virtues of that 'mixed' education of which the National School system was intended to be a demonstration, was inclined towards a solution that would allow Catholics and Protestants to meet within the confines of the same university. This was the vision which inspired that apostle of mixed education, Sir Thomas Wyse; it was no less the vision which guided that more mundane statesman, Sir Robert Peel. And it was Peel who in 1845, on the very eve of the Famine, carried through two measures which, had they had time and opportunity to fructify, might well have transformed the situation. One, the Maynooth Act, carried government recognition of Maynooth much further, giving the College a large capital sum for building and increasing its annual grant from £9,000 to £26,000. But more far-reaching even than this placatory gesture towards Irish Catholics was Peel's second measure, the Provincial Colleges Act, establishing three new colleges at Cork, Galway and Belfast. Theoretically undenominational, the first two were clearly intended to serve the largely Catholic hinterlands of the south and west, while the Belfast college was just as obviously designed to meet the insistent Presbyterian demand for higher education.

These were the 'godless colleges' denounced by O'Connell (in a phrase borrowed from the High Tory, Sir Robert Inglis). More ominous than the Liberator's diatribes, however, was that not only the Pope, but also the Catholic hierarchy (after considerable internal divisions of opinion) came out against them. Thereafter, in the second half of the nineteenth century, although the university question was always, as we shall see, an integral part of Irish politics, university education itself was condemned to move along three quite different paths. One was the traditional, though increasingly isolated, road followed by Trinity College. Trinity was still attended by the flower of Anglo-Irish youth (and by many of the Catholic upper and middle class as well until it was formally denounced by the hierarchy in 1875 as dangerous to faith and morals), but the university remained aloof from the main stream of Irish life – wealthy, international in its reputation, contemptuous of the claims of nationality, and adamantly opposed to all efforts to submerge its identity in any federal or conglomerate structure.

A second path was hacked by Cardinal Newman through the jungle of conflicting Catholic ideas and demands. The Catholic University properly so called was founded at Dublin in 1854 largely on the initiative of Archbishop Cullen. When he obtained the services of John Newman as first Rector it seemed as if he had pulled off a major coup. Yet the results were disappointing. Newman, it is true, was stimulated into writing the famous discourses later published as *The Idea of a University*, but, aside from his initial and invaluable impulse towards making the new college on St Stephen's Green a place both of wide and of modern learning, he had little enough to contribute. This was partly because of temperamental differences between Cullen and himself. There were grievances on both sides. The distinguished visitor had always intended that his appointment should be part-time, whereas Cullen not unnaturally wanted a Rector who was permanently and visibly at his post. Newman, as one who had after all known the great world, was perhaps also irked by the peasant shrewdness of the Archbishop, especially in money matters, and money was always tight. At any rate, the Rector abandoned his experiment within five years, while the poverty which had dogged his infant university continued, and indeed intensified, after his departure. Except for the Medical School in Cecilia Street, which predated it (having been founded in 1837) and which prospered exceedingly, the Catholic University had a struggle to survive, let alone make an impact on the educational world around it. In 1882 it was reorganised as University College, Dublin, and the following year it passed into the hands of the Jesuits who controlled it for the next quarter of a century.[28] In that time some of the ablest young men in Ireland passed through its doors (this was the era of James Joyce, Francis Sheehy-Skeffington, T. M. Kettle, F. Cruise O'Brien, C. P. Curran, to name only a few), yet numbers remained small – in the 1890s little more than a hundred – and the activities of the College continued to be severely limited by the fact that, as a privately founded and exclusively denominational institution, it did not qualify for public money.*

Not indeed that those institutions which did qualify for public money – the Queen's Colleges, representing the third avenue of Irish university development – had a much easier time of it. The one situated in Belfast was the most thriving of the three and it did achieve a measure of genuinely mixed education, though that was perhaps not too difficult where Presbyterians accounted for sixty-five per cent of the students at the mid-century and Catholics for only five. This was not to say that Presbyterians had grown any less denominationally-minded. On the contrary, in 1853, just a few years before the Ulster revival, they created their own theological school (the General Assembly's College which, until disestablishment, received an annual subvention from the state) and were also able, through the munificence of a certain Mrs Magee, to launch another embryonic university at Londonderry in 1865 – Magee College – teaching arts subjects and theology, the latter very decidedly under Presbyterian auspices.

It was clearly desirable, both to counter the fissiparous tendencies of religious difference, and also to make the individual colleges more

* It may seem inconsistent that Maynooth had received substantial grants earlier in the century whereas the Catholic University got nothing. The explanation is that the endowment of Maynooth as a *theological* college (not as a university in any broad sense of the term) was seen as a counterpoise to the wealth of the established Church of Ireland. When that Church was disestablished in 1869 the opportunity was taken to discontinue all denominational endowment, though Maynooth was compensated by a sum of almost £370,000, equivalent to fourteen years' annual grant.

viable in institutions, that an effort should be made to bring the three Queen's Colleges into some closer relationship. This was in fact done in 1850 when they were linked together as constituent colleges of what was called the Queen's University, with power to conduct examinations and to award degrees. Yet even that, though undoubtedly an improvement, was far short of a final solution. The colleges continued to struggle, partly because the government held them on a tight rein financially, but mainly because they were individually and collectively boycotted by the vast majority of Catholics. As late as 1869, when the Queen's University had been in existence for nearly twenty years, Cardinal Cullen was able to claim that in that year only thirty-seven Catholic students were working for their arts degrees there – eighteen in Cork, sixteen in Galway and three in Belfast.[29] By then, however, the whole question was about to enter a new phase. In 1873 Gladstone, as part of the Irish reforms of his first administration, attempted to create a genuinely national and non-sectarian university by abolishing the Queen's University and one of its constituent colleges (Galway) and by bringing together within a single framework Trinity, the Catholic University, Belfast, Cork and Magee. With the massive insensitivity which that most subtle of men could sometimes display, he thus succeeded at a single stroke in alienating every section of Irish opinion and his proposal was resoundingly defeated. Next, it was Disraeli's turn, and he at least succeeded in effecting some change, though on a modest scale. By the University Education (Ireland) Act of 1879, he contrived to abolish the Queen's University – it was formally dissolved in 1882 – and to replace it by a purely examining body, the Royal University, which was empowered to confer degrees upon all who had passed its prescribed examinations, with the proviso that medical degrees could only be conferred upon those who attended approved medical schools. The old Catholic University was simultaneously reconstituted so as to comprise all Catholic colleges deemed to rank as institutions of higher learning – at that time the list included not only Newman's foundation (renamed University College in 1882) but also the Cecilia Street Medical School; Maynooth; the French College, Blackrock; St Patrick's College, Carlow; and Holy Cross College, Clonliffe; and later, St Kieran's College, Kilkenny, the Carmelite College, Terenure, and St Ignatius's, Temple Street, Dublin.[30]

The new arrangement, as it developed in the thirty years after 1879, still fell far short of the Catholic demand – which remained as always a fully denominational university entitled to state aid – but in two ways it marked a significant advance. First, it provided at long last a common meeting-ground for Catholics and Protestants: not only did they compete for scholarships and prizes on equal terms, but they were also eligible for Fellowships of the new university, and even though the title had a certain air of unreality in a non-teaching institution, the fact that half these posts were assigned to professors of the Catholic University represented a real, if indirect, endowment of Catholic higher education. And secondly, it is probably true to say that the standard imposed by the Royal University – which was both high and seen to be fairly administered – helped in the short run to benefit university education itself, and in the long run to improve the quality of the teaching in the schools. Moreover, the new reform, coming as it did hard on the heels of the changes in secondary education, could scarcely have been better-timed to offer the chance of pursuing a course of higher learning to the more gifted pupils thrown up by the intermediate system. And, increasingly, they began to take advantage of the opportunity, the number presenting themselves for the Royal University's examinations rising from 748 in 1800 to 2,658 in 1900.[31]

Yet the heart does not instinctively warm to a university which is at bottom no more than a board of examiners and the real problem still remained unresolved – how at the same time to meet the Catholic demand and to rescue the individual Queen's Colleges from an extinction which the statistics revealed to be coming steadily nearer decade by decade. Even the Belfast College itself fell in numbers from 567 in the session 1881-2 to 347 in 1899-1900, while in the same period Cork dropped from 404 to 171 and Galway from 208 to 83. Indeed, the entire university membership of Ireland was pathetically meagre. According to the Census of 1901 it totalled 3,200, of whom about 1,000 attended Trinity College.[32] It was not surprising, therefore, that in the last decade of the nineteenth century and the early years of the twentieth schemes of further reform should have proliferated. Yet one after another they failed to issue in any practical improvement and always the failures echoed two constantly recurring themes.

The first was the apparent inability of church and state to find any common ground whatever in this most sensitive area, an inability which seemed to become greater rather than less as time went on and Catholic expectations grew higher. The root cause of the difficulty in reaching a satisfactory compromise is to be found in the second theme that dominated this period of anxious inquiries and abortive proposals. It was of course the simple fact that the university question at bottom was not just an educational question, nor even a religious question, but a political one. To Unionists, whether British or Irish, who believed, or affected to believe, that Home Rule meant Rome rule, the spending of public money to endow a Catholic university seemed at best an exercise in masochism, at worst a form of Protestant self-destruction. And if this was felt by the Unionist rearguard to be true of attempts to endow a *separate* Catholic university, it was felt to be even more true of the suggestions circulating in the early 1900s about merging Trinity in any reconstructed federal University of Dublin. That particular solution had to be laid aside in the face of a violent 'Hands off Trinity' campaign, though it has yet to be seen whether the reprieve then obtained was total or merely a stay of execution for seventy years.*

* It is proper to record that two of the most distinguished members ever to represent the University of Dublin in the House of Commons – Sir

When in 1908 a settlement was at last reached, almost through exhaustion, it resulted in the south, at least, in defeat for the concept of 'mixed' education. Trinity was left to go its own way alone (except that Magee developed a special relationship with it, whereby students from the Londonderry college were able to complete their courses in Dublin and qualify for the degrees of Dublin University), the Royal University was abolished and two new universities were created in its place. One of these, the Queen's University of Belfast, was the old Queen's College of that city writ large, and was destined in time to become large and flourishing and famous. The other, the National University of Ireland, was a federation of which the University Colleges of Cork, Dublin and Galway were to be the component parts, with Maynooth linked to the main body as a recognised college. Although the principle that the National University should be undenominational was enshrined in the act of parliament which created it, it was in effect a Catholic university in receipt of substantial government funds – starting with a capital grant of £170,000 and a recurrent grant of £74,000 per annum. Such was the outcome of nearly a century of agitation, but although the settlement was widely hailed at the time as a wise solution – it was in fact probably the only acceptable solution – it registered a deep and enduring division within the country and was, as the leading modern authority has remarked, 'in a profoundly significant sense the prelude to the partition of Ireland in 1921'.[33]

(v)

If the stormy history of Irish education in the nineteenth century serves to expose some of the limitations of state intervention, especially when the state attempted to step outside the sphere of amenity and to enter that of belief or opinion, this should not be allowed to obscure the central and most important fact about the intellectual history of Ireland in the post-Famine period – that the battle against illiteracy had been virtually won before the time came for the British authorities to hand over their responsibilities to a native administration.

Nor should the endless politico-religious controversies that raged round schools and universities blind us to the fundamental benefits that more and better government had brought to the country during those years. Allied to the change in the economic environment described earlier, these experiments in the 'social laboratory' of Ireland had

Edward Carson and the historian, W. E. H. Lecky – were both supporters of a separate Catholic University. No doubt they were not uninfluenced by the realisation that to concede this claim would be to safeguard the status quo of their own college, but no-one who reads their speeches can fail to be struck by their genuine concern for the educational needs of the Catholic majority.

beyond question improved the quality of life for a great many Irish men, women and children. Of course, there was a dark side to the picture. Much of the improvement was only possible because of the continuing drain of population through emigration. Development was lop-sided, favouring the towns at the expense of the countryside, or the more prosperous at the expense of the less prosperous. Within each sector dangerous social tensions still persisted, tensions that would be brought to the surface in the countryside by the Land War of the 1880s, and in the towns and cities by the labour troubles of the years 1907 to 1914. Not even the proliferation of boards and councils was able to banish abject poverty from the land – rural labourers in their unhygienic cottages, city-dwellers in their decaying tenements, continued to live in a wretchedness that perpetually staggered outside observers. Standards of health and housing, despite some real advance, remained deplorably low and in some districts, and for more than a few individuals, starvation itself was never far away.

Yet when the worst is said, and every allowance made for the apparently incurable residuum of human misery, the signs of general improvement among the population at large are too numerous and too striking to be mistaken. It is true that the absence of some essential statistics – not to mention the dearth of reliable research on the existing statistics – makes it notoriously difficult to quantify this improvement. We should expect, for example, to see it registered in a steady growth of Irish income – both national and individual. Such growth there undoubtedly was, though its nature and extent are still in large degree surrounded in mystery. Thanks, however, to a recent and perceptive – though also extremely hypothetical – attempt by Professor Larkin to penetrate this mystery, it is possible to sketch in a very tentative and provisional fashion how Irish income changed during the nineteenth century.* On the evidence available he estimates that the national income increased from about £35 million per annum at the beginning of the nineteenth century to perhaps £82 million a year at the end. Any facile enthusiasm which this increase may evoke can easily be held in check by a reference to the comparable British figures which recorded a growth from £232 million in 1801 to £1,643 million in 1901. However, that there *was* an Irish increase, though a very modest one, seems indisputable. What is more difficult is to determine how this was distributed per head of the population. According to Professor Larkin (and it must be stressed that this part of his calculations is very speculative) the per capita income of the Irish population rose from £6·7 per annum

* See the article by E. Larkin, 'Economic Growth, Capital Investment, and the Roman Catholic Church in Ireland', in *American Historical Review* (April, 1967), lxxii, especially pp. 870-83. Professor Larkin readily concedes the lack of reliable information and the necessarily hypothetical character of some of his assumptions and conclusions, but in the absence of any more detailed analysis, all Irish historians will remain in his debt for a pioneering study of outstanding originality.

in 1801 to £7·9 in 1851; thereafter it grew more markedly until in 1901 it was of the order of £18·4. That this was unevenly divided between Catholic and Protestant goes almost without saying, but Professor Larkin's calculations indicate that the difference between the two religious groups may perhaps have been greater than was previously realised. Assuming for the first half of the nineteenth century a subsistence figure of £5 a year for the individual he reckons that throughout that period the Catholic population as a whole fell regularly below that amount. But in the second half of the century, with his notional subsistence rate rising steadily decade by decade until it reached £10 a year in 1901, his conclusion is that in each decade the Catholic per capita income was above the margin, rising, he would suggest, from £5·1 in 1851 to £12·4 in 1901. The Protestant minority, on the other hand, never came remotely within sight of the subsistence border-line and their income per head, on the basis of Professor Larkin's figures, was generally triple, sometimes quadruple, that of the Catholic majority.

Yet although these differences may well have reinforced religio-political rivalries by a sense of deprivation among Catholics, and of privilege among Protestants, the fact remains that even for the depressed majority the condition of their lives was improving. This, no doubt, was partly because the government, as we have seen, spread a steadily expanding safety-net beneath the most vulnerable sections of the population in its provisions for poor relief, medical care, housing and pensions. That these were scanty enough by modern standards cannot be denied, but in these matters the post-Famine period should properly be compared, not with the second half of the twentieth century, but with the first half of the nineteenth. Such a comparison can only show that things were slowly but surely changing for the better, even having regard to the areas of deep poverty and near destitution of which mention has already been made.

Although the visibility of change was perhaps more evident in the towns, or rather in a handful of the larger centres of population, it was apparent also in the countryside where, after all, the vast majority of Irish families still had to earn a living. By the beginning of the twentieth century the tenant-farmer had either become, or was well on the way to becoming, the owner of his holding, and a peasant proprietary, with all the virtues and vices that the term implies, was gradually emerging. Conservative, ignorant, technically incompetent as many of these small farmers may have been, their achievement of independent status nevertheless marked an important stage in the country's development from which there was no going back. Irish agriculture would still have to fight its way into the markets of the world outside, and in the process learn how far it had to travel before it became fully competitive, but at least the future was in its own hands and it could face that future unencumbered by an antiquated and vicious system of land-tenure. And deficient though he might be in modern methods, the Irish agriculturist, cashing in as he so often did on the relatively high and easy returns of pasture-farming, found himself able to accumulate a modest supply of capital, even if that capital was often used, as we have seen, as a dowry to promote an advantageous marriage, rather than as an investment to improve the quality of his land or stock.

Moreover, although the countryman had his share of economic depression in the latter part of the nineteenth century. It seems probable that during those years – though more strikingly, perhaps, in the subsequent period between 1896 and 1913, except where agricultural prices were outpaced by general prices – his individual purchasing-power increased. The evidence for this is derived from many sources – from the growth of a money economy itself, from the development of retail trading, from greater variety of diet, from additional earnings in cottage-industries, and from the corresponding growth of post office savings and bank deposits. Some of this improvement came, of course, from the operation of external factors – mainly the government land legislation and the beneficent activities of the Congested Districts Board, the Department of Agricultural and Technical Instruction, or the new-fangled co-operative societies that Sir Horace Plunkett was, not without success, endeavouring to promote. But partly also, no doubt, the slow accretion of prosperity was a consequence of greater mobility. This could be both local and general. At the local level the increasing use of the bicycle (as, later, of the bus), brought the farming community nearer to the market-town and this, while adversely affecting the remoter village shops or the pedlars who had for so long served the needs of the most isolated families, introduced a growing proportion of the rural population to the attractions of a wide range of consumer goods and therefore to the uses of a money-economy. In another and wider sense, better rail and sea transport was a solvent of many of the problems of the countryside simply by bringing the surplus labour-force within reach of other sources of livelihood, whether seasonally, in harvest work across the Irish Sea, or permanently, through emigration to foreign parts.

Often, no doubt, movement was merely movement from the countryside to the town. More accurately, perhaps, it was movement towards Dublin or Belfast, for apart from those two giants only a few other places (notably Londonderry) showed any remarkable or sustained growth; most of the smaller towns actually declined in numbers and many retained, as some do even to the present day, a spacious emptiness which had changed little since the eighteenth century. Nevertheless, the rural exodus was such that the urban population accounted for a steadily growing proportion of the whole, from about one-eighth in 1841 to about one-third in 1911. Apart from the northeast, where heavy industry offered reasonable chances of regular employment (though both this and the rate of remuneration varied between the comparative affluence of, say, the shipping or engineering industries, and the often sweated conditions of the hard-pressed linen industry), the working-class population of the towns tended to have to rely upon the insecure and poorly-paid jobs associated mainly with the building or distributive trades – the men were dockers, carters, porters or general labourers, while the women for the most part went into service. The tendency in Ireland since before the Famine, as Charles Booth had noted in 1891, had been for the percentage of the population productively employed to decline, and for the number of those engaged in distribution, service and general labour to increase.* 'These', as a French observer remarked acutely if unkindly of the general labourers, 'are men without any definite trade, ready for anything and good for nothing.'[34] They were to remain a high proportion of the labour-force up to 1914 and even beyond it.[35]

Over this working class, so often precariously poised on the verge of destitution, there rose a middle class which, though never large by the standards of more heavily industrialised countries, was steadily increasing in numbers and prosperity. In its lower reaches – as among the various clerks employed in business or in government offices – it could still be poorly enough paid, but for those who were self-employed in commerce – builders, grocers, drapers, publicans and the like – movement up the scale of well-being and respectability was evident, both from their growing prominence in the economy, and, more visibly, from the spreading suburbs which they inhabited on the fringes of the cities and the larger towns. Fewer in numbers, but superior in social status, and generally also in their style of living, were the owners of the larger businesses and the professional men. These formed an element in society which was not only prosperous, but becoming less exclusive in its prosperity. It is true that some of the larger enterprises in the south (Guinness's brewery, Jameson's distillery, Jacob's biscuit factory, to name only the more obvious examples) were owned by a relatively small number of Protestant families, as was by far the greater part of the heavy industries in the northeast, but Catholic membership of the medical and legal professions, which had long been important, had become dominant by 1914. And although in the inner circles of the civil service, Protestants, as we have seen, were represented to a disproportionately high degree, the tendency in the previous fifty years had been towards a growing involvement of Catholics in government both at the centre and in the provinces.

It is tempting to contrast the rising importance and prosperity of this middle class, modest though that class remained in size, with the declining significance of the aristocracy and the landed gentry. In retrospect, of course, it is easy to see that the social balance in Ireland was undergoing a profound change between the Famine and the First World War.

* In agriculture Booth reckoned the proportional decline between 1841 and 1891 to be from 50·9 to 43·7 per cent and in industry from 29·3 to 20·4 per cent. The corresponding increases in commerce were from 2·6 to 5·4 per cent and in domestic service from 9·4 to 12·2 per cent. Cited in W. P. Coyne (ed.) *Ireland: Industrial and Agricultural* (Dublin, 1901), p. 55. For wage-rates among Irish urban workers, see pp. 69-70 above.

The position of the old Ascendancy was being steadily undermined, both by the transfer of their lands to the new farmer-owners, and by the administrative reforms which placed more and more local government and law enforcement in the hands either of elected bodies or of officials drawn from the ranks of management rather than from county families. Yet this picture of a governing class in full retreat needs to be qualified in three respects. First, so long as a Viceregal Court remained, so long would the old élite gather round it, and so long, too, would many members of the professional middle class – 'Castle Catholic' as well as 'Castle Protestant' – be attracted into that charmed but gimcrack circle. Secondly, it has to be remembered that the actual process of decline was very gradual and that the social prestige of the 'Big House' and all it stood for lingered on long after its economic foundations and its administrative functions had been eroded. Right up to 1914, it is probably not too much to say, most of the Anglo-Irish were blissfully unaware that their day was ending. If Irish society had a 'tone' in the early years of the twentieth century, that tone, however nationalist critics might deplore the fact, was still being dictated by the descendants of those who had dictated it for over two hundred years.

But there is a third and all-important way in which any analysis of change in the Ireland of those years has to be qualified. Because the Anglo-Irish governing class virtually disappeared in the revolutionary storm which broke over it between 1914 and 1921, it is easy to exaggerate the degree to which that political revolution was paralleled by either an economic or a social revolution. True, the vacuum left by the 'Big House' was filled to some extent by the Catholic professional class and by the substantial farmers, the publicans and the shopkeepers. But society itself was to change remarkably little. In their continuing reliance upon the efficient functioning of a more or less benevolent government, in their reluctance to innovate in either industry or agriculture, in their attachment to their religion, and in their unchanging moral and social attitudes, the Irish presented to the twentieth century world the strange and paradoxical spectacle of a people who, having pursued with immense tenacity and a great measure of success the goal of independence, were content to rear upon the foundations of that independence one of the most conservative states in Europe.

4. Variations on the Theme of Nationality

Against the dark and tragic background of the Great Famine the pos-
turings of most of the individual actors in the drama seem unimportant and almost ludicrously irrelevant. When it became clear in the
autumn of 1845 that the potato crop was doomed Irish politics were
still the politics of repeal, not of hunger. Ever since his towering success in winning Catholic Emancipation in 1829, the 'Liberator', Daniel
O'Connell, had aimed avowedly at ending the Union between Great
Britain and Ireland, but for the ten years after the triumph on which
his reputation still largely depends he had spent most of his vast energy
in winning administrative and social reforms for his country by exerting
upon English political parties whatever pressure was open to him in the
House of Commons.[1] In 1840, however, at the age of sixty-five, he had
launched a new organisation, the National Repeal Association, designed
to bring the question of repeal vividly before his fellow-countrymen by
the same technique of mass-agitation which had served him so well in
the Emancipation campaign. After a slow start – repeal was too abstract
a question for the peasantry and had few obvious attractions for the
middle class or the gentry – O'Connell's movement began to gather momentum, partly because he succeeded in winning the support of an
important section of the clergy, but still more because he was powerfully reinforced by an unlooked-for ally, the group that soon became
known as 'Young Ireland'.

The initial impetus behind this group came from three men, two of
them not long graduated from Trinity College, Dublin. One, Thomas
Davis, was a Protestant of mixed English and Anglo-Irish parentage.
His father, who was a surgeon with the British Army, died just before
the boy was born (at Mallow, county Cork) in October 1814, but the
young Thomas Davis was brought up in comfortable circumstances by
his mother. Entering the university in 1831, he graduated four years
later and then turned to legal studies. Although called to the bar, he
did not practise and continued to play a part in the affairs of the main
student debating-club in Trinity, the College Historical Society. It was
to this society that he announced himself, in an address delivered in
1840, as a nationalist dedicated to the service of his country. It was at
Trinity also that Davis met the second of the trio who were to make
such an impact on their own and subsequent generations. This was
John Blake Dillon. Born in 1814 at Ballaghaderrin, county Mayo, of
tenant-farmer origins, his initial destination had been the priesthood.

Finding he had no vocation, he made the transition, unusual then and since, from Maynooth to Trinity College, graduating in 1840 and following Davis as president of the College Historical Society. Together they dabbled in political journalism and together they joined O'Connell's Repeal Association in 1841. But what really took them out of their academic ivory tower was their decision in 1842 to start a newspaper of their own – the *Nation*. In making this decision, and in carrying it out, they owed much to the journalistic skill and organising ability of the third member of the triumvirate, Charles Gavan Duffy. Gavan Duffy was a northern Catholic, born in Monaghan in 1816 into a middle-class background. He had no university education, but even as a very young man had worked on newspapers in Belfast and Dublin; more experienced than either of his friends, he was the driving force behind the paper once it was actually launched, though its intellectual tone was set primarily by Davis.[2]

Almost at once the new paper gained a wide following among educated men and women (and presently, also, among the people at large) for a doctrine of nationality which Davis himself described as 'a nationality of the spirit as well as of the letter', a nationality that would embrace all creeds, races and classes within the island, 'not a nationality which would prelude civil war, but which would establish internal union and external independence'.[3] The elaboration of this doctrine was to be an essential part (though still only a part) of the legacy Young Ireland was to bequeath to posterity, but before exploring it further we must first place the group in its historical context. Although the founders of the *Nation*, and most of the eager band of contributors they soon gathered round them, were initially supporters of the Repeal Association, they were divided from O'Connell by age, by background, by attitudes towards public life, above all by the simple fact that he, though growing old and surrounded by sycophantic hangers-on, could still dominate the masses and the rising Catholic middle class, whereas they, though increasing steadily in influence, as yet exerted that influence only upon a relatively small minority of intellectuals.

It was not surprising therefore that friction should soon have developed between 'Old Ireland' and 'Young Ireland', nor that this should have emerged openly not very long after O'Connell's great year of mass demonstrations ended in fiasco, when in October 1843 he abandoned his much-advertised 'monster meeting' at Clontarf under pressure from the government. Convicted of conspiracy the following February, he emerged after some months of imprisonment (which had been made as comfortable for him as possible) with a clear determination to revert to his former policy of parliamentary opportunism. This did not mean, as has sometimes been suggested, that his influence declined overnight. On the contrary, he retained much of his old magnetism for his fellow-countrymen for at least another two years and some of the most successful of his 'monster meetings' were held as late as 1845.[4] Nevertheless, the Young Irelanders, though as reluctant as most nationalists to detect flaws in the great man, began nevertheless to become increasingly disenchanted with him. They were alienated by his apparent, if transient, readiness to consider a federal solution to the Irish demand which fell far short of repeal, by accusations from his family and followers that they themselves were anti-Catholic and irreligious, and most of all by his attitude towards Sir Robert Peel's Colleges Bill of 1845, which was an attempt to provide university education for those whose needs were not, or could not, be met by Trinity College. Peel's aim, it will be recalled, was to establish three colleges at Belfast, Cork and Galway, the first intended mainly for Presbyterians, the latter two for Roman Catholics. The essence of the scheme was that the colleges were to be free from all denominational tests and that any religious or moral instruction given in them was to be financed by private and not public sources. The Irish bishops were somewhat divided in their reactions to this offer, but showed signs of wanting to use it as a base for further negotiation. O'Connell, however, came out strongly against the 'godless' colleges, as they were termed, and against the whole principle of mixed education of Catholics and Protestants at the same institutions. Since this principle lay at the very heart of Young Ireland doctrine a collision was unavoidable and the two sides clashed openly at a meeting of the Repeal Association in May 1845. To some extent the dispute was academic, for Peel refused to make the concessions the bishops wanted and the Queen's Colleges came into existence under an ecclesiastical cloud, but its importance was real enough – henceforward, however the cracks might be papered over, the fissure in the repeal movement was deep and irremovable.[5]

It was to be intensified still further the following year. By then Thomas Davis, who might have been a moderating force, was dead, stricken down by scarlet fever when still only thirty-one. But even Davis might have been able to do no more than postpone an outright split, for by 1846 it was becoming steadily clearer that two different concepts of nationality were confronting each other – O'Connell's moderate constitutionalism and the much more intransigent creed of Young Ireland, which did not rule out the possibility that in certain circumstances freedom might have to be won by force of arms. In July O'Connell forced the issue to a head by presenting to the Repeal Association a resolution rejecting the use of force other than for self-defence in extreme necessity. This, though it may have been to some extent a tactical device whereby he sought to re-establish control over Young Ireland, was with him a genuine and deeply felt principle.* Unable to

* The fundamental difference between O'Connell and his Young Ireland critics may not at first have been very clear to most contemporaries, but one perceptive English student of Irish affairs, Frederick Lucas (for whom see pp. 116-20 below), laid his finger on it within weeks of the split. Writing in *The Tablet* (8 August 1846), he emphasised that O'Connell's great and abiding concern was to obliterate 'the instinct of physical force' which Young Ireland, while themselves disclaiming any revolutionary

accept this policy the Young Irelanders withdrew from the Association, the lead in this secession being taken by Gavan Duffy and by William Smith O'Brien. O'Brien, who was forty-three years old at this time, was a Protestant landowner (though descended from the ancient Irish family of O'Brien of Thomond and very conscious of the fact) who had been elected to parliament as far back as 1828, when he had distinguished himself by his support for Catholic Emancipation. He only joined the Repeal Association in 1843 and although he deputised for O'Connell while the latter was in prison, his sympathies lay increasingly with the idealism and religious tolerance of Young Ireland. Consequently, when the secessionists set up their own organisation, the Irish Confederation, at the beginning of 1847, he found himself unable to resist the pressure from Gavan Duffy and others that he should place himself at its head.

At that point, with the country reeling under the impact of the Famine, the initiative passed decisively into the hands of Young Ireland. O'Connell's death later in the year removed at one stroke whatever cohesive force still remained in the Catholic mass-movement and it soon appeared that his sons and followers were quite unable to maintain the sort of control the old man had done even during his last anti-climactic years. But Young Ireland itself spoke with more than one voice. Those, like Smith O'Brien and Gavan Duffy, who followed closest in the foot-steps of Thomas Davis, while theoretical revolutionists, were in fact much more wedded to Davis's doctrine of reconciliation, and since they attached great importance to winning over men of property (many of whom, of course, were Protestant landlords) they were only prepared to permit the use of force as a last resort. On the other hand, these were years of rapid and cataclysmic change. It was not just that in Ireland the whole structure of society seemed to be threatened by the Famine, but that in Europe at large red revolution stalked through country after country. And as Irishmen watched closely what was expected to happen in England (like many Englishmen they over-esti-mated the strength of Chartism) and what actually did happen in France and central Europe, some of them began to consider whether the time might not be ripe for a similar outbreak in their own country. Yet was there really a basis for a successful insurrection in Ireland in

intent, were constantly resuscitating by the warlike imagery of their prose and verse. 'Never,' wrote Lucas, 'was there a clearer duty marked out for any man than that marked out for O'Connell. It was simply and nakedly to take the first seasonable opportunity of raising before the public this question of physical force between himself and his antagonists; and so to raise it as, if possible, to crush the very life out of this hostile doctrine, put the people permanently on their guard against its advocates, and prevent it ever being seriously raised again.' I am grateful to Professor Maurice O'Connell of Fordham University for drawing my attention to this article, and for allowing me to see in typescript an essay in which he developed this theme himself and which he pub-lished in the *Irish Times*, 30 Dec. 1971.

1848? Those who thought there was looked not merely to a political motivation, but to an economic one as well. For out of these troubled times emerged a theory of action which was to cast a long shadow over Irish nationalism for many years to come. Its progenitor was James Fintan Lalor. Born in 1807, Lalor was the son of an O'Connellite MP who had been active in the anti-tithe agitation of the 1830s, and it was precisely in the land question that Lalor discerned the Achilles' heel of the existing regime. During 1847 he emerged from total obscurity (fragile in health, he lived nearly all his short life in his native Queen's County) with a series of open letters to the *Nation* in which he developed his central thesis that repeal of the Union was a matter of secondary importance compared with the protection and well-being of the Irish tenant-farmers. Lalor was not, as is sometimes supposed, against private property in land, but he did hold that such property should be conditional, not absolute. In his view, all title to land derived ultimately from the people, and although he did not carry this view to the logical conclusion that the landlords ought therefore to be expropriated *en masse*, he made it quite clear that only those who gave adequate security to their tenants could expect to be saved. The strength of Lalor's case derived mainly from his realisation that the Famine had created, potentially at least, a new situation:

> Society [he wrote in the second of his letters] stands dissolved. In effect, as well as of right, it stands dissolved, and another requires to be constituted. To the past we can never return, even if we would. The potato was our sole and only capital, to live and work on, to make much or little of; and on it the entire social economy of this country was founded, formed and supported. That system and that state of things can never again be resumed or restored; not even should the potato return.[6]

Appealing to the landlords to help in the transformation of society if they did not want to be for ever thrust aside, he summed up his doctrine in one emphatic proposition:

> Its theory contains itself in a single principle; its practical solution is comprised and completed in a single operation. Lay but the foundation and the work is done. . . . Lay deep and strong the only foundation that is firm under the foot of a nation – a secure and independent agricultural peasantry. A secure and independent agricultural peasantry is the only base on which a people ever rises or ever can be raised; or on which a nation can safely rest.[7]

Time was to show that the old society was more resilient than he imagined, but in 1847 it was reasonable enough to suppose that the slate had been wiped entirely clean. Few, however, grasped the implications of this supposition as clearly as Lalor and few, certainly, moved as quickly from theory to policy. Hard on the heels of his diagnosis came his drastic suggestion for a cure – that the tenants should be organised as a prelude to a general strike against rent and, alternatively or additionally, a refusal to pay poor rates.[8] To the more moderate Young Irelanders this was wild, anarchic talk, but there were others who came, albeit gradually, to see in it a genuine means of exerting pressure that might well turn an abortive rebellion into a social revolution. The most important of these was John Mitchel. Mitchel was, like Gavan Duffy, a northerner, but a much more pugnacious one. Born in 1815 the son of a Presbyterian minister, he qualified as a lawyer and joined the Repeal Association in 1843. Two years later he came south to Dublin, became a writer for the *Nation*, and rapidly emerged as among the two or three most forceful and effective journalists to write for Irish newspapers during the nineteenth century. Mitchel, once he had become convinced that a revolution was necessary and that Lalor had the key to it, took this policy to the Irish Confederation early in 1848, demanding that that body begin to organise the country for a campaign to prevent the payment of rents or poor rates. Instead, the Confederation backed Gavan Duffy's alternative proposal for a strong and independent parliamentary party to put the country's case at Westminster. In disgust Mitchel resigned from the Council of the Confederation and started his own paper, the *United Irishman*, advocating armed insurrection to achieve an Irish republic which would destroy landlordism and secure 'the land for the people'.

When the news from Paris showed that revolution might indeed be a real possibility, the ranks of the Confederation began to close again and the *Nation* became nearly as militant as the *United Irishman*. There remained, nevertheless, a significant difference. Those who looked to Smith O'Brien for leadership hoped for a political, not a social revolution; but for those who followed Mitchel and his friends a political revolution was only a step towards the entire recasting of society. This in itself would undoubtedly have driven a fresh wedge between the two wings of the movement, but before the situation could develop further the British government intervened in May 1848, arresting both O'Brien and Mitchel, together with one of the fieriest of the Young Ireland orators, Thomas Francis Meagher. O'Brien and Meagher were discharged, but Mitchel, who had certainly been outspoken enough in his language, was convicted of treason and sentenced to fourteen years' transportation.* From this the authorities proceeded in July to the arrest of

* Mitchel escaped from Tasmania (whither he had been transported) in 1853 and lived as a journalist in the United States for over twenty years. He won notoriety by his support of the South in the American Civil War and by his defence of the South's 'peculiar institution' – slavery. Mitchel retained an interest in Irish politics of the extremer variety and in February 1875 was elected to a Tipperary seat after he had indicated that he would not take his place in parliament. Unseated as a convicted felon he was again returned in March. He travelled to Ireland for the election but died at Newry within a few days of his success.

Gavan Duffy, the seizure of the *Nation* offices, and the suspension of *habeas corpus*, this last extreme measure enabling them to suppress the political clubs that the Confederation had sought to establish in various parts of the country. There seemed no way to hit back at this coercion except by force and so, later that month, the Young Irelanders stumbled, or were pricked, into insurrection. But whatever hopes they might have had of posing a serious threat to the regime vanished in the face of their own inefficiency and the vast indifference of a population too confused by faction and demoralised by hunger and disease to have any will to fight. Here and there a few sporadic outbursts occurred, but although individuals like Smith O'Brien and John Blake Dillon showed personal gallantry, their attitude to war was much too genteel to offer the slightest prospect of success. Smith O'Brien in particular was adamant that as little damage as possible should be caused to property and his own surrender to a body of armed police at Ballingarry in county Tipperary after less than a week of entirely ineffectual campaigning virtually brought the rising to an end.[9] By the autumn of 1848 most of the leaders were either in prison or on their way to exile.*

'Young Ireland', it has been well said, 'was a movement at its weakest in action'.[10] And certainly, when it did finally lurch into its high-principled and futile rebellion it exhibited all the classical symptoms of romantic idealism totally out of touch with the world of reality. Yet it would be foolish to condemn the men of 1848 as of no account because their venture ended in fiasco. Their physical revolution may have foundered in the Widow McCormack's cabbage-patch, but their ideological revolution lived on long after they were gone. Even though, in reaction against their political failure, their intellectual contribution may have been disregarded by those who came immediately after them, we can see now that they bequeathed to later generations three important doctrines. One of these, John Mitchel's insistence upon the need to achieve a republic entirely independent of England, was not of course a new idea (he only arrived at it himself as late as March 1848), but his enunciation of it struck with particular force upon a generation that had grown up under the shadow of O'Connell and his very different programme of constitutional nationalism. Mitchel looked back to Wolfe Tone and this was his central significance in the movement, for in doing so he linked the dispirited and famished Ireland of his own day with the most formidable uprising in modern Irish history and through it with the fountainhead of the republican tradition. Of course Mitchel

* Of the two principal leaders one, Smith O'Brien, was transported to Tasmania but returned to Ireland after his release in 1856; he took no further part in politics. The other, John Blake Dillon, escaped to America after many adventures and practised as a lawyer in New York for some years. Returning to Ireland in 1855 he became drawn into moderate politics and was returned to parliament in 1865, but died of cholera a year later before he had had time to make his mark in the arena where his son John was to be a leading figure for nearly forty years.

did more than look back to the past, he held a lesson for the future as well, a lesson absorbed equally by the Fenians in 1867 and by Connolly and Pearse in 1916. But what especially distinguished Mitchel in this revolutionary progression was the violence of the hatred he managed to convey in his Carlylean prose. This was not, as he himself was at pains to make clear, a hatred of particular individuals, but a hatred of that generalised concept of oppression to which he gave the name England. It was no accident that in the last pamphlet he wrote before going out to proclaim the republic in Easter Week 1916, Patrick Pearse should have quoted with approval these words of Mitchel's:

> I do believe myself incapable of desiring private vengeance. . . . The vengeance I seek is the righting of my country's wrong, which includes my own. Ireland, indeed, needs vengeance; but this is public vengeance, public justice. Herein England is truly a great public criminal. England! all England, operating through her government; through all her organised and effectual public opinion, press, platform, parliament, has done, is doing and means to do, grievous wrong to Ireland. She must be punished; that punishment will, as I believe, come upon her by and through Ireland; and so Ireland will be avenged.[11]

Mitchel's own view of revolution was coloured, as we have seen, by the writings of Fintan Lalor, and Lalor's emphasis upon the primacy of the land war was the second of the legacies passed on by Young Ireland to their political heirs. Lalor himself was as dedicated an insurgent as Mitchel. Not only did he help to launch the *Irish Felon* (a newspaper intended to carry on the work of the *United Irishman* after Mitchel's arrest), but, although swept into prison in 1848 only to be released as a dying man, he spent his last months before his death in December 1849 trying to foment a new outbreak in the south. His lasting influence, however, was in the interplay of economic thought and action. In this he influenced equally Michael Davitt and the Land League, James Connolly (who saw him as a solitary peak in nineteenth century Irish thinking about the economic factor in history) and Patrick Pearse. Lalor's doctrine was fragmentary, hasty and ill-considered – everything he had to say was said between 1847 and 1849 – but it powerfully reinforced the Wolfe Tone tradition which looked to the sovereignty of the people as the basis of nationality. Here is how he stated it in his first letter to the *Irish Felon*, in a passage that was later to become perhaps the most quoted of all his writings:

> The principle I state, and mean to stand upon, is this, that the entire ownership of Ireland, moral and material, up to the sun, and down to the centre, is vested of right in the people of Ireland; that they, and none but they, are the land-owners and law-makers of this island; that all laws are null and void not made by them; and all titles

to land invalid not conferred and confirmed by them; and that this full right of ownership may and ought to be asserted and enforced by any and all means which God has put into the power of man.[12]

Yet in the end, though Young Ireland may stand in the eyes of later generations for its advocacy of a people's republic, it stands still more for the gentler, reconciling ideals of Thomas Davis. Davis, too, could be extreme, and did not rule out the use of force, but his vision of the future was essentially a vision in which the different and warring elements of Irish life would be fused into a higher, nobler whole. It is easy in the light of subsequent events to dismiss such a vision as fantasy and the accusation that has often been levelled against Davis and his school – that their nationalism was too romantic, too literary – is not without foundation. 'Yet', as an acute critic has observed,

it has a dignity of aspiration, if not of enunciation. Surrounded by evidences of the erosion of things Irish all round him, aware of Irish linguistic change, constant imitation of English fashions and attitudes . . . and conscious that even the national leader, O'Connell, was committed to English Utilitarianism, Davis struggled manfully to recall his countrymen to a sense of pride in being Irish.[13]

This is indeed the essential message of Davis, one might fairly say the essential message of the Young Irelanders as a group. Pointing as they did to the whole past civilisation of their country – its language, its history, its literature, its laws and monuments – they insisted that this was something to which *all* Irishmen were heirs, the common ground on which conflicting sectional interests might eventually unite. Nowadays this seems naive and too facile in its optimism, and Davis has been condemned by some as too much the Anglo-Irish Protestant liberal and too little the Irish nationalist, as too superficial in his approach to the complex Gaelic and Catholic roots of Ireland's culture, in short as almost irrelevant to the great debate about what constitutes a nation. But this is to do violence to history by the cardinal sin of omitting whatever may not fit into some latter-day stereotype. It is to overlook the fact that his teachings moved many of the best minds and most generous spirits that came after him. It is to ignore that he was named as master by men so diverse as the Fenian, John O'Leary, Arthur Griffith and Patrick Pearse. If the reality of Irish life came to bear little relation to Davis's dream, the fault may be in the reality, not in the dream.

(ii) THE QUEST FOR AN INDEPENDENT PARLIAMENTARY PARTY

Throughout the period of the Union Irish nationalism expressed itself politically in three main ways – armed revolution, mass agitation, and parliamentary pressure. Which of these methods would be used at any particular moment, and whether they would be used singly, in combination, or in competition, depended very much on the circumstances of the time, but there was an important difference between parliamentary pressure and the other two modes of expression. Whereas mass agitations could only be called into being with great difficulty and under some exceptional provocation, and whereas armed revolution was by definition a final and desperate expedient, the fact that Irishmen were permanently represented, year in year out, in the House of Commons meant that they had ready to their hands an instrument which, if they could only master it, could be used at any time to extract concessions for their country.

To master this instrument, however, was precisely the problem. The Irish seats, which in the post-famine period amounted to 105 (later reduced to 103), constituted less than a sixth of the total strength of the House of Commons, so that even if all the Irish members were to be united on any one policy they could still only hope to sway the balance if English parties were so closely matched that the government of the day was dependent on the Irish vote to stay in office. But of course the Irish members never were united on any one policy. On the contrary, for the first three-quarters of the nineteenth century many of them faithfully reflected both the attitudes and the organisation, or rather lack of organisation, of their English counterparts, and Irish constituencies were generally occupied by Whigs, or Liberals, or Conservatives, in much the same way as constituencies in other parts of the United Kingdom.

Yet it would be misleading to draw the parallel too exactly. For although Irish members might usually be indistinguishable from other members it remained true that they were at Westminster under rather peculiar conditions and that some at least persisted in believing that they should not be there at all. To separate such members from the common herd, to give them an identity of their own, in short to create an independent Irish parliamentary party, was therefore a constantly recurring dream with those who wanted to use Irish representation in the Commons as a means of redressing Irish grievances or even of ending the Act of Union that bound the two countries together. Daniel O'Connell had had some, admittedly transitory, success during the 1830s and 1840s in creating a party pledged to reform and ultimately to repeal, but it had been based mainly on personal allegiance to himself and, as he declined, so too did it. The Young Irelanders also had been attracted by the idea of forging an effective parliamentary weapon and until the pull, or drift, towards revolution had become irresistible Charles Gavan Duffy, as we have seen, had for a time championed this policy against Mitchel's intransigent republicanism.

With the collapse first of O'Connell's mass agitation for repeal, and then of the uprising of 1848, parliamentary pressure seemed, in the immediate future at any rate, to be the only channel left open for practical political action by nationalists. Yet, ironically enough, in the immediate aftermath of '48 popular attention was centred not upon putative political action, but upon existing economic grievances. Even though the Famine years, as we saw earlier, had reduced the population so drastically, this had not, in the short term at least, improved the position of those tenants who had survived hunger and disease and had not used the escape hatch of emigration. On the contrary, their position seemed almost worse than before. Rents which might not have been excessive in good times now pressed hard upon the impoverished farmers and even those landlords who had had a reputation for kindliness in times past were themselves so hard pressed that they were driven to resort more freely than before to evictions for non-payment, which remained, it is fair to add, by far the most common ground for eviction. But evictions were becoming a matter not just of retribution but of policy. Landowners, both the old landowners and those who had bought up land under the Encumbered Estates Act, were seizing the opportunity to clear small-holders off the land and to consolidate their tenements into larger and, it was hoped, more economic farms. The tenants, lacking any kind of security, were only too vulnerable to this kind of pressure—in 1849 no less than 16,686 families were known to the police to have been evicted, and in 1850 the total had gone up to 19,949.*[14] It is true that in the former year 3,302 families—and in the latter, 5,403—were reinstated as caretakers, but this still left a substantial number who were cut adrift from their holdings, especially if they had the misfortune to be tenants of the smaller and more impecunious landlords, who were often, to use a country saying, pulling the devil by the coat-tails. Efforts to organise some sort of resistance had begun as far back as 1847—Fintan Lalor had been involved in one of them—but it was not until 1849 that the first Tenant Protection Society with any pretensions to permanence was organised at Callan, county Kilkenny, with the two-fold aim of obtaining rents fixed by independent valuation, and of pledging the farmers themselves not to take the land of any evicted tenant who had been prepared to pay a rent so valued.[15]

This initiative was soon followed elsewhere in the south and by 1850 there were twenty similar societies scattered through Munster, Leinster and Connaught. In Ulster, meanwhile, an agitation, superficially similar but fundamentally different, had simultaneously been gaining ground. In that province the tenants were to some extent already protected by the 'Ulster tenant-right' which gave them a reasonable expectation of

* In the thirty years after 1849 about five million acres, roughly a quarter of the land of Ireland, changed hands under the Encumbered Estates Act (L. M. Cullen, *Life in Ireland* (London, 1968), p. 144). This was not only the time when evictions were at their height, but it also fell within the period (extending from the Famine through the decade of the fifties) when many of the rents were fixed which survived unchanged for twenty years only to become the target of the Land League. (For illustrative figures, see B. Solow, *The Land Question and the Irish Economy, 1870-1903*, pp. 71-2.)

remaining undisturbed in their holdings so long as they paid their rent, and which also allowed them to sell the right to occupy their holding to anyone whom the landlord was prepared to regard as an acceptable tenant. These, probably over-rated, privileges were widely regarded at the time as putting the Ulster farmers in a somewhat more secure, and therefore prosperous, situation than their fellows in the south, but the 'custom' suffered precisely from the fact that it was a custom not a law, and one which landlords who were themselves under economic pressure might be tempted to abrogate. To remove this uncertainty and to convert their privilege into a right protected by the courts therefore became a fundamental objective for the northern farmers. As early as 1847 W. Sharman Crawford, MP for Rochdale but an Ulsterman by birth, had introduced a bill into the House of Commons to legalise the Ulster custom, or 'tenant-right' as it was often called, only to meet with ignominious defeat. This defeat had exposed the vulnerability of the farmers' case and almost at once tenant-societies began to be founded in various parts of the province in support of Sharman Crawford. The fact that in the next two years Ulster, the 'custom' notwithstanding, began to suffer from the same maladies of high rents and frequent evictions as the rest of Ireland intensified the agitation and by 1850 it had not only become geographically widespread, but had attracted the powerful support of the Presbyterian Church.[16]

The emergence of these tenant-right movements in so many different parts of the country at a time when repeal was apparently dead and damned pointed the way towards the kind of agrarian combination of which Fintan Lalor had written so passionately and perceptively only three short years before. And when in August 1850 representatives of the various tenant-right societies met in Dublin to form the Tenant League it seemed as if an agrarian combination was precisely what they had in view. The aims of the League were declared to be the winning of fixity of tenure, lower rents and legal protection for Ulster tenant-right, and for a moment it looked as if here was a platform on which farmers from every part of the country could unite. Yet in reality this was not so and the potentially formidable threat of a national strike against rent never materialised. For this there seem to have been two main reasons. One was that although the Tenant League was optimistically called by its historian, Charles Gavan Duffy, 'The League of North and South', the title was always something of a fiction.[17] Individual northerners, like Sharman Crawford himself, were enthusiastically loyal to the tenant-right movement, but the Ulster societies as a whole had less drive and less staying-power than those in the south – understandably so, since the grievances of the northern farmers, though real enough, were still less urgent than those of the tenants in most other parts of the country. There was, therefore, little likelihood that even if an agitation were to develop it would become a truly *national* agitation.

But here the second factor militating against any such agitation asserted itself. There was no widespread agrarian campaign mainly because the two principal leaders of the Tenant League were determined to try to solve this essentially economic question by political means. One of them, Gavan Duffy, the only Young Irelander of note free to engage in politics after 1848, reverted almost by instinct to the idea he had been pressing on his friends almost up to the eve of the abortive rising of that year – that the best way of exerting pressure and winning positive reforms for Ireland was to return to parliament a party independent of all other groups in the House of Commons and able, by its unity and solidarity, to exercise an influence out of all proportion to its numbers. The other outstanding figure in the League – possibly, indeed, the more outstanding of the two – shared the same idea. This was Frederick Lucas, an Englishman, born in 1812 and thus four years older than Gavan Duffy. A Quaker by origin, Lucas had become a convert to Catholicism and in 1840 had founded his paper, the *Tablet*, designed to speak for his new-found co-religionists. He transferred his headquarters to Dublin in 1849 and at once became immersed in the problems of the Irish poor. But for Lucas, as for Duffy, the answer to these problems was primarily political. While living in England he had sought to organise Catholic voters as a separate, independent body and the idea of an Irish party quite distinct from all others was one to which he readily responded. Consequently, when the new League, having defined its objectives, went on to outline its methods of attaining them, the emphasis was placed firmly upon political propaganda and the formation of a political party pledged to oppose any government which did not accept the principles of tenant-right and tenant-security for which the League itself stood.

By a curious chance, quite unconnected with Irish affairs, this impulse towards parliamentary action was intensified by the crisis which blew up in 1850 and 1851 over the Pope's decision to institute in England a regular diocesan organisation with an Archbishop and Bishops. This at once provoked a storm of Protestant indignation and led to the introduction into parliament of the Ecclesiastical Titles Bill, repeating in more precise terms the prohibition already contained in the Emancipation Act of 1829 against the assumption of territorial titles in England by Catholic prelates. Most of the Irish members who represented Catholic constituencies voted against the Bill and though this in itself was not sufficient to prevent it from passing into law, their action was significant in two respects. First, since they were themselves for the most part Liberals and since the government responsible for the legislation was itself a Whig one, they were asserting their separate identity in the most marked manner available to them. And second, they combined among themselves to attack the ministry not just on the Ecclesiastical Titles Bill, but on every possible occasion, and in so doing gained a degree of unity and cohesion, which they sought to perpetuate beyond the parliamentary session by forming in Dublin in August 1851 a kind of extra-mural organisation, the Catholic Defence Association.

These independent Irish members were not numerous – only about two dozen out of some sixty Irish Liberals adopted the new policy – but they were sufficiently effective to attract considerable attention and sufficiently conscious of their own militancy to assume the flamboyant title, 'the Irish Brigade'.* They contained, also, men of substance and of considerable influence in Ireland. Three in particular were destined to stand out. One was the fiery and cantankerous Mayo landlord, George Henry Moore, more famous perhaps as the father of the novelist George Moore, but himself the subject of an affectionate portrait by his other son, Maurice.[18] A second was an ambitious barrister and able debater, William Keogh, MP for Athlone. And the third was John Sadleir, MP for Carlow, a rich man by Irish standards, heavily – and time would reveal disastrously – involved in a variety of business undertakings.

Here then was an independent Irish party in the making, but it was a party which had fashioned its precarious unity out of a religious issue, and a religious issue seemed hardly the best basis on which to knit together Ulster Presbyterians and southern Catholics. Should the Tenant League therefore shun the 'Irish brigade' or should it try to make use of this weapon placed almost providentially within its grasp? Gavan Duffy, whose ecumenical Young Ireland instincts were still strong, feared that the admixture of a religious issue with an agrarian one would only prejudice the latter. Lucas, on the other hand, drawn by his own previous history to see an independent party as essentially a Catholic one, had no qualms and it was his policy that prevailed. In August 1851 the leaders of the 'Brigade' and the League came together and formulated a common policy which embraced two of the League's original aims – lower rents and protection of tenant-right – while dropping the difficult question of security of tenure for the time being.

This, it must be emphasised, was not much more than a loose alliance which happened to be convenient to both parties, but events almost immediately conspired to make it rather more than this. Early in 1852 the Whig government fell, giving place to a Conservative ministry under Lord Derby. The Conservatives were a minority in the House and counted on a general election in July to improve their position. In the interval, however, they bade fair to outdo the Liberals in the strenuousness of their Protestantism, issuing a proclamation in June enforcing the prohibition already imposed by the Emancipation Act of 1829 on Catholic processions. This in itself would have inflamed Irish opinion, but when serious riots broke out at Stockport in Cheshire a couple of weeks later, after Catholics who had disregarded the ban had been set upon by Protestant mobs, the natural reaction in Ireland was to blame the entire incident upon the reactionary policy of the government. With Liberals and Conservatives both tarred with the same brush

* They were later to attract a less flattering description – 'the Pope's brass band' – but there seems little evidence that this was contemporary usage.

of religious bigotry the prospect of an independent Irish party seemed more than ever enticing.

It was just such a party that the election of 1852 seemed to have produced. Not only were the Brigade returned in force, but the League leaders were elected as well, and in most parts of the country, with the significant exception of Ulster, the principle of independent opposition appeared to have carried the day.* Following the election two conferences were called in Dublin in the autumn of 1852. At the first of these it was decided that the MPs, who had been returned on tenant-right principles, should hold themselves 'independent of and in opposition to' all governments which did not fully meet the demands of the Tenant League. And at the second conference, which dealt with the religious question, it was equally decided that Irish Liberal MPs should be asked to remain 'independent of and in opposition to' all governments which did not proceed to repeal the Ecclesiastical Titles Act and disestablish the Church of Ireland. In total, the number of Irish members who pledged themselves to independent opposition in support of these agrarian and religious policies was forty-eight. This made them the largest party in Ireland, for at the recent election the Conservatives, even after the most strenuous efforts, had been unable to muster more than forty-one, the balance being made up of fifteen Whigs and a solitary Peelite.

But was this new 'independent party' really a party at all in any recognisable sense of the term? The sequel suggests that it was not. At the end of 1852 the Conservative government fell from power (not without a strong push from the Irish party) and a Whig-Peelite coalition under Lord Aberdeen took its place. Two members of the Irish party – William Keogh and John Sadleir – were offered posts in the new administration and both of them accepted. At once they were violently attacked in Ireland as pledge-breakers and renegades which, on any reckoning, was precisely what they were. Their defection was not the end of the independent party, but that two such prominent members had deserted at the first opportunity was disconcerting on a double count. First, it indicated how difficult it was going to be to persuade able and ambitious men to confine themselves to the stony and sterile path of independent opposition which, however admirable in principle, offered those who trod it virtually no chance of advancing their own careers. And secondly, and in more practical terms, the action of Sadleir and Keogh proved infectious. Other Irish Liberals moved quietly over to support of the ministry and even in the constituencies the disillusioned electors began in some instances to turn again to well-tried

* The situation in Ulster was radically different partly because the influence of the landlords was countered less by the influence of the priests than elsewhere, partly because the religious issue which agitated the south left Ulster Presbyterians unmoved (except, perhaps in the opposite direction) and partly because times were beginning to improve and the need for agitation seemed no longer pressing.

Whigs rather than continue the experiment with unreliable independents. By 1853 the Irish party was down to twenty-six members, with three others doubtful. This was still more than half the original total, but it was a sad thinning of the ranks to have occurred in so short a time.

To contemporaries, and to many subsequent historians, the brazen departure of Sadleir and Keogh from the pledge-bound party seemed to constitute such a dramatic repudiation of the doctrine of parliamentary independence that it has been given a more central position in the story than it really deserves. Far more serious for the future of the party was the next crisis that assailed it two years later. Predictably enough, this arose out of the party's preoccupation with the religious issue. Because that issue had been so prominent at the election of 1852 it had been almost a matter of course for the parish clergy up and down the country to take a prominent part in electioneering. In this there was nothing either novel or surprising. In a poverty-stricken and backward countryside they had long represented a natural counterpoise to the landlords and were generally and readily accepted as political as well as spiritual mentors to their flocks. So in 1852 they had bent themselves with a will to the task of arranging meetings, canvassing electors, even transporting voters to the polls. Since there was no secret ballot it was obvious that opportunities for intimidation were very great and a bishop anxious that his priests should keep their spiritual leadership unstained by contact with the gross world of politics might reasonably look askance at such whole-hearted involvement by the parish clergy in the heady excitement of a general election. Such a prelate was Paul Cullen, who, after a period as head of the Irish College in Rome, had become Archbishop of Armagh in 1850, being rapidly translated to Dublin where he remained at the centre of all the controversies swirling round the Church during his long tenure of the Archbishopric from 1852 to 1878.

When the Irish independent party had first come into being Cullen, like the majority of the Irish bishops, had preserved a cautious neutrality towards it, though he was reckoned to be not unsympathetic either towards the Tenant League or towards the Catholic Defence Association. Gradually, however, his attitude became distinctly cool. It was noticeable that he did not join in the general condemnation of Sadleir and Keogh and this warning sign was soon followed by others which indicated that he was preparing to bring pressure on the clergy to abstain from the kind of political intervention which so many of them had come to take for granted. There were excellent pastoral reasons for inducing the priests to moderate their ardour and during 1853 and 1854 the Church as a whole, both at a national council of bishops and at the Armagh and Dublin synods, had been addressing itself to this very problem. Nevertheless, given the central part played by the clergy in elections, any limitation of their right to participate freely was bound to have unpleasant consequences for the independent party, and it was not surprising that its leaders reacted strongly against what the Archbishop seems quite genuinely to have regarded as an eminently reasonable exercise of his authority.

Unhappily, the role of the parish priests and curates at the hustings was not the only bone of contention between Cullen and the party leaders. He, for example, with his lively appreciation of the need for turning every twist in British politics to Catholic advantage – especially in the sphere of education – was made increasingly uneasy by the whole concept of independent opposition which he regarded as not only impracticable, but dangerous. 'If all Catholics were to unite in adopting such principles', he wrote agitatedly to Rome in 1855, 'I am persuaded that the English government in self-defence would have to expel them from parliament and begin to renew the penal laws.'[19] This was certainly a gross, almost a ludicrous, overstatement of the case, but the touch of hysteria the passage betrays may be due at least in part to the fact that both the Tenant League and the independent party were linked in Cullen's eyes with red revolution by reason of the fact that Charles Gavan Duffy was prominent in each of them. Cullen had been in Rome in 1848–49, had been most powerfully and disagreeably impressed by the uprising of that time, and by some curious logic of his own never ceased thereafter to equate Young Ireland with Young Italy, or Gavan Duffy with Mazzini. The comparison was grotesquely inept at either the general or the personal level, but it was real enough to the Archbishop and certainly helped to shape his attitude towards both League and party.

Yet it was not Duffy but Lucas who turned out in this instance to be his chief adversary. Convinced, unjustly it would now appear, that Cullen was bringing pressure to bear exclusively upon priests who had been prominent in support of the independents, Lucas eventually took the very extreme step of appealing to Rome in the winter of 1854–5, partly to win support for the policy of independent opposition, partly to secure freedom of political action for the clergy. On the first point he was predictably unsuccessful, for the Papacy quite naturally refused to budge from neutrality in what was, from its point of view, an essentially domestic matter. On the second point he seems to have met with at least a reasonably sympathetic hearing and may even have been instrumental in securing a relaxation of the rules governing the making of political speeches by priests in Ireland. But this gain, if it was a gain, was more than outweighed by the added hostility with which Cullen repaid him for his manoeuvre, and by the steady drift away from the party of laymen and priests, both shocked by the temerity with which he had tried to strike at the Archbishop through the Vatican. By 1856 the parliamentary strength of the party had dwindled to a dozen, and since Lucas had died the previous year, and Gavan Duffy had gone off in despair and frustration to begin a new career in Australia, it seemed as if the once promising movement of independent opposition had come to an ignominious end.

This was not quite the case. The embers of independence were not entirely extinct and for a few years more they were occasionally capable of flickering into life. But the party as such was never again able to rise above a total of twelve members and found it difficult enough to maintain even that number. What finally broke it was the overwhelming strain of continuing the austere policy of parliamentary aloofness when the political situation cried out for the very different policy of playing one English party off against the other. In 1858 the Conservatives had again taken office without a stable majority and the temptation to trade Irish votes for Irish concessions became in the end irresistible. But the mere fact of yielding to this temptation exposed the hollowness of the independent party's pledge. If Irish members, sworn to fight all governments which would not meet their full demand, in practice supported a Conservative government in the hope of receiving much less than that demand, what then became of independent opposition? The answer was not long in coming. In 1859 the ministry introduced a bill for parliamentary reform. Was the Irish party to support this desirable measure or should it adhere to its principles and side with the Liberal opposition? Perhaps it was characteristic of the confusion into which the Irish independents had fallen that half of them answered this crucial question one way and half the other. The split thus indecently made public was never mended, the Tenant League ceased thereafter to exist, and though independent members still haunted the House of Commons they sat as individuals, not as a party.

Thus ended an interesting but vain experiment to break out of the straitjacket which the Act of Union seemed to have imposed on Irish politics. By whatever test one cares to apply the Irish party was a failure. It did not achieve a single item in its programme. It made little impact in parliament. In Ireland it was beset throughout its career by problems and crises and lost ground almost as rapidly as it had originally gained it. Worst of all, by its very ineffectiveness it killed for nearly a generation any belief in the value of parliamentary pressure and set up a current of scepticism, even of cynicism, towards constitutional methods that was to run through Irish politics until the British connection was finally broken by other means. To use those other means – to turn again to armed rebellion, however doomed and futile – now became the guiding ideal of all those impatient young men for whom the defection of Sadleir and Keogh epitomised everything that was base and weak in parliamentarism.

To lay the blame for this melancholy situation upon the leaders of the independent party is legitimate, but only so long as it is realised that, their personal inadequacies apart, they were to some extent the victims of circumstances beyond their control. It was, for example, their misfortune but not their fault that in the mid-nineteenth century all the jobs and promotions conferred by patronage were monopolised by those who contrived to be on good terms with whatever government was in power. But an independent Irish party, and still more its hungry followers in the constituencies, could never hope to share in the spoils precisely because it *was* independent. It was asking a lot of local patriots to demand that they remain faithful indefinitely to a political party that could not reward its own – indeed, the sequel showed that it was asking too much. Moreover, in the country at large the party was ill-placed to resist the still powerful influence of landlords who might favour Whigs or Tories, but never independents. This influence might have been balanced by that of the priests – in fact, was balanced in 1852 – but after the quarrel with Archbishop Cullen even this hope proved vain. And if that were not enough, it has to be remembered that the business of getting elected to parliament, and staying there once elected, was extremely expensive. Throughout the brief history of their movement the leaders of the independent party were plagued by the impossibility of obtaining sufficient candidates of wealth and calibre. This difficulty was so pervasive and so crippling that it has been described by the leading authority on the subject as 'probably the most serious obstacle' to the building up of an independent Irish party.[20]

One moral may perhaps be drawn from the story. The history of the Tenant League and the Irish Brigade suggests very strongly that the leaders had mistaken their priorities. They hoped to remove economic grievances by parliamentary pressure; but they failed to realise that an Irish party was only effective in the House of Commons to the extent that it was backed by a powerful movement at home. O'Connell in his prime had glimpsed that fundamental truth of Irish politics, but Lucas and Gavan Duffy and George Henry Moore all ignored it. When it was rediscovered a generation later by Parnell and Michael Davitt a startled world learned for the first time how explosive a combination a mass agrarian movement and a tightly disciplined party under leadership of genius could prove to be.

(iii) THE PHOENIX FLAME*

The emblem of insurgent nationalism in Ireland has traditionally been the phoenix, the bird which, springing eternally from its own ashes, has symbolised for over a hundred years the determination of Irish revolutionaries to mount on stepping stones of their dead selves to higher things. It is peculiarly apt that this symbol should have been so closely associated from the beginning with the Fenian movement which, as surely as any phoenix from its pyre, rose from the ruins of the insurrection of 1848. In both a personal and an ideological sense Fenianism was the successor to, or continuation of, Young Ireland – at least of that militant section of Young Ireland which, not content with making its

* By way of tribute to the late Desmond Ryan, who did so much to illuminate the history of the Fenian movement, I have borrowed for the heading of this section the title, *The Phoenix Flame*, which he used for his study of John Devoy and Fenianism published over thirty years ago.

own futile contribution to the year of revolutions, set to work as soon as that was stamped out to plan another outbreak.

A second attempt to establish an independent Irish republic within a few months of the failure of 1848 was never much more than a fantasy, and in fact, as we saw earlier, Lalor's attempt to bring about a rising in 1849 was virtually still-born. In this there was nothing surprising. The government was on the alert and ready to bring superior force quickly to bear wherever a crisis threatened. The people were confused and disheartened, intent mainly upon the brute business of physical survival. The leaders themselves were not only few in numbers at the outset but had been further reduced by imprisonment, transportation and exile. Yet, ironically enough, in this diaspora lay the seeds of the next manifestation of the will to independence. For it was in America and in France that the movement, apparently crushed out of existence in Ireland, still lived on. America was important to the continuity of revolutionary nationalism primarily because of the number of Irish people who went to live there in the Famine years and after. In 1851 alone 221,000 had left for the United States and three years later the emigration rate was still running at over a hundred thousand. By then there were about a million men, women and children of Irish birth who had made their way across the Atlantic and somewhat more than a quarter of a million were to be found in Britain. These emigrants, or refugees as they might well be called, were mostly very poor, they encountered great difficulty in establishing themselves in their new environments, and all too often they gravitated to the bottom of the social and economic scale. Not surprisingly, the hatred they carried in their hearts against the cause, as they understood it, of all their sufferings was intensified by their experiences, and the Irish ghettoes in the cities of the United States, and to a lesser extent those of England and Scotland, rapidly became centres of virulent anti-British feeling.

The role of France in the complex politics of revolutionary Ireland was quite different – less permanent, but nevertheless important. Where the British and American cities provided the mass-feeling which in time might generate active support (and not least financial support) for a new attempt at independence, France – more specifically Paris – afforded a haven to some of the leaders who ceaselessly plotted and schemed for a new day of reckoning. Among the flotsam and jetsam of revolutionary movements from all over Europe that fetched up in the French capital in and after 1848 two Irishmen in particular stood out. One, James Stephens, though very explicit about his own genius for leadership, was all his life something of a mystery. We know, for example, that he was born in Kilkenny in 1824, and educated at St Kieran's College there, but we know little else about his early days. It seems that his family background was comfortably bourgeois, that he himself was trained as a civil engineer, and that he worked for some time on railway construction in the south of Ireland.[21] Like so many other young men of his generation he was deeply influenced by the

Nation newspaper, and by the whole Young Ireland movement. He appears to have taken part in secret drilling with the Confederate clubs in the neighbourhood of Kilkenny and when the rising came he acted as *aide-de-camp* to Smith O'Brien, being seriously wounded at Ballingarry. After many adventures he escaped to France with a companion, Michael Doheny (who has left a memorable record of these wanderings), arriving in Paris in September 1848.[22] There, he eked out a precarious existence as a teacher of English and a student of many subjects. According to his own account, he mixed freely with the leading European revolutionaries and deliberately resolved to become a professional in the art and science of conspiracy.

His chief friend in Paris was John O'Mahony. O'Mahony had been born about 1815 near Mitchelstown, in county Cork, of an ancient and prosperous land-owning family. It was a family with a rebel background, since O'Mahony's father and uncle had both been 'out' in 1798. O'Mahony himself was educated in Cork and at Trinity College, Dublin. He left the university without taking a degree but not before he had become something of a specialist in languages, including Irish, and in the ancient history of his own country. (Later, in exile and under conditions of great hardship, he achieved a famous translation of Keating's *History of Ireland*.) Unlike Stephens, O'Mahony had first been drawn towards politics by O'Connell's repeal movement. Then, following a familiar progression, he had come under the spell, first of Thomas Davis and the *Nation*, and afterwards of Fintan Lalor and John Mitchel. Almost more than anyone else, indeed, O'Mahony was to carry into the new phase of the movement Lalor's vision of a social-democratic republic, though he managed to combine this, in a fashion characteristically his own, with what Stephens called an 'intense nostalgia' for the Gaelic past. Tall, athletic, inordinately handsome, O'Mahony was at once a fighter and a dreamer. In later years the latter trait was to predominate, but in 1848 his temperament responded enthusiastically to the opportunity of action offered by the rising. When that opportunity evaporated he, too, contrived to escape to Paris and at once joined that little group of Irish conspirators who drew from the recent fiasco only the moral that next time there must be more intensive and secret preparation. Sharing this view, O'Mahony refused to countenance the premature and ill-conceived attempt at insurrection in 1849. Instead, after several penurious years in Paris, he moved in 1854 to New York, where he found not only a large Irish population (more than a quarter of the city's total) but also another group of exiled Young Irelanders, among them Michael Doheny.

In New York O'Mahony gradually emerged as the most dedicated, if not perhaps the most efficient, of the refugee leaders, but for the time being the movement's centre of gravity shifted back to Ireland. It did so because in 1856 Stephens himself had returned home to reconnoitre the situation. It was depressing enough. A gargantuan tour on foot (the famous 'three thousand mile walk') showed him that the old Confederate clubs had vanished and that it was necessary to build again from the foundations. Spurred on by suggestions from O'Mahony and Doheny that he should himself begin the work of renewal, Stephens undertook, with characteristic self-confidence, to enrol 10,000 men within three months if he could be guaranteed a hundred pounds per month and also, and still more typically, if his own dictatorial control of the organisation were accepted. His emissary to America, Joseph Denieffe, was only able to bring back four hundred dollars, but even with this small fund Stephens was prepared to make a start. On St Patrick's Day, 1858, he launched a new secret society with the old aim, 'to make Ireland an independent democratic republic'. In form, this society closely followed the contemporary continental model. Security, so it was fondly hoped, was to be preserved by the division of the membership into 'Circles'. A Circle consisted theoretically of 820 men commanded by a 'Centre' and organised in multiples of nine. Under each Centre (A) were nine B's (captains), under each B were nine C's (sergeants), and under each C were units of nine D's (privates). The intention was to maintain secrecy by allowing the rank and file member to be aware of his own immediate group and therefore incapable of betraying the larger ramifications of the movement. Unhappily, this did not occur in practice and few conspiratorial societies can have been so easily and frequently penetrated by informers and secret agents as this one.*

From this small beginning sprang the movement we know as Fenianism. That was not Stephens's name for it. At first, indeed, his secret society had no name, being called variously 'The Society', 'The Organisation', or 'The Brotherhood'. Gradually the 'Brotherhood' theme became predominant, though until 1873 no-one seems to have been clear whether the Brotherhood was to be described as Revolutionary or Republican. It was only after the reorganisation of the society in that year that the initials IRB., which were to weave themselves into the very fabric of Irish history, came to stand definitively for Irish Republican Brotherhood. The designation, Fenian, came, as might have been expected, from O'Mahony's preoccupation with the Gaelic past, for he wished to apply to the members of his parallel American organisation (whence it spread to include the Irish wing of the movement

* The oath, as revised by Stephens in 1859, ran as follows: 'I, AB, in the presence of Almighty God, do solemnly swear allegiance to the Irish Republic now virtually established; and that I will do my very utmost, at every risk, while life lasts, to defend its independence and integrity; and finally, that I will yield implicit obedience in all things, not contrary to the laws of God [or, sometimes, 'the laws of morality'], to the commands of my superior officer. So help me God. Amen.' This oath was substantially changed upon the reorganisation of the republican movement in 1873 and frequently taken in a shortened form, of which the following is an example: 'I agree to become a member of the IRB, and I swear to do all in my power to establish the independence of Ireland and to keep secret all things relating to the organisation.'

also) the name that had been carried by the warrior-caste of the heroic legends of ancient Ireland.

The time was soon to come when the American organisation, the Fenian Brotherhood properly so called and founded, like Stephens's society, in 1858, would make most of the running. But in the immediate future the initiative lay with Stephens and with a young man who had shared with him the launching of the new secret society. The young man was Thomas Clarke Luby, on the face of it a most improbable conspirator. Born in 1822, the son of a Church of Ireland rector married to a Catholic, and the nephew of a much respected Fellow of Trinity College, Dublin, Luby clearly sprang from even more of an 'establishment' background than Thomas Davis himself. Following a somewhat desultory study of the law, Luby had made the fashionable pilgrimage from the literary revivalism of the *Nation* to Lalor and Mitchel, from the oratory and journalism of Young Ireland to the Confederate clubs and the rising of 1848. Luby's part in the rising was marginal, but he had become more deeply involved in the efforts of Lalor and others to make 1849 a more significant date in the revolutionary calendar. When this, too, ended in failure, Luby turned up in Paris, intending to join the Foreign Legion to learn infantry tactics. But this proved impossible, and after a year in Australia he returned to Ireland and began to dabble in political journalism. He first met Stephens on the latter's reappearance in Dublin in 1856 and two years later helped him to found the 'Brotherhood' and to tour the country seeking recruits.[23]

Almost at once they met with unexpected success. By the summer of 1858 Stephens had penetrated into Cork and found there a thriving literary and political group – the Phoenix Society – which had been founded about the year 1856 by Jeremiah O'Donovan. O'Donovan, or O'Donovan Rossa as he was more usually called, was born at Rosscarbery in county Cork in 1831 and had grown up as an Irish speaker in an area that was still predominantly Gaelic in its culture. He came of petty bourgeois stock and set up in business as a grocer in the town of Skibbereen where he founded his society. The impact of Stephens upon O'Donovan and his little band of enthusiasts was immediate and powerful. They were swept into the secret republican organisation and from that moment the organisation began to spread rapidly. Even at this early stage, however, it was by no means so secret as its leaders liked to assume. Within a few months of Stephens's mission to county Cork the local parish priests were warning their flocks against becoming involved in the movement and the *Nation* newspaper – since Gavan Duffy's departure to Australia in the hands of a journalist from Bantry, Alexander Martin Sullivan – was emphatic in separating its brand of constitutional nationalism from what it took to be the politics of the Phoenix Society. When this pointed attack on extremism was followed immediately afterwards by the arrest of several Phoenix men in Bantry and Skibbereen it was easy to jump to the conclusion that Sullivan had been in touch with the authorities, and Stephens at once spread the story that he was a 'felon-setter', that he had pointed out members of the society to the police. There was no convincing evidence to substantiate the charge (the arrests were in fact based upon word received from a priest and from an informer), but a more damaging indictment it would have been impossible to make and there can be little doubt that Stephens used the incident to destroy Sullivan's known ambition to rebuild the constitutional party.[24]

The Phoenix trials did not have the desired effect of nipping the separatist revival in the bud. On the contrary, they gave it priceless publicity and it continued to grow, though it is difficult to establish just how many separatists, or Fenians as we may now begin to call them, there actually were at any one time. This is partly because of the mystery in which the conspirators attempted to shroud their activities, still more because Stephens himself is one of our main sources of information and where his own exploits were concerned the Chief Organiser was not backward in claiming credit. His estimate was that in Ireland and Great Britain together about 80,000 Fenians had been enrolled by 1865; in addition, there were perhaps several thousand among the Irish soldiers in the British army and of course large numbers in the United States. The very vagueness of these estimates is significant, and it is probable that the numbers actually on the ground in Ireland fell far short of Stephens's ambitious calculations; indeed, we shall see presently that when an insurrection did eventually break out, it was a very small-scale affair.

Insurrection, all the same, remained the goal. But the approach to this grand, climactic event was marred by bitter disagreements within the movement, by personal rivalries, by hesitancies and last-minute changes of plan, and, it must be added, by moments not far removed from farce. The would-be revolutionaries had really two problems to contend with. One was the problem of mobilising their forces, widely scattered as these were and lacking in almost every means of waging effective warfare. The other was the problem of extending the movement in Ireland not only by secret organisation, but by public propaganda aimed both at stating their case and at refuting the charges of atheism and socialism levelled against them by an alarmed and largely hostile Church.

The second of these problems, though difficult, was not insuperable and in attempting to solve it the Fenians, if they did not achieve complete success, at least called into play men of exceptional intellectual calibre and produced a notable contribution to Irish political writing which, indeed, had an influence, perhaps its chief influence, far beyond their own time. It was Stephens's idea that the movement needed a newspaper if it was ever to reach the mass of the Irish people and if it was ever to raise enough funds to keep afloat. A secret revolutionary organisation proclaiming its doctrines within a stone's throw of Dublin Castle is not without its comic side. But it was not without its dangerous side either, and a main cause of the friction that arose just at this time between Stephens in Ireland and O'Mahony in America was precisely the fact, which O'Mahony seized on immediately, that this kind of publicity, however useful in the short term, would ultimately prove incompatible with the underground movement as they had originally conceived it. Characteristically, Stephens disregarded these warnings, and in November 1863 his newspaper, the *Irish People*, duly appeared. Equally characteristically, his grandiose conception of what his own share in the enterprise should be dwindled to a few painfully written leading articles, and the main burden of running the paper fell upon O'Donovan Rossa, as business editor, T. C. Luby and two important late-comers to the scene, John O'Leary and Charles Kickham. Both were Tipperary men and both were sons of shopkeepers. Kickham was the older of the two and in a literary sense the more distinguished. Born at Mullinahone in 1828, he was handicapped from childhood by a shooting accident which left him almost totally blind and deaf. Nevertheless, he entered vigorously into the politics of his day, becoming first a Young Irelander and then the organiser of a Confederate club in his home town. Physically incapable of an active part in the rising of 1848, he later joined the Tenant League and seems to have been attracted into the republican movement – but only in 1860 – by O'Mahony, to whom he was related by marriage. Although in later days Kickham was to personify the rigid intransigence of a republicanism that refused to be compromised by any dealings with constitutional nationalism, he lives in the memory of his countrymen mainly by his novel, *Knocknagow*, and by a handful of poems and ballads. *Knocknagow* was first published in 1873 and has been in print ever since. Few Irish novels have commanded such a faithful public among successive generations, but this may be because for most readers it portrays with pathos and insight a rural society that has vanished for ever. Such readers, however, tend to miss the chief message of the novel, which is Kickham's fundamental conservatism. For him the Famine had marked a watershed in Irish social history because it had wiped out a paternalism which, if sometimes vicious, could also be benevolent, and had substituted in its place the cash nexus. In Kickham's view the outwardly successful men of the post-Famine era – the new landlords and the rising shopocracy of the towns – were also the most tainted, and he spared neither Catholic nor Protestant in his contempt.

If in Kickham, despite his own middle-class background, there was a certain aristocratic disdain, this was carried still further by his friend and fellow-worker, John O'Leary. O'Leary was born in the town of Tipperary in 1830 and at seventeen went up to Trinity College, Dublin to study law. Converted to Young Ireland by the *Nation* (ever afterwards Davis was a holy name to him), he soon gravitated into the Confederate clubs. His attempt to join the 1848 rising in Tipperary was foiled by its speedy collapse, but he was active in the efforts to resuscitate the movement the following year and was briefly imprisoned for his pains. He then resumed his studies, transferring from law to medicine and from Trinity to the Queen's Colleges of Cork and Galway. He never qualified, however. Instead, he drifted first to Dublin, then to Paris, next to America and back to Paris again, until he finally settled in Ireland to work for Stephens on the editorial staff of the *Irish People*. But although that in itself committed him to Fenianism it was characteristic of him that he refused to take the secret oath of allegiance. This was symbolic of his whole attitude towards revolution. For him the spirit of independence was the essence of nationalism, not the deeds through which men might seek to make the spirit manifest. The revolutionary must cultivate an inner stoicism, must abide by a stern code of conduct imposed by himself upon himself. 'He had grown up', Yeats later recalled, 'in a European movement when the revolutionist thought that he, above all men, must appeal to the highest motive, be guided by some ideal principle, be a little like Cato or like Brutus, and he had lived to see the change Dostoievsky examined in *The Possessed*.' Yet he retained his own fastidiousness to the end. 'There are certain things a man must not do to save a nation', he once told the poet. When Yeats had asked what things, O'Leary replied 'to cry in public', and in that single phrase summed up all his own uncompromising, honourable integrity.[25]

Upon these two men, principally, fell the burden of combating the attack on Fenianism which developed in the early 'sixties. That this attack should have come mainly from the Church was not in itself particularly surprising. Secret societies were, after all, no new thing in Ireland and long before national revolution had begun to engage men's attention, the peasants had formed their own underground conspiracies to mete out rough justice to unjust landlords, harsh agents or land-grabbing fellow tenants. 'Ribbonism', to use the collective name often applied to these violent products of rural tension, had quite naturally attracted ecclesiastical condemnation, since it had led all too often to murder and every kind of bestial brutality. It was equally natural that the emergence of an oath-bound political society like the IRB should attract similar condemnation, but just at this time the clerical onslaught was greatly strengthened by two circumstances. One was the fact that the Roman Church, not just in Ireland but in Europe at large, had reacted to the revolutionary outbreaks of 1848 in general, and to the rise of Italian nationalism after 1848 in particular, by a vigorous counterblast against what Pope Pius IX lumped together in the Syllabus of Errors of 1864 as the principal evils of the age – Socialism, Liberalism, Freemasonry, secret societies of various kinds and especially those which were anti-clerical in intent.

The second circumstance affecting the Catholic attitude to rebellion in Ireland was the influence of Archbishop Cullen, or Cardinal Cullen as he became in 1866. Cullen, some of whose most impressionable years had been passed, as we have seen, as Rector of the Irish College in Rome at a particularly disturbed period, shared to the full the horror of conservatives everywhere at the progressive dismantling of the temporal power of the Pope. But whereas many Irish Catholics saw no further than that they ought to go in person to the aid of His Holiness (an Irish brigade was hastily recruited in 1859 with clerical blessing, but reached Rome too late to be of any effective help), Cullen was no less preoccupied with the causes of the collapse of the papal power, seeing in this disaster the triumph of the enemies of religion and especially of secret societies such as the Carbonari. An ecclesiastic who had already condemned the moderate Gavan Duffy as an Irish incarnation of Mazzini was not likely, in the changed and deteriorating circumstances of the 1860s, to take a lenient view of Fenianism. And in fact Cullen struck at it whenever and wherever it appeared, leaning heavily on the existing papal condemnation of clandestine organisations. These organisations were not censured simply because they were secret (though it was a sin to join a secret society), but because, as a modern authority has pointed out, 'they were, in technical language, occult, that is to say they were unlawful combinations of private individuals against the legitimate public authority of Church or State'.[26] In the most complete summary of his views on the subject, the famous pastoral of 10 October 1865, Cullen not only denounced the Fenian Society as 'a compound of folly and wickedness', but also warned his people against conspiring to overthrow the government and against swearing obedience to strangers who might not be men of religion, might indeed be enemies both of the Church and of the existing structure of society. Besides these spiritual admonitions there was a prudential argument which many bishops stressed, and to which Cullen himself was not blind, that an armed uprising in existing circumstances could only end in failure and suffering, perhaps even death, for those who took part in it.

The Church was by no means monolithic in its condemnation of the Fenians. Eventually, it is true, Cullen succeeded in massing the great majority of the bishops behind him, but few were as unsparing in their comments as he was and probably only one exceeded him. Since this was Dr David Moriarty of Kerry, whose politics were indistinguishable from Unionism, the exception was no help to Cullen's case. A number of the bishops, and still more of the parish clergy, it is fair to say, could only have been repelled by Moriarty's famous sermon delivered early in 1867 after a premature uprising in his diocese, in which he described the Fenian leaders as 'criminals' and 'swindlers', and called down upon them 'God's heaviest curse, his withering, blasting, blighting curse', adding for good measure the phrase that has haunted his reputation ever since – that for their punishment 'eternity is not long enough, nor hell hot enough'.[27]

Outward opposition to what might be called the Cullen doctrine was not, perhaps, widespread, but there were some dioceses where, with or without the bishops' knowledge, the sacraments were not withheld from practising Fenians. And in one diocese – that of Tuam – the archbishop himself, the redoubtable John MacHale, stubbornly refused to toe the line. It is true that this may have had at least as much to do with his long-standing rivalry with Cullen as with any deep-seated sympathy for the Fenians (though he was no friend to British rule), but it had one unfortunate consequence, since the most outstanding case of a priest defending the organisation in the teeth of his superiors came from within his jurisdiction. The culprit, or hero according to the point of view, was Father Patrick Lavelle, an able but contentious man, whose academic career at the Irish College in Paris had been abruptly ended after he had become involved in disputes with the Rector. Exiled to the remoteness of Partry in county Mayo, he emerged into national prominence when in 1861 he defied Archbishop Cullen by preaching at the funeral of a well-known Young Irelander, Terence Bellew Mac-Manus, after Cullen had refused a lying-in-state at the Pro-Cathedral on the well-founded suspicion that the whole affair was being stage-managed by the Fenians. Not content with this, Father Lavelle a few months later delivered a lecture, again in Dublin, with the provocative title, 'The Catholic doctrine of the right of revolution'. The essence of his argument was that against misgovernment Ireland had a right to revolt and that because this was justified, the Church could not refuse to sanction it, and certainly ought not to condemn it. Since Lavelle further added to his defiance by becoming a vice-president of the 'National Brotherhood of Saint Patrick', an 'open' society which was little more than a front-organisation for Fenianism, Cullen was resolved to discipline him. Yet, though a meeting of bishops decided that he should be silenced this was not easy to achieve. Even after repeated appeals to Rome and angry altercations between the two archbishops, the intrepid priest continued to expound in the newspapers the message that men had the right to rebel against a tyrannical government.

It was not perhaps a very tyrannical government that allowed Kickham and O'Leary to conduct their counter-campaign in the *Irish People* for nearly two years without interruption. They themselves were less concerned with arguments between ecclesiastics as to whether or not there was such a thing as a right of revolution against a legitimate government, than with making the point that the priest as such, whether sympathetic or unsympathetic, had no place in politics. It was a point they, and especially Kickham, made again and again with almost brutal clarity. Drawing on past history – on 1798, on the passing of the Act of Union, on 1848, even on the melancholy fate of the Tenant League – the columns of their paper each week beat out the steady refrain 'no priests in politics'. If the priests had betrayed the people on these occasions, argued Kickham, what guarantee was there that they would not do so again? Could they, indeed, help doing so? Not only were they without experience, they were not even free agents and, if so commanded by Rome or by their bishops, would have to abandon the people's cause the moment they were ordered to do so. In earlier times, perhaps, it had been different. Then the people, sunk in ignorance and in apathy, had looked to their clergy as the only educated class willing and able to help them. 'But', Kickham insisted, 'times are changed. The people are now comparatively educated, and demand the right possessed by the people of other Catholic countries of acting according to the dictates of their own judgment in all worldly concerns.'[28]

It is unnecessary to follow the controversy in all its acrimonious detail. Superficially, it seemed to end in a clerical victory when in 1870 the Papacy, after some earlier vagueness on the subject, produced a condemnation of Fenianism categorical enough to satisfy even Cullen. How far this was in response to Cullen's own pressure, or to the simultaneous and possibly more effective pressure applied by the British government, is still disputed by historians, but if the dispute is academic so in a sense may have been the original condemnation. By 1870, after all, the immediate crisis of Fenianism was past and the people were beginning to turn to the new Home Rule movement and to look for redress of grievances by constitutional means. Yet the quarrel between the Fenians and the Church went far beyond the immediate issues of the day and was to have a permanent importance in the history of Irish nationalism.

For both sides the clash illustrated the difficulty of trying to conduct a revolutionary movement in a Catholic country. From the Church's point of view the condemnation of Fenianism on the grounds that it was secret, anti-government, anti-clerical and dangerous to society, was well-founded, even if intemperately expressed. It was demonstrably true that the republican movement *was* anti-governmental, *was* frequently anti-clerical, and *was*, ultimately, concerned not just with the overthrow of a regime, but with a remodelling of society. Kickham, O'Leary and O'Mahony might nurse their nostalgia for an aristocratic past, but too many others had drunk too deep of Fintan Lalor's doctrines for their projected revolution to be other than social as well as political. It was far from coincidental that their appeal should have been mainly to the artisan class and the school teachers in the towns and to the small farmers and labourers in the countryside. And although the intimate connection between the struggle for the land and the struggle for independence was to be reformulated some years later in the 'New Departure', such a connection was already implicit – sometimes, indeed quite explicit – in the programme of the revolutionary movement.[29] Those who genuinely believed, as most clergy did, that such an onslaught on existing institutions would cause untold misery and suffering even if it were successful, would naturally find themselves on the side of conservatism and the preservation of the *status quo*. But since in general they believed also that the onslaught never could be successful this caused them to redouble their strictures, for in their view it could only be a sin to lead out ignorant and ardent young men to a struggle that might well end in their extermination.

Yet if religion and prudence alike pointed towards condemnation, the fact that many priests were close to their flocks in origin and outlook made them reluctant to go the whole way, and allowed them to turn a not unsympathetic ear to the seductive Fenian argument that love of country was in itself a transcendent virtue and that a man who was ready to die for his country ought not to be convicted of mortal sin. Moreover, the differences of opinion within the ecclesiastical camp seemed to many contemporaries to leave the question open, enabling some laymen at least to exercise the right of choice, either with a clear conscience or on the pretext of reasonable doubt. The situation of the rest has been well described by a modern writer: 'Many . . . felt that ecclesiastical opinion, whether favourable to Fenianism or not, was altogether irrelevant. Some, who believed that they could not serve two masters, chose Fenianism and dropped away from the practice of their religion. Others held simply that churchmen were acting *ultra vires* in a political question.'[30]

In the last analysis the principal importance of the conflict may not have been that it resulted in the triumph of one side over the other – it clearly did not result in a triumph for either side – but rather that it showed both religious devotees and political zealots how far they could afford to go. The Church in particular quietly and gradually absorbed the lessons of the crisis and learned to make its political comments with greater discretion. It was significant, for example, that when the next uprising came in 1916, only seven bishops denounced it, but twenty-two remained silent, one hesitated, and one defended it. The contrast with the Fenian period could not have been more pointed. But even more striking than this was the way in which the collision of the 'sixties averted what had threatened to be the increasing sectarianism of Irish politics. There had been a moment in the 'fifties when it had seemed as if the terms 'Catholic' and 'nationalist' might end by becoming synonymous. The dispute over Fenianism averted this danger, partly because the Fenians themselves were determinedly non-sectarian in the tradition of Tone and Davis, still more because by the very firmness with which they confronted the leaders of their own Church they showed that the Irish laity was not subservient in political matters to its religious mentors. For them the separation of Church and State was no empty phrase, but a principle which lay at the very heart of their programme. By maintaining that principle in circumstances of great difficulty they made a contribution of incalculable value to the development of Irish nationalism.[31]

The struggle with the Church was confused and prolonged. But the struggle of the Fenians to organise their own forces for actual insurrection, though no less confused, was brief and disastrous. Essentially it was a question of combining the efforts of the American and of the Irish movements. At any time this would have been difficult because of distance, but co-operation was made still more hazardous by a clash of personalities which resulted in Stephens being reduced from his self-assumed dictatorship to headship of the European wing only, O'Mahony retaining control of the American wing. This, however, did not really alter the terms of the problem, which remained how best to bring American aid – money primarily and later, it was hoped, men – to Ireland. That problem still awaited solution when at last, and well primed by informers, the government struck. On the night of 15 September 1865 the offices of the *Irish People* were raided and most of the leaders, including O'Leary, Luby and O'Donovan Rossa, were arrested. Stephens, living in seclusion on the outskirts of Dublin, managed to evade capture for another two months. The continuity of the movement thus came to depend largely on one man, John Devoy. As the crisis developed, he emerged as the strongest advocate of action, proposing, early in 1866, a desperate scheme for an uprising based on an appeal to the Irish soldiers in the British regiments then stationed in the country.

The scheme may not have been quite so desperate as it seemed, for Devoy knew what he was about. At this time only twenty-three years of age, he came of a farming family from county Kildare. In 1861, spurning the constitutional politics in which A. M. Sullivan was trying to interest him, he succeeded in doing what Luby had earlier failed to do, joining the Foreign Legion in order to learn infantry warfare. Having got what he wanted, he deserted in 1863 and joined the group of journalists working for the *Irish People*. Devoy at this stage of his career was a romantic nationalist, caught up in the dream of an armed insurrection and the establishment of an Irish republic. The dream was to remain with him all his long life, but the man himself was gradually to change from the enthusiastic amateur of the 'sixties into a bitter, irascible, unforgiving, but always intensely professional revolutionary. Between October 1865 and February 1866 he took a major part in the risky business of swearing Irish soldiers into the Brotherhood, especially those of the Dublin garrison.[32] The success with which he carried out this task gave a peculiar authority to his advice, even if it was the advice of a young man who had been only an infant when Stephens had first begun his conspiratorial career.

The advice was not taken. Whether it was because Stephens's vanity was irked by this bold initiative from one so young, whether it was because he doubted the readiness of the Irish soldiers to mutiny, or whether it was because he believed at bottom that a successful rising depended on more American aid than had so far manifested itself, it is impossible to say for certain. But what does seem certain is that, however desperate the chance, those winter months of 1865–66 were his *only* chance. The moment passed almost as soon as it had presented itself. On 11 November Stephens himself was arrested and all seemed at an end. Yet even then there was one last flicker of hope. Only a fortnight after he had been seized, Devoy, with great daring, engineered his escape from Richmond jail in Dublin, hoping that now at last the 'Chief Organiser of the Irish republic' would do something to bring that republic to birth. But all was in vain – Stephens still refused to authorise a general rising and had instead to be smuggled out of the country to America. Devoy, who was himself seized in February 1866 and imprisoned until 1871, never ceased to believe that a golden opportunity had been squandered and before long was to be found publicly accusing his former leader of cowardice. Historians have been a little kinder in their estimate of Stephens than Devoy could bring himself to be, but they have tended to agree with the younger man that 1865 marked the high point of the movement and that, the chance of a rising once missed, circumstances were never again to be so favourable.

This, admittedly, was far from clear at the time. Following his successful escape, Stephens made his way to New York, where it was reasonable to hope the main effort might still be organised. In one sense this was an accurate enough assessment. The ending of the Civil War had released hundreds of Irishmen, trained in the use of arms, unfitted for peaceful work and eager to strike a blow for Ireland. Unhappily, there was acute disagreement among these American Fenians as to how that blow might best be struck. There were two main schools of thought. One, which in 1865 was still headed by O'Mahony, was, theoretically at least, committed to a rising in Ireland, but O'Mahony himself had come under heavy criticism, partly because he was a bad judge of character and relied, even against the advice of friends, on thoroughly untrustworthy men, some of whom turned out to be informers. But partly also his position was undermined by the fact that while he apparently wished to maintain his personal dictatorship intact, he had no dynamic policy to justify this dictatorship. Confronting him, therefore, was a group of dissidents, called the 'senate wing' because of their demand that the organisation should be controlled by a senate, not an autocrat. This faction nursed the hope – which seems ludicrous in retrospect but has to be seen against a background of existing Anglo-American tension – that a Fenian invasion of Canada might provoke a favourable setting for an Irish revolt. During 1866 they tried to carry this policy into effect and an armed party of Fenians actually crossed the Canadian border, only to be rounded up by government forces, well warned in advance. The incident did not provoke a war between Britain and the United States, and though the proponents of a Canadian invasion were so enamoured of it that they tried it twice more, in 1870 and 1871, the experience of 1866 was enough in itself to show that Irish freedom was not to be won on the banks of the St Lawrence.

Stephens, on his arrival, at once assumed the leadership of the section that advocated direct intervention in Ireland. But although he displaced O'Mahony in the process he was no more successful than his old friend in launching the long looked-for assault. Indeed, his very arrogance and self-confidence made the situation even worse, for having repeatedly promised that 1866 would be *the* year, he allowed it to pass with nothing more aggressive than speeches and declarations. For this there were in fact good enough reasons. The situation in Ireland was difficult and confused, with the leaders for the most part in jail and the army in firm control of the 'Fenian regiments'. And in America, though money was subscribed and arms were collected and desperate men clamoured to be able to use them, those who felt that these preparations were utterly inadequate to the immense task of overthrowing British power in Ireland had logic on their side. Had Britain been involved in a major war things might have been otherwise, but so long as she remained at peace an American Fenian attempt upon Ireland could never be more than a bow drawn at a venture.

Nevertheless, even though the odds against them were so heavy, the Irish-American veterans of the Civil War moved restlessly to and fro between the United States and Ireland, bringing the prospect of rebellion steadily nearer. There were not very many of them – perhaps no more than 150 – and the police were able to follow their activities in meticulous detail, but they supplied the essential fuse for what had long been an explosive situation. Foremost in the group was Thomas J. Kelly, a Galwegian by birth, a printer by trade and a colonel by courtesy. He had been in Ireland in 1865 and had taken part in the Stephens rescue. A year later he displaced Stephens from the leadership of the 'O'Mahony wing' and was entrusted with the command of the Fenian forces in Britain and Ireland. Early in 1867 he arrived in England with a band of fellow-officers (others went direct to Ireland) and, after consultation with the remaining Irish leaders, decided to launch a rising without delay. Planned originally for February, the outbreak was called off, partly on account of the difficulty of organising the Fenian forces in Ireland at such short notice, and partly because the leaders realised how thoroughly their secrets had been penetrated by informers. The countermanding order reached the remote parts of Kerry too late and there was a small demonstration on the Iveragh peninsula, but it speedily collapsed when those involved found that they were completely isolated. A simultaneous attack on Chester Castle (to obtain arms) had also been intended, but this too petered out in face of the unmistakable preparedness of the garrison. Alike in England and in Ireland it had become painfully obvious that Fenianism, which had begun with the specific object of achieving secrecy, was honeycombed with government agents (some of whom, like J. J. Corydon, became legends in their own lifetime) and that this, combined with the lack of arms, money and organisation, would be fatal to any attempt.

Yet the attempt was made in the end. It was made on the night of 5–6 March 1867 which, with the ill-luck that so often seemed to dog Irish rebellions, chanced to be a night of bitter cold and heavy snow. There was no coherent plan of operations, nor perhaps any policy other than the desperate hope that the insurgents might hold out long enough to be accorded belligerent rights by the USA and thus precipitate that long cherished Anglo-American war which had become so embedded in Fenian mythology. Groups of brave, unorganised, miserably armed men turned out in Dublin, Cork, Tipperary and Limerick, and to a lesser extent in Clare, Waterford and Louth. In Dublin, going against the normal revolutionary grain, the insurgents moved out of the city, instead of striking from within. The police and troops were glad to let them go, rounding them up at leisure as they floundered in the snowdrifts of the Dublin hills. In the Dublin area it is possible that as many as two thousand men were involved in this hopeless endeavour, with perhaps twice that number in county Cork and some hundreds elsewhere.

Defeat was followed, as usual, by widespread arrests and heavy sentences for those convicted. Public opinion in Ireland, which had been apathetic, if not hostile, towards the rising was sensitive on the subject of punishment. To this the government was not unresponsive, in that all death sentences were commuted, but imprisonment for long periods and in harsh conditions was the lot of most of the leaders. In the result, the very brutality of their treatment created perhaps more sympathy for Fenianism than had existed even in its heyday and within two years of the insurrection a powerful movement demanding amnesty for political prisoners had developed in Ireland. For years to come 'amnesty' was to be a means of keeping the cause of irreconcilable republicanism vivid in the minds of the people.

Indirectly, also, the arrests after the collapse helped to bring the whole problem of the Fenian movement nearer to the mainstream of British politics. In September 1867 the 'Chief Organiser', Colonel Kelly himself, was seized with another Fenian in Manchester. Their comrades succeeded dramatically in rescuing them by attacking the van in which they were being brought to prison. One of the police-guards was accidentally shot dead while the lock was being blown off and five men were arrested. After an unsatisfactory trial, and on evidence that, to say the least, was dubious, three men – Allen, Larkin and O'Brien – were executed. These were the 'Manchester Martyrs' who at once became symbols of resurgent nationalism. In England, on the other hand, the events in Manchester strengthened the impression that Fenianism was a powerful and sinister force at work in the very heart of English society, an impression still further reinforced by the gunpowder explosion at Clerkenwell prison in London at the end of 1867, when an attempt to blow up part of the prison wall killed a number of innocent people. The mingled horror and anger which these events aroused could work, however, in two quite different ways. It could intensify the determination of those who believed that firm, repressive government was what Ireland needed and must have. But it could equally well prompt thoughtful men to look beyond the violence at what had created the violence and to wonder if the time had not come to woo Ireland from the paths of desperation by a sustained attempt at constructive reform. That one of those who now began to think in this way was Gladstone was not the least, if perhaps the most unexpected, of the legacies left by the Fenians to posterity.

There were other legacies as well. Although as an attempt at insurrection Fenianism was totally inadequate, as a phase in the evolution of Irish nationalism it was of central importance. Not merely was it a vital link in the chain connecting the men of 1848 with the men of 1916, but in its brief high noon it established, or restated, certain fundamentals of the separatist ideal. By its resistance to ecclesiastical censure and its rigorous attempt to separate Church and State it proclaimed that the independence for which it fought was intellectual, even spiritual, as much as political. By its appeal to the lower classes it indicated that, however innocent of Marxist theories of society it might be, it had grasped where the real base for a genuinely radical movement might lie in the future. By its reliance on American aid it demonstrated that the Irish question had become irrevocably international, with consequences that were to reverberate through the next half century. But finally, and perhaps most important of all, Fenianism, by its call to arms, reiterated for its own generation the old, harsh maxim that freedom had to be fought for, while by their integrity and bravery in hopeless circumstances its champions passed on to their successors like a living flame the lesson that to sacrifice himself for his country was the highest good to which a man might aspire. Fifty years later the full meaning of that lesson would be made plain.

PART II

The Union under Strain

1. Genesis of Home Rule

Futile as the Fenian insurrection of 1867 had seemed to be, yet its reverberations above and below ground were to echo through Irish and English politics for years to come. In the long run its influence on the secret revolutionary movement aiming at the achievement of an independent republic by force of arms was probably more significant, but in the immediate aftermath it was the public impact that mattered most. 'Violence', a later Irish agitator was to say, 'is sometimes the only way to secure a hearing for moderation', and this, though small comfort to Fenians languishing in prison or in exile, sums up the catalytic effect of their protest on both sides of the Irish Sea.

In England and in Ireland, it is fair to say, the prospects of securing a hearing for moderation, even without violence, were better than they had been at almost any time since the Famine. In Ireland the total, almost ludicrous, failure of the Fenian rising had cleared the way for a recrudescence of constitutional agitation pointed towards specific and realisable reforms. And in England, where in the final analysis the initiative still rested, the long confusion of mid-Victorian politics seemed at last to be coming to an end. Something approaching a modern division of political groups into two main parties – recognisably Liberal and Conservative – was beginning to emerge and at the head of these rival parties stood leaders of national reputation, Gladstone and Disraeli. Both men had long understood the danger a discontented Ireland could be to English security. As far back as 1844 Disraeli had diagnosed the Irish question as 'a starving population, an absentee aristocracy, and an alien church, and in addition the weakest executive in the world'.[1] The very next year Gladstone, travelling in France, had met the statesman and historian, Guizot, and had heard him say that England would have the support of Europe if she gave justice to Ireland. To one who was as responsive to European opinion as Gladstone – who was, indeed, European rather than insular in his whole life-style – this remark conveyed a challenge and a reproach, both implicit in a famous passage he wrote in a letter to his wife just at that time: 'Ireland, Ireland! that cloud in the west, that coming storm, the minister of God's retribution upon cruel and inveterate and but half-atoned injustice! Ireland forces upon us these great social and great religious questions – God grant that we may have courage – to look them in the face and to work through them.'[2]

Yet the years had passed and neither man had taken up the challenge.

The explanation is no doubt to be found in the pressing urgency of English, European and colonial business beside which the claims of Ireland seemed insignificant and peripheral. Disraeli, when he finally did climb to the top of the greasy pole, was too old and too preoccupied with other and more glamorous issues to do more than try and hold the Irish question at arm's length, though even he could not prevent it from casting a long shadow over his last years of power. Gladstone was in a different position. Younger, sensitive not just to the criticisms of Europe but to the more insistent promptings of his own conscience, moving steadily after Palmerston's death in 1865 to a dominant position amongst that medley of Whigs and Radicals, churchmen and non-conformists, bourgeoisie and working-men, out of which a great Liberal party was to be fashioned, he could turn at last to 'look in the face and work through' the problems Ireland still presented.

For such a man it was possible to see the Fenian outbreak not just as a series of acts of terrorism, but as the symptom of a deeper malaise, and in an important speech in December 1867, only a few days after the Clerkenwell explosion, he tried to pass on to his English audience his own conviction – antedating Fenianism by many years – that Irish violence was the product of Irish grievance. Remove that grievance and 'instead of hearing in every corner of Europe the most painful commentaries on the policy of England towards Ireland we may be able to look our fellow Europeans in the face'.[3] The timing of this speech was significant on two counts. First, because Gladstone was addressing himself to a general public which had that year become politically much more important through the extension of the franchise downwards to include what were taken to be the more responsible elements of the working-class. How this leap in the dark might affect domestic English politics no one could foretell, though all sorts of alarms were being sounded in various directions. But one consequence of this electoral reform was to induce among party leaders a mood of caution which extended even as far as the House of Lords. That there might be a conflict between peers and people was no longer an academic speculation. It was a frightening possibility which, if it did not exactly transform the upper House into a model of sweet reasonableness, at least made it for the time being less ready to veto controversial legislation than it had been in the past or was to be in the future. For a statesman shaping his course toward Irish reform – controversial by definition – this relative quiescence of the House of Lords provided a golden opportunity.

The second sense in which the timing of the speech was important was that it was delivered in the knowledge that before long an election would be held on the new register. Gladstone could anticipate no more than anyone else what the result might be, but it is significant that early in the session of 1868 he challenged the government, and in the end brought it down, on the general proposition that the time had come to sever the connection between church and state in Ireland. The privileged position of the 'alien church' (that is, the Anglican Church of Ireland) was certainly a long-standing Irish grievance and Gladstone had accepted in principle twenty years earlier that it must be ended. But in retrospect this reform hardly seems to have contained in itself the whole answer to Fenianism. It did not. Nor did Gladstone think it did. He was drawn to it as a point of departure, however, both by temperament and by expediency. If, as has so often been said of him, religion was the lodestar of his life, then it followed that there could scarcely be a more important question in politics than the relationship between the ecclesiastical and the civil power. If he felt this to be true in England (and it was a lifelong preoccupation with him) it was even more imperatively true in Ireland where the religion of the vast majority of the population was greatly inferior in status and resources to that of the small Ascendancy class. And just how great was the numerical disparity between the two religions was starkly revealed by the Census of 1861, which gave for the first time reliable information about denominational affiliation. It showed that out of a population of $5\frac{3}{4}$ million, Roman Catholics accounted for $4\frac{1}{2}$ million and Anglicans of the established church for just under 700,000. Here, apart altogether from questions of principle or conscience, was a political reason for change. And there were others. An assault on the Church of Ireland would be popular not only with the underprivileged majority in Ireland, but also with nonconformists in Britain. Conservative churchmen – whether they called themselves Liberal or Tory in politics – might view the precedent with a shudder, but there could be no doubt that Irish disestablishment was a game that more than one could play.

It was in fact a game which helped to produce one of the most remarkable, if transient, partnerships of the nineteenth century – that between the Irish hierarchy and the Liberal non-conformists. That the Protestant Church of Ireland should be disestablished was a natural objective for the Irish Roman Catholic bishops; that this should be promoted as a useful experiment to be repeated elsewhere was an equally natural objective for the British Liberation Society. Disestablishment had been a main plank in the platform of the National Association ever since its formation in Dublin in 1864* but close contact with the Liberation Society both before and after that event had helped the Irish bishops and their lay supporters to define with increasing precision what they meant by disestablishment. This was not just the sundering of church and state in a legal sense. It involved also the disendowment of the Church of Ireland. But further, it involved a determination that the funds set free by this disendowment should *not*, as some Catholics argued, be redistributed amongst the various de-

* A moderate, Catholic pressure-group, sensitive to the views of Archbishop Cullen. For the Liberation Society, founded in 1844 but increasingly active in the years after the Crimean War, see J. R. Vincent, *The Formation of the Liberal Party* (London, 1966), pp. 68-76. Its central aim was the disestablishment and partial disendowment of the Church of England.

nominations (the policy of 'concurrent endowment'), but should be *secularised* – put, that is, to non-religious purposes. The endorsement of this determination had involved the Irish hierarchy in a delicately ambiguous position. To demand secularisation was to demand the very thing Pope Pius ix had so desperately attempted to resist in Italy. 'The Irish bishops', it has been well said, 'therefore flew in the face of the *Syllabus of Errors* in a campaign to attain that which the Papacy most dreaded: a "free church in a free state".'[4] They were, or seemed to be, working for a state neutral among competing religions, in effect a liberal state. They did this in full consciousness of the possible danger because the alternative seemed to them a greater danger – that the Roman Catholic Church in Ireland, if it sought to win endowments from the expropriation of the Church of Ireland would, by accepting what the hierarchy eventually spurned as 'state pensions and government gifts', be riveting the collar of an alien authority round its own neck.

With the cry for reform rising louder and louder in Ireland, and striking a sympathetic chord in England, it was not surprising that in both countries Irish issues should have dominated the election campaign, or that Gladstone, swept into power with a large majority, should have turned at once to the redress of Irish grievances. Ireland was not his only concern, of course, but it bulked large enough in his programme to occupy the main part of his energies in the first two sessions of the new parliament. His Irish policy, however, was not restricted solely to disestablishment. With church reform he wanted to combine a generous measure of protection to the tenant farmer and also to give to Catholics that university of their own which they had been seeking for so many years and for which Newman's precarious experiment in Dublin had not proved an adequate substitute.

This last objective eluded him, remaining to plague Anglo-Irish relations for another forty years. But the Irish Church Act of 1869 and the Irish Land Act of 1870 were driven through by Gladstone himself with tremendous vigour and parliamentary skill. He succeeded first in disestablishing the Church of Ireland on terms sufficiently fair to Irish Protestants as to make nonsense of their Archbishop of Dublin's forecast that 'every man among them who has money or position, when he sees his church go, will leave the country'. Briefly, what the Act did was to break absolutely the legal connection between Church and State, making of the Church of Ireland in effect a voluntary body as from 1 January 1871. In a more material sense disestablishment meant that the property of the Church was confiscated and vested in a Temporalities Commission specially set up to administer the revenues accruing. The annual grant to the Catholic college at Maynooth was discontinued, as was also the *regium donum* to the Presbyterian Church, though in both cases compensatory payments were made. Ecclesiastical courts ceased to operate, but a new organ of government, the Representative Church Body, was set up to receive the churches and burial grounds in use at the time of the passing of the Act, and also to buy from the

Temporalities Commissioners the parsonages and glebes belonging to the Church. The life-interest of clergy, school-masters and other officials of the old establishment was carefully protected and a considerable part of the funds realised by disestablishment was absorbed in this way. It has been estimated in fact that of the property in land, buildings and tithe which the state took into its possession by virtue of the Act about ten million pounds may have been returned in one form or another to the Church of Ireland. This still left a substantial 'church surplus' for use on secular purposes and with judicious management this was eventually made to yield about thirteen million pounds, which was paid out between 1871 and the ending of the Union in relief of poverty, for the encouragement of agriculture and fisheries, the endowment of higher education, and other purposes.[5]

One intention of the Act which was perhaps less regarded at the time was to facilitate the purchase of church lands by their tenants with state aid. About 6,000 farmers took advantage of this offer and the subsequent history of the land question was to show that here was the germ of a permanent solution of the landlord-tenant relationship. At the time, though, this was not apparent. Not only was the experiment thought to be on a scale too small to be significant, but in many cases the landlords themselves bought out the church lands and the tithe rent charge that went with them; where this happened rents were not observed to suffer any magical diminution and the essential structure of the system remained unimpaired.[6] Perhaps it was not surprising, therefore, that when Gladstone himself took up the question in 1870 he went upon a very different tack. His primary aim was to achieve a more just relationship between landlord and tenant, but to do so without affronting the susceptibilities of men of property in either country. Borrowing to some extent from the ideas of his Chief Secretary, Chichester Fortescue, he made his legislation turn on two key points. One was that the Ulster custom, or any essentially similar custom prevailing elsewhere, should be given the force of law wherever it existed.* And the other was that a tenant who did not enjoy the benefit of the custom – and that meant the great majority – should be given increased security in his holding. This was to be done in two ways. First, if he surrendered his farm his right to compensation for improvement was made more extensive, improvements now being held to be the work of the tenant whereas hitherto they had been accredited to the landlord. But second and more important, Gladstone hoped to restrain landlords from evicting their tenants unjustly by cutting their hands 'with the sharp edge of pecuniary damages'; in other words, eviction for causes other than the non-payment of rent would involve compensation for 'disturbance'.

* For the Ulster custom, see pp. 114-16 above. And for a penetrating criticism of the assumptions on which the 1870 Act was based, see B. Solow, *The Land Question and the Irish Economy, 1870-1903*, chaps. 2 and 3; also E. D. Steele, 'Ireland and the Empire in the 1860s: Imperial Precedents for Gladstone's First Irish Land Act', in *The Historical Journal*, xi, 1 (1968), pp. 64-83.

These were the main innovations of the Act but it also, due largely to the insistence of John Bright, took another small step in the direction of land purchase, since it permitted tenants to borrow from the state two-thirds of the cost of their holdings, repaying the debt by five per cent annuities spread over thirty-five years.

In practice the Land Act of 1870 was a disappointment. The Ulster custom proved difficult to define in law and when so defined was often defined restrictively. And although the provisions governing compensation for improvements do seem to have had a beneficial effect, the principal purpose of the Act – to protect tenants who had no custom to safeguard them – was defeated, largely because the landlord's power to raise the rent remained untouched and tenants evicted for non-payment of rent were in most cases beyond the power of the courts to help them; so also was the large class of tenants who held by leases of thirty-one years or more, and were not entitled to compensation for disturbance if their leases were not renewed. The real solutions still lay in the future – co-partnership between landlord and tenant on the short-term, the transfer of ownership from landlord to tenant in the long run. But just as the Act failed to achieve the first of these solutions, so it proved inadequate to the second. The 'Bright clauses' remained little more than a pious gesture. There was no real incentive for landlords to sell and the burden of purchase was too heavy for most tenants to want to buy, so that less than a thousand took advantage of the facilities offered. This was many fewer than had purchased under the Irish Church Act, but in the latter instance, of course, the conditions of sale were easier and the Commissioners had fewer qualms about selling than had private landlords.

Nevertheless, Gladstone's Irish legislation, though a long way short of revolutionary, had a symbolic significance far beyond its immediate effects. It signalled a fresh way of looking at Irish problems. It marked a new (if rather suspect) harmony between English Liberalism and Irish Catholicism. Above all, it gave notice that the Protestant Ascendancy was no longer immutable and invulnerable. 'In future', Cardinal Cullen had reported to Rome after the passing of the Church Act, 'the Protestants will find themselves without any privileges . . . The poor Protestants are all very irritated. They never did imagine that England would have abandoned their cause.'[7] In the first part of his diagnosis he was prematurely optimistic; the Protestant hold on power and privilege had been loosened, but another generation would have to pass, and much more violent storms beat about their heads, before they would finally begin to yield their long and deeply entrenched supremacy. But the second part of the Cardinal's analysis was certainly correct. The 'poor Protestants' were not only irritated, but also confused and apprehensive. The English connection, which since the Union had been their sheet-anchor, now suddenly seemed to be less permanent and less secure than they had hitherto taken for granted. Angrily and nervously some of them began to reconsider their position and to cast about them for an alternative stay and prop.

It is against this background of Protestant disillusionment and uncertainty that the unlikely origins of the Home Rule movement must be sought. Yet if Home Rule was the product of a new situation, it was also, initially at least, very much the creation of one man – Isaac Butt. Butt was a lawyer, a persuasive – even passionate – advocate who had earned reputation and respect in defending first Young Irelanders in 1848 and then Fenians after the mass arrests of 1865 which had preceded the abortive insurrection of two years later. On the face of it they could scarcely have had a more unexpected defender. Born in 1813, the son of a Church of Ireland clergyman in county Donegal, Butt had been educated at Trinity College, Dublin, and grew up in an atmosphere of conservatism that was to remain with him all his life. Graduating in 1836 after an outstanding academic career, he stayed on at Trinity to teach political economy, but abandoned this shortly afterwards to embark on the practice of law. At that stage, he was firmly convinced that the Union with Britain was necessary and desirable for Ireland, giving her peace and stability; so impeccable was his conservatism, indeed, that he also accepted unhesitatingly the link between the Church of Ireland and the state as no less essential to the well-being of the country.

These, however, were difficult propositions for an intelligent and ardent young man to hold for long. And even during his brief spell as an academic economist, Butt had begun to move away from the comfortable certainties of his class and environment. He could not close his eyes to the poverty of the masses around him and gravitated easily towards that familiar panacea of discontented Irishmen – the necessity for separate tariffs to allow industry to root itself in Ireland and agriculture to be free to exploit the market on its own doorstep. The onset of the Famine gave these abstract economic doctrines a new urgency, but that unparalleled disaster also led Butt to realise that it was not enough simply to blame the *laissez-faire* policies of the government. It was the fundamentally unsound relationship between landlord and tenant that lay at the root of the trouble. His conservatism now began to take on a more dynamic character. He was still for the Union, he was still for the preservation of property, but in the most remarkable of his early pamphlets – The Famine in the Land (1847) – he coupled a demand for positive action by the authorities to relieve distress with a warning that to neglect Ireland was to risk creating a coalition of the very classes and creeds whose mutual antagonism had hitherto been the basis of British rule. The next year, defending the Young Irelanders, he went beyond his customary attack upon the economic consequences of the British connection to suggest that possibly the solution might lie in a form of federalism which would give Ireland a separate and subordinate parliament without endangering the Union.

Little more was heard of this for another twenty years, or of Butt either. Elected to a seat in parliament he spent most of the time in

England between the Famine and the Fenian outbreak. From this period dates apparently a certain moral degeneration which was later to have a crippling effect upon his career. A man of winning disposition and great natural kindliness, he found temptation irresistible. This element of weakness in his character, combined with total disorganisation in money matters, drove him steadily to the poverty and degradation in which eventually he was to founder. Obliged to repair his fortunes at the bar, he returned to Ireland in time to win renewed acclaim for his defence of the Fenians, which in turn led him on to a further campaign – only partly successful but nevertheless helpful to his own popularity – for amnesty for the political prisoners.

Meanwhile his own political ideas had been maturing. Now more than ever he felt that co-operation between men of property regardless of religious differences was the best defence against revolution in Ireland and radicalism in England. But the men of property would have to show an intelligent appreciation of realities; in particular they would have to understand that stability in Ireland could only be achieved if the Church of Ireland were disestablished, if Catholic claims in regard to denominational education were firmly met, and if landlords dealt more generously with their tenants. By the late 'sixties these were already familiar concepts. The general election of 1868 had been fought in Ireland mainly on these very issues and the Irish Liberals who captured 65 of the 105 seats in that election had gone to Westminster pledged to support Gladstone in carrying through precisely such a programme. Now these Liberals, scarcely less than the Conservatives who occupied the other forty seats, were indubitably men of property. Out of their total of sixty-five members no fewer than thirty-seven were from the landed class (a landlord being defined as one in possession of land valued at one thousand pounds or upwards), ten were from the professions and seventeen from commerce.[8] For them a programme of moderate reform was the right road to salvation. But, like the Irish Conservatives, though for opposite reasons, the Irish Liberals found cause for dissatisfaction with Gladstone. Where the former were outraged by the Church Act, the latter were hurt by his inadequate response to the amnesty movement and deeply disappointed by the failure of the Land Act to cut to the heart of the problem of tenant-right.

A favourable opportunity had thus been created for Butt to advance his own cherished solution to the Irish problem – federalism. And it was not surprising that when he and his friends called a meeting in Dublin on 19 May 1870 to discuss a policy for the future it should have been attended by representatives of a wide spectrum of opinion. Of the sixty-one people who either attended the meeting or later allowed their names to be added to the committee which was set up on that occasion, twenty-eight were Conservatives, seventeen were moderate or 'constitutional' nationalists, ten were Liberals and six were either Fenians or Fenian fellow-travellers. In terms of religion, so far as this can be ascertained, thirty-five were Protestant and twenty-five were Catholic.[9] The purpose of the meeting was to create a new body, the Home Government Association, to mobilise opinion behind the demand for an Irish parliament with, as Butt put it, 'full control over our domestic affairs'. The presence of so many Protestant Conservatives at this meeting impressed contemporary observers and has fascinated students of Home Rule ever since. But this element of genuine Protestant 'conservative nationalism' in the Home Government Association should not be overestimated, and this for three reasons. First, those Protestants who dabbled in Butt's movement were never more than a small minority of the whole; the bastions of the Ascendancy – the big houses in the countryside, the Church of Ireland, Trinity College, those business interests which depended on close economic ties with Britain – these all remained loyal to the Union, however disgruntled by Gladstone's embarrassing insistence that property had duties as well as rights. Secondly, what looked like a stampede towards Home Rule was in reality a recoil from the way in which, as it seemed to nervous Protestants, the British authorities, who should have been preserving their status, seemed bent on undermining it. These Protestants were reacting to insecurity – of course within a very different context – much as their forbears had reacted in the eighteenth century. If the British connection could not be made to serve their purpose, then they would rough-hew their destiny themselves. But just as the 'Protestant nation' of the eighteenth century had found it impossible to judge how far it dared go in conciliating the Catholic majority without damaging its own ascendancy, so too in the late nineteenth century, the Anglo-Irish gentry and middle class were unlikely to dally long with even conservative nationalism if it seriously looked like upsetting the status quo.

And this leads us to the third reason for their reluctance to commit themselves too deeply. It was that Butt himself, despite his fundamentally conservative cast of mind, had already moved further in some respects than his fellow-Protestants. He aimed at a movement which would be genuinely comprehensive and which would bring under the same banner not just disappointed Conservatives, but also Liberals, constitutional nationalists and even Fenians. As the composition of his committee of sixty-one indicates, he had some initial success in attracting individuals from these very diverse backgrounds. And it is fair to add that in the first year of its existence the Home Government Association gathered an increasing amount of support not only in Dublin but in other parts of the country as well.[10] Yet it is easy to see now what became clear very soon to many contemporaries – that the Home Government Association could never really be much more than a bundle of jarring incompatibilities. Butt was trying to drive three horses in troika, but they were horses that were used to running in quite different directions. The Protestants, as we have seen, were nervous from the beginning and any widening of the basis of the organisation to include a sizeable representation of Catholic nationalism, or even Catholic Liberalism, was bound to intensify that nervousness. In fact it was not long before the Conservative element began to fall away from the Association, especially after the passing of the Ballot Act in 1872 when men of property in general, an˙ landlords in particular, were confronted for the first time with the disagreeable prospect that the lower orders would henceforward be able to vote as they pleased. Nor were the Catholic Liberals or moderate nationalists much more amenable to Butt's persuasions. So long as the Association seemed little other than a vehicle for Protestant discontent, so long would Catholics, whatever their political persuasion, fight shy of it. Moreover, many Liberals – and also Gladstone's as yet faithful ally, the Irish hierarchy itself – still hoped for a favourable settlement of the question of denominational education. Until they knew the mind of the British government on that they would hang back from Home Rule.

The third of Butt's wayward horses was even harder to drive than the other two. There was no doubt that individual Fenians respected him for his work at the state trials and in the amnesty movement, but it was extremely unlikely that they would ever accept federalism as a substitute for independence, or that they would ever regard the Home Government Association as more than a front organisation through which it might or might not suit them to work for the time being. There have been suggestions, indeed, that either Butt himself, or G. H. Moore – the old stalwart of the 'independent' party of the 1850s, who might well have elbowed Butt out of the Home Rule leadership had he not died in April 1870 – had some sort of understanding with the Fenian leaders that the new agitation should operate for a trial period only, and that if it proved unsuccessful traditional methods should be resumed. If such a compact did exist then it was an interesting anticipation of a much more far-reaching development that was to occur a few years later, but it is hard to see that any 'new departure' based on co-operation between physical force men and constitutionalists had much future within the context of Butt's extremely limited conception of Home Rule. Even so, there were a few straws in the wind pointing to such co-operation. We know, for example, that when Butt formed an organisation – the Home Rule Confederation of Great Britain – to push his ideas among the Irish in England, Wales and Scotland this organisation was speedily infiltrated by Fenians. There are indications also that on the fringes of the Home Rule movement in Ireland – and soon very near the centre of it – were to be found individuals who seemed intent upon maintaining a connection between Fenianism and constitutional politics, though whether this was to convert Fenians or to subvert moderates is more difficult to determine. Finally, we have at least the suggestion of some kind of agreement with the Fenians from Butt himself when at the very start of his new organisation he was able to say : 'As for the men whom misgovernment has driven into revolt, I say for them that if they cannot aid you they will not thwart your experiment.'[11]

But the weakness of the Home Government Association stemmed from the inadequacy of its programme as well as from the heterogeneity of its composition. The leader himself was responsible for this by insisting that it should not be a political party, simply a pressure-group to propagate the federal gospel. Its business was not to fight by-elections, not to cover the country with a network of elaborate organisation, not even to be diverted into agitation for tenant rights or denominational education; its business was federalism and nothing but federalism.

What did federalism mean and how did it differ from repeal of the Union? It was something more, but also something less, than repeal. As Butt defined it in his speeches and in his pamphlet, *Irish Federalism*, it envisaged the restoration of an Irish parliament consisting of Crown, Lords and Commons, with jurisdiction over the internal affairs of the country and control over local resources and taxation. Superficially a re-creation of the constitution of 1782, Butt's proposals, as he frequently pointed out, actually went further than that constitution, since there would now be an Irish executive directly responsible to the Irish parliament in the Canadian or Australian fashion.* Where his scheme fell short of the 1782 constitution, and of the idea of repeal which had dominated constitutional politics in Ireland since O'Connell's time, was that he insisted on regarding federalism as an imperial and not just an Irish panacea. The parliament at Westminster would, he thought, be the great council for the whole empire and as such, Irishmen, as well as Englishmen, Scotsmen or Welshmen, ought to be represented in it. And because it was to be an imperial parliament it must retain authority over foreign policy, defence, war and essential taxation.[12] It was this insistence on continuing Irish representation at Westminster that divided him most sharply from his nationalist contemporaries and it was significant that when, during 1871, Home Rule began to register its first electoral success, the demand that simple legislative independence be substituted for federalism began immediately to be heard.

These early divergences within the Home Rule movement were symptomatic. Throughout its long history and despite all the different formulations of what self-government ought to comprise, the question of whether or not Irishmen should still sit at Westminster if they had a parliament of their own was never properly resolved. On the short term, however, and so long as Butt remained at the head of the agitation, Home Rule continued to mean federalism. And although there were

* The constitution of 1782, which we shall presently see Arthur Griffith demanding as the basis for his Sinn Féin movement, had been extracted by the Protestant Ascendancy in Ireland from an English ministry debilitated by the loss of the American colonies. It was less a constitution than a redistribution of the respective legislative powers of the Westminster and Dublin parliaments. It suffered from many defects of which perhaps the two outstanding were that the acts of the Dublin parliament were still subject to veto in London and that Irish government was still in the hands of a Lord Lieutenant appointed on the advice of English ministers and in effect responsible to them.

always die-hard repealers who cast a cold eye on his enthusiasm, yet events were beginning to play into his hands. Up to 1873 he had still lacked approval from the bulk of the Irish bishops, who remained loyal to Gladstone in the expectation that he would give them the denominational university they yearned for. But when in that year his long-awaited University Bill proved unsatisfactory, they threw their influence against him and the opposition of the Irish Liberals in the House of Commons contributed directly to the fall of the ministry which rapidly followed.[13] And if that were not enough, the very next year Gladstone launched forth on his polemical campaign against the decrees of the Vatican Council with a fine disregard for the susceptibilities of his late allies. It seemed as if the strange honeymoon between the Irish hierarchy and English Liberalism was finally at an end.

The bishops' disenchantment with Gladstone turned them cautiously towards Butt who, at the end of 1873, felt strong enough to replace the old Association with a new body – the Home Rule League. Its programme was not essentially different from that of the Association, but it provided the basis for a genuinely national organisation. Anyone could become a member if he paid one pound per annum, and later the door to associate members was thrown open for only one shilling a year. By this time enough MPs had become affiliated for the inaugural conference to toy with the idea that all members elected on a Home Rule platform should be asked to agree to concert their efforts in the House of Commons and to vote, or abstain from voting, in a body as the majority might decide. Here, all unknown, was the germ from which a great parliamentary party was to grow. But the time was not yet ripe. The members, indignant at this proposed limitation on their independence and integrity, rejected the proposal out of hand. Butt's speech against it was, however, significant in quite a different sense. He had always been a reverent House of Commons man and now that he was back at Westminster again (he had been elected for Limerick city in 1871) he made it plain that he would have no truck with independent opposition of the kind suggested. If such opposition meant 'a system of indiscriminate voting against every ministry upon every occasion that could turn them out', he would not accept a seat on those conditions. 'To bind himself to such a pledge', he said, 'would destroy every particle of moral influence which any action of his would have in the House of Commons.'[14]

This was not merely an academic debate. The very next year the trickle of by-election victories swelled to a flowing tide in the general election. In this, the first election since the adoption of the secret ballot in 1872, constitutional nationalism, it has been said, returned to the centre of the stage. No less than fifty-nine members were elected on a Home Rule platform and the old polarisation of Irish politics between Liberal and Conservative had apparently gone for ever. Conservatism as such was still important – it accounted for thirty-three seats in 1874 – but simple Gladstonian Liberalism in Ireland had begun its swift plunge into oblivion, only ten Liberals not committed to Home Rule being successful. Yet the decline was not quite as catastrophic as it seemed. The election had followed so close on the heels of the formation of the Home Rule League that Butt and his friends had been unable to find a sufficient supply of impeccable federalists. Counting, as they necessarily had to do, upon clerical support in many constituencies, they were obliged to accept a number of candidates who were essentially Liberal in background or sympathy and who had qualified as Home Rulers only by a late and hasty declaration for the cause. In one or two instances, indeed, popular feeling was strong enough to elect a keen nationalist in the teeth of clerical opposition (as in Limerick) or (as in Louth) to divide parish clergy enthusiastic for Home Rule from their more cautious bishops, but such cases were still exceptional. A recent analysis has even suggested that out of the fifty-nine nominal Home Rulers, probably only twenty were deeply committed. Of the remainder, nineteen were either former Liberals, or in one way or another tarred with the Gladstonian brush, and twenty were newcomers about whom it was impossible to say for certain which way they would jump, except that some of them were unlikely to jump far in the direction of Home Rule.[15]

Moreover, in social composition the fifty-nine members of the Home Rule group were still overwhelmingly of the upper or middle class. There were twenty-three landowners or sons of landowners, seven 'rentiers' (men of means but no paid occupation), eight merchants, bankers and newspaper proprietors, and nineteen professional men including, of course, a strong contingent of lawyers. Yet if this still seems a very gentlemanly kind of representation, there were indications of change. Landlords, though numerous, were less numerous than they had been in 1868. By contrast the professional and mercantile elements had markedly increased. Most striking of all, the election of 1874 had produced two tenant-farmers among the Home Rulers where none had been before. It would be too much to say that the advent of the Home Rule agitation had democratised Irish politics, but it would not be unfair to say that this platform, combined with the effect of the Ballot Act upon the electorate, had opened the way for the rise of a politically active middle class.* The process was later to be carried much further; in 1874 it had scarcely begun to take effect and the party which Butt began to organise directly the election was over remained uneasily divided between a landed and a middle-class section. From this significant social division was to spring at least part of its later paralysis.[16]

* Recent research suggests that in England the Ballot Act may not have put an immediate end to influence and intimidation, especially in the countryside. (See Henry Pelling, *Social Geography of British Elections, 1885-1910* (London, 1967), pp. 11-13.) In Ireland too, no doubt, there was still scope for landlord or clerical pressure, but the important fact that the social composition of the Home Rule representation *was* changing has nevertheless to be insisted upon.

But a more important cause for that paralysis was that the fifty-nine Home Rulers did not in fact form a party in any recognisably modern sense of the term. Although most of them met in Dublin before the new session and agreed, or seemed to agree, on a policy of independence of either of the great English parties, many of the new members had promised the electors that they would work for other causes – land reform, amnesty, denominational education – besides Home Rule. The only thing they had in common, and the only thing on which Butt held them to any kind of conformity, was that they had all espoused some form of self-government. Yet even this had its obscurities. The old fissure between federalists and repealers had only been papered over in 1874 and it was significant that the best the new party could do by way of a formula for joint action ran as follows:

That deeply impressed with the importance of unity of action upon all matters that can affect the parliamentary position of the Home Rule party, or the interests of the Home Rule cause, we engage to each other and to the country that we will use our best endeavours to obtain that unity by taking counsel together, by making all reasonable concessions to the opinions of each other, by avoiding as far as possible isolated action, and by sustaining and supporting each other in the course which may be deemed best calculated to promote the grand object of national self-government which the Irish nation has committed to our care.[17]

If this meant anything it meant a polite agreement to differ on fundamental issues. It was abundantly clear that members were still free to take an individual line when they chose and time was to show that this was precisely what many of them were prepared to do. It has to be admitted, however, that even had they been willing to pledge themselves firmly to more disciplined action they would have found such action difficult to take. This was partly for external reasons, partly because of the inherent defects of Butt's own approach to parliamentary politics. Externally, the situation in England had changed very much to Ireland's disadvantage. The Conservative victory in the British elections had brought to power a Disraeli whose attention was occupied at this time mainly by the disturbed condition of world affairs. War or rumours of war in the Balkans, in Africa, in Afghanistan, overclouded these years and by comparison with such great events Irish problems easily came to seem peripheral. And anyway, apart from these international issues, parliamentary time was to a large extent taken up with English domestic legislation. Ireland had had her turn under Gladstone, now it was time to attend to the needs of others. It was still, of course, open to Butt and his party to introduce Irish legislation themselves and they did so repeatedly – especially on the land question – but they had always to reckon with the indifference of the Commons and the active hostility of the Lords.

And this was where the inherent weakness of Butt's movement, and of Butt himself as a political leader, stood most starkly revealed. Irish legislation was frustrated in the years after 1874 not just because British attention centred itself elsewhere, but because of Butt's inability to centre it on Ireland. Not only did his party lack cohesion, lack conviction, lack the driving power of a profound movement of discontent at home; his own view of the parliamentary role of an Irish member remained incorrigibly conservative. Sympathetic as always to the needs of the Irish masses, he failed utterly to see that the only way to satisfy those needs through legislation was by the pressure of a tightly controlled Irish party. To be fair, most of his fellow Home Rulers would have resisted any such control to the uttermost, for they agreed with their leader that excessive discipline was incompatible with the dignity and independence of representative men. In any event, since Butt himself had a certain sympathy for the imperial policies of Disraeli, whereas many Home Rulers remained essentially Liberal in their outlook, there was little enough common ground between them. Butt's own personality, moreover, precluded vigorous leadership. He sincerely believed that it was important for Irish MPs to show by their decorum and sense of responsibility in the House of Commons that their country was fit for self-government and that this policy – essentially a policy of conciliation – was the only possible path to parliamentary influence. Unfortunately, while he himself embodied this policy to perfection, the continuing disarray of his private life made it hard for him to offer constant precept and example to his colleagues. Too often he was absent, trying to repair his shattered fortunes by spasmodic attention to his law practice, or simply because absence was the only way of avoiding his creditors. Perhaps it was not surprising that some of the party, though lacking his excuse, imitated his behaviour, with the result that before long complaints began to be raised in Ireland about persistent absenteeism among the Home Rulers.

There were, however, a few who held that politeness, moderation and due attention to the niceties of House of Commons procedure were not the only way to educate English opinion about Irish needs. If Irish members used their position to be obstructive rather than co-operative might this not succeed in drawing attention to their existence better than any amount of genteel but ineffective debating? Such at any rate was the view of one of the most remarkable of the recent additions to the party. This was J. G. Biggar, a Belfast provision merchant, Protestant in origin and later a convert to Catholicism. Biggar had taken a prominent part in the founding of the Home Rule League and had distinguished himself by demanding from the outset that Home Rule candidates for election be asked to give written pledges that if returned to parliament they would act together. Elected to parliament himself in 1874, he clashed with Butt over discipline in the very first session and in 1875 made himself widely unpopular by using the rules of the House to compel the Prince of Wales to withdraw from the public gallery.

But unpopularity at Westminster held no terrors for him. Unprepossessing in appearance, in fact almost a hunchback, delivering his opinions abruptly in a harsh Belfast accent, Biggar was nevertheless a man with valuable qualities. Tough-minded, shrewd, loyal once his loyalties had been engaged (which to Butt they never fully were), he represented a very different tradition from that to which so many of his colleagues belonged. He had recently joined the Irish Republican Brotherhood (in which he was rapidly elevated to the Supreme Council) and, like several other 'advanced' nationalists just at this time, seemed to be groping his way towards some as yet ill-defined alliance between the Fenian and the parliamentary traditions. Such a man was unlikely to spend much time conciliating English opinion. Contempt for that opinion was, on the contrary, one of his leading characteristics and it led him easily into a policy of obstructing English business as a means of ventilating Irish grievances. It was this policy that caused his first collision with Butt and which, undeterred, he developed in subsequent sessions. He was not alone in pursuing it and was supported on occasion by nine of his colleagues; indeed, by 1876, so disillusioned had Ireland become with the non-success of Butt's gradualism that even the normally circumspect newspaper, the *Nation*, began to advocate obstruction as the only means of overcoming the indifference of the House of Commons.

Yet Biggar, though a mainspring of the new policy, was unlikely to supersede Butt. Given the social composition of the party at that time, to say nothing of his own rasping individualism, a Belfast tradesman of plebeian background and appearance could never hope to mount into the highest place. What was needed was a new leader of impeccable origins and unmistakable dynamism. And the hour was about to produce the man. In April 1875 a by-election victory in Meath resulted in the advent of a new recruit to the Home Rule party, Charles Stewart Parnell. On the face of it he hardly seemed the timber of which Irish nationalists were made. A landlord, a Protestant, educated in England, deeply attached to his family and to the life of a country gentleman, extremely reserved in manner and (in his early days) reticent in speech almost to the point of unintelligibility, he seemed to combine most of the obstacles to political success in Ireland. On the other hand, he had the appearance and the temperament of a leader. He was strikingly handsome, with eyes of peculiar intensity, and seemed to exercise an equal fascination upon men and women. Capable alike of charm and ruthlessness, he had a strong, if narrow, intelligence and, though never a spell-binding orator, still less a wit, or even at bottom a sympathetic personality, he imposed himself upon his world by a self-confidence so intense as to be regarded later by his fellow-countrymen as almost superhuman. This self-control, however, had only been achieved after a struggle, for he was a nervous and superstitious man who disliked noise, large crowds and all the drudgery of public speaking. Yet he forced himself to become proficient and the bungling novice who was the despair of his first backers very rapidly grew to be a master of the art of communicating in terse and simple phrases his own passionate convictions to vast audiences. For passion, it must be emphasised, was the key to his nature. To those who only saw him from the outside, as it were, cold, calculating judgment seemed his dominant characteristic. He did indeed have that kind of judgment – at certain points in his career he displayed a genius for it – but time was to show that passion, combined with an almost demonic pride, was the force that ruled his life.

He was, of course, partly the product of his heredity and his environment. The family had a history of political nonconformism. An ancestor, Sir John Parnell, had opposed the Act of Union, and others of his name had subsequently supported Catholic emancipation. More immediately important was the fact that his mother, born Delia Stewart, was the daughter of a famous American admiral who had fought against England in the war of 1812. Married into this Anglo-Irish ascendancy family, she fell in with its traditions sufficiently to dine at the Viceregal Lodge, entertain English officers at the Parnell estate of Avondale in county Wicklow, send her son Charles to Cambridge and have her daughters presented at Queen Victoria's court. But most accounts agree that she combined these proprieties with an American heritage, duly passed on to her children, of extreme anti-English feeling. This expressed itself most forcibly in a sympathy for Fenianism which was certainly shared by Charles. Parnell was not himself a Fenian (he was only twenty-one when the abortive rising of 1867 broke out) but long afterwards he testified that it was Fenianism which had first turned him towards politics – that, and memories of the 1798 rebellion which still lived in the Wicklow countryside around his home.

Yet all this, though part of his personality, does not explain fully why he should have become an active nationalist. There was something else at work inside him – a deep, enduring, curiously personal, dislike of England and Englishmen. His experiences at Cambridge may have contributed to this – he got into trouble with the authorities and left without taking his degree – but beneath everything was a feeling very characteristic of the Anglo-Irish stock to which he belonged, an angry reaction against the complacent air of superiority so many Englishmen adopted in their attitude towards Ireland. 'These Englishmen', he once said to his brother, 'despise us because we are Irish, but we must stand up to them. That's the only way to treat an Englishman – stand up to him.'[18]

For such a young man, proud, emotional, spoiling for action, the policy of obstructionism had obvious attractions. Before long Parnell was acting closely with Biggar and a handful of other obstructionalists, and although he can scarcely be said to have impressed the House as an orator in his first two sessions, one of his interventions was notable – when in 1876 he intervened to assert that the Fenians who had killed a policeman at Manchester in 1867 when attempting to rescue two of their comrades had committed no murder. This, together perhaps with his associations with Biggar, brought him to the attention of leading Fenians and ex-Fenians in England, with the result that in 1877, after one famous outburst of obstructionism in parliament which precipitated an open breach between Butt and his tormentors, Parnell replaced his leader as president of the Home Rule Confederation of Great Britain. For the old Home Ruler this was the writing on the wall. He still retained enough authority in the party and in the League to stave off final disaster for another year, but all through 1878 his position continued to deteriorate, as did his health also. The Balkan crisis of that year (following on the Russo-Turkish war of 1877) seemed to him a national emergency in which it was the duty of responsible men to rally behind the government. To his Irish critics, on the contrary, it was an ideal opportunity for the Home Rulers to demonstrate that they had no 'community of interest' with England in her foreign adventures by leaving the House in a body before the division on the Balkan crisis was taken. This drastic action, which was proposed at a Home Rule Conference in Dublin in January 1878 by a fiery young medical student, John Dillon, of whom much more was to be heard in the future, was violently resisted by Butt and not in fact adopted. And for the rest of that session Butt continued to ignore pressure for independent and united opposition, reserving his right to vote for the government if and when he thought it desirable. It was no surprise, therefore, that at the end of the year Dillon again attacked the ageing leader for his reluctance to embarrass the government, then involved in the Afghan war, by hostile action in the House of Commons. It was against the younger nationalists at home that Butt finally turned to bay at a meeting of the Home Rule League in February 1879. He had there to face what was in effect a motion of no confidence (and a charge from Dillon that in his subservience to the government he was virtually behaving like a traitor) but although he scraped home with a majority of thirty-two votes to twenty-four in his favour, he left the meeting a beaten man. Already seriously ill, he declined rapidly and by May he was dead.

There was now no obstacle in Parnell's path. But which way would he turn? Was he to use the Fenians or be used by them? Would he continue to work through the House of Commons, or would he, under Fenian pressure, be tempted or driven back to Ireland to lead an extra-parliamentary, and even in the end, revolutionary agitation? These were not abstract questions. They seemed rather to call for immediate and practical decisions, for a choice to be made between two quite different traditions of nationalism. Some, indeed, were already making that choice, or having it thrust upon them. Thus in 1877, the very year of Parnell's rise to prominence, Biggar and John O'Connor Power (another of those who walked the shadowy line between the physical force and the constitutional movements) were expelled from the Supreme Council of the IRB because of their parliamentary activities, and two others, John Barry and Patrick Egan, resigned from that body about the same time. Would Parnell be confronted with a like dilemma, or was it conceivably a dilemma that had no real meaning for him? Had conditions similar to those of 1877 persisted into subsequent years he might have had to answer such questions sooner or later. But the conditions of 1877 did not persist. On the contrary, as the fight against Butt ground on towards its inexorable end that fight came to be seen as only a fraction of a larger situation, a situation that was rapidly being transformed by two startling new developments.

2. Land and Politics

The first of the two new developments which were to change Irish politics so radically occurred not in Ireland but in America. Irish-American nationalism, which, as we have already seen, had exercised a powerful influence on Fenianism in the 'sixties, now again became a force to reckon with. The collapse of the Fenian rising in 1867 had had the same disintegrating effect upon the Irish in America as upon the Irish at home. But whereas in Ireland the effect of this had been to open the way for a revival of constitutional politics, in the United States the reaction of extreme nationalists was to establish a new and more effective secret organisation. This was the Clan na Gael (or United Brotherhood as it was less frequently called) which was founded in 1867 by Jerome J. Collins, an Irish-American journalist employed by the newspaper tycoon, James Gordon Bennett. The most powerful individuals in the Clan were, however, William Carroll, a doctor from Philadelphia, and John Devoy. Devoy had, of course, been deeply involved in Fenianism himself before seeking refuge in America. He, too, became a journalist (and a very able one) in Bennett's empire, but for the next fifty years a large part of the inexhaustible energy of this tenacious, bitter and altogether formidable man was to be poured into the double task of making Irish-American nationalism a force in the politics of the United States and of forwarding the cause of revolution in Ireland.

With the domestic preoccupations of the Irish-Americans we are not here concerned, though for a proper understanding of their actions it has to be realised that these preoccupations were intensely important to them. Starting, as most of them had done, from the lowest abyss of poverty, they wanted desperately to climb up to acceptance and respectability. For them the American Declaration of Independence was not a tired formula, but an ideal to be reached out for and grasped. Moreover, it was an ideal that was as valid for their native as for their adopted land. Irish independence would allow them to enter more freely into the benefits of American independence. 'You want to be honoured among the elements that constitute this nation', a visiting Irishman told them in 1880. 'You want to be regarded with the respect due to you; that you may thus be looked on, aid us in Ireland to remove the stain of degradation from your birth.'[1] But independence for Ireland and respectability in America could only be won by discipline and cohesion; it was these qualities above all that the Clan sought to instil into its members.

Within ten years of its foundation the Clan numbered perhaps 10,000 – mainly working-class in the rank and file, mainly middle-class in the leadership. After 1877 it was formally linked with the IRB in Ireland by a joint revolutionary directory containing three representatives of each organisation and a seventh chosen by the other six members. At that time the policy of the leaders was to plan another insurrection in Ireland, ready to break out whenever England was next involved in a major war, a possibility which, at the height of the Balkan crisis in 1877–8, seemed by no means remote. The Clan, however, had no monopoly of Irish-American support. To some, its schemes seemed much too ponderous and unrealistic to offer any reasonable hope of immediate action and wilder spirits, like the Fenian, O'Donovan Rossa, pinned their hopes on direct action in the form of terrorist activities financed from 1875 onwards by a so-called 'Skirmishing Fund'. When this Fund grew to sizeable proportions it was in effect taken over by the Clan, but the impulse towards terrorism remained and sporadic outbursts of violence originated by, or linked with, Irish-American extremists, were to complicate Anglo-Irish relations for many years to come. At the opposite pole from the extremists were the great mass of Irish immigrants, preoccupied with making a living in a time of economic depression, marked to some extent by the social radicalism bred of that depression, but above all faithful sons and daughters of the Church and unlikely to be swept into a mass movement unless under the stimulus of a nationalist revival in Ireland.

In 1877 there was little overt sign of any such revival. Nevertheless, Parnell, as we have seen, was beginning to emerge as a distinctive figure among the constitutionalists and to attract the attention of extreme men on both sides of the Atlantic. As early as August of that year the Fenian J. J. O'Kelly (later to be one of his most devoted followers) had met him in Paris and reported to Devoy that he was 'cool – extremely so and resolute'. And in January 1878 Dr William Carroll interviewed him in London and found him, so he believed, in favour of the absolute independence of Ireland. Two months later Parnell, accompanied by two other parliamentary obstructionists, was brought by Carroll face to face with John O'Leary and John O'Connor, both high in the leadership of the IRB. It was a crucial meeting in two respects. On the one hand, it confirmed the uncompromising determination of the IRB to have no dealings with constitutional nationalists; the previous year O'Connor Power and Biggar had been expelled, and John Barry and Patrick Egan had withdrawn from the supreme Council precisely on this issue, and the meeting of March 1878 made it abundantly clear that for Irish revolutionaries to work with parliamentarians would be to risk a fatal contamination. On the other hand, the meeting also revealed that the Irish-American view was by no means so rigorous. Perhaps because they were further removed from the scene of action, perhaps because in America they had absorbed a pragmatic tradition which predisposed them to action more readily than the barren idealism of the IRB,

Carroll and Devoy saw in Parnell an ally through whom and with whom they could work. This is not to say that the Clan na Gael was blowing cold on revolution – merely that in the search to unify and strengthen Irish nationalism in both countries it was prepared to contemplate the mobilisation of a far wider range of forces than any the limited and fanatical vision of the IRB could comprehend.

Parnell's own most remarkable contribution to these negotiations seems to have been his silence. If he had other notions of the proper relationship between the extreme and the constitutional movements he did not choose to reveal them. But neither, at this stage, did he choose to cut himself off from the knights of the Fenian Holy Grail. On the contrary, only a couple of months after his meeting with the IRB representatives, he told an audience of Lancashire Irishmen (at St Helen's in May 1878) that if Irish members were expelled from parliament for their obstructionist tactics, then the Home Rulers should formally secede in a body and assemble in Ireland as the provisional government of the country. There was nothing particularly novel in this idea – it had been suggested by Charles Gavan Duffy as far back as 1848 and was in the minds of many writers and speakers in the late 1870s – but what was specially interesting about Parnell's speech at this particular juncture was that it chimed with, and may even have been suggested by, parallel Irish-American pronouncements.

Yet about all these notions there was a haunting air of unreality. The Irish-Americans, indeed, were impatient for action. The centenary of the 'legislative independence' of 1782 was approaching and they hoped to celebrate it with a victory not less complete than Grattan's. But the basis for such a victory was nowhere apparent. Parnell might or might not be a desirable ally, but he still lacked substance. Even amongst Home Rulers there was only a handful of obstructionists, and in the country at large any mass withdrawal from parliament (had it been remotely feasible) would probably have been greeted by total confusion and bewilderment. What was needed, therefore, was a policy that would engage the sympathy and active support of the Irish people as a whole.

Slowly and tentatively the Irish-Americans were groping their way towards such a policy. One of the most extreme of their newspapers, Patrick Ford's *Irish World*, had been for some time labouring the point that to work for Irish independence without at the same time, or even previously, providing for the economic security of the great majority of Irishmen by abolishing the existing system of landownership would be futile. This policy was taken up by Devoy during 1878 in circumstances that were confusing at the time and which have only gradually been elucidated by historians. At the end of the previous year a young Fenian, Michael Davitt, had been released from prison. Born, like Parnell, in 1846, Davitt was the son of a tenant-farmer who, having been evicted from his county Mayo holding, emigrated with his family to Lancashire. There the young Davitt worked in the mills as a child labourer, losing an arm in an industrial accident when only eleven years of age. Sensitive, intelligent, intensely aware of his country's history, he was almost inevitably drawn as a young man into the IRB. Acting as an arms agent for the organisation, he was arrested in 1870 in the act of trafficking in arms for allegedly unlawful (i.e. Fenian) purposes and was sentenced to fifteen years' penal servitude. Released after surviving seven years of extremely harsh conditions, he at once rejoined the IRB and to all appearances was ready to take up once more the threads of insurrection where he had had to drop them at the time of his seizure.

Later he was himself to give currency to the notion that these appearances were deceptive and that, on the contrary, he had occupied his years of solitude in fashioning a plan whereby, as the Young Irelander, Fintan Lalor, had prophesied long before, the land question would become the engine that would drag the national question in its train. But of this, which he was soon to present as his alternative to the futility of yet another ill-planned and under-manned rebellion, there was little sign in 1877 or 1878. In the latter year he arrived in America mainly to visit his mother. He met Devoy as a matter of course and no doubt learnt from him and others how Irish-American nationalism was shaping. Davitt's own preoccupation at that time, apart from earning a living as a public lecturer, seems still to have been with strengthening the forces of revolution and preparing the ground for another uprising, should the international situation make this possible. But by October 1878 he had so far absorbed the doctrine of combined action between parliamentarians and more extreme nationalists that in a lecture in Brooklyn he urged that Irishmen at home should seek to penetrate every elective office (which, he considered, it was open for them to do since the Ballot Act) and support every kind of reform in order to prepare the way for independence. Among the reforms he advocated was a solution of the land question along the lines of co-partnership between landlord and tenant. This, however, fell short of the Irish-American demand and at that same meeting Devoy came out uncompromisingly for the total abolition of landlordism, though, since this was by definition a long-term solution, he was prepared to agree with Davitt that the immediate target should be to protect tenants from arbitrary eviction. And like Davitt, though if anything more emphatically, he insisted that the only way in which extremism could make an impact was by a policy of permeation, not isolation.

Less than two weeks after these declarations Devoy – having consulted other members of the Clan, though not Davitt who was absent on a lecture tour – elaborated these hints and nods into something much more explicit. Misled, apparently, into thinking that Parnell was about to make the irrevocable break with Isaac Butt which in fact only came in the next year, he sent him a telegram promising him support if he in his turn would adopt unequivocally the two major Irish-American objectives. The first of these was that 'federal' Home Rule should be dropped, and a general commitment to Irish self-government (purposely not defined too exactly) substituted in its place. And the second was that the land question should be vigorously pushed at both its levels – that is, immediate protection for the tenant, followed ultimately by the creation of a peasant proprietorship. The day after the dispatch of this telegram (26 October 1878) Devoy made it clear in a series of press interviews that this 'New Departure', as he called it, was not a change of ends, only of means. Those who were revolutionaries would remain revolutionaries. By emerging into the open they would be educating Irish opinion and thus bringing nearer the day when a fully informed and articulate people would demand of their representatives that they withdraw from the parliament at Westminster and set up their own legislature in Ireland. If this should lead to violence and a war of independence then that was a logic with which old Fenians would be well content.[2]

To talk of a New Departure was one thing. To translate it into action was quite another, and the effort to do so led to confusions and contradictions which have ever since bedevilled the history of this crucial episode. Briefly, what happened was that Devoy and Davitt (who, once he learned of it, subscribed to the New Departure programme) sailed to France, where in January 1879 they met the leaders of the IRB. Once more, as Carroll had done the previous year, they encountered the unwavering opposition of what one might not unfairly call revolutionary conservatism. The president of the Supreme Council, the ageing novelist Charles Kickham, would not hear of any deviations into parliamentary politics or land reform and closed all discussion of the subject by the simple but symbolic gesture of removing his ear-trumpet. Individual Fenians, it was conceded, might possibly participate at their own risk in 'open' agitations (and even this concession was withdrawn the following year), but there could be no question of a formal alliance.[3] Such intransigence, perhaps, was only to be expected. More might be hoped from Parnell. Devoy and others met him in March (again in France) but had an inconclusive interview at which the parliamentary leader showed himself as difficult to pin down as ever, though apparently leaving Devoy with the impression that he was not averse to the use of force and not circumscribed in his views about the kind of self-government Ireland should be aiming at.

At this point events began to impose a pattern of their own. Irish politics were about to be transformed by the second of the new developments of these critical years. The root of the trouble, as so often before, lay in the poverty and insecurity of the Irish tenant-farmer. The Act of 1870 was too limited in scope to have made any great inroads on agrarian distress even in good times, but from the mid-seventies onwards the times had been bad and getting worse. Agricultural depression, due mainly to American competition, resulted in a serious decline in prices of farm produce and, since the depression was equally severe in Britain, the earnings of migrant labour, upon which many Irish families depended to eke out the meagre living they scratched from their own holdings, fell off very markedly. In Ireland itself the value of the principal crops produced fell by nearly fourteen million pounds between 1876 and 1879, and in Connaught – the poorest of the provinces – the latter year saw a loss of earnings from England of no less than £250,000. Inexorably the peasants were driven to seek credit where they could find it – the banks for the more substantial, the village money-lender or the 'gombeen man' for the impoverished majority. But this was at best a temporary expedient and when the hard-bought money was exhausted rents – even relatively moderate rents – could not be paid. Inevitably, evictions followed; in 1879, for example, over 1000 families numbering nearly 6000 people were turned off the land.[4] Equally inevitably, these evictions produced 'outrages', varying from the maiming of cattle and the burning of haystacks or farm-buildings, to attempts on the lives of landlords and their agents, all this complicated by the village vendettas of tenants against other tenants who could not resist the temptation to become 'land-grabbers', occupying farms from which their fellows had been driven.

Neither the causes of this unrest nor its consequences were new. What was new, or rather unprecedented in scale since 1847, was the extent to which the depression was accompanied, especially in the west of Ireland, by actual starvation. Many families still depended heavily on the potato as a staple crop and when it failed – as between 1877 and 1879 it did fail – they were in dire trouble. Just how serious was their plight may be judged even from the impersonal statistics issued by the government. Whereas in 1876 more than four million tons of potatoes worth nearly £12½ milion had been produced, in 1879 this had declined in quantity to just over one million tons and in value to less than £3½ million.[5] This was the situation that confronted Davitt when, after the abortive Paris meeting, he visited his native Mayo. To a man of his origins and temperament the misery of these poor people made an immediate and, as it turned out, decisive appeal. At once (April 1879) he joined in a demonstration at Irishtown to demand justice for the tenant farmer and was soon led on to place this demand in the very centre of his own programme. Next, he attempted to persuade Parnell to throw his energy and growing influence behind the new campaign and in Dublin at the beginning of June the two men, together with John Devoy, discussed this possibility. Parnell's own views on the land question, though unlikely to be as radical and emotional as Davitt's, had nevertheless been developing fast. When he first entered politics in 1875 he had been content to argue for fixity of tenure and fair rents, but by 1877 he was already moving towards the idea of peasant ownership as the ultimate solution. He was certainly speaking in Ireland on these lines by the end of 1878 and in the spring of 1879, even before Davitt had held his demonstration at Irishtown, Parnell at Cavan was looking forward to the time 'when by purchasing the interests of the landlords it might be possible for every tenant to be the owner of the farm which he at present occupies as tenant-at-will or otherwise'.[6]

There was thus some reason for Davitt to hope for Parnell's involvement. And, at that June meeting the tenant's son did in fact persuade the landlord to come down to Westport with him the following week to attend a further meeting to demand social justice for the farmer. But did Parnell, at this conference with Devoy and Davitt, promise more than merely to lend his aid to a rapidly developing agrarian agitation? Devoy always maintained that he did and that the conference resulted in a grand alliance to carry the New Departure into effect – resulted, that is, in an agreement to push on both the Home Rule and the land movements, but to regard them as means to the greater end of freedom to be won, if necessary, by armed revolution. Parnell and Davitt emphatically denied that any such hard and fast arrangement was ever reached. As no written records were kept, the debate has continued in one form or another ever since, but the weight of the evidence supports the view that there was no alliance as such, simply a provision for, as Davitt expressed it, 'an open participation in public movements by extreme men . . . in friendly rivalry with moderate nationalists'. One can see, of course, why each of the three participants had his own view as to what the conference really achieved. For Devoy, if he was to be able to face the Clan on his return, it was essential to be able to claim that sooner or later Parnell would proceed beyond reform to revolution. There is unmistakable evidence that Devoy genuinely believed this; had he not believed it, he would not have thrown Irish-American support behind Parnell as whole-heartedly as he did in the succeeding years. But this was surely wishful thinking. Parnell had so far shown no inclination to abandon parliamentary action and, genius that he was in not committing himself, it was highly unlikely that he would have tied his hands in this particular way. Davitt's motivation was possibly more complex, but when in 1888 he embarked on his great *apologia pro vita sua* before the Special Commission appointed to inquire, among other things, into possible links between Irish nationalists and American revolutionaries, he was anxious to demonstrate in all sincerity that he himself had left the paths of secret conspiracy far behind him and had become a man imbued with a passion to right the wrongs of the poor, be they Irish farmers or English working-men. By 1888 he was indeed transparently such a man and it was natural for him to deny with all his force that only nine years earlier he had entered into a secret alliance with his old Fenian comrades. So far as the Dublin meeting went, he may well have been correct. But before the Dublin meeting, and while he was still in America, he, unlike Parnell, had accepted the New Departure. His absorption in the land question forced him steadily towards a breach of that previous understanding. American Fenians never forgave him for this, but to Davitt, obsessed as he became with the fate of the Irish peasant, even the good will of his former associates dwindled into secondary importance.

Did Parnell come in the end to share Davitt's obsession? The answer can only be that he did not, but that his involvement in the 'land war' (as it came almost immediately to be called) while undoubtedly tactical was also something more than tactical. Justice for the tenants was a policy to which passion as well as intelligence compelled his assent. But, characteristically, it was an assent tinged with the caution that came partly from his ability to see things in the long view and partly from an innate social conservatism. Thus, although he took the plunge at Westport by urging the tenants in a famous phrase to 'keep a firm grip of their homesteads' he qualified his acceptance of land purchase as the final solution by remarking that it would be highly beneficial if this could be carried through 'without injury to the landlord'. His own ideas of how purchase could be arranged were complex, and irrelevant for us because never put to the test, but it was noticeable that whereas he regularly held up to his audiences the prospect that the farmers must eventually become the owners of their holdings, he did not disdain whatever lesser substitutes in the way of greater security for tenants English governments might have to offer. Neither, for that matter, did he endorse the doctrine of compulsory purchase except in very limited and specialised circumstances or under the momentary pressure of public opinion.

Parnell was able to take a more realistic view of the land question than Davitt, who eventually arrived at a policy of land *nationalisation* rather than peasant *ownership*, both because he had a better understanding of the farmer's hunger for the soil, and because for him the settlement of the land question was only part of a much larger complex. 'I would not have taken off my coat and gone to this work', he said in 1880, 'if I had not known that we were laying the foundation in this movement for the regeneration of our legislative independence.'[7] Holding this ultimate goal firmly in his mind and sensing the enormous driving power of the land question ('I am only sorry to say that I think they [the people] would go to hell for it,' the old Fenian, Charles Kickham, had told him) he was bound to identify himself with it. In the autumn of 1879 he accepted Davitt's invitation to become the president of a new organisation, the Irish National Land League. The two objectives of the League – preserving the tenants from being rack-rented and unjustly evicted in the short term, and making them owners of their farms in the long term – offered a programme which not only he, but a great many of his fellow-countrymen could accept. Moreover, as the League developed its campaign for 'the land of Ireland for the people of Ireland' in the succeeding two years, it assumed the character of a mass-movement based primarily on moral force. Brilliantly led by a handful of devoted men – several of them, like Davitt himself, Fenians or ex-Fenians – the League set itself to give the peasantry not only protection but self-respect. In its earliest phase concerned largely with the relief of starving and destitute people, it developed naturally from this into an agency for succouring families evicted for non-payment of rent. But it did not stop at that. From the very beginning one of its main functions was to organise popular demonstrations against evictions and to mobilise public opinion against any man who dared to take a farm from which another had been evicted. Even as early as October 1879 the young John Dillon, who after the destruction of Isaac Butt had flung himself eagerly into the struggle, was instructing the farmers as to what this might mean. After suggesting to them that they should offer their landlords a reduced rent and pay none at all if this was refused, he urged them not to touch the land from which a farmer had been evicted because of such non-payment. 'If any man then takes up that land let no man speak to him or have any business transaction with him.'[8]

This was in embryo the policy of social ostracism which Parnell was to enunciate with such devastating clarity a year later, when, in one of the most famous speeches of his career, he told a gathering of farmers at Ennis that if there was to be land reform in the coming session of parliament it would be the measure of their determination not to pay unjust rents. 'It will be the measure of your determination not to bid for farms from which others have been evicted, and to use the strong force of public opinion to deter any unjust men amongst yourselves – and there are many such – from bidding for such farms.' Any one who transgressed the code should be placed in a 'moral Coventry', shunned by his neighbours 'as if he were a leper of old'. A few days later this policy began to be applied not just to tenant-farmers but to Lord Erne's agent, Captain Boycott, the breaking of whose nerve after a long struggle not only gave a new word to the language but also provided an object-lesson to a closely observant peasantry.

It was all very well to insist on the importance of moral suasion, but a movement of this kind, touching as it did upon the deepest passions and needs of desperate men, was not likely to avoid violence for long. And in fact, though the leaders constantly urged the methods of peaceful persuasion, a penumbra of outrage surrounded the League from the very beginning. All the old ruthlessness of agrarian vendettas reappeared and intimidation, cattle-maiming, burnings and shootings, spread through the countryside. Usually, it must be said, these crimes were closely related to the progress of evictions. Thus, in 1877, 463 families were evicted and the number of outrages was 236; in 1878, figures were 1,238 and 863. And in 1880, at the very height of the agitation, when over 2,000 families were driven from their homes outrages totalled 2,590.[9]

In one sense, obviously, violence, provided it did not get entirely out of hand, was a source of strength to Parnell. Not only did a number of Irish Fenians become heavily involved in the League, but Irish-Americans as well became convinced that this social convulsion was contributing to the ultimate objectives of the New Departure. Visiting the United States early in 1880, Parnell had a great personal success and, despite some setbacks, raised nearly £30,000 for the relief of Irish distress. This was but a foretaste of what was to come, however, and the money subscribed, not just by Clan na Gael but by a steadily widening circle of Irish-American sympathisers, rapidly came to occupy a place of central importance in Parnell's calculations. It might be thought that this accretion of strength on the left wing would have been more than counter-balanced by a recoil on the right. No doubt there were good, sober nationalists who viewed the Land League with horror, but the contemporary evidence suggests that even among those most likely to be alienated by violence, support for the League rapidly became formidable. The parish clergy, who knew the sufferings of their flocks at first hand, were for the most part sympathetic to the agitation, as were a number of the bishops. At the same time many of the Home Rule members of parliament, their constituents, and the newspapers which spoke for them, were all swept up in what was fast becoming a genuinely national movement.

For this concentration of diverse forces behind the League there were three main explanations. The first and most obvious was that the landlords were a small and deeply hated Ascendancy class; to oppose them was an almost instinctive reaction, but a reaction greatly stimulated by the simple visibility of the miseries of the poor :

> I must say, [wrote General Gordon to Gladstone at the end of 1880] from all accounts and from my own observation, that the state of our fellow countrymen in the parts I have named [he was referring to the west of Ireland] is worse than that of any people in the world, let alone Europe. I believe that these people are made as we are, that they are patient beyond belief, loyal, but, at the same time, broken spirited and desperate, living on the verge of starvation in places in which we would not keep our cattle.[10]

If this was the verdict of a compassionate outsider, it may be imagined how much more fiercely burned the resentment of Irishmen themselves.

The second factor affecting the balance of power in Ireland was the remarkable change in Parnell's own position made manifest by the general election of 1880. This election, which brought Gladstone back to power, was dominated in Britain by his Midlothian campaign against 'Beaconsfieldism', but was fought in Ireland mainly on the land issue. It was nothing less than a personal triumph for Parnell, who was returned for three seats himself and who obtained increasing support from the newly elected Home Rule MPs. That support was enough to carry him into the chairmanship of the parliamentary party, though it was not yet enough to give him unquestioned authority. In the early summer of 1880, it has been reckoned, he could only count with certainty upon twenty-four members as against twenty-one of the old style Home Rulers; the balance was held by fourteen uncommitted members, most of whom moved over to the Parnellite camp as time went on. In social composition the party of 1880 continued the swing towards the middle-class that had first become apparent in 1874, but more striking even than this was the fact that among the new members were several – of whom John Dillon was perhaps the most conspicuous – who were much more bellicose and outspoken in the House of Commons than even the obstructionists of a few years before. Some of Parnell's most zealous adherents, indeed, were duellists or military adventurers who had a record of actual physical violence behind them.[11] Such an accretion of parliamentary strength was made possible for Parnell partly by the operation of the Ballot Act, but still more by the impetus he had gained from his leadership of the Land League. This was, however, a two-way process. For if the land agitation had now increased his stature as a parliamentary leader, he was soon to demonstrate that it was precisely as a parliamentary leader that he could exercise most influence upon the land agitation.

And here the third factor affecting the consolidation of Irish nationalism entered in. If Irishmen of such varying backgrounds co-operated as closely as they did between 1880 and 1882 it was at least in part because British policy drove them to it. For although Gladstone was in power again, and was generally – and rightly – held to be sympathetic to Ireland's needs, he had also a responsibility for law and order which he was not likely to shirk. The main aim of Parnell and his followers was to win from the government some promise of redress for the evicted tenants. At first the omens were propitious. In the summer of 1880 a bill to award compensation to certain classes of evicted tenants out of the Irish Church surplus actually succeeded in passing the House of Commons. It was then promptly rejected by the House of Lords, with the natural and inevitable consequence that the agitation in Ireland began ominously to boil up once more. The membership of the League increased by leaps and bounds, the number of its meetings went up sharply, money for its support poured in from the United States (where Davitt had launched an American Land League earlier in the year), special land courts were set up by the League's organisers to settle agrarian disputes in total disregard of the ordinary law of the land, and the leaders of the movement went from county to county encouraging and stimulating the resistance of the tenants to eviction. Not unnaturally, agrarian outrages increased; of the 2,590 listed for 1880, nearly 1,700 were committed in the last three months of the year. And there was a further conclusion to be drawn from this situation – hopeful or sinister according to the point of view. As outrages mounted, so evictions diminished. During 1880 there were in all 2,110 ejectments, but only 198 occurred in the last quarter.[12]

This was something no government could afford to ignore and although Gladstone and the Chief Secretary, W. E. Forster, were feeling their way towards a major reform of the Irish land law there was strong pressure on them to restore order first. A preliminary attempt to do so at the end of 1880 – by prosecuting the leaders for a conspiracy to prevent the payment of rent – was a predictable fiasco, since no Dublin jury could be found to return a verdict against them. But early in the new session of parliament the government confronted them with a much more serious threat when the Chief Secretary announced his intention to secure special powers to deal with agrarian violence. Parnell and his band of supporters at once responded by dogged and angry obstruction, prolonging the debate on the Address in reply to the Queen's Speech for eleven nights. When immediately afterwards the first of Forster's two Coercion Bills – the Protection of Person and Property Bill – was introduced, Irish opposition was intensified to such a degree that the other business of the House was completely disrupted and one sitting was spun out for no less than forty-one hours. To meet this campaign the Speaker authorised the use of the closure of debate and the Bill was able to resume its passage, but not before there had been another formidable demonstration of Irish indignation. The day after the closure was first applied the government announced the arrest of Michael Davitt. At once the Irish benches erupted, the Prime Minister was halted in mid-speech and calm was not restored until thirty-six Home Rulers, including Parnell and Dillon, had been first suspended and then ejected from the House.

This head-on clash with the government confronted Parnell with a major crisis. Feeling among his followers and in the country at large was so inflamed that if he had chosen then and there to withdraw with his party from the House of Commons and place himself at the head of a no-rent campaign in Ireland he would have attracted formidable support. This was indeed what Davitt himself had urged as the right policy to follow immediately the Coercion Bill became law. True, the Bill had not yet been enacted, but Davitt's arrest provided just as good a *casus belli*. And there is no doubt that Parnell was under heavy pressure to secede from parliament. Just before and just after Davitt's arrest two alternative courses of action were being urged upon him. One, Davitt's own policy of so-called 'dispersion', called for Parnell and three or four colleagues to go to America to collect funds, for others to stay in England to work upon public opinion there, and for the League leaders to fight the battle against coercion in Ireland. The other alternative – the policy of 'concentration', of which Dillon was the leading advocate – simply demanded that the whole party should come home and promote an all-out campaign against the payment of rent. Although Parnell seemed to lean for a moment towards the latter suggestion, it was not one that was likely to appeal to the bulk of the Home Rule party, or even to all the members who habitually supported him. But in fact he adopted neither the policy of dispersion nor the policy of concentration. On the contrary, he let it be known that, however disagreeable the task, he intended to stay at his post in the House of Commons and to devote himself to 'widening the area of the agitation', by effecting a junction 'between the English masses and Irish nationalism'.

In making this crucial decision Parnell was apparently opting for a constitutional rather than a revolutionary role, and most students of the period have seen this choice as a turning-point in his career. No doubt it was, in the sense that it demonstrated that for him as a leader practicality was the touchstone of success. Had he thought a social revolution in Ireland, flaming perhaps into actual war, the best way of getting what he wanted, then a social revolution or an actual war there would have been. But even the fiery Dillon realised how one-sided such a fight must necessarily be and in his calmer moments still urged the tenants to use only the non-violent weapon of the boycott. Parnell was certainly as well aware as Dillon of the dangers of hurling an unarmed peasantry into open conflict with the law, but he had a further motive for not leaving the House of Commons at this juncture. This was simply that he remained convinced that there was more to be gained by staying where he was. What he had in mind was not just the continuing duty of opposing coercion (a second measure, the Peace Preservation Bill, was introduced in March) but also the knowledge that the government had always intended to accompany its punitive legislation by substantial land reform.

This reform, as it was gradually revealed in the early months of 1881, was in no sense a final solution to the land question – indeed, it may even have impeded such a solution since it concentrated on controlling rent rather than on stimulating the economy – but it went a long way to meet the immediate demands of the tenants. Essentially it established the principle of co-partnership in the soil between landlord and tenant. It did this by giving the tenant the famous 'three F's' – fair rents, fixity of tenure and free sale. The first of these presumed boons would, it was hoped, be achieved by setting up a special Land Commission to which the tenants would be encouraged to apply and where the rents payable to their landlords would be fixed by judicial arbitration for a period of fifteen years; the clauses providing for security of tenure and for free sale were intended both to guard against unjust eviction (broadly speaking the tenant who paid his judicial rent would be protected in his occupancy) and to entitle the farmer, when he vacated his holding, to the right to obtain a fair price for the improvements he had made in it. The Bill was extremely complicated and after it became law led to an immense amount of tedious and vexatious litigation; worse still, more than half the tenants who had holdings of over an acre were excluded from its operation, the most hard hit in this respect being the 150,000 leaseholders and the 130,000 occupiers who were in arrears with their rent.

Nevertheless, even though these and other deficiencies stamped the Land Act of 1881 as clearly inadequate to meet the challenge with which the agricultural depression was confronting Ireland – it was, for example, virtually useless to the overpopulated and infertile west – to condemn it on economic grounds is to miss the point. The legislation, as a recent authority has pointed out, was recommended (by the Bessborough Commission) 'less as an economic policy than as a political stroke'.[13] Whether Parnell fully appreciated the Act's practical and technical inadequacies may be open to question, but he could recognise a major concession when he saw one. It is not in the least surprising, therefore, that he should have been determined to see it through the House of Commons and to improve it wherever possible. There was, however,

172

one danger implicit in this eminently sensible line of action. This was that if he proved too co-operative he might lose ground in Ireland. Yet paradoxically, if he was still to be effective at Westminster he must remain in touch with the agrarian left wing. This was made more difficult by Dillon's intense opposition to the proposed land reform and although he was swept into prison for his extreme language between May and August 1881, he represented a current of feeling Parnell could not ignore. But neither could Parnell, as a parliamentary leader, ignore the reactions of moderate nationalists – the clergy, the more substantial tenants, the *Freeman's Journal* – to whom the Land Act would come as an unmitigated blessing. Characteristically, Parnell solved his problem by balancing between the two extremes, thrusting in either direction as circumstances seemed to demand. Thus, whereas on the second reading he tried (though with only partial success) to persuade his followers to abstain from voting for the Bill, the party were encouraged to work hard at amending it during committee. On the third reading, however, it was left to their own discretion whether to vote for it or not and Parnell himself, once it was safely through the Commons, got himself suspended for the rest of the session by a carefully calculated outburst against the government. This left him free to return to Ireland to mend his fences, which he proceeded to do with his usual ingenuity. On the one hand, he persuaded the League not to reject the Act *in toto*, but rather to test it by bringing certain specified cases to the new tribunal, a manoeuvre which had the further advantage of restraining the tenants from rushing to the Land Commission in their thousands. And on the other hand, in order to keep the agitation alive, he explained to the left wing both at home and in America that these test-cases were designed to expose the 'hollowness' of the Act. At the same time he launched a newspaper, *United Ireland*, under the editorship of an intrepid young Cork journalist, William O'Brien, which at once became the spearhead of a continuous and violent attack upon coercion in every shape and form.

Since Parnell was no less intransigent in his own speeches that autumn, it was natural for the government to believe that he was after all opposed to the Land Act (it had become law near the end of August) and was bent on using the League to frustrate it. 'He desires', said Gladstone at Leeds on 7 October, 'to arrest the operation of the Land Act, to stand as Moses stood, between the living and the dead; to stand there, not as Moses stood, to arrest but to extend the plague.' This warning went unheeded. Two days later, at Wexford, Parnell replied with a deliberately wounding speech in which he described Gladstone as, among other things, 'a masquerading knight-errant'.[14] The cabinet, now convinced that he meant to wage war upon the Act, decided at last to arrest him and on 13 October he was lodged, with other 'suspects' imprisoned under the coercion laws, in Kilmainham jail.

It has been suggested that in shutting him up in prison the government got Parnell out of most of his difficulties, investing him with the halo of an agrarian martyr while at the same time absolving him from all responsibility for what happened to the Land League in his absence. Even to contemporaries it seemed that Parnell was courting arrest that autumn with the object of reuniting the constitutional and the agrarian wings of the national movement behind him. But although this may be the truest explanation of his policy, it leaves unsolved the question of how he hoped to lead that movement from a prison cell. To this the answer may well be that while he certainly still intended to lead the movement, he did not wish or intend it to be the same movement that it had been between 1879 and 1881. As he himself wrote to his mistress, Katharine O'Shea, on the very day of his seizure: 'Politically it is a fortunate thing for me that I have been arrested, as the movement is breaking fast and all will be quiet in a few months, when I shall be released.'[15] To put the matter more bluntly, he had already grasped the central fact that the Land Act had beaten the Land League and that there was no future for a predominantly agrarian agitation.

This reading of his motives may seem to be at variance with the fact that after his arrest he and the other principal Land Leaguers (who followed him to Kilmainham within a few days) signed a manifesto calling for a general strike against rent. Yet the contradiction is more apparent than real. The evidence suggests that both he and Dillon were reluctant to issue the manifesto because of the dangers to which it might expose a virtually leaderless peasantry. But since there was now no way of 'testing' the Act it would have been difficult to deny the No Rent enthusiasts a chance to try their alternative policy which had, besides, the added attraction of appealing strongly to Irish-American extremists. In the event, however, this call to direct action (which appeared in the newspapers on 19 October) proved futile, as Parnell had in all probability anticipated. It was roundly condemned by most responsible nationalist opinion, and it seems to have helped the government to make up its mind to suppress the Land League altogether on the following day. Consequently, the manifesto, in the absence of any organisation to carry through its policy of withholding rent, fell on the deaf ears of tenants who had their own ideas about the future and were already preparing to 'test' the Land Act by taking full advantage of its terms.[16]

Although the Land League was thus effectively broken by the end of 1881 this did not mean an end to agrarian outrage and disturbance. On the contrary, the imprisonment of the leaders opened the way for a new phase of violence. Between January and October 1881 there were forty-six individual attacks, consisting of nine murders, five cases of manslaughter and thirty-two of firing at the person. Between mid-October 1881 and the end of April 1882 (the period of Parnell's imprisonment) there were seventy-five similar attacks – fourteen murders and sixty-one cases of firing at the person.[17] Much of this, as the Chief Secretary himself pointed out, was due to the growth or revival of secret societies, though it may also to some extent have been the product of the irresponsible behaviour of the Ladies Land League, organised by Anna Parnell to keep up the running while her brother was in prison, but regarded by him as so reprehensible that one of the first things he did on his release was to suppress it.

The moral of this was clear. At the time of his arrest Parnell was said to have remarked that 'Captain Moonlight' (i.e. the waging of secret and uncontrolled vendettas by desperate men or groups of men) would take his place and this was precisely what seemed to be happening. The country was never more in need of firm leadership than during those months and the only man who could provide it was locked up in jail. Clearly there was a case for releasing him, the more so since the Land Act was running into serious trouble (as Parnell had predicted) because of its failure to provide adequately for tenants who were in arrears with their rent, often through no fault of their own. There was here the basis for a possible bargain between a government wanting to restore peace and quiet to the country and a leader wanting to resume his leadership. For Gladstone, the only reason for putting Parnell in prison in the first place had been his apparent hostility to the Land Act; once it could be seen that that hostility no longer existed there was no reason why he should not be released. For Parnell, too long a spell in prison involved a serious risk of losing his grip upon the Irish situation. It involved also a private grief. During his imprisonment he had been allowed out briefly on parole and had used this liberty to pay a secret visit to Katharine O'Shea, who had just given birth to their first child. The child died soon after he saw it and there was an obvious compulsion for him to get out of Kilmainham as soon as he could to be with the bereft mother.

Yet the negotiations needed to get him out – complex and highly secret as they were – took long to complete. At the end of them he had reached an understanding with the government, the so-called Kilmainham 'treaty', that the arrears question would be dealt with, that leaseholders would be admitted to the benefits of the Land Act, and, by implication at least, that coercion would be dropped. For his part he agreed to regard the Act, if amended, as 'a practical settlement of the land question', to use his influence against intimidation and outrage in Ireland, and 'to co-operate cordially for the future with the Liberal party in forwarding Liberal principles and measures of general reform'. With both sides thus disposed to conciliation there seemed no reason to keep the prisoners any longer in jail, and at the beginning of May Parnell and his principal colleagues were set free.

To disappointed agrarians of the left the Kilmainham 'treaty' was a bitter blow and though loyalty to the leader and the cause prevented open disruption, several of the most important of them dropped, temporarily or permanently, out of the movement. Davitt, to whom the 'treaty' was a turn 'in the wrong direction', became increasingly absorbed in his own panacea for the land question – nationalisation – but was prepared to stifle his criticisms in the interest of unity. The treasurer of the Land League, Patrick Egan, resigned later in 1882 and departed for a new and distinguished career in America. Dillon also left for the United States a little later, partly because he was quite genuinely threatened with tuberculosis and needed a drier climate, partly because, although he too kept his feelings on a tight rein, he could not bring himself to approve of Parnell's one-man 'new departure'.[18]

There was, however, another reason besides personal loyalty for the failure or refusal of the agrarians to erupt in condemnation of the Kilmainham 'treaty'. Parnell, Dillon, and J. J. O'Kelly were released on 2 May. On 3 May they crossed to England where they made a brief but spectacular appearance in the House of Commons, and on 6 May they escorted Davitt from Portland prison back to London. That very day a new Chief Secretary, Lord Frederick Cavendish, arrived in Dublin to replace W. E. Forster who had resigned in protest at the Kilmainham 'treaty'. Later on the evening of his arrival Cavendish and his Under-Secretary, T. H. Burke, were set upon by a band of assassins while they were walking in the Phoenix Park in Dublin and stabbed to death. The murderers belonged to a secret society, the Invincibles, and the deed so shocked Parnell that he actually proposed to Gladstone that he, Parnell, should withdraw from public life. The Prime Minister declined to accept this offer (there was indeed no technical sense in which he could accept it) but the force of English public opinion drove him into a further Coercion Act for Ireland. This had the inevitable effect of banishing internal discord among Irish nationalists, who joined (even Dillon) in resisting the new legislation. In this way, though only for a few months, the disintegration of the old agrarian-parliamentary alliance was postponed.

At first sight it seemed as if the Phoenix Park murders must destroy the Kilmainham 'treaty'. This was a natural enough view to take at the time and has since been adopted by more than one historian, including the author of the most recent study of this episode.* But in reality it did not do so. Once the initial shock and revulsion had passed Parnell was able to continue with his drive towards an 'open' constitutional movement in which he would be free to use his extraordinary talent for political manoeuvre. Did this emphasis upon constitutionalism betoken any real shift towards the right? Different answers to this central question have been given by different writers at different times, but perhaps the key lies in the distinction between tactics and strategy. Tactically, Parnell did appear to have moved decisively towards moderation. Time was to show, for example, that although the land question still had explosive possibilities, when the next crisis in the affairs of the tenants came round he was conspicuous by his absence. For him, apparently,

* T. Corfe, *The Phoenix Park Murders* (London, 1968). This is an exciting account of the crime and its unravelling but in my view overestimates the political effect of the assassinations. G. M. Trevelyan put forward the same interpretation in a rather more simplified form (*Sir George Otto Trevelyan: A Memoir* (London, 1932), p. 108).

the pressures of social revolution were no longer a necessary or desirable lever in the political game. Yet the *end* of that game, the grand strategy which determined his subsequent moves, was the same as ever. Parnell still wanted legislative independence, as much of it as he could get and with no preferences as to the donor. It remained to be seen, however, whether the change of means might not ultimately affect the end to be achieved, whether parliamentary politics without a revolutionary situation in Ireland would give him a strong enough base from which to negotiate.

3. Parnell: Zenith and Nadir

Even if Parnell's ultimate objective remained the same after 1882, the shift of emphasis from agrarianism to constitutionalism inevitably had profound, and in some ways permanent, effects upon his movement. This was almost immediately apparent both at the national and the parliamentary levels. Before 1882 was out the defunct Land League had given way to another organisation, the Irish National League, which, unlike the old one, put Home Rule in the forefront of its programme and relegated 'land law reform' to second place. From the beginning the National League was dominated by the parliamentary party in a way the old Land League had never been. In fact, one of the most important functions of the new body was precisely to prepare the constituencies for elections and to set up machinery – the county conventions – for the selection of prospective candidates. This, it must be admitted, did not prevent Parnell, acting sometimes on his own or with a small party committee or caucus, from firmly indicating in advance which particular candidates he wanted chosen, but the conventions were genuinely representative of local nationalism and in ordinary times close co-operation between the party and the leading men in the constituencies allowed the machinery to work smoothly and efficiently enough.

A secondary function of the National League, but still an important one, was to raise funds for the conduct of the cause as a whole and for the maintenance of the parliamentary party in particular. Between the founding of the Land League in 1879 and the Kilmainham 'treaty' in April 1882 the total receipts of the League, so far as they can be accurately known, were £233,420, of which almost all seems to have come from America (Davitt, indeed, estimated that by October 1882 the American contribution alone had gone up to £250,000). After the agrarian agitation had died down, the flow of American money diminished, as did the aggregate revenue of the new organisation. In the first four full years of its operation this amounted to £109,734 and for much of that time the contribution from the United States apparently did not rise above thirty per cent and may even have been less. This threw a heavy responsibility upon the National League – in itself no bad thing as part of the country's long-neglected training in self-government – which, on the whole, it discharged very successfully.[1]

The financial burden upon the National League was, ironically enough, increased by the very effectiveness with which it organised the constituencies. The full effects of this were seen for the first time at the general election of 1885, when the franchise reform of the previous year had trebled the Irish electorate and when a combination of enthusiasm, good management and political excitement enabled Parnell and his party to win every seat in Ireland outside eastern Ulster and Trinity College, Dublin. The party he led back to Westminster was a world away from the party that had existed when he first entered politics, or even the party of which he had become chairman in 1880. Not only was it eighty-six members strong (eighty-five Irish members, plus T. P. O'Connor, who was elected for the Scotland division of Liverpool), but it was a much more disciplined and tightly knit party, bound by the parliamentary 'pledge' which had been evolved *pari passu* with the convention system and which committed members to 'sit, act and vote' with the parliamentary party, and to resign if a majority of the party should decide that the obligation had not been fulfilled.

This was not only a larger and better disciplined group, it was also more homogeneous. It contained, naturally, fewer landlords and was even more emphatically middle-class in composition than its predecessor, though it was noticeable that the lower, as distinct from the higher, middle-class was increasingly represented. In 1880 the sixty-one Home Rulers had been composed of eight landowners (with over 1000 acres each), nine of the more substantial business class, twenty-one of the higher professions (chiefly lawyers and doctors), eight of the lower professions (mainly journalists), two of the farmer-shopkeeper category, and three with undefined occupations. In 1886 the comparable figures were: five landowners, fifteen substantial business men, twenty-two from the higher professions, nineteen from the lower professions, twenty-two from farmers, shopkeepers or wage-earners, and three with undefined occupations.[2] Many of these men had close connections with their constituencies, and about half the entire total needed financial support from the party funds if they were to keep up a regular attendance at parliament. It was significant that the growth in the farming and shop-keeping element coincided with a decline in the number of extremists in the party ranks. There were still a few ex-Fenians – though not so many as previously – and although a considerable number of these new members were destined to go to prison when the land war flared up again, it seems not unfair to suggest that the political and social attitudes of the bulk of the members were distinctly conservative. So, at any rate, it seemed to those excellent judges of conservatism, the Irish hierarchy. Already by 1884 the bishops had brought themselves to trust the party to represent their views on educational matters in the House of Commons, and at the general election of 1885 Catholic clergy were authorised to participate as delegates at the county conventions and did so in large numbers, often exerting very considerable influence upon the proceedings.

Even before that crucial general election English parties had begun to be uncomfortably aware that, with Ireland still unsatisfied and an extended franchise in prospect, Parnell and his followers might well find themselves before long able to hold the balance of power at Westminster, exercising that power both through their own augmented numbers and through the influence (variously estimated, but generally regarded as important) which Irish votes might have upon the election results in certain English constituencies. For the Liberal government there was the further complication that the coercive legislation of 1882 was due to expire at the end of the 1884–5 parliamentary session and that any attempt to renew it, at least without some compensating concession, would arouse fierce Irish opposition, possibly prejudice harmless English measures, and place the Liberal party in the embarrassing position of fighting the coming election with coercion still fresh in the memories of the electorate.

It was not surprising, therefore, that ministers faced with the need to renew coercion (for the state of Ireland still seemed disturbed enough for them to consider this desirable) should have begun to consider how best they could sugar the pill. It was still less surprising that the initiative should have been taken by Joseph Chamberlain, who had been consistently uneasy about coercion without redress of grievances and who had been meditating 'a modified form of Home Rule' as far back as 1879. It was not, however, until the winter of 1884–5 that he was able to find an opportunity to formulate his alternative and put it to the test. Known by various names, but usually called the 'central board' scheme, it was essentially an essay in the devolution to an Irish council – or 'central board' – of certain powers of legislation in regard to education and communications (land was originally included, but subsequently dropped), together with a comprehensive overhaul of local government at the county level. This was, no doubt, an advance on anything that had hitherto been offered, but it was still a long way short of legislative independence and Chamberlain himself made it plain at this very time that, while he had no objection to Home Rule in principle, he objected to it as defined by Isaac Butt, 'because I believe it would not work, but would infallibly lead to a demand for entire separation'.

Unhappily, Chamberlain miscalculated the Irish reaction to his proposals, partly because he may have relied too much on the approval shown by the Irish hierarchy for his scheme, and partly because his main contact with Parnell – Captain O'Shea, of all people – misled him into thinking that the Irish leader would accept the scheme as a final settlement, which the latter had no intention of doing. There were difficulties within the cabinet as well and in the end it was decided not only not to proceed with Chamberlain's proposals, but to introduce a new Coercion Bill without adequate remedial legislation. Chamberlain, following the lead of his friend, Sir Charles Dilke, resigned on 20 May 1885 and they in their turn were joined a day later by a third minister, G. J. Shaw Lefevre. These resignations had neither been accepted nor withdrawn when the Liberal government, which had been on the verge of collapse for some time under accumulated foreign disaster and internal stresses, was defeated by a combined vote of Conservatives and Parnellites on June 8.[3]

This was a strange, and on the face of it unlikely, combination. Yet in reality it was not so very surprising. The Kilmainham 'treaty' had indeed committed Parnell to 'forwarding Liberal measures' in a very general way, but he was, after all, only at Westminster to forward the interests of his own people and must hold himself at liberty to do this by whatever means presented themselves at any given time. His strength lay precisely in his freedom to throw his weight in this direction or in that as political strategy might dictate. The time was coming when a Liberal alliance would be an integral part of parliamentary nationalism, but that time was not yet. In the meanwhile there seemed strong reasons for seeing if the Tories could do any better than the Liberals. Even before Gladstone's government fell, Parnell had had a strong hint from Lord Randolph Churchill that this might be so – more specifically, that a Conservative ministry would not consider it necessary to renew coercion. Churchill, it is true, was speaking without the authority of his chief, Lord Salisbury, but since the latter had agreed to form a caretaker (in effect, a minority) government until the general election – still some months away – it was elementary prudence to placate Parnell, especially if, as Churchill gathered from a meeting with him, the Irish leader was prepared in return to throw the Irish vote in Britain on the Conservative side when the election eventually came. Parnell, for his part, had no reason not to do business with the Tories if business could be done.[4] Apart from the fact that Salisbury, if he were really in earnest about an Irish settlement, would have a far better chance than Gladstone could ever hope to have of getting it through the House of Lords, it would be, to say the least, convenient to be allied for the time being with the party which Irish Catholics in England regarded as the protector of their denominational schools.

At first the omens for such an alliance seemed propitious. The Conservatives not only dropped coercion, they also went so far as to pass very rapidly a Land Act – the Ashbourne Act – which marked a significant step along the road to land purchase. The essence of the Act was that the government would provide five million pounds to enable tenants to borrow the *whole* of the purchase price, which would then be repaid by four per cent annuities over a period of forty-nine years. Three years later the initial sum of five million pounds was expanded by a further Land Act to ten million pounds and as a result of these two measures over 25,000 tenants were enabled to buy their farms.[5] All this represented solid, long-term gain. More immediately suggestive was the fact that the Earl of Carnarvon was appointed Lord-Lieutenant with a seat in the cabinet. Carnarvon was keenly anxious for a settlement based on some acceptable form of self-government for Ireland, but his tragedy was to be that he was never able to find one equally acceptable to Salisbury and Parnell. Salisbury did allow him, however, to have an interview with Parnell, an interview shrouded in such melodramatic secrecy that it was not even known to most of Carnarvon's fellow-ministers. Each man seems to have been well-impressed by the other, but they reached no positive agreement. Indeed, it was hard to see how they could, since their views on what constituted adequate Home Rule were probably much further apart than Carnarvon, for one, realised. Nor for that matter was Carnarvon typical of the cabinet as a whole. Salisbury, certainly, was far from convinced that Conservatives should entangle themselves in a far-reaching Irish settlement and it is difficult to resist the conclusion that the approach to Parnell was probably little more than an attempt to beguile him into swinging the Irish vote behind the Conservative party at the coming election.

If this was the intention then it met with a certain measure of success. But that is not to say that Parnell fell headlong into any carefully laid trap. No altruist himself, he was unlikely to make the elementary error of expecting political altruism in others. If he was prepared at this stage to dally with the Conservatives, it was because in doing so he was manoeuvring steadily nearer the ideal position of balance which would allow him to play one English party off against the other. And in fact his immediate impulse was to turn to the Liberals to persuade them to raise the bidding. But he turned in vain. Gladstone recoiled from such naked political bargaining, partly because it seemed to him improper, but partly because both he and his colleagues were still in search of a coherent Irish policy. In the event, Parnell did ultimately throw the Irish vote behind the Tories. His control over that vote was not absolute and on this particular occasion his advice chimed so closely with the wishes of the Catholic clergy (looking, as usual, to the Conservatives for succour on the educational question) that it is not always easy to discern where his instructions ended and those of the clergy began. Moreover, not only did he himself in a few instances authorise his people to vote for carefully selected Liberals, but in some other constituencies the Irish still went bull-headed for the Liberal candidates regardless of orders or pressures to the contrary. All the same, and even with these reservations, the swing was perceptible and a number of seats – Chamberlain put it at twenty-five, but it may have been more – did pass from Liberal into Tory hands. The overall result of the election could not have been more dramatic. The Liberal majority over the Tories was eighty-six, but since eighty-six was also exactly the number of Parnell's party, the coveted balance of power was now within his grasp.[6]

Yet there were some who said at the time that this result represented a serious setback for Parnell and that by his order to the Irish in Britain to vote Tory he had robbed the Liberals of the vital seats that would have given them a clear majority for Home Rule. Apart from the fact that Home Rule was a dominant issue only in Ireland, and had not been accepted as a viable policy by either Liberals or Conservatives, the argument that a Liberal majority would have been a majority favourable to the Parnellite demand seems excessively naive. The greater the Liberal independence of Parnell, the less likely Gladstone was to do his bidding. Conversely, the closer the totals of the two English parties, the greater the leverage for the Irish.

Events soon showed what this might mean. The Conservatives, realising that the Irish vote had not won them the majority they needed, abandoned with suspicious readiness the wearisome pretence of negotiating with Parnell. Carnarvon's high ideals were unceremoniously jettisoned and with unblushing cynicism Lord Salisbury's government indicated at the opening of the new parliament in January 1886 that a return to coercion in Ireland was in prospect. The Irish riposte to this was obvious and swift. Combining with the Liberals, they defeated the Conservatives on an amendment to the Address and Lord Salisbury resigned two days later. The ball was now once more in Gladstone's court, but what he might do with it baffled all conjecture. It was, in fact, only in December 1885 (that is, after the election was over but before parliament had met) that his son Herbert had flown the famous 'Hawarden Kite', by publishing in the press what amounted to a strong indication that his father was moving steadily towards Home Rule, but by what stages and to what extent were still obscure when the change of government occurred.

The timing and motives of Gladstone's conversion lie outside the compass of a history centred on Ireland, but so important were the repercussions of that conversion that one or two comments upon it must be made. First, it is not enough simply to explain it by the pressure of Parnell's eighty-six members. Had Gladstone been thinking solely in terms of political calculation, the potentially disintegrating effects of Home Rule upon his own party would surely have weighed with him more heavily than the prospect of opposition, even obstructionist opposition, from the admittedly formidable Irish party. He was, it is true, deeply anxious that a settlement of the problem of Ireland should not, as he put it, 'fall into the lines of party conflict' and to contemporaries, always ready to suspect the purity of his motives, this seemed merely an oblique method of shovelling off the responsibility onto the Conservatives. Yet this was hardly fair. Gladstone would certainly have preferred the Conservatives to settle the Irish question because he genuinely believed they had a better chance of settling it, but his cogitations of the summer and autumn led him inexorably to the decision that if they would not attempt it, he must. For there was a moral imperative involved in this decision. He had arrived at it, as he had arrived at others of the cataclysmic decisions of his lifetime, by asking himself what was the right, ultimately the Christian, solution. Now, it was a central tenet of his faith as a Liberal that enlightened self-government was the highest stage of political evolution that man could reach. Holding this view, he had been in the past the champion first of Italian, then of Balkan, nationalism. Was he justified in denying to Ireland the right to travel the same road? Perhaps, so long as he could genuinely believe what so many of his fellow-countrymen still believed – that the Irish were a backward people and fundamentally unfit for self-government. But he had lived for years close to the heart of the

Irish problem. He had seen how deep-rooted and tenacious the demand for self-government really was, he had marked the change from agrarianism to constitutionalism, he had noted the rise of a disciplined and highly effective parliamentary party, and he had recognised in that party's leader a man with whom it was possible to negotiate. Could it seriously be maintained any longer that these people were unfit for self-government?

For Gladstone to journey to Damascus was one thing, for his party to follow him was quite another. And in the event, hard upon his discovery that Home Rule was the only way to pacify Ireland, his party began to break up. Some of the Whigs on whom he had leaned so heavily in the past would not join his government at all, but worse even than this was that when he began to disclose his Irish policy to his cabinet colleagues he at once lost Chamberlain and G. O. Trevelyan. The break with Chamberlain was crucial – crucial to both men and to the future prospects of Ireland. Chamberlain had immense ability, was a formidable House of Commons man, and had hitherto gone out of his way to show sympathy to the Irish cause. Yet now he was alienated beyond recall and was soon to justify Parnell's description of him as the man who killed Home Rule. The story of his breach with Gladstone is a part of English rather than Irish history – it owed perhaps as much to temperament as to Ireland – but the fact of Chamberlain's opposition needs some explanation, not just because of the effect it had upon the immediate situation, but for what it symbolised. One suggestion, Marxist in conception, has been that a factor that weighed very heavily with him was Parnell's demand – made repeatedly during 1885 – that an Irish parliament must have the right to protect Irish industries. It is certainly true that Chamberlain reacted very strongly against this demand and there is no reason to doubt that in doing so he spoke for many British industrialists to whom Irish protection would have closed a market they had long regarded as their own. But this superficially attractive argument is hardly conclusive, for it ignores two important facts. One was that Parnell, under direct pressure from Gladstone, agreed to abandon protection as a part of the settlement of 1886; and the other is that although a good deal of lip service was paid in Ireland to the idea of protection, such industries as existed at that time were themselves dependent on the British market and notably unenthusiastic about proposals to erect tariff barriers between the two countries.[7]

It seems probable, in reality, that Chamberlain's motives were less economic than personal and political. They were personal in the sense that the collapse of his 'central board' scheme in 1885 had left him with the conviction that Parnell had first accepted and then rejected the scheme, and was therefore not to be trusted. If there was deception during that episode, it came from O'Shea, not Parnell, but one can see that Chamberlain might well have thought otherwise. Chamberlain, however, felt himself humiliated as well as deceived by the events of that summer. He had intended to make a tour of Ireland and had counted on a friendly reception. Instead, the nationalists, having in the mean-time set their course towards a Tory alliance, received his overtures with such scorching contempt that the trip had to be abandoned. He had held out, his biographer mournfully remarks, 'a generous and manly hand. The hand he thought would be clasped was bitten to the bone.'[8]

Personal resentment may thus have been an element in his opposition to Home Rule – and may have accounted for the exceptionally bitter tone of some of his speeches – but it was hardly enough to cause him to abandon a high and promising position in the great Liberal party and go into a wilderness which might have ended his political career. Con-temporaries, indeed, were puzzled as to why he should take this risk when he was already identified with Irish reform. The answer seems to be that although the differences between the 'central board' scheme and Gladstone's Home Rule Bill of 1886 do not seem so vast in retro-spect they were real enough at the time. Essentially they were the difference between local government and self-government. Chamber-lain, like many others, seems quite genuinely to have believed that what Gladstone was proposing would lead to grave internal dissensions in Ireland and would also be disruptive of the Empire. On the face of it this seems an exaggerated fear. The Bill provided for an Irish parlia-ment of two 'orders', which would not be separate houses, though they could vote separately when desired and each would have a suspensory veto over measures introduced by the other. There was to be an Irish Executive responsible to this legislature, but certain very important sub-jects were reserved to the control of the Imperial Parliament – the chief of these being the Crown, peace and war, defence, foreign and colonial relations, customs and excise, trade and navigation, post office, coinage and legal tender. One-fifteenth of the charges in the United Kingdom budget for 'imperial purposes' were to be met by Ireland, but the re-mainder of the revenue raised there was ultimately to be at the dis-posal of the Irish parliament and government. Irish judges would be appointed and paid by the Irish government and would hold office on the same terms as English judges, but there would be a right of appeal to the Judicial Committee of the Privy Council, which would also have the right to decide whether any act of the Irish parliament or govern-ment was *ultra vires*. Gladstone had also originally intended that Irish representation in the House of Commons should cease. This was prob-ably unwise in view of the continued interlinking of Irish and British finance and it also alarmed some members as indicating an intention to abdicate control over Ireland. The Prime Minister offered to reconsider the point, but too late to affect the issue. Equally, perhaps more, im-portant was his intention to couple with Home Rule a Land Act which would apply the principle of purchase on a grand scale. This was in-tensely disliked even by the Liberals who remained loyal to him – it affronted their ideas of political economy and they resented subsidising a class which in Ireland was overwhelmingly Unionist – and though Gladstone was probably right in thinking that to buy out the landlords was essential to the success of his scheme, in this he was still some years ahead of his time, or at least of his party.

It will be obvious that Gladstonian Home Rule fell a long way short of full self-government and, to a later age, what it withheld seems almost more significant than what it bestowed. So modest do these proposals appear, that it requires an effort of the imagination to understand the uproar they caused at the time. From the babel of confused and sometimes inconsistent argument against Home Rule three lines of opposition are clearly discernible. The first – of which both Lord Randolph Churchill and Chamberlain made full use – was that there was not one Ireland but two, and that it would be both dangerous and unjust for the Imperial parliament to hand over Irish loyalists (or Unionists as they could now be called) to the mercy of a native government for which they felt only revulsion. The roots of this hostility went deep and, although consistently misjudged by nationalists, were a product of the real fears of Unionists about their economic well-being, their political security and their religious freedom.* In 1886 these fears, which were especially prevalent in northeast Ulster, were brilliantly exploited by Churchill and his slogan, 'Ulster will fight and Ulster will be right', was no mere catch-phrase. Already in that year symptoms were appearing of what was to become a raging fever between 1912 and 1914 – already there was drilling, already there were proposals for a solemn oath of resistance and for the purchase of arms to make that resistance effective.[9]

The two remaining arguments against Home Rule were to some extent inter-related. The first of these maintained that Irish self-government would lead to total separation and thence to the dismemberment of the Empire. Shorn of its more hysterical arabesques this argument had at least the justification that Parnell's own position on the matter was distinctly equivocal. As recently as January 1885 he had made one of the most famous of all his speeches and uttered those words which are now inscribed on his monument in Dublin: 'No man has the right to set a boundary to the onward march of a nation. No man has a right to say: "Thus far shalt thou go and no further." '[10] But in the Home Rule debates, when asked point-blank if he accepted the Bill as a final solution he had replied 'Yes' and had later made that pledge, if anything, more explicit. 'I accept this Bill', he said, 'as a final settlement of our national question and I believe the Irish people will accept it'. This *may* have been a tactical manoeuvre, and if he had survived to head an Irish government responsible to an Irish parliament, he might not have been able to resist either the temptation or the pressure to move further towards independence. Since he was never in a position to have to make that choice we cannot tell what he would have done, but it is not surprising that his opponents regarded the suddenness and finality of his conversion with some scepticism.

* The theory of the 'two Irelands' is further considered in chap. 8 below.

This scepticism was reinforced by the widely prevalent notion that, whatever Gladstone might say and think, the Irish were still not to be trusted to rule themselves. There was, a recent authority has suggested, 'a deep chasm between the Anglo-Saxonists, who argued that Irish character made the Irish unfit for self-government, and the environmentalists, who believed in the potential equality of mankind and contended that historical circumstances had made the Irish what they were'.[11] The suggestion here is that the opponents of Home Rule were, consciously or unconsciously, permeated by 'Anglo-Saxonist' attitudes which assumed an inherent superiority for those of Anglo-Saxon stock and a corresponding inferiority for others, including of course the 'Celts'. Considerable evidence has been adduced to indicate that such ideas were more widely held by Victorian intellectuals than has generally been supposed, but of course racism was no monopoly of the educated classes. It reflected, also, popular prejudices about the Irish in Britain, working often at lowly and ill-paid employment, living in squalor, by turns sycophantic and aggressive, suspect in their religion, despised (and sometimes feared) as drinking too deep and quarrelling too often. It fed also on the incidents inseparable from agrarian warfare – on the atrocities against animals, on the boycott, on the shootings and stabbings of Irishmen by other Irishmen. It was by no means impossible for ordinary British citizens, whatever their politics, to feel at one and the same time that the Irish were deeply to be pitied for their poverty and sufferings, but also that because of their backwardness, their illiteracy, their supposed domination by their priests, they were fundamentally unsuited to have charge of their own affairs. This was a jaundiced view that could be changed, and presently would be changed, but it was unreasonable to expect it to change overnight or to find either in parliament or in the constituencies much sympathetic understanding of Gladstone's insight into the Irish question.[12]

The result when it came was close, but decisive and not unexpected. The Tories, their numbers swollen by defecting Liberal Unionists, were able to defeat the Home Rule Bill on its second reading by thirty votes. Gladstone thereupon resigned and the subsequent general election, though not affecting Home Rule solidarity in three-quarters of Ireland, returned a strong Conservative and Liberal Unionist majority in Britain. Lord Salisbury at once formed a government dedicated to the proposition that what Ireland needed was twenty years of resolute government and the first major crisis of Home Rule was over. The tradition which sees that crisis as a great divide in British as in Irish politics is not without foundation. The events of 1885 and 1886 had in a sense clarified what had become a very confused situation. At last the issue of Home Rule had been forced into the open and the two great parties had had to declare themselves. Gladstone's conversion, bringing with it the loyal support of most Liberals, seemed to the nationalists a great triumph. So no doubt it was. Parnell, as Gladstone himself said long afterwards, had 'set the Home Rule argument on its legs'. But for this achievement the Irish leader paid a heavy price. This was partly because it was no longer open to him to balance between Liberals and Conservatives, bringing pressure on each as circumstances might dictate. Partly also, it was because dependence on the Liberals brought its own limitations, since, if the alliance was to be continued, Parnell would have to pay more attention to the susceptibilities and wishes of his English friends than he had thought it necessary to pay between 1882 and 1885.

If the ultimate result of the climactic year of 1886 was thus to limit Parnell's freedom of manoeuvre, this was not immediately apparent. So far as he himself was concerned, the sequel to the furious activity of the Home Rule crisis was a period of withdrawal and quiescence. This was to some extent necessitated by his deteriorating health (which continued to trouble him until the end of his career), but it also owed something to his increasing involvement with Mrs O'Shea, for, as we shall presently see, 1886 had also been a crisis year in his private life.*
Events, however, did not stand still just because he disappeared for the time being from the scene. On the contrary, in Ireland the old agrarian storm was brewing again, had begun to gather, indeed, even before the result of the Home Rule battle was known. The country was deep in agricultural depression and there was about the findings of a new Royal Commission (the Cowper Commission) a sad familiarity. When that Commission reported early in 1887, it revealed that the prices of crops and of livestock had been falling catastrophically during the two previous years and that this was due in part to American competition, in part to soil exhaustion and in part to the restriction of credit. The consequences were equally familiar and equally lamentable. Tenants, squeezed from so many different directions, were unable to pay the judicial rents fixed by the Act of 1881 – others who were still outside the operation of that Act were even worse off – and eviction followed as the night the day. As far back as January 1886 there had been indications on the Galway estates of the Marquess of Clanricarde that the tenants were ready to turn and fight. An explosion was avoided so long as Home Rule was in the balance, but in the autumn, after Parnell had failed to persuade the House of Commons to accept a Tenants' Relief Bill, the situation rapidly became more critical.

The leader himself, however, took little part in what followed. Instead, the direction of this new phase fell into the hands of three men – John Dillon (who had returned from America in 1885 in time to re-enter parliament for the Home Rule debate), William O'Brien (still the presiding genius of *United Ireland*) and Timothy Harrington, the secretary of the Irish National League. It was they (and more specifically Harrington) who devised the scheme known as 'the Plan of Campaign' which was published in *United Ireland* in October 1886. It can best be described as a device for collective bargaining on individual estates. Where a landlord refused to lower his demands voluntarily **the tenants**

* For this relationship, see pp. 195-6 below.

were to combine to offer him reduced rents. If he declined to accept these, they were to pay him no rents at all, but instead to contribute to an 'estate fund' the money they would have paid him if he had accepted their offer. This fund was to be used for the maintenance and protection of the tenants who were morally certain to be evicted for putting this policy into practice. If the estate funds proved insufficient – they soon did – the resources of the National League were to be mobilised. As for land-grabbers, for them there remained, as before, the boycott. 'That the farms thus unjustly evicted will be left severely alone, and everyone who aids the evictors shunned, is scarcely necessary to say.'[13]

The advice contained in the Plan of Campaign and urged in person on the tenants by Dillon and O'Brien was seized upon by the farmers of the south and west with all the desperation of drowning men clutching at a straw. The organised movement that resulted was more than a straw, but it was hardly a lifebelt. It never assumed the proportions or the savagery of the earlier phase of the land war between 1879 and 1881, and although it certainly caught the imagination of the country and caused the government a great deal of trouble, was in fact confined during the years of its effective operation (1886-90) to 116 estates. On sixty of these estates peaceful settlements were reached, and on a further twenty-four terms were agreed after a clash; on fifteen estates the tenants went back on the landlords' terms and on eighteen no agreement had been achieved up to 1891. The number of evicted tenants and their families involved in the Plan of Campaign probably did not exceed 1,400 at any one time, but the cost of looking after them was very heavy, amounting to more than a quarter of a million pounds between 1886 and 1893, at which latter date a special commission was set up to inquire into the condition of the tenants still unrestored to their holdings.[14]

Yet if this was not a large scale movement it developed in some parts of the country – notably Tipperary, Limerick and Kerry – into a very bitter and potentially dangerous conflict which destroyed the health of one Chief Secretary, Sir Michael Hicks Beach, and made the reputation of his successor, Salisbury's nephew, Arthur Balfour. We shall see presently that 'Bloody Balfour', as his Irish enemies called him, played a conspicuous part in developing a constructive Unionist policy for Ireland, but in his early years as Chief Secretary his fame, or notoriety, rested upon his exceptionally ruthless and consistent use of coercion. In 1887, indeed, he took the principle of special legislation a stage further than his predecessors by bringing into operation a new Crimes Act which was not only drastic in itself, but did not require frequent renewal by parliament and so was denounced by its critics as 'perpetual'. Gradually it began to take effect and, over the three years between 1887 and 1890, undoubtedly had a weakening effect upon the agitation.

It was not, however, the only weapon the government employed. We know now that in one key instance – the Ponsonby estate in county Cork – Balfour himself encouraged other landlords (English as well as Irish) to take the estate off the near-bankrupt owner's hands. Enough leaked out to the nationalist press about this for the tenants of A. H. Smith-Barry, the leader of the syndicate, to withhold their rents out of sympathy for the Ponsonby tenants. Smith-Barry, part of whose property included the town of Tipperary, responded with wholesale evictions, so that the leaders of the Plan were drawn into the desperate expedient of building a substitute town, New Tipperary, which turned out to be a disastrously expensive venture. This is but one example – though admittedly an extreme one – of the kind of financial stress under which the Plan constantly laboured and which in the end proved more debilitating even than coercion.[15]

No less insidious and difficult to combat was the government's other stratagem, which was to enlist the aid of the Church, and of Rome itself, against the agitation. In this, it is true, they were not alone, for two Irish bishops independently complained to the Vatican that boycotting was rife in the country and that parish priests were becoming too much involved in the struggle. It was certainly true that priests in many parts of Ireland did take the side of the tenants, and that some of them went to jail for doing so, but it was also true that two archbishops (Cashel and Dublin) had given their support to the movement. In response to these baffling and conflicting reactions the Pope sent his own emissary, Monsignor Persico, to Ireland during 1887, and although his report was by no means wholly unfavourable to the tenants' cause, Leo XIII was sufficiently perturbed about the situation to issue in April 1888 a 'rescript' condemning the Plan and boycotting as illegal, and in effect warning the Irish Church to stand clear.

This at once produced an immense outburst of feeling in Ireland. The hierarchy ostensibly bowed to the papal command, but made it sufficiently clear that they were unwilling to commit themselves to rigorous opposition to the tenants' movement. The Catholic members of the parliamentary party went out of their way to denounce interference by the Holy See 'with the Irish people in the management of their political affairs'. Numbers of the parish clergy – except in some dioceses, such as Limerick, where a strong bishop still stood out against the Plan – continued to take part in it and to suffer imprisonment for their pains. And, finally, the leaders of the agitation, especially John Dillon, were moved to formulate a doctrine of political liberalism which went far beyond the immediate point at issue. In speech after speech Dillon laid down the basis for what he conceived to be the proper relationship between Church and State in a Catholic country, giving his views lapidary expression on a memorable occasion at Drogheda a few weeks after the rescript had been published :

Are we to be free men in Ireland [he asked] or are we to conduct our public affairs at the bidding of any man who lives outside Ireland ? We owe it to ourselves, we owe it to our friends in England, we owe it to the ancient traditions of our country, we owe it to our Protestant fellow-countrymen, who expect they are about to share with us a free Ireland, that it will not be an Ireland that will conduct its affairs at the bidding of any body of cardinals . . . That is the principle of Irish liberty, and I say without fear that if tomorrow, in asserting the freedom of Ireland, we were to exchange for servitude in Westminster servitude to . . . any body of cardinals in Rome, then I would say good-bye for ever to the struggle for Irish freedom.

The Catholic priest, he insisted in another speech shortly afterwards, had always in Ireland been regarded as a citizen as well as a priest. 'The attachment of the Irish people for their priesthood and for the See of Rome has survived the rack and the gibbet, but I doubt very much whether it would survive if we were to see the priests forbidden to sympathise with the poor and, as they were told to do by the Great Master, to denounce iniquity even when it was in high places.'[16]

As the Plan of Campaign pursued its hectic course, stroke followed swiftly by counter-stroke, it began to seem, for the time being at least, that Parnell was being eclipsed by his fiery subordinates. Dillon, O'Brien and Harrington, assisted by a number of other MPs, came to dominate the popular imagination. Identifying themselves as they did with the tenants, defying secular and ecclesiastical authorities on their behalf, going to prison for them, sacrificing health and risking life so that the movement might somehow still continue, they gained enormously in influence and prestige from the part they played in these years. But what was the reaction of their titular leader to this unexpected, and in a sense unintended, challenge to his supremacy? He made his attitude clear before the agitation was three months old and held to that attitude through all the storms that followed. In December 1886 he sent for William O'Brien and warned him not to extend the Plan beyond its existing limits and to avoid violent speeches (Dillon had just made a particularly extreme one) in the future. It appears that he issued this warning after consultation with the Liberals and that his disapproval of the Plan was based primarily upon the fact that a new agrarian war might endanger the Liberal alliance which, he assured John Morley, was 'the fixed point in his tactics'. Eighteen months later, in a celebrated speech to a Liberal audience at the Eighty Club, he again made it abundantly clear that all the furore about the papal rescript, or for that matter about the Plan itself, should not be allowed to distract attention from the main objective of Liberals and nationalists alike – the winning of Home Rule.

To the leaders of the agitation this speech, which was almost a disavowal, came as a wounding blow and Dillon had a hard time of it to persuade William O'Brien not to throw his hand in there and then. But in fact Parnell had overestimated the adverse effect the agitation might have upon English opinion. As Balfour applied his coercion more and more relentlessly and as stories of police brutality filtered across the Irish Sea – the most notorious instance being the Mitchelstown 'massacre' of September 1887 when the police fired on a large crowd, killing three and wounding two – a wave of sympathy for the tenants' plight swept through the Liberal party. And since the leaders of the Plan lost no opportunity of pointing out that what they were attempting was to win for the Irish peasant the right of collective bargaining that the trade union movement had won for the English workingman, a more genuine solidarity began to underpin the Liberal-nationalist alliance, and it came to seem that the Plan, so far from jeopardising Home Rule, was actually helping forward that 'union of hearts' which both sides were so assiduously cultivating.

This solidarity was strengthened by another but quite different development – the ferocious attack upon Parnell and his followers by *The Times* newspaper in its articles 'Parnellism and crime'. These first appeared in March 1887, timed to appear just as the Coercion Bill was on its way through parliament. The object of the articles was to establish a connection between the Irish leader and terrorism. The most damning link appeared to be a letter purporting to have been written by Parnell on 15 May 1882, in which, allegedly, he expressed his regret for having had to denounce the Phoenix Park murders. In the House of Commons Parnell denounced this letter as a forgery, but a libel action taken by one of his former colleages, F. H. O'Donnell, who conceiving himself to have been implicated by the allegations, allowed *The Times* to produce what seemed to be further incriminating evidence. Parnell repeated his denials and asked for a Select Committee of the House of Commons to inquire into the authenticity of the letters. He did not get this. Instead, the government, acting it must be said in a very partisan manner, set up a special commission to investigate not the letters but the various charges that had been made by *The Times* against Parnell and his party, and also against others – notably Michael Davitt – who had been involved in the land war. This was tantamount to putting the whole nationalist movement on trial.

The sequel is too well known to need more than the briefest summary. During 1888 and 1889 the commission minutely investigated the history of the previous decade and turned up a great deal of interesting information about a great variety of subjects. But to the public at large there was only one question that mattered. Were the letters said to have been written by Parnell and others genuine or not? In February 1889 the question was answered in the best traditions of Parnellite melodrama. A Dublin journalist, Richard Pigott, cracked under examination in the witness-box, admitted to having forged the letters himself, fled from England and then shot himself in Madrid. Although the commission's findings were not published for another year this incident was rightly regarded at the time as the turning-point in the inquiry and as the vindication of Parnell. When the report finally appeared it exonerated the Irish leaders in all essentials from the main charges against them, though it found that they had promoted an agrarian agitation in which crime and outrage had been committed by persons whom they had incited to practise intimidation. This, however, was merely to labour the obvious and the last word remained with Parnell. 'Well, really, between ourselves', he said to his colleagues, 'I think it is just about what I would have said myself.'[17]

The failure of the attempt to discredit the Parnellite movement resulted inevitably in a great access of popularity for the leader of that movement. Parnell now became for a brief space the darling of English Liberalism and there seemed no limit to what the Liberal-nationalist alliance might soon expect to achieve. Never had the 'union of hearts' seemed so permanent or so hopeful. And with Parnell's visit to Gladstone at Hawarden in December 1889 to discuss the possible shape of the next Home Rule bill that union looked to be on the verge of a spectacular triumph. Later, it is true, what passed at the meeting between the two men became the subject of bitter controversy, but at the time both expressed their satisfaction and Parnell even went so far as to admit in private that Gladstone's proposals 'meant a most satisfying solution'.

There remained, however, the shadow of the Plan of Campaign. While it was true that coercion was not the only governmental reaction to the agitation – in 1887 a further Land Act had extended the protection available to tenants and had brought leaseholders at last within the scope of the Act of 1881, while in 1888 yet another Land Purchase Act increased the money available to tenants for buying their farms – the burden of looking after 'the wounded soldiers of the land war' remained crushingly heavy. In 1889, despite a fund-raising mission by Dillon to Australia, the final crisis seemed at hand. In their desperation the leaders turned to Parnell. They found him as forbidding towards the Plan as he ever had been. William O'Brien tried to explain to him that they needed at least £30,000 in addition to the further £30,000 Dillon was expected to raise in Australia. At first he received a flat refusal, even though he plied the leader with lurid details of imminent collapse on several key estates. Deeply wounded, O'Brien (who had more affection for, and received more affection from, Parnell than perhaps any other Parnellite) then told his leader that he and Dillon would have to consider withdrawing from a situation that had become intolerable. 'He said', reported O'Brien, 'with the most brutal frankness that we could not get out of it – that we had got ourselves into it, adding, "you forced me to say that" '. In the upshot Parnell agreed to allow a new organisation to be formed to make a systematic appeal for funds, but despite all O'Brien's entreaties, refused to place himself at its head or indeed to take any part in its activities. The Tenants' Defence Association, as the new body was called, was at once put in motion and within a few months had produced £61,000 for the relief of the tenants, but to this Parnell had contributed little more than his name. It is scarcely correct, therefore, to argue, as has been argued, that in 1889 he was reproducing on a smaller scale the agrarian-constitutional balance of ten years earlier. On the contrary, his disapproval of the Plan of

Campaign was consistent and unwavering, and remained so to the end of his life. Almost certainly this was because he continued to regard it as a dangerous irrelevance. The game had become political and he intended to play it in exclusively political terms.[18]

This did not in itself mean that he was prepared to play it in strict accordance with rules laid down by his Liberal allies. He was well aware that there were mutterings on the left – in Ireland and in America – about the corrupting effects of constitutional politics, and it was commonsense also to remind his English friends that he was still the head of an Irish nationalist movement. This may explain, therefore, why in May 1889 he used in one of his rare speeches in Ireland a tone that seemed to belong to a totally different phase of his career. It was nothing less than a warning to his fellow-countrymen not to expect too much of constitutionalism. Suppose, he said, that it turned out that Home Rule could not after all be won in parliament:

> I for one would not continue to remain for twenty-four hours longer in the House of Commons at Westminster. . . . The most advanced section of Irishmen, as well as the least advanced, have always understood that the parliamentary policy was to be a trial and that we did not ourselves believe in the possibility of maintaining for all time an incorruptible and independent Irish representation at Westminster.[19]

It has been suggested that this curious speech was not so much a reversion to his earlier intransigence as an attempt to prepare in advance a line of attack he was to follow after his party had split asunder in circumstances to be described in a moment. This may be so, though it seems an excessively Machiavellian explanation; even Parnell could scarcely have foretold in May 1889 all the twists and turns of the next eighteen months. It is on the whole more likely that he was trying to do two things. One was to warn his own parliamentary followers that too much fraternisation with the Liberals – symbolised for many Irish MPs by their membership of the National Liberal Club – could have a debilitating effect upon their nationalism.* And the other was to re-assure his fellow-countrymen in general (and perhaps also some of his Irish-American supporters) that although the Liberal alliance seemed the best hope for Home Rule, it was an alliance that could be ended at any time if policy so dictated. True, he gave no indication of wishing to end it – and in hard fact he had nothing to put in its place save an independent and barren opposition – but one can see that it was important to his authority that he should at least appear to have the free-

---

* It was characteristic that Dillon who, through his wife, had access to the innermost circles of political Liberalism, should later have chosen to join the Bath Club where he could be certain that members' views would be so far to the right of his own that no dialogue could even be attempted. Unlike Parnell in many things, he shared his contempt for nationalists who showed too great a fondness for the amenities of Liberal society.

dom to choose. That freedom, however, was soon to be compromised by his private liaison far more than by his public alliance. At long last the black cloud that had hung over so much of his career was about to eclipse him. In December 1889 Captain O'Shea filed suit for divorce from his wife, citing Parnell as co-respondent, and in November 1890 the case came to trial.

Parnell had first met Katharine O'Shea as far back as the summer of 1880 and for both of them it had been virtually a case of love at first sight. She had then been married to Captain W. H. O'Shea for thirteen years and although she had borne him three children their marriage had ceased to have much reality by the time she met Parnell. The couple lived increasingly apart and both of them – she at Eltham, he in a London apartment – were dependent on the benevolence of Katharine's wealthy aunt, Mrs Wood. Mrs O'Shea had looks (a little overblown perhaps), vivacity and charm, but what she gave to Parnell was more important to him than any of these. She gave him, besides a genuinely passionate love, the atmosphere and comfort of a home, the feeling – which he had lacked all his life – that there was one place at least where he could leave politics behind, lower his guard, and be at peace. By 1881 they had begun to live together for short periods and in 1882, as we have seen, she gave birth to the child which died shortly afterwards and which he always believed to be his. In 1883 and 1884 two other children were born – both of them Parnell's beyond any doubt – and in 1886 they took the crucial decision to live together continuously and permanently. There are strong indications that members of the Liberal government knew something of what was going on as early as 1882 (when Parnell was under close surveillance) and it seems that some at least of his own parliamentary party were aware of the affair by 1885 or 1886. Yet O'Shea did not bring his action until December 1889, even though, as he admitted in the divorce court, his suspicions had been aroused in 1886, when he had subsequently forbidden his wife to have anything more to do with Parnell. O'Shea's story was accepted by the court – it was not contested by either Mrs O'Shea or Parnell, since their one ambition was to get married – and O'Shea duly received his decree.

Was he really deceived by his wife and his political leader for so long as he swore he had been? Katharine's account of the triangular relationship, which she told to the young MP, Henry Harrison, in 1891 and which he published forty years later in a book, *Parnell Vindicated*, suggested that he knew perfectly well what was happening almost from the beginning and was prepared to close his eyes to it if connivance was made worth his while. He had political ambitions and up to 1885 had been able to cut something of a figure as the principal (and almost wholly unreliable) intermediary between Parnell and Chamberlain. Even as late as February 1886 Parnell took an enormous risk in forcing O'Shea as an 'unpledged' candidate on Galway City in the teeth of a virtual mutiny by J. G. Biggar and T. M. Healy, which very nearly blew the lid off the scandal. But O'Shea's parliamentary career as an Irish MP petered out a few months later after his refusal to vote for the Home Rule Bill, so that politics alone do not account for his strange acquiescence. He had, however, a second motive – money. It seems to have been generally accepted in the family circle that Mrs O'Shea's aunt would leave her a large fortune when she died, provided, of course, that Katharine did not disgrace the family name in the meantime. Now in 1881, from which time Mrs O'Shea dated her husband's acquiescence, the aunt was already eighty-eight years old. It seemed therefore as if the *ménage à trois* would have to last only a very short time. In fact it had to last for eight years, since the old lady did not die until May 1889. The fortune was duly left to Mrs O'Shea, but in such a way that the Captain could not get his hands on it. So when other aggrieved relatives decided to challenge the will, O'Shea joined forces with them. Obviously he had a strong card to play, for if in divorcing his wife he could demonstrate that Mrs O'Shea had for years been deceiving the aunt who had left her all her money, then the case for overturning the will might be strengthened. Or if not this, then at least the threat of divorce might be used as blackmail to extort a handsome sum in settlement. According to what Katharine told Henry Harrison, O'Shea would have called off his suit (and even allowed her to divorce him!) if she could have paid him £20,000. This she could not do – her inheritance being in jeopardy – and so the case went to court.

Although Mrs Parnell's version (she had become Mrs Parnell when Harrison interviewed her) leaves some things unexplained, it does at least provide a possible reason for what would otherwise seem Parnell's extreme foolhardiness in assuring several people before the case came on that he would emerge from it without a stain on his reputation. Had O'Shea withdrawn his suit no doubt this would have been so. But he did not withdraw; on the contrary, as the trial progressed and his story was told without any defence being offered by the other side (Parnell being passionately anxious for the divorce so that he could make Katharine his wife), all the shabby paraphernalia of marital deception was publicly displayed – the false names, the frequent changes of address, the undignified entrances and exits.

Parnell, in short, had committed the unforgivable sin of being found out and in England this in itself, even without the squalid details provided by the divorce proceedings, would have been enough to damn him. At once it became apparent that an intolerable strain was being put upon the Liberal alliance. Gladstone came under pressure from many quarters, but especially from the non-conformists, to make a decisive break with the discredited Irish leader. At length, on 24 November 1890, he saw the vice-chairman of the Irish party, Justin McCarthy, and told him that if Parnell did not retire from politics the Liberals might expect to lose the next election with the inevitable consequence that Home Rule would be postponed probably beyond the time when Gladstone himself would be there to help it through. McCarthy promised to convey this solemn warning to Parnell, but Gladstone, to make assurance doubly sure, wrote a letter in similar terms for John Morley to show to Parnell the following day. In this letter Gladstone emphasised that if the Irish leader did not withdraw then Gladstone's own leadership of the Liberals would become 'almost a nullity'.

What gave these exchanges their particular urgency was that the Irish parliamentary party was due to meet in London on 25 November. Up to that time the Irish reaction to the news had been extraordinarily well controlled. So great was Parnell's ascendancy that the instinct of his followers was to remain true to him and several leading parliamentarians, who were later to eat their words, declared their loyalty in the days immediately following the verdict in the divorce court. The only discordant note came from Michael Davitt, who had believed his earlier assurances, and now urged him to retire; even Davitt, however, envisaged only a temporary withdrawal until Parnell was able to marry Mrs O'Shea. Amongst the Irish bishops there was, of course, great perturbation, and some would have liked to speak their mind freely. But they relied heavily on the advice of Archbishop Walsh of Dublin and that sagacious man counselled caution, at least until the Irish party held its fateful meeting on 25 November.

When the party assembled Parnell – characteristically – had managed to avoid receiving, or at least acting upon, Gladstone's ultimatum. The party, quite in the dark about the Liberal pressure, re-elected Parnell with acclamation. Motives, no doubt, were mixed. Some acted out of simple faith; others felt that in some mysterious way this cloud would be dispelled as had the Pigott forgeries; yet others seem to have been naive enough to believe that after he had been re-elected, he would then gracefully retire. But he had no intention whatever of retiring even when Morley confronted him with Gladstone's letter after the meeting. Gladstone then took a very serious decision. Although he knew that the Irish party had elected Parnell in ignorance of his views he made up his mind to publish his letter to Morley immediately. By doing so, of course, he confronted Irishmen, and not just the parliamentarians, with a choice between Parnell and himself – in effect a choice between Parnell and Home Rule.

It was an excruciating choice. Ever since 1886 the Liberal alliance had seemed absolutely essential to Home Rule – could it now be sacrificed out of loyalty to one man, even though it was that one man who had brought Home Rule so nearly within reach? On the other hand, Parnell had done more than anyone else to impress upon his party and his country the principle of independent opposition and to throw him over now, at the public insistence of the Liberal leader, would be to lay themselves open to the charges of basely betraying both the principle and the man who most embodied it. Almost immediately there were signs that some would be swayed one way, some another. To resolve the confusion it was decided, after a second meeting of the party, when Parnell made it clear that he would not resign, to adjourn until 1

December in order to allow time to ascertain the views of some members, including Dillon and O'Brien, who were in America collecting money for the evicted tenants. Both sides used the interval to prepare for battle, but it was Parnell who forced the pace. Two days before the party was due to meet he published in the newspapers his 'Manifesto to the Irish People'. In this extraordinary document he chose, with his accustomed audacity, to ignore the divorce issue altogether, and instead accused a section of his party of having themselves been corrupted by the Liberal alliance. Not only that, but he also gave a version of his famous conversation with Gladstone at Hawarden in 1889 (which Gladstone at once contradicted in detail) designed to reveal that the Liberals were unsound on Home Rule and on practically every aspect of Irish policy. Perhaps these charges had some effect on Irish opinion at large, though even this is doubtful, but they finished Parnell forever in the eyes of the Liberals. Now, still more than before, the party would have to choose between him and Home Rule. The manifesto also completed the alienation of influential Irishmen. It evoked a strong condemnation from the Irish delegation in America, and still more important, it gave the signal to the bishops to come into the open and throw their powerful weight against a leader who seemed to have taken leave of his senses.

Yet, though the forces gathering against Parnell were rapidly becoming formidable, the party could not brace itself to break with him until after a week of intense and tortured debate in Committee Room Fifteen. It was a debate conducted – apart from a few unhappy allusions to the divorce – at a high level of political argument and the case was stated on both sides with conspicuous ability. Those who were for Parnell condemned 'Liberal dictatorship' and insisted on the principle of independent opposition, reckless of what this might mean to the cause of Home Rule. Parnell himself, however, took a different line, suggesting with great astuteness that if he was to be sacrificed then the party should at least get a good price for him by exacting guarantees from the Liberals about disputed points in the projected Home Rule Bill. The anti-Parnellites (as they soon came to be called) threw back at him the needless provocations of his Manifesto, insisting that the cause was more important than the man and that if Home Rule really did depend on the Liberal alliance then the Liberal alliance must be maintained.

When at the end of that week the party split in two a majority went with the vice-chairman, McCarthy (forty-five in all), and twenty-seven stayed with Parnell.* He was himself quite unshaken by this result and proceeded at once to carry the war to Ireland. Undoubtedly he had at the outset considerable support, especially in Dublin and one or two other cities, but against the personal devotion he knew so well how to

* To these totals need to be added the members who were absent. So far as I can ascertain the whole party divided in the proportion of thirty-two for Parnell and fifty-four against him.

inspire were massed powerful voices and deep anxieties. Not only Davitt, not only the influence of the Church, not only the votes of most of the leading members of the party, but also the fears of ordinary decent people for the welfare of the evicted tenants and for the whole future of Home Rule combined to overwhelm him.

But the agony was bitter and long drawn-out. On three occasions — North Kilkenny, Carlow and North Sligo — the issue was fought at by-elections and in each case Parnell's candidate was decisively defeated. This made, or seemed to make, no appreciable difference to him and over and over again he declared his resolve to fight on, alone if need be. It was noticeable, however, even from the moment he arrived back in Ireland that he passed easily from the theme of independent parliamentary opposition to language that could bear a very different interpretation. In Dublin for example, after observing truly enough that what was at stake was the life and death of the constitutional movement, he continued: 'If our constitutional movement today is broken, sundered, separated, discredited and forgotten, England will be face to face with that imperishable force which tonight gives me vitality and power and without which we are broken reeds. . . . And if Ireland leaves this path upon which I have led her . . . I will not for my part say that I will not accompany her further.' If he really meant what he seemed to be saying then it did indeed look as if he were turning away from constitutional politics and becoming, as has been well said, 'what he had always condemned — an "Impossibilist", harking back to the pre-party period and neo-Fenianism'.[20]

This was certainly the impression he conveyed to many contemporaries, an impression strengthened during the Kilkenny by-election when both he and his supporters seemed to be appealing directly to 'the hillside men', that is, to the Fenian tradition. Moreover, it seems to have been the impression conveyed to the Fenians themselves, and one after another — in Ireland, in England and in America — they came out in his support. Yet these appeals need to be read with caution. Parnell had never been one voluntarily to diminish his freedom of action more than he had to, and in practice he did not diminish it even after his party had broken in two. If these were revolutionary speeches they were nevertheless marked by his habitual ambiguities. Had he lived longer he might have had to resolve those ambiguities, but the fact remains that while he did live he did not abandon constitutional methods and repeatedly referred to the coming general election as his great opportunity to restore his authority.

Perhaps what those wild speeches indicated was not so much his conversion to the ways of physical force, as his own degeneration as a leader. Even those who loved him and were close to him in the last months of his career were shocked by the change in him. This was partly physical; he had not been in good health for years, and the strain of his campaign in Ireland rapidly wore him down. But the change was psychological as well. His sensitivity as an individual and his pride as a leader had both been deeply wounded and in his fierce reaction to his tormentors he himself lost all moderation. On the personal plane, the vilification of Katharine O'Shea (whom he married in June 1891) was an unendurable affront which provoked him in his turn into violent and insulting language about his former colleagues which they could scarcely be expected to forgive. Equally, on the political plane, the very fact that the great parliamentary party – so much his own creation – had splintered in his hand under English pressure, and the even more terrible realisation that because of this he could never hope to lead his country towards Home Rule, together contributed to the strange errors of judgment which disfigured the last phase of his career.

Of these, the most important was his refusal to accept extremely favourable terms for his temporary retirement. In the early weeks of 1891 William O'Brien, and later John Dillon, met him in France in an attempt to link his withdrawal with the concession by the Liberals of the kind of guarantees about Home Rule which Parnell himself had suggested in Committee Room Fifteen. Considerable progress was in fact made towards obtaining these guarantees and Parnell himself was consulted at every turn. Yet even so he broke off the negotiations on what appeared to be extremely trivial grounds. Why he did this we cannot be sure even to this day, but it seems probable that he was convinced there could be no such thing as a temporary retirement. 'If I go, I go for ever', he had said, at the beginning of the quarrel, and this he would never accept. So it remained, as it had begun, war to the death. But death was nearer than anybody thought and on 6 October 1891, aged only forty-five, he died at Brighton in the arms of his wife, Katharine.

He left behind him not just the bitter rancour of the split but also the memory of great and long-enduring achievements. Three in particular stand out. One was the fact that the land problem – though far from its final solution – had been revolutionised by the Act of 1881 which, as Parnell himself had prophesied, was the measure of the determination and tenacity of the tenants acting through the Land League. But the Land League, much though it owed to Davitt's passion for social justice, would hardly in itself have secured that revolution without Parnell's superb ability to combine the explosive force of agrarianism with a mastery of parliamentary pressure at Westminster. His second achievement was to bring Home Rule from a vague aspiration into the forefront of practical politics and in doing so to win the support of one of the two major English parties. In this, it may be said without exaggeration, he changed the whole basis of the relationship between Britain and Ireland not only for his own generation but for the one that came after him. And finally, and perhaps most significant of all, was his creation of a disciplined, efficient and pledge-bound parliamentary party which, by its performance at Westminster, offered a living proof that Ireland was ripe for self-government, and through its elaborate machinery for political self-expression in the constituencies provided the country with essential experience in the democratic process. Nor was this all dissipated when he himself was deposed. In a sense, indeed, the party, by deposing him, revealed its political maturity, for his deposition was nothing less than the reassertion of majority rule over the dictatorship of a single individual. It is true that the party was fearfully damaged by the years of furious internecine dispute which followed his death, but the principles and the practice of parliamentary politics survived, to re-emerge powerfully in the years between 1900 and 1914.

Yet when all is said about Parnell's constructive policies the truth may still be that it was his myth rather than his record that most influenced posterity. To the generation that grew up in the poisonous atmosphere of the split which persisted for nearly ten years after his death, Parnell stood out as a towering figure, far above the politicians whom he had created and who had repaid him – so the argument went – with betrayal. To this new generation the Parnell of the land war, or the Parnell of the last great struggle, seemed more fundamental, more real, than the Parnell of the Liberal alliance or the Kilmainham 'treaty'. It was easy from his own extremer speeches, from his intense hatred of all things English, and from the drama of his fall to picture him as an archetypal revolutionary leading yet another forlorn hope against the British connection, and the victim – like so many before him – of English guile, ecclesiastical interference and Irish feebleness. To see him thus was of course to oversimplify a great deal and to omit at least two important considerations. One was that for almost his entire career – and perhaps even for the whole of it – he was not a physical force man, not a separatist, not the leader of any forlorn hope. He was for winning the maximum self-government by the most efficient means and, given the environment within which he had to work, parliament seemed to him – at least during the years of his greatest effectiveness – the road by which Ireland could best come at Home Rule. The other defect of the conventional view of him as the hero betrayed was that it failed to recognise that he was himself responsible for his own disaster – responsible in the narrow sense by accepting for so long the dangerous O'Shea liaison, and responsible in the broader sense by refusing to withdraw in circumstances that were specially designed by some of the most respected and devoted men in his party to make withdrawal easy for him. But myths operate at levels far removed from reason and it was as the proud man overthrown by base men that Parnell's name was to echo through Irish literature and politics with a passion that has not even yet entirely died away.

4. Constructive Unionism

The period between the death of Parnell in 1891 and the re-emergence of the Irish parliamentary party nineteen years later as a key factor in the balance of power at Westminster is often dismissed by historians as a kind of political vacuum, to be passed over as swiftly and silently as possible. From the viewpoint of the parliamentary pursuit of Home Rule, but from that viewpoint only, there is some truth in this assessment. The effect of Parnell's catastrophe both upon his party and upon the prospects of Home Rule was entirely disastrous. It is true that when the general election came at last in 1892 the Liberals, though outnumbered by Conservatives and Liberal Unionists, were able to scrape together a small majority in the House of Commons with the support of the Irish nationalists and of a solitary Independent Labour member. Gladstone, though shaken by the precariousness of this majority, braced himself with Homeric courage to the task of piloting his second Home Rule Bill through the House of Commons in the following year. As he and everyone else had anticipated, it was then quickly knocked on the head by the House of Lords and with Gladstone's retirement from politics a few months later it was evident that Home Rule was dead and buried without hope of any speedy resurrection. The Liberal party, almost as deeply divided among themselves about leadership and policy as were their Irish allies, went out of office in 1895 and for the next ten years the combination of Conservatives and Liberal Unionists ruled supreme.

Even a united and disciplined Irish party would have found it difficult to maintain a high morale in this bleak situation. But Parnell's heirs were so thoroughly demoralised by their own internal divisions that they did not cease their quarrelling even while the Home Rule Bill itself was at stake in 1893, and in succeeding years things seemed to get worse rather than better. There were in the 'nineties three separate groups, owing allegiance respectively to John Redmond (elected by the Parnellites to the leadership vacated by the dead chief,) to T. M. Healy and to Justin McCarthy (replaced from 1896 onwards by John Dillon). Ostensibly the line of division was still that between those who had sided with Parnell in 1890 and those who had gone against him. The general election of 1892 had greatly reduced the strength of the Parnellites, who succeeded in salvaging only nine seats, as against their opponents' seventy-one, from the wreckage. They did a little better in 1895, eleven against seventy, but the results indicated that although a stubborn and insuppressible minority, they *were* nevertheless a minority and doomed apparently to continue so. This, however, was cold comfort to the anti-Parnellites, whose ranks were split by enmities almost as deep as, if not deeper than, those between themselves and the Parnellites. It was partly a clash of personalities – John Dillon and William O'Brien *versus* Tim Healy – partly a clash between rival concepts of discipline and freedom, but most of all a struggle to determine whether or not a clerical-political party would rise out of the ruins of the Parnell split. This or something like it had seemed to be taking shape in the last months of the fight against Parnell, when, in the absence of Dillon and O'Brien (both in prison between February and July 1891 for offences connected with the Plan of Campaign) Tim Healy had attracted much support from the clergy for his frenetic attacks upon the fallen leader. Even before they came out of prison Dillon and O'Brien, whose anti-clericalism (not to be confused in either case with irreligion) had been well-known for years, had recognised that they would have a fight with Healy on their hands as well as with Parnell's followers. They fought that fight inch by inch during the next nine years in a series of struggles involving control of newspapers, of party committees, of the constituencies themselves, and in the end they won it. The details of this verbal civil war are squalid and unedifying and need not concern us here, but the final result was important. When the party did eventually achieve unity in 1900 under the Parnellite John Redmond, it stood ready to fight in the same fashion and on the same lines as it had fought in Parnell's prime – a party predominantly Catholic but not subservient to the Church, and a party genuinely nationalist without being either sectional or sectarian.[1]

Even though we can see now that much hung upon the conflict between Healy and his enemies, this was not so obvious at the time. It was not surprising that many contemporaries, seeing only the surface manifestations of the quarrel, should have turned in disgust from the vituperative vulgarity of the parliamentarians and that the most significant developments of these years should have been entirely divorced from, and frequently antagonistic to, what seemed the tasteless and futile charade of Irish attendance at Westminster. These developments – notably the emergence of a new and more sharply defined cultural nationalism and the rise of the movement called Sinn Féin – will be dealt with shortly.* In the meantime it is necessary to insist that during this same period of apparent sterility in the aftermath of Parnell, the face of Irish society was being slowly and steadily changed by agencies which owed nothing to cultural nationalism, nothing to crusades for 'Irish Ireland', and very little even to parliamentary pressures from Redmondites, Healyites or Dillonites.

We do not have to look very far for the origins of this change, though to explain it is more complicated. It sprang essentially from the Conservative or Unionist doctrine that Home Rule was at bottom a 'knife and fork' question, in other words that the impetus behind nationalism could be halted by social amelioration. This may in the end have seemed

* See below, chaps. 5 and 6.

a tragically mistaken doctrine – historians still differ as to whether it was the doctrine that was mistaken or the circumstances that were unpropitious – but it had nevertheless almost revolutionary consequences for Ireland. Moreover, and this is what gives it its interest as well as its complexity, it was not simply an official or governmental doctrine, but came simultaneously to be held by a number of Irish landlords who discovered at this late stage in the history of their class, a mission – baffling to contemporaries but perfectly genuine all the same – to work for the betterment of their country and the welfare of their fellow-Irishmen.

Historically, it was the governmental drive towards reform which came first, and it was the Chief Secretary, Arthur Balfour, in the popular mind the very personification of coercion, who was mainly responsible for converting the spasmodic impulses of Unionists towards reform into a settled and consistent policy. We have seen already that in 1887 he succeeded in drastically overhauling the Land Act of 1881 and that in 1888 he had augmented by another five million pounds the money provided under the Ashbourne Act of 1885 for land purchase. To Balfour, to his uncle Lord Salisbury, and ultimately to most Unionists except the naturally nervous Irish landlords, the creation of a stable peasant proprietary had come to seem the only permanent solution of the problem. The principle of dual ownership established by Gladstone in 1881, while undoubtedly improving the position of many tenants, had provided untold opportunities for friction between the two interests involved. If the landlords could be persuaded to sell on terms which were reasonable for both sides then, so the Unionist argument ran, at one stroke a fundamental cause of Irish lawlessness would have been removed and a new element of social, and perhaps also political, conservatism – the small farmer with a stake in the soil – would have been introduced into the Irish countryside. Or, as a modern authority has well put it, it was hoped that land purchase 'would disconnect Fintan Lalor's agrarian engine from the rest of the train and sidetrack the Home Rule carriages for ever'.[2]

Time would tell whether the argument was fallacious or not. But it could not even be posed until the policy itself had become more of a reality. By 1890 the moment seemed ripe for another step forward, and Balfour proposed to seize the chance by bringing in an 'heroic measure' which would include some system compelling reluctant or unco-operative landlords (like the Marquess of Clanricarde) to sell. This, however, was too ambitious and he had to drop it. The Act he did introduce was delayed and obstructed in parliament (Parnell's opposition to it was probably a direct outcome of the Liberal alliance) and it was not until 1891 that, in a slightly altered form, it finally became law. The amount of money provided for the financing of land purchase was much greater than under any previous Act – no less than thirty-three million pounds – but the process of buying was hedged around with so many complicated regulations that tenants were easily discouraged. Moreover, the Act introduced a new and unpopular principle in stipulating that the landlords should be paid not in cash but in land stock which was liable to fluctuate with the state of the market. As the land stock fluctuated so did the volume of land sales and despite an amending Act in 1896 the amount advanced under this scheme was only just over £13½ million. The number of purchasers was 47,000, but by 1898 applications had fallen away sharply and it seemed as if Balfour's elaborate machinery must shortly grind to a halt.[3]

Yet if the Act of 1891 did not justify all Balfour's hopes of effecting a revolution in land purchase, it did mark a significant new departure in quite a different direction. Its purpose was not only to create a race of peasant proprietors in the future, but to relieve existing poverty in the poorer districts of the west and south of Ireland. These were the areas where 'distress' – near or sometimes actual starvation – was most endemic and where the population, still heavily dependent upon the potato, was most vulnerable to the bad seasons that came with such appalling frequency along the Atlantic coast. The root cause of the trouble was that too many people were trying to live on too little land. It was, however, less a problem of over-population than of population unevenly distributed. These districts were 'congested' in the official jargon, not because perhaps half a million people lived there, but because too many of them were trying to scratch from bog or stony mountain land a living which was at best precarious and sometimes non-existent. In formulating a policy to deal with this intractable problem Balfour was almost certainly influenced by Joseph Chamberlain. Chamberlain, though adamantly opposed to Home Rule and swinging year by year further from his Liberal origins, had never abandoned his conviction that coercion in Ireland must always be accompanied by conciliation in the form of improved economic and administrative efficiency. His ideas, as outlined in 1888 in the pamphlet 'A Unionist policy for Ireland', were characteristically grandiose, ranging from land purchase and local government to railway building and industrial development.

As a responsible minister Balfour could scarcely be as sweeping in his approach as Chamberlain, but his solution had a Birmingham stamp upon it. Grasping the central fact that assistance of various kinds had to be proffered to people who were beyond helping themselves, he set up a new administrative agency, the Congested Districts Board. It consisted of two land commissioners, five experts appointed by the government and the Chief Secretary himself as an *ex officio* member. The Board's objects, broadly speaking, were four-fold: to promote local industries by subsidies and technical instruction; to amalgamate uneconomic holdings by land purchase; to assist migration from impoverished areas to the newly amalgamated holdings; and finally, to improve the quality of agriculture in the congested areas. At the outset the CDB (to adopt the initials that soon became very familiar to Irishmen) was rigidly limited in its geographical operation by the decision to define a congested district as one in which the total rateable value divided by the number of inhabitants amounted to less than thirty shillings per person. In 1891 this definition produced an area of just over 3½ million acres and a population of about half a million spread over parts of the counties of Donegal, Leitrim, Roscommon, Sligo, Mayo, Galway, Kerry and Cork; gradually, however, the Board's frontiers were extended until by 1910 it had doubled the acreage to which it ministered. As with frontiers, so with finance. Starting life with a modest income of just over £41,000 (drawn from the Irish Church surplus), the Board attracted to itself all sorts of supplementary revenues until by 1912 its income was over £530,000, though even this was probably too small for it to discharge its manifold responsibilities to its own satisfaction.

From an administrative point of view the most valuable contribution of the CDB was the tradition it built up of meticulous investigation of conditions in the smallest subdivisions – the Poor Law Unions – of the various congested districts. This not only secured for the government far more accurate and detailed information than ever before, it also made for intelligent application of existing resources. These were expended in a multitude of different, but generally constructive, projects – the encouragement of cottage industries, the building of roads, bridges and harbours, the stimulation of a fishing industry, the provision of expert advice on the raising of crops and livestock, above all, perhaps, land purchase and resettlement. This last function, the key to ultimate success, at first proceeded fitfully enough, but when in 1909 the Board at last obtained compulsory powers things moved more swiftly and when in 1923 it handed over its responsibilities to the Irish Free State it had bought more than two million acres at a cost of over nine million pounds.[4]

The work of the Congested Districts Board was inevitably long-term in its effects and the full fruits of Balfour's initiative were not garnered until long after he had ceased to be Chief Secretary. But in the meantime there was always the fear of famine to contend with; in 1890 the reappearance of potato blight turned that fear into a reality. At once Balfour launched a programme of relief which, characteristically, rapidly became not just another administrative improvisation but a permanent addition to the amenities of the west. Some direct assistance – outdoor relief and the provision of seed-potatoes – to starving people was inevitable, but the Chief Secretary was anxious to avoid the demoralising effect of a dole and so far as possible restricted the distribution of food to the disabled and the aged. What was most needed was employment and this was found partly through an increase in the road and bridge-building programme, but even more through a radical extension of a scheme for light railways first set on foot in 1889. Despite the considerable expense of building these railways in difficult and sparsely populated country (a factor that has since led to their abandonment), Balfour pressed on with his plans, which resulted in the creation of a dozen different lines and the employment of 16,000 people. Despite the grumbles of professional railway experts and the alarming scale of costs – in some instances £5000 a mile – few things contributed more to 'opening up' the west than this swift and resolute exploitation of what was almost a chance opportunity. Those of his critics who were obsessed by the coercionist aspect of his regime and derided his policy as one of 'light railways and heavy punishments' had missed a good deal of the point.

But although Balfour's achievement was enough to rank him among the most successful Chief Secretaries to hold office during the Union, his was not a record of unmixed success. He failed, for example, to carry through a measure of local government which would have given Ireland county councils on the lines of those already established in the United Kingdom in 1888, though with the significant difference that in Ireland not only was there to be special representation for sectional interests, but the government was to have the power to dissolve councils for financial irresponsibility or for oppression of minorities. Naturally, when a Bill to this effect was introduced early in 1892 (by Balfour though he had ceased to be Chief Secretary) the Liberal and nationalist opposition was bitter. And since Unionists were not friendly to it either it was eventually dropped. Balfour himself was probably more enthusiastic about his second forlorn hope – to meet the oft-repeated demand by Irish Catholics for a university of their own. His motives were not entirely divorced from politics – he hoped in effect to bribe the bishops into taking a severe line on agrarian agitation by dangling a Catholic college in front of them – but he was enough of an educationist to want the new university for its own sake, and to want it without the tight ecclesiastical control for which the hierarchy was hankering. Unfortunately, the mere mention of any such concession was enough to arouse vehement anti-Catholic prejudice amongst Unionists and although Balfour would have liked to bring in a Bill in 1889 or 1890, the reception he got from his own party was such that he had to abandon the idea with undignified haste.

The fate of these measures was a salutary reminder of the prejudice and passion still rampant in a deeply divided society. But not all Unionists, nor for that matter all nationalists, were caught in this web of hereditary hatred. And the closing years of the nineteenth century saw the emergence of a new and startling phenomenon – the attempt by men of different religions, backgrounds and political convictions to forget for the time being the things that separated them and to concentrate instead on the work of social regeneration that cried out to be done. Pride of place in this movement towards rconciliation belongs beyond question to Sir Horace Plunkett.[5] Born in 1854, the third son of the sixteenth Baron Dunsany, he had had a conventional enough education at Eton and Oxford. The threat of tuberculosis drove him to the American west and for ten years (1879–89) he lived the life of a rancher in Wyoming. Family circumstances brought him back to Ireland in 1889 and although he retained some business interests in, and a lifetime's affection for, the United States, his father's death saddled him, though not the heir, with heavy responsibilities which included the management not just of the Dunsany estate, but of land and coalmines in England and Wales. Unmarried, vigorous, free from money-troubles, with an intense zest for the practical details of administration, he found these private commitments insufficient to absorb his energy and soon began to look about for some other means of satisfying his compulsive urge for work.

He found it in the countryside around him. Like most intelligent landlords he could see that while in one sense the countryside was changing rapidly, in another sense it was still embedded in the past. Men's minds had been obsessed by the land question, but, for obvious historical and indeed economic reasons, they had seen it primarily as a *tenure* question, not as a question of how the soil might best be cultivated and the rural economy be made resistant to ruinous foreign competition. With the landlord-tenant relationship on the way to solution, Plunkett felt that the time had come to concentrate attention increasingly on production and distribution. For him this policy was summed up in the single word – co-operation. But co-operation was not just a more efficient way of utilising the resources of the country, it was also a means of restoring the Irishman's self-respect, sapped, so it seemed to Plunkett, by many years of coercion and eviction and also by the demagoguery of nationalist politicians. Excessive preoccupation with political pressure – whether for Home Rule or for lesser objectives – had, in his opinion, led to a weakening of moral fibre and self-reliance. 'Whatever may be said of what is called "agitation" in Ireland', he once wrote, 'as an engine for extorting legislation from the Imperial Parliament, it is unquestionably bad for the much greater end of building up Irish character and developing Irish industry and commerce.'[6]

In politics Plunkett was a Unionist (though in his later years he accepted dominion status as a workable solution), but a Unionist who sat very loose to his party. Believing as he did that the contemporary involvement in Home Rule and the 'tenure' question were distractions from the essential task of social and economic reform, he castigated his fellow-Unionists for their refusal to participate in the great work of regeneration He blamed the landlords for thinking only of their own short-term interests and he blamed the industrialists for sticking so closely to business that they had failed to make an adequate impact on Irish Unionism, which represented not a coherent policy but rather the creed of a social caste dedicated to the status quo both in politics and in economics. 'The result', he commented acidly, 'has been injurious alike for the landlords, the leaders of industry, and the people. The policy of the Unionist party in Ireland has been to uphold the Union by force rather than by a reconciliation of the people to it'.[7]

With that detached impartiality which made him at times one of the best-hated men in Ireland, Plunkett turned his guns with equal severity upon the nationalists. He regarded them as primarily responsible for imbuing their fellow-countrymen with two damaging ideas. One was that the whole system of English government in Ireland was so bad that it must be overturned before constructive policies would have any chance of success. The other was that if anyone tried to put such policies into effect before Home Rule was achieved, he was to be opposed on the ground, as Plunkett put it, 'that . . . any non-political movement towards national advancement, which in its nature cannot be linked, as the land question was linked, to the Home Rule movement constitutes an unwarrantable sacrifice of ends to means.' The results of this negative attitude of mind were not only that nationalism seemed bereft of constructive policies of its own, but that the constant emphasis of the leaders upon the necessity for solidarity and conformity bred the very qualities which Plunkett found so objectionable – 'the lack of initiative and shrinking from responsibility, the moral timidity in glaring contrast with the physical courage', the intense dread of public opinion which the practice of boycotting had done so much to develop.[8]

Such comments were not likely, or indeed designed, to please, and the nationalist leaders repaid Plunkett's bluntness with bitter hostility. Unfortunately for the success of his schemes he also contrived, with a touch of that unearthly genius he had for alienating influential sections of opinion by his uncompromising zeal for the right as he saw it, to arouse further enmity by criticising the Roman Catholic Church with the same frankness he had used towards the politicians. There was no sectarianism in this – although he was a Protestant himself, two branches of his family were Catholic – only sublime tactlessness. He could answer in self-defence that he dealt equally frankly with Ulster Protestantism, which he accused of bigotry, but this did not save him from the consequences of his temerity. Concerned as he was to make Irishmen more capable of standing on their own feet, he attacked Catholicism as being too authoritarian, too liable to induce fatalism in the devout, too little concerned with economic realities and too much concerned with raising money for church-building.[9] When he published these strictures in 1904 (in his book *Ireland in the New Century*) the counterattack he provoked – by the press, from the pulpit, even in the House of Commons – may have surprised him by its ferocity but did not disturb his serene self-confidence. He would have done well to pay it more attention than he did.

His ideas, however, like his fame, matured slowly. Although he was sufficiently interested in co-operation to start a little co-operative store on the family estate at Dunsany before he left for America, it was not until he settled permanently in Ireland in 1889 that he began to think of it in wider terms. The problem of the Irish agrarian economy, as he saw it, was not just the endemic depression caused by the influx of cheap food from abroad, but the fact that the products which Ireland herself might reasonably have expected to sell to the outside world – notably butter and eggs – were so poorly packed and graded as to be utterly uncompetitive. Yet new methods and new machinery (for instance the mechanical cream separator and churn) were at hand if only the farmers could be persuaded to use them. Here and there a few parish priests, conscious of the danger to their flocks if these new means of production fell into the hands of middlemen, had tentatively experimented with the notion of dairies – or 'creameries' as they were called in Ireland – on a co-operative basis, but when Plunkett seriously began to interest himself in the plight of Irish agriculture there was nothing remotely approaching a co-operative movement.

He started his first society (at Doneraile in county Waterford) in 1889, but it was an uphill struggle and he had to address more than forty meetings before he registered even this single success. From the outset he encountered stubborn opposition – sometimes the deadly lethargy of the small-minded and suspicious peasant, sometimes the jealousy of priest or curate, sometimes the belief (by no means wide of the mark) that he was trying to stultify nationalism by distracting attention towards economics. However, there were compensations. Gradually he began to gather allies – Lord Monteagle in Limerick, the young land-agent, R. A. Anderson, who became one of his most devoted disciples, and the able Jesuit, Father Tom Finlay, who combined the Professorship of Moral Philosophy at the Catholic University with a first-hand knowledge of agricultural co-operation on the continent.

With this kind of support the idea, once launched, began to spread and both creameries and co-operative societies appeared in different parts of the country. Within five years there were thirty-three – mainly in Cork, Tipperary and Kilkenny – and by 1894 progress was far enough advanced to encourage Plunkett to attempt some kind of national consolidation. In that year he founded the Irish Agricultural Organisation Society with himself as president and Anderson as secretary. The Society was intended both to develop links between the existing societies and to carry the gospel still further afield, but it was essential to Plunkett's concept of co-operation that while the IAOS should be propagandist in the agricultural sense, it should be politically neutral. Propaganda was powerfully reinforced by the foundation of a journal, the *Irish Homestead*, in 1895. It was edited at first by Father Finlay and later by one of Plunkett's great discoveries, George William Russell, better known as the poet AE. Russell was a northern Protestant, born in Lurgan in 1867. He had come south to Dublin to study art, but entered Pim's drapery store in Dublin as a clerk at the age of seventeen. He was a mystic, a visionary, a painter and poet of uneven talent, an encourager of genius greater than his own, an original thinker on social problems, a first-rate journalist, and a gentle, lovable man who for the next thirty years was to occupy a central place in the cultural and intellectual life of Dublin. Plunkett appointed him as one of his organisers in 1897 and his entry into the co-operative movement coincided with its period of most dramatic growth. Within ten years of the foundation of the

* For a very different contribution by the Monteagle family to Irish affairs see the account of the Howth gun-running, pp. 325-6 below.

IAOS there were 876 societies with an annual turnover of about three million pounds.[10]

Perhaps it was inevitable that Plunkett should move sooner or later from this still rather obscure private sphere into public life. As early as 1891 Arthur Balfour had singled him out to become a founder of the Congested Districts Board, and although the Board laid too much emphasis on paternalism and too little on self-help for Plunkett to take very kindly to its work, it at least allowed him to move nearer the frontier between administration and politics. The following year he took a decisive step across that frontier by entering parliament for South Dublin. It was one of the few constituencies outside Ulster that had a heavy concentration of Unionists and it was as a Unionist that Plunkett won the seat. But he was, as his constituents soon found out, a highly unorthodox Unionist and it was not long before they were at odds with their member. Still, he was returned a second time at the general election of 1895 and almost at once began to cut across the normal party lines. In August of that year he published in the newspapers 'a proposal affecting the general welfare of Ireland'. Given that a Unionist government was now in power and presumably would be for the next five years at least, there was, he suggested, a chance to think about other things besides Home Rule and he instanced two of his own hobby-horses – the need to create a Board of Agriculture for Ireland, and the necessity to promote technical, or 'practical', education. He suggested, therefore, that the leaders of the various Irish parties should come together to form the nucleus of a committee to press for these and other similar projects. The response to this initiative was remarkably favourable, at any rate from some Unionists, notably Liberal Unionists, and Parnellites, though the nationalist majority (dominated by Dillon who never relaxed his inveterate hostility to landlords in general and regarded reforming landlords with more than ordinary suspicion) threw cold water on the idea, as did also the leading Irish Unionist MP, Colonel E. J. Saunderson. Meetings were held during the parliamentary recess – hence the name, Recess Committee, by which this body was always known – and in 1896 a unanimous report was issued. This document, based both on Plunkett's own thinking and on research stimulated by him, contrasted the backwardness of Irish agriculture with what was being done elsewhere, and drew the moral that although voluntary self-help must still be the basis of progress, the time had come for the government to step in and provide the necessary financial and administrative underpinning for thoroughgoing agricultural development.

Out of this initiative there came in due course nearly everything he has asked for. It was a triumph of skilfully directed pressure, but also the happy outcome of an exceptionally favourable conjuncture of circumstances. The Chief Secretary in the new government was Balfour's brother, Gerald, and although he had not the drive or ability of Arthur, he shared his view that the coin of Irish government had two faces, amelioration as well as coercion. In 1896 he successfully carried through a Land Act which increased the amount available for purchase under the 1891 Act and dropped some of the safeguards embodied in that Act which had frightened off the peasantry in the previous five years. The approach to purchase was still piecemeal and the solution was to be much more drastic than any the Balfours had been able to propose, but at least the new measure showed that the government impetus towards reform had not been stifled by the Unionist success in the elections. On the contrary, two years later (in 1898) Gerald Balfour triumphantly carried through an Irish Local Government Act which deservedly ranks as one of the most important measures of conciliation passed during the whole period of the Union. Abandoning the checks and balances which had made the Bill of 1892 so unpopular, it gave Ireland a system of local government on the British model, with county councils, urban district councils and rural district councils. These were elected bodies chosen on a wide franchise which included women and peers. The new councils took over the administrative and fiscal duties of the old grand juries (but not their judicial functions) and were eligible to receive grants from the Treasury as well as to impose their own local rates. Once they began to operate they were, of course, dominated by the Catholic and nationalist majority who found in them an invaluable training-ground for self-government. In social terms, also, the effect of the Local Government Act was not far short of revolutionary, for it marked a decisive shift in power and influence over the country at large away from the landlord ascendancy class and towards 'the democracy' of farmers, shopkeepers and publicans.

Side by side with this governmental solicitude, and quite distinct from Plunkett's own initiative, nationalists and Unionists were stirred to joint action by the report of a Royal Commission on the financial relations between Britain and Ireland. This Commission, promised by Gladstone in 1893, began work in 1894 and two years later produced a massive survey which did indeed seem to indicate that Ireland had been seriously overtaxed since the Union. True, there were minority reports which qualified this conclusion, but the general reaction in Ireland was that what had been suspected for years had now turned out to be correct. At once a great movement of protest was set on foot and by February 1897 this had issued in an All-Ireland Committee which proceeded to summon a conference of Irish parliamentarians to discuss what action could be taken. The circular calling the conference was signed by Colonel E. J. Saunderson, John Redmond, T. M. Healy and, it is hardly necessary to add, by Horace Plunkett. Dillon, by this time titular leader of the anti-Parnellites, at first hung back, sceptical as always of landlords bearing gifts, but in the end he too participated and pressed for early legislation to implement the report. That was too extreme for the Unionist members of the conference and no formula acceptable to everyone could be found. This, however, was less serious than it might have been, for it soon became clear that the government had no intention of doing anything about the matter. What *was* significant, and far transcending the differences of opinion at the conference, was that Unionists and nationalists had again found a common meeting-ground and a common cause.

This augured well for the success of the Recess Committee's plans. And in fact, in 1899, they won from the government an Act creating a Department of Agriculture and Technical Instruction for Ireland. When at the end of that year Plunkett himself took office as Vice-President of the Department (in effect as a minister, though responsible to the Chief Secretary) it seemed that all his dreams for a new Ireland were about to come true. Yet the reality somehow failed to live up to his expectations. This is not to say that a great deal was not achieved. The new Department did certainly make an impact both upon the Irish administration and upon the Irish countryside. Administratively, it led to some much-needed rationalisation in that a variety of different functions, previously performed by separate and unco-ordinated bodies, were gathered under its wing. It assumed responsibility not only for agriculture and technical instruction, but for fisheries, the collection of statistics, the prevention of animal and plant disease, the supervision of the National Museum and the National Library, and (from 1905 on) the geological survey of Ireland. With this rationalisation went also a degree of constitutional innovation. In order to bring the Department closer to the people it was designed to serve, the government equipped it with three semi-representative advisory bodies, a Council of Agriculture, an Agricultural Board, and a Board of Technical Instruction. The Council of Agriculture, which met infrequently and was intended mainly as a forum for discussion, had a strong county council element in its composition, and in the Board of Technical Instruction local government authorities were also heavily represented; the Agricultural Board was smaller, consisting as it did of the President (the Chief Secretary), the Vice-President, four persons nominated by the Department, and two members from each province elected by the Council of Agriculture. There was thus a real attempt to link the headquarters in Dublin with the farmers and shopkeepers who stood to gain most from the work of the Department. Perhaps the attempt was over-elaborate and the machinery too intricate. The Department grew very fast (by 1914 it had a staff of 370, over 700 if associated enterprises are included), and as it grew complaints of bureaucratic delay became louder, though contemporaries were very ready to lay at least some of the blame for this on the Department's Secretary and not on the Department itself. This was T. P. Gill, a former nationalist MP, who had been secretary of the Recess Committee and whom Plunkett had chosen for the new post in the teeth of Unionist disapproval. He was honest and hard-working, but excessively cautious and sadly lacking in imagination.*

* One of the great set-pieces of George Moore's *Hail and Farewell*, the *chronique scandaleuse* of Dublin at this period, is his dual portrait of Plunkett and Gill as an Irish 'Bouvard et Pécuchet'. The portrait is

Nevertheless, in its practical work the Department made its presence felt. The business of agricultural and technical education was taken seriously, and in time ten separate institutions were brought under its control, including the Royal College of Science, the Albert College (of agriculture) and the forestry centre at Parnell's old home, Avondale; in addition, it maintained a staff of peripatetic lecturers (138 of them by 1914) giving 'itinerant instruction' in agriculture, horticulture, poultry breeding, and butter manufacture. It was no less active in other directions – devising experimental schemes for the improvement of livestock and crops, making agricultural loans, encouraging afforestation, wrestling with problems of animal disease, stimulating fisheries, and collecting and publishing a vast amount of information on many different aspects of Irish economic life.[11] Much of this was unquestionably valuable work, and T. P. Gill, in giving evidence to the Commission on Agriculture of 1923 (when many things in Ireland had changed) was moved to claim that the Department had been mainly responsible for a substantial increase in crop yields during the period of its operation. There had been some increase, indeed, though since most of the important crops (with the notable exception of potatoes) had in fact been registering relatively high yields in the half century before the Department was set up, it is at least possible that the other factors which made for stability – and which were discussed earlier in this book* – had as much to do with the increase as the labours of Gill and his minions.[12] The really important question which seems not to have occurred to the Department – or for that matter to its successor for several decades after 1923 – was whether it was enough to improve the technique of the individual farmer without assessing more carefully than seems to have been done the economic environment in which he was operating or the kind of growth that would be most beneficial in the future. And even at the level of technique it is doubtful that in the generation between the setting up of the Department and the creation of the Irish Free State the travelling inspectors and instructors did more than scratch the surface of that conservatism which, even in the mid-twentieth century, still seemed to observers, both foreign and domestic, the most deeply ingrained characteristic of the Irish farmer.†

In this there is nothing very surprising. Agricultural revolutions do not happen overnight, even when imposed from above by far more ruthless methods than were available to Plunkett's Department, and he himself no doubt would have been content to claim only that he was pointing out the way for others to follow. Yet he cannot avoid some of the blame for the inescapable fact that his exciting new initia-

---

entirely malicious and extremely funny, but just close enough to the truth to be damaging.

* See Part I, chap. 2.

† For the evidence and consequences of this conservatism in the post-1923 period, see Part IV A, chap. 4.

tives, both at the co-operative and at the governmental level, did not catch fire in the way he had hoped. Part of the difficulty came from within, part from without. He was an indifferent judge of men and although some of his appointments turned out very well, others were disastrous. But what was worse than this was that he was an indifferent judge of ideas as well. He seems quite genuinely to have believed that once co-operative methods had established themselves in a given country, they would only come to their full fruition with liberal aid from the State. For him, therefore, the creation of the Irish Agricultural Organisation Society and of the Department of Agriculture and Technical Instruction were two aspects of a single unified conception. For AE, on the other hand, the two bodies stood for quite different, and possibly antagonistic, conceptions; co-operation meant self-help, state aid meant state domination. In the long run, Plunkett's notion that self-help and state aid were complementary, not conflicting, might have turned out to be the right one, but his tragedy, and that of his movement, was that he never had the long run he needed. Indeed, for most of the eight years that he was at the head of the Department, he was in a peculiarly vulnerable position. At the general election of 1900 he was unseated in Dublin by another Unionist and, after a futile attempt to find an alternative seat in Galway, had to reconcile himself to the fact that he would never sit in parliament again. Technically, he did not have to be an MP to be Vice-President of the Department, but it was galling to be exposed to attack without being able to answer back, and when in 1906 the Liberals came to power he could only expect his appointment to be terminated. This duly occurred – though not until 1907 and then mainly as a result of nationalist pressure – and his dual experiment thereupon came to an abrupt end.

The results were immediately apparent. His successor as Vice-President, T. W. Russell, an Ulster Liberal and a stalwart defender of tenant-farmers, made it clear that in future there would be no partnership between the IAOS and the Department. Not only was the former to be a subordinate body, its activities restricted and its accounts supervised by the government, but from 1908 onwards its grant from the Department was cut off. Personal relations between Russell and the IAOS became extremely bad and from 1909 to 1913 the co-operative movement in Ireland depended largely on Plunkett's own resources to stay alive. In the latter year, however, the IAOS received the first of a series of annual grants from the newly established Development Fund and entered on a fresh period of expansion. By 1914 it had over a thousand affiliated societies with a turnover of more than £3½ million, of which the creameries accounted for £2½ million.

It seemed a happy ending – but was it? In one sense, no doubt, it was. Plunkett's brain-child clung tenaciously to life and, despite many vicissitudes, the co-operative movement still exists and still has its Dublin headquarters at the same house in Merrion Square which his admirers donated to the IAOS in 1908. There has even been growth, though growth in the last half-century has been measured less in the number of the societies (for a process of amalgamation soon began) than in the amount of the turnover. Among the creameries, for example, the increase between 1931 and 1951 was from £4·7 million to £23·8 million and while the other societies were on a decidedly smaller scale they too registered advance, even though much more modest advance.[13]

Yet although Plunkett had clearly established something with an element of permanency about it, the results in his own life-time were less spectacular than he might have looked for. 'Beyond effectively re-organising the dairying industry', it has been said, 'it [co-operation] made little impact on the economic or social life of the country.'[14] If this judgment, though harsh, now seems irrefutable, it was perhaps because Plunkett made one miscalculation more fundamental than any that have yet been mentioned. Because Home Rule was moribund when he entered public life he assumed that politics had become less urgent and vital for Irishmen than economics. But here he was profoundly mistaken. In the very years when he was launching his movement the whole political situation was in ferment and out of that ferment would come a mood and temper sharply inimical to the well-meant efforts of Protestant landlords to lead their fellow-countrymen by co-operative paths to quiet pastures.

Moreover, even within his own immediate sphere of interest, Plunkett underestimated the extent to which traditional patterns of agitation and unrest still survived. He thought the land question had changed from a problem of tenure to a problem of technique. But the farmers thought otherwise and his beloved Department actually came to birth in the midst of an agrarian upheaval which portended a renewal of the land war. It began, as the Land League had done, in Mayo. This time, however, the impetus came not from Davitt but from William O'Brien, who had settled near Westport in the mid-nineties and had been painfully struck by the contrast between the poverty-stricken tenants in their small holdings and the relatively affluent graziers on the neighbouring grass-farms or 'ranches'. To him the remedy was 'as luminously self-evident as the disease'. It was to redistribute the population by buying out the ranches. This was, of course, one of the objects of the Congested Districts Board, but an object that was never adequately fulfilled because the Board lacked compulsory powers of purchase. The failure of a private member's Bill to give it such powers helped to convince O'Brien, who probably required no urging, of the necessity to launch a thoroughgoing agitation in order to bring pressure on the government. Accordingly, in January 1898 he started a new body which, in commemoration of the 1798 centenary celebrations, he called the United Irish League. At first very small and much absorbed in the local and particular problems of the west, the League gradually grew to formidable proportions. In doing so, it provided O'Brien, who had almost certainly intended this from the outset, with an instrument of salvation not only for the tenant-farmers but for the divided parliamentarians as well. And he had this much justification that when at the beginning of 1900 the Irish party was reunited, it was reunited under the shadow of the League and with the various protagonists very well aware that the current of opinion in the country was running strongly from them and towards O'Brien's new agitation.

But it was as an agitation, not as the political force it eventually became, that the League initially attracted the attention equally of tenants and police. The latter reckoned that whereas by mid-summer 1899 the UIL had no more than 33,000 members, in June 1900 the total had gone up to 63,000 and by August 1901 was almost 100,000. At that time there were nearly a thousand branches and what had started as a western movement had spread to many parts of the country. As it spread, so its policy developed from the simple redistribution schemes of the early days to a sustained and highly articulate demand for the ending of 'dual partnership' and the buying out of the landlords by compulsory purchase. Although for much of its history the United Irish League was decidedly less violent than the Land League, it did use some of the same weapons – notably the boycott and various kinds of intimidation. To meet this the government resorted to the time-honoured expedient of coercion, with such effect that by the autumn of 1902 more than half the country had been 'proclaimed' because of the illegal activities of the League and a number of MPs had served terms in prison.

Yet although there seem to be obvious parallels here with 1879 and 1886, they are misleading. Coercion was no doubt a reality in 1901 and 1902, and the agitation was certainly intensive and widespread enough for the authorities to take it seriously while it lasted, but the Chief Secretary who had to administer the dose was a very different man from either W. E. Forster or Arthur Balfour. George Wyndham, who succeeded Gerald Balfour at the Irish Office in 1900, was in fact very close to the Balfour brothers and had served an Irish apprenticeship as Arthur's private secretary. Romantic, poetic (indeed a minor poet in his own right), with Irish blood in his veins, he came to Dublin Castle imbued with the notion that he would build on the earlier foundations of constructive Unionism and not leave his post until the Irish problem had been solved and his own reputation made in the process. Unhappily, he was impulsive, uncertain in judgment, and lacked stamina. He was undeniably brilliant, but time was to show that this very brilliance in a curious way reflected a fundamental instability.

Wyndham's heart was never in coercion and he only employed it, it seems, to placate his cabinet colleagues while he prepared for an all-out assault on the land problem. His first attempt in 1902 was an ill-considered measure which was wisely dropped, but before he could gather himself for a much more comprehensive bill in 1903 the entire situation was dramatically changed by another of those independent and unofficial Unionist initiatives of which Sir Horace Plunkett had hitherto had almost a monopoly. This time, however, the credit belonged not to Plunkett, but to the scion of another Protestant landlord family, Captain

John Shawe-Taylor. It was perhaps not altogether a coincidence that Shawe-Taylor's aunt was Lady Gregory who, as we shall see presently, had already shown herself as careless of the conventional pieties of her class as her nephew now proved himself to be. On 2 September 1902 he wrote a short letter to the newspapers inviting certain named representatives of landlords and tenants to meet in conference to bring about a settlement of the long struggle between the two classes. For the landlords he invited the Duke of Abercorn, Lord Barrymore (the former Smith-Barry of Plan of Campaign days), the O'Connor Don and Colonel E. J. Saunderson, at that time the leader of the Irish Unionist MPs. As the tenants' representatives Shawe-Taylor suggested the chairman of the Irish parliamentary party, John Redmond, together with William O'Brien, T. C. Harrington and T. W. Russell. This letter, coming as it did from an unknown private individual, might well have been ignored had not Wyndham given it a benediction the moment it appeared. The landlords as a body remained deeply suspicious of the proposal and the representatives named in the letter refused to act. Others, however, were found to take their place – the Earls of Dunraven and Mayo, Colonel Hutcheson-Poe and Colonel Nugent-Everard. The tenants' representatives, encouraged by the warm reception given to the scheme in most nationalist quarters, accepted the invitation and in December the Land Conference assembled in Dublin. The chairman was the Earl of Dunraven, celebrated internationally as a yachtsman, but known in Ireland as an improving landlord whose estate at Adare, county Limerick, was a model of its kind. After only a fortnight's discussion the Conference produced a unanimous report which, though brief, was comprehensive enough. It ranged widely over the whole agrarian scene, calling for thoroughgoing reform of the Congested Districts Board, for the settlement of the evicted tenants question, and for better provision of housing for labourers. But public attention was centred from the start on the Conference's main proposal, which was that a massive scheme of land purchase should at once be undertaken by the government. This was not to be compulsory, but the landlords were to be guaranteed a fair price through state aid to purchasers who would repay by annuities extending over 68½ years. The details, of course, would have to be left to the government, but the Conference was agreed upon the three overriding principles which should be applied – that the new owners should have a fair start and a reasonable prospect of success; that the landlords should receive some special inducement to sell; and that for the benefit of the whole community 'it is of the greatest importance that income derived from the sale of property in Ireland should continue to be expended in Ireland'.[15]

The report formed the basis of the Land Act Wyndham triumphantly passed through parliament during the session of 1903. This Act, which has ever since borne his name, carried the principle of land purchase further than it had ever been carried before and to that extent, though its financial provisions later proved inadequate, it deserves to be called revolutionary. Briefly, what Wyndham proposed was that landlords should be encouraged to sell entire estates, not just piecemeal holdings, and that sales should proceed if three-quarters of the tenants on any given estate acquiesced. The prices to be paid would range from 18½ years' purchase up to 24½ years' purchase on first-term rents (rents fixed by the Land Courts under the Act of 1881), or from 21½ to 27⅔ years' purchase on the lower second-term rents fixed in or after 1896. The money was to be advanced to the purchasers by the state and repaid over 68½ years by annuities at the rate of 3¼ per cent. The incentive to the landlord called for by the Conference report was to be provided by a bonus on each sale to be paid out of Irish revenues. There were some features of these proposals that nationalists strongly disliked – they thought the purchase-price too high and the regulations governing rent-reductions too complex – but there was no denying that a great opportunity now presented itself to the tenants which cried out to be seized. And seized it undoubtedly was. Even though compulsory purchase was *not* conceded until the amending Act of 1909 (and then only in minimal form) the pace of land transfer was greatly accelerated by the Wyndham Act and its later sequel. When in March 1920 the Estates Commissioners summed up the effect of this legislation they found that the two Acts together had led to a total of eighty-three million pounds being advanced (another million having been lodged by purchasers in cash payments) and that sales totalling a further twenty-four million were pending. Between 1903 and 1920 nearly nine million acres had changed hands and two million acres more were in the process of being sold.[16]

With the Wyndham Act the coping-stone was placed on the whole edifice of constructive Unionism, but while the Act undoubtedly fulfilled the immediate and urgent need of ending the land war, it did not, as its sponsors had hoped, inaugurate a new era in Irish politics. Wyndham himself wanted to march on from this triumph to the solution of the university problem, and some at least of the members of the Land Conference were no less eager to see if the same technique of friendly bargaining round the table could be applied to other vexed questions.* For a brief period in 1903 and 1904 it seemed, in short, that Ireland might witness a new and staggering phenomenon – the emergence of a third force divorced equally from orthodox Unionism and orthodox nationalism and pledged to the settlement by consent of all contentious issues short of Home Rule.

The history of this experiment was short, squalid and, in a wider sense, tragic. Each conciliatory group in turn was struck down within its own camp. O'Brien was the first to feel the weight of his colleagues'

* Captain Shawe-Taylor did actually send another letter to the press in September 1903 proposing a further conference – this time on the university question. The Earl of Dunraven was also known to be interested in settling that question by consent and Wyndham himself only abandoned the idea very reluctantly.

disapproval. The running criticism which had accompanied the passage of Wyndham's legislation through parliament became louder and more precise once the Act had passed into law. O'Brien, who had become obsessed with the great future he predicted for the policy of 'conference plus business', was too ready to dismiss this criticism as factious. But it was not. It was, on the contrary, extremely formidable, since its chief exponents were Michael Davitt, John Dillon and the *Freeman's Journal*. We can see now that their objections to the terms offered to the landlords, and to the financial clauses of the Act in general, had more substance than O'Brien was prepared to allow, but he was right in diagnosing their opposition as much more than technical. What they, and Dillon in particular, were attacking was the doctrine which underlay the Land Conference, the doctrine that it was possible to settle the great issues that divided Irishmen by the methods of conciliation. What Dillon feared especially was that this process of progressive amelioration of specific grievances would lead in the end to a weakening of the national demand and that the Home Rule movement itself would be undermined by the insidious effects of co-operation with Unionists who, however benevolent, were and remained dedicated to the maintenance of the British connection. When in 1903 Redmond, confronted with this new split in his party, threw in his lot with the critics of landlordism, O'Brien retaliated by resigning. For a time he was absent from politics through ill-health and although after his return he was re-admitted to the party for a brief space, he soon withdrew again to pursue in increasing isolation a policy which, though generous and honourable in itself, seemed as time went on more and more unrelated to the ugly facts of Irish political reality.

The landlords with whom O'Brien had hoped to inaugurate a new golden age of co-operation were the Earl of Dunraven and his friends. This group, calling themselves the Land Committee, had kept up their contacts with each other during 1903 and 1904. The success of the Conference, Dunraven later recalled, had set them thinking 'whether the political problem . . . might not be solved by the same means'.[17] Accordingly in 1904 the Committee reconstituted itself as the Irish Reform Association and in August of that year issued a preliminary report describing the aims of the new body. These could be summed up in the single word 'devolution'. All that this meant in effect was that while proclaiming their loyalty to the Union, these reforming landlords wanted to see Ireland given more extended powers of local government. In drafting their proposals, and especially a more detailed second manifesto issued in September 1904, the Reform Association enlisted the aid of the Under-Secretary at Dublin Castle – that is, the permanent head of the Irish administration. This was Sir Antony MacDonnell, an Irish Roman Catholic who had had a distinguished career in the Indian Civil Service. In 1902 George Wyndham persuaded him to come and help him in Dublin even though he knew that MacDonnell had a brother in the Irish parliamentary party and was a self-confessed Liberal in politics with 'strong Irish sympathies'. MacDonnell was a forceful and choleric character (even his friends called him 'the Bengal tiger'), but he was a very able man and seems to have accepted the Irish appointment mainly because it offered exceptional scope for his undeniable administrative talent. But Dublin Castle was less exalted than the Council of India, on which he had been offered a seat, and he only agreed to come to Ireland in the belief that he would have a greater say in policy-making than Under Secretaries were usually permitted.

The document which MacDonnell helped Dunraven to produce (perhaps it would be more accurate to say, produced for him) looked forward to the creation of financial and legislative councils for Ireland, to be endowed with considerable powers of local government and the ability to raise and spend certain categories of revenue. This was still not Home Rule, but it was a considerable step in that direction. MacDonnell believed that he had covered himself with his superiors by telling the Lord Lieutenant what he was doing and by writing to Wyndham explaining that he was helping Dunraven. He was considerably taken aback, therefore, when Wyndham at once publicly repudiated the devolution proposals in a letter to *The Times*. Apparently, he had not grasped the import of MacDonnell's letter; worse, he had mislaid it so effectively that it was not found until several years afterwards. What made the gap in communication between the two men so serious was that from the moment the detailed scheme appeared it came under fire from almost the entire body of Irish Unionism, affronted both by the scheme itself and by the well-founded suspicion that Sir Antony MacDonnell, whose official business it was to uphold the existing form of government, had been at the bottom of the Irish Reform Association's proposals. That any government, much less a Unionist government, should even seem to countenance devolution was at once interpreted as an incipient surrender to Home Rule and all through the autumn and winter of 1904–5 the agitation against the Under Secretary and his supposed nefarious plans grew and swelled. It had in the end two major consequences. One was that in Ulster – where feeling ran particularly high – an Ulster Unionist Council was set up with the object of linking the main organs of Unionism in the north – especially the local constituency associations and the Orange lodges – in a common organisation 'with a view to consistent and continuous political action'. The Council, which took shape at the end of 1904 but was only formally constituted in March 1905, at once became the rallying-point of the more intransigent Unionists and if, in years to come, *Ulster* Unionism seemed to be both more articulate and more forceful than *Irish* Unionism, some at least of the explanation is to be found in the stimulus provided by the devolution crisis.

The second consequence of that crisis was entirely predictable. When parliament assembled early in 1905 and the attack on Sir Antony reached a new crescendo of violence, he naturally defended himself by obliging his superiors to admit the steps he had taken to keep them informed. For them, and for Wyndham especially, to make this admission was in effect to admit responsibility, and when it emerged in the course of debate that the Under Secretary had been encouraged on his appointment to believe that he would exercise an influence on policy greater than that normally allowed to permanent officials, the fury of the Ulster Unionists knew no bounds. Wyndham, his health and nerve both broken, was obliged to resign and his career never recovered from this disaster. Sir Antony remained in office, and was indeed to help the Liberal government to plan an alternative scheme of devolution only two years later, but for the remainder of the Unionist tenure of power – that is until the end of 1905 – strict orthodoxy was the order of the day.[18]

In retrospect the devolution crisis may seem a storm in a teacup. The devolution proposals were an interesting new departure, but they were a long way from Home Rule and in any event never came remotely near being put to the test. Yet in reality the episode was one of fundamental importance, for it demonstrated conclusively the limits of constructive Unionism at both the official and the unofficial levels. Part of the apprehensions which sprang into life in 1904 and 1905 probably owed their origins to an increasing distrust amongst the mass of ordinary Unionists of the extent to which the government, at least from the time of Gerald Balfour onwards, had seemed bent on placating the spirit of nationalism. And it was in the nature of things that just as Dillon, on the one side, distrusted the policy of conciliation as undermining the demand for Home Rule, so on the other side, the Ulster Unionists saw in it a direct threat to the Union. The whole affair was a classical instance of the kind of fate that lies in wait for moderation in a political climate where extremes predominate.

The collapse of the devolution proposals marked also the effective end of the unofficial thrust towards constructive Unionism. Lord Dunraven did not, indeed, surrender easily and he continued for several years to attempt to reach a *modus vivendi* with William O'Brien. But it was a vain endeavour, since each of them was to all intents and purposes an outlaw from his own side. Even at the height of his expectations Dunraven had never succeeded in converting the great bulk of the Ascendancy class. The Irish Reform Association attracted consistent support only from about thirty landlords and the motives of its members in supporting devolution are by no means clear.* But in the present state of our knowledge it is reasonable to suppose that they, like Sir Horace Plunkett, had realised that the changes in local government and in land ownership had set a term to the social and administrative dominance of the gentry in the Irish countryside. If there was to be any future for them and their descendants it must be a future not only within the empire (on this they were all agreed) but a future in which Ireland would

---

* The history of the Irish landed gentry at this crisis in their affairs is at present being investigated by Professor L. P. Curtis and we may expect the whole question of 'constructive Unionism' to be illuminated by his researches.

have the kind of institutions and governmental structure that would allow them to participate and contribute from the by no means contemptible expertise which they, as a governing class of long standing, possessed. The tragedy of Irish Unionism is that so few of this class could see the writing on the wall, or could react to it in any way but by clinging stubbornly to a status quo which many of them must have known in their hearts was doomed. With a dour, indomitable spirit they dedicated themselves to the simple proposition that the Union must be maintained in all its integrity and that anything that weakened it must be *ipso facto* opposed. Or, as one of the most literate of them – Edward Dowden, in his day a celebrated Professor of English at Trinity College – put it in a single lapidary sentence: 'The logic of the situation will not be altered; two ideas, essentially antagonistic, will confront each other – now as in 1886 – until one or the other has obtained the mastery.'[19]

5. The Battle of Two Civilisations

Nineteenth century Europe produced many instances of the importance of language, literature and history in the awakening or resurrection of a sense of nationality amongst oppressed or subject peoples. Of this general tendency Ireland is usually held to be one of the supreme examples, but, although there is a basis of truth to the claim, it cannot be accepted without some qualification. In its simplest form the claim is based on the argument that in the 1840s Thomas Davis and his friends did for their country what Mazzini had done for his, and this is an argument not to be despised. Most historians would probably agree that the tradition which looks back to the young men of the *Nation* newspaper, and to Davis in particular, as the first to recognise, in Patrick Pearse's later phrase, that a 'nationality is a spirituality', is a well-founded tradition.

Yet it was not a tradition that rooted itself immediately in the popular mind or imagination. On the contrary, for forty years after Davis's death, the forces destructive of Irish nationality seemed far stronger than those working in its favour. When Davis wrote in praise of the Gaelic tongue it was still the language of perhaps a million and a half of his fellow-countrymen. But even then the position of Gaelic in the cultural life of Ireland was being undermined and the events of the next few years completed its downfall. With the peasantry decimated by famine, disease and emigration, with the growth of a system of primary education deliberately modelled on that of England, and with English beckoning as the only avenue to profitable employment at home and abroad, it was no wonder that Irish retreated to the more inaccessible parts of the west and south, or to the surf-bound islands off the Atlantic coast. To all intents and purposes it must have seemed by the third quarter of the nineteenth century that the tongue of the foreigner had finally triumphed.

However, at the very time when Irish was ceasing to be the possession of the people, it was passing into the care of the scholars and antiquarians, not to be mummified, but to be revivified by new discoveries and publications. An interest in the Irish past, and especially in Irish literature and antiquities, stretched as far back as the seventeenth century, and although some of this enthusiasm – provoked, at least in part, by a reaction against the Ossianic cult – was dilettante and jejune, it produced a notable institution, the Royal Irish Academy (founded in 1785) which was to stand at the centre of much of the serious research done on the sources of Irish civilisation during the nineteenth century.*

* The part played by James Macpherson's *Lays of Ossian* in influencing

As that century progressed, scholars, working either as individuals or in groups, or through specialist societies – ranging from the Gaelic Society (founded in 1806) to the Irish Archaeological Society, the Celtic Society and the Ossianic Society (the last three active mainly between 1840 and 1860) – began to uncover more and more of what slowly came to be seen as the evidence of a rich and splendid history. Whether they were men of native stock, like John O'Donovan and Eugene O'Curry, or Anglo-Irish like George Petrie, Sir Samuel Ferguson, Sir William Wilde and Whitley Stokes, or philologists of the German school from Jakob Grimm to Ernst Windisch and Kuno Meyer, they were driven by the same passion – to secure for the language, the monuments and the literature of an ancient country their proper place in the history of western culture.[1]

This was work of fundamental importance, and out of it was later to come a much more dynamic movement, but in the short run it had little to offer the spirit of nationality, since its leading figures were either academics or men of letters, unwilling or unable to emerge from their libraries into the hurly-burly of political life. What was most needed, therefore, was some new development which would appeal directly to the mass of the people. Attempts were made to reach them, it is true, through the more popular newspapers of the 'sixties – the *Nation*, for example, or the *Shamrock* – and about the same time the Fenian, O'Donovan Rossa, taught Irish classes at the Mechanics' Hall in Dublin before more violent patriotism absorbed him, but all such efforts, sporadic and ill-organised as they were, were doomed to failure. When a significant success was at last achieved, it came about in quite a different way. While the Irish language had faded, the playing of Irish games, especially hurling, had never completely died out, for in the country districts such games offered one of the few forms of entertainment to be had. In the towns, on the other hand, although Trinity College had a hurling club dating from the 1860s, the games and sports that tended to be most played were those of English origin. Athletics particularly, since the military and the police took them seriously, and also because they were inexpensive, spread far and wide. But athletic meetings were conducted, naturally enough, under the rules of the Irish Amateur Athletic Association, an Anglo-Irish body concerned, obviously, with the development of what were in reality English sports. In short, the same fate of Anglicisation which had already overtaken academic education, seemed likely to overwhelm physical recreation also.

At this point, however, an organised resistance began to develop. It was led by a remarkable man, Michael Cusack. An Irish-speaker and a

poetic taste in England is well-known; what is less well-known is that in constructing his pseudo-Scottish epics he used Irish material which stimulated Irishmen to look more deeply into their own past. One of those so stimulated was a Limerick doctor, Sylvester O'Halloran, who played a notable part in the foundation of the Royal Irish Academy.

native of county Clare, he had built up in Dublin what was in effect a cramming school, the Civil Service Academy, turning out candidates for the various branches of government service. In 1883, under his auspices, the Civil Service Academy Hurling Club was founded and the following year, after a newspaper controversy over the control of athletics by the Irish Amateur Athletic Association, Cusack declared his intention of creating a rival organisation to foster native games and sports. Cusack was a large, bearded, tweedy and altogether formidable man. He appears as 'The Citizen' in Joyce's *Ulysses*, and no doubt many experienced the same sort of treatment that he meted out to Leopold Bloom. Indeed, so dictatorial was he that his resignation from his own organisation was forced only eighteen months after he had launched it. But he had drive and ability – and he also had contact with the Fenians. When, on 1 November 1884, he founded the Gaelic Athletic Association at Thurles in county Tipperary at least four of the seven men who attended the meeting were Fenians. This connection between the GAA and the extreme wing of the nationalist movement was never lost. The police no doubt attached an exaggerated importance to the connection when they included, as they consistently did, reports on the GAA among their files relating to secret societies, but they were perfectly right in recognising the potentially revolutionary spirit that permeated this outwardly innocent association.[2]

This is not to say that revolution was regarded as in any sense an immediate objective. Two thousand GAA hurlers might march at Parnell's funeral in tribute to his supposed extremism in the last months of his life, and many were to be found amongst the militants when the critical moment came. But that critical moment was still a generation away, and in the meantime the GAA, as it spread rapidly through the country, achieved three very different purposes. In the first place, it encouraged local patriotism. Competitions on a county basis were organised in both Gaelic football and hurling and these soon became, as they still are, the focus of passionate enthusiasm. Secondly, the GAA inculcated among its members an uncompromising hostility to foreign games. The tone for this was set from the start by Archbishop Croke, the first patron of the infant association. For him the prevailing fashion for English sports was part and parcel of a general betrayal of the national heritage:

Indeed, [he wrote] if we continue travelling for the next score years in the same direction that we have been going in for some time past, condemning the sports that were practised by our forefathers, effacing our national features as though we were ashamed of them, and putting on, with England's stuffs and broadcloths her masher habits, and such other effeminate follies as she may recommend, we had better at once, and publicly, abjure our nationality. . . .[3]

The consequences of this attitude were more extreme than Croke, or perhaps even Cusack, had anticipated. For the GAA developed this anti-English conception to an almost fanatical degree, initiating a highly controversial ban upon all English games – that is to say prohibiting its members either from playing such games or becoming in any way associated with them.

There remains one final achievement of the GAA. It not only revived the Irishman's local pride in his county, but his national pride in his country. The currents of thought and feeling that were beginning to excite the intellectuals, the thrill of participation in great events that could occasionally come to the townsman, were not for him, living out his laborious life in a fast-emptying landscape. What he needed was something that would catch his imagination by its colour and movement and at the same time recall to him an aspect of the Irish civilisation to which he was, however impoverished, the heir. This, more than any other agency, the Gaelic Athletic Association achieved, and this was its chief contribution to the revival of national feeling in rural Ireland.

But revolutions are made with ideas, not hurley sticks. It was still necessary to give to Irish nationalism an intellectual basis more profound and exacting than an amiable enthusiasm for Gaelic pastimes or a less amiable detestation of 'foreign' games. Such a basis was soon to be provided with the launching of the Gaelic League in 1893. Of all the factors influencing the rise of a new and urgent sense of nationality at the end of the nineteenth century, this has come to be regarded as perhaps the most significant, though at the time of its foundation that would have been difficult to predict. In its earliest days there was little to show that it was any different in character, or likely to have any different future, from the scholarly societies already mentioned. Indeed, its progenitors sprang from an environment very similar to that of the earlier enthusiasts for the language. Three stood out above all others. One, Father Eugene O'Growney, was Professor of Irish at Maynooth and author of one of the best-known textbooks for the study of the language. The second was Eoin MacNeill. MacNeill was born in 1867 at Glenarm, county Antrim, a small Catholic island in a sea of Protestantism. Educated privately and at St Malachy's College, Belfast, his bent was towards Irish history and literature even while, as a young man, he had to earn a living as a junior clerk in the civil service. It was MacNeill who first suggested the formation of a new movement to take the Irish language to the people, but it was the third member of the triumvirate, Douglas Hyde, who was to be its most persuasive apostle. Hyde, the son of a Church of Ireland rector, was born in Sligo in 1863, and grew up at French Park in the neighbouring county of Roscommon. He first learnt Irish from the country people round his home and when he went to Trinity College, Dublin, drifted naturally enough into the Society for the Preservation of the Irish Language, which had been founded in the capital in 1877. When that body went the way of so many others – split into dissident fragments – Hyde transferred his allegiance to the Gaelic Union and under its aegis began to write the first of his poems in Irish. Being, however, a member of the Anglo-Irish ascendancy, he was also open to the influences – soon to be discussed – which at that very time were drawing the young Yeats, T. W. Rolleston and some others towards the notion of a literature which, while written in English, should owe its inspiration to the Irish past. This group of writers mingled in yet another tiny association, the Pan-Celtic Society, and also collaborated in producing in 1888 a volume, *Poems and Ballads of Young Ireland*, dedicated to the old Fenian, John O'Leary.

Out of these slight beginnings Yeats and Hyde hoped to evolve a whole school of literature and as a means towards that end they founded the Irish Literary Society in London at the end of 1891, followed in May 1892 by the National Literary Society with its base in Dublin.* It was to the latter group that Hyde delivered, in November 1892, the lecture which first won him a wide audience.[4] It was called 'The Necessity for de-Anglicising Ireland', and it was from first to last a plea to his fellow-countrymen to turn away from things English before they lost irretrievably the sense of a separate nationality. 'It has always been very curious to me', he observed, 'how Irish sentiment sticks in this half-way house – how it continues to apparently hate the English, and at the same time continues to imitate them; how it continues to clamour for recognition as a distinct nationality, and at the same time throws away with both hands what would make it so.'[5] The remedy, he insisted, was to recover as much as possible from the native past of the country, its language, its manners and customs, its games, its place-names and surnames. But his principal point was that Irishmen should forthwith abandon English books and periodicals as their staple reading. What should they put in place of this 'garbage', as he called it? Hyde's answer is illuminating. He did not suggest the classics of Gaelic literature because he knew very well that they were out of reach of all save a tiny minority. Instead, he recommended to them the works of Tom Moore and of Davis – in other words, the precursors of the Anglo-Irish literature to which Hyde himself at that time was committed. From this, he asserted, Irishmen would derive a sense of what was 'most racial, most smacking of the soil', and this would be the best protection against English influences. But if this protection were not achieved, 'we will become what, I fear, we are largely at present, a nation of imitators,

* The inaugural lecture to the Irish National Literary Society (16 August 1892) was delivered by Dr George Sigerson who besides being a celebrated Dublin doctor and an even more celebrated Dublin host, linked in his own person the beginnings of the climax of the literary revival. Born in 1839, he was Hyde's predecessor in the collection and translation of Irish poetry, his *Poets and Poetry of Munster* having appeared as early as 1860 (in continuation of a similar volume compiled by James Clarence Mangan, the tortured and gloomy poet of the 1830s who died young and is remembered chiefly by one poem 'The Dark Rosaleen' and by the fact that both Yeats and Joyce were influenced by him in their early days). A few years after the foundation of the Literary Societies Sigerson produced (in 1897) his *Bards of the Gael and Gall*, an astonishing feat of exact, yet musical, translation from Irish into English.

the Japanese of western Europe, lost to the power of native initiative and alive only to second-hand assimilation'.[6]

In reality, the attempt to cultivate Irish patriotism through the medium of the old-style Anglo-Irish literature was a compromise which pleased nobody. It certainly did not satisfy the language enthusiasts, nor, as we shall see presently, did it satisfy Yeats, to whom the 'de-Davisisation' of literature was coming to seem just as important as the de-Anglicisation of Ireland was to Hyde. When, therefore, the following year MacNeill made his proposal for a popular language movement, Hyde, whose genuine enthusiasm for Irish no-one could doubt, eagerly fell in with it, and on 31 July 1893 the Gaelic League was founded, with Hyde as its first president. Its aims were simply and briefly stated. There were, originally, only two – first, the preservation of Irish as the national language of the country, and the extension of its use as the spoken tongue; and second, the study and publication of existing Gaelic literature, and the cultivation of a modern literature in Irish. The new body was to be primarily propagandist and to Hyde himself it was of cardinal importance that it should not be identified with any particular political group or allegiance. If he had abandoned Davis's notion of an Irish literature in English, he still clung, and was always to cling, to Davis's other and more comprehensive concept of a national regeneration that should find room for men of all origins, creeds and classes.

In later years this doctrine of political neutrality became more and more difficult to maintain – it had its critics from the beginning – and Hyde himself was eventually (in 1915) to resign the presidency on this issue. But that was for the future. First there were to be the golden, strenuous years of growth, slow at first then steadily accelerating until by 1908 there were some 600 registered branches. By that date one of the League's key practical objectives – the introduction of the teaching of Irish into the National (i.e. primary) Schools – had been effectively achieved. And not only that, but a successful battle had also been fought against an attempt to exclude Irish from the programme of the secondary schools. More striking still, Hyde himself in 1909 led the victorious campaign to include Irish as a compulsory subject for matriculation in the newly established National University.

All this activity brought Hyde and his friends – their protestations notwithstanding – very close to politics, but there were those who said they should be closer still. The young William Rooney, for example, who was with Arthur Griffith one of the progenitors of Sinn Féin,* pointed out at the turn of the century that to avoid politics was a mistake 'in an organisation which has charged itself with the promotion of Irish nationality'. If they really wanted to make Irish the language of the country that would mean agitation, 'but agitation means politics, more or less, and the movement has got to face it, if it is not to come to a standstill'.[7] Yet Rooney, like Hyde, was realist enough to know that the country could not be expected to become Gaelic overnight and,

* See pp. 248-9

again like Hyde, he saw in the Anglo-Irish literature that was already available a substitute, at least for the time being:

Nothing less than a miracle, [he truly observed] could give us at once Gaelic readers; and we must read something if we are to remain reasonable beings. This Anglo-Irish literature, which certainly mirrors the life of the Ireland that is presently ours provides us with the necessary material. It is not perfection of Irish thought . . . but it is a saving salt that will secure the heart of the country from complete decay.[8]

There were others, however, who saw in the Anglo-Irish tradition only a threat to true nationality, the more dangerous precisely because it was so appealing. Early in the new century they found a trenchant spokesman. This was D. P. Moran, a Waterford man by birth, but a London journalist by profession. It was a profession in which he became highly expert, writing a sharp, pugnacious prose that reflected a sharp, pugnacious mind. Moran had made contact with the Irish Literary Society in London in the 'nineties and when he returned to Ireland it was with the avowed object of fostering the language. But it was characteristic of him that his approach was totally different from that of the scholars and men of letters who had so far dominated the movement. Moran's object was to destroy the comforting vagueness in which so many nationalist aspirations were shrouded. Sham patriotism, muddled thinking, ill-directed enthusiasm, cant (or *ráimeis*, to use the Irish expression which he succeeded in making almost a household word) of all kinds – these were the enemies he attacked and in attacking them spared neither institution nor individual, however venerable or venerated. Something of his quality appeared in articles he published in the *New Ireland Review* from 1898 onwards, but it was with the foundation in 1900 of his own weekly paper, the *Leader*, of which he remained editor and proprietor for the next thirty-six years, that he first began to strike home to a wider audience.

Moran's interest in the language was genuine and very fundamental to him, but it was by no means the only facet of his nationalism. On the contrary, he saw the language revival essentially as the means to a greater end. That end was the recreation of Irish independence, interpreted not in terms of political gestures, however extreme, but rather in terms of independence of mind and attitude. Moran's nationalism, or, as he called it in his best-known work, his 'Philosophy of Irish Ireland', had both its positive and its negative aspects. On the positive side, in addition to encouraging the language enthusiasts he opened his columns to the efforts of Edward Martyn and others to improve the standards of Irish taste in music, architecture, sculpture, stained-glass and painting, especially where these were connected, as they mostly were, with church-building. More than this, he conducted a running fight against the social evils he saw around him – drunkenness, slum-housing, recruitment of ignorant youths into the British Army, malnutrition and the manifold diseases that carried off the poor in their thousands. Above all, he identified himself with what might be called 'voluntary protectionism'. Week in, week out, he urged his readers to buy Irish wherever possible, and contemporaries, when they regarded him, even more perhaps than Griffith, as the chief protagonist of the Irish industrial movement, showed a sound instinct. Here again, industrial initiative, like linguistic initiative, was for him part of a larger pattern which he summed up in the very first number of the *Leader*. The Irish nation as he conceived it would be, he wrote.

a self-governing land, living, moving and having its being in its own language, self-reliant, intellectually as well as politically independent, initiating its own reforms, developing its own manners and customs, creating its own literature out of its own distinctive consciousness, working to their fullest capacity the material resources of the country, inventing, criticising, attempting, doing.[9]

But the negative side to Moran's philosophy was no less important. Vigorous assailant of *ráimeis* that he was, he was sharply critical of what passed for patriotism in his day. This criticism took several forms. One was a campaign of constant denigration of the Irish parliamentary party at Westminster whom he regarded as imitation Englishmen making ludicrously ineffective attempts to play the game of English politics. Just as much as Griffith, Moran must be regarded as one of those most instrumental in undermining the whole constitutional movement, a fact only realised by the parliamentarians themselves, if at all, when it was too late. It was not just the Home Rulers who aroused his ridicule. Sinn Féin, with its strongly political programme, seemed to him equally at sea, even though he agreed with Griffith's economic objectives. The 'Green Hungarian Band', as he contemptuously christened the Sinn Féiners, had gone astray, he suggested, when they nailed their flag to the masthead of the 1782 constitution: *

When we look back upon 1782 from 1899, we see it not in the halo of a glorious victory, but in the shape of an animated skull grinning at us, an emblem of victory perhaps – the victory of death. It did not mark a noble but a disastrous epoch and turning point in Irish history. It sent us adrift in a new world by which we were first corrupted and then eaten up; it set up a new temple before which we have burned incense, and have made the greatest sacrifice in our power – the sacrifice of our national character.[10]

In attacking the constitution of 1782 Moran had at least this much historical justification, that insofar as it was a victory at all, it was a victory for the Protestant Ascendancy and not for the Irish nation. But when he went on from there to attack the whole range of nationalist activity from Wolfe Tone to Parnell he put himself at risk. To *épater les bourgeois* was one thing, to deride the entire nationalist canon was quite another. And it led him into palpable absurdities. It was, perhaps, just

* For the 1782 constitution, and its importance to Griffith, see below, chap. 6.

possible to uphold the paradox of defining Wolfe Tone as a Frenchman born in Ireland of English parents, but to say of him that he was no more extreme a rebel than the Bishop of Derry was to make nonsense of history.* O'Connell got off more lightly, but even he was condemned for turning his back upon the language. 'He was a giant, but like all of us he was hood-winked by the new interpretation of nationality sprung upon the country by the Glorious Constitution of 1782. He did more than any other man, because he was a giant, to kill the Gaelic language and the distinctive character of the people.'[11] As for 'the second-rate 48 men', they were 'large-hearted, well-intentioned fools whom we magnify into great heroes', and whose only achievement was to knock a few more nails into the Gaelic coffin. Even Fenianism, though men had died or gone into jail for it, was empty, operatic gesturing which had led nowhere and never would.[12]

Why all these sweeping condemnations? For one central reason – because, in Moran's view, all the political solutions that had been proposed hitherto had been concerned essentially with independence, not with the re-creation of nationalism. 'We are proud', he wrote, 'of Grattan, Flood, Tone, Emmet, and all the rest who dreamt and worked for an independent country, even though they had no conception of an Irish nation; but it is necessary that they should be put in their place, and that place is not on the top . . . The foundation of Ireland is the Gael and the Gael must be the element that absorbs.'[13] Or, as he put it in that most seminal of all his essays, 'The Battle of Two Civilisations':

In Grattan's time Irish civilisation was thrown overboard; but Irish 'nationality' was stuck up on a flag of green – even the colour was new fledged – and the people were exhorted to go forward and cover themselves with glory. If I am right in equating nationality with a distinct civilisation, we get now a vivid glimpse of the first great source of the insincerity – all the more insidious because unconscious – the muddled thinking, the confusion of ideas, the contradictory aims which even the most cursory observer discerns in the Ireland of today. Since Grattan's time every popular leader, O'Connell, Butt, Parnell, Dillon and Redmond, has perpetuated this primary contradiction. They threw over Irish civilisation whilst they professed – and professed in perfect good faith – to fight for Irish nationality.[14]

This conception of two civilisations – the Pale (or the British connection) versus the Gael, the Anglo-Irish versus the Irish – was absolutely fundamental to Moran's thought and it accounts for much of the intransigence, even bitterness, to be found in his writings. Sometimes this expressed itself in tasteless and rather childish name-calling. Protestants

* The reference here was to Frederick Augustus Hervey, the wealthy and eccentric Earl of Bristol and Bishop of Derry. He had taken a characteristically extravagant part in the Volunteer movement which had led to the winning of the 'constitution of 1782' but he was a lightweight in politics and is better remembered as an inveterate traveller who has given his name to innumerable 'Hotels Bristol' all over Europe.

were 'sour-faces'; the Anglo-Irish were 'West-Britons'; persons of native Irish stock who committed the unforgiveable sin of aping English or West-Briton manners and attitudes were 'shoneens', and so on. But this was only a surface manifestation of something far deeper – Moran's intense conviction of the necessity to throw off every kind of attachment to things English. This led him to look with the most implacable intolerance upon the Anglo-Irish, and especially upon those who sought to involve themselves in the life of the country.

At any time such rebuffs would have been injurious, but coming just at that precise moment they had important and unforeseeable consequences. For at last and after many generations some at least of the Anglo-Irish were deliberately cutting themselves loose from the prejudices and interests of their class and beginning, slowly and painfully, to make common cause with those amongst whom they had lived for so long as an alien garrison. Broadly speaking this movement 'to the people' took two forms – one primarily social and economic, the other primarily intellectual and artistic – though in such a small and closely interwoven minority the same people were sometimes to be found active on both fronts. We have already seen something of the socio-economic movement of which the chief monuments were Sir Horace Plunkett's pioneering work in agricultural co-operation, the creation of the Department of Agriculture and Technical Instruction, and the conciliatory policy of Lord Dunraven and other landlords leading to, and stemming from, the Land Conference. Now it is time to consider the other aspect of this Anglo-Irish metamorphosis, which revealed itself in essence as a prolonged and brilliant attempt to create an Irish literature – predominantly poetic and dramatic – in the English language.

Why at the turn of the century there should have been such a remarkable outpouring of Anglo-Irish talent, even of genius, still remains something of a mystery. It has been plausibly suggested that the artists and writers who were most productive at this period were the first generation to have grown up in the realisation that the ascendancy of the caste to which they belonged was no longer secure and inevitable. The disestablishment of the Church of Ireland in 1869, the Land War, Gladstone's legislation of 1881 making the tenant a partner in the soil with the landlord, the growth of land purchase under subsequent Tory governments, the coming of the county councils in 1898, above all the adoption of Home Rule as official Liberal policy – all these things, it is argued, were the writing on the wall for a whole social order, in fact for a whole way of life. That there was malaise and uneasiness, and even an anxiety to come to terms with the new situation before it was too late, is not to be denied. Nor can it be denied that this anxiety reflected itself not just among landlords with an eye to the main chance, but among men of intellect and imagination as well. It was no accident, for example, that the summons to the Land Conference which prepared the way for the far-reaching Wyndham Act of 1903 came from Lady Gregory's nephew, Captain John Shawe-Taylor, nor that a few years later the magnificent conception to create and endow a gallery of modern art in Dublin came from another of her nephews, Hugh Lane. It was no accident either that Sir Horace Plunkett, of all Anglo-Irish landlords the most active and fertile in reform, should have been in touch with Lady Gregory and her circle as early as 1896, that in 1897 he should have enlisted the poet and mystic George Russell (AE) to help in his co-operative work, and that by 1899 he should have been characteristically organising 'a dinner-party with an object, viz. the further promotion of co-operation between the practical men and the dreamers of Ireland, George Moore, Yeats and Edward Martyn, Lady Betty [Balfour] and Lady Gregory'.[15]

It would be a mistake, however, to attribute the cultural renaissance simply to a sudden access of patriotism, or to a death-bed repentance, on the part of the entire Anglo-Irish ascendancy. For one thing, most of them – landlords and middle-class alike – remained serenely wedded to their traditional life-style, as loyal as ever to the Union, and as blind to Irish Ireland as if it had never existed. And for another thing, the renaissance itself was the work of a quite small and closely-knit group who were exposed to certain very specific influences. Briefly, these might be described as theosophy, occultism and magic, Irish fairy-tales and folklore, the Celtic sagas, geography and politics. Esoteric Buddhism, or Madame Blavatsky's version of it, might seem a far cry from a literary revival, but the mysticism which informs, say, Yeats's early Irish plays or the poetry of AE, owes much to the capacity of both men to see visions and dream dreams, a capacity powerfully reinforced in AE's case by his theosophy and in Yeats's case by the ease with which he passed and repassed from theosophy to occultism and thence to the cabbalistic magic of the Hermetic Students of the Golden Dawn. On the more mundane level, the societies or organisations thrown up in the 'eighties and 'nineties to propagate these various doctrines provided a whole series of meeting-places at which the devotees could test their theories and share their experiences. Such, especially, was the Dublin Hermetic Society, founded in 1885 and becoming a Theosophical Lodge the following year, which brought together such diverse characters as W. K. Magee (John Eglinton) whom Yeats had known at the High School, Dublin; AE, whom he had first met at art school; and the old Fenian, John O'Leary, who had returned to the city from exile in 1884 and to whose romantic nationalism Yeats was soon to succumb. Yeats himself did not join the Dublin lodge – his family went to live in London in 1887 and he took his theosophy neat from the fountainhead at Madame Blavatsky's London lodge, just as he got his magic direct from the society of The Golden Dawn when it was founded early in 1890.[16]

These preoccupations with mysticism and magic would in themselves have been an unpredictable force. What gave them potency and purpose was that Yeats and others – especially AE – allied to them a discovery both of the old heroes of the Irish sagas and of the wealth of fairy-tale material still extant in the countryside. From their theo-sophical inquiries, and particularly from Madame Blavatsky's *Secret Doctrine*, they had derived notions of the coming of a Messiah, and of a new revolutionary epoch springing from a great international war which both Yeats and AE had seen foreshadowed in separate visions in the year 1896. The visions, though fundamental to the artistic development of both men, do not concern us here except in one respect, that they linked the poets to an underground tradition in Ireland, cherished by the Fenians and eventually acted upon by the men of 1916, that the Irish would seize the chance of such a conflagration to assert their freedom.[17] That their dreams and musings upon the ancient gods be-came rooted in Celtic rather than eastern mythology was due primarily to the work of yet another Anglo-Irishman, Standish James O'Grady. His *History of Ireland* (the so-called 'Bardic History') had appeared in 1878 and 1880, opening the whole shadowy but exciting world of the sagas to the literary imagination. O'Grady was a Unionist in politics, and in some ways a rather reactionary one, but this early work of his was nevertheless of fundamental importance. No-one has described its effect better than AE:

> Years ago, [he wrote in 1902] in the adventurous youth of his mind, Mr O'Grady found the Gaelic tradition like a neglected antique *dun* with its doors barred, and there was little or no egress. Listening, he heard from within the hum of an immense chivalry, and he opened the doors and the wild riders went forth to work their will. Now he would recall them. But it is in vain.[18]

The other source, fairy-tale and folk-lore, was to be sought for not in libraries but in the homes of the people. Douglas Hyde had blazed the trail when he published his first volume of folk-stories (in Irish) in 1889. He had followed this in 1890 with a further instalment, and three years later, in Irish and in translation, with his beautiful *Lovesongs of Connacht* which, as Yeats remarked, 'were the coming of a new power into literature'. Yeats himself, though knowing no Irish and far less in-timate with peasant life than Hyde, had ventured into the field with two collections of tales published in 1888 and 1892. He continued this interest intermittently during the next few years, but it was not until he met Lady Gregory in 1896 and began to stay regularly at her home at Coole Park in county Galway, that he learned at first hand what a wealth of experience lay waiting to be transmuted into poetry and drama. Later, when their Irish theatre had become an established fact, Yeats and Lady Gregory would have to withstand the ironic criticism of Dubliners who rated each new play by PQ – peasant quality. But peasant quality, for good or ill, was embedded from the very beginning at the centre of the Anglo-Irish literary movement. The attitude of these early explorers towards the peasant was essentially romantic, for they saw in him a primal innocence miraculously preserved from the con-taminating influences of civilisation. It was reserved for the one dramatist of genius the movement produced, John Millington Synge, to present an earthier view of the countryman a few years later, but Synge, no less than the others, fell greedily upon the resources of idiom and rhythm this newly discovered world revealed.

The very fact that Hyde, Yeats, Lady Gregory and Synge should all have found the idiom and the rhythm so accessible was in itself no accident. It was a remarkable feature of their movement – and perhaps a partial explanation not only of its success, but of its *limited* success – that they should all have had, as did also George Moore and Edward Martyn, a common root in the west of Ireland. Hyde, as we have seen, grew up in Sligo and Roscommon. Yeats's family was based on Sligo town. George Moore, though long expatriate, was in fact an absentee Mayo landlord, and Edward Martyn's Galway estate was only a few miles from Lady Gregory's Coole Park. Even Synge, though his home was on the outskirts of Dublin, was a countryman by inclination, immersing himself in the life of the Wicklow glens or the Aran islands with a completeness his colleagues in the movement could never achieve. Although the group was divided by religion (Martyn being a fervent Catholic, Moore a lapsed Catholic, and the rest Protestant) all – save Yeats and AE – belonged to the gentry. They not only shared a common background of country life, they were in close physical communication with each other. It was precisely this intimacy, this possibility of discussing and planning in private without the distraction of public meetings and committees, which allowed the new movement to develop so fast and which also, it must be said, gave it from the outset a distinctly autocratic character.

One further element in the situation remains to be mentioned – the political vacuum created by Parnell's death and the breaking of his party into fragments which were still bitterly at war with one another at the very moment the new movement was being launched. The direct and powerful effect of the fall of Parnell upon the writers of the generation which came after him is one of the truisms of Irish literary history and the Parnell myth was to be as potent in the work of Joyce as in that of the Anglo-Irish group. For the latter the stricken leader was easily identifiable with the Celtic hero, Cu Chulain, to whom Standish O'Grady had introduced them, and the composite figure that emerged from their heightened imaginations prefigured the political Messiah implicit, and sometimes explicit, in so much of the writing of this time.*

Not, indeed, that the progenitors of the movement agreed among themselves about what their own political role should be. On the contrary, they diverged so much that no common role was possible. Hyde, as we know, was neutral. Martyn was attracted by Sinn Féin, though not permanently so. Yeats was for a time deeply involved – emotionally at any rate – with the republicans, partly because John O'Leary satisfied his romantic conception of a hero, and partly because after he met and fell in love with Maud Gonne in 1889, her commitment to extremism swept him, at first ecstatically then more reluctantly, in its train. Lady

* For the later influence of the Cu Chulain cult, see Part III, chap. 2.

Gregory, though broadly sympathetic to nationalism, was perhaps more interested in reconciling opposites than in defining differences and this was true of AE also. George Moore was incapable of a sustained political attitude and Synge was almost totally uninterested in such matters. But it was not the intention of these writers to appeal to particular sections or to specific political passions. On the contrary, the very fact that such passions seemed to them to be dead, and the residual controversies so stale, encouraged them to create a literature which would move men's minds and imaginations anew. Yet, because it was a literature about Ireland, whether based on the mythical hero or the actual peasant, it could not but rouse passions of its own.

Were these passions to be enlisted in support of the new movement or were they to be mobilised against it? In the answer to this question lies the key to a great part of the debate between the two civilisations which dominated Irish intellectual life between the death of Parnell and the Easter Rising. And it was not long before the question began to thrust itself forward. As we have seen, Yeats together with T. W. Rolleston (another young Irishman who had been influenced by Standish O'Grady), founded the Irish Literary Society of London in 1891, following it next year with the National Literary Society in Dublin. The intention was to win a public for the literature, folk-lore and legends of Ireland – at first sight nothing could be more worthy or more uncontroversial. Yet in reality it was not so. There was indeed an Irish public ready to turn from politics to literature. But by upbringing, education and inclination they understood by this the patriotic literature of Young Ireland – literature in English certainly, but recalling the Gaelic past and harnessing it to a doctrine of re-emergent nationality. Thus, when Yeats proposed an eminently practical scheme for setting up travelling libraries to circulate literature to the people, the battle was immediately joined on what literature this should be. There was a strong party, headed by Sir Charles Gavan Duffy and the cantankerous lawyer, J. F. Taylor, which took it for granted that all that was needed was to make the legacy of Young Ireland available as widely and cheaply as possible. Already, it seems, Yeats felt instinctively that the harking back to the stereotypes of the past would paralyse him or any other poet who strove to create something new and different. Argument raged furiously between the factions, but Yeats was overborne and when a scheme to publish works of Irish interest was transferred from his hands to those of Gavan Duffy he withdrew to London in disgust. The episode, trivial in itself, has a wider significance. It was the first note of discord in what was to become a cacophony. Yeats approached the Irish past not primarily as a patriot (though, since this was the period of his connection with the IRB, he could have claimed that his patriotism was ardent enough) but as an artist concerned above all to create. Those whom he sought to convince, however, were too long habituated to regard art as propaganda to be able to think of it as anything other than subservient to nationalism.[19]

It was this fundamental difference of conception that burst into the open with the launching of a far more ambitious project, the Irish Literary Theatre. Although Edward Martyn had confided to George Moore his ambition to write plays in Irish as far back as 1894, it was not until Martyn had made contact with Yeats, and both of them with Lady Gregory in 1897–8, that the idea of establishing a theatre began to take shape. It was decided to begin the experiment with Yeats's symbolic play, *The Countess Cathleen*, and an Ibsenite play by Martyn, *The Heather Field*. Even before it was produced, *The Countess Cathleen* aroused controversy and the actual first performance was a stormy foretaste of what was in store for any independent-minded dramatist who chose to interpret Irish themes in his own way. In his play, written several years earlier, Yeats had imagined two devils coming to Ireland to tempt the starving peasants to sell their souls for gold. The Countess Cathleen sacrifices her possessions so that she may buy food for the people, and is in the last resort prepared to sell her own soul for them. To Catholic nationalist opinion the very notion of any Irish man or woman agreeing to sell his soul was utterly repugnant and here, on the very first night of the new theatre, a central dilemma presented itself not merely for Yeats, but for all those members of the ascendancy class who were striving to express themselves in a way that should be nationalist but not subservient to any hallowed shibboleth. The problem was really twofold. First, it was the problem of securing a hearing for new ideas or new modes of expression which did not conform to the traditional Catholic and nationalist sanctities. And second, and not less important, it was the problem of securing a hearing for such work without it being condemned, not on aesthetic but on political grounds, as emanating from the Anglo-Irish who, by definition, were to be regarded as anti-Irish and hostile to everything that Irish Ireland stood for. Ominously, in 1899, just when *The Countess Cathleen* added fuel to the flames, that apostle of Irish Irelandism, D. P. Moran, was already attacking the very notion that 'the Celtic note' in literature could be the symbol of a national intellectual awakening. On the contrary, it was, he wrote, 'one of the most glaring frauds that the credulous Irish people ever swallowed'.[20]

What made the quarrel so bitter and confused was that it was really about two separate issues. One was the question of whether or not there could be an Irish literature in English. The other concerned the freedom of the artist to write what he liked and to use his art, in a phrase Yeats was fond of at that time, as 'a criticism of life'. Yet, although these were different issues, it was hard to keep them apart since the same people were involved in both sets of arguments and what started as a dispute about language was liable to end in a controversy about the function of art in relation to nationalism. Thus, while Hyde or William Rooney or Gavan Duffy might plead for a literature in Irish as the ultimate goal, they were all realistic enough to know that this was impossible in the immediate future, and that in default of a native

Gaelic literature Ireland must make do for the time being with the patriotic literature – in English – of Young Ireland. But to those who fought for the right of the artist to express himself in English as he wished this attitude was doubly offensive. Not only did the protagonists of Young Ireland glibly assume that art must of necessity minister to patriotism, but by postulating that it would eventually do so in Irish they set their course towards what seemed to Yeats and his group – ambitious to create a literature which, while Irish, would reach out towards Europe – a stifling parochialism. And it was, in fact, Yeats's school-friend John Eglinton who pointed out that this tendency, if pressed to its logical conclusion, would divide the country into two separate nationalities. 'Sooner or later', he added, 'Ireland will have to make up its mind that it is no longer the old Gaelic nation of the 5th or 12th, or even of the 18th century, but one which has been in the making ever since these islands were drawn into the community of nations by the Normans.'[21] To this the answer was that of course Ireland was not the Gaelic Ireland of earlier centuries, but neither was she part of the 'imperial people' of Britain. 'We are working', wrote W. P. Ryan* in reply to Eglinton, 'for a new Irish civilisation, quite distinct from the English'. It was, he said, the Gaelic Leaguers 'who see that once we are "at home" in our own language and literature, we may naturally and profitably proceed, if we have time and opportunity, to the acquisition of quite a number of others . . . But without our own we may be but cultured slaves and polished *seonini*.'[22]

Not so, replied Eglinton. The modern Irishman, whether he liked it or not, was the son of the *mariage de convenance* of the Union. As such he was in a perpetual dilemma :

On the one hand, the ties of nature, his chivalrous sense and compassion, constrain him to espouse the cause of his mother. On the other hand, it is easy to see that, however picturesque his mother may be as she sits crooning songs of hatred against her betrayer, a young nationality, with a world of new enterprise and purpose in his soul, new thought and invention in his brain, passion as yet unexpended in his heart, must find something lacking in a mental and spiritual attitude so uncompromisingly negative.

Was not the solution, therefore, an Irish literature in English and had not the great names of the past, Tom Moore and James Clarence Mangan, Samuel Ferguson and John Mitchel, provided the model?[23]

Did this, therefore mean that Eglinton, unlike Yeats, saw in Young

* W. P. Ryan was a journalist as able as D. P. Moran and in some ways resembling him in his enthusiasm for the Irish Ireland movement. For a time in the early years of the new century he ran a widely read paper, the *Irish Peasant*, until it fell foul of the Church and was obliged to close down, an episode described by Ryan himself in a novel, *The Plough and the Cross*. Ryan subsequently migrated to England and joined the staff of the *Daily Herald*, but his son, Desmond Ryan, was educated at Pearse's school, St Enda's, later becoming a leading authority on the Easter Rising and indeed on the whole Fenian tradition.

Ireland and that tradition the model for the future? In fact it did not, as he made plain a month or so later in an essay – 'The de-Davisisation of Irish Literature' – which defines as clearly as anything written at this time the standpoint of the Anglo-Irish. Davis, he pointed out, had reacted violently away from 'that damned thing, call it Yankeeism or Englishism . . . which measures prosperity by exchangeable value, measures duty by gain and limits desire to food, clothes and respectability'. Against this materialism Davis had evoked an image of Celtic Ireland, but in doing this 'he gave a sort of religious or idealistic status to modern Irish patriotism which it has retained: for since Davis the true religion of the Irish nationalist has been patriotism'. To insist, however, that 'Irishness' should be the touchstone of whatever new literature was to be written, was 'to transport literature in this country back to that point where Davis left it, to that region . . . in which all private differences are sunk and in which the Irishman has to speak in his national rather than in his human capacity'. But, Eglinton insisted, that was not good enough. And he continued:

> Literature must be free as the elements; if that is to be cosmopolitan, it must be cosmopolitan . . . and I should like to live to see the day of what might be called, without any disrespect to Davis, the de-Davisisation of Irish national literature, that is to say, the getting rid of the notion that in Ireland a writer is to think first and foremost of interpreting the nationality of his country, and not simply of the burden which he has to deliver. The expression of nationality, literature cannot fail to be; and the richer, the more varied and unexpected that expression, the better.[24]

Ironically, at the very same moment that Eglinton was indicting Davis and his school for subordinating art to nationalism, others were preparing to attack the Young Ireland tradition precisely because it had not been nationalistic enough. It was D. P. Moran, characteristically, who put this argument in its most uncompromising form. W. P. Ryan had written a little book criticising Davis on the ground that he did not at bottom stand for Irish Ireland. Quite right, said Moran:

> The Young Irelanders carried on a great error that had like to kill this nation. . . . One does not necessarily reflect on the nobility of character, the brilliant intellect, the courage of the Young Irelanders, when he asserts today that their efforts were vitiated in consequence of a fundamental error. Their country was Anglo-Ireland, but they called it in perfect good faith Ireland.[25]

It is easy to see what was happening. Young Ireland represented middle ground between the two civilisations; Davis, surely, if he stood for anything, stood for the reconciliation of the two civilisations. But in a time of increasing national self-consciousness this was no longer enough and the Davis tradition came under fire from both extremes – from those who found it fell short of their nationalist ideal, and from those who found it constricting precisely *because* of its intense preoccupation with nationalism.

It was perhaps inevitable that, having, as they believed, demolished Davis, the two extremes should then collide, and it was doubly inevitable that they should collide in the arena of the theatre which was to be the *national* theatre. In the years after its first stormy launching, it had in fact gone from strength to strength. There were still occasional growls from the Irish Irelanders – the version of Diarmuid and Grania which Moore and Yeats put on in 1901 was dismissed by Moran as 'a rather heartless piece of vandalism on a great Irish story' – but since they simultaneously produced *The Twisting of the Rope* (Hyde's Irish play) it seemed clear to the language enthusiasts that the theatre was serving at least some useful purpose. Indeed, the very next year Yeats himself achieved perhaps the apogee of his career as a nationalist writer with *Cathleen ni Houlihan,* the play he wrote for Maud Gonne, in which the old woman who symbolises Ireland, speaks of those who have helped her in the past and may yet die for her in the future. The emotional impact on contemporary audiences was intense and at least one observer went home asking himself if such plays should be produced 'unless one was prepared for people to go out to shoot and be shot'. The same thought troubled Yeats in old age when he asked himself the famous question which is neither so arrogant nor so pointless as it seems:

> Did that play of mine send out
> Certain men the English shot?[26]

In *Cathleen ni Houlihan* Yeats was able to write out of his own imagination upon a theme to which his audience was bound to be sympathetic. But what if he, or some other, were to claim the same freedom with themes that were unsympathetic, were to write of the peasantry, for example, without enchantment? The tempest that broke the following year over the head of J. M. Synge supplies the answer. Synge, born in 1871 and therefore six years younger than Yeats, had taken rather longer to arrive.[27] After attending Trinity College, Dublin, he had migrated to the continent, anxious only to become a writer and attracted, in the first instance, to French literature. Yeats, meeting him in Paris, may have had some share in diverting him to the Aran islands, but once there Synge was transformed by his environment. He already had a passion for solitude – had sought it constantly in the Wicklow glens – but the remoteness and strangeness of the islands conquered him. Out of his visit came not only a remarkable account of life on Aran, but new sensitivity to peasant speech and a new resolve to render it into English. But – and the point is crucial – Synge's peasants were not to be idealised peasants, they were earthy men and women differing from their kind elsewhere only in the beauty of the language Synge put into their mouths, or rather adapted from the Irish he heard them use. Thus, in the first of his two controversial plays – *In the Shadow of the Glen* – performed in 1903 by the Irish Literary Theatre (as it had now become) Synge, after depicting the loneliness and frustration of a young wife married to an old man and condemned to the empty monotony of life in a remote Wicklow cottage, ended his play by having her elope with a 'travelling man' or tramp, and in so doing unleashed an immediate and entirely predictable storm.

Arthur Griffith took the lead in denunciation, declaring that Norah Burke, the errant wife, was 'a lie', because, he said, 'all of us know that Irish women are the most virtuous in the world' and 'in no country are women so faithful to the marriage bond as in Ireland'. Synge, he suggested, was passing off as Irish an old Greek tale, 'The Widow of Ephesus'; there was no warrant for laying this travesty at Ireland's door. The attitude of mind behind this criticism was revealing. It showed an instinctive desire to repudiate whatever did not square with the accepted stereotype of what an Irish peasant home should be. Even more significant, however, was Griffith's attack, as the controversy developed, upon what he held to be the falsity of Yeats's definition of a nationalist as one 'who is prepared to give up a great deal that he may preserve to his country whatever part of her possessions he is best fitted to guard'. 'But', said Griffith, 'that definition is not ours. He who is prepared to give up a great deal for his country is no doubt a good man, but unless he is prepared to give up all we do not deem him a nationalist.' 'Cosmopolitanism', he added bitterly, 'never produced a great artist nor a good man yet and never will . . . If the Irish theatre ceases to reflect Irish life and embody Irish aspiration the world will wag its head away from it.'[28]

The same basic argument – that the artist should subordinate himself totally to the cause – was repeated on all sides. As an Irish critic, James Connolly (not to be confused with the Labour leader of the same name) explained, if Ireland were free then things might be different. 'But at present we need a national theatre not for the purpose of enlarging our national vanity, but of restoring our national pride.' 'The theatre', he insisted, 'possesses to a great degree a power of indoctrinating good and evil principles of life and thought, of ennobling or degrading civic and national spirit, and because of these potentialities it has seldom been left to its own device.' And, unkindest cut of all, the point was driven home by Maud Gonne, since earlier in the year the wife of Major John McBride. 'Mr Yeats asks for freedom for the theatre, freedom even from patriotic capitivity. I would ask for freedom for it from one thing more deadly than all else – freedom from the insidious and destructive tyranny of foreign influence.'[29]

Against this subservient role of the artist Yeats had been rebelling even before the advent of Synge. We have seen that from the time he fell under the spell of John O'Leary he had immersed himself in Irish politics, joining and working with the Irish Republican Brotherhood. Dr Conor Cruise O'Brien, in his searching account of this episode, is surely right in emphasising that this involvement predated his falling in love with Maud Gonne, though there can be little doubt that the fact that she herself was so deep in conspiratorial politics acted as a powerful magnet to the poet and held him fast bound longer than might otherwise have been the case.[30] Even as late as 1901 he could still persuade himself that a writer, and especially an Anglo-Irish writer, had a clear-cut choice to make:

> All Irish writers have to choose whether they will write as the upper classes have done, not to express but to exploit this country; or join the intellectual movement which has raised the cry that was heard in Russia in the 'seventies, the cry 'to the people'.

And again:

> Moses was little good to his people until he had killed an Egyptian; and for the most part a writer or public man of the upper classes is useless to this country till he has done something that separates him from his class.[31]

But already by that time the political situation was changing. The Irish party, split asunder by the Parnell crisis, had reunited in 1900 and conservative, middle-class nationalism was again in the ascendant. Romantic nationalism was at a discount and the Irish movement 'needing no longer great sacrifices, nor bringing any great risk to individuals, could do without exceptional men, and those activities of the mind that are founded on the exceptional moment'.[32] For Yeats, therefore, it had lost its savour. Worse, to the extent that political nationalism might actually hinder the free expression of the artist's mind, its revival was potentially dangerous. Of that conservative, middle-class nationalism, the *Irish Independent* was a characteristic organ. Founded initially as a pro-Parnellite paper, it had been taken over in the mid-nineties by William Martin Murphy, a wealthy industrialist and, as a former member of the parliamentary party, one of those who had taken a prominent part against Parnell at the time of the split. The *Independent* had come out against Synge even before *In the Shadow of the Glen* had been performed and this had given Yeats his cue. Always a formidable fighter, he now saw his enemy clear:

> If [he wrote] we think that a national play must be as near as possible a page out of *The Spirit of the Nation** put into dramatic form, and mean to go on thinking it to the end, then we may be sure that this generation will not see the rise in Ireland of a theatre that will reflect the life of Ireland. . . . Literature is always personal, always one man's vision of the world, one man's experience, and it can only be popular when men are ready to welcome the vision of others. A community that is opinion-ridden, even when those opinions are in themselves noble, is likely to put its creative minds into some sort of prison. If creative minds preoccupy themselves with incidents from the political history of Ireland, so much the better, but we

---

* The title of a collection of the patriotic verse of Davis and other contributors to *The Nation* newspaper, first published in 1843 and many times re-issued in the next half century. Yeats, it is fair to add, though deeply critical of Davis's influence on literature, paid tribute on the centenary of his birth to the Young Irelander's devotion to his country and especially to his moral courage (*New Ireland*, 17 July 1915).

must not enforce them to select those incidents.[33]

A week later, after the storm had broken, he returned to the theme, chastising what he called 'the chimeras' of pulpit and press:

> Certain generalisations [he observed scornfully] are everywhere sub-stituted for life. Instead of individual men and women and living virtues differing as one star differeth from another in glory, the public imagination is full of personified averages, partisan fictions, rules of life that would drill everybody into the one posture, habits that are like the pinafores of charity schoolchildren.[34]

In his next diatribe, only a week later, he was even more specific, singling out 'three sorts of ignorance' that afflicted the theatre, con-trasting them with the politics of extremism as he had known them. Once (and he spoke as John O'Leary's pupil) extreme politics were 'the politics of freedom' but now they seemed 'about to unite themselves to hatred of ideas'. The three kinds of obscurantism which he identified were, first, that of 'the more ignorant sort of Gaelic propagandist, who would have nothing said or thought that is not in country Gaelic'; next, that of 'the more ignorant kind of priest who, forgetful of the great traditions of his Church, would deny all ideas that might perplex a parish of farmers or . . . half-educated artisans'; and finally, that of 'the politician, and not always of the more ignorant sort, who would reject every idea which is not of immediate service to his cause'. And he added passionately:

> Now, I would suggest that we can live our national life without any of these kinds of ignorance. Men have served causes in other lands, and gone to death and imprisonment for their cause without giving up the search for truth, the respect for every kind of know-ledge. . . .[35]

This episode, though less well-known than the famous riots when *The Playboy of the Western World* was performed four years later, has seemed worth dwelling on because 1903 was a turning-point, not only in Yeats's own life, but in the battle of the two civilisations. For the poet that year brought with it the loss of Maud Gonne by her marriage to a man he was unable to respect, a blow which no doubt reinforced – though it did not cause – his decision to withdraw from the grimy world of politics. He did not cease to be a nationalist and he did not cease – he and Lady Gregory – to fight for the theatre (recreated as the Abbey Theatre in 1904) that meant so much to them both. Indeed, the furore roused by the *Playboy* in 1907 gave his formidable talent for contro-versy a fresh outlet which he accepted, one suspects, not without relish. All the same, it is from this time that he began that withdrawal into aristocratic contempt for what he saw as the base and squalid elements in Irish life which was to become so central to his later attitudes. A new bitterness enters his writing and informs especially his view of that Catholic and nationalist middle-class whose star was rising as that of the Protestant Ascendancy was waning. By a curious chance, just as Maud Gonne's marriage had fallen in the same year as the first Synge crisis, so the death of John O'Leary in 1907 coincided closely with the *Playboy* riots, both events separating Yeats still further from the nationalism of his youth. With the death of Synge in 1909 and George Moore's departure from Dublin two years after that it began to seem as if the impetus behind the Anglo-Irish literary movement was dying away.* And when in 1912–13 Hugh Lane's project for a splendid gallery of modern art in Dublin was brought to nothing, partly because of the reluctance of rich men like the Unionist Lord Ardilaun and the nationalist William Martin Murphy to make an adequate contribution until there was evidence of public demand, and this in turn was followed by Murphy's attempt to break James Larkin's Irish Transport and General Workers' Union, Yeats's indignation overflowed in an angry public letter about the labour dispute and, more importantly, in the great, bitter poetry of *Responsibilities*. It was this poetry which, more clearly perhaps than anything he had yet written, marked his instinct to recoil in anger and disgust from the mean-spirited world he saw about him.†

For Yeats this recoil was not to be permanent, but for the movement of which he was, in a sense, the most representative figure, it was nevertheless symbolic. He, with Lady Gregory, Synge and the rest, had come to be identified with the deliberate and intensive effort to create a modern Irish literature in English. In little more than ten years they had enriched the experience of their fellow-countrymen by the extraordinary variety and abundance of their talent. The results have passed into literary history and have become part of the European inheritance. The poems of Yeats himself, the plays of Synge and Lady Gregory, Eglinton's essays and AE's verse, the stories of George Moore and his irreverent chronicle of the whole movement, *Hail and Farewell* – all this (which is by no means the whole canon) represents a staggering achievement reached in an almost incredibly short span of time.

Yet, although nothing can take from the quality of the achievement, those who made it possible were in the long run the losers in the battle of the two civilisations. Even by 1903, more clearly by 1907, beyond

* It is worth recording that it was in 1912 that James Joyce also left Dublin for the last time. He had been a spectator – sometimes indignant, sometimes ironic – of the battle between the two civilisations which, however, he had come to regard as irrelevant to his own artistic future. But his departure at that particular moment adds to the stronge sense one already has of change and movement, even perhaps of the passing of an era.

† For the labour dispute, see chap. 8 below. The poems of Yeats which most directly reflect the poet's mood at this time are 'To a wealthy man who promised a second subscription to the Dublin Municipal Gallery if it were proved the people wanted pictures'; 'September 1913'; 'Paudeen'; and 'To a Shade'. The last of these, marking the re-entry of the Parnell theme into his work, gained additional force from the fact that Murphy, with his friend T. M. Healy, had been in the van of the movement to depose the leader in 1890.

any conceivable doubt by 1913, it had become evident that their movement could not succeed on their terms, only on terms which seemed to
them humiliating and dishonourable. The truth was that their initiative,
like the parallel initiatives of Plunkett and Dunraven, was founded on a
false assumption, an assumption easily enough made in the silence that
had followed the fall of Parnell. It was the assumption that in art, as in
society, collaboration between classes, religions and races would fill the
political vacuum. But in reality there was no vacuum. The political
issue – the issue of separation from Britain – remained the central issue
and everything else would continue to be judged according to whether
it added to or subtracted from the national demand. Between 1906 and
1914 this demand was still predominantly a demand for Home Rule,
the kind of moderate nationalism on which Yeats as a good Fenian
cast an indifferent eye. But as the Home Rule crisis reached its climax,
and as the possibility of a violent solution once more asserted itself, the
lines of demarcation – already deeply etched by the Gaelicising tendencies of the preceding years – became more profound than ever. Yeats
himself was to find that 1916 reawakened, if only for a time, his revolutionary ardours, but for the class of which he was so proud a
member the end of their supremacy was at hand.

6. The Rise of Sinn Féin

In the years immediately following Parnell's death the discomfiture of the parliamentary party and the disillusionment of the electors seemed equally complete. And although, as we shall see, the party did eventually drag itself back by slow and painful stages to a position of authority and power, it is arguable that constitutional nationalism suffered a permanent, and perhaps in the end a fatal, injury from the split which had destroyed the leader and then divided his followers into three warring factions for nine long years. But the very fact that the disaster was so total had a consequence that is hardly surprising. Young people did not cease to be interested in politics simply because Parnell was no more, or because his lieutenants seemed bent on mutual extermination. They simply turned in a different direction. If, as seemed evident, the parliamentary movement had come to grief through excessive reliance on English parties, then the time had come to think again of self-reliance. Self-reliance could mean different things to different people, but to every eager nationalist disgusted by the squabbles of the Home Rulers it meant as a minimum a return to the conception of Ireland as a nation with its own individuality and identity.

This conception could be expressed in all sorts of different ways—culturally, economically and politically. As time went on new organisations evolved, new personalities emerged, stressing one aspect more than another, but in the 'nineties this kind of differentiation was not to be looked for. Instead, small groups of patriots drew together to form little clubs and societies dedicated to the discussion of ways and means of resurrecting—perhaps one should say, creating—a sense of Irish nationality. Many of these pioneers were influenced by the language revival and practically all of them looked back to a political tradition which owed far more to Wolfe Tone or the Fenians than it did to Isaac Butt or Parnell. The societies were never numerous and were located chiefly in the larger cities—the Celtic Literary Societies of Dublin and Cork for example, or the Oliver Bond Society of Dublin—but they soon began to have an influence out of all proportion to their number or size.

This was partly due to personalities, but partly also to an exceptionally favourable combination of circumstances. The revolutionary tradition of 1798, the tradition which pointed to Ireland's destiny as an independent sovereign republic, celebrated its centenary in 1898 and inevitably there was great excitement. Every kind of nationalist paid homage to the United Irishmen including, no doubt, many who would have recoiled in horror from any re-enactment of Tone's insurrection. But, though most of the pious exhortation was froth, not all of it was.

A new generation had been reminded of an old faith and the lesson was eagerly absorbed. Hard on the heels of this celebration came the outbreak of the Boer War. Again, all kinds of nationalists had no difficulty in agreeing to condemn it, but some, closely watching the struggle of the South African republics against what seemed overwhelming force, began to question the legend of British invincibility, and two small Irish brigades, commanded by John MacBride and Arthur Lynch, actually took part in the war on the Boer side.*

All this upsurge of a more aggressive sense of nationality might, however, have spent itself ineffectively, had it not been for the emergence at this point of a remarkable man, Arthur Griffith. Griffith was born in Dublin in 1871 and trained as a printer. Economic necessity drove him in his mid-twenties to South Africa, but he returned at the request of his friend William Rooney, to edit a new weekly paper, *United Irishman*. This was to become for Griffith's contemporaries as potent a force as the *Nation* had been for the contemporaries of Thomas Davis, whom Griffith claimed as his master to the end of his days. That *United Irishman* made the impact it did was largely due to the editor himself. The pen-name under which he often wrote – Cuguan, meaning a dove – was curiously inappropriate. There was always more of the hawk than the dove about Griffith. A silent, reserved man, he was loved by a handful of intimates, but kept the rest of the world at arm's length. His public attitudes were often harsh, for he could be aggressive and quite merciless in his criticism of what he took to be the servility or toadyism of those who were content with a political settlement which still left the British connection intact. He was not an easy man to work with and Patrick Pearse spoke for others besides himself when he reproved him for being too hard, too obstinate, too narrow and suspicious, too self-opinionated. Yet if all this was true, it was true also that Griffith was an inspired journalist who combined style and temper in a way no-one else could match. He recalled both the savagery of Swift and the ruggedness of John Mitchel, but to these he added his own intensity and his own intimate knowledge of the political and economic environment about him.

It goes almost without saying that Griffith and his earliest collaborators were separatists in the fullest sense of the term. This much he made clear in the very first issue of his paper (4 March 1899). 'To be perfectly plain', he declared, 'we believe that when Swift wrote to the whole people of Ireland 170 years ago that by the law of God, of nature and of nations they had a right to be as free a people as the people of England, he wrote commonsense.' But how was that freedom to be achieved? Griffith was equally clear and equally emphatic: 'Lest there might be a doubt in any mind, we will say that we accept the nationalism of '98, '48 and '67 as the true nationalism and Grattan's cry "Live Ireland – perish the Empire!" as the watch-word of patriotism.'

* As will be seen below, pp. 260-1, both the '98 centenary and the Boer War affected parliamentarians as well as more extreme nationalists.

In practice, of course, as Griffith very well knew, 'the policy of '98, '48 and '67', the policy of armed uprising, was not feasible.* His immediate objective was therefore primarily propagandist, even educative. He wanted his fellow-countrymen to recover their self-respect, to cherish their language, literature and history, to foster their own industries, above all to cease to look to England with slavish gratitude for every slight improvement in their condition. Inevitably, this process of education involved also chastisement, and few of the devotees of orthodox nationalism escaped the lash of Griffith and his friends. William Rooney, who before his death in 1901 at the age of twenty-seven had become, as Griffith himself said, the Thomas Davis of the new movement, summed up this criticism when he dismissed the various nationalist causes then before the public as all falling short of 'the national ideal':

Of course there are ideals of all possible forms. There is the ideal of the land reformer which masquerades as a national ideal, 'Ireland for the Irish – the land for the people', blazoned on all its banners and declaimed from all its platforms. There is the Home Rulers' ideal – a parochial body meeting within the shadow of Grattan's statue, under the fold of the Union Jack, and passing a series of harmless bills for the better government of Ireland – a body of green-liveried henchmen of the British connection, with the spoils of office for their faithful stewardship. There is the ideal of the Irish agricultural reformer, whose soul yearneth for a millenium of practical poets and poetical dairy boys. And there are again the academic language enthusiasts who look to the resurgence of Gaelic to dissipate all our megrims. Now each one of these possesses elements of a national ideal – but none of them can reasonably be allowed to be *the* ideal . . . many of the movements before the public are in a sense national – but when they admit the supremacy and acknowledge the right of British law in Ireland, they cannot claim to be the national ideal, which, rightly interpreted, ought to mean an Irish state governed by Irishmen for the benefit of the Irish people.[1]

There was, however, a limit to criticism which tended, after all, to be too often negative. It was about a year after his paper was first launched that Griffith began to move towards a more constructive approach, opening his columns to discussion about the possibility of a new organisation which would link together the scattered literary and political societies and produce a practical programme for the future. During that first year, although the *United Irishman*'s circulation

* Griffith joined the IRB and appears to have been a member up to about 1910, though this date has recently been disputed (see Ernest Blythe's review of K. B. Nowlan (ed.), *The Making of 1916* (Dublin, 1969), in *Irish Times*, 3 Apr. 1969). Thereafter, his contacts with revolutionary nationalism (though not with its innermost circles) remained close. It would be fair to say that his objections to the use of force were not objections of principle, but rather that in the circumstances in which Ireland was placed, it did not seem a practical proposition.

was still small, Griffith's fame had begun to grow, not only because he was in and out of trouble with the police through his vigorous campaign against recruiting in Ireland for the British army, but also because of his scathing comments on Queen Victoria's last visit to the country in 1900, when she came, or was sent, over, as the paper truly enough remarked, 'in her dotage . . . to seek recruits for her battered army'.

Griffith himself was too much of an individualist to be an ideal organisation man. It was only very slowly that the projected new body came into being, and then only after he had stressed that it was to be federal in structure and not highly centralised. Moreover, when advocating it in his newspaper, he made it clear that those who joined it should openly acknowledge 'its present inability to lead Ireland to victory against the armed might of her enemy', and should confine themselves to 'the disciplining of the mind and the training of the forces of the nation'. No secrecy would be needed and all that would be required of members was that they should declare themselves advocates of an Irish republic and that they should be persons of 'decent character'.[2] When the much-discussed organisation finally took shape in the autumn of 1900, it was not therefore surprising that its publicly advertised programme should not have been very much more than the sum of what other bodies had previously put forward. It was given the name 'Cumann na nGaedheal' and its declared object was to be to advance the cause of Irish independence by 'cultivating a fraternal spirit amongst Irishmen'. And if this seemed a little vague, there followed a list of other aims which included the support of Irish industries, the study and teaching of Irish history, literature, language, music and art, the cultivation of Irish games, resistance to everything tending towards the anglicisation of Ireland, the nationalising of public boards and the development of what was rather hopefully called 'an Irish foreign policy'.[3] There was nothing here that pointed towards separatism in the full sense of the term and although the new organisation chose John O'Leary as its first president, this was a gesture towards the past rather than the future, for the veteran Fenian was long retired from revolutionary politics and had but a short while to live.

As a programme it was high-minded, though not perhaps calculated to cause much uneasiness either to the government or to the old-style parliamentary nationalists. One of those who was powerfully attracted by Griffith has later caught its spirit exactly in a few sentences :

It was a sober and a sparsely-smoking movement, very much in earnest, and rather puritanical, which was one of its great strengths. . . . Some of its practices may be small beer and may raise a smile in an age which has not known what the captivity was like, but they were seriously meant and seriously undertaken, and they had their value at the time.

No doubt this was true and no doubt members experienced a glow of virtue when they used Irish manufactures, smoked Gallaher's tobacco or even submitted to the not too onerous discipline of drinking only Irish liquor.[4] But something more was needed and Griffith was gradually feeling his way towards supplying it. It was typical of him that what he produced was a policy, or rather two policies, which at that moment seemed wholly ideological and impracticable, but which time, after many strange adventures, was to vindicate in the end.

The first of these – and the one with which his name will always be associated – was the conception to which he himself gave the baffling name of 'the Hungarian policy.' By this he meant the policy successfully pursued by the Hungarian patriot, Franz Déak, who organised a massive abstention of Hungarian representatives from the Imperial Diet at Vienna in order to secure the re-establishment of a separate Hungarian parliament in Budapest. The Ausgleich of 1867, which conceded this right to the Hungarians, and which made Austria and Hungary two separate entities linked by the Emperor, seemed to Griffith to offer an important parallel for the relations between England and Ireland. The fact that Griffith underestimated the complexity of the Ausgleich and failed to realise how the existence of common ministries of war and foreign affairs and the retention of close economic ties between the two parts of the Empire diminished Hungarian autonomy, may reflect upon him as an historian, but not as a propagandist. For he had grasped the central lessons of the Ausgleich for Ireland – that it had been won for the Hungarians by a masterly display of parliamentary non-co-operation. It was this lesson that he now began to expound in response to the demand for leadership. His new doctrine first saw the light at a convention of Cumann na nGaedheal on 26 October 1902 when, after a scathing attack upon the Irish nationalist representatives at Westminster, he proposed this resolution :

That we call upon our countrymen abroad to withdraw all assistance from the promoters of a useless, degrading and demoralising policy until such time as the members of the Irish parliamentary party substitute for it the policy of the Hungarian deputies of 1861, and refusing to attend the British parliament or to recognise its right to legislate for Ireland remain at home to help in promoting Ireland's interests and to aid in guarding its national rights.[5]

The curious point about this resolution is that a perfectly respectable Irish pedigree could have been found for it without confusing honest nationalists with obscure Hungarian analogies. O'Connell had toyed briefly with such a policy in 1843, Thomas Davis had advocated it on behalf of the Repeal Association in 1844 and nearly forty years later it was urged on Parnell by his left wing in the critical winter of 1881. No doubt it was important to Griffith to show the policy in action, not just in contemplation, and he was led on to elaborate his analysis of the Ausgleich in a series of newspaper articles in the first six months of 1904, publishing them in book form later that year as *The Resurrection of Hungary.* In the closing pages of his book he not only drew the parallel for Ireland, but went a stage further by pointing to a critical moment in Irish history when legislative independence had been, or seemed to have been, achieved. This was, in Griffith's view, the meaning of the 'constitution of 1782' and of the Renunciation Act passed by the British parliament the following year. Linking the Irish experience of the eighteenth century with the Hungarian experience of the nineteenth, Griffith's programme was seen to be a policy of abstention from Westminster, of the re-creation of a native parliament or its equivalent on Irish soil, and the carrying through of an Anglo-Irish Ausgleich whereby the only institutional tie between the two countries would be the Crown itself. And, drawing on O'Connell's ill-fated scheme of 1843, Griffith called for the setting up in Ireland of a Council of Three Hundred which would become the policy-making assembly for the whole country, and whose decrees would be carried out by the county councils and other locally elected bodies.

Looking at this scheme in the cold light of history, it is difficult to avoid the suspicion that Griffith's knowledge of eighteenth century Ireland was nearly as sketchy as his understanding of nineteenth century Hungarian politics. He seems to have had an idea of Grattan's parliament which bore little resemblance to reality. Corrupt, unrepresentative, unable to control the executive, its very laws still subject to a royal veto exercised on the advice of the British government of the day, the glorified colonial assembly which was snuffed out by the Act of Union was far from the ideal parliament Griffith held up to his countrymen's admiration. From another viewpoint also his doctrine was bound to be suspect to those who believed in their hearts that separation from Britain would only be won by force of arms. Griffith put forward his Hungarian policy to show, as he said himself, 'that the alternative of armed resistance to the foreign government of this country is not acquiescence in usurpation, tyranny and fraud'.[6] True, when letters began to pour in begging him to take up the role of an Irish Déak, he replied that this would not be possible. Had he been a Hungarian he would have followed Kossuth the rebel rather than Déak the constitutional statesman. For him the Hungarian policy was not the final Irish demand. He had put it forward as an alternative to parliamentarism as well as to actual revolution, and he would loyally support it so long as circumstances prevented any more positive advance, but its natural leader, he thought, should be someone whose whole ambition for the country would be fulfilled by the restoration of Grattan's parliament.[7]

In the event, however, there was no one else who could lead as effectively as Griffith. This was partly because the Hungarian policy was so very much the child of his own brain, but it was also because he coupled with the Hungarian policy a second line of argument which was calculated to appeal much more directly to many of his readers than abstruse and sometimes difficult argument derived from the shadowy recesses of Central Europe. This other string to his bow was quite simply the development of Irish industries behind an effective tariff barrier. Here again Griffith was no innovator. The encouragement and use of Irish manufactures had been part of the common coin of patriotism since the days of Swift and Berkeley. More recently, in the 1840s, Sir Robert Kane had published a massive – and excessively optimistic – survey of Ireland's potential economic wealth and Parnell, who had included Kane's book in his own sparse reading, had put industrial development very high on his programme. Such a policy, however, was doomed to failure unless it was accompanied by tariff autonomy. That could not exist under the Union and it had been a main object of Irish nationalism to achieve it as an essential part of self-government. But this was difficult, partly because English manufacturers would not surrender free entry to the Irish market unless forced, and partly because wherever Irish industry had developed on a sufficient scale to look outwards, as in the Lagan valley, or among some of the brewers and distillers of Dublin and the south, the attraction of belonging to a prosperous free trade area such as the United Kingdom had hitherto far outweighed the dubious benefits that *might* accrue if a native tariff reserved for them an impoverished and mainly rural clientele. Even Parnell in his prime had found the obstacles to tariff reforms insuperable and in 1886 had agreed – reluctantly, and only after extreme pressure from Gladstone – to drop the claim for tariff autonomy from the Home Rule bill of that year.

Griffith was unmoved by this previous history of frustration. Characteristically, he had his eye, not on the hated parliamentarians, but on yet another foreign mentor. This was the great German apostle of protection, Friedrich List, whose *National System of Protection* came to be Griffith's gospel, a book, as he himself wrote, that he would like to see in the hands of every Irishman. For Griffith, no doubt, List's significance was two-fold. On the one hand, Bismarckian Germany could be regarded as a monument to his ideas; protectionism, in other words, was not just a beautiful dream, but could be, and had been, made to work. And on the other hand, perhaps even more importantly, List insisted that a protective tariff was as much a factor in emergent nationalism as a country's language, literature or history. Indeed, Griffith went so far as to adopt List's definition of a nation as his own. A nation, List had written:

. . . should possess a common language and literature, a territory endowed with manifold natural resources, extensive and with convenient frontiers and a numerous population. Agriculture, manufactures, commerce and navigation must all be developed in it proportionately, arts and sciences, educational establishments, and universal cultivation must stand in it on equal footing with material production. Its constitution, laws and institutions must afford to those who belong to it a high degree of security and liberty, and must promote religion, morality and prosperity. It must possess suffi-

253

cient power to defend its independence and to protect its foreign commerce.[8]

Griffith felt this emphasis upon manufactures to be all the more urgently necessary, partly because of the long habit of the people to think of the land as their only major resource, and also because this very habit had led them to link the question of national independence too intimately with the solution of the land question. To Griffith this was a gross over-simplification. 'We in Ireland', he wrote bitterly, 'have been taught . . . that our destiny is to be the fruitful mother of flocks and herds – that it is not necessary for us to pay attention to our manufacturing arm, since our agricultural arm is all-sufficient.' 'The fallacy', he continued, 'dissolves before reflection':

With List I reply: A nation cannot promote and further its civilisation, its prosperity and its social progress equally as well by exchanging agricultural products for manufactured goods as by establishing a manufacturing power of its own. A merely agricultural nation can never develop to any extent a home or a foreign commerce, with inland means of transport and foreign navigation, increase its population in due proportion to their well-being, or make notable progress in its moral, intellectual, social and political development, it will never acquire important political power or be placed in a position to influence the cultivation and progress of less advanced nations and to form colonies of its own.[9]

Needless to say, Griffith did not nurse any such imperialist ambitions as the last sentence might seem to imply. But he did emphasise over and over again that real independence for Ireland must be economic as well as political and that this could never be complete so long as the country depended on its powerful neighbour for the bulk of its manufactures. It can be made an objection against him that, like many others, he fell into the trap of over-estimating Ireland's resources and that his blissful calculations of the number of extra millions of people the country could support ignored the possibility that the existing low population might itself be important evidence about the numbers that Irish resources were really capable of maintaining. On the other hand, he was surely right to press for the development of a native mercantile marine, for the reafforestation of large tracts of the countryside, and above all for the withdrawal of Irish funds from English enterprises and their employment in promoting Irish industry. In all of this he may have been ahead of his time, but such themes were to have a long career after his death; indeed, it is not too much to say that they, and others deriving from them, still stand at the centre of much economic thinking in Ireland.

The economic nationalism which thus emerged as one of the most important elements in Griffith's writing had been implicit in his attitude to Irish affairs from the time he had first begun to make an impact on the public. What made this doctrine explicit was the growing need for a more formal organisation and a more coherent programme of action. Cumann na nGaedheal was never intended, as we have seen, to be more than a loosely co-ordinating body, to which other societies might be affiliated and through which they might keep in touch with one another. In the first years of the new century, and partly under Griffith's inspiration, these societies began to multiply. He himself was responsible for one new group, the so-called National Council, which was formed in the early summer of 1903 to organise protests against the visit of King Edward VII to Ireland. It had no constitution and no special conditions of entry, being open to all those 'who believe in the absolute independence of their country for one purpose on which both can agree – the stamping out of flunkeyism and toadyism in the land'.[10] It attracted an extraordinary variety of supporters – the playwright and Irish Maecenas, Edward Martyn, was chairman; Maud Gonne was one of the honorary secretaries; W. B. Yeats, inevitably, was not far away, but there were other members – the old Fenians, John Daly of Limerick and Dr Mark Ryan of London – who were attracted less by the theories of Griffith or the charms of Miss Gonne, than by the possibility of using this new group, or any group, to forward the separatist ideal. The immediate agitation against the royal visit produced results of a kind – Dublin Corporation, for example, decided (though only by three votes) against a loyal address and the existence of a formidable anti-English sentiment was signalised by the holding of one of the largest public meetings to take place in Dublin for many years. More important, the National Council remained in being after the king had departed in order to serve as a forum in which representatives of the various nationalist societies could meet to discuss policies and problems. These societies were reinforced from 1905 onwards by the formation of the 'Dungannon Clubs', commemorating by their name the Volunteer Convention which led to the winning of the constitution of 1782. The first of these was founded by two young Ulstermen, Bulmer Hobson and Denis McCullough. Both were members of the IRB and were to figure largely in the revolutionary movement in the years ahead. But the Dungannon Clubs, though separatist in intent, were not secret organisations. They were openly recruited and advertised and their main purpose was to educate the rising generation in the gospel of independence. The first of the clubs was based on Belfast and although branches were formed in Dublin, London and Glasgow, the main support for the new movement was, and remained, in Ulster.

All this activity was a sign of life, but it carried with it the danger of excessive proliferation of small and overlapping bodies, competing with each other for the allegiance and support of what was still only a tiny minority of the population. To avoid confusion and waste of effort Griffith, albeit somewhat reluctantly, decided to take the initiative. Accordingly, in November 1905, at the Annual Convention organised by the National Council, he outlined a detailed policy for the future. It was to this policy that one of his supporters, Máire Butler, a well known Gaelic Leaguer (and cousin to Sir Edward Carson of all people), gave the name by which it was ever after to be known – Sinn Féin. The words, meaning simply 'Ourselves', sometimes mistranslated 'Ourselves alone', summed up admirably the central tenet of Griffith's thought – the concept of national self-reliance. His speech to the Convention (later reprinted as *The Sinn Féin Policy*) elaborated the economic ideas already summarised and called for the creation of a Council of Three Hundred, composed of MPs who would agree to abstain from Westminster together with delegates from local bodies, to assume the power of a *de facto* parliament.

Nothing in 1905 seemed more unlikely than that an Irish parliament not far removed from this ideal should actually come into being within fifteen years. At the time the more urgent necessity was not to draw up imaginary constitutions for improbable assemblies, but to bring about some sort of formal unity between the various groups attracted by Griffith's ideas and looking to him increasingly for a lead. Gradually, such unity was achieved. In April 1907 the Dungannon Clubs and Cumann na nGaedheal came together to form the Sinn Féin League, and in September 1908 these in turn joined with the National Council to form the body known simply as Sinn Féin. The grand object of the organisation was defined as 'the re-establishment of the independence of Ireland', but quite what this meant was ambiguous. As Griffith observed at the time : 'I am a separatist. The Irish people are not separatists. I do not think that they can be united behind a separatist policy. But I do think that it is possible to unite them on this policy.'[11] 'This policy' declared first that Ireland was 'a distinct nation', to which pious assertion every brand of nationalist could subscribe. But it then went on to state that Sinn Féin would make no voluntary 'compact' with Britain until she honoured the compact she had made in 1783. This, if it meant anything, meant the restoration of legislative independence to the King, Lords and Commons of Ireland. But, since many of those who were becoming interested in Griffith's ideas – especially the young men of the Dungannon Clubs – were also being permeated by republican doctrines, to define independence in terms of the 'constitution of 1782' as a *maximum* demand would have made it impossible for extreme separatists to work with Griffith thereafter. It was to meet their objections that the opening clauses of the constitution demanded, as already stated, 'the re-establishment of the independence of Ireland'. Thus early in its career did Sinn Féin hesitate between two quite different conceptions of Irish nationality, a hesitation which, magnified and distorted as it was to be by the events of later years, was to have a momentous influence upon modern Irish history.

But this was still far in the future. On the short run, the constitution declared that it was the business of Irishmen to use what powers they had, or might obtain, to work for 'the creation of a prosperous, virile and independent nation'. To bring this about the locally elected bodies, and especially the county councils (through their General Council) must play a leading part, since they were after all the only representative institutions actually at work in Ireland and dominated by nationalists. They were adjured to take into their purview every question of national interest and, as an aid to their deliberations, an appendix to the constitution laid down a list of fifteen severely practical objectives which, by a not very remarkable coincidence, closely resembled Griffith's original *Sinn Féin Policy*. These included protection for industry and commerce; the establishment of an Irish consular service, of a mercantile marine, of a national bank, a national stock exchange, a national system of insurance; the setting up of national arbitration courts and of a national civil service; the institution of national control over transport, waste lands and fisheries; the reform of education and of the poor laws; the prosecution of a policy of non-consumption of articles paying duty to the British Exchequer; the withdrawal of all voluntary support to the British armed forces; and, finally, the non-recognition of the British parliament.

The enunciation of this policy and the unification of the various societies into Sinn Féin, was intended to be only a beginning. In reality, however, it marked the high-point of a movement which now began quite rapidly to decline. About this apparent reversal of fortune there need be no mystery. Great though the excitement and enthusiasm might be among the converted, it has to be remembered that the great mass of Irishmen remained entirely unmoved. Statistics of the membership of the various Sinn Féin bodies are difficult to measure, but it does not seem that even in its pre-war heyday – between 1908 and 1910 – there were more than 150 of these clubs and societies at the very outside, and the total may have been nearer 100; all of these were very small and Griffith himself found it hard to maintain his newspaper, which, after 1906, was no longer *United Irishman*, but *Sinn Féin*.[12]

It may be argued against this that just at this time, 1907–8, Sinn Féin had made its first incursion into national politics with not unimpressive results. An MP, C. J. Dolan, resigning his seat in North Leitrim, partly in disgust at the failure of the Irish party to commit their Liberal allies to Home Rule, and partly under the influence of Griffith's *Resurrection of Hungary*, stood as a Sinn Féin candidate on a platform of abstention from Westminster. After a hectic campaign, in which, significantly, he received considerable support from the IRB, Dolan polled 1,157 votes against 3,103 for the Irish party's official nominee. This was certainly a portent and at least one of the parliamentary leaders, John Dillon, was prepared to take Sinn Féin seriously from that moment onwards. Yet in reality Dolan's candidature was premature and his quite substantial showing at the polls only a flash-in-the-pan. The votes he received were at least as much an expression of discontent with the ineffective manoeuvres of the Home Rulers as an affirmation of belief in Sinn Féin. There had been widespread disappointment that after nearly two years of pressure on an allegedly sympathetic Liberal government, the most the Irish party had been able to extort was an Irish Council Bill which was no more than a measure of expanded local government. The bill itself was rejected by an irate National Convention and, although the parliamentarians did not escape their share of the blame, the upsurge of indignation which the incident produced may even have helped them by enabling them to take a more intransigent tone in the House of Commons in the future.*

At all events Dolan's candidature remained the solitary excursion of Sinn Féin into the larger world of politics. That it was not followed by others was due to several factors operating independently but simultaneously. For one thing, an extended parliamentary election campaign needed funds and these were never plentiful. Indeed, they were soon to become less plentiful.[13] For about six months, from August 1909 to January 1910, Griffith tried to run a Sinn Féin daily paper; the attempt was a lamentable and expensive failure, discouraging to all concerned and draining the movement of money that might have been used for other purposes. Moreover, in the field of 'advanced' nationalist journalism there were formidable competitors, such as W. P. Ryan's *Irish Peasant* in 1909 and 1910, and the IRB paper, *Irish Freedom*, from 1910 onwards. Apart from this competition, though not entirely unconnected with it, was the steady growth in the power and influence of the IRB itself. After the return to Ireland of the veteran Fenian, Tom Clarke, in 1907 and the reorganisation of the brotherhood in that year, it became a much more active proselytising force and many who might have been attracted to Griffith's programme of slow and steady nation-building – and some, also, who remained attracted to it – were swept by a natural enthusiasm for the activism of the republicans.

Finally, the long moribund Home Rule movement sprang into new life when the budget crisis of 1909, leading on to the curbing of the veto power of the House of Lords, at one stroke gave Redmond the leverage he needed to bring his policy back to the centre of the stage and also removed the chief constitutional obstacle to a Home Rule Bill being carried into law.† With this opportunity opening out before the country it was natural that attention should once again, if only for a time, be concentrated on the parliamentary battle, and Sinn Féin could do little more than stand watchfully on the sidelines, insisting that it was not a party but a demand. As one of its pamphlets put it just at this time:

> Above the cries of contending parties we raise the cry of Ireland and Irish independence. . . . Not an Ireland for a class or for a creed, but an Ireland for the Irish, and the whole of the Irish, not an Ireland fettered and trammelled by England, but mistress of her own destinies, evolving her own national life and building for herself an ever-increasing prosperity. . . . We have to recognise the nation, rather than parties within the nation; for it is greater than any party, and in

* The episode of the Irish Council Bill is dealt with in the context of parliamentary politics in the next chapter.

† For the republican and parliamentary rebirths, see chap. 7 and Part III, chap. 1.

the service of the nation all men have an equal right as well as an equal duty.[14]

It was not the least of the ironies in the history of Sinn Féin that when eventually its hour did strike it achieved its triumph in an era of unexampled party strife and as itself a party intensively conscious of its own special role.

7. Home Rule Revived

Although the manifestations of a political and cultural renaissance described in the previous chapters may seem in retrospect to have been the points of departure for a new and ultimately triumphant surge of nationality, this was by no means clear at the time. The new movements were highly articulate, they were attractive to the rising generation, and they captured some of the best minds of the time, but up to 1914, or even up to 1916, they remained minority movements. For the great mass of those whose political hopes for the future were summed up in the programme of Home Rule, the old parliamentary party still held the centre of the stage.

That party had made a remarkable recovery from the long agonies of the split, even though time was to reveal that it had never regained quite the authority or *élan* of its Parnellite heyday. The reunion it painfully achieved between 1898 and 1900 was less spontaneous than imposed from without. Reunion came partly because even the most purblind politicians could not but be aware that their internal struggles looked cheap and trivial in the context of the centenary of the 1798 rebellion. It came partly because the outbreak of the South African War offered a chance for nationalists of different persuasions to combine in opposition to a British policy which all of them deeply and instinctively abhorred; the contrast between the undignified squabbles of the Irish and the spectacle of the Boers fighting for their independence was painfully apparent to the parliamentarians, as to others, and a powerful incentive to unity. But most of all, as previously suggested, reunion occurred because if it had not done so there was a real threat that the United Irish League would supplant the divided party in the public esteem and might even in a short time obliterate it altogether.

The process of healing the wounds left by the split was undoubtedly made easier by the decision of the anti-Parnellites to accept as chairman of the reunited party one of Parnell's few surviving followers. That the chairman actually chosen was John Redmond was almost an accident, but for the success of the policy of reconciliation it was a happy accident. Even today it is difficult to arrive at a just assessment of this man who knew the extremes of success and failure and whose career was to end in unrelieved tragedy.[1] His reputation in Ireland has been overshadowed both by his own failure to win Home Rule and by the repudiation of constitutional methods which began to be widespread after 1916, and which had convinced Redmond himself by the time of his death in 1918 that the movement to which he had given his whole life was irretrievably doomed. But in 1900 this was mercifully hidden.

At the time of his election as chairman he was only forty-four and his great parliamentary talents were just coming to full flower. He had a fine presence and a fine voice – was, in fact, one of the best orators produced by the Irish party during its whole existence. Steeped to a greater extent even than Isaac Butt in the ways of the House of Commons, he became one of its most distinguished members – patient under provocation, adroit in debate, capable at times of rising to the heights of emotional intensity. Deeply marked throughout his life by loyalty to Parnell, he shared many of his leader's attitudes and was, like him, a Wicklow country gentleman at heart. But unlike Parnell – and in the end this may have contributed to his undoing – he seems to have found it difficult to hate Englishmen and things English. On the contrary, he appears always to have been more conscious than any of his Irish colleagues of Britain as the centre of a great empire where, for white men at least, self-government was a natural and realisable objective. This vision of a community in which Ireland, Home Rule at last conceded, would have an honoured place, was fundamental to his political thinking and was to colour his action at the most decisive crisis of his life.

In private a courteous but retiring man, Redmond in his official capacity was a firm and highly competent chairman – wise, constructive, nearly always a moderating influence. The newly united parliamentarians, nerves on edge and old animosities only half-buried, tested these qualities to the uttermost, but though he had to ride out storms from every quarter of the political compass, he gave the party a stability and buoyancy it had lacked for many years. Not the least of his gifts, essential indeed to his survival, was his ability to choose the right side. Having been for nearly ten years the leader of a tiny group, he showed as chairman of the whole party a highly developed flair for consensus politics. A cynic might say that he simply put into practice Mr Pickwick's immortal advice that when caught between two crowds one should shout with the larger, but there was more to Redmond than this. Having realised in 1900 that the United Irish League held the key to the future, he threw in his lot with Dillon and O'Brien, not just because they controlled the big battalions, but because the League offered the promise of a nationwide organisation which would do for the constituencies what the Irish National League had done under Parnell (and to a lesser degree under Redmond himself in the limited areas where his writ still ran) and what the hastily improvised Irish National Federation had vainly tried to do for the anti-Parnellites during the years of division. Before 1900 was out the UIL had finally been accepted as the legitimate heir of the previous organisations and from then until the end of the whole constitutional movement its fortunes were intertwined with those of the parliamentary party.

O'Brien himself, it is true, had hoped at the outset that the party would be subordinate to the League, but although the rules for the selection of parliamentary candidates seemed to give more freedom to the constituencies than before, and although the party was solemnly called to account each year at a National Convention held under the auspices of the UIL, it was not long before the popular body was in thrall to the parliamentarians as much as the Irish National League had ever been. This was partly because of O'Brien's own withdrawal into political isolation in 1904 and again in 1909, but partly also it was because the secretaryship of the United Irish League was held by Joseph Devlin. Devlin, who started life as a bar-tender in Belfast (where he was born in 1871), and lived to become the doyen of Ulster nationalists, was perhaps the ablest newcomer to be recruited into the party after its reunion. An outstanding public speaker, the 'pocket Demosthenes' was popular in the House of Commons and loved and respected by his fellow-Catholics in the north. He was, in addition, a first-class organiser, who took from Redmond's shoulders the business of local and sometimes grubby negotiation which the chairman found repugnant and was not well-fitted to conduct. Less happily, Devlin's administrative talent overflowed into another body, the Ancient Order of Hibernians, in which he served as Grand Master of the Board of Erin. This was a confessedly sectarian institution, deriving from the eighteenth century, which drew its main strength from Ulster, where it represented the Catholic reaction to the Orange Order.* Although it was undeniably valuable in getting out the vote at elections, it came to be identified with machine-politics of a peculiarly narrow and bitter kind, and even amongst the party's own supporters, especially the younger men, it was regarded with misgiving and sometimes active distaste.[2]

With the support of the League and the Hibernians, the backing of the *Freeman's Journal* and the loyal, if at first cool, co-operation of John Dillon, Redmond slowly consolidated his position as a national leader. He was never fated, however, to control a completely cohesive party. He came nearest to doing so at the general election of 1900, when the nationalists won eighty-one Irish seats, but one of these seats was occupied by T. M. Healy, who, though instrumental in Redmond's election to the chair, was unable to adapt himself to the new situation that had resulted from the coalescence of the party and the UIL. He refused to dissolve the organisation he had built up during the split – the People's Rights Association – and was formally expelled from the fold in December 1900. Thereafter he remained – with a brief interval

* Descended from the Ribbon Societies of pre-Union days, the order took its modern name about 1838. Its career, both in Ireland and in America, was marked by bitter internal disputes and within the Irish wing of the movement, the Board of Erin, unity was only restored (and even then not completely) in the early years of the century. It was no accident that the revival of its fortunes coincided with Devlin's rise to prominence in national politics; by about 1909, it has been estimated, the main body had about 60,000 members in Ireland, the dissidents about 4,000 (J. J. Bergin, *History of the Ancient Order of Hibernians*, Dublin, 1910). See also A. C. Hepburn, 'The Ancient Order of Hibernians in Irish Politics, 1905-14', in *Cithara*, vol. x, No. 2 (St Bonaventure University, May 1971).

between 1907 and 1909 – in independent opposition. This was not in itself a serious threat to the party, though it was a great waste of exceptional ability. Healy was not only an outstanding advocate, he was a brilliant debater who at his peak could hold the House of Commons in the hollow of his hand. Unfortunately, his brilliance had always been coupled with political unreliability. Ambitious, vain, bitter-tongued, he was never an easy colleague and could find no resting-place between leadership and outlawry. Yet although his personal following was small after 1900, he remained formidable for two reasons. One was that he was closely allied to the former MP, William Martin Murphy, who had shared with him the burden of the attack on Parnell. Murphy was one of the leading businessmen in Dublin – we shall meet him again in that role – and he was also the owner of the *Irish Daily Independent*, bought, ironically enough, from the Parnellites in 1900. Murphy used this paper not merely to support Healy, but to harass Healy's opponents at every turn, and since the *Independent* was widely read by the Catholic middle-class, its constant nagging in time affected the party's popularity, with ultimately dire results.

But if Healy was formidable, or potentially so, the second reason was that adversity made him a bedfellow of that other political nonconformist, William O'Brien. In his dealings with O'Brien, as with Healy, Redmond showed an acute awareness of where, in the party and in the country, the centre of gravity really lay. The chairman had acted with O'Brien at the Land Conference and, in the teeth of criticism from some of his colleagues, had collaborated closely with Wyndham during the passing of the Land Act in 1903. But beyond that he was not prepared to venture. The game of working hand in glove with landlords would not be worthwhile if it were to isolate him from the most influential nationalists in the country, or if it were to lead to a fresh fragmentation of the parliamentary party. The withdrawal of O'Brien after his policy of conciliation had been rejected did of course represent a new fragmentation, but though Redmond was much shaken when it occurred, it was not a major split. Even though O'Brien was subsequently joined in the wilderness by other dissident MPs, the number of independent Nationalists did not rise above the eleven who were returned at the January election of 1910. Several of these had left the party with private grievances of their own, but while O'Brien did admittedly control some seven seats, these were confined to the city and county of Cork. He still had nuisance value but he could hardly be considered a seriously disruptive force – unless something went very badly wrong with Redmond's leadership.

That leadership would ultimately depend upon whether or not the party could deliver Home Rule. So long as the Unionist hegemony lasted this was clearly out of the question. But although the landslide victory won by the Liberals in the election of January 1906 ended the long Unionist reign with a vengeance, Irish hopes that this presaged a revival in the fortunes of Home Rule were decidedly premature. There were three reasons why this should be so. One was that the very size of the Liberal majority made that party independent of all others in the House of Commons and thus denied Redmond the leverage he needed. A second was that the Liberals, immediately after their great triumph, found their hopes of passing constructive legislation constantly foiled by the veto of the House of Lords which the Tories seemed bent upon using as a counterpoise to their numerical inferiority in the Commons. Since the Liberal success in 1906 had roused great expectations of reform in many quarters, it would only be a matter of time before this deliberate policy of using the hereditary chamber to block the measures passed by the elected one created a major constitutional crisis.

This in itself would have made it very difficult for the Irish party to press the demand for Home Rule with any hope of rapid success. But a third discouraging feature of the situation was that the probing operations of the Nationalists to discover the intentions of the Liberals even before the election had taken place had revealed quite unmistakably that with Gladstone's passing there had passed also much of the old fervour to pacify Ireland. In fact, it became very clear that although the Liberal leader, Sir Henry Campbell-Bannerman, and some other influential figures such as John Morley and Earl Spencer, remained true to the Gladstonian conception, there were others, of whom Lord Rosebery was the most candid spokesman, who felt that it was high time the whole policy was dead and buried. Most Liberals, probably, stood between the two extremes and were ready enough to accept a formula evolved by Campbell-Bannerman's eventual successor, H. H. Asquith, and by Sir Edward Grey, as far back as 1901 and described by the latter in these words: 'Things must advance towards Home Rule, but I think it must be step by step.' It was this essentially gradualist doctrine to which Sir Henry Campbell-Bannerman pledged himself in public and in private when he assured his nationalist friends that although Home Rule was not itself an immediately feasible proposition he hoped to be able to pass some serious measure which would 'be consistent with and lead up to, the larger policy'.[3]

What this meant in practice was that the Irish got nothing at all in 1906 and that in 1907 they were offered an Irish Council Bill – in effect a Liberal version of the old devolution scheme, which owed nearly as much to Sir Antony MacDonnell as Lord Dunraven's ill-fated project had done. However criticised, amended and redrafted by the nationalist leaders the Council Bill remained a sadly inadequate substitute for Home Rule, described even by the sympathetic Campbell-Bannerman as a 'little, modest, shy, humble effort to give administrative powers to the Irish people'. The Council, part nominated but mainly elected, was to be given control over eight departments of the Irish administration, including education, local government and Plunkett's Department of Agriculture and Technical Instruction. The funds necessary to service these departments were to be transferred to the Council, but the Lord-Lieutenant was to be left with wide powers of veto, and of course the overriding authority of the cabinet and, ultimately, the Imperial Parliament, was to remain intact. Redmond and Dillon were understandably cool towards the proposals, but for tactical reasons were reluctant to condemn the Bill out of hand. In Ireland, however, such niceties were little understood and the predominant reaction was one of deep disappointment. It was morally certain that when a National Convention met in May 1907 to determine what action should be taken, the call for rejection would be irresistible. In fact, even before the Convention met the two leaders had come to the conclusion that the Bill was hopeless and the almost universal condemnation of it in the country only strengthened their determination. Redmond himself took the bull by the horns and at the Convention denounced the Liberal offer as totally unacceptable. It was withdrawn immediately and the net result of the episode seemed to have been to produce a great deal of friction to no purpose.[4]

In reality, the fiasco of the Irish Council Bill went deeper even than its melancholy public manifestations. It had starkly revealed what many middle-of-the-road nationalists had hitherto failed to realise, the vulnerability of the party in a situation where it was dependent on the *beaux yeux* of its Liberal allies, without being able to bring to bear the pressure which a more evenly balanced House of Commons would have allowed it to exert. Redmond's was indeed an unenviable position. The Liberal alliance was the only hope for Home Rule, yet if it failed to produce the desired solution then it, and those who supported it, would come under heavy fire from public opinion at home. The reception accorded to the Irish Council Bill showed just how serious this could be. Not only were the party leaders furiously criticised by the fierier members of the United Irish League (they were concentrated mainly in Dublin and nearly all belonged to the 'ginger-group' known as the Young Ireland branch of the League), but within the party itself a small section – probably not much more than half-a-dozen – suggested that the time had come to reunite with Healy and O'Brien and to withdraw temporarily from the House of Commons. This was, of course, nothing less than the policy of Sinn Féin – diluted, no doubt, by a tincture of constitutionalism, but still recognisably the doctrine Griffith had been preaching for years past. Redmond was strong enough to ignore the proposal, but, as we saw earlier, one of those associated with it, C. J. Dolan, resigned to contest his old seat as a Sinn Féin candidate. He was defeated without too much difficulty, but nothing could alter the fact that the idea of abstention from Westminster had for the first time been made the central issue in an Irish election.

The only answer the party could doggedly make to the critics in its rear was the two-fold one that Home Rule was not prejudiced by the withdrawal of the Irish Council Bill because that Bill had never been intended as a substitute for 'the larger policy', and that until the moment was ripe for that 'larger policy' it was the duty of Nationalists to work for other and much needed reforms. And in fact the Liberals, although so disappointing on the main question, did not cease during these years to add to the sum of constructive Irish legislation. In rapid succession, Acts were passed between 1906 and 1909 to improve the housing of the working-classes in the countryside and in the towns, to protect the interests of town-tenants, to settle the still outstanding question of the evicted tenants and to amend the defective finances of the Wyndham Act. Perhaps even more important in its long-term effects than any of these was the Irish Universities Act of 1908 which, while it did not resolve the differences between the University of Dublin (Trinity College) and the Catholic majority in Ireland, did at least go a long way towards giving the latter what they wanted. The Royal University (never, in effect, more than an examining body) was abolished. In its place two new universities were set up. One, the Queen's University, Belfast, was the old Queen's College writ large and, by a curious freak of timing, anticipated by a few years in the sphere of education the coming political division of the country into north and south. The other new creation, the National University of Ireland, brought together in a federal structure the University Colleges of Cork, Galway and Dublin. This, although technically non-denominational, was intended by the Chief Secretary, Augustine Birrell, as a gesture to Irish Catholicism and was generally accepted as such in Ireland.*

This career of beneficent legislation was halted in 1909 by the crisis which arose over the budget of that year. Faced with the need to find more money for social services – e.g. old-age pensions and the extension of social insurance – and for defence, the Chancellor of the Exchequer, Lloyd George, brought in a budget which, in scope and severity, seemed almost revolutionary. He proposed to increase income tax, to levy a super-tax, to introduce a series of land taxes and to raise death duties, liquor licences and the imposts on spirits and tobacco. The budget was intensely unpopular in Ireland, especially those parts of it which struck at the distillers and publicans upon whom the party depended so heavily for financial contributions and local support. But to attack the Chancellor was not so easy as it seemed, for it soon became obvious that the Conservatives were prepared to go to the uttermost to resist his assaults upon property by using the House of Lords to veto the budget. Here was the climactic incident in the long and bitter conflict that had raged between the two Houses ever since the Liberals had returned to power. If now the Lords actually did reject the budget then clearly a major constitutional crisis would result. From that crisis might emerge an abolition, or at least a limitation, of the veto power of the Lords over legislation passed by the Commons. In such a situation, and with such a prize to play for, the nationalist leaders could not join uninhibitedly in the campaign against the budget. True, they could criticise it – and did so – and they could threaten to oppose it unless it were accompanied

* For the university question in its educational context, see above, Part I, chap. 3.

266

by a really satisfactory reduction in the power of the House of Lords, but they had at the same time to realise that if they did oppose the budget then the Liberal government would infallibly fall and the prospect of Home Rule in any forseeable future would be correspondingly diminished.

For Redmond and Dillon, therefore, the budget, disagreeable as it was, was of secondary significance; or rather, its chief importance was that it gave them a means of bringing pressure to bear on their Liberal allies so to restrict the Lords' veto as to remove that last constitutional barrier from the path of Home Rule. Unfortunately, there were dangers here as well as opportunities – dangers at home and also at Westminster. At home the party leaders had to reckon not only with an indignant public reaction against the new impositions (quite uninhibited by the fact that Ireland had accepted Old Age Pensions with alacrity), but also with the fact that the 'independents', of whom the most important were William O'Brien and T. M. Healy, stood ready to make capital out of this indignation. O'Brien and Healy, together with the other dissidents, had re-entered the party after a solemn truce had been concluded in the winter of 1907–8. Almost immediately, however, a rift had opened again on the very same issue that had provoked O'Brien's resignation in 1904. This was the need to carry further the process of land purchase, which by 1908 was running into financial difficulties. O'Brien at once suggested a new Land Conference on the lines of the original one held in 1902. This proposal was decisively defeated at a party meeting and O'Brien was obliged to face the fact that his policy of conciliation held no appeal for the great majority of his fellow-nationalists. Worse still, when in the following year he put forward basically the same idea to the National Convention of the UIL while it was considering the Land Bill then pending, he was not only outvoted but was actually shouted down. Characteristically, he reacted by forming a new organisation, the All-for-Ireland League, through which he hoped to campaign for 'conference plus business', and when this organisation was denounced by the party leaders he responded by once more leaving the party, followed in due course by his little coterie of Cork 'independents' and by the inevitable Tim Healy.

O'Brien and his group remained small in numbers, but their capacity for mischief was not to be underestimated, especially when an issue like the budget gave them a golden opportunity to take the parliamentary party in the flank. But this hostility, vexatious as it was, was for Redmond and his friends far less nerve-racking than the complex manoeuvres resulting from the constitutional crisis itself. The nationalist policy was to extract what concessions they could on the details of the budget, but to support it as a whole provided they received in return a sufficiently firm guarantee of the abolition or effective limitation of the veto power of the House of Lords. All through 1900 they strove for this objective with little enough success. But at the end of November the Lords finally did reject the budget and in so doing miraculously transformed the situation. Parliament was at once dissolved and a general election followed immediately. The Irish leaders were now in a much stronger position to exert leverage and the first sign of this was a public statement by the prime minister, Asquith (made in the knowledge that if he was not explicit enough the Irish vote in Britain would be thrown against the Liberals), that the problem of Ireland would only be solved 'by a policy which, while safeguarding the supremacy and indefeasible authority of the Imperial Parliament, will set up in Ireland a system of full self-government in regard to purely Irish affairs'.

That the election itself would destroy the overall Liberal majority was predictable. But that it would create virtual parity between the two major parties – Liberals 275 against Unionists 273 – and place the balance of power in the hands of the forty Labour members and the Irish was something nobody could have foreseen. In fact, Redmond, with his seventy-one votes, could make or break the government, though he had always to keep in mind that if he did break the government he would simultaneously postpone Home Rule indefinitely. Moreover, his own freedom of manoeuvre was further circumscribed by the virulent hostility towards the budget which the election campaign in Ireland had brought to the surface and which the eleven 'independents' returned at the polls were certain to exploit to the full. In short, the Irish party could only support the Liberals in their drive to force the budget through if Asquith gave them convincing proof that he would be able that same session to limit the veto power of the House of Lords, the underlying assumption being that once the veto question was satisfactorily settled, Home Rule would be the next item on the agenda.[5]

The business of screwing the courage of the Liberals to the sticking-point was excruciatingly difficult and was still further complicated by the death of King Edward VII in May 1910. His successor, George V, was well-meaning but totally inexperienced, and there was a widespread feeling that he ought not to be subjected at once to the rigours of a full-scale constitutional conflict. Accordingly, the Liberal and Conservative leaders agreed to meet, four-a-side, in private conference with a view to breaking the deadlock. The Nationalists were of course excluded from its sessions and while it lasted – from June to November – they were extremely nervous lest some agreed solution should be reached at their expense. They were right to be nervous because, although they were not in a position to know anything about the matter one of the Liberal representatives, Lloyd George, dangled before the Unionists the prospect of a coalition government to settle the outstanding issues of the day. The chief of these was the great question of tariff reform, but Lloyd George was also prepared to settle the Irish question by consent, and to settle it, if need be, by a federal arrangement such as many moderate Unionists were drawn towards at that time. These manoeuvres, like the conference itself, collapsed because the chief Unionist delegate, Arthur Balfour, resolutely refused to accept either a settlement of the House of Lords question, or of the Irish question, on any basis that would, in his opinion, imperil the unity either of his party or of the empire. To accept a federal solution would be to alienate Irish Unionists without satisfying Irish separatists and would thus be the worst of both worlds. 'No man', he ruled, 'has a right to destroy the property of which he is a trustee [or] to throw over its [his party's] strongest convictions.'[6]

In the end, therefore, no agreement at the conference or between individuals was possible and the Liberals moved one stage nearer to their final confrontation with the House of Lords. This did not come, however, until after a second general election which only served to strengthen Redmond's position. This time the Liberals and the Unionists were exactly equal with 273 seats each. Labour went up to forty-two, and the Irish Nationalists accounted for eighty-three, of whom seventy-three were followers of Redmond. The pressure could now be resumed with greater severity and in the end, though only after extreme tension and under the threat of a mass creation of Liberal peers, the House of Lords capitulated. The government's solution – embodied in the Parliament Act of 1911 – was to reduce the absolute veto of the Lords to a delaying power of two years. Any measure that had passed in three successive years through the House of Commons would thus automatically become law. With this clarification of the situation, and with Redmond still holding the balance at Westminster, it was clear to all beholders that the first serious test of the new procedure would be Home Rule.

8. Labour in Ferment

No one who casts even the most cursory glance over modern Irish history can fail to be struck either by the slowness with which anything remotely recognisable as a labour movement emerged, or by the relative feebleness of that movement when it did emerge. Yet the reasons for such delayed and stunted growth are obvious enough, and spring directly from the economic and political circumstances of the country. In economic terms, the absence of a labour movement of the conventional kind reflected the absence of a conventional industrial revolution. Except for the special case of northeast Ulster, industry remained, as we have seen, essentially small-scale and closely linked to the needs and products of a predominantly agricultural country. Here and there, it is true, and particularly in the brewing and distilling industries, larger businesses were successfully established, but these, no less than the smaller industries, depended in the main upon processing and selling what the farmer had to offer. Industries catering primarily for the consumer in a small, poor country are not likely to be large industries and Ireland was no exception to the rule. The opportunities of employment were limited, and were to be found mainly in a number of skilled or semi-skilled trades – building, distributive work, tailoring, hairdressing, saddlery, cabinet-making etc. – and in unskilled labour which was used mostly for road and rail work, at the docks and in general transport.

A labour situation where the demand was generally less than the supply and where, consequently, there was a large pool of unemployment, or at best underemployment, was not conducive to the growth of organisation either at the trade union or at the political level. Nor is there much evidence that the leaders of public opinion – even nationalist public opinion – concerned themselves to any marked degree with such organisation for most of the nineteenth century. This was partly, but only partly, because of the overwhelming emphasis laid by all nationalist movements, whether constitutional or otherwise, upon the repeal of the Union. By the side of this dominant political issue, questions of industrial welfare, of hours and wages, of workers' solidarity, seem to have been regarded as of only minor importance; or, if of major importance, as questions not to be answered until after independence had been won. In practice, of course, the political struggle could never for long be divorced from its economic context. Only that context was agrarian, not urban. Nineteenth century Ireland did not lack her class war, but it was a war that was aimed at bringing about what Michael Davitt called 'the fall of feudalism'. Davitt himself had a vision of the collective ownership (land nationalisation) which he wanted to substitute for that feudalism, but it was a vision few of his countrymen shared. The feudal aristocracy gave way, not to any proletarian dictatorship, but to a rural bourgeoisie, in its own way as conservative as the landlords it had displaced – a bourgeoisie composed for the most part of small farmers clinging immovably to their patches of ill-cultivated land, and small shopkeepers adding 'the halfpence to the pence and prayer to shivering prayer'. A proletariat did indeed exist – it included both the farm-labourers in the countryside and the slum-dwellers in the towns – but it was ignored by contemporaries and has not yet found its historian.*

This did not mean, however, that there was no industrial organisation at all. On the contrary, workers' combinations, which had survived repressive legislation throughout the eighteenth century, responded in the nineteenth to the more favourable opportunities created by the repeal of the combination laws and the onset of industrial progress. Even though, as we have seen, this was not extensive over much of Ireland, there was enough new economic activity to bring into being fresh unions or, as became increasingly common in the middle years of the century, branches of English unions. Because of the absence of heavy industry outside the northeast, these unions were mostly small groups of craftsmen and, except in Dublin and one or two of the bigger towns, they led a precarious and rather intermittent existence. In outlook they were the reverse of radical, and although they naturally concerned themselves with questions of wages and conditions of work, they seem broadly to have accepted the framework of capitalism; for them, as for most Irishmen who thought about the matter at all, the most urgent economic task was to create more jobs and if this could only be done by an influx of capital they were certainly not going to prejudice that possibility by stirring up bad relations with the employers.

Thus, when in 1863 some of the Dublin unions came together to form the United Trades' Association, they did so not only to protect 'the rights of labour', but also to encourage native manufactures. 'The association', it was stressed, 'had not been formed to interfere with the

* Even during the Land War there were indications of friction between the tenant-farmers and the farm-labourers and as late as 1910 John Dillon was noting it apprehensively as a future storm-centre. In 1890 Devitt vainly attempted to interest Parnell in a nascent organisation of workers – the Irish Federated Trade and Labour Union – and some fifteen years later William O'Brien took up with enthusiasm another abortive body, the Land and Labour Association. Both of these attempts failed to make any serious impact on the labour problem, partly because their members were too few and too poor, but even more because the political leaders of the day regarded them as dangerous deviations from the party line – which was Home Rule. The various attempts to form more than purely local labour associations in the 1880s have been described by J. W. Boyle, 'The rise of the Irish Labour Movement, 1888-1907', pp. 122-44 (unpublished doctrinal thesis, Trinity College, Dublin, 1961).

legitimate progress of trade – on the contrary, their desire was to push trade in every manner possible.'[1] Once in being, the Dublin Association was soon drawn on to think in larger terms; by 1864 it was not only in correspondence with a similar body in Cork, but was looking forward to the creation of some form of national organisation. This seemed less urgent, however, when in 1868 the Trades Union Congress was established in Britain. Since many Irish trade unionists belonged to 'amalgamated' unions with their headquarters in Britain, the prospect of belonging to a potentially powerful organisation already in existence, was much more attractive than the task of having to build one themselves from the foundations, and for the next quarter of a century the Irish labour groups dwelt more or less contentedly under the shadow of their more prosperous and more highly developed neighbours.*

But as time passed, in this sphere, as in politics, the demand for Home Rule began to be heard. Irishmen were the poor relations of the British labour world and were made to realise it. They felt themselves under-represented in the amalgamated unions and at the TUC, and at both levels were resentful of the emphasis – in itself natural enough – that was placed upon British rather than upon Irish problems. This did not prevent the drift towards amalgamation. On the contrary, so far as collective bargaining was concerned, the weak Irish unions could only benefit from association with their opposite numbers in Britain, and so usual had this kind of association become that by 1898 there were only ninety-six independent unions, with a membership of 13,077, in the whole of Ireland.[2] Nevertheless, the hankering for an organisation of their own continued, and in 1894 a conference in Dublin, attended by 119 delegates from all over the country, decided to establish an Irish Trades Congress. Thenceforward, Irish delegates played little part in the proceedings of the parent British body. Paradoxically, their own Congress continued to depend for a good deal of its support upon the amalgamated unions to which so many Irish trade unionists still belonged. By the end of the century about 60,000 workers were represented at the annual meetings of the Irish Trades Congress (rising only to about 70,000 in 1910) and most of these came from some fifty unions of which roughly half had their headquarters in Great Britain.[3] It was not surprising, therefore, that the unions which dominated these gatherings were the skilled crafts (where the 'amalgamateds' were very strong) and that up to 1906 the British-based unions supplied approximately fifty per cent of the 'sustentation' on which the Congress depended.

* Within individual Irish cities consultation and co-operation between unions was carried on through the medium of Trades Councils. One such body was founded at Belfast in 1881 and another in Dublin in 1886: several smaller towns followed suit in due course. In Dublin the craft unions predominated, but elsewhere general labourers' unions seem to have participated from time to time. By 1894 both the Belfast and Dublin Trades Councils claimed to have 15,000 affiliated members each (J. W. Boyle, op. cit., pp. 146, 148).

Nor was it surprising that the tone of debate in Congress should have been of the most decorous conservatism. A resolution in favour of the nationalisation, not just of the land, but also of the means of production, distribution and exchange, was defeated at Cork in 1895 by fifty-seven to twenty-five and most members present seemed to agree with the dictum of William Field, MP, a butcher by trade and a member of the Irish parliamentary party, that 'the theory of socialism was all right if they had to deal with angels and not with human nature'. Yet the very next year the first ripples of impending change were to spread across the placid surface of the Irish labour movement, for it was then that James Connolly arrived in Ireland. Born in Edinburgh in 1868 of Irish parents forced to emigrate through sheer economic necessity, Connolly's early life was spent in the lower depths of poverty and deprivation. He who was to become the foremost Irish socialist theoretician was virtually self-educated. As a young boy he went from one dead-end job to another, even serving in the army for a time but leaving it abruptly before his time had expired. At the age of twenty-one he married and settled down in Edinburgh as a carter employed by the Corporation. Then began his indoctrination with the two creeds that were to dominate his life – socialism and nationalism. For both of them he was in large measure indebted to John Leslie, of Scottish birth but partly-Irish origin, who combined a lifelong attachment to socialism with an encyclopaedic knowledge of Irish revolutionary movements. From him Connolly learnt much theory, much history and also, though not without difficulty, the art of public speaking.

It was Leslie, too, who directed Connolly towards Ireland. Having stood as a socialist for Edinburgh Town Council and been defeated, the neophyte had no future as a Corporation employee. He had to emigrate to survive and through Leslie's agency was saved from going to South America by an offer from the Dublin Socialist Society to come and act as their paid organiser at what turned out to be the highly precarious wage of a pound a week. The title of the Society was rather more grandiose than the reality and for the next seven years Connolly had uphill work to make a living for his family and to spread the word among a dulled and unresponsive proletariat. Yet within a few weeks of his arrival he succeeded in launching the Irish Socialist Republican party. It consisted at the outset of a few kindred souls and was never a very thriving organisation; indeed, when Connolly had to leave Dublin for America in 1903 – again because of the impossibility of providing for his wife and children – the spark he had lit flickered and almost went out altogether. The real significance of this little party, however, had nothing to do with its numerical strength, its open-air meetings or its occasional forays into municipal politics. The ISRP was important primarily because it gave James Connolly a platform and allowed him in his speeches, and in the first of his newspapers, the *Workers' Republic*, to evolve his doctrines not from theory alone, or by observation from afar, but through direct experience of what it meant to be a poor

273

man living in the Dublin slums.[4]

From the very outset Connolly addressed himself to the double task that was to occupy him for most of the rest of his life. On the one hand, he had to try to wean the Irish worker from a dumb acceptance of the status quo and move him sharply leftwards towards a more dynamic programme – in effect, towards socialism. But on the other hand, he had to reckon with a powerful nationalist tradition and to define his own attitude towards that tradition. His solution to the first of these problems is to be found in the inaugural manifesto of the new party, which looked boldly to the establishment of an Irish Socialist Republic 'based upon the public ownership by the Irish people of the land and instruments of production, distribution and exchange'. This general principle was developed in more detail in the 'programme' which formed the main part of the manifesto – a programme calling for the nationalisation of railways and canals; the supplanting of private banks by state institutions; a graduated income tax on higher incomes to finance pensions for widows, orphans and the aged; restriction of the working week to forty-eight hours and the establishment of a minimum wage; free maintenance for all children, public control of the National Schools by popularly elected boards, and free education up to and including the university level; gradual extension of public ownership 'to all the necessaries of public life' and the adoption of universal suffrage.

How did Connolly propose to reconcile this thoroughgoing socialism with the nationalism in which his fellow-workers were immersed and by which he was himself so profoundly influenced? His aim was to demonstrate that the two currents of thought were not antagonistic but complementary. As he put it in a statement issued just before the launching of the manifesto:

> The struggle for Irish freedom has two aspects; it is national and it is social. The national ideal can never be realised until Ireland stands forth before the world as a nation, free and independent. It is social and economic because no matter what the form of government may be, as long as one class owns as private property the land and instruments of labour from which mankind derive their substance, that class will always have it in their power to plunder and enslave the remainder of their fellow creatures.

From this it seems that although he might regard the two currents as complementary, he was quite clear that, as he phrased it in later years, 'the Irish question was at bottom an economic question', and indeed, in the manifesto itself he made this very explicit. Private ownership, he contended, was 'the fundamental basis of all oppression, national, political and social'. Yet when he went on to define how independence was to be achieved, he left open the path for political action. 'The Irish Socialist Republican holds', he wrote:

> That . . . the national and economic freedom of the Irish people must be sought in . . . the establishment of an Irish Socialist Republic

and the consequent conversion of the means of production, distribution and exchange into the common property of society, to be held and controlled by a democratic state in the interests of the entire community.

That the conquest by the Social Democracy of political power in parliament, and on all public bodies in Ireland, is the readiest and most effective means whereby the revolutionary forces may be organised and disciplined to attain that end.[5]

This passage suggests that while Connolly had recognised thus early the problem that was to haunt him right up to 1916 he had not really succeeded in solving it. The Irish question was at bottom economic, but political action, it appeared, would be 'the readiest and most effective means' of preparing to deal finally with it. This was the so-called social democratic approach (as opposed to syndicalism which looked to the use of economic power – for example, the general strike – as the means of overthrowing the capitalist state) and Connolly was in the end to give his life for it when he marched out to take his place in the Rising of 1916. He was not unaware of syndicalism, nor uninfluenced by it at one stage of his evolution, but in choosing to place political action first and the reshaping of society second in his order of priorities he was surely obeying a sound instinct. In the circumstances of the time, indeed, he could hardly have done otherwise. Yet, whether he fully realised it or not (and at the end of his life he almost certainly did) a socialist movement that became involved in a nationalist revolution stood in grave danger of being swallowed up. And although Connolly would no doubt have justified the means in terms of the ultimate end, he failed to realise how often the end is shaped by the means. Had he lived, of course, things might have been different. But this we cannot know. All that the historian can say is that the record of the Irish labour movement after 1916 was to be less a monument to him than a demonstration of the insolubility of the problem he had seen so clearly at the threshold of his career.

Even at the time he made his original diagnosis the cure Connolly proposed must have seemed hopelessly Utopian, not in the strict Marxist sense, but because so many alternative panaceas were competing for public attention at that time, and still more because the bulk of the workers were not attuned to his message. Organised labour, it is true, was not unmindful of the need for political action and in the early years of the new century was groping its way towards the notion that the needs and interests of workingmen might be better catered for by a distinctive labour party rather than, as hitherto, by the Irish parliamentary party. The latter certainly contained a sprinkling of artisans, but seldom more than three or four and it was trying the credulity of Congress a little high for one of them, J. P. Nannetti, to say in 1906 that 'the Irish parliamentary party were the Labour party'.[6] In fact, from the turn of the century there had been increasing pressure among the more advanced trade unionists not so much to create a separate (party of their own, which they were not equipped to do, but to affiliate with the Independent Labour Party in Great Britain. In 1892 an infant Belfast Labour Party was founded, becoming in 1893 a branch of the I.L.P. It faded away about 1897, to be followed (for about a year) by the first Belfast Socialist Society. From this environment there sprang the leading exponent of the idea of parliamentary representation for trade union interests, William Walker. Walker, born in 1870 and only twenty-four when he went as a Belfast delegate to the first Irish Trades Union Congress, was a joiner by craft, with a flair for trade union affairs and a natural gift for the Old Testament style of oratory that was almost a *sine qua non* of public life in Belfast at that time. He found no apparent difficulty in combining Ulster Unionism with international socialism and was able to gather enough support to win a seat on the Belfast Corporation. In 1904, as president of the ITUC, he carried the members with him in recommending affiliation with the Labour Representation Committee in Britain and the following year was largely instrumental in resurrecting the Belfast Labour Party which had fallen on evil times during the previous decade. Under its aegis Walker campaigned for one of the Belfast parliamentary constituencies three times in the next two years, coming within three hundred votes of victory on one occasion.[7]

All this was evidence of life, but not, it must be admitted, of very vigorous life. Nor could it be vigorous until the 'old unionism' of the craft unions was reinforced by the 'new unionism' reaching down to the sweated and unskilled workers in Belfast, Dublin and other cities, where the employers were still able to profit from the abundance of cheap labour to exact long hours for low wages. The next phase of the Irish labour movement was to see precisely this grafting of the new unionism upon the old – a revolutionary development which will always be associated with the name of one man, James Larkin. Larkin was born in Liverpool in 1876 of Irish parents who, like Connolly's parents, had been driven through poverty to emigrate. Larkin – again the parallel with Connolly is close – spent much of his childhood earning a few shillings a week in blind-alley jobs to eke out the family income, and, like Connolly once more, he picked up what education he could how he could. He was never to be the intellectual that Connolly became, but he read widely and used his reading to fortify a vivid imagination and a natural gift, or rather genius, for flamboyant oratory. Larkin's speeches were larger than life because Larkin himself was larger than life. Physically a very powerful man, he had a big presence and an even bigger voice which allowed him to dominate vast meetings even in the open air. He himself asked little enough of existence – he was simple in his tastes, simple in his religion (he may have remained a Catholic though he castigated the Church for its attitude to social problems), simple in his vision of a society that would bring beauty as well as security to the workingclass home. 'Here', as Sean O'Casey summed him up, 'was a man who would put a flower in a vase on a table as well as a loaf on a plate.' But his emotions, too, seemed more intense than those of ordinary men. He was driven by a deep compassion and tenderness for the poor to preach 'the divine gospel of discontent'. The other side of that gospel was a *saeva indignatio* against employers who exploited their workers or against trade union officials who failed to protect their members. Larkin, once enraged, respected neither laws nor conventions nor individuals, and his creative years were passed in a frenzy of passionate involvement and controversy. He was the archetypal bull in a china-shop and it was a moot point whether irate industrialists or staid trade unionists were more alarmed by his irruption onto the Irish scene.

He arrived in 1907, sent by the National Union of Dock Labourers to organise the dockers in the various Irish ports, but more especially Belfast and Dublin. He began work in Belfast and within a few months the city was in turmoil with strikes and lockouts affecting not only the dockworkers, but also the carters and coal-men, and even a section of the police. The most remarkable, if temporary achievement of Larkin's first crusade in Ireland was to still for a brief space sectarian rivalries amongst Catholic and Protestant workmen, who were persuaded to present a common front to the employers.* The economic benefits of this joint action were, however, marginal. The carters and coal-men did certainly receive some increase of wages but the employers reserved the right to employ whom they chose – thus frustrating Larkin's ambition to force the 'closed shop' upon them – and the dockers were obliged eventually to capitulate and creep back to work hat in hand.[8]

What Belfast had really demonstrated was not the power of Larkin, but the weakness and poverty of the men he had been sent to lead. Yet Belfast, for all its harsh conditions and its sweated industry, seemed almost a paradise for the workingman compared with Dublin. When 'the strike organiser from England' – as Arthur Griffith was soon to christen him – arrived in the capital to set up his headquarters there in 1908 he was taken aback by the poverty, disease and degradation he found in the slums which housed the greater part of the working population. Between then and 1914 the conditions prevailing in Dublin were pitilessly exposed in a series of reports which painted a fearful picture of what life in that beautiful but decayed city was really like for its poorest citizens. From these reports it is enough to select a few of the more terrible details in order to establish the atmosphere in which Larkin was to pass the most creative period of his life. About thirty per cent (87,000) of the people of Dublin lived in the slums which were for the most part the worn-out shells of Georgian mansions. Over 2,000 *families* lived in single room tenements which were without heat or light or water (save for a tap in a passage or backyard) or adequate sanitation. Inevitably, the death-rate was the highest in the country, while infant mortality was the worst, not just in Ireland, but in the

* In this he received some help from the nationalist MP, Joe Devlin, and also from the Independent Orange Institution; for the latter, see pp. 295-7 below.

British Isles. Disease of every kind, especially tuberculosis, was rife and malnutrition was endemic; it was hardly surprising that the poor, when they had a few pence, often spent them seeking oblivion through drink.

The problems of Dublin was, however, economic as well as social. Or rather, it might have been easier to grapple with social degradation if the economic base had been sounder. The city had for decades been attracting population from the rural districts without being able to provide sufficient employment. Being a commercial and distributive, rather than an industrial, centre, most of its labour was employed in the carrying trade. In 1901, for example, out of a total male labour force of 40,000, only about a quarter were employed in skilled trades such as printing, engineering, leather-work or clothing. Over 7000 of the 40,000 just mentioned were 'carriers' in one form or another and no less than 23,000 were labourers, whether builders' or general. Most were in fact general labourers who could hope for only casual work. The precise amount of unemployment in Dublin is impossible to estimate; informed contemporary estimates at the time Larkin arrived in the city put it at anything up to twenty per cent, though in the skilled trades the figure would have been appreciably less, perhaps as low as ten per cent. And this, it must be emphasised, relates to men only. Unemployment, or underemployment, among women was in all probability as bad and the prevalence of prostitution may well have been a consequence of this. In such circumstances wages could not have been high. We know, indeed, that apart from being irregular, they were very low. Most slum families seem to have earned less than a pound a week in 1909 and virtually all of this went on the barest necessities of life.[9]

It was against this background that Larkin set to work to organise dockers, carters and labourers just as he had done in Belfast. Initially, he met with more success in Dublin than in the north and in 1908 alone conducted three successful strikes which led to higher wages for the men. In doing so he had quarrelled with James Sexton, the General Secretary of the English-based Dockers' Union by which Larkin himself was employed. Sexton, not surprisingly, found Larkin unamenable to discipline and too fond of calling Irish strikes which had to be financed from English pockets. Suspended at the end of 1908, Larkin at once proceeded to found his own Irish Transport and General Workers Union, which gradually attracted into its ranks the majority of carters and dockers in Belfast, Dublin and other ports, though not without a struggle from the National Dockers' Union, especially in Belfast, where Sexton and Larkin fought each other for mastery. There followed several years of intense activity marked by frequent strikes and constant turmoil. Sometimes, as in Cork in 1909 – where Larkin received a jail sentence for his activities – these strikes were disastrous, sometimes they were relatively successful. But for Larkin the essential point was that his union was beginning to give the most down-trodden of the workers a sense of identity and of self-respect. He was, in short, driving home to them by practical example the force of that aphorism of Camille Desmoulins' which Connolly had put at the head of his manifesto twelve years earlier: 'The great appear great because we are on our knees: let us rise.'

Naturally, Larkin made enemies and not just among employers. He incurred the displeasure of the Irish parliamentary party when in 1908 he re-established the Dublin branch of the Independent Labour Party. He was pursued by the fierce and rancorous hostility of Griffith and Sinn Féin, partly because Griffith persisted in regarding him as the embodiment of English trade unionism, but still more because the constant stoppages engineered by the 'strike organiser' were disrupting industry, and 'whatever causes the area of manufacturing to contract in Ireland dangerously affects the future as well as the present prosperity of the country'.[10] More ominous even than this was the opposition Larkin encountered among the leaders of the conservative 'old unions' who still dominated the Irish TUC and who were still, many of them, members of English-based amalgamated unions. In the quarrel between Larkin and the National Union of Dockers enough of these leaders had sided with the latter to secure Larkin's expulsion from Congress in 1909. Even they, however, were amenable to the argument of solidarity and when Larkin was imprisoned the following year for his part in the Cork strike his fellow-unionists rallied to his support. In 1911 he himself was rehabilitated and the Irish Transport and General Workers' Union was allowed to become affiliated to Congress.

This reconciliation should not be allowed to conceal the fact that just as Larkin was a very different kind of agitator from the run-of-the-mill official, so his union was a very different kind of organisation from those with which it had now been aligned. To say that the difference lay in the fact that Larkin was a syndicalist and that ITGWU was a prototype of the 'one big union' beloved of American syndicalists is an over-simplification, but it is an important part of truth. For what distinguished Larkin from other, more conventional, trade unionists was not just a question of temperament, but a question of approach. Although a man of action rather than of ideas, and human enough to sacrifice long-term consistency to short-term advantage whenever it suited his book to do so, Larkin was not untouched by the new ideas of direct action that were flowing through the labour movement at that time. These have been labelled 'syndicalism', but the term meant so many things to so many different people that it has long lost whatever precision it may once have had. In France, for example, the stress was laid upon direct action by the proletariat through its principal weapon, the withdrawal of its labour. By repeated strikes, 'sympathetic' strikes, refusals to handle 'tainted goods', and ultimately by the general strike, the workers would simultaneously destroy capitalism and prepare the way for their own assumption of power. But whereas in France the 'syndicate' or union was to provide a *local* basis of power, in the United States, where industry itself was so massive, the emphasis of syndicalist thinking was upon trade union centralisation, upon the concentration of the labour force into large agglomerations, culminating in 'one big union'.

More important than these differences of emphasis between localism and centralism was the fact that syndicalists, however divergent their views might be about the structure of the movement, agreed on the necessity for 'industrial unionism' – that is the extension of trade unionism to the hitherto unorganised masses – and agreed also that it was essential to imbue these masses with militant class-consciousness. Clearly, Larkin, without having to intellectualise about the matter, had acted on these two principles from the outset of his career and had indeed anticipated in Ireland the great wave of strike action, more or less syndicalist in character, which swept over Britain in 1911 and 1913.

The theoretical basis for promoting and using industrial unionism as Larkin had done was provided, if theory were needed, by James Connolly. After he had gone to America Connolly had become an organiser and propagandist for the Industrial Workers of the World, the spearhead of industrial unionism in the United States, and in this capacity he had absorbed the current syndicalist ideas, which he expressed with his usual clarity in his paper, *The Harp*, and in a pamphlet later published as *The Axe to the Root*. At this stage of his career he seems to have turned away from the political preoccupations of his earlier Irish manifesto and to have been possessed by the idea that the conquest of economic power by the workers was the all-essential thing. 'The first act of the workers', he wrote, 'will be through their economic organisations seizing the organised industries; the last act will be the conquest of the political power'; and again: 'The struggle for the conquest of the political state of the capitalist is not the battle, it is only the echo of the battle. The real battle is being fought out, and will be fought out, in the industrial field.'[11]

By 1910 Connolly, disillusioned with the rivalries and jealousies of the American sects, was ready to come home. He came back primarily to revive socialism, but in 1911 was appointed an organiser for Larkin's union, with Belfast as his base and Ulster as his main responsibility. Just before his return he had completed the main literary work of his life – *Labour in Irish History* – which clearly established his intellectual superiority over his fellow-workers, and he now at once took his place as a major figure in the labour movement. In his book, the first sustained attempt to apply a Marxist interpretation to the past experience of his native land, he found in the economic factor the key to all that had gone before. 'The Irish question', he insisted, 'is a social question, the whole age-long fight of the Irish people against their oppressors resolves itself, in the last analysis, into a fight for the mastery of the means of life, the sources of production in Ireland.'[12]

But although *Labour in Irish History* bore the marks of syndicalist influence – only gradually did its author move back towards the endorsement of political revolution that led him into the GPO in 1916

– it would be wrong to assume that Connolly, any more than Larkin, was imprisoned in an iron cage of doctrine. On the contrary, though they were poles apart in temperament and not always the happiest of bedfellows in the labour movement, they had this in common, that they were both prepared to use whatever means came to hand in the particular situation in which they found themselves. As Larkin once remarked: 'Why use one arm when we have two? Why not strike the enemy with both arms – the political and the economic?' This was the position that Connolly came ultimately to share. Even in 1910, indeed, he accepted – perhaps for the sake of unity – a manifesto issued by the Socialist Party of Ireland (his old party under a new name) which, after defining the party's aim as being to gain control of 'the entire resources of the country', went on to declare that the method would be to use the ballot box to secure the election of socialist representatives on all elective bodies 'and thus gradually to transfer the political power of the state into the hands of those who will use it to further or extend the principle of common or public ownership'.[13] And in 1912, at the Irish Trades Union Congress, it was Connolly who carried the motion that 'the independent representation of labour upon all public boards' should be part of Congress policy, a policy which in 1914 resulted at last in the formal creation of the Irish Labour Party, in such close communion with Congress that the latter was renamed the 'Irish Trades Union Congress and Labour Party'.[14]

Yet, paradoxically enough, it was industrial rather than political action that now opened out before them. The industrial unrest that racked Britain in 1911 spread rapidly to Ireland and Larkin, ever ready to use the weapon of the sympathetic strike, was soon heavily involved in disputes affecting dockers, carters, coal-men and eventually railwaymen. In terms of wage-increases these stoppages produced very mixed results, but their real significance was not the money that accrued to the workers, but the power that accrued to Larkin's union. More and more it became obvious – to the employers as well as to Larkin himself – that so long as he could maintain his remarkable personal ascendancy over the dockers he held the port of Dublin (and other ports, too) at his mercy. During 1912, with trade moving briskly and business eager to recoup its losses of the previous year, the Irish Transport and General Workers' Union met with little resistance. Some of his most effective peaceful bargaining was achieved at that time – the most notable example being his reorganisation of the labour force in the port of Dublin – and it was not surprising that the numbers joining his union rose dramatically from 4000 in 1911 to 8000 in 1912 and thence to about 10,000 in the middle of 1913.[15]

At first it seemed as if nothing could stop this mounting tide of success. Between January and August 1913 Larkin pulled off two more coups by gaining substantial pay-rises for his dockers from some of the most important shipping companies in Dublin, and by bringing the agricultural labourers of the surrounding countryside into his union to

281

such effect that at harvest-time they were able to hold the farmers to ransom and extract from them what seemed the princely sum of seventeen shillings for a sixty-six hour week. But then Larkin turned his attention to a far more formidable foe – the Dublin United Tramways Company. This was part of the commercial empire of one of the wealthiest magnates in the city – William Martin Murphy. Murphy had many interests – he was a pioneer of tramways and electric railways in several countries, he owned a big hotel and a large department store, and in the *Independent* newspaper, as we have already seen, he had a powerful propaganda weapon. The *Independent* appealed primarily to the more substantial sections of the Catholic middle class and Murphy himself was well placed to become the paladin of the Dublin employers. The latter had formed a defence organisation of their own, the Employers' Federation, as far back as 1911, but it was only now in 1913 that Murphy managed to give it some backbone. Before Larkin could press home his attack, the Tramway Company forestalled him by declaring that it would not recognise Larkin or his union. Larkin at once struck back by calling out the tramwaymen on 26 August, during Horse Show week, the peak of the social season in Dublin and therefore the moment of maximum inconvenience.

The strike was only partially effective, since the company had been dismissing Larkinites for some time before it occurred, but it rapidly spread to other parts of Murphy's empire. Larkin attempted to infiltrate the distribution department of the *Independent*. His men were promptly locked out. He then requested the principal newspaper distributors in the country – Eason's – not to circulate the *Independent*, and when they refused Larkin called a strike there too. Next, his dockers began to refuse to handle 'tainted' goods, i.e. goods destined for Eason's, and Murphy gathered himself for the counterattack. After intensive discussion at the end of August, the Employers' Federation, some 400 strong, decided to break Larkin's union by locking out all their employees who belonged to it. Since the Coalowners' Association had just done the same, and the builders, timber and cement merchants, and even the farmers, speedily followed suit, the end result was that by the end of September some 25,000 men were off work. As most of them had families it would probably be no exaggeration to say that close on 100,000 men, women and children faced a grim winter if strike and lockout continued. They did continue – in an atmosphere of increasing bitterness and violence. Larkin intensified his warlike speeches and was arrested for his pains on charges of seditious libel and seditious conspiracy. Released on bail, he repeated his violent language as if nothing had happened. Threatened with re-arrest he disappeared for twenty-four hours, only to re-emerge, heavily disguised, on the balcony of Murphy's Imperial Hotel in O'Connell Street. He was seized by the police before he could utter more than a few words to the Sunday morning crowd, but scuffles broke out and the police, who had already been in frequent collision with pickets from Larkin's unions, turned on the crowd with savage baton charges. These in turn provoked mob rioting and at the end of it all two people had been killed and many hundreds wounded, including two hundred policemen. The shock to Dublin feeling was profound, and scarcely had it been absorbed when tension in the city was further increased by the news that two tenement houses had collapsed, killing seven of the inmates and injuring a number of others.

The immediate outcome of these days of crisis was an impressive demonstration of labour solidarity. With the principal Irish leaders arrested (including Connolly), the resistance to the employers was organised by two able trade unionists, P. T. Daly and William O'Brien.* They at once dispatched emissaries to the British Trades Union Congress which responded with massive grants of money and food. Congress alone granted nearly £100,000 of the £150,000 which was subscribed by British sympathisers while the lockout lasted. But as the tragic dispute, with its attendant miseries of cold, starvation and destitution for thousands of Dublin families, dragged on, it became a question how long British unions would be prepared to finance their Irish brethren. Hopes of a settlement faded when the employers rejected the report of a government inquiry in October and tempers began ominously to rise. Special bitterness was caused by the action of the Roman Catholic clergy in preventing the departure to temporary homes in England of children from the tenements, who were starving through no fault of their own. This scheme, entirely benevolent in intention, was opposed on the ground that the children's faith would be endangered if they were sent out of the country. So emphatic and well-organised was the hostility that the rescue operation had to be abandoned and the children left to wither in the sanctity of their slums.

Such bigotry moved Larkin, who had been released from prison after a brief incarceration, to furies of denunciation. So also, unfortunately, did the failure of the British labour movement to go beyond its contributions of food and money and back the Irish struggle with sympathetic strike action. Carrying his 'fiery cross' to England, Larkin soon over-reached himself and alienated those without whose support the resistance of his union would have crumbled within a very few days. Why did he do it? The answer lies only partly in his personality. He was a violent, tempestuous man at the crisis of his career, and was naturally prone to think that those who did not adopt his methods were *ipso facto* against him. But behind this question of temperament lay something more profound, something which existed at two quite different levels. At one level Larkin stood for a militant conception of trade unionism which the more moderate British leaders were at that moment striving to contain. The Dublin dispute of 1913 was, therefore, for them

* This William O'Brien is not to be confused with the parliamentarian of the same name. A tailor by trade, O'Brien became one of the most prominent trade unionists of his generation and ended as a bitter foe of Jim Larkin's. For his subsequent career, see below, Part IV A, chap. 5, section iv.

an extreme instance of the kind of injury that aggressive industrial unionism could bring upon those who meddled with it. Consequently, while they recognised a need to help working-men in their struggle to survive, they closed ranks instinctively against Larkin's crude attempts to bully them into endorsing his kind of unionism. At another level altogether, Larkin's movement was an Irish movement which was, potentially at least, a seedbed of revolution. It has to be remembered that the Dublin lockout took place in an atmosphere of gathering tension over the Irish question as a whole, when Ulster opposition to Home Rule had declared itself in no uncertain terms and when it had begun to seem as if Ireland might dissolve in civil war, dragging Britain after her into the abyss. English labour leaders were hardly to be blamed if they shrank back from the brink of that abyss and refused to hurl their own followers over it for a cause that had nothing to do with the movement as a whole and seemed to promise little enough success even for its Irish adherents.

All explanations of Larkin's breach with the English unions must be speculative, so impulsive and unpredictable a man was he, but the results of that breach are beyond argument. Contributions from Britain dwindled to a trickle in the New Year of 1914, and in the course of January and February, the men gradually drifted back to work. Connolly later described the result as 'a drawn battle' and in the sense that the employers did not achieve their total objective – the destruction of Larkin's union – this was a fair verdict. But Murphy and his associates had achieved a good deal nevertheless. Many employees were only taken back on condition that they did not join the union, that they did not engage in sympathetic strikes, and that they would not refuse to work with non-unionists. It might be possible to build the Transport and General Workers' Union again in the future, but the work would have to be begun once more almost from the foundations. And if Connolly, writing at a distance from the event, was prepared to draw some comfort from the result, it was Connolly, writing immediately after the event, who found the bitterest and truest words to describe what had happened. 'And so', he wrote, 'we Irish workers must again go down into Hell, bow our back to the lash of the slave driver, let our hearts be seared by the iron of his hatred, and instead of the sacramental wafer of brotherhood and common sacrifice, eat the dust of defeat and betrayal. Dublin is isolated.'[16]

Yet the legacy of 1913 was not solely a legacy of isolation and defeat. Two consequences flowed from the crisis which within three years were to have an importance no-one could have foreseen at the time. The first was a shift in the leadership of the Irish labour movement. Larkin emerged from the quarrel not without honour – his courage had been as conspicuous as his judgment had been faulty – and in 1914 he served as president of the Irish Trades Union Congress. But his temper, never of the sweetest, had notably disimproved. Moody and impatient of criticism, he even threatened to resign from his own union in June 1914.

This catastrophe was averted, but he became increasingly restless and in October left for a lecture tour in America. By a series of mischances he did not return to Ireland until 1923, and when he did return was never again to achieve his old unquestioned dominance. The vacuum left by his departure was immediately filled by James Connolly, but a Connolly who was deeply disillusioned by the collapse of international socialism after the outbreak of the war and whose mind was turning steadily towards the political revolution that was to engulf him and everything he stood for in 1916.

Yet Connolly was no longer just an organiser, just a journalist, just a theoretician. For the second consequence of 1913 was that this man, who was to emerge as the most able and indomitable strategist of armed insurrection, was given, as a result of the lockout, a weapon that he could fashion to his own use. This was the tiny force, numbering only about 200 men, known as the Irish Citizen Army. It had come into being during the labour dispute partly to enable the locked-out men to defend themselves in clashes with the police, and partly to combat the demoralising effects of unemployment by giving them some cohesion and sense of purpose. It was suggested by an ex-Army officer, Captain J. R. White, that a course of drilling would help to occupy the men usefully and in November 1913 he put his plan into effect with the approval of Larkin and Connolly. Since the Irish Volunteers were being founded at the same time, it was unlikely that the Citizen Army would attract many recruits and in fact, when the men went back to work, their little force almost disappeared. That it was resuscitated was due largely to the initiative of one of the most remarkable individuals that the Dublin slums ever produced – Sean O'Casey. At that time a general labourer and an admirer of Larkin's, O'Casey – or O Cathasaigh as he signed himself then – was instrumental in bringing together a small group which launched the revivified Citizen Army at a public meeting in 1914. The principle to which above all it stood committed was that 'the ownership of Ireland, moral and material, is vested of right in the people of Ireland'. In more practical terms, the aims of the Army were to equip and train Irishmen to enforce and defend its basic principle of public ownership; 'to sink all differences of birth, privilege and creed under the common name of the Irish people'; to maintain 'the absolute unity of Irish nationhood' and to stand for recognition of the rights and liberties of the world's democracies.[17]

Membership of the Citizen Army was open to all who accepted the concept of equal rights and opportunities and who were prepared to work with organised labour to that end. At Larkin's instance a further clause was added, laying it down that every member must be, if possible, a member of a trade union recognised by the Irish Trades Union Congress. Yet one who was present at the inaugural meeting, and who was to become the most flamboyant of all the soldiers of the Citizen Army, was as far removed from a trade unionist as it was possible to be. This was Constance, Countess Markievicz. Born in 1868 (actually in London), a Gore-Booth of Lissadell in county Sligo, she had departed early from the quiet paths of the Anglo-Irish Ascendancy class to which she belonged by marrying a Polish count, Casimir Markievicz, who, apart from a passion for the theatre and a modest talent as a painter, had not much to offer her. Tall, beautiful, dynamic, eccentric even by the relaxed standards of her class, she overflowed from domesticity into public affairs. Interested above all in women's rights – it was the suffrage question that first caught her interest – she had a deep compassion for the poor, who loved her for it to the end of her days. She joined Sinn Féin, but recoiled from Griffith – the distaste, it seems, was mutual – and poured part of her energy into Maud Gonne's women's organisation, Inghinidhe na h Eireann, and part into her own creation, the boy-scouts or Fianna.* But it was always the poor that drew most from her and during the lockout she had worked ceaselessly at the task of providing food for the workers' families. She had sheltered Larkin before he made his speech from the balcony of the Imperial Hotel, and when Larkin left for America her home in Dublin became a *pied à terre* for Connolly in his turn. She was not easy to work with – voluble, seemingly arrogant (though perhaps this masked the loneliness of a déclassée), and, as the years went on, becoming more and more bitter and intense. O'Casey disliked her – and indeed withdrew from the Citizen Army because of her† – but she had many of the attributes of a soldier and her fondness for uniform was not mere exhibitionism. She was to play a man's part in and after 1916.[18]

Connolly, however, remained the brains and the driving force behind the Army, as he did behind the Transport and General Workers' Union and the labour movement as a whole. And Connolly, from the moment the war broke out, and he realised that all the fraternal declarations of international socialism had been powerless to stop it, bent all his formidable powers of persuasion and organisation towards the Irish insurrection which thenceforward it became the main business of his life to bring into being.

* For the Fianna, see below, p. 317.

† The ostensible cause of the quarrel was that the Countess also belonged to the Volunteers which, just at that time – the summer of 1914 – had had to submit to Redmond's dictation (see pp. 327-8). It was impossible, O'Casey argued, for the Countess to belong both to the Citizen Army and to a body dominated by those who had not the interests of labour at heart. O'Casey was narrowly outvoted and resigned, but the conflict of policy was not the sole issue, there were differences of temperament as well.

9. Ulster Blocks the Way

If for Irish nationalists the destruction of the veto power of the House of Lords removed the last constitutional obstacle to Home Rule, Irish Unionists drew from the crisis of 1909–11 a very different moral. For them the Parliament Act was the signal that the threat to their status and security which had been in abeyance for a generation had once again become urgent and formidable. Their reaction, as we shall presently see, was to take steps for their own protection that were to lead them in the name of loyalty far along the road to civil war. But although many contemporaries were taken aback by the vehemence and bitterness of their resistance, to those whose memories went back twenty years there need have been nothing strange or novel about the phenomenon.

The historical factors which separated Unionists from other Irishmen of course went back centuries rather than decades – but the differences of origin, of religion and of social and economic development which produced this fundamental cleavage in Irish society were focused more sharply than ever before by Parnell's success in bringing Home Rule into the realm of practical politics in 1885–6. More specifically, it was his triumph at the general election of 1885 (fought on a new and extended register) which both defined the threat to Unionism and helped to determine its character. Up to 1885 the Irish constituencies had been divided amongst Liberals, Conservatives and Nationalists, but the campaign of that year changed this traditional picture in three important respects. First of all, outside the nine counties of Ulster and the two seats allotted to Dublin University, no Conservative candidate gained a victory at all, with the result that while it was still permissible to speak of Irish Unionism as an entity, in parliamentary terms the running was increasingly made by Ulster Unionism. But second, because in Ireland the issue at the 1885 election was clearly seen as the preservation or destruction of the Union, a process of polarisation almost inevitably set in, constituency after constituency being won by representatives of either of the two extremes. The effect of this was to obliterate Liberalism – formerly well represented, especially in Ulster – as a political force in Ireland. It was not completely wiped out and individual Liberal Home Rulers would still for some time yet scramble home for particular seats, but from 1885 until the end of the Union there was to be no room for a third party in Irish politics.

The final consequence of Parnell's victory was perhaps the most important of all because it served to distort and prejudice the nationalist view – and to some extent the British view also – of the real balance of power in Ireland. For nationalist successes in the nine counties of Ulster, though not as staggering as elsewhere, were nevertheless very considerable. In fact, out of thirty-three seats in the province they won seventeen as against the Conservative total of sixteen. These figures were to be substantially repeated – with marginal variations in the Conservatives' favour – in subsequent elections, and they had two opposite but equally important effects. On the one hand, by exhibiting the province as evenly divided in its political loyalties, they led Home Rulers, Irish as well as British, to underestimate the strength and tenacity of Ulster Unionism and therefore to assume that while that Unionism might be coerced it did not need to be conciliated. And on the other hand, the Unionists themselves, confronted with this irrefutable evidence of the enemy in their midst, were naturally driven to exaggerate the siege mentality to which, for historical reasons, they were already prone and to answer the implied menace to their security by even tighter organisation and even greater intransigence.

This movement towards organisation and intransigence was beyond doubt the chief political legacy of the Home Rule crisis of 1885–6, but before considering how Unionism was institutionally transformed during that crisis, it is necessary to be clear about its aims and composition. In a sense, of course, it had only one aim – to preserve the Union. But what did the Union mean? What was its value to Unionists? More precisely, what did it protect them against? Different individuals would no doubt have given different answers to these questions, but most of their answers would have related to three main preoccupations – religious, economic and political – which sometimes overlapped, sometimes not. Of these three preoccupations the religious factor, though the most difficult to measure, was by no means the least significant. Traditionally, it has been hard for those outside Ireland, or even for many Irishmen themselves, to realise the intensity and passion of the Unionists' cry that Home Rule meant Rome Rule. Their insecurity sprang partly from the realisation of their numerical inferiority over the country as a whole, partly from the fact that even where they had a majority – in the north-east – they had still to reckon with a large Catholic population, but most of all from the evidence, which seemed to them convincing, that the Catholic Church was already a power in nationalist politics and might become an even greater power in the future. Where they were in a minority fear counselled caution, but where they predominated their hatred readily vented itself in the aggressive intolerance which characterised the extremer forms of Ulster Protestantism for most of the nineteenth century and which to this day embitters the political, as well as the religious life of the province. At the present moment, with the entrails of Ulster bigotry laid bare to the world as never before, it is perhaps easier to understand the reality of this religious tension, though it is still difficult to explain it.

It is not enough to explain it simply in terms of the friction between religious majorities and minorities, nor even on the ground – valid
288

thought this may be – that Irish Catholicism and Irish Protestantism (and especially the more extreme Presbyterian variants of the latter) have been, partly by reason of their juxtaposition, faiths held with strong personal conviction.* The slogans with which each side has abused the other, savage and primitive though they seem, have no doubt represented genuinely held beliefs. But in the north at least they gained an additional explosive force from their connection with deep underlying economic tensions as well. Nothing more strikingly illustrates the difference between Unionists in northeast Ireland and in the rest of the country than the fact that these economic tensions showed themselves most plainly in the towns, especially Belfast and Londonderry. Whereas outside the northeast Unionism was identified mainly with the landlord caste and a thinly spread professional and commercial middle class, in the six counties Unionism was the political creed not only of the gentry, not only of many businessmen, lawyers, doctors and Protestant clergy, but of a substantial number of farmers, agricultural labourers and industrial workers as well. Since the large Catholic minority, about a third of the total population at the end of the nineteenth century (and about the same proportion of the population of the city of Belfast) had a high percentage of families which were either working-class, or engaged in the lower reaches of commerce (publicans, grocers etc.) and of agriculture, it followed that in lean times competition for jobs and land frequently became competition between Catholics and Protestants, overflowing often enough into violence and bloodshed.

There was, however, quite another sense in which economic factors affected political alignments. For most of the nineteenth century the Union represented security for property not only for Protestant landlords but for Protestant businessmen as well. Yet here again the passage of time revealed a difference of interest and emphasis between the Unionism of the northeast and the Unionism of the rest of the country. So far as the gentry were concerned, although obviously the safety of their houses and demesnes was still important to them, their broad economic interests had been more than adequately protected by the land purchase legislation culminating in the Acts of 1903 and 1909, which had allowed them to sell out on what were, initially at least, favourable terms. But amongst the industrialists of the northeast, directly dependent as they were upon external markets and sources of raw material, membership of the great British free-trade area was vital. For them the nationalist emphasis on tariff autonomy under Home

* This may be the place to recall once more the point commonly made by all Irish historians, that it would be misleading to make a complete equation of the terms Protestant=Unionist and Catholic=nationalist; there were, of course, some Protestant nationalists, even extreme nationalists, and there were some 'loyal' (or 'Castle') Catholics. Nevertheless, it remains true as a broad generalisation that Catholicism was identified with nationalism, and Protestantism with Unionism.

G

Rule spelt ruin, since it would condemn them – so they believed – to a protectionist regime that would expose them to retaliatory discrimination in the world outside, offering them as recompense only the impoverished Irish hinterland.*

To these religious and economic apprehensions was added a third, and more directly political, motive for resisting Home Rule. Fully to understand the hysterical intensity with which Irish Unionists opposed even the very modest degree of self-government that either Gladstone or Asquith was prepared to offer, it is necessary always to remember how the whole history of the Union had been dogged by violence and bloodshed, whether agrarian in its motive or aimed at the overthrow of the British connection. In 1886, for example, the Phoenix Park murders were only four years old, and although quieter times had eventually come round, the memory was not easily eradicated. Nor was it likely to be, so long as constitutional nationalism was obliged to compete with the republican tradition which looked to the ending of the Union by an armed insurrection. It did not matter that this was a minority movement menacing nationalist parliamentarians as much as it menaced the British connection. Many Unionists refused to distinguish between degrees of nationalism and were content to oppose Home Rule not just on its own merits, but because they believed it would be used merely as a springboard for something much more extreme. The importance of this belief was that it raised the whole issue from a provincial to an imperial plane. If complete separation was the ultimate aim, then Unionists could argue that they were fighting, not just for their own sectional interests, but for the integrity and safety of the empire. It was this aspect of their cause which more than any other single factor attracted to their side the powerful forces of British Conservatism and so ensured that the battle would be fought on a wide front and with the maximum of bitterness.

But how to conduct the battle? How to establish Irish Unionism as the standard-bearer of order and conservatism in an Imperial as well as in an Anglo-Irish sense? It was not the least of Gladstone's contributions to the Irish question that he contrived to provide just the spur that was needed. First the realisation that the widening of the franchise in 1884 struck at their electoral position in the country, and after that the shock of seeing Home Rule suddenly elevated from an idea to a policy, galvanised Unionists north and south into a frenzy of organisation. This took place simultaneously at several different levels. In the countryside the most dramatic and probably the most effective outcome of this new burst of activity was the revival of the Orange Order.

* This attitude was shared by those – again mainly Protestant – who controlled the few large-scale enterprises in the south. Three in particular – to name only the most obvious Dublin examples – leaned heavily on the export market. These were Guinness's brewery, Jameson's whiskey distillery and Jacob's, the biscuit manufacturers.

Founded in 1795 as the vehicle for militant Protestantism, the Order had been formally dissolved in 1836. In fact, it had never really disappeared and the smaller farmers, agricultural labourers, and city workers had remained intensely loyal to it. Now, in the mid-'eighties, the gentry and the middle classes returned to it once more and its lodges came to provide not only the nucleus for local Protestant patriotism, but also a meeting-ground where men of different social backgrounds could come together on a basis of equality and in pursuit of a common aim. That it would have a significant political role in the future was assured by the fact that the leadership of the Order fell increasingly into the hands of Orangemen who were also MPs – notably the famous William Johnston of Ballykilbeg, W. Ellison Macartney and Major (later Colonel) E. J. Saunderson.

The function of the Orange Order was to serve, in the words its historian has applied to an earlier phase of its career, as 'a barrier to revolution and an obstacle to compromise', but it operated most effectively by generating mass emotion amongst the rank and file of Ulster Unionists.[1] Being essentially a northern phenomenon, and being also singularly unsubtle in its approach, it did not, despite its undoubted importance as a psychological weapon, meet all the needs of Irish Unionism for political machinery adequate to withstand the pressures of resurgent nationalism. To provide at least part of this machinery a group of southern Irish Unionists – landowners, businessmen and academics – met privately in May 1885 to form a new organisation, the Irish Loyal and Patriotic Union. Their immediate intention was to contest as many seats as possible in the three southern provinces at the general election of 1885. They did actually fight in fifty-five constituencies, but the result was such an unmitigated disaster – no Unionist winning a seat in the whole of the south except Dublin University – that they turned their energies towards propaganda, more especially propaganda designed to persuade British voters and British politicians that the Union must be preserved. Their original aim had been to establish an all-Ireland body, but although they claimed to speak for Irish Unionism as a whole it was significant that almost from the outset the Ulster Unionists insisted on maintaining a separate body of their own. The Irish Loyal and Patriotic Union – or Irish Unionist Alliance as it became in 1891 – was never very large and even as late as 1913 had less than 700 members. But it was wealthy, close-knit (since its adherents came mainly from a small minority in which there was a good deal of intermarriage) and influential out of all proportion to its numbers. This was partly because its finances enabled it to keep up a constant flow of information for the use of Unionists in both countries (often very effectively presented), but still more perhaps because among its members were some – such as Lord Lansdowne or Lord Midleton – who were leaders not just of Irish but of British Unionism.[2]

The Irish Unionist Alliance by itself could never provide an entirely satisfactory framework for Irish Unionism in its entirety because so

few of its members represented Irish seats in the House of Commons.*
It is not surprising, therefore, that as soon as the dust of the 1885
election had settled, the Ulster Unionists, encouraged by the Grand
Orange Lodge of Ireland, should have taken the initiative in constructing the first rudimentary model of a Unionist parliamentary party.
This was in January 1886, at a meeting which, though held in Dublin
and attended by some southern Unionists, was dominated by the
northern representatives. With the election of party whips and a chairman, the nascent party can be said to have become institutionalised;
a certain amateurism persisted for a while and the chairmanship was
apparently intended to be a rotating office. Very soon, however, it became attached to one individual. This was the redoubtable E. J. Saunderson, a wealthy Cavan landlord, a stalwart Protestant, a fire-eater in
manner and appearance, and one of the wittiest and most popular
speakers in the House of Commons.³ Simultaneously with this new
departure Ulster Unionism was evolving its own local organisation,
founded in Belfast in January 1886 and called originally the Ulster
Loyalist Anti-Repeal Union. Although landowners and businessmen were
prominent in it from the start, leading Protestant churchmen also took
a major part in its proceedings, which were quite openly directed towards arousing religious passion, not only in Ireland but in Britain as
well. As one of its strongest supporters, James Henderson, the owner
of the conservative *Belfast Newsletter*, put it in a speech at Newry a
few weeks after the new body had been started : 'I believe myself that
if we can stir up the religious feeling in Scotland we have won the
battle . . . if we excite this feeling among the Scotch, that they ought
not to leave us to be destroyed, it will be one of the most important
points in our favour.'⁴

The Anti-Repeal Union grew very rapidly. It had to do so because
it had only a few months in which to organise resistance to Gladstonian
Home Rule. The climax of this resistance, which was stage-managed
by the Anti-Repeal Union, was the visit of Lord Randolph Churchill to
Belfast in February 1886, the visit that enabled him, as he described it
himself, to 'play the Orange card'. He played it, it is important to remember, not merely by urging Ulstermen to fight against Home Rule,
but by assuring them that if the dark hour came when they had to
defend themselves 'there will not be wanting to you those of position
and influence in England who are willing to cast in their lot with you –
whatever it may be – and who will share your fortune'. Thus early in
the struggle the correspondence of interest between Unionists in Ireland

* In the parliament elected in 1886 no fewer than twelve Irish Unionists
took refuge in British constituencies – the great majority of these were
from the south. No doubt this gave them some weight in the Unionist
party of Great Britain, but it did not lessen their isolation in Ireland.
The structure and organisation of southern Irish Unionism are thoroughly
dealt with in a recently published book by P. J. Buckland, *Irish Unionism I:
The Anglo-Irish and the New Ireland, 1885 to 1922* (Dublin, 1972).

and in Britain was being emphasised, a correspondence resting on the assumption, which Lord Randolph also made very plain, that what was at stake was an imperial, not just an Irish issue. 'Like Macbeth before the murder of Duncan, Mr Gladstone asks for time. Before he plunges the knife into the heart of the British Empire, he reflects, he waits . . .'[5] While he reflected, the Anti-Repeal Union, working closely with the ILPU, continued its campaign of propaganda and pressure against Home Rule, reaching a crescendo of activity during the months – April to June 1886 – which saw the introduction and defeat of Gladstone's Bill. Nor did the Unionists rest content with persuasion. The Anti-Repeal Union and the Orange Order vied with each other in breathing threats of defiance if ever an Irish parliament should come into existence. They were prepared indeed to go beyond threats and there is evidence that they were thinking seriously in terms of armed resistance and were hoping that in this they would have the support of Field-Marshal Lord Wolseley.

The rejection of the Home Rule Bill in June absolved the Ulstermen from having to act out their dire threats, but in view of what was to happen later, it would be unwise to assume that had the Bill passed their resistance would simply have collapsed in a flurry of violent language. On the contrary, the outbreak of serious rioting in Belfast, just as the Home Rule debate reached its climax, was an ugly reminder of the religious and economic rivalries endemic in Ulster society. A hard winter had produced greater than usual distress and unemployment. This had been aggravated by discrimination against Catholics, leading to renewed friction between the workingmen of both religious persuasions, which in turn was intensified by the inflammatory and provocative oratory and journalism of the preceding months. Trouble broke out in the docks on 3 and 4 June. A few days later a Protestant mob ran wild and the army had to be called in to restore order. Despite this, there was sporadic fighting in Belfast and other towns through the rest of the summer and at the end of it thirty-two people had been killed, 442 arrested and 377 police injured.

These disturbances coincided with the election of July 1886, necessitated by the fall of Gladstone's government after the defeat of Home Rule. This did not change in any essentials the balance of power between nationalist and Unionist (in Ulster only a handful of marginal seats were contested) but by emphasising the rigidity of the electoral structure in Ireland (and it was not to change its pattern significantly right up to 1918) the campaign of 1886 helped to draw more clearly and precisely than before the real lines of division in the country. From quite another standpoint the 1886 election had an additional significance. It completed the work of 1885 by registering the virtual eclipse of Irish Liberalism. It did this in two ways. On the one hand, it demonstrated that there was no place at the polls for a Liberal Home Rule party as such.* And

* Individual Liberal Home Rulers still could capture an occasional seat for some time to come and they could still cut a considerable figure in

293

on the other hand, it drove Liberals who were opposed to Home Rule inexorably closer to the Unionists. The most striking indication of this was the fact that in 1886 there were no cases where Liberal Unionists and Unionists competed for the same seat. This seems to have been largely due to the initiative of the Duke of Abercorn in bringing both groups into a body – the Northwest Loyal Registration and Electoral Association – specially designed to prevent clashes in the debatable territory of Donegal, Tyrone and Londonderry. It served its purpose well – perhaps almost too well, for Liberal Unionists insisted on safeguarding their identity by creating their own organisation, the Liberal Unionist Association, which was still in being in 1914. But it may be doubted whether it ever gave them much more than psychological satisfaction, since the polarisation of politics which was the chief legacy of 1885–6 ensured that in moments of crisis it would be their Unionism rather than their Liberalism that they would be obliged to emphasise.

Moments of crisis were not lacking in the twenty years after Gladstone's failure, but they did not produce the same frenzy of innovation that the advent of his first Home Rule Bill had done. The explanation is simple enough. It was partly because once the political machinery for resisting Home Rule had been established it was a relatively easy matter to keep it in readiness for action; partly also, of course, the relative stability of Irish Unionism in the twenty years after 1886 derived from the generally favourable political climate. With nationalism in disarray and Home Rule in abeyance there was no real need for Unionists to excite themselves. Not, indeed, that they failed to generate excitement on the two occasions when this seemed particularly to be called for. The first was in 1893, when Gladstone earned his second Home Rule Bill through the House of Commons. As before, there were mass demonstrations in Ulster, sporadic outbreaks of violence and threats of armed resistance. No doubt all these were perfectly genuine, but few of those who vented their hatred of Irish self-government so fiercely could seriously have believed that they would have to back up their words with actions in 1893. And of course there was no necessity for them to do so, since the House of Lords gave the Bill a quick, and on the whole merciful, dispatch.

It was otherwise with the second alarm which set Irish, more specifically Ulster, Unionism in motion during those years – the devolution crisis of 1904–5. As we saw earlier, the fear that a Conservative government was actually preparing to tamper with the sacred British connection provoked an outburst of such sustained ferocity that the Chief

public life. One of the most remarkable of them was Lord Pirrie who succeeded the founders of the famous ship-building partnership of Harland and Wolff as head of the firm. A Unionist, then a Liberal Unionist, and finally a Liberal, in a Belfast which had little use for political evolutionists he remained to the end of his life something of an anomaly.

Secretary, George Wyndham was driven from office.* We may doubt that the Union was in as grave danger as Wyndham's critics believed it was, but what is important is the fact of that belief and the consequences which flowed from it. Unionists, waking from their nightmare, reacted to it by trying to achieve a tighter and more efficient organisation of their forces. This they largely achieved through the creation of the Ulster Unionist Council. As originally established it consisted of 200 members, half to be nominated by the local Unionist associations, fifty by the Orange Grand Lodges, and the remaining fifty to be divided among MPs, peers and *ex officio* members; in 1911 it was enlarged to include Unionist Clubs and the militant Derry Apprentice Boys, an organisation recalling by its very name the Protestant resistance to James II and 'popery' in 1689. The aims of the Council were to organise 'consistent and continuous political action' among Ulster Unionists, to frame the policy of the parliamentary group, and generally 'to advance and defend the interests of Ulster Unionism in the Unionist party'. In these aims, as we shall see presently, it was to be conspicuously successful when the climax of the Home Rule agitation was reached between 1912 and 1914, but although the events of those critical years made plain as never before what an Ulster poet has called

> The hard cold fire of the northerner
> Frozen into his blood from the fire in his basalt

it would be wrong to deduce from this either that the Unionism of the north was by then the only Unionism that mattered, or that that Unionism was quite as monolithic as it seemed.[6]

It may even be that part of the hysteria aroused by the Wyndham-MacDonnell affair derived from the realisation that while Unionism outside Ulster was clearly divided, Unionism inside Ulster did not speak with one voice either. The appearance of 'deviationist' tendencies simultaneously in north and south was hardly accidental – in both instances it was only made possible by the temporary relaxation of the normal Unionist-nationalist tensions – but deviation naturally took different forms in different places. Where in the south the threat to orthodoxy came from landlords coquetting with the conciliationist policies of William O'Brien, in the north friction arose – as might indeed have been expected – because of a growing feeling among some industrial workers in Belfast that their social and economic interests were being sacrificed to the maintenance of a narrow and rigid political creed. The spokesman for this latter discontent was a shipyard worker,

---

* See chap. 4 above. When collecting material for my article, 'The Irish Unionist Party and the Devolution Crisis of 1904-5' (*I.H.S.*, vi (Mar. 1948), 1-22), I had occasion to correspond with the two MPs – Charles Curtis Craig and William Moore – who had led the attack on Wyndham and had been mainly responsible for setting up the Ulster Unionist Council. Although this was more than forty years after the event, and both were very old men, I was left in no doubt about either the reality or the vehemence of their fears for the safety of the Union at the time of the crisis.

T. H. Sloan, who besides being a temperance enthusiast and evangelical preacher, was an outspoken critic of the dominance of the landed gentry and big business in the counsels of official Unionism. On the death of the redoubtable Johnston of Ballykilbeg in 1902, Sloan contested his vacant seat in South Belfast and won it. Very soon, however, he quarrelled with the leader of the parliamentary group, Colonel Saunderson, whom he suspected, of all people, of being 'soft' on Catholicism.* Expelled from the Orange Order for this act of insubordination, Sloan, in the best Ulster tradition, at once founded his own Independent Orange Institution, which combined an aggressive Protestantism with a genuine concern for the workers.[7] Left to himself Sloan might not have amounted to much, but his break-away movement was greatly helped by the adhesion of an exceptionally able journalist, Robert Lindsay Crawford, then editor of a Dublin paper, the *Irish Protestant*, which was so Low Church that it even succeeded in detecting ritualist tendencies in the Church of Ireland. Crawford himself, however, was much more liberal in his outlook and in 1905 provided the Independent Orangemen with a statement of policy – the so-called Magheramorne Manifesto – which attempted to lift the new movement out of sectarian politics. It was in fact an appeal for religious toleration, for men to realise 'that the Irish question is not made up of Union and Repeal', and for a programme which would include not only a measure of devolution but also improvements in the material prosperity of the people.

Sloan put his name to this document (though with the important reservation that he was not to be taken as agreeing to anything in it that might be construed as 'antagonistic to the settled policy of the Unionist party in Ulster'), and it attracted enough support to make possible a rough working alliance between Labour, nationalist and Independent Unionist candidates in Belfast at the general election of 1906. At that election Sloan retained South Belfast, and the nationalist, Devlin, won West Belfast. In addition, another Independent captured North Antrim, and T. W. Russell, standing on a platform of compulsory land purchase, was returned for his old constituency of South Tyrone, also as an Independent Unionist. Russell, admittedly, was *sui generis*, and continued to evolve until he ended as a Liberal Home Ruler. Still, the fact that official Unionism not only faced Independent candidatures in several other constituencies, but came out of the election with a

---

* It was characteristic of the small-minded bigotry of the extremer forms of Ulster Protestantism that Sloan's allegation against Saunderson was that the latter had voted against a clause calling for the inspection of convent laundries in a recent Laundry Bill. Inspection of Catholic institutions was a standard demand among Protestant militants, but in this instance there were good grounds for it; a factory report in 1905 revealed deplorable conditions of work in some of these institutional laundries. Colonel Saunderson indignantly denied the charge, but this did him little good and he was sufficiently harassed to resign his position as Grand Master of the Belfast Lodge.

firm grip on just fifteen of the thirty-three Ulster seats was an indication of how far disruption had gone.[8]

Yet it would be easy to exaggerate the importance of this Independent Unionism. It served, certainly, to demonstrate in a new field a constantly recurring factor in Ulster history – the tendency of tough-minded, argumentative people to go their own way – but such autonomy was sharply limited by the overriding need to maintain the Union intact. This not only made it impossible for dissident Unionists to work in any fundamental way with nationalists, it also restricted the extent to which they could differ from their own more orthodox brethren. Thus, Lindsay Crawford, who in 1906 had returned to his native province to edit a Liberal paper in Belfast, was promptly deprived of his editorship the following year and expelled from the Independent Orange Institution partly because he had openly advocated Home Rule, and partly because he had been tactless enough to expose sweated labour conditions in the linen industry. Deprived of his backing, Sloan reverted to the narrow sectarianism from which he had started, was unable to hold his seat in January 1910, and failed, this time decisively, to regain it in December. Under the impact of the constitutional crisis, Ulster Unionism had closed its ranks again.

It was, indeed, not only Ulster Unionism, but Irish Unionism that had closed its ranks. As far back as 1907 increased co-operation between the two sections had been sought for by the creation of a Joint Committee of Unionist Associations, designed to harmonise the work of the Irish Unionist Alliance and the Ulster Unionist Council. Much of this work was propagandist and between 1907 and 1914 the larger part of it seems to have been undertaken by the southern organisation, the Irish Unionist Alliance. This body used its considerable resources to finance a steady stream of publications, to arrange tours for British politicians in Ireland, to contest seats, to subsidise Ulster Unionism, above all to send its missionaries far and wide through Britain, helping at elections, speaking at meetings, nursing contacts with Conservatism at every level, and always preaching the simple gospel that the Union, and with it the empire, must be preserved. These tasks were not in themselves dramatic and when the situation began to grow tense from 1910 onwards public attention was caught by the much more flamboyant behaviour of the Ulster Unionists, but in fact each wing had its part to play. The southern Unionists, being a small and scattered minority, had no hope of taking the direct action which appealed so strongly to their northern brethren, yet this did not mean that their influence was negligible. On the contrary it was not only very considerable but also peculiarly intractable. Ulster Unionists, secure in the knowledge that if the worst came to the worst they had a strong fortress in the northeast, could afford to treat with the enemy, as eventually they did. No such luxury was open to southern landlords and businessmen who were convinced, however mistakenly, that Home Rule meant extinction for them, and that it must therefore be fought tooth and

297

nail without any thought of compromise.

This was a fight which, despite their numerical inferiority, they were exceptionally well placed to carry on. It is sometimes forgotten how intimately involved they were in the affairs of British, and not just Irish, Unionism. Apart altogether from the fact that their principal leaders, the Marquess of Lansdowne and the Earl of Midleton, were both prominent in the Conservative party, they contributed eighty-six to the total of 104 peers in the House of Lords who had Irish interests, and it was typical of their 'international' character – if one may use a term they would emphatically have repudiated – that whereas in 1914 they held only two southern Irish constituencies, eighteen of them occupied British seats. When one adds to this ties of marriage and the fact that some individuals held property in both countries, it is evident that the southern Irish Unionists were in some important respects almost indistinguishable from their British counterparts. Ulster Unionists, by contrast, were much less closely integrated into the main body of Conservatism. This was partly because, with their own strong territorial base in the northeast of Ireland, they did not need to be integrated, but also perhaps because in temperament and social composition they had little enough in common with Unionists in England, whose attitude towards them was often a strange and baffled mixture of admiration, alarm and cold distaste. It was not without significance that the Ulstermen in 1914 held sixteen seats in their own province and only two in Britain, or that their share in the Irish representation of the House of Lords was no more than eighteen out of the 104 already mentioned.

But leaving aside these numerical considerations, it can be argued that the general situation of British Conservatism between 1906 and 1914 allowed a compact and highly articulate group such as the southern Irish Unionists to exert more pressure than might have been the case in quieter times. The deep divisions within the party over tariff reform and also, to a degree, over the future of the House of Lords, left a vacuum in policy which the Home Rule issue – clear-cut and heavily charged with emotional overtones – was admirably qualified to fill. Moreover, the argument that the threat to the gentlemen of Ireland was but a part of the larger peril to which men of property were exposed on both sides of the Irish Sea, was highly seductive and gave the role of opposition a kind of sanctity in the eyes of many Tories. They forgot, of course, that 'constructive Unionism' in the previous twenty years had probably done more than anything else to undermine the position of the Irish ruling caste; their concern was with the present, and they needed little persuading that the cause of Irish Unionism in general, and of southern Unionism in particular, was identified with the defence of the landed interest, with the unity of their party, and the preservation of the empire.[9]

The growing co-operation between the two wings of Irish Unionism, and between Irish Unionism and British Unionism, was powerfully helped from 1906 onwards by the Irish choice of leaders. After Saunderson's death in 1906 his vacant chair was filled for four years by Walter Long, an English country gentleman *par excellence*, but deeply – almost romantically – attached to Ireland, and during that four-year period representing South Dublin, one of the only two constituencies in southern Ireland (outside Trinity College) which Unionists could hope to hold. Long was thus well placed to maintain close contact between the Conservative forces in both countries, but when he found a London seat at the election of January 1910 it became necessary to replace him as leader of the Irish Unionists. The unanimous choice of the party – and a momentous choice it was – fell upon Sir Edward Carson.

Carson was a quintessential southern Unionist. Born in Dublin in 1854 and educated at Trinity College, he had been called to the Irish bar in 1877 and began a meteoric climb to the top of his profession. He first achieved fame, or notoriety, as a Crown prosecutor at the time of the Plan of Campaign. This brought him to the notice of Arthur Balfour, then Chief Secretary. 'I made Carson, and Carson made me', Balfour declared in later years. 'Everybody right up to the top was trembling . . . Carson had nerve however.' It was Balfour who recommended that his still young assistant be made Irish Solicitor-General in 1892. This necessitated a seat in parliament and at the general election of that year (which brought the Liberals back and abruptly ended Carson's tenure of office) he was returned as one of the members for Dublin University, a seat he was to hold without interruption for the next quarter of a century. It was at this time also that he made one of the crucial decisions of his life, transferring his law practice to London and taking silk in 1893. Almost at once he began to make his name in a series of celebrated cases and became a leader of the English bar, indeed one of the most powerful and persuasive advocates in an age of great lawyers. His technique of cross-examination was formidable (as Oscar Wilde, among others, learned to his cost), his mastery of a brief meticulous and complete, his oratory terse, lucid and compelling. These were gifts that were to stand him in good stead in politics as well as in the law, but he fascinated contemporaries by his personality as much as by his ability. Tall, grim, hatchet-faced, with a sallow complexion and a saturnine expression, he looked, and frequently was, a dyspeptic pessimist. He was, in addition, a hypochondriac who enjoyed his ill health to the full, though this did not prevent him, like many hypochondriacs, from getting through an immense amount of work and living to a ripe old age on the strength of it. In the House of Commons, as in the courts, he made his impact by his conciseness and clarity, his ruthlessness in argument, his impatience of compromise. He had, besides, a flair for the theatrical or flamboyant gesture which was out of place in parliament (though he used it even there to good effect), but which enabled him in the years after 1910 to play like a virtuoso upon the emotions of mass-audiences, especially in Ulster.

His own politics, however, were more complex than either his critics or his supporters quite realised. It was significant, for example, that although he sat for an ultra-conservative university, he remained a Liberal Unionist. He did not hesitate to quarrel with his party on points of principle, or even, later, to resign office, and in his sympathy for the nationalist demand for a Catholic university he stood far to the left of the Ulster Unionists whom he was to lead for so long. But then – and this is essential to an understanding of the inner tragedy of his career – he had only a limited amount in common with those same Ulster Unionists. For Carson the maintenance of the Union was, as he called it, 'the guiding star of my political life', and if he came to appear increasingly as the champion of Ulster Unionism this was in one highly important respect an illusion. Ulster gave him his base, his striking-force, the ultimate sanction behind his speeches of defiance, but in his strategy the aim of Ulster resistance should not be to secure some special status for the north, rather to make Home Rule impossible for any part of Ireland. Time was to bring him to the cruel understanding that his vision of Irish Unionism as a seamless robe was not shared by those on whom he most relied.

This, it is true, was far from apparent in 1910. On the contrary, it was in the following year, with the Parliament Act on the statute-book and Home Rule looming appreciably nearer, that Carson's honeymoon with the Ulster Unionists really began. In July 1911 he met the Ulster Unionist Council and in September 1911 he paid to Belfast the first of those semi-regal visits, and undertook the first of those exercises in mass-hypnosis, that were to punctuate the years of crisis that lay ahead. It was not without significance that this new departure was stage-managed for him by the man who more than any other came to symbolise the very soul of Ulster intransigence. This was James Craig, later Lord Craigavon. Born in Belfast in 1871, the son of a wealthy whiskey distiller, Craig's early life was uneventful, save for a spell of service in the Boer War, where he displayed that personal courage which was to be one of his outstanding characteristics throughout his life. Uninterested in business, well-provided with money, profoundly attached to his city and his province, he gravitated naturally enough towards politics, entering parliament as member for East Down in 1906. Craig's record in the House of Commons was respectable, but scarcely impressive. His real strength lay in organisation and administration, and in his capacity to inspire his fellow-Unionists by his rock-like resistance to any attempt to coerce Ulster. He was a large man, physically – with heavy features, pale eyes, a military moustache and a disconcertingly blunt manner – but intellectually he was a man of one idea, to preserve the character and integrity of the Ulster he knew and loved. For this he was prepared, if necessary, to go into armed re-bellion; failure to appreciate this fundamental fact about him was to cost many people dear in the future.

It was therefore fitting that Carson's first great Ulster demonstration should have been in the grounds of Craigavon, Craig's house just outside

Belfast. And no less fitting that almost his first words to the vast audience drawn from Orange lodges and Unionist clubs all over the province were a promise not only to resist 'the most nefarious conspiracy' to bring in Home Rule, but to carry that resistance to extremes. 'We must be prepared', he warned them, 'in the event of a Home Rule Bill passing, with such measures as will carry on for ourselves the government of those districts of which we have control. We must be prepared . . . the morning Home Rule passes, ourselves to become responsible for the government of the Protestant province of Ulster.' This was not just the rhodomontade that Liberals and nationalists claimed it to be. Two days later Carson was in consultation with the Ulster Unionist Council and a commission of five, with James Craig at its head, was appointed 'to frame and submit a Constitution for a Provisional Government of Ireland, having regard to the interests of the loyalists in the other parts of Ireland'.[10]

These steps, it is well to remember, were taken months before a Home Rule Bill of any description was before the House of Commons. But it was morally certain that one would be introduced in the new session and Unionist opposition began to harden in advance still further. The process was hastened by the fact that in November 1911 Balfour was replaced in the Conservative leadership by Andrew Bonar Law. Law had been born in Canada, but was of Ulster stock, and had made his fortune in the iron trade. He was a dour and somewhat depressing man, though an able speaker and a ruthless, not to say unscrupulous political opponent. His Ulster heritage was important to him – passionately important, if such a low-keyed man could be said to have a passion – and while he would have preferred to use Ulster as a means of destroying Home Rule *in toto*, he was in the end, if the worst came to the worst, prepared to bargain on the basis of the exclusion of the province (however it might be geographically defined), even if this should entail the abandonment of the southern Unionists. And at the very outset, in April 1912, two days before the Home Rule Bill was introduced, he made his position clear. Speaking to an audience of 100,000 Ulstermen just outside Belfast, he appealed directly to their historical consciousness by comparing their situation with that of the beleaguered city of Londonderry in 1689. 'Once again', he declared, 'you hold the pass for the empire. You are a besieged city. Does not the picture of the past, the glorious past with which you are so familiar, rise again before your eyes . . . The government by their Parliament Act have erected a boom against you, a boom to cut you off from the help of the British people. You will burst that boom.'[11]

The long-awaited Bill, when finally unveiled by Asquith, hardly seemed to call for such heroics. It proposed to give Ireland a separate parliament with jurisdiction over her internal affairs, but it withheld from that parliament not only large issues of policy (for example defence, peace or war, relations with the Crown, even, initially, the control of the police) but also effective control of revenue which, including the vital customs and excise department, were reserved to West-minster. Partly for this reason, partly because it was envisaged that in the future Ireland would be called upon to make a contribution in return for the 'imperial services' she shared (e.g. defence), Asquith pro-posed that a certain proportion of Irish members should continue to represent their country in the British House of Commons. On the face of it, it is more difficult to see why Redmond should have been prepared to accept such a modest form of self-government than why the Unionists should have been prepared to take arms against it. The answer in both cases may be the same – that such a measure could hardly, of its very nature, be other than provisional. Asquith had not solved, any more than Gladstone had solved, the impenetrable problem of what to do about Irish finance. To concede full financial autonomy would be to allow Ireland not merely to discriminate against British goods, but to conclude tariff treaties with other countries, from which it would be a short step to the demand for a separate foreign policy, with all the progressive loosening of the imperial structure which, it was as-sumed, this would involve. Yet without financial autonomy could Home Rule really work? John Redmond thought not, and in the de-bate on the Bill expressed Irish misgivings when he pointed out that it did not give the 'complete and immediate control' over finance that he would have wished. 'Admittedly', he added, 'it is a provisional settle-ment . . . When the time for revision does come . . . we will be en-titled to complete power for Ireland over the whole of our financial system.' 'When the time for revision does come'! It was precisely this that Unionists most dreaded, it was for that very reason they opposed Home Rule to the uttermost from the moment it entered the realm of political possibility. As Carson put it: 'We see, as Irish ministers saw in 1800, that there can be no permanent resting place between com-plete union and total separation . . . If there were no other objection to the establishment of a separate government in Dublin, it would be impossible because legislative autonomy can only be coupled with financial independence.'[12]

If neither side even at the time could see the Home Rule Bill as other than a posting stage to more complete independence, it is hardly sur-prising that historians have tended to dismiss the debates as unreal. They were indeed unreal, but not just on that ground alone. Even if the Bill as originally introduced had been satisfactory in its financial clauses, it would still have been unacceptable for two further reasons. One was that it contained no safeguards for Ulster. The other, and more profound, reason was that with the House of Lords unable to do more than delay it, the likelihood, or rather certainty, was that the real pressures would come from outside parliament and that the crisis would take the form, not of reasoned argument in the constitutional mode, but of a gigantic war of nerves carried on in an atmosphere of mount-ing hysteria and bitterness.

During 1912 the Unionists made it plain enough that for them this was a totally exceptional issue to be settled by totally exceptional methods. In July they held a great demonstration at Blenheim Palace which was attended by Bonar Law, Carson, and Carson's friend and rival at the bar, F. E. Smith. It was at this meeting that Bonar Law made an attack upon the Liberal government and its policy which went far beyond anything that had yet been said in the controversy. The government, he said, was 'a Revolutionary Committee which has seized upon despotic power by fraud', and the Conservatives, in their opposition, would not be bounded by the restraints that would influence them in an ordinary constitutional struggle. Even if the Home Rule Bill was carried through the Commons 'there are things stronger than parliamentary majorities'. As for the Ulster Protestants,

if an attempt were made to deprive these men of their birthright – as part of a corrupt parliamentary bargain – they would be justified in resisting such an attempt by all means in their power, including force . . . I can imagine no length of resistance to which Ulster can go in which I should not be prepared to support them, and in which, in my belief, they would not be supported by the overwhelming majority of the British people.[13]

Such a tone, as Law's biographer truly remarks, had not been heard in England since the debates of the Long Parliament, and it is important to be clear why the leader of the Conservative party, traditionally the party of law and order, should have felt impelled to make it. There seem to have been two main explanations. One was the conviction, widely held among Conservatives, that the Liberals, since they could only hold power with the support of the nationalists, had been in effect blackmailed by Redmond – the 'corrupt parliamentary bargain' – into putting forward a scheme of Home Rule which took no account whatever of the rights and interests of the Protestant minority and consigned them without adequate protection to the mercy of their hereditary enemies. Linked with this conviction was the second reason why the Conservative leader was ready to go outside the bounds of the constitution. This was the belief, again widely held, that the issue of Home Rule had not been fairly submitted to the British people; the two elections of 1910, it was contended, had been fought on the question of the House of Lords. Home Rule ought now to be put before the electorate on its own merits. This argument, however, was of very dubious validity. Home Rule had certainly figured in the elections – Asquith's pledge in December 1909 had been made during the first of the two campaigns – and it would have been a very naive elector indeed who did not realise that much of the bitterness over the Lords' veto was engendered less by the veto itself than by what lay immediately beyond it – i.e. Home Rule. Moreover, the principal Conservatives who had taken part in the constitutional conference during 1910 knew very well not only that attempts had then been made to settle the Irish problem by consent, but that it was essentially that problem which had led to the break-down of the conference. Of course, it could be argued that what was known to the inner circle of the leaders was not known to the rank-and-file or to the people in general, and that only an election devoted specifically to Home Rule could really produce a decision, the implication here being that a 'decision' could only be a decision if it were reached by a majority of British, as distinct from Irish, voters. To this the Irish answer was that while the Conservatives claimed to uphold the Union, they were refusing to abide by its rules. If Ireland was part of the United Kingdom, then a Liberal majority depending on the Irish vote was just as legitimate as any other kind of majority and there could be no question of a 'corrupt parliamentary bargain'. As for the other Unionist contention, that a minority was being sacrificed to a hostile majority, the nationalist counter-argument was that this notion was based on the theory that in Ireland there were two distinct nations. It was a notion that was completely unacceptable to Redmond and his friends, and even, initially, to his Liberal allies, for at much the same time as Bonar Law was endorsing rebellion at Blenheim, Asquith in Dublin was declaring his conviction that 'Ireland is a nation, not two nations, but one nation'.[14]

Obviously the two sides were so far apart that for most of the crisis they seemed not even to be talking the same language. More and more it became clear that deeds, not words, would decide the issue. What this meant in practice was that the reaction of the Liberals, caught between two opposing forces, would be determined by the degree of pressure each of these forces could bring to bear. There was a hint of the form that reaction would take in the decision adopted by the cabinet and conveyed to Redmond as early as February 1912 – three months before the introduction of the Home Rule Bill – that if it became necessary to make concessions to Ulster the government must hold itself free to do so. The first parliamentary suggestion of such special treatment for Ulster came on 11 June when a Liberal member, T. G. Agar-Robartes, proposed the exclusion of the four most Protestant counties – Antrim, Armagh, Londonderry and Down. Carson and the Ulster Unionists voted for this for tactical reasons. Believing as they did that a partitioned Ireland would not be economically viable, they had only to take Ulster, or even a significant part of Ulster, out of the scheme for the scheme itself to collapse. 'If Ulster succeeds', said Carson bluntly, 'Home Rule is dead.'

There were in fact enough other votes to defeat the motion and the great debate continued on the assumption that Ireland would still be regarded by the government as a single entity to which, as the timetable slowly unrolled, Home Rule would be applied in the course of 1914, after the Government of Ireland Bill had completed its third circuit of the parliamentary process. But, as the debate inside the House of Commons became increasingly unreal, so the debate outside grew fiercer and more strident. The pressures exerted by the Unionists against the Liberal-Nationalist alliance were two-fold. On the one hand Bonar Law attempted to persuade the King that he should, if necessary, use the royal veto against Home Rule when the time came. This suggestion was first made in May 1912 and came to nothing in face of George v's impeccably constitutional behaviour, but it was a worrying indication of how far the monarchy itself was likely to be involved in the crisis. On the other hand, the Unionists in general, and Carson in particular, devoted themselves to raising the tension in Ulster to a new high pitch. In September 1912, amid scenes of deep emotion, Carson led a vast concourse of Ulstermen in signing the Solemn League and Covenant. As loyal subjects of the King they pledged themselves, without any evidence of conscious irony, to oppose the King's government and to use all necessary means 'to defeat the present conspiracy to set up a Home Rule Parliament in Ireland. And in the event of such a Parliament being forced upon us we further solemnly and mutually pledge ourselves to refuse to recognise its authority.'

What gave this tribal ritual its real menace was the fact, insufficiently appreciated either by the government or by the nationalists, that the Ulstermen were beginning to drill and to organise in support of their threats. As far back as Carson's Craigavon meeting of 1911 a Tyrone detachment of Orangemen had impressed all observers by their smartness which, it appeared, was the result of conscientious drilling. During 1912 it was discovered that Justices of the Peace could authorise such drilling 'for the purpose of maintaining the constitution of the United Kingdom as now established' and more and more groups of ardent Unionists took up the idea. In January 1913 the Ulster Unionist Council made the crucial decision to form these groups into a coherent body – the Ulster Volunteer Force – to be limited to 100,000 men and organised on a military basis. To help them they had a retired Indian army general, Sir George Richardson (recommended by no less a person than Field Marshal Roberts) assisted by an able staff officer, Captain Wilfred Spender. The fact that the Volunteers drilled openly was ominous, but since they drilled for the most part with wooden rifles it was still open to the nationalists to laugh at them and to persist in the dangerous belief that they were bluffing. The time was fast approaching when this belief would become much more difficult to sustain.

Meanwhile, in parliament and behind the scenes the pressure for some sort of compromise was mounting. Early in January 1913 Carson proposed in studiously moderate tones that the whole nine counties of Ulster be excluded from the Bill. It was, of course, a totally unacceptable suggestion and Carson himself made it plain that he was still not prepared to compromise on the main issue, but at least it indicated a willingness to talk about possibilities. And although his motion was rejected, when Winston Churchill, then First Lord of the Admiralty, met Bonar Law at Balmoral in the autumn he found him also prepared to negotiate on the basis of some kind of exclusion. The hope of agreement was faint, but it was enough for the Prime Minister himself to hold three meetings with the Leader of the Opposition between

305

October 1913 and January 1914, to explore the possibility of six or even four Ulster counties opting out. They were not, in fact, able to reach any settlement, but it was perhaps an indication of the way the wind was blowing in government circles that Winston Churchill, in a much publicised speech at Dundee in October, made out a case for the special treatment of northeast Ulster. True, he qualified this by remarking that special treatment for a limited area was 'very different from the claim . . . to block the path of the whole of the rest of Ireland', but the nationalist leaders immediately responded that it was not in the least different and that they could not give any countenance to the idea of partition. 'Irish Nationalists', said Redmond a few days later, 'can never be consenting parties to the mutilation of the Irish nation.'[15]

Yet it was becoming increasingly clear that this was what they were going to be expected to be. Towards the end of 1913 the Liberal government began itself to exert pressure on the Irish leaders to accept some form of temporary partition. The latter's reaction – which now seems naive in the extreme, but was beyond any reasonable doubt perfectly genuine – was to urge their allies to stand firm, not to make offers to the Unionists, and to disregard Ulster protests as bluff. 'I must express the strong opinion', wrote Redmond to Asquith in November, 'that the magnitude of the peril of the Ulster situation is considerably exaggerated in this country.' Since simultaneously Asquith was unable to make any headway with either Bonar Law or Carson, no offer beyond a very tentative suggestion for the temporary exclusion of a part of Ulster was made by the Liberals, and since this was almost equally displeasing to all parties, the situation drifted on towards the explosive year of 1914 with no peaceful solution whatever in sight.

We know now that even by the end of 1913 the government had become seriously worried that what Redmond was still dismissing as Ulster bluff might turn out to be Ulster rebellion. Evidence had been reaching the authorities that arms and ammunition were being brought secretly and in increasing quantities into the north of Ireland. This evidence was only too well-founded. During the year one of the most fanatical of the Ulstermen, Major Fred Crawford, had organised the smuggling of several thousand rifles, a number of machine guns and a large quantity of ammunition, but when in December the government prohibited the import of weapons and ammunition into Ireland, Crawford's aim – which was to equip the entire Ulster Volunteer Force – was still far from realised. Accordingly, he obtained the permission of the Ulster Unionist Council to buy what he needed in Germany and to plan, in his own secret and highly melodramatic fashion, to run the guns – 20,000 of them, together with three million rounds of ammunition – into a northern port or ports when opportunity offered.[16]

While Crawford was away on his mysterious expedition, the situation changed yet again. The formation of the Ulster Volunteers had been answered in the south by the establishment, in November 1913, of the Irish Volunteers. This, as we shall see presently, marked the beginning of an important shift in the balance of power within the nationalist movement, and although that only gradually became apparent, the proliferation of private and unofficial armies was enough in itself to make it imperative that the Liberal government should act quickly either to produce a settlement or to quell the gathering storm.* In fact they tried to do both. Asquith, who was under heavy pressure from the King to offer adequate safeguards to Ulster, at last got Redmond and his friends to agree to the proposal that individual Ulster counties might be allowed to opt out of Home Rule for a period of three – almost immediately raised to six – years, after which they would automatically come under the Irish parliament. Even this temporary expedient was a highly dangerous concession for Redmond to make, inviting as it did the criticism that if, despite all his protestations that Ireland was one nation, he was prepared to this limited extent to recognise that it was two nations, he was in effect conceding the principle for which Carson had all along been fighting and which, once conceded, was capable of being exploited still further. Against this it has to be remembered that only by a show of reasonableness could Redmond hope to hold a divided cabinet and a wavering monarch in line, and that if the cabinet broke on this issue, or if the King dismissed his ministers (as was not outside the bounds of possibility), there would in either event be an end of Home Rule. Besides, there was a good tactical reason for making the offer, in that it put the onus of rejection on the opposition. Not indeed that the opposition had any qualms about accepting that responsibility. When Asquith put it to the Commons on 9 March Carson threw it back in his teeth, with the contemptuous comment that Ulster would not accept 'a sentence of death with a stay of execution for six years'. A week later he stormed out of the House declaring that his place was at the head of his people. He crossed to Belfast at once and, so great was the prevailing uncertainty, many believed he had gone there to set up a provisional government.

He did not in fact do so – though the previous autumn the Ulster Unionist Council had prepared the ground for just such a contingency – and the next heightening of the almost unbearable tension came, not from recalcitrant Ulstermen, but from the Liberal Government's decision at long last to take the necessary military and naval steps to strengthen its position in the north. This was a grave, if necessary decision, and turned out to be even graver than could have been anticipated. For some time past there had been rumours that the army might be disaffected – nor were these rumours idle, for the officer class as a whole was Unionist in its sympathies, many of its members being themselves Irish or having Irish connections. More ominous even than that was the fact that the Unionist leaders were at this very time

* For the Irish Volunteers see Part III, chap. 1 below. The emergence of the Citizen Army, as described in the previous chapter, was of course additional evidence of the trend towards direct action.

seriously considering whether they might not cause the House of Lords to refuse to pass the annual Army Act, without which no government could exist, since in the absence of an Army Act the Army itself could not be paid or even kept in being as a regular force. That the Conservative party should have come to this pass, at a time of deep international tension in Europe, was a staggering indication of how far the Irish crisis had corroded all the ordinary decencies and conventions of constitutional government. But before Bonar Law and his associates had made up their minds to reject this desperate plan, the initiative was seized by a group of Army officers stationed at the Curragh camp in Ireland. In a state of dire confusion – due partly to the highly charged atmosphere of the time and partly to a misunderstanding of orders – some fifty-eight officers proffered their resignations rather than face the prospect of having, as they believed, to 'coerce' Ulster. Worse still, one of the generals in Ireland, Sir Hubert Gough (himself a member of the Anglo-Irish Ascendancy caste) proceeded to London and, aided by the Director of Military Operations (Sir Henry Wilson, another Anglo-Irish soldier), extracted from the Secretary of State for War, Colonel J. E. B. Seely, a pledge that the government had no intention of using the Army 'to crush political opposition to the policy or principles of the Home Rule Bill'. This was too much even for the patient Asquith to stomach. Seely was obliged to resign, as were two generals, and Asquith himself took over the War Office for the time being. He at once repudiated Seely's pledge, but nothing could conceal the fact that he had very nearly had a mutiny on his hands and that he could not count upon the loyalty of the Army if he now moved to coerce Ulster. He did not move to coerce Ulster.*

It was against this background of ever growing passion and bitterness that Major Crawford now reappeared upon the scene. He had carried out his arms purchases in Germany (enabled to do so by large sums subscribed to a Defence Fund by English as well as Irish Unionists) and on the night of 24–25 April these were landed at three harbours on the east coast of Ulster (Larne, Bangor and Donaghadee) and distributed with extraordinary speed and efficiency all over the province inside twenty-four hours.[17] It is hard to say which impressed contemporaries more – the fierce determination that had inspired this

* What happened at the Curragh was not a 'mutiny' as it was once usual to call it. It was resignations in anticipation of unwelcome orders, not refusal to obey such orders once issued, that the government was faced with. Even so, it was clear enough that the situation was critical and might get out of hand very easily if a clash were actually to occur between the Ulster Volunteers and the forces of the Crown. In such circumstances Asquith, as was his natural bent, thought discretion the better part of valour. The episode is well described in Sir James Fergusson, *The Curragh Incident* (London, 1964), though an earlier work, A. P. Ryan, *Mutiny at the Curragh* (London, 1956), shows greater insight into the underlying political realities.

coup, or the inability of the government either to prevent it taking place or to punish those who had perpetrated it. These two events – the Curragh incident and the Ulster gun-running – had, as we can now see, a double effect upon the situation. On the one hand, the gun-running restored the military supremacy in Ireland to the Ulster Volunteers with the inevitable result that the Irish Volunteers in the south were moved at once to imitate the northern initiative. And on the other hand, with the situation deteriorating as fast as it was doing, the government had more reason than ever to work for a settlement and, since it could not coerce Carson, attempt to coerce Redmond.

In June 1914, therefore, Asquith, groping desperately for a compromise, even if only a temporary one, decided on an Amending Bill to deal separately with Ulster. As introduced in the Lords, it provided for county option for six years – precisely 'the stay of execution' already rejected by Carson. But since the Unionist majority in the upper House promptly altered the proposals so as to provide for the exclusion of all nine counties for an indefinite period, it was plain that nothing was to be hoped for from this device. Reluctantly, and dreading the failure which was almost inevitable, Asquith allowed himself to be pushed inch by inch nearer to the conference between the two parties that the King had been anxiously urging upon him for some time. The conference duly held its first meeting on 21 July at Buckingham Palace, bringing face to face Asquith, Lloyd George, Redmond and Dillon on the one side, and on the other Bonar Law, Lord Lansdowne, Carson and James Craig. After a few days of intensive but entirely fruitless negotiation discussing maps and figures but always getting back, as Asquith wrote to a friend, 'to that most damnable creation of the perverted ingenuity of man, the county of Tyrone', the Conference ended in deadlock. It had proved quite impossible to agree on areas of exclusion which would not do injury to either Catholic or Protestant.

The breakdown of the Conference was announced on 24 July. Two days later the Irish Volunteers carried out their gun-running on the Ulster model, but improved upon the occasion by doing it in broad daylight. This, too, was a decisive event, more decisive than was realised at the time, even in Ireland. Superficially, the southern Volunteers were under Redmond's control, for the previous month he had insisted that his nominees should be given what he believed would be a predominant voice in the Provisional Committee which governed their organisation. His action earned him deep resentment but little real influence. The gun-running was planned and carried out without his knowledge, and although the intention of most of those who participated was probably no more than to restore the balance between their force and the Ulster Volunteers, the residuary legatees of this operation were the IRB, who had already permeated the Irish Volunteers for purposes of their own.* The greater part of the guns were landed at Howth, on the north side of Dublin Bay, so that they could be distributed with the maximum speed. This was done despite the authorities' decision to call out the troops, but when the latter were returning to barracks a further incident occurred of precisely the kind calculated to do most damage to Anglo-Irish relations. Harassed by a hostile but unarmed crowd, the troops turned and fired, killing three people and injuring thirty-eight.

The immediate political effect of this tragedy was to make it more impossible even than before for the nationalist leaders to compromise. Since Carson was equally adamant, there seemed no way out short of that civil war which had been threatening for so long. But quite suddenly the domestic quarrel was submerged in the vaster European crisis. With the international situation worsening almost hour by hour, Asquith abandoned his intention of pressing on with an Amendment Bill. But would this mean also the abandonment of the Home Rule Bill itself, now so near the end of its long and weary course? The British arguments in favour of this were strong. With war imminent it would be folly to aggravate the internecine conflict. But a European war did not seem to nationalists a sufficient reason to baulk them of what seemed to them their just expectations. If Redmond did not succeed in getting Home Rule onto the statute-book he might not be able to hold back the surge of indignation that would sweep over Ireland. He himself was in a dilemma. Home Rule was the ultimate objective of his whole political career and naturally he did not want to jettison it at this eleventh hour. On the other hand, his sympathies with Britain in the war now breaking out were strong, far stronger than were those of most of his colleagues or of the country he led. At this agonisingly difficult moment in his career he took a momentous decision, one that in the long run was to cost him dear. On 3 August, in an emotional speech to the House of Commons, he pledged Ireland's support for the war and urged the government to leave the defence of Irish shores to Irishmen, to the Volunteers from north and south.

This generosity seems to have been, if not quite spontaneous, at least without political calculation, though it was a reasonable supposition that it might make Asquith a little more amenable to the demand that Home Rule should go on the statute-book. Whether this was so or not, or whether the Prime Minister was more impressed by the impassioned warnings Redmond addressed to him in private that the loyalty of the south could not be relied on if Home Rule were denied, it is impossible to say. He was, of course, being simultaneously pressed in the opposite direction by Bonar Law and Carson, and it was not until September that

* The complex cross-currents that swirled round the Irish Volunteers are dealt with below, Part III, chap. 1. It was typical of the confusion of life in Ireland at the time that the purchase of the arms in Germany and their transport to Dublin were carried out by sympathisers who were mainly members of the Anglo-Irish Ascendancy class.

he finally escaped from his predicament by agreeing to place the Government of Ireland Act on the statute-book, but with two provisos. One was that it should not come into operation until after the end of the war; and the other was that it would not come into operation until after parliament had had an opportunity of making provision for Ulster by special amending legislation. And thus it came about on 18 September that the nationalists and their allies found themselves in a House of Commons almost denuded of Unionists, welcoming the news that the royal assent had at last been given. And amid cheers and the singing of 'God Save the King' a long, bitter chapter in the history of two countries seemed to have been ended. Yet nothing could have been further from the truth. Asquith might have bought time by his compromise, but he had bought little else.

PART III

The Union Broken

1. Phoenix Resurgent

So much was happening in Ireland, so many new movements were competing for a share of the limelight, in the decade before the First World War that it is hardly surprising that what in the end was to be the most significant of all these developments escaped the attention of most contemporaries. Admittedly, it was designed to escape their attention, for it was nothing less than the revival of the old, secret, separatist movement, the awakening into life once more of that phoenix which had been the emblem of the Fenians fifty years earlier. At the beginning of the twentieth century such a resurgence seemed, on the face of it, impossibly remote. The ashes of revolt had long since grown cold. The Irish Republican Brotherhood had become old and flabby, its leaders elderly *apparatchiks* content to take refuge behind a convenient clause in their constitution which stated that 'the IRB shall await the decision of the Irish nation as expressed by a majority of the Irish people as to the fit hour of inaugurating a war against England'.[1] Since the Irish people had not for a long time shown the slightest inclination to inaugurate a war against England, the Supreme Council of the IRB had been able with a clear conscience to devote itself mainly to the fascinating trivia of Dublin municipal politics.

Understandably, such trivia lost some of their fascination when viewed from Belfast. And it was in Belfast, where so much of the future of Ireland was being decided in these years, that the inevitable reaction of the younger generation against their supine elders first showed itself. Essentially it was the work of three men – Denis McCullough, Bulmer Hobson and Sean MacDermott.* The first of these, McCullough, was born in Belfast in 1883. His father, who owned a public house in that city, had himself been a Fenian and arranged for the boy to be admitted when he was on the verge of eighteen. His enthusiasm only momentarily quenched by the fact that his initiation had been hurried through at the side door of a Belfast pub by an IRB man who had more urgent business inside, McCullough threw himself eagerly into the business of recruiting for 'the organisation' and in 1904 was responsible for the admission of the man who was to share with him the day to day work of revival. This was Bulmer Hobson, born the same year as

* MacDermott was born John MacDermott and in later life signed himself Seán MacDiarmida. Sean MacDermott is a barbarous marriage of the English and the Irish forms of his name, but since it has long been popular usage it seemed pedantic not to continue to employ it here.

McCullough, but into the very different background of a Quaker middle-class family. From childhood he had been attracted by the Irish Ireland movement and had been an enthusiastic member of both the Gaelic League and the GAA. He seems to have had remarkable organising ability from the very start of his career and while still in his teens had founded a debating club for boys and also a propagandist body called the Protestant National Association which was, among other things, the somewhat improbable forbear of the Ulster Literary Theatre.

The first achievement of this partnership between McCullough and Hobson was the creation in 1905 of the Dungannon Club, intended by its name to evoke memories of the Volunteer movement of 1782 and the winning of Irish legislative independence at that time. Although, as we saw earlier, the Dungannon Club, and others of the same name which sprang into existence elsewhere in the next year or so, were merged in Griffith's Sinn Féin organisation in 1907, the ultimate aim of these young enthusiasts was even then more specific and more outspoken than Griffith would have found acceptable for his movement. That aim was summed up in the title of the weekly paper – *The Republic* – they started in 1906, and in the leading article Hobson contributed to the first number. 'We stand for an Irish republic', he wrote, 'because we see that no compromise with England, no repeal of the Union, no concession of Home Rule, or Devolution, will satisfy the national aspirations of the Irish people . . . National independence is our right; we ask no more and we will accept no less.'[2]

The Dungannon Clubs, apart from their general purpose of propagating the ideas of Irish Ireland, had both a negative and a positive function. The first was to discourage recruiting into the British Army, the second was to encourage recruiting into the IRB. Of all the eager young men they attracted into their movement by far the most striking was Sean MacDermott. Born in 1884 the son of a small farmer in county Leitrim, he had had to earn his own living from an early age, drifting from Ireland to Glasgow and then back to Belfast in search of precarious and mostly dead-end employment. Gay, good-looking, highly intelligent but without much formal education, a born intriguer and quite ruthless in attaining any goal he set himself, he had at first been attracted by the sectarian politics of the Ancient Order of Hibernians. Weaned from this by Hobson and McCullough, he soon became their closest colleague and in 1906 was sworn into the IRB. In 1908, following the merger with Griffith's movement, he and Hobson moved to Dublin, and while the latter began to establish himself as a journalist, MacDermott became a full-time organiser for Sinn Féin, travelling all over the country and laying the foundations of that intimate knowledge of nationalism in its extremer forms which was to make him such a formidable figure a few years later. Meanwhile, the third member of the trio, McCullough, stayed in

Belfast, reorganising the IRB there, and moving so rapidly up the ladder that in 1908 he became the Ulster representative on the Supreme Council.[3]

During his years in Belfast Hobson had included among his multifarious activities one which went almost unnoticed at the time, but which was to provide a precedent for a development of great importance. In 1902 he had formed a rudimentary boys' movement, called Na Fianna Eireann, primarily to promote a Junior Hurling League and to interest Ulster youths in the Irish language. When he came to Dublin Hobson mentioned this small-scale experiment to the Countess Markievicz, who at once suggested that they start a national organisation on the same lines. She hired a hall at her own expense and about a hundred boys turned up to an inaugural meeting in August 1909. The new Fianna which resulted from that meeting was, however, a very different organisation from its Belfast prototype. From the beginning it was intended as a youth movement to train boys for participation in a war of liberation. Each boy, on joining, made the following declaration: 'I promise to work for the independence of Ireland, never to join England's armed forces, and to obey my superior officers.' The training he received was partly academic – in Irish history and the Irish language – but more importance was attached to physical fitness, scouting and even military exercises.[4] With this sort of background it was inevitable – as Hobson intended – that a number of the Fianna should graduate into the ranks of the IRB. Within a few years he was able to form a Dublin 'circle' of IRB members who had begun their careers in the Fianna. Many of these became officers in the revolutionary forces, two were executed after the Rising and, as we shall see, the boys themselves had a habit of being on hand whenever disciplined action was required.

But no amount of recruiting, no amount of training, would achieve anything until there had been changes at the top. The IRB was governed at this time by a constitution last amended in 1873. This had laid down the conditions for admission and had prescribed the following oath to be taken by newly initiated members:

In the presence of God, I . . . do solemnly swear that I will do my utmost to establish the national independence of Ireland, and that I will bear true allegiance to the Supreme Council of the Irish Republican Brotherhood and Government of the Irish Republic and implicitly obey the Constitution of the Irish Republican Brotherhood and all my superior officers and that I will preserve inviolable the secrets of the organisation.[5]

According to this constitution the IRB was to be locally established in county centres or district centres (for the towns), and these in turn were to be grouped into seven electoral divisions – Leinster, Ulster, Munster,

Connaught, North of England, South of England and Scotland. Each electoral division was to choose one representative to sit on the supreme council. These seven members were then to choose four other members whose names would only be known to the seven. The total strength of the Supreme Council or Government of the Irish Republic was, therefore, eleven, but, since members were necessarily scattered and could not meet together very often, effective power was concentrated into the hands of three officers elected from within the eleven – the president, the secretary and the treasurer.

It was this innermost citadel of power that had to be forced if the new generation were ever to breathe fresh life into the organisation. By the early 1900s three men – Fred Allen, P. T. Daly and John Hanlon – had grown old in the exercise of the central authority in the organisation and to get rid of them, or at least to outvote them, became the main objective of the reformers. Because the IRB was a secret organisation it is not possible even yet to trace the stages by which this was achieved. but we do know that a major reason for the success of the young men was that one old man was on their side. This was Thomas James Clarke, whose revolutionary career went back over twenty years. In actual fact he was not really an old man at all, since he had been born in 1857, but in terms of experience, service and suffering he seemed to belong almost to another age. In his twenties he had become involved in the dynamite campaign in England and for this was sentenced to penal servitude for life in 1883. After serving fifteen years of this sentence in conditions of brutalising harshness, he was released and went to America, where he worked closely with John Devoy. In 1907 he returned to Ireland and soon afterwards was co-opted onto the Supreme Council. Outwardly no man could have seemed less of a desperado. His prison experiences had left him looking delicate and much older than his years. He kept a tobacconist's and newsagent's shop in North Great Britain Street and with his large, cheap spectacles, his drooping moustache and frail figure, he looked the small tradesman's part to perfection. Yet appearances could not have been more deceptive. Clarke was to play a central role in the coming struggle and was to be indispensable in two quite different ways. First, he was the all-important link between the IRB and the Clan na Gael in America, and time was to show just how vital this was. But second, beneath his mild exterior there burned the fanaticism of a totally committed patriot. Narrow, rigid and a man of one idea he may have been, but that one idea – the independence of Ireland as a sovereign republic – gave meaning to his own life and inspiration to the few whom he allowed to come to close quarters with him.

Among those few were the activists of the new generation who between 1908 and 1914 came to dominate the Supreme Council. They included not only McCullough, Hobson and MacDermott, but also Patrick McCartan, another northerner and ultimately a doctor by profession; P. S. O'Hegarty, a brilliant journalist (later an eminent civil servant and bibliophile); and Major John MacBride, who had fought with the Boers in South Africa and who, by marrying Maud Gonne, had earned from the poet W. B. Yeats an hostility that lasted until MacBride's death before a firing-squad in 1916 transmuted it into homage. Against this concentration of talent the older generation could offer only a crumbling defence. One of them, P. T. Daly, was expelled from the Supreme Council in 1910 for alleged misuse of American funds, and another, Fred Allen, resigned in 1912 after a series of quarrels arising partly out of financial matters, but partly out of the demand by the young men that the IRB should sponsor a militantly republican newspaper.[6] This, which was mainly Hobson's idea, was carried through in the teeth of conservative opposition on the Supreme Council and by November 1910 the first number had appeared. The paper, *Irish Freedom*, was managed by MacDermott, but mainly written by Hobson and O'Hegarty. From the outset, until its suppression by the government in 1914, it took an advanced republican line, advocating, as Hobson has lately recalled, 'the independence of Ireland by every practicable means, including the use of physical force'.[7]

But although these developments presaged a new spirit in the IRB, they could not conceal the fact that the organisation remained small and poor. True, it received three hundred pounds a year from the Clan na Gael, but apart from this had only the modest subscriptions of its members to fall back on. Since the total membership in 1912 was about 2,000, it followed that revenue, and consequently action, was circumscribed.[8] If the organisation were ever to break away from the stultifying routine of small-scale polemical journalism and endless internal disputes about doctrine and personalities, the opportunity would have to come from without, not from within. How that opportunity occurred is a familiar story which need only be briefly sketched here. The years of change inside the IRB were also years of change in the Irish situation as a whole. From the viewpoint of the extremists what was important about those years was that they marked not just the climax of the parliamentary drive for Home Rule, but also the extra-parliamentary reaction of Ulster against Home Rule. With the signing of the Solemn League and Covenant, the formation of the Provisional Government and the launching of the Ulster Volunteers it was becoming steadily clearer that the whole struggle was passing out of the sphere of peaceful argument and into the sphere of physical force. To the republicans in the south the most significant of these developments was the emergence of the Ulster Volunteers as a disciplined body in 1913, following a year of scattered and unorganised drilling and arming. It was not unfitting, therefore, that it should have been an Ulsterman, the ubiquitous Hobson, who set a similar ball rolling in Dublin. During the summer of 1913 (a summer charged, as we have seen, with the passions aroused by the industrial war between Larkin's union and the employers*) he began to prepare for the development he saw coming – the formation of a similar force on the nationalist side – by arranging for the secret drilling of IRB men so that they might be ready to control this force if and when it came.[9] But such a force could hardly come through the direct agency of the IRB itself, which did not have sufficient following in the country and which, as a secret society, was naturally unwilling to move into the open until `the right psychological moment. What was needed was some independent initiative that the extreme men could then exploit for their own ends.

This initiative was supplied by the article, 'The North Began', which appeared on 1 November 1913 in the Gaelic League paper, *An Claidheamh Soluis*, and became famous overnight. It was written by Eoin MacNeill, in response to a request for an article 'on matters of general public interest' from a young man whose own life was to be completely changed by what happened in the next few weeks. This was Michael Joseph Rahilly, or The O'Rahilly as he had taken to calling himself by this time. Born in 1875 of a well-to-do Kerry family, he was educated by the Jesuits at Clongowes Wood College and later at University College, Dublin, which, however, the threat of tuberculosis obliged him to leave before graduating. For some years he led the life of a country gentleman and was even a Justice of the Peace for a short time. Later, after a spell in the USA (he married an American girl), he settled in Dublin and became attracted by Griffith's teachings. He began to write regularly for Sinn Féin newspapers and continued to work for Griffith's movement, even in the years of its relative decline between 1910 and 1913. From Sinn Féin he passed to the Gaelic League (reversing the normal nationalist order of progression) and became a member of its central executive in 1912. When in the following year *An Claidheamh Soluis* was reorganised, The O'Rahilly became its managing director. It was in that capacity that he asked MacNeill to contribute the article from which, it has been said, a whole new chapter of Irish history derives.[10]

It is important to be clear at this point about the significance of the fact that it was MacNeill who took this particular initiative at this particular time. By 1913 Eoin MacNeill was one of the best known men in Ireland. His work for the Gaelic League had taken him all over the country, while his scholarship, which had been recognised by his appointment to the chair of Early Irish History at University College, Dublin, had made him a familiar figure among intellectuals. But, although everywhere identified with the Irish revival, he was also regarded as a moderate in politics, in fact as a Home Ruler of the school of John Redmond. This meant not only that many people were prepared to pay attention to what he said, but that when what he said turned out to be different from what he might have been expected to say, the impact was all the greater.

* See Part II, chap. 8.

In 'The North Began' his purpose was to make his readers see that, properly understood, the emergence of the Ulster Volunteers represented not so much a threat to nationalists as an opportunity for them. The Ulstermen, he asserted, had made 'the most decisive move towards Irish autonomy since O'Connell invented constitutional agitation'. The northern movement, he claimed in a paradox that was more apparent than real, was a genuine Home Rule movement since it demonstrated the determination of Ulster Unionists to be masters of their own fate whatever might be decided in the British Parliament. In taking this line, he suggested, they were only following the earlier precedent of the Volunteers of 1782. But from that precedent there was a moral to be drawn. 'Their disbandment led to the destruction alike of self-government and of prosperity, and the opportunity of rectifying a capital error of this sort does not always come back again to nations'. Ulster, however, had shown the way and made it clear that 'the British army cannot now be used to prevent the enrolment, drilling and reviewing of Volunteers in Ireland'. 'It is evident', he concluded, 'that the only solution now possible is for the empire to make terms with Ireland or to let Ireland go her own way. In any case it is manifest that all Irish people, Unionist as well as Nationalist, are determined to have their own way in Ireland'.[11]

Outspokenness such as this, coming from a man known to be impeccably moderate, provided the physical force party with exactly the lever they were seeking.* Within a few days of the article appearing Bulmer Hobson had asked The O'Rahilly to see MacNeill and find out if he was prepared to take the matter further. MacNeill agreed and invitations went out to a select few to meet at Wynn's Hotel in Dublin on 11 November for discussions about how best to build on this initiative.[12] The select few were selected mainly by The O'Rahilly and Bulmer Hobson, though the latter did not himself come to the meeting lest the appearance of one so identified with extremism should frighten away more constitutionally minded nationalists whose support at

* It should be mentioned here that an independent, if short-lived, initiative had been taken at Athlone as early as September-October 1913, when a group calling themselves the Midland Volunteer Force had begun to drill and organise in imitation of the Ulster Volunteers. The 'Force' seems to have had its share of internal friction and it was in any event swallowed up by the larger movement controlled from Dublin, but it is interesting that MacNeill, in a covering letter he sent with his article to The O'Rahilly, showed himself aware of the experiment and expressed his 'firm conviction that free-soldiers [Volunteers] will have to be established throughout Ireland as soon as possible, as has been done at Athlone'. (The original of this letter is in the possession of Mr Aodhogan O'Rahilly; for its context see Oliver Snoddy, 'The Midland Volunteer Force, 1913', in *Journal of the Old Athlone Society* (1968), pp. 39-44; see also the same author's article in *Studia Hibernica* (1965), pp. 113-22.) The police, however, did not take it seriously; see the RIC report in PRO, co/904/91.

this stage was essential. Nevertheless, of the ten who were present on that day, four were members of the IRB and it is quite clear that the physical force men had already begun to sense the possibility that a 'front' organisation might soon emerge which they must at all costs control.[13]

During the next few days more meetings were held and the basis of the organising or 'provisional' committee was widened to include some who could be regarded as broadly representative of parliamentary nationalism. Soon the committee numbered thirty members, but this did not mean that the IRB had relaxed its vigilance. Of the thirty members twelve were then in the IRB and several others were shortly afterwards to be sworn into the organisation. Finally, on 25 November, scarcely more than three weeks after MacNeill's article had appeared, a vast public meeting was held at the Rotunda Rink in Dublin to launch the new movement. MacNeill had composed a manifesto for the occasion, driving home the points he had made in 'The North Began'. The Tory party's policy in Ulster, he declared, had been deliberately adopted 'to make the display of military force and the menace of armed violence the determining factor in the future relations between this country and Great Britain'. If Irishmen acquiesced in this new policy they would be surrendering their rights as men and citizens. 'If we fail to take such measures as will effectually defeat this policy', he warned, 'we become politically the most degraded population in Europe and no longer worthy of the name of Nation . . . In a crisis of this kind the duty of safeguarding our own rights is our duty first and foremost. *They have rights who dare maintain them.*' But rights could only, in the last resort, be maintained by arms. And now, in their present situation, 'at the mercy of almost any organised aggression', it was time to form 'a citizen army' or body of Irish Volunteers.* The object of such a force would be 'to secure and to maintain the rights and liberties common to all the people of Ireland'. 'Their duties', he emphasised, 'will be defensive and protective, and they will not contemplate either aggression or domination.'[14]

The meeting was enormously successful. An eruption of Jim Larkin's supporters, then locked in their long and bitter struggle with the Dublin employers, caused some confusion but did not prevent the enrolment of between 3,000 and 4,000 enthusiastic recruits. And this was only the beginning, for by the following May numbers had risen

* The phrase 'citizen army' had been used by Jim Larkin in a labour dispute as far back as 1908. More to the point, only a few days before the Rotunda meeting, on 13 November, James Connolly had called for the workers to drill and train 'as they are doing in Ulster'. Five days later he used the actual phrase 'citizen army' and on 27 November there began the first drilling of what was to become the workers' own force. In the early stages Larkin was more directly involved than Connolly in the affairs of the Citizen Army. See Part I, chap. 8.

to about 75,000 and were to grow still further in circumstances soon to be described. It was clear beyond question that yet another private army had arrived on the scene.

But was it to be a real army with teeth or just an army of paper tigers? The answer depended on one crucial factor – the supply of arms. The difficulties in the way of obtaining weapons in any adequate quantity were almost insuperable. Money was lacking and would remain lacking while the parliamentary leaders made up their minds how to deal with this new phenomenon. But even if money had been plentiful the government, only a few days after the Rotunda meeting, had issued a proclamation prohibiting the import of arms, so adding greatly to the perplexities of the Volunteer leaders. The Provisional Committee was still in being – it was to remain the governing body of the movement until October 1914 – but in the early months of growth effective power was in the hands of the original triumvirate, MacNeill as chairman, The O'Rahilly as treasurer, and Bulmer Hobson as secretary. The first two of these acted as an arms sub-committee and by April 1914 The O'Rahilly was emphasising to John Devoy in America that money was still the crux of their problem – 'it is NOT the proclamation that prevents us going ahead but lack of funds.'[15] That very month the Ulster Volunteers demonstrated conclusively that the proclamation was indeed no hindrance. But their successful *coup* in landing a cargo of guns and ammunition along the north-east coast on the night of 24 April was more than just an illustration of how an efficient organisation could outwit the lethargic authorities. It was a deliberate and successful attempt to regain the initiative and to tilt the balance of power in Ireland once more in their favour. If the Irish Volunteers were ever to make a reality of their movement they must have arms urgently and in large numbers. In other words, they must not only raise the indispensable funds, but they must also somehow or other engineer a gun-running exploit in the south comparable with what the Ulster Volunteers had just achieved.

The money problem was solved – for the time being, at least – in an unexpected way. The prime movers were two Anglo-Irish enthusiasts for the nationalist cause. One was Alice Stopford Green. Born in 1847 the daughter of a Church of Ireland Archdeacon, the Reverend E. A. Stopford, she married the historian J. R. Green in 1877. After his death six years later she turned to the writing of history herself and in 1908 published her most famous work, *The Making of Ireland and its Undoing*. That book revealed her as 'a passionate historian' who, like so many of the Anglo-Irish, had been led by her reading of history into an active sympathy with the Irish demand for a separate national identity.[16] She was a woman of charm, wit and intelligence who gathered round her in London a circle of friends ranging from Arthur Balfour on the right to Beatrice Webb on the left and including several members of the Liberal government of the day. She was also a patron of humanitarian movements and this brought her into contact with such champions of the oppressed as E. D. Morel and Sir Roger Casement. Her ties with Casement were particularly close and her influence over him was very great. Like her, Casement was Anglo-Irish. The son of an army officer, he was born at Sandycove, just outside Dublin, in 1864. His parents died when he was very young and he was brought up in the rigorous Protestantism of county Antrim. After a varied career in West Africa he entered the British Foreign Service in 1892 and in the next twenty years won an international reputation for his work in exposing the exploitation of natives by European employers first in the Congo and then in Peru. He received the KCMG, but in 1913 retired from his post. Long before that he had become deeply involved in Irish affairs. This was partly due to friendships formed in Belfast when home on leave from abroad. He is known to have met Bulmer Hobson as early as 1904 and in later years his main base in the north was the house of a well-known solicitor, F. J. Bigger, who was also a friend of Hobson's. It was in 1904 also that Casement first met Mrs Green and although their initial concern was with the Congo, the following year they both collaborated with Hobson in producing an anti-recruiting pamphlet, the circulation of which was one of the earliest achievements of the Dungannon Club.[17]

Casement, then at the height of his career, was a striking figure. Tall and extremely handsome in a dark, romantic style, he was gentle in manner and entirely selfless in doing what seemed to him best for whatever cause he was serving. However, he suffered from poor health, was very highly strung, and had a tendency towards melancholia which had probably been accentuated by the horrors he had seen on the rubber plantations. It was later to be charged against him, mainly on the basis of the so-called 'black diaries', which passed into the British government's hands after his arrest in 1916, that he was a homosexual. Nationalist writers have generally found it impossible to accept this evidence, though some of it is formidable, and they tend to dismiss the accusation as a monstrous slur upon a man who was loved and honoured by a great variety of men and women in his own lifetime. For the historian writing long after the event it is perhaps permissible to suggest that the question of whether or not Casement was a homosexual is not directly relevant to the part he took in the Irish revolution – or rather it would only be relevant if anything in his conduct had suggested that his private life was influencing his public actions. Since there appears to be no firm or clear-cut evidence that was actually the case, the question of homosexuality loses much of its historic importance, except, of course, to those who subscribe to the doctrine that every patriot must be like Caesar's wife.[18]

His retirement from the Foreign Service left Casement free to devote himself entirely to Irish affairs. By the end of 1913 he was a member of the Provisional Committee of the Irish Volunteers and in the spring of 1914 he was largely instrumental in persuading Mrs Green to form a small 'London committee' to raise funds for the purchase of arms. Very quickly £1,500 was collected and plans began to be laid for obtaining the necessary weapons and getting them to Ireland. Since the whole venture was illegal the strictest secrecy had to be maintained. In Dublin only MacNeill, Hobson and The O'Rahilly knew what was afoot, and in London knowledge of the plot was confined to those who had a definite function to perform. It was agreed that Darrell Figgis, an Anglo-Irish journalist with a good knowledge of the continent, should be the chief agent for purchasing rifles and ammunition. He was accompanied to Germany at the end of May 1914 by Erskine Childers. Childers was destined to play a major role, not just in this escapade, but in the subsequent history of Ireland. At this point he was forty-four years old and already had a varied career behind him. Educated at Haileybury and Trinity College, Cambridge, he had fought in the British army in the Boer War and had written much on military matters. He had been a clerk of the House of Commons for some years, but although he did not abandon this neutral coign of vantage until 1910, he appears to have become a convinced Home Ruler about 1908. With this kind of background he seemed to superficial observers no more than an English sympathiser for the cause and even in later years, when he was deeply involved in Irish politics, his enemies were to revile him as 'the Englishman'. This was unfair. His mother was a Barton of Glendalough, county Wicklow, and for most of his life he regarded the family's beautiful house there as his home.

But Childers, man of many talents as he was, had one talent in particular that was essential to the success of the Volunteers' plan. One of those active on the London committee, Mary Spring Rice (a daughter of Lord Monteagle and, such was the paradoxical nature of the times, a first cousin of the British ambassador at Washington, Sir Cecil Spring Rice), had suggested that the best way to bring home to Ireland the weapons purchased in Germany was to sail them back in private, and therefore unobtrusive, yachts. Now Childers was a superlative yachtsman who had already spent a great deal of time sailing along the German North Sea coastline while gathering material for his famous book, *The Riddle of the Sands*, an early and classic example of the novel of espionage. It was decided therefore that once the arms were bought in Germany (and the money available secured 1,500 Mauser rifles and 45,000 rounds of ammunition) they should be brought by a German tug from Hamburg to a point of rendezvous off the Belgian coast. There they were to be met by two yachts. One was Childers's own boat, the *Asgard*; the other, the *Kelpie*, belonging to a cousin of Mary Spring Rice, Conor O'Brien. The crews of the two vessels consisted mainly of Anglo-Irish or English gentry and three women were aboard – Erskine Childers's semi- crippled American wife, Mary Spring Rice and her cousin, Kitty O'Brien.

Why, it may be asked, was this strange episode, on which, it can be said without exaggeration, turned the whole future of the Irish insurrection, so largely in the hands of the Anglo-Irish Ascendancy class? The answer is certainly not that they were fanatical republicans. Casement, it is true, had already written articles looking forward to an Anglo-German war as Ireland's opportunity, and had developed bitterly anti-British feelings while still in the Foreign Service, but he was not in the confidence of extreme nationalists and was never a member of the IRB. Most of the others concerned in the gun-running (apart from Mrs Green whose nationalism, while intense, was for obvious reasons mainly theoretical) were either Liberal or vaguely Home Rule in their sympathies. Their initiative seems to have been an almost instinctive reaction to what had already happened in Ulster. To such people, generous-minded and idealistic, it was not difficult to believe that the scales were being unfairly weighted against Home Rule. In England the government vacillated and seemed endlessly vulnerable to the threat of force. The Ulster Volunteers had used that threat with absolute impunity and complete success. Why should it not be employed in the south, where it might help to stiffen the determination of Asquith and his colleagues in following out the policy to which they were in honour committed? And, of course, if shipping arms illegally to Ireland added a spice of excitement to comfortable aristocratic lives, so much the better. But that the guns they were planning to bring in might actually go off, and go off in other hands than theirs, seems not to have entered into their calculations.[19]

Such an adventure, so much at the mercy of wind and tide and accident, seemed bound to fail. In fact, it succeeded brilliantly. The arms and ammunition were divided into two cargoes. That carried by the *Kelpie* was transferred off the Welsh coast into another yacht, the *Chotah*, owned by an eminent Dublin surgeon, Sir Thomas Myles, and landed safely at Kilcoole in county Wicklow at the beginning of August. But for the cargo carried by the *Asgard* an altogether more daring and flamboyant plan had been devised by Bulmer Hobson. He proposed that the yacht sail in to Howth Harbour on the north side of Dublin Bay, and that the Volunteers rapidly unload her and march away with their rifles. There was a dual intention behind this audacious plan – to demonstrate that the Ulster Volunteers had no monopoly in outwitting the authorities and, by gaining maximum publicity, to encourage recruiting.

Both aims were amply achieved, though not without bloodshed. By a miracle of timing, the *Asgard* arrived at Howth at the appointed hour on 26 July 1914 and was there met by the Volunteers, together with the devoted Fianna. The guns and ammunition were speedily unloaded and distributed, but on the march back the way was blocked by police and soldiers of The King's Own Scottish Borderers. There were some scuffles, but while the Volunteers' leaders engaged the authorities in prolonged argument, the rank and file slipped away with their weapons, the great majority of which escaped seizure. Later that afternoon, however, triumph was tinged with tragedy. As the troops made their way back to barracks along Bachelor's Walk beside the Liffey they were baited by the crowd. Owing, probably, to a misunderstanding of orders, the rear files turned to retaliate. Shots were fired, bayonets were used, three people were killed and thirty-eight wounded. Had it not been that Europe was then moving almost hour by hour closer to war, this terrible end to the episode might well have led to an explosion in Dublin.

That it did not lead to an explosion may, however, have been due at least in part to the internal tensions existing within the Volunteer movement at that very moment. For between the end of May, when the guns were bought in Hamburg, and the end of July, when they were landed at Howth, there had been a major crisis over the control of the Volunteers. As this private army had grown in numbers the parliamentary leaders became anxious and during May John Redmond, John Dillon and Joseph Devlin put heavy pressure on MacNeill to amend the composition of the Provisional Committee in their favour. From their viewpoint this was a perfectly justifiable demand. They were approaching the very climax of the Home Rule campaign, they might shortly expect to have the responsibility for governing Ireland, therefore, they could argue, they must be in a position to dominate the Volunteers. But they found MacNeill, professed Home Ruler though he was, curiously difficult to pin down. This was not surprising, for, as we now know, although one or two of his associates (notably Casement and the Inspector-General of the Volunteers, Colonel Maurice Moore) were vaguely aware of what he was about, he had not consulted the Provisional Committee as a whole. MacNeill, clearly, was in a fearsome dilemma. On the one hand, Redmond still possessed the allegiance of the vast majority of nationalists and could very probably ruin the whole Volunteer movement if he chose to instruct his followers to boycott it. On the other hand, if the movement were handed over to him lock, stock and barrel, the more advanced nationalists would move out at the precise point when, unknown to them, the weapons which were to give the Volunteers real power and authority were still on the high seas.

Naturally enough, MacNeill temporised. Naturally enough, the parliamentarians grew impatient. They thought him vain, confused and unbusinesslike. He was none of these things, but was simply playing a waiting game. Yet time was running out. It was known that Home Rule would not reach the statute-book without the special problem of Ulster being reserved to be dealt with separately and it was more than ever necessary for Redmond to have behind him the same kind of disciplined force that Carson had had at his disposal for so long. Eventually, brushing on one side a proposal for an elected executive,

Redmond published his ultimatum in the newspapers on 9 June 1914. In this – which came as a complete surprise to most of the Volunteers – he demanded that twenty-five persons nominated by the Irish parliamentary party should be added to the Provisional Committee. Even though his ultimatum looked forward to an eventual election for the governing body of the Volunteers, it was clear that on the short term the inclusion of twenty-five moderate Home Rulers would give him virtual control. The Volunteer leaders were faced with an agonising decision. Either they allowed their organisation to remain intact under Redmond, or they rejected his demand and so risked what Hobson later called 'a disastrous, and, indeed, a fatal split'.[20] In the end, after angry discussion, those who put unity above everything else carried the day and the ultimatum was accepted. It seems that MacNeill was able to secure acceptance of this policy mainly because he had the support of Casement and Hobson; the latter, no doubt preoccupied by the fate of the guns then stowed away in *Asgard* and *Kelpie*, was especially emphatic that the 'bitter pill be swallowed. He was probably right in his contention that the Redmondites on the Committee could easily be outmanoeuvred by their more experienced colleagues but this did not save him from the wrath of his comrades in the IRB. Tom Clarke never spoke to him again and his old friend Sean MacDermott was also permanently estranged. So impossible did Hobson's position become, indeed, that although he remained a member of the IRB, he resigned from the Supreme Council and ceased to edit *Irish Freedom*.[21]

Yet he had his reward. When the arms did arrive they were delivered to a body of Volunteers who though inwardly divided had at least managed to avoid the ultimate humiliation of a public split. And, as Hobson himself had anticipated, the success of the gun-running exploit reverberated through the country so that recruiting, which had become sluggish, recovered to such an extent that by September 1914, the force numbered 180,000.[22] By then, however, the war had intervened and the history, both public and secret, of the Volunteers had entered a new phase.

2. The Road to Revolution

Every revolution has a secret history difficult to discover and to disentangle. The Irish rising of 1916 is no exception. Indeed, it is more
complicated than most because the insurrection developed at several
levels which came to have less and less contact with each other as
time went on. Moreover, the complexity of the situation was increased
by the fact that affairs moved towards their climax in the midst
of a great war and were at certain vital moments influenced by events
far beyond the frontiers of Ireland.

The key to the understanding of the rising lies in the fact that from
the very beginning of the war the open and the secret nationalist
movements began to draw apart. Later, and in dramatic circumstances,
they were to converge again, but in the interests of clarity it is pre-
ferable to consider them separately at the outset. So far as the open
movement was concerned, the hard-won unity bought at the price
of yielding to Redmond's demands in June 1914 did not last long.
Redmond himself, as we saw earlier when considering the final stages
of the Home Rule agitation, had taken a momentous initiative when,
at the outbreak of the war, he had declared his sympathy for
Britain in the coming conflict and had asked the government to
entrust the defence of Ireland to the Volunteers of north and south.
At that time, and apparently for some weeks afterwards, he intended
that the Volunteers should not be required to take an oath of
allegiance and should not be called upon to serve outside Ireland,
even though it was pointed out to him by the military authorities
that the war was in fact going to be decided on the battlefields of
Flanders.

Then on 20 September, in a speech at Woodenbridge, county Wicklow, which seems to have been quite spontaneous, he suddenly
reversed his policy and called on the Volunteers not just to fight for
Ireland, but to go 'wherever the firing-line extends'. What prompted
him to take this grave step is still a matter of argument. It may have
been a reaction of gratitude for the fact that Home Rule had at
last actually reached the statute-book, it may have been a gesture
of competition with the Ulster Volunteers whom Carson had already
urged to fight overseas, it may even have been – as his biographer
suggests – a desire to provoke a crisis within the Provisional Committee. A crisis there certainly was. Four days later the bulk of the
members of the original executive issued a statement repudiating both

Redmond and his nominees on the Provisional Committee. The Volunteers at once split in two and although the great majority, about 170,000, stayed with Redmond to form the National Volunteers, the remainder – perhaps 11,000, representing on the whole the more active and extreme section of the movement – kept the name Irish Volunteers and in October 1914 formed their own separate organisation.[1] In this organisation the Provisional Committee was replaced by a General Council consisting of one representative from each of the thirty-two counties and one from each of the nine chief cities and towns. In addition there was to be a President and eight other members elected by annual convention of the Volunteers from candidates resident within ten miles of Dublin. These nine members were to form a Central Executive, and since the election of local representatives proceeded very slowly it was obvious that the Central Executive would be the real power to create a headquarters staff for the purpose of putting the Volunteers in a state of proper military preparation. MacNeill himself was Chief of Staff, Bulmer Hobson was Quartermaster, and The O'Rahilly was Director of Arms. But, as events turned out, it was the holders of three other posts who were to exercise supreme authority at the critical moment. These were Patrick Pearse (Director of Military Organisation), Thomas MacDonagh (Director of Training) and Joseph Plunkett (Director of Military Operations).[2] Since all three were either then, or soon afterwards, members of the IRB, it is clear that the open movement was already being penetrated by the secret society; indeed, it seems that even on the General Council itself the IRB had, unknown to MacNeill, a controlling majority.[3]

But Pearse, MacDonagh and Plunkett were more than a secret revolutionary cell operating within the Volunteer movement. Collectively and individually they represented one strand in the making of the revolution of 1916 which, though baffling to some contemporaries and often afterwards to posterity, was nevertheless of great importance. They were all poets, they were all Gaelic enthusiasts, they were all consumed by the same fire of revolutionary romanticism. Plunkett was the youngest of the three. He was born in Dublin in 1887 into a well-known Irish family. His father was a papal Count who had been attracted by Griffith's Sinn Féin doctrines but was, at least until 1916, essentially non-political, and fully occupied with his duties as Director of the National Museum. The son, Joseph, was delicate from childhood and spent much of his youth out of Ireland – in Sicily, Malta and Algeria – seeking the sunshine he needed. Precociously intelligent, he was interested in philosophy and poetry – and in soldiering. In 1910 he met MacDonagh for the first time, when the latter was asked to tutor him in Irish. Soon the two were collaborating in theatre work and in the production of the *Irish Review*, one of those weeklies, part-political and part-literary, which abounded in Ireland at that epoch. The periodical was suppressed in November 1914 largely because of Plunkett's violent language, and from then on he threw himself into the work of the Volunteers, whom he had joined at their inception the previous year. There was a certain theatricality about Plunkett which was apt to deceive the casual observer. He was addicted to wearing large rings and bracelets, he loved conspiratorial devices like pass-words and disguises – yet at the same time he had considerable military ability and by the end of 1914 he was already devising plans for street-fighting in Dublin.[4]

His teacher and collaborator, Thomas MacDonagh, came of a different background and was moulded on a large scale. Born in county Tipperary in 1879, he was educated at Rockwell College and worked as a schoolmaster first at Kilkenny and then at Fermoy. While still scarcely more than a student he became deeply involved in the Gaelic revival and in 1908 helped Pearse to set up his bilingual school at St Enda's. He combined this with study for a degree at University College, Dublin, and proved sufficiently outstanding a scholar to be appointed an assistant lecturer in English at University College, Dublin, at the end of 1911. Of the three poets MacDonagh had perhaps the greatest promise and as early as 1908 the Abbey Theatre had produced his play *When the Dawn is Come*. Prophetically, it dealt with a war against England in which the command was vested in a council of seven men. It was not, however, until 1913 that MacDonagh was drawn out of what looked like becoming a pleasant donnish and literary existence by his concern at the violence with which the police dealt with the Larkinite strikers. Like Plunkett he developed an interest in military tactics and like him he was one of the first to join the Volunteers, though he does not appear to have been admitted into the IRB until 1915. By then he had established his reputation as a formidable organiser, having helped Bulmer Hobson to carry out the landing of the guns at Howth and having, in August 1915, planned the massive demonstration at O'Donovan Rossa's funeral which gave Pearse the chance to make his famous invocation to the spirit of Fenian revolution.[5]

Pearse himself, although the same age as MacDonagh, had lived already more in the public eye. Born in Dublin in the street which now bears his name (it was then Great Brunswick Street) in 1879, his father was an English monumental sculptor who had settled in Ireland some years before Patrick Henry Pearse's birth. James Pearse married twice and Patrick Henry was a son of this second marriage from which came also his brother William and two sisters.[6] Patrick Pearse was educated by the Christian Brothers in Dublin and took his BA in 1901 through the old Royal University. Soon afterwards he was called to the bar, but he seems to have been an almost briefless barrister and his real interest – education – soon revealed itself. For him, as for so many of the generation of 1916, the path of genuinely national education lay through the revival of the Irish language and

331

culture. Pearse was not a native speaker, but he began to learn Irish as a child of eleven or twelve and for the rest of his life it became a part of his very being. When he was only seventeen he started the New Ireland Society to popularise Irish poetry and folk-lore and as early as 1897, in one of his presidential addresses to that Society, the essentially mystical character of his nationalism began to reveal itself. 'The Gael is not like other men', he declaimed, 'the spade, and the loom, and the sword are not for him. But a destiny more glorious than that of Rome, more glorious than that of Britain awaits him: to become the saviour of idealism in modern intellectual and social life. . . .'

It was precisely this idealism which Pearse carried into his educational work. To instil into the rising generation a love for their own past, and for their language and literature, was impossible, he believed, in the context of the existing educational system which was English-oriented and dominated by the examination fetish. In 1908, therefore, he founded St Enda's, that bilingual school in which MacDonagh was one of his earliest helpers. Originally in Cullenswood House at Rath-mines, it was moved two years later to The Hermitage at Rathfarn-ham. From the outset it was a financial burden and Pearse was several times on the verge of having to abandon his experiment. He was saved by the devotion of his own family, who helped to run it without receiving any pay, and by the friends who came to his rescue with credit from time to time. He had intended to break entirely with the 'murder-machine', as he called the existing system in one of his pamphlets, but he was obliged to compromise with it to the extent of agreeing to prepare at least some of his pupils for public or university examinations. This, however, did not prevent him from taking his own often very modern ideas as far as he could. His aim was to kindle enthusiasm rather than to impart information, to inspire rather than to discipline.

With this went an element of propaganda. As was only to be expected from his own background, it was propaganda in the first place for the Irish revival. The school language and games were Irish, and everything except languages and scientific subjects was taught bilingually. But this was not all. Pearse's propaganda was not merely Gaelic in an abstract sense, it was nationalist as well. The boy who entered the school would find confronting him a fresco with these words emblazoned round it: 'I care not though I were to live but one day and one night, if only my fame and my deeds live after me.' This was a saying attributed to Cú Chulainn, the legendary hero of Ulster, who in the Irish sagas was depicted as fighting to the death against the invaders of his country.

The words expressed what came to be the ruling passion of Pearse's life and he was to repeat this theme again and again in the few years that remained to him. But in the days when he was struggling to keep St Enda's in existence romantic nationalism seemed far away. His own most public sphere at that time was the Gaelic League, of which he was an enthusiastic member, editing the League's weekly paper, *An Claidheamh Soluis*, from 1903 until the pressure of his school responsibilities obliged him to give it up in 1909. The Gaelic League was of course at that time non-political – it remained so until 1915 – and Pearse's own politics were not very different from MacNeill's. As late as 1912 he spoke (in Irish) on a Home Rule platform in Dublin, though anyone who studied his speech on that occasion might have noticed in it an important qualification. 'Let the foreigner understand', he said, 'that if we are cheated now there will be red war in Ireland.'[7] Even this reservation, however, did not save him from being regarded askance for some time afterwards by extreme republicans to whom any gesture of support for Redmond's policy was anathema.

Curiously enough it was his oratorical talent that ultimately helped him to convince the extreme men that he was one of themselves. Conquering a slight stammer, and a very considerable degree of shyness, Pearse had made himself over the years a speaker of extraordinary power and magnetism. Even as early as 1911 he had impressed Tom Clarke – not usually one to suffer orators gladly – by these qualities and in the summer of 1913 he was chosen to give the oration at the annual commemoration of Wolfe Tone, a ceremony of which the IRB were the devoted guardians. Pearse chose to recall not only Tone's objectives but his methods. 'To break the connection with England, the never-failing source of all our political evils, and to assert the independence of my country – these were my objects. To unite the whole people of Ireland, to abolish the memory of all past dissensions, and to substitute the common name of Irishmen in place of the denominations of Protestant, Catholic and Dissenter – these were my means.' The phrases were well-worn certainly, but Pearse gave them a new urgency when he called on his audience to pledge themselves to fight as Tone had fought, even if for some of them, the fight would end as Tone's had done. 'Such', he said, almost as if he were musing aloud, 'is the high and sorrowful destiny of the heroes: to turn their backs to the pleasant paths and their faces to the hard paths, to blind their eyes to the fair things of life . . . and to follow only the far, faint call that leads them into the battle or to the harder death at the foot of a gibbet.'[8]

If this meant anything it meant that Pearse was moving towards the physical force camp and the series of articles he contributed later that year to Bulmer Hobson's *Irish Freedom* pointed in the same direction. It was the time of Larkin's fight against the Dublin employers and this set Pearse on a train of thought which in the end was to bring him into close sympathy with that other great original thinker in the revolutionary group, James Connolly. But it was an instinctive, not a doctrinal, sympathy. 'I am nothing so new-fangled as a socialist or a syndicalist', Pearse wrote in October 1913. 'I am old-fashioned enough to be both a Catholic and a Nationalist.' Nevertheless the existence of so much suffering and starvation in the city moved him to a sense of burning injustice. Larkin might be wrong in some of his methods, 'but this I know, that here is a most hideous wrong to be righted, and that the man who attempts honestly to right it is a good man and a brave man'.

But it was typical of him that he did not see the Dublin slums in Marxist terms. 'We have not great cities', he wrote, 'we have not dense industrial populations; we have hardly any ruthless capitalists exploiting immense masses of men.' Yet there was dire and desperate poverty. Why? 'Before God, I believe that the root of the matter lies in foreign domination. A free Ireland would not, and could not, have hunger in her fertile vales and squalor in her cities.' From this it was but a step to consider the conditions under which freedom might be obtained. And in November, with the example of the Ulster Volunteers before him, he was already beginning to preach the doctrine that the only serious nationalism was armed nationalism. 'Personally I think the Orangeman with a rifle a much less ridiculous figure than the Nationalist without one.' 'For after all', he wrote in December, 'may it not be said with entire truth that the reason why Ireland is not free is that Ireland has not deserved to be free? Men who have ceased to be men cannot claim the rights of men; and men who have suffered themselves to be deprived of their manhood have suffered the greatest of all indignities . . . For in suffering ourselves to be disarmed . . . we in effect abrogate our manhood.'[9]

It was in the nature of things that a man of such ability, holding such views, should not only join the Volunteers but rise rapidly to the top, and in fact Pearse was a founder-member of the Provisional Committee. Then, by what seems now an almost inevitable progression, he was admitted about a month later (probably in December 1913) to the IRB. He departed almost immediately to America to raise funds for St Enda's, where he was taken under the wing of John Devoy and made as favourable an impression upon that cast-iron revolutionary as any poet or orator could reasonably be expected to make. Each step he took now seemed to bring him further from contemplation and nearer to action.

(ii)

But although Pearse in 1913 had clearly reached the point where an armed insurrection was presenting itself to him as in the logic of events, his own thought was still evolving. And before we can trace the actual development of the conspiracy in which he was so soon to be involved it is necessary first to be clear about his doctrine of revolt. As he revealed it in his writings, and as MacDonagh and Plunkett to a rather lesser extent revealed it in theirs, it was a Messianic doctrine combined with a doctrine of sacrifice.[10] All these three writers were intensely Catholic, and Plunkett in particular was deeply influenced by mysticism, especially by the writings of St John of the Cross. In the years immediately before 1916 we find each of them, emphatically and deliberately, giving to his nationalism a religious quality:

Like a divine religion [as Pearse wrote] national freedom bears the marks of unity, of sanctity, of catholicity, of apostolic succession. Of unity, for it contemplates the nation as one; of sanctity, for it is holy in itself and in those who serve it; of catholicity, for it embraces all the men and women of the nation; of apostolic succession, for it, or the aspiration after it, passes down from generation to generation from the nation's fathers.[11]

But theirs, though often expressed in mystical terms, was not a religion of meekness. It was a religion of Apocalypse; they came bringing not peace but a sword. What MacDonagh, for example, emphasises in 'Wishes for my son' is not divine love but divine justice:

> Wild and perilous holy things
> Flaming with a martyr's blood,
> And the joy that laughs and sings
> Where a foe must be withstood,
> Joy of headlong happy chance
> Leading on the battle dance.[12]

For Plunkett also, though to combine an essentially contemplative mysticism with a nationalism that called for action created all kinds of tensions in his verse, the final resolution of his problems was to merge his mysticism in his nationalism. Thus, in 'The Little Black Rose Shall Be Red At Last,' Plunkett, whose own last act upon earth was to marry Grace Gifford in his cell the night before his execution, addressed himself as a lover to the dark rose, the traditional image of conquered Ireland:

> Because we share our sorrows and our joys
> And all your dear and intimate thoughts are mine
> We shall not fear the trumpets and the noise
> Of battle, for we know our dreams divine,
> And when my heart is pillowed on your heart
> And ebb and flowing of their passionate flood
> Shall beat in concord love through every part
> Of brain and body – when at last the blood
> O'er leaps the final barrier to find
> Only one source wherein to spend its strength
> And we two lovers, long but one in mind
> And soul, are made one only flesh at length;

335

Praise God if this my blood fulfils the doom
When you, dark rose, shall redden into bloom.[13]

The theme of the blood-sacrifice is clearly apparent in these lines, but it was of course from Pearse that it received its most powerful and direct expression. As early as November 1913, when he had reached the crossroads in his career, he announced the fact in 'The Coming Revolution'. In this essay, written just after MacNeill's article 'The North Began', Pearse commences with a declaration deliberately intended to have a shattering effect upon those who had hitherto identified him with the non-contentious activities of the Gaelic League:

> I have come to the conclusion [he wrote] that the Gaelic League, as the Gaelic League, is a spent force; and I am glad of it . . . The Gaelic League was no reed shaken by the wind, no mere *vox clamantis*: it was a prophet and more than a prophet. But it was not the Messiah. I do not know if the Messiah has yet come, and I am not sure that there will be any visible and personal Messiah in this redemption: the people itself will perhaps be its own Messiah, the people labouring, scourged, crowned with thorns, agonising and dying, to rise again immortal and impassible.

The Gaelic League, he explained, had been a necessary stage in the education of those who wanted to serve Ireland, but it was only a stage. 'We never meant to be Gaelic Leaguers and nothing more than Gaelic Leaguers' – now it was time to look forward to the task of the future, which was 'to accomplish the revolution'. And so, he said, whenever Dr Hyde produced his dove of peace at a meeting, 'I have always been careful to produce my sword; and to tantalise him by saying that the Gaelic League has brought into Ireland "not peace, but a sword".'

But how was the revolution to be accomplished? Pearse had his answer ready. 'A thing that stands demonstrable is that nationhood is not achieved otherwise than in arms.' Whether that meant actual bloodshed or not, time alone would tell, but Irishmen must accustom themselves 'to the thought of arms, to the sight of arms, to the use of arms'. 'We may', he concluded philosophically, 'make mistakes in the beginning and shoot the wrong people; but bloodshed is a cleansing and a sanctifying thing, and the nation which regards it as the final horror has lost its manhood. There are many things more horrible than bloodshed; and slavery is one of them.'[14]

A man who could write such language in a time of peace could only respond in one way to the heavily charged atmosphere of war. And it is clear from Pearse's writings and speeches from 1914 onwards that the theme of bloodshed was becoming dominant, even obsessive. A recent critic has seen in this a deterioration from the serenity and lyricism of his earlier work. 'The human voice', he has suggested, 'is replaced by the shrill screech of crowd rhetoric. The imagery shows an almost pathological lust for violence.'[15] This is, of course, a literary judgment which may be challenged by other critics on its own ground. But for the historian it is an inadequate judgment because it does not take sufficient account of context. What Pearse wrote and said, in 1915 and 1916 especially, is important both because of his own position as a revolutionary leader and because of the growing tension of the Irish situation. And what he said pointed inescapably towards an insurrection in arms. It was implicit in his graveside panegyric on O'Donovan Rossa in August 1915 when he spoke on behalf of 'the new generation that has been re-baptised in the Fenian faith'. 'Life springs from death', he proclaimed, 'and from the graves of patriot men and women spring living nations.'[16] More explicit, because even more emphatic, was the language of the article 'Peace and the Gael' he wrote at the end of the year. This was an open and exultant hymn to war. 'The last six months', he declared, 'have been the most glorious in the history of Europe.' And he continued : 'It is good for the world that such things should be done. The old heart of the earth needed to be warmed with the red wine of the battle-fields. Such august homage was never before offered to God as this, the homage of millions of lives given gladly for love of country.' War, he admitted, was indeed a terrible thing, but it was also a 'sacred duty'. And again he returned to the religious motif :

Ireland will not find Christ's peace until she has taken Christ's sword. What peace she has known in these latter days has been the devil's peace, peace with sin, peace with dishonour . . . Christ's peace is lovely in its coming, beautiful are its feet on the mountains. But it is heralded by terrific messengers; seraphim and cherubin blow trumpets of war before it. We must not flinch when we are passing through that uproar; we must not faint at the sight of blood. Winning through it, we (or those of us who survive) shall come unto great joy.[17]

'We, or those of us who survive.' No man contemplating the odds against a successful rising in Ireland could have counted with any certainty on surviving. But Pearse, it seems, went further and contemplated the possibility of achieving his real victory by *not* surviving. In after years one of his sisters was to recall that her brother's greatest devotion was to Calvary, 'to Christ Crucified and to the Crucifix', and there seems little doubt that for him both the crucifixion and the legend of Cú Chulainn pointed the way to the sacrifice of one man for the benefit of the people. In several of his later poems he faces this prospect with sadness, but with tranquillity. Thus in 'Renunciation' the poet renounces the senses one by one until only death confronts him : **H**

> I turned my back
> On the vision I had shaped
> And to this road before me
> I turned my face.
>
> I have turned my face
> To this road before me
> To the dead that I see
> And the death I shall die.[18]

Similarly, Pearse, whose love for his mother was intense and who, in fact, wrote her a most moving poem, 'To my mother', during the last days before his execution, had already anticipated the event in another poem called 'The Mother' where he makes her accept the death of himself and his brother:

> I do not grudge them; Lord, I do not grudge
> My two strong sons that I have seen go out
> To break themselves and die, they and a few,
> In bloody protest for a glorious thing.[19]

The sacrificial element here is obvious and Pearse himself did not shrink from carrying it to its most extreme conclusion by seeing the hero's death as, in the most literal sense, an *imitatio Christi*. The most celebrated instance of this is his last play, *The Singer*, which forecasts almost uncannily the course of his own career. In that play the hero, MacDara (who is Pearse himself) is forced into exile because of his patriotic songs. In his travels he comes to learn that to be truly wise one must abandon the wisdom of the world and become what the world calls foolish. He returns home to comfort his mother and impart his new knowledge to the people. But the Sassenach (the English) are about to invade the country and the word to organise the fight against them has not been given. Ordinary men and women hang back, but MacDara will go forward alone: 'One man can free a people, as one Man redeemed the world. I will take no pike, I will go into the battle with bare hands. I will stand up before the Gall as Christ hung naked before men on the tree.'[20] Blasphemy, heresy? Again, Pearse is ready with his answer, for in 'The Fool' he had already anticipated such charges from the lawyers in council, 'the men with the keen, long faces', and those who pity the fool for having tried to give life to a dream:

> O wise men riddle me this: what if the dream come true?
> What if the dream come true? and if millions unborn shall dwell
> In the house that I shaped in my heart, the noble house of my
>   thoughts?
> Lord, I have staked my soul, I have staked the lives of my kin

*On the truth of Thy dreadful word. Do not remember my failures,
But remember this my faith.*[21]

Yet if Pearse, and some others, expected that an insurrection would lead to a blood-sacrifice which in time might inspire a revivified nation to wage a more successful war, this was not the view of all the revolutionaries, nor did it mean that even those who held the sacrificial doctrine went into the struggle without doing what they could to plan for victory. And however deficient their planning may seem in retrospect to have been, it was done in deadly earnest and in full knowledge of the consequences of failure.

The earliest initiative appears to have been taken in America, where in August 1914 a special committee of Clan na Gael met the German ambassador in New York to tell him of their intention to organise an armed revolt in Ireland and ask for military assistance. This news was at once communicated to Ireland and the Supreme Council of the IRB decided, within a month of the outbreak of war, that there should indeed be a rebellion but that it should take place even if German aid was not forthcoming. Early in September at least one conference was held in Dublin with 'advanced' nationalists who were not members of the IRB in order to discuss the prospects of a rising. Arthur Griffith and the two labour leaders, James Connolly and William O'Brien, are known to have been involved in these discussions which, however, may have been premature, since they did not produce any overt result except the formation of a short-lived Irish Neutrality League that seems to have concentrated its attention mainly on an anti-recruiting campaign.[22]

There was a kind of historical inevitability about the fact that the very first move in organising a revolt should have been an approach to Germany, for an alliance with England's enemy in a great war was the traditional opening gambit in Irish revolutionary tactics. But that the attempt to form a close link with Germany should have been pressed forward so insistently was due mainly to the accidental circumstance that Sir Roger Casement happened to be in the United States when war broke out. For years past he had been maintaining in private and in public that a war between England and Germany was bound to come and that this would be Ireland's opportunity. He at once saw himself in the role of Irish ambassador to a friendly ally and although John Devoy, with ample justice as it turned out, distrusted his competence for the task, he could scarcely disown a man who was deliberately putting his neck in a noose for the sake of the cause. Casement went off to Germany, therefore, financed by Irish-American money, and charged with a three-fold task – to recruit an Irish brigade from among prisoners of war in Germany, to secure general German support for a declaration of Irish independence, and, more specifically, to arrange for arms to be shipped to Ireland.

His mission was an almost unrelieved disaster. It even began badly with his insistence upon taking with him a Norwegian seaman, Adler Christensen, whom he had met casually in New York. Christensen travelled as Casement's servant, but he seems to have been treated more as a companion and the unsavoury rumours that soon leaked out about him – with their markedly homosexual overtones – did nothing to improve Casement's standing as an ambassador. On the way to Germany, so Casement was convinced, the British minister in Norway (M. de C. Findlay), offered Christensen a bribe of £5,000 to help in kidnapping his master or 'knocking him on the head'. Casement may have been right in his suspicions – stranger things have happened in war-time – or, as Devoy suspected, the plot may have been an invention of Christensen's to feather his own nest, but whatever the truth of the matter its real importance was that Casement allowed it to become an obsession, blinding him at a crucial moment to far larger issues. Probably also, it contributed directly to the intense depression and frequent illness to which he was subject throughout his stay in Germany.

At the end of 1914, it is true, he had his brief moment of triumph when he did elicit from the Germans a high-sounding declaration – or 'treaty' as Casement preferred to call it – permitting the formation of an Irish brigade, promising arms and ammunition for Ireland (with the substantial reservation that these would materialise after a German naval victory) and pledging German recognition of and support for an independent Irish government, should the revolutionaries succeed in setting one up. Such was Casement's achievement, but it was hollow from the start. The recruitment of an Irish brigade was an almost complete failure even when his labours were reinforced by those of a very competent assistant, Robert Monteith, sent out specially by Tom Clarke, or by the more spasmodic efforts of Joseph Plunkett who visited him briefly in 1915. Arms, indeed, were sent eventually, but Casement, as we shall see presently, was left in the dark about the arrangements for their dispatch and in the end there was little left for him to do but to hazard his own life in an attempt to halt at the last minute an insurrection he had come to believe was doomed to failure.[23]

Until he re-entered the conspiracy at that late stage Casement's activities in Germany were peripheral, as they surely would have remained even had he been much better suited to his work. Because, although he had been quite logical in thinking of an Irish revolt in the context of help from Britain's enemy, there was still no disguising the fact that the revolt itself could only be planned and carried out by Irishmen in Ireland.

In effect this meant Dublin, and it was there that the next act in the drama now unfolded. What happened was complex and is not even now fully documented, but the key to understanding is to keep constantly in mind that preparations proceeded at two distinct levels. We have to deal not only with a secret movement (indeed, with a secret movement within a secret movement), but also with an open movement which, unknown to its leader, was being penetrated by the secret movement. The Volunteers who had remained loyal to MacNeill had increased during the latter part of 1914 from 11,000 at the time of the split with Redmond to 13,500. Numbers then apparently fell off for a while, but began to pick up after a recruiting drive was launched in the spring of 1915 and by April 1916 the total had reached about 16,000.[24] This, together with the tiny Citizen Army of not much more than about 200 men, was to provide the striking force for the insurrection. That, however, was not how MacNeill himself saw it. His strategy, which seems also to have been that of Bulmer Hobson and of The O'Rahilly, was that the Volunteers should be kept intact as a highly organised and well-disciplined force, not to be thrown into a hopeless struggle *during* the war, but to act as a pressure-group *after* the war. Joined, it was hoped, by disillusioned ex-soldiers, they would then be able to demand the implementation of the Home Rule Act which had been placed on the statute-book in September 1914 and simultaneously suspended.

But even those who favoured this kind of waiting-game realised that they might not be allowed to play it. Consequently, MacNeill and his colleagues had to frame a provisional plan of action to be put into operation in either of two circumstances – if the Volunteers themselves were threatened with suppression or disarmament, or if the country as a whole was faced with the possibility of conscription. To meet these contingencies, each of which would have been recognised as a *casus belli*, the Volunteers had to continue to arm, to train and to make their strategic dispositions. These, it is interesting to note in the light of later history, did *not* envisage pitched battles based on the seizure of key points in Dublin, but rather the development of guerrilla warfare throughout the country.[25]

Thus the Volunteers presented an outwardly warlike front without, so long as MacNeill could prevent it, being committed to an immediate and desperate uprising. But could he prevent it? Although he was not himself apparently aware of the fact, the IRB had a majority of the crucial positions within the movement. And on the all-important headquarters staff three out of the original six members – Pearse, Plunkett and MacDonagh – were all committed to the idea of a war-time insurrection, as was also Eamonn Ceannt who was added to the staff as Director of Communications in August 1915.* Even before

---

* Ceannt (or Kent) has remained a more shadowy figure than the other leaders. Born in Galway in 1881 he lived most of his life in Dublin and worked in the Treasurer's department of the Corporation. He came to extreme nationalism by way of the Gaelic League and Sinn Féin, and

the end of 1914, it appears, some of the extremer members of the Volunteers – and this included not merely Pearse and Plunkett but also Ceannt, who was a member of the General Council at that time – began to discuss the possible form a rising might take; it is not clear whether this would have been confined to Dublin or would also have involved the provinces.[26] That seems to have been an independent and unauthorised initiative, which was soon scotched by the IRB, but it had its importance in the scheme of things, partly because the tactics then worked out foreshadowed those adopted in 1916, and partly because the men involved were soon to be involved again in a much more official capacity. For in the spring of 1915, as a result of intensive negotiations between Devoy and the Germans, Joseph Plunkett was sent to Berlin to arrange for the shipment of arms to Ireland in the following year. And not only this, but in May 1915 the executive of the Supreme Council of the IRB decided (probably on the prompting of Tom Clarke) to set up a military committee. The first members of the committee were Pearse, Plunkett and Ceannt, even though none of them was at that time on the Supreme Council. In September, Sean MacDermott and Tom Clarke joined this special committee, or Military Council as it came to be called. It was reinforced in January 1916 by the inclusion of James Connolly and in April by the co-option of Thomas MacDonagh. These seven men were to be the signatories of the Proclamation of Independence.

That, however, was still far in the future. The date of the rising had not been fixed when the Military Council was first formed and it was not until the end of 1915 that Easter 1916 was finally decided upon. Even then, so secret were the plans of this group that although in January 1916 the Supreme Council of IRB took a general decision that there should be a rising as soon as possible, the actual date was not disclosed to them. Indeed, the president of the three-man executive of the Supreme Council, Denis McCullough, was also kept in the dark, though this could be explained by the fact that he lived in Belfast. Recent research suggests, however, that the activities of Clarke and MacDermott had not only had the effect of excluding members of the Supreme Council from what was going on, but had also weakened the chain of command within the IRB itself. By departing radically from the standard mode of 'swearing in' to the organisation, and by imparting their secrets (or such as they chose to impart) to a rigorously selected few, they certainly preserved their plot from the traditional betrayal by informers, but only at the price of ultimate

was sworn into the IRB by Sean MacDermott. He was a founder member of the Volunteers and was described by one who knew him well as 'more naturally a physical force man than any of the other leaders' (F. O'Donoghue, 'Ceannt, Devoy, O'Rahilly and the Military Plan', in F. X. Martin (ed.), *Leaders and Men of the Easter Rising*, pp. 195-6).

confusion among IRB men in the country at large.* Effectively, therefore, control was vested in these two members of the executive (Tom
Clarke and Sean MacDermott) and to a possibly lesser degree in their
colleagues on the Military Council – Pearse, Plunkett, Ceannt and, later,
Connolly and MacDonagh.[27]

To fix dates and make plans was one thing – to bring men into the
streets was another. The only men worth bringing into the streets
were the Volunteers and the Citizen Army. But how was this to be
done? So far as the Citizen Army was concerned the problem was not,
indeed, to bring them into the streets but to keep them off them. Ever
since James Connolly had arrived in Dublin to take up permanent
residence in October 1914 he had been growing steadily more militant.
He had made up his mind on the outbreak of war that he would
work for an insurrection to proclaim an independent republic and
in his paper, the *Irish Worker*, he had openly stated that the working-
class would be perfectly entitled to join a German army, were such
to land in Ireland, 'if by doing so we could rid this country once and
for all from its connection with the Brigand Empire that drags us un-
willingly into this war'.

Connolly, however, was faced with a theoretical problem that did
not trouble his future colleagues in the rising. As a socialist he had to
define his position towards what he was bound to regard as an imperialist war. It would not be enough simply to regard Irish independence as an end in itself; he could only justify fighting for this if he
could persuade himself and the workers that an Irish revolution might
be a factor contributing to the general overthrow of capitalism. If the
workers, he wrote wistfully in that same article, were to disrupt the
war effort all over Europe 'rather than slaughter each other for the
benefit of kings and financiers', Ireland would do well to contribute
what she could to the common cause. Indeed, she might even be a
forerunner. 'Starting thus, Ireland may yet set the torch to a
European conflagration that will not burn out until the last throne and
the last capitalist bond and debenture will be shrivelled on the funeral
pyre of the last war lord.'[28]

But the European conflagration did not burn as Connolly had hoped.
International solidarity among the workers was conspicuous by its
absence, and so far from strengthening fraternal bonds between
socialists in different countries the war seemed to be loosening them
more than ever. Connolly, therefore, was thrown back upon the

* For this interpretation, and especially for the crucial importance of the
part played by MacDermott, see F. X. Martin, 'The 1916 Rising – a *coup
d'état* or a "bloody protest"?' in *Studia Hibernica* (1968), No. 8, pp. 132-7,
also Maureen Wall, 'The Background to the Rising: from 1914 until the
issue of the countermanding order on Easter Saturday, 1916', in K. B.
Nowlan (ed.), *The Making of 1916* (Dublin, 1969), pp. 157-89. For Mac-
Dermott's biography, see C. J. Travers, 'Seán Mac Diarmada, 1883-1916',
in *Breifne* (1966), pp. 1-46.

Irish situation and obliged to look at it in local, not universal, terms – or rather to adapt the universal to the local. He had, that is to say, to reckon with Irish national feeling, which he fully shared, but at the same time to ensure that that feeling, if and when it exploded into action, would concern itself not simply with forms of government, but with underlying social and economic realities. He would fight for a republic, yes, but it must be a people's republic, designed to achieve certain minimum demands for the working-class. As he defined those demands at the end of 1915 and the beginning of 1916 they pointed towards a collectivist state:

We want and must have economic conscription in Ireland for Ireland. Not the conscription of men by hunger to compel them to fight for the power that denies them the right to govern their own country, but the conscription by an Irish nation of all the resources of the nation – its land, its railways, its canals, its workshops, its docks, its mines, its mountains, its rivers and streams, its factories and machinery, its horses, its cattle, *and* its men and women, all co-operating together under one common direction that Ireland may live and bear upon her fruitful bosom the greatest number of the freest people she has ever known.[29]

And if this language seemed a little more high-flown than his readers were accustomed to hear from him, he followed it a few weeks later with a much more explicit programme:

All the material of distribution [he wrote] – the railways, the canals and all their equipment will at once become the national property of the Irish state. All the land stolen from the Irish people in the past, and not since restored in some manner to the actual tillers of the soil, ought at once to be confiscated and made the property of the Irish state . . . All factories and workshops owned by people who do not yield allegiance to the Irish government immediately upon its proclamation should at once be confiscated, and their productive powers applied to the service of the community loyal to Ireland, and to the army in its service.[30]

Holding these views, it is hardly surprising that Connolly found it difficult to reach common ground with the Volunteers, even with those of their leaders who owed their primary allegiance to the IRB. Of those who were to sign the proclamation with him in 1916 only Pearse came near to a conception of the material basis of freedom which would have satisfied Connolly. Pearse's master in this was James Fintan Lalor, who in the days of Young Ireland had swept the idea of a purely political revolution on one side and had warned his fellow-countrymen not to be deceived by 'constitutions, and charters, and articles, and franchises'. 'Let laws and institutions say what they will, this fact will be stronger than all laws . . . the fact that those who own your lands will make your laws, and command your liberties and your lives.'[31] In the last of the trio of important pamphlets he devoted to the definition of Irish freedom in the early months of 1916, Pearse accepted Lalor's logic and gave it, if anything, a wider connotation. National sovereignty, he claimed, must be exercised for the good of the people – that is, of *all* the men and women who make up the nation. Sovereignty extends, therefore, to the material possessions of the nation and 'no private right to property is good as against the public right of the nation'. He reduced this thesis to a few simple propositions, which he stated as follows:

1. The end of freedom is human happiness.
2. The end of national freedom is individual freedom; therefore, individual happiness.
3. National freedom implies national sovereignty.
4. National sovereignty implies control of all the moral and material resources of the nation.

But, he hastened to add, 'to insist upon the sovereign control of the nation over all the property within the nation is not to disallow the right to private property'. On the contrary, it was for the nation itself to determine the balance between public and private resources. He could, he admitted, conceive of programmes involving the nationalisation of land, or transport, or even all the sources of wealth, but he took up no doctrinaire position towards them. 'There is nothing divine or sacrosanct', he wrote, 'in any of these arrangements; they are matters of purely human concern, matters for discussion and adjustment . . . matters in which the nation as a whole can revise or reverse its decision whenever it seems good in the common interests to do so'.[32]

There was in all this an obvious lack of system or of the rigorous analysis to which Connolly had trained himself, and had they lived to argue the matter out the debate between them would doubtless have disclosed sharp divergences of philosophy and of objective.* Nevertheless, each of them was committed to the idea of a revolution that should be social as well as political. That idea they embodied in the Proclamation of Independence and for it in the end they died.

Yet although Pearse and Connolly did ultimately agree upon a formula, it seemed at one time impossible that they would ever be

---

* Connolly's Marxist biographer concedes that Pearse 'reached a similar definition of the progressive camp in *The Sovereign People*'. But he continues: 'where Connolly differed from Pearse was in resolving the "people" into its component parts, and seeing the leading role of the working class within the class alliance' (C. D. Greaves, *The Life and Times of James Connolly* (London, 1961), p. 288). Pearse, with his ecumenical view of the nation as *all* the people, would probably have regarded this distinction as a compliment.

able to agree upon the plan of action without which the formula would be mere empty verbiage. After the preliminary discussions of September 1914 the planning of the insurrection went underground and, as we have seen, was effectively restricted to the members of the Military Council set up by the IRB. Since Connolly remained outside that charmed circle for the whole of 1915, he was not in a position to know what was going on. He seems, on the contrary, to have believed that the impulse towards revolution had died away, and although he had discussions with some of the Volunteer leaders in the autumn of that year about joint action against 'economic conscription' (that is, economic pressure being put upon workers to enlist), the failure of any positive policy to result from these meetings only confirmed him in his intention to go on alone if necessary. 'The Irish Citizen Army', he wrote, 'will only co-operate in a forward movement. The moment that forward movement ceases it reserves itself the right to step out of the alignment, and advance by itself if needs be. . . .'[33]

This was not rhetoric. The drilling and training of the Citizen Army intensified almost week by week, battle exercises were arranged (one of them under the very walls of Dublin Castle) and it began to seem as if Connolly might launch an insurrection with his 200 men, doubtless in the hope that others would be drawn in, but, even if they were not, still determined to strike a blow on his own. Such a development would have been disastrous, not only to the secret plans of the Military Council, but also to the Volunteers, since it could so easily have been made the occasion for a general disarmament of the force and perhaps also for the seizure of the leaders. It was, therefore, in the interests of MacNeill as well as of Pearse that Connolly should be restrained from rash and premature action. About the middle of January 1916, accordingly, MacNeill saw Connolly in the presence of Pearse and urged him to be cautious. Connolly was completely impervious to argument and pressed for an immediate insurrection, repeating his by now well-worn theme that whether or not the Volunteers came out, the Citizen Army would fight in Dublin. 'I said', MacNeill recalled some months later, 'that, if he counted in that event on compelling us to fight rather than stand by and see his men destroyed, he was mistaken. We came to no agreement.'[34]

After this interview Pearse stayed behind, telling MacNeill that he agreed with his attitude, and that he believed he could get Connolly to abandon his scheme. 'Very shortly afterwards', continues MacNeill's note of the interview, 'he assured me that he had succeeded with Connolly.' Behind that simple sentence lies one of the strangest episodes in the pre-history of the rising. So obscure is it that some of the facts are not known even yet and may never be known. We do know, however, that on 19 January Connolly disappeared from view and that neither his family nor his closest colleagues had any

346

news of him until on 22 January he reappeared as suddenly and mysteriously as he had vanished. He had spent the intervening time in close and arduous discussion with members of the Military Council. They told him of their plans for an Easter revolt and persuaded him to agree to act with them. From that time forward he was entirely in their confidence, was sworn into the IRB and became a member of the Military Council. It was not therefore very difficult for Pearse to reassure MacNeill that he had 'succeeded with Connolly', though hardly in the sense that MacNeill had intended.[35]

But the Citizen Army was not the only, or even the main, threat to MacNeill's control over the Volunteers. There is evidence, scattered but cumulatively impressive, that the IRB had been infiltrating the organisation at the local level as well as in headquarters. Indeed, it was necessary that they should do so, since if they were ever to use the Volunteers in battle the chain of command must be complete.* MacNeill himself had discovered as early as September 1915, when present at a muster of Volunteers in county Limerick, that instructions had been sent down by Pearse to several senior officers to make certain military dispositions in the event of a war breaking out.[36] For reasons that have never been adequately explained – though the explanation may simply be that MacNeill was not a military man – the Chief of Staff took no firm action then to restrain his impetuous colleagues. Nevertheless, rumours of an impending rising continued to grow and to reach MacNeill. He sought for assurances – from Pearse, Plunkett, and MacDonagh according to his account of May 1916 – and duly received them. He questioned MacDonagh more than once – they were after all both on the staff of University College[37] – and MacDonagh reproached him for not believing what he had already been told.[37]

Disturbed not only by the rumours but also, it would seem, by arguments then appearing in print that it was essential to strike before the war was over and that there must be a sacrifice of life to move the mind and imagination of the people, MacNeill in February wrote Pearse a long letter which, though intended to be personal, was actually read out in his, MacNeill's, absence at a meeting of the Volunteer executive, producing the usual crop of disclaimers that any action was intended.[38] About the same time MacNeill drew up a memorandum, cast apparently in much the same terms as the letter, which, since its publication a few years ago, has established beyond any reasonable doubt his attitude towards the whole concept of a rising. The document is particularly valuable because it was written two months *before* the event and cannot therefore be regarded as an apologia for his own actions on the eve of the outbreak. As one would expect from a man of his intellectual calibre it was at once a

---

* But, as we saw earlier, the activities of Clarke and MacDermott had in fact weakened the efficacy of the chain of command.

balanced and admirably perceptive analysis of the motives which were prompting men to demand an immediate rebellion and a dispassionate plea for common-sense.

MacNeill started from the proposition that the only justification for a rising would be 'a reasonably calculated' prospect of success – without that it would not only be militarily but morally wrong to move. And that success, he insisted, must be 'success in the operation itself, not merely some future moral or political advantage which may be hoped for as the result of non-success'. In estimating the chances of succeeding it was not enough to be dependent on instinct or premonition or on the adoption of *a priori* maxims such as that Ireland should take action during the present war, Ireland has always struck her blow too late, or in military matters the advantage lies with the side that takes the initiative. 'To put forward these or any other dogmas of the kind', he wrote firmly, 'without associating them with the actualities, or so as to overrule the actualities, would be a proof of mental incapacity. To act on them would be madness, to act on them without otherwise justifying the action would be criminal.'

In these few sentences he defined the whole case against a rising at that particular point in time and his own policy in the subsequent critical weeks becomes much clearer in the light of the thesis here laid down. Yet what of the other argument – the argument not of the poets only, but of Connolly as well – that action *was* necessary, that lives must be sacrificed to produce an ultimate effect on the national mind?* This MacNeill admitted to be 'a sounder principle' than any of the others he had dealt with in his memorandum and he conceded that 'if the destruction of our nationality was in sight, and if we came to the conclusion that at least the vital principle of nationality was to be saved by laying down our lives then we should make that sacrifice without hesitation'. How far did he realise that by this admission he was opening the door to the eager young men who saw in the existing situation just such a threat to 'the vital principle of nationality' as he had described and who were prepared to sacrifice their lives to safeguard that principle? Preoccupied as he was by military actualities, MacNeill, indeed, seems not remotely to have understood how deeply those who subscribed to the blood-sacrifice

* We have seen above how Pearse, Plunkett and MacDonagh regarded the doctrine of the blood-sacrifice. Here is how Connolly in February 1916 expressed himself on the same theme: 'But deep in the heart of Ireland has sunk the sense of the degradation wrought upon its people – so deep and so humiliating that no agency less powerful than the red tide of war on Irish soil will ever be able to enable the Irish race to recover its self respect . . . Without the slightest trace of irreverence but in all due humility and awe, we recognise that of us, as of mankind before Calvary, it may be truly said "without the shedding of blood there is no Redemption".' (C. D. Greaves, *The Life and Times of James Connolly*, pp. 318-19).

doctrine were committed to letting that doctrine govern their actions. He himself dismissed it in his memorandum as not coming within the scope of their military planning and urged his readers to trample on their own personal feelings and think only of the country's good.

In effect this meant assessing the position in terms of power, not of emotion. And, even though the war was not going well for the Allies at that moment, no rational estimate of the forces deployed by the government in Ireland in the early part of 1916 could have produced any other conclusion but that the Irish Volunteers and the Citizen Army would be hopelessly outnumbered in the event of a rising. In fact, when the rising came in April there were about 6,000 effective British troops in Ireland, together with a considerable number of war-wounded. In addition, of course, the authorities could count upon 9,500 members of the armed RIC and slightly more than 1,000 of the unarmed Dublin Metropolitan Police. On the nationalist side, the vast majority of the old-style Volunteers (in 1916 about 105,000) were still loyal to Redmond and were not likely to be involved in a revolt. The maximum striking force available to the conspirators consisted, therefore, of the MacNeill Volunteers (the Irish Volunteers properly so called) numbering about 16,000 and the Citizen Army of just over 200. The disparity of strength is further emphasised if it is remembered that many of the Volunteers, especially outside Dublin, had no guns at all, and that their battalions were often much thinner on the ground than they were on paper.[39]

The conclusion MacNeill drew from his own analysis of the situation was eminently sensible, but psychologically unsound. It would be easy, he argued, for the British forces to overwhelm the Volunteers at any moment. Therefore, it was the business of the Volunteers not to give provocation, but to build up their numbers and above all to hold on to their weapons. On this last point he was most emphatic (as he was also in the pages of the *Irish Volunteer*) that here, if anywhere, a genuine *casus belli* would exist. 'I have not the slightest doubt . . .', he wrote, 'that we are morally and in every way justified in keeping by all necessary force such arms as we have got or can get. I hold myself entitled to resist to death any attempt to deprive me of any arms or ammunition or other military materials that I have or can protect for myself or for the Irish Volunteers.' Yet this argument, which remained throughout the basis of his whole position, was for two reasons much more dangerous than he seems to have realised. One was, that by stating so clearly that the seizure of arms would be the signal for fighting to begin, he put himself at the mercy of every rumour or false alarm, deliberately contrived or not, that this was about to happen, and thus committed the Volunteers in advance to a battle of which he would have chosen neither the time nor the place. But the second danger was even greater. It came from the fact that he was asking desperate and excitable men to observe *indefinitely* an unnatural restraint. In asking this he was underestimating the amount of tension and aggression that the mere possession of arms can engender. That the corollary to giving men weapons is to arouse in them an overwhelming urge to use those weapons was, apparently, not dreamt of in his philosophy.

(iv)

The outcome was that although he professed himself satisfied with the reception of his memorandum by the executive of the Volunteers, nothing was really changed. The underground conspiracy did not cease; on the contrary, it now began to move faster and faster towards the climax. The crux of the matter, as always, was the extent to which the Germans would be prepared to help and the degree to which it would be possible to co-ordinate their assistance with an uprising in Ireland. At one time there had been wild talk of a German expedition on the large scale. Casement is said to have believed that no insurrection could succeed without the aid of perhaps 50,000 German troops, and even when the rising had actually started without sight or sign of a single German the strangest rumours still circulated about the presence, or imminence, of such reinforcements.

Given the naval situation, a landing of foreign troops was virtually impossible and the Germans, it can reasonably be argued, were being no more than realistic when they eventually agreed, after considerable badgering, to send only arms and ammunition. Unfortunately, not only did the method of shipment vary at different stages of the negotiations, so also did the timing. From these confusions dire consequences were to spring. Early in February 1916 the Military Council had told Devoy that the rising was to take place on Easter Sunday. His dispatch to the Germans changed this to Easter Saturday and suggested that the arms should be landed 'between Good Friday and Easter Sunday'. The German response was a cable to America on 4 March undertaking to convey 20,000 rifles and ten machine-guns to Tralee Bay 'between 20th and 23rd April'. Since Easter Sunday was 23 April it was clear that already a large and potentially dangerous gap had appeared in the timetable. Not surprisingly the cable drew an urgent demand from Devoy (18, 19 and 20 March) that the arms should if possible be landed on Easter Sunday. For good measure he asked also that a submarine be sent to Dublin Bay and that Germany attempt to land some troops 'possibly from an airship'. Even Devoy, it seems, was not immune from fantasy, but the Germans lost no time in impressing on him that submarines and troops were both out of the question. In the end, however, they relented and did send one submarine, not to effect a diversion in Dublin Bay, but to land Sir Roger Casement on the coast of Kerry. The arms were loaded aboard a steamer, the *Aud*, which left Lübeck on 9 April, reaching the Kerry coast on the afternoon of 20 April where her captain, Karl Spindler, expected to meet a pilot-boat which would bring him in to Fenit pier to unload, and also to rendezvous with the submarine bringing Casement.

No pilot-boat appeared, for a reason that was as tragic as it was absurd. Collaboration between the Military Council and the Germans had always been difficult because of the necessity of communicating with each other via America, either in cables sent to and from the German embassy in Washington or by agents travelling as ordinary passengers on the ships still plying between Germany and neutral America. Both these methods had serious disadvantages. If the latter was too slow and cumbersome, the former was almost suicidal since, unknown to the conspirators, British naval intelligence had broken the German code and was thus able to interpret the messages passing between Berlin and Washington. And, as if this were not enough, a German agency in New York was raided on 18 April by the American secret service. Almost the first thing they found was the transcript of a message just received in cipher from Dublin and wirelessed immediately to Berlin, a message so important that it was at once passed on to the British authorities. This message contained a specific demand by the Military Council that the arms should not be landed in Kerry until the night of Easter Sunday, 23 April. What had happened, apparently, was that the Irish leaders had become convinced that to allow the Germans a choice of dates – between Thursday 20 April and Sunday 23 April – would be too dangerous, since it would mean that the arms would be in process of distribution through the southwest perhaps three days before the rising was timed to break out; and this would be impossible to disguise from the British authorities. Therefore, the arms landing and the rising must be synchronised as closely as possible. This was, from their point of view, a reasonable demand. But from the German point of view it was highly unreasonable, since to pinpoint the end of a long and dangerous voyage to one single time – the night of 23 April – left no margin at all for error.

Captain Karl Spindler, admittedly, was a skilful seaman and, if warned in time, he could very probably have re-organised his timetable to fit the new instructions. But the new instructions only arrived in Berlin long after he had left Germany and as his ship, incredibly enough, had no wireless it was impossible to make contact with him.* No doubt some blame attaches to the German author-

* It should be mentioned here that on 6 April Casement received a message from Count Plunkett (father of Joseph Plunkett) sent via the German embassy in Berne to Berlin. This confirmed that the rising was to be on Easter Sunday. Two versions of this document exist, one asking that the arms be delivered not later than Easter Saturday, the other stipulating Easter Monday. Even if we accept Easter Saturday as more likely to be the correct date, the phrase 'not later than' did not convey the real intention of the Military Council, which was that the arms should not be landed *before* Sunday night. Consequently the Germans saw no

ities for sending him out so ill-equipped. But the Military Council cannot escape censure either. Quite unjustifiably, they assumed that their amended date – 23 April – had been accepted and took no precautions to meet the *Aud* any earlier, though ordinary common-sense might have suggested that absolute precision could hardly be looked for in a matter of this kind. True, the Germans had informed Devoy that they could not countermand the *Aud's* orders at this late stage and Devoy, it seems, did try to get a message to this effect through to Ireland. But this was never received and the Military Council went on their way unsuspecting. It was not until Friday that Plunkett at headquarters sent his agents down to Kerry to complete the arrangements for the reception of the arms and by that time it was too late. Having cruised up and down the coast in dangerous prominence and, it would now seem, considerable confusion about where he actually was, from Thursday night until Friday morning, Spindler was at last intercepted by British warships. It was most surprising, indeed, that he had managed to stay at large for so long, since for the previous month there had been intensive naval activity off the west coast in readiness for precisely this eventuality. The *Aud* was ordered into Queenstown Harbour and on Saturday morning (22 April) at the approaches to the port, Spindler abandoned his ship and sent her and her cargo of weapons to the bottom. With her disappeared whatever slender hope the Irish insurgents had had of mounting an insurrection on a scale large enough to have even the faintest prospect of success.*

Meanwhile the German submarine, with Casement on board, had arrived at the same place at almost the same time as the *Aud*. Casement, accompanied by Robert Monteith and by Daniel Bailey (one of the Irish 'brigade' formed in Germany) was put ashore at dawn on Good Friday, 21 April. Casement had left Germany in great confusion of mind, not fully aware of recent twists and turns of policy or complexities of timing, but with two simple objects in view. The first was to use his influence to call off a rising which he now believed was doomed to fail, and the second was to die fighting beside his comrades if, despite his warnings, the rising nevertheless took place. He succeeded in neither. Almost drowned as he came ashore, he was rounded up in a matter of hours, sent to Dublin and thence to London, where in due course he stood trial for treason.[40]

---

need to change their plans and the *Aud* sailed with her original instructions.

* Spindler's own subsequent account, *The Mystery of the Casement Ship* (Tralee, 1965), has generally been accepted as accurate. However, J. de Courcy Ireland, in *The Sea and the Easter Rising* (Dublin, 1966), has shown it to be unreliable in its references to the crucial night of April 20-21. See also the same author's 'New Light on the 1916 Naval Action', in *Irish Independent*, 3 Aug. 1966.

Unfortunately these mishaps were only part of a larger pattern of confusion and division at headquarters. To understand the effect of this confusion and division upon the country at large it must be remembered that the military plan for the insurrection had been drawn up by a very small group – Pearse, Ceannt, Plunkett and Connolly – and that in the interests of security it was kept highly secret, so secret that even the provincial leaders of the Volunteers were given only a very general notion of what they were to do and even that at what was, for some of them, extremely short notice. Yet they had an essential part to play, although the key to the plan was, and remained, Dublin. There, it was intended that the insurgents should seize a ring of fortified positions in important and strategically placed buildings which would then be defended against the full strength of the British counter-attack. If it proved impossible to hold the city, a corridor was to be kept open to the west, so that the revolutionary forces might fall back behind the line of the Shannon. In the meantime it was to be the function of the Volunteer forces in the south and west – the Cork, Kerry and Limerick commands – to land, protect and distribute the precious arms which were to come in through Fenit on Tralee Bay. The Galway brigade was simultaneously to be mobilised along the Shannon and the remaining Volunteers, mainly in Munster and Leinster, were to devote themselves to disrupting communications and preventing as far as possible the movement of British reinforcements towards Dublin. It was not proposed to stage any major outbreak in the north, though there was a grandiose and quite impracticable notion that the Volunteers from Belfast, Derry and Tyrone should converge on Dungannon and move westwards to reinforce the Shannon garrison.[41]

Put thus baldly it sounds a desperate scheme. And, given that when it was drawn up the Volunteers had not a single machine-gun, or heavier weapon, and that outside Dublin only one man in five had a service rifle, it will be seen that it was a desperate scheme indeed. It was, of course, precisely this scarcity of weapons that gave the mission of the *Aud* its crucial importance. Once the German rifles and ammunition had been sunk, there was no *military* justification for proceeding with the rising and the aspect of blood-sacrifice came to be all-important.

It is necessary to bear this background in mind when considering the paralysing conflict that developed at headquarters in the days immediately before the die was finally cast. It was the conflict, long foreshadowed, between those – MacNeill, Hobson and The O'Rahilly – who would launch the Volunteers only if a governmental attempt were made to suppress them or to impose conscription on Ireland, or in the much more remote event of a German landing in the country, and those – Pearse, Plunkett and Ceannt (fortified after January 1916 by the adhesion of Connolly) – who would force on a rising, whatever the odds, as the sole means of regenerating Irish nationalism. By the beginning of April, despite all the disclaimers he had received, MacNeill was again becoming anxious about the rumours of an impending outbreak and on the fifth of that month he secured the consent of the headquarters staff that, apart from routine matters, no order would be issued to the Volunteers without being countersigned by him. It appears that once again he received an assurance from Pearse that no independent action was being contemplated.[42]

But no sooner had he taken these precautions than he was confronted with what, on the face of it, seemed to be exactly the *casus belli* he had predicted in his memorandum of February. On 19 April was published the so-called 'Castle Document'. It purported to be a government instruction for the suppression of the Volunteers, the occupation of various key points where sedition was thought to be being hatched, and the arrest of various disaffected persons. True, the credibility of the document was somewhat tarnished by the fact that it apparently called for the house of the Roman Catholic Archbishop of Dublin to be surrounded – a bizarre precaution if ever there was one, for Dr Walsh's behaviour, though sometimes dictatorial, was never treasonable. The government at once denounced it as a forgery, but although the matter has been keenly disputed ever since it is still not possible to say for certain whether it was wholly genuine, fancy mixed with fact, or a complete fabrication. The balance of opinion, however, is heavily in favour of its having been a forgery. Those who knew most about it – Sean MacDermott and Joseph Plunkett – took their secret to their graves, but it is easy to see that what mattered at the time was not whether it was true or false, but its psychological impact in helping to create the kind of atmosphere most calculated to bring all the Volunteers swarming into insurrection. Certainly, its immediate effect upon MacNeill (though he later came to regard the document as false) was all that the war party could have desired. Having seen it, apparently, ahead of publication, he held rapid meetings of the headquarters staff and the executive of the Volunteers and then sent out a general order warning his men to prepare themselves to resist suppression.[43]

This was on Wednesday, 19 April. Late on Thursday night, at Volunteer headquarters, Bulmer Hobson learnt by chance from two of the officers that orders were going out, or had already gone out, to the various commands to prepare for an insurrection the following Sunday. Hobson, together with his informants (they were J. J. O'Connell and the writer, Eimar O'Duffy) went straight to MacNeill's house at Rathfarnham to tell him what they had learnt. MacNeill, though he had actually gone to bed and came down to open the door for them in his pyjamas, insisted on going at once to St Enda's to demand an explanation from Pearse. 'Then for the first time', runs MacNeill's memorandum, 'I learned by Pearse's admission that the rising was intended.' This led, naturally, to a direct clash between the two men. MacNeill declared he would do everything he could –

354

short of informing the government – to stop the outbreak. Pearse replied that he was powerless to do so and that interference now would only cause confusion. To his chief's reproaches about keeping him in the dark Pearse replied – a little lamely – that he and his friends had found MacNeill difficult to approach, but also and more brutally, that the Volunteers were really the creation of another organisation, and had found it desirable to make use of him.

MacNeill was as good as his word and prepared to send out orders countermanding those previously issued by Pearse. J. J. O'Connell was dispatched south to control the situation there, but before the countermanding orders could be distributed the situation had changed again. On the morning of Good Friday (the same morning that the *Aud* had been intercepted and Sir Roger Casement captured), Pearse, Mac-Donagh and MacDermott all came out to MacNeill's house and persuaded him that any commands he might convey to the country would either be ignored or else cause dangerous confusion and in any case would not prevent the rising. For MacNeill the clinching argument seems to have been the revelation (entirely new to him) that a German ship with arms was on the high seas; none of the Dublin leaders, of course, knew then that the ship was no longer a factor in the situation. Lacking this knowledge, MacNeill agreed not to interfere and to let the arrangements for the following Sunday stand. In fact, he went further and wrote out a circular for general distribution to the Volunteers warning them that government action to suppress the Volunteers was 'inevitable' and 'may begin at any moment'. But that afternoon, to make assurance doubly sure for the activists, Bulmer Hobson, upon whom would have devolved the responsibility for sending out any further countermanding orders, was decoyed to a house in another part of Dublin and there kept prisoner by the IRB until the critical point had passed.[44]

This point was fast approaching. Late on that same Good Friday evening Pearse received a summons to attend an urgent conference at Liberty Hall, the headquarters of Connolly's Citizen Army. There he seems to have had the first news that things had gone badly wrong in Kerry. This did not affect his resolve – nor Connolly's either – to lead out the Volunteers on Easter Sunday, but it needed little imagination to forecast what the effect on MacNeill would be. He, however, was still wavering. On the Saturday morning he was visited separately by Joseph Plunkett (barely out of a nursing-home where he had had an operation on his throat, and already a dying man) and by Thomas MacDonagh. MacNeill, though unaware of the true gravity of the situation, had seen in that morning's paper news of the arrest of an unknown stranger (Casement) in Kerry and this increased his uneasiness. 'This news', he recorded later, 'helped to persuade me that the situation was beyond remedy – though I was then ready to take part in the rising I did not see the least prospect of success for it. I consented because I held that we were entitled to protect ourselves in the most effective way and to the utmost in our power.'[45]

But there was much worse news to come. On Saturday evening he had two more visitors, The O'Rahilly and a Volunteer officer, Sean Fitzgibbon, who had managed the Kilcoole gun-running with great ability and whose views coincided with those of MacNeill, and indeed, of The O'Rahilly also. Earlier that week Fitzgibbon had been sent by Pearse to the south with orders for the local leaders who were to handle the landing of the expected German arms, and had been assured by Pearse that the orders had MacNeill's approval. On his way back on Saturday he met another Volunteer, Colm O Lochlainn, one of MacNeill's own UCD students, and learnt from him what O Lochlainn had only just picked up by accident – that the *Aud* was sunk and Casement arrested.* Back in Dublin that evening Fitzgibbon and O Lochlainn took their story to The O'Rahilly, then recovering from a heavy cold. At once he drove them to Rathfarnham where they repeated their story to MacNeill, Fitzgibbon adding for good measure evidence which convinced MacNeill that the 'Castle document' was a forgery. The Chief of Staff was thus confronted simultaneously with the crushing news that he had been deceived right, left and centre by Pearse and his friends, and at the same time with the realisation that if the 'Castle document' really was a forgery, then the authorities had *not* made up their minds to strike and his warning to the Volunteers had been unnecessary.[46]

His instinct was again to throw everything into reverse. But first he determined to have it out once more with Pearse. He drove immediately with his visitors to St Enda's and a brief but angry scene followed. According to the later recollections of O Lochlainn, who witnessed it, Pearse was highly excited and declared to MacNeill: 'We have used your name and influence for what they were worth, but we have done with you now. It is no use trying to stop us: our plans are all made and will be carried out'. MacNeill retorted that he was still Chief of Staff and would forbid the mobilisation. Pearse told him the men would not obey him, whereupon MacNeill replied that if they did not the responsibility would be Pearse's.[47]

These exchanges make painful reading in retrospect. Here were two good and honourable men caught in a web of distrust and mutual recrimination at the most critical moment in the modern history of their country. Each was intensely, selflessly patriotic, yet the gulf between them was unbridgeable. The deception of MacNeill cannot have been other than distasteful to Pearse and his friends, but they had

* O Lochlainn had been one of a group instructed to disable the government wireless station at Cahirciveen and set up a transmitter of their own at Tralee. The expedition ended in tragedy when a car containing the wireless expert took the wrong road and drove off the pier at Ballykissane; three of the four occupants, including the expert, were drowned.

learnt quickly in the hard school of conspiracy that devotion to the cause cancels out friendships, old loyalties, all the ordinary ties that bind men to one another. Given that they honestly believed a rising to be necessary, and believed also that MacNeill was the chief obstacle in their path, they easily convinced themselves that to deceive him became a revolutionary duty. Men who were leaving mothers, wives and children behind them were unlikely to quail at this additional load upon their consciences.

The conspirators recognised that MacNeill, in trying to stop the rising, was acting consistently and courageously along the lines he had publicly and repeatedly laid down. And so, although his counter-manding orders of Easter Sunday struck a fearful blow at their plans, Pearse, MacDermott and MacDonagh all in their last hours were careful to exonerate him from any charge of disloyalty or lack of patriotism. And MacNeill for his part, deeply injured though he was at the moment when he faced his crisis of confidence, steadfastly defended the honour of his former comrades at his own court-martial and in later life.[48]

When the last confrontation between MacNeill and Pearse took place it was already late on Saturday evening and the mobilisation was due the next day. Hurriedly MacNeill arranged for as many helpers as possible to converge on the temporary headquarters he established at the house of a friend, Dr Seumas O'Kelly, in Rathgar Road. The meeting which then occurred went on until about one o'clock on Sunday morning and was attended by The O'Rahilly, Arthur Griffith, Fitzgibbon, O Lochlainn, Sean T. O'Kelly and various others, including MacDonagh and Pearse, who came and went without effecting any change in the situation. Messages countermanding the rising were sent in all directions and, as the outbreak was not fixed to begin until late on Sunday evening, there was enough time to reach most, if not all, the Volunteer corps. The order which went out this time was at last clear and unequivocal. 'Volunteers completely deceived', it ran. 'All orders for special action are hereby cancelled, and on no account will action be taken.'[49] Finally, after waiting as long as he dared for some sign that Pearse and his group had altered their minds, MacNeill took the last decisive step of publishing in the *Sunday Independent* for 23 April an order prohibiting all Volunteer movements whatsoever for that day.

This, he might reasonably have thought, would be the end of the matter. It was indeed the end of any prospect of a country-wide rising, but it was not the end of the plan for a blood-sacrifice, and it was not the end of the deception of MacNeill. On the Sunday morning, with MacNeill's countermanding order staring up at them from the *Sunday Independent*, the leaders of the war party met at Liberty Hall. There, although it was perfectly plain that they were committing military suicide, they decided that they would begin the insurrection on Monday at noon and, with whatever forces they could lay their hands on, attempt to carry out the initial plan of occupying key buildings in Dublin.* But, in order to prevent any further checkmating by Mac-Neill, Pearse wrote to him and sent MacDonagh to his house with the message that the Dublin parades for Sunday had been countermanded according to MacNeill's instructions. So indeed they had, but MacNeill was not to know until the morrow what had been decided in their place. And by then it was too late.

* Tom Clarke, that inveterate fire-eater, was for coming out on Sunday as planned, but was over-ruled on the grounds of sheer impracticability.

3. The Rising

Hindsight has its defects as well as its advantages. Because the 1916 rising has lodged itself so firmly in the mythology of Irish revolution it has been easy to regard it as inevitable. But it was far from inevitable. Apart altogether from the internal divisions among the leaders which, as we have seen, almost paralysed it at the start, the conditions precedent for a truly national insurrection were simply not in evidence. This was the point above all others that MacNeill had tried to drive into the heads of his colleagues when in February 1916 he set down on paper the pros and cons of a rebellion:

> I do not know at this moment [he wrote] whether the time and the circumstances will yet justify distinct revolutionary action, but of this I am certain, that the only possible basis for successful revolutionary action is deep and widespread popular discontent. We have only to look around us in the streets to realise that no such condition exists in Ireland. A few of us, a small proportion, who think about the evils of English government in Ireland, are always discontented. We should be downright fools if we were to measure many others by the standard of our own thoughts.[1]

There were not many matters on which MacNeill's own thoughts ran parallel with those of the authorities in Dublin Castle, but on this topic they were in broad agreement. Between the outbreak of the war and the early months of 1916 the police reports flowing in to the Castle painted the picture of a country which was not only peaceful but also relatively prosperous. True, there was some unemployment in industries that could not be adapted to the war effort, there was a growing shortage of consumer goods and prices were steadily rising. On the other hand, the demands of the war itself had created alternative opportunities for labour, not just in Ireland, but also in the munitions industries of England. Even enlistment in the forces, though by 1915 this was becoming highly unpopular, had produced economic dividends of a sort. The mere fact that by April 1916 there were 150,000 Irishmen on active service, of whom two-thirds had joined up since August 1914, meant a considerable influx to Ireland of separation allowances and other remittances. Sean O'Casey's Bessie Burgess was not just a lone, lorn widow, she was representative of a type.

But the war did not only provide more jobs, it provided a generally favourable economic environment for Ireland. The farmers, naturally, reaped the reward of food scarcity and high prices, and in 1916 from county after county came news of booming times. In Armagh farmers were 'more than compensated for any deficiency in yield by the high prices obtainable for farm produce and stock'. In Down 'industrial employment is very fair and wages are good'. In Tyrone 'agricultural interests were never so prosperous'. In Carlow 'the farmers are making a good deal of money by cattle'. In Louth they were enjoying a period of 'unexampled prosperity'. So also in Wexford, Cork and some other counties.[2]

This contemporary evidence is reinforced by a survey made by a distinguished economist, C. H. Oldham, just after the end of the war. Studying the behaviour of the principal Irish exports in the period between 1904 and 1916, he noticed a general increase not just in the value of these exports (which could partly have been accounted for by the rise in prices), but in their quantity as well. In terms of value most kinds of agricultural produce had gone up almost astronomically. Linen exports, for instance, were worth £9 million in 1904 but in 1916 valued at nearly £20 million. Cattle exports had jumped by almost exactly the same amount. Bacon had gone up from £2¼ million to £7 million, poultry from £3 million to £8 million, butter from £3¼ million to nearly £7 million, brewing from almost £2 million to £3½ million, woollen goods from less than a million to just over £3 million and sheep from £1¾ million to nearly £2½ million. Quantitatively the increases of course were not so large, but they were nevertheless considerable. If the year 1904 be taken as base=100, then linen exports in 1916 stood at 114.5, cattle at 142.9, bacon at 150.8, poultry at 146.5, butter at 156.3, brewing at 171.8 (though whiskey was down to 45.6), and woollen goods at 332.2.[3]

But if, as these figures suggest, prosperity was widely diffused among the chief industries of Ireland and there was no groundswell of economic discontent, no one can read the documents of the time, or the correspondence of the responsible officials, without becoming aware of a growing sense of uneasiness, not only in government circles but also among the parliamentary nationalists. At first sight this uneasiness seems out of proportion to its possible causes. The police reports for 1915 and 1916 do indeed mention 'Sinn Féin' activity, generally against recruiting, in various parts of the country, though always as being on an insignificant scale. Yet it was from these small beginnings that much greater trouble was to flow. The very same reports that speak disparagingly of Sinn Féin frequently refer to a falling-off in recruiting quite apart from any contribution agitators might have made to that result. The fact is that whereas in the autumn of 1914 there had been quite considerable enthusiasm for the war, by 1915 that enthusiasm had already died down. Partly this may have been the perfectly human reaction of individuals to the slaughter on the western front – the young man who is alleged to have replied to a girl who came recruiting to his house 'Enlist? Is ut me enlist? An' a war going on!', may have spoken for a good many of his generation.[4] Partly also, no doubt, Irishmen in general shared the disappointment of John Redmond that Kitchener had made hardly any concessions to national sentiment and very little effort to attract the Volunteers *en masse* to specifically Irish brigades. But more than this there was a feeling, widespread if often inarticulate, that the war, while undeniably good for business, was not Ireland's affair. The suspension of the Home Rule Act during the war, and the knowledge that the Ulster problem remained to be dealt with, had not only created a sense of political anti-climax, but had left the Irish little disposed to take an active interest in the fate of Belgium when their own future still seemed so obscure.

If, however, recruitment languished, and if the wastage of manpower on the battlefield continued at its appallingly high level, then another and altogether more explosive question loomed ahead. Failing voluntary enlistment might not the government feel impelled to introduce conscription? This had first begun to be discussed in the cabinet in June 1915 – not just for Ireland but for the whole United Kingdom – and the issue was to continue to plague the coalition government up to the very moment of the Easter rising. But although in January 1916 Redmond had secured exemption for Ireland from the measure conscripting bachelors which had then been passed, the broader threat of generalised compulsion still hung over the country. It is hardly surprising that a policy which aroused such bitter feelings even in England, deeply committed as she was to the war, should have been received with execration across the Irish Sea where the sense of detachment from what was going on in Europe was so much greater.

The emergence of the conscription issue during 1915 confronted the authorities in Ireland with a great problem. On the one hand, the very existence of the threat of compulsory military service was a powerful cohesive force binding the Volunteers together – we have seen already that even MacNeill was prepared to bring his men out if the threat was translated into action. On the other hand, since compulsion had not yet been applied to Ireland, it was difficult for the government to move against those who openly opposed it. For that matter, it was hard, if legally permissible under the Defence of the Realm Act, to move against those who were openly pro-German without giving them the publicity they craved and thus achieving a result precisely the opposite of what was intended.

The decisions on these grave matters were made in effect by three men. Of these, one, the Lord Lieutenant, normally functioned only in a formal or decorative capacity, though decorative was hardly the word Dubliners would have used to describe the parsimonious and bourgeois court held by Lord and Lady Aberdeen. The Aberdeens, however, were prised, with difficulty, out of the Viceregal Lodge during the winter of 1914-15, to be succeeded by Lord Wimborne, a younger, more thrustful man, with some Churchill blood in his veins and a Churchillian itch to involve himself in matters that were not strictly his concern. Effective political power rested, of course, with the Chief Secretary and since Augustine Birrell was on friendly terms with Asquith, had a seat in the cabinet, and had immense experience of Irish affairs, he remained, as he had been since 1908, the man ultimately responsible for government policy. But he was by 1915-16 very much an absentee Chief Secretary. Holders of that office habitually spent a large proportion of their time in London and Birrell was no exception. Never very happy on the Irish Sea, he found it less attractive than ever with war-time hazards added to its other rigours, and consequently he tended to leave the day-to-day conduct of Irish affairs to his permanent Under-Secretary.

Since October 1914 this had been Sir Matthew Nathan. Nathan came to Ireland after a career of conscientious, indeed distinguished, public service and on arriving at Dublin Castle assumed that his chief task would be to prepare the way for a Home Rule government to take office in Dublin when the war was over. To this end he had several conversations with Redmond and Dillon, and grew to have particularly close relations with the latter, since Dillon spent much more time at home in Dublin than he did in England. True to his principles the old Home Ruler would not visit Nathan in an official building and their meetings were either on neutral ground or in Dillon's house in North Great George's Street. Very early in their acquaintance it became clear that Dillon was at least as much exercised about the existing political situation in Ireland as he was about the future of Home Rule. Soon after the outbreak of war the government had closed down the most extreme of the nationalist newspapers – *Irish Freedom* and *Sinn Féin* for example. Others, which were often the same papers under a different name, soon sprang up again and Dublin Castle was gradually drawn into a tedious and not very rewarding campaign against subversive and irrepressible journalists. Such a campaign seemed to have little enough effect either on the journalists or on the movements they represented, but it had a very bad effect on Dillon. It was a constant theme with him in his dialogues with Nathan that to drive the extremists underground would only be to render them more dangerous. Far better, he insisted, to leave them alone.

Both men were in fact involved in the same dilemma, or rather in two different aspects of the same dilemma. Dillon could not support the government in suppressing extremist organisations, or even newspapers, for no nationalist, however wedded to constitutional methods he might be, could ever act with the British against his fellow-countrymen. At the same time he knew very well that these particular fellow-countrymen were bent on the destruction of the English connection and the Irish party alike, and the more licence they were given the greater threat to the parliamentarians they would become, particularly as the latter were already gravely handicapped by Redmond's continued support for a thoroughly unpopular war.

362

For Nathan the dilemma resolved itself into a choice of evils. Either he must let the extremists have their heads, trust the police reports that they had no large following, and gamble that war-time prosperity would cancel out their propaganda. Or else he must clamp down on them and risk a major explosion which might actually finish by strengthening them and further weakening the orthodox Home Rulers.

In the end, as might have been expected, he compromised and had Birrell's approval for doing so. From time to time he swooped on the errant newspapers, from time to time agitators were deported from one district to another or even sent out of the country altogether, but no all-out offensive was launched against the Irish Volunteers and no attempt was made to seize the leaders. The consequence was that recruiting-agents for the Volunteers (and also, *sub rosa*, for the IRB) went steadily ahead with their work and, as the danger of conscription came nearer, the stock of the parliamentary party continued to sink. To Nathan himself, and even it seems to Dillon also, it was clear that extremism was definitely on the increase in the last months of 1915.

This tendency continued into the early part of 1916 to such a degree that the Volunteers were now openly drilling and parading in a manner that struck the military, at least, as highly provocative. So much so, indeed, that about the end of March Sir John French, at that time in command of Home Forces, pressed the Irish government to say if they were satisfied there was no likelihood of an Irish rising. But in asking this he had more than the recent excess of the Volunteers in mind. On 22 March he had been told by the Director of Military Intelligence in Britain that the latter had received information 'from an absolutely reliable source' that a rising was being contemplated in Ireland and that the Irish extremists were expecting German assistance. The rising was timed to break out on 22 April and German arms, it was believed, were to be landed at Limerick by that date. Almost certainly this information, which came into the hands of the military authorities a full month before the rising occurred, was derived from the navy's interception of German code messages between the United States and Berlin and although it was not completely accurate – the later changes in the plans of the insurgents seem not to have been known to, or grasped by, British intelligence – it was near enough to the mark to have constituted a serious warning. As such it was passed on to General Friend, the officer commanding in Ireland, and although he was not apparently over-impressed with it, he did make certain tentative arrangements with his superiors in England for strengthening the British garrison and making available reinforcements if necessary. These discussions had not produced any positive results before the rising occurred, but it is possible that they may have contributed to the speed of the British counter-stroke after the event.

It is not known whether the civil authorities – Wimborne, Birrell or

Nathan – ever saw the secret intelligence report, since, incredible as it may seem, there was no direct communication between the Admiralty, which was the source of this intelligence, and the Irish government, which, one might have thought, had the most direct interest in it. If the information of March 1916 reached Dublin Castle at all it presumably did so through General Friend, but if Nathan knew of it he appears not to have taken it very seriously. At any rate on 10 April he wrote to the Adjutant General a reply to French's query about the possibility of an insurrection which was to cost him dear in a few weeks' time. 'Though the Irish Volunteer element has been active of late, especially in Dublin', he commented, 'I do not believe that its leaders mean insurrection or that the Volunteers have sufficient arms if the leaders do mean it.'[5]

Less than a week after he had given this assurance Nathan was handed (on 17 April) a letter General Friend had received from the officer commanding the defences of the port of Queenstown on the coast of Cork. It mentioned the possibility of a landing of arms and ammunition on the southwest coast and of a rising for the following Saturday (22 April) now only five days away. Nathan showed the letter to the head of the RIC, Sir Neville Chamberlain, and although they were both sceptical about the 'rumour', as they considered it, Chamberlain thought it desirable to put his men on the alert in the southern and southwestern counties, while the Chief Commissioner of the Dublin Metropolitan Police took similar precautions in the capital. Their scepticism was, if anything, increased by the conflicting reports they were getting from informers inside the Volunteer movement. One said that nothing was known about the importation of arms, another that Thomas MacDonagh had warned his men to be ready for a rising on Easter Sunday. What neither Nathan nor the police realised was that informers whose only source of evidence was from among the Volunteers were as ignorant as they were themselves. The initiative, as we now know, rested with the Military Council of the IRB, and in that group there were no informers.

But on Saturday – that 22 April which had been mentioned as the key date – all uncertainties seemed to be resolved at last. By then the *Aud* had been sunk, Casement had been captured, and the whole insurrection apparently scotched. That same day Nathan felt able to write to Birrell, still detained in London by a cabinet crisis on conscription, that he could 'see no indication of a "rising" '. And if, in the light of what actually happened, this now seems the extreme of folly, it has to be remembered that not only Nathan, but also the military authorities in Ireland, believed that Casement was a much more important figure than he really was, and also that no rising could possibly occur without a landing of arms and ammunition. The latter judgment was eminently sensible – MacNeill, after all, took the same view – but the miscalculation about Casement stemmed from simple ignorance. The Irish government would have been considerably taken aback to learn that he had come to stop an outbreak, not to lead one. At any rate, his capture and the sinking of the *Aud* had so swung the balance of military advantage against any likely insurgents that General Friend felt quite justified in going on leave. And when on the morning of Sunday, 23 April, MacNeill's order cancelling the mobilisation of the Volunteers appeared in the *Sunday Independent*, it certainly seemed as if such optimism was not misplaced.

Nevertheless, even if events in Kerry had seemed to destroy all chances of an insurrection, they might still be turned to further advantage. By early on Sunday morning Nathan had before him the report of a statement by one of Casement's companions (Bailey) revealing what had been intended. It would now be possible to implicate the leaders of the Volunteers and to seize them. This at any rate was Lord Wimborne's view. When Nathan went to see him before noon on Sunday the Lord Lieutenant urged him to round up the ringleaders 'who, having countermanded their Easter Day parade, are probably sitting in conclave conspiring against us'.[6] This was precisely what they were doing at that very moment, but Nathan – even though he had word that a quantity of gelignite had just been carried off from a quarry to Liberty Hall – still hesitated. Good civil servant that he was, he needed to have the consent of his political master, the Chief Secretary, and wired at once to Birrell for permission. 'Can this be proceeded with', he added with typical caution, 'subject to concurrence of the Law Officers, Military Authorities and Home Office?' Later that evening the various officials concerned met again at the Viceregal Lodge and Wimborne had to listen not only to Nathan's plea that everything should be done with a decent legality, but also to demands from the military for adequate time to make their preparations. The Lord Lieutenant wanted action at once but allowed himself to be persuaded that the next day, Easter Monday, would be a bad day to attack Liberty Hall (regarded as the headquarters of the conspiracy) with the city on holiday and too many Volunteers at leisure. Besides, a short delay would have the additional advantage of giving Nathan time to get Birrell's blessing. But Birrell did not receive Nathan's request until Easter Monday – and by then the initiative had been seized by other hands.

The decision which the prime movers of the insurrection had taken on Sunday – that they would start the rising on the morning of Easter Monday – condemned them, as they well knew, to an enterprise that was doomed to disaster before it had even begun. The hurried and secret messages sent out to selected Volunteer Officers were not enough to cancel out the effects of the sudden and repeated changes of plan right up to the last moment and from this central fact flowed two consequences which in themselves largely determined the pattern of what was to follow. One was that it was simply not possible to involve the country at large to any significant extent. In the south, for example, there was utter confusion and although some of the leading Volunteers in Cork, especially Terence MacSwiney and Tomás Mac Curtain, were certainly eager for action, their instructions miscarried until it was too late for them to do anything. The Volunteers rose in Wexford, it is true, and even had local successes in Enniscorthy and Ferns, but precisely because they *were* local these successes led to nothing and the contagion of revolution was easily enough contained. Similarly in Galway, where Liam Mellows, one of the ablest graduates from Countess Markievicz's Fianna, led a force of about 1,500 Volunteers into the field and actually managed to hold the town of Athenry for a brief period; lacking contact with any other forces, and lacking also an adequate supply of arms, Mellows could not sustain his offensive and within a few days had to disband his little army. Only in the neighbourhood of Ashbourne, in the north of county Dublin, did the Volunteers achieve what might fairly be described as a victory. There, an outstanding guerrilla leader, Thomas Ashe, at the head of less than fifty Volunteers won a pitched battle with the RIC, captured four police barracks, together with large quantities of arms and ammunition, and was still undefeated when he received Pearse's order to surrender. But this achievement was altogether exceptional – over most of Ireland the Volunteers remained miserably, but necessarily, passive, without either the means to make their presence felt or much notion of what was happening in Dublin.

It was in Dublin nevertheless that the second fatal consequence of the earlier confusion revealed itself. Although it was obviously easier to reach the various Volunteer and Citizen Army units in and around the city it was still not possible to reach them all in time. The result was that numbers were seriously depleted and although men – and women – converged on Liberty Hall in a steady stream from early on Monday morning, when the various detachments set out on their missions between eleven and twelve o'clock the forces involved were extremely small, even if we include those who joined the insurgents after the fighting had started. The Citizen Army contributed 219 and the Volunteers probably about 1,300; even when allowance is made for other possible additions, the entire total seems not to have exceeded 1,600. From this it followed that the original plan of operations had to be severely modified. The most that could now be done was to seize certain key buildings and hold them for as long as possible – either in the hope that the fire might spread to the rest of the country, or that a prolonged resistance might qualify the survivors to be represented as belligerents at the Peace Conference (at the end of the war, whenever that might be), or quite simply in the belief that a sacrifice in arms would have that regenerative effect on Irish nationality to which so many of the leaders had looked forward for so long. 'We are going out to be slaughtered', said Connolly to his friend William O'Brien, and he and the other leaders accepted their fate calmly and with dignity as the fulfilment of an expected destiny.[7]

In one sense, of course, the very desperateness of their undertaking gave them an initial advantage. That fine holiday morning the crowds were utterly unaware of what was brewing and although the authorities, as we have seen, meditated their own plan of attack, the series of setbacks the Volunteers had suffered during the previous few days had lulled them into a false sense of security. The benefit of surprise rested, therefore, with the insurgents and they used it to establish themselves firmly in their chosen strong-points before any counter-stroke could be delivered against them. The centre of operations was to be the General Post Office at the north end of Sackville Street (now O'Connell Street) and the other strategically placed garrisons were to occupy the Four Courts, the South Dublin Union, the Mendicity Institution, Jacob's biscuit factory, Boland's Mills and St Stephen's Green. The first shot was actually fired by the Citizen Army, which launched an attack on the heart of government, Dublin Castle itself, at mid-day. The policeman on guard was shot dead, but although the insurgents penetrated inside they did not press home their attack. This was probably because they had, understandably enough, failed to realise that the garrison was much reduced because of the number of men on leave and that the Castle – with Sir Matthew Nathan inside – was theirs for the taking. On the other hand, though the psychological impact of such a capture would have been immense, the military arguments against trying to hold that widely dispersed conglomeration of buildings were decisive, and the attackers contented themselves with occupying the City Hall nearby and some other buildings commanding the main entrance to the Castle.

Elsewhere in the city the occupation went very much as planned, though even at the outset the plan itself revealed manifest deficiencies. In Stephen's Green, for example, the Citizen Army officer, Michael Mallin, with Constance Markievicz as his second-in-command, wasted valuable time digging trenches in the little park, oblivious of the fact that it was overlooked by buildings on all four sides. They remedied this in time and retreated to the College of Surgeons on the west side of the Green, which they occupied for the remainder of the week, but even here their planning was defective. They should have seized the tallest building in the neighbourhood, the Shelbourne Hotel, but having lost their first opportunity they were never allowed a second. It was speedily occupied by troops who dominated the rebel position in the College of Surgeons from that time forward. An even greater weakness in the overall planning was the failure to establish a base of operations in the real heart of the city, College Green, by taking over either the Bank of Ireland or Trinity College. The latter might have presented the same problem as the Castle, since it covered too much ground to be easily held by the small number of insurgents available, but, manned as it was by its own Officers Training Corps and the military, it sat astride the rebel communications, in the end seriously disrupting them.

The General Post Office, by contrast, was never a satisfactory headquarters, for it was very difficult to maintain contact with the other outposts, especially once the military counter-thrust began. On the other hand, it was spacious and solid and well-adapted to withstand siege. It was destined, therefore, to be not merely the military centre of the rising, but also the seat of the provisional government, headed by Patrick Pearse, who combined his putative civil function with the actual one of commander-in-chief. With him in the building were other members of the government – Tom Clarke, Sean MacDermott, Joseph Plunkett and James Connolly. Connolly, like Pearse, had a double role, for he was commander of the Dublin forces and, until incapacitated by wounds, the real driving-force behind the military efforts of the insurgents. Joseph Plunkett had taken a major part in the initial planning, but by the time the rebellion had begun he was too ill to do little more than lie on a mattress while the tide of action ebbed and flowed about him. The party in the Post Office included others who either had played, or were later to play, important parts in the movement. One was Michael Collins, already at the age of twenty-six one of the most competent of the Volunteer officers. Another was Desmond FitzGerald, only just out of prison where he had been serving a term for ignoring a banishment order, and destined to take a large share in the founding of the Irish Free State. A third was James Ryan, at that time a medical student and subsequently a staunch follower of Mr de Valera and a durable minister in his governments after 1932. A fourth was Desmond Ryan, one of Pearse's favourite pupils at St Enda's, who was later to become one of the principal historians of the rising and perhaps the chief author of Pearse's posthumous reputation. There are many others, men and women, who deserve to be mentioned, but one of them stands out in retrospect and stood out even at the time. This was The O'Rahilly who, although he had been MacNeill's right-hand man in the attempt to stop the rising, had felt it his duty to join it once it had been started, despite the wounding fact that the insurrectionary plan had been kept secret from him. Many years later Yeats, in a famous ballad, caught admirably the full tragedy of his position:

> 'Am I such a craven that
> I should not get the word
> But for what some travelling man
> Had heard I had not heard?'
> Then on Pearse and Connolly
> He fixed a bitter look;
> 'Because I helped to wind the clock
> I come to hear it strike'.[8]

Just as the purpose of seizing the Post Office was to house a provisional government as well as a military staff, so the purpose of the rising was not merely to make a protest in arms, but formally to declare the existence of an independent Irish republic. In political terms indeed, this was the principal achievement of the insurrection, the point of departure, it is hardly too much to say, for all subsequent Irish history. It was, therefore, a climactic moment when Pearse stepped out in front of the Post Office and read aloud the famous proclamation to a sparse and almost completely uncomprehending audience. It ran as follows:

POBLACHT NA EIREANN
THE PROVISIONAL GOVERNMENT
OF THE
IRISH REPUBLIC
TO THE PEOPLE OF IRELAND

IRISHMEN AND IRISHWOMEN: In the name of God and of the dead generations from which she receives her old tradition of nationhood, Ireland, through us, summons her children to her flag and strikes for her freedom.

Having organised her manhood through her secret revolutionary organisation, the Irish Republican Brotherhood, and through her open military organisations, the Irish Volunteers and the Irish Citizen Army, having patiently perfected her discipline, having resolutely waited for the right moment to reveal itself, she now seizes that moment, and supported by her exiled children in America and by gallant allies in Europe, but relying in the first on her own strength, she strikes in full confidence of victory.

We declare the right of the people of Ireland to the ownership of Ireland and to the unfettered control of Irish destinies, to be sovereign and indefeasible. The long usurpation of that right by a foreign people and government has not extinguished the right, nor can it ever be extinguished except by the destruction of the Irish people. In every generation the Irish people have asserted their right to national freedom and sovereignty; six times during the past three hundred years they have asserted it in arms. Standing on that fundamental right and again asserting it in arms in the face of the world, we hereby proclaim the Irish Republic as a Sovereign Independent State, and we pledge our lives and the lives of our comrades in arms to the cause of its freedom, of its welfare and of its exaltation among the nations.

The Irish Republic is entitled to, and hereby claims, the allegiance of every Irishman and Irishwoman. The Republic guarantees religious and civil liberty, equal rights and equal opportunities to all its citizens, and declares its resolve to pursue the happiness and prosperity of the whole nation and of all its parts, cherishing all the children of the nation equally, and oblivious of the differences carefully fostered by an alien Government, which have divided a minority from the majority in the past.

Until our arms have brought the opportune moment for the establishment of a permanent National Government, representative of the whole people of Ireland and elected by the suffrages of all her men and women, the Provisional Government, hereby constituted, will administer the civil and military affairs of the Republic in trust for the people.

We place the cause of the Irish Republic under the protection of the Most High God, Whose blessing we invoke under our arms, and we pray that no one who serves that cause will dishonour it by cowardice, inhumanity, or rapine. In this supreme hour the Irish nation must, by its valour and discipline, and by the readiness of its children to sacrifice themselves for the common good, prove itself worthy of the august destiny to which it is called.

Signed on behalf of the Provisional Government:

THOMAS J. CLARKE,

SEAN MAC DIARMIDA,	THOMAS MacDONAGH,
P. H. PEARSE,	EAMONN CEANNT,
JAMES CONNOLLY,	JOSEPH PLUNKETT.

In this short document the hopes and plans of the small revolutionary minority at last reached their fruition. Technically the work of all seven signatories, the language bears the hall-marks of Pearse's style, though MacDonagh may also have been concerned in the writing. Four points about it are of special interest. First, it is essentially historical in conception. The intention is to link the present with 'the dead generations' and to establish 1916 as the latest link in a chain stretching back over three centuries. *This* insurrection was not to be regarded as a sudden, opportunist explosion, but rather as the logical development of a long-established nationalist tradition. Second, that tradition itself is firmly stated to be the republican tradition – a fact underlined not merely by the references to the Irish republic in the title and in the body of the document, but also in the very explicit declaration that Ireland's manhood had been organised by the Irish Republican Brotherhood as well as by the Volunteers and the Citizen Army. Evidence has lately come to light which suggests that this emphasis on the republic was the affirmation of an ideal rather than the definition of a prosaic, working form of government. During occasional lulls in the fighting at the Post Office Desmond FitzGerald talked with both Pearse and Plunkett of what the future might have been, or what it might still be if Germany won the war. He found them both quite ready to envisage the possibility of a German prince – they even named Prince Joachim as a candidate – being installed as king of an independent Ireland, in the expectation, presumably, that this ruling family would in time become as identified with Ireland as the Hanoverians eventually had been with England. Nor, apparently, was this an idle or isolated dream, for Mr Ernest Blythe has published his own recollection that a similar idea was put forward by Mac-Donagh and Plunkett in a discussion at Volunteer headquarters in January 1915.[9] That some of the leaders of the rising should have contemplated an actual monarchy instead of the ideal republic to which they committed themselves on the morning of Easter Monday does not, of course, rob the Proclamation of its central significance. The schemes for an imported German princeling mooted in 1915 and 1916 were very vague and depended anyway on Germany winning the war. What would matter in the end would not be prognostications about a future that never happened, but the fact that a republic had been declared and that men and women had been found ready to die for it.

Nevertheless, though the idea of a German monarchy was visionary, that of a German alliance was not and it was this – the third significant feature of the Proclamation – that probably did most to damage the revolutionaries in the eyes of their contemporaries. The claim that the Irish forces were supported 'by gallant allies in Europe' was more fantasy than fact, though it was fantasy based on fact. This alone would have exposed the leaders to the penalties of treason, but it was a risk which, from their viewpoint, had to be taken if ever the representatives of an independent Ireland were to obtain recognition from that hypothetical Peace Conference to which, it was still fondly assumed, the defeated Allies would eventually come to beg terms from a victorious Germany.

Finally – and it is the fourth point in the Proclamation that needs to be emphasised – the influence of James Connolly is to be seen in the passage relating to political, civil and social rights. These were vaguely enough defined in all conscience, but they were also precise enough to foreshadow the rise of an Irish state which would actively oversee the welfare of its citizens, which would 'pursue the happiness and prosperity of the whole nation and of all its parts, cherishing all the children of the nation equally and oblivious of the differences carefully fostered by an alien government, which have divided a minority from the majority in times past'. Here was the brightest hope for the future; here also was the seed of the deepest disillusionment.

What followed after the occupation of the various strongpoints has been many times retold, much of it by the participants themselves.[10] It is unnecessary, and would be impertinent, to follow in their footsteps. But really the pattern of the tragedy was simple and can be briefly described. It was determined by the interplay of four factors. The first was the numerical weakness of the insurgents. The second was their inability – partly because of their lack of numbers, partly because of the confusion in the country – to deny their enemy the opportunity of reinforcing his strength, which he did rapidly by moving troops from other parts of Ireland and later by bringing in large numbers from England. The third was the essentially defensive posture adopted by the Irish forces in their fixed positions. This, while also partly a product of their numerical inferiority, in fact condemned them to a static role, waiting for their fortified posts to be isolated and reduced one by one. The fourth factor was the ruthless and effective use the British commanders made of artillery. Connolly, in one of those rare moments when the tactician in him was submerged by the doctrinaire, had forecast that the army of an imperialist, capitalist power would never resort to the wholesale destruction of property. Perhaps in his heart of hearts he did not believe this and was only trying to reassure his inexperienced men. But if he did believe it he could not have been more wrong, for if one single factor can be adduced as the really decisive one in the crushing of the rising, it was precisely the superiority of the field-gun over the rifle.

Even when the rising began the insurgents were outnumbered by between two and three to one; within forty-eight hours the odds had lengthened to twenty to one and on succeeding days troops continued to pour into the city. So heavily weighted were the scales, indeed, that the real miracle of Easter week is not that the rising was suppressed so soon, but that it lasted as long as it did. This was partly due to the caution of the military leaders, but partly also to the fierce resistance put up by insurrectionary forces. Some strongholds, like Jacob's factory or the College of Surgeons, were left almost untouched to the very end. But in other areas there was most bitter hand to hand fighting – in the South Dublin Union, at the Mendicity Institution, at the City Hall and in the neighbouring buildings, and in the outlying positions guarding the Four Courts. The most extraordinary achievement of all, however, was not in one of these heavily defended points, but at the approaches to Mount Street Bridge. There, on Wednesday, 26 April, a dozen well-placed and very brave men for a whole day prevented the advance of British reinforcements from Kingstown by the direct route into the city. Almost half the entire British casualties during the week were incurred in this engagement, when several companies of the Sherwood Foresters were hurled repeatedly against accurate and sustained rifle-fire which kept them at bay until the Volunteers were finally overwhelmed by weight of numbers. This single action suggests that had the insurgents' tactics been based upon street-fighting rather than upon the defence of large public buildings the task of putting down the rising would have been still bloodier and more difficult than it actually was.

Even as things were troops trained for the trenches found it a nerve-wracking business to fight a largely unseen enemy who was difficult and sometimes impossible to identify by uniform. It was not surprising that ugly incidents occurred, two of which in particular were singled out for public inquiry. One of them, admittedly, was the work of a man mentally unhinged, an Irish officer, Captain J. C. Bowen-Colthurst. This was the murder of Francis Sheehy-Skeffington and two journalists, Patrick Mackintyre and Thomas Dickson. Sheehy-Skeffington was one of the best-loved figures in Dublin and a notable champion of all sorts of minority causes. He was a teetotaller, a vegetarian, a worker for women's rights, a socialist, above all a pacifist. Intensely opposed to the rising, though sympathetic to the fundamental objects of the Volunteer movement, he had gone into the city to help the wounded and to try to restrain his fellow-citizens from looting. Returning home on the night of Tuesday, 25 April, he was arrested at Portobello Bridge. That night he was brought out as a hostage on a raiding-party and saw Bowen-Colthurst shoot dead an unarmed youth. The next morning, without any sort of trial or chance to vindicate himself, he was taken out, with the two journalists, and executed. The bodies were buried in quicklime and Bowen-Colthurst himself led a raid on the dead man's home in a vain attempt to procure incriminating evidence which might in some way mitigate his crime. It was only after some days, and the direct intervention of Major Sir Francis Vane, that Bowen-Colthurst, who had in the meantime committed other atrocities, was removed from his post.[11]

Because Sheehy-Skeffington was well-known his case became a *cause célèbre* and Bowen-Colthurst was eventually found guilty of murder while insane. It was otherwise with the dark and mysterious stories emanating from North King Street. North King Street was part of the out-defences of the Four Courts and the troops had to work through it house by house. Civilians were almost bound to suffer in such an operation, but the tale was that deliberate reprisals had been taken against them by men of the 2/6th South Staffordshire regiment. At the time it was alleged that fifteen people had been done to death, and after two bodies had been recovered from a hasty grave in a cellar an official inquiry was held. It did not succeed in identifying any culprits, but the circumstantial evidence was formidable and the impression indelibly graven on the minds of Dubliners was that something like a massacre had indeed occurred.

It must be emphasised, however, that the hatred of the soldiers which such events and suspicions engendered came late and was largely confined to those who had suffered directly from their attentions. For the citizens in general the rising began as a spectacle, became an inconvenience and ended as a tragedy. During the week that fighting continued the normal life of the city was paralysed, communications were interrupted, food soon grew scarce and privations among the poor were especially severe. This did not prevent civilians from moving about the city and constantly getting in the line of fire while gratifying that insatiable curiosity which is a leading

373

characteristic of the Dubliner. Unfortunately, they were not always content to remain spectators. Since the forces of the law – in the shape of the Dublin Metropolitan Police – had been withdrawn from duty at the outset there was nothing to prevent criminals, or simply the very poor, from making the most of their opportunity. And so for the first few days of its brief existence the Provisional Government of the republic looked out from the Post Office at a saturnalia of looting and wrecking – sweetshops, toyshops, shoeshops, grocery stores, wine-merchants were broken into indiscriminately and some were set on fire.

It was only in the latter part of the week, when the fighting was intensified, that these terrible scenes came to an end. But they were replaced by others still worse. The introduction of artillery – first used to sweep barricades off the streets on Tuesday evening, next on Wednesday morning by the gunboat *Helga* to destroy the empty Liberty Hall, and after that systematically at each stage of the operations – meant that the damage to housing by direct hits and still more from incendiary shells, was immense. Sackville Street, one of the most magnificent streets in Europe, became by Friday one vast lake of fire and many other parts of the city were nearly as completely destroyed. When all was finished, rebuilding grants worth £¾ million were made in 212 cases, and a further £1 million was paid out in compensation for damages. It is safe to say that this by no means covered the losses the city had incurred.[12]

It was the scorching, all-consuming fire which eventually drove Pearse and his immediate followers out of the Post Office. By Friday evening their position had become untenable. Leaving the doomed building by Henry Street they turned into Moore Street, striving to break northwards through the encircling military cordon in the vague and desperate hope of turning westwards to join forces still holding out in the Four Courts. But Moore Street was dominated by a military barricade and The O'Rahilly, leading a forlorn charge against it, was shot down and killed. The remainder of Pearse's party took refuge in houses further down the street, but it was plain that their situation was hopeless. Connolly, gravely wounded earlier in the week, had been cruelly tried as he was jolted on a stretcher from the Post Office to Moore Street, most of the men were weak with exhaustion and strain, and Pearse could no longer find it in himself to ask more of them. On Saturday, therefore, Elizabeth O'Farrell, one of three brave women who had stayed with the headquarters staff through all vicissitudes (the others were Julia Grenan and Connolly's secretary, Winifred Carney), carried messages to and fro until Pearse and Connolly finally agreed to sign a cease-fire order on the basis of unconditional surrender. This was then conveyed to the various posts still in rebel hands. The last capitulations took place on Sunday, 30 April, and although a few snipers continued to be troublesome during that night, by 1 May the rising was to all intents and purposes at an end. All told, it had cost 450 persons killed, 2,614 wounded and 9 missing – the vast majority of all these casualties occurring in the city of Dublin. Military losses were 17 officers killed and 46 wounded; 99 other ranks killed, 322 wounded and 9 missing. The RIC lost 13 killed and 22 wounded, the DMP 3 killed and 7 wounded. The official estimate lumped together civilian and insurgent casualties, giving a total of 318 killed and 2,217 wounded.[13] Such was the cost in blood of the actual fighting, though the full price had yet to be paid.

As the military commitment during the week had grown heavier so the chain of command had grown more exalted. Operations had at first been in the hands of Brigadier-General W. H. M. Lowe, but on Thursday Major-General Sir John Maxwell arrived to take over control. He had been specially selected by the government and was given absolute powers, as he lost no time in making plain to civil authorities and Dublin citizens alike. Martial law had already been proclaimed in the city on Easter Monday and the following day this had been extended to the rest of the country, but it was not until the rising had actually been crushed that Irishmen learnt what this might mean in practice. The surrender of the leaders was followed at once by large-scale arrests in Dublin and in the provinces, and also by the setting-up of general courts martial. In all 3,430 men and 79 women were taken into custody. Of these, 1,424 men and 73 women were released after investigation. A total of 170 men and one woman (the Countess Markievicz) were tried by courts martial and of these the one woman and 169 men were convicted. The remainder of the prisoners, 1,836 men and 5 women, were sent to England and interned there, but of these 1,272 were discharged after further inquiry and most of the others were released at Christmas.[14]

These are very considerable numbers when seen in relation to the strength of the insurgent forces during the rising itself. It is plain that the military were bent on doing what the civil government had so signally failed to do – destroy revolutionary nationalism root and branch. In fact, as was obvious enough to intelligent people even at the time, such wholesale seizures and deportations had exactly the opposite effect. We know from contemporary evidence that the insurrection did present the British with a real chance to discredit not only the IRB, the Volunteers and the Citizen Army, but also Sinn Féin and every form of extreme nationalism. People were angry at the ruin of their city, many were hungry, some faced unemployment, and the middle classes – who in the end would have to pay for a good deal of the damage – were bitterly resentful, as may be seen from the condemnation of the rising by the Dublin newspapers and from the clamour raised by one in particular – the *Irish Independent* which had some claim to represent the views of Catholic businessmen – for condign punishment to be meted out to the rebels.[15] And as the leaders were marched off to prison to await court-martial, they were marched through crowds that were at best apathetic, at worst thoroughly hostile.

Among those arrested and deported were many who had had nothing to do with the rising and probably even some who were completely nonpolitical. Their experiences in prison and internment camps did nothing, however, to strengthen their attachment to British rule in Ireland. On the contrary, numerous young men were now exposed as never before to political indoctrination, with effects that were to be felt before many years had passed. Even in the months that lay immediately ahead the parliamentarian, John Dillon, was to complain repeatedly that the government seemed bent upon 'manufacturing Sinn Féiners'. It is not too much to say that the process began immediately the fighting stopped.

Yet the most powerful impulse towards a nationalist resurgence was not to be found in the prison camps but in the Dublin courts-martial. The most fearful rumours stalked through the city about what was happening at these secret trials of which the only outward sign was the summons to priest or relative at dead of night and the laconic announcement next morning of death sentences carried out. No fewer than ninety prisoners were initially sentenced to death. Of these, seventy-five had their sentences commuted to various terms of penal servitude. The most eminent of those who escaped shooting were Countess Markievicz and the Commandant at Boland's Mill, Eamon de Valera. Both exchanged execution for penal servitude for life, the Countess because of her sex (to her great indignation) and Mr de Valera partly because of representations made by the American Consul in Dublin that he was an American citizen; this was not strictly accurate, but it may have helped to save his life and so alter the course of Irish history. On the other hand, it is fair to add that his own view has always been that he escaped simply because the British authorities had decided that enough was enough.

Nevertheless, fifteen of the death sentences were carried out and it was these executions, spun out from 3 May to 12 May and involving some instances of what seemed unnecessary ferocity, which more than anything else served to sway Irish opinion towards the insurgents. Pearse himself, of course, expected to die and Tom Clarke, it is said, thought better of committing suicide in the Post Office so that the onus of shooting him should fall on the British. Probably also the leaders of the various detachments in different parts of the city had anticipated that death might be their portion. After all, theirs had been a serious insurrection causing the diversion to Ireland of a large body of troops at a time when they were desperately needed elsewhere, and it was hardly surprising that General Maxwell's reaction should be to match the gravity of the punishment to the gravity of the outbreak. All the same, he misjudged the situation and went too far. Some of those who were shot – for example, Michael Mallin, Edward Daly, Eamonn Ceannt, Con Colbert and Sean Heuston – had fought as soldiers and had fought cleanly, even chivalrously; they deserved a better fate. An arguable case could have been made out for executing the signatories of the Proclamation, for these men represented the very fount and origin of the conspiracy, and their traffic with Germany, however futile, exposed them to the penalty for treason. But even here – to shoot James Plunkett, who was dying anyway, and James Connolly, who was so seriously wounded that he had to be tied to a chair, was not only grossly inhumane, it was psychologically inept. And if this was true of those two key figures in the rising, how much more true was it of the gentle Willie Pearse whose only crime it was to have loved his famous brother enough to be at his side wherever he went and whatever he did.*

The immediate shock and horror aroused by these killings was felt mainly in Ireland (though there were violent repercussions in the USA too) since the names of most of the victims were little known elsewhere. But it was far otherwise with Sir Roger Casement, who, after trial at the Old Bailey, was hanged at Pentonville prison on 3 August despite an outcry by his friends in England and by powerful sections of American opinion. The fact that at the time of his trial copies of the 'black diaries' were privately shown to various influential people to counteract the sympathy so widely felt for his tragedy may not have been generally known at the time, but to those who were aware of it, this manoeuvre added a new dimension of horror to the darkening scene, a new bitterness to the hatred that was fast coming to be the chief legacy of the Easter rising.

But Ireland could not be ruled by executions and by martial law for ever. True, the rising had destroyed the effectiveness of the civil authorities and Wimborne, Birrell and Nathan had all to resign, only Wimborne being later reinstated. Yet, despite these dislocations it might still be possible, before the hatred and the horror had bitten too deep, for the situation to be turned to political advantage. Such at least was the Prime Minister's conclusion when, after visiting the country between 12 and 19 May, he asked Lloyd George to initiate discussions with the Ulster Unionists and the leaders of the Irish parliamentary party, to see if even at that eleventh hour a Home Rule settlement might not be snatched from the ruins of the government's Irish policy. For the parliamentary nationalists this development presented a fearsomely difficult problem which almost at once opened up a serious divergence of views between John Redmond and his ablest colleague, John Dillon. Alone of the party leaders Dillon had

* The names of those executed in Ireland were: P. H. Pearse, Tom Clarke, Thomas MacDonagh (3 May); Joseph Plunkett, Edward Daly, William Pearse, Michael O'Hanrahan (4 May); John McBride (5 May); Eamonn Ceannt, Michael Mallin, Con Colbert, Sean Heuston (8 May); James Connolly, Sean MacDermott (12 May). In addition, Thomas Kent, whose family had conducted a private battle of their own against the RIC in county Cork during the mopping-up operations after the rising, was executed at Cork on 9 May.

actually lived through the experience of the rising, being marooned with his family in their house at North Great George's Street, only a few hundred yards away from the General Post Office. He was therefore in a unique position to judge the temper of the city and to report on the feelings aroused by the executions, arrests and deportations, being indeed inundated by requests for help from families of many of the victims. Thus, whereas Redmond's first comment on the outbreak, made in London to the House of Commons, was an outright condemnation expressing his own feelings of 'detestation and horror', Dillon, while agreeing with the condemnation, was from the beginning much more concerned with the dire political consequences that would follow if the suppression of the rising were to be mishandled. Already by 30 April he was urging Redmond to impress on the government the necessity for caution. 'The wisest course', he wrote, 'is to execute *no one* for the present . . . If there were shootings of prisoners on a large scale the effect on public opinion might be disastrous in the extreme.'

Redmond did his best, but made little enough impression on Asquith who, however, seemed scarcely in control of events, for despite his assurances the executions continued. So, while the Irish leader issued to the press a statement about 'this insane movement' blaming it primarily on Germany, Dillon in Dublin grew steadily more enraged at the shootings and arrests and more convinced that if there was insanity anywhere it was to be found in government policy. At last he came over himself to London in a state of extreme nervous tension and intervened in the Commons debate of 11 May on the Irish situation with a speech which at once became famous. His immediate purpose was to stop the executions at all costs, but, sympathetic to the Fenian tradition as he had been since the days of his youth, he could not conceal his admiration for those who had made their protest in arms. On the one hand, he charged the government with 'letting loose a river of blood' and undoing the whole life-work of the parliamentary party by this policy of ruthless punishment. And on the other hand he shocked the House, first by his exposé of the Sheehy-Skeffington case, which he had made peculiarly his own, and then by his praise of the insurgents – not murderers, he insisted, but men who had fought a clean fight, a brave fight, however misguided, 'and it would have been a damned good thing for you if your soldiers were able to put up as good a fight as did these men in Dublin'.[16]

To make such a speech in a hostile House of Commons was a very courageous act, but it was much more than that. By making it Dillon was, to an even greater extent, perhaps, than he was himself aware, pointing out to the followers of the constitutional movement the only road to salvation. Ever since the formation of the coalition government the previous year and the consequent admission of Carson to the cabinet, he had been pressing Redmond to adopt a more independent and critical attitude. After the rising he was more than ever convinced that the Irish party should play the part of a vigorous opposition at Westminster, since this, however unpopular it might make them in the House of Commons, would be the only way of retaining popular support at home. True, the immediate effect of the speech, so the police reports flooding in from all over the country seemed to indicate, was to rouse sympathy for the insurgents.[17] This, however, was an oversimplification. Sympathy *was* aroused, no doubt. But that, as the contents of Dillon's own mailbag showed him, would not involve a transfer of allegiance from the parliamentary party if it became once more intransigent and vigorous. Still less would it involve a transfer of allegiance if the party could somehow conjure Home Rule out of the surrounding chaos.

The next two months were filled by negotiations with Lloyd George to achieve precisely this end. Wary after his experiences in 1914 he dealt separately with Redmond and his friends on the one side and Carson and his friends on the other. By this device he persuaded them to agree individually to terms which would not have stood up for long if he had gathered the two parties round the same table.* Broadly speaking, his 'Headings of a settlement as to the government of Ireland' proposed that the Government of Ireland Act of 1914 should be brought into operation 'as soon as possible' for the twenty-six counties, the six northeastern counties to be excluded. Redmond accepted this on the *understanding* that exclusion would be temporary, whereas Carson accepted it in the *knowledge* that it would be permanent, for he had received a written pledge to that effect from Lloyd George. Even with these diametrically opposing reservations each leader had great difficulty in persuading his followers to agree. Redmond had to threaten his own resignation before Ulster nationalists would swallow the bitter pill of separation from their co-religionists, and Carson, though carrying Ulster Unionists with him, had to reckon on the fears and apprehensions of Southern Unionists.†

It was, therefore, peculiarly fitting that it should have been a member of the old Ascendancy landlord caste, Lord Lansdowne, who (aided and abetted by that personification of the English squirearchy, Walter

* There was a joint session at the outset, but the crucial negotiations were separately conducted.

† It was symptomatic of the disillusion of northern nationalists with the parliamentary party that the 1916 Home Rule negotiations were quickly followed by the formation of a splinter group, the Irish Nation League, pledged to oppose partition in any shape or form. It was almost entirely confined to Ulster and had only limited influence even there. But it had a two-fold significance in the wider context of the post-1916 situation. First, it represented *overt* dissatisfaction with constitutionalism and its subsequent evolution was an ominous indication of how easily disgruntled supporters of Redmond could become proto-extremists. And second, in the course of its evolution the Irish Nation League contributed directly, and sometimes abrasively, to the general confusion which reigned among militant nationalists for more than a year after the Rising.

Long) took a major part in obliterating Lloyd George's precariously balanced house of cards. Not only did he oppose the solution vehemently in cabinet (where he denounced it as a surrender to force which could lead to more violence to extract further concessions), but he also attacked it openly in the House of Lords, and this after Redmond had himself agreed to additional safeguards for Britain's military and naval interests in Ireland. Lansdowne's speech (on 11 July) made it brutally clear that the partition of the country would be 'permanent and enduring', and for good measure it indicated in language deliberately offensive to nationalists that Britain would make her own defence dispositions in the twenty-six counties with which a Home Rule government would be unable to interfere. After some further vain exchanges with the government Redmond washed his hands of the proposals and was left to nurse the bitter realisation that he had dealt the popularity of his own party at home a well-nigh fatal blow in order to obtain a settlement that had turned out to be no settlement at all.[18] 'Enthusiasm and trust in Redmond is *dead*, so far as the mass of the people is concerned', wrote Dillon to his friend T. P. O'Connor that autumn. But with Redmond he might have coupled the whole constitutional movement for, in the last analysis, it was the chief casualty of 1916.

4. Sinn Féin Transformed

One of the strangest features of the rising of Easter week was that almost before it had ceased it was being described as a Sinn Féin rebellion. This curious misconception, which was shared by many Irish as well as by British observers, probably derived from the simple fact that whereas the secret springs of the insurrection were known to hardly anyone, the name of Sinn Féin as an open, separatist movement had been familiar for at least a decade. Yet to saddle Sinn Féin with the responsibility, or credit, for what had happened was a travesty of the truth. Individual Sinn Féiners did indeed take part in the fighting, but they did so as Volunteers or Citizen Army men, not as members of Griffith's organisation. Griffith's own attitude to the plans of the IRB, when he learnt of them on the Saturday before the revolt began, had been the same as MacNeill's and he had hoped that the latter's countermanding order would be effective in preventing an outbreak. Moved by the heroism of the insurgents after the fighting had begun, Griffith had offered to join them but had been asked by the leaders in the Post Office to stand aside, as his propagandist services in the future would be of greater value.[1]

Fortunately for his reputation this did not save him from the arrest and imprisonment which, in the circumstances of the time, were fast becoming the sole passport to political respectability in Ireland. Released towards the end of 1916, he at once resumed publication of his paper, *Nationality*, and with all his old vigour began not only to attack the proposed partition of the country and the menace of conscription, but also to advocate something that was soon to become an integral part of Sinn Féin policy – the proposition that Ireland should be allowed to put her case for independence to the Peace Conference when the war was over.

By the end of 1916 the internees were home again and only the hard core of revolutionary leaders who had received long prison sentences remained shut up in Britain. The men who had been deported after Easter came back at Christmas to a country which seemed in the interval to have undergone some strange enchantment. But there was nothing magical about the transformation. All that had happened was that the revulsion of feeling brought about initially by the executions had been intensified by subsequent events. As early as June 1916 Dillon had warned Lloyd George that 'the temper of the country is extremely bad – and the temper of this city *ferocious*'.[2]

Many different factors had contributed to bring this about. One was the growth of what one can only call a cult of the dead leaders, a cult centred round the frequent commemorative Masses held in the churches of Dublin. Relatives of the dead men emerging from these churches were greeted with cheers by crowds which developed the dangerous habit of marching in vast processions singing provocative political songs. It did not need much imagination to see where this might lead. 'One of the half-mad officers of whom Dublin seems to have an inexhaustible supply,' wrote Dillon in another letter to Lloyd George, 'might any day in connection with these church demonstrations bring about a regular massacre and the worst of the situation is that some of those who are working up the demonstrations – particularly the women – would I am convinced be well pleased if a collision took place.'[3]

A second factor in producing this militant mood, especially in Dublin, was the continuance of martial law. The semblance of civil government had been restored with the appointment of H. E. Duke as Chief Secretary, but General Maxwell was still the real power in the land and Maxwell was not withdrawn until November. While he remained there could be no tranquillity in Ireland. Not that his presence was the only affront to public opinion in those months after the rising. There followed one on top of the other the failure of the Home Rule negotiations, the trial and hanging of Sir Roger Casement and the publication of the report of the inquiry into the Sheehy-Skeffington case. And if this were not enough there was always in the background the nagging fear that conscription was about to be imposed on Ireland.

There was yet a third element – and time was to show that it was the most important of all – in the new situation confronting the men who were released at the end of the year. This was the fact that the organisations which had prepared the way and provided the striking-force for Easter week had not been destroyed then or afterwards. They had merely been driven underground and waited only for a favourable opportunity to reappear. Indeed, within a few days of the executions, a group of IRB men had secretly begun the business of reactivating the physical force movement. Meanwhile, on the surface, the formation of an Irish National Aid Association and an Irish Volunteers' Dependants' Fund helped both to knit together those who wanted to do something for the families of the dead, the wounded and the prisoners, and also to provide a focus for the hatred and bitterness which seemed to grow greater not less as the rising receded into the past.

But could this hatred and bitterness be harnessed to some constructive political purpose? Quite suddenly, in January 1917 a by-election in North Roscommon suggested an answer. It was decided by the advanced nationalists to put up a candidate against the nominee of the Irish parliamentary party and they chose George Noble, Count

Plunkett, the father of the executed Joseph Plunkett. Count Plunkett stood ostensibly as an Independent, but he was vigorously supported by Sinn Féin and won with ease. On being elected he declared (not, it would appear, without some pressure) that he would not take his seat at Westminster. This result created an entirely new situation in Irish politics and the parliamentary leaders were in no doubt at all about the gravity of the situation confronting them. Redmond himself was so shattered that he drafted a memorándum for publication in which he sought to justify the party's record and to warn the country against the alternative policy its enemies were encouraged by the election to assert – separation from the empire, withdrawal from the House of Commons, the establishment of a republic and the use of force, if need be, to achieve these aims. It would not be unnatural he admitted, if the electors had grown tired of being served in parliament for so many years by the same men and he would make no complaint if replaced. 'Let the Irish people replace us, by all means, by other and, I hope, better men, if they so choose. But, in the name of all they hold most sacred, do not let them be led astray by any passion of resentment or will-o'-the-wisp of policy into courses which must end in immediate defeat of their hopes for the present and permanent disaster to their country.'[4] Appalled by this document, which they rightly regarded as enough to destroy the party if made public, Redmond's colleagues persuaded him not to give it to the newspapers. Nevertheless, the fact that he had written it at all after only *one* election defeat was evidence of how far he had already given way to despair.

There were to be many moments in the next few months when despair seemed the only sane reaction. Hard on the heels of the election the government began to re-arrest some of the more recklessly vociferous ex-prisoners. Not surprisingly, when three other by-elections occurred – in May, July and August – Sinn Féin candidates won them all. In the first of these, at South Longford, Dillon himself took charge of operations, realising how essential it was to wipe out the effects of the previous defeat. 'We have the bishop, the great majority of the priests and the mob – and four-fifths of the traders of Longford', he wrote to Redmond. 'And if in face of that we are beaten, I do not see how you can hope to hold the party in existence.' Yet they *were* beaten and though the margin was only thirty-seven votes, the party as a whole was so deeply affected by the disaster that the idea began to circulate among members that they should resign in a body. Redmond was able to scotch this notion promptly, but that it had even been mooted was a further ominous storm-signal.

Still more significant, though for a different reason, was the East Clare election later that summer. It was significant because it was Mr de Valera's first parliamentary battle and because, newly released from prison, he took his stand on the Proclamation for which Pearse and the other leaders had died. He was careful, however, not to adopt too doctrinaire a position. 'We want an Irish republic', he said, 'because if Ireland had her freedom, it is, I believe, the most likely form of government. But if the Irish people wanted to have another form of government, so long as it was an Irish government, I would not put in a word against it.'[5] At the time, perhaps, the qualification was less noticed than the assertion. What really mattered was that in de Valera the electors saw the senior surviving Commandant of the Easter rising and realised that a vote for him was not just a vote against the parliamentary party but a vote for 1916. The parliamentary party itself was in no condition to make a fight and had so far abdicated its responsibilities that it had not even chosen the candidate who undertook the forlorn task of opposing him. The result was a foregone conclusion, though the scale of de Valera's victory (he received 5,010 votes against 2,035) was such as to suggest to many observers inside and outside the country that the parliamentarians had gone into irretrievable decline. This was in fact not yet quite true, but the East Clare result did show beyond a shadow of doubt that the old party could no longer claim to speak for nationalist Ireland as a whole, and to that extent its stock was fatally weakened both at home and in the House of Commons.

But East Clare was more than just another nail in the coffin of the Home Rule movement. In a longer perspective its greatest significance was that it marked the emergence of de Valera as a national leader. Hitherto, he had remained a rather shadowy and relatively unknown figure, partly because of his temperament (which was austere, aloof and somewhat forbidding) and partly because his career up to about 1913 had been that of a dedicated intellectual rather than an active revolutionary. Born in New York in October 1882, the son of a Spanish father and an Irish mother, Katherine Coll, de Valera had spent his childhood with his mother's family at Bruree, county Limerick. Educated at the local National School, then by the Christian Brothers at Charleville and finally at Blackrock College, he had taken a degree through the old Royal University and had then become a teacher of mathematics, for which subject he was always to retain a tenderness. He approached nationalism through the Gaelic League, and a love of the Irish language was to become one of his most abiding passions. He joined the Irish Volunteers at their foundation, trained himself with characteristic thoroughness to be an efficient officer and was in due course entrusted with the command of the Boland's Mills sector. During the rising he emerged as a humane and efficient, if also a rather tense and overwrought commander. Saved almost accidentally from execution, as we have seen, he first began to emerge as a man of marked authority and capacity in the various prisons to which he was assigned during the year of his captivity. His gifts for leadership and discipline helped prisoners who might otherwise have become demoralised to preserve their independence of spirit and they repaid him with a devoted loyalty which was to carry some of them into strange and stormy waters.

While these by-elections were being fought two major developments had transformed the whole situation. The first was the entry of the United States into the war in April 1917. Inevitably, this gave great encouragement to those Irishmen who advocated complete independence for their country. Long before the United States became a belligerent, as far back as May 1916, President Wilson had declared his belief that 'every people has the right to choose the sovereignty under which they shall live' and also that small states had the right to the same respect for their sovereignty and territorial integrity as the great powers insisted upon for themselves. Such language, though perhaps more concerned with Wilson's need to get re-elected in 1916 than with the realities of Irish politics, was music to the ears of the homecoming Irish prisoners. On his very first night in Dublin after his release Mr de Valera, along with Eoin MacNeill and some twenty-four others, signed a message to the American president (by then safely installed in the White House for another four years) which echoed almost the very words Wilson had used the previous year and informed him that the Irish people were intent upon establishing their right to defend themselves against 'external aggression, external interference and external control'.[6]

When this message was sent to Wilson America was already in the war, the war which Wilson himself had declared (on entering it) to be 'a war for freedom and justice and self-government amongst all the nations of the world'. But if the United States was to give of her best in this crusade then it was even more necessary than before to appease Irish-American opinion. This could only be done if the British government abandoned coercion and made yet another attempt to establish a satisfactory form of self-government for Ireland. Heavy American pressure was exerted in the spring of 1917 to bring this about and it was largely in response to this pressure (though there are indications that in March the cabinet had independently been groping for a more constructive policy) that Lloyd George launched the second new development of this crucial year. This was, in its first form, the renewal of his old offer to Redmond of immediate Home Rule for the twenty-six counties. When this was flatly refused he seized on a suggestion of Redmond's that a conference or convention of Irishmen should be held in the hope that they might be able to work out their own salvation. That Redmond should ever have thought such a gathering would produce anything but stalemate is a measure of his desperation, just as the history of the Convention when it did meet was to be the measure of his own personal tragedy. Its first sessions were held in July but, while it was driven hard by its enthusiastic though too loquacious chairman, Sir Horace Plunkett, and continued to meet until the spring of 1918, it achieved nothing.

Two things damned it from the start. One was that it was boycotted by Sinn Féin and by organised labour. The other was that the Ulster Unionists remained just as inflexibly opposed to any form of Home Rule as they had always been. In a despairing effort to isolate them and force Lloyd George into coercing them Redmond tried to make common cause with the Southern Unionists, even to the extent of contemplating the abandonment or limitation of the right of the prospective Irish parliament to levy its own customs duties. The only effect of this was to open a gulf between himself and his closest colleagues and when he died in March it was in the bitter knowledge that his lifelong struggle to reconcile nationalist with Unionist and Ireland with England had ended in unrelieved failure.

(ii)

Nevertheless, the Convention affected the Irish situation in two important, if negative ways. In the first place, as we can now see, it finally disposed of the myth that any settlement was possible, as conditions then were, on the basis of an Ireland which would be at once united and self-governing. This was a harsh doctrine and it is not surprising that contemporaries refused to accept it. For a few years more parliamentarians, Sinn Féiners and British government alike would go on insisting that *some* settlement (though their definitions of such a settlement were worlds apart) could and must be found which would apply to the whole of Ireland. Yet, in the light of the proceedings at the Convention, such a faith, however admirable, seems quite inexplicable. The time had surely come to realise that Ulster Unionists were not bluffing and that when they said they would not be party to any scheme of Home Rule they meant precisely what they said.

The second negative consequence of the Convention was rather more immediately obvious. This was that in the already uneven battle that was developing between Sinn Féin and the parliamentary party, the scales were now more heavily weighted against the latter. So long as the Convention continued in being, the parliamentarians were obliged to fight on the defensive, unable even to redefine what they meant by Home Rule lest it should prejudice the discussions then in progress. Worse even than that, Redmond had exactly repeated the mistake of the previous year in committing his party's prestige to a policy which was no better than a gamble against the odds. And when the policy crashed the party crashed with it. Sinn Féin, in contrast, by holding aloof from the futilities of the Convention, not only retained its own freedom of manoeuvre, but stood to gain immeasurably from the discomfiture of its rivals.

It must be said, however, that while it used the breathing space afforded by the Convention to extend its own organisation and propaganda, Sinn Féin received a great deal of assistance from the government. With almost inconceivable foolhardiness the authorities that summer resorted to the old policy of pin-pricking coercion – 'proclaiming' meetings, prohibiting the wearing of uniforms or the carrying of weapons, and arresting some of the more prominent and articulate opponents of the regime. Among these was Thomas Ashe who, when sent to Mountjoy jail in Dublin went, with some others, on hunger-strike. The prison officials resorted to forcible feeding and as a result of this treatment Thomas Ashe died in hospital on 25 September 1917. His funeral was at once made the occasion for a political demonstration unexampled since the rising. In deliberate defiance of the government regulations the Volunteers marched in uniform and with their rifles, and neither police nor troops dared intervene to stop them. It seemed almost as if Ireland were back at the point in 1915 when Patrick Pearse had reminded his fellow-countrymen at O'Donovan Rossa's funeral that 'life springs from death; and from the graves of patriot men and women spring living nations'. But this time there was no oration – just three volleys over the burial-place and two sentences spoken by a young man still unknown to the world at large. The young man was Michael Collins and his two sentences were in their way as heavy with meaning as Pearse's panegyric. 'Nothing additional remains to be said. The volley which we have just heard is the only speech which it is proper to make above the grave of a dead Fenian.'[7]

The prominence of Collins on this occasion had a double significance. First, it symbolised the re-emergence of the IRB as a force in Irish politics. It was the IRB, thinly disguised as the 'Wolfe Tone Memorial Committee', which had organised the funeral demonstration and though Collins wore the uniform of the Volunteers, it was his membership of the Brotherhood that gave him his real authority.* And it was precisely this – that Collins was now seen to be a man of authority – that was the other significant thing about the part he played in the ceremony. At this time he was still only twenty-seven years of age. Born in 1890 at Clonakilty, county Cork, he received his only formal education at the local National School. At the age of sixteen he had emigrated to London where he worked for a time in the British postal service and later for a firm of bankers. In London he was attracted into the GAA and the Gaelic League, going on from there, like so many others, to join the IRB to which he was admitted in 1909. When a company of Irish Volunteers was started in London in 1914 he joined

* The odd title 'Wolfe Tone Memorial Committee' recalls, in the oblique-ness of its terms of reference, the old Emmet Monument Association of Fenian days. Emmet, in his speech from the dock, had said: 'When my country takes her place among the nations of the earth, then, and not till then, let my epitaph be written'. Since Tone's objective had been the same, the 'Memorial Committee' had presumably a similar monument – a free country – in mind for him.

it too. In January 1916 he had returned to Dublin where he found employment with the chartered accountants, Craig, Gardner and Co. He then became heavily involved in the work of both IRB and Volunteers, was chosen by Joseph Plunkett to be his *aide-de-camp* and fought in the GPO in Easter week, where Desmond FitzGerald found him 'the most active and efficient officer in the place'. Being unknown to the Dublin police he was not court-martialled after the surrender, but was sent with the other internees to the camp at Frongoch in North Wales. There his talent for leadership rapidly asserted itself. Not only did he take a main part in organising resistance to prison regulations, but he also, under the very noses of the authorities, set up a branch of the IRB. Released at the end of 1916, he threw himself with characteristic energy into the work of the Irish National Aid Association (by then amalgamated with the Irish Volunteers Dependants Fund) and also into the reorganisation of the IRB. He became a member of the Supreme Council and worked with Ashe and Diarmuid Lynch, among others, to revise the constitution of the secret society.

As a man Collins was a strange mixture, almost a divided personality. 'There were two Micks', as Desmond Ryan later recalled '. . . one, the jolly gasconading, hard-swearing, good fellow; the other a dour, quiet man who lived with his life in his hand, heroic, dignified, a thinker, a fighter, a mystery.'[8] Well-built, athletic, with immense powers of work, he performed whatever he had to do with formidable efficiency and punctuality. But the lack of these qualities in others moved him easily to loud and blasphemous rage which made him many enemies. Those who met his exacting standards, however, grew to love him for his physical courage, his coolness in the face of danger and for his loyalty to his comrades. But behind the larger than life figure of 'the Big Fellow' was the political realist, the ruthless conspirator who had no time for high-flown sentiment or romantic idealism. It was not for nothing that Sean MacDermott had been his revolutionary mentor.

Yet, although by the autumn of 1917 Collins had gone a long way with the reorganisation of the IRB and was also rising fast within the hierarchy of the Volunteers, the relations of these two bodies with each other, and of them both with Sinn Féin, were confused and unhappy. In a sense the situation in 1917 resembled that on the eve of the rising, in that there was no clear division between the functions of the secret society and those of the more or less open organisation. But in 1917 there were two complications which had not existed earlier. One was that some of those who had been 'out' in Easter week were reluctant for various reasons to see the IRA regain its former importance. Cathal Brugha, for example, one of the most inveterate fighting-men produced by the rising, believed that the IRB had served its purpose, that next time the whole country would be in arms and that no secret initiatives would be needed.

Others, like de Valera, who had only joined the IRB reluctantly before the rising and pointedly declined to rejoin it after his release, disliked the Brotherhood partly because of the Church's ban on such societies, and partly perhaps because the miscarriage of the 1916 plan had revealed what chaos could be caused by open and underground movements pulling different ways.

The other fresh complication was that whereas in 1916 Griffith's organisation had stood somewhat apart from the mainstream of the revolutionary movement, in 1917 – partly because of the arrests and deportations, partly because of a genuine confusion in the public mind – the entire complex of 'advanced' nationalism was labelled with the name Sinn Féin. It was important, if the future was not to be bedevilled as the past had been by different policies pursued at different levels, to bring some order and unity into the existing chaos. And chaos is the only word which describes the situation that had begun to develop immediately after Count Plunkett's victory at the North Roscommon election. Part of the blame for this has to be laid at the door of the Count himself, who has been not unfairly described by a recent writer as 'an elderly, erratic *enfant terrible*'.*
A late-comer to politics who lacked judgment, and indeed ordinary common-sense, the Count was misled by his victory into imagining that in some fashion he had become the very incarnation of Sinn Féin. Nothing could have been further from the truth, but even if it had been the case the term Sinn Féin itself was in grave danger of coming to mean so many different things to so many different people as to have little political weight or significance. As for the original Sinn Féiners who had not been 'out' in 1916 – and these, of course, included Griffith himself – they were resented and scorned by IRB men, and also by some Volunteers, for what was taken to be their pacifism and because Griffith's solution – to use abstention from Westminster as the means of regaining 'the constitution of 1782' – was no longer acceptable to the devotees of the republic.

These incompatibilities crystallised at a convention called by Count Plunkett in April 1917 with the dual object of framing a national policy and closing the gaps between the various groups sheltering under the somewhat tattered umbrella of Sinn Féin. But unity was not helped by the Count's declared intention to do away with the umbrella altogether and in place of the existing Sinn Féin organisation, with its network of local branches, to create a new body, to be called the Liberty League, which would take over the functions both of

* M. Laffan, 'The unification of Sinn Féin in 1917', in *I.H.S.* (March 1971), xvii, 360. The account given above of the fortunes of Sinn Féin owes much to Mr Laffan's article and to two other studies also published since the first edition of this book appeared. These are B. Farrell, *The Founding of Dáil Eireann* (Dublin and London, 1971), chap. 2; and P. Pyne, 'The Third Sinn Féin Party, 1923-26', in *Economic and Social Review* (1969-70), vol. 1, Nos. 1 and 2.

Sinn Féin and of the Irish Nation League.* The debate that followed was acrimonious and confused, but an outright split was avoided by a compromise solution patched up by Griffith and Count Plunkett's supporter, the radical Father Michael O'Flanagan, in a hurried conversation at the back of the platform, the assembled delegates regaling themselves with patriotic songs while these important deliberations were going on.

The outcome was that the various groups were to be allowed to retain their separate identities but that they were to maintain contract with a new central body, later called the Mansion House Committee, on which were included Plunkett and Griffith with an equal number of their respective supporters, William O'Brien of the Labour movement (though he later resigned) and a representative of the Irish Nation League. Despite this surface agreement, Plunkett went ahead with the formation of his Liberty League and before long his followers and Griffith's were busily competing up and down the country in the establishment of fresh branches of their rival organisations. The spring and early summer of 1917 were marked by intensive activity at the constituency level – due, it would appear, much more to local initiative than to leadership from Dublin – and whereas in April 1917 there may have been no more than 166 'Sinn Féin Clubs' with a membership of perhaps 11,000, by October the corresponding figures had shot up to 1,200 clubs and a quarter of a million members. It seems that Griffith was the principal beneficiary of this expansion, partly because his organisation was better and his writings widely read, but partly also because of the simple fact that he still retained as it were the copyright of the magical name, Sinn Féin. In the end, after brisk but wasteful competition, the Liberty League was abandoned in late May or early June 1917 and the two sets of clubs amalgamated. Although an augmented Mansion House Committee was retained as the central directing body for the movement as a whole (the new members significantly included some of the more eminent of the recently released prisoners, notably de Valera and W. T. Cosgrave), the merger marked, or seemed to mark, a triumph for Griffith.

But if so, it was a strictly qualified triumph. With the arrival of the new men from the prisons of England both Plunkett and Griffith inevitably suffered some eclipse. It was ironical, but in retrospect seems almost inevitable, that no sooner had Sinn Féin been restored to health by its founder than it should have been calmly taken over by the men who brought with them the aura of 1916. The process of absorption continued quietly between June and October 1917, but it gradually became clear that at the convention, or Ard-Fheis, which was due to be held in the latter month, a confrontation of some kind would be difficult to avoid. The convention itself was

* For the Irish Nation League, see the second footnote on p. 379 above; also M. Laffan, op. cit., p. 355.

preceded by strenuous negotiation at a committee charged with drafting a new constitution for the organisation and it was in this committee rather than the full convention that the battle was fought out. In essence, it was a battle between republicans and non-republicans, Cathal Brugha being the most irreconcilable of the former group, Griffith still dominant among the latter in defending the doctrines he had laid down a dozen years before. Disagreement was so acute that at one time it seemed as if the meeting must break up. Then at the last moment Mr de Valera produced the formula which, for a time at least, was to win general agreement. It ran as follows:

Sinn Féin aims at securing the international recognition of Ireland as an independent Irish Republic.

Having achieved that status the Irish people may by referendum freely choose their own form of government.

When the full Ard-Fheis met on 25 October it was attended by over a thousand delegates who were well aware that their actions and decisions would be critical for the whole future of the movement. Yet despite this the proceedings were more harmonious than might have been expected. This was partly due to Griffith's own magnanimity. Although the voting for the presidency of the organisation was likely to be close, he could reasonably, as the original founder of Sinn Féin, have expected to be elected. He stood down, however, as did also a third candidate (Count Plunkett) and Mr de Valera was unanimously chosen. But partly also the unexpected harmony of the meeting was due to the committee's magical formula which seemed so exactly to suit the needs of republicans and non-republicans alike. 'This is not the time for discussion on the best forms of government', their new president told the delegates. 'But we are all united on this – that we want complete and absolute independence. Get this and we will agree to differ afterwards.' No doubt he was sincere in this. No doubt the delegates accepted the compromise embodied in the formula as a heaven-sent escape from an intolerable dilemma. First win your republic and then decide whether that or some other form of government suits you best. It seemed so simple and so logical. Yet in reality it was neither. Men who were still so close to the blood-sacrifice of Pearse and his comrades might have reflected how a cause is hallowed by the deaths of those who perish for it. Suppose more fighting were necessary to establish the republic – would men who had taken arms on its behalf ever be content with anything else? In 1917, it is fair to say, such a question seemed academic. Few people were thinking then of another insurrection, and even the word republic, though widely used, seems at this stage to have been often a synonym for independence rather than a definition of status. Most probably hoped that the time-honoured methods of Sinn Féin would suffice – passive resistance, non-attendance at Westminster, self-reliance in every aspect of the country's existence. Yet the question still persisted and the time was fast approaching when it would have to be answered.

The reorganisation of Sinn Féin was matched by the simultaneous reorganisation of the Irish Volunteers and, immediately following his election as President of Sinn Féin, de Valera was elevated to the Presidency of the Volunteers, so that at least two of the three bodies pledged to Irish independence would run in tandem under the same leadership. Yet even here there was the germ of future confusion. Just as the IRB had moved rapidly into key positions in the original Volunteer headquarters staff, so now they did precisely the same thing with the reconstituted executive. Thus Collins became Director of Organisation, Diarmuid Lynch, Director of Communications, and another IRB man, Sean McGarry, General Secretary. On the other hand, since Cathal Brugha, now a convinced opponent of the IRB, was Chief of Staff, there was obvious scope for future friction.

These developments within the Sinn Féin and Volunteer movements had done much to give 'advanced' nationalism shape and purpose and discipline, but although the long-term programme of seeking international recognition of an independent Irish republic had been enunciated clearly enough, it was not clear how this was to be achieved in the immediate future. Nor did it become clear during the ensuing winter, a period when the fortunes of Sinn Féin seemed to be flagging, when the Irish parliamentary party won three by-elections in a row, and when some of the wilder spirits on the left began, to the embarrassment of their leaders, to raid private houses in search of arms, and to break up large grazing farms in the west and south of the country for the purpose of arbitrarily assigning plots of land for tillage to small farmers and labourers. This last manoeuvre – an interesting throw-back to the aims and methods of the land agitations of the past – was carried out on the ground that there was an incipient food shortage in the country, but if it had been allowed to spread it would have confronted Sinn Féin with a serious dilemma and might even have brought to the fore that awkward problem which had so far been glossed over – did political revolution also mean social revolution or did it not?

(iii)

The problem did not have to be faced at that moment because the government, as so often before, came to the rescue of its opponents. With the unleashing of the German offensive of March 1918 the need for more and yet more men on the western front became imperative and the demand that conscription be extended to Ireland naturally grew more urgent than ever. For several weeks the cabinet threshed about in an effort to get the 150,000 men they so badly wanted from

Ireland without at the same time creating a major political crisis in that country. They had ample warning that to apply compulsory service to Irishmen would, as the Chief Secretary remarked, be tantamount to recruiting Germans and that additional troops would probably have to be sent to Ireland to enforce conscription. Yet ministers who were contemplating the recruitment of Englishmen up to the age of fifty or even fifty-five, would be unlikely to shrink from sweeping into the army the young men so temptingly within reach across the Irish Sea.

Lloyd George's own view was that conscription and Home Rule hung together. Up to the beginning of April he was still clinging – with what, in retrospect, seems to have been quite unjustifiable optimism – to the hope that the Irish Convention would produce recommendations for Irish self-government on which he could then proceed to act. Even without such recommendations he apparently intended to go ahead with some sort of Home Rule offer in which, of course, special provision would have to be made for Ulster. It was on this basis that he finally took the plunge and on 10 April introduced in the House of Commons a Military Service Bill which, while it did not impose conscription directly and automatically on Ireland, gave the government power to apply it by Order in Council whenever the necessity arose. But although he coupled with this a pledge to introduce a Home Rule measure before military service began to take effect, his promises were – in Irish eyes, at any rate – already such a debased currency that attention was centred from the start entirely on the conscription issue.[9]

'All Ireland will rise against you', Dillon (who had just taken Redmond's place at the head of the Irish party) warned him, and when, on 16 April, the bill passed through the House of Commons, the parliamentarians withdrew from Westminster and returned to Dublin. There they at once made common cause with Sinn Féin and the other opponents of military service in what became, almost overnight, the most massive demonstration of nationalist solidarity that had been seen since the beginning of the war. From every part of Ireland, except the north-east corner, support for an anti-conscription campaign poured in. It came not only from the different sections of the parliamentarians, from the trade unions and from Sinn Féin, but also from Cardinal Logue and the Standing Committee of the Irish bishops, who issued a public statement declaring that 'conscription forced in this way on Ireland is an oppressive and inhuman law which the Irish have a right to resist by every means that are consonant with the laws of God'.[10]

The qualification contained in the last phrase of that declaration was possibly intended as a warning not to go too far or too fast, but if so it went unnoticed in the fever of preparations to organise resistance to the conscription that now at last and so suddenly appeared imminent. On 18 April an imposing conference of representative men

393

was called together at the Mansion House by the Lord Mayor of Dublin. Sitting round the same table were Dillon, Joseph Devlin, de Valera, Griffith, T. M. Healy, William O'Brien (of the All-for-Ireland League) and the other William O'Brien (the labour leader) together with several of the latter's colleagues. Not even in his most strenuous endeavours to solve the Irish problem had Lloyd George ever come near producing such uniformity of views amongst so diverse a group of Irishmen as he did by this one action. The Conference agreed upon a pledge, drafted by Mr de Valera, which was to be taken in every parish on the following Sunday. It ran as follow: 'Denying the right of the British government to enforce compulsory service in this country, we pledge ourselves solemnly to one another to resist conscription by the most effective means at our disposal.' This pledge, which was duly taken at the church doors by thousands of people on 21 April, was at the same time reinforced by practical measures to make resistance effective. Hostilities between Sinn Féin and the parliamentary party were temporarily suspended (the party even withdrew a candidate from a by-election to give the seat to Sinn Féin), in each parish a 'committee of defence' was to be formed to obstruct conscription, a National Defence Fund was launched and plans were laid to present the Irish case to the President and Congress of the United States. In addition, a special meeting of the Irish Trades Union Congress decided on a token general strike of twenty-four hours and on 23 April this was held with paralysing effect everywhere except in Belfast.[11]

All this was impressive evidence of unity. But it was a precarious unity, as no one understood more clearly than the parliamentary leader, John Dillon. Convinced as he had been since the failure of the 1916 negotiations that Lloyd George was intent upon clearing the ground for a stand-up fight with Sinn Féin and that the Prime Minister now regarded the Irish party as a tiresome irrelevance, Dillon realised all too clearly the dilemma now facing him and his colleagues. On the one hand, they had to be as adamantly opposed to conscription as any other group in Ireland and there is no reason to doubt that this opposition was completely sincere. On the other hand, the whole issue might have been expressly designed to promote extreme nationalism in Ireland and, as Dillon was well aware, this could only be at the expense of the parliamentarians. 'All I can safely say', he wrote to his friend T. P. O'Connor while the Mansion House conference was still in being, 'is that enough has transpired already to make it quite clear that the purpose is to swallow us up and that the "tiger" should emerge from the conference with the constitutional party inside.'[12]

In the circumstances it was hardly surprising that the truce between the party and Sinn Féin should soon have broken down. In fact, it broke down within a fortnight of the Mansion House Conference when both sides decided to contest a by-election at East

Cavan, a seat held by the party for many years. The contest was given heightened importance by the fact that the Sinn Féin candidate was none other than Arthur Griffith who, from the beginning of his career, had been a bitter critic of the parliamentarians and who now in his election campaign declared that before any real unity could be established between the party and Sinn Féin, the party 'would have to accept the Sinn Féin programme of absolute independence for Ireland, abstention from the British parliament and that the Peace Conference was the place where freedom was to be won'. This indeed would have been the 'tiger' walking off with the constitutional movement inside, and since Dillon shortly afterwards denounced these grandiose objectives as 'a policy of lunatics' it was clear that what little common ground the anti-conscription movement had provided had now disappeared completely.[13]

Left to themselves the two opposing sections might have made a close fight of it in East Cavan. But they were not left to themselves. Yet again the government intervened in the way most calculated to rally maximum support for Sinn Féin. Anticipating vigorous resistance to conscription, the cabinet had been considering for some time the possibility of arresting the leaders and on 11 May dispatched Field-Marshal Lord French to Dublin to replace Lord Wimborne as Lord Lieutenant. As a military man it was judged that he would have a better chance to put conscription into force when needed, and he was given wide powers to suppress disorder, though Lloyd George tried hard to impress upon him the elementary political wisdom of putting the onus for shooting first on the 'rebels'. Before he went Lord French had told the cabinet that he proposed to issue a proclamation and arrest 'those against whom evidence of intriguing is produced'. On 15 May the terms of the Proclamation were approved by the cabinet, on the night of 17 May almost the entire leadership of Sinn Féin and the Volunteers (with the important exceptions of Michael Collins and Cathal Brugha) was seized, and on the morning of 18 May the newspapers carried the details of the proclamation which stated, among other things, that Sinn Féin had been engaged in a treasonable conspiracy with the Germans.

Such was the so-called 'German plot'. Few people outside official or Unionist circles believed in it at the time, and it has generally been scouted by historians since, especially as the authorities refused to produce the evidence on which they had acted. There was, in fact, rather more to the matter than met the eye. Bits and pieces of information had been reaching the government from time to time that the American Irish, more specifically the irrepressible Devoy, had renewed their contacts with Germany within a few weeks of the rising, that there had been discussions about further landings of arms in Ireland, even that some German weapons had been sent to that country but had failed to arrive. Apart from this fairly steady exchange of messages between the Irish-Americans and the Germans, there were scattered indications that U-boats had been in contact with agents off the west coast of Ireland, and there was what seemed more substantial proof when one of Casement's ill-fated Irish Brigade, James Dowling, was arrested in Galway after having landed from a submarine. He had in fact been sent by the Germans on their own initiative to try to discover whether there were any prospects for a rising. His mission was to convey a code message to this effect to the IRB and such a message, it seems, did reach Michael Collins. It is doubtful if Collins ever attempted to send a reply, but if he did, the answer would certainly have been noncommittal since the whole policy of the IRB and of the open movement alike was at that time one of conservation not insurrection.[14] But in all of this there was no sign of a concerted 'plot' and no evidence that the Sinn Féin leaders were in any way implicated. What the government needed was a colourable excuse for shutting up the principal opponents of conscription and this the 'German plot' provided.[15]

There is strong evidence that the Sinn Féin leaders had had advance warning that their arrest was imminent, but that they deliberately decided to let themselves be taken, partly because they well knew the effect their imprisonment would have upon public opinion in general, and more specifically because of the effect it would have upon the East Cavan election.[16] In this latter calculation they were certainly justified. The election, which had been in the balance, went decisively in Griffith's favour and from prison he had the satisfaction of learning that he had won by over a thousand votes. Dillon, who was in the best position to know, blamed the result partly on 'spiritual intimidation' by the younger priests, but also upon government policy. Intimidation, he wrote to T. O. O'Connor, 'combined with the cry – who wants the blood of Griffith? – and the desperate hatred of LG and the government formed an accumulation of forces which it was impossible to overcome.'[17]

East Cavan, as we can now see, was a dress rehearsal for the general election which came immediately after the war ended in November. But before that happened Lord French's military rule had pushed the country still further into a mood of dangerous irritation. The arrests had proved merely the signal for the old cycle of intermittent and largely ineffective coercion to begin again. On 3 July the Volunteers, the Gaelic League and the various Sinn Féin organisations were 'proclaimed' as 'a grave menace'; not only were their meetings declared illegal, but all public gatherings were prohibited unless with police authorisation. Yet, although during these months over a thousand arrests were made, Sinn Féin was not destroyed. It was merely driven underground where it became, if anything, more menacing than before. That this was so was due mainly to the small group of leaders who had managed to escape the police net and who, though often in imminent danger of arrest, managed not only to keep their organisation intact but actually to expand it. The dominant figure in this group was Michael Collins, whose pre-eminence in the struggle for independence dates from this period when, combining the Volunteer posts of Adjutant-General and Director of Organisation, he not only revitalised the movement in the country, but also built up an intelligence service – with contacts in the post office, the prisons, and even the G Division of Dublin Metropolitan Police detectives – which was to prove invaluable in the perilous times that lay ahead. There was, of course, far too much for one man to do and a great deal of the business relating to the military training, discipline and tactics of the Volunteers was in the hands of his immediate colleagues, Cathal Brugha (Chief of Staff), Brugha's deputy Richard Mulcahy, Rory O'Connor (Director of Engineering) and the journalist, Piaras Béaslaí who became editor of the revived Volunteer journal, *An t Oglàch*, which first reappeared in August 1918 and rapidly became the mouthpiece for the most violent antagonism to conscription. On the political side a similar work of organisation and propaganda was carried on by the Sinn Féin officers who had hitherto avoided arrest. The most important and effective of these was the Dublin tailor, Harry Boland, whose energy and powers of work rivalled those of Collins himself. It was largely due to his initiative that the number of members of Sinn Féin clubs up and down the country continued to grow rapidly despite the extreme difficulty of the situation.[18]

The immediate impulse behind this furious activity was not revolution, but simply the determination to be ready to resist conscription at all costs. For so long as the war lasted, and while the results of voluntary enlistment were as meagre as the figures showed them to be, the cloud of conscription hung over the country. It was this which gave cohesion to the nationalist effort, and it was this also which inevitably brought nearer the possibility of an armed conflict between the Volunteers and the military authorities. 'It is our duty', wrote Béaslaí in his paper, 'to resist conscription actively, working together as an armed, organised and disciplined body . . . in an emergency every true Volunteer should know how to act for himself; it is his duty to resist to the death . . . to make his death or capture dearly purchased by the lives of his enemies.' And a few weeks later an anonymous writer (in fact, Ernest Blythe) went even further in an article entitled 'Ruthless Warfare'. This called on the Volunteers to recognise that the imposition of conscription would be an act of war which must be met by war:

If England decided on this atrocity, then we, on our part, must decide that in our resistance we shall acknowledge no limit and no scruple. We must recognise that anyone, civilian or soldier, who assists directly or by connivance in this crime against us, merits no more consideration than a wild beast, and should be killed without mercy or hesitation as opportunity offers . . . Thus the man who serves on an exemption tribunal, the doctor who treats soldiers or

397

examines conscripts, the man who voluntarily surrenders when called for, the man who in any shape or form applies for an exemption, the man who drives a police-car or assists in the transport of army supplies, all these having assisted the enemy must be shot or otherwise destroyed with the least possible delay.[19]

Much of what was soon to happen in Ireland becomes plain in the light of this article. On the short view, admittedly, it seemed irrelevant, for within a month of its publication the war was over and the danger of conscription vanished overnight. Nevertheless, it expressed a mood of cold savagery which more than almost anything else written at the time marked out the distance Ireland had travelled since 1916. Meanwhile all the passion, all the determination which Sinn Féin had been able to mobilise against the threat of military service, was thrown behind it in the general election that followed hard on the heels of the Armistice. It did not matter that many of the Sinn Féin candidates were still in prison, that their director of elections was arrested three weeks before polling day, or that their manifesto was heavily censored by the authorities. On the contrary, these governmental attentions were an added advantage and certainly did not prevent them from getting their message home to the electorate.

What was that message? In essence it was a reaffirmation of the republican ideal, which was to be achieved by a four-point policy. These four points were first – withdrawal from Westminster; second – 'making use of any and every means available to render impotent the power of England to hold Ireland in subjection by military force or otherwise'; third – the establishment of a constituent assembly, as 'the supreme national authority'; and finally – to appeal to the Peace Conference 'for the establishment of Ireland as an independent nation'.[20] Such a programme proved irresistible. In vain the parliamentary party raised its sights to what appeared to be a demand for dominion status. The lure and glamour of the republic – which, apart from its intrinsic attractions, was the natural focus for the all-prevailing hatred of England – carried everything before it. On the eve of the dissolution of parliament Dillon's party held sixty-eight seats, William O'Brien's following and a handful of Independents together accounted for ten, the Unionists numbered eighteen and Sinn Féin seven. After the election, while the Unionists had increased their strength to twenty-six, the Independents and O'Brienites were completely wiped out and the once great parliamentary party was reduced to six seats, of which four were held in border-constituencies which Sinn Féin and the party had agreed to divide among themselves without contests so as not to risk Unionist victories. Apart from these, all other seats, seventy-three in number, went to Sinn Féin.*

* Owing to the fact that individual candidates (e.g. Mr de Valera) were returned for more than one seat, the seventy-three constituencies won by Sinn Féin were represented by sixty-nine members. Because of redistribution,

It is true that this landslide was not, in electoral terms, quite as impressive as it seemed on the surface. Nearly a third (thirty-one per cent) of the electors did not vote, and only 47.7 per cent of the votes cast were votes for Sinn Féin, though against this must be set the fact that in twenty-five constituencies they were returned unopposed. It is important to note, also, that the election was the first at which a virtually new generation of voters had had a chance to express their views, and there is no reason to doubt that a great many of these young people plumped for Sinn Féin. The Irish electorate rose from 700,000 in 1910 to just under 2 million in 1918; a very large part of this increase was registered in the boroughs where the trebling of voting strength was a common occurrence. It seems inescapable that this worked to the advantage of Sinn Féin. Indeed, if one takes as a realistic basis for study only the twenty-six counties which were presently to form the Irish Free State, the Sinn Féin proportion of the votes cast rises from the 47.7 per cent mentioned above to almost 65 per cent. It is significant, in this context, that in certain seats the candidates of the parliamentary party actually *increased* their votes in 1918 as compared with the previous election in 1910, but these gains were nevertheless wiped out by the large increase in the electorate of which a sufficiently large proportion may be presumed to have voted for Sinn Féin. One further factor which prepared the way for this striking result was the decision by Labour – after much havering, and secret negotiations with Sinn Féin which might have produced a 'seats deal' – not to stand as a separate interest at the polls, mainly, it would seem, so as not to prejudice 'a clear expression of the people's opinion upon the question of self-determination.'[21] There were, admittedly, complaints of intimidation, and even of impersonation, on behalf of Sinn Féin, and it would have been surprising if some of these had not been justified, especially if it be remembered that passion was running high, and that the Sinn Féiners, as a virtually outlawed party, fought under very great difficulties, their literature liable to seizure, their meetings often broken up, their offices raided and their agents frequently arrested.[22] It was, in short, a bitter and ugly election, with no holds barred on either side. Yet none of this can take away from the fact that, in political terms, the result had completely transformed the face of Irish politics. Nothing would ever be the same again.

---

the total number of Irish seats at the election was 105, not 103 as previously.

5. The Struggle for Independence

Sinn Féin had won an overwhelming triumph at the general election, but what would they do with it? What *could* they do with it, indeed, since most of their leaders and many of their newly elected members remained locked up in British jails? The world did not have to wait long for an answer. True to their election pledges, they turned their backs firmly on Westminster and began, such of them as were at liberty, to prepare the ground for the creation of a separate Irish parliament. A private meeting of Sinn Féin representatives was held on 7 January 1919 to make the necessary arrangements and from this meeting went out invitations to the members elected for *all* constituencies at the recent election to attend on 21 January the first session of the Assembly of Ireland, or Dáil Eireann as it was known from the very beginning. The Unionist members and the survivors of the old parliamentary party ignored the summons, so in practice the new Dáil consisted only of Sinn Féiners. And since thirty-four of them were in prison and eight others absent for other reasons the number of members actually present on this historic occasion was no more than twenty-seven.[1]

The proceedings, which were mostly in Irish, did not take more than two hours, but they were nevertheless momentous. After Cathal Brugha had been elected as presiding officer for the day, the roll was called, temporary clerks were appointed and a short provisional constitution adopted. This called for the setting up of an executive government, consisting of a Prime Minister (Priomh-Aire) chosen by the Dáil and four other ministers (Finance, Home Affairs, Foreign Affairs and Defence) nominated by the Prime Minister and dismissible by him, but subject to ratification by the Dáil after their nomination. The whole government, or individual ministers, could be dismissed by the Dáil on the basis of a unanimous resolution and since the provisional constitution also gave the Assembly full powers of legislation and absolute control over finance, it was clear enough that the framers of this brief document had fully grasped the essence of the doctrine of popular sovereignty then coming into vogue among the new nations of Europe.[2]

The same preoccupation with sovereignty, though linked in this instance with traditional Irish historicism, was manifest in the first of three major statements read to the Dáil and approved by it. This – the Declaration of Independence – began by recalling that 'whereas the Irish people is by right a free people', for seven hundred years it had not ceased to repudiate 'foreign usurpation', nor to protest in arms against it. More specifically, the Declaration looked back to the recent past, asserting that 'the Irish Republic was proclaimed in Dublin on Easter Monday, 1916, by the Irish Republican Army, acting on behalf of the Irish people'. The Declaration of Independence was accordingly presented to the Dáil not as a new departure, but rather as a re-affirmation:

Now, therefore, we, the elected Representatives of the ancient Irish people in National Parliament assembled, do, in the name of the Irish nation, ratify the establishment of the Irish Republic and pledge ourselves and our people to make this declaration effective by every means at our command.

The emphasis in this passage on 'the Irish people' and 'the Irish nation' was echoed in the preamble and elsewhere in the body of the Declaration. Thus, in the preamble it is 'the Irish people' that is 'resolved to secure and maintain its complete independence', to undertake all the responsibilities of nationhood and 'to constitute a national policy based upon the people's will, with equal right and opportunity for every citizen'. Likewise, it was the elected representatives of the Irish people who alone had power to make laws for Ireland, for 'the Irish Parliament is the only Parliament to which that people will give its allegiance'.[3]

The Declaration of Independence was intended for foreign as well as for home consumption and contained not only a demand for the evacuation of the country by 'the English garrison', but also a claim for the recognition and support of all free nations. This claim and this demand were repeated at greater length in a 'Message to the Free Nations of the world' where both were linked with that fundamental aim of Sinn Féin – 'to be confronted publicly with England at the Congress of the Nations [the Peace Conference], in order that the civilised world having judged between English wrong and Irish right may guarantee to Ireland its permanent support for the maintenance of her national independence'.[4] That the confrontation might be translated into action the Dáil in this same opening session appointed three delegates – Mr de Valera, Arthur Griffith and Count Plunkett – to be its delegates to the Peace Conference.

Hitherto the proceedings had followed a course which, if highly idealistic, was at least predictable. But idealism did not stop short at declaring a republic nor appealing to the free world. It penetrated also the third and very different document to which the Dáil that day gave a hearing. This was the 'Democratic Programme' which started from the premisses enunciated by Pearse in his last major pamphlet, The Sovereign People, but went on to make much larger and more specific assertions. Echoing Pearse (but significantly avoiding any mention of Connolly) the Programme declared that the nation's sovereignty extended to all its material wealth and resources and reaffirmed with him that 'all right to private property must be subordinated to the public right and welfare'. The country, so the Programme continued, was to be ruled in accordance with 'the principles of Liberty, Equality and Justice', and it called upon every man and woman to spend his or her strength in the service of the people. 'In return for willing service, we, in the name of the Republic, declare the right of every citizen to an adequate share of the produce of the Nation's labour.' Then followed a passage to which later generations were to look back in irony and anger:

It shall be the first duty of the Government of the Republic to make provision for the physical, mental and spiritual well-being of the children, to secure that no child shall suffer hunger or cold from lack of food, clothing, or shelter, but that all shall be provided with the means and facilities requisite for their proper education and training as Citizens of a Free and Gaelic Ireland.

How this millenium was to be achieved the Programme naturally enough did not set out in detail. But it anticipated a whole series of social and economic reforms which would presumably help to produce the desired result. The 'odious, degrading and foreign Poor Law System' was to be abolished; the physical and moral well-being of the nation was to be safeguarded by appropriate legislation; the natural resources of the country – its soil, its minerals, its fisheries, even its bogs – were to be exploited; there was to be (in the tradition of Sinn Féin) a drive to develop industry, to promote foreign trade and create an extensive Irish Consular Service; finally, the government would co-operate with the governments of other countries 'in determining a standard of social and industrial legislation with a view to a general and lasting improvement in the conditions under which the working classes live and labour'.[5]

Before trying to discover how the high ideals and intense emotions expressed in those two hours of 21 January fared in the bleak world outside the Mansion House, two comments have to be made about the theoretical positions to which the Dáil now stood committed. One is that it was highly unfortunate that, as the late P. S. O'Hegarty put it, 'this assembly took place with so little of the intelligence of the Dáil being present'.[6] Since de Valera and Griffith were both in prison the restraint they might have imposed on the exuberance of their followers was lacking. It was significant that the presiding chairman was Cathal Brugha, an *enragé* if ever there was one, and it was surely no accident that the declaration of the republic was made in such forthright terms. The 'strait-jacket' of which Mr de Valera was later to complain so bitterly had already begun to be fashioned. On the other hand, although so many of the responsible leaders were absent, it would be going too far to say that the assembly was dominated by its extremists. Quite the contrary. As has been pointed out by a recent writer, the Sinn Féin representatives who brought the First Dáil into existence were far removed from the modern stereotype of the guerrilla freedom-fighter. 'Taken together with the Executive of Sinn Féin at this time', he suggests, 'they must be seen as a group fully committed to independence but moderate in their perception of what that independence might mean.'[7]

The other point is that the Democratic Programme attracted criticism even before it was presented to the Dáil. It was in fact a rather mysterious document for which different people have been given the credit at different times. It appears to have been drafted in its original form by Thomas Johnson, either in response to a request from Sinn Féin or, as another and on the whole more probable account has it, as an initiative taken by the Irish delegation to the forthcoming International Socialist Conference at Berne, apparently in the hope that they might be able to win support from the Conference for Irish independence by demonstrating that although Labour might not be directly represented in the Dáil as a political party, it had sufficient influence with that body to ensure its acceptance of a predominantly socialist programme. It appears that discussions did take place between Sinn Féin and Labour representatives, but that the notes recording the course of the discussions were so inchoate and so unacceptable to leading members of Sinn Féin and of the IRB (including, it seems, Michael Collins) – both on ideological grounds and because they were regarded as running counter to the grand strategy of independence – that Sean T. O'Kelly was deputed to produce a modified version for the Dáil's consideration. This he did with only a few hours to spare and the resulting document was the one which the Dáil in due course adopted.[8] In retrospect, it must be said, the apprehensions of Collins and his friends seem to have been needless. The promised social revolution soon became what Professor Patrick Lynch has called it, 'the social revolution that never was'. In the immediate future the struggle for independence, as Collins had foreseen, was too intense to allow time or energy for experiments in welfare, and when peace finally returned after 1922 the dominance of the property-owning classes and the internal divisions of the workers combined to draw a veil of oblivion over the Democratic Programme.[9]

Oblivion – though much speedier – was also the fate of the appeal to the Peace Conference. Mr Sean T. O'Kelly was duly dispatched to Paris as an envoy charged with obtaining admission to the Conference for the three delegates appointed by the Dáil, but despite many months of effort he never came remotely within reach of his objective. The only possible hope of recognition would have been if the Irish case had been backed by the United States, but of this there was no sign. True, the Irish-American organisation, the Friends of Irish Freedom, was prepared to do what it could to bring pressure to bear upon President Wilson. But as a pressure-group it suffered from the disadvantage that since its formation in 1916 it had been dominated by the two pillars of Clan na Gael, John Devoy and Judge Daniel Cohalan. Both of them, and Cohalan in particular, had incurred Wilson's enmity, largely it would seem because their support for Irish independence expressed itself in pro-German and virulently anti-British sentiments, but partly also because of their opposition to the President's *idée fixe* of a League of Nations. Nevertheless, their influence among Irish-Americans was very great and in February 1919 they were able to evoke a massive demonstration of sympathy for the Irish cause at an Irish Race Convention in Philadelphia. This Convention sent a delegation to interview the President before he sailed for Europe, but Wilson, already irritated by the passing of a House of Representatives resolution calling for the Peace Conference to consider favourably the Irish claim to self-determination, was frigid in the extreme. He would only agree to see the delegation after Cohalan had absented himself from the room, and when he did finally grant an interview he refused absolutely to be drawn either on Irish self-determination or on the admission of Irish delegates to the Peace Conference. Unabashed, the Convention sent three representatives of its own to Paris in an effort to secure a hearing for Ireland but they were no more successful than O'Kelly had been. They did, however, visit Ireland during their travels and brought home an impression of conditions there so lurid that Irish-American opinion became even more inflamed against Britain – and against Wilson for his non-co-operation – than before.[10]

(ii)

But Irish independence would in the end turn on what happened in Ireland, not Paris. And in Ireland the most urgent problem was to come down from the emotional heights of 21 January to the practical problems of organising a government most of whose potential members were already in prison and the remainder likely to be before long. In a private session held on the day after the inaugural meeting a temporary ministry was appointed, with Cathal Brugha as Prime Minister, Eoin MacNeill as Minister for Finance, Michael Collins as Minister for Home Affairs, Count Plunkett as Minister for Foreign Affairs and Richard Mulcahy as Minister for Defence. At that time, these proceedings were widely regarded as an elaborate charade, totally unreal and futile, though, as the *Freeman's Journal* prophetically observed, if what had taken place was seriously meant then Ireland was on the eve of one of the most tragic chapters in her history.

For the time being, however, the British government, which seems to have been in two minds about whether or not to suppress this new assembly at the outset, held its hand. Indeed, so far from adding to its roster of distinguished prisoners, it was not proving very successful at holding on to those it had already got. Early in February Michael Collins and Harry Boland succeeded in rescuing Mr de Valera from Lincoln jail by the time-honoured device of smuggling into the prison keys hidden in cakes. Shortly afterwards Robert Barton, a Sinn Féiner who was soon to attain high prominence, escaped on his own from Mountjoy prison in Dublin, followed shortly afterwards by some twenty other prisoners who climbed over the wall of the same jail in broad daylight. During March, prompted partly it seems by the influenza epidemic then raging, the government decided to release its prisoners and Mr de Valera, who since his escape had remained in hiding in England, was free to return home.

When the Dáil next met, therefore, on 1 April, it was attended by a much larger gathering of Sinn Féin members. Fifty-two members answered the roll-call and from the proceedings of this second session dated what might be called the permanent constructive work of the Dáil. As might have been expected in a revolutionary body it was very much an assembly of young men. About a third of the members were under thirty-five years of age and nearly three-quarters of the whole total were under forty-five. It was also – and in Irish conditions this, too, was predictable – preponderantly Roman Catholic in religion; in fact there were only two Protestants in the first Dáil, Robert Barton and Ernest Blythe. More unexpectedly – but again explicable in the circumstances of the time – there was much less connection between members and their constituents than had been normal under the parliamentary party or was to be normal in later and more settled times. Nearly fifty per cent did not live in their constituencies (though many had some sort of family connection with the areas they represented). Moreover, only ten per cent had any experience of local government. These two facts together suggest that many of the new men had risen to prominence in one or other of the nationalist organisations and, since these all had their heaquarters in the capital, a high proportion had become Dubliners by adoption. It is less surprising – given the strong vein of cultural nationalism in the Sinn Féin movement – to find that sixty per cent at least had had a secondary education and rather more than a quarter had had a university or professional training. In terms of occupation – so far as these can be accurately judged at a time of upheaval – it was strikingly evident that the major industry of the country – agriculture – was grossly under-represented. There were only seven farmers (i.e. ten per cent of the total membership) in the first Dáil, whereas the professional and commercial classes loomed large, accounting for no less than sixty-five per cent of the whole. But this did not make it an assembly of the men of property of the country. On the contrary, among the professional men it was the journalists and teachers who predominated, while the commercial representatives were nearly all shopkeepers and employees. 'The core of the republican movement', it has been well said, 'was constituted from among the lower social groups within the middle class.'[11]

After the formal opening of the session Sean T. O'Kelly was unanimously chosen as Speaker (Ceann Comhairle), two deputy Speakers were nominated and clerks of the House appointed. Then, after several amendments to the constitution had been passed – the most important of them allowing for a larger executive – Mr de Valera was elected Prime Minister. The following day he submitted his ministerial nominations to the Dáil. The choices were even more significant than most members perhaps realised at the time, for Mr de Valera had intimated to Collins and others, from the moment he got out of jail, that he believed his place in the immediate future should be in America organising support and gathering funds for the cause. To his colleagues it seemed a strange decision with matters so delicately poised in Ireland, but he was immovable and it was only after some difficulty that they persuaded him to spend at least a short interval in Ireland setting up his government. The composition of that government was, therefore, of crucial importance since effective power would be in its hands during Mr de Valera's absence. Apart from himself – usually designated President of the Dáil rather than Prime Minister – eight Ministers were appointed. These were Griffith (Home Affairs, acting also as the President's deputy), Collins (Finance), Brugha (Defence), Plunkett (Foreign Affairs), Countess Markievicz (Labour), Cosgrave (Local Government), Eoin MacNeill (Industries), and Robert Barton (Agriculture). Lawrence Ginnell, formerly a somewhat erratic member of the Irish parliamentary party but returned as a Sinn Féin candidate at the general election, was appointed Director of Propaganda for the time being. With the exception of Ginnell, who, on his arrest in May 1919 had to be replaced by Desmond FitzGerald (until, after *his* arrest in February 1921 he was succeeded by Erskine Childers), these were the people on whom rested the primary responsibility for carrying out the fundamental Sinn Féin policy of providing an alternative government in Ireland to which, rather than to the régime centred on Dublin Castle, Irishmen would naturally and instinctively turn.

The difficulties of such a task were enormous. Even though the Dáil itself was not formally suppressed until September 1919, individual members of it were frequently 'on the run' from the police and from about May of that year onwards the Assembly was virtually driven underground. By the autumn of 1919 it had even become necessary to ask some key figures in the movement *not* to attend meetings in case they should be arrested, and in November the headquarters staff of the Dáil was seized, together with many important papers. The Assembly continued to meet in secret but the hazards of its career were reflected in the decline in the number of its sittings; whereas in 1919 there were six sessions, there were only three in 1920 and three in 1921. Taken together these made up a total of twenty-one actual meetings of which fourteen were held in 1919, three in 1920 and four in 1921.[12] It followed from this fugitive kind of existence that normal parliamentary work was impossible. There was little in the way of legislation, little even of constructive debate or opposition. Indeed, there could scarcely be an opposition in any recognisable sense of the term, since the Dáil was a one-party legislature. Organised labour, which might have provided such an opposition, and was to do so after 1922, had, as we have seen, deliberately not contested the election of 1918 (nor did it contest that of 1921) in order to leave the field clear for the great and over-riding issue of national self-determination to be fought out.

The consequence of this almost complete absence of ordinary parliamentary usage was that there was very little check upon ministers who, for their part, were also having to operate in secret, and to improvise desperately. There were no formal government offices and the various departments moved about from house to house often only a few hours, or even minutes, ahead of the police. That they should achieve anything at all in such circumstances was remarkable, and some of them, it must be admitted, achieved very little. A great deal depended on individuals, and the Dáil Ministries flourished or faded in proportion to the qualities, or lack of qualities, of those who headed them. In the Ministry of Finance, for example, Michael Collins was conspicuously successful in raising a 'Dáil Eireann National Loan' of close on £358,000.[13] Robert Barton at the Ministry of Agriculture was likewise effective in setting up a Land Bank which began, on a modest scale, to advance loans to farmers and thus carry on the process of land purchase; following disturbances by landless men in the west in 1920, a land commission was set up to administer a scheme of land acquisition and distribution which was to be the basis for more extensive reforms after independence had been achieved. In the Ministry of Local Government W. T. Cosgrave and his young assistant, Kevin O'Higgins, both earned the reputations and gained the experience that were to take them to the highest levels of power in the years ahead. Gradually, they built up close contacts with local councils and officials all over the country and when at the local elections of January and June 1920 Sinn Féin won a sweeping victory that task was made much easier. Out of 127 corporations and town councils they controlled 72 completely and shared their authority with other nationalists in a further 26. They dominated 28 out of 33 County Councils, 182 out of 206 Rural District Councils and all but 16 of the 154 Poor Law Boards. Even the fact that proportional representation gave considerable weight to other parties and sections could not disguise the extent of the republican triumph.[14] As a result, in mid-summer of that year the Dáil felt strong enough to recommend the councils to break off their connection with the existing Local Government Board and by October practically all of them outside northeast Ulster had done so, despite the considerable financial risks to which they were exposing themselves through the loss of their grants and in aid. The final blow at the old system was struck when the republican forces burned down the Customs House in which the Local Government Board was housed; such at least was the justification offered for the destruction of the most beautiful building in Dublin.

Even more striking than the development of Sinn Féin control over local government was the way in which, for a time, the British machinery of justice was supplanted by a system or hierarchy of 'Dáil Courts'. They began at first in a rather haphazard fashion as 'arbitration courts' on a model first operated in West Clare and spreading rapidly during 1919 and early 1920. In addition, to meet the flood of litigation in connection with land, special land courts were set up under the Ministry of Agriculture and a special republican police force was formed to execute the decrees of these various courts. In June 1920 it became necessary to systematise the administration of the law by a decree of the Dáil which at the same time laid down that land claims could in future only be brought into court by licence from the Minister of Home Affairs. Within three months of this decree there had emerged (a) Parish Courts, consisting of three members, meeting once a week and dealing with small civil and criminal cases; (b) District Courts of five members meeting once a month and dealing with more important civil and criminal cases, or with cases coming to them on appeal from the Parish Court; (c) special sessions of the District Courts three times a year, presided over by a 'circuit judge' and having unlimited civil and criminal jurisdiction – there were four circuit districts and four circuit judges; (d) a Supreme Court sitting in Dublin and composed of not less than three members appointed for three years and functioning both as a court of first instance and as an appellate tribunal. The legal system applied in all these courts was the law as it stood on 2 January 1919, save as amended by Dáil Eireann, though citations from 'the early Irish law codes', Roman law and even the decisions of continental courts were permissible. The very existence of such strange innovations confronted the conservative legal profession with a vexing problem which they solved realistically by turning a blind eye whenever solicitors and barristers appeared before the new courts. In due course these various tribunals were declared illegal by the government and were to some extent driven underground. The system itself was not destroyed, however, and it has been estimated that by July 1921 there were over 900 Parish Courts and over 70 District Courts in operation.[15]

But over all this furious activity there hung a grave question. How long could the Dáil and its Ministries carry on work which was illegal in the eyes of the British government without coming into direct and violent conflict with that government? In fact, and by a curious coincidence, such conflict had already broken out on the very day on which the Dáil met to proclaim Irish independence. For it was on 21 January 1919 that the first shots were fired in what gradually became an Anglo-Irish war. The scene was Soloheadbeg, in county Tipperary, the occasion an ambush organised by a group of Volunteers belonging to the 3rd Tipperary Brigade and containing three men who were to become almost legendary figures in the guerrilla warfare of which this was the first ominous indication. They were Seumas Robinson, Sean Treacy and Dan Breen, and their objective was a cartload of explosives being escorted to a neighbouring quarry by two policemen of the RIC. It was not intended that the police should be killed, but the gunmen were young, impetuous and perhaps tense: the call to surrender was followed rapidly by a fusillade of shots and the two constables fell dead. The raiding party seized the explosives (needed for making homemade bombs) and disappeared into hiding for the next three months.

Outwardly there was nothing to distinguish this ambush from other acts of terrorism of a pattern with which the authorities had been only too familiar for many years. And indeed, even though this attack was followed by others aimed directly at the RIC and resulting frequently in the capture or destruction of their barracks, the government attitude was that these were crimes of violence, outrages, murders – but not acts of war. There were, doubtless, political reasons why the suppression of this kind of disorder should be treated by the British authorities as an extended and intensified police exercise and not as a war against a republic which had not been recognised and did not officially exist. But on the Irish side it *was* regarded as a war from the very beginning and it was not long before responsible Sinn Féin leaders began first to encourage and then to organise the attacks on the police. As early as 31 January, for example, the official organ of the Volunteers, *An t Oglách*, proclaimed that every Volunteer was entitled to use 'all legitimate methods of warfare against the soldiers and policemen of the English usurper, and to slay them if it is necessary to do so to overcome their resistance'. And in April, just after a magistrate had been killed at Westport and another RIC constable at Limerick, Mr de Valera himself proposed to the Dáil that a policy of social ostracism be carried out against the police force. 'Their history', he said, 'is a continuity of brutal treason against their own people.' 'They must be shown and made feel,' he continued, 'how base are the functions they perform and how vile is the position they occupy.'[16]

In this it must be said there was an element of exaggeration. Of course the RIC were not, as he rightly pointed out, an ordinary body of police. They were armed and they had been used repeatedly in the past to carry out harsh, unpopular and sometimes violent policies. On the other hand, they *were* Irishmen and in many parts of the country had established friendly relations with the people amongst whom they lived. Moreover, although Sinn Féin could hardly be expected to know this, they were by 1919 already in the twilight phase of their existence, which had begun from the moment the Liberals had seriously braced themselves to prepare for Home Rule before the war. The presumption was that once a native government ruled at Dublin Castle the RIC would be disbanded and the prospect was hardly one to encourage efficiency; even more dispiriting, no doubt, had been the growth of private armies between 1912 and 1916 which the authorities seemed to have neither the will nor the capacity to check.[17]

Yet, however weakened they might have been by past events, the RIC stood full in the path of the revolutionaries and must expect to bear the brunt of the coming storm. They were vulnerable on two counts – because theirs was the primary responsibility for maintaining law and order, and because they were the nearest and most accessible source for the arms and ammunition which the Volunteers so desperately needed. It was this latter fact that gave Mr de Valera's denunciation of the police its deadly significance, for what was said in the Dáil could not go unnoticed at Volunteer Headquarters. The evidence is still too scanty for us to be able to define with any exactitude the relations between the civil government set up in 1919 and the military arm, especially when it is remembered that some of the leading members of the military arm belonged to the IRB while others did not. But certain things stand out amid the confusion. One is that when Cathal Brugha, who had been Chief of Staff of the Volunteers, became Minister of Defence he worked to bring the Volunteers under the control of the Dáil and to counteract the influence of the IRB. A second is that as late as April 1919 Mr de Valera himself admitted in the Dáil that the Minister of Defence was 'in close association with the voluntary military forces which are the foundation of the national army' – in other words that no civil control had as yet been established.[18] And a third indisputable point is that in August of that year Cathal Brugha did at last succeed in winning the approval of the Dáil for a resolution imposing on all members of that assembly and of the Volunteers the same oath of allegiance to the state. Each deputy and each Volunteer had to swear to 'support and defend the Irish Republic and the Government of the Irish Republic, which is Dáil Eireann, against all enemies, foreign and domestic . . .'[19] It seems to have been intended at the time to summon a Volunteer Convention to endorse this action, but the danger of mass arrests was too great and in fact, although the Volunteers took the oath as individuals, their organisation never formally ratified the change in status which the oath implied. That change is best summed up by saying that they were now the standing army of the republic, in recognition of which they came to be called the Army of the Irish Republic, more popularly the Irish Republican Army, more popularly still the IRA.[20]

So much is clear enough. What is less clear is how far, in the struggle now about to develop, the IRA evolved its strategy and tactics independently of the civil government and how far the Minister of

Defence really was in control of his military subordinates. We may never know the full truth about this vitally important matter, but we do know that as the guerrilla war unrolled considerable tension developed between Brugha and Michael Collins. Collins was not the Army Chief of Staff (this post was filled by Richard Mulcahy after Brugha moved to Defence) but as Adjutant-General, Director of Organisation and Director of Intelligence he was at the very centre of military planning and, with his immense energy and drive, was undoubtedly the mainspring of the military effort. Even if a recent biographer's suggestion is true – though this seems, on the face of it, unlikely – that 'the most lethal weapon ever carried by Collins was a fountain pen', his coolness in danger, his innumerable hairbreadth escapes, the very richness and diversity of his personality, caught the imagination of his contemporaries and made him into a myth long before the Anglo-Irish war was over.[21] All the evidence suggests that Brugha, and some other republican zealots – for example, Austin Stack – did not take kindly to this myth, and the personal animosity felt by Brugha in particular was later to have very serious consequences. It was not, however, entirely a question of personal jealousy. Just as Collins was himself a very complicated man, so also he occupied a very complicated position. If in a military sense he was subordinate to Brugha, in a civil sense he was his equal, since he sat in the same cabinet as Minister for Finance. And behind his two public roles there remained his secret role as a member (and eventually President) of the Supreme Council of the IRB. And while there was no question whatever of the loyalty of Collins and other IRB men to the régime inaugurated in 1919, their constitution declared that the Supreme Council was 'in fact as well as right the sole government of the Irish Republic until Ireland secures absolute national independence and a permanent republican government is established'. To those who were suspicious of the IRB – and to ex-IRB men like Brugha in particular – this polity within a polity must always have been a source of uneasiness and if, as has recently been suggested, Collins had expressed doubts (on military grounds) about bringing the army so directly under the Dáil, one can see how this uneasiness might have been increased.[22]

(iii)

It is time now to turn to the conduct of the war itself. Broadly speaking, the hostilities fell into three phases. During the first of these, which occupied virtually the whole of 1919 and the early months of 1920, the pattern of events emerged only very slowly and incidents, though numerous, were mostly on a small scale. The second phase, filling the latter part of 1920, saw the British counter-measures taking shape and terror and counter-terror reaching a crescendo with the fearful blows struck by both sides in November and December. The final phase occupied the first six months of 1921 and although over-shadowed by the long-awaited truce in July of that year, it witnessed the systematic exploitation by the Irish flying columns of the tactics of ambush, the development of guerrilla war à l'outrance. The massive retaliation which this would have involved (perhaps on the lines of the scorched earth and concentration camp policies of the Boer War) was still being meditated by the British government when peace came.[23]

The first phase of the war was in essence a struggle between the IRA and the police. The latter were handicapped because their uniforms made them conspicuous (whereas their opponents frequently wore no uniforms at all), because their barracks were often isolated, and because there was a long tradition in the countryside that the police were the natural enemies of the people. In addition, they were by 1919 somewhat under strength and although individual men and units often fought bravely against heavy odds the force as a whole, for reasons stated earlier, was psychologically on the defensive even before the fighting began. Faced with nearly 1,500 barracks and huts to defend they could dispose of from 9,500 to about 9,700 men who, in addition to preserving law and order over the whole of Ireland outside Dublin, had also to attend to a multiplicity of ordinary police duties. In some of the three or four-man stations, as their own journal querulously pointed out in September 1919, these duties could not have been properly discharged even if all the men had been kept continu-ously awake.[24]

Actual losses in the latter part of 1919 were not unduly heavy. Eighteen RIC men were killed between 1 May and the end of the year and although a number of the smaller barracks in the south and west had become so vulnerable to attack that they had to be evacuated there is no serious evidence of any widespread panic among the police. There were, of course, some resignations, but not as many as has some-times been suggested, mainly, it would seem, because of a pay rise that year and an official inquiry into conditions which, it was hoped, would lead to improvements. The real difficulty at that early stage in the struggle was not so much retirement as recruitment. This, perhaps, was where Mr de Valera's policy of ostracism was most effective, though no doubt the fact that by then the force offered little prospect of a permanent career was an added disincentive. Yet events in that winter of 1919-20 indicated that recruitment there would have to be if the situation in Ireland was ever to be brought under control. The IRA attacks – upon troops as well as police – became steadily more frequent and more daring. In December 1919 they had even become so confident that they attempted the assassination of the Viceroy, Lord French himself, on the outskirts of Dublin. The attack failed, but it had been a near thing and there were soon to be other incidents. Michael Collins had already formed his group of agents – the Squad as it was called – dedicated to the cold-blooded elimination of the G-men, the detectives of the Dublin Metropolitan Police whose knowledge of the IRA personnel was uncomfortably accurate and whose information led to frequent arrest of Sinn Féiners. By the end of 1919 most of the G-men had been stalked through the streets and systematically shot down and the Squad was believed to have co-operated with the Tipperary Brigade in the attempt on Lord French's life.

Not indeed that Lords Lieutenant or detectives were the only ones in danger of assassination. In March 1920 occurred two incidents which shocked opinion not only in Ireland but in England and abroad. One was the murder of Tomás MacCurtain, Lord Mayor of Cork and Commandant of the Cork No. 1 Brigade of the IRA. He was killed in his own house by a gang of masked raiders and there was enough circumstantial evidence that the raiders had been the police themselves for a jury to bring in a verdict of murder against the British government and its local agents, the Lord Lieutenant, District Inspector Swanzy, and other members of the RIC. The case was by no means completely proven – Lord French stoutly maintained that MacCurtain had been killed by Irish extremists because he was too moderate – but the general impression left on most people's minds was that the Lord Mayor of Cork had been the victim of a deliberate police reprisal. This was certainly Collins's view and he had no hesitation in ordering Swanzy's execution, which was duly carried out a few months later, even though that officer had been moved to the north of Ireland for his own protection. The other incident, which occurred a few days later, took place in Dublin in broad daylight. A Dublin Castle official, an elderly magistrate named Alan Bell, had been assigned the duty of uncovering Sinn Féin funds lodged in various banks under different names. He had been altogether too successful in this task and it was decided to put an end to his activities. Accordingly, he was taken out of a crowded tram by half a dozen young gunmen and shot dead by the roadside.

It is against this background of blow and counter-blow pushing Ireland nearer and nearer to a reign of terror that Lloyd George's policy must be judged. Essentially his reaction to the situation was much what the reactions of most British statesmen to Irish violence had been since the days of Gladstone – to combine redress with coercion. Redress took the form of a Government of Ireland Bill, designed to carry into effect the partition of the country which had been implicit in so much of the debate about Home Rule since 1914. This measure, which passed into law during 1920, was virtually ignored by Sinn Féin, but it did nevertheless effect a profound change in Irish politics, the consequences of which are still working themselves out to this day. Briefly, it proposed to set up two Home Rule parliaments in Ireland, one for the six north-eastern counties and one for the remainder of the country. The powers to be remitted to these local parliaments were not very extensive and the important control of finance still remained with the imperial parliament at Westminster.* Much was made at the time of an ingenious device included in the Bill whereby a bridge between the two parts of the country would be provided by a Council of Ireland representative of the two parliaments; it was to be given certain modest powers of its own and these, it was hoped, might be increased with the consent of north and south. The Bill also envisaged that partition should end, and a single parliament take over responsibility for the whole country, whenever the two regional parliaments should vote that this be done.

Totally divorced as it was from the realities of political life in Ireland, Lloyd George's offer had no effect whatever on the deadly struggle then moving towards its climax in the south. In northeast Ulster on the other hand it was accepted, albeit grudgingly, as the form of government which would least disturb the connection with Britain. That the settlement should apply to six counties rather than to the nine of the historic province was seen by Ulster Unionists – with that cold realism they managed to combine at critical moments with fanatical passion – as the only effective way of maintaining a permanent dominance over the Catholic and nationalist minority which, whatever the geography of partition, was bound to remain large. How difficult it would be to govern that minority, let alone assimilate it, was demonstrated by the serious religio-political riots which occurred in Londonderry, Belfast and elsewhere that summer while the Bill was still on its way through parliament. To some extent provoked by IRA attacks on the police and on Protestant workmen, the temper of Ulster Orangemen was whipped to a frenzy by the re-organisation of the Ulster Volunteers and Sir Edward Carson's promise to use them for the protection of the province against Sinn Féin. There followed an ugly and protracted campaign of terrorism in which many Catholic families were driven from their homes, 62 people being killed and 200 wounded. Long before the Government of Ireland Act came into force the following year there had thus been established the sad and bitter pattern which from the beginning was to dominate the life of the new state.

But northern riots – grim though they were – were only a fraction of the problem facing the government. The main enemy was still the republican regime in the south and its military arm, the IRA. The methods adopted to deal with them were rigorous coercion and the strengthening of the government forces, especially the police. Coercion was directed towards the suppression of organisations declared to be illegal, the imprisonment of men and women convicted, or even suspected, of political 'crimes', and the stamping out of all revolutionary propaganda. None of these aims was achieved. The illegal organisations, from the Dáil downwards, simply went underground; some of them, like the Sinn Féin courts, did not find it necessary

* For what this involved in practice see Part IV B, chap 1.

to do even that. Again, though hundreds of arrests were made, and some of the leading revolutionaries seized, there were always others ready to step into the gap and the continuity of republican government was never really broken. Nor was the censorship, rigorous as it was, able to prevent the dissemination of republican propaganda. The cyclostyled newsheet, the *Irish Bulletin*, though produced at great danger and often in almost impossibly difficult circumstances, proved virtually irrepressible and copies of it, sent regularly to English newspapers and to MPs and other public figures, did much to create a sympathetic public opinion for the Irish cause. But this, it is fair to add, would probably have been created anyway by the reports sent back by visiting English journalists, especially those from the Liberal press – the *Daily News*, the *Manchester Guardian* and the *Westminster Gazette*, supported by *The Times* which, under a great editor, Wickham Steed, worked hard and consistently for reconciliation between the two countries. No doubt these were counter-balanced to some extent by the cries for blood and vengeance resounding from the right – notably *The Spectator*, the *Morning Post* and the *National Review* – but, as we shall see presently, English horror at what was happening in Ireland was to be a major factor in eventually bringing the struggle to an end.[25]

Nothing contrived to bring this horror home to decent people in England more than the behaviour of the recruits enlisted at the beginning of 1920 as a reinforcement for the RIC. The first of these, who began to arrive in Ireland in the early spring, were at once nicknamed the Black and Tans. The name, deriving originally from a famous hunt in the south of Ireland, was bestowed on them as a witticism because a shortage of equipment obliged them to wear khaki uniform with the black-green caps and belts of the police, but it soon became a synonym for terror. Yet they were not, as the contemporary legend had it, the sweepings of English jails, sadists and perverts let loose upon an innocent countryside. Their admission to the force, at least in the early months of recruitment, was governed by the strict rules the RIC had always applied to the selection of candidates, though as numbers rose fast in the winter of 1920-21, it is hard not to believe that the rules were relaxed to some extent, and that some individuals with criminal tendencies did not slip through the net. But the Black and Tans were for the most part young men who found it hard to settle down after the war, who had become used to a career of adventure and bloodshed, and who were prepared to try their luck in a new sphere for ten shillings a day and all found. They were the same type, and produced by much the same circumstances, as the Congo mercenaries of our own day. Their ruthlessness and contempt for life and property stemmed partly from the brutalisation inseparable from four years of trench warfare, but partly also from the continual and intense strain imposed upon them by service in Ireland. They were vulnerable to every kind of sudden attack by bomb or rifle-fire and since their opponents seldom wore uniform and could vanish into the empty countryside, or into the crowded streets of the cities, it is not surprising that the 'Tans' should before long have come to regard the whole population as hostile, which, certainly, once it had experience of the methods of the new police, it very soon became.

A similar judgment may be made upon a second group of specially recruited men who began to appear in Ireland during the summer of 1920. This was the so-called Auxiliary Division of the RIC, more familiarly known as 'the Auxies'. For the most part they were ex-officers who received a pound a day and had their own dark-blue uniform with Glengarry caps. Contemporary opinions of them are interestingly divergent, but in action they seem to have been every bit as tough and uninhibited as the Black and Tans, if not more so; indeed, their own commanding officer, Brigadier-General E. F. Crozier, eventually resigned his post rather than go on leading what he described as a drunken and insubordinate body of men.[26]

These special forces were augmented by additions to the troops already stationed in Ireland until by the time the truce came in July 1921 the military effort being deployed was quite formidable. There were then about 1,400 Auxiliaries and although the Black and Tans had originally been intended merely to fill up the vacancies in the ranks of the regular RIC – numbering approximately 1,500 at the beginning of 1920 – the worsening situation led to more and more of them being taken on. Altogether, it has been reckoned that between 1 January 1920 and the end of August 1922 (when the RIC was formerly disbanded) 12,000 men enrolled, of whom perhaps 7,000 were taken into service, many of these being replacements for men of the regular RIC who, from the summer of 1920 onwards, had begun to resign in large numbers. Estimates of the combined forces of police and troops vary. The Irish figure of 15,000 police and 50,000 soldiers is probably too high and the computation of General Sir Neville Macready (appointed Commander-in-Chief in Ireland in 1920) that the combined total was 40,000 is likely to be nearer the mark.* Against this the IRA could muster forces which, though theoretically large, were in practice limited by the shortage of arms and ammunition and also by the fact that their tactics were to use small bodies of men and avoid general engagements. Thus, though the full strength of the IRA may have been as much as 15,000, the most that were on active service at one time was probably about 5,000. Michael Collins, who was in a better position to know than most, put the 'working' force

* Contemporary estimates – even official ones – of the number of police involved do not usually distinguish between regular RIC and Black and Tans. The RIC totals for 1920 and 1921 were 11,056 and 14,174 respectively; it has been suggested that the Auxiliaries may have numbered about 770 in October 1920; by January 1922, they were 1,418. For this information I am deeply indebted to Colonel Dan Bryan and Mr Richard Hawkins.

of the IRA much lower – at about 3,000.[27]

Yet the struggle was not so one-sided as these figures might seem to indicate. The IRA, concealed among a population which was either friendly or too frightened to appear unfriendly, had the advantage of surprise and cover. The war which now developed, therefore, took on a pattern that was soon to become drearily familiar. It was not, it must be stressed, a total war affecting the whole country; on the contrary, in many areas life went on as usual, but in the cities of Dublin, Cork and Limerick, and throughout the counties of the south and west, violence was always liable to flare up and to be met by counter-violence. The police remained, as before, the chief target of the IRA and, in the year 1920, 176 were killed and 251 wounded; the military, who were rather more difficult to surprise, suffered smaller losses, but even so, 54 soldiers were killed and 118 were wounded during the same months. Irish losses during the worst part of that year amounted to only 43 killed, but casualties among the IRA and civilians became heavier as the war went on, and for the whole period between 1 January 1919 and the truce in July 1921 are calculated to have been 752 killed (IRA and civilians) and 866 wounded.[28]

How best to meet these sudden onslaughts, when the attackers appeared out of nowhere and disappeared just as quickly, was the central problem confronting the Irish administration during that year. It was a problem that was never to be solved, but during 1920 two different solutions – one official, the other highly unofficial – were attempted. The official answer was the Restoration of Order in Ireland Act, which in the second half of 1920 gave wide and exceptional power to the military commander. General Macready would have preferred a simple regime of martial law for the whole country, but this was not acceptable to the cabinet. Instead, he was given authority to arrest and imprison without trial anyone suspected of Sinn Féin associations, to try prisoners by court-martial and to institute military inquiries into violent deaths rather than coroners' inquests. The seizure of suspects under this law was, of course, one of the primary duties of the Black and Tans and the Auxiliaries. Much of the work was done at night and the cities, Dublin especially, learned to dread the sight of their Crossley tenders – a motor chassis fitted with the body of a lorry and capable of holding eight or ten fully armed men – roaring through the night with their headlights blazing, to stop in front of a house where wanted men were believed to be hiding. Then would come a thunderous knocking on the door and a room by room search of the inhabitants. Anyone whose credentials were dubious would be whisked away in the lorry and could disappear, perhaps, for months. The other solution was even more brutal. It was to answer terrorism by reprisal. There was much debate at the time about the difference between 'unauthorised' and 'authorised' reprisals and the cabinet at one stage went so far as to consider a memorandum from Churchill as to the possibility of using the latter in direct retaliation for individual attacks by the IRA.[29] This was felt to be inopportune, but it is doubt-ful if the victims of such attacks – their houses burned down or looted and members of their families sometimes shot in front of their very eyes – would have been much impressed by these metaphysical dis-tinctions.* For, as the year 1920 wore on, it was becoming harder and harder to contain the violence of the new police. At Tuam in county Galway, and at Newport and Templemore in county Tipperary, shoot-ing incidents were followed by wholesale destruction of property, including the burning of creameries; the attack on the creameries, large numbers of which were eventually to be destroyed, was an ironic comment on the futility of the whole struggle, since they were the fruit of one of the few constructive policies that had had a chance to take root in Ireland before 1914.

These outbreaks were followed by others later in the year when the town of Balbriggan was terrorised and partly destroyed by a band of drunken Black and Tans – after the death of an RIC officer from fearful wounds caused by expanding bullets had inflamed his men – and by other similar attacks in county Clare and in county Meath. The fact that the first action of these raiding parties was usually to loot the public-houses added to the chorus of disapproval now rising from liberal circles in England, but it is at least possible that for some of these men the excitement of drink was the only way they could nerve themselves for what they were about to do, just as afterwards the oblivion of drink may have been the only way they could live with what they had done.

Yet the attacks by the IRA continued, despite the growing fury of the reprisals. Even in Dublin itself a party of British soldiers was shot down by Volunteers in plain clothes. One of the latter, an eighteen-year-old student, Kevin Barry, was captured in this affray and after court-martial was sentenced to death by hanging. His case aroused deep emotion in Ireland and a widely-backed appeal for mercy, but the sentence was nevertheless carried out. This execution, coming only a week after the death in prison of Terence MacSwiney (who had succeeded MacCurtain as Lord Mayor of Cork and had been arrested the previous August), following a hunger-strike lasting no

* 'Official' reprisals – mainly the destruction of houses belonging to people known or suspected to be implicated in Sinn Féin activities – were in fact sanctioned by General Macready in martial law areas, but since the IRA retaliated in kind against government sympathisers – sometimes burning two loyalist houses for every Sinn Féin home destroyed – the policy was not pressed home very forcibly. As late as June 1921 the military were still demanding the right of 'authorised', i.e. official, reprisal, though the Commander-in-Chief, General Sir Neville Macready, had admitted that the Sinn Féin counter-reprisals were effective. The Cabinet's dis-cussion of the matter was somewhat inconclusive, but it did indicate a desire on the part of the Chief Secretary to bring General Macready under tighter control. (Thomas Jones, *Whitehall Diary: Vol iii. Ireland 1918-1925*, ed. K. Middlemass (London, 1971), pp. 72-3.)

less than seventy-four days, set the stage for the terrible events of November 1920, by any reckoning the worst month in the entire Anglo-Irish war. The climax was reached on 'Bloody Sunday', 21 November, when the IRA, with the knowledge and approval of the Minister of Defence, Cathal Brugha, planned and carried out a simultaneous attack against Englishmen living in various parts of Dublin who, though apparently ordinary civilians, were believed to be intelligence agents of the British Army. The killings were organised by Collins and two officers of the Dublin Brigade of the IRA and though the officers – Peadar Clancy and Dick McKee – were themselves arrested on the night before the blow was to be struck the operation went ahead as directed. On Sunday morning, therefore, armed men broke into the houses and hotels where the men were staying and shot eleven of them, some in front of their wives. Four officers were wounded and two Auxiliaries who had attempted to intervene were killed, as was another officer who was shot by mistake. How many of those eliminated in this cold-blooded manner were really intelligence agents it is not possible to say with certainty, but Collins's own intelligence system – which had its representatives at the Castle and among the DMP detectives – was extremely acute and it is unlikely that he had been misinformed. 'I found out', he told General Crozier after the truce, 'that those fellows we put on the spot were going to put a lot of us on the spot, so I got in first'.

This multiple shooting spread a wave of horror through both England and Ireland, but the horror was redoubled by the revenge the Black and Tans took that same afternoon when they invaded the sports ground of Croke Park where a Gaelic football match was being played and fired indiscriminately on the players and the crowd; twelve people died and sixty were wounded. And, as if this were not more than enough, that same day McKee and Clancy, though their complicity in the attacks on the intelligence officers was not then known to their captors, were shot while attempting to escape from Dublin Castle. The phrase has an ugly ring about it, and at the time was frequently enough used as a euphemism for murder, but in this instance, it may well have been strictly applicable, since the two men had nothing but execution to look forward to if they remained in custody. Nevertheless, as so often before, it was the *fact* of the shooting and not the *motive* which burnt deep into the popular mind.[30]

Even with this blood-letting November had still not closed its account of death and terror. At the very end of the month there occurred an event which was significant not just because it provoked one of the most savage reprisals of the war, but because it provided perhaps the first major illustration of what were increasingly to be the Irish tactics as the struggle entered its third and final phase. At Kilmichael, near Macroom Castle in county Cork, Tom Barry – Commandant of the Cork No. 3 Brigade of the IRA and beyond question one of the most ruthless and successful of all the guerrilla leaders

– placed his flying column of less than forty men in ambush to await the return to their barracks of two lorry-loads of Auxiliaries. The lorries were slowed down by a ruse and as the police climbed down from them they came under heavy fire; only one man survived and he had been left for dead. Almost at once – on 10 December – martial law was proclaimed in Cork and the neighbouring counties. The very next day another ambush only a few miles from Cork City caused more Auxiliary casualties and that night Auxiliaries and Black and Tans poured into the town, looting, wrecking, drinking and burning – burning to such effect, indeed, that a large part of the centre of the city was completely destroyed, while the fire brigade were deliberately obstructed as they sought to bring the flames under control. In the House of Commons the Chief Secretary – at this time Sir Hamar Greenwood, a Canadian believed by the government to have the qualities necessary to rule Ireland with an iron hand – protested that Cork had been burnt by its own citizens, but a private military inquiry was so damaging that the cabinet decided that 'the effect of publishing the report if Parliament was sitting would be disastrous to the government's whole policy in Ireland'.[31] Meanwhile, the Auxiliaries made their own comment on the affair when they swaggered about the streets of Dublin with burnt corks in their caps.

Although there were no more catastrophes quite as bad as this, it would be wrong to say that the worst was over by the end of 1920. On the contrary, the next six months witnessed some of the most intensive fighting and some of the most savage incidents of the whole struggle. The depredations of IRA flying columns and the use of ambushes if anything increased, as did also the shooting of frequently unarmed individuals who for one reason or other had become pawns in the game. Both sides used essentially the same tactics and the difference between them seemed only semantic – though in reality it went much deeper. To the Irish every incident that occurred – even the massacre of a harmless tennis party in Galway or the shooting of a seventy-year-old lady, Mrs Lindsay of county Cork, who had warned the British forces of an impending ambush – was an act of war which violent and desperate men sought to justify by the simple proposition that they were fighting for the freedom of the country as a republic entirely independent of England. From this point of view the very fact that the flying columns were now engaging in larger-scale operations and tying down great numbers of troops, still more the success, if success it can be called, of the carefully planned operation to burn down the Customs House in the heart of Dublin (May 1921) were taken as additional evidence that what was in progress was, in sober truth, a war. To their critics and opponents – who included some of their fellow nationalists, among them more than one bishop – their so-called guerrilla campaign was no war at all. It was simply a series of murderous attacks, cowardly, brutalising and productive only of a vicious circle of savagery.

Yet there was an important sense in which the conflict was less terrible than it had been the previous year. It was less terrible because at last there was a gleam of hope that the fighting might be brought to an end by a negotiated truce. It was no accident that the re-entry of the political factor into the situation coincided with de Valera's return to Ireland. After setting up his government in the spring of 1919 he had left for America in June and had remained away for the next eighteen months, his place as head of the government being taken first by Arthur Griffith and then, after Griffith's arrest in November 1920, by Michael Collins. The President of the Dáil (or President of the Republic as he was usually called in the States and did not deny the soft impeachment) had four main objectives in visiting America – to gain sympathy for the Irish cause, to commit one, or preferably both, of the political parties to self-determination for Ireland; to secure governmental recognition of the republic, and to raise money for the prosecution of the war effort at home. In the first and last of these objectives he brilliantly succeeded, though the second and third proved to be beyond him. Amongst the rank and file of Irish-Americans he had an astonishing success and was rapturously received at meeting after meeting up and down the country. This rapture, admittedly, was not shared by the 'professional' Irish-Americans, Devoy and Judge Cohalan, the dominant figures in the Friends of Irish Freedom.* That organisation, after the fashion of Irish organisations whether in America or Ireland, was already deeply divided before de Valera arrived, both on the theoretical question of whether it should endorse an Irish republic, or simply Irish self-determination, and on the more practical issue of whether the 'Victory Fund' then being raised in aid of the Irish cause should be sent to Ireland or retained for use in America for forwarding causes – such as opposition to the League of Nations – which might, indeed, be linked with Ireland's destiny but looked suspiciously like a further round of Judge Cohalan's feud with President Wilson.

For de Valera these internal dissensions were a distraction from the main purposes of his visit, but he could not avoid them entirely, and gradually he became drawn into bitter and undignified disputes with both Devoy and Cohalan. This was partly due to his own ignorance of the American scene and even more perhaps to his evident immaturity when called upon to play a part in what was after all a much wider theatre than any he had yet known. Partly also, however, it was due to a clash of personalities. Both Cohalan and Devoy had been so long dominant in Irish-American affairs that they were not prepared

* For this organisation, see pp. 403-4 above.

to yield authority even to the 'President of the Irish Republic' if he sought to intervene in what they regarded as their own preserve. It was a collision of two stiff-necked, strong-minded individuals with another stiff-necked, strong-minded individual, and it is not surprising that deadlock resulted. But behind these personal rivalries and dissensions was a deep difference of policy. For Devoy, and more especially for Cohalan, the great fact of the future, as they believed, was that sooner or later Anglo-American trade rivalry would provoke a war between the two countries. Welcoming this prospect, Cohalan saw the League of Nations as a hindrance to America's freedom of manoeuvre and part of an insidious design to entangle the United States in the web of European, more specifically British, diplomacy. President de Valera, on the other hand, had no objection to the League of Nations, provided Ireland was a member; and he saw no reason to look forward to perpetual discord with England. On the contrary, while he was still in America he gave an interview (February 1920) to the *Westminster Gazette* in which he suggested that an independent Ireland would be prepared to offer Britain guarantees against foreign attacks based on the republic analogous to those the United States had obtained from Cuba. The Cubans, sheltering under the umbrella of the Monroe Doctrine, had undertaken not to let themselves be used by foreign powers against the United States. 'Why,' asked de Valera, 'doesn't Britain make a stipulation like this to guard herself against foreign attack . . . Why doesn't Britain declare a Monroe Doctrine for the two neighbouring islands? The people of Ireland so far from objecting would co-operate with their whole soul.'[32]

To his American opponents this suggestion seemed to indicate that the President was beginning to back away from his republic and recriminations became more bitter than ever. In reality, it indicated nothing of the kind – he had been careful at the time, and continued so afterwards, to emphasise that what was in question was British security *after* Irish independence, not Irish independence itself. Nevertheless, in a quite different direction this interview has a historic significance of its own, for in it may be discerned the germ of the doctrine of external association of which so much was to be heard during the next thirty years. Unhappily this was by no means the only occasion of friction. President de Valera's probably misguided decision to attend the National Conventions of both the Republican and Democratic parties was a direct involvement in internal American politics which aroused the anger of others besides Devoy and Cohalan. He failed signally to get either party to include Irish independence in its election programme and at the Republican Convention had the humiliation of seeing a milder resolution by Judge Cohalan preferred to his. Nor did he meet with any more success in approaching Cohalan's old enemy, President Wilson. Wilson, indeed, was past help himself. Stricken by paralysis during the election campaign, he was in no position to deal with de Valera's plea for recognition when it reached the White House in October 1920. Even had he been in full health he could scarcely have made a favourable reply; as things were, no reply was given at all.

If de Valera's critics attacked him for political maladroitness he himself had legitimate grounds for complaint in the way in which Irish-American financial contributions to the Irish cause had hitherto been handled. Up to the end of 1920 the Irish Victory Fund had produced nearly a million dollars, of which about three-quarters had been retained in the United States to be used in the campaign against the League of Nations. But during that same year the President launched his own campaign to sell Irish bonds to a public which seemed to have an inexhaustible appetite for them. The Victory Fund was closed down and money poured into de Valera's bond-drive. Five million dollars was raised in this way, of which four million was actually spent in Ireland. Without this money it would have been impossible to continue the war in Ireland for so long, and even with it there were signs of shortage when the truce was signed in mid-1921.[33]

The determining factor in the timing of de Valera's return to Ireland (which he reached at Christmas 1920) was probably the arrest of Arthur Griffith the previous month, though, as the President told the Dáil when he addressed it for the first time after resuming his position as head of the government, he was also influenced by the length and severity of the Anglo-Irish war. So impressed was he by the bitterness and harshness of the struggle that on this occasion he alarmed some of those present by suggesting that the Irish forces were not strong enough to push an aggressive warfare to the point of decision and that, to ease the burden on the people, this might necessitate 'a lightening off' of attacks against the enemy.[34]

But there was another and more substantial reason for looking at the war with fresh eyes. Even before the President had left America there had been signs – faint and wavering, but unmistakable – that a truce might be on the way. In England the pressures against the war and all the savagery it brought in its train were mounting. Leading politicians of different parties, eminent churchmen, newspapers of various complexions, the influential Labour party commission of inquiry which was active in Ireland in the autumn of 1920 – all these combined in condemning the methods that were being used by the forces of the Crown and which, so far from crushing Irish resistance, served only to blacken Britain's name in the eyes of the world. Accordingly, Lloyd George, though in October he was still speaking of the IRA as 'the small body of assassins, a real murder gang', and in November was proclaiming publicly that 'he had murder by the throat', was simultaneously allowing tentative inquiries about a truce to go forward. Early in December (only a fortnight after Bloody Sunday) the most substantial of these efforts took shape when the Roman Catholic Archbishop of Perth, Dr P. J. Clune – whose nephew, incidentally had been killed in Dublin Castle at the same time as McKee and Clancy – was dispatched to Dublin to sound out the Irish leaders, seeing first Collins and then (in Mountjoy jail) Griffith and Eoin MacNeill.[35]

But the truce negotiations thus initiated soon broke down. The main reason appears to have been that Lloyd George – who had both vengeful soldiers and die-hard Unionist politicians to consider – insisted that the Irish must give up their arms before peace could be seriously considered. This, of course, they absolutely refused to do. On the Irish side, when these discussions were subsequently debated in the Dáil, considerable stress was also laid on the fact that independent initiatives by Father Michael O'Flanagan (a 'political' priest who was a Vice-President of Sinn Féin but in no sense a representative figure) and by a few Galway county councillors, had helped to harden the British government's resolve to see the war through to the bitter end.[36] And indeed, as we have seen, martial law was at once proclaimed in large areas of the south and west and the struggle entered on an even more intensive phase.

Yet the very fact that talks had begun at all made it easier to take up the threads again when opportunity served. The return of President de Valera to the scene, uninvolved as he had been in the prosecution of the war and therefore, perhaps, capable of some degree of detachment, seemed to Lloyd George to present just the opportunity that was needed. Thus, when the President was arrested, almost by accident, on 22 June, this embarrassing mistake was hastily rectified the next morning, and British officials – notably Alfred Cope, the Assistant Under-Secretary at Dublin Castle – were encouraged to persist in their efforts to make contact with the republican leaders all through the early months of 1921. At one time, indeed, so many balls were simultaneously in the air that de Valera had to insist firmly that the only valid negotiations would be negotiations conducted through him. But when he did enter into discussions – first with Lord Derby in April and then with Sir James Craig (who was about to become Prime Minister of Northern Ireland) – the results seemed entirely negative.

Nevertheless, that an attempt should have been made to bring the leaders of north and south together was a significant pointer to how urgent the necessity for a settlement was becoming. For in the same month of May that saw the strange confrontation between de Valera and Craig, the general elections to the two Irish parliaments called for by the Government of Ireland Act were due to be held and the partition of the island would then be an accomplished fact. If the two men could have found any sort of common ground this would have been an indication, however meagre, that the Act might yet work as intended, and the two parts of the country co-operate with each other through the Council of Ireland – that product of British ingenuity so cherished in conception, but ultimately so barren in result. But of course there was no common ground. Each man held resolutely to his own view of the Irish past and the Irish future; in fact, so far from the situation having been improved by the meeting, the republicans continued, and, if anything intensified, the boycott against goods from Belfast which they had initiated the previous August in reprisal for the anti-Catholic riots of that summer.

The elections duly took place and produced an entirely predictable situation. In the six counties of Northern Ireland Sir James Craig and his Unionists were firmly entrenched with forty out of fifty-two seats. In the rest of the country the election machinery was used by the republican government not to create a parliament of southern Ireland but simply as a means of choosing a new Dáil. This assembly, strictly the second Dáil Eireann, was much larger than the first, for the Government of Ireland Act had provided for 128 Irish seats together with thirty-three allotted to the south in the imperial parliament. Seats in the imperial parliament were, of course, an irrelevance, but the outcome of the election in the Irish constituencies was a clean sweep for the republican candidates, many of whom were IRA officers. In every single constituency – except for the University of Dublin which elected four members, ostensibly non-party but in fact Unionist – the republican or Sinn Féin candidates were returned *unopposed*. Such unanimity was in itself suspicious and one can hardly doubt that while there was much genuine support there was also a degree of intimidation. The new Dáil, however, though much bigger than the old, closely resembled its predecessor in composition. It is true that the proportion of members non-resident in their constituencies fell from forty-six to twenty-five per cent, but in other respects the two bodies were very alike. The second Dáil had an even higher proportion of young men than the very young first Dáil, but in terms of education, occupation and social origin there was little essential difference, though it is perhaps worth noting (in the light of the bitterness of subsequent debate) that whereas the first Dáil contained only two relatives of those who had died for the cause in 1916 or afterwards, the second Dáil had seven, of whom four were women. In general, the assembly remained predominantly urban and composed mainly of the lower groups within the middle class. Farmers were still under-represented with ten per cent of the total, and organised labour, by its self-denying ordinance not to contest the elections, had with the best intentions helped to perpetuate a situation where there was still no formal or effective parliamentary opposition.[37]

But from a British point of view the real problem presented by the new 'parliament' was its political, not its social composition. Clearly it was as intransigently republican as ever, but if on the appointed day for its opening (28 June) less than half the members attended – and, given their republicanism, this was certain to happen – then the Government of Ireland Act laid down that the parliament would be dissolved and southern Ireland would have to be ruled as a crown colony. In effect this would mean additional coercion and plans were actually made to extend the area of martial law from 12 July. It was a grim prospect, bristling with every kind of difficulty. Public opinion was sure to be outraged, so also would be the Dominion Prime Ministers due shortly to assemble for a Colonial Conference, while at a more practical level the government recoiled from military estimates that if the Irish resistance was to be seriously tackled then 80,000, perhaps even 100,000, troops would be needed. It was not surprising, therefore, that efforts to achieve a truce should have been redoubled, and that Lloyd George and at least some of his colleagues should at last have begun to realise that what they had been fighting was not just a murder-gang, but a formidable movement. The aim for which that movement fought, an independent Irish republic, was still as unacceptable to British eyes as ever, but there had been signs as early as the previous April that the Prime Minister had been groping towards the idea that a solution modelled on, or analogous to, dominion status might be the way out. On the other hand, Irish stubbornness for the republic was matched by the Unionist determination to crush rebellion before negotiating and it would require all his adroitness to walk the tightrope between these two extremes.

Yet in the end, after all the secret and semi-secret discussions, the truce came quite suddenly and openly. The catalyst that set everything free to move has generally been regarded as the famous speech which George v made in Belfast on 22 June in which he used these words:

> I speak from a full heart when I pray that my coming to Ireland today may prove to be the first step towards an end of strife amongst her peoples, whatever their race or creed. In that hope I appeal to all Irishmen to pause, to stretch out the hand of forbearance and conciliation, to forgive and forget and to join in making for the land which they love a new era of peace, contentment and goodwill.[38]

Even though, as is well known, General Smuts (who had, incidentally, been kept carefully informed of events by the Irish republican leaders even before he left South Africa, and had visited Dublin earlier that month) took a large share in the drafting of the King's speech, George v's evident emotion and long-expressed desire to have done with terrorism in Ireland had a notable effect in England and helped to give Lloyd George the impetus he needed. Mr A. J. P. Taylor, a historian not prone to sentiment, even goes so far as to suggest that this initiative of the King's 'was by far the greatest service performed by a British monarch in modern times'.[39] This may well be true in the English context, for it was followed immediately by an offer from Lloyd George to de Valera of a tripartite conference between the British government and representatives of northern and southern Ireland. But Dáil Eireann and the ministry responsible to it were unlikely to have been much influenced by a royal declaration delivered in Belfast, of all places, and, of all occasions, at the opening of a parliament which seemed to set the seal on the partition of their country. For them two other factors were surely more significant. One was that Lloyd George's overture, shorn of previous conditions demanding the surrender of arms or barring certain individuals from the conference table, did seem to indicate a real desire to make peace and had therefore to be taken more seriously than before. And the other was that a breathing-space in the long war of attrition was badly needed. The IRA, though still full of fight, was facing critical shortages of men and materials. The burning of the Customs House, for example, had cost five killed and eighty prisoners and even if this dire blow to the beauty of the city could be classed as a victory, the republic could not afford many more of the same kind. Weapons were even scarcer than men and, since the guerrillas had necessarily to rely on rifles, machine-guns and home-made bombs, they were unable, as General Mulcahy was to point out later, to drive the British forces from anything more substantial than a police-barracks. Collins himself, it has been said, remarked to the Chief Secretary afterwards, that the Irish resistance could not have lasted more than another three weeks. 'When we were told of the offer of a truce we were astounded. We thought you must have gone mad.'[40]

Both sides were thus being pushed towards negotiation, though the highly complex manoeuvres de Valera found it necessary to go through before the parties could sit down at the same table were an ominous presage of what was to come. At length, after the President had established that there must be an actual truce *before* he went to London, and that when he did go he must negotiate with Lloyd George without the necessity of having Sir James Craig present at their discussions, the long-awaited truce came into operation at noon on 11 July 1921. De Valera arrived in London on the following day, accompanied by Griffith, Robert Barton, Austin Stack and Erskine Childers, and met Lloyd George four times in the next ten days. The Irish leader also met Sir James Craig who gave him a piece of advice he might have done well to heed. 'Are you going to see Lloyd George alone?' the Unionist asked him. 'Yes', replied de Valera. 'Are you mad?' said Craig. 'Take a witness. Lloyd George will give any account of the interview that comes into his mind or that suits him.'[41] Nevertheless, the meetings were *tête à tête*, de Valera reporting on them afterwards to his colleagues.

The essence of what Lloyd George had to offer was dominion status but this, though much more than had ever been offered before, was seriously diminished by several vital qualifications – a limitation on the size of the Irish Army, the continuance of voluntary recruiting in Ireland for the British forces, the granting of air and naval facilities to Britain, the payment by Ireland of a contribution to the British war debt, above all the stipulation that any settlement reached 'must allow for full recognition of the existing powers and privileges of the parliament of Northern Ireland, which cannot be abrogated except by their own consent'. President de Valera's instinct was to reject all this, which fell so far short of the republican demand and virtually perpetuated partition into the bargain, without even going through the formality of taking it home to be considered by the Dáil. But Lloyd George warned him that the alternative would be a resumption of war and the Irish leader in the end agreed to submit the terms to his own cabinet.

As was to be expected that cabinet reacted much as he had done – the first impulse of members was to turn them down flat. But it was agreed to submit them to the second Dáil. This body, composed of all the members elected to the 'Southern Ireland Parliament' the previous May except the four members for Dublin University, had not yet had an opportunity of meeting since many of those chosen had been in prison. With the coming of the truce the prisons were opened and the assembly could begin to function above ground and at full strength. At its first sessions in August several significant new departures were to be observed. First, de Valera was now accorded the title of President of the Irish Republic in place of his previous description as President of Dáil Eireann. Second, all deputies (members) took an oath to 'bear true faith and allegiance' to 'the Irish republic and the Government of the Irish Republic which is Dáil Eireann'. Third, de Valera nominated a new cabinet containing only senior ministers. These were Griffith (Foreign Affairs), Stack (Home Affairs), Brugha (Defence), Collins (Finance), Cosgrave (Local Government), and Barton (Economic Affairs). Two former cabinet ministers, Count Plunkett and the Countess Markievicz, were given ministerial posts outside the cabinet and Kevin O'Higgins began his swift ascent to power by achieving ministerial status (but also without cabinet rank) while remaining subordinate to his old chief, Cosgrave.[42]

After hearing de Valera's statement on the truce negotiations the Dáil agreed to confirm the cabinet's rejection of them. This did not mean, however, a resumption of the war. On the contrary, the next two months were filled with correspondence between the British Prime Minister and the Irish President in an effort to find some formula which would perform the apparently impossible and allow the two parties to advance from a precarious truce to a negotiated settlement. But it was hard to see how this could be achieved, since de Valera was committed to the concept of independence and Lloyd George could not contemplate an Ireland outside the empire. Yet there was a loophole which, if it did not offer a solution to the problem, at least allowed discussions to proceed. It was noticeable in the correspondence that while the President made little reference to the republic *per se*, he did hold out some prospect that an independent Ireland might be in some form associated with the empire. Dominion status itself he considered illusory because of the proximity of Britain, and anyway, as he rightly pointed out, it was not real dominion status that Ireland was being offered. What then was the alternative? He put it to Lloyd George as follows:

A certain treaty of free association with the British Commonwealth group, as with a partial league of nations, we would have
been ready to contemplate, and as a government to negotiate and
take responsibility for, had we an assurance that the entry of the
nation as a whole into such association would secure for it the
allegiance of the present dissenting minority, to meet whose
sentiments alone this step could be contemplated.[43]

Even such a formula as this raised as many problems as it attempted
to solve, but at least it indicated a willingness on de Valera's part to
consider some form of connection with Britain. And there were
other hopeful signs. At the opening of the new Dáil a few days later
he stressed that the setting up of the first Dáil had been a vote for
freedom and independence rather than for a particular form of
government, 'because we are not republican doctrinaires'.[44] And the
next day, talking at large about future relations with Britain, he
seemed not to rule out 'an association that would be consistent
with our rights to see that we were the judges of what was our own
interests, and that we were not compelled to leave the judgment
of what were our own interests to others'.[45] This was not, perhaps,
a great deal, but it was enough to encourage Lloyd George to persist and
at last, at the end of September, he found the formula he needed.
President de Valera was invited to send delegates to London on 11
October 'with a view to ascertaining how the association of Ireland
with the community of nations known as the British empire may best
be reconciled with Irish national aspirations'.[46]
This invitation it proved possible to accept. But contrary to all
expectations de Valera himself was not one of the delegates. Why he
should have remained at home has been a matter for conjecture
ever since. No doubt he felt it desirable to emphasise his position as a
Head of State who did not enter into negotiations. Probably also he
visualised a situation where the negotiations in London might have
to be broken off – in which case it would be better that they should
be broken off by a moderate like Griffith rather than by the seemingly inflexible President who had already once rejected Lloyd George's
terms. Again, there were extreme republicans inside his own cabinet
– Brugha and Stack, for example – upon whom he would be likely
to exert more influence if he were not directly involved in whatever
settlement might emerge from the London talks. But it may be that
his chief preoccupation was to ensure, by his presence in Dublin,
that his colleagues would be careful to refer back to him before
making any vital decisions.* If this was so, however, then there

* The recently published *Private Sessions of the Second Dáil* (Dublin, n.d.
[1972]), pp. 95-6, confirm that a major motive, perhaps the major motive,

was an inexcusable – and in the event, tragic – ambiguity about the instructions issued to the delegates. According to their credentials – approved by the cabinet and the Dáil but not, for obvious reasons, formally accepted by the British government – they were 'envoys plenipotentiary from the elected Government of the Republic of Ireland to negotiate and conclude with the representatives of His Britannic Majesty George V a Treaty or Treaties of association and accommodation between Ireland and the Community of Nations known as the British Commonwealth'. If this meant anything it meant they had power to sign on their own responsibility. But before they left home they also received explicit orders to submit to Dublin the complete text of any draft treaty about to be signed and to await a reply. From this initial confusion much bitter recrimination was to flow.

The delegation that did go was nevertheless a very strong one. It was led by Arthur Griffith and consisted in addition of Michael Collins, Robert Barton and two lawyers, Gavan Duffy and Eamon Duggan. Griffith was an obvious choice and – since economic issues would be involved – so also was Barton. But Collins was intensely unhappy at the prospect and only went out of a profound sense of duty – and with a profound anticipation of what the future might hold in store. The other two delegates were there primarily in their capacity as legal experts, but Gavan Duffy, who had practised as a solicitor in London and had acted for Casement at his trial in 1916, was much more than a lawyer. He had drafted the Dáil Declaration of Independence in 1919 and in that same year had gone as a Dáil envoy to the Paris Peace Conference. A high-principled and tenacious man, he was in fact to be the last to sign the Treaty on the Irish side. But, inevitably, it was Griffith and Collins who had to bear the main burden of confronting a formidable British team led by the Prime Minister and including Winston Churchill, Austen Chamberlain, Lord Birkenhead, Sir Laming Worthington-Evans, Sir Hamar Greenwood and the Attorney-General, Sir Gordon Hewart. Three further points have to be made about the negotiating position of the Irish delegates. The first is that Griffith, although he fought his corner as hard as any man could, went to London in the almost certain knowledge that he could not bring back recognition for the republic and dubious even about de Valera's alternative device of 'external association'. The second is that since the two most rigid republicans in the cabinet – Brugha and Stack – had refused absolutely to serve on the delegation, this, added to de Valera's abstention, meant that while the extreme repub-

---

for de Valera's refusal to be part of the delegation was his conviction that, as Head of State, he was the symbol of the republic and that the symbol should be kept 'untouched' and 'uncompromised'. His private correspondence at this time echoed the same theme – see Earl of Longford and T. P. O'Neill, *Eamon De Valera* (London, 1970), p. 146.

lican case was possibly under-represented among the ministers who travelled, it was decidedly over-represented among those who stayed at home. The fact that friction already existed between Brugha and Collins made this alignment of forces specially unfortunate. And the final point is that among the secretaries the Irish took with them was Erskine Childers, whose attachment to the Irish cause, dating as we have seen from before the First World War, had hardened into an intense, fanatical republicanism. Griffith, unhappily and also unjustly, regarded him as an Englishman intruding into Irish affairs and the abrasive hostility between them was to darken both men's lives as time went on.

It is not necessary to tell again in detail the story of the arduous negotiations.* Three issues, briefly to summarise a complex situation, were involved. These were – the status of the new Irish polity; the question of whether Ireland was to be reunited or remain partitioned; and the requirements of British security and defence. Curiously enough, this last problem was disposed of relatively amicably, arousing less discussion than might have been expected either at the conference-table or afterwards in the Dáil debates. Yet in retrospect the Irish agreement to allow Britain the use of certain naval bases even in peacetime would seem to have made nonsense of any claim to real independence, for such an arrangement would in any major war have made it wellnigh impossible for Ireland to preserve that neutrality which is the ultimate hall-mark of sovereignty.† At the time, no doubt, this may have seemed a remote contingency compared with the urgent and baffling problem of what sort of Ireland was going to emerge from the conference.

The general strategy of the Irish delegation was that if they had to break off the negotiations they would do so on the question of Ulster. It was a cardinal point with them to insist on the essential unity of their country and at all costs to avoid if they could the mistake of the parliamentarians five years earlier in agreeing to partition, however hedged about with qualifications. But for the British the relationship of Ireland to the empire, including the fearsomely difficult questions of sovereignty and allegiance to the Crown, was as crucial, if not more so. It was at the seventh plenary session – on 24 October – that this latter issue first became critical when Griffith produced a scheme, approved by the Dáil cabinet, for external association, the

* The most complete account is in F. Pakenham (now the Earl of Longford), *Peace by Ordeal* (London, 1935); his considered second thoughts should also be consulted in T. Desmond Williams (ed.), *The Irish Struggle*, pp. 107-15. To these sources should now be added: Earl of Longford and T. P. O'Neill, *Eamon De Valera*, chaps. 12 and 13; Thomas Jones, *Whitehall Diary: Vol. iii, Ireland 1918-1925*, ed. K. Middlemass, pp. 119-83; M. Forester, *Michael Collins: The Lost Leader* (London, 1971), chaps. 14 and 15.

† For the later history of this aspect of the settlement, see Part IV A, chap. 2.

same concept that was to run like a thread through Anglo-Irish relations for nearly three decades. 'On the one hand', ran the formula, 'Ireland will consent to adhere for all purposes of common agreed concern to the League of Sovereign States associated and known as the British Commonwealth of Nations. On the other hand Ireland calls upon Great Britain to renounce all claims and authority over Ireland and Irish affairs.' But, asked Lloyd George immediately, did this mean that Ireland accepted the Crown or did it not? Griffith fenced with him. Ireland, he said, could not accept the Crown for her own internal purposes and must be free to choose her own head of state, but she might recognise the King as head of the association [of the empire]. Cross-examined by a baffled Lloyd George as to whether this meant that the Irish would be foreigners or British subjects Griffith replied with a definition of reciprocal citizenship essentially the same as that which exists today. 'We should be Irish, and you would be British, and each would have equal rights as citizens in the country of the other.'[47] This scheme of association, though at first hearing incomprehensible to the British representatives, seemed on reflection not unhopeful if only it could be amended to bring Ireland clearly inside the empire. But to de Valera in Dublin the very fact that the position of the Crown had already begun to loom large in the discussions was a danger signal. There must, he wrote, be no question of any allegiance to the King. 'If war is the alternative we can only face it.'

The conference then split into sub-committees and in some of its less controversial aspects began to make rapid progress. This, however, only threw into high relief the large constitutional questions still remaining unsolved. More and more it began to seem that the twin dilemmas – over status and over Ulster – were in fact Siamese twins, passing the wit of man to separate. Each side had its own extremists to reckon with and this made movement in any direction almost impossible. By the end of October Lloyd George, faced with a resolution of censure in the House of Commons moved by 'die-hard' Unionists, was ready to woo Griffith with the promise that if the Irish delegation met him satisfactorily on the constitutional question he would fight the die-hards to secure 'essential unity' on Ulster. Griffith was prepared to fall in with the suggestion (conveyed to him by Lloyd George's secretary, Tom Jones) that he write the Prime Minister a letter explaining just how far he would be prepared to go in return for Lloyd George's best efforts to bring Ulster somehow into line. Even the contemplation of such a move aroused alarm among his colleagues but when finally a letter was written it seemed cautious enough. In it Griffith pledged himself, provided he was satisfied on all other points, to recommend that Ireland should accept recognition of the Crown as head of the Association of Free States [of the empire] and that she should join in 'free partnership' (the terms of which were

later to be defined) with the British Commonwealth. Later, he was persuaded by the British negotiators to change this to free partnership
with the states *within* the British Commonwealth, something decidedly
different. At the time, however, this seemed of small importance compared with the fact that Lloyd George was at last apparently ready to
stake his career and the fate of his ministry on pushing Ulster towards
a settlement satisfactory to the Irish delegation.

In retrospect it seems astonishing that the delegates, Griffith
especially, should have placed so much reliance upon the British
government's ability to coerce the Ulster Unionists. This had not
worked in 1914, 1916 or 1917 and it was even less likely to be effective
in 1921 when an Ulster government was actually established in
Belfast – a government, moreover, which still had substantial backing
from English Conservatives, some of them actually members of
Lloyd George's coalition cabinet. Sir James Craig had in fact only to
sit tight, and at sitting tight he was an acknowledged master. Lloyd
George saw him twice early in November and found him predictably
adamant against any sort of connection with a Dublin parliament
or against any tampering with the border of the six counties.

If Lloyd George meant what he said about resignation this was
surely the moment for him to go. Instead he tried another approach
which, as we now know, first occurred to him on November 7
and which was put to the Irish delegation the next day by his emissary, Thomas Jones, as if it were the latter's own suggestion.[48] What
would the Irish delegation think of a Boundary Commission to determine the frontier between north and south and which, the delegates
found it only too easy to believe, might well award such substantial
areas of the six counties to them as would make a 'Northern Ireland'
impossible as a separate, political entity? Griffith's reply is recorded in
a report he sent to de Valera. 'We said it was their proposal, not ours',
he wrote, 'and we would therefore not be bound by it, but we
realised its value as a tatical manoeuvre, and if Lloyd George made
it we would not queer his position.' It has been charged against
Griffith that in making even this cautious admission he was in effect
releasing Lloyd George from his promise to resign if Ulster did not
co-operate. This is true, but against it has to be set the fact that
Griffith was face to face with the same dilemma that had confronted
Redmond in 1914. If Griffith now forced the resignation of Lloyd
George, or if Redmond had then forced that of Asquith, the only consequence would have been the return to power of intransigent Unionism incarnate in the obdurate shape of Bonar Law.

Intransigent Unionism, indeed, was already uneasy enough. There
was to be a Conservative Party Conference at Liverpool on 17
November and although Lloyd George's ministry had triumphantly
survived its vote of censure in the House of Commons, if the
Liverpool Conference 'bolted' on the subject of Ulster then it would

be all up with the coalition. The Prime Minister's task, therefore, was to keep the Irish delegation in play while he continued his discreet pressures on Ulster. But Craig remained impervious to pressures, discreet or otherwise. The idea of a Boundary Commission he found as odious as any of the others that had been put forward. Instead, he proposed – tongue half in cheek, perhaps – that a fairer solution would be to give dominion status to north as well as south. Lloyd George at once brushed this aside with the prescient remark that 'frontiers once established harden into permanence', and still hammered away at his proposal for a Boundary Commission. On 12 November he saw Griffith and explained that Ulster would be offered an all-Ireland parliament with the right to opt out of it within twelve months. But if this right was exercised then Craig would have to accept a Boundary Commission. Again, Griffith responded that this was Lloyd George's responsibility, not his. Agreed, replied Lloyd George, but he must at least be sure that when his Conservative friends fought for his policy at Liverpool they would not be repudiated by the Irish delegation. Griffith, according to one account, conceded that he would not 'let Lloyd George down' in such circumstances. From his own report to de Valera it appears that while he did not guarantee to accept the new proposal, 'I would guarantee that while he was fighting the "Ulster" crowd we would not help them by repudiating him.' But actually he went further than this. When on 13 November Lloyd George's emissary, Tom Jones, showed him a draft of what had passed on the previous day, Griffith assented to it as a correct record. This document – containing as it did the promise that if Ulster declined to belong to an all-Ireland parliament, then her frontiers would be revised by a Boundary Commission 'so as to make the boundary conform as closely as possible to the wishes of the population' – seemed to Griffith so routine as not to be worth mentioning to his colleagues, but was later to be used against him with devastating effect.

Meanwhile all went well at Liverpool. The chairman of the Conference, Sir Archibald Salvidge, was secretly visited by Lord Birkenhead, who assured him that whatever settlement was reached it would not be prejudicial to Ulster, and he was able to guide the Conference away from a revolt against the government, which, to be fair, it seems to have been in his mind to do anyway. But Lloyd George was no sooner out of trouble in this direction than it cascaded onto him from another. On 16 November he had submitted to the Irish delegation a rough outline of the progress he considered to have been made so far. This contained the Boundary Commission proposal, but while it seemed unequivocally to place Ireland inside the empire, there was no mention of oath, or allegiance, or even of the Crown itself. Six days later the Irish delegates (after ominous internal friction between Griffith and Childers, the latter standing firmly as ever on the rock of the republic) produced their own memorandum in reply. Although in many ways a moderate and constructive document, it offended

Lloyd George in two ways. It was silent about the Boundary Commission – though insistent on the 'essential unity' of Ireland – and it did not move any closer towards the empire than association. It appears that the British Prime Minister very nearly broke off the negotiations at this point and when, after some difficulty, a plenary session was arranged for 23 November the atmosphere was stormier than it had been for some time. He did, however, win the delegation's consent to the idea of a Boundary Commission for Ulster, so that what now remained to be settled was the constitutional relationship between the new dominion and the empire, the Irish still insisting that within Ireland the Crown should have no significance at all.

Their attitude was reinforced by a visit to Dublin that weekend. It was useless, Griffith argued on his return to London, to hold Canada up as the dominion model for Ireland. The insistent pressures of geographical propinquity could not be denied and the Crown in an Irish context would not just be a symbol, it would 'continue to possess the real power of repression and veto which Ireland knows'. The British met this objection handsomely, offering to draft a more innocuous form of the Oath of Allegiance and also inviting the Irish to invent any phrase they liked which would ensure that the Crown would in practice intrude no more in their internal affairs than it did in those of Canada or any other dominion.

Events now moved rapidly towards a climax. Lloyd George had promised to send Sir James Craig in Belfast the final decision not later than 6 December and although presumably there was no real reason why this deadline could not have been extended, the very fact that it existed meant that it came to be regarded as the terminal date for a conference which had, indeed, already gone on dangerously long. Before there could be a conclusion, however, the Irish delegates had to return once more to Dublin with the terms that had so far been hammered out. Almost all day on Saturday, 3 December, the cabinet – sometimes with others present, sometimes not – sat in bitter and contentious debate which foreshadowed much that was to come. The case for accepting the British terms was in essence that they were the best that could be obtained, that the safeguards surrounding the Crown were adequate, and that if the Crown were not accepted in some way then the foothold in Ulster afforded by the Boundary Commission would be lost. Against this it could be argued that the 'essential unity' of Ireland had been fatally compromised, that the British were bluffing and could be pushed further on the constitutional question, above all that the Holy Grail of the republic was vanishing in the midst of discussion. All present were under great strain – the delegates themselves were near the point of exhaustion – and this partly explains the sharpening of tempers and especially Brugha's offensive remark that in dealing mainly with Griffith and Collins 'the British government selected its men'.* But partly, of course, the harshness of

* Later in the Dáil he qualified this by saying that the British government.

435

these discussions sprang from the realisation that the ideal was not attainable and from a deep division among those present as to whether the substitute that was now within grasp was worth the taking. Eventually, after Griffith had made it clear that he personally would not take the responsibility of breaking on the question of the Crown, and after de Valera had re-drafted the Oath of Allegiance so as to make the concept of external association more rather than less emphatic, the delegates were hastily given their instructions only a few minutes before they were due to travel back to London. These stated that they were to carry out their original instructions with the same powers; that they were to say to the British 'that the cabinet won't accept Oath of Allegiance if not amended' and 'to face the consequences assuming that England will declare war'; that Griffith was to tell Lloyd George that the proposed agreement could not be signed – 'to state that it is now a matter for the Dáil, and to try and put the blame on Ulster'; finally, that if the delegation should think it necessary, they were empowered to meet Sir James Craig.[49]

This, it must be admitted, was hardly an illuminating brief for hard-pressed negotiators to carry to one of the most crucial confrontations in the history of their country. If it made anything clear it was that the original confusion was even further confounded. The delegates were still plenipotentiaries, but they were plenipotentiaries still tied to Dublin. And although their discussions and subsequent instructions had foreseen some of the circumstances that were likely to arise, they had not – as events were soon to show – foreseen them all.

Arrived in London they plunged at once – 4 December – into hard and tense discussion with Lloyd George. They found him tough and unyielding, ready to believe, or to persuade them that he believed, that their attitude could only lead to a final rupture. They themselves reflected the deep divisions that had emerged at the Cabinet meeting the previous day and Griffith was so uneasy about the terms they were expected to present that almost up to the last minute he was threatening not to lead the delegation. He did lead it, and with great ability, but apparently in vain. Despite his efforts to centre the discussions on Ulster the question of Ireland's relationship with the empire kept rearing its head. 'Our difficulty', said Gavan Duffy at one point, 'is to come into the empire, looking at all that has happened in the past.' This was honest, but hardly politic. 'That ends it', cried Austen Chamberlain, jumping to his feet, and at once the negotiations were broken off.

But Lloyd George's resources were not yet exhausted. He was well aware that the delegation was now divided and his strategy was to play upon those who were closest to the British position. On 5

---

had selected them, not as dishonourable men, but as the weakest members of the team. This was merely to substitute fatuous offensiveness for angry offensiveness.

December he saw a reluctant Collins and found him anxious about the form of the Oath and still more about the question of Ulster. There was little common ground between them on the former question, but on the latter it seems that Collins was only too ready to let himself believe that after the Boundary Commission had done its work economic pressures would bring about the 'essential unity' of Ireland.[50] Later that afternoon he, Griffith and Barton were summoned to meet the Prime Minister, Chamberlain, Birkenhead and Churchill. Although the discussion ranged widely over various aspects of the proposed agreement the crucial question was the position of Ulster. Griffith tried desperately to bring Lloyd George to the point of asking Sir James Craig to agree to the essential unity of Ireland before the Irish delegation committed themselves irrevocably to any particular form of association with the empire. But Lloyd George checkmated him by producing the document Griffith had approved on 13 November. On the basis of that document he had understood Griffith to have agreed that if Ulster opted out of the proposed all-Ireland Parliament then the boundary of Northern Ireland would have to be revised by a Boundary Commission. Eventually Griffith, soul of honour that he was, capitulated. He had said he would not let Lloyd George down and he would be as good as his word. 'I have never let a man down in my life', he said, 'and I never will.' It was clear that there would be no break on Ulster from him.

The discussion then veered towards the Oath. De Valera's formula had been simple: 'I . . . do solemnly swear true faith and allegiance to the constitution of the Irish Free State, to the Treaty of Association and to recognise the King of Great Britain as head of the Associated States.' This, however, was too clearly a restatement of the doctrine of external association to be palatable to the British representatives. They could not accept it, but they did go a considerable distance towards meeting the Irish demand. 'I . . . do solemnly swear true faith and allegiance', ran their version, 'to the Constitution of the Irish Free State as by law established, and that I will be faithful to H. M. King George v, his heirs and successors by law, in virtue of the common citizenship of Ireland with Great Britain and her adherence to and membership of the group of nations forming the British Commonwealth of Nations.' Irish acceptance of this depended, of course, on Irish acceptance both of dominion status in general and of the Boundary Commission solution for Ulster in particular. Griffith was prepared to sign an agreement on these lines. But what, asked Lloyd George, of the rest of the Irish delegation? 'The Irish delegates', he said at last, 'must settle now. They must sign the agreement for a Treaty or else quit . . . and both sides would be free to resume whatever warfare they could wage against each other.' Brandishing two letters in their faces he reminded them that he had to send one of them to Sir James Craig that night. Would it be the letter confirming that agreement had been reached or would it be the other saying that the Sinn Féin representatives refused to come within the empire? 'If I send this letter it is war, and war within three days. Which letter am I to send?'[51]

At 7.15 that evening the Irish withdrew to consider this ultimatum. As they rose to go Churchill was struck particularly by the ravages the discussions had wrought upon Collins. 'In all my life', he wrote afterwards, 'I have never seen so much passion and suffering in restraint.' Nevertheless it seems that Collins on the way back to their quarters made it clear that he would sign. Duggan intimated that he would go with Griffith and Collins, but it needed several hours of argument before Barton and Gavan Duffy agreed. Thus they all took up their great responsibility and decided to accept the Treaty. To this day historians have reflected with amazement on their failure to communicate with de Valera even by telephone. The explanation for this was mainly physical – he was in Limerick at the crucial moment and not easily accessible. But the delegates' decision to sign without struggling for yet another adjournment sprang essentially from more profound, if incalculable causes, of which the chief seem to have been the mesmeric intensity of Lloyd George's personality, their own weariness combined with the willingness of the most eminent among them for a settlement which, while not conceding the republic, was still far more generous than any Britain had previously been brought to make, and especially perhaps Collins's conviction that a resumption of the war would be disastrous – these things all pointed them along their *via dolorosa*. And so three of them – Griffith, Collins and Barton (the others signed later) – returned late that night to Downing Street and, after some minor amendments had been dealt with, signed at 2.10 a.m. on 6 December 1921 the Articles of Agreement for a Treaty which conferred upon southern Ireland, or 'the Irish Free State', the status of a dominion and in so doing brought one stage nearer the conflict which, as Cathal Brugha had prophesied, would 'split Ireland from top to bottom'.*

* The application of the Treaty, and its relation to the constitution of the Irish Free State are discussed in Part IV A, chap. 1.

6. The Great Divide

'When you have sweated, toiled, had mad dreams, hopeless nightmares, you find yourself in London's streets, cold and dank in the night air.

'Think – what I have got for Ireland? Something which she has wanted these past seven hundred years. Will anyone be satisfied at the bargain? Will anyone? I tell you this – early this morning I signed my death warrant. I thought at the time how odd, how ridiculous – a bullet may just as well have done the job five years ago.'[1]

Thus Collins, writing to a friend on the day the Treaty was signed. The note of sombre foreboding that dominates this letter dominated also the agonising debate in Ireland to which the signature of the agreement gave rise. The news, which reached Dublin piecemeal and more slowly than might have been expected, was received by de Valera and the other ministers who had stayed at home with grim dissatisfaction. A cabinet meeting to discuss the action of the plenipotentiaries was immediately summoned for Thursday, 8 December, by which time it was expected that Griffith, who had stayed on in London to give certain assurances about the future to representative southern Unionists, would be back in Dublin with his colleagues.* When all seven ministers finally did meet (with Gavan Duffy and Erskine Childers also present) the debate was long and anxious. For several hours the issue of acceptance or rejection hung in the balance and it was only when Robert Barton reluctantly cast his vote for the Treaty (largely because he felt this was the only honourable course after having signed it in the first place) that the delegates won a majority for their policy. In that majority were Griffith, Collins and Cosgrave, as well as Barton; against them were de Valera, Brugha and Stack.

These were only the opening shots in what was soon to become a general engagement. The real test would be the meeting of the Dáil which would have to decide on ratification or rejection, and both sides at once began to prepare the ground for what everyone realised would be a crucial debate. President de Valera was first in the field with a Proclamation to the Irish People issued on the evening of the day in which he had found himself in a minority at the cabinet. 'I

* The southern Unionists were anxious to secure adequate representation for their minority viewpoint in the parliament of the Free State. For Griffith's solution of the problem, see Part IV A, chap. 1.

feel it my duty to inform you', he said, 'that I cannot recommend the acceptance of this treaty either to Dáil Eireann or to the people.' Griffith, for his part, countered next day with a statement anticipating the line he was to cling to tenaciously during the weeks ahead. The Treaty, he maintained, would lay the foundations for peace between Ireland and England. 'What I have signed I will stand by, in the belief that the end of the conflict of centuries is at hand.'[2]

The Dáil was due to meet on the following Wednesday, 14 December, and until then there was a period of confusion and uncertainty. Press opinion in general was in favour of accepting the bargain so hardly won in London. So too were many of the bishops. Ordinary people, who wanted only to be allowed to sleep quiet of nights and earn an honest living, probably saw no further than that this had suddenly become possible; for them, and for many others, the immediate release of prisoners held by the British authorities was a fact more potent than any abstract conception of an ideal but unrealisable republic. Among the fighting-men, naturally, a more intransigent attitude was to be expected. A number of the IRA leaders were prepared to take their cue from de Valera or Brugha and it has even been suggested that the latter had to restrain certain commandants from arresting the delegates for treason the moment they landed in Ireland. No doubt also, many of the rank and file, though little troubled by high politics, had small enthusiasm for settling down to a humdrum existence after all the excitements of the past two and a half years. But the Army was by no means monolithic. On the contrary, cracks and fissures were already beginning to appear as other officers, for whom Collins could do no wrong, looked to him rather than to Brugha for leadership. In another sense, also, Collins's influence made itself felt. The Supreme Council of the IRB, of which he was President, issued a statement to members of the organisation giving its opinion that it was in Ireland's interest that the Treaty should be agreed. True, no order was issued and every member of the IRB who was also a member of the Dáil was left free to act and vote according to his conscience, but, given Collins's immense personal ascendancy within the IRB, it was not difficult to guess how many of his fellow-members might use their freedom of action.*

But all these currents of opinion for and against the Treaty were held in suspension until the Dáil should decide. And the Dáil found

---

* It may be, as Mr Ernest Blythe has recently suggested, that the influence of the IRB after 1916 has been exaggerated by historians. No one doubts its crucial role in 1916, but thereafter, as the struggle for independence became more open and more widespread, the conspiratorial element may have become less significant. Yet even if this was so, any organisation with which Collins was intimately involved derived a measure of importance from the very fact of his involvement; in reality not only between 1919 and 1922, but even up to 1924 (see below, pp. 488-9) the IRB was a complicating factor in the inner history of the Army.

it agonisingly difficult to decide. During twelve public sittings (and one secret session), spread over nearly a month and interrupted by an adjournment for Christmas, the long and sad debate continued. It is scarcely an exaggeration to say that these discussions were as important for the future of Ireland, as were those of the Federal Convention after the American War of Independence for the future of the United States of America. They did not indeed produce a Constitution, nor even the basis for a secure future, but in Dublin in 1921-22, as in Philadelphia in 1781, one has the same sense of ordinary citizens consciously responding in their diverse ways to extraordinary events. And although there was a notable lack of eighteenth century urbanity in Dáil Eireann there was the same passionate concern for fundamentals, the same desire to probe to the bottom the very meaning of independence.

There was also a great deal of irrelevance, much platitude and – especially towards the end – outbursts of rancorous bitterness between individuals. At the outset an inordinate amount of time was consumed, and ill-feeling engendered, by a wrangling argument over the instructions issued to the delegates and about whether they were or were not plenipotentiaries in the full meaning of the term. It was in fact only at the secret session of 15 and 16 December that debate first began to be centred on the really vital question of what sort of independent status Ireland could hope for. Even then much of the time of that private session was occupied with a discussion of a proposal put forward in very general terms by de Valera, not to assert the republic pure and undefiled, but rather to rewrite the Treaty according to his own favourite nostrum of external association.[3]

Not surprisingly, deputies were puzzled. To the republican zealots it can only have seemed irrelevant, to the proponents of the Treaty it was unnecessary. A great deal more was to be heard of it in the future, but when public sittings were resumed on 19 December the debate swung back, as sooner or later it was bound to do, towards the central issue – was what had been brought back from London a worthy return for all the bloodshed and suffering of the Anglo-Irish war? Griffith, in proposing the motion that the Dáil approve of the treaty, made it clear that he had signed the agreement 'not as the ideal thing' but believing that it marked an honourable peace and that it safeguarded Ireland's vital interests. It was not the case, he insisted, that they had compromised the demand for a full republic. 'In the letters that preceded the negotiations not once was a demand made for the recognition of the Irish republic. If it had been made we knew it would have been refused. We went there to reconcile the two positions and I hold we have done it.' President de Valera's alternative, Document No. 2, which had been before the Dáil in private session but which at this stage of the debate he was still withholding from public discussion, did not, as Griffith pointed out, represent the 'uncompromising rock' of the republic; it was, on the contrary 'merely a quibble of words' about the way in which the King should be recognised as head of the Commonwealth and certainly not enough to justify throwing away the Treaty and resorting once more to war. For what, after all, was the real achievement of the Treaty?

It is the first Treaty between the representatives of the Irish Government and the representatives of the English Government since 1172 signed on equal footing. It is the first Treaty that admits the equality of Ireland . . . We have brought back the flag; we have brought back the evacuation of Ireland after 700 years by British troops and the formation of an Irish army [applause]. We have brought back to Ireland her full rights and powers of fiscal control. We have brought back to Ireland equality with England, equality with all nations which form that Commonwealth, and an equal voice in the direction of foreign affairs in peace and war.

As for the Oath of Allegiance, it was, he maintained, an oath any Irishman could take with honour, for it was in the first instance an oath to the constitution of his own country, and only afterwards a declaration of faithfulness to the head of the British Commonwealth. True, he admitted, 'we took an oath to the Irish Republic, but, as President de Valera himself said, he understood that oath to bind him to do the best he could for Ireland. So do we. We have done the best we could for Ireland. If the Irish people say "we have got everything else but the name Republic, and we will fight for it", I would say to them that they are fools, but I will follow in the ranks.' He did not think, however, that they would do this and he ended with the proud claim that they had 'translated Thomas Davis into the practical politics of the day' and had carried through the great revolution 'of seeing the two countries standing not apart as enemies, but standing together as equals and as friends'.[4]

Griffith, when he sat down, had made the pro-Treaty position absolutely clear and other speakers on his side, with the towering exception of Collins, did little more than embroider the themes he had marked out. But for de Valera, who led the attack against the Treaty, such clarity was more difficult to achieve. This was partly because his own obsessive preoccupation with the meaning of words led him into intricacies of speech where deputies found it hard to follow him, but still more because he laboured under the disadvantage of having to attack the Treaty without having yet convincingly demonstrated that what he put forward in its place was sufficiently different to justify throwing overboard the London agreement. In the debate on 19 December he dwelt less on his own alternative proposals than on the defects of the Treaty itself as he saw them. 'I am against this Treaty', he declared, 'because it does not reconcile Irish national aspirations with association with the British government . . . I am against this Treaty because it will not end the centuries of conflict between the two nations of Great Britain and Ireland.' A war-weary people, he acknowledged, might indeed accept at the moment things that did not accord with their national aspirations, but what sort of foundation to build on was that? 'I will tell you that Treaty will renew the contest that is going to begin the same history that the Union began, and Lloyd George is going to have the same fruit for his labours as Pitt had.'

Much of his attack was concerned with the Oath of Allegiance, that same Oath which was to bedevil his own career for the next decade. To him it was mere sophistry to contend that swearing faithfulness to the King was a secondary matter, and that the Oath to the Constitution was what really counted. The King would *be* head, not just of the Commonwealth, but of Ireland. Irish Ministers would be His Majesty's Ministers, the Army would be His Majesty's Army. His fundamental objections to what they were being asked to do were, in essence, expressed in this series of propositions.

> . . . I am once more asking you to reject the Treaty for two main reasons that, as every Teachta [deputy] knows, it is absolutely inconsistent with our position; it gives away Irish independence; it brings us into the British Empire; it acknowledges the head of the British Empire not merely as the head of an association, but as the direct monarch of Ireland, as the source of executive authority in Ireland.[5]

It was one thing, however, to say that the Treaty gave away Irish independence. It was quite another to postulate that that independence should take a republican form. De Valera did, it is true, argue that to swear an Oath of Allegiance to the King would be 'inconsistent with the Republic', but (with Document No. 2 still held in reserve) he had not committed himself to the republic *pur sang*. His aim was still, by whatever desperate sleight of hand, to reconcile the republic with Commonwealth Association. But Austin Stack, the Minister for Home Affairs, who followed him, swept these arabesques impatiently to one side. The Treaty, he said, was based essentially on conceding dominion status for Ireland, on giving Ireland full Canadian powers, 'I, for one', he said roundly, 'cannot accept full Canadian powers, threequarter Canadian powers, or half Canadian powers. I stand for what is Ireland's right, full independence and nothing short of it.' He stood, as he truly said, in the Fenian tradition and, in an ominous passage, he looked towards what might happen in the future. 'If I, as I hope I will, try to continue to fight for Ireland's liberty, even if this rotten document be accepted, I will fight minus the oath of allegiance and to wipe out the oath of allegiance if I can do it.'[6]

In such an attitude as this, instinct with the death-wish as it might seem to less inflexible men, there was at least a rough and brutal logic not without great persuasive power. It needed, therefore, a compelling speech from Collins – to whom parliamentary orations were generally anathema – to restore the balance. He pointed out at once that the exchanges that had taken place between de Valera and Lloyd George *before* the delegation went to London had made it perfectly clear that the conference did not take place on the basis of any English readiness to recognise the republic, 'and I say if we all stood on the recognition of the Irish republic as a prelude to any conference, we could very easily have said so, and there would be no conference'. 'What I want to make clear', he continued, 'is that it was the acceptance of the invitation that formed the compromise.' And then he used a phrase that was to become famous, for it summed up in a few words the whole doctrine of constitutional development that was to guide the new state long after he himself was dead. He recommended the acceptance of the Treaty, he said, because it gave freedom, 'not the ultimate freedom that all nations aspire and develop to, but the freedom to achieve it'. Hardly anyone, he observed a moment later (after digressing to deny that any of the delegates had been intimidated into signing the document), really understood the Treaty or the immense powers it actually conferred upon the Free State. The true conquest of Ireland, he suggested, had been its economic exploitation by England, an exploitation resting ultimately on military force. Now that force would be withdrawn and Ireland could develop in freedom. She would remain a weak country for a long time to come, however, and for him this was the chief justification of membership of the Commonwealth with the same status as the other dominions. The very fact of being associated with Canada, South Africa and the rest, would safeguard the Irish position. 'They are, in effect, introduced [into the Treaty] as guarantors of our freedom, which makes us stronger than if we stood alone.' He was even prepared to argue – though with a more doubtful logic – that the most obvious derogation from Ireland's dominion status, the continued occupation of the Treaty ports by British forces, would not lead to any British re-occupation of the country precisely because Ireland now formed one of a group of self-governing countries. 'Associated in a free partnership with these other nations it is not a danger, for their association is a guarantee that it won't be a jumping-off ground against us.'

Trying hard to inject into the debate that realism which was one of his own outstanding characteristics, Collins turned near the end of his speech to the question of the six separated counties of the northeast. He wanted to persuade the Dáil that Northern Ireland presented a complex problem not to be solved by any crude frontal attack. 'We have stated we would not coerce the northeast', he said. 'What was the use of talking big phrases about not agreeing to the partition of our country?' Partition was a fact, it existed, and the only way of dealing with it was to try to reach mutual understanding between the two parts of Ireland. This, he believed, the Treaty had made possible. In retrospect that may seem an excessively naïve reaction, indicating that even Collins was falling into the old nationalist fallacy of underestimating the stamina and intensity of Ulster Unionism. But there was another explanation. Before signing the Treaty he had, it will be remembered, been led to believe that the Boundary Commission would render 'Northern Ireland' a non-viable entity and that a merger with the south would follow.[7] We know from the evidence of one of his friends, P. S. O'Hegarty, that Collins – and others close to Collins – at the time of the Treaty debates still believed from his conversations with Birkenhead and Churchill, that the northeast would be left with only four counties and that *they* (meaning apparently the British) would make a four-county government impossible.[8] If Collins thus believed the Boundary Commission would prove a trump-card, it is not surprising that most other speakers, less well-informed, left the question of partition very much on one side (with the conspicuous exception of a long and moving speech by Sean MacEntee) and that the debate continued to revolve around questions of status and association rather than what a later generation might be inclined to regard as the more fundamental problem of the division of the country.*

Collins was followed by Childers, intellectually one of the most formidable opponents of the Treaty and at odds with Griffith, as we have seen, even before the negotiations had been concluded. In a long, lucid speech – doubly exasperating to his victims precisely because it was so meticulous – Childers exposed what he took to be the defects of the settlement, though he agreed with Collins that there had never been any question during the London talks of 'an isolated republic standing alone. . . .' 'The sole question before the nation, . Dáil Eireann, and the delegation was how is it possible to effect an association with the British Commonwealth which would be

* It has been estimated that of 338 pages of debate printed in the Dáil report only nine are devoted to the question of partition; of these nine pages two thirds were contributed by three deputies from county Monaghan (near the northern border). It is also worth pointing out that in Document No. 2 de Valera made no new proposals for Ulster, apparently accepting the Boundary Commission solution (Maureen Wall, 'Partition: the Ulster Question', in T. Desmond Williams (ed.), *The Irish Struggle*, p. 87). Since the above was written, the publication of the secret debates of the Dáil indicates that in August 1921, during the truce, Mr de Valera pointed out that Republicans had not the power 'and some of them had not the inclination' to use force against Ulster. 'For his part,' he said a little later, 'if the Republic were recognised, he would be in favour of giving each county power to vote itself out of the Republic if it so wished.'

honourable to the Irish nation.' External association, if it had been strictly adhered to, would have solved the problem, but what they had got was totally inadequate and in actual practice less than Canada had, despite the great play that had been made with the Canadian model. At once he put his finger on the strategic weakness of the Treaty, the cession of the ports, and in effect, the abdication of Ireland's right to defend her own coasts. With pitiless logic he traced the effect this – 'the most humiliating condition that can be inflicted on any nation claiming to be free' – would have on Irish foreign policy. 'What is the use', he asked, 'of talking of equality, what is the use of talking of a share in foreign policy, what is the use of talking of responsibility for making treaties and alliances with foreign nations which may involve a country in war?' How could Ireland make such decisions when she was denied effective power to implement them, and especially when – unlike Canada, vast and geographically remote – she remained immovably under the shadow of Britain? About the fundamental nature of the Treaty, he insisted, there should be no doubt in anybody's mind. 'It places Ireland definitely and irrevocably under British authority and under the British Crown.'[9]

With this speech, one of the ablest delivered on either side, the case against the Treaty had been presented in all its important aspects. But if Childers so to say wound up for the opposition – though there were of course many speakers and many days of debate still to come – the pro-Treaty case received the same kind of comprehensive and lucid treatment from the deputy who came immediately after him. This was Kevin O'Higgins, still just short of thirty, but with considerable experience of government behind him and his characteristic powers of intense concentration and brutal logic already well developed. For him the acceptance of the Treaty was essentially a matter of practical politics. The terms that had been won in London were the best that could have been got without a resumption of war – 'a war in which there would have been no question of military victory'. 'For God's sake', he urged, 'let us not waste time in irrelevancies respecting our keen desire for better terms . . . Deputy Childers, to my mind, took a lot of unnecessary time and trouble in explaining how much nicer it would be to get better terms than these. He did not tell us, as an authority on military and naval matters, how we are going to break the British Army and Navy and get these better terms.' They had been right to fight in the first place for the republic as their full demand, but, he added shrewdly, the very fact of agreeing to negotiate had compromised that full demand. Then, in a passage remarkable from a man who was to do perhaps more

This remarkable admission aroused some, but not much, criticism, in a Dáil so sluggish that Mr de Valera himself observed that 'there did not seem to be much desire on the part of the members to speak' (Private Sessions of Second Dáil (Dublin [1972], pp. 29, 32).

than any other single individual to make the Treaty work, he admitted that he did not want to be forced into a stronger advocacy of it than he felt. It was not ideal, it was not everything that Ireland wanted, *but* 'it represents such a broad measure of liberty for the Irish people and it acknowledges such a large proportion of its rights, you are not entitled to reject it without being able to show them you have a reasonable prospect of achieving more.' He made it plain enough that he resented the element of compulsion that had entered into the last stage of the negotiations – but even with this reservation he still thought entry into the Commonwealth was worth while and that for a very interesting reason.* 'I believe', he said, 'the evolution of this group must be towards a condition, not merely of individual freedom but also of equality of status.' If any single sentence could sum up the policy of the Irish Free State towards the Commonwealth in the decade after the Treaty it would be this one, and O'Higgins himself was to play a main part in transforming his instinctive feeling about the Commonwealth into accomplished fact. And for Ireland also, he was convinced, gradual development was the key to the future. 'I hardly hope', he said, 'that within the terms of this Treaty there lies the fulfilment of Ireland's destiny, but I do hope and believe that with the disappearance of old passions and distrusts, fostered by centuries of persecution and desperate resistance, what remains may be won by agreement and by peaceful political evolution.' And, practical as always, he ended with an impassioned plea to the Dáil not to sacrifice people to doctrine. 'The welfare and happiness of the men and women and the little children of this nation must, after all, take precedence of political creeds and theories.'[10]

But it seemed as though theories, if not creeds, would prevail for some time longer. As the debate went on, day in and day out, before and after Christmas, its quality notably declined. The main positions had been taken, and the principal actors in the drama had said their say, in the early part of the proceedings. Thereafter there was much tedious repetition, much irrelevance and also, unhappily – though understandably in the conditions of almost intolerable strain to which the Dáil was subjected – much personal abuse, aimed especially at Collins, though by no means at him alone. It is important to realise, however, that the bitterness which now began to erupt uncontrollably sprang from convictions deeply held, from a republican faith hallowed by the blood of those who had died in 1916 and afterwards. It was not surprising, therefore, that the women members of the Dáil should have been among the most uncompromising opponents of the Treaty, since

* O'Higgins, like other deputies, attributed to Lloyd George the threat of 'immediate and terrible war'. In fact, as we have seen, the Prime Minister had used somewhat different language, though no doubt the effect of it was the same. Within a few minutes of O'Higgins's speech, deputies were to hear from Robert Barton a moving explanation of why

upon them had fallen so much of the suffering that flowed from the Anglo-Irish war. And even though Mrs O'Callaghan, widow of the murdered Mayor of Limerick, protested that no woman in the Dáil would vote 'because she is warped by a deep personal loss', she herself, and Tom Clarke's widow, and Terence MacSwiney's sister, were adamant for the republic whatever the cost.

Had a vote been taken before the Christmas adjournment it is possible that this uncompromising view might have prevailed and that the Treaty might then have been rejected. The interval for reflection was, on the whole, an interval favourable to the settlement – it produced many resolutions from public and other bodies in favour of acceptance and very few against – and it is significant that no sooner had the Dáil reassembled on 3 January than Collins sought to substitute some positive action for the endless stream of words. What he had in mind was that the opponents of the Treaty could refrain from voting in the division (this would allow them to preserve their principles intact) and enable the Provisional Government to come into existence for the purpose of taking over the administration of the country from the British. Afterwards, Collins suggested, in words that have an ominous ring in retrospect, 'you can fight the Provisional Government on the republican question'. This led to intensive and semi-private negotiation for two days, but it proved unacceptable to de Valera, who dismissed the proposal with some justice as an invitation to let the Free State take root and then try to pull it up again. He himself was still manoeuvring for a favourable opportunity to introduce into the debate his alternative to the Treaty. This was the scheme, embodied in the famous but elusive Document No. 2, which had been discussed previously at the private session and which pro-Treaty speakers had repeatedly tried to bring within the ambit of the public debate so that the people should realise that de Valera's substitute for the Treaty was not the republic properly so called, but external association. At one point, on 4 and 5 January, it seemed as if it would at last be discussed, but even then confusion still persisted about what the document really contained. At the private session it had numbered twenty-three clauses. When circulated again to the Dáil on 4 January, six of these clauses had been dropped. Griffith at once protested that they were being asked to consider an essentially different document and after the Dáil had adjourned he took the drastic step of sending the original Document No. 2 to the press.[11] In reality, the difference between the two versions was not so extreme as he made

he signed the Treaty in violation of his oath to the republic. 'Speaking for himself and his colleagues, the Prime Minister with all the solemnity and the power of conviction that he alone, of all men I have met, can impart by word and gesture . . . declared that the signature and recommendation of every member of our delegation was necessary or war would follow immediately.'

out, for in both of them the President had been striving to make the same two fundamental points. The first of these concerned status and declared quite simply that 'the legislative, executive and judicial authority of Ireland shall be derived solely from the people of Ireland.' The second had to do with Ireland's relation to the Commonwealth and, after defining how matters of 'common concern' would be handled, put the crucial question of the Crown in a single lapidary phrase: 'That, for purposes of the Association, Ireland shall recognise His Britannic Majesty as head of the Association.' With this ingenious formula it would have become possible at one stroke to abolish the Oath and to exclude the Crown completely from the internal affairs of the country. Whether such ingenuity would have commended itself to the British negotiators of the Treaty was, of course, another matter.

It was not, however, a matter that was to be put to the test there and then. The chief importance of Document No. 2 is that it makes intelligible much of de Valera's subsequent career. It also explains why for him, as much as for Griffith and Collins, the rupture over the Treaty that was then, on 4 January, only a few days away, was an unmitigated disaster, since it was bound to lead both sides to harden into extreme attitudes. Not surprisingly, therefore, when he rehearsed the history of the document to the Dáil on 6 January his speech showed evidence of severe strain. In a sense it was a speech of self-justification designed both to show that the concept of external association was *not* incompatible with the existence of the republic, and also that he himself was not just an intellectual spinning abstractions in his study, but was close to the thoughts and desires of ordinary citizens. 'Whenever', he said in a phrase that was to haunt him for many years, 'I wanted to know what the Irish people wanted I had only to examine my own heart and it told me straight off what the Irish people wanted.'[12] He still, he assured the Dáil, stood for the republic as it had been proclaimed in 1916, but he stood also for peace and reconciliation with Britain. Both of these could be achieved by Document No. 2, but Document No. 2 could only be put to the House by a new and undivided Cabinet. Since the present Cabinet was now 'divided fundamentally' he proffered his resignation and that of his ministers. When it was objected that this was out of order in the midst of a motion on whether or not the Treaty should be accepted, he burst out petulantly that he was 'sick and tired of politics – so sick that no matter what happens I would go back to private life'. But he agreed to let the debate go on and finally on 7 January came the long-awaited decision – sixty-four votes for the Treaty, fifty-seven against.

This was indeed an historic moment and realised as such even at the time. But it was also a moment which seemed only to intensify the gathering confusion. The way was clear now for de Valera to resign and this he duly did. But who or what should take his place? And with the resignation of the President of the republic, what became of the republic itself? What, for that matter, was to be the fate of the Dáil which, if there was any logic to what had just happened, had, by approving the Treaty, voted for its own speedy extinction? These questions were not academic. They assumed a frighteningly practical form when de Valera proceeded to stand for re-election as President of the republic. If he won, then the entire agony of the Treaty debate would seem to have been in vain. And he very nearly did, for the motion was only defeated by sixty votes to fifty-eight. There followed a long and involved discussion as to whether or not Griffith was the appropriate man to take his place and, if so, whether he could justly be described as President of the republic when he had signed a Treaty incompatible with the existence of that republic. Inevitably, there was ill-humour and bitterness, though the principals in the argument behaved with dignity, even with magnanimity. Griffith spoke of his 'love and respect' for de Valera while the latter, after warning deputies against fratricidal strife, promised the pro-Treaty party that 'we will be there with you against any outside enemy at any time'. He and his friends would co-operate provided they did not compromise their principles in doing so. 'We will not interfere with you', he said, 'except when we find that you are going to do something that will definitely injure the Irish nation.' How significant a reservation this might be time was soon to tell.

(iii)

The transition could hardly have been other than difficult and painful. So much was evident when de Valera and his associates ostentatiously withdrew from the Dáil while Griffith was being elected to the Presidency. The opponents of the Treaty returned again immediately afterwards, it is true, but already by then it was apparent that the time for parliamentary debate was over and that the shape of the future would be determined by the answers to two questions. Could the new government really govern? And what would be the attitude of the Army to the outcome of the marathon argument in the Dáil?

Before long it would be clear that these two questions were in effect one question and that the durability of the civil government would depend upon the loyalty of the Army. At the end of the Dáil discussions, the new Minister of Defence, General Mulcahy, had assured the House that the Army would remain the Army of the Irish Republic. But would it remain one Army? Given the divisions that were now opening between friends, even between members of the same family, it would have been too much to expect that the soldiers should remain silent and neutral. On the contrary, they were as deeply split as any other section of the community. Of the headquarters staff a majority favoured the Treaty, but it had also some redoubtable opponents, including such ardent republicans as Rory

O'Connor, Liam Mellows and Sean Russell. In the provinces, likewise, the same confusion prevailed and here also some of the most able Commandants – for example, Liam Lynch and Ernie O'Malley – held fast to the republic. This was a particularly dangerous situation because of the past history of the military arm. The force from which it sprang, the Irish Volunteers, had originally had its own government or executive and had only come under the control of the Dáil at the moment when Cathal Brugha had insisted that deputies and soldiers alike should take the oath of allegiance to the republic. Now that the republic itself had come to seem so shadowy, would the Army still hold itself bound by this oath? Soon it appeared that it – or at least a section of it – might not. On 12 January (only two days after the debates had concluded) a group of officers – including Rory O'Connor, Liam Mellows, Oscar Traynor and Liam Lynch – wrote to the Minister of Defence demanding the summoning of an Army Convention. At this Convention it was proposed to introduce resolutions not only reaffirming the Army's allegiance to the republic, but also entrusting supreme control to an executive of its own choice – in effect to a government independent of the civil authorities. Mulcahy's instinct was to resist this pressure, but since it was obvious that the convention would be held anyway he decided in the end to accept the proposal and it was agreed that a meeting should be held within two months. Meantime, however, and as an obvious precaution, he went ahead as rapidly as he could with the formation of a regular national army drawn from cadres whose loyalty to the Treaty was deemed to be impeccable.

In these preliminary exchanges, discreet and muffled though they were, we can now detect the first premonitory rumblings of the coming Civil War. But at the time, naturally, it was the assumption of power by the first native Irish government for 700 years that caught the imagination of the public. Yet even here there was complexity. When Griffith was elected President in de Valera's place he at once formed his own ministry, consisting, besides himself, of Collins, Gavan Duffy, Duggan, Cosgrave, Kevin O'Higgins, General Mulcahy, P. J. Hogan, Joseph McGrath, Michael Hayes, Desmond FitzGerald and Ernest Blythe. But essentially this was a caretaker government which was responsible to a dying Dáil. The business of actually taking over from the British authorities could only (under Articles 17 and 18 of the Treaty) be done by a different government constituted by a meeting of the Southern Ireland Parliament elected under the Government of Ireland Act of 1920. This Parliament, as we have already seen, was identical with the Dáil, except that it also contained four representatives of Dublin University. But when its members were summoned on 14 January to approve the Treaty and to constitute the Irish government, de Valera and his supporters stayed away, so that the brief business of the Southern Ireland Parliament was done by sixty pro-Treaty representatives together with the members for Dublin

University. Collins became Chairman of this Provisional Government and several of his colleagues in the Dáil Ministry joined him in the Provisional Government – Cosgrave, Duggan, O'Higgins, Hogan and McGrath; in addition, Eoin MacNeill and Finian Lynch were members of the Provisional Government but not of the Dáil Ministry. This duplication was certainly complicated, but it worked better than might perhaps have been expected, due partly to the very fact that some of the most important and forceful advocates of the Treaty figured in both ministries, and partly to the practice of holding joint meetings whenever circumstances demanded.[18]

Because it was the specific function of the Provisional Government to take over from the British it followed that the main administrative burden fell on Collins, who now carried an appalling load of responsibility. It was to him that Dublin Castle was surrendered on 16 January and it was he who shuttled back and forth between London and Dublin arranging the final details of the transfer of power. Soon the outward and visible signs of imperial withdrawal began to manifest themselves. British troops marched away from their barracks for the last time, the Black and Tans and the Auxies were sent home, the disbandment of the RIC was set in train and a new unarmed Civic Guard was formed to replace both them and the republican police. Relations with the British government were the least of Collins's worries. Far more immediately pressing – once the evacuation of the troops and special police was well under way – were the two problems of Northern Ireland and the deepening internal division in the south. That Northern Ireland would hold firmly to its own parliament was only to be expected and Collins, like other pro-Treaty Ministers, was probably prepared to put up with this in the expectation that the Boundary Commission would end such independent capers. But in the meantime there was a large Catholic and nationalist minority in the six counties dangerously exposed to the kind of pogrom that had been unleashed in 1920. If this should happen again it would be difficult for an Irish government in the south, whether pro- or anti-Treaty, to stand aside. Both Collins and Sir James Craig stood to gain from peace and on 21 January they reached agreement in London on a promise by Craig to protect the northern Catholics from persecution, and by Collins to end the boycott of Belfast goods which had been the south's retaliation for the previous anti-Catholic attacks. But the border was a standing provocation to the IRA, and raiding and shooting continued sporadically, always with the promise of something much more serious behind it. During February and March cases of arson and killing multiplied. The northern government sought to bring lawlessness under control by a Special Powers Act which imposed stringent regulations about curfew, illegal drilling and the wearing of illegal uniforms, and also made the possession of firearms punishable by death. All this, together with the appointment of that arch-Unionist, Sir Henry Wilson, as Northern Ireland's military adviser on his retirement from the British Army, pointed towards a desire to shatter IRA attacks on the north once and for all. True, at the end of March another and more elaborate north-south agreement was negotiated which began with the optimistic declaration: 'Peace is today declared.' But this did little or nothing to check the mounting campaign of brutality against Catholics, several thousands of whom were driven out of Northern Ireland altogether. So terrible was the situation that in the spring of 1922 it seemed that the IRA might forget its own internal divisions and strike at the common foe.

Had it done so the outcome of the Treaty might have been a different kind of Civil War, a religious war, a war of north and south, rather than a war between old comrades. But in fact, even before the crisis in Northern Ireland had developed, the dissensions within the IRA had already gone almost beyond the point of no return. For both sides this was a catastrophe, but for Collins it was a peculiarly personal tragedy, since he had done so much to build up the Army and still regarded himself as at heart a soldier. It was difficult for him to believe that the weapon he had forged was breaking to pieces under his very eyes, and contemporary accounts suggest that he was so obsessed with the dangers and heartbreak of a split in the Army, and indeed in the whole Sinn Féin movement, that in trying to avoid such a break he found his relations even with Griffith less easy than they had formerly been.[14] Griffith, with that power of incisive leadership which came so naturally to him, wanted to scotch the trouble whenever and wherever it showed itself. Unhappily, there were all too many places and occasions where division within the ranks of the Army could easily arise. Military depots and barracks were taken over usually by the local IRA forces as soon as the British evacuated them, but whether they held these strong-points for the Provisional Government or for the republic depended on a host of circumstances over which neither Griffith nor Collins had any control. An example of the potentially fatal confusion that could arise in such a situation was provided at Limerick in late February and early March when two different contingents disputed the control of the town. At the last minute a settlement was patched up, but it is significant that Griffith was for strong action at once. In this instance, it seems, Collins was prepared to go with him, but it was noticeable that when General Mulcahy suggested that the pro-Treaty forces were in no position to force the pace, he jumped at the chance of another breathing-space before violence took over.[15]

Limerick, as Griffith seems instinctively to have grasped, was a portent, likely to be followed by other similar incidents. To grasp the nettle was essential – but also dangerous. Just how dangerous the month of March was to reveal. Two separate and at first unrelated developments threatened the position of the Provisional Government. The first was the re-emergence of de Valera on the political scene at the head of what was ostensibly a new party – Cumann na Poblachta

(League of the Republic) – but was in reality the main body of his supporters in the Treaty debates. The former President celebrated the event by a series of speeches which, according to his friends, were a statesmanlike warning against the dangers of physical force, but which, to his critics, looked remarkably like an appeal to that very policy. Thus on 16 March, the day after his new party was launched, he denounced the Treaty as barring the way to independence. 'It was only by Civil War after this that they could get their independence.'[16] And on three occasions in the next three days he declared that if the Treaty were accepted then the fight would have to go on, even if it had to be fought over the dead bodies of Irishmen slain by Irishmen.*

However well-intentioned, this would still have been dangerous language in any circumstances. It was particularly dangerous in view of the second and almost simultaneous development of that month – the crisis in the Army. It was brought to a head by the action of the Minister of Defence (Mulcahy) in forbidding at the last moment the holding of the long-promised Army Convention for fear it would result in the setting up of a military junta. Since, however, he was in no position to enforce obedience to his edict, he suffered the humiliation of seeing the Convention take place in spite of him. True, it was not attended by the pro-Treaty men and it did contain some IRA officers who had not yet despaired of reaching an accommodation with the government, but there was no gainsaying that it was dominated by the out-and-out republicans amongst whom Rory O'Connor was rapidly emerging as one of the most intransigent leaders. The result of the convention was to confirm the allegiance of the Army – or that section of it which O'Connor and his friends controlled – to the republic and to vest authority in an executive consisting of sixteen officers and including, besides O'Connor himself, such redoubtable fighters as Lynch, Mellows and O'Malley. O'Connor, in a specially summoned press conference, made it perfectly plain that they would not obey Griffith or his ministers and that they repudiated the Dáil. 'Do we take it that we are going to have a military dictatorship, then?' he was asked. To which he replied: 'You can take it that way if you like.'

It soon became clear what this would mean in practice. Within a few weeks of the convention the forces of the executive – or 'Irregulars' as we may now begin to call them – seized the Four Courts and

* One quotation will suffice: 'If they accepted the Treaty,' he said at Thurles, 'and if the Volunteers of the future tried to complete the work the Volunteers of the last four years had been attempting, they would have to complete it, not over the bodies of foreign soldiers, but over the dead bodies of their own countrymen. They would have to wade through Irish blood, through the blood of the soldiers of the Irish Government and through, perhaps, the blood of some of the members of the Government in order to get Irish freedom . . .'

certain other buildings in Dublin which they turned into strongly held military posts.[17] At the same time incidents multiplied throughout the country as government troops and Irregulars manoeuvred for possession of important strategic points, and it seemed only a matter of time before serious fighting would break out. The situation was delicately poised and yet extremely complex. There were now in effect four governments in the same small island. One of these, Sir James Craig's in Northern Ireland, was determined to preserve its separation from the rest of the country, but in these spring months of 1922 it was an open question whether or not it could do so. Riven as the province was by internal divisions between Catholics and Protestants, its border by its very existence was a standing affront to the south. And, as we have seen, one of the factors preventing the two sections of the IRA from flying at each other's throats was the possibility of combining to go to the aid of their co-religionists and fellow-nationalists in the north. Of the other governments, two – those of Griffith and of Collins – were both in the strictest sense of the term 'provisional', Griffith's because it would die when the Dáil gave place to a newly elected parliament, and Collins's because it was never intended to do more than prepare the way for the new dominion and would have completed its task when the Irish Free State came formally into being at the end of 1922. The fourth government – the Executive of the anti-Treaty IRA forces – had of course no legal status at all, but it was armed and resolute, and in a violent time that might yet render it formidable. This four-fold division of authority did not, however, exhaust the political confusion or near anarchy into which the country was drifting. For in addition to the anti-Treaty Irregulars, and as yet quite distinct from them, stood de Valera's Cumann na Poblachta, unreconciled to the Treaty and a potential source of trouble should the efforts of Griffith and Collins fail to preserve the authority of the pro-Treaty party.*

It was small wonder that the British cabinet, reviewing the situation in April, was doubtful if the Provisional Government could survive. Even if civil war did not erupt in the south, it was still possible, Churchill suggested in a memorandum for his fellow-ministers, that the whole twenty-six counties might go over to the republican side and that an attack would be made upon Northern Ireland. In such a situation the role of the British forces would be to hold the best military line in Ulster 'irrespective of the boundary', while at the same time flying columns of troops should attack republican centres of government in Dublin or elsewhere. Air power and economic sanctions

* Mention should also be made at this point of the revitalised women's organisation, the Cumann na m Bann, with Countess Markievicz at its head. It was fiercely, even virulently, republican, and followed closely the line taken during the Treaty debates by such speakers as Kathleen Clarke, Mary MacSwiney and Erskine Childers. For this reason it was christened by the wags the 'women and Childers party'.

would also have to be used against the insurgents but – and here was a change from the conditions of the previous three years – republican troops in uniform ought not to be treated as rebels.

Churchill thought that April would mark the turning-point in Ireland. The next ten days, he told the Cabinet on 10 April, would show 'whether the leaders of the Free State were prepared to fight or to endure without resistance the insults now being offered them'.[18] In this, however, he was premature and reckoned without Collins's almost desperate insistence on exhausting every possible line of peaceful settlement before resorting to force. In pursuing this policy to such lengths as to endanger his relations with his own colleagues, Collins may to some extent have been actuated by military caution – the government forces were still too small and disorganised to be sure of success – but it seems probable that it was a political factor that was uppermost in his mind. The time was fast approaching when a general election must be held for a new parliament to hammer out a constitution for the Irish Free State so that the dominion status promised by the Treaty could come into operation by the end of the year. As far back as February, before the split had gone too deep, Griffith and de Valera had been able to meet at the Ard-Fheis of Sinn Féin and agree that no election should be held for three months, by which time it was hoped that there would be a draft constitution for the new state upon which, as well as upon the question of whether or not to accept the Treaty, the electors would be asked to vote. But conditions had radically changed in the interval and for such an election now to take place in the midst of a civil war (assuming such a thing even to be practicable) would be from every point of view disastrous. Collins, therefore, still clung to the hope that the election might take place either under truce conditions or after some preliminary agreement between the rival sections so as to limit the extent of the actual contest at the polls. This explains the frantic negotiations out of which was to emerge in the end the so-called Collins-de Valera pact, so puzzling at the time and so much denounced ever since.

(iv)

The situation in which Collins and his fellow-members of the Provisional Government found themselves was excruciatingly difficult. On the one hand, the executive of the IRA had set up their headquarters in Dublin under the very noses of the supposedly responsible authorities, had then proceeded to recoup their funds by the simple process of robbing banks, and had even made their presence physically felt by posting snipers in a position to dominate both the government buildings and the official Army headquarters at Beggar's Bush. On the other hand, the Provisional Government was simultaneously trying to work out a constitution which would be acceptable not only to a highly critical British cabinet, but also to the anti-Treaty followers of de Valera. To put down the military challenge presented by Rory O'Connor at the Four Courts might well involve the country in a general conflagration; not to put it down might equally well lead to the disappearance of the Provisional Government. On the political front the dilemma was no less acute. To adopt a constitution which did not square with the Treaty would mean trouble with Britain; yet to adopt one which did not square with the concept of external association would mean trouble with de Valera.

It is against this bafflingly complex situation that Collins's man-oeuvres must be judged. But it has to be borne in mind that all the time he was a soldier who could not for long lose sight of old loyalties and of military objectives. Old loyalties drove him to negotiate with the anti-Treaty forces up to the very last minute; military objectives – more specifically the possibility of mounting an attack on Ulster – led him to co-operate closely with IRA leaders along the northern border at the very time when non-military politicians like Griffith or Kevin O'Higgins were demanding that the Army in every shape or form should be brought properly under civil control. It was natural, therefore, that when a conference at the end of April, arranged by the Archbishop of Dublin, and attended by de Valera, Brugha, Griffith, Collins, the three principal Labour leaders, the Lord Mayor of Dublin and the Mayor of Limerick, failed to reach agreement on the conduct of the forthcoming election, Collins should have turned to his former comrades. The result was the promulgation at the beginning of May 1922 of the so-called Army Document, signed by representatives of pro- and anti-Treaty forces. It called for a political and military reunification and demanded 'an agreed election' leading to the forma-tion of a government that would have the confidence of the whole country. However, since it also proceeded from the assumption that 'the majority of the people are willing to accept the Treaty', it is not surprising that it was immediately denounced by O'Connor as 'a political dodge intended to split the Republican ranks'. Nevertheless, it commanded enough respect even among anti-Treaty men for a truce of a kind to be patched up – not before it was time, for at the moment the document was being drawn up fighting was actually going on in Kilkenny and there were reports of sporadic violence from other places.[19]

Out of this truce came yet more negotiations between the politicians, who met several times during May. Some progress was made towards the idea of a 'panel' election, with a coalition government to follow it, but the talks broke down over the apparently insoluble problems of whether, and if so in what circumstances, the Treaty could be made an issue at the election. In the end Collins took the matter into his own hands and had a personal meeting with de Valera on 20 May at which their seven-point 'pact' was concluded. The essence of it was that there would be a national coalition panel, representing both the existing sections in the Dáil and in Sinn Féin. All on the panel would stand as Sinn Féin candidates and the number allowed to each section would be the same as its existing strength in the Dáil. After the election a coalition would be formed with an elected President, a Minister of Defence representing the Army and nine other ministers, five from the majority, four from the minority. This was, of course, a thoroughly undemocratic procedure and the only gesture made towards allowing free choice to the electors was the proviso that 'every and any interest is free to go up and contest the election equally with the National Sinn Féin panel'.[20] In an election where armed men were certain to be much in evidence this was not, perhaps, much of a concession, but in the event it was to have more significance than had been anticipated.

This pact, to which Collins no doubt put his name with the best of intentions, was by any odds a deplorable document and it seems that when it was submitted to a joint meeting of the Provisional Government and the Dáil Cabinet, Griffith came within an ace of repudiating it. 'When voting commenced and his name was called', Mr Blythe remembers, 'he sat silent in apparent distress for about two minutes before giving his assent.'[21] He had good cause for distress. The pact was not just a travesty of the electoral process, it represented a major tactical victory for the opponents of the Treaty. No one summed up its likely consequences better than Churchill in a report to the British Cabinet ten days later: 'It prevented an expression of opinion on the Treaty; it gave the Provisional Government no further representation of strength or authority from the Irish people; it left the Government in its present weak and helpless position; it ruptured Article 17 of the Treaty.'[22] The reference to Article 17 of the Treaty was inspired by the supposition that if four republicans were to sit in the coalition government after the Irish election they would refuse to fulfil the obligation imposed on ministers of signifying in writing their acceptance of the Treaty. But in fact much more than Article 17 was at issue. The whole Anglo-Irish settlement hung in the balance and the British government were to find in June, when they came to look seriously at the draft constitution proposed by the Provisional Government, that even Irishmen like Collins and Griffith, who had staked their lives on the settlement of December 1921, were capable of producing an instrument of government which departed in important particulars from that settlement. Straining as they were to avoid civil war, the Provisional Government went as far as they dared in approximating their constitution to the concept of external association. They reduced the Crown to a cipher, they dropped the Oath, they excluded appeal to the Judicial Committee of the Privy Council, they claimed the right (which no other dominion then had) of making their own treaties, and they did not recognise the special position of Ulster. In short, their draft constitution was eloquent of their dilemma. Either they made a constitution that conformed with the Treaty and quarrelled with de Valera; or else they made a constitution which amended the Treaty in a republican sense and risked an open breach with London.

The way out of the dilemma was, however, predictable enough. Lloyd George could still exert more pressure than de Valera and, after some hard bargaining, Griffith and Collins accepted amendments which brought their draft firmly once more within the confines of the Treaty. Had this amended draft been published any reasonable length of time before the election it would presumably have destroyed the pact. For purely technical reasons it did not appear until the voting day and practically the entire campaign was fought on the basis of the Collins-de Valera agreement that the purpose of the election was to produce a coalition of the two opposing parties 'without prejudice to their present respective positions'. However, less than forty-eight hours before polling Collins himself made a speech advising the electors in plain terms to vote for whatever candidates they thought best. This was widely regarded as a virtual repudiation of the pact and although opinions still differ as to the effect, or even the exact meaning, of Collins's speech, it is probably fair to say that for most people, the pact notwithstanding, the central issue was the Treaty. On the other hand, it is essential to a proper understanding of subsequent events to realise that in Republican eyes the pact remained in existence and the election was still an election designed to produce a coalition. When the results were announced on 24 June it was found that the pro-Treaty panel had won fifty-eight out of the 128 seats, whereas the anti-Treaty panel had won only thirty-five; there were in addition seventeen successful Labour candidates, seven Independents, seven Farmers,* and four members for Dublin University. Perhaps the most striking feature of the election was not that the panel arrangement did indeed leave a considerable number of seats uncontested, but rather that other parties of varying origins had asserted their right to compete and that Labour especially was at last emerging as a potential party of opposition. All told 620,283 votes were cast. Of these, the pro-Treaty panel candidates won 239,193 and the anti-Treaty panel candidates 133,864. The remaining candidates – Labour, Independents, Farmers – between them polled the largest total, 247,226 votes. It began to seem as if there was a substantial proportion of the electorate which would like to cry a plague on both the pro- and anti-Treaty houses and which perhaps might in the future find the strength and courage to do so.[23]

But that future was not yet. Once again violence was to distort the pattern of events and to sweep all carefully laid plans for pacts, coalitions, and constitutional oppositions ruthlessly on one side. On 22

* This was a group which represented, on the whole, the larger and more prosperous farmers. It took the pro-Treaty side and later was to give steady support to the Cosgrave government.

June Field Marshal Sir Henry Wilson – that archetypal Unionist who had opposed every form of Irish self-government since before the First World War – was assassinated on his own doorstep in London. His murderers were Commandant Reginald Dunne and Joseph O'Sullivan, of the London battalion of the IRA. Both men were duly hanged and went to their deaths without revealing on whose orders they had acted. Like so many of the shootings of those troubled years this episode was shrouded in mystery when it happened and has even yet resisted all attempts at final elucidation. It has to be said, though, that a substantial body of evidence has been accumulated (most of it from IRA officers who were acquainted with various circumstances surrounding the murder) which points to the fact that the two assassins 'executed' Wilson in response to a military order and that this order emanated from Collins himself. One version has it that he had issued the command during the Treaty negotiations and subsequently forgot to cancel it. This seems unlikely for a man normally so meticulous about detail, and another account would suggest that the order was given only about two weeks before it was carried out. Some commentators, it should be added, refuse to accept that Collins, holding the responsible position he did at that time, could have taken the appalling risk of setting in motion a violent act which, if his complicity had been discovered, would have ruined both him and the entire Provisional Government. Responsibility, such writers assert, should be laid elsewhere – perhaps at the door of the IRB, perhaps even, as Mr Ernest Blythe has lately suggested, upon individuals unknown who were enemies of Collins and wanted both to stab him in the back and also to sabotage the Treaty.[24] But to repeat, the bulk of the evidence points towards Collins, who was not only ruthless enough to give the order, but was also at that time particularly incensed by the attacks upon northern Catholics made by the very Ulster Unionists with whom Sir Henry Wilson had always identified himself.[25]

No such evidence, it need hardly be said, was available at the time either to Collins's own colleagues or to the British government. Griffith condemned the assassination outright (Collins joined him in drafting a statement for publication) and the British authorities, largely, it would seem, because of the known fact that the assassins were IRA men, jumped to the conclusion that it was the executive still lodged in the Four Courts that was responsible. This assumption was not without a certain logic. For the extreme wing of the IRA, an incident of this kind, if it were to provoke strong British action in reprisal, might bring on again a state of war between the two countries and in so doing mend the rift which had opened between Irishmen who supported and Irishmen who opposed the Treaty. The fact that, in the IRA hierarchy, Rory O'Connor was commanding officer of the Irish 'forces' in Britain to which Dunne and O'Sullivan belonged might seem on the surface to give further colour to the theory that the deed was done at his command. But in reality this was merely a coincidence and his military title a largely nominal one so far as Britain was concerned. And, although O'Connor would certainly have welcomed a renewal of the war with Britain, he at once issued a public statement that he had had nothing to do with the shooting. 'If we had', he said, with a candour that compels belief, 'we would admit it.'

Yet a war with Britain was what he nearly got all the same. The British government at once recalled General Macready from Ireland and asked him to prepare an assault upon the Four Courts, though it was as apparent to Macready as it was to Rory O'Connor that any such action would precipitate a reunion of the divided Irish forces. In the event the instructions were cancelled next day and the government contented itself with a warning to Collins that the 'ambiguous position' of the IRA could no longer be ignored. 'Still less can Mr Rory O'Connor be permitted to remain with his followers and his arsenal in open rebellion in the heart of Dublin . . .' The Provisional Government must end this state of affairs and the British authorities would be prepared to lend them the necessary artillery to do it.

This was virtually an ultimatum requesting one set of Irishmen to fire upon another set of Irishmen at the behest of the British cabinet. As such, it could very easily have had an adverse effect, had not events in Dublin independently pushed the Provisional Government in the direction Churchill and Lloyd George wanted them to go. On the night of 26 June a raiding-party from the Four Courts garrison, intent upon 'acquiring' transport from a garage, was intercepted by government troops and its leader captured. Not to be outdone, others of the Four Courts garrison that same night kidnapped the Deputy Chief of Staff of the pro-Treaty Army, General J. J. O'Connell. This was a challenge which not even Collins could any longer shrug off. It was at once decided to proceed against the Four Courts and, although British guns were indeed to be used against the recalcitrant O'Connor, it was the internal stresses and strains of the Irish situation, not the external British pressure, that brought on the final clash.

The attack on the Four Courts – which began on the morning of Wednesday, 28 June 1922 and ended on Friday, 30 June when flames made the building untenable, thus obliging the garrison to surrender – was not, as is still sometimes said, the beginning of the Civil War. The country had in fact been drifting in that direction almost from the beginning of the year. But the siege of the Four Courts *was* a dramatic demonstration that the struggle was about to become more serious, more systematised, more deadly. Its immediate effect was to polarise the conflict and end many of the existing uncertainties. Thus, although the anti-Treaty section of the IRA had begun to be deeply divided both over the prolonged efforts to reunite the armed forces by agreement and over an alternative suggestion to secure *de facto* reunification by provoking the British Army into offensive action, these dissensions vanished as if by magic once the guns began to boom.

Equally, the political opponents of the Treaty, hitherto quite separate from the anti-Treaty IRA, were pulled along in the wake of violence. Mr de Valera at once condemned the attack on the Four Courts as a fatal breach of the pact, saluted the occupying garrison as 'the best and bravest of our nation', and identified their resistance with the defence of the republic. Simultaneously, Liam Lynch, who only a few days previously had resigned as Chief of Staff because of disagreement with the Four Courts garrison, made his way south, resumed his post and prepared for war. Soon many of the old warriors of the republic were in the field again – Brugha, Stack, Countess Markievicz, de Valera, all hastened to the Dublin headquarters of the Irregulars. But as fighters they seemed to have learnt nothing and forgotten nothing. Once again, as in 1916, they occupied prominent buildings in the heart of the city mainly – as if to make the parallel complete – in O'Connell Street, and once again their enemies methodically blasted and burnt them out of their fixed positions. There was a certain symbolical aptness in the fact that when this phase of the war ended after a week of fighting, it ended with the shooting down of Cathal Brugha, that legendary warrior of Easter week, as he emerged, gun in hand, from the ruins of a burning building.

The war which now became general fell into two main phases, the first consisting of a series of direct confrontations and the second of a resumption by the Irregulars of the guerrilla warfare which had served so well against the British. The first phase, though bloody, was also brief, and lasted no more than two months. During that time the government forces steadily drove their opponents from one stronghold after another until by the end of August all the large towns and cities were in their hands.

On the face of it, this was an unexpectedly rapid and complete victory, for at the outset the balance of forces seemed strongly in favour of the Irregulars. Accurate figures are hard to come by, but some estimates of the government forces place them at no more than 7,000 when the Dublin fighting started. A recent and well-informed study suggests that this figure should probably be doubled, but that even so the anti-Treaty troops may at that stage have out-numbered them by four to one.[*] This, however, did not long remain the case. An energetic recruiting campaign found a ready response from young men reared on the violence of the Anglo-Irish

[*] E. Neeson, *The Civil War in Ireland, 1922-1923* (Cork, revised paperback ed. 1969), pp. 118-19. Since anti-Treaty calculations of the strength of the whole IRA at the time of the Army Convention in March 1922 indicated a total of over 100,000 it would seem, as Mr Neeson points out, that considerable numbers of the IRA remained neutral (ibid., p. 89). In addition to Mr Neeson's book, the history of the struggle can be followed in C. Younger, *Ireland's Civil War* (London, 1968) and (with a strong Republican bias) in D. Macardle, *The Irish Republic* (New York, 1965 ed.), parts xii to xiv. The political background has been explored by Professor

war and now ready to compete with the veterans, from the unemployed (of whom, in the summer of 1922 there were reckoned to be 150,000) and from Irishmen demobilised from the British Army whose expertise in killing was their only saleable asset. Enlistment in the pro-Treaty forces soon reached the rate of 1,000 a day and before long the government could deploy in the field an army of 60,000 men.[26] Against these resources the Irregulars had no adequate counter-weight. This may partly have been because they were apparently reluctant to accept ex-soldiers from the British Army (though one of their most notable commanders, Tom Barry, belonged to that category) but, as the fight wore on, it seems to have been due still more to their failure to win over the population to their side. Indeed, there is evidence that in some areas, so far from being won over, the inhabitants were deeply alienated by the cavalier attitudes of certain local commanders and were also, naturally enough, bitterly resentful when their towns and villages were occupied and thus made the target for the superior weapons of the government forces. Since these weapons included artillery, in which the anti-Treaty forces were markedly deficient, the damage to property was frequently severe and the resentment of the property-owners correspondingly magnified. This resentment was not, on the whole, switched to those who used the big guns to dislodge the IRA, because the guns were seen as the harbingers of a return to law and order and thence to more settled economic conditions.

The anti-Treaty section's failure to win wide-spread support from the population was itself symptomatic of a deeper malaise. While both sides had drifted into Civil War, the government, precisely because it was the government, had at its disposal the whole administrative machine, a regular if not very imposing revenue, and a power of initiative which enabled it to fight the war largely on its own terms – which terms included not only a fairly rigorous censorship of news but also, as we shall see, the adoption of extreme coercive methods. The Irregulars, on the other hand, lacked the sinews of war, lacked organisation, and lacked even a credible policy. They had a policy, indeed – to reassert in arms the indivisible republic. Unfortunately for them, it was a republic which was more invisible than indivisible, and the sincere and moving idealism with which its champions sought to evoke it roused little echo in a war-weary country bent upon as

---

T. Desmond Williams in his essays 'From the Treaty to the Civil War' and 'The Summing Up' in the volume *The Irish Struggle, 1916-1926* (London, 1966), edited by himself. Further light on individual attitudes is shed by two biographies, the Earl of Longford and T. P. O'Neill, *Eamon de Valera* (London, 1970) and M. Forester, *Michael Collins: the Lost Leader* (London, 1971). In general, though, it must be stressed that a mature judgment must await the release of material which is still locked up in the archives of the Bureau of Military History and which is unlikely to be available for many years to come.

speedy a return to normality as possible. As for the organisation which might have presented a more immediately attractive programme to the people, it was virtually non-existent. The political leader of the anti-Treaty party was still Mr de Valera, but when Mr de Valera attached himself to the Irregulars he soon found, as many another civilian has found in like circumstances, that when the shooting starts the military are singularly deaf to the promptings of the politicians. Thus, although Mr de Valera made his first attempt to end the war as early as mid-July, when the anti-Treaty situation had already begun to deteriorate, and repeated his efforts at frequent intervals thereafter, he was consistently overruled by the soldiers.

Military intransigence was personified by one man, Liam Lynch. Although other commanders were no doubt as unyielding, his attitude derived particular importance from the fact that such strategy as the Irregulars were able to improvise depended largely upon him. As Chief of Staff he was primarily concerned with attempting to co-ordinate the activities of the various IRA brigades which had come out against the government and before the war had ended he was also acting as a *de facto* Commander-in-Chief. Difficulties, partly logistic, partly arising from the tendency (in which GHQ had perforce to encourage them) of local officers to regard their posts as in effect independent commands, made it impossible for him ever to effect a concentration of the forces allegedly at his disposal big enough to secure a decisive superiority. It has been argued that had he been able to do this, his best plan would have been to march on Dublin and there put the issue to a final test. But this ignores both his un-certainty about his rear – the position in the key city of Limerick, for example, was extremely confused in the early days of the war – and underestimates his own initial reluctance to believe that the war would have to be fought *à l'outrance*. It did not take him long to realise that this was indeed so and once he had accepted the in-evitability of bitter conflict no man became more fanatically committed to the pursuit of a victory which week by week receded further from his grasp.

The plan of campaign he adopted, or which was forced upon him by circumstances, was to attempt to hold a line stretching from Water-ford to Limerick. Behind this line were grouped the main anti-Treaty forces and it was a not unreasonable assumption that, if their efforts over most of the rest of Ireland could only be sporadic, they would at least be able to defend what was known – half in jest, half in grim earnest – as 'the Munster Republic'. But even this limited and essen-tially defensive strategy was a vain illusion. Lacking adequate numbers, lacking transport, lacking artillery, the Irregulars were driven from town after town, sometimes by outflanking movements, more often after heavy bombardments and direct assaults. The fall of Limerick and of Waterford on successive days – 20 and 21 July – virtually sealed the fate of 'the Munster Republic', and although stubborn resistance was offered first in county Tipperary and later along the approaches to Cork, the end of organised resistance in the south came when on 12 August that city was captured by a sea-borne force taking it in the rear.

These reverses effectively ended the first phase of the war. The steady attrition of the Irregulars in the south had made concerted counter-attack impossible and although some leaders elsewhere – notably Frank Aiken during his adventurous career in and around Dundalk – had gained occasional local successes, the government's rolling up tactics in Munster had been repeated (or in some areas anticipated) in the midlands and the west with similar results. Nothing remained for the most resolute of the anti-Treaty leaders but to resort to guerrilla tactics. Increasingly, from late August and September onwards they took to the mountains, especially in the wilder parts of the south-west. This was a desperate expedient and it was not made any less desperate by a steady hardening of public opinion which was both reflected in and influenced by the Church's severe condemnation of the anti-Treaty position. As far back as April, the Irish hierarchy had criticised the action of the anti-Treaty officers in setting up their own executive, but in October they far exceeded these strictures. 'They carry on what they call a war', said the bishops of the Irregulars, 'but which in the absence of any legitimate authority to justify it is morally a system of murder and assassination of the National forces.' It is impossible to estimate what this and the threat of excommunication which accompanied it may have cost the anti-Treaty cause in terms of lost allegiance or diminished resolution (though some of the bolder spirits may well have been fortified, not weakened, in their resistance by this ecclesiastical intervention), but upon a population which was devoutly Catholic it could not fail to take effect.

As winter approached the situation of the guerrillas deteriorated still further, and it was not surprising that the methods by which the war was fought should also have degenerated. A struggle carried on by ambush and counter-ambush, with death liable to come suddenly from any quarter, preyed on men's nerves and drove them to extremes of cruelty. Soon rumours, and also some apparently well-authenticated stories, began to abound of torture inflicted by government troops, of reprisals by the guerrillas and even of the massacre of anti-Treaty prisoners by chaining them to landmines.

In such circumstances it was inevitable that whatever faint hopes of a negotiated peace might have existed in mid-August should have vanished by Christmas. Even on the pro-Treaty side, although military success was undeniable, it had been overshadowed by disasters of a different kind which, however, operated upon the government as defeat in the field had operated upon their opponents, strengthening their resolution to carry on the struggle to the bitter end. Scarcely had the war of confrontation entered its closing stages when the two pillars of the pro-Treaty side crashed to the ground inside a single fortnight. On 12 August died Arthur Griffith, barely fifty years old but worn out by the strains, disappointments and sheer exhaustion of the previous three years. Ten days later Collins perished in an ambush laid by Irregulars, shot through the back of the head on what can only be described as a characteristically reckless expedition in which no ordinary Commander-in-Chief would have involved himself for a moment. But Collins was no ordinary man and the likelihood of a violent death was something he had lived with for years and of which, on this occasion, he may even have had a premonition.[27]

With Collins and Griffith both dead the burden of government fell mainly upon Cosgrave, the young O'Higgins and General Richard Mulcahy, who succeeded Collins as Commander-in-Chief. When the Dáil elected in June finally met in September, it confirmed Cosgrave in office as head of the administration and he and his gifted group of ministers began the final operation to bring the Free State at last to its painful and protracted birth. But the Dáil itself remained a depleted body. De Valera and his supporters not only refused to recognise it – arguing that the Second Dáil, which was to have met on 30 June in order to dissolve itself but had never been allowed to do so, had no legitimate successor – they joined with the Irregulars' Executive to set up in October their own republican government of which de Valera was President and which included, as Minister of Defence, Sean Lemass, destined to serve many years as his right-hand man and in the fullness of time to take Ireland a long step away from memories of the Civil War. But the formation of such a government was a measure of the anti-Treaty party's desperation rather than of its confidence in the future. The civilians remained as much in thrall to the soldiers as ever and Mr de Valera's fugitive months as head of a virtually non-existent government are rightly described by his biographers as his 'darkest hour'.[28]

In the short term, of course, the proclamation of a rival government merely heightened the bitterness of the struggle. But, because the Irregulars were difficult to pin down, or even to identify, it ceased to be a struggle conducted on military lines, degenerating into a series of attacks and reprisals which more than anything else led to estrangements persisting sometimes to this day. To deal with its enemies the government took exceptional and very severe powers including the right to try before an Army Court, and if necessary to execute, persons found in unauthorised possession of arms or ammunition. One of the first and most distinguished victims of this policy was Erskine Childers and it did not lessen the bitterness with which this blow was received by his comrades to reflect that 'the Englishman' had long been a particular enemy of Griffith and of O'Higgins, both of whom, it is fair to say, seem to have regarded him as a far more powerful, and from their point of view more baneful, influence in Irish affairs than he really was.

Violence of this kind although itself provoked by violence, begot, as always, more violence in return and so the vicious cycle revolved. The atmosphere of deepening horror was, if anything, intensified, by the fact that when at the end of the year the Irish Free State was duly set up, with a Dáil and a Senate, the members of those two bodies were at once threatened by their opponents with death and the destruction of their property.* On 7 December one of the deputies in the Dáil, Sean Hales, was shot dead in Dublin. The next morning four republican leaders were taken out and shot in reprisal. The group included Liam Mellows and Rory O'Connor (who had been best man at O'Higgins's wedding scarcely a year before) and the decision was only taken after dire heart-searching by the government.[29] But once taken it was acted upon repeatedly thereafter, until in various parts of the country a total of seventy-seven prisoners was shot in reprisal for outrages (murder, attempted murder, and arson being the chief) committed by the Irregulars. Apart from those who were executed, many others, estimated at 11-12,000, were shut up for varying periods in government prisons.† They included names famous in the republican roll of honour – Mary MacSwiney, Grace Plunkett (who had married Joseph Plunkett in prison the night before his execution in 1916), James Connolly's daughter Nora, and eventually, though some months after the ceasefire, de Valera himself.

These terrible events and decisions – productive as they were of enmities that still divide family from family – played their part in the war of attrition that was steadily wearing down the republican forces. When their most outstanding leader, Liam Lynch, was killed in action in April 1923 the end was seen to be near. His successor as Chief of Staff of the Irregulars, Frank Aiken (years later to become Minister for External Affairs of the Irish Republic), agreed with de Valera that it was time to negotiate a truce and on 24 May the cease-fire came at last. The republican troops did not, however, surrender their arms. They were told to conceal them where they might be recovered if needed, for despite the surrender the republic lived on in the eyes of its supporters, even though its President was on the run and it had no effective machinery of government. To what tragic ends this visionary republic was to lead its adherents will later appear.

* The first election under the constitution of the Irish Free State was held in August 1923. But the new state was brought into being by the Dáil which had been elected in June 1922, minus Mr de Valera and his colleagues. This truncated Dáil acted as a Constituent Assembly from September onwards; as such it was responsible for the establishment of the Senate which, for its first three-year term, consisted of thirty members nominated by the government (the intention being to secure a sufficient representation of ex-Unionists) and thirty elected by the Dáil; given the non-attendance of the Republicans this first election 'contained', as even the historian of the Senate admits, 'many elements of farce' (D. O'Sullivan, *The Irish Free State and its Senate* (London, 1940), p. 92.

† It is more difficult to estimate the total number of deaths on each side. The pro-Treaty forces lost nearly 600 men in July and August 1922

But in May 1923 it seemed for all practical purposes to be dead. Power now rested firmly in the hands of the companions and political heirs of the men who had signed the Treaty and brought the Irish Free State into being. What they would make of their opportunity remained to be seen.

---

alone and the anti-Treaty losses were almost certainly heavier. A recent, but admittedly approximate, calculation places the combined losses at about 300 a month, or just under 4,000 in all. The cash cost to the government of crushing the resistance of the Irregulars was reckoned by Kevin O'Higgins to be about £17 million, but the material damage to property probably exceeded £30 million (for these estimates, see E. Neeson, *The Civil War in Ireland*, p. 291; D. Macardle, *The Irish Republic*, p. 861, and D. O'Sullivan, *The Irish Free State and its Senate*, p. 115).

PART IV

The Partitioned Island

A. FROM FREE STATE TO REPUBLIC

B. NORTH IRELAND UNDER
HOME RULE

It is the paradox of all revolution that it paralyses the creative impulse from which it sprang. Its origin a principle, its end a formula – such is its fatal cycle.
L. KOHN, *The Constitution of the Irish Free State*, p. 108

1. Building the New State

(i) THE FOUNDATIONS

That the revolutionary of today is the conservative of tomorrow is a truism of politics in no way contradicted by the recent history of modern Ireland. But it is, perhaps, less often observed that the revolutionary becomes a conservative, not just because of the sobering influence of power upon responsible individuals, but also because revolutions, even when they appear to be most successful, frequently preserve as much as they destroy. The Irish revolution, though it succeeded to a far greater extent than had at one time seemed remotely possible, nevertheless ended in compromise and if the compromise seemed then, and has proved since, ephemeral, yet its very existence helped to bring into play that tension between the revolutionary and the conservative elements in Irish society which dominated the political life and institutions of the new state in its earliest years.

The most striking illustration of this is to be found in the Constitution itself. The Constitution of the Irish Free State (Saorstát Eireann) Act of 1922 embodied a highly ingenious attempt, if not to have the best of both worlds, at least to bridge those two worlds in such a way as to reconcile the ideals of the recent revolutionary past with the necessity of a continuing British connection. Thus, on the one hand, the preamble to the Act echoed the revolutionary doctrine of popular sovereignty in the phrase 'all lawful authority comes from God to the people', a doctrine restated more concretely in Article 2 of the actual Constitution, where it was laid down unequivocally that 'all powers of government and all authority legislative, executive and judicial in Ireland, are derived from the people of Ireland'. On the other hand, not only was the Crown retained at various points in the document, but the second clause of the Act made it clear that the Constitution was to be construed 'with reference to the Articles of Agreement for a Treaty between Great Britain and Ireland . . . which are hereby given the force of law, and if any provision of the said Constitution or of any amendment thereof or of any law made thereunder is in any respect repugnant to any of the provisions of the Scheduled Treaty it shall, to the extent of such repugnancy, be absolutely void and inoperative'. In short the Treaty, which was intended to hold the new dominion within the confines of the Commonwealth, was made a part of the municipal law of the state – so much so that when the new Constitution was being debated in the Dáil members were informed

471

that the articles implementing the Treaty (and also certain others designed to safeguard the rights of minorities) were regarded by ministers as so vital that their rejection would involve the resignation of the government.[1]

From the very beginning, therefore, the Constitution seemed to point in two quite different directions. But its contradictions did not end there. For not only did it seek to harmonise republican ideals with membership of the Commonwealth, it also attempted to combine the pragmatic British approach to the business of government with an attachment to those ringing declarations of human rights which were common to so many revolutionary constitutions in various parts of the world after 1918 and of which the Democratic Programme of the first Dáil had been an early example. It must be admitted, however, that the Constitution of 1922 fell a good deal short of the Democratic Programme and it was perhaps significant of the way in which the first, fine, careless rapture of revolutionary radicalism was already fading that the attempts made by some Labour members to bring the social content of the Constitution more into line with the doctrines of James Connolly came to nothing.[2] In fact, only two 'programmatic' declarations were embodied in the Constitution – one asserting the right (in practice it turned out to be a compulsion) of all citizens to free elementary education, the other providing for the legal succession of the Free State to all rights in lands, waters, mines and minerals within the territory of the Free State previously held by the Crown or a Department of State, and also investing the Free State with a general title to the control of all natural resources of the country and of all franchises and royalties to be derived from their exploitation. Although in practice the latter article was rarely invoked, and then on a very limited scale, it opened the way to a thoroughgoing policy of nationalisation of the country's resources should that ever be deemed necessary; so to this extent the old radicalism, if muted since 1919, still made itself heard.[3]

But it was not just social rights that the Constitution undertook to protect. In addition, by Articles 6 to 9, it expressly guaranteed such personal rights as *habeas corpus*, the inviolability of the citizen's dwelling, freedom to practise any religion ('subject to public order and morality'), freedom of expression and freedom of association. There was, of course, nothing particularly novel about these provisions; they were simply the embodiment in a written instrument of a familiar liberal tradition and did not involve any departure from the legal framework within which the authors of the Constitution themselves had grown up. But it was felt necessary – chiefly for the reassurance of the Protestant minority – to go rather further and to prohibit the state from endowing any religion, imposing any disability on account of religious belief or status, affecting prejudicially 'the right of any child to attend a school receiving public money without attending the religious instruction at the school', discriminating between schools managed by different denominations, or acquiring church property by compulsion except for certain clearly defined public purposes and then only after payment of compensation.[4]

This, however, was not the only protection minorities received under the Constitution. The very day the Treaty was signed Arthur Griffith had met three representative Unionists and had, it seems, given them two assurances. One was that proportional representation would be used for elections to the Dáil, and the other was that they should have due representation in the upper house, the Senate. A few weeks before his death in August 1922 Griffith met the southern Unionists again and concluded with them what were later called 'Heads of Agreement' relating more specifically to the composition and powers of the Senate, upon which many of the Protestant minority were coming to pin their chief hope for the future. Griffith's proposal that the Senate should be elected by proportional representation from a panel two-thirds nominated by the Dáil and one-third by the Senate itself was extremely cumbersome and had soon to be simplified. Of more immediate importance was the concession that in the *first* Senate half the sixty members would be elected by the Dáil and half would be nominated by the President of the Executive Council (Prime Minister) 'in manner calculated to represent minorities or interests not adequately represented in the Dáil'. The Unionists fought hard to secure that the Senate would have an effective power of suspending legislation, but the best they could achieve was the right to hold up bills for 270 days instead of the year they had sought for. They would have liked also, in cases of disputed legislation, to press for a joint sitting of both houses with joint voting; they were allowed the empty formula of a joint session, but the withholding of a joint vote deprived this of much of its meaning.

Although the Unionist minority professed themselves disappointed with the outcome, they recognised nevertheless that there had been a genuine effort to meet their demands and to integrate them into the new state. That such an effort had been made was emphasised by Kevin O'Higgins, who had shared with Griffith in the later stages of the negotiations, when he spoke in the Dáil about the minority problem shortly after Griffith's death:

> These people [he said] are part and parcel of the nation, and we being the majority and strength of the country . . . it comes well from us to make a generous adjustment to show that these people are regarded, not as alien enemies, not as planters, but that we regard them as part and parcel of this nation, and that we wish them to take their share of its responsibilities.[5]

The government was as good as its word. Of the first thirty senators to be nominated, sixteen could be said to have been broadly Unionist in their sympathies, and a seventeenth, W. B. Yeats, though certainly no Unionist, was very conscious of his Anglo-Irish heritage. The group included a number of those 'constructive Unionists' who had tried to bridge the gap between their order and the rest of the country before 1914 – for example, Sir Horace Plunkett, the Earl of Dunraven, the Earl of Mayo, the dowager Countess of Desart – and the high quality of debate in the Senate owed a great deal to them. But nothing could conceal the fact that debate did not often issue in action, and that the special position the Unionists had achieved in the Senate was not much more than a special position enabling them to watch the work of the dominant lower house from close quarters.[6]

The Dáil was deliberately intended to be dominant, not just over the Senate, but over the executive government as well. Its membership, being determined by the size of the population, was subject to periodic revision, but during the first decade of the Constitution's working was fixed at 153, including three representatives for each of the two universities then existing. The members were elected by proportional representation (the single transferable vote) on the basis of universal adult suffrage for a normal term of six years. The rules governing procedure followed British practice very closely (those governing privilege were more narrowly drawn) but although the convocation and dissolution of parliament were nominally vested in the representative of the Crown (i.e. the Governor-General), again on the British model, the exercise of those powers was expressly vested in the Dáil itself. Thus, while the Executive Council (cabinet) could advise a dissolution it could only do so when it had a majority. If it lost its majority then the Executive Council had no option but to resign and leave the task of forming a new government to its opponents.[7] This was a notable departure from English and dominion practice and was inspired at least in part by the desire to demonstrate the supremacy of the legislature over the executive.

This desire expressed itself also in other ways, some of them novel and even bizarre. The framers of the Constitution appear to have recognised that they needed cabinet government more or less after the British fashion, but at the same time to have recoiled from entrusting to ministers the degree of independence which that implied. Thus, while provision was made for the Executive Council to consist of a President and certain other ministers, not only was the President himself to be chosen by the Dáil, but his nominations for the various posts in the Executive Council had also to be approved by the lower house. This emphasis upon the authority of the Dáil was, however, only partly a tribute to the concept of popular sovereignty. It seems to have sprung also from a feeling that the effect of proportional representation would be to do away with large and strong parties on the British model. Even Kevin O'Higgins, who, as we shall see, was more closely identified with strong government than anyone else, appears to have shared this feeling. 'We will have groups here', he said in the Dáil on one occasion, 'small groups of seven or eight. We will not have parties on definite lines of political cleavage.' The moral he drew from this was that they would not have cabinet government either. Wanting, as he claimed, the maximum of individual liberty for deputies in the Dáil, he maintained that this could not be achieved 'by adhering to collective responsibility'.[8]

What this meant in practice was a strange departure from the cabinet system as ordinarily understood. In the draft Constitution submitted to the Constituent Assembly it was proposed, in addition to the 'parliamentary' type members of the Executive Council, to have certain others – 'extern' ministers – who would not be subject to collective responsibility with the rest of the Council, but would be directly and individually responsible to the Dáil. The practical reason for having them was the perfectly laudable one of bringing people with specific expertise into the work of government, but there was also a doctrinaire reason – that through such ministers it would be possible for the Dáil to exercise very direct control over the departments for which they would be responsible. Since the original draft envisaged, apart from the President, only four ministers of the normal 'parliamentary' kind and no less than eight 'extern' ministers, it can be seen how strong was the urge to turn the Executive Council away from the more conventional lines of cabinet development.

It is rather harder to see how this device can ever have been expected to work satisfactorily and it was, perhaps, the measure of the immaturity of the new government that it could have imagined it would be possible to accommodate, as it were on two separate planes, the technical ministers and those who controlled the purse-strings and the other realities of power. Not surprisingly, the scheme was modified in debate, emerging in the Constitution as a provision for a normal cabinet of not less than five and not more than seven (all members of the Dáil and collectively responsible to it), together with such other 'extern' ministers (doubly extern in that they were no longer to be members of the Executive Council) as would provide a total ministry of not more than twelve. Moreover, the appointment of the extern ministers was to be permissive only, not mandatory as had first been proposed. These extern ministers were to be chosen by the Dáil but need not be members of that body. Whether such a device as the two-tier executive could ever have been fitted into the machinery of parliamentary government, even in the most favourable circumstances, is highly problematical. As things were, the circumstances could hardly have been more unfavourable. Not only the fact that clearly-defined parties at once emerged in the Dáil (contrary to the expectations of the 'experts'), but also the need to govern strongly in a time of serious unrest, led the President of the Council, Mr Cosgrave, to rely much more upon his ordinary ministers and much less upon his extern ones. The latter did, indeed, play a considerable part in the administration of the country, and one of them, Patrick

Hogan, was an outstanding Minister of Agriculture, but the whole concept soon changed its character under the impact of experience. Not only were the extern ministers in actuality government nominees backed by the government majority in the Dáil, they were also expected to observe practical, if not theoretical, cabinet responsibility like their more conventional colleagues. It could hardly have been otherwise. The original idea behind the innovation had assumed a Dáil where there would be no rigid parties and a great deal of free voting. But once a party system of the old, familiar kind emerged the extern ministers rapidly became superfluous. The experiment was virtually abandoned after a constitutional amendment in 1927 and from 1928 onwards no more were appointed.[9]

Much the same fate befell the two other provisions of the Constitution intended to emphasise the doctrine of popular sovereignty – those relating to the referendum and the power of initiative. Both of these devices were intended to associate the people directly with the legislative process. They had a long history behind them but had suddenly become fashionable after 1918 when so many of the new constitutions then being worked out laid deliberate emphasis upon this aspect of democracy. The framers of the Constitution of the Free State were no doubt aware of, and perhaps to some extent influenced by, the experiments that were taking place more or less simultaneously in other countries, but it has been suggested by Professor Mansergh that, in spirit at least, the Irish provisions looked back to an earlier and more individualist tradition. In Ireland, as he rightly says, there was no general acceptance of an organic view of the state and the rules in the Constitution governing direct legislation by referendum and initiative were intended, as he puts it, 'to provide, not a representation of the people's will, but rather a safeguard for individual rights'.[10] Such an interpretation fits well with the Irishman's traditional attitude towards government. Like Calvin Coolidge's preacher on the subject of sin, he was, in general, 'against it'. The insertion of machinery for direct legislation with the Constitution, therefore, served two purposes. On the one hand, in theory at least, it provided a popular check on what might become an over-mighty government. And on the other it could be argued, and was argued during the constitutional debates, that 'personal actual contact between the people and the laws by which they are governed' was highly advisable in a country where the laws and those who had administered them had for so long been regarded as alien, and when, for this very reason, political education and experience were conspicuously lacking.

Alas for these great expectations. Referendum and initiative alike had a short life and a dismal one. It was indeed laid down that after a preliminary period of eight years (later extended to sixteen) no amendment of the Constitution could take place without a referendum, but on ordinary legislation the procedure was optional.[11] And even this optional procedure was limited by the two important qualifications that Money Bills were excluded from it, and also 'such Bills as shall be declared by both Houses to be necessary for the immediate preservation of the public peace, health or safety'.[12] In the early years of the Free State the government had frequent recourse to this escape clause and the elaborate machinery provided by the Constitution was left to rust. It had been intended that this machinery should allow the government's opponents in either house of the Oireachtas an opportunity of submitting any ordinary Bill of which they disapproved to the people at large. Such a Bill, even if it had been passed by the government majority, could be suspended for ninety days on the written demand (presented to the President of the Executive Council not later than seven days after the Bill had been passed) of two-fifths of the members of the Dáil or a majority of the members of the Senate. During this period of suspension the Bill might be submitted to a referendum, but only if the Senate passed a resolution demanding this and assented to by three-fifths of its members, or, alternatively, if a petition were presented signed by not less than one-twentieth of the voters. In the event, the Senate never used the power conferred on it by the Constitution – there would have been a most dangerous collision with the lower house if it had done – and although a minority in the Dáil did employ the suspensory weapon to hold up the Electoral Amendment Act of 1927 (the cause of a major party battle which will be described in the next section) it proved impossible to obtain the necessary number of signatures for a petition demanding a referendum.

The referendum has sometimes been described as the way in which the people can rectify their representatives' sins of commission. Likewise, the initiative, the power to propose new legislation, can be seen as the people's opportunity to rectify their representatives' sins of omission. But in the light of experience in many countries the tendency has been to regard such 'direct' legislation – whether by referendum or initiative – with diminishing enthusiasm. It has been criticised as crude, ill-informed, incoherent and even anarchical in its interference with the normal working of representative institutions, intolerant of racial and religious minorities and – worst of all, perhaps – as opening the way to the irresponsibility of the anonymous legislator.[13] The authors of the Free State Constitution seem to have shared these misgivings, for Article 48 of the Constitution begins with the permissive phrase – 'the Oireachtas may provide for the initiation by the people for proposals for laws or constitutional amendments'. Should it fail to do this within two years (and it did fail) then it was laid down that on a petition signed by not less than 75,000 voters – of whom not more than 15,000 were to belong to one constituency – the Oireachtas would then be obliged either to set up the necessary machinery or to submit the question to a referendum, and even this was hedged round with qualifications to make difficult the initiation of laws or amendments of the constitution.

On the other hand, Article 48 did open the way for a very small minority to raise fundamental issues and in a deeply divided country such as the Irish Free State that could have all sorts of repercussions. Realising this, a cabinet sub-committee recommended as early as 1924 that both the referendum and the initiative should be abolished. Nothing was done, however, with the result that three years later the government was confronted with a major crisis. By then Fianna Fáil had emerged as a large and potentially powerful party and after its entry into the Dáil it proceeded to carry out an intense propaganda campaign in the country, which resulted in a petition signed by 96,000 voters being presented to the Dáil in May 1928, demanding the abolition of the parliamentary oath, and so presaging a general attack upon the Treaty.* The government countered by introducing a Bill – of which, admittedly, it had given notice at the preceding general election – for the abolition of the referendum and initiative. There followed three weeks of intense and bitter debate which, though ostensibly devoted to the merits and demerits of direct legislation, was, as everyone well knew, simply a continuation of the old quarrel over the Treaty. In the end, the government, by frequent use of the guillotine, fought its measure through both houses. It was still open to the opposition to demand a referendum under Article 50 of the Constitution, but here too, Mr Cosgrave and his colleagues outflanked their opponents by declaring the Bill to be 'necessary for the immediate preservation of the public peace and safety' and as such not to be referred back to the people. The referendum (save for such constitutional amendments as might be enacted after a further period of eight years from 1929) and the initiative thereupon both disappeared from the law of the land.

It has been necessary to dwell at some length on these intricate details of the Constitution because they point to a conclusion of the highest importance for the future of the Irish Free State. It is clear that the events of the period up to 1927 had belied Kevin O'Higgins's expectation that the Dáil would be made up of small groups of deputies independent of party ties. It is hard, indeed, to see how such a prophecy could ever have been realised in the existing conditions of the time. The sort of 'deliberative assembly' that O'Higgins envisaged might conceivably have been possible, though even this is arguable, had there existed in the country a large measure of agreement about the sanctity of the Treaty and the future of the Irish Free State as a developing dominion within the framework of the British Commonwealth. But of course there was no consensus. The split that had led to the Civil War remained unhealed. All that had really happened was that the main opponents of the new regime – Mr de Valera and his friends – by refusing to take the parliamentary oath of allegiance had allowed the pro-Treaty party or parties to

* For the political background to the constitutional crisis, see below, pp. 498-9.

govern without exposing the weaknesses and deficiencies of the Constitution. When Fianna Fáil eventually did decide to enter the Dáil, it was natural that they should want to exploit these weaknesses and deficiencies, with the inevitable result that the period 1927-32 was one of almost incessant crisis.

However, from Mr de Valera's decision to participate in constitutional politics a second and even more far-reaching consequence was to flow. The very fact that after 1927 two major parties, deeply divided on fundamental issues and by passionately held principles, confronted each other in parliament could only serve to reduce the margin for constitutional experimentation. What mattered most was not that some delicately balanced lever should be pulled to elicit a free vote in the country or the Oireachtas on this issue or on that, but that a government should either rule on the basis of a well-organised majority in the Dáil, or else get out and make way for another that could. In short, a two-party dialectic became the norm of Irish politics and with it the acceptance of that fully-fledged cabinet system from which the founders of the state had been struggling to escape. As has been well said, 'the logic of the British system reasserted itself'.[14]

It was a logic that dictated continuity, not change. And if this were true of parliamentary institutions, it was even more true of other areas of government where any kind of violent break with the past was an invitation to anarchy. We find, therefore, that the same ministers who established the Constitution engaged almost simultaneously in an intensive programme of legislation to set the day-to-day administration of the country on a sound footing. By any standards this programme would have been a formidable achievement, but at a time when much of Ireland was still in the grip of Civil War or its aftermath, it was an astonishing performance. Some aspects of it will be dealt with later, but here it is necessary to single out the measures which laid the foundations for the firm and efficient government that rapidly became the hallmark of the Free State. The most important of these concerned the civil service, the police, the law courts and the whole domain of local government. It was decided by the new regime to take advantage of the transfer of power in order to make an end of the old jumble of boards and councils and put a more coherent structure in its place. This was the intention behind the Ministers and Secretaries Act of 1924 which brought all the various administrative bodies together into a system based on eleven ministerial departments – those of the President of the Executive Council, Finance, Justice, Local Government and Public Health, Lands and Agriculture, Industry and Commerce, Fisheries, Posts and Telegraphs, Education, Defence, and External Affairs. A little later (in 1928) Agriculture became a separate department and Lands and Fisheries were amalgamated, but apart from that the structure remained unchanged up to the Second World War. During and after the war other departments were added, mainly to deal with enlarged social services, but in essence the system introduced in 1924 has survived to the present, though it has latterly been subjected to criticism as being too rigid and too conservative for the rapidly changing circumstances of the modern age. Following a recent exhaustive inquiry (the Devlin Report), it is to be expected that the 'seventies will see considerable modernisation and also, no doubt, the expansion in size which always seems to follow civil service reform.

In two respects this system, while improving on the haphazard arrangements inherited from Britain, yet followed British precedent. First, the Ministry of Finance rapidly established a dominance over other departments reminiscent of the Treasury's supremacy in Whitehall. And second, the government acted quickly (by the Civil Service Regulation Act of 1923 and by other subsequent legislation) to set up Civil Service Commissioners to supervise the recruitment of candidates into the service. The establishment of this body, which has acted with great efficiency and impartiality ever since, did more than anything else to ensure that the new state would escape, at least in its central administration, the worst evils of the spoils system. It was a help, of course, that many of the senior officials appointed under British rule agreed to stay on, so that some years later a Commission of Inquiry was able to report that there had been no disturbance 'of any fundamental kind' and that 'the same main tasks of administration continued to be performed by the same staffs on the same general basis of organisation and procedure'.[15] At the time of the changeover there were 21,000 civil servants and while some of these left and others were hastily recruited under what amounted to war-time conditions, the service did not change either its character or its numbers. In the mid-thirties it was still no more than 20,000 strong and even by the mid-fifties numbered about 33,000, of whom roughly a half were in the Post Office.[16] On this stable, and by no means excessively broad base, has been reared, it is not too much to say, the entire edifice of Irish central government.*

Simultaneously with their drive to create a more coherent system of administration, ministers were turning their attention to the courts and to the police. It was a remarkable gesture of confidence in the future that in 1923, although the country was still deeply disturbed, Mr Cosgrave and his colleagues took the decision to create in the Free State an unarmed police force that would contrast favourably with the old semi-military RIC and with its lineal descendant, the RUC, which was at that time being set up in Northern Ireland.

---

* It has been pointed out that if those employed by local authorities and the state-sponsored bodies are included, the total in the public service rose from about 90,500 in 1940 to 134,200 in 1965; the percentage share of the total labour force absorbed by the public service went up in the same period from 6.9 to 12.1 (B. Chubb, *The Government and Politics of Ireland*, p. 222).

This force, the Garda Siochana (or Civic Guard), was at first a temporary improvisation but was given permanence by an Act of 1924 and, almost from the start, was an unqualified success, vanquishing by its record the fears of those who had predicted that a national police force would become an instrument of government tyranny.

The Civic Guard derived originally from republican police called into being by the exigencies of the Anglo-Irish war. The same exigencies had led, as we have seen, to the emergence of so-called 'Dáil Courts' administering the law at various levels in increasingly successful competition with the established courts which still functioned under British rule. Once power had been transferred, however, the government lost no time in getting rid of the Dáil Courts and the last of them was abolished before the end of 1922. The following year parliament made provision for the formal winding-up of their proceedings and the way was clear for a thorough-going reconstruction of the ordinary courts of law. This in its turn was carried out by the Courts of Justice Act of 1924, establishing a hierarchy ranging from the District Courts at the bottom, through the Circuit Courts, the High Court, and the Court of Criminal Appeal to the Supreme Court at the top. The new hierarchy differed in some significant ways from the old. For example, the time-honoured Justice of the Peace disappeared, as did the more recent and more disliked Resident Magistrate, and the old Petty Sessions gave place to District Courts presided over by paid District Justices.[17] Again, the familiar County Court was abolished, to be replaced by Circuit Courts, each Court being assigned a circuit representing about 400,000 people and having very considerable jurisdiction in both civil and criminal matters. These two reforms between them went far to achieve the main object of government policy which was, by decentralising the administration of justice, to give the citizen quicker and less costly access to the law. At the centre also there was considerable rationalisation. Here the main innovations were the creation of the Court of Criminal Appeal; the position given to the High Court by the provision (Article 65 of the Constitution) that in all cases respecting the provisions of the Constitution it alone should have original jurisdiction; and the setting up of the Supreme Court as the final court of appeal, not only from the High Court (and in certain circumstances from the Court of Criminal Appeal as well) but also as the final arbiter in matters respecting the constitutionality of legislation.[18] The right of the individual to apply for leave to appeal to the Judicial Committee of the Privy Council was, of course, expressly safeguarded by the Constitution and nothing in the powers of the Supreme Court was to be allowed to impair this right.

It should be stressed that these changes, far-reaching though they were, were essentially changes of practice and procedure rather than of principle. The Free State still retained much in its legal system that was inherited from Britain. The tenure of judges during good behaviour, for example, was carried over into the new structure, though it was not until 1946 that this was extended to District Justices. The legal profession continued to be recruited and trained, and even to dress, much as before. Above all, the law that they professed was still essentially the common law as it had evolved over the centuries.[19]

In local government, as in the central administration, the new broom swept relentlessly clean. Over much of Ireland the local authorities, which even at the best of times had often been too small and too poor to be very effective, had been hard hit by the insecurity of life and property during the turbulent years between 1919 and 1923. What was most urgently needed was to reorganise the system brought into being by the Act of 1898 so as to create units of government which would be both competent and economically viable. At first, too, it was hoped that in this sphere, as in the law, real decentralisation would be feasible. In practice this proved to be difficult, partly because the country continued disturbed for so long, partly because local authorities came to depend increasingly upon the government in Dublin for a large part of their revenue, and partly also, it must be said, because it was not always possible to root out incompetence, corruption or simple self-interest from the local administration.

As we have already seen, the Ministers and Secretaries Act of 1924 set up the Ministry of Local Government and Public Health as a new department. Very soon it acquired a wide variety of functions, but from the outset its main concern was with the local councils and their constant struggle to deal with the often urgent problems of the poor law, public health, housing and the upkeep of roads – to name only a few of their most important responsibilities. So that these problems might be tackled with more resources and better hope of success the Local Government Act of 1925 remodelled the whole system. Negatively, it got rid of the Rural Districts, those small and generally impoverished sub-divisions of the counties which had been spawned by the Act of 1898. Positively, the new legislation provided for a different kind of administrative unit – the County Health District. In most parts of the Free State the County Health Districts coincided with the boundaries of the actual counties (though urban districts were excluded from their purview) and the County Councils (which had been in existence since 1898) were made the sanitary authorities for the County Health Districts, exercising their power through Boards of Health composed of ten members from each Council; to these Boards also, in most cases, was entrusted the business of administering public assistance to the very poor. So long as British rule had lasted, this assistance had been closely linked to the nineteenth century workhouse system and although outdoor relief had become more common as time went on, so far as the destitute were concerned (and many of the sick and mentally afflicted as well), the workhouse had continued to overshadow their penurious lives. By an Act of 1923 the new government remodelled this system also. Public assis-

482

tance was organised on a county basis, most of the old Poor Law Unions were amalgamated and many of the workhouses were closed. Some were metamorphosed into the County Homes which the Act undertook to provide for the aged and infirm. In addition, County and District Hospitals were to be made available to the sick, while the able-bodied poor were to be relieved as far as possible in their own homes. To be poor in Ireland would still be a bleak enough fate after 1923 – and to be poor and ill would be still worse – but at least it could be claimed that the state was making a determined effort to break away from the Victorian conception which for so long had seemed to assume that poverty was *prima facie* evidence of some delinquency or deficiency in the pauper.

The changes brought about by the new Local Government Act produced a pattern of twenty-seven administrative counties and four county boroughs, each electing its own Council as the rate-levying authority and as the body responsible for the efficient discharge of all the multifarious duties of the local authorities; in addition, there were sixty-five urban sanitary districts charged with the care of health in their respective towns and cities.* Local government elections were, like general elections, held under a form of proportional representation, but with a property qualification which in effect limited the vote to owners or tenants (and their wives) of any land or premises with an annual rateable value of ten pounds. The effect of this was to produce an electorate which in 1929 was considerably smaller than that for the parliamentary constituencies – roughly a million as against a million and a quarter.

The local Councils were expected to raise the greater part of their revenue from the rates, but increased expenditure led to a steady growth in the contribution made by the central government. Thus, whereas in 1923-4 the revenue from rates totalled nearly 72 per cent of local government funds and the contribution from the Exchequer only 22.5 per cent, in 1931-2 the respective percentages were 52 and 42. It was not surprising, therefore, that the Act of 1925 gave the Minister of Local Government the power, not only to inquire into the conduct of a Council, but to dissolve it if such inquiry showed this to be necessary in the public interest. Out of this provision was to come what has been called 'perhaps Ireland's major invention in the field of government'.[20] The Act laid it down that where a Council was

* To these authorities must be added the borough corporations of certain specified towns, the urban district councils and the town commissioners. After various emendations of local government law and practice, the total of local authorities was officially listed in 1961 as consisting of twenty-seven councils, four county borough corporations, seven borough corporations, forty-nine urban district corporations and twenty-eight town commissioners. The seven borough corporations and the forty-nine urban district councils were linked with the county managers whose functions are described overleaf (John O'Donnell, *How Ireland Is Governed*, chap. lx; B. Chubb, *A Source-Book of Irish Government* (Dublin, 1964), p. 264).

dissolved the Minister could appoint Commissioners to exercise its duties for a period not exceeding three years when, it was hoped, a new and suitably chastened Council would be elected. This device, though intended to be punitive, turned out to be extremely popular and cases were known of the electorate refusing to choose another Council so as to force the central government into reappointing its Commissioners. This may have shown a deplorable lack of civic spirit among the inhabitants, but it accurately reflected at once the desire for greater efficiency and the serious lack of real administrative experience in most parts of Ireland.

The popularity of the Commissioners was by no means confined to the smaller and more backward Councils. In 1929 the city of Cork blazed a new trail with the appointment of a City Manager modelled to some extent on the existing Commissioners but intended to co-operate with the City Council, not to replace it. Dublin and Dun Laoghaire soon followed suit and it was probably inevitable that sooner or later the fashion would spread to the countryside as well. In 1940 provision was duly made for this by the County Management Act which laid upon all counties the obligation to have or share a manager. These officials were permanent, full-time, well-paid administrators, but the financial and legal responsibility of the Councils was carefully and elaborately preserved. In practice, of course, both because of his expertise and because he enjoyed the priceless advantage of continuity, the Manager, especially if he had the rudiments of tact, was in a position to influence very powerfully the course of local government. And if that government gained in maturity and competence over the years the 'managerial revolution' may take a large part of the credit.[21]

Thus, advancing simultaneously on many different fronts, the new and untried Ministers sought to enter into their inheritance and build upon the foundations laid by their British predecessors. At any time this task of rebuilding virtually the entire administration of the country would have been tremendous. But to begin it in the midst of a Civil War and to carry it on despite the sullen opposition of bitter, inveterate enemies was to take a fearful gamble. How nearly this gamble came to disaster we can only realise if we turn to the political history of that angry and desperate time.

(ii) THE EXERCISE OF POWER

When in the spring of 1923 Mr Cosgrave and his colleagues launched their political party – Cumann na nGaedheal – it was intended not merely to be the rallying-point for those who took the Treaty side in the Civil War, but also to bring together men of different classes, origins and creeds who were prepared to contribute to the building of the new state within the framework of the Constitution as approved in October 1922. The party did not, of course, absorb everyone who was prepared to work within the Constitution and the first general election held under the new dispensation in August 1923 produced, as might have been expected under proportional representation, a Dáil which represented a very wide spread of opinion. Apart from forty-four Sinn Féin members who had no intention of taking their seats, there were four main groups and one Independent Labour member. Of the four groups Cumann na nGaedheal, with sixty-three members, was much the largest, having in the absence of Sinn Féin a majority over all the other groups put together. The other three consisted of Independents (sixteen), Farmers (fifteen) and Labour (fourteen). The first two of these groups, while pledged to pursue and safeguard their own particular interests (extremely various in the case of the Independents) were free to give some support to the government from time to time, and the main burden of official opposition fell, therefore, upon the Labour members, led with conspicuous ability by Thomas Johnson and Cathal O'Shannon.

The new government was headed, as before, by Griffith's successor, W. T. Cosgrave, as President of the Executive Council. His Vice-President and Minister of Home Affairs was Kevin O'Higgins and his Minister of Finance was Ernest Blythe. The four other members of the Executive Council were Joseph McGrath (Industry and Commerce), Eoin MacNeill (Education), Desmond FitzGerald (External Affairs) and General Richard Mulcahy (Defence). There were, in addition, four 'extern' ministers who were not members of the Executive Council. These were Patrick Hogan (Agriculture), J. A. Burke (Local Government), J. J. Walsh (Postmaster-General), and F. Lynch (Fisheries).

Upon this small group of men rested a fearful responsibility. For although, as we saw earlier, Mr de Valera had in effect ended the Civil War some weeks before the general election with his 'proclamation' to his followers of 24 May, there was not the slightest indication that the ending of the physical struggle would lead to any easing of the tensions between the Republicans and those who had accepted the Treaty. Indeed, there was not even certainty that the Civil War itself was permanently finished, since the Irregulars had only dumped their arms, not surrendered them. Moreover, the very fact that the political exponents of republicanism, Sinn Féin, had a big enough following to win forty-four seats at the election served notice on the government that any failure of nerve on their part, any evidence that the job was too big for them, might lead, at the very least, to the destruction of the whole pro-Treaty position, at worst to a headlong plunge into anarchy.

Yet, whatever the risks, and however unpromising the circumstances, the manifold problems of reconstruction had to be faced. Four tasks in particular loomed ahead of Mr Cosgrave and his fellow-ministers. One was the reconstitution of the entire machinery of government – how this was set on foot during the Civil War and driven through to a conclusion after it was over has already been described. A second was the assertion of the status of the new dominion as a member nation of the Commonwealth, and a third was the economic regeneration of the country. Both these will be dealt with later in this book.* At this point it is the fourth objective of the government that demands our attention, since unless it had been achieved there would have been no hope of success in any of the others. This was nothing less than the restoration in the Free State of a respect for law and order, the demonstration, ruthless if need be, that here at last was a government that was prepared to govern.

Since the restoration of law and order was primarily the responsibility of the Ministry of Home Affairs it was natural that the holder of that office, Kevin O'Higgins, should seem to dominate the political stage. In fact, that remarkable man was of such a calibre that he would have played a leading role whatever post he had been assigned. In 1923 O'Higgins was still only thirty-one years old, but like many others in those revolutionary times, had matured rapidly under the responsibilities thrust upon him. Joining the Irish Volunteers while still a student, he had been swept into prison in the spring of 1918 during the government purge occasioned by the 'German plot', and later that year was elected as a Sinn Féin member for Queen's County. As such he took part in the proceedings of the first Dáil, gaining his initial experience of administration as assistant to W. T. Cosgrave when the latter was appointed Minister of Local Government in the underground movement that Sinn Féin was then developing in opposition to British rule. Later he came much under the influence of Michael Collins, an influence that was, indeed, to be the most permanent one in his life. 'I try to do what I think the Big Fellow would have done', he said once and in this sentence epitomised his whole career. O'Higgins himself was a man of contrasts. He could be gay (as a student he had been a good deal more than gay), he could be taciturn. In public he was ruthless and often careless of the enemies he made by the roughness of his tongue; in the intimacy of his family no man could be more affectionate. Deeply religious, even puritanical in some of his views, there was, however, nothing of the mystic about him and of all the heirs of Griffith and Collins he was probably the most unflinching political realist. He had great intelligence, great courage, great self-control, and powers of work which staggered his contemporaries. So much did he impress by his industry and drive that it was even the fashion, before the implications of the phrase could be fully realised, to call him 'the Irish Mussolini'. Nothing could have been further from the truth. He was inclined, certainly, to be dictatorial with his colleagues and with the Dáil, but he believed profoundly both in the parliamentary process and in the sanctity of contracts. Both beliefs led him to take his stand

* Relations with the Commonwealth are discussed in the next section; for economic policy, see chap. 4 below.

on the Treaty and perhaps no other single individual did more between 1922 and 1927 either to ensure its acceptance or to enable the country to turn its back on the rancorous past and begin a new life.[22]

But – and here we come back to the *leitmotiv* of O'Higgins's later ministerial career – that life could not begin until the ordinary conditions of civilised intercourse had been re-established. During the Civil War O'Higgins had not hesitated to accept his share of the responsibility for the extreme steps taken by the Free State government, even when these included the execution by way of reprisal of Rory O'Connor, who had been best man at his wedding but a short time before. When the war was over he did not relax his vigilance and at once took steps to obtain special powers under the Public Safety Act of 1923, enabling the government to continue the internment of such of its prisoners as it was deemed necessary to keep in jail in the public interest, and also to arrest and detain anyone suspected of being a danger to the public safety. The Minister was given wide scope under the Act – but this could be justified on two grounds. One was that the Republicans, notwithstanding the cease-fire, continued to regard themselves as *the* government and the pro-Treaty majority in the Dáil as usurpers. It was only common sense, therefore, for the government to look to its own defence. And the other was the simple fact that violence and lawlessness of all kinds continued to flourish. Between August 1923 and February 1924 there were, for example, no less than 738 cases of arson and robbery under arms, and on 21 March 1924 there occurred an incident which could easily have created (as was no doubt intended) a serious crisis in Anglo-Irish relations. A number of unarmed British soldiers, accompanied by civilians, were proceeding by boat towards the harbour of Queenstown (nowadays called Cobh) when they were fired upon by a group of men in Free State Army uniforms. The men got away in a car, leaving behind them one dead and over twenty casualties in the British party. Since Queenstown was one of the 'Treaty ports' to which Britain had right of access for defence purposes, this attack was clearly meant to embroil the two governments. Restraint on both sides ensured that this did not happen, but it was ominous that even an official reward of £10,000 did not lead to the discovery of the assassins.

Scarcely less ominous, from the point of view of the internal recovery of the country, was the difficulty that was simultaneously being experienced in the legal recovery of debts. This was partly due to the confusion bred by the Civil War, but partly also to continued intimidation after it had ended, with the result that by March 1924 there were some 7,000 decrees outstanding, representing £170,000 of debts. The figure may not seem excessive – though in a poor country like Ireland it was serious enough – but O'Higgins put his finger on its real significance when he remarked that 'the ceasing of the bailiff to function is the first sign of a crumbling civilisation.'

Against this background he did not hesitate to reach for a prolongation and extension of his powers. The year 1924 therefore saw a further Public Safety Act continuing the regulations for arrest and detention, the re-enactment of the penalties (including flogging) previously imposed for arson and armed robbery, the renewal of the control over firearms that had been temporarily enacted in 1923, and the passing of another measure to strengthen the powers of sheriffs in the recovery of debts. Gradually, these draconian measures took effect. By the end of 1924 conditions were stable enough for most of the internees to be set free – including Mr de Valera who had been arrested in his constituency at the time of the general election in August 1923 but was released the following July – and in the countryside at large commercial conditions had so far returned to normal that by the beginning of 1926 debts outstanding had been reduced to less than half the 1924 figure.[23]

Unfortunately, the government itself was not immune from the confusion and passion that were the two principal legacies of the Civil War. Mr Cosgrave's ministry, indeed his party too, was, in the phrase Burke had used long ago about Lord Chatham's administration, 'a tessellated pavement without cement'. Or rather, the cement that had held it together had been the pressures of the Civil War and the necessity of standing by the Treaty. Once the immediate physical danger was over the cement began to crack and the differences within the Executive Council began to be more and more publicly paraded. It was not merely that ministers were, for example, divided on economic policy and were capable of standing up in the Dáil and speaking one in favour of free trade, another in favour of tariffs. This, though embarrassing, at least did not threaten the foundations of the state. But when, quite suddenly, in March 1924 a mutiny broke out in the Army, then truly a chasm opened at the government's very feet. Ostensibly, the mutiny was caused by the fact that the ending of the Civil War had led to a considerable reduction in the Free State forces, culminating in the demobilisation of nearly 2,000 officers at the beginning of March. This in itself would have produced some discontent, for many of them had been bred to the gun and had little talent for anything else. They resented the dismissals and they resented even more the fact that several former British officers had been recruited into the Army in recent years. But the roots of the trouble lay deeper. Some of the soldiers and their officers had only come down on the pro-Treaty side out of devotion to their leader, Michael Collins, and they still believed that Collins, had he lived, would somehow or other have gone beyond the Treaty to secure the republic. These men had formed part of the Irish Republican Army that had fought the Anglo-Irish war, but, since the title IRA was annexed by those who had fought with Mr de Valera in the Civil War, the men who gave their loyalty to the Free State went by the name of 'old IRA'. It was, however, a very conditional loyalty, and when by 1924 it seemed clear that the Cosgrave government had no intention of going beyond the Treaty, their impatience boiled over. The result was an ultimatum (dated 6 March 1924) which was sent to Mr Cosgrave, and was signed, on behalf of these 'old IRA' veterans, by two of their officers, Liam Tobin and C. F. Dalton. It demanded the removal of the Army Council and that demobilisation should be suspended, but also, and here was the sinister note, reminded the government that the IRA had only accepted the Treaty as a stepping-stone to the republic.

What made this threat potentially so serious was that there were already serious divisions within the Executive Council about the relations between the Army and the civil power. O'Higgins, as a devoted constitutionalist, was emphatic that the military must be brought under the control of the properly constituted government of the country and he had already complained repeatedly – and emphatically – about lack of discipline. Inside the cabinet the spokesman for the Army was General Richard Mulcahy. But he, while sensitive to criticism of the armed forces, was himself in a difficult position. It appears that the doyen of all revolutionary movements in Ireland, the Irish Republican Brotherhood, was steadily establishing its influence among the Army officers. The IRB, following Collins, had accepted the Treaty, and at the time of Collins's death, General Mulcahy had been a member of the Supreme Council of that body. If, therefore, there was IRB infiltration of the Army it was not unreasonable to suppose that he might be sympathetic to it. The old IRA, on the other hand, regarded this infiltration as a threat to their own ascendancy and this explains their demand for the removal of the Army Council, on which the IRB was strongly entrenched. Where the IRB officers looked to Mulcahy as their spokesman in the government, the old IRA looked to the Minister for Industry and Commerce, Joseph McGrath, to safeguard their interests.

On receipt of the ultimatum the government acted promptly. The signatories of the document were arrested, and the Chief of Police, Eoin O'Duffy, was brought in to command the defence forces. The mutiny itself was not on a large scale, although there were some desertions, and before it had a chance to grow to dangerous proportions Mr McGrath was able to assure the mutineers that there would be an inquiry into the administration of the Army, that the Army Council would be remodelled, that there was to be no victimisation, and that deserters could return in safety to their posts. McGrath himself, however, was by that time a private individual, since he had resigned at the beginning of the affair in protest against the way in which the Ministry of Defence had, in his view, precipitated the crisis by neglecting the grievances of the old IRA, grievances which had been before the government in one form or other since the previous year and which, if promptly met, would have rendered the mutiny unnecessary.

But the incident did not end there. A few days later Free State troops surrounded a building in Dublin which contained some of the mutinous officers. The latter were armed and a grim street-battle was avoided only by the intervention of the ubiquitous McGrath. The action of the troops, it later emerged, had been ordered by the Adjutant-General who had consulted the Minister of Defence, but not his superior officer, General O'Duffy. In the absence of Cosgrave through illness, it fell to O'Higgins to resolve this latest phase of the crisis. He did so with characteristic incisiveness. Not only the Adjutant-General, but two other high-ranking officers were called on to resign, and O'Higgins was preparing to put the same pressure on the Minister of Defence when General Mulcahy forestalled him by offering his own resignation. The episode had not only cost the government two ministers, but had also shaken its authority in the Dáil. Perhaps, though, the lesson, if expensive, was cheap at the price. For what these tangled transactions had ultimately revealed was the extreme difficulty in the aftermath of a revolution of mastering the forces that have carried through that revolution. The problem had been complicated by the struggle for power within the Army, but in essence it was simple enough – could a civilian government impose its authority on those who, in effect, had brought it to power? O'Higgins had no doubt about the answer. 'Those who take the pay and wear the uniform of the state', he told the Dáil, 'be they soldiers or police, must be non-political servants of the state.' In this faith, and with equal impartiality, he stood over not only the dismissal of the generals, but also the ruling that absconding officers who had not returned to their posts were to be regarded as having 'retired' from the Army. This firm action, together with the concessions earlier made to the legitimate grievances of the mutinous troops, ended an affair which, if O'Higgins had not shown his quality at the critical moment, might well have resulted in the fall of the regime.[24]

While the government was extricating itself from this predicament another crisis was working slowly to a climax. It developed out of a subject even more explosive if possible than the relations of the Army with the civil power, the relations between the Irish Free State and Northern Ireland. It will be recalled that during the Treaty negotiations Griffith's intention 'to break on Ulster' had been thwarted by the British delegation, and by Lloyd George in particular, who persuaded him to sign the Treaty on the understanding that if the north refused to form part of a united Ireland, then a Boundary Commission would be created to determine the frontiers between the two areas of Ireland. Both Griffith and Collins, it seems, anticipated that such a Commission would recommend large transfers of territory to the Irish Free State. Article XII of the Treaty, therefore, contained the proviso that if Northern Ireland decided to opt out of the suggested union with the south, then the Boundary Commission, consisting of three persons, would be set up to 'determine, in accordance with the wishes of the inhabitants, so far as may be compatible with economic and geographic conditions, the boundaries between Northern Ireland and the rest of Ireland'.

Later, the Free State signatories to the Treaty were to come under heavy fire for agreeing to an Article cast in such vague terms and containing, in the phrase relating to economic and geographic conditions, an almost infinitely exploitable area of disagreement. At first, however, there appears to have been a general disposition only to constitute the Boundary Commission as a last resort and several attempts were made to reach agreement by direct negotiations between the parties concerned. But when by 1924 it became clear that no progress could be made along these lines Mr Cosgrave agreed with the British government not only that the Commission should be set up, but also that Britain should appoint the Northern Ireland representative which Northern Ireland itself had resolutely refused to do. As finally established, therefore, the Commission consisted of a neutral chairman, Mr Justice Feetham, of the South African Supreme Court; Mr J. R. Fisher, a prominent northern Unionist nominated by the British government to represent Northern Ireland; and finally, for the Free State, the Minister of Education, Eoin MacNeill, himself, it will be remembered, an Ulster Catholic from the Glens of Antrim.

For most of 1925 the Commission perambulated the border, taking evidence from all and sundry, but giving no inkling of how it was going to report. The Commissioners, oppressed by the gravity of their task, had agreed among themselves not to disclose their deliberations but, unhappily for his own future peace of mind, MacNeill agreed also that the Commissioners should sign a joint report and that it should not be published unless it was one which all the Commissioners could sign.[25] There can be little doubt that, like Griffith and Collins before him, he had believed that the outcome of the Commission could only be to the advantage of the Irish Free State which might, perhaps, be assigned large parts of Fermanagh and Tyrone. Then, suddenly, on 7 November the *Morning Post* published an apparently inspired statement to the effect that the Commission would leave the frontier much as before, except that an area of Donegal would go to the north and that the south would make minor gains elsewhere. Again there was a deep silence. It was broken at last on 20 November when MacNeill resigned from the Commission. Explaining his action in the Dáil a few days later, he asserted that while he had agreed in principle to sign a joint report before knowing what it was going to contain, he had come to realise that his interpretation of Article XII was quite different from Judge Feetham's and that, in consequence, he could not possibly subscribe to the report about to be issued. He had accordingly resigned from the Commission and, recognising the logic of his situation, followed this by resigning from the Executive Council a few days later.

These resignations were the acts of an honourable, but, some people could not help feeling, also a much confused and misled man. Whether they would suffice to save the government of which he had been a member was, however, another matter. Certainly, if the Commission's report was as damaging as MacNeill had indicated, and if, as was apparently the case, his resignation was no bar to the other two Commissioners publishing their findings, then the Irish Free State would be faced with the worst crisis in its short history, for its own representative would be open to the charge, however unfair, that he had spent long months *buttressing*, not diminishing, partition, and this without a word to his cabinet colleagues. The situation was made even worse by the presumption, which the Free State and the British government seemed to share, that once the Commission had presented its report, they would be bound to implement it forthwith. There was a moment in October 1925 when the British looked as if they might retreat from that position, but it is fair to say that both governments were hagridden by the fear that administrative chaos, or even bloodshed, might result from immediate implementation of the report. To prevent this happening urgent action was essential. Accordingly, on 28 November representatives of the Irish Free State government – Cosgrave, O'Higgins, Patrick McGilligan (who had succeeded McGrath as Minister for Industry and Commerce) and the Attorney-General – crossed to England and met the Prime Minister, Stanley Baldwin, at Chequers. Next day, the Northern Ireland Prime Minister, Sir James Craig, arrived and the Free State ministers met him also, finding him, it is said, as intransigent as ever where the six counties were concerned, but distinctly cool towards the British negotiators. 'Anything I can do', he said to O'Higgins, 'to help you get what you can off *those fellows*, I will.'[26]

He could, of course, afford to be generous at the expense of the British government. Had the report of the two Commissioners been promulgated and become law, Northern Ireland might have gained considerably and would not in any event have been seriously reduced. But to prevent the report being promulgated the Free State representatives consented to a tripartite agreement which was signed in London on 3 December 1925. Its purpose was in effect to amend the Treaty in respect of Article XII, but advantage was taken of the opportunity to deal at the same time with Article V, which had left the Free State liable for an unascertained share of the British public debt and also for the payment of certain war pensions. The essence of the Agreement was contained in three points. First, the existing boundary between Northern Ireland and the Irish Free State was to remain unaltered. Second, the Irish Free State was to be released from its liabilities under Article V. (By the same token, Northern Ireland was also released from its share of the British debt.) Third, the powers of the Council of Ireland relating to Northern Ireland under the Government of Ireland Act of 1920 were to be transferred to the Northern Ireland government, and the two Irish governments were to meet together in the future to settle matters of common interest. The Council of Ireland had originally been intended as a means of bringing the two parts of Ireland closer together, but it had never in fact been other than mythical. The provision for future meetings of the two governments was a much more rational approach to the problem of co-operation. Indeed, it was all too rational, since passions ran so high on both sides of the border that heads of government could not meet without committing political suicide. Forty years were to pass before the leaders of Northern Ireland and what had then become the Republic were to face each other again at a conference table.[27]

Perhaps the settlement was the best the Free State delegates could have obtained under the circumstances, but nothing could hide the fact that this agreement gave, or seemed to give, an element of permanence and stability to the border that had not been there before. The only reason Griffith and Collins had assented to the Treaty, in the last resort, had been their understanding that a door had been left open by Article XII for the reunion of the country. Now that door had been slammed in the faces of their successors the division of the country, which had been at the heart of so much of the history of the previous twenty years, seemed deeper than ever. It could be said, of course, that all that had happened was that the Irish Free State had at last been brought face to face with the ultimate reality which nationalists had always been curiously reluctant to confront – the fact that there was a solid phalanx of Ulstermen deeply and immovably attached to the Union and utterly unaffected either by threats or cajolements from the south. Southerners, very naturally obsessed by the possible fate of Ulster nationalists condemned to minority status in the six counties, could never reconcile themselves – and still cannot do so – to the notion that Northern Ireland intended to remain a separate entity. Nevertheless, in the short run, and whatever the future might hold, this was what the failure of the Boundary Commission entailed.

It was inevitable that the government which had negotiated such an agreement should be fiercely assailed at home, and it was small comfort that, had the actual report of the Commission been published then (it only appeared in 1969) the uproar might have been still worse. Even as it was, the fissiparous tendencies within Mr Cosgrave's party were intensified. Not only did he lose a prominent supporter (Professor William Magennis, one of the members for the National University), but he was faced with a rash of new parties which aimed at drawing support away from Cumann na nGaedheal. They were too small to present much of an immediate threat, but as a symptom of the loss of confidence in the government engendered by the boundary fiasco they were distinctly ominous.*

* *Report of the Irish Boundary Commission*, 1925 (Dublin, 1969). See especially the introduction by G. J. Hand and also the same author's

Far more important, of course, was the reaction of Mr de Valera to this turn of events. It was a strictly predictable reaction, in that the failure of the Commission gave him an ideal opportunity at one and the same time to point to this disaster as a natural consequence of the Treaty and correspondingly to belabour the government for dismembering the country. All the same, he made less capital out of the incident than might have been expected, for the very good reason that simultaneously with the border crisis he was faced with a crisis of his own. His theoretical (or metaphysical) position during the years since 1922 had been that he was still President of the Republic. His 'government' therefore claimed to control the Irish Republican Army through the agency of the 'Minister for Defence' (Mr Sean Lemass) and the 'Chief of Staff' (Mr Frank Aiken). But the IRA had become impatient with a government that had nothing to govern and no way of making its presence felt. Consequently, at a Convention held in November 1925 it withdrew its allegiance from Mr de Valera and his colleagues, and an Army Council was set up to direct the future activities of the IRA which were more and more devoted in the future to the idea of ending partition by force.

This secession left Mr de Valera in a very exposed position. His Sinn Féin party did indeed enjoy considerable support in the country, but that could give him no political leverage so long as the party professed itself unable to enter the Dáil because of the oath of allegiance to the Crown. There soon began, therefore, the elaborate manoeuvres which were destined within a few years to bring him to power as a constitutional leader. In March 1926 the Sinn Féin party organisation met to discuss its attitude towards the oath. It had before it a motion in Mr de Valera's name to the effect that if the oath was removed it would become a matter of policy rather than principle as to whether a Republican could enter the Dáil (or for that matter the Northern Ireland parliament). This motion encountered considerable opposition and it was clear that many of those present still preferred the pure milk of revolutionary gospel – that it was incompatible with the principles of Sinn Féin to send representatives into any 'usurping' legislature. The motion was accordingly defeated by 223 votes to 218.

Regarding this, quite correctly, as in effect a vote against his policy, Mr de Valera at once broke with Sinn Féin. This marked the virtual end of what has been described as 'the third Sinn Féin party'. During its brief life – it lasted only from 1923 to 1926 – it could reasonably claim to have been the logical successor to the two earlier move-

'Eoin MacNeill and the Boundary Commission', in F. X. Martin and F. J. Byrne (ed.), *The Scholar Revolutionary: Eoin MacNeill, 1867-1945, and the Making of The New Ireland* (Dublin, 1973). The British government's role in the crisis is in part revealed in Thomas Jones, *Whitehall Diary*, vol. iii, *Ireland, 1918-1925*, edited by Keith Middlemass (London, 1971), pp. 220-46.

ments – Griffith's original foundation, the so-called 'monarchial' party which monopolised the Sinn Féin label from 1905 until 1917, followed by the second or 'national' party resulting from the fusion with de Valera's forces in that year. This second Sinn Féin party was, as we saw, shattered by the split over the Treaty. Now in 1926 there was to be a further split. The die-hard Republicans remained outside constitutional politics to form the fourth or 'fundamentalist' Sinn Féin party which, denied all chance of power and responsibility, tended to become steadily more intransigent in its attitudes. There is a real sense in which it can be regarded as the ancestor of the present Sinn Féin organisation. At the time, however, it seemed to have no prospect but to perish in the wilderness, for Mr de Valera, having broken with the extreme men, lost no time in building an alternative power-base.[28] In May he formally launched a new party to be called Fianna Fáil – nowadays, of course, a powerful and well-organised force in Irish politics, but at the time a somewhat exotic growth whose very name – Warriors of Fál (Fál being a poetic symbol for Ireland) – seemed to look towards the mists of antiquity than towards any ascertainable future. Nevertheless, the party attracted into its ranks most of Mr de Valera's more moderate Sinn Féin adherents and its formation was seen even at the time to be the portent of a significant new departure, since it indicated that at last the most formidable opponent of the Treaty was moving once more into the arena of practical politics.

There remained, however, the stumbling-block of the oath and as the next general election approached – it was due in 1927 – it became obvious that this would be, for Fianna Fáil at any rate, the main issue on which it would appeal to the country. Meanwhile, Mr Cosgrave's government, with that characteristic stoicism which was as morally admirable as it was politically suicidal, continued to give hostages to fortune. In March 1926 it had concluded with Britain the so-called 'Ultimate Financial Agreement' which confirmed an undertaking given in 1923 that the Irish Free State would pay to the British government the land annuities arising out of the land legislation of the late nineteenth and early twentieth centuries; in addition, the Free State accepted responsibility for the payment of certain RIC pensions, the total obligation from these two commitments being about five million pounds a year. This agreement, though regarded by Mr Cosgrave's government as an obligation of long standing, offered nevertheless a broad target for attack, partly because it had not been submitted for parliamentary approval, but even more because it could be represented as involving the Free State in payments from which, so it was argued, the previous agreement of 1925 had released her. Either way, it was an unpopular settlement and helped to weaken the government's position in the country.*

But this was not all. Towards the end of 1926 the IRA attacked twelve police barracks in various parts of the country, killing two

* For further discussion of the financial question, see chap. 2 below.

unarmed Civic Guards. The government at once reacted strongly with a new Public Safety Act, bringing back the old powers of detention and of suspending *habeas corpus*. It was intended only for use in emergency but it could very easily be attacked as a further exercise of power by tyrannical ministers. And, as if this were not enough, O'Higgins, with his fierce integrity, proceeded to alienate an extremely influential section of the electorate by passing rapidly through both houses an Intoxicating Liquor Act which aimed at limiting the number of public houses and reducing the hours of opening. As a social reform this was probably long overdue – it had been recommended by an impartial commission of inquiry – but to drive through parliament on the eve of an election a measure that was certain to infuriate the drink trade seemed, even to some of O'Higgins's faithful supporters, not so much a vindication of principle as an exercise in masochism.

O'Higgins and his fellow-ministers fought the election on their own past record. Given the kind of situation they had inherited, it was an impressive record, and they could point with justifiable pride to such achievements as the virtual completion of land purchase, the development of agriculture and the launching of the Shannon electrical project.* All this had been achieved within the framework of what was then regarded as an impeccable financial orthodoxy and if, to a later generation, Mr Cosgrave's government stands open to the charge that it spent too little on the welfare of its citizens, then it can be replied that not only is the charge anachronistic (it is unhistorical to judge the 1920s in terms of the 1960s) but that small spending was balanced, to some degree at least, by light taxation. Income tax had fallen from six shillings to three shillings in the pound, the duties on tea and coffee had been abolished, and the duty on sugar lowered. And if it be true that Cumann na nGaedheal was coming to be seen increasingly by its enemies as the party of hard-faced business men who, to adapt Stanley Baldwin's phrase about the post-1918 House of Commons, looked as if they had done well out of the Civil War, then these important reductions in the cost of the poor man's comforts have also to be remembered.[29]

It was doubtful, however, whether sober rectitude and efficient but conservative government would suffice. Passion was not yet all spent in Ireland, it had only been deflected. The many opponents of the government tried, in their different ways, to stir that passion again and to focus it on parliamentary politics. Broadly speaking, their efforts took two forms. One was to suggest that Cumann na nGaedheal had become too committed to membership of the British Commonwealth and had ceased to be – some of its extremer opponents would have said it never had been – a truly national party. The other was to assail its economic policies as inadequate to cure the two major and continuing evils of unemployment and emigration. The great panacea – held out mainly by Fianna Fáil, but attractive to some of the smaller parties

* For the government's economic achievement, see below, chap. 4.

also – was to be a programme of economic development behind high tariff barriers, a programme conveniently calculated to appeal not only to those who had genuine doubts about the continuing validity of free trade in the post-war world, but also to that very considerable section of the public which had been brought up to believe that economics was simply an extension of nationalism.

When the election came at last in June the results were intriguingly inconclusive. The government party, though still the largest individually with forty-seven seats, was closely followed by Fianna Fáil with forty-four. The Labour party came next with twenty-two seats – an upsurge in its fortunes due partly to increasing public interest in economic and social issues, but partly also, perhaps, to the reluctance of some of the electors to vote for Fianna Fáil so long as they persisted in their policy of abstention; for working class voters unsure of the future of Fianna Fáil, the natural alternative would certainly have been to go for Labour. There were in addition fourteen Independents and eleven of the Farmers' party. Apart from these, Sinn Féin had five, and the independent Republicans two, seats. One other party – the National League – returned what were likely, in the prevailing conditions of uncertainty, to be eight very important members. It had been founded the previous year by Captain William Redmond, son of the old parliamentarian John Redmond, and its programme of full co-operation with Britain and Northern Ireland appealed most to older voters who still had some nostalgia for the great days of the Home Rule movement; it had some following also amongst ex-soldiers and amongst publicans disenchanted with the reforming zeal of O'Higgins. In its social attitudes the National League leaned towards the right and only a very naïvely enthusiastic supporter could have seen in it much prospect of future growth.

Everything turned, therefore, upon Mr de Valera's reaction to the electoral stalemate. His first step was to lead his entire party to the Dáil and seek admittance. When the Clerk drew his attention to the 'little formality' of the oath which had to be 'taken and subscribed by every member of the Oireachtas before taking his seat therein', the Fianna Fáil deputies declared their intention of entering the Dáil without the oath. The doors of the chamber were then locked against them and they withdrew to their headquarters, where Mr de Valera delivered the standard philippic against the oath. 'They pledged themselves to the people', he was reported as saying, 'that as long as they were representatives of the people they would never take an oath of allegiance to a foreign king. They had been prevented because they would neither take a false oath nor prove recreant to the aspirations of the Irish people and renounce their principles.'[30] Since the second largest party was thus still immobilised, Mr Cosgrave again took office, with Kevin O'Higgins acting not only as his Vice-President, but combining also the offices of Minister for Justice and Minister for External Affairs; the remainder of the Executive Council was much as before and gave promise of a further period of stable and efficient government.

Yet in fact the situation was very serious. So long as Fianna Fáil remained outside the Dáil what went on inside the Dáil was bound to have an air of unreality. And a political situation where one large party governed because among the welter of smaller parties there was no coherent opposition to take its place was in itself unhealthy. How this situation might have developed no one can tell, for suddenly, and out of a seemingly clear sky, it was transformed by tragedy. On 10 July 1927, barely two weeks after the new government had been formed, Kevin O'Higgins was walking alone, unarmed and unguarded, to Mass at a church a short distance from his home in Blackrock, near Dublin. Three assassins, who had been lying in wait in a motor-car, opened fire on him. He ran for cover but was hit and fell, seriously wounded, to the ground. The men then stood over him, fired repeatedly into his body, and made off at high speed in their car. Their identity was unknown and has remained so (officially at least) to this day. O'Higgins was found by his old colleague, Eoin MacNeill, and taken back to his own home, where he died some hours later.[31]

This terrible stroke removed at the age of thirty-five the most brilliant and most fearless of those who had come to power after the Civil War. Had O'Higgins lived we can hardly doubt that the pattern of Irish politics would have been very different. Even his death transformed the entire balance of parties. The government at once introduced yet another Public Safety Act, giving it power to declare unlawful any association that aimed at the overthrow of the state by force and laying down severe penalties for membership of any such association; the Act gave the authorities drastic powers of search and also made provision for the setting up of a special court with power to inflict death or penal servitude for life upon those convicted of the unlawful possession of firearms. It marked, undoubtedly, a severe encroachment on the liberty of the subject and was repealed in December 1928. But the government went beyond the immediate crisis by passing two other measures which struck at the whole abstentionist policy of Fianna Fáil. The first of these, the Electoral Amendment Bill, provided that every candidate for election to either House should, when nominated, swear that if elected he would take the oath as prescribed by the Constitution. Every elected member who failed to do this within a given time would be disqualified and his seat vacated. Coupled with this was another Bill which proposed (a) to restrict the right of members to demand a referendum (under Article 47 of the Constitution) to those who had taken the oath, and (b) to abolish the initiation of laws or constitutional amendments by the people.

The Electoral Amendment Bill was clearly a deliberate attempt to oblige Mr de Valera to resolve his dilemma, and in doing so to establish in the country, virtually for the first time since the Civil War, the possibility of the peaceful evolution of a two-party system. It is hardly credible that Mr Cosgrave and his colleagues did not foresee what they were doing or did not anticipate that a direct consequence of this measure would, sooner or later, be the assumption of power by Fianna Fáil. But, as men pledged to the Free State Constitution and anxious above all to establish a working parliamentary democracy in the country, they were bound by the logic of their position to persuade Mr de Valera and his followers into accepting a full share of responsibility, even if that meant the end of Cumann na nGaedheal's ascendancy.

Whatever the motives behind the Bill it soon produced its predictable effect. Faced with the disagreeable alternative of either maintaining his aloofness on a point of principle which was beginning to strain the patience of his adherents (two of whom had in fact broken with Fianna Fáil and taken the oath and their seats), or coming to terms with political realities, he did not hesitate much longer. To get round the oath was, indeed, no insuperable obstacle to one who has some claim to be regarded as the constitutional Houdini of his generation. Mr de Valera at the time, and on many subsequent occasions, described with exquisite subtlety how he and his party reached the conclusion that the oath was simply an empty political formula which, being so regarded even by their opponents, could be taken by Fianna Fáil 'without becoming involved, or without involving their nation, in obligations of loyalty to the English Crown'.[32] He explained this in greater detail to the Dáil after he had come to power, again emphasising that because others had admitted the oath to be merely a formality he had felt justified in testing the position, by confronting the Clerk of the Dáil in a manner he described as follows:

I have here [he told the Dáil in 1932] the original document written in pencil, and in Irish, of the statement I made to the officer who was supposed to administer the oath. I said, 'I am not prepared to take an oath. I am not going to take an oath. I am prepared to put my name down in this book in order to get permission to go into the Dáil, but it has no other significance.' There was a Testament on the table and in order that it could be no misunderstanding I went and I took the Testament and put it over and said, 'You must remember I am taking no oath.'[33]

The immediate consequence of Fianna Fáil's entry into parliamentary politics was to imperil the precarious supremacy of Mr Cosgrave's party. The distinct possibility emerged that the Dáil might divide into two broad groups – on the one hand the government party plus the Farmers and most of the Independents, on the other hand Fianna Fáil in uneasy alliance with Labour and with the eight stalwarts of Captain Redmond's National League. But the latter were not quite so stalwart as they seemed. When negotiations were started to form an anti-government group in order to defeat Mr Cosgrave on a vote of no confidence, one of the eight National League members, Mr Vincent Rice, transferred his vote to the other side, on the grounds that the National League was being made the puppet of Fianna Fáil. Even so, the voting resulted in a tie and might well have gone against the government but for an incident that demonstrated the truth of the old axiom that in Ireland farce follows hard upon the heels of tragedy. Another National League member, Alderman John Jinks of Sligo, was intercepted by two Sligo friends, Major Bryan Cooper, an Independent member, and the editor of the *Irish Times*, R. M. Smyllie, who prevailed on him to absent himself from the critical division. Accounts differ as to whether they achieved this result by an excellent luncheon which the alderman was obliged to sleep off in his hotel, or whether they simply sent him home on the next train to Sligo. Either way, there was deadlock in the Dáil which was resolved by the chairman giving his casting vote in favour of the government. Mr Jinks, his moment of fame fulfilled, passed from the political stage, though not entirely from memory, since his name was carried for several years by a very successful racehorse.[34]

A Dáil so evenly divided gave no party a chance to govern and, inevitably, there had to be a second general election barely three months after the previous one. The issues were the same, but the parties were all short of funds and the smaller ones suffered as a result. Sinn Féin disappeared from view altogether, the National League was almost wiped out (it was reduced from eight to two seats), the Farmers fell from eleven to six, and, most striking of all, Labour – deeply divided between its own moderates and extremists – lost nine seats, including those of the leader, Thomas Johnson, and the influential trade unionist, William O'Brien, general secretary of the Irish Transport and General Workers' Union.[35] In contrast to the shattered fortunes of the lesser parties, the two big ones both strengthened their position – Cumann na nGaedheal winning sixty-seven seats and Fianna Fáil fifty-seven. Already, it seemed, the logic of a two-party system was beginning to assert itself, although, in order to secure himself in power, Mr Cosgrave was obliged to form an alliance with the Farmers' party. The addition of those six seats, together with the support of a number of Independents, allowed him a further lease of life for four and a half years.

Nevertheless, although the government went on much as before, and still contained most of the same able men, the gap left by Kevin O'Higgins seemed to yawn wider and wider as time went by. The administration continued to be efficient and economical, and abroad, especially in the Commonwealth, its prestige steadily increased, but it fatally lacked appeal in its own country. This was not entirely its fault, of course. It was caught, like other governments all over the world, in an economic depression so severe that copybook finance suddenly came to seem irrelevant and ministers, who knew no other kind of finance, soon found themselves in deep and stormy water. Moreover, the entry of Fianna Fáil into parliament had not solved, and could scarcely have been expected to solve, all the problems of accommodating the revolutionary spirit within the framework of constitutional politics.

In the end it was this nagging question of domestic security that did more than anything else to unseat Mr Cosgrave. The economic situation certainly became increasingly serious as the depression deepened, but we shall never know how successfully the government would have grappled with that, or how flexible it might have become in adapting traditional policies to new circumstances, because it was never able to give the matter its full attention and was overtaken by political disaster while the economic crisis was still at its height. In essence, the problem it was faced with was the problem it had been faced with ever since 1922—how to defend the Treaty and the Constitution which was based upon the Treaty. In a sense that problem had been complicated rather than simplified by the emergence of Fianna Fáil as a constitutional party and by the split in the Republican forces which had preceded it. Formerly, it had been easy to define one's opponents and, if one had the courage, simple enough to deal with them. But now it was no longer so straightforward, for the enemy was within the gate as well as outside it.

It was true, no doubt, that the Fianna Fáil programme was perfectly explicit on the constitutional issue—they stood for the abolition of the oath. But where precisely would they go from there? How wholeheartedly constitutional had they really become? It was difficult to be clear about the answer. Difficult, for example, when Mr Lemass told the Dáil in March 1928 that Fianna Fáil was 'a slightly constitutional party'. 'We are', he continued, 'perhaps open to the definition of a constitutional party, but before anything we are a Republican party. . . . Our object is to establish a Republican government in Ireland. If that can be done by the present methods we have, we will be very pleased, but, if not, we would not confine ourselves to them.'[36] Even more difficult, when in 1929 Mr de Valera himself, while admitting that some one had to keep order in the community and that the government, by virtue of what he called its 'de facto position' was the only body that could do so, still continued to deny its legitimacy. 'You brought off a *coup d'état* in the summer of 1922', he accused them. As for himself, while he had come into the Dáil as a matter of practical policy. 'I . . . stood by the flag of the Republic, and I will do it again.' And then he added a striking remark which must have haunted him more than once in the years to come. 'Those who continued on in that organisation which we have left can claim exactly the same continuity that we claimed up to 1925.'[37]

This remark has to be seen in the context of what was actually happening in the revolutionary movement at that very time. It was suggested earlier that, with the withdrawal of Mr de Valera and his

501

followers into constitutional politics, the IRA became to all intents and purposes a military organisation dedicated to the establishment of a republic for the whole of Ireland. But while it still contained some remarkably able men it was by no means as monolithic in its structure as apprehensive outside observers sometimes imagined. Although its objective was primarily political, it was also sensitive to economic and social problems, partly because some of its members looked back to Connolly for their inspiration, and partly for the sound revolutionary reason that unemployment and discontent were the ideal recruiting-sergeants for an underground movement. Consequently, while some of the leaders remained steadfast to the old Fenian tradition, others leaned in varying degrees to the left. One such was Peadar O'Donnell, who had been much involved in a campaign to prevent the payment of land annuities long before this became part of Fianna Fáil's official policy. O'Donnell belonged to a group with socialist leanings which in 1931 founded a new organisation, Saor Eire, whose objectives, as well as the eternal republic, were to overthrow 'Irish capitalism' and to provide 'an independent revolutionary leadership for the working class and working farmers'. Saor Eire was promptly denounced as communistic and suppressed later in 1931, but, although it is likely enough that there were some communists among its members, neither communism as such, nor, for that matter, Marxism in any shape or form, made any significant headway among the Irish workers for reasons that will be discussed later.* Institutionally, Marxism expressed itself through the Irish Workers' League, founded by James Larkin in 1923 on his return from America, and more briefly through the Communist Party of Ireland which emerged into the open ten years later, but neither of these bodies made much impact on Irish public opinion.[38]

It was otherwise with the political activists. When the Public Safety Act passed after O'Higgins's death was repealed at the end of 1928, it was noticeable that crimes of violence and intimidation – especially of juries – began to increase. This seems to have been connected with the foundation of yet another revolutionary group (the Central Council of the Republic or Comhairle na Poblachta) which in its official weekly paper, *An Phoblacht*, carried on a ceaseless campaign of vituperation against the government. To meet these threats, and especially the attacks upon jurymen, the Juries Protection Act was passed in 1929, though only under guillotine procedure in the teeth of fierce opposition from Fianna Fáil; originally limited to two years, it had later to be extended. This, however, did not prevent the situation from deteriorating still further. Illegal drilling continued in many parts of the country, and, during 1931 especially, the number of shootings became very alarming, even if some of these shootings were 'executions' by the IRA of members who had turned informers or were in other ways deemed to have betrayed the organisation. Not

* See chap. 5, section iv below.

the least disturbing feature of this grim recrudescence of violence was that in June of that year (1931) the Republicans and Fianna Fáil marched together in the annual pilgrimage to Wolfe Tone's grave at Bodenstown. Fianna Fáil, it seemed, was still only 'a slightly constitutional' party.

It was hardly surprising in the circumstances that the government should resolve to meet extremism with extreme measures. In October 1931 it introduced the Constitution (Amendment No. 17) Bill, which was really a Public Safety Bill of a most ferocious kind. The Bill set up a military tribunal of five members, empowered to deal with political crime and to punish it with the death penalty if necessary, the only appeal being to the Executive Council. The Executive Council itself was given authority to declare associations unlawful by a simple order, and wide powers of arrest and detention were conferred on the police. These regulations did, it must be admitted, mark an unprecedented limitation of the liberty of the subject and they could only be justified by the gravity of the threat to public order. The Bill was strenuously opposed by Fianna Fáil, as was only natural, but Mr de Valera was to find before long that a military tribunal had its uses; even at the time he conceded that 'if there is no authority in this House to rule, then there is no authority in any part of the country to rule'. On 17 October this exceptional measure became law, provoking, it is said, an exodus of extremists from the country that same night. Three days later the government used its powers to declare twelve organisations illegal, including Saor Eire and the IRA, thus enabling members of these organisations, if arrested, to be brought before the military tribunal.[39]

Without doubt this legislation contributed much to the government's unpopularity and it certainly helped to align the IRA behind Fianna Fáil when the election came in 1932. By that time, however, Mr Cosgrave and his colleagues were faced with a sea of troubles – mainly economic, but partly stemming from the simple fact that a party which has been ten years in office is bound to alienate some parts of the electorate and bore others. With that Roman austerity which had characterised them at so many critical moments in the past, the ministers faced the election committed to a policy of rigorous retrenchment. To a country deep in unemployment and poverty Mr Cosgrave held out the prospect of reduced pay for national school teachers and for the police. Moreover, and almost as if its aim was to produce an ecstasy of unpopularity, the government chose this moment to prosecute Mr de Valera's paper, the *Irish Press*, for seditious libel, and to prosecute it not in the ordinary courts but before the military tribunal. The result was predictable – odium for Cumann na nGaedheal and advertisement for Fianna Fáil.

Fianna Fáil's own approach to the election was exceedingly circumspect. There were many, and not only ex-Unionists, who were quite sure the heavens would fall if Mr de Valera were to obtain power.[40]

It was important to allay their fears and this the Fianna Fáil manifesto was well-calculated to do. The abolition of the oath was, of course, still in the forefront, but it may well have been the economic sections of the document that the electorate found more enticing. The land annuities and certain other charges were, it was promised, no longer to be paid to Britain (the annuities would be retained in the state treasury) and this was popular with the farmers. But even more popular – both with them and with other sections of the electorate – was the vigorous programme of economic self-sufficiency which the manifesto set out in terms alluring both to the agricultural and the industrial interests. How a mainly exporting country without adequate fuel or raw materials was to win through to such independence of the outside world was a little less than clear, but in this, as in so much else, actual experience of administration would be the great educator. The immediate effect was certainly remarkable. Fianna Fáil blossomed as a constitutional party (the republic was not mentioned in the manifesto) while Mr Cosgrave and his followers obligingly fell upon their own swords. Even so, the results of the election were by no means conclusive. Fianna Fáil, indeed, became the largest single party with seventy-two seats as against fifty-seven for Cumann na nGaedheal, but there were still eleven Independents, seven Labour, four Farmers and two Independent Labour to be taken into account. Relying upon the support of Labour Mr de Valera could reckon upon a *bloc* of seventy-nine supporters, Mr Cosgrave upon seventy-four if he could hold the other groups in line. This was certainly no landslide and he would have been a bold prophet who would have forecast for Mr de Valera sixteen uninterrupted years of office. Yet such was to be the sequel and 1932, whether contemporaries realised it or not, was to take its place as one of the great divides in Irish history.

(iii) IN PURSUIT OF STATUS

The first two articles of the Treaty, providing that 'Ireland', or 'the Irish Free State' (both terms were used, with characteristic ambiguity), should have the same constitutional status in the empire as the other dominions, and, more specifically, that her relationship to the imperial government and parliament should be that of Canada, must strike the modern historian as strangely, almost grotesquely, inadequate. The facts of the case were quite otherwise. The Irish situation could not be defined by analogy because the Irish Free State was not a dominion like the rest. This was partly because history and geography had together placed her in a far closer relationship with Britain than had ever been possible for any of the other dominions. But much more was it because she was simply a different kind of country from all the others. Where they had been countries of settlement, and, except for South Africa, countries of predominantly British settlement, Ireland was an ancient nation which was a motherland second only in the Anglo-Saxon world to England herself. Moreover, although it was true that the other dominions were at that very time moving rapidly towards wider self-government – as, for example, in their conduct of foreign policy – their progress towards dominion status had been a process of evolution, subject no doubt to setbacks and crises, but registering nevertheless a steady and peaceful advance. The Irish, by contrast, had arrived at dominion status by revolution, and thwarted revolution at that. For them such status represented not growth, but arrested development, not fulfilment but frustration. In short, to admit into the family circle an Ireland which had not only been denied its republic, but had had to submit to partition as well, was at most to reduce an impossible situation to a barely tolerable compromise. It did not, in the long run, settle anything. To its detractors the Irish Free State remained an abortion and even to its supporters it symbolised desire unappeased.

On the other hand, if, as Kevin O'Higgins pointed out, Ireland had been forced into 'this miniature League of Nations', it could be argued, as O'Higgins himself argued, that it was at any rate a League which had no fixed or rigid constitution and therefore offered the possibility of further evolution.[41] True, some of the dominions, New Zealand especially, and to a lesser extent Australia, were satiated, or very nearly satiated powers, for, as the Australian prime minister, W. M. Hughes, put it at the Imperial Conference of 1921: 'We have been accorded the status of nations . . . What greater advance is conceivable? What remains to us? We are like so many Alexanders. What other worlds have we to conquer?'[42] But there were others, notably Canada and South Africa, which shared, though less intensely, the Irish impatience with the lack of precision which seemed to prevail in all statements of what dominion status really involved. There were in fact, even in 1921, powerful pressures, of which General Smuts was the most eloquent spokesman, in favour of a clearer definition of dominion status. In a private memorandum, 'The Constitution of the British Commonwealth', which he circulated to the United Kingdom and other Commonwealth governments in 1921, and which was not published until long afterwards, he urged the necessity for rounding out dominion status and cited the Irish example as a warning that this was a question of the utmost urgency:

> . . . Unless dominion status was quickly solved in a way that would satisfy the aspirations of these young nations, separatist movements were to be expected in the Commonwealth . . . The only way to meet such movements is not to wait until they are fully developed and perhaps irresistible in their impetus, but to anticipate them and make them impossible by the most generous concession of the dominion's nationhood and existence as a state. The warning against always being too late with a proper solution, of which Ireland is an

example to the whole Commonwealth, is one which we can ignore only at our own peril.[43]

The essential point that Smuts was here concerned to make was that while the dominions did indeed already enjoy most of the essentials of equality with the United Kingdom, in law and constitutional form there were still elements of subordination. If the effect of definition would be to remove these elements then South Africa could certainly look to the Irish Free State as a valuable ally.

This turned out to be the case. It is probably true that in any event the decade after the Treaty would have been a period of rapid change for the empire – the dominions had grown greatly in power and self-confidence as the result of the war and this was bound to reflect itself sooner or later in constitutional advance – but there can be no doubt that this process of change was greatly assisted by the presence at Imperial Conferences of Irish delegates who were under all sorts of pressures to enlarge the freedom implied by dominion status, and who had always at their backs the unrepentant and unrelenting guardians of the republican ideal. From the very outset the presence of the new dominion began to affect the external forms, and more subtly the inward essence, of the empire. For one thing, the term 'empire' itself began to go out of fashion and its successor, 'British Commonwealth of Nations', which had been experimentally used in other contexts, made its first official appearance in Article IV of the Treaty. Further, the oath of allegiance which members of the Dáil were required to take, deeply repugnant though it was to Mr de Valera and his followers, was nevertheless significantly different from the oath which was the rule in Britain or the other dominions. The Irish parliamentarian did not in fact swear direct allegiance to the King. He swore true faith and allegiance to the constitution of the Irish Free State as by law established, and only after that did he swear to be faithful to the King and his successors 'in virtue of the common citizenship of Ireland with Great Britain and her adherence to and membership of the group of nations forming the British Commonwealth of Nations'.[44]

Even more striking than these formal changes was the fact that the Irish Free State achieved dominion status by means of the 'articles of agreement for a treaty between Great Britain and Ireland'. This had a dual significance. On the one hand, the Treaty, as a distinguished historian has remarked, 'gave to Ireland a legal guarantee' of its status of equality, thus marking 'an important step in the process by which the customary content of dominion nationhood was transformed into positive law'.[45] And on the other hand, the remarkable admission that the Treaty was between 'Great Britain and Ireland' went, from the British viewpoint, perilously close to recognising Dáil Eireann's claim to speak for the whole country. Of course, in practice provision was made for Northern Ireland to preserve its separate status, and the

British government also quickly sought, as has been said, to close 'the moment of ambiguity' about the meaning of the word 'Treaty' by passing two statutes in 1922 which, from the British viewpoint, made full provision for the new dominion. One, the Irish Free State (Agreement) Act, incorporated the Treaty as a schedule, and the other, the Irish Free State (Constitution) Act, which ratified the Treaty, also contained the Constitution as *its* schedule. Both the Treaty and the Free State Constitution were thus embodied in British statutes and in this way, it was hoped, a veil of constitutionality would be cast over the complex legal issues raised by the way in which the Anglo-Irish settlement had been reached. Discussion has continued ever since among jurists and others about the nature of the settlement, and especially about the legal basis of the Treaty. We are not here concerned with these highly technical questions, but it is necessary to stress that from the Irish point of view the Treaty was a recognition of national sovereignty and that, even among those who accepted it, and the membership of the Commonwealth which went with it, there was a determination to press the implications of this fact as far as they could be pressed. It was entirely logical, therefore, that in 1924 the Free State government should have made an issue of registering the Treaty with the League of Nations at Geneva. It was in vain that the British government protested that the Covenant of the League was not intended 'to govern relations *inter se* of various parts of the British Commonwealth'. The Irish remained adamantly of opinion that what they had signed with Britain in 1921 was an international treaty and as such came within the purview of the League. The same logic operated in 1929 when the other dominions agreed with Britain that when accepting the obligation to refer disputes to the Permanent Court of International Justice, in certain circumstances they would reserve disputes between members of the British Commonwealth. The Irish Free State made no such reservation, thus emphasising once again the fact of separate nationhood.[46] 'In the garb of "Dominion status" ', it has been well said, 'a nationally self-conscious European state was introduced into the symmetry of the Empire, a dominion neither in form nor in substance, bound indeed to transform the entire framework of dominion association by its revolutionary origin and nationalist aspiration.'[47]

The Irish Free State, admittedly, was not the only problem child with which the British government had to deal. The South Africans, too, as we have seen, were deeply concerned with questions of equality and separateness, though, in the immediate post-war years, more with equality than with separateness. At the Imperial Conference of 1921, for example, General Smuts had urged that the status of Governor-General be changed, so that in future he should only be the representative of the Crown and not an agent of the British government – a proposal which carried with it the important corollary that dominion governments should henceforth have direct access to the King.[48]

Smuts, also, had been anxious that the right of dominions to control their own foreign policy should be more precisely defined, and here too the implication was clear – definition meant, or was intended to mean, an expansion of dominion responsibility and autonomy. Smuts did not continue long in power, but his successor, General Hertzog, was even more insistent in emphasising South African nationalism. Consequently, the Imperial Conference of 1926 brought together South Africans and Irish in a common endeavour to define the nature of the Commonwealth and in so doing to place beyond argument the freedom and equality of the dominions. What emerged from that Conference is familiar history. There was heavy pressure from both delegations to produce a formula adequately descriptive of the Commonwealth as it was in 1926, and, after much discussion and many drafts and amendments, Arthur Balfour, as presiding chairman, produced the lapidary phrases which form one of the great landmarks in the constitutional history of the empire. Great Britain and the dominions alike were defined thus:

. . . autonomous communities within the British Empire, equal in status, in no way subordinate one to another in any aspect of their domestic or external affairs, though united by a common allegiance to the Crown and freely associated as members of the British Commonwealth of Nations.[49]

It is difficult even at this distance of time to be sure how to distribute the responsibility for achieving this advance, for advance it certainly was to have the equality of the dominions with Britain stated so unequivocally. Kevin O'Higgins, who was one of the leading Irish delegates to the conference, was quite clear in his own mind that the Irish contribution had been decisive. 'The onus of the "status" push . . . has fallen very largely on ourselves', he wrote from London to his wife, and afterwards, when General Hertzog returned in triumph to South Africa declaring that he had 'brought home the bacon', O'Higgins's characteristic comment was – 'Irish bacon'.[50] But Professor Mansergh, one of the most eminent historians of Commonwealth affairs, interprets the Conference rather differently. He sees the South African pressure as more significant, partly because the South Africans had been longer in the game and were therefore more experienced, and partly because, in his view, a South African secession (which was always a possibility) would, at that time, have been far more disastrous to the whole conception of the Commonwealth than an Irish secession. Professor Mansergh, indeed, would go further and assign the most influential role neither to South Africa nor to the Irish Free State, but to Canada, which he regards as having held the balance between the pro-British Pacific dominions on the one side, and nationalist South Africa and the Irish Free State on the other.[51] But this is perhaps an over-simplification, for it is known that relations between the Irish and the Canadians were very close at the Conference, and that in Dr O. D. Skelton, the secretary to the Canadian delegation, O'Higgins had an ally after his own heart. They both recognised that the Irish Free State, as a very recent member, was unlikely to win general assent for some of its more advanced proposals and it was agreed between them that the Canadians should put forward some of these as of their own initiative. 'Many of the balls fired at the Conference by the Canadians', says O'Higgins's biographer, 'were, unknown to the other delegations, manufactured by the Irish.'[52] This has been confirmed by the more recent researches of Dr D. W. Harkness whose work, incidentally, demonstrates not merely the ubiquity but also the ability of the Irish delegation.[53]

The essential achievement of the 1926 Conference had thus been to state in broad terms the concept of co-equality. What this was to mean in more specific legal senses was gradually worked out in succeeding years and after a meeting of experts in 1929 and a further Imperial Conference in 1930 (in which Irish delegations again took a prominent part) the Statute of Westminster of 1931 summed up, as it were, the accumulated changes of the previous decade and, in the light of the principles established in 1926, made clear the extent of the powers the dominion parliaments enjoyed. Starting from the assertion in the preamble that the Crown was 'the symbol of the free association of the members of the British Commonwealth of Nations', it went on to lay down that, in future, legislation by the parliament of the United Kingdom would only apply to dominions at their request and with their consent. It was also enacted that henceforward dominions would be competent to legislate in those matters affecting them which had previously been regulated by the legislation of the United Kingdom parliament and that they would have the power to repeal existing legislation by that parliament on such matters. In addition, they would have full authority to make laws having extra-territorial operation.[54] So extensive were the powers now attributed to the dominion parliaments that, in the House of Commons debate on the Statute, Winston Churchill pointed out the particular dangers this held for Anglo-Irish relations, since, he alleged, it would now be possible for the Dáil at any time legally to repudiate every provision of the Treaty. To prevent this he was prepared to move an amendment inserting a restrictive clause, but the mere threat of such a clause evoked from Mr Cosgrave a letter reminding the British government that the Treaty rested on the assent of both parties, and depended essentially upon the good faith of each towards the other. 'We have reiterated time and time again', he wrote, 'that the Treaty is an agreement which can only be altered by consent.' Any attempt to safeguard it by legislative enactment, he added, would have an effect quite opposite from that intended. The letter was actually read out in the course of the debate, but it proved to be unnecessary, since Stanley Baldwin himself urged upon the House that a restrictive clause of this kind would offend not only the Irish Free State, not only Irishmen all over the world, but other dominions as well. The Statute of Westminster had to be an act of faith or it was nothing. This was the view that prevailed and the Statute, without a restrictive clause, passed into law at the end of 1931.[55]

There was a curious irony about the timing of this event. It marked, after all, the climax of a decade of achievement in which Irishmen had taken an honourable share and for which, in a sense, Kevin O'Higgins might be said to have died. Few now would deny that the presence of the Irish representatives at the Imperial Conferences which had led up to the Statute of Westminster not only helped to shape the instrument itself, but also influenced the pace and development between 1921 and 1931. Yet the coping-stone had hardly been placed in position when Mr Cosgrave's government fell from power. With the Fianna Fáil victory in the general election of 1932, and Mr de Valera's assumption of office, the stage was set for a new phase in Ireland's relations with the Commonwealth. At the very moment when the Statute had made clear the full extent of the legislative freedom the dominions possessed, a leader had come to power who, if the past meant anything, was certain to use that legislative freedom to the full

2. The Ascendancy of de Valera

(i) DISMANTLING THE TREATY

Mr de Valera was not more than a few days in office before he began his long-awaited assault upon the Treaty and all that it implied. As it developed that assault initially took two forms – the removal of the Oath of Allegiance from the Constitution and the suspension of land annuity payments to the United Kingdom Exchequer. The history of the land annuities and of the resulting 'economic war' is discussed later in this book.* Here it is enough to make the point that the coupling of the land annuities issue with the constitutional dispute had an unfortunate, but predictable, effect upon the British government, and especially upon the responsible minister, J. H. Thomas, Secretary of State for the Dominions. This, to him, sinister conjunction of an attack upon legal forms with a disavowal of financial obligations, betokened that something more than a mere readjustment of the relations between Britain and the Irish Free State was in question. He sniffed the approach of treason in every tainted breeze and saw in the return to power in 1932 of the intransigent republican of 1922 a direct threat to the whole basis of the settlement so painfully reached in the Treaty.

In this he was both right and wrong. Wrong in that he underestimated the internal factors in Irish politics which imposed a limit upon Mr de Valera's freedom of action. Right in the sense that the arguments about the Oath and the annuities did before long broaden out to embrace other and more fundamental questions. This was apparent from the moment (22 March 1932) that the British government received its first official intimation of Mr de Valera's intentions. In the opening salvo of what became before long a general engagement the Irish leader went far beyond the technical question of whether or not the Oath was mandatory in the Treaty. He was, in fact, prepared to maintain that it was not mandatory, but what concerned him much more was to ground his attack on the basis of

* See chap. 4 below. The reactions of the British government to Mr de Valera's assault upon the Treaty position in and after 1932 have been traced by D. W. Harkness in an article, 'Mr de Valera's Dominion: Ireland's Relations with Britain and the Commonwealth, 1932-8', in *Journal of Commonwealth Political Studies* (Nov. 1970), viii, No. 3, pp. 206-28. This article, based as it is upon Cabinet papers lately made available, throws much light upon the British attitude as revealed in the proceedings of the 'Irish Situation Committee' between 1932 and 1938. I am grateful to Dr Harkness for allowing me to see his article in advance of publication.

popular sovereignty. The Constitution of the Irish Free State was the people's Constitution, he declared, and the people had a right to modify it when they chose. As for the Oath itself, it was a relic of medievalism and an intolerable burden. It had been at the root of all the civil dissension in Ireland for the past ten years and had made impossible the development of friendly relations with Britain. It had, anyway, been imposed under the threat of immediate and terrible war, and now that the people had spoken, it must go.

Not unnaturally, Mr Thomas registered shocked incredulity. He at once denied the legal argument that the Oath was not mandatory and denied even more strenuously that a general election and a change of government could cancel an agreement which Mr Cosgrave but a few months earlier had said could not be altered except by consent. But Mr de Valera swept his expostulations on one side. Replying on 5 April to the British protest, he virtually ignored the legalistic aspects of the dispute and went straight to what was, for him, the heart of the matter. 'Whether the Oath was or was not "an integral part of the Treaty made ten years ago" [he said] is not now the issue. The real issue is that the Oath is an intolerable burden to the people of this state and they have declared in the most formal manner that they desire its removal.' Such language was far removed from the diplomatic niceties that usually soften the abrasive remarks governments may feel compelled to make to each other, and it was even more alien to the careful formalism of the constitutional lawyers. Yet Mr de Valera's passionate outbursts supply the essential key to our understanding of this crucial episode. There was, indeed, to be a great deal of legal argument, for each side had an elaborate case to make. But, given the ambiguities surrounding both the Treaty and the Irish Constitution, it is not surprising that the legal argument was conducted in a fog, and though, as has been well said, 'the fog which impeded the defence was favourable to the assault', Mr de Valera showed by his actions that he was prepared to disregard the fog and drive on hard towards his objective.[1]

What exactly was his objective? When he met Mr Thomas in June in an abortive attempt to reach agreement – ostensibly over the economic dispute – Mr de Valera apparently told him that his 'ultimate' aim was the unity of the country, the recognition of Ireland as a republic, some form of association with the Commonwealth and the recognition of the King as head of the association. This was not essentially different from the programme of the famous Document No. 2 of ten years earlier, but Mr de Valera admitted that the election of 1932 had not given him this kind of mandate. For the moment, therefore, he limited his scope to achieving two main purposes – first, to remove the Oath, and second, to delete from the Constitution Act and from the Constitution itself the provisions which had made the Treaty a part of Irish municipal law. It may be contended – and the point was constantly made against him in debate – that while the first of these purposes had certainly figured in his election manifesto, the second as certainly had not. But while his opponents argued that he had no power to amend the Constitution Act, it was clear enough that his second purpose followed quite logically from the first. If he succeeded in deleting the Oath it was necessary that he should remove at the same time those parts of the Constitution Act and of the Constitution itself which might have led the Irish courts to declare the Removal of Oath Act invalid on the ground that it was repugnant to the Treaty. The second section of the Constitution Act, it has to be remembered, had contained a very specific repugnancy clause around which fierce disputes had rolled in days gone by. It ran as follows:

The said Constitution shall be construed with reference to the Articles of Agreement for a Treaty between Great Britain and Ireland . . . which are hereby given the force of law, and if any provision of the said Constitution or of any amendment thereof or of any law made thereunder is in any respect repugnant to any of the provisions of the Scheduled Treaty, it shall, to the extent only of such repugnancy, be absolutely void and inoperative . . .

It was proposed, accordingly, to delete this section from the Constitution Act in order to remove the obstacle of repugnancy. And for the same reason Article 50 of the Constitution, which had provided for amendments of the Constitution by the Oireachtas up to a period of sixteen years 'within the terms of the Scheduled Treaty' had to be amended by the deletion of the offending phrase. Even with these precautions, it is worth adding, the Irish judges in the Supreme Court were still maintaining more than a year after the new measure had become law that the legislature had no power to amend or repeal the Constitution Act. Perhaps it was fortunate that no case directly involving the constitutionality of the Removal of Oath Act ever came before them.

What the judges might or might not do and say had no observable effect upon Mr de Valera. His Bill passed the Dáil in May 1932. It was then debated by the Senate, which returned it to the lower house with certain amendments, the most important of which was designed to prevent the measure from coming into force until agreement had been reached between the Irish Free State and the British government. The Dáil, as was to be expected, disagreed with all the Senate's amendments, but when the Bill came back to the Senate a second time, the latter insisted upon the amendments. In the normal course this deadlock would have resulted in the suspension of the Bill until November 1933, unless a general election intervened. An election did intervene (in January 1933) and resulted in a decisive victory for the government. Fianna Fáil now numbered exactly half the House (excluding the chairman), but with the support of eight Labour members had a working majority of sixteen.* When, therefore, Mr de Valera resumed the struggle in the New Year after his position had been strengthened at the polls, he was able to press home his policy. When the Removal of Oath Bill again came before the Senate in March the upper House could do no more than retard its progress for sixty days after which, in May 1933, it became law.

The removal of the Oath was only one prong of an attack which was now developing on several fronts. This attack had two main targets – the Governor-General's position as representative of the Crown, and the citizen's right of appeal to the Judicial Committee of the Privy Council. So far as the first of these was concerned, it was understandable that a government bent upon taking the Crown out of the Constitution should wish to diminish the powers of the Crown's representative. It was less understandable that it should seek to achieve its purpose by first mounting a campaign of petty insult against the individual concerned. From 1928 onwards the post originally held by T. M. Healy had been occupied by James MacNeill who, after a distinguished career in the Indian Civil Service, had been for a time High Commissioner for the Irish Free State in London. A series of provocations in the spring of 1932 led him to publish on his own responsibility the acid correspondence he had had on the subject with Mr de Valera and not long afterwards he was dismissed, or allowed to resign. His place was taken by Domhnall Ua Buachalla. Mr Buckley (to use the English version of his name) had been a country shopkeeper and was, as may be deduced, an enthusiast for the Irish language, but he possessed no very evident qualifications for the post of Governor-General. However, it was speedily made clear that no special qualifications were required. Mr Buckley was installed, not in the Viceregal Lodge, but in a suburban villa, and his main function was to affix his signature to acts of parliament. For this it was sufficient to be, as Mr Buckley was, a faithful adherent of the party in power.[2]

Larger constitutional issues were raised when in 1933 Mr de Valera moved on to strip from the office of Governor-General the power of recommending the appropriation of money and also the power to withhold the King's assent to Bills and to reserve them pending the signification of the King's pleasure. These powers had in fact been purely formal and it could be said of the two Constitutional Amendment Bills introduced to deal with them that they were only bringing constitutional forms into accord with constitutional reality. But linked with these was a third amendment, abolishing the right of appeal to the Judicial Committee of the Privy Council. In Britain these developments were greeted with alarm as indicating a fresh assault upon the Treaty and two ministers – one of them the much-tried J. H. Thomas – even challenged the right of the Free State government to act as it had done. In this they were probably reflecting accurately

* For the circumstances of the 1933 election, see below, pp. 526-7.

enough a view that was widely prevalent in Britain at the time. This was that, notwithstanding the powers conceded to dominion legislatures by the Statute of Westminster, and notwithstanding the equality of status so memorably defined at the Imperial Conference of 1926, the parliament of the Irish Free State was debarred from the enlargements of dominion status achieved since 1922 whenever such enlargements clashed with limitations existing at the time of the Treaty and written into that document.

A crucial instance was the right of appeal to the Judicial Committee of the Privy Council. This was not mentioned directly in the Treaty at all, but since the Treaty had defined the relationship of the Free State to 'the Imperial Parliament and Government' as being that of Canada, and since Canada in 1922 did not have the right to abolish by legislation the right of appeal to the Privy Council, the presumption was that the Irish Free State did not have it either. In fact, the Free State Constitution made provision for appeal, albeit in a rather back-handed fashion. Article 66, after declaring that the decision of the Supreme Court should be 'final and conclusive' and not 'capable of being renewed by any other Court Tribunal or Authority whatsoever', then went on to add the seeming contradiction that nothing in all this was to impair 'the right of any person to petition His Majesty for special leave to appeal from the Supreme Court to His Majesty in Council or the right of His Majesty to grant such leave'. From early in the history of the Free State this provision was a source of irritation and Kevin O'Higgins made it clear in 1922 that in practice the model Ireland would follow would be that of South Africa rather than Canada, in other words that appeals would not be allowed as of right, but only in exceptional cases raising international issues.

For several years the Privy Council accepted this restriction and agreed that 'as far as possible' finality and supremacy were to be given to the Irish courts. But in 1925 it agreed to admit an appeal in a case turning on the interpretation of a Land Act – a domestic issue if ever there was one. The Free State Government was galvanised into action and rapidly passed legislation affirming its view of the law, whereupon the petition was withdrawn. That same year the Privy Council admitted another appeal (this time affecting the position of British civil servants who had retired after the change of government) and, since this related directly to Article X of the Treaty, the Privy Council felt justified in reversing the decision of the Irish Supreme Court. The Free State government met this by declining to give effect to the Privy Council's decision but, as it later turned out that the Privy Council's decision had been dubious in law anyway, it proved possible to settle the matter, not in the courts, but by agreement between the governments. A few years later, in 1930, when a third case was taken to the Privy Council, the Irish parliament again passed legislation forestalling the Privy Council's judgment.

'Only one conclusion', it has been well said, 'can be drawn from a consideration of these cases, namely the uselessness of the appeal to the Judicial Committee.' Certainly, the Irish experience had shown the machinery to be extremely ineffective and quite incapable of operating when a dominion government was determined to prevent it. The Imperial Conference of 1926 had gone some way towards anticipating this by declaring that it was no part of the British government's policy that appeals to the Judicial Committee should be determined other than in accordance with the wishes of the parts of the empire primarily affected, but it had also added a warning that any changes in the system ought only to be made after consultation and discussion. Four years later the Irish Free State delegates to the next Imperial Conference sought to obtain the right to abolish the appeal and, on failing to get this concession, seriously considered introducing unilateral legislation. It will be seen then that Mr de Valera's action in 1933 can scarcely have taken British ministers by surprise. His legislation was no more than the climax of a long history of Irish objection to a court which even Kevin O'Higgins, that devoted defender of the Treaty, had stigmatised as 'a bad court – a useless court and an unnecessary court'.[3]

Nevertheless, the reaction of the British government to the new legislation of 1933 was remarkably – indeed excessively – sharp.* This may partly have been because Mr Thomas and his advisers saw behind it what they took to be Mr de Valera's grand design for an unfolding republic, but it sprang partly also from a certain uneasiness about the extent to which the Statute of Westminster itself had opened the way for the Free State to abrogate the entire Treaty settlement. After all, both the Treaty and the Irish Constitution were, as we have seen, contained in British acts of parliament. The Statute of Westminster empowered the legislature of the Irish Free State to amend British acts of parliament. Therefore the legislature of the Irish Free State was empowered to alter the Treaty and the Constitution. Against this logic, the British sought to argue that the Statute of Westminster, so far as the Irish Free State was concerned, had been 'conditioned by the terms of the treaty under which the Irish Free State was granted the *status* which it enjoys'.[4] Apart from the exceedingly dubious question of how far a statute can be 'conditioned' by anything, this argument rested on very shaky ground when it attempted

* For Thomas's reaction in November see N. Mansergh (ed.), *Documents and Speeches on British Commonwealth Affairs, 1931-52* (London, 1953), pp. 301-3. Dr Harkness, in the article already cited, reveals further that when Mr de Valera sought an assurance that secession from the Commonwealth would not expose him to 'war or other aggressive action' from Britain, the initial British impulse was to reply simply that Ireland would become a foreign country and her citizens treated as aliens in Britain with all that that implied; in the event, fearful apparently that such an answer would merely intensify Mr de Valera's intransigence, the British government contented itself with a refusal to forecast what its action might be in hypothetical circumstances.

– as it seemed to do – to set limits to the development of the Irish Free State as a dominion on the same footing with other dominions because of what had been written into the Treaty. This was to make nonsense of everything that had happened since 1922. Either the Irish Free State was a dominion co-equal in status with the other dominions or it was not. If it was, then the Statute of Westminster applied to it in exactly the same way as to other dominions. If not, then there was little point in further association with the Commonwealth and Mr de Valera's departure from it would be, if anything, accelerated.

In the end the issue was resolved, ironically enough, by the Judicial Committee of the Privy Council itself. In 1935 it heard on appeal a test case designed to elicit whether or not the Irish legislation abolishing the appeal was valid or not.[5] The judgment then delivered made it abundantly clear that whereas before 1931 the Irish Free State parliament had not been competent to abrogate the Treaty, as a result of the Statute of Westminster it had obtained the necessary power to do so. This effectively cut the ground from under the British government's feet. It was difficult to substitute another argument which had something to be said for it – that the Treaty was an international agreement and as such ought not to be unilaterally demolished – if only because in earlier years Britain had spent a great deal of energy denying that the Treaty *was* an international agreement and asserting that it was essentially a domestic matter. The only resort left was to fall back upon international morality and to maintain, though with signs of desperation, that 'there must be some obligations that are binding other than legal obligations'.[6] But in the mid-1930s ministers had only to raise their eyes from the Anglo-Irish Treaty to the Treaty of Versailles to see how inhospitable the climate had become to that kind of plea.

More immediately to the point, the judicial decision of 1935 had left the initiative with Mr de Valera and he needed no urging to exploit it to the full. That same year, for example, he passed through the Free State parliament two measures – the Irish Nationality and Citizenship Act and the Aliens Act – which not only defined Irish nationality and made provisions for reciprocal citizenship between the Free State and other countries, but also continued still further to inflame British opinion by including British subjects in the definition of an alien as anyone who was not a citizen of the Free State. The details were technical, but the direction was unmistakable. Even though British subjects were in fact exempted from the operation of this legislation by executive order, the language used in the Acts pointed not towards membership of the Commonwealth, but towards 'external association' as Mr de Valera had sketched it long ago in Document No. 2.[7]

The very next year the abdication of King Edward VIII gave him the opportunity to make this concept much more explicit. In a sense, no doubt, the abdication crisis only precipitated what was already in train. It had been known for some time that Mr de Valera was at work on a new Constitution and it was widely assumed that this Constitution would remove the Crown, thus at long last giving a republican form to the government of the country. However, since Edward VIII had removed himself from the throne before Mr de Valera had had an opportunity of removing him from the Constitution, it was necessary to face the situation thus unexpectedly created. Mr de Valera faced it by introducing two measures. The first was designed to take the Crown out of the internal government of the Free State by abolishing virtually all the functions of the Governor-General. The second, by an apparent sleight of hand, conjured the Crown into existence again for purposes of external relations, so long as the other nations of the Commonwealth continued to recognise it as 'the symbol of their co-operation.'[8]

Of these two measures the first was not much more than the embodiment in an Act of what had been the effective practice of the government for some time past – or, more accurately, it was the culmination of a policy deliberately embarked upon when Mr MacNeill was replaced as Governor-General by Mr Buckley. The second, however, marked a genuine new departure. It had, indeed, little enough to do with the present predicament of the British monarchy, but it had a great deal to do with the past history of the Irish republic. What it did in effect was to clear the way for the Constitution of 1937, which was to be a republican Constitution in everything but name, and to retain the King merely for certain limited purposes.* These purposes were specified in Clause 3 of the Act, which used terminology of far-reaching importance. The exact wording was as follows:

> It is hereby declared and enacted that so long as Saorstát Eireann is associated with the following nations, that is to say, Australia, Canada, Great Britain, New Zealand, and South Africa, and so long as the King recognised by those nations as the symbol of their co-operation continues to act on behalf of each of these nations (on the advice of the several governments thereof) for the purposes of the appointment of diplomatic and consular representatives and the conclusion of international agreements, the King so recognised may, and is hereby authorised to, act on behalf of Saorstát Eireann for the like purpose as and when advised by the Executive Council to do so.

The phrasing of this Clause indicated that the use of the Crown, even for such limited purposes, was to be both permissive and conditional. The procedure it outlined *might* be followed by the Free State government, but there was nothing to say that this would always be

* For the general significance of the Constitution of 1937 see section iii below.

the case; likewise, the procedure, if it was followed, would only be followed *so long as* the Commonwealth countries named therein continued to recognise the Crown as the symbol of their co-operation. Another way of putting this is to say that relations between the Free State and the Commonwealth had been taken out of the Constitution, where they had been a bone of contention for so many years, and had become, in effect, matters of external policy. This, as a modern authority has well said, was 'the most significant development' of the whole period since equality of status had been defined in 1926.[9]

By these manoeuvres, which to orthodox imperialists must have seemed a veritable rake's progress, Mr de Valera was not just stripping away the Treaty settlement item by item. He was doing two things of far wider significance. On the one hand, he was demonstrating the difficulty – which in the last analysis the Treaty had only papered over – of accommodating as a dominion a country which was not a 'natural dominion', in the sense of being predominantly British by settlement, but which thought of itself rather as a separate nation. And on the other hand, by bringing off these coups so successfully one after the other, he was revealing how almost infinitely elastic the Commonwealth was becoming, how far it was capable of being stretched beyond what could have been imagined twenty or even ten years earlier. Now, there were already stirring in the womb of time other territories which were clearly not 'natural dominions' and which in due course were also to regard themselves as separate nations. On them the Irish precedent had a profound influence, most marked, perhaps, in the case of India which, when deciding in 1949 to remain in the Commonwealth (as a republic), adopted a formula acknowledging the King as head of the Commonwealth virtually identical with that proposed by Mr de Valera as far back as 1922 and in essence incorporated by him in the legislation of 1936.[10]

By contrast with the hectic events of 1936, the appearance of the new Constitution in 1937 was, from the viewpoint of Commonwealth relations, almost an anti-climax. True, it contained no reference to dominion status, it dropped the names Irish Free State and Saorstát Eireann, and Article 5 declared flatly that Eire or Ireland (the two versions of the name were embodied in Article 4) was 'a sovereign, independent, democratic state'. Nevertheless, the principle of external association was carried over into the document, though it was phrased only in a very permissive fashion. The conduct of external affairs was vested in the government, but Article 29 qualified this as follows:

For the purpose of the exercise of any executive function of the State in or in connection with its external relations, the Government may to such extent and subject to such conditions, if any, as may be determined by law, avail of or adopt any organ, instrument, or method of procedure used or adopted for the like purpose by any group or league of nations with which the State is or becomes associated for the purpose of international co-operation in matters of common concern.[11]

Even this proviso, it should be stressed, was hedged round with further safeguards for the country's sovereignty. Since the Constitution could be amended by referendum there was nothing to prevent the people, if they so wished, from deleting Article 29. Moreover, the Constitution provided that every international agreement to which the state became a party should be laid before the Dáil and that war should not be declared without the assent of the Dáil. For that matter, and apart altogether from what was specifically laid down in the Constitution, it was open to the Irish parliament, as we shall presently see, to repeal the External Relations Act when circumstances appeared to demand it.

The Constitution, therefore, was emphatic in the stress it laid on sovereignty. No less emphatic, though implicit rather than explicit, was the essentially republican character of the document. But why was this character implicit rather than explicit? Why, when he had gone so far, did Mr de Valera not carry his logic to the extreme of embodying the sacred word in the written instrument? We are still too close to the event to be able to answer these questions with certainty, but one reason why the sacred word did not appear may well have been precisely because it was so sacred. Many times during his career Mr de Valera made it clear that for him the ideal was a republic of thirty-two counties, not twenty-six. To give the name to a truncated Ireland was in a sense to betray the men of 1916. But there was not only a question of doctrine, there was a question of policy. If Mr de Valera's policy was – as he and his ministers frequently affirmed – to pursue the unity of Ireland, then a republic would surely intensify rather than diminish the existing partition. And while it might be argued – and was to be argued again later – that northern Unionists had shown so little sign of wanting to join the south at any time and under any guise that the declaration of a republic was unlikely to make much difference to their attitude, those whose passion for unity blinded them to this attitude might well have felt that such a declaration in 1937, with its presumed sequel of a complete break with the Commonwealth, would only have had the effect of locking and barring a door already hard enough to open.

Further, the pursuit of unity involved not merely unity for all Ireland, but unity within the territory for which Mr de Valera was himself at that moment responsible. To a man of his antecedents – haunted as both he and his opponents were by the memory of the Civil War – it was essential to be seen to have passed as it were from the revolution to the state, to have become a national leader and to have cast off his old role as chieftain of an implacable faction.[12]

It was important for him, therefore, to steer between the Scylla of republicanism and the Charybdis of dominionism. On the one hand, he must strain to reach as many of the objectives of the republic as possible – how else could he justify his whole career? On the other hand, if he did not wish to perpetuate the divisions of the 1920s, he must do this without decisively breaking with the settlement of 1921 and so inflaming the very substantial minority which had built its whole political world upon that settlement. The Constitution of 1937 was a determined and largely successful attempt to achieve this balance. It allowed him to meet all but the diehards of the left with the plea that in its essentials the republic had been achieved. It allowed him equally to meet all but the diehards of the right with the argument that he was only using the legal forms which they themselves had bequeathed to him, to advance nearer to that ideal of sovereignty that all had held before the Treaty had been signed. They might protest, and did so most strenuously, that he was using these forms for purposes which had not been foreseen or intended, but it was difficult for them to accuse him of anything worse than consistency to his own past. No doubt they would have been ready to declare that this was accusation enough, though he, on his side, could point to the fact that in not making the republic explicit he had left himself open to the charge of *inconsistency* from his own former associates. The middle road he was taking inevitably exposed him to these fusillades from both sides but, having grasped the substance, he could afford to let his critics spend themselves on the shadow.

Internal factors such as these may have had a bearing on the decisions taken in 1936 and 1937, but it may well be that external factors were no less important. Since it was generally assumed that the declaration of the republic at that time would involve exit or expulsion from the Commonwealth, it behoved the Irish government to consider what the consequence might be. Unfortunately, this was impossible to predict. There *might* be difficulties for Irishmen living in Britain, though there was a tendency at the time to exaggerate such difficulties; there *might* be disagreeable economic results; there *might* be all sorts of legal complications; there *might* even be, in the sphere of external relations, the unpleasant necessity to walk naked and alone in a world ill-disposed towards the sovereign independence of small, unprotected states. It was impossible to tell how things would turn out, but all these considerations counselled caution.

And caution, in the end, was well rewarded. The British government's public reaction to the Constitution was phlegmatic to a degree that would have excited the envy of Phileas Fogg. In private, it is now known, the Cabinet agonised a good deal about whether the new Constitution left 'Eire' inside the Commonwealth or signalled her departure. However, it – and, after consultation, the dominions also – decided 'to treat the new Constitution as not effecting a fundamental alteration in the position of the Irish Free State . . . as a member of the British Commonwealth of Nations'.[13] This was no doubt untidy, inconsistent and perhaps even an extreme example of a deep-seated tendency in the Commonwealth to hope that awkward problems would either solve themselves or disappear if they were ignored long enough. Certainly, it created a situation which, in theory at least, was absurd enough. For the next twelve years Britain and the dominions were to go on regarding Eire (to adopt the Irish usage embodied in the Constitution) as a member of the Commonwealth. For the next twelve years Mr de Valera was to go on maintaining that, on the contrary, she was outside it and only externally associated with it for limited purposes.

But what is theoretically absurd can sometimes produce strangely practical results. So it was with the Irish imbroglio. The very tolerance with which Britain absorbed the new situation so improved relations between the two countries that the very next year it was possible to end the economic war. And not only that. By the Anglo-Irish Agreements of 1938 the British government undertook to evacuate the bases in the twenty-six counties which had been guaranteed to them by the Treaty. The motives which inspired this action of Neville Chamberlain's, and the bitter criticism it provoked from Churchill and others, do not here concern us. What is relevant is that the return of the Treaty ports enormously fortified Mr de Valera's contention that Eire was a genuinely independent state by making possible for the first time an independent Irish foreign policy. That foreign policy, as we shall presently see, was a policy of neutrality. The British concession over the ports did not in itself mean that that neutrality would be observed in the coming war, but at least it may be said to have improved the chances of such an experiment being successful.

The Agreements of 1938 did not solve everything, of course. The problem of partition still remained to bedevil Anglo-Irish relations and the fact that the south did in the end achieve its neutrality while the north became deeply involved in the war certainly made that problem, if possible, even more intractable than before. Yet there is a sense in which 1938 marks the end of a chapter not just of Commonwealth history, but of the history of the reluctant dominion itself. The dismantling of the Treaty did not end overnight the quarrel between those who had taken opposite sides in the Civil War. That quarrel, one sometimes feels, will never be ended until the last of the revolutionary generation is below ground, and perhaps not even then. Nevertheless, the progressive advance in status and the rounding out of sovereignty had removed from dispute many of the things that had divided the nation for so long. Indeed, it is permissible to go further and to ask whether one of the great ironies of Irish history was not implicit in these transactions. If in 1948-9 the political heirs of Cosgrave and O'Higgins brought themselves to make the formal and final transition to a republic in name as well as in fact, was not this only possible because the foundations had been so firmly laid between 1932 and 1938 by the political enemies of Cosgrave and O'Higgins?

(ii) THE NEMESIS OF CIVIL WAR

If, as has been alleged, Mr de Valera and his followers entered the Dáil to take up office on 9 March 1932 with revolvers in their pockets and fearful of some counter-stroke from their opponents or the Army, then their behaviour had a symbolic significance.[14] Those who had made war upon the state now controlled the state – but could they be sure that the tide of violence which had swelled so angrily for so long would now subside? For that matter, were they correct in assuming that the main threat would come from the recently defeated protagonists of the Treaty rather than from their own irreconcilable left wing? The political history of the Irish Free State during the next six years was to revolve largely round these questions, to which the passing of the years was to provide some strange answers.

At first the assumption seems to have been that the victory of Fianna Fáil would usher in a second honeymoon between Mr de Valera and the zealots of the republic. The influence of the IRA had been thrown behind him at the election in the expectation that, if returned to power, he would 'open the jails' and release the prisoners convicted by the Military Tribunal. Sure enough, on 9 March the Minister for Defence in the new government, Mr Aiken, proceeded from the Dáil to Arbour Hill Barracks where he had an apparently cordial meeting with an imprisoned IRA leader, George Gilmore. The next day all the prisoners were released, on 12 March *An Phoblacht* (the weekly paper of the extremists) reappeared and on 18 March the government put an end to the Military Tribunal and allowed the order outlawing the IRA to lapse. Almost immediately drilling and recruiting by the physical-force men commenced again and, ominously, threats to deny to Mr Cosgrave and his friends freedom of speech and of the press became increasingly frequent. To prevent their public meetings from being broken up the former government party began to organise in their own defence. Some weeks previously a new organisation, the Army Comrades Association, had made its appearance on the scene. Springing initially (February 1932) from the energy and enthusiasm of Commandant Edmund Cronin, its first president was a distinguished soldier, Colonel Austin Brennan. Its objectives – to uphold the state and to honour Irish Volunteers who had died in the Anglo-Irish war – were unexceptionable and it seemed no more than a club or friendly society for ex-officers and men of the Free State Army. But in August the new body opened its ranks to the public and soon was claiming a membership of 30,000. Not only that, but the ailing Colonel Brennan was replaced as president by one of the leading pro-Treaty politicians, Dr T. F. O'Higgins, the brother of Kevin O'Higgins. Although still emphasising the non-political character of the Association, Dr O'Higgins made it clear that he and his friends would regard it as their prime duty to ensure freedom of speech for all and that to this end they were preparing to enrol volunteers. Thus, within a few months of Mr de Valera's coming to power two extra-parliamentary bodies – the IRA and the ACA – were already exerting a direct and potentially sinister influence upon politics.

These developments were the more disturbing because within the parliamentary system itself there was deadlock and confusion. Mr de Valera's majority, as we have seen, depended upon the support of the small group of Labour members. Their support was conditional upon Fianna Fáil adopting a vigorous programme of social reform. During the election Mr de Valera and his colleagues had made a direct and largely successful appeal to the poorer sections of the electorate. The time was coming when this image of the poor man's party would be harder to sustain, but in 1932 it had considerable validity. Broadly speaking, it was justifiable at that period to claim that Fianna Fáil drew most of its support from small farmers, shopkeepers, and sections of the artisan and labouring classes, whereas Cumann na nGaedheal represented to a much greater degree the more conservative, propertied interests in the country – the large farmers, the leaders in industry and commerce, the established professional men.[15] It may seem strange that it was Fianna Fáil rather than Labour that secured the greater part of the working-class vote, but for this there were several explanations. One was that the Labour movement suffered from deep internal divisions. Between 1918 and 1930 the Labour party and the Trade Union Congress formed a single organisation and it was unfortunate that this was a period of acute and bitter rivalries within the trade unions themselves. These will be considered later in a different context,* but to the extent that they hindered the growth of a vigorous and unified workers' movement they militated against the political effectiveness of the parliamentary Labour party. However, even when the unions and the party went their separate ways in and after 1930, the electoral showing of the Labour candidates remained unimpressive and in 1932, though they held the balance of power, their own strength had been reduced from ten effective members before the dissolution to seven in the new parliament. This failure to make headway suggests that they faced more fundamental difficulties than those caused by their own disunity. In fact, they faced three such difficulties, any one of which would have been crippling.

The first was simply that the political situation in 1932, as in all the previous elections in the history of the Free State, was inimical to the growth of a Labour party. So long as men spent their passions

* See below, chap. 5, section iv.

and their energies on the legacy of the Treaty and the Civil War—so long, that is, as the lines of division in Irish elections continued to be political rather than social, so long would Labour be doomed to sterility. But the second obstacle in their way was scarcely less immovable. Given that Ireland remained predominantly agricultural, with hardly any concentrations of industrial population, the solid proletarian basis for a Labour party was lacking. And this in turn helped to explain the third disadvantage under which the workers seemed condemned to fight their political battles—the absence of a clear, coherent ideology. Lip-service was regularly paid to James Connolly, of course, but the party never allowed its enthusiasm for the dead socialist to commit it to a living socialist faith. It was for social reform, certainly, but not apparently for the total reconstruction of society. Although it was, naturally, critical of capitalism, it rejected in 1930 a proposal to include in its constitution the objective of the ownership and control by the workers of Ireland of the whole produce of their labour. This, it must be said, was not wholly the consequence of the party's own conservatism, it was to some extent also a reflection of the conservatism of the society in which the party lived. More specifically, it was a reflection of the difficulty which many working men experienced in reconciling a deeply-felt Catholic faith with an advanced socialist programme. In 1936, for example, William Norton, who had led the party in the campaign of 1932 and was to remain at its head for many years, seemed to have succeeded in moving his colleagues to the left when he persuaded them to incorporate into their new constitution not only the 1930 resolution on public ownership, but also a demand for 'the establishment in Ireland of a Workers' Republic founded on the principles of social justice, sustained by democratic institutions and guaranteeing civil and religious liberty and equal opportunities to achieve happiness to all citizens who render service to the community'. It is true that these vaguely benevolent phrases smacked more of the Cheeryble brothers than of Karl Marx, but the use of the phrase 'Workers' Republic' was highly significant, for this, more than any other phrase that could have been used, brought the party once more close to Connolly. Uncomfortably close, as it turned out. Three years later, after a lengthy correspondence on the subject, the Roman Catholic hierarchy declared its objection to this aim of achieving a Workers' Republic and the Labour party obediently deleted it from its constitution.[16]

Even with the support of this tiny and not very effective Labour group, Mr de Valera had too small a margin for comfort if the opposition parties pulled together. At first, admittedly, there was not much evidence that they would do so. Mr Cosgrave, with his great experience and judgment, was still at the head of his party, but it was a party for the time being demoralised by defeat. History, perhaps, has not yet done justice to the man who may well ultimately stand to Irish politics in the same relation as Attlee to British politics – an astute, tenacious chairman, excellent in cabinet but lacking in charisma. Now a party in power may consent to be led by a good chairman, but a party in opposition needs a man of action. Mr Cosgrave supplied the opposition with neither the dynamism nor the colour it craved and almost immediately dissatisfaction began to show itself.

It appeared first among the farmers whose normal export market had been drastically reduced by the 'economic war' with Britain, and some of whom had a hankering to carry Mr de Valera's policy on the land annuities to what seemed to them the logical conclusion of withholding payment from the Irish, as well as from the British, government. In the autumn of 1932 they, with some other support, began to grope their way towards a new party under new leaders. One of the new leaders was Mr Frank MacDermot, a member of an old Roscommon family. He was at that time in his mid-forties, and had had a varied career. Educated in England, he had fought in the British Army during the war, and had later spent some time with a firm of New York bankers. He was highly intelligent, almost too articulate, and a firm believer in the necessity of a Commonwealth connection.* Closely associated with him was a younger man who had also entered the Dáil for the first time in 1932. This was Mr James Dillon. The son of the last chairman of the old Irish parliamentary party, he was, though still barely thirty, no stranger to politics which, from childhood up, had been part of the very atmosphere he breathed. He had important business interests (being mainly responsible for running the family firm at Ballaghadereen, county Mayo) but by inclination and inheritance he was closely drawn to the farming community. In later years he was to become an outstanding Minister for Agriculture, but even in opposition he was a striking figure, with some claim to be considered the only real parliamentary orator produced by any party since the setting up of the Free State.

Under the guidance of these two men – both elected initially as Independents – a new political party emerged before the year was out. Originally saddled with the impossible title of the National Farmers' and Ratepayers' League, it soon became much better known as the National Centre Party. It was pledged to help the farmers recover their prosperity, to obliterate the bitterness of the Civil War, to end the Anglo-Irish dispute and to pursue a policy of friendliness towards Northern Ireland. It rapidly gathered support – to such an extent, indeed, that many well-wishers, especially among professional men, began to speak of a new party alignment which would bring under one banner all those in favour of improved relations with

* The present writer can recall, on going to live in Boyle, county Roscommon, as a child of ten just after the 1933 election, seeing on a bridge over the river the legend: 'Frank MacDermot – British spy'. It was incomprehensible to him then – and still is.

Britain. But before this movement could develop, Mr de Valera, whose sense of timing had always been one of his most remarkable attributes, suddenly dissolved parliament and plunged the country into a new election only ten months after the previous one. He had, as we have already seen, clashed with the Senate over the Removal of Oath Bill, and one object of the dissolution was to abolish the upper house 'as at present constituted'; if it was decided to retain it, he said at the outset of the campaign, its numbers would be reduced, as would also those of the Dáil. For the rest, he reiterated his previous programme for industrial development, increased tillage and the retention of the land annuities – though, as a sop to the farmers, he announced that the amount of the annuities payable to the home government would be reduced by half.[17] The labourers and small farmers were likewise wooed by promises of relief schemes and increased bounties. Against these blandishments the opposition parties offered little coherent counter-attraction and it was not surprising that Mr de Valera improved his position very considerably. The results were as follows: Fianna Fáil seventy-seven; Cumann na nGaedheal forty-eight; National Centre Party eleven; Labour eight; Independents eight; and Independent Labour one.[18]

Yet, while the election strengthened the government in parliament, it was becoming steadily clearer that the real struggle between parties was being fought out in the country at large. It was a struggle that rapidly threatened to get out of hand. After the election the IRA embarked openly on a campaign of recruitment and violent incidents began to multiply. It was at this moment that the government which, to its credit, had resisted earlier pressures to make extensive changes in the police, now decided to dismiss the Commissioner, General O'Duffy himself. O'Duffy had initially been appointed by Kevin O'Higgins in the early days of the state and to the leaders of the opposition his removal was a confirmation of their worst fears. Their reaction was to organise their own forces for a struggle that might become critical at almost any moment. Just after the election, between February and April 1933, the Army Comrades Association had been re-modelled with a view to greater discipline. The outward and visible signs of this discipline was the wearing of a blue shirt, and the be-wildered onlooker might have been forgiven if he saw in this emergence of private armies on the left and on the right an extension to Irish politics of the clash of ideologies then in full career on the continent. Such an interpretation, though too simple, would not have been entirely unfounded. There were symptoms of class war in Ireland at that time and there were men on both sides who were more or less consciously seeking to identify with one or other of the European movements. We have already seen that the IRA did contain an influential section (small in numbers, perhaps, but highly articulate), which was either communist or sympathetic to communist ideals. And even though the name communist was certainly thrown about very loosely by contemporaries, the tone of *An Phoblacht*, with its demand for war on the ranches and the banks and its condemnations of 'the economic stranglehold of imperialism', has a very familiar ring to the student of Marxist history.

But how far did this leftward tendency of the IRA call into being an equal and opposite reaction towards fascism? Some intellectuals, certainly, were obsessed by the danger of communism and one of the most outspoken of them, Professor James Hogan of University College, Cork, not only warned against the supposed impending peril in a famous pamphlet – *Could Ireland become Communist?* – but did not hesitate to draw the logical conclusion from what he saw, or seemed to see, under his very eyes. 'It was the growing menace of the Communist IRA', he declared, 'that called forth the Blueshirts as inevitably as Communist anarchy called forth the Blackshirts in Italy.' Nor did he stop there. Both Professor Hogan and Professor Michael Tierney of University College, Dublin, writing in *United Ireland* – which was the organ of the Cosgrave party – paid tribute to the corporate state in its Italian form. It was this, rather than the crude dictatorship of Mussolini, that Professor Tierney saw as the permanent legacy of fascism. The corporate state had evolved, he considered, a scheme of social and political organisation so suited to modern conditions that every civilised country would adapt it to its own needs. For him, as for Professor Hogan, the logic was clear. 'The corporate state must come in the end in Ireland, as elsewhere.'[19] In fact, as critics have since pointed out, the doctrines formulated in *United Ireland*, and even appearing in the Cosgrave party programme of 1933, owed as much to another Italian as they did to Mussolini. The teaching of Pope Pius XI in the encyclical *Quadragesimo Anno* laid heavy emphasis upon vocational organisation and representation within the state and it was this stream of thought that was likely to be more influential in Catholic Ireland. Indeed, its influence was not confined to any one party and, as we shall see, vocational ideas were to figure prominently in the Constitution of 1937.*

In the immediate future, however, it did seem for a brief moment that fascism might produce in Ireland not just abstract corporative

* For a full investigation of the attractions of fascism for some Irish intellectuals at this time, see M. Manning, *The Blueshirts* (Dublin and London, 1971), especially pp. 211-50. His summing-up of the political ideas of the Blueshirt movement as a whole cannot be improved upon: 'While the corporate ideas developed by Tierney and Hogan did give to the Blueshirt movement a distinctive ideology, it is clear that for the great majority, both of leaders and of rank-and-file supporters, this issue was largely an academic one. The issues which gave Blueshirtism its impetus, which concerned the minds and activities of its members and which determined the manner in which it developed, were far from academic. Blueshirtism was essentially the product of Civil War memories, fear and distrust, and the threat of economic collapse. Beside these, the promise of a new corporate state counted for very little.' (*The Blueshirts*, pp. 230-1).

doctrines, but a flesh and blood dictator. Once relieved of his police duties, General O'Duffy turned towards the Blueshirt movement. In July 1933 Dr O'Higgins handed over the leadership of the Army Comrades Association to him and the organisation itself was renamed the National Guard. Its supporters insisted (with a vehemence that is perhaps a little suspect) that it was unarmed, although its members were certainly proficient in the use of batons and knuckledusters.[20] The government strove to ensure that it remained without lethal weapons, by cancelling all licences to possess firearms and thus with-drawing from the former ministers, and from General O'Duffy, the right to carry revolvers, which most of the leaders had done since the assassination of Kevin O'Higgins. It is doubtful, in fact, whether the National Guard surrendered *all* their arms, but even so they were less well-equipped than the IRA, and, from the very fact that they wore uniforms of blue shirts, much more easily identifiable by the author-ities.

Nevertheless, the government persisted in regarding the new move-ment as a menace. Almost at once an occasion arose for a trial of strength between O'Duffy and the authorities. In August 1933 (only a few days after the firearms licences had been withdrawn) the General announced a mass march to Glasnevin cemetery on a route which would pass the parliament buildings at Leinster House. The purpose of the march was to commemorate the deaths of Griffith, Collins and O'Higgins, but, with fascist analogies so much in fashion, it was not surprising that to the fevered official imagination this looked like a deliberate attempt to reproduce Mussolini's march on Rome. Hurriedly, the government brought the old emergency regulations of the Cosgrave regime into force again, thus enabling it to ban the march only a few hours before it was due to start. At the same time, it recruited into the police forces a body of auxiliaries drawn mainly from the ranks of former IRA men and equipped them with guns and armoured cars. Known from the start as the Broy Harriers (after the new Commissioner of Police, Colonel Eamonn Broy), they were formidable evidence of the lengths to which the authorities were prepared to go to prevent the *coup d'etat* that was believed to be im-minent.* But O'Duffy was no Mussolini. At the last moment he cancelled the march, protesting to the end that no political stroke had been intended. All the same, the government followed up its precautionary measures by resurrecting the Military Tribunal and declaring the National Guard to be an unlawful association.

Had the fiasco of August 1933 led to the disappearance of O'Duffy from public life at that moment it might have been better for all con-cerned. Instead, however, it had the unexpected consequence of

---

* The name Broy Harriers recalled that of the famous county Wicklow hunt – the Bray Harriers. But it did not escape contemporaries that the nickname of the much hated British auxiliary force in the Anglo-Irish war – the Black and Tans – had similarly derived from the hunting-field.

causing him to deviate into precisely those party politics he had earlier condemned. The following month saw a remarkable fusion of the three main groups which felt themselves to be most threatened by the recent developments. Thus out of the junction between Cumann na nGaedheal, the National Centre party, and the National Guard arose a new body, which, characteristically, could not even agree upon a common name. In its early days it was known both as the United Ireland party and as Fine Gael (Tribe, or Family, of Gaels), though in practice the Irish title soon supplanted the English one. General O'Duffy became its leader (though he had no seat in parliament) and Mr Cosgrave, Mr MacDermot and Mr Dillon agreed to serve under him as Vice-Presidents. To comply with the law the National Guard changed its name and to some extent its character. It became the Young Ireland Association and blossomed – briefly – as a youth movement clearly owing a good deal to continental examples.

The policy of the new party was very much what that of Mr Cosgrave and his colleagues had been since their fall from power. 'United Ireland' stood for a united Ireland within the Commonwealth. It stood also for the ending of the economic war, for the abolition of proportional representation in its existing form, and, as a gesture to the prevailing fashion for corporative doctrines, it advocated the establishment of agricultural and industrial corporations with statutory powers. It must be said at once, though, that the new party began disastrously. The alliance with O'Duffy was a grave error of judgment. This was not, as some feared at the time, because he was still at heart a potential dictator. In his own mind, indeed, he may have nursed such ambitions long after they had become impracticable and it is probably true that some among his followers would have liked to see him sweep to power over the corpse of constitutionalism. But the real trouble with O'Duffy was not that he was cold-bloodedly authoritarian, but that he was warm-heartedly incompetent. A good police chief, he was a child in politics and, being a vain man with no judgment, was easily betrayed into wild language and false positions. Thus, the undoubted tendency in some quarters to see him as a 'Führer' received no encouragement from his actual performance. Whether for reasons of euphony or of irony, the chant of 'Hail O'Duffy' seemed somehow to lack the hypnotic effect of 'Heil Hitler'.

The single practical issue on which the General had a policy was, characteristically, the one most likely to separate him from his constitutional colleagues. It concerned the growing unrest among farmers whose plight was still deteriorating under the effects of the economic war. When some of these withheld payment of their local rates and of land annuities to the government, their cattle were impounded and auctioned at a fraction of their value to buyers who, naturally, were so unpopular that they had to be closely guarded by police, usually the armed Broy Harriers. O'Duffy's notion was that the new party should capitalise on this discontent and in August 1934 he presided at a convention of his movement (under government pressure, it had changed its name yet again to the League of Youth) which passed a resolution calling on farmers not to pay the land annuities and on labourers not to pay their rates. For a constitutional opposition this was, of course, a totally untenable position since, if taken seriously in the country, it could only have led to anarchy. Even as it was, some Blueshirts showed themselves more than ready to lend a hand to irate farmers in resisting cattle auctions by blocking roads and railways. As for the General himself, not content with bestowing his approval on this wrecking policy, he spoke a few days later about the possibility of a war with England over partition – into which, it appeared, he would be ready to lead his Blueshirts – and this despite the fact that he was the nominal head of a party pledged to continue within the British Commonwealth. These *gaffes* were at once followed by the resignation of Professor Hogan as a protest against O'Duffy's 'destructive and hysterical leadership' which made him 'utterly impossible' as a political colleague. 'It is about time', he said, 'the United Ireland party gave up its hopeless attempt of saving General O'Duffy from his own errors.'[21]

Apparently this was also the feeling of the other leaders of the party and on 21 September 1934 the General was obliged to resign the leadership which, after being left vacant for some months, was taken over by Mr Cosgrave the following spring. It was not clear whether or not O'Duffy had also resigned as head of the League of Youth. His opponents said he had and elected Commandant Cronin (the originator of the idea of the blue shirt) in his place. General O'Duffy denied that he had resigned both posts and some of the Blueshirts split off from the main body out of loyalty to him. He set up a rival League and followed this with a so-called National Corporative party which, however, never really struck root. There remained for him one tragi-comic episode. When in 1936 the Spanish Civil War broke out O'Duffy (who had never lacked courage or a kind of consistency of his own) led his Blueshirts to fight on Franco's side. After about a year there he returned home and to political obscurity, dying in 1944 at the early age of 52.

Meanwhile the problem that had called the Blueshirts into being was as far as ever from being settled. The years 1933 and 1934 were marked by numerous outrages and several murders or attempted murders which were unmistakably political in motive. Many of these attacks were directed either against leaders of the opposition, or against individual Blueshirts, and it became essential for the government to impose its authority upon both sides.[22] Since the Blueshirts were an open organisation it was relatively easy to keep them under supervision, but the IRA was a very different problem. Different in a technical sense because, as an underground organisation without uniform, it was hard to combat. Different in a political sense, because the ties between Fianna Fáil and the Republicans were still so close that it was difficult for Mr de Valera to bring himself to use the full force of the law against them. In fact he only did so after other methods had failed. During 1934, for example, a new Volunteer Force was created as a branch of the Army and commissions in this new body were given to ex-members of the IRA. Again, later that year, the Military Pensions Act was passed in order to provide pensions for men (and women) who had fought with the IRA in the Civil War. It is likely enough that these measures weaned some – perhaps a considerable number – away from the underground movement, but the extremists were unimpressed, denouncing the pensions as 'an attempt to buy off the hostility which exists against the rewarding and subsidising of treason'.[23] Towards the end of the year, therefore, Mr de Valera sent for one of the leaders, Sean Russell, and asked for the surrender of the IRA's weapons. This elicited the predictable reply that the arms had been retained from 1922 onwards on Mr de Valera's own order for the purposes of the republic. Would the IRA then not refrain at least from armed drilling and parading in the open? But Russell would consider nothing short of a declaration of the republic within the next five years. There was no doing business with him on such terms and he went away as secretly as he had come.[24]

The government was thus left with no option but to use the same machinery – the Broy Harriers and the Military Tribunal – against the IRA as it had done against the Blueshirts. To some extent, no doubt, its task was made easier by the splits developing among the Republicans themselves. The main division appeared to be between those who were primarily concerned with the attainment of the republic and those who wished to emphasise its character as a *workers'* republic by dwelling on the need to overthrow not just the regime in Northern Ireland, but capitalism throughout the whole country. The former section (which was the larger) was led by Maurice Twomey and Sean Mac-Bride and it retained control of the weekly newspaper *An Phoblacht* – until this ceased publication from lack of support in 1935. The dissident minority broke away to form the Republican Congress, of which the leading spirits were Michael Price, Sean McGuinness, Peadar O'Donnell, George Gilmore and James Connolly's daughter, Mrs Nora Connolly O'Brien. All but the last-named had been active in the now defunct Saor Eire* and they carried into the new body the same old disputatious fanaticism. Unedifying quarrels broke out between the two groups, resulting even in scuffles during the annual commemoration ceremonies at Wolfe Tone's grave in 1934 and again in 1935. By the latter date, however, the Republican Congress itself had split in two on the issue of whether to concentrate on the fight against imperialism or on the narrower goal of establishing a workers' republic. In practice the left-wing group found itself unable to con-

* See p. 502 above.

centrate on either since it did not receive enough support to run a newspaper or an organisation – both of which were virtually extinct by the end of 1935.

Yet, although these fissiparous tendencies may have helped the government in one way, in another way the lack of any unified control over the IRA increased the risk of serious incidents. Such incidents continued during 1935 and 1936 and three barbarous murders in particular shocked the entire country, opening the way for Mr de Valera to act more decisively than he had yet done. The first of these occurred in February 1935 at Edgeworthstown, county Longford, where Richard More O'Ferrall, the son of a local land-agent, was fatally wounded by four gunmen who had intervened in a dispute on the estate for which More O'Ferrall senior was the agent. The second (in March, 1936) was the cold-blooded murder on his own door-step of Admiral Somerville, brother of Edith Somerville, the co-authoress of *Some Experiences of an Irish R.M.* and many other books. The Admiral, seventy-two at the time of his death, had retired to Castle-townshend, county Cork and his only 'crime' had been that, when asked by local youths for help in joining the Navy, he had been glad to give them references. The horror of this cowardly assassination was still fresh in the public mind when the third murder occurred a month later. This time it was the shooting down, in Dungarvan, county Waterford, of a young man, John Egan, who had been a member of the IRA and who, having incurred the displeasure of his former associates, was 'executed' by them – possibly, it has been conjectured, because he had refused to take part in the murder of Admiral Somerville. It is instructive to observe that the four men who were accused of the Edgeworthstown murder were discharged 'not guilty'; that one man was convicted of the Egan murder, but, after sentence of death had been commuted to life imprisonment, was in fact released after two years; and that the murderers of Admiral Somerville were never traced. Nevertheless, despite, or perhaps because of, the strange workings of justice, the government dared hesitate no longer. On 18 June 1936 the IRA was at last declared an illegal organisation and shortly afterwards its Chief of Staff, Maurice Twomey, previously arrested, was sentenced by the Military Tribunal to three years' hard labour.[25]

The IRA was driven below ground by this action, but it was not destroyed. Its policy, however, underwent some startling changes of direction. In the immediate sequel, the will-o'-the-wisp of the Spanish Civil War beckoned it as it had beckoned O'Duffy and, as if to perpetuate the folly and futility of their own Civil War, Irishmen fought on opposite sides in Spain – about 200 to 300 of the IRA for the republican side as against some 700 Blueshirts for Franco – in a cause that had nothing to do with any of them.

Much more significant than this was the development of a new wave of hostility towards England. The war, it seemed, was to be carried right into the enemy's own territory. The responsibility for this fresh campaign rested mainly with the new Chief of Staff of the IRA, Sean Russell, who in 1938 persuaded the remnants of the Sinn Féin representatives in the old Dáil – it was part of their mystique that they still called themselves the Second Dáil – to renew the link with the IRA which had previously existed. Thenceforward the army council of the IRA was, for Russell and his associates, the lawful government of the country. In January 1939 they dispatched an 'ultimatum' to Britain demanding her withdrawal from 'every part of Ireland', that is, from the north and from the Treaty ports. No doubt they would have been astonished if they had received an answer (they got none) for they had already decided on a plan of action which was immediately, and despite the objections of some more clear-sighted members, put into action. The plan consisted simply of arranging a series of explosions in various places in England, partly to advertise the very existence of the IRA and partly with the confused notion that this might bring home to the English people the hatred which partition kept alive in Ireland. Ostensibly it was to be a campaign of sabotage against factories, communications and power installations, but for the most part it degenerated into a series of squalid exploits that seldom rose above the planting of bombs in post-boxes and public lavatories, or in suitcases at railway luggage offices. In the first six months of 1939 over 120 such incidents had occurred at the cost of one life and fifty-five people wounded. Then came serious explosions at two railway termini and, worst of all, an outrage at Coventry where a bomb went off in a crowded street, killing five people and injuring seventy others.

What did these lethal activities achieve? The short answer is that they achieved no positive results whatever.* But on the negative side they served to inflame British public opinion as it had not been inflamed for many years. Whenever caught, IRA men received stiff prison sentences and two were hanged for their part in the Coventry explosion. Irishmen living in Britain but who had been born in Ireland were compelled to register with the police and many hundreds were sent back to their native land, where Mr de Valera was taking his own precautions. In rapid succession, in mid-summer 1939, the Dáil passed a Treason Act prescribing the death penalty for acts of treason and an Offences Against the State Act, enabling the government to reintroduce the Military Tribunal and to intern prisoners without trial. Even this did not prevent the IRA from carrying out its most remarkable coup of that year – the raid, just before Christmas, on the Army's own supply of ammunition in a heavily guarded fort at the Phoenix Park in Dublin. It was, however, a Pyrrhic victory. Most of the ammunition was recovered, many arrests were made, and the

* Unless the education of Brendan Behan be reckoned a positive result. His autobiography, *Borstal Boy*, and the play, *The Quare Fellow*, throw a curious light on the IRA mentality of the time.

government secured yet more legislation – the Emergency Powers Act – allowing it to open a special internment camp at The Curragh in county Kildare for the imprisonment of those who were in a certain sense its own spiritual and political heirs.[26]

So the wheel came full circle and the logic of the Civil War was worked out to its own grim conclusion. The men who had upheld the revolution against the state now upheld the state against the men who still believed that revolution was a sacred duty. That legacy of continuity which Mr de Valera had conceded to those who would not follow him into parliamentary politics in 1927 was now asserted against him. 'Recognition of the Free State – with or without an oath – is treason to the republic.'[27] Thus wrote one of the most fanatical republicans, Mary MacSwiney, and by that simple test she condemned not just Griffith and Collins, not just Cosgrave and O'Higgins, but de Valera and Lemass as well. To the extremists it followed that if the republic was the only lawful government in the country, then they had the right to attack – to shoot down, if need be – any traitor who claimed to be exercising authority either in the Free State or in Northern Ireland. They saw themselves, in short, as the soldiers of a perpetual revolution, or rather of a revolution which would end only when all thirty-two counties entered the republican fold.

But if the logic of principle was with them, the logic of fact was against them. Whatever they might say or do, romantic Ireland *was* dead and gone. We can see now what was hidden from them, that Mr de Valera, by dismantling the Treaty and advancing constitutionally ever nearer towards a *de facto* republic, had cut the ground from beneath their feet. The balance of forces, so evenly poised at the time of the Civil War, had been tilting against them ever since. The IRA, formerly at the centre of events, now found itself peripheral and regarded by most Irishmen as irrelevant.* No longer enjoying broad-based support in the country, no longer able to mount major campaigns in the style of the Anglo-Irish war, its members were driven inexorably back upon isolated acts of terrorism which, as in the bomb outrages of 1939, had no military objective and resulted only too often in the murder or mutilation of innocent civilians. Harried by the government, split by their own dissensions, they seemed to have come to the end of the road. Yet they were only forced underground, not completely destroyed. So long as the border existed, so long as the indivisible republic beckoned, so long would young men answer the call of their blood and their history. Neither Mr de Valera nor his opponents had heard the last of the IRA.

It has been necessary to dwell at some length on the futile violence of these years because it was an integral part of the pattern of politics between the accession to power of Fianna Fáil and the out-

* Estimates of its strength in the late 'twenties and early 'thirties vary from 15,000 to 30,000, but internal feuds and arrests and internments, especially between 1938 and 1940, reduced this figure drastically.

break of the Second World War. As one looks back upon it, it is clear that that pattern owed its distinctive character more to Irish than to European conditions. It was natural, of course, that it should take some colouration from what was happening abroad and it was certainly true, as we saw earlier, that some of the economic stresses and ideological conflicts which were tearing the continent apart made their presence felt in Ireland also. Nevertheless, they were not the preoccupations of the great majority of Irishmen. The coshes and knuckledusters, the programmes and slogans, the posturing of O'Duffy, the gang warfare between the Blueshirts and the IRA, these were not the death-agonies of a Gaelic Weimar, they were rather the last convulsive spasm of the fever that had been wasting the land since 1922 – they were the nemesis of Civil War.

(iii) THE NEW CONSTITUTION

'Ireland', it has been said, 'got a new Constitution in 1937 because Mr de Valera and the Fianna Fáil party were dissatisfied with the Constitution of the Irish Free State, but this dissatisfaction . . . was centred mainly on Commonwealth status and symbols.'[28] It is certainly true, as we saw in a previous section, that the progressive dismantling of the Treaty had left the Constitution of 1922 in a decidedly threadbare condition. However, it is equally true that internal amendments, no less than external ones, had radically changed the character of Irish government and these alterations, too, pointed to a complete re-drafting of the Constitution. This radical change of character, it needs to be stressed, had not affected the essentials of the cabinet system which, as Professor Chubb has pointed out, tended towards an even closer approximation to the British model under Mr de Valera than under his predecessors, but it had affected very drastically the structure of parliament as a representative body.[29] As his administration consolidated its position it became more and more impatient with the checks and balances that had been introduced into the Constitution mainly, though not entirely, to quieten the apprehensions of ex-Unionists in 1922. In practical terms this had meant not only that ministers came into frequent collision with the Senate, but also that they looked with a jaundiced eye upon university representation in the Dáil, and upon that peculiarity of the electoral system which ordained that there should be a fairly high percentage of constituencies with more than five members each, on the assumption (perhaps less justified in practice than its admirers imagined) that in this way proportional representation would safeguard the interests of minorities.[30]

Historically, it was the collision with the Senate that came first. We have seen already that in 1932 the upper house had blocked the

Removal of Oath Bill and that the Fianna Fáil election programme of 1933 had looked forward to a reduction in its numbers, possibly even to its complete elimination. Long before that, indeed, Mr Sean Lemass had stated his party's view of what an ideal Senate should be with a frankness that left nothing to the imagination. Speaking in 1928 in support of a motion that the Senate should be elected solely by the Dáil, he explained that the purpose of this proposal was to ensure that if there had to be a Senate it would be entirely subordinate to the lower house, 'held tight in the grip of this body and unable to wriggle unless this body so permits it'. 'We are in favour, of course', he added, 'of the abolition of the Senate, but if there is to be a Second House let it be a Second House under our thumb. Let it be a group of individuals who dare not let a squeak out of them except when we lift our fingers to give them breath to do it.'[31]

In practice, it must be said, the Senate was far from being the haven for ex-Unionists that some of its detractors alleged. It had, on the contrary, become increasingly political in its make-up and the triennial elections had come more and more to follow party lines. It was true that Fianna Fáil, though its strength in the upper house steadily increased from 1928 onwards, did not command a working majority there. On the other hand, party discipline was less rigid than in the Dáil and for non-controversial measures the government could usually get sufficient support in a Senate which took its function as a revising chamber very seriously indeed. Nevertheless, for an administration bent on rapid and revolutionary constitutional change, an upper house which still retained an independent outlook was an obvious embarrassment and it was a matter of no great surprise when in March 1934 Mr de Valera introduced a Bill for its abolition. The Senate fought vigorously against its own destruction, and even while under sentence of death fought equally vigorously during 1935 against the removal of university representation and the reduction in the number of constituencies with five members or more from eighteen out of twenty-eight to eleven out of thirty-four. This, however, as its members well knew, could be no more than a delaying action, and in May 1936 the Senate ceased to exist.

It was, therefore, under single-chamber government that Mr de Valera carried through the important legislation of 1936 defining the external association of the Free State with the British Commonwealth, and it was under single-chamber government that he added as it were the decorative frieze to this achievement by abolishing the Governor-Generalship in June 1937.[32] But by that time the draft of a new Constitution was already before the public. It was debated in the Dáil during the early summer and submitted for referendum to the people on 1 July 1937, a general election being held the same day to replace the old Dáil which had been dissolved in mid-June. The voting, both in the referendum and the election, was closer than the government would no doubt have wished, but it was decisive enough to maintain Fianna

Fáil in power, though somewhat precariously, and to bring the Constitution into force at the end of 1937.*

What was it to which the Irish people had thus lukewarmly committed themselves? The Constitution was a remarkable document – remarkable for what it contained and for what it omitted, remarkable still more because, as we now know, it was very largely the work of one man, Mr de Valera himself. It has been well described as attempting 'to reconcile the notion of inalienable popular sovereignty with the older medieval conception of a theocratic state'.[33] The notion of popular sovereignty, inherent in Irish revolutionary thought from the days of Wolfe Tone onwards, was to be balanced by the principle that in the last analysis such sovereignty could only be exercised under God. Hence the emphatic language of the preamble:

In the name of the Most Holy Trinity, from whom is all authority and to whom, as our final end, all actions both of men, and states must be referred,

We, the people of Eire,

Humbly acknowledging all our obligations to our Divine Lord, Jesus Christ, who sustained our fathers through centuries of trial,

Gratefully remembering their heroic and unremitting struggle to regain the independence of our Nation,

And seeking to promote the common good, with due observance of Prudence, Justice and Charity, so that the dignity and freedom of the individual may be assured, true social order attained, the unity of our country restored, and concord established with other nations,

Do hereby adopt, enact, and give to ourselves this Constitution.[34]

In the circumstances of 1937 and of the recent past it was inevitable that this doctrine of popular sovereignty should express itself in a deliberate turning away from the dominion type constitution under which the Free State had struggled towards the assertion of its independent status. Thus the very first Article declares that 'the Irish nation hereby affirms its inalienable, indefeasible, and sovereign right to choose its own form of Government, to determine its relations with other nations, and to develop its life, political, economic and cultural, in accordance with its own genius and traditions'. The second Article – in intention at least – is no less assertive of sovereignty, claiming as it does that 'the national territory consists of the whole island of Ireland, its islands and the territorial seas'. This, it is true, was far removed from contemporary reality – Article 3 came down to earth

* The results of the referendum were 685,105 for the Constitution, 526,945 against; it appears that some thirty-one per cent of those entitled to vote did not in fact do so. The general election gave Fianna Fáil exactly half the seats in the Dáil and left them more than ever dependent on Labour. The figures were: Fianna Fáil, sixty-nine; United Ireland (Fine Gael), forty-eight; Labour, thirteen; Independents, eight.

with the proviso that 'pending the re-integration of the national territory' the laws enacted by the parliament to be established under the Constitution would apply only to the twenty-six counties – but to Mr de Valera and his associates it was of the highest importance, psychologically as well as politically, that what they conceived to be the fundamental unity of the country should be emphasised in the most solemn fashion. It was no less important that when the state – as distinct from the nation – was being defined, popular sovereignty under God should again be stressed. 'Ireland', ran Article 5, 'is a sovereign, independent, democratic state', and the next Article expressed this, if anything, even more forcibly. 'All powers of government, legislative, executive and judicial', it laid down, 'derive, under God, from the people, whose right it is to designate the rulers of the State and, in final appeal, to decide all questions of national policy, according to the requirements of the common good.' And, so that political independence might receive the same sort of emphasis that popular sovereignty did, Article 7 provided for a separate Irish flag (the green, white and orange tricolour) and Article 8 stated in its first clause that the Irish language, 'as the national language', was *the* first official language, and in its second clause that English was 'recognised' as *a* second official language.*

Yet, despite all this elaboration, political independence did not extend to calling the state by name what it quite evidently was in fact – a republic. That this gap remained was due in a double sense to the existence of partition. Mr de Valera himself was deeply reluctant then, as later, to identify the republic with anything less than the thirty-two counties for which the men of 1916 had died. At the same time, it seemed prudent (though in practice, perhaps, a little naive) to leave open a loophole for the reunification of Ireland by deliberately not writing into the Constitution the one word which of all others was anathema to the men of the north. 'If the Northern problem were not there', Mr de Valera admitted in debate, '. . . in all probability there would be a flat, downright proclamation of a republic in this [Constitution].'[35]

Of course the absence of the word did not impede the actuality. This was made clear enough in the system of government embodied in the document. And nowhere was it made plainer than in the Articles relating to the office of President. The President was a head of state, but he was also more than this. Elected by popular suffrage for seven years (and eligible for re-election for a second term only), he could not be removed from office except by impeachment and even then the proposal to prefer a charge against him, which could be made in either House, had to be supported by not less than two-thirds of the members of the House in which it had been preferred.[36] His duties were intended to be – and in practice mainly have been – formal, but Mr de Valera himself regarded the President as the

* My italics.

guardian both of the people's rights and of the Constitution.[37] To this end he was entrusted with special, discretionary powers which differentiated him sharply from, say, the Governors-General of Commonwealth countries. Thus, first, he had the power to refer any Bill other than a Money Bill or a Bill proposing to amend the Constitution to the Supreme Court for a decision as to whether or not any part of it was repugnant to the Constitution – this procedure has been used three times.[38] Second, if asked to do so by joint petition from a majority of the Senate and not less than one-third of the Dáil, he could refuse to sign a Bill dealing with a matter 'of such national importance that the will of the people ought to be ascertained', until the will of the people had been ascertained by referendum.[39] And in the specific case of amendments of the Constitution – which could only be carried out after referendum – the President was enjoined by Article 46 only to sign the resulting law to change the Constitution after he had satisfied himself that the provisions for a referendum had been complied with. Third, the President had power at any time to convene a meeting of either or both Houses or to communicate with the Houses 'by message or address' on matters of national or public importance.[40] Finally, he had the power – which, if party strength in parliament was evenly balanced, could become important – to refuse a dissolution to a prime minister (Taoiseach) who had ceased to command a majority in the Dáil and who had asked for such a dissolution.[41] If the President did refuse a dissolution then the Taoiseach would have no option but to resign, leaving it to the Dáil to nominate his successor. Such a situation might easily lead to a serious constitutional crisis and it seems unlikely that any President would in practice make use of this particular weapon. So far, in fact, none has done so.

In this last function, and also in his supervisory role at times of referendum on amendments to the Constitution, the President was able to act on his own. But in the exercise of his other powers he was obliged to consult the Council of State, a body of notables comprising certain office-holders and such other individuals up to the number of seven as the President might think fit to appoint.[42] The Council, however, was assigned a very minor place in the scheme of things, for although it was there to advise the President, he was under no obligation to accept its advice. In the event it has met very seldom, being summoned mainly to be consulted as to whether or not certain legislation should be referred to the Supreme Court for a decision on the question of repugnancy. It will be seen, therefore, that although in normal times the President would not be expected to go outside his purely formal and ceremonial duties, yet potentially he could play a significant part in a moment of crisis. This was not so obvious in the beginning, when the first President was the aged and infirm Gaelic scholar, Dr Douglas Hyde, but in recent years Presidential elections have been fought on party lines and the fact that the President is now none other than Mr de Valera himself (at the time of writing in his second term) gives a certain piquancy to the way the office has been defined.

It would be wrong, however, to deduce from the rather elaborate mode in which the President's powers were woven into the Constitution that he was exalted at the expense of the working government, the Taoiseach and his fellow-ministers. On the contrary, particular attention was paid to the Taoiseach in the document and powers which had perhaps been implicit earlier in the office of President of the Executive Council (at least while Mr de Valera held it), were now made explicit. Thus, not only was it laid down that his advice must be sought in virtually all matters of importance, but he was also given the power of recommending in his own right that the President should dissolve parliament.[43] In addition, he could advise the President to accept the resignations of individual ministers or even to dismiss them if necessary. His powers in relation to the legislature were, if anything, even more extensive. He was to decide the date of assembly for the Dáil; he could nominate his ministers without being obliged to tell the Dáil to which departments they were being assigned – though in practice he did do so, of course; no motion or grant to appropriate funds could be considered by the Dáil except on a message from the government signed by him; it was he who presented all Bills to the President for signature; and the eleven nominated members of the Senate were in fact nominated by him.[44] Since the Constitution also provided for what is, by modern standards, a not unduly large government of not less than seven or more than fifteen members, it is clear that the Taoiseach, with no pressing necessity to delegate his very considerable powers to worry him, was well placed to dominate his colleagues. Indeed, as has been justly said, 'there can be no doubt that the intention of the 1937 Constitution was to elevate the Taoiseach formally and in practice to the position of a strong British Prime Minister'.[45] That appellation might not have pleased Mr de Valera, but it describes his own tenure of the office accurately enough. It may be a rather less exact description of his successors, with the possible exception of Mr Sean Lemass, who, despite, or perhaps because of, his readiness to act on a majority vote rather than wait for unanimity, exerted such a personal ascendancy over his own cabinet as to seem at times *plus roi que le roi*, more chief-like than de Valera himself. Nevertheless, as a modern authority (Mr Brian Farrell) has suggested, the framework within which the cabinet operates in Ireland is such as to reserve to the Taoiseach a predominant role in government. 'Given', he writes, 'parliamentary representatives whose main concerns are local, even parochial, and parties sensitive to established community interests and values, the main restraints on executive policy-making spring less from the institutions of politics than from the value systems of the community. No other body in the society can compare in potential influence and power with the state-machine; the cabinet holds within itself a near-monopoly of major public decisions and, with rare exceptions, it is clear that what it decides will be accepted by the Oireachtas [parliament] and implemented loyally by the public service. Within the cabinet no single actor – irrespective of office, personality or power base – can compare in influence with the Taoiseach; what he says, with rare exceptions, will be listened to and what he wants achieved.'*

Compared with the change of emphasis from Governor-General to President, and from President of the Executive Council to Taoiseach, the powers and functions of the Oireachtas, or parliament, were little altered in essentials from what they had been in the 1922 Constitution. True, there was provision for direct popular participation in legislation – as there had been in the earlier Constitution until it was removed in 1928 – but this was limited to referenda on constitutional amendments and to the discretionary power of the President to submit proposed legislation to the people in certain exceptional, not to say unlikely, circumstances. Nevertheless, even though limited, the power of referendum was potentially important and on two occasions – in 1959 and 1968 – has resulted in significant defeats for a government bent upon the abolition of proportional representation. More recently – in May 1972 – a referendum on the question of Irish entry into the Common Market has provided the government of the day (Mr Lynch's Fianna Fáil administration) with a majority in favour of 'going into Europe' so massive as to astonish all beholders.

The structure of parliament bears superficially more resemblance to what had been envisaged in 1922 than to the single-chamber government Mr de Valera had created by the abolition of the Senate in 1936. Though himself still apparently unconvinced of the necessity for a second chamber, he was prepared to 'give way to the people who are anxious for it'.[46] But he did not really give way very far. There was to be a Senate of sixty members consisting of eleven government nominees, six university representatives and forty-three members elected on a vocational basis from five panels of candidates 'having knowledge and practical experience of' National Language and Culture, Literature, Art, Education and certain professional interests; Agriculture and Fisheries; Labour; Industry and Commerce; Public Administration and the social services.[47] Despite its echoes of the corporative state and the papal encyclicals – or perhaps because of

* B. Farrell, *Chairman or Chief?: The Role of Taoiseach in Irish Government* (Dublin and London, 1971), pp. 82-3. This volume, the first in a series of 'Studies in Irish Political Culture', of which Mr Farrell is editor, contains a useful, and to a certain extent a comparative, account of the careers in office of the five men who have occupied the post of Taoiseach (or its equivalent) since 1922. For two views of the 'cabinet timber' available for the construction of Irish governments, see B. Chubb, *The Government and Politics of Ireland* (London and Stanford, California, 1970), pp. 171-6, and A. Cohan, *The Irish Political Elite* (Dublin and London, 1972), vol. 4 of 'Studies in Irish Political Culture', especially chaps. 1 and 2.

them – this aspect of the Senate's structure seems never to have worked nor to have been given much chance to work.[48] The upper house, it has been said, has to some extent become 'a refuge for meritorious and disappointed candidates of the Dâil'.[49] Most critics would agree with that, though some might cavil at the word 'meritorious'. The crucial question for a second chamber is of course the extent to which it can revise or hold up legislation transmitted to it by the lower house. By this acid test the Senate of the 1937 Constitution was but a shadow of its predecessor. It could suspend ordinary Bills for only ninety days, and Money Bills for no more than twenty-one days, and even these periods, as we have seen, could be 'abridged' in emergency by a certificate of the Taoiseach, a resolution of the Dáil and the concurrence of the President.[50]

The Dáil, which inevitably remained the predominant partner in the legislative process, was, as before, to be elected by proportional representation on the basis of not less than one member for each thirty thousand of the population or more than one member for each twenty thousand of the population.[51] The total number was to be revised every twelve years and the movement of population resulted in a reduction from 40 constituencies and 147 members in 1947 to 38 constituencies and 144 members in 1961.[52] Although the Constitution allowed it rather less scope than formerly for intervention in the routine business of government, the Dáil was still beyond question the chief source of legislation and it retained, naturally, its superior powers in regard to Money Bills and Bills to amend the Constitution.[53] Its procedure approximated to British practice in some, though not all, respects, even if the niceties of debate have tended – still tend occasionally, indeed – to be disturbed by bitter echoes of the Civil War. In recent years it has averaged rather more than 70 sittings, totalling over 500 hours, a year. Of this time about half has been given to financial business and only a very tiny fraction to private members' Bills.[54] Party discipline has been, on the whole, fairly rigid – no doubt because governments have usually had very small majorities – but though members can be vociferous on occasions (especially at question-time) the predominance of complicated official business has meant that relatively few back-benchers say very much. Perhaps they have not very much to say, but whether they have or not, it is difficult to avoid the conclusion that their two main functions are to vote as they are told in the House, and outside it to bring what pressure they can to bear upon ministers in the interests of their constituents. In a small, intimate country like Ireland this latter function is exceedingly important and a number of members have built their reputations less on what they do in the chamber, than on their success in obtaining jobs, pensions and so on for 'the boys' at home; in the process, it is only fair to say, the constituency as a whole often benefits as much as individuals.

All the same, one is left with an abiding impression of a parliamentary system which, however important as a forum for expressing opinions or voicing grievances, is scarcely adequate to the needs of a modern society whether in its function of criticising the government or in the sphere of creative legislation. It has, in fact, been condemned by a leading expert in this field as deficient on three counts. 'First, its procedures and techniques are archaic and ineffective; second, the staff and facilities available to members are meagre; and, third, too few of the members are equipped by education or experience to make the kinds of inquiries that are necessary or to appreciate the kind of data that ought to be made available in order to judge performance. Thus, neither the methods employed nor the personnel involved, whether representative or professional, are adequate to appraise large programmes of public expenditure upon an ever increasing range of economic and social objectives, including long-term capital programmes and extensive subsidies. Even if they were, the style and demeanour of opposition . . . and the conception members generally have of their function do not favour really effective or hard-hitting criticism.'[55]

The same conservatism which dictated that there should be little fundamental change in the legislature ensured that the law courts and the whole judicial machinery inherited from the 1922 Constitution should be carried over intact into the new dispensation. It was expressly stipulated in 1937 that 'subject to this Constitution . . . the laws in force in Saorstát Eireann immediately prior to the date of the coming into operation of this Constitution shall continue to be of full force and effect until the same or any of them shall have been repealed or amended by enactment of the Oireachtas'.[56] Similarly, it was provided by Article 58 that the pre-1937 courts were to continue in existence and with the same jurisdictions as before, 'subject to the provisions of this Constitution relating to the determination of questions as to the validity of any law'.[57] The reference here, of course, was to the power of the President to refer Bills to the Supreme Court for an opinion on the question of repugnancy. That this was something more than an interesting piece of constitutional decoration has been demonstrated by the fact that on three occasions important legislation has been so referred to the Supreme Court which in one instance (the School Attendance Bill of 1942) found parts of the measure to be unconstitutional.[58]

Mr de Valera, however, did not confine himself to questions of government and jurisdiction. He included also in his Constitution two features which then and subsequently attracted much attention both inside and outside the country. One was the declaration of certain 'fundamental rights' to which the citizen was entitled, and the other was the insertion – largely, it seems, for the guidance of the legislature – of what he called 'directive principles of social policy'. These formulations were not in themselves particularly novel. Fundamental rights are explicitly stated in many modern constitutions, and not only rights but social principles also, had appeared in one form or another in the 1916 proclamation, the Democratic Programme of 1919, and the Constitution of 1922. What gave Mr de Valera's provisions their particular interest was the way they attempted to combine the liberal, democratic mode in which such declarations were commonly expressed with a very specific Catholic content.[59]

These two aspects rubbed shoulders in the group of Articles (40 through 44) devoted to fundamental rights. Article 40, which dealt with 'personal rights', was very much in the liberal, almost one might say the egalitarian, tradition, with its opening statement that all citizens 'shall, as human persons, be held equal before the law', its explicit commitments to habeas corpus, its guarantees of freedom of speech, peaceable assembly and association, its promise that private dwellings should be inviolable and its proviso that laws regulating the rights of free assembly or of forming associations and unions should not contain any political, religious or class discrimination. It is true that these particular rights were made 'subject to public order and morality', and that this qualification was regarded by Mr de Valera's critics as characteristically devious, but in fact Article 40, together with certain other safeguards laid down in Articles 34 to 38, dealing with the law-courts, did reflect a serious concern for individual liberty. Irish lawyers, it is only fair to add, have not been slow to point out what is, technically, a greater qualification of these rights than the formula about 'public order and morality' – the ability of the government in time of war or national emergency to take powers that would nullify much of what is conceded in Article 40. On the other hand, the 'emergency' which was declared when war broke out in 1939 is still legally in existence and no law-abiding citizen seems any the worse.[60]

The other fundamental rights (Articles 41 to 44) refer successively to the family, education, private property and religion. Here if anywhere, as all accounts agree, does the Constitution take on a specifically Catholic flavour, or, as has sometimes been suggested, a Thomist and scholastic flavour. These Articles, it seems, owe much to the encyclicals of Pope Pius XI, especially *The Christian Education of Youth* (1929), *Christian Marriage* (1930) and *Quadragesimo Anno* (1931), though in all probability we should look beyond the encyclicals to that synthesis of Catholic social principles published by the International Union of Social Studies of Malines in Belgium in 1927 and known as the Social Code.[61] It is against this background that Article 41 in particular must be read. This opens with the remarkable declaration that 'the State recognizes the Family as the natural primary and fundamental unit group of society, and as a moral institution possessing inalienable and imprescriptible rights, antecedent and superior to all positive law'. From this it follows that the state guarantees to protect the family as the basis of the social order and to guard the basis of marriage. To that end it is laid down that 'no law shall be enacted providing for the grant of a dissolution of a marriage'. Furthermore, recognising that 'by her life within the home, woman gives to the State a support without which the common good cannot be achieved', the state itself was 'to endeavour to ensure that mothers shall not be obliged by economic necessity to engage in labour to the neglect of their duties in the home'.[62] These phrases, uncomfortably reminiscent of the Hitlerite formula for women of *Kinder, Küche, Kirche*, are not, however, to be seen (as feminists, understandably, might see them) simply as the expression of a paternalistic dictatorship. Not only were they in line with Catholic thinking, they corresponded to an ideal with which many Irish men and women would have been in instinctive sympathy. This is not necessarily to say that the reality approximated even remotely to the ideal. Children would still go hungry, women would still lose their youth prematurely rearing large families in the Dublin slums, marriages would still often produce more suffering than bliss – nevertheless, even though this was the burden of daily existence, the affirmation had been made, the state had committed itself publicly to upholding a pattern of life that the majority of its citizens felt to be the right pattern for them.

The emphasis on the importance of the family is carried over into Article 42, where the state acknowledges it to be 'the primary and natural educator' of the child. Parents were free to provide this education as they wished, subject to the insistence of the state on 'a certain minimum education'. To provide for this it was laid down that 'the State shall provide for free primary education and shall endeavour to supplement and give reasonable aid to private and corporate educational initiative, and, when the public good requires it, provide other educational facilities or institutions with due regard, however, for the rights of parents, especially in the matter of religious and moral information'.

When it turned (Article 43) to deal with property the Constitution trod a carefully drawn line between the rights of the person and the responsibilities of the state, though even here, as commentators have insisted, the over-riding concern was not to balance nineteenth century individualism against twentieth century collectivism, but rather to accord closely with Catholic teaching on the subject at that period. Thus, while the Article began by recognising rights to private property, it went on to declare that these ought to be regulated 'by the principles of social justice', and from this proceeded to the major qualification of what had been conceded already by enabling the state to 'delimit by law the exercise of the said rights with a view to reconciling their exercise with the exigencies of the common good'. This was not simply, however, to take back with one hand what had been given with the other. It was, on the contrary, to recognise that in such a matter hard-and-fast doctrinaire positions could not be taken up in advance, and that in its attitude towards private property a government responsive to Catholic doctrines would be guided by expedience and human welfare, conditioning factors which might easily change from time to time.[63]

It would be reasonable to suppose that a Constitution so sensitive to the social teachings of Catholicism would accord to the Catholic Church itself a specially favoured position. This it did, but only up to a point – and the reservation was deliberate and significant. The state, declared Article 44, 'recognises the special position of the Holy Catholic Apostolic and Roman Church as the guardian of the Faith professed by the great majority of the citizens', but it also recognised the Church of Ireland, the Presbyterian Church, the Methodist Church, the Society of Friends, the Jewish congregations and 'the other religious denominations existing in Ireland at the date of the coming into operation of this Constitution'. Not only this, but the next clause guaranteed freedom of conscience to every citizen and also repeated in detail the prohibitions of the 1922 Constitution against religious discrimination and interference with church property, save for 'necessary works of utility and on payment of compensation'. The broad toleration revealed by these clauses no doubt had, at least in part, a political motivation. They were as necessary in 1937 as they had been in 1922 to reassure the minority within the twenty-six counties and also to convince doubting Protestants in the six counties (if, indeed, any convincing was possible) that Home Rule had not, after all, meant Rome rule. But it is proper to add that Article 44 was not just a form of religious propaganda. It did no more than represent what had been the actual situation in the Irish Free State from the beginning, and to embody in the written document what southern Protestants had gratefully experienced in their own lives. Nor is there any reason whatever to doubt that these provisions corresponded to Mr de Valera's own deepest convictions.

It should be added that at the time of writing (1972) there is considerable pressure to change or reform the Constitution. Apart from the fact – in itself of the utmost significance – that the recent decision to join the European Economic Community will almost certainly lead to some reassessment of the concept of sovereignty, there would seem to be two other factors influencing the desire for change. One is the altered climate of religious feeling since the Second Vatican Council.* The other is the growing realisation in some quarters that if the ideal of a reconciliation between north and south is ever to be more than a pious platitude then it would sooner or later be necessary to overhaul those Articles of the Constitution which were most likely to grate upon Protestant susceptibilities. It was probably this realisation which prompted the then Taoiseach, Mr Lemass, to

* This is referred to briefly below, pp. 686-9. For a full treatment of the subject, see the admirable study by John Whyte, *Church and State in Modern Ireland*, 1923-1970 (Dublin and London, 1971), especially chap. 11.

appoint an all-party committee to review the Constitution as long ago as 1966. The Committee's report was published at the end of 1967 and although the ensuing debate was at times rather desultory and inconclusive the eruption of the northern crisis has given the whole matter a fresh urgency.

The articles in this particular context which were singled out by the report were Article 41 (which prohibited divorce) and, of course, Article 44 defining the 'special position' of the Roman Catholic Church. Linked with these in public discussion – to an extent unimaginable even ten years ago – has been the Criminal Law Amendment Act of 1935 which forbade the sale and import of contraceptives. Since the issues have still to be resolved, no conclusion can yet be drawn from the ebb and flow of public argument. Two comments may, however, be made on the situation as it stands at present. First, it is evident, as was only to be expected, that the ecclesiastical reaction to proposals to relax the law relating to divorce and to contraceptives has been decidedly hostile, a reaction which, in the case of contraceptives, has been strongly reinforced by the promulgation in 1970 of the papal edict, *Humanae Vitae*. But secondly, it is equally clear that the Church has not shown itself by any means wedded to the special position guaranteed to it by Article 44. On the contrary, as recently as September 1969, Cardinal Conway openly declared that he 'would not shed a tear' if the controversial clauses disappeared and shortly afterwards this position was officially endorsed by the hierarchy as a whole.*

Although the fundamental rights provisions of the Constitution did, as already suggested, attempt to combine liberal principles with Catholic social teaching, they did so in a way which strongly suggests that what was really intended was to provide a framework within which society could evolve, without the necessity of further rapid or drastic change. To say this is to say in effect that the purpose behind these Articles was essentially conservative. No less conservative was the intention underlying the 'Directive Principles of Social Policy' embodied in Article 45. Here too a balance was delicately maintained between the rights of the individual and the needs of the community. Here too the influence of Catholic thought made its influence directly felt. Thus the state was to promote the welfare 'of the whole people' by securing and protecting 'a social order in which justice and charity shall inform all the institutions of the national life'. To achieve this the state was so to direct its policy that citizens 'may through their occupations find the means of making reasonable provision for their domestic needs'. And not only that, it was 'to safeguard with especial care the economic interests of the weaker sections of the community, and, where necessary, to contribute to the support of the infirm, the widow, the orphan and the aged'. Likewise, it was 'to endeavour to ensure that the strength and health of

* The relevant clause has now been abolished after a referendum.

workers, men and women, and the tender age of children shall not be abused and that citizens shall not be forced by economic necessity to enter avocations unsuited to their sex, age or strength'. Even in the realm of property and business enterprise the state was to enter in to prevent the exploitation of man by man – to guard against monopoly, to control credit for 'the welfare of the people as a whole', to supplement private initiative in industry and commerce wherever necessary, to settle as many families on the land as might be practicable, to ensure that the ownership and control of the material resources of the community be so distributed amongst individuals and classes 'as best to subserve the common good'.

There is a vague benevolence about some of these phrases that could easily move the critic to scepticism. And his scepticism might be fortified by the discovery that these 'principles of social policy' were intended only for the general guidance of the Oireachtas and were not cognisable by any court. Nor can it be affirmed with confidence that actual policy has to a significant degree been shaped by these principles or that the poor and the weak have become any less poor and weak because of the existence of Article 45. It is only fair, however, to make two points on the other side. One is that even though the Article is not enforceable in the courts, and even though every clause of it is so vague and imprecise as to drive a lawyer to distraction, yet it is not unfitting for a society which does broadly accept the principles embodied in the Article to display them boldly in its Constitution where they may be read and pondered not only by the legislators of the present but by the legislators of the future, who may some day come closer to translating them into reality.

And the other point that needs to be made is that these very directives, though occasionally derided by the sophisticated, were deeply admired and closely studied by some of the newly emerging nations after the Second World War, to such an extent that not only the principles of social policy, but also the fundamental rights, were incorporated in whole or in part into the Constitutions of India and Burma. Partly because of this, and partly because it provided a model for a written constitution, republican in character and containing the essentials of parliamentary democracy, the Irish Constitution of 1937 had, according to a modern authority on the subject, 'a wide significance in relation to those parts of the Commonwealth in which nationalist aspirations demanded a precise formulation of the political practices, aims and ideals they were to adopt'.[64]

Yet in the last resort the Constitution of 1937 must be judged less by what it did for an evolving Commonwealth than by what it did for Ireland. And what it did for Ireland can be summed up in a single sentence. It achieved stability. After nearly thirty years of incessant war, revolution and political change the twenty-six counties had at last reached a kind of equilibrium so profound and so firmly based that even the final step towards the formal realisation of the republic, when it came in 1948-9, could be taken by the passing of a simple act of parliament and without the necessity of far-reaching constitutional amendment. It is too soon yet to say what the verdict of history upon Mr de Valera will be. But it may well be that when the verdict has to be given the two fruits of his pre-war policy – the External Relations Act and the Constitution of 1937 – will come to be seen as the most remarkable achievement of a most remarkable man.

(iv) NEUTRALITY AND ISOLATION

It is probably inevitable that a small nation which has just achieved self-government should be preoccupied with its own affairs to the almost total exclusion of what is happening in the rest of the world. In the Irish Free State this natural preoccupation was heightened by the persistence of the deep internal divisions dating from the Civil War, but although it is no doubt true that most of the population *were* completely absorbed in their own affairs, it was never possible for the leaders of either of the two main parties to ignore for long the existence of international tensions and the effect these might have upon their country.

For Irishmen striving to assert their national identity within a Commonwealth which, however benevolently disposed, they still found restrictive, the League of Nations at Geneva was an obvious counterpoise. Even to join the League, as the Irish Free State did in 1923, was in a manner to assert separate nationhood, as was also the decision to register the Anglo-Irish Treaty at Geneva the following year in the teeth of British objections. But it was not the Irish intention simply to use the League as a convenient means of scoring points against Britain in the elaborate game of Commonwealth relations. The Free State was a member, as other small countries were members, because the League seemed – for a brief while at least – to offer some alternative to the old power-balance dominated by the great nations. Once inside the League, therefore, the Irish were prepared to take their full share of the responsibilities of membership. In 1926, for example, the Free State stood for election to the Council but, partly through lack of preparation, partly because of British opposition (on grounds of expediency, not principle, her leaders were assured), was defeated.[65] The Irish candidature was successful, however, in 1930 when it received considerable, and perhaps decisive, backing from other Commonwealth countries.[66]

Even a very brief acquaintance with what went on at Geneva was enough to induce disenchantment. Kevin O'Higgins, admittedly a man to whom scepticism came easily, expressed this disenchantment as early as 1925, in a letter to his wife written while attending an abortive disarmament conference:

> On the whole [he wrote] I am, I fear, inclined to be mildly cynical about this 'League of Nations' without denying that it has certain advantages. Personal contact between representatives of Governments is good. It breaks down prejudices and insularities . . . but don't let anyone convince you that the League – whatever its germs and possibilities – is a temple of justice where great and small can meet on equal terms and only right prevails. It simply imposes the necessity for hypocrisy – vice's tribute to virtue – but once that is paid, then *sicut erat in principio*, etc.[67]

But if O'Higgins was a realist who, so far as the future of the League was concerned, took refuge in cynicism, Mr de Valera, no less a realist after his own fashion, was prepared to react very differently. His instinct was not to write off the organisation, but rather to lecture it for its own good. And by chance it happened that only a few months after coming to power he had an unrivalled opportunity to do so. In September 1932 he took office as President of the Council of the League and, discarding the well-tried platitudes offered to him by his advisers, spoke out with devastating frankness. It was a critical moment in Geneva. The Japanese aggression in China was less than a year old and everywhere men, as Mr de Valera said, were looking to the League to see how it would meet this threat to peace. He warned the astonished delegates that they were, after all, answerable at the bar of world opinion and that this opinion was becoming increasingly critical, if not hostile:

> People are complaining [he said] that the League is devoting its activity to matters of secondary or very minor importance, while the vital international problems of the day, problems which touch the very existence of our peoples, are being shelved or postponed or ignored. People are saying that the equality of States does not apply here in the things that matter, that the smaller States whilst being given a voice have very little influence in the final determination of League action . . . Finally, there is a suspicion abroad that little more than lip-service is paid to the fundamental principles on which the League is founded; there is a suspicion that the action of the League in the economic sphere can be paralysed by the pressure of powerful national interests, and that if the hand that is raised against the Covenant is sufficiently strong, it can smite with impunity.[68]

That these misgivings were only too well founded the Italian invasion of Abyssinia demonstrated three years later. Here a great power, Italy, did indeed 'smite with impunity' and in doing so showed with bleak clarity just how easily the economic sanctions imposed by the League could be paralysed. For Mr de Valera (who was, incidentally, his own Minister for External Affairs) this situation posed a special difficulty. Not only was the Roman Catholic Church in Ireland uneasy about the imposition of sanctions on Italy, but the very fact the chief protagonist of a sanctions policy was Great Britain exposed him to the taunt that by supporting that policy he was kowtowing to the enemy with whom at that very moment he was engaged in an economic war. He was able to dispose of the latter argument by the famous retort that 'if your worst enemy happens to be going to Heaven by the same road you are, you don't for that reason turn around and go in the opposite direction'.[69] But the widespread anxiety in the country about getting involved in what might become an actual war with Italy was something much harder to combat.

It was, he freely admitted, a painful dilemma. Either the Free State must be 'thrown into a position of enmity with those with whom we wish to be on terms of friendship', or else it must face the terrible alternative – 'the abandonment of duty and the betrayal of our deepest convictions and of our word solemnly given'. At such a moment that rigid adherence to principle which had been the bane of his domestic opponents showed itself in its most admirable form. Convinced as he was that collective security was the only hope for the world – for great nations as well as for little ones – he realised that the League was unlikely to withstand a second crisis of confidence. What the Japanese had begun the Italians might well complete. 'The final test of the League and all that it stands for has come', he warned the Assembly in September 1935. 'Make no mistake, if on any pretext whatever we were to permit the sovereignty of even the weakest State amongst us to be unjustly taken away, the whole foundation of the League would crumble into dust.' The pledge of security, he insisted, had to be universal. 'If the Covenant is not observed as a whole for all and by all, then there is no Covenant.'

Why [he concluded passionately] can we not at least place this League of Nations on a stable foundation? Why can we not free the fundamental instrument of the League from its association with political arrangements which are universally recognised as unjust? Why can we not endeavour to forge an international instrument, not merely for settling international disputes when they arise, but for removing in advance the causes of those disputes?[70]

In the light of subsequent events, and of the suicidal stampede of Europe over the precipice of the Second World War, these read like rhetorical questions. Perhaps they seemed so even at the time, but in the evolution of an independent Irish foreign policy they have an important place. For if they could not be properly answered the moral was clear. And Mr de Valera was quick to draw it in a broadcast to his own people on his return home. If Italy succeeded like Japan in violating the Covenant, then the League of Nations would disappear as an effective safeguard. 'It becomes, in fact', he said, 'a source of danger – a trap for States trusting in it, leading them to neglect adequate measures for their own defence.'[71] This was still his view the following year and in the Dáil he actually went so far as to speculate if the time had not come to withdraw altogether from the League.[72] He was reluctant to do so, for any forum where statesmen could meet was better than no forum, but his own thoughts were turning more and more insistently towards neutrality. 'All the small States can do', he said in Geneva in 1936, 'if the statesmen of the greater States fail in their duty, is resolutely to determine that they will not become the tools of any great power, and that they will resist with whatever strength they may possess every attempt to force them into a war against their will.'[73]

It was this insistence upon neutrality that led him to resist pressure at home to recognise General Franco's regime in the Spanish Civil War. The Irish people, he freely admitted to the League in 1937, were far from indifferent to some of the issues then being fought out in Spain, but his government believed in non-intervention, both because the form of government to be adopted in Spain was a matter for Spaniards only, and even more because intervention could set off a chain-reaction leading to 'a general European disaster'.[74] But while it was relatively easy to maintain this attitude of aloofness towards a remote and obscure struggle for power in Spain, would it be possible to do so when the great storm finally broke upon Europe and all the major powers were swept into the conflict? For Mr de Valera the key to this question was the relationship of Ireland with Britain. So long as his powerful neighbour was in possession of the Treaty ports, and entitled to demand certain other facilities in time of war, there was an obvious risk that a foreign enemy might consider Irish protestations about neutrality a trifle academic, and that Ireland would find herself involved in a major struggle without having been able to exercise the smallest influence on her own fate.

That is why the return of the ports in 1938 marks so important a turning-point in the relations between the two countries. Neutrality at once became a more practicable policy and the causes of friction between Britain and Ireland were correspondingly reduced at a vital moment in history. This did *not* mean that Irish policy would then box the compass from isolation to involvement on Britain's side. Mr de Valera made it abundantly clear that so long as partition lasted there could be no question of Irish co-operation with Britain, or for that matter with other Commonwealth countries, in matters of defence. On the other hand, the logical corollary for him of the Agreements of 1938 was that his government would never permit any part of Ireland to be used as a base for attack against Britain. This, as has been truly said, 'assured Britain for the first time in modern history of a friendly neutral responsible for the defence of nationalist Ireland'.[75]

Mr de Valera has testified more than once to his appreciation of the part played by Neville Chamberlain in the dramatic improvement of Anglo-Irish relations during 1938 and he seems to have been no less favourably disposed towards the British Prime Minister's policy of appeasement. By a curious chance that year found the Irish leader President of the Assembly of the League of Nations (his candidature having been strongly supported by Britain) which met in September while the Munich crisis was actually unrolling. When on 30 September Chamberlain reached agreement with Hitler on the dismemberment of Czechoslovakia, it fell to Mr de Valera to announce the fact to the Assembly. 'All honour', he said, 'to those who . . . strove – as we now know, thank God, successfully – for such a solution.'[76] The 'solution', temporary as it was, had of course been reached outside the League and with absolutely no reference to it. And whatever Mr de Valera might have felt it necessary to say in public, the events of 1938 can only have confirmed him in his opinion that as a force for peace the League of Nations was finally discredited. Thenceforward the only hope for small countries – and a precarious hope at that – was neutrality. 'I have stated here in this House', he told the Dáil in April 1939, 'and I have stated in the country, that the aim of government policy is to keep this country out of war, and nobody, either here or elsewhere, has any right to assume anything else.'[77] As war came closer month by month this attitude hardened, receiving full support in parliament from all the other parties.* Indeed, the very fact that Britain now seemed certain to be drawn in strengthened the Irish determination to be neutral. For neutrality, after all, was not just the instinctive reaction of a small power to keep clear of the quarrels of big powers, it was the outward and visible sign of absolute sovereignty. To be free to choose between peace and war was the mark of independence, to be free to choose between peace and a *British* war demonstrated to all the world just how complete that independence really was.

Yet there went with it an air of unreality which the actual outbreak of war served only to intensify. Neutrality was a fine sentiment, but the harsh fact was that it could only be enjoyed on sufferance. That the twenty-six counties passed through the war – in neutral jargon it was called the 'emergency' – unviolated, was due partly to British forbearance and partly to the success of first British, and later Allied, arms. This forbearance was severely taxed several times. Even before the fighting started the British representative in Ireland, Sir John Maffey (later Lord Rugby) took private soundings from the editor of the *Irish Times* – still, at that time, reckoned to be a pro-British newspaper – to see what the Irish reaction to a landing by British troops

* It is proper to record that a leading member of Fine Gael, Mr James Dillon, took a different view and eventually (in 1941) resigned from his party on this issue, only rejoining it ten years later.

in certain circumstances might be.[78] He was left in no doubt that the reaction would be violently hostile, but the temptation to re-occupy the ports must have been very severe during the critical stages of the Battle of the Atlantic; indeed, had it not been that bases were available in Northern Ireland, and especially at Londonderry, it is hard to see how Britain could have avoided taking some desperate action to secure her western approaches.* The entry of America into the war did not ease matters, for although the United States was, almost by definition, friendly to Ireland, the American ambassador, Mr David Gray, had no hesitation in recommending the seizure of bases in the south to President Roosevelt and in 1944, with the Normandy landings imminent, it was the Americans rather than the British who wanted pressure to be brought upon Ireland, mainly with a view to preventing the leakage of vital information to the Germans. It is probably too early yet to say for certain why the Allies held their hand. No doubt they were influenced to some extent by the adverse reaction such an occupation of a small neutral country would have provoked from world opinion; though any sane calculation of risks would also have warned them that resistance would have been so fierce as to defeat the object of the manoeuvre. The regular Irish army was indeed tiny – only about 7,000 regulars with a reserve of 14,000 – and very poorly equipped, but with additional recruitment and the formation of a local defence force, there were a quarter of a million men under arms by the end of the war and capable of mounting an effective guerrilla campaign. The lessons of 1919-21 were not, after all, distant enough to have been forgotten by either side.

But if there was no Allied occupation what were the chances of a German attack? The answer appears to be that a direct invasion as a means of striking at Britain from the rear was ruled out. On the other hand, had Operation Sealion succeeded in 1940 and Britain been overrun, there can be little doubt that Ireland would have suffered the same fate. German documents captured after the war revealed

* Since the above was written the Cabinet records for 1939 have become available. These indicate that there was very strong pressure inside the government (especially from Churchill as First Lord of the Admiralty) to demand naval facilities and to take them by force if need be. In the face of Mr de Valera's adamant refusal to compromise his neutrality, the British government finally decided not to use force unless the U-boat menace became literally a matter of life and death, but it is clear from the arguments in the Cabinet that the decision might very easily have gone the other way (for a brief summary of this episode see the articles in *Irish Times*, 1 and 2 Jan. 1970). Further Cabinet papers released as this book went to press (for summary see *Irish Times*, 1 Jan. 1971) indicate that British warnings of an imminent German attack on Ireland, coupled with a rather vague promise by Britain to accept the principle of Irish unity if Eire entered the war alongside the Allies, left Mr de Valera and his policy of neutrality equally unmoved.

that plans had been laid, or at least discussed, to that end.[79] It is fair to say, therefore, that Irish neutrality depended not alone upon the Allies observing it, but upon their forces being strong enough to prevent the Germans from infringing it.

Of course, since both Germany and Britain maintained diplomatic representation in Ireland throughout the war, Dublin became, like Lisbon, one of the whispering-galleries of Europe and a natural centre for intrigue and spying of every kind. Amid all this the Irish government trod its thorny neutral path as delicately as possible and developed a remarkable capacity for not noticing disagreeable facts. Thus on the one hand it turned a blind eye to British aircraft flying over Donegal, or to the return of stranded British airmen across the border, and on the other hand it managed to ignore for a considerable time the existence of a wireless transmitter in the German embassy. The latter, admittedly, was closed down in 1944 at Allied insistence, but the rumours and the espionage continued. Even before the war the Germans were in touch with the IRA, and it has been suggested that German intelligence officers had had a hand in planning the bombing campaign in England in 1939 which, however, they would have preferred to restrain until war had actually broken out.[80] When it did break out they not only hoped to make use of two IRA leaders then in Germany – Sean Russell and Frank Ryan – but also, through an agent, Herman Goertz, to make contact with the organisation in Ireland itself.* Goertz, a brave man but not overwhelmingly competent, was taken aback by the disarray and inefficiency he found among his supposed allies. 'You know how to die for Ireland', he told them, 'but how to fight for it you have not the slightest idea.'[81] Goertz landed by parachute in May 1940 but was arrested the following February. In 1947, rather than face deportation to Germany, he committed suicide. His mission, so far as one can judge, had been entirely futile.[82]

It is doubtful whether the IRA, even if they had been more efficient or the Germans had paid them more attention, could have achieved very much. The mood of the country was set on neutrality and the harassing of control-points along the northern border, the main objective towards which the Germans sought to direct IRA efforts, commanded no widespread support in the twenty-six counties. Such raids did certainly take place, but the north was so well armed (it was, after all, on a war footing), the south was so much on the alert, and the IRA itself was so much split by internal divisions, that the

* Russell, the former Chief of Staff of the IRA, had gone to America in 1939 to raise funds. In 1940, rather than return to internment in Ireland, he went to Germany. Ryan had been imprisoned by Franco for his part in the Spanish Civil War, but his escape was engineered by the German Abwehr and by the Spanish secret police. He was then taken to Germany and he and Russell were sent together by submarine to land in Ireland. Russell died en route and Ryan, having returned without landing, died in Dresden in 1944.

effect of these attacks was simply to ruin the resources of the organisation. Apart from Russell and Ryan, twenty-six IRA men lost their lives between April 1930 and May 1946. Of these, nine were executed, five killed in gun-battles with the police on both sides of the border; six died in prison hospitals; three died on hunger-strike; two were killed in explosions and one was shot by military police at the internment camp in The Curragh.[83]

On the whole it would be a fair verdict to say that Irish neutrality, even though carried to the scrupulously correct lengths of a visit of condolence by Mr de Valera to the German embassy on the death of Hitler, favoured Britain rather than Germany. As we shall see presently the war brought the British and Irish economies even closer together than they had been before, and although Ireland's imports were hard hit by British blockade regulations (and by the desperate shortage of shipping) her own exports of cattle and meat products rose steeply. So, of course, did emigration and the amount of money sent home by the many thousands of men and women who went to work in the United Kingdom.* And not only to work, but to fight as well – during the whole period of the war some 50,000 persons from the twenty-six counties volunteered to serve in the British forces.

For those who stayed at home the war made itself felt in two main ways. One – which was more obvious at the time, but was in fact less important – was the inevitable consequence of inhabiting a small under-developed island in a hostile world. All sorts of commodities ran rapidly out of supply and various kinds of rationing had to be imposed. Private motoring virtually ceased in 1943 and long-distance travel even by public transport was not easy.[84] Gas and electricity consumption was heavily cut and coal was at times almost unobtainable. There was clothes rationing, bread rationing, and a steady reduction of other foodstuffs until at one stage the weekly allowance per person was ½ oz. of tea, 6 oz. of butter and ½ lb. of sugar. There can be no doubt that this created real hardship, especially for the poor, many of whom depended very largely on bread, butter and tea and could ill-afford to buy more expensive but still available meat. Nevertheless, the great effort to achieve self-sufficiency, wasteful of natural resources and uneconomic as it may have been in the long run, did at least keep starvation at bay.

It was the other consequence of the war – psychological rather than material – that was eventually to prove far more significant for Ireland. This was, quite simply, her almost total isolation from the rest of mankind. At the very moment when she had achieved stability and full independence, and was ready to take her place in the society of nations, that society dissolved and she was thrown back upon her own meagre resources. The tensions – and the liberations – of war, the shared experience, the comradeship in suffering, the new thinking about the future, all these things had passed her by. It was as if an entire

* For the effects of the war on the Irish economy, see pp. 622-3 below.

people had been condemned to live in Plato's cave, with their backs to the fire of life and deriving their only knowledge of what went on outside from the flickering shadows thrown on the wall before their eyes by the men and women who passed to and fro behind them. When after six years they emerged, dazzled, from the cave into the light of day, it was to a new and vastly different world.

3. New Beginnings

Since, when the war ended, Mr de Valera and some of his senior colleagues had been in office for thirteen years, it would not have been surprising if the strain of carrying such a burden for so long had begun to tell. The will to rule, no doubt, was as strong as ever, but the capacity to do so was less evident. And as problems thickened round the tired and harassed government the notion that it was time for a change began to gain ground in the country.

The task of post-war adjustment in a period of continuing, or even accentuated, scarcities would have been difficult enough even under the most favourable conditions, but the conditions turned out to be as unfavourable as they well could be. Apart from the obvious problems staring everyone in the face – that industry was lacking in raw materials, fuel and capital equipment, that the consumer was hungry for manufactured goods of all kinds, and that the long wage-freeze of the 'emergency' years had built up tremendous pressures for pay-increases in all sectors of the economy, the Irish weather now added its own complications. The summer of 1946 was one of the wettest on record, so wet as to wash away all Mr de Valera's earlier appeals for increased wheat production, with the results that the meagre harvest left the government with no option but to resort once more to bread-rationing. Hard on the heels of the wretched summer came one of the hardest winters of the century. Fuel supplies, already perilously low, sank to critical depths in the early months of 1947, industry and transport were brought almost to a standstill, and the miseries of the long-suffering population were intense.

It was entirely predictable, but economically disastrous, that people, irked by these new hardships coming on top of the wartime restrictions, should have rushed to buy what little there was in the shops. Inevitably, prices rose while wages still lagged behind, and the demand for imports threatened rapidly to outpace the assets available to pay for them. Little though contemporaries may have realised it, they were already caught in the first of a recurring series of economic nightmares in which an underdeveloped economy was to be exposed to galloping inflation. The government was aware of at least some of the dangers and in an attempt to check wage advances made strenuous efforts to hold back prices; but, since the most radical of these – the introduction of subsidies to keep down the cost of essential foodstuffs – necessitated a supplementary budget in the autumn of 1947 to impose further taxes, it was obvious that, electorally speaking, Mr de Valera was giving a dangerously large number of hostages to fortune.

Almost at once fortune began to claim them. The war was not long over before scattered signs appeared in the constituencies of a kind of cumulative boredom with the old party machines, the old party slogans, even the old party leaders. The hour was ripe for a new departure in politics, and the hour duly produced the man. This was Mr Sean MacBride, son of Major John MacBride, one of the insurgents executed after 1916, and of the beautiful Maud Gonne, who had enslaved W. B. Yeats in the early years of the century. Born in 1904, Mr MacBride had grown up, naturally enough, in a republican atmosphere. Educated partly in France, he had joined the anti-Treaty side during the Civil War and never lost touch with the extreme movement thereafter. Called to the Irish bar, he became an eminent Senior Counsel, with a reputation for successfully defending IRA men who had fallen foul of the government. It was from die-hard republicans of this sort – whether survivors of the old Saor Eire movement or members of a group known as Coras na Poblachta which had split off from Fianna Fáil – that the nucleus of a political party calling itself Clann na Poblachta began slowly to be formed. As the name (literally 'Republican Family') indicates, the adherents of the new party were dedicated to the establishment of an Irish republic, but to this ambition they added, with no apparent sense of incompatibility, a burning passion to end partition.

It is doubtful, however, if a new party would have had much success at that particular point in time if it had put all its eggs in the republican, anti-partition basket. Clann na Poblachta did not in fact commit that elementary error. What attracted some of the abler young men in the country towards the Clann was not just that it was republican, but that it was – or appeared to be – radical as well. Of this social radicalism Dr Noel Browne may be regarded as the leading – though not, as events were to show, the most representative – exponent. Dr Browne was totally inexperienced in politics, but his views might have been described as Christian Socialist, had not that label been annexed by the large, highly organised European parties with which his lonely individualism had little enough in common. But this very loneliness, though it left him fatally vulnerable in a parliamentary sense, was to make him in time a great symbolic figure of the Irish Left, one of the few, indeed, to have appeared since the formation of the state. Born in 1914, the son of a former policeman in the Royal Irish Constabulary, his childhood was overshadowed by the menace of tuberculosis, which carried off his father and then, after the family had moved to London, his mother and a brother and sister. Noel Browne himself attracted the favourable notice of the Jesuits, who educated him at Beaumont. Next, through the benevolence of a wealthy Dublin family, he was enabled to go to Trinity College, where he qualified as a doctor. Soon after this, he too contracted tuberculosis and on recovery made the eradication of the disease in his home country the prime business of his life. In 1947 he was introduced to MacBride – at that time framing the programme of Clann na Poblachta with Mr Noel Hartnett and Mr J. McQuillan – and from this meeting came at least a part of the welfare proposals with which the party was prepared to go to the country when the time came.[1]

That time came sooner than perhaps even the most optimistic opponents of Fianna Fáil could have expected. In the autumn of 1947 the government's always precarious control of the balance of power was suddenly endangered by the loss of two by-elections, one of them to Mr MacBride himself. Mr de Valera attempted to restore the situation, and perhaps also to nip the growing threat from the Clann in the bud, by holding a general election in February, 1948. He failed, narrowly but decisively. On a register slightly larger than at the last war-time election of 1944 which had confirmed his party in office, and with a redistribution of seats which increased the number of deputies in the Dáil from 138 to 147, the best that Fianna Fáil could muster was sixty-eight seats. To retain power Mr de Valera would have needed to share it with one or more of the other parties. They, however, were dazzled by the possibility of forming among themselves a coalition from which the veteran of so many electoral triumphs would at last be excluded, and at length, after several days of negotiation, an 'inter-party' government emerged to the astonishment of all beholders. It was a justifiable astonishment, for under the same umbrella sheltered not only Fine Gael (which, with thirty-one seats was still the second largest party in the Dáil) but also a farmers' party (Clann na Talmhan), the two groups in which the Labour party was then divided, an Independent (Mr James Dillon), and, of course, Clann na Poblachta. The Clann had won ten seats at the election and this, though far from the avalanche which some had predicted, was enough to give them two places and great influence in the cabinet that resulted from the elaborate negotiations.*

* The election resulted in the following distribution of seats: Fianna Fáil, sixty-eight; Fine Gael, thirty-one; Labour, nineteen; Clann na Talmhan, seven; Clann na Poblachta, ten; Independents, twelve. Clann na Talmhan must not be confused with the old Farmers' party which was represented in the Dáil between 1922 and 1932. The latter derived its support mainly from the larger and more prosperous farmers. It was conservative in its attitudes and a handful of its surviving members were attracted into the short-lived National Centre Party in the early 'thirties, but thereafter the wealthier members of the farming community tended to identify with Fine Gael. Clann na Talmhan, on the other hand, was launched in 1938 primarily as the vehicle for western small farmers dissatisfied with the treatment they were receiving from Fianna Fáil, the party they had consistently supported since its foundation. During the war years it was vocal and by no means ineffective, winning ten seats at the election of 1943. The unsettled climate of Irish politics in the decade after the war gave

It could hardly be called a cabinet of all the talents, for it contained too little experience (to say nothing of a modicum of incompetence), but the key posts were filled by undeniably able men eager to make the most of office after the long frustrations of opposition. The leadership, and most of the ministries, fell to Fine Gael as the strongest member of the coalition, but it was perhaps symptomatic of the difficulties lying in wait for the new government that the Taoiseach was not the man who had led the party since Mr Cosgrave's retirement in 1944. That man, General Richard Mulcahy, had been altogether too effective a leader of the Free State Forces in the Civil War for him to preside comfortably over a cabinet that contained the political heirs of the men he had fought against a generation earlier. And so, although he himself is said to have taken the initiative in the negotiations that produced the inter-party government, he emerged from those negotiations in the somewhat improbable role of Minister for Education.[2] The headship of the patchwork coalition went instead to Mr John A. Costello. Mr Costello, at that time fifty-seven years of age, was a distinguished lawyer who had served as Attorney-General during the last six years of the Cosgrave regime. Mr Costello's tenure of office was to be controversial in the extreme, but even those who differed most sharply from him admitted his skill and patience as a chairman who could, most of the time, bring order and reasonable harmony into the proceedings of his variegated and highly temperamental team.

Apart from General Mulcahy and Mr Costello, Fine Gael was powerfully represented in the cabinet by another of Cosgrave's colleagues, Mr P. McGilligan, who presided with stern austerity over the Ministry of Finance; by Dr T. F. O'Higgins, a civilian charged with Defence; by General Sean MacEoin, a soldier responsible for Justice; and by Daniel Morrissey, a refugee from Labour to whom was entrusted the important office of Minister of Industry and Commerce. The other posts were carefully distributed according to the bargaining power of the parties represented in the coalition. Mr MacBride took External Affairs, Mr Joseph Blowick (Clann na Talmhan) took Lands and Fisheries, while Mr William Norton of the Labour party took Social Welfare and acted as deputy (or Tanaiste) to Mr Costello. His Labour colleague, T. J. Murphy, went to Local Government and J. Everett (National Labour) to Posts and Telegraphs. Those appointments were all more or less predictable, but two of the most interesting were also two of the most experimental. One was that of Mr James Dillon, who had left Fine Gael in 1942 over the issue of neutrality and was not to rejoin it again until 1952; having gained a prodigious

_____

it perhaps more importance than it deserved and it was to supply ministers to both the inter-party governments. However, with the recovery of Fianna Fáil after 1957, Clann na Talmhan dwindled and by the mid-sixties had ceased to exist.

and colourful reputation in opposition he was now, as an Independent, to have the chance (which, as we shall see, he seized with both
hands) to establish himself as an imaginative and constructive Minister
for Agriculture. And the other was Dr Noel Browne, whose career
as a deputy and as a minister began on the same day. Assigned to the
Ministry of Health, he was admirably placed to launch those schemes
of social welfare which had led him in the first instance into the arms
of Clann na Poblachta.

With so much ability available, and with such a wide field of initiative in reform opening out before it, the inter-party government
seemed poised to give a decisive new turn to the development of
modern Ireland. As we shall see presently, it did achieve in that
direction more than posterity has been inclined to give it credit
for, but it is one of the ironies of history that its fame – or ill-fame,
according to the point of view – has come to depend less on a variety
of domestic successes than on one domestic failure and on the
dramatic change which it introduced into the country's relationship
with the British Commonwealth.

It was this last issue that dominated the early months of the
coalition's existence. Given the preoccupations of Clann na Poblachta
with the republic, it was inevitable that the question of Ireland's status
should have come up at the general election. Even as late as 1947 Mr de
Valera was still expounding the doctrine of external association and
still insisting that under his External Relations Act Ireland was to all
intents and purposes a republic, in fact, if not in name.[3] During the
election campaign Clann na Poblachta had of course put the repeal of
that act and the declaration of the republic in the forefront of their
programme. Fine Gael, on the other hand, although some of its
members (including Mr Costello himself) where uneasy about the
ambiguities of the existing situation, was widely regarded in Ireland as
still being in some sense a 'Commonwealth' party and the election
speeches of the leaders, though well-stocked, like everyone else's,
with the explosive vocabulary of 'anti-partition', stopped short of
the republican demand, which, indeed, was only too likely to rivet
northern Unionists even more closely to the Crown and the British
connection.

Nevertheless, despite this fundamental incompatibility between the
achievement of a republic and the removal of the border, the government decided to repeal the External Relations Act. We are still too
close to the event to be able to dogmatise about the factors which
had most influence upon this decision, but three points can be made
with reasonable certainty. One is that the presence of Mr MacBride in
the cabinet, pledged as he was to work for a republic, was bound to
bring the issue to the fore sooner or later. A second is that the balance
of parties within the Dáil was so even that the inter-party coalition
was highly vulnerable to an initiative from what Mr Costello (in a
letter to the present writer) has called 'some person not well disposed

to the government'.[4] Had such a person – say, an Independent deputy – brought forward of his own volition a proposal to modify the External Relations Act in the direction of a *de jure* rather than a *de facto* republic, the effect of this upon the coalition might well have been catastrophic.* In the absence of any agreed policy among its members, Fine Gael might well have voted one way and Clann na Poblachta another, with the result that their partnership would have ended almost before it had begun.

It may be asked why, granted that it was necessary to agree upon a policy, should that policy have been the policy of the Clann rather than the policy of the status quo? The answer may be partly in the leverage that the Clann's ten seats gave to Mr MacBride, but – and here is the third point that has to be made – it may be found also in Mr Costello's own attitude of mind. For although his main interest when taking office seems to have been in economic reform, it is undoubtedly true not only that he found the External Relations Act untidy and inadequate, but that he was deeply conscious of the way in which the idea of the republic had haunted and divided Irishmen ever since the Civil War. To take the gun out of politics by settling this problem – so far as it could be settled – was for him an act of statesmanship that would justify even the traumatic break with his own party's history which it would entail.[5]

As is well-known, he announced his intention of doing this in September 1948 while on a visit to Canada. The dramatic and seemingly sudden character of this announcement gave rise immediately to a chaos of conflicting rumours, some of which, despite frequent refutations, still circulate to this day. The most notorious of these alleges that Mr Costello – or as one version has it, Mrs Costello – was insulted by the Governor-General of Canada, who happened to be that distinguished scion of Ulster Unionist stock, Field-Marshal Earl Alexander of Tunis, and that in consequence Mr Costello stormed off in a rage to a press conference where he 'declared' the republic forthwith. Apart from the fact that this would have been constitutionally impossible, the story is completely false. The truth, however, is no less strange and absorbing.

First, it is necessary to emphasise that before Mr Costello left for Canada at all there had been a cabinet decision to repeal the External Relations Act. There is still some uncertainty about the precise date, and some confusion of ministerial recollections about the occasion (not unnatural after a lapse of twenty years), but Mr Costello himself, and his Minister for External Affairs, Mr MacBride, have both gone on record that the decision was taken that summer – in all probability in August. Not only that, but Mr MacBride and the Tanaiste (Deputy

* This is not so hypothetical as it may sound. It was believed by political commentators at the time that the cabinet had in mind specifically the possibility of intervention by the late Captain Peadar Cowan (*Irish Times*, 10 July 1962).

Prime Minister) Mr Norton, had made it quite clear in the Dáil that the External Relations Act would be repealed before long and had elicited indications from Fianna Fáil that on that side of the House there would be no opposition to such a move. In July, for example, Mr MacBride had remarked – and the significance of what he said had not gone unnoticed – that there was no parallel between the history of the Commonwealth countries and that of Ireland. 'The Crown and outworn forms that belong to British constitutional history', he added, 'are merely reminders of an unhappy past that we want to bury, that have no realities for us and only serve as irritants.'[6] And less than three weeks later Mr Norton roundly declared that the External Relations Act was 'a fraud on the people' and that 'it would do our national self-respect good both at home and abroad if we were to proceed without delay to abolish the External Relations Act'. To which Mr de Valera replied: 'Go ahead. You will get no opposition from us.'[7]

It seems clear, therefore, that by August 1948 the scene had been set for a radical change of policy. This still does not explain, of course, why the change was announced in Canada. It arose indirectly out of the accidental circumstance that Mr Costello had been invited as a distinguished lawyer to address the Canadian Bar Association. He arrived in Montreal on 30 August and while he was their guest (until he left for Ottawa on 4 September) he deliberately refrained from making what he has since called 'comments of a political character'. Nevertheless, the speech which he delivered to his Canadian hosts – on 'Ireland in international affairs' – had been regarded at home as sufficiently important to have been read and approved by the cabinet before his departure. For the most part it was an able and objective account of the way in which the constitutional relations of Ireland with the Commonwealth had changed since the Treaty, but Mr Costello did allow himself to refer to the 'inaccuracies and infirmities' of those sections of the External Relations Act which dealt with the position of the Crown.[8] This was in no sense a declaration of the republic, but at least it indicated to all and sundry that Mr Costello was not exactly wedded to the Act. And the very next night he himself had evidence of one of these 'infirmities'. At the Bar Association dinner, after the toast of 'The King' had been given, the Canadian Minister for External Affairs said to him, 'Doesn't that cover you?' 'I had to argue', Mr Costello subsequently recalled, 'that it did not, because we were not real members of the Commonwealth.'[9]

This was confusing enough, but worse was to come. On 4 September Mr Costello was the guest of the Canadian government at an official dinner in Ottawa. This was the famous occasion round which legend has gathered, and although the legend is far removed from the truth, during the dinner Mr Costello did have two unpleasant experiences.*

* In my account of this dinner I have drawn heavily on an essay of mine. 'The Years of Adjustment, 1945-1951', in T. Desmond Williams and

565

One was that at the Governor-General's table he was confronted with a replica of 'Roaring Meg', the famous cannon used in the defence of Derry in 1689 and ever since an almost sacred symbol to Ulster Unionists. This was hardly the most tactful gesture to make to a nationalist prime minister, but while it is doubtful whether the green, white and orange flower-arrangement which Earl Alexander later claimed had also been set before Mr Costello had the desired emollient effect, the incident was hardly likely to lead to the secession of Ireland from the Commonwealth. The other incident, admittedly, was more vexatious. It had been arranged by the Irish High Commissioner with the Canadian government that two toasts would be drunk – 'The King' and 'The President of Ireland'. Yet, when the time came, only 'The King' was proposed. In retrospect, so Mr Costello told the present writer, he was satisfied that this was probably no more than an error of protocol but it was a slightly ominous coincidence that a few months earlier the same thing had happened to him in Downing Street when dining with Mr Attlee. Such an omission, twice repeated, and involving in effect a denial of the existence of the republic, was yet one more illustration of the ambiguities embalmed in the External Relations Act. Even so, and although he had come believing that both toasts would be proposed, Mr Costello did not – as the story subsequently went – leave the dinner in a rage and he did not straightaway summon a press conference to make any dramatic revelations about Ireland's status in the Commonwealth.

What really precipitated his action in Canada was not these dinner irritations, but rather the appearance in next morning's *Sunday Independent* of the headlines: 'External Relations Act to go'.[10] This referred to Mr Costello's speech to the Canadian Bar Association, and also to those of Mr MacBride and Mr Norton already quoted. Whether the decision to run the story at that particular time was 'inspired' or not must remain a matter of speculation, though it is perhaps not altogether irrelevant to note that the paper was usually regarded as being particularly close to Mr Costello's own party. Reverting to the topic fourteen years later, the *Sunday Independent* itself declared that its headline had derived from 'an intelligent reading' of ministers' speeches and this judicious comment may be as near to the truth as we are likely to get.[11] Mr Costello only learnt of this development by telephone late on Sunday afternoon. He was due to give a press conference on Tuesday, 7 September, and had therefore no more than thirty-six hours in which to decide how to answer the questions he

K. B. Nowlan (ed.), *Ireland in the War Years and After* (Dublin and London, 1969). I am grateful to the editors and to Mr Michael Gill, the publisher, for permission to use this material. For the background to the whole affair see also the quotations from a memorandum by Mr Costello in B. Farrell, *Chairman or Chief?: the Role of Taoiseach in Irish Government* (Dublin and London, 1971), pp. 47-50.

would now inevitably have to face. Sheer distance made consultation with his ministers virtually impossible – at least in any satisfying depth – and in fact he appears to have come to his decision on his own, but with the memory of the cabinet discussion before he left home very much in the forefront of his mind. 'If no decision had been made before I left', he has since written, 'it would be quite improper for me to have made the statement that I did and it would have been very easy for me to deal with the matter referred to in the *Sunday Independent* of 5 September, 1948.'[12]

Knowing what he did know about the decision made before he left, he felt that he had no alternative but to speak out frankly and say, as he did say, that it was his government's intention to repeal the Act. This was the declaration which caused such a stir in Ireland, even among ministers for whom the timing of the announcement probably came as much as a surprise as for anyone else.* What gave it real significance, of course, was that it was not just a statement of intent to repeal the offending legislation, for in reply to a specific question from a foreign correspondent Mr Costello made it perfectly clear that repeal meant also secession from the Commonwealth.[13]

In accordance with his decision the Republic of Ireland Bill was introduced in the Dáil in November 1948 and had passed through all its stages by the end of the year, leaving the way clear for the republic itself to be formally inaugurated on the symbolic date of Easter Monday, 1949. In the debates Mr Costello stressed that his party had a dual intention – to put an end to ancient rancours within the country and at the same time to establish Anglo-Irish relations on a better, because a less ambiguous, basis. In reply to the obvious objection that this step would make the ending of partition even more remote than before, he contended that refraining from it in the past had not evoked a friendly gesture from Northern Ireland – why then continue to refrain from it in the hope of a reconciliation that never came?[14] This was an argument of very doubtful validity. Repeal might not make a bad situation worse, but it surely meant that it would be harder thenceforward to make that bad situation better.

* Interviewing Dr Noel Browne on 3 January 1967 I had a clear impression that the announcement had taken him by surprise. And five years earlier Lord Rugby (who, as Sir John Maffey, was the much respected British Representative to Eire in 1948) in giving his recollections of the incident had recalled that Mr MacBride also had looked surprised when receiving the news of the announcement on the evening of 7 September. Mr MacBride's comment on this, however, was that if he looked surprised, it was because he was astonished that anyone should regard the news of Ireland being ready to repeal the External Relations Act as in any way sensational (*Irish Times*, 10 July 1962). On the other hand, it is fair to add that the Irish people had a reasonable right to expect that an announcement of such momentous import might most appropriately have been made on their own soil.

And indeed, in the short run at least it must have seemed that the Irish action did make the bad situation worse, for the British riposte followed swiftly. When in 1949 the imperial parliament passed the Ireland Act with a view to regularising the position, it included in that Act a proviso that Northern Ireland would never be detached from the United Kingdom without the consent of the Northern Ireland legislature. It is true that recent events have indicated that Northern Ireland autonomy is a more precarious thing than it was then assumed to be, but this does not alter the fact that the pledge given in 1949 seemed – and was intended – to lock and bolt the door against the anti-partition movement, thus confirming the critics in all they had said about the incompatibility between the two goals of ending the border and establishing the republic.

This, however, was still in the future. So far as the Dáil was concerned, coming events cast no shadows and the government's legislation went through without let or hindrance. Fianna Fáil could scarcely oppose it, though they might have been excused for feeling that the government had caught them bathing and stolen their clothes. Moreover, the clothes did not fit very well. Mr de Valera's lifelong ideal had been an all-Ireland, not a partial, republic, and what was solemnly celebrated in April 1949 fell far short of that ideal. Perhaps, indeed, the curious sense of disenchantment that can be observed in the generation that has grown up within the boundaries of this mutilated polity is in part a consequence of the very fact that a twenty-six county republic was seen and felt to be a second-best solution – a sentiment summed up in two bitter lines of a not very popular song parodying the unofficial national anthem 'God save Ireland' inherited from the nineteenth century:

> God save the Southern part of Ireland
> Three-quarters of a nation once again.[15]

Whatever the reaction in Ireland – and there was, of course, some enthusiasm along with a good deal of indifference – the ultimate success of the government's policy depended not just on its own unilateral action, but upon the response of Great Britain and the other Commonwealth countries. By a curious coincidence, a conference of Commonwealth prime ministers was due to assemble at London in October 1948 – that is, between Mr Costello's Canadian announcement and the introduction of repeal legislation in the Dáil. Although not enough is yet known about the private reactions of the British government to the proposed Irish secession to admit of any confident generalisations, it would not have been surprising if, in the light of all that had passed between the two countries for so many centuries, some alarm and disapproval had not been voiced, or even expressed in some kind of retaliatory action. That this proved not to be the case may have been due in part at least to the good offices of the dominion members of the Commonwealth Conference. While that Conference was in progress Irish representatives met representatives of the British, Canadian, Australian and New Zealand governments at Chequers and at Paris. As a result of these meetings – at which the influence of the Australian and Canadian statesmen is believed to have been especially powerful – the view emerged, to all intents and purposes unanimously, that Ireland's withdrawal should not be allowed to affect the friendly relations existing between that country and the nations of the Commonwealth.

In practical terms this meant, and has meant ever since, that in the two areas – citizenship and trade – where the Irish were most vulnerable they had nothing to fear. So far as the former was concerned, it was mutually agreed between Britain and Ireland that the British Nationality Act of 1948 – passed, ironically enough, just before the crisis – should still apply. The effect of this was that citizens of Eire, although no longer British subjects, would, when in Britain, be treated as though they were British subjects – a fact of enormous significance for the large numbers of Irish men and women living and working in the country; by the usual device of reciprocity British subjects when in Ireland would be accorded the same treatment as Irish citizens. No less important than reciprocity for individuals was preference in trade. Here the anxious questions were whether the preferential arrangements then existing between the two countries would be annulled by the fact of Ireland's secession, and whether they would be held to clash with the General Agreement on Tariffs and Trade negotiated at Geneva in 1947. On both counts the verdict was favourable to Ireland and the special economic relationship already established between the two countries survived intact, to grow even closer as time went on.[16]

Yet, if the net result of all this furious activity, apart from reinforcing the connection between Northern Ireland and the rest of the United Kingdom, was apparently to make very little positive impact on Anglo-Irish affairs, there could be no denying that Ireland – albeit no more than 'three-quarters of a nation once again' – had, in breaking the last tenuous link that bound her to Britain, reached a turning-point in her own history. Even here, however, the spirit of paradox that had so often entered into her dealings with her powerful neighbour made one last appearance. For by a strange irony, in the very year when Ireland left the Commonwealth as a republic, India, which had also become a republic, was recognised at her own request as remaining within the association. Why then, it may be asked, if republican status was no longer to be a bar to membership, did Ireland take her final and decisive step?

It may well be that the answer to this question can only be given, not in constitutional or legal terms, but in the language of political psychology. The experiment of dominion status laboured, it has been well said, under three overwhelming liabilities. 'The first was that it came too late, the second that it came as a result of violence, and the third that as a result of partition it was deprived of strong, coherent support.'[17] Nothing, not even the labours of the pro-Treaty party, not even the sympathy of other dominions, not even the belated generosity of Britain herself, could surmount these fatal defects. Ireland remained deaf to the siren voices of the Commonwealth and in the end heard only the ghosts of Roger Casement and all those other dead men knocking on the door. Equality, it seemed, was no substitute for nationality, and in the case of Ireland too much blood had flowed too often for nationality to be satisfied by any kind of connection or tie with Britain, however widely drawn or however magnanimously conceived.

This is not to say that Ireland's brief career, whether as a dominion or in external association with the Commonwealth, was therefore entirely barren. On the contrary, it is reasonable to suggest that the history of Anglo-Irish relations in this century has burned so deep into the British official mind that the post-1945 Commonwealth has provided a much kindlier climate for emergent nations than might otherwise have prevailed. It is the fate of pioneers to be forgotten by those who come after them, but it is not altogether fanciful to see in these territories which have moved so swiftly in the last twenty years from colonial status to full independence, the chief beneficiaries of what happened in Ireland between 1916 and 1949.

If, then, Ireland has not only saved herself by her exertions, but profited others by her example, this may well turn out to be her chief positive contribution to the modern Commonwealth. Yet the lurking suspicion remains that the negative contribution may ultimately be more significant – the demonstration that not even the most imaginatively conceived association of states can fulfil the inner demands and compulsions of a passionate sense of nationality. If the Commonwealth should disappear – and recent prime ministers' conferences have brought this within the realm of possibility – it will disappear because it will have been proved that political independence is not enough. Just two months before the Easter Rising Patrick Pearse expressed this fundamental truth in words that go far beyond the immediate Irish context in which he wrote them. 'Independence', he declared, 'one must understand to include spiritual and intellectual independence as well as political independence; or rather, true political independence requires spiritual and intellectual independence as its basis, or it tends to become unstable, a thing resting merely on interests which change with time and circumstance.'[18]

(ii) POLITICS IN FLUX

Looking back nearly twenty years after the event, Mr Costello claimed the declaration of the republic as perhaps the biggest achievement of the inter-party government.[19] Certainly, it is likely to be the one for which it is most remembered. But there were others, less dramatic and less controversial, which also deserve to be recorded. Broadly, these fall into two categories – those that made an immediate impact and those that sowed a harvest others were to reap long after the coalition was no more. In the former category, four developments stand out, two of them associated with Mr James Dillon, who proved himself to be a dynamic Minister of Agriculture. The first of these was the 1948 trade agreement with Britain which obtained more favourable terms for Irish farm produce, especially by linking the price of store cattle and sheep to the guaranteed price received by British farmers for their fat cattle and sheep. The second of Mr Dillon's initiatives – and one that brought the government considerable popularity – was the launching in 1949 of the ambitious Land Rehabilitation Project, a determined effort to bring back into full production land which had remained idle through lack of capital or for other reasons. It was intended that the Project should extend to about four million acres and that the scheme, spread over about ten years, would cost the state some forty million pounds, to be met in part from United States loans under the European Recovery Programme. Even now, two decades later, it is perhaps premature to pass judgment on the economic viability of the Land Rehabilitation Project, but in terms of electoral psychology it made excellent sense, for it brought the first faint stirrings of hope to many districts long assumed to be stagnant if not dying.* As a modern economist has well said: 'Removing the rocks from Connemara may have been bad economics for Irish adherents of the Manchester school, but to many people emotionally involved in the west of Ireland and its people it was the best news since the activities of the Congested Districts Board.'[20]

If Mr Dillon's scheme for reclaiming derelict land had social as well as economic implications, the concern for welfare which the inter-party government displayed was even more evident in the other two practical reforms it managed to carry through in its three years of office. One was the remarkable improvement in the provision of houses, especially in the countryside. By the end of the war the situation in the twenty-six counties had become so bad that 110,000 new dwellings (in town and country together) were required to meet the immediate need. By 1950, largely through the enterprise of Mr T. J. Murphy as Minister for Local Government, the rate of building had reached 12,000 a year, which was far higher than anything attempted before 1939. This did not solve the problem of the Dublin slums, of course, but it began that transformation of rural housing which to the traveller revisiting the remoter parts of Ireland after a

* The difficulty of assessing the Land Rehabilitation Project is increased by the lack of reliable statistics on the subject, but for some general comments on the policy of state aid to agriculture, see below, chap. 4, section v.

lapse of ten or twenty years is one of the most exciting signs of progress.

Even more striking, and so complete that nowadays it is taken almost for granted, was the virtual eradication of tuberculosis that Dr Noel Browne succeeded in carrying through with extraordinary rapidity. This disease, which for generation after generation had eaten into the already declining population, was particularly dire in its effects because its incidence was always heaviest in the twenty to thirty-four age-group. As recently as the decade 1911-20 it had claimed 205 victims per annum for each 100,000 of the population.[21] Thereafter the situation slowly improved, though when Dr Browne came into office it was still killing between 3,000 and 4,000 people every year.[22] Although the introduction of mass radiography by his predecessors had improved diagnosis, treatment was still hampered by the lack of hospital beds. To remedy this deficiency and build enough modern sanatoria to cope with the onset of the disease even in its early stages was Dr Browne's main problem and he solved it brilliantly by a radical redeployment of his Ministry's finances. Liquidating its assets of twenty million pounds and mortgaging the next ten million pounds that could be expected to accrue, he spent the money on a vast project of supplying and staffing sanatoria throughout the country.* Admittedly, advances in medical research coincided providentially with his campaign and the introduction of BCG, together with the use of Streptomycin, brought not only cure but prevention at last within range. The combination of these four factors – mass radiography, the new sanatoria, modern methods of treatment, and vaccination, combined to produce some astonishing results. It was in 1949 that the death-rate from tuberculosis first fell below one hundred per 100,000 population and by 1952 this proportion had fallen as low as fifty-four; five years later it had been reduced to twenty-seven.[23]

Apart from these obvious and demonstrable successes, the inter-party government also set in train other reforms which, in the sphere of economics, were destined to have consequences far greater than could have been foreseen at the time. It would be a naive over-simplification to say of this patchwork coalition, composed as it was of men of widely differing ideas on almost all economic questions, that it produced anything coherent enough to be called a common view, but as some of the ideas thrown up by new men worked their way into practice it began at least to seem as if Mr Costello and his colleagues did have a recognisably different outlook from that of Fianna Fáil. This has been concisely defined by a distinguished Irish economist as a belief that the best recipe for the cure of unemployment and emigration was a rigorous application to Irish conditions of the Keynesian

* The chief source of revenue was the Hospitals' Sweepstake. For this and for the general framework of health legislation within which Dr Browne had to work, see chap. 5, section iii.

doctrines on government spending. 'State spending', he has written, 'was to become the conspicuous feature of inter-party economic policies.'[24] But if this investment were to be used to the best effect expert advice would be needed. To obtain it two new organisations were created, each of which was in due course to make a notable contribution to the growth of economic planning in Ireland. One, the Industrial Development Authority, brought together a group of influential men with wide experience of financial and industrial matters and gave them the task not only of planning and assisting industrial growth, but also of scrutinising the protectionist structure within which industry had for so long been sheltering. The other, Coras an Trachtala, was the offspring of a committee originally set up to examine ways and means of reducing the serious dollar deficit. The new organisation – a strikingly successful example of the state-sponsored bodies described below*was established primarily to promote Irish exports to the United States and Canada, but proved to be so efficient that it became a permanent institution which extended its operations all over the world.

It would be wrong, however, to equate these initiatives, valuable though they were in themselves, with anything approaching an industrial boom. There was increased activity, indeed, and there was undeniable growth. Between 1946 and 1953 industrial production increased by nearly sixty per cent and nearly 50,600 new jobs were created in industry. This was certainly an improvement on past performances, but it remained, nevertheless, subject to serious reservations. One was that the growth-rate, although superficially impressive, appeared so partly because of the low level from which development had started; if the surrounding plain is flat enough, even a mole-hill will seem imposing. A second reservation concerns the job situation. Not only was the increased industrial labour force still less than half that employed in agriculture, it represented only twenty per cent of the entire working population, a dangerously low proportion by contemporary European standards. Moreover, the continuing drain of emigration very nearly offset the new opportunities created in industry. In 1951 the total number of persons at work was only 12,000 more than in 1926. The net increase of 159,000 in industrial employment over that period had been almost wiped out by a decrease of 147,000 in agricultural employment. Even in the period of so-called expansion between 1946 and 1951, and taking the wastage from emigration into account, the Irish economy was able to create new jobs for no more than 800 people each year.[25]

Nor were these the only items on the debit side. Apart from the familiar weaknesses of the economy – the scarcity or timidity of its private capital, the conservatism of its agriculture, the poverty of its internal market, and its lack of exports – the government had to con-

* See chap. 4, section ii.

573

tend with a variety of pressures both foreign and domestic.* To the devaluation of sterling in 1949 and the inflationary effects of the Korean war were added pressures from all sides for wage-increases to chase, if not to surpass, the rising spiral of prices. The coalition had inherited from Fianna Fáil a wrangling dispute with the national school teachers (who had actually gone on strike in 1946) and growing unrest among white-collar workers which culminated in a bank strike in 1950. It was becoming clear, in short, that even among the more secure section of the community the increasing cost of living, together with the absence of social services comparable with those in Britain or Northern Ireland, was causing real hardship. The government was well aware of the problem and did what it could to solve it. In his very first budget Mr McGilligan cut expenditure in defence and other departments in order to increase the pensions payable to old people, widows and orphans. But this, though certainly overdue, was only a palliative and gradually, after much heart-searching, the government groped its way towards an elaborate and comprehensive scheme of social welfare which formed the basis of legislation introduced in the Dáil early in 1951. On 11 April this passed its second reading, but this triumph was no sooner secured than it became irrelevant, for on that very day the coalition was paralysed by the revelation of an internal crisis which was destined in the end to destroy it.

The storm had been brewing for some time. During the war years and immediately thereafter the vast and complex issues raised by the necessity to improve the health and welfare services in the twenty-six counties had been widely discussed. From the impetus provided by these discussions had sprung the legislation enacted by Fianna Fáil in 1947 which had set up separate departments of Health and Social Welfare and which had also been intended to lay the foundations for a national health service.† The health service proposals, though modest enough compared with what Britain and Northern Ireland were just then being equipped, were far-reaching enough to cause intense alarm in conservative circles and to bring about a clash between the government and its critics. This might, to some extent, have happened anyway, but two circumstances combined to make the clash unexpectedly severe. One was the fact that in the preceding twenty years Catholic thinking in Ireland had taken an increasingly 'integralist' form – that is to say, it had fallen much under the influence of continental ideas stressing Catholic concepts of the moral law and the need for thorough commitment to Catholic social teaching, and in general emphasising the special position the Catholic Church ought to occupy in the community. In the sphere of welfare, Irish Catholic writers had accorded particular weight to the papal encyclical

* For a survey of the general situation of the Irish economy at this time, see chap. 4, section v.

† For this legislation and its significance, see chap. 5, section iii.

of 1931, *Quadragesimo Anno* (itself an adaptation or revision of the celebrated encyclical, *Rerum Novarum*, issued by Pope Leo XIII forty years earlier). Both encyclicals were devoted to mitigating, or removing, the evils alike of unregulated capitalism and of excessive state intervention. Thus, not only did they seek instead to promote the formation of vocational groups but they also attached particular importance to the 'natural unit' of the family. In consequence, they were deeply opposed to any contemporary trends which could be interpreted as transferring responsibility for the health and welfare of children from their parents to an impersonal and external authority.

But – and this was the second circumstance liable to lead to a collision between Church and state – the long-established Fianna Fáil government seemed – perhaps because it was so long-established – to be developing an excessively paternalistic tendency. In this it may have been following rather than leading a civil service which at the time was attracting widespread criticism for its brusque and sometimes overbearing attitude towards the public, but the end result was the same. The forces of vocationalism saw themselves as leading a crusade against the bastions of bureaucracy and even before the health service provided its sensational *casus belli* the antagonists had already clashed over the decidedly short shrift given by the government to the *Report of the Commission on Vocational Organisation* (issued in August 1944) and to the Social Security Plan based on proposals for National Health Insurance published by Dr John Dignan, Bishop of Clonfert, two months later.*

It is against this background of intermittent controversy that the Fianna Fáil Health Act of 1947 has to be seen. From the outset it aroused intense opposition inside and outside the Dáil. Some of this came from the medical profession, but most of it derived from critics who insisted that the liberty and privacy of the individual would be invaded by the state to an intolerable degree if the Act became law. The storm centred round three points in particular – that in the reorganised health service free choice of doctor would not be available, as it was in the health services of most other highly developed countries; that there was a high degree of compulsion, for example in the medical inspection of schoolchildren and in the powers given to the responsible Minister to order the disinfestation – and, if need be, the detention – of persons suspected of being sources of infection; and thirdly, that the scheme, by increasing the authority vested in the

* For the intellectual and the political backgrounds to the events of 1947-1953, see J. H. Whyte, *Church and State in Modern Ireland, 1923-1970* (Dublin and London, 1971), especially chaps. 3, 4 and 5. This work, which is incomparably the best contribution to the writing of contemporary Irish history known to me, is essential to an understanding, not merely of the public role of the Catholic Church in Ireland, but also of the evolution of modern Irish Catholicism. In addition, it contains (chaps. 6, 7, 8 and 9) a masterly analysis of the 'mother and child scheme' crisis of 1951 to which my account in the following pages is greatly indebted.

Minister of Health, contributed to a further centralisation of governmental power. In addition – and, in the light of subsequent events, most important of all – the provisions relating to the establishment of a scheme for maternity and child welfare (including the education of women 'in respect of motherhood'), to be available to mothers and all children up to the age of sixteen, regardless of means, provoked from the Roman Catholic hierarchy a letter of remonstrance to Mr de Valera. This letter, private but none the less formidable for that, condemned the scheme on various grounds, but most significantly as being 'entirely and directly contrary to Catholic teaching on the rights of the family, the rights of the Church in education, the rights of the medical profession and of voluntary institutions'.

The crisis, however, did not come in 1947. Before it had had time to develop Mr James Dillon, at that time an Independent member of the Dáil, determined to test the constitutionality of the Act. It was therefore possible for Mr de Valera to temporise. This he did by informing the bishops in February 1948 that he would defer a full reply to their protest until after the courts had ruled on the validity of those sections of the Act which had been impugned. But at that very moment the electorate was ruling on the validity of his own government. In the election which had just been fought he had failed to win an overall majority and within days of his letter having been dispatched to the bishops the inter-party government had taken over the reins.

Dr Browne thus inherited a situation full of possibilities – and of dangers. His preoccupation with the campaign against tuberculosis meant that he was unable to address himself immediately to the health service problem, though soon after taking office he announced that some of the sections of the Act which had been most criticised as infringing parental rights would be repealed or amended. So far as the mother and child scheme itself was concerned, the cabinet decided in June 1948 to retain a 'free for all' scheme and not to attempt to mollify the doctors by introducing a means test. It was not in fact until June 1950 that Dr Browne began to brace himself to implement the scheme, but by that time the inter-party government had already had an ominous foretaste of the weight of 'integralist' opinion when two of its other proposals – one dealing with social insurance and one with legal adoption – encountered such opposition that the latter had to be dropped and the former had not reached the statute-book when the government fell from power in 1951.

When eventually Dr Browne was able to bring forward his draft proposals it soon appeared that the mother and child scheme in its essentials followed the precedent set by Fianna Fáil in 1947. It was ambitious by Irish standards and, since it was intended to make it available without charge to all mothers and to all children under the age of sixteen, it was certain to involve heavy expenditure. Not surprisingly it immediately came under attack from two quite different directions. The medical profession, like their colleagues in similar situations in other countries, smelled 'socialised medicine' from afar and made no secret of their distaste; they were particularly suspicious of the absence of a means test and they seem also to have feared that under a strong minister the scheme would lend itself to excessive political control. Dr Browne would certainly have had a fight on his hands to persuade his fellow-doctors into accepting the scheme, but precisely because he was a strong minister he might well have succeeded in doing so.

Unhappily, he had simultaneously to fight on a second front against a more powerful enemy. Dealing as they did with the most intimate aspects of maternity, the new proposals by their very nature impinged directly upon the family which, as we saw earlier, was enshrined in the Constitution as 'the natural primary and fundamental unit group of society', possessing 'inalienable and imprescriptible rights, antecedent and superior to all positive law'.[26] Since the family was seen as a moral as well as a social institution it could count, of course, not only upon the support of the courts but that of the Church as well. And the more the Church considered the implications of the proposed service the more uneasy it became. As far back as October 1950 the bishops had made their anxieties known to the Taoiseach. They feared that any scheme framed on the lines Dr Browne was known to be pursuing would result in an invasion of family rights and would lead to a deterioration in the confidential relations that ought to exist between doctor and patient. In addition, they were apprehensive of the results which might flow from sex education by medical officers possibly not of the same religion as their patients and they took their stand on the broad principle that provision for the health of children was an essential part of the responsibilities of parenthood. The state, they concluded, 'has the right to intervene only in a subsidiary capacity, to supplement, not to supplant'. Dr Browne attempted to meet these objections in an elaborate memorandum (he had himself taken theological advice, though it did not do him much good) and by confronting the bishops' representatives face to face. Through a series of misunderstandings that would have been farcical were not the consequences so tragic, Dr Browne believed he had satisfied the hierarchy when in fact he had done nothing of the sort.

In March 1951, when Dr Browne, having failed to reach agreement with the Irish Medical Association, published an outline of his scheme, the crisis deepened. For a few weeks there was frantic activity as ministers sought to bridge the gap between an adamant minister and a rock-like Church, but all was in vain. Once the hierarchy had made it clear that vital questions of faith and morals were involved, the resistance of the government crumbled and Dr Browne found himself increasingly isolated, even from his colleagues in Clann na Poblachta. It is fair to say that for some time past relations had been deteriorating, not merely between Dr Browne and his colleagues from other parties, but also between Dr Browne and the leader of his own party, Mr MacBride. The disenchantment of his colleagues with Dr Browne may have been partly on general grounds – he was a highly-strung man under great pressure and this no doubt made him difficult to work with – but, more specifically, it seems also to have sprung from the fact that some ministers were having second thoughts about a means test, whereas he was as firmly set as ever on making his scheme free without any discrimination. The breach with Mr MacBride was by all accounts more fundamental, based as it appears to have been on Dr Browne's increasing conviction that Clann na Poblachta was being corrupted by office and was in danger of losing its radical soul. On 10 and 11 April a sharp exchange of letters took place between Dr Browne and Mr MacBride, as a result of which, and at Mr MacBride's insistence, Dr Browne sent his resignation to Mr Costello on 11 April.[27]

The most immediate casualty, apart from Dr Browne himself, was the mother and child scheme, though a little later Fianna Fáil succeeded in passing some of its provisions into law. There is clear evidence, however, that had it not been for Mr de Valera's expert guidance, Fianna Fáil, too, might have been involved in a head-on collision with the bishops.[28] But what chiefly alarmed contemporaries was less the individual fate of the minister (there were those who said he had gone the wrong way about his business, even that he was bent upon a clash) than the way in which a difficult question of principle had been resolved. It had been resolved, apparently, by the abject capitulation of the secular to the spiritual power. The *Irish Times*, pointing out the disastrous effect that this example of ecclesiastical intervention would have upon the movement to end partition, concluded bitterly that 'the Roman Catholic Church would seem to be the effective government of this country'. This, no doubt, was an exaggeration, and it would have been exceedingly naive for any layman to have expected the Church to keep silent upon such a matter, where, after all, questions of faith and morals clearly *were* at issue.* But what was, and still is, alarming about the crisis was that it demonstrated the extreme difficulty in a Catholic country of drawing the line between morals and politics – the difficulty, if one follows the affair to its logical conclusion, of reconciling parliamentary democracy with ecclesiastical authority. But perhaps the very violence of the controversy had its own salutary effect. Such a collision was too dangerous to be repeated – and has not been repeated.

The inter-party government itself did not long survive Dr Browne's departure. Indeed, even before the quarrel over the mother and child scheme, Mr Costello's coalition had shown signs of breaking up. It had been exposed to ridicule – in Ireland always a deadly weapon – over the so-called 'Battle of Baltinglass', where the hapless Minister of Posts and Telegraphs was forced to withdraw his nomination to a

* The arguments on both sides are fully and fairly set out by J. H. Whyte in *Church and State in Ireland, 1923-1970*, chap. 8.

village postmastership in face of spirited, and richly comic, local resistance. More serious, the government was still baffled by the phenomenon of inflation and early in 1951 was driven to the desperate expedient of freezing prices at the level obtaining in the previous December. And if this were not enough, Clann na Poblachta, the lynch-pin of the coalition, was itself in dissolution. In February 1951, *before* the mother and child scheme had reached crisis point, one of the most influential members of the party, Mr Noel Hartnett, had resigned on the ominous grounds that the Clann had become obsessed with power and had abandoned 'any political or social philosophy'. When, on top of this, Dr Browne's resignation was followed by others – some inspired by rural dissatisfaction at the government's failure to solve its economic problems – it became clear that the coalition was fast losing its hold on power and in May Mr Costello decided to go to the country.

The ensuing election was decisive in one sense, indecisive in another. Fianna Fáil only marginally improved its position, winning sixty-nine seats as against sixty-eight three years earlier. Had the other parties been able to agree among themselves as before, a new coalition might have resulted, led once again by Fine Gael which, with forty seats, had emerged from the election nine stronger than in 1948. But the dynamism which Clann na Poblachta had provided in the previous election was sadly lacking in 1951. The party was reduced from ten seats to two and, in view of its virtual extinction, the balance of power was held momentarily by the fourteen Independents. When the Dáil assembled they used that power (Dr Browne voting with them) to replace the coalition by Fianna Fáil.*

Yet, although Mr de Valera was thus able to form a government, it was always a minority government with little real stability. True, it lasted for nearly three years and, as we shall see later, made a determined attempt to grapple with some of the problems of social reform left unsolved by its predecessor, but like that predecessor, it was dogged from start to finish by inflation and an adverse balance of payments. Domestic politics in these years of stagnation came indeed to be dominated by an unending, and often ill-informed, debate about how the economic malaise could best be cured. Some clamoured loudly for 'repatriation' of sterling assets, others blamed the rising prices on excessive capital investment by the coalition, while amid the babel of conflicting voices the government dourly addressed itself to the bleak task of restoring financial probity through high taxation and reduced expenditure. Even in this it was not very successful, for while the country groaned under a tax burden that increased from £98 million to £103 million in the year 1953-4, public spending in the same period rose from £107 to £121 million.

* The distribution of seats in 1951 was as follows: Fianna Fáil, sixty-nine; Fine Gael, forty; Labour, sixteen; Clann na Talmhan, six; Clann na Poblachta, two; Independents, fourteen.

Inevitably, by-elections began (early in 1954) to go against Fianna Fáil, but Mr de Valera's usual conditioned reflex – to call another general election – did not produce its usual results. Whereas his own party dropped to sixty-five seats (its worst showing since 1932), Fine Gael improved strikingly from forty to fifty, while Labour recovered the three seats it had lost in 1951. Between them these two parties dominated the situation and were able without too much difficulty to construct another coalition government.* But it was far from being a replica of the old, either in composition or in energy. Admittedly, Mr Costello was again at its head and Mr Norton, as Minister for Industry and Commerce, was still his deputy; Mr Dillon presided as before over Agriculture, Mr Blowick over Lands and Fisheries and General Mulcahy over Education. Moreover, although Mr McGilligan was conspicuous by his absence, there were new names and rising reputations to be accommodated – notably Gerald Sweetman (Fine Gael) who took Mr McGilligan's place as Minister of Finance, Mr B. Corish (Labour) who became Minister of Social Welfare, and Mr Liam Cosgrave (Fine Gael) who filled Mr MacBride's old berth at the Ministry of External Affairs. This last appointment – through no fault of Mr Cosgrave's, who, indeed, made an admirable debut – revealed one fundamental weakness in the coalition's situation. Mr MacBride, though pledging support to the new government, refused to join it, and since Dr Browne for obvious reasons was not available either, much of the colour and initiative which had characterised the first coalition at its best was absent from the second.

As it turned out, this reconstructed inter-party government had but a short, bleak existence. No more than Fianna Fáil was it able to damp down inflation and its efforts to do so by the old conventional methods of cutting expenditure and increasing taxation brought it the same harvest of unpopularity that Mr de Valera and his colleagues had reaped in the previous three years. Furthermore, the new coalition had to contend with a much more critical domestic situation than the old. It had not been long in power before it was confronted by an ominous revival of IRA activities. This may in part have been a by-product of the years of economic stagnation, but it was connected both with the rise and the decline of Clann na Poblachta. During the first inter-party government, it was difficult for the police to deal as firmly as they had been in the habit of doing with the 'illegal organisation' while republicans were firmly entrenched in the citadels of power. Even the close co-operation that had grown up in the recent past between law-enforcement authorities on both sides of the border had necessarily languished when the fever of 'anti-partition' had been at its height. Under these circumstances, a new generation of extremist

* The distribution of seats in 1954 was: Fianna Fáil, sixty-five; Fine Gael, fifty; Labour, nineteen; Clann na Talmhan, five; Clann na Poblachta, three; Independents, five.

leaders found it relatively easy to regroup and rebuild. And although they might just conceivably have been prepared to hold their hand so long as Mr MacBride and his colleagues were in office, once that happy condition of affairs had ceased they were free to revert to the hallowed policy of trying by force to bring about the all-Ireland republic of their dreams. As early as 1952 arms raids on military barracks in Northern Ireland, and even England, signalled a return of violence. Not for the first time, activism, however extreme its methods and impracticable its aims, reawakened enthusiasm for the cause. Subscriptions multiplied, in America as well as in Ireland, and by 1956 the IRA felt strong enough to open a veritable campaign against police-barracks and other 'strategic' objectives. The government, though unwilling to take special powers to deal with this fresh outbreak, had no option but to use the due process of the existing law against those who were bringing the gun back into politics. Although time was to show that more drastic methods were required, Mr Costello soon found that those he did use were too drastic to command the support he needed in the Dáil. Early in 1957, his administration was suddenly faced with a vote of no confidence moved by none other than Mr MacBride. The ostensible basis of the motion was a condemnation of the government's failure either to unify the country or to achieve an acceptable level of prosperity in that part of it for which ministers were responsible.* But Mr Costello, looking back ten years later, had little doubt that a no less significant factor influencing Mr MacBride's withdrawal of support was the attitude taken by the coalition towards the IRA.[29]

Whether this was the crucial factor, or whether, as is more likely, the government fell because of an accumulation of infirmities, it is impossible yet to decide with any real certainty. What is indisputable is that it not only fell but in doing so opened the way for a new chapter in the political dominance of Fianna Fáil. In the general election which followed in March 1957 Mr de Valera's party swept into power with a total of seats (seventy-eight) which freed it from humiliating dependence on any other party. Fine Gael sank back to its 1951 figure of forty seats, Labour was reduced from nineteen to thirteen, and Clann na Talmhan from five to three. Independent representation improved slightly from five to eight, but this modest advance was completely overshadowed by two other results. One was the virtual obliteration of Clann na Poblachta as an electoral force. It polled a beggarly 22,000 votes and though this was enough to allow it to

---

* It is only fair to point out that the coalition did have some success in closing the trade gap, in fact reducing the balance of payments deficit from £35 million in 1955 to £14 million in 1956. But to achieve even these results it had to resort to such draconian devices – for example, stringent import levies – that it seemed at the time only to be adding to the general sum of dreariness without offering any real hope of future improvement.

salvage one seat from the wreckage, that seat was not occupied by Mr MacBride.* His strange venture into Irish politics was to all appearances over, and before long he was to be found carving out a new career as Secretary-General of the International Commission of Jurists. The other new phenomenon which the election produced was the return of four Sinn Féin members. True to the traditional policy of their party, they refused to take their seats in the Dáil, but that they should have captured as many as four constituencies was a warning that could not much longer be ignored. Either there must be a rapid and perceptible improvement in the country's general situation, or the bankruptcy of the existing leaders, and perhaps even of the existing parties, would be manifest, with incalculable consequences for the peace and stability of the country.

In fact, as is already evident at this short distance of time, the general election of 1957 was, so far as such things can be, a turning-point in the recent history of Ireland. Admittedly, this was not immediately apparent. Mr de Valera, though then seventy-five years of age, once more took office as Taoiseach and gathered round him a team of seeming Bourbons, the very roll-call of whose names sounded as if the party had learnt nothing and forgotten nothing in the two and a half decades since it had first come to power. Yet in reality this was not so. Between 1957 and the next election in 1961 the situation was transformed in four important respects. First, the government acted promptly to deal with the activities of the IRA. The detention camp at The Curragh which had been used to detain activists during the war was reopened for the same purpose, and in July 1957 the notorious Part II of the Offences against the State Act was reintroduced, thus giving the government power to arrest and detain without trial. By the end of the year 100 people were interned in the south and perhaps twice that number in the north, where a combination of firm police action and remarkable civilian restraint gradually enabled the authorities to get the upper hand. It was a slow and painful process – the IRA did not abandon its campaign officially until 1962 – but there can be little doubt that in the Republic the evident readiness of the government to act ruthlessly whenever necessary brought the situation under control much more quickly than in the six counties.

A policy of simple repression, however, would hardly in itself have sufficed to deal with the growing unrest and discontent in the country. More constructive, and ultimately far more important, was the second major innovation of these years – the long-awaited leap forward into an era of unimagined – if, as events turned out, precarious – prosperity. Ironically enough this was in part a legacy of the second inter-party government. Preoccupied, as the earlier one had been, with the problem of how best to obtain and to deploy capital, it had

* The subsequent electoral history of Clann na Poblachta is soon told. It secured one seat at each of the elections of 1961 and 1965 and thereafter vanished from the scene.

appointed a Capital Advisory Committee which had not been long in existence before it urged that a programme for economic development should be drawn up with a view to directing investment, especially public investment, into productive channels. The coalition collapsed before any such report could be produced, but by a curious chance it bequeathed to its successors the man most capable of drafting such a document. This was a civil servant, T. K. Whitaker, who, at the early age of forty, had been selected in 1956 by the Minister of Finance, Gerald Sweetman, to fill the key post of secretary of his department. He did not begin work on the report until late in 1957 but then, with direct encouragement from his new political masters in Fianna Fáil, wrote it so rapidly that it was published in May of the following year, forming the basis for the Programme for Economic Expansion adopted by the government in November 1958. The well-nigh revolutionary implications of this new expansionist outlook will be considered later in this book.* Here it is sufficient to stress the psychological rather than the economic consequences of what was happening. In place of the old orthodoxies and the old introspection, Ireland seemed at last to be moving towards participation in the world of the mid-twentieth century. The new emphases on attracting foreign capital, developing a wider range of exports, modernising agriculture, were all designed to lift the country out of its nerveless dependence on external factors over which it had no control, and to accustom it to exercising independent judgment and initiative. Of course, there were hazards as well as advantages in this policy, and the decade of the 'sixties was to show that the economy was far from rolling forward on oiled castors. Moreover, although the Irish government did seem to speak with a more individual voice than formerly in matters of trade and finance, it could not escape the inexorable lesson of geography – that as a small and not very wealthy island it was bound to go on being deeply affected by the economic vicissitudes of its near neighbour and biggest customer, Britain, and also by the changing pattern in the larger entity of Western Europe, of which, however humble and remote, it remained inescapably a part. Yet, even though expansion for Ireland in the circumstances of the time could only mean involvement – to be expressed not just in renewed Anglo-Irish trade agreements, but in aspirations towards the Common Market – this does not alter the fact that after the Whitaker Report the former aimlessness and hopelessness had begun to give way to a drive and optimism previously unknown.

Of course, this could not have come about through the work of one man, or on the basis of a single document. It was only made possible by reason of the third of the changes we have to consider in these crowded years. This was the final replacement of the old guard by the rising generation of Fianna Fáil politicians. In 1959 Mr de Valera at last retired from the active leadership of his country, though not from

* See below, chap. 4, section v.

public life. The manner of his going was strange, but not uncharacteristic. Early in the year the Senate, normally a docile enough assembly, braced itself to reject a government proposal to hold a referendum with a view to abolishing proportional representation. Since the rejection amounted to no more than a ninety-days suspension, the Bill eventually became law and the referendum was fixed for 17 June. By a piece of rather too obvious sleight of hand the presidential election which fell that year was arranged for the same day, and to drive the point home to anyone obtuse enough not to have grasped it already, Mr de Valera stood as, in effect, the Fianna Fáil candidate. He was successful – defeating an old rival, General Sean MacEoin, by 538,000 votes to 417,536 – but the electorate refused to play politics with proportional representation and the government proposal was defeated.*

Mr de Valera's removal to Phoenix Park – where, up to the time of writing, he has filled the office of President with great dignity and distinction for two full terms – left the way open for a complete reconstruction of the government. The bridge with the past essential for a party with its roots deep in the conservative countryside was provided by the new Taoiseach, Mr Sean Lemass. Although he had had to wait for the highest office until he was almost sixty, his political education had commenced at the age of sixteen when he was one of those who occupied the General Post Office. He fought on the anti-Treaty side in the Civil War, but had followed de Valera after the latter opted for constitutional politics in 1927. When Fianna Fáil took office five years later, Mr Lemass served as Minister for Industry and Commerce, rapidly earning a reputation for ruthless efficiency which was formidably enhanced by his performance as Minister of Supplies in the difficult years of the emergency. Scarcely less significant was the fact that he had been the principal architect, with Gerald Boland, of Fianna Fáil's constituency organisation – generally regarded as far superior to that of its rivals – and that he was personally responsible for the reconstruction and revival of the party after the defeat of 1948, with consequences which are still making themselves felt to this day. Intelligent, pragmatic, with an almost instinctive understanding of economic problems (he could have made his fortune many times over in private business), the new Taoiseach was admirably equipped to preside over a period of rapid expansion. It is no mere exercise in public relations which links his name indissolubly with the forward policy of these years. To his predecessor, Dr James Ryan, and to Mr de Valera himself, may belong the credit for the initially favourable reception the government gave to the Whitaker Report, but the responsibility of implementing it fell squarely upon Mr Lemass. Characteristically, he shared it with a group of able young

* Reintroduced in 1968 by another referendum the proposal was once more rejected and it seems unlikely that proportional representation will be challenged again in the near future.

men who between them were to take over the direction of the party after his own retirement from the leadership in 1966, having fought and won two further leases of power for Fianna Fáil in 1961 and 1965.* From this group — which included his successor, Jack Lynch, his son-in-law Charles Haughey, P. J. Hillery, Brian Lenihan, George Colley and the late Donough O'Malley — were to be drawn the makers of policy in the 'sixties and, it may well be, far into the 'seventies as well.

The advent of a new generation in Fianna Fáil was matched by similar developments in the other two main parties. General Mulcahy retired from the leadership of Fine Gael within a few months of Mr de Valera leaving Fianna Fáil for the Presidency. His successor, Mr James Dillon, who had rejoined Fine Gael in 1952, served for that party the same function of bridging the present and the past as Mr Lemass did for Fianna Fáil. But whereas Mr Lemass, dominant as always over his colleagues, was able to look to the future right up to the moment of his resignation, Mr Dillon had a much more difficult task in trying to hold together a party which, while retaining its middle-class conservative bias, was under pressure from some of its younger supporters to change with the times. For a while it seemed that the mantle of power would descend on Mr Costello's son, Declan Costello, a young barrister who in the early 'sixties attempted to convert the party to a more progressive social policy. The embodiment of that policy — the programme called *The Just Society* — was, however, accepted by Fine Gael only a few weeks before the general election of 1965, and the reluctance of the electorate to swallow reforms which the protagonists themselves had quite evidently only half-digested, did much to reinforce the conservative leanings of the party. The younger Costello subsequently withdrew from politics and in 1965, when Mr James Dillon suddenly resigned the leadership, it passed to Liam Cosgrave, son of the perdurable politician who had seen the Free State through its first and stormiest decade. It should be said, though, that Fine Gael has shown greater resilience than this brief account would indicate

* In the process, however, Fianna Fáil lost its unassailable majority and held office with Independent support. At the most recent election (1969) it succeeded in the face of strong opposition and against all the odds in retrieving its independence of all other parties in the Dáil. The tenacity of its hold on power may be due partly to the very wide spectrum of support it can draw on — from a section of the farming community, from shopkeepers, from industrialists, and also from many who look to it for improved social services — but it is no doubt a product, too, of the fact that power generates its own momentum; in a country like Ireland, where patronage has always had an important function in government, to be in office is a great help towards staying in office. It would seem also that in 1969 the redrawing of constituency boundaries ensured for Fianna Fáil a 'bonus', estimated — admittedly by one of its opponents — as five or six more seats than it might otherwise have expected to win. (G. Fitz-Gerald, *Towards a New Ireland* (London, 1972), p. 43.)

and that the party has continued to attract some of the best minds in the country; an opposition front bench which includes Dr Garret FitzGerald cannot be considered less than formidable.

Almost simultaneously a change had taken place in the leadership of the Labour party when in 1961 the veteran William Norton gave place to a much younger man, Brendan Corish. It may be, though, that in the long run a much more significant event was Dr Noel Browne's decision in 1963 to throw in his lot with Labour. After his dramatic departure from the inter-party government in 1951, he had taken temporary and somewhat uncomfortable shelter with Fianna Fáil which ended with his defeat in the election of 1954. Thereafter, he attempted to establish a party of his own, the National Progressive Democrats, but lacked the funds to build up any permanent organisation. His joining Labour in 1963 may have seemed at the time an act of political desperation, for that party was still far to the right of Dr Browne's own socialist standpoint. Three years later, however, the party formally pledged itself to 'a coherent, socialist philosophy'. In the evolution of that policy not only Dr Browne, but other intellectuals who had descried in Labour the only hope for a new radicalism – for example, Dr Conor Cruise O'Brien, Dr David Thornley and Mr Justin Keating – have played and are playing, especially since their election to the Dáil in 1969, an increasing part.* At the time of writing (summer, 1972) the Labour party appears to be in some disarray. This is partly because of differences of opinion between Dr Thornley and some of his colleagues over the crisis in Northern Ireland and, perhaps more fundamentally, because the urban radicalism of the intellectuals is rather strong medicine for a party which still draws its main support from non-industrial sources and which for that reason sometimes gives the appearance of being obliged to sail at the speed of the slowest ship in its variegated convoy.

The three developments here briefly summarised – the restoration

* This formidable accretion of intellectual strength has not yet been matched by a comparable increase in voting-power. Between 1965 and 1969 Labour representation in the Dáil declined from twenty-two to eighteen and at the general election in the latter year the Labour party could do no better than hold its figure at eighteen, compared with Fianna Fáil (seventy-five) and Fine Gael (fifty) – the remaining seat going to an Independent. This may simply mean that the electorate has not yet had time to evaluate the changed character of the Labour party, but it underlines the continuing difficulty of a workers' party in establishing itself in a country where the industrial population is still relatively small. For two interesting recent prognostications about the party's future, see M. Viney and O. Dudley Edwards 'Parties and Power', in O. Dudley Edwards (ed.), *Conor Cruise O'Brien Introduces Ireland* (London, 1969), pp. 95-103; and C. Cruise O'Brien, 'Ireland, 1969', in *Irish Times*, supplement, 21 Jan. 1969. Dr Browne's role as a socialist pioneer is perceptively analysed by M. McInerney, 'Noel Browne: Church and State', in *University Review*, vol. v, no. 2 (summer, 1968).

of public order, the new economic policy, the emergence of a new generation in politics – together pointed towards a fourth development which time may show to have been the most important of all. No one who has lived in Ireland, or studied Irish conditions, in recent decades can have failed to realise that, at least until the political explosion of 1968-9 in Northern Ireland, the Republic had begun to turn its back upon the legacy of bitterness bequeathed to it by the partition of the country and the Civil War. So far as the first of these is concerned, the exchange of visits between the two Prime Ministers of north and south (Captain Terence O'Neill and Mr Lemass) in 1965 – the first such exchange since the division of the island has become an accomplished fact – was widely seen at the time as an indication that old animosities were quietly being laid aside. And though the recent revival of sectarian and political violence in Ulster had obviously shattered the accord which seemed to have been established five years ago (the accord itself, indeed, may have contributed to Captain O'Neill's fall from power in 1969), a longer perspective may yet reveal that the precedent then established offers a foundation on which to build if, but only if, a profoundly altered regime should emerge from the present turmoil in Northern Ireland.

The crisis in the six counties – apart from the appalling dangers it holds for all those directly involved in it – carries also, of course, the risk that, if it intensifies, the hard-won stability of the other twenty-six may also be disrupted. Indeed, there have been signs that this is already happening. That the exponents of physical force, the IRA, should have been deeply stirred by what was happening in the north was only to be expected; and that their movement should rapidly have split – between the 'official' IRA who have so far tended towards caution, and the 'provisional' who have been clamant for thoroughgoing intervention – was also predictable. But potentially more serious are the stresses and strains which have emerged within the governing party in the Republic. Firm evidence, naturally, is still lacking, but there are strong indications of deep divisions in the cabinet over the question of whether or not the Republic should have taken more direct and positive action when the Ulster situation deteriorated so disastrously in August 1969. More recently still, in May 1970, the Taoiseach, Mr Lynch, was faced with an even graver crisis which led to the resignation of two ministers, Mr M. O'Morain and Mr K. Boland, and the dismissal of two others, Mr Charles Haughey and Mr Neil Blaney. The two dismissed ministers' names had been persistently mentioned in connection with an alleged plot – in which the IRA was rumoured to have been involved – to smuggle arms into Northern Ireland, with the obvious intention that these would find their way into nationalist hands, and one of them, Mr Haughey, was brought to trial on charges arising out of the allegations. He was subsequently acquitted, but this was far from being the end of the crisis. As the northern situation steadily worsened between 1970 and 1972 there were many occasions when it seemed that Mr Lynch must fall from power, either because of his inability to bridle the private armies of the IRA, or because the unity of his party was subjected to almost intolerable strain. In fact, despite resignations, expulsions, and the formation by Mr Boland in 1971 of a new party, Aontacht Eireann, calculated to appeal especially to Fianna Fáil dissidents, Mr Lynch has so far managed to survive. It is true that early in 1972, after the shooting of thirteen people in Derry city on 'Bloody Sunday' (30 January) as a result of action by Paratroops, and the subsequent burning of the British embassy in Dublin by an infuriated crowd, Anglo-Irish relations reached their lowest ebb for many years.* Yet within a few months of these grave events Mr Lynch registered three successes which would have been unthinkable at the beginning of the year. These were the establishment of special courts in an endeavour to deal with the gunmen; the winning at the referendum of 10 May of a crushing victory in favour of entry into the European Economic Community† and, in August 1972 the retention, again by a large majority, of a crucial seat, thus enabling Fianna Fáil to maintain a precarious lead over the combined forces of the Fine Gael and Labour.‡

The fact remains, nevertheless, that in existing circumstances Mr Lynch's options in regard to the northern crisis are distinctly limited. Given the past record of his own party (and, it would seem, the present inclinations of a section of it), together with the absence of sufficient force, or sufficiently reliable force, in the Republic to deal with the IRA, there appears to be little he can do save to maintain his contacts with the main opposition party (the Social and Democratic Labour Party) in the north, to seek to strengthen the rule of law at home, and to bring to bear in London whatever pressure is open to him for a conference aimed at producing a permanent and all-Ireland solution. But the future is so dark and uncertain that only one firm conclusion can be drawn at the present time. It is surely this – that different though the paths of north and south have been in the last fifty years, the demands of blood and history are still insistent; the island remains one island, and neither part of it can fail to be vitally affected by what happens in the other.

* For the events of 'Bloody Sunday', see below pp. 778-9.

† In a poll of about seventy per cent of the total electorate, just over a million votes were cast in favour of entry and almost 212,000 against. In each of the 42 constituencies there was a majority of over 70 per cent of those voting in favour.

‡ The traumatic experiences of the last two years have helped to whittle away the *overall* majority Mr Lynch won at the general election of 1969. In August 1972, after the Mid-Cork by-election, party strength was as follows: Fianna Fáil 70, Fine Gael 51, Labour 17, Independents (of various shades) 6.

War-time neutrality, most Irishmen would agree, had been a blessing to their country. But it was a blessing that had to be paid for, not merely in terms of a stagnant, or even retrogressive economy, but in terms of increasing psychological as well as physical isolation. Although Ireland could not be completely unaware of the new world that was coming so painfully to birth between 1939 and 1945 – Dublin, as we have seen, ranked with Lisbon as one of the key listening-posts in Europe for allied and axis powers alike – none of those who experienced what life was like in the twenty-six counties during the emergency years are ever likely to forget the intense introspection and gathering sense of unreality which geography, policy and censorship together conspired to produce.

Once hostilities had ended there was, of course, a reaction. People who had been starved for so long of contact with other countries were eager to renew their links with what had once passed for civilisation and even to play a part in building a new international polity on the ruins of the old. For individuals, it is true, the difficulties of travelling far afield, especially to the war-battered countries of Western Europe, meant that the process of emerging from isolation was a slow one, but at the government level involvement was more rapid. The reasons for this were partly political, partly economic. The economic reason was simply that, as we saw earlier, the effort to overcome the shortage of houses, fuel and manufactures caused by the war, together with the natural impulse of consumers to buy greedily whatever was available, had combined by 1947 to produce a major financial crisis. In consequence, Ireland soon found herself in the queue for Marshall Aid and, on receiving it, was inexorably caught up in the machinery of European economic reconstruction, becoming in due course a member of the Organisation for European Economic Co-operation. Participation in this sphere of post-war activity brought with it two advantages. In the short run, Ireland benefited immediately and massively from American aid which by 1950 amounted to nearly 150 million dollars in grants and loans.* But in the long run, and even more important, the country was brought into close contact with other European states, large and small, at a period when economic stringency was giving place to economic expansion and when new techniques of economic analysis and planning, as well as new extensions

* It could be argued, of course, that the injection of this amount of unearned capital into the economy not only created a false sense of security, but also, where it was not deployed on genuinely productive enterprise (and this sometimes happened) helped to intensify the inflation that became a never-ending feature of those years. But even the critics of Marshall Aid have not cared to contemplate what life would have been like without it.

of state enterprise, were being widely adopted. For the Irish economy this was both a chastening and exhilarating experience. Chastening because, as the early OEEC reports on Ireland made icily clear, standards of productivity and efficiency were among the lowest in Europe, but exhilarating also because the links with Europe, and even the opprobrious reports themselves, brought with them the possibility of change and improvement, opening the way for the genuine and sustained advance that came at the end of the 1950s.

If the economic motives for Ireland's increased participation in international affairs stemmed from her wartime experience, so also, though more obliquely, did the political ones. The neutrality of the country, as Mr de Valera had shaped and defined it even before the war had broken out, had been an expression, one might say the ultimate expression, of Irish independence. During the struggle itself, however, and especially after the entry of the United States into the war, it became necessary to find a more cogent and specific reason to explain why Ireland was not fighting by the side of the great country to which she had in the past contributed so much of her own blood. The reason which was advanced was the reason most likely to find favour with Americans in general and Irish-Americans in particular – that Ireland, as herself, a truncated state, could not join a grand alliance of which Britain, the power ostensibly responsible for the partition of the country, was a leading member.[30]

There is no reason to doubt the genuineness of this argument – however little ice it may have cut with critics like Churchill who, understandably obsessed with the strategic implications of Irish neutrality, remained obstinately blind to the connection between that neutrality and events in which he himself had played no inconsiderable part – but it had one consequence that in retrospect can only be seen as unfortunate. The linking of neutrality with partition served within Ireland to reanimate the whole issue of the border to such a degree that by 1945 the reunification of the country had come to seem for many well-intentioned people, both inside and outside official circles, the keystone of whatever tremulous arch of foreign policy the government might seek to throw across the chasm that separated a small neutral from the recently belligerent powers. And so it came about, with an irony that might have been ludicrous had it not had tragic undertones, that at the very moment when the rude surgery of partition was being used all over the world to 'solve' problems that had shown themselves insoluble, at the very moment when Europe itself was being partitioned by the Iron Curtain, the Irish signalled their return to the comity of nations by what was intended to be a powerful propaganda drive to awaken the conscience of the world to the plight of their sundered country. What began as an uproar of voluntary bodies – among which the Anti-Partition League that emerged early in 1947 was perhaps the most vociferous – became, however, much more serious when Mr de Valera fell from power in 1948 and proceeded to use his enforced leisure to conduct a tour of the United States, Australia and Britain, devoting countless speeches and the whole force of his formidable personality to 'anti-partition'.

Where Mr de Valera led, the inter-party government which had succeeded him in office could ill afford not to follow. The ending of partition was, of course, an article of faith with that government and although, as we have seen, the declaration of the republic scarcely contributed to this end, the unofficial propaganda campaign rapidly became official. Irish representatives at international gatherings were instructed to pursue what has since been aptly, if inelegantly, called 'the policy of the sore thumb' – that is, the raising of the partition issue on every conceivable occasion with the double aim of embarrassing Britain and enlisting foreign sympathy for the Irish case. But if Britain was embarrassed (which is doubtful) her embarrassment was as nothing compared with that of some of the able and intelligent Irishmen who were condemned to walk this futile treadmill.* Nor is there much evidence to show that foreign sympathy was in fact enlisted to any marked degree. At Strasbourg certainly, where Ireland became a founder member of the Council of Europe in 1949 and used the Assembly for some years thereafter as one of the main platforms for anti-partition speeches, the reaction among other delegates seems to have been one of boredom mingled with bewilderment.

But, there was one sphere in which this generally unproductive policy did directly affect – and still affects – the status of Ireland in the western world. As international tension was accentuated in the immediate aftermath of the war and the threat of a renewed communist advance across Europe seemed to become steadily more imminent, there emerged not just a local alliance of the powers that felt themselves to be in particular danger – the Brussels Pact of 1948 – but a larger grouping, the North Atlantic Treaty Organisation, which came into being the next year. There were many reasons why Ireland might have been attracted into the orbit of NATO. Geographically, she was an integral part of the Atlantic community. Ideologically, she was as deeply opposed to communism as any member of the Alliance and did not even maintain diplomatic relations with the Soviet Union. Politically, the cohesive power of NATO and its military effective-

* The chief of them, Dr Conor Cruise O'Brien, has written recently that he 'blushes to recall' the amount of his professional time that was devoted between 1947 and 1951 to 'anti-partition'. 'The only positive result of this activity, so far as I was concerned [he adds] was that it led me to discover the cavernous inanities of "anti-partition" and of government propaganda generally.' (C. Cruise O'Brien, 'The Embers of Easter', in O. Dudley Edwards and F. Pyle (ed.), *1916: The Easter Rising*, p. 233.) It is fair to add, however, that once the anti-partition fever was over, Ireland became a model member of the Council of Europe, being the first country to accept the jurisdiction of the European Court of Human Rights.

ness were alike supplied by the United States, of all powers the one with which Ireland might have been expected to be most *en rapport*.

Yet, despite these inducements, Ireland declined the invitation to join the alliance. The decision not to accept was taken in the first instance by the inter-party government and it was a decision which may well have been directly influenced by the charter of that government. Had the senior partner in the coalition – Fine Gael – commanded sufficient seats in the Dáil to allow it to dispense with the inter-party arrangement and rule independently, its history and inclinations might well have taken it into NATO. But in practice Fine Gael had little freedom of manoeuvre. This was partly because it depended so heavily on the support of Clann na Poblachta, which, being almost by definition a party wedded to the concept of ending partition, would have found it difficult to sanction membership of an alliance wherein the 'author' of that partition, Britain, took a prominent part. Partly also, of course, the inter-party government as a whole, and not merely Mr MacBride's segment of it, was bound to fight shy of NATO, if only because it could not appear to be less intransigent on the subject of the border than Mr de Valera, then busily engaged in 'putting an anti-partition girdle round the earth'.[31]

Accordingly, when in February 1949 Mr MacBride, as Minister for External Affairs, was asked in the Dáil about the government's attitude to the Atlantic alliance then taking shape he was able to make this categorical reply: 'As long as partition lasts, any military alliance or commitment involving joint military action with the state responsible for partition must be quite out of the question as far as Ireland is concerned.'[32] The same answer, more impersonally worded, was returned to the formal invitation to join the alliance, with the rider that to join any military grouping of which Britain was a member would be to expose the Irish government to the risk of civil conflict within its own jurisdiction. For Ireland, it was made plain, the correct approach to North Atlantic security must involve the ending of a situation which was a standing threat to the peace of Britain and Ireland alike.[33]

The decision once made has never been reversed. Nor is this surprising. Apart from a second brief spell of inter-party government between 1954 and 1957, Fianna Fáil has remained continuously in power from 1951 until the time of writing. For much of that period the ideas of Mr de Valera remained dominant and these ideas – which in matters of foreign policy had acquired exceptional authority in the light of Ireland's wartime experience – continued to revolve round the doctrine of neutrality. But it was, nevertheless, neutrality with a difference. At the time of a great world conflict to stand aside had seemed the last, desperate resource open to a small nation, a gamble that had to be taken against the odds, and which paid off largely for reasons outside the control of the government. But in the Cold War which developed in the decade after the fighting had ended, neutrality, or neutralism as it was becoming fashionable to call it, had gained respectability as a way of life, almost a philosophy of international relations, for those countries – especially the 'emergent nations' of Asia and Africa – which had no desire to be caught up in-great-power politics. Individually, their desires were doubtless of little account, but what gave them more weight than they would otherwise have had – though even that was hardly excessive – was the existence of the United Nations which, from its war-time beginnings as an attempt to give the victorious alliance some permanent status, had emerged in and after 1945 as the successor to the League of Nations.

Ireland, as a small power which had taken an honourable part in the affairs of the defunct League, might have been expected to be one of the first to apply for membership of the new organisation. And in fact such application was duly made in August 1946, to be at once vetoed by the Soviet Union on the ground that that country had no diplomatic relations with the applicant. Subsequent attempts to gain admission were regularly vetoed in the same way (though this did not apply to Irish membership of the specialised agencies of the United Nations) and it was not until after the 'package deal' of 1955 that Ireland, along with numerous other countries from both sides of the Iron Curtain, took her seat in the session of 1956, the session racked by the simultaneous Suez and Hungarian crises. The head of the Irish delegation was Mr F. H. Boland, a sagacious and experienced diplomatist who was at the time of his appointment the permanent head of the Foreign Service. That service had been much expanded over the years, notably by Mr MacBride between 1948 and 1951, and it now contained a considerable number of able young men, an astonishingly high proportion of whom were simultaneously making reputations as poets, critics and historians.

The appearance of this versatile delegation at the United Nations coincided with the brief term of office of the second inter-party government and it fell to Mr Liam Cosgrave, as Minister for External Affairs, to lay down the guiding-lines of Irish policy. The policy he enunciated – and in the formulation of which it may be conjectured his permanent officials took their share – was based upon what Dr Cruise O'Brien, at that time one of those officials, has described as the 'three principles'. Briefly, these were: first, scrupulous fidelity to the obligations of the Charter; second, that Ireland should try to maintain an independent stance, with the intention 'to avoid becoming associated with particular blocs or groups so far as possible'; but finally, and notwithstanding the second principle, Ireland was to do what she could to preserve Christian civilisation and to support wherever she could those powers primarily charged with the defence of 'the free world' against communism. 'We belong', as Mr Cosgrave observed in the Dáil, 'to the great community of states made up of the United States, Canada and Western Europe.'[34]

How far this third principle seriously compromised the second principle remained to be seen, though not to be seen by Mr Cosgrave who, with the fall of the inter-party government, gave place to Mr Frank Aiken. Mr Aiken, who became Minister of External Affairs in 1957 and retained the office until his retirement from politics in 1969, was one of Mr de Valera's oldest associates – old enough, certainly, to recall that his leader's reputation at Geneva before the war had been based on the independent attitude he had then so clearly displayed. That attitude Mr Aiken was prepared to try to reproduce in New York. For several years he did so with remarkable success and the Irish delegation – intelligent, articulate, extremely well-prepared – played a part in the world of the Assembly far out of proportion to the size or international importance of their country. One has only to read the speeches the Minister delivered between 1957 and 1961 – some of them on issues still as crucial as when he first addressed himself to them – to understand the extent to which a genuinely Irish foreign policy was beginning to emerge during those years. In some respects – as, for example, in the annual plea that Mr Aiken made for the nonproliferation of nuclear weapons – it was a policy common to all small, exposed countries. In other respects, again, in its generally anti-colonialist tone, it was a policy Ireland shared with the new Afro-Asian states and to which Mr Aiken was able to give an historical depth denied to all save, perhaps, the Americans:

We know [he said in 1960] what imperialism is and what resistance to it involves. We do not hear with indifference the voices of those spokesmen of African and Asian countries who passionately champion the right to independence of millions who are still, unfortunately, under foreign rule . . . More than eighty years ago the then leader of the Irish nation, Charles Stewart Parnell, proclaimed the principle that 'the cause of nationality is sacred, in Asia and Africa as in Ireland'. That is still a basic principle of our political thinking in Ireland today, as it was with those of my generation who felt impelled to assert in arms the right of our country to independence.[35]

But there was a sense in which Irish policy at the United Nations in those early years went beyond concern with nuclear proliferation or even with anti-colonialism. The test case was China – more precisely, whether the question of the admission of the People's Republic of China ('Red China') ought or ought not to be discussed in the Assembly. For a small neutral this was a potentially explosive issue, since American influence was totally committed to reserving the Chinese place in the Assembly and on the Security Council for the Chiang Kai Shek regime based on Formosa. As early as 1957 the Irish vote was cast with the minority which favoured such discussion, and although American pressure was at once brought to bear in a manner which

Dr Cruise O'Brien has amusingly described, Mr Aiken returned to the charge repeatedly between then and 1961.[36]

Not surprisingly, his independence exposed him to attack from two quite different directions. Critics in America – and some in Ireland also – refused to recognise that there was an important difference between *discussing* Chinese representation and voting for the admission of 'Red China'. Yet when in 1955 Mr Aiken showed that there could be a very real difference by coupling a renewed plea for discussion with a strong condemnation of recent Chinese aggression in Tibet, he was at once assailed by the Soviet Union with the accusation that in raising the Tibetan question he was acting at the behest of another [i.e. the American] delegation. Not at all, he replied: 'We believe that whenever the rights of a small people are forcibly violated in this manner, the representatives of other small peoples in this Assembly have the duty to speak out.' And later in the same session, again referring to China's violation of human rights, he made in effect the same point that Litvinov had made long ago in the League of Nations, that peace is indivisible:

If the Assembly [he said in October 1959] demonstrates that it is prepared to condemn wholesale violations of human rights, wherever they are perpetrated, it will be maintaining intact that invisible but effective barrier against further acts of aggression which is constituted by a vigilant world public opinion. If, on the other hand, it chooses to ignore a flagrant denial of human rights to an entire people, then it weakens that barrier and must render further violations of human rights a little easier and a little more likely.[37]

In practice, it must be admitted, Irish speeches in the Assembly, however eloquent and however independent, were unlikely to have a very direct effect upon the course of world affairs. In some spheres – notably the prevention of nuclear proliferation – Mr Aiken's initiatives were indeed made the basis for serious discussion, but this could not hide the stark and disagreeable fact that in a world of giants pigmies have only a limited role to play. And although Ireland, known to be both anti-colonialist and anti-communist, was better placed than most to follow a neutralist policy, it became increasingly difficult to do so as time went on. By 1961, certainly there were clear signs that the second and third principles of Irish policy at the United Nations were at last beginning to demonstrate their incompatibility, and this at a time when 'second principle' forces inside the Irish delegation were weakened by the resignation of Dr Cruise O'Brien, following his experiences in the Congo.* In the session of that year, faced with a situation where the China question was at last

* Dr Cruise O'Brien had been selected in 1961 by the then Secretary-General of the United Nations, Dag Hammarskjöld, to represent the organisation in Katanga with a view to ending the secession of that

on the agenda (the United States having already manoeuvred the Chinese into declaring that they did not recognise the Charter or regard previous decisions of the United Nations as binding) Mr Aiken went on record as not being prepared to support China's admission until her government gave guarantees against further aggression, withdrew from Korea and respected the rights and liberties of the Chinese people. Since the guarantees were not forthcoming there was no longer anything to prevent the Irish delegation from voting on this matter in the same lobby as the United States.

That this perceptible movement towards 'westernism' was not an isolated phenomenon was made almost brutally clear the following year when the Taoiseach, Mr Lemass, carried his party with him at its annual conference in a speech which saluted the United States as the guardian of the 'free world', while at the same time condemning the communist bloc in language that would have been music to the ears of John Foster Dulles had he lived to hear it. The American orientation which this implied was greatly reinforced by the triumphant visit of President Kennedy to Ireland in the summer of 1963, and the bond of sympathy between the two countries which he then established or renewed was not to be broken even by his assassination a few months later.

Nevertheless, despite the strong gravitational pull exerted by Washington, the limitations of the Irish role at the United Nations should not be overemphasised. Even if there had been a shift from 'second principle' to 'third principle' (and the extent of that shift may have been exaggerated) Ireland remained a conscientious and generally respected member of the organisation. She showed this most effectively not in words but in deeds, by assuming on several occasions the burdensome duty of contributing a contingent of troops to the United Nations peace-keeping forces. It is true that these excursions provided occupation for an otherwise unemployed army which the troops themselves gratefully seized upon as giving meaning to their existence, but the Congo episode of 1960 showed that something more than a military promenade could be involved. In the summer of that year an

province from the central government. The story of his mission – at first seemingly successful, but ultimately abortive – and the whole strange train of events that led to his own resignation and Hammarskjöld's death belong to international history and to the biographies of the principal figures involved. They have no place in this narrative, though it is relevant to point out that the affair had a powerful impact in Ireland, where, apart from providing a superb opportunity for Irishmen to indulge their national habit of taking sides *con brio*, it helped to bring home to a startled public both the extent of their country's involvement in world affairs and the risks inherent in playing for such large stakes. Dr Cruise O'Brien's account of the crisis is in his book, '*To Katanga and Back*. To this fascinating, though necessarily subjective, record should be added his recently published play, *Murderous Angels* (New York and London, 1969).

Irish force was sent out to join the United Nations troops of whom General Sean MacEoin was the commander-in-chief. A few months later a party of these Irish soldiers was ambushed by Baluba tribesmen, and ten men were killed. The shock to Irish public opinion was intense, but despite a rumour (happily unfounded) nearly a year later that a much larger Irish force had been massacred at Jadotville, the country did not retreat, and has not retreated, into isolationism.* On the contrary, not only have Irish troops continued to serve overseas – in Cyprus, for example, or Kashmir – but at the United Nations itself the Irish delegation as recently as 1965 put forward drastic amendments to the existing methods of financing peace-keeping operations. These were designed to ensure that the permanent members of the Security Council who had approved of a given operation should assume responsibility for seventy per cent of the cost, the remaining thirty per cent to be provided by other member-states, in the proportion of twenty-five per cent from the wealthier, and five per cent from the poorer, countries. Predictably, this proposal fell foul of the Security Council and has not yet been found acceptable; in consequence, and as a protest against the voluntary system of financing these operations which still prevailed, Ireland decided to pay for a time the cost of its Cyprus contingent out of its own exchequer.[38]

In the last analysis, however, the chief beneficiary from the new international role of Ireland may not have been the Congolese or the Cypriots but the Irish themselves. Although no doubt there is still considerable indifference to foreign affairs in the country. There is at the same time an increasing awareness of the smallness and oneness of the world and a growing realisation that to opt out from that world, or to sit by the turf-fire crooning over ancient and still unrectified grievances, is no longer possible. Partly, no doubt, this increased awareness is a result of the tendency of people to go abroad for their holidays far more than before, but it is also an inevitable outcome of the country's heady, if sometimes chastening, experiences at the United Nations. Without these experiences it might have been much more difficult than it actually proved for the government to take a further step – perhaps the most crucial step of all – when on 1 August 1961 Mr Lemass announced that Ireland would apply for membership of the European Economic Community. The fact that she subsequently shared in the rebuffs administered to Britain by General de Gaulle may have deprived the gesture of much of its significance at the time, and may even have contributed to the air of unreality which has often since seemed to overhang such public debate as there has been on 'going into Europe'. Nevertheless, although one may suspect that for many voters the specific issues at stake may have seemed – and may still seem – too complicated to grasp, the massive vote in favour of entry registered at the 1972 referendum can neither be ignored, nor explained away as essentially a vote on domestic

* The total of Irish soldiers killed in the Congo was twenty-six.

597

politics – i.e. against Sinn Féin, which has always opposed the Common Market on the ground that it constitutes a threat to political independence – rather than on the larger European question.[*]

Despite the prognostications of stark ruin and abounding prosperity with which the opponents and supporters of the Common Market have respectively bombarded a bemused public, the consequences of joining the Community are incalculable. As with so much else that vitally affects the future of Ireland, the historian can only wait upon events and judge them in the light of what has yet to be experienced. All the same, the very fact that entry into Europe has been approved by such a vast majority does in itself suggest that Irish foreign policy may now be moving perceptibly in a direction which could scarcely have been predicted as recently as a decade ago. Up to about 1960 neutralism, combined perhaps with a discreet determination not to prejudice a future solution of partition by adopting a stance on most international questions too far removed from that of Britain, restricted Irish diplomacy to a somewhat limited range of choices. To support institutions such as the United Nations or the Council of Europe, to conform on the large issues there to be decided to an increasingly 'western' line, but at the same time to maintain a rigorous boycott of NATO – these seemed almost the only available options. But it is possible, even probable, that in an enlarged European Community Ireland will in future be considerably less under the influence of either Britain or America than hitherto and reasonably certain that if belonging to the Common Market can be shown to produce benefits, there will be no reluctance on her part to assume the corresponding responsibilities.[†] There are, after all, good historical grounds for arguing that to the Irish entry into Europe will be a homecoming as much as a new departure.

[*] For the extent of the victory, see p. 588, note above. It should be noted that although the Labour party was opposed to joining the Common Market (partly on economic grounds) the two largest parties, Fianna Fáil and Fine Gael, were both in favour of entry.

[†] It is also arguable that in areas such as agriculture, regional policy, or even representation in Community institutions, the effect of Irish membership of EEC may be to reveal that the common interest of Northern Ireland and the Republic will be greater than the common interest of Northern Ireland and the rest of the United Kingdom. For the development of this argument, see G. FitzGerald, *Towards a New Ireland* (London, 1972), especially chap. 6.

4. The Quest for Prosperity

We affirm the duty of every man and woman to give allegiance and service to the Commonwealth, and declare it is the duty of the Nation to assure that every citizen shall have opportunity to spend his or her strength in the service of the people. In return for willing service, we, in the name of the Republic, declare the right of every citizen to an adequate share of the produce of the Nation's labour ('Democratic Programme', *Dáil Eireann, Minutes and Proceedings*, 21 Jan. 1919, pp. 22-3).

After 35 years of native government people are asking whether we can achieve an acceptable degree of economic progress. The common talk amongst parents in the towns, as in rural Ireland, is of their children having to emigrate as soon as their education is completed, in order to be sure of a reasonable livelihood (T. K. Whitaker, *Economic Development* (1958), p. 5).

(i) ECONOMIC INTERDEPENDENCE

The years of the First World War, of the War of Independence and of the Civil War had altered so much in Ireland that it was difficult at once to realise that in economic matters continuity not change was to be the order of the day. True, the context in which economic policy had to be formulated and applied was very different from what it had been under British rule. Since Ireland was no longer a single entity, the industrial northeast – traditionally, if over-optimistically, regarded as a source of strength – was no longer available. Moreover, the disturbed condition of the rest of the country from 1919 onwards had led to much physical damage and dislocation of trade; worse still, perhaps, it had created an atmosphere of confusion and unsettlement in which business could hardly be expected to thrive. Yet the most important new development, after all, was that at last an Irish government sat in Dublin, and since it was a government reared on Griffith's economic ideas and composed of his political heirs, it was reasonable to suppose that the vigorous growth of an autonomous Irish economy would be its most urgent task.

So no doubt it was. But the Irish government, like the Irish people, was faced with certain inexorable and unpalatable facts. The first of these was that political independence, even in the sense in which that had been achieved by the Treaty, was no guarantee of economic independence. On the contrary, the pattern established in the latter half of the nineteenth century proved hard to break. The Irish Free State remained part of an economic complex of which the United Kingdom was, as before, the predominant partner. The Irish monetary system was firmly tied to sterling, Irish commerce continued, for the time being at least, to be conducted within the framework of free trade, and ninety or more per cent of Irish exports still looked to Britain and Northern Ireland for their market.

Moreover, if the harsh realities of life in the great world had not been noticeably changed by the excitements of the previous decade, neither had the internal structure of the Irish economy. The new national government, like the old British one, saw in agriculture the basis of the country's existence and addressed itself at once to the problems of that key sector. This preoccupation may help to explain why Griffith's followers hesitated to follow Griffith's recipe of self-sufficiency through the development of native industries behind high tariff walls. 'The propagandist writings of one man', observed Kevin O'Higgins with characteristic bluntness, 'cannot be accepted simply as revealed truth, requiring no further investigation . . .'[1] Further investigation in fact suggested that if agriculture was the economic basis of the state, and if it depended upon exports for its well-being, then it was only common sense to seek to make Irish farmers competitive by improving the standard of their produce, if necessary by legislation aimed directly at regulating the breeding of livestock and raising the quality of dairy products. Not only that – if, as was the case, the great bulk of agricultural exports came from livestock and dairy products, then the trend must be towards encouraging this specialisation, even if that involved a growing dependence upon imported food-stuffs.

Now, since such an agricultural policy was aimed at developing the export trade, it followed that tariffs for the protection of home industries were largely inhibited by the fear of foreign retaliation. Far better, so it seemed, was it to rely upon the benefits of agricultural prosperity percolating through to other sections of the community, leading in course of time, perhaps, to a modest expansion of home industries. A few pre-existing tariffs were indeed taken over by the new government (notably those on tobacco and motor cars). Some additional ones were incorporated in the budgets of 1924, 1925 and 1926 (on such articles as boots and shoes, glass bottles, soap and candles, clothing and confectionery), but it remains true to say that up to 1926 the attitude of the Free State government was one of extreme caution towards the whole concept of industrial protection. In that year a Tariff Commission was set up to examine the case for extending duties to cover additional industries. Up to 1931 the results of its labours were scarcely impressive – a mere handful of relatively unimportant industries (with the exception of butter which received assistance actually in 1931) obtained some tariff benefits and even these only after searching inquiry. It is proper to add, however, that the few large-scale enterprises in the country – brewing, distilling and biscuit-manufacture – were themselves so dependent upon the export market that a protectionist policy would for them have been irrelevant, if not positively embarrassing.

Some expansion, no doubt, there was. Over a hundred new factories were said to have been opened in the protected industries by 1930, giving increased employment in those industries to just over 13,000 people. It can be claimed also that the Censuses of Industrial Production which began to be taken in 1926 showed an improvement for the years after the Tariff Commission had begun its work. The value of the net output in the industries covered by these Censuses (that is the gross value of output less cost of materials, fuel, light and power) went up from just over £23 million in 1926 to £25.6 million in 1931. Even these figures, not in themselves calculated to fire the blood of an economic nationalist, are too favourable, since they include a wide variety of what might more properly be classed as services. Annual inquiries into industries producing transportable goods elicited a more accurate, if bleaker, picture. The net output of those industries was valued at £16.4 million in 1916 and £18.2 million in 1931.[2] By no stretch of the imagination can this be regarded as an industrial renaissance.

Nor did it give rise to any radical redeployment of labour. The increase of the labour-force in the industries selected for annual review (in effect, the main factory-based industries) was a little under 5,000 during the five years 1926-31. In the whole range covered by the Census of Industrial Production there was an increase during the same period of from 102.5 thousand to 110.6 thousand. And if this total is swollen by the inclusion of other marginal industrial workers (as it was in the 1926 Census of Population) to 164,000, this was still only 13.5 per cent of the persons at work in the country that year. Ten years later this had gone up to 16.7 per cent, but that increase was due, as we shall presently see, to a deliberate policy of industrialisation much more forcefully pursued than any before 1932. Even within this small percentage of the total work-force, the emphasis was overwhelmingly upon production for the home market. In 1929 concerns producing goods for domestic consumption accounted for no less than eighty-five per cent of the labour employed in industry. And in that year the value of domestic manufactures exported (excluding tractors and other vehicles where imports were also involved) was only worth £1.6 million. By 1935 this figure had fallen to just over £600,000; since in the same period prices of industrial goods were estimated to have fallen by not more than seventeen per cent, there was evidence here of considerable decline in physical volume. Small wonder that the Secretary of the Department of Industry and Commerce, giving evidence to the Banking Commission, observed that there was 'no immediate propect at the present time of establishing a substantial export trade in the new industries; that is, in the new industries that are established behind customs protection'.[3]

So far as Mr Cosgrave and his ministers were concerned, then, upon the well-being of agriculture rested the well-being of the country at large. They inherited an agriculture which, as we have seen, had achieved a certain stability about the turn of the century. This stability – its critics might have called it stagnation – did not change to any marked degree during the first decade of the Irish Free State, nor for that matter, for many years thereafter. The total agricultural area of the twenty-six counties (that is the area occupied by tillage and pasture) had been just over twelve million acres in 1910. Over the next twenty years it declined to about 11¾ million acres, though some, perhaps most, of this change was due to the fact that a proportion of what had formerly been reckoned as marginal pasture land had been put aside as rough grazing and so left out of calculation. The relative shares falling to tillage and pasture had not altered drastically since the great adjustment of the second half of the nineteenth century. The tendency of the area under grain to decline steadily, which had been so marked a feature of the post-Famine years, continued to be manifest under a native government. The total of just over a million acres of grain crops in 1921 (itself somewhat swollen by the recent war demand) contracted to 763,284 acres by 1931. Adding in the figures for root and green crops and flax (also declining as a group) the entire acreage of tillage may be said to have fallen from 1.8 million acres in 1921 to 1.4 million ten years later. During the same period the combined totals of hay and pasture rose roughly from 10 million acres to 10.3 million.[4] In other words, though pasture remained dominant in the agricultural economy, it had not greatly enlarged its actual area. Indeed, the full force of this central fact in the life of the country can only be realised by seeing it in a longer perspective:

Area under Crops and Pastures[5]
Percentage Distribution

	1851	1901	1931
Ploughed Land	29	14	12
Hay	9	14	20
Pasture	62	72	68
Total	100	100	100

But, while pasture was still supreme after 1921, there was no great variation in the number of animals it supported. The number of horses declined marginally between then and 1931 and so, more important, did the number of cattle – from 4.4 million in 1921 to just over 4 million in 1931. The relative decline in milch cows was slighter than in dry cattle, but the latter still accounted for three-quarters of the total.

In two instances – pigs and poultry – there was a sharp increase (poultry went up by nearly six million in the decade) and although some of this may have been due to a readiness to pay more attention to these branches of production on large farms, and to the low price of imported feeding-stuffs, poultry especially remained *par excellence* a small-farm activity.

Ireland, indeed, was still a country of small holdings, though the size of the holdings was tending to grow and the proportion of agricultural land occupied by very small farms to diminish. It is true that as late as 1931 there were still nearly 45,000 under one acre, and also true that although this was about a third less than the 1910 figure, the total was later to rise again. Such small plots of land, however, can scarcely be regarded as farms in any meaningful sense. For farms over one acre, on the other hand, the trend was undoubtedly towards consolidation. Thus, as late as 1917, holdings between one and thirty acres were about 65 per cent of the total; by 1951 they had dropped to 58 per cent and this tendency was to continue. But these small holdings under thirty acres only occupied 24 per cent of agricultural land in 1917 and 22.5 per cent in 1931. Farms between thirty and a hundred acres occupied 38.5 per cent in 1917 and 42.8 per cent in 1931. Although farms of a hundred acres and over occupied 37.4 per cent of the agricultural land in 1917, their share had fallen back to 34.7 in 1931. Over the forty years between the end of the First World War and the publication of the report on Economic Development in 1958 the most marked movements were away from farms *under* fifteen acres and *over* two hundred acres, and towards an intermediate range of between thirty and a hundred acres. By the mid-fifties farms in that range accounted for 45 per cent of the whole area under crops and pasture.[6]

But this process of consolidation has to be seen in the context of a declining rural population. Between 1926 and 1936 the total of men and women at work in agriculture fell from just over 644,000 to just over 605,000. This trend was to be greatly accelerated in succeeding years (for reasons partly connected with emigration during the Second World War), with the result that over the twenty years between 1926 and 1946 there was a total decline of 85,400; of this total no less than seventy per cent occurred on farms of less than fifteen acres.[7]

Consolidation did not necessarily mean increased efficiency, though in many cases it might be a pre-condition for it. It has been estimated, for example, that although the gross value of the output of agriculture in the Irish Free State increased from £57.8 million in 1926-7 to £61.4 million in 1929-30 (falling back thereafter under the combined effects of the depression and the Anglo-Irish economic dispute, but reviving with the onset of war), nearly all of the increase was due to the movement of prices. It has been suggested, indeed, that although the volume of agricultural output in the area of the twenty-six counties increased by perhaps twenty-five to thirty per cent between 1861 and

1909, since then (at least until the mid-fifties) there had been no significant change of volume. In fact, as the Emigration Commission Report puts it, 'during the past hundred years . . . the disappointing record of agriculture shows only a total increase of 25 per cent in the volume of output, all of which had taken place by the first decade of this century'. So small had this increase been that the Commission reckoned that despite the drift from the land the existing volume of output could have been produced by about two-thirds of the workers actually on the farms.[8] It may be argued, as a counterbalance to this rather bleak analysis, that at least it can be shown that even if volume did not rise significantly the yield of crops per acre did do so. It is certainly true that this happened between the second half of the nineteenth century and the early years of the twentieth at a rate comparable with similar developments elsewhere in Europe. But between about 1919 and the middle 'thirties there was, except for the production of potatoes, a marked slowing down. The following table will show something of this movement:[9]

Estimated Annual Average Yields Per Acre

Years	Wheat (cwt)	Oats (cwt)	Barley (cwt)	Potatoes (tons)	Hay (cwt)
1850–59	13·0	13·4	16·7	4·6	38·7
1900–09	19·1	16·7	18·3	4·2	45·2
1910–19	19·9	18·0	18·9	5·1	40·9
1932–36	20·4	19·5	20·5	7·7	41·3

We are dealing, therefore, with an agriculture which had become stabilised over a long period of years. Not only that – this stabilisation had taken place at the point in history where the tenant-farmer was at last becoming the owner of his holding as a result of the land legislation in the two generations before the First World War. The small or medium farm worked mainly as a family concern thus became the stereotype; even in the mid-1920s only nineteen per cent of the labour-force on farms in the Irish Free State consisted of paid employees. It has been suggested with some plausibility that this social pattern imposed upon Irish agriculture (or rather, reinforced) a deeply conservative approach to farming, characterised above all by a passion to acquire or to retain land almost regardless of its economic potentiality.* No doubt the farmer gained in security from becoming

* It is important to remember, however, that the conservatism of Irish agriculture was not a new phenomenon, springing solely from peasant ownership. 'Agriculture', it has been well said, 'would be plagued with the self-same problems to-day were Ireland still a tenancy at will, for these problems were inherited, not created by peasant proprietors' (Joseph

an owner; probably also, at least while agricultural prices remained buoyant, he gained in income once the land legislation began to take effect, for his judicial rents or land annuities were generally lower than the old rents in the competitive market. And although it is true that during the 1920s the cost of living index was rising faster than agricultural prices, and that those prices were severely hit at the end of the decade by the world depression, the worst effects of this were not felt in Ireland until the 1930s because, during the first decade of the Free State's existence, the prices of foodstuffs of animal origin held up rather longer than the prices of cereals.[10]

It did not follow, however, that the tenant transmogrified into owner necessarily changed his attitude towards farming – if he had more money this did not mean that he was going to invest it in improving his holding. The very stability of Irish agriculture which we have just been considering suggests, indeed, that he did not. We have seen already that in the first half of the twentieth century the area of tillage was declining, while pasture remained more or less static. It is no less significant that there was also a slowing down in the rate at which farms were being stocked with cattle and sheep. Whereas during the Famine years (1847 to 1851) livestock increased at the rate of 4 per cent per annum, the corresponding rates for 1901-21 and 1921-61 were 0.4 and 0.2 per cent respectively.[11] This is not in itself surprising; it simply means that given the kind of equilibrium between tillage, dry cattle and dairy farming that had been established, the opportunity for profitable investment was not obvious. Where such an opportunity did offer itself, as in poultry-farming, full advantage was no doubt taken of it, but there are indications that lacking any obvious outlet, and lacking also the economic spur of a rent economy, the farmer was beginning to use some at least of any increased income that might accrue to him to achieve a higher standard of living for himself and his family. That this was happening is suggested by the findings of the Commission on Derating, which reported in 1931 that there had been a marked improvement in living conditions on many Irish farms.[12] It is suggested still more by the fact that the dowry-system for farmers' daughters, though going far back into Irish social history, developed very significantly at this time. It has been observed that before about 1880 dowries were very frequently paid in kind, but that from then onwards (with the land legislation starting to take effect) sums of three or four hundred pounds began to change hands; in more recent times dowries of one thousand or even two thousand pounds have been not unknown.[13] Since in many cases the dowry of a daughter-in-law was used as a means of 'fortuning-off' the daughter of the house in her turn, it follows that this bride-price

Lee, 'Irish Agriculture', in *Agricultural History Review* (1969) xvii, part 1, p. 73). For the nineteenth century background to this subject, see Part I, chap. 2.

was not necessarily (though sometimes, no doubt, it was) an addition to the capital of the farm. Indeed, even if it did not go out again in this form, it could be, and often was, used to assist the emigration of other members of the family, in which case it was, of course, carried out of agriculture altogether.

But not only did Irish farmers cling to their land and not only were they reluctant to invest heavily in it. Their tendency towards inertia was powerfully reinforced by another factor – which was that they were growing older. In 1881, 34.7 per cent of Irish farmers were under forty-five years; 43.5 per cent were between forty-five and sixty-five, while 21.8 per cent were over sixty-five. Women farmers accounted for only 13.5 per cent of the total, and of these no more than 3.6 per cent were over sixty-five. But by 1946 a situation had been reached where a third of all farmers were over sixty-five. Women accounted for one-sixth of the total; nearly half of these were over sixty-five and three-quarters were widows.[14] It would be difficult to imagine a more infallible recipe for rural conservatism.

How far did the state in the first decade after the Treaty seek to counteract this conservatism, how far was it even felt that it needed to be counteracted? The answers to these questions cannot be simple and clear-cut, because the lines of official policy are themselves confused. Politically, the structure of Irish agriculture was sacrosanct – owner-occupancy had been the ark of the covenant for so many years that to tamper with it would have been suicide for any politician. No politician in fact showed the slightest sign of doing so. On the contrary, a continuing preoccupation of governments for at least twelve years after the Treaty was to round out the process of land purchase. The most important step towards the completion of purchase was the Land Act of 1923 (amended in 1925) under which all land where landlord and tenant still had a dual interest was ruled to pass automatically into the hands of the Land Commission, to be vested in due course in the tenants as proprietors, subject to payment of the appropriate annuities. A system of standard prices was laid down, and in addition the vendor received from the state a bonus of ten per cent of the standard price. Untenanted land in the Congested Districts was to be taken over by the Land Commission (inheriting the functions of the old Congested Districts Board) which also had power – subject to certain exceptions – compulsorily to acquire untenanted land outside this area if such land was needed either to relieve congestion or facilitate the resale of tenanted land. The problem was complex and progress slow, but the Minister for Agriculture, Mr Patrick Hogan, a man of exceptional drive and ability, achieved substantial success; nevertheless, two further acts, those of 1933 and 1934, were needed after the change of government to wind up the business and even these left some serious problems of congestion unsolved. The end result was that between 1923 and 1937 the transactions authorised by these various measures involved advances of

£27¼ million, affected the ownership of 117,000 holdings, and covered an area of 3.6 million acres.[15]

It has to be emphasised that the same government which took a fundamentally conservative view of the structure of rural society was equally orthodox in its economic attitudes. It aimed at – and largely achieved – a frugal and efficient administration. Almost Gladstonian in its approach to public finance, it exerted itself to deep taxation down to a minimum and to regulate expenditure accordingly. How far it succeeded may be judged from the fact that in 1931 exchequer receipts were, at twenty-four million pounds, only fifteen per cent of the national income, and that when Mr Cosgrave yielded office to Mr de Valera in 1932 the entire public debt of the Irish Free State was only thirty-five million pounds, which was about one-fifth of the annual national income.[16]

Against this background of impeccable financial probity has to be seen the government's campaign to improve agricultural standards. Clearly, such improvement as might be achieved would come not from any revolutionary approach – Keynesian or otherwise – to the economy as a whole, nor from any massive increase in public spending. Rather was it to be conjured out of the countryside by providing better technical education, by imposing stricter marketing regulations, and by making available to farmers the credit which in the past had either been denied them by the banks or supplied at an extortionate price by the gombeen men. The first of these policies, better education, had been the goal of all Irish agricultural reformers for many years and the new Department of Agriculture was just as much concerned as the old Department of Agriculture and Technical Instruction had been with teaching and demonstration. How effective this was has been questioned. Even as early as 1923 the Department was being criticised as unrealistic in its advice and out of touch with actual conditions on the farms, and as recently as 1958 the deficiencies of agricultural education were trenchantly exposed in the Whitaker Report. More effective, because backed by the sanctions of the law, were the series of acts passed between 1924 and 1930 regulating standards of cleanliness, purity, packaging and marketing in the branches of the industry dealing with pork, bacon, eggs and dairy produce, and also the important advance embodied in the Live Stock Breeding Act of 1925, under which every bull and boar used for breeding purposes had to be licensed by the state. Inevitably, all this cost money and even a government obsessed with the necessity of balancing budgets had to accept steadily increasing expenditure on agriculture, apart altogether from land purchase. The amount so expended rose from just under a million pounds in 1925 to £2.7 million in 1931. Much of this, it must be added, went not on directly productive work, but on expanding and continuing the old device of granting farmers relief from rates on agricultural land; the grant for this purpose was doubled in 1926 and continued to rise at intervals thereafter.[17]

The most striking new departure, however, was the decision to make available to farmers loans for productive purposes on reasonable terms. In 1927 the Agricultural Credit Act provided for the setting up of an Agricultural Credit Corporation as a limited company with a nominal share capital of £500,000, later much increased as its operations grew in scale. Its finances were guaranteed by the state and it was empowered to lend money to farmers, usually on the security of a first mortgage of their land. Up to 1936 the Corporation had advanced loans on this basis of just over a million pounds, plus a further quarter of a million on other security. Individual transactions were generally small. Of a total of 16,719 in the first nine years of operation, all but 239 were for sums under five hundred pounds and the overall average was eighty-two pounds. No doubt this reflects the scale of operations on a typical Irish farm, but perhaps it reflects also a deep-seated reluctance on the part of the farmer to cumber himself with debt charges even in the interests of efficiency. It is perhaps significant that although most of these small loans were repayable over a period of five to ten years there was evidence of a good deal of unpunctuality, leading sometimes to actual default. By 1936 almost £30,000 of bad debts had had to be written off and an additional £70,000 set aside for similar contingencies in the future. Yet despite this unpromising beginning, the Agricultural Credit Corporation had a significance that went far beyond its immediate modest operations. With the Electricity Supply Board, also established in 1927, it shared the distinction of being the first visible evidence of a trend that was to become more and more important as time went on. These two organisations were the first of a whole line of similar bodies whereby the state was increasingly drawn to intervene in various sectors of the economy into which private capital had been unable or unwilling to enter. The main development of this tendency belongs to a later period which is dealt with below, but it is strikingly indicative of the kind of pressures that were being generated in the Irish economy that even a government so little *dirigiste* as that of Mr Cosgrave should have felt it necessary to take these first faltering steps along the primrose path of state intervention.[18]

To strike a balance of profit and loss on the free trade era of the Irish Free State is not easy, the more so as policy was overtaken, not to say overwhelmed, by the onset of the world depression. And even though, as already mentioned, livestock prices held up longer than those of cereals, the crisis was only postponed. Thus, the value of agricultural exports (of which livestock and livestock products accounted for about ninety-eight per cent) fell from £35.8 million in 1929 to just under £14 million in 1935.[19] This, it is true, was not just a consequence of the depression; it was partly due also to the economic war with Britain and it is clear that the worst of the storm came after the change of government. But already by 1931 the agricultural price index number (base 1911-13=100) had fallen to 110 from the high point of 139.2 reached in 1929. Agricultural wages, naturally, had also declined, though this was offset by a reduction in the cost of living. Taking the country as a whole, money incomes had suffered a sharp fall between 1929 and 1931, but since the index of general prices had gone down even further the effect was to produce a slightly higher real income in 1931 than in 1929.[20]

Against this, however, must be set the fact that the number of persons receiving home assistance under the Poor Law had gone up steadily in the last years of the Cosgrave regime. In 1925-6 the total had been 47,963; in 1930-1 it was 77,474. And to this has to be added the further fact that already in the mid-twenties unemployment was running at the rate of six per cent of the total working population. The data for assessing unemployment before 1932 are inadequate and it is probable that a more accurate calculation would give a higher percentage; even as it stands, the figure of six per cent does not take into account the problem of under-employment, especially in agriculture.[21]

The indictment could be taken further. As we have seen, agriculture, despite all the efforts of an energetic Minister, had not fundamentally changed its character and still remained in many ways underdeveloped. Industry, also, though it had expanded somewhat, was still essentially small-scale and – save for a few long-established enterprises – quite unable to compete in the open market. Worst of all, the government had not succeeded in arresting the decline in population. From a total for the twenty-six counties of 3.1 million in 1911, it had fallen to 2.97 million in 1926 and this decline was to continue. What was particularly serious for a state that set so much store by agriculture was that this loss fell mainly upon the rural areas. The rural decline between 1911 and 1926 was from 2.2 million to 2.0 million and this had fallen still further to 1.9 million by 1936. Although the town population actually took an upward turn in 1926 (reaching its highest total since 1851) this was not enough to compensate for the drain from the countryside. Inevitably linked with this overall decline was emigration. The period during which the Irish Free State was founded saw a heavy outward movement. Net emigration between 1911 and 1926 (admittedly a fifteen-year period) was 405,029. That terrible momentum was indeed slowed down in the next decade to 166,751, but neither the Cosgrave nor the de Valera government could take much credit for this. Emigration fell off largely because the outlets for it diminished, but when the outlets were once more available after 1936 the old wound began to bleed again as heavily as before.[22]

On the credit side it has to be remembered that a great work of restoration and reconstruction had confronted the government after the Civil War. Understandably, its energies had been devoted primarily to creating once more in the country the conditions for economic advance in the future. By 1931 this task had been effectively carried out. The rule of law had been upheld, the Free State's international standing as a creditor nation had been maintained, budgets had been scrupulously balanced and taxation held firmly in check, administration had been frugal but competent, and if the economic ideas of ministers and their advisers savoured more of Adam Smith than of J. M. Keynes, no-one could deny that within the limits this implied, their policies had been remarkably effective.

In the last resort, Mr Cosgrave and his colleagues could with some justice have defended their decade of power on the ground that in a period of almost unprecedented difficulty they had enabled the country simply to survive. But by 1932 new pressures were demanding new responses which they were ill-fitted to provide. Their economic policy had assumed the continued existence of an international free trading system in which Ireland's principal role, as hitherto, would be to export foodstuffs and import manufactures. But that delectable, if unsophisticated, nineteenth century world had dissolved in ruins around them. Interdependence had suddenly come to mean participation in losses as well as in profits. And, as confidence in the old economic order drained away, and protectionist policies proliferated all over the world, economic nationalism became once more respectable.

In Ireland, of course, economic nationalism had been respectable for a long time and in a world of rising tariffs Arthur Griffith's doctrines began to seem increasingly relevant. An independent Ireland, he had claimed, must be free to impose its own tariffs and must use that power to develop, not only agriculture, but industry also so as to achieve the great end of economic nationalism, which was self-sufficiency. By one of those familiar ironies of Irish history the men who repudiated Griffith's political settlement inherited his economic ideas. Fianna Fáil, from the moment of its foundation, identified itself with the doctrine of economic nationalism and one of the first important interventions in the Dáil of Mr Sean Lemass, who in due time was to assume a large share of the responsibility for the industrial development of the country, was to enunciate this doctrine, when in 1928 he attacked the Tariff Commission for not going far or fast enough. 'We believe', he said, 'that Ireland can be made a self-contained unit, providing all the necessities of living in adequate quantities for the people residing in this island at the moment and probably for a much larger number.'[23] Here, in a sentence, was the germ of a new departure, looking to the creation of an Ireland that would be both politically and economically freer of the British connection than the men of the Treaty had ever been able to make her. With the electoral victory of Mr de Valera in 1932 the way was clear for the testing of this new concept against the harsh realities of a world plunged in dire depression.

(ii) STRIVING FOR SELF-SUFFICIENCY

It is perhaps unfortunate, though inevitable, that the history of the drive towards self-sufficiency should have become inextricably intertwined with the history of the financial dispute, or 'economic war', with Britain. Yet, since that dispute with the country's leading customer had a direct effect upon the economy at large, it cannot be ignored. Its full consequences can only be seen in the context of the general economic policy of the new government. But its history may be disposed of more briefly. Fianna Fáil came to power in March 1932. Immediately, they introduced much more extensive tariffs, the first budget (March 1932) containing no less than forty-three new duties. Simultaneously, on taking up office, Mr de Valera announced that his government would not transmit the land annuities accruing under the Irish Land Acts; later he added certain other items to this programme.

What precisely was involved? In 1923 the then government of the Irish Free State had undertaken to collect and pay to the United Kingdom the moneys due from tenant-purchasers – that is, the annuities in respect of holdings purchased under the Land Acts; to pay a contribution towards the interest due on additional Land Stock previously issued; to pay a proportionate share of the cost of RIC pensions and those of certain other retired public servants; and to continue payments of certain annuities arising out of expenditure on public works. This 'provisional' agreement was not actually published until 1932, but in 1925 a further settlement was reached arising out of the discussions on the border questions. By its terms the United Kingdom waived any claim to an Irish Free State contribution to the public debt of the United Kingdom, as had been provided for by the Treaty, but *per contra* the Irish Free State agreed to pay £250,000 p.a. for sixty years in discharge of compensation paid out by the United Kingdom for damage to property in Ireland between 1919 and 1925. This in turn was followed by a further 'ultimate agreement' in 1926 which, like the agreement of 1923, admitted the liability to pay the land annuities.

Mr de Valera's case was that the agreements of 1923 and 1926 were invalid because they had never been ratified by the Dáil. The burden of the annuities, he constantly insisted, had never been more than a contingent liability for a share of the United Kingdom public debt from which the Free State had been specifically released by the agreement of 1925. Attempts to settle the dispute broke down in June, whereupon the British government rapidly imposed duties of twenty per cent *ad valorem* on Irish cattle and on the other main Irish agricultural exports to the United Kingdom, with the object of recovering by this means the money withheld by the Free State. These duties were later increased in severity and between July 1932 and 31 March 1935 had produced a revenue of £10.7 million against the alleged Irish default of £14.5 million. Nor was this the only weapon used against the recalcitrant Irish government. Because of the dispute, the Ottawa Conference, which later that year produced a whole crop of preferential tariff agreements amongst members of the Commonwealth, could have no ameliorating effect on Anglo-Irish economic relations; on the contrary, Irish Free State goods entering the United Kingdom became subject to the general scale of import duties laid down in the British Import Duties Act of 1932. Between that date and March 1935 these duties had produced a revenue of just over a million pounds. Finally, Britain's need to protect her own agriculture led her in 1934 to restrict the import of Free State cattle by a quota system limiting fat cattle to fifty per cent of the 1933 figure, imposing a one hundred per cent restriction on store cattle and prohibiting the entry of Irish beef and veal. At the beginning of 1935 this policy was somewhat relaxed by an agreement – the so-called Coal-Cattle Pact – whereby the quotas for Irish cattle were raised by a third in return for an Irish promise to take all coal from United Kingdom sources, thus involving an increase of United Kingdom coal into the Free State of 1¼ million tions a year. The following years (1936 and 1937) these relaxations were further extended.

Against such pressures the Free State government had naturally retaliated by imposing its own duties on imports from Britain – the most important being five shillings a ton on coal and coke, and twenty per cent *ad valorem* on cement, electrical goods, machinery, iron and steel. These, in their turn, were subsequently extended to other goods as part of the general tariff policy initiated by Mr de Valera's government, for even the relaxations of 1935 and 1936 could not alter the fact that a protectionist regime was now fully entrenched in Dublin.[24]

What were the principal economic consequences of this nagging dispute between the two countries? There can be no denying that they were serious, even allowing for the complicating effects of the general collapse of world agricultural prices. We have seen already that the value of Irish agricultural exports (a great part of which went to Britain) fell from £35.8 million in 1929 to £13.9 million in 1935. The total of all Free State exports to the United Kingdom in 1929 had been worth £43.5 million – in 1935 it was worth just under £18 million. Value, admittedly, is an unsure guide at a time of rapidly falling prices. Volume is apt to be more illuminating, but volume, too, tells a sorry tale. Sorriest of all, perhaps, in the vital livestock trade, where it showed that while in 1929 775,000 cattle had been exported (the vast majority to Britain), by 1934 the figure had dropped to just over half a million.[25]

It is no exaggeration to say that the cattle industry, the very life-blood of the country's economy, was threatened with collapse. Moreover, since there were certain commodities – for example, tea, petroleum, coal – which the Free State had still to import from Britain, there was every prospect that the adverse balance of trade, which the country had learned to live with since the Treaty, would become more serious. Whereas in 1929 imports had exceeded exports by about fourteen million pounds, this margin had increased to over twenty-one million pounds by 1934. A contemporary calculation of the real 'terms of trade' (having regard, that is, to the movement of import and export prices) suggests that up to the early months of 1932 export prices resisted the general decline a little better than import prices, but that in the latter half of that year export prices fell far below those of imports. 'This decline, which has since persisted', commented the Banking Commission report six years later, 'must largely be attributed to the imposition of the special duties and restrictions by the United Kingdom.'[26] To some extent this adverse movement was offset by invisible earnings, but even allowing for these, the deficit on current account went from £3¼ million in 1931 to £6⅓ million in 1934.[27] It recovered somewhat thereafter, but this sort of balance of payments situation, continued year after year, was bound to lead to a deterioration of the Free State's jealously guarded external assets. Precise calculations in this field are notoriously hard to come by, but perhaps it is enough to say that the best available figures indicate that there was a net decrease in the Free State's sterling holdings of just over nine million pounds in the four years ending 31 December 1935.[28]

Clearly, although even in 1935 the reserves were still substantial, alternative policies to diminish the drain were necessary. These, in fact, fitted in well enough with the programme of self-sufficiency about to be described. But before turning to that it is necessary to trace the history of the Anglo-Irish dispute to its conclusion. Although each side undoubtedly inflicted damage on the other, the effect of the quarrel seemed to be to emphasise economic interdependence rather than economic separateness. This was obviously less true of Britain than of the Free State, though Britain could ill-afford to fall from supplying the Free State with 75.8 per cent of its imports in 1932 to little more than 54 per cent in 1935. But for the Irish disputants the quarrel, bitter and prolonged as it was, could not be allowed to alter the direction of trade; indeed, there was no other direction in which trade could go. Irish exports were still utterly reliant upon the British market. In 1932 over ninety-six per cent went there and at no time up to 1938 did the percentage fall below ninety.[29]

The really serious effect of the 'economic war' upon the Free State was not just that the depression of agriculture, and of the cattle industry in particular, reduced the incomes of the farmers, but that this reduction was likely to affect other sectors of the economy as well, by reducing the demand of the agricultural population for whatever home industry might have to offer. 'Indeed', as the Banking Commission observed, 'an industrial programme has hardly had a fair chance of succeeding at a time when a large section of the market for industrial goods is severely curtailed.'[30] When, therefore, political developments at last opened the way for a settlement in 1938 the chance was firmly seized.* In their financial and economic aspects the agreements then

* For the political background, see Part IV, A, chap. 2.

reached provided that the Irish government would pay the United Kingdom ten million pounds in final settlement of all claims by either government arising out of the dispute. Mr de Valera had therefore won his battle over the land annuities. But so far as Anglo-Irish trade was concerned, the basic principle was that of a return to the pre-1932 position. The special duties imposed by each side were to be withdrawn, with the result that Irish agricultural produce was to be admitted henceforward to the United Kingdom market free of duties, while the British government obtained a virtually complete monopoly of the Irish market for British coal. Both sides accepted the Ottawa concept of equal opportunity, and preferential duties were re-established by the two governments; in effect, while each country still retained protection for certain of its own products, the agreement allowed them to develop most-favoured nation treatment on a reciprocal basis. Both, however, reserved the right to apply a quota-system to certain of the other's products should home producers be endangered by excessive competition, and in this proviso lay the real threat to Irish agriculture in the future. Initially, the agreement was to run only until August, 1940, but by then of course the whole context of the question had been drastically changed.[31]

Important though the Anglo-Irish economic war undoubtedly was, it would be wrong to allow it to loom too large in the history of the 1930s. There is, on the contrary, some truth in the contention that world conditions, apart altogether from the predilections of Fianna Fáil, were pushing Ireland along the road to protection and that the economic war itself 'was incidental to, and not a condition of, the protective policy of those years'.[32] That policy, as we have seen, started out as a policy of economic nationalism – that is to say, an attempt to break the Free State's commercial dependence upon Britain. But the conception behind the campaign for this new departure that Fianna Fáil waged ceaselessly from 1927 was broader than a mere extension of an old political quarrel into the world of business. It involved also a serious and prolonged attempt to redress the balance between the different sectors of the economy – to free the countryside from the dominance of the cattleman, to extend the area of tillage, to develop home industries and thus provide employment for those who might otherwise be obliged to emigrate.

An essential key to much of this programme is to be found in the tariff. Immediately Mr de Valera took office numerous duties at very high rates were imposed on a wide variety of goods, and this policy was continued over the years, more than 1,000 items being affected by 1936.[33] In addition, a complicated quota and licensing system was introduced to control the amounts and value of particular imports. Such steps, though they may have helped to reduce expenditure on foreign goods, were in themselves negative and in the long run could only be justified if behind this protective barrier there grew up 'infant industries' capable of holding their own in the future.

To help these to develop was therefore a prime object of government concern. This expressed itself in several ways. One was to ensure, by means of the Control of Manufactures Acts, 1932-4, that Irish industry should as far as possible be concentrated in the hands of Irish owners. Another was to provide, through the Industrial Credit Company, for the financing, at least in part, of such transfers of ownership to Free State nationals. Founded in 1933, the Company's capital was almost entirely subscribed by the state – a considerable expenditure since, in the first four years of its operation, it made capital issues amounting to nearly £6½ million. Yet a third device was also aimed at providing credit on reasonable terms to manufacturing enterprises which showed some promise of providing speedy employment. This was the system of trade loans provided for by the Trade Loans (Guarantee) (Amendment) Act of 1933. The system had its origins in an Act of 1924 which had empowered the government to guarantee repayment of the principal of, and payment of the interest on, certain types of loan which, it was hoped, would lead to substantial capital expenditure with consequential increases in the number of jobs available. Initial experience of this kind of encouragement had proved disappointing. Between 1925 and 1929 £317,000 had been lent to eighteen interested parties and by 1936 half of them were in default to the extent of nearly £200,000. The Act of 1933 gave further hostages to fortune by relaxing the conditions so that loans might in future be made not just for capital expenditure, but for working capital as well, which was obviously a much greater risk. When examined before the Banking Commission on this matter, the Secretary for the Department of Industry and Commerce was almost fatalistically resigned to a fresh crop of failures, leading to yet more expenditure by the state. Predictably, the Commission was considerably shocked by the story he unfolded and drew, with unwavering firmness, the classical conclusion that 'the government should not seek to deal directly with individual businesses in providing assistance for long term credit.'[34]

But the government showed itself little impressed by such doctrines. On the contrary, since it was evident that private capital was neither very extensive nor very adventurous, the state was drawn steadily further and further along the road of direct intervention in various fields of enterprise. One such field was housing. Although the primary responsibility for this belonged to the local authority, the burden of debt which this laid upon them (over £20 million by 1937) was so great that the central government had to come to the rescue. The Housing Act of 1932 provided that the state could contribute from one-third to two-thirds of housing-schemes operated by the local authorities. Up to March 1937, £3.4 million had been used for this purpose and a further £6 million was ear-marked for future expenditure along the same lines. In effect a housing subsidy, this kind of assistance really amounted to a public works policy, designed not merely to provide more houses but more employment as well.[35]

Far more important than this, however, and in the long run destined to have a much greater effect upon the social and economic life of the country, was the increasing tendency to create what have been called state-sponsored bodies for specific purposes, a tendency which, as we saw earlier, was already beginning to show itself in the 1920s, but which, after the change of government, was to be very much intensified. Almost from the earliest days of independence it had become clear that there were certain kinds of economic activity which either required too much capital or involved too much risk for private companies to venture upon. Yet often these very activities were themselves essential to further economic growth and as such the state could not ignore them. On the contrary, it became more and more deeply involved in supplying the deficiencies of the private sector.

One of the earliest and most celebrated of these state intrusions into the world of business was the development of a nationwide supply of electricity. The possibility of using the abundant water resources of Ireland as a means of providing electricity had been tentatively explored in the years immediately after the First World War, but the initiative in bringing these vague ideas to the point of practicality belonged to Dr T. A. McLaughlin, an Irish graduate of electrical engineering in the employment of the German firm of Siemens-Schuckert. His dream was of a great system of electrification based on the river Shannon. Other schemes and other interests competed with this conception, but after exhaustive inquiry the government adopted the Shannon scheme. The construction of the main power station at Ardnacrusha, near Limerick city, began in August 1925 and was completed towards the end of 1929. While it was being completed an Act of the Dáil set up the Electricity Supply Board as a statutory body with wide powers to control the generation, distribution and sale not only of Shannon electricity, but of electricity throughout the country. At that time such electrical power as the country possessed was in the hands of a number of small producers and the Act gave the Board the right to acquire either compulsorily or by agreement any electrical undertaking then in existence. In practice, compulsion was sparingly used, mainly perhaps because the superior efficiency and resources of the Board gradually drove its competitors out of the market.

In framing the Board's constitution the government was influenced to some extent by foreign, especially Swedish, experience. There was to be a full-time chairman and from two to six, later seven, ordinary members appointable for five years and eligible for renewal. The Board was responsible to the Minister for Industry and Commerce and its reports to him were to be published and laid before both Houses of the Oireachtas. From the beginning it proved to be a highly dynamic organisation. Even though demand before the Second World War roughly doubled every five years, that demand was met to such effect that by 1939-40 the Board was generating 407 million units, though the war, with its fuel shortages, led to an actual drop in consumption. After 1945 the advance was resumed and the first steps were taken to utilise turf (peat) as a fuel for generating stations, additional to coal and water-power. By March 1961 the Board's total installed capacity was 723.5 megawatts, of which steam plant (coal or oil-fired) accounted for almost forty per cent, hydro-electric plant for about a third, and steam plant using peat for the remainder. Despite the fact that industrial demand was low for most of this period and that the consuming public was not very wealthy, the Board contrived to carry out its expansion and yet keep the cost to the consumer lower than that in most European countries. In the earlier years, naturally enough, attention had been concentrated upon the towns and villages. By 1943 about ninety-five per cent of this urban and semi-urban population was being supplied, but, even with such penetration into the countryside as had then been achieved, still only about fifty per cent of the total population had electricity. It was not until after the Second World War that rural electrification began in earnest. The work was difficult and expensive, but by March 1964 out of nearly 800 areas requiring service only eight remained to be dealt with. Consumption over the country as a whole had risen to nearly 3,000 million units – almost fifty times what it had been in 1929-30.[36]

The Electricity Supply Board has been described in some detail not just because of its own achievements – though these were remarkable – but because in many ways it blazed a trail which has become a broad highway. The use of state-sponsored bodies for a variety of purposes, economic and other, has developed to such a degree that they are now so numerous, and fulfil such a variety of functions, that to generalise about them is virtually impossible, and even to define a state-sponsored body is almost beyond the wit of man. For the purposes of this study, however, it is enough to accept the recent description made by an authority on the subject – that they are 'autonomous public bodies other than universities or university colleges, which are neither temporary in character nor purely advisory in their function, most of whose staff are not civil servants, and to whose board or council the government, or ministers in the government, appoint directors, council members etc'.[37] Although this definition excludes many types of organisation in which the state takes an interest, the number coming within it is still formidable. During the period when economic self-sufficiency was being most strenuously pursued – from 1932 up to the end of the Second World War – thirteen such bodies were added to the six which had been inherited from the previous regime and five more were added during the war years. In the post-war period the pace accelerated so that by the early 'sixties there were no less than fifty-five.

Not all of these, of course, were intended to perform economic services and though there are various ways of classifying them, the most convenient for our purposes is the distinction between 'trading enterprises' and the rest. Trading enterprises may be defined as state-sponsored bodies which have significant sources of revenue other than grants-in-aid from the central government or from local authorities.[38] On this reckoning thirty-four out of the fifty-five bodies listed up to 1963 qualify as trading-enterprises, though even they, it must be added, generally derived a much larger share of their capital directly from government grants than from their own profits or from the external sources of borrowing which were occasionally open to them.

As the practice of state intervention in this way became more familiar, so did the range and scope of the state-sponsored bodies become steadily wider. Nowadays they are concerned not only with directly productive enterprises, but with radio and television, the encouragement of the arts, the prosecution of research, the control of horse-racing and betting thereon, hotel management, tourism and a wide variety of matters affecting health and the medical profession. Initially, as might be expected, the emphasis was predominantly economic, which, on the whole, it has remained. Of the nineteen bodies formed between 1927 and 1939, apart from those already referred to (the Agricultural Credit Corporation, the Industrial Credit Company and the Electricity Supply Board) the following 'trading enterprises' were created – the Industrial Alcohol Board, the Irish Sugar Company, the Dairy Disposal Company, Aer Rianta (for the management of Dublin airport), Aer Lingus (European Air Services), Milk Boards for Cork and Dublin, and the Irish Life Assurance Company. Non-trading enterprises of the same period included Bord Fáilte Eireann (tourism), the Hospitals Trust Board and the Medical Research Council. During the war years the most important of the new bodies dealing with economic matters were Irish Shipping, the Central Bank of Ireland and the Pigs and Bacon Commission. After 1945 the area of state activity continued to expand – among the most important of the new bodies then established were Coras Iompair Eireann, charged with the almost impossible task of rescuing the public transport system from bankruptcy, and Bord na Mona, which within fifteen years of its foundation in 1946 had revolutionised the production of turf or peat for both domestic and industrial purposes.

It is not necessary to seek any profound philosophy of state socialism behind the emergence of this variegated collection of organisations. They were essentially individual responses to specific situations – the intentions of the government were strictly pragmatic. This has not, of course, exempted the state-sponsored bodies from all kinds of criticism. At different times it has been said that they took too large a share of the managerial talent available in the country, that they competed too much with the private sector, that they hold the consumer to ransom, and that there is inadequate public control over their activities. Whether such charges are valid it is not for a study of this kind to determine. Just as the state bodies defy generalisation in describing them, so they defy it in judging them No doubt some of these accusations have been true some of the time; it is harder to believe that all of them have been true all of the time. But of the importance of these organisations to the economy there can be no doubt. By the early 'sixties they employed some 50,000 people (over thirty-five per cent of all the workers in state employment and some seven per cent of the total number of employees in the country), possessed assets of about £230 million and paid out over £35 million a year in wages and salaries.[39] In a sense the very criticisms that were levelled against them were a measure of their success. When they first appeared they appeared because of economic need, not as part of any deeply reasoned governmental plan. The lack of private capital, the timidity of private capitalists, the necessity to supply some public services and rescue others – these were the fundamental reasons for the formation of the state-sponsored bodies. And if latterly private capital has been critical of these public concerns, it is well to maintain historical perspective by recalling the years when the state had little alternative but to call into existence a new world of initiative to redress the deficiencies of the old.

In the period before and during the Second World War state intervention of this kind had clearly to be seen in the broader context of the pursuit of self-sufficiency. It remains to ask how far self-sufficiency was actually achieved in the two spheres which were central to the whole policy of the government – industrial development and a reorientation of agriculture by means of an intensive drive to expand the area of tillage, and especially of wheat.

In the industrial sector, certainly, both the volume and the value of production, as well as the numbers employed, increased between 1931 and 1938. The value of net industrial output rose from £25.6 million in the earlier year to £36 million in the later, while industrial employment went up from 111,000 to 166,000.[40] On the other hand, a price had to be paid for this achievement. The few large export industries which already existed were emphatically not helped by a protective tariff and the amounts earned by the export of, for example, biscuits, porter, and beer all fell sharply in the 'thirties. Indeed, there was a marked decline in the whole total of non-agricultural exports, which fell between 1932 and 1938 from £6.4 million to £4.4 million. The unpalatable fact was that the new Irish industries were unlikely to make much headway in foreign markets, for reasons which the Report of the Banking Commission makes abundantly clear. First, they were likely to be costly, since in order to attract capital at all, interest rates had to be high. Second, wages in the Irish Free State were also relatively high, high enough at all events to make it unlikely that mass-produced Irish goods would be at all competitive with those of low-wage countries such as Japan. And again, the home market was so restricted that this in itself inhibited the development of businesses large enough to trade successfully in the outside world.[41]

Not, indeed, that the creation of small, home-based industries was enough to make Ireland self-sufficient, even behind tariff barriers. Lacking most kinds of cheap fuel or raw materials, the very fact of industrialisation meant for her a larger import bill – the value of imports other than foodstuffs rose from £27.6 million in 1932 to £30 million in 1938.[42] Some of this was accounted for by the import of machinery or semi-manufactured goods to be worked up in Ireland, though some of it, it is only fair to add, may have been due to increasing sophistication among consumers as a slowly rising national income put more commodities within their reach. There was, it seems, considerable rigidity in the wage-structure which, in industry, changed very little between 1932 and 1935, even though the cost of living for most of that time had been steadily going down; the latter did, it is true, begin to rise again from 1935 onwards, but so also did industrial wages, though apparently to a lesser extent.[43]

Given the restricting conditions within which industry had to work, it was clear that any real advance in the economic life of the country would, as always, be bound up with the condition of agriculture. Only in this sector was there any real potentiality for developing the export trade, and it was only by developing that trade that purchasing power within the economy could be generated.* Yet in the 1930s, in the midst of world depression complicated by the economic war with Britain, the prospects of agricultural prosperity could hardly have seemed grimmer. Irish exports (mainly agricultural) had dropped from forty-seven million pounds to thirty-six million pounds even between 1929 and 1931. Between then and 1934 they fell by a further eighteen million pounds, or by twenty-seven per cent in volume.[44] In such a situation self-sufficiency became less a policy of economic advance than a vast rescue operation. The most desperate efforts were used to re-orientate agriculture – to make the country less dependent on the badly injured cattle industry, while at the same time preventing that industry from collapsing into total ruin. All sorts of devices were used – a guaranteed price for wheat, import controls on flour and bacon, export subsidies on butter, bacon and sheep offals, compulsion to use a quantity of home-produced grain in animal feeding-stuffs, bounties on cattle exports, the development of the beet-sugar industry, the halving of land annuity charges to farmers.

Yet, despite these varied inducements, the overall volume and structure of Irish agriculture showed remarkably little change during

* It has been estimated that in 1934-5, when the national income was about £140 million, the farming community in Ireland had only about £10.5 million to spend on household necessities, a figure which improved to £20 million in 1938 and £70 million in 1950. The same authority reckons that national income, which rose from £158.2 million in 1938 to £363 million in 1950 at current prices, in real terms actually advanced by only twenty-four per cent in the period 1938-50. See the able and suggestive article by R. C. Geary, 'Irish Economic Development Since the Treaty', in *Studies* (Dec. 1951), xl, pp. 399-418.

the decade as a whole. Net agricultural output (that is, everything consumed on, or sold off, the farm less the value of feeding-stuffs, seeds and fertilizers) reached a peak in 1935-6, but was actually at a lower level in 1938-9 than in 1929-30. There had, it is true, been a substantial increase in the output of crops and the dramatic increase in the acreage of wheat is perhaps the best known fact in the economic life of the country in the pre-war years. From just under 21,000 acres in 1931 it had increased to 255,000 acres in 1936. Taking as base-year 1930=100, the index number for the acreage of wheat in 1936 was 952, falling back somewhat in the next two years and rising to 955 in 1939.[45]

But this movement is in reality misleading. More wheat was grown, certainly, and the time was fast approaching when the country would be grateful for it, but the acreage under wheat represented in the main a switch out of other crops. The overall increase in tillage had in fact been very small. Again taking the year 1930 as 100, the index number for the total area of tillage was 111 in 1936 and only 102 in 1939. What seems to have been happening was that whereas the cattle crisis, combined with government encouragement of other forms of agriculture, had caused a swing towards tillage (and to some extent dairying also) in the early part of the decade, as soon as the coal-cattle pacts gave grounds to hope for better times, farmers began thankfully to revert to their old pattern. Indeed, by 1937-8, although the value of cattle exports was still much below what it had been in 1929-30 (an annual average of £8.5 million as against £14.2 million) cattle now took 50.8 per cent of agricultural exports compared with 43.8 per cent in the earlier years; the percentage share of every other significant agricultural export except horses had declined in the interval.[46]

It is difficult, therefore, to avoid the conclusion that all the efforts of the government had done little to change the real terms of the problem. That problem has been admirably stated by a recent writer:

Manufacturing industry was geared to the small protected home market and because of this its costs were too high to warrant any hope of a substantial export trade. Agricultural exports depended to a greater extent than ever on cattle, and against an expansion of cattle production there were formidable and well-nigh impenetrable barriers. An increase in non-cattle exports implied an increase in subsidies, which in turn implied a further reduction in living standard.[47]

The consequence was that although Irish incomes were increasing slowly during the decade, the gap between those and British incomes was widening. Whereas in 1931 the average income per head in Ireland was sixty-one per cent of that in Britain, by 1939 the corresponding figure was forty-nine per cent.[48] It was hardly surprising that emigration, which had slowed down, now again accelerated, leaving two dire consequences in its train. One was that domestic demand for the products of Irish industry and agriculture was to that extent further diminished. The other, even more serious, was that while protection had created a whole complex of vested interests not necessarily compatible with present efficiency or future prosperity, emigration, by removing some of the pressures for change, contributed its share to what seemed the immutable inertia of Irish economic life.

Nor was this situation significantly altered by the war years. In a sense, indeed, they may be said to have intensified it. For the war in its turn had three principal effects upon the Irish economy. In the first place, by imposing a state of siege upon the country, it gave more emphasis than ever to the policy of self-sufficiency. Second, because of the inevitable shortages of fuel, raw material and semi-manufactured goods of all kinds, any significant industrial advance was virtually ruled out. And finally, and perhaps most important of all, the safe stagnation of Irish neutrality was more than counterbalanced in the eyes of an increasing number of young people by the swollen wage-packets of wartime Britain. In a recent, moving account of the de-population of a Mayo town, Mr John Healy recalled that his first reaction, listening as a boy to Neville Chamberlain's voice on the radio announcing the outbreak of war with Germany was: 'A war! Maybe the Germans will blow up the school above.' And he continues: 'They didn't, of course: instead the war which never touched our shores eroded our town more completely and insidiously than if it had been subjected to a one-night blitz.'[49]

To some extent this is emotional over-simplification. Emigration from Mayo was no new phenomenon, though, as Mr Healy points out, in the past it had tended to be rural rather than urban. During the war years it was both rural and urban. And the evidence of the travel documents issued during the war certainly gives point to his lament. It indicates that Mayo headed the list of counties with the greatest number of emigrants, both male and female. Between 1940 and 1951 it lost a greater total (43.4 thousand) than any other county except Dublin, while the average annual rate of 27.8 per thousand was far ahead of that of all the other counties – the nearest rivals, significantly, being those other remote and beautiful corners of the western world, Donegal and Kerry. Travel documents, obviously, are no more than a broad guide to the number actually leaving the country as permanent emigrants, but the evidence of the first two Censuses after the war suggest that net emigration for the whole of the twenty-six counties was just over 187,000 between 1936 and 1946 and 119.6 thousand in the next five years.[50]

It could be argued, almost in Malthusian terms, that, leaving aside the long-range social, economic and human problems of emigration, the exodus of so many young people helped the country in two ways to survive during the war years. On the one hand, the remittances they sent home were a much needed addition to private resources and, ultimately, to the national income. On the other hand, there were, to put the matter brutally, that many fewer mouths to feed. And feeding the existing population was, naturally, the obsessive preoccupation of the government.

To achieve this end what had to be done was to intensify the policies initiated in the pre-war years, but to do this without benefit of foreign animal feeding-stuffs, farm machinery or fertilizers. Despite these handicaps the volume of net agricultural output increased very considerably. Taking 1938-9 as 100, the index rose fairly steadily until by 1945 it had reached 116.8. There were several reasons for this. One was that output was ruthlessly maintained at the expense of the soil. Lack of fertilizers and intensive exploitation of the land meant that even during the war years the yield in starch pounds per acre fell sharply; had this been continued much longer the effects would have been ruinous. A second reason for the increase in output was the official policy of compulsory tillage. In 1940 it was made obligatory to till one-eighth of the arable land in each holding; by 1944, and until the policy was abandoned in 1948, the proportion was as high as three-eighths. A third factor affecting the volume of agricultural production was the drive to replace almost non-existent coal by turf; production of this fuel went up from just under 3.9 million tons in 1939 to 4.4 million in 1943. Finally, of course, it has to be remembered that since the main sector of Irish agriculture was and remained grass-based dairying, cattle and sheep production, the raw material, so to speak, was already there in abundance and unlikely to be too much affected by the shortage of fertilizers or machinery.[51]

In practical terms the most significant feature of the war-time years was the rise in the area of tillage and especially of that devoted to wheat. The total area of tillage (including not only grain but root and green crops and flax), which had been 1.5 million acres in 1939, had expanded five years later to 2.6 million. Wheat, which had accounted for about 250,000 acres in 1939, reached 662,000 acres in 1945 – the largest figure ever reached since agricultural statistics first began to be collected in 1847.[52] Even this vast effort did not suffice to avoid bread-rationing, which was imposed in 1942. Other commodities to be rationed were tea, sugar and butter; meat not only remained plentiful, but the export of live animals and meat products continued to be the staple of Irish trade with Britain and the principal means whereby neutral Ireland managed to build up large external assets during the war. The percentage of agricultural output exported during the war naturally declined, but the decline was not as catastrophic as might have been feared. It fell from an average of 34.3 per cent in the five years preceding the war to an average of 26.3 per cent between 1939 and 1945, reaching its lowest point, 20.6 per cent, afterwards, in the bleak year of 1947 when the British market was in various ways deeply depressed. Thereafter it revived, though even by the early 'fifties it had barely reached its immediate pre-war level.[53] But by then external conditions, and indeed internal ones also, had changed so greatly that Ireland was confronting a different world.

(iii) POST-WAR VICISSITUDES

For a time at least this different world was a world where the surpluses of the 'thirties had given place to widespread scarcity, offering a greater outlet for Irish farm produce. It was also a world where governments were deeply concerned with full employment, even if this entailed large public spending. For Ireland there was both opportunity and danger in this situation. Opportunity, in that there was now a climate of opinion very different from the rigid financial orthodoxy still prevalent in the earliest years of the Free State, and consequently an increasing pressure on governments to spend more. But danger, also, in that full employment with high wages in Britain not only continued to attract Irish men and women to the honey-pot, but created similar expectations amongst those who stayed at home.

How well equipped was Ireland to satisfy those expectations? Superficially, she was in a strong position, with large external assets (worth £270 million in 1946) and the prospect of a constant demand for her exports. On the other hand unemployment still continued at a high level and, in the immediate aftermath of the war, the natural desire of the population for an end to austerity and the pressure of long pent-up wage claims created very rapidly an inflationary situation. As early as 1947 there was a balance of payments deficit of nearly thirty million pounds and this was no isolated phenomenon. By 1956 recurrent deficits had 'more than offset the surpluses earned during the last war'.[54]

The unpleasant fact was that the economy had not fundamentally changed since the war and that its inherent weaknesses had not been eradicated. One way of illustrating this is to consider the slow growth of that entity, notoriously elusive and difficult to measure, the Gross National Product (defined as national income plus depreciation plus indirect taxes minus subsidies). Between 1949 and 1956 the *volume* of GNP grew by perhaps eight per cent, compared with twenty-one per cent for Britain and forty-two per cent for the countries grouped in the Organisation for European Economic Co-operation. But in terms of *rate of growth* the story is even more revealing. Between 1926-1938 the percentage rate of increase may have been no faster than 1.2 per cent per annum, though this can be no more than a tentative estimate. During the war, and up to 1947, it was apparently nil. Between 1947 and 1953 the rate was 1.8 per cent per annum, levelling out at about 2 per cent during the next decade.[55]

This was a perceptibly slower rate of growth than the British and quite markedly slower than those prevailing in the OEEC countries.

And even this growth owed an unhealthily large proportion to heavy state spending, directed mainly towards social welfare. What was happening in the decade after the war was that the government was making frantic attempts not merely to provide work for the population and in so doing to reduce emigration, but also to provide amenities and services of a kind that were coming to be normal elsewhere but of which Ireland was still largely innocent.

It must be said that to a certain extent, though at the cost of a mounting deficit, this policy took effect. Farm incomes improved with an expanding market, rising cattle prices, and heavy government expenditure on agriculture, and the demand for goods and services increased. Since a protectionist tariff was still jealously maintained, home industry could not but benefit. The volume of production of transportable goods in 1953 was nearly twice what it had been in the war years and the numbers employed in the industries producing such goods went up by about a third. Even so, this growth was not well sustained, at any rate beyond 1955, and it was certainly insufficient to staunch the flow of emigration. Not only was there a steady decline in the number of people working (in agriculture it dropped from 597.2 thousand in 1946 to 378.7 thousand in 1961, and in manufacturing industry from 187.6 thousand to 179.4 thousand between the same two dates) but the number leaving the country continued to be formidable. Net emigration for 1951-6 was 196,763, for 1956-61 it was 212,003.[56] These rates were nearly three times the pre-war rates and for the decade 1951-61 in particular were higher than for any other comparable period in the twentieth century.

Some at least of the current explanations for the slow growth of Irish industry are all too familiar – it still suffered from a shortage of private capital, it was still unable to develop any extensive range of competitive exports, it was still inhibited by the smallness and relative poverty of its domestic market. But in the 1950s, no more than in the 1930s, could these defects be separated from the most deep-seated problem of all – the condition of Irish agriculture. Because of her small internal market and her lack of fuel and raw materials, Ireland could not achieve Western European living standards without selling abroad. For her, to sell abroad meant in effect to sell her agricultural produce. In the last resort everything depended upon that. And it was in this sector that the government made its most determined efforts at stimulation.

In terms of policy there was no revolutionary change of direction, but there was a striking increase in the amount of money the government was prepared to spend on agriculture. This went up from about £4⅓ million in 1939 to £13¼ million in 1952; in the latter year that amounted to just over 10 per cent of total state expenditure and the proportion tended to grow as time went on, rising (with occasional set-backs) to 18.7 per cent in 1962.[57] Yet, despite this spending, the return was hardly impressive, indeed distinctly unimpressive by comparison with those Western European standards by which Ireland was beginning to measure herself. If the immediate pre-war period be taken at 100, then in 1947-8 the index number for Ireland's volume of gross agricultural production was 90, compared with a combined OEEC figure of 83. But by 1959-60, while the Irish figure had gone up only to 97, the OEEC figure stood at 139. In fact, as has often been observed, the volume of Irish agricultural output had remained virtually static since 1909, and there are grounds for believing that it was then not significantly greater than it had been in 1861.* It is true that the *net* output (that is all output consumed on, or sold off, farms less the value of feeding-stuffs, seeds and fertilisers bought by farmers) increased by about twenty per cent between 1929-30 and 1963, but a considerable part of this may well have been due to the widespread introduction of tractors (40,000 during that period) and other kinds of mechanisation.[58]

An essential feature of the 1930s had been the guaranteeing of minimum prices to the growers of particular crops. This was continued into the post-war years, though sometimes with odd results. Wheat, for example, which was *par excellence* the crop so singled out, expanded so fast that in 1957-8 there was an embarrassing surplus which had to be disposed of at an estimated loss to the exchequer of nearly £1½ million; in consequence, the government had hurriedly to revise its policy, applying the guaranteed price to a reduced tonnage and 'marrying' the price received by the growers to the total receipts for the sale of wheat. So also with sugar-beet, which in the 'fifties was approaching a position of surplus, with the result that in 1959 the Irish Sugar Company had to take steps to restrict the acreage. More significant than these variations in the yield of specific crops was the fact that because wheat and sugar-beet were economically attractive by reason of the price-supports they enjoyed, less of the available tillage was allotted to oats, potatoes and green crops. Further, with the protection of barley mainly for the benefit of the maltsters, the import of cheaper foreign barley and maize was stringently controlled. This in turn had its effect on the smaller farmer, showing itself in a marked decline of the pig industry and in the even more drastic decline of poultry.

In the broader terms this readjustment was tending to increase the country's reliance upon dairy-produce, cattle and sheep and especially the last two. Whereas in 1937-8, cattle, beef and veal had together accounted for 50.8 per cent of Irish agricultural exports, by 1960-1 this had gone up to 70.2 per cent. The rise in sheep, mutton and lamb exports was only of the order of 1 per cent, but the share of pigs, poultry and dairy-produce together had fallen from 36.3 per cent to 16.7.[59] More and more they had to find their satisfaction in the home market – the export battle on which so much depended was to be

* See above, p. 603; the estimated increase in gross volume between 1861 and 1909 was twenty-five to thirty per cent.

fought mainly by the cattle industry. What seemed to be happening was that in the old tug-of-war between intensive and extensive farming, the latter was once more gaining an ascendancy. And while this may have made sound economic sense, it was more questionable in social terms. No doubt the intention behind state aid to agriculture was to improve farm incomes, but there remains some doubt as to how far this really happened. The increase of food prices fell upon the countryman as upon the town-dweller, and so did the consequential increase in the price of consumer goods. Since Irish population was still preponderantly rural, it followed that the farmer paid heavily for his price-supports. True, there were profits to be made, but with the renewed emphasis on extensive farming, these tended to be made on the larger farms. It was not merely that the best prices were obtained for the products of the bigger grass-farms, or even that the increased price of feeding-stuffs adversely affected characteristic small-farm lines such as pigs and poultry; it has also to be remembered that technological change was at last beginning to have its impact upon Irish agriculture and that, as always, it was the larger farms that could best afford, and stood most to benefit from, mechanisation.

It would therefore be dangerous to assume that however fervently government policy may have been aimed at transferring wealth from the non-agricultural to the agricultural population, this actually happened in the way intended. We are too close to these events to be dogmatic about them, but it must be said that it is at least as possible that the real transfer of wealth may have been from small farmers to large farmers, a transfer which cannot be divorced from one of the great social problems of the post-war years – the problem of rural depopulation. It can scarcely be a coincidence that the movement towards consolidation, already well-established, continued steadily. In 1931 farms of one to thirty acres accounted for 57.9 per cent of all holdings and 22.5 per cent of farming land; by 1960 the comparable percentages were 49.6 and 17.4. Even more striking than this was the decline in the number of males engaged on small farms. Between 1931 and 1960, while the total number of males engaged in all forms of agriculture had dropped by 24 per cent, those working on farms of one to thirty acres fell by 50 per cent as compared with a 12 per cent drop on farms of a hundred acres or over.[60] Now, rural depopulation tends to be most directly influenced by the disparity of prices between rural and other incomes and by the possibility of bridging that gap through moving either to the towns or across the sea. A modern writer has put this controversial point thus : 'To the extent to which the policy of farm produce price support depressed the real income of the agricultural community, particularly of those on small farms, it must be held responsible for rural depopulation.'[61] But how far the policy of price support really has led to this result still remains a matter of debate.

The picture of a depleted countryside and of an agriculture which, despite its considerable internal changes of structure, had not succeeded in raising its volume of output to any significant degree, must be seen against the background, already sketched, of a national economy that was finding it exceedingly difficult to adjust to the post-war world. By the middle 1950s a serious crisis of confidence had developed, caused partly by the specific and recurring nightmare of a balance of payments deficit (between 1947 and 1956 the surpluses accumulated during the war were more than wiped out, and although a small surplus was in fact achieved in 1957 this was only by most stringent economies), and even more by a widespread anxiety that the general performance of the economy was so poor that the country was falling behind Western Europe standards, not only in productivity but in the social benefits that productivity might be expected to confer. In 1955, therefore, a Capital Investment Advisory Committee was appointed to examine especially the position with regard to public investment. It recommended, as was to be expected, that a greater proportion of this investment should in future be directed to productive ends, and with this in view urged that a programme for economic development be drawn up. This was entrusted to T. K. Whitaker, the secretary of the Department of Finance, with results that historians may yet come to describe as revolutionary.

(iv) TAKE-OFF?

After a few months of intensive work, Dr Whitaker presented his report, entitled *Economic Development*, to the government in May 1958: on its publication at the end of that year it was at once recognised not merely as an important contribution to the economic debate, but as offering a way out of the economic impasse. It is hardly too much to say, indeed, that even today it can be seen as a watershed in the modern economic history of the country. On the one hand, it looked forward to a prosperous future which, given certain conditions, might be – as in many ways it has been – achieved in a relatively short time. But on the other hand it offered a telling indictment of all the inadequacies which the record of the previous forty years had revealed so starkly – the backwardness of agriculture, the meagreness of industry, the decline in population, the shadow of emigration, the scarcity and timidity of private capital, and the tendency of public capital to be expended on projects that were without doubt socially desirable, but were also too often economically unproductive. For the classic symptoms of low income per head combined with a consistently adverse balance of payments, Dr Whitaker offered remedies that may at first sight have appeared startling, but were in reality no more than the intelligent application to the local Irish situation of doctrines that had been current among economists elsewhere for many years.

So persuasive were his arguments that, with relatively minor exceptions, they were reproduced in their essential terms in the First Programme for Economic Expansion which the government laid before the Oireachtas in November 1958. It was in effect a five-year plan for expansion – expansion which was to involve many sectors of the country's economy, but principally agriculture and industry. So far as agriculture was concerned, the main effort was to go into improving grassland farming, so as to achieve an increase in output and in exports. Linked with this there was to be a campaign for the eradication of bovine tuberculosis, more efficient marketing and more intensive development of agricultural education. The amount of money spent on agriculture, which was already estimated to be nineteen million pounds for 1958-9, was to go beyond the twenty million pounds mark in succeeding years, and some price supports were still to be maintained for wheat, beet, milk and eggs.

In industry, the primary aim was seen to be the stimulation of 'a vast increase in private industrial investment while maintaining the supply of capital for productive state enterprises'. This did not mean a cessation of state intervention on the industrial front – far from it, the number of state-sponsored bodies (almost all concerned with finance, production or communications) increased by twelve between 1958 and 1961 – but it did mean that traditional policies would be re-assessed. Foreign capital, already wooed by the coalition government in 1956 and more systematically by the Industrial Development (Encouragement of External Investment) Act of 1958, would be further enticed by tax concessions and other facilities. And not only that, protection for protection's sake would no longer be tolerated. The Programme took it for granted that before long Ireland would be participating in some form of European Common Market and that to aim at self-sufficiency in the old style was simply not realistic. 'Hence', it continued, 'it must now be recognised that protection can no longer be relied upon as an automatic weapon of defence and it will be the policy in the future *in the case of new industries* to confine the grant of tariff protection to cases in which it is clear that the industry will, after a short initial period, be able to survive without protection.' There were, of course, other ways of assisting infant industries, and the government pledged itself to help in the starting of new projects, the purchase of machinery, the cost of technical assistance schemes, the siting of industry in underdeveloped areas and always and above all, in the promotion of exports.

The cost of this 'leap forward' was substantial, but, as the Programme insisted, it was a time when risks had to be taken. Adding the various kinds of promised aid together it seemed that the *new* government expenditure would amount, for the full term of the plan (from 1959-60 to 1963-4) to £53.4 million. And if this in turn were added to the cost of the existing schemes the formidable total for the five years would be £220.4 million.[62]

How far did success attend these undoubtedly strenuous efforts? It is too early to give a considered answer to this question, though some of the signs are at least encouraging.* The Gross National Product, for example, rose over the period of the plan by more than four per cent per annum instead of the modest two per cent aimed at in the Programme, though it has been pointed out that external conditions were particularly favourable at that time, that the stimulus of the prospect of entry into European Common Market may also have played a part, and that, anyway, there existed in the country unutilised capacity which only waited opportunity. Be that as it may, the fact remains that investment was almost doubled, despite an increase in savings. Most remarkable of all, the long drawn-out fall in the population seemed at last to have been halted. The Census of 1966 showed an actual increase in the population of 62,411 persons, while emigration reached a new low level. The total for the five years 1961-6 was 83,855, little more than a third of the previous intercensal period, and the annual net rate per 1,000 had fallen from the disastrous 14.8 of 1956-61 to 5.7 between 1961 and 1966. It was notable also that the increase in population manifested itself most strikingly in the lower age-groups; if this were to continue it might have profound implications for the marriage rate.[63]

The new programme, however, was not free of criticism. Although it did indeed seem to have precipitated, or at least coincided with, an industrial boom of which the evidence was clearly visible in the form of new factories, increased employment and a higher standard of living, it was evidently less effective in the agricultural sector on which so much attention had been lavished. Thus, whereas net agricultural output was only one per cent higher in 1963 than in 1957, industrial output in 1963 was forty-seven per cent above its 1957 level. The relative failure in the farming sector seems to have been in part due to inadequate and rather unsophisticated planning, in part to exceptionally adverse market conditions. The agricultural expansion envisaged in the Programme laid most weight on the development of beef production, though it was also intended to shift the increasing amount of state expenditure into more constructive projects by granting subsidies rather to means of production (such as fertilizers) than to finished products (for example bacon or butter), and by gradually transferring the Agricultural Grant away from rate-relief and towards increased research, education, and advisory schemes. Hopefully, it was also suggested that the number of cows might be increased by 50,000 a year, to reach a total of 1½ million by 1964. In fact the number of cows did rise, but only from 1,235,700 in 1957 to 1,318,000 in 1963. At the same time the number of horses fell by 76,000 and the contraction of tillage, and corresponding expansion of grassland, amounted to 251,000 acres.

* The best analysis known to me is that by Garret FitzGerald, *Planning in Ireland* (London and Dublin, 1968), chap. 4; see also J. Meenan, *The Irish Economy Since 1922* (Liverpool, 1970), chap. 16.

As part of the campaign for agricultural improvement, state spending on fertilizers was raised during the five year period covered by the Programme from under £1 million to £3.6 million and the cost of these to the farmer dropped by over a third. Between 1957 and 1962 consumption of fertilizers went up by about two-thirds. If this sounds impressive it has to be remembered that the rate of increase was much the same in the bad years 1948-57, when the price of fertilizers was rising. This suggests that fertilizer use may be determined more by farm structure than by its own cost. In Ireland fertilizers have traditionally been much less used on grassland than on tillage – consequently the increase in grassland during the period of the First Economic Programme was likely to have affected adversely the consumption of fertilizer.

An integral part of the plan to develop the cattle industry still further was the scheme for the eradication of bovine tuberculosis. This was pursued with great vigour and before the Programme was completed the disease had been virtually stamped out in twenty of the twenty-six counties, though since the remaining six included some of the key dairying counties, success could hardly be called complete. Still, if the campaign had not been undertaken and carried through so swiftly, the bulk of Irish store cattle might have been banned from entering the United Kingdom. Whether the effect of such a ban might not have been to stimulate an equally lucrative trade in carcasses has been, and still is, much argued. What cannot be disputed, however, is that despite all the efforts made, the rise in the net agricultural output of the country was in reality very small. Taking as the base year 1953=100, the index of volume increased from 106.8 to 108 between 1957 and 1963. These are hardly the statistics of an agricultural revolution.[64]

Before the First Economic Programme had run its course the government was laying its plans for a Second Programme which was introduced in 1963 and intended to cover the period up to 1970. Whereas the First Programme had been deliberately flexible and reluctant, in view of the external pressures to which Ireland was exposed, to set specific targets, the Second Programme did commit itself to more precise objectives. It was intended that the Gross National Product should increase, in real terms, by fifty per cent in the decade of the 1960s – more precisely that the GNP, which in 1960 was £669 million at the prices then prevailing, should by 1970 reach £1,000 million, valued at the prices that ruled in 1960. To achieve this it was proposed that the growth rate for the economy as a whole between 1964 and 1970 should not fall below what it had been under the First Programme – i.e. 4 per cent per annum – though individual sectors were expected to grow at different annual rates, the industrial target being fixed at 7.1 per cent and that of agriculture at 3.8 per cent. It was anticipated also that exports of goods and services would rise by 75 per cent during the decade, that there would be a net increase in employment of 81,000, and that net emigration would by 1970 be reduced to 10,000 a year.[65]

These were hostages proffered to fortune, with a vengeance. And how very much Ireland was at the mercy of fortune's wheel was brought home to the country immediately after the Second Programme had got under way, when Britain, herself in the throes of economic crisis, included Ireland in the fifteen per cent levy on imports she imposed in October 1964. The Irish government protested in vain, although some of the damage was repaired by the trade agreement signed between the two countries in December 1965. By that agreement Britain undertook to remove almost all restrictions on Irish goods by July 1966 and Ireland agreed to remove hers on British imports over a period of ten years. British import quotas for Irish bacon and butter exports, which had been damaging, were to be increased and Irish exports of live animals and meat products were also to be gradually raised. In return, Ireland undertook a progressive dismantling of the special terms granted to foreign investors and management. Since at the same time Irish tariff policy was still being shaped both by the commitment to participate in the 'Kennedy round' of general tariff reductions, and by the assumption that sooner or later entry into the Common Market must come, it is obvious that her exposure to external forces, always great, was being intensified.*

Experience has shown, alas, that the high expectations of the Second Programme were somewhat over-optimistic. This was partly due to difficult economic conditions in the world at large, partly to internal strains and stresses, some of them probably inseparable from the unprecedentedly rapid economic advance the country was undergoing. Thus, while industrial development continued to make headway, unemployment (especially in agriculture) remained higher than expected, there was a heavy deficit in the balance of payments of £41.8 million in 1965 (though by 1967 this had been converted into a modest surplus of £10 million), and emigration continued at an embarrassingly high level which did not fall below 15,000 in any year between 1963 and 1967, actually rising in 1965 to over 20,000. In addition, government expenditure – partly to finance development and partly to increase social services – grew faster and consumed a greater share of resources than had been foreseen, with the result, among other things, that the tax burden on the citizen was correspondingly increased.[66] The cumulative effect of these disappointments was to produce

* The intimacy of the economic connection with Britain was probably inevitable in the circumstances, but it is well to remember that it could be dangerously one-sided. Irish agriculture, for example, has been vulnerable for some twenty years to the British policy of buying food in the cheapest market, a policy which could be pursued with few inhibitions once the decision had been taken – as it was after the Second World War – to cushion British farmers against its effects by compensating them with so-called 'deficiency payments'.

a major readjustment in the national plan, signalised by the ending of the Second Programme before its term and the introduction of a Third (and supposedly more realistic) Programme to cover the years 1969-72.

How this will turn out it is obviously much too soon to be able to say, though it requires no great insight to predict that it, like its predecessors, will continue to be at risk so long as there remains the present pervasive uncertainty about the kind of international frame-work to which this essentially exporting country is going to have to accommodate itself. Nevertheless, even though no quantitative test can be applied at this stage, no-one who knows the country in the mid-sixties well and compares it with what it was twenty years earlier can fail to be struck by the change. In part the change is visible and material – more factories, more office-blocks, new housing estates, better kept country cottages, an absence of barefoot children, a presence of supermarkets, television sets and family cars. But the change is more than just the emergence of a consumer society with debit as well as credit in the ledger. It is something impalpable and impossible to measure – a change of attitude, perhaps a change of heart. One can best describe it as a sense of new life and vigour, a stirring of hope, even a belief that the future will be better than the past has ever been.

Yet the last word must be one of caution. Not merely is the country faced with the great leap in the dark of entry into the Common Market, but the Third Programme has run into difficulties which, if they have little to do with the uncertainties of the European future, have a great deal to do with the realities of the Irish present. Although we are too close to events to be able to comment in any but the most tentative fashion, it is already clear that the pace of economic growth slackened between 1968, when national production rose at a record rate of 8 per cent, and 1970, when the rate of growth had declined to 2.5 per cent. The pattern for the latter year was admittedly distorted by damaging strikes in cement and banking, and there were signs of modest improvement by 1971, but how far these are the portents of a more general recovery is still (in the summer of 1972) an open question. Not only does the international economic environment remain somewhat bleak, but the continuing crisis in Northern Ireland has inevitably had an impact upon the south as well. The most obvious casualty has been the tourist industry – where, indeed, it is possible that no real growth at all will have been achieved by the end of the Third Programme in 1972 – but in general the widespread anxiety abroad as to whether violence might not spread to the Republic as well did nothing to foster foreign confidence in the Irish situation. Moreover, the country continued to be plagued by rising prices, and by the consequential wage demands, to such an extent that industry seemed to be becoming less rather than more competitive. Certainly, a comparison with certain major industrial powers for the period 1963-71 suggests that although output per man-hour had undoubtedly increased in Ireland, earnings per hour had also gone up so far and fast that Irish wage-costs per unit of output had by 1971 placed the Republic at a severe disadvantage.[67]

It was not therefore surprising that economic policy in 1971 should have had to be framed to meet a depressing combination of sluggish growth, rising prices and a large balance of payments deficit on current account. The situation might have been much worse had not agricultural exports reached a record figure of £221 million (industrial exports also rose, though not so steeply), but even so the government was obliged to resort to what looked suspiciously like an Irish version of 'stop-go', a cautious budget in the spring being followed by a dose of reflation in the autumn. It is too early yet to be able to say what the effect of these measures may be, or whether such improvisatory tactics will enable the Third Programme to get back on course, but the official forecast is not optimistic. For 1972 it anticipates a rate of increase in the volume of national production of no more than 2 to 2.5 per cent, with the implication that overall growth for the period 1969-72, instead of the 17 per cent originally projected, may be nearer to 12 per cent.[68] We can but conclude, therefore, that while entry into the Common Market may operate as a great liberating-force in succeeding years, the independently-functioning economy – so far as the Irish economy can truly be said to function independently – is still, despite the evidence of advance in many sectors, faced with large and intractable problems. The crock of gold at the foot of the rainbow remains tantalisingly elusive, and the rainbow itself seems to presage as much storm as sunshine.

5. Problems of Social Policy

'Ireland . . . not free merely, but Gaelic as well; not Gaelic, merely, but free as well.'[1] With these words Patrick Pearse consecrated, as it were, the union of language and nationality which had been the lodestar of his life and which, largely through his own efforts, had given a new depth and intensity to the revolutionary movement that culminated in the Easter Rising. And even though at that time enthusiasts for the Irish language were, like the revolutionaries themselves, in a small minority, the swing towards Sinn Féin between 1916 and 1918 which we observed earlier necessarily involved increased emphasis upon cultural no less than political independence. It was accepted in principle, even if practice lagged far behind, that Irish was an essential element in the establishment of a separate national identity and from the moment the first Dáil assembled in January 1919 the revival of the language became a major object of policy.

For obvious reasons it was not until the Anglo-Irish war was over that the Free State government could address itself to the formidable task of translating the ideal of a Gaelic Ireland into some kind of recognisable reality. Not much investigation was required to indicate just how formidable that task was. In the primary schools, where the main hope for the future must lie, less than a quarter of the total were giving any attention to Irish at all at the time of the transfer of power in 1921-2. It is true that at the secondary level, mainly because of the decision of the National University in 1913 to make Irish a compulsory subject for matriculation, an undoubted stimulus had been given to the teaching of the language – more precisely, perhaps to cramming it for examinations – but in the country as a whole the proportion of Irish speakers at the last Census before the war had been only 17·6 per cent of the total population.[2]

The new government did not lack advice as to how to go about the business of revival. It had before it two sets of suggestions, one emanating from the Gaelic League, the other from a conference convened by the Irish National Teachers' Organisation. The Gaelic League had not passed through the time of troubles unscathed. It had suffered a serious split in 1915 when a majority at the Dundalk Ard Fhéis (annual convention) had carried the famous resolution to include the political independence of Ireland among the League's objectives. Since it had been founded as a non-political body, Dr Douglas Hyde, its great father-figure, resigned and various other moderates followed his example.

Apart from these losses, some of the leading activists – Pearse, Mac-Donagh, Cathal Brugha – perished in or as a result of the fighting between 1916 and 1922 and the League itself, like most other nationalist institutions, was torn by the Civil War. It was, however, in 1920, with the Anglo-Irish war just beginning and the dissensions over the Treaty still far in the future, that the League issued its proposals for the future of the language, embracing all levels of education. So far as national schools were concerned it recommended that a distinction be made between three different categories – those in the Irish-speaking areas (the *Gaeltacht* properly so-called), those in partially Irish-speaking areas and those in English-speaking areas. In the first category all subjects should be taught through the medium of Irish; in the second, Irish should be regarded as the principal language of the school, and bilingual programmes should be adopted wherever possible; finally, in the English-speaking areas (which of course accounted for much the greater part of the country) Irish should still rank as the principal language and should be taught as a *spoken* language for an hour 'a day wherever teachers were available. It was further proposed that Irish be taught to all children in secondary schools; in the Gaeltacht it was to be the medium of instruction for other subjects and the remaining secondary schools elsewhere (again, the vast majority) were to be instructed to be in a position to do likewise at the end of five years. The universities for their part were to provide vacation courses to help teachers to reach the required level and were themselves to be prohibited from conferring degrees on students in any branch of learning who could not speak Irish fluently.[3]

This was certainly a far-reaching, not to say draconian, programme – much too much so to be practicable, given the fact that for over a hundred years the entire educational system had been exposed to pressures in favour of English less direct, perhaps, but no less effective, than those the Gaelic League would have liked to exert in favour of Irish. More significance, therefore, attached to the second set of suggestions aimed at the government in these early, formative years – the suggestions embodied in the 1921 report of the Conference organised by the Irish National Teachers' Organisation. The Conference was far from being fully representative of educational opinion in the country, but its proposals were sufficiently realistic to be taken seriously. Like the Gaelic League, the Conference was prepared to recommend compulsion, but in a modified sense. In the higher standards (classes) of the national schools Irish and English were both to be obligatory subjects, but Irish was to be the medium of instruction for the history and geography of Ireland and also for singing and drill. More radical even than this, and ultimately to be of great importance, was the recommendation that in infant classes *all* work done was to be in Irish – this despite the fact that English was the home language of ninety per cent of these small children. Since, however, at that time the country had not been finally partitioned and the Dáil might, in theory at least, be supposed to be legislating for all thirty-two counties, an escape clause was added to the effect that 'in the case of schools where the majority of the parents of the children object to having either Irish or English taught as an obligatory subject, their wishes should be complied with.'[4]

It was, of course, for the government to decide how far and how fast to adopt the principle of compulsion. It began, certainly, with a number of impressive gestures. The constitution of 1922 declared that Irish was 'the national language' and steps were taken to make at least some knowledge of it compulsory for civil servants, members of the Army and the Garda Síochana as well as in the Law Courts. This policy met with greater success than has sometimes been allowed, but since the great majority of the servants of the state in the early years of independence had been recruited under an English-speaking regime, it was asking too much to expect them to become bilingual overnight. Indeed, it may be that after nearly forty years it was still asking too much. A survey in 1959 indicated that the policy of making a knowledge of Irish essential for admission to certain grades of the civil service had resulted in some 4,000 civil servants (fourteen per cent of the total) achieving fluency, and a further 14,000 (fifty per cent of the whole) attaining a 'reading and writing' knowledge of it. The disconcerting fact that a further 10,000 were returned as having little or no Irish at all may perhaps partly be explained by the fact that the qualifying examination in the language was only imposed on about a third of the personnel, but it is less easy to understand why in the Gaeltacht itself as late as 1951 the effort to ensure that all public officials would have a competent knowledge of the language was reckoned to have been 'not more than half successful'. For the civil service as a whole it would appear (according to inquiries made in 1956) that outside those departments having particular need to use Irish the proportion of official business transacted through the language scarcely amounted to as much as two per cent of the total.*

The real battle for the language, however, has not been in the service of the state, but in what successive governments have regarded as its two principal nurseries – the schools and that dwindling area of the country where Irish is the everyday language of the people. If there was ever to be a truly national solution to the problem, the revival of Irish in the schools was obviously crucial and this was realised from the very beginning. The Provisional Government of 1922 had not been more than a few weeks in office when it ordained that as from 17 March

* It has been estimated that by a curious coincidence the amount of space annually occupied by Irish in the Dáil and Senate debates was less than two per cent though the number of deputies and ministers with a good knowledge of Irish was perhaps as high as one third. (*Commission on the Restoration of the Irish Language*, English summary of Final Report, pp. 21-23.)

of that year Irish should be taught or used as a medium of instruction in all primary schools for not less than one hour a day during the ordinary school hours where there was a teacher competent to do so.[5] In this last proviso lay the rub. For a survey of schools carried out that very year revealed that of some 12,000 teachers then employed in the national schools of the Free State, only 1,107 had certificates to show that they could teach bilingually; true, nearly another 3,000 had certificates indicating they could teach Irish and a further 922 had what were mysteriously described as 'temporary' certificates in the subject, but this still left a great many teachers totally unable to meet the government's requirements. Inevitably, there was a frantic rush to achieve a basic competence through summer courses and visits to the Gaeltacht. In 1922 alone £75,000 was paid out in grants for this purpose and, after the courses had been continued for another three years, it was reckoned that by the beginning of 1926 about 6,200 out of a total of primary teachers that had grown to 13,000 had reached a satisfactory standard.[6] So that the supply of teachers well versed in Irish might not only be maintained but increased, the Department of Education established in that year the first of a series of residential preparatory colleges for teachers which eventually were sited in Galway, Dublin, Ballyvourney, Donegal, Dingle and Tourmakeady.[7] Whether as a result of this initiative, or as a simple consequence of the passage of time, it has recently (1960-1) been claimed that ninety-six per cent of primary teachers are now qualified to teach Irish and eighty-nine per cent to teach other subjects *through* Irish, though it is not made clear how many of those qualifications are at pass and how many at honours level.[8]

The massive transformation that these figures suggest was no more than was necessary if government policy in the schools was to be implemented. In 1925-6 this policy was revised in the light of a second programme put forward by a further – and much more representative – Conference organised by the Department of Education. The principal recommendations were that where a teacher was competent and where children could assimilate the instruction so given, then Irish should be extended as a medium of instruction in other subjects as far as possible, though it was not to be obligatory where these provisions did not apply. Where the full use of Irish was not feasible, then a policy of gradual introduction was to be adopted. What this appeared to mean was that in infant classes all instruction was to be given through Irish regardless of the home-language of the children, and that further up the school time spent on a variety of subjects – for example, history, geography, algebra and geometry – was to be reduced to allow more class-hours to be spent on Irish. After fifteen years of this policy the Irish National Teachers' Organisation came out strongly against it and published a report indicating widespread dissatisfaction with the practice of teaching other subjects – especially arithmetic and algebra – 'through the medium'. In practice, it must be said, the regulations actually in force were not so rigorously applied as this would seem to indicate and from the late 1940s onwards progressive relaxations could be observed.* And although the government commission on the restoration of the Irish language took its stand unequivocally on the principle of bilingualism, its own figures indicated how far that principle was from being observed in the schools. Outside the Gaeltacht (where Irish, naturally, was the medium of all instruction) there were in 1960–1 only 183 schools in the whole of the Republic where all teaching was given through Irish; of these, 47 were special infant schools and most of the remainder were in areas bordering on the Gaeltacht.[9]

But the government did not rely entirely on the stick; the carrots also provided were not inconsiderable. This was particularly true of the secondary schools. As we saw earlier, Irish, as an optional subject, was already well established before independence and this situation continued after the transfer of power to such a degree that in 1924 (the last year in which the old system operated) eighty-six per cent out of a total of nearly 10,000 candidates presented Irish at the Intermediate Examination. Official policy was directed towards sustaining and encouraging this tendency by financial inducements of various kinds. Thus 'Class A schools', where Irish was the normal medium of instruction, Class B (1) schools, where the teaching given through Irish was not less than the teaching given through English, and Class B (2) schools where at least one other subject besides was taught through that medium, were all eligible for varying increases on their capitation grants up to a maximum of twenty-five per cent.† Teachers who could give instruction through Irish received a fifty pound increment, government grants for textbooks were made available, and, as an incentive to the pupils themselves, Irish was made an essential subject to qualify for scholarships at both the Intermediate and Leaving Certificate level. A proportion of

* Latterly there have been scattered signs of further efforts towards a more flexible policy. The government has adopted a new spelling (Litriú Nua), intended to come generally into use between 1962 and 1972), with the aim of bringing the written language nearer to daily speech. On the other hand, there is still strong feeling against teaching 'through the medium', which has found vehement expression in the recently formed Language Freedom movement. In their electoral platform in 1961, Fine Gael held out hopes of a more permissive attitude in the future, but though this may have helped them to pick up votes, they are still out of office. Even among devotees, it seems, there is a less dogmatic insistence on speaking the language at all times than formerly. The sign of such intention, the gold ring or Fainne, is sometimes nowadays replaced by the Fainne Nua, which indicates that the wearer can and will speak Irish, but does not feel bound to do so on all occasions.

† For the financing of secondary education after 1922, see the following section. It should perhaps be mentioned here that in the rare cases where a child does not include Irish in his secondary-school curriculum, the parent is normally expected to pay to the school an increased fee equivalent to the capitation fee so lost.

such scholarships have been set aside for children from the Gaeltacht, where in addition the parents or guardians of children between the ages of seven and seventeen years attending as day-pupils at national, secondary or technical schools, received a grant (initially two pounds, then five, later raised to ten pounds) for each child, provided that Irish was the language of the home and that the child spoke it fluently. It was, however, ominously significant that the number of children qualifying for such grants declined from 9,844 in 1955–6 to 9,158 in 1962–3.[10]

This decline is but one small illustration of the problem that has confronted the state for nearly half a century (and the language revival movement for a generation longer than that) – the problem not merely of restoring Irish outside the Gaeltacht, but of keeping it alive within the Gaeltacht. It is a problem complicated by the fact that the native-speaking areas (nearly all concentrated along the western seaboard) were precisely the areas that were economically least viable and were therefore being emptied faster by emigration – the haemorrhage there as elsewhere being mainly of the young blood upon which the continuity of the language in the last resort depended. That the problem was at bottom economic and social as well as linguistic has been recognised in official circles for at least forty years. As long ago as 1925-6 a special commission on the Gaeltacht urgently pointed out that it was necessary not just to prop up the language along the western seaboard, but to adopt a wide-ranging policy of welfare and employment in order to ensure that native-speakers were not driven out of the area by sheer economic necessity.

For many years, however, no very positive steps were taken. The seemingly insoluble difficulties of the Gaeltacht were passed nervously from one ministry to another and it was not until 1956 that a special Department was set up to look after the area.* The following year legislation was passed through the Dáil to develop and assist local industries in the area and in 1958 a state-sponsored body, Gaeltarra Eireann, was established to act as the main channel of government assistance, though the Gaeltacht continued also to benefit from the activities of other Departments as well, especially those concerned with

* Incredibly enough, it was not until that same year, 1956, that an agreed geographical definition of the Gaeltacht was arrived at. It was then declared to cover an area of 1,860 square miles (less than six per cent of the land surface of Ireland) which, however was not a homogeneous unit, but scattered along the western seaboard (Donegal, Mayo, Galway, Kerry), Cork and a district (Ring) in county Waterford; to this should be added two tiny colonies transplanted to county Meath. The total population was then 78,524, but the number actually at work in the Gaeltacht in 1961 was only 27,282, three-quarters of them employed in agriculture. (Even after 1956, such is the ineradicable conservatism of the official mind, it seems that some government departments still continued to cling to their own cherished and diverse definitions of what actually constituted the Gaeltacht.)

the well-being of depressed areas. On its establishment, Gaeltarra Eireann took over assets valued at £700,000 and in addition received £100,000 a year, primarily to finance the production and marketing of tweed, knitwear, embroidery and toys at thirty-four centres located in or near the Gaeltacht. By the early 1960s it had 700 full-time employees and another 1,000 part-timers on its books. Sales amounted in 1963–4 to £750,000 but only the tweed industry was paying its way; the others made such heavy losses that the trading deficit for that year was just over £100,000. Part of this deficit was undoubtedly due to the absence of industrial centralisation, but, since Gaeltarra Eireann has the social function of keeping the Gaeltacht in existence, as well as the economic function of making it more prosperous, these losses have hitherto been regarded as part of the price that has to be paid if the language is to be saved from extinction. In many other ways and from many other sources, assistance has been, and still is being, poured into the area, in some instances at a higher rate than for other parts of the country. Thus under the Land Project three-quarters of the cost of reclamation is provided by the state, compared with two-thirds elsewhere; animals for breeding purposes are provided at a reduced rate; the maximum grant for a new house was a hundred pounds more than it was for small farmers in other parts of the country, and the amount advanced for the reconstruction and improvement of old houses was markedly larger in the Gaeltacht; payments for road-building, for fishing-boats, for water-supply and sewerage were all on a relatively generous scale.[11]

Still more recently (in 1969), a council – Comhairle na Gaelige – was appointed by the government to help it towards a review of policy on the language question and to advise on future implementation of such policy, particularly in regard 'to the use of Irish as a medium of general communication'. An important part of its work since then has been the investigation of what is nowadays called 'sociolinguistics', and one of its first publications was a scholarly investigation of the problems presented by bilingualism in the Irish context.* In addition, the new council itself examined the possibilities of making local government more responsive to the needs of the Irish-speaking districts, and of securing for the Gaeltacht an adequate share of the energy – and the

* M. O Murchú, *Language and Community*, Comhairle na Gaelige, 'Occasional Paper No. 1' (Dublin, 1970). The paper advocates the attainment of an Irish-English 'diglossia' – that is a linguistic situation in which two languages may be used in different but overlapping domains (or spheres) of the individual's life in society; the implication for Irish in its present circumstances would seem to be that the revival of the language does not depend upon fostering it in one particular domain, but in all, with perhaps special emphasis upon the public rather than the home-neighbourhood domains. It is worth noting that the current emphasis on bilingualism is in marked contrast with the impracticable and chauvinistic ideas of the early language enthusiasts who wanted to uproot English altogether.

cash – which in the next few years, under the impetus both of the Buchanan Report* and of entry into the Common Market, is likely to be expended on regional development. The principal specific recommendations of Comhairle na Gaelige were that in each county containing a Gaeltacht area there should be established a Gaeltacht Area Committee consisting of representatives of the local electoral districts; that the business of the Committees and their offices should be conducted in Irish; that certain functions of the county councils should be transferred to the Area Committees and that, so far as possible, the latter should be empowered to act in their own areas for the Departments of State; that a Central Council for the Gaeltacht Area Committees should be established; finally, and from the development point of view, that Gaeltarra Eireann and the Shannon Free Airport Development Company should be asked to form a working party 'to furnish an early report on the requirements, objectives and implications of development in the Gaeltacht areas, the constituents of a co-ordinated set of development policies, the organisational structure suitable for their implementation, and the new powers and additional financing required'. It is obviously too soon yet to say what may be the effect of these recommendations – which would seem to represent a rather desperate attempt to halt the juggernaut of centralisation in its tracks – but at least it should be recorded that the government, much criticised as it often is for its alleged indifference to Gaeltacht problems, has already begun to implement some of the council's recommendations. Local government organisation is in the process of being reorganised along the lines suggested and provision is being made for Gaeltacht Area Committees and for a Central Council of those Committees; the working party on the future development of the Gaeltacht has submitted its report, which is being considered by the government; and, in the meantime, apart from assistance from the Special Regional Development Fund of nearly £2 million, the resources available to the Department of the Gaeltacht and to Gaeltarra Eireann have been increased to £4 million for the year 1972–3.[12]

Yet although this is evidence of effort and concern, critics have repeatedly urged that it is not enough. The Gaeltacht, in fact, is faced with two quite different dangers. On the one hand it has continued inexorably to shrink and by 1961 had a population of less than 80,000 native Irish speakers (a 1969 estimate puts it as low as 50,000), figures which put it within measurable distance of extinction. And on the other hand, some of the very measures now being taken to revive its material prosperity – most notably the development of tourism – threaten its linguistic integrity. The pressure on the native-speaker to become bilingual is overwhelming, and since the language of commerce

* Regional Studies in Ireland. A report commissioned by the United Nations on behalf of the Government of Ireland and prepared by Colin Buchanan and Partners, in association with Economic Consultants Ltd. (Dublin, 1968).

and of intercourse with the outside world is English, the inducements to give English the major place are well-nigh irresistible. 'If the present population trends and the present rate of language change continue', a modern writer has warned, 'there will be no Gaeltacht at all – not even the present bilingual semi-Gaeltacht – in another 20 years. If these factors intensify, the final demise will be swifter still.'[13]

This brings us to the crux of the problem. 'The preservation and the strengthening of the Gaeltacht', as the recent Commission on the restoration of the Irish language observes, '. . . must not be approached as if it were an attempt to preserve the Irish language and spread it as the normal language of Ireland. . . . There can be no survival, we fear, without revival.'[14] And although no doubt it is true that government support could be much more emphatic than it has been, it would be a kind of abdication – and, indeed a recrudescence of the 'slave-mentality' of an earlier age – if the revival were simply to be left in official hands.* It is, after all, in the ordinary habit and style of life that the battle must in the end be won or lost and the issue of that battle can only be decided by people, not governments. For it is not just impersonal economic factors, but intimate social and personal ones that press inexorably against the revival. Newspapers, books, the radio, the cinema, television, the motor-car, the tourist – all combine to lure native-speaker and non-native speaker alike towards the seeming delights of a mass civilisation from which, in their naïvete, they regard it as a badge of inferiority to be excluded. And just as in the days of Douglas Hyde the Gaelic League set itself towards the de-Anglicisation of Irish life and literature, so in the past decades not only the still-surviving League, but a multiplicity of other organisations as well, have followed, faint but pursuing the same objective. Only a few of these agencies can be mentioned here, but even a selection will serve to indicate their variety.

There are, for example, several newspapers and periodicals devoted to the language – the chief of them, *Inniu* ('Today') was founded in 1943 as a monthly, but became a weekly three years later and has a circulation variously estimated at between 11,500 and 17,000. There are several publishing houses, one of them run by the government, and a book-club, *An Club Leabhar*, with about 1,500 members. And although the demand for literature in Irish is clearly limited, a school of writers has grown up whose best work has received critical acclaim. They include an outstanding playwright, Mairéad Ní Ghráda, novelists and short-story writers such as Maírtin O Cadhain and Díarmaud O Súilleabhaín, together with several notable poets, among them Máire Cruise O'Brien. But it is ironic, and symbolic, that two works which in English translation had a wide circulation outside the country – *Twenty*

* The careful reader of the government White Paper of 1965 on the restoration of the language will observe that while the vast majority of the Commission's 288 recommendations are accepted in principle, the official attitude towards implementation seems decidedly cautious.

Years Agrowing by Muris O'Súileahbáin and *Peig* by Peig Sayers were both about the Blasket Islands off Kerry, which now have not only no Irish-speakers, but no inhabitants at all.

Apart from the printed word, music and sport have secured a fairly firm base in popular affection.* The Gaelic Athletic Association still continues to flourish and the All-Ireland competitions in hurling and Gaelic football attract vast crowds and enormous local patriotism.† Similarly, the music festivals (Fleadhs) organised from 1951 onwards by Comhaltas Ceoltoírí Eireann (Traditional Music Society of Ireland) have not only reawakened interest in the old songs and ballads at the parish level, but once a year bring together audiences of up to 100,000 at the All-Ireland Fleadh. More comprehensive in its appeal than either of these, and possibly the key to the whole future of the movement, is an organisation which was founded just over twenty-five years ago. This is Comhdáil Náisiúnta na Gaelige (National Gaelic Congress) created in 1943, but dominated since 1946 by a very powerful and energetic pressure-group, An Comhchaidreamh; originally composed mainly of students, several of its members have since attained to positions of considerable influence in Irish educational and intellectual circles. It was from this body that there sprang in 1953 one of the most interesting and successful initiatives in the revival movement – the organisation known as Gael Linn. Its primary purpose has been to use modern media to reach a wider public through Irish. To that end it has launched a football pool, has staged new plays, has provided gramophone records and has made two fascinating films, *Saoirse?* (Freedom?) and *Mise Eire* (I am Eire) with musical scores by the composer, Séan O'Riada, that have deservedly become famous.[15]

All this is certainly a sign of life, but the haunting question returns – how vigorous is that life and how far does this manifold activity serve to arrest the onset of ultimate extinction? No question is more bitterly debated in modern Ireland and the difficulty of arriving at a just assessment of the balance between the Irish-speaking and non-Irish-speaking sections of the population is greatly complicated by the fact that no satisfactory definition of what constitutes 'Irish-speaking' has yet been arrived at. Professor Brian O Cuiv, of the Dublin Institute of Advanced Studies, has estimated that by 1951 no more than 35,000 used Irish as their ordinary medium of speech and that no more than 3,000 people in the whole country were ignorant of English.[16] Official figures, which are sometimes criticised for being unduly over-optimistic, if not actually tendentious, do not paint so black a picture, but even so indicate a

* To the developments listed here should be added a new venture, Radio na Gaeltachta. This came on the air for the first time on 2 April 1972, largely because of the pressure of a group of dedicated individuals.

† The GAA continued to 'ban' its members from playing or attending foreign games on pain of expulsion from the Association, though this was only confirmed in 1965 after hot debate. Since then the ban has been removed.

grim enough situation. It has been reckoned that in 1936, of the population of three years and over, 660,601 – or 23·7 per cent of the whole – could speak Irish, but that this figure had fallen by 1946 to 588,725, or 21·2 per cent of the then population of three years and over. In 1961, on the other hand, it is claimed that the number of speakers has actually increased to 716,420 and that this amounts to 27·2 of all the people three years of age and over.[17]

It may be doubted, however, if this total is composed entirely of Irish-speakers who might by any stretch of the imagination be called fluent. On the contrary, most of the ordinary experience of life goes to suggest that not merely in Dublin, but even in Galway itself, English comes more readily to the tongue of most inhabitants.* Certainly, those who feel the language to be threatened have lost none of their sense of urgency, and schemes now being canvassed – for example, the use of language laboratories and the possibility of learning from the Israeli experiment in Hebrew – have about them an air of almost frantic enthusiasm as if their promoters knew – indeed, they must know – that time is inexorably running out. The future of the language, in short, remains as before balanced on a knife edge.[18]

(ii) EDUCATION

If the language enthusiasts sought to preserve and cherish what they had inherited from the past, the problem Irish educationists had to face presented itself in exactly opposite terms – to throw off the dead hand of history and create for their country a system of education that should be not only indigenous but modern as well. Yet for forty years after the foundation of the state, successive governments, so far from solving this problem, seemed scarcely to be aware that it even existed. And if it seems strange that Ireland, after passing through a period of intense political upheaval, should have rested content for so long with an educational structure of extreme conservativism, then one can only answer that the element of paradox in this situation was more apparent than real. As we saw earlier, almost from the moment schooling began to be organised on a national scale during the nineteenth century it took on a predominantly denominational character, both at the primary and the secondary – indeed also at the university – level. Nothing in the stormy years between 1916 and 1922 changed this situation in the slightest. True, the transfer of power resulted in a degree of centralisation, whereby the general responsibility for all kinds of education outside the universities which had been previously parcelled out

* In all fairness two points should be made here to redress the balance. One is that even if Galway city is much anglicised one does not have to go far along the coast to be in genuinely Irish-speaking country. And the other is that in Galway itself the University College has long been – and still remains – the only centre of higher education where a wide range of courses is taught and studied at degree level through the Irish language.

among the various Boards was vested in a Minister, operating from 1924 onwards through a newly created Department of Education. But although Professor Eoin MacNeill, who was Minister at the time of the reorganisation, spoke feelingly about the segregated and fragmented system he had inherited, that system was beyond his power to change. Neither the primary nor the secondary schools were state-owned, and although the government each year paid out considerable sums in teachers' salaries and – to the national schools – in building grants, direct control of the schools, including the appointment and removal of the teachers, remained in the hands of the managers. These, as before, were still overwhelmingly clerical, subject only to their bishops or to boards of trustees, as denominational practice might dictate.

This is not to say, of course, that the role of the state in education was restricted simply to that of milch cow. On the contrary, apart from a general responsibility for ensuring that the schools should provide adequately for the needs of society, the Minister had a primary duty to see that value was received for the money he dispensed. And although critics were in time to become vociferous about what seemed to constitute the official view of 'value', there can be no denying that, apart altogether from the financial pressures it could bring to bear, the Department's power to inspect schools and to conduct the public examinations gave it a decisive influence over the development of both the national and the secondary programmes. To understand the full extent and effect of that influence it will be necessary to look separately at the two levels, because, although it was a declared aim of policy to bring them into closer relationship with each other, they remained, and still remain, very different entities.

So far as the national schools were concerned, the government appears to have had four main objectives. The first was to revise the syllabus, partly, as we have seen, by the introduction of compulsory Irish, but partly also by the broadening of courses through the introduction of a wider range of optional subjects. After much experimentation the national school programme in the early 'sixties, on the eve, that is, of what may in time come to be called the educational revolution, was based on a five or six hour day, five days a week, for a minimum of 190 days in the year. Instruction was given in religion and in Irish, English, arithmetic, history, geography, music and (for girls) needlework; optional subjects (whose availability varied enormously, however, from school to school) included rural science or nature study, drawing, physical training, cookery or laundry or domestic economy for girls, and manual instruction for boys. Algebra and geometry were taught in some schools, but were not obligatory in the smaller ones or in classes taught by women. Of the working week about two and a half hours was spent on religion, about ten hours on vernacular languages (Irish and English in the approximate ratio of two : one), five hours on arithmetic and five hours on other subjects, with about one hour each for history and geography in the upper standards.[19] Such was the education received free of charge week by week by some 472,000 children between the ages of six and fourteen in 4,800 national schools.*

Linked with revision of the syllabus was the second objective of government policy – to facilitate movement from the primary to the secondary schools. Since the latter were fee-paying institutions (at least up to the beginning of the reform era in the mid-1960s) the most urgent need was to provide for an adequate number of scholarships to enable poor but able pupils to extend their education beyond the age of fourteen. To this end, legislation of 1921 and 1923 (the Intermediate Education Act and Local Government (Temporary Provisions) Act) empowered local authorities to levy a rate not exceeding a penny in the pound to finance such awards. The value of these scholarships was not large (varying from fifteen pounds to fifty pounds), but it underwent no significant change for forty years until the Local Authorities (Education Scholarships) Amendment Act of 1961 established the new principle whereby the state contributed an annual subvention amounting to at least half the value of the scholarships. In fact, the state tended to contribute more than the minimum amount and local authority scholarships soon rose dramatically in consequence – from 621 in 1961 to 1,775 in 1963.[20] The scholarships were of course for the exceptional minority, but for less gifted pupils the Department in the late 1920s instituted the Primary School Certificate examination, partly as a qualification to ensure admission to a secondary school, and partly in the hope that it would be of value to school-leavers seeking employment.† In practice this amiable intention resulted, as might have been anticipated, in a sacrifice of education to cramming and was condemned by the teachers themselves on more than one occasion. So long as the test was voluntary the issue was largely academic (between 1929 and 1942 only about twenty-five per cent of those eligible took it), but in 1943 the Department, in the teeth of strong criticism, made it compulsory for all who had reached the sixth standard, and by the early 'sixties some 40,000 children a year were thus committed to the examination mill.[21]

The third target at which the government aimed in these early years was one that had already attracted attention in the nineteenth century. Soon after the new Department was set up a determined attempt was made to carry forward the principle of compulsory attendance which had been half-heartedly introduced by the Irish Education Act of 1892. In 1926 the School Attendance Act only laid down that attendance should be compulsory on all school days for children between the ages

* There were in addition some 192 non-aided and fee-paying primary schools catering for about 21,000 children; these included the preparatory departments of secondary schools and were mostly in or near Dublin.

† A Primary School Certificate was not, however, essential for entry to a secondary school. Many of them held their own examinations at which the standard was notoriously low – a fact not uninfluenced, perhaps, by the system (described below) relating their government grants to the number of their pupils.

of six and fourteen, and that this should be enforced by special officers appointed by local School Attendance Committees and the police. In practice, it must be admitted, this requirement was somewhat vitiated by the right of the parent to give his child 'compulsory' education outside the state system (in his own home, if he so desired), and also by the inadequacy of the fines imposed and the slackness of the authorities themselves. Nevertheless, a perceptible improvement in average daily attendance has been registered – from 73.5 per cent in 1925-6 to 88.1 per cent in 1963.[22]

The question of school attendance was inextricably bound up with the fourth, and in some ways the most intractable, of the problems with which the new Department had to wrestle. Partly because education had developed along denominational lines, partly also because of the unavoidable effects of a declining population, a great deal of wasteful duplication had occurred over the years in the building and maintenance of the national schools. All sorts of related difficulties had arisen from this situation. Too many schools were understaffed, classes were frequently far too large, or else uneconomically small, buildings were old-fashioned and heating, lighting and sanitation were often totally inadequate. Between 1926 and 1932 efforts were made to amalgamate some of the smallest schools, but how ineffective these were may be seen from the fact that as late as 1962-3 there were still in the Republic 736 schools with one teacher each and 2,458 with two teachers each – the pupil-teacher ration being 17.9 in the first instance, and 26.3 in the second. Nor was the situation any better in the larger schools – indeed, it was actually worse, for the pressure of population was not matched by an adequate supply of teachers, with the result that the pupil-teacher ratio sometimes rose to over 40.[23] This serious imbalance – which not only affected the quality of the teaching, but also the well-being of the pupils, and in addition may often have accentuated the harshness of the discipline – was extremely difficult to rectify because of the fact that although the state paid by far the greater proportion of the cost of building (latterly its contribution compared with that of the local school authority has been in the ratio of 11 : 2), the schools nevertheless remained the property of the churches. The replacement of defective buildings, or even the provision of proper heating and water-supply, rested in the last analysis with the managers, and since many of these were old and conservative clergy it frequently followed that even though aid was freely available, interminable delays interposed before anything constructive was done. In recent years, it is true, more rapid progress has been made and attractive schools are to be seen in many parts of the country, but although in the decade 1953-4 to 1962-3 grants amounting to over sixteen million pounds were sanctioned for building or improvement, about 2,400 schools – roughly half the total – still occupied accommodation that dated from the nineteenth century.[24]

Despite its archaic features, primary education in Ireland has been able to call upon the services of a body of devoted teachers (14,000 of them according to a survey for 1962-3) who have undoubtedly done a great deal, despite the difficulties just described, to lay the foundations of a sound, if somewhat old-fashioned education. But it is when we seek to peer beyond this level, into the dark and confused world of secondary schooling, that the indications of strain and stringency become more apparent. At first sight, indeed, the unsatisfactory pattern which had emerged during the nineteenth century appears to have changed remarkably little in the first half of the twentieth.* Secondary schools remained firmly in private hands, owned and run either by religious orders, or boards of governors, or in very rare instances by individuals. Nevertheless, even in this sector the state during the past fifty years has steadily become more and more intimately involved, not merely in the financial provision for these schools, but in their staffing and teaching arrangements.

The first important break in the old pattern occurred as early as 1924 when the Intermediate Education (Amendment) Act repealed the clauses in previous legislation which had tied grants to secondary schools to the results obtained by their pupils in the public examinations. Instead, the new act provided that financial assistance to the secondary schools should be given in two main ways. First, a capitation fee was to be paid in respect of each recognised pupil, a pupil being 'recognised' if he had a Primary School Certificate or had otherwise satisfied the (normally very low) entrance requirements of the school. And second, the state paid the major part of secondary teachers' salaries, with bonus payments for those who taught through the medium of Irish.[25] The appointment and dismissal of these teachers continued to rest with the school authorities, but the Department's regulations required that schools in receipt of grants should employ a certain minimum of 'registered' teachers related to the number of pupils in the school, and that they should pay these teachers, if lay, a fixed minimum basic salary. Qualifications for registration included a degree from a recognised university, a recognised graduate qualification in the theory and practice of education, evidence of a year's satisfactory experience of teaching, and oral competence in the Irish language. By 1964, of 5,000 teachers employed in state-aided secondary schools about 4,000 had achieved these qualifications and were on the register – a striking improvement on the meagre array of qualifications that category was able to offer before 1914.[26]

In addition to this basic financial assistance, the government over the years was gradually committed to giving special grants to aid in the development of science teaching, domestic economy, manual instruction and music. It was not, however, until 1964 that the far-reaching and long overdue decision was taken to make capital grants for the building of new schools and the improvement of old ones. It is too soon to say yet how radically this will change the situation in the republic, but it may have come just in time to enable the schools to

* For the nineteenth century developments, see above. Part I, chap. 3.

accommodate the steep rise in secondary schooling which has recently been projected. At the time of the 1964 decision there were 569 state-aided secondary schools catering for some 88,000 pupils, but by 1970 it was a anticipated that space would be needed for perhaps 114,000 pupils.* If this estimate is correct, the building programme will indeed have been a race against time.

Scarcely less important than the schools we have been considering, which represent the Irish equivalent of a grammar-school, was the other branch of secondary education concerned with vocational training. As we saw earlier, this kind of training – then called 'technical education' – had only reached a very rudimentary stage by the time of the transfer of power.† Such as it was, the Department of Education took it over in 1924 and two years later set up a commission to investigate the whole field. From its recommendations, which were largely implemented by the government in the Vocational Education Act of 1930, have stemmed most subsequent developments. Under the general control of the Minister, Vocational Education Committees were to be selected by the local rating authorities; the Committees were to be representative of educational, cultural, commercial and industrial interests in the area, but the local authorities themselves were limited to not more than eight seats out of a minimum total strength of fourteen. These new bodies were to be given wide powers of initiation and control over the courses offered, subject to the Minister's approval. The all-important finance was to be provided partly from local rates, partly from government subventions which were intended to be on a *pro rata* basis, but have in fact often outpaced the local contribution. Fees were payable by the students participating, but they were deliberately fixed at a very low level and accounted probably for not more than ten per cent of income.

Under this stimulus there emerged thirty-eight Vocational Education Committees which between them covered the whole country. Their main responsibility was – and still is – to provide two quite different kinds of education – 'continuation' and 'technical'. 'Continuation' education was defined in the act as 'education to continue and supplement education provided in elementary schools, and [it] includes general and practical training in preparation for employment'. This was in effect full-time education for boys and girls, beginning usually at fourteen years and lasting for two or three years – the emphasis being on woodwork, metalwork, mechanical drawing and mathematics for the boys, domestic economy and commercial subjects for the girls. Irish and

* Non-aided secondary schools (apart from a handful of specialised institutions) were only three in number in 1964 and catered for no more than 250 pupils. If the specialised schools were added the total of pupils accommodated would amount to 2,600; it was not anticipated that there would be any significant increase in this figure by 1970 (*Investment in Education*, pp. 4, 36 and 58).

† See Part I, chap. 3.

English were taught in all the schools, art and science in some, and other options according to the resources at the Committee's disposal. The numbers attracted by this kind of opportunity have steadily grown and in 1964 there were nearly 250 schools catering for some 29,000 students; attendance was voluntary, save in the county boroughs of Cork, Limerick and Waterford.[27]

Side by side with 'continuation' education, 'technical' education has simultaneously been developed. Defined as 'education in or pertaining to trades, manufactures, commerce and other industrial pursuits', it has come to embrace a wide variety of activities, from training for apprentices to courses leading to professional qualifications; inevitably, as most of those coming to the schools were already in employment, the great bulk of the teaching was done through evening classes. It has to be said, however, that outside Dublin, Cork, Limerick and Waterford, facilities were limited and advanced technological training over a wide field was really only possible in Dublin and to a lesser extent in Cork. The discrepancy between the demand and the supply was to lead, as we shall see in a moment, to radical rethinking of this whole subject.

Radical rethinking, indeed, was to be the keynote of the 1960s in almost every field of Irish education, but before turning to these revolutionary new developments, one fundamental change, almost coeval with the creation of the Department of Education itself, remains to be mentioned. In 1924 the old Junior, Middle and Senior Grade examinations were swept away, to be replaced by the Intermediate Certificate (usually taken by pupils leaving school at about sixteen) and by the Leaving Certificate, which was intended to be the culmination of the pupil's secondary education and to fit him for admission to a university. In preparing for these examinations all students were required to undergo a curriculum which must include Irish, English, history and geography, mathematics, another language or science or commerce, domestic science (for girls). It soon became the general tendency at both examinations to present five or six subjects and in the Leaving Certificate separate papers are set at the pass and honours levels. The most striking conclusion to be drawn from a study of the papers actually taken by the students at the Leaving Certificate – the more important of the two examinations from the career point of view – is that secondary education in Ireland retains to the present day a strong literary bias. A survey based on the 1962–3 examination, which is presumably not untypical, indicates that apart from Irish (the only 'essential' subject for the examination), boys almost all took English and mathematics and eighty-eight per cent of them took Latin. Physics and chemistry on the other hand were taken by about thirty per cent of candidates from boys' schools and French by only twenty-one per cent. Among girls a similar pattern declared itself, except that more of them (sixty-four per cent) took French and even fewer of them took any scientific subject – the percentages being 4·8 per cent for chemistry, 4·7 per cent for physics and 4·7 per cent for the combined physics and chemistry paper.

Only one per cent of all girls taking mathematics in that year obtained honours in the subject.[28]

There are of course obvious explanations for this bias. Partly, no doubt, it was due to the prohibitive financial cost of providing adequately for science teaching, partly to the shortage of good teachers, and partly also, perhaps, to the tendency of Church-run schools to favour the old and well-tried subjects. It is at any rate significant that Latin stands so high on the list and that modern languages are by comparison neglected. To some extent this latter phenomenon reflects the difficulty of obtaining modern language teachers who also fulfil the requirement to have a competent knowledge of Irish, but it may also be a consequence of the natural tendency of pupils, confronted by strong pressures to take Irish and Latin, to limit their commitments to those two languages. For a country that is committed to the European Community this would seem to be an unfortunate development, which has been accentuated both by the failure to develop any marked skill in speaking languages, and by the relapse – after fifteen years of free experimentation between 1925 and 1940 – into the system of set-texts which Patrick Pearse long ago denounced in The Murder Machine as one of the worst features of the old examination system.[29]

It is against this background of a school system that had struggled for forty years to produce an acceptable minimum of education for its children in the teeth of poverty, public indifference and official complacency that the exciting new developments of the last decade have to be seen. Without doubt the changes that have been set in motion are part and parcel of the expansionist mood through which the country has been passing. Certainly, they could not have been envisaged without the notable upsurge in the Irish economy which followed – or, as some would say, coincided with – the adoption of the Whitaker Report. But no less important than the readiness of the government to pour money into education has been the psychological impulse towards reform which derives from the increasing tendency of Irishmen to measure their achievements by the standards of Western Europe. There was a curiously apt symbolism in the fact that the first scientific study in depth of the educational situation in Ireland – Investment in Education – should have been produced under the joint sponsorship of OECD and the Department of Education. Appointed in 1962 and reporting some three years later, the survey team provided at long last the statistical and factual basis for the schemes of practical improvement which have proliferated since the publication of their findings.*

The impact of this report – at least upon informed opinion – was in many respects shattering. It was difficult to decide which of its reve-

* The group responsible for this epoch-making document were Mr Patrick Lynch, Director (University College, Dublin); Mr W. J. Hyland (Statistics Office of the United Nations, formerly of the Central Statistics Office, Dublin); Dr Martin O'Donoghue (Trinity College, Dublin); Mr P. U. O'Nualláin (Inspector of Secondary Schools).

lations was the more alarming – the extent to which the needs of the present had not been fulfilled, or the extent to which the needs of the future had not been anticipated. Central to both these deficiencies was the fact, which the survey demonstrated with crushing finality, that the 'flow' into secondary education was far below what was either desirable or needful. On the basis of its findings it has been estimated that of the 57,000 children who left primary schools in 1957, only about 40,000 went on to some form of post-primary education. Of these, only some 10,000 would sit for the Leaving Certificate and fewer than 2,000 would end in the universities.[30] Not only that, but the report also uncovered important regional and social distinctions, though in this it did no more than give substantial foundation to what might in any event have been supposed. Post-primary education, it pointed out, was more readily available in the prosperous and populous parts of the country which, naturally, had more and better equipped schools. Similarly, the professional and white-collar workers, who were twenty per cent of the working population in 1961, were shown to have obtained sixty-five per cent of the university places awarded on the result of the Leaving Certificate examination of that year, whereas the manual workers, accounting for twenty-five per cent of the working population, gained only two per cent of university places.[31]

For these phenomena – not all of them peculiar to Ireland by any means – there are various, as yet insufficiently investigated, explanations. The fact that Irish secondary education – and still more, university education – traditionally rested partially on a fee-paying basis is no doubt one reason for the imbalance which has resulted, but it is not a completely convincing one, since Irish school fees are in general very low. University costs are, of course, heavier and the lack of adequate state or local government aid must certainly have had an inhibiting effect upon university applications.* Nevertheless, other reasons for the 'wastage' among school-leavers have to be found and they are not obscure. The lure of paid employment, geographical remoteness from centres of good teaching, the liability of school careers to be interrupted by family emigration, an inherited suspicion in certain classes of the community that secondary or higher education is at worst useless, at best for 'them' and not for 'us' – all these have played, and still play, their part in preventing the country from tapping all the resources of talent at its disposal.[32]

To evoke this talent and to give it the opportunity it needs has become the dominant concern of the Department of Education, which has been fortunate in attracting for this very reason some of the best of the

* In secondary day-schools in the early 1960s they ranged from as little as £10 per annum to £100; in boarding-schools the range was from about £75 to £150 per annum and upwards. At universities tuition fees in most subjects worked out at between £50 and £65 for arts, £80 for applied sciences, and around £100 for medicine and allied subjects. But to these would have to be added the cost of subsistence in and out of term.

younger politicians to have achieved office during the past decade. These new developments are so very recent that it is quite impossible at the time of writing to assess them in terms of results, but the mere list of the major schemes emanating from successive ministers from about 1963 onwards conveys something of the atmosphere of urgency that has suddenly pervaded this hitherto quiescent area of Irish life. The list, then, includes a much more determined drive than hitherto to consolidate and amalgamate the small or rural schools; the building of comprehensive schools designed to combine both grammar-school and vocational courses for scattered communities; a massive development of vocational education in general, with particular emphasis upon the establishment of regional Colleges of Technology; the provision of free secondary education, though on terms that make the participation of Protestant schools difficult, and also of free transportation; the allocation of much larger funds for scholarships, especially to the universities; the revision of the Leaving Certificate syllabus to allow of greater specialisation.

Not all of these proposals, of course, have met with unqualified approval. Local patriotism has put up a sturdy rearguard defence against the suppression of the smaller schools; secondary school authorities (especially those which run the more expensive schools) have anticipated serious difficulties in implementing free education; and educationists generally have looked askance at the Department's lurch towards specialisation at a time when elsewhere the tendency has been in the opposite direction. More recently, in 1971, considerable friction was aroused by the proposal of the Minister for Education to rationalise post-primary instruction in twenty-five centres throughout the country by merging publicly-owned (and multi-denominational) vocational schools with private schools run by Catholic religious orders. The new schools were to be vested in trustees to be appointed by the Catholic bishops in whose dioceses they were located, and on their managing committees the private school owners were to have two thirds of the representation. Despite these supposed concessions, the private schools remained unappeased by a scheme which so obviously struck at their autonomy, while Protestants were not unnaturally uneasy at the prospect of their children being placed under predominantly Catholic management. While the issues were still being debated, the Minister acted in the spirit of his proposals by creating in two rapidly-expanding Dublin suburbs what were called 'community schools', but which in effect involved the submersion of the existing public vocational schools in new units to be created with the co-operation of the religious orders, and to be, in the main, under Catholic ownership and control. After pressure in the Dáil from both Fine Gael and Labour, the Minister modified his plan to admit a broader base both for the trustees and the board of management, but the episode had given a painful shock to Protestant susceptibilities at the precise moment when it seemed more urgent than ever to convince northern

Unionists that the Republic was not a theocratic state and that their co-religionists were not exposed to sectarian pressures.[33]

But all these controversies have been over-shadowed by the high drama which since 1967 has surrounded the question of future university development. The 'solution' of the university question that had been reached in 1908 had proved much more enduring than it looked at the time. As we saw earlier, this had created a National University, consisting of the three University Colleges at Dublin, Cork and Galway, while leaving the independent status of Dublin University intact. The three University Colleges, after a period of slow growth and financial stringency, began to expand very rapidly from about the time of the Second World War, but while they were rooting themselves more and more deeply in the life of the country, the position of Trinity College remained embarrassingly anomalous. The end of British rule had left that ancient foundation impoverished and exposed, yet although it remained firmly embedded in the popular mind as an 'anti-national' institution, successive governments, genuinely anxious to promote good relations with the Protestant minority, had almost ostentatiously refrained from any interference with the College. The same, however, could scarcely be said of the Roman Catholic hierarchy, which at frequent intervals reminded the faithful that they were forbidden, without a special dispensation, to attend the university With or without a dispensation, some did in fact continue to come to Trinity, but never in sufficient numbers to enable the university to fill all its available places, and the authorities were increasingly drawn to rely upon the foreign – more specifically, British – connection that had always been important to them. Even with this reinforcement, however, the College remained poor, isolated and in a state of apparent decline until the end of the Second World War. Thereafter, the influx of students from outside grew much greater. By 1952–3, out of a student population of 2,000, slightly more than a third came from outside Ireland. Ten years later, in a student population of 3,000, the foreign proportion had gone up to nearly fifty per cent.

It began to seem in fact as if one of the two fully autonomous universities in the republic was becoming little more than an annexe of the English educational system. This was never the university's own intention and from 1962 onwards the most strenuous efforts were made to reduce the non-Irish element.* There was a sound prudential reason

* Commentators from outside Trinity College seem to find difficulty in accepting this. The present writer, who became Senior Tutor responsible for admissions at this very time, can testify that a rapid reduction in foreign numbers was the prime objective; this policy has since been carried much further. It is also important to remember in the context of partition that of all the universities in the Republic, Trinity has much the closest connection with Northern Ireland. In 1952-3 students from the six counties numbered 386 (as against a total of 111 for the three Colleges of the National University combined); in 1962-3 the respective totals were 472 for Trinity, 128 for the National University.

for doing so, for almost simultaneously with the rise in foreign students had come an important new development in government policy. Until just after the Second World War, whereas the three Colleges of the National University had been heavily financed by the government, the grants paid to Trinity had been negligible. In 1947, recognising that the old foundation was, or could become, a national asset, the then government began to put its payments to Trinity on a different basis. By 1952–3 the university was receiving £100,000 a year and ten years later this annual grant had gone up to £250,000. This put it above University College, Galway, roughly on a par with University College, Cork but still decidedly below University College, Dublin. At the latter date (1962–3), student numbers were 1,785 for University College, Cork, 1,471 for University College, Galway, 3,188 for Trinity College, Dublin and 6,272 for University College, Dublin.*

With the demand for university places rising and government expenditure increasing, it was perhaps inevitable that the long and calm autonomy the universities had enjoyed should sooner or later be broken into by a commission of inquiry. Such a commission – a very powerful one – was appointed in 1960 to investigate not merely the universities, but the whole field of higher education. It worked long and laboriously, eventually in 1967 producing an admirable and far-reaching report. It recommended among other things that the federal structure of 1908 should be dissolved and that UCC, UCG and UCD should be established as independent universities; that the constitution of Trinity College, should be 're-stated' – with the implication that it should remain a separate entity; that no new university should be established, but that 'New Colleges' should be established in various centres, commencing with Dublin and Limerick; that increased financial aid be provided to open the universities 'as fully and freely as possible' to all qualified students; that a Technological Authority be established to promote and assist technological training and research and that a permanent Commission for Higher Education should be set up to keep the problems of university finance and expansion under constant review.[34]

Almost at the very moment when this long-considered document was being made public the then Minister for Education – the late Mr Donogh O'Malley – made his own independent foray into the field. In an announcement that immediately became famous, and which has dominated discussion of the whole question of higher education ever since, he declared that the time had come to end the isolation of Trinity from the mainstream of national life, and that he proposed to achieve this by promoting a merger of the two Dublin colleges – Trinity

* The totals include part-time and full-time students for all save Trinity, which lists only the full-time students. The actual grants in 1962-3 were: £193,380 for Galway, £209,000 for Cork, £275,250 for Trinity and £942,500 for University College, Dublin. This last figure is swollen by a capital grant of £424,000, and the Trinity figure included a capital grant of £50,000 for repair of historic buildings.

College and University College – to form a new University of Dublin.*
Many explanations have been advanced to explain the Minister's
dramatic and unilateral intervention, and as he died suddenly the following year it may be that we shall never know the whole truth. He
himself presented it as a determination, not only to give Trinity the
opportunity of 'taking the final step across the threshold of the mansion to which it properly belongs, the Irish nation', but also to ensure
that the universities used money provided by the state to the best advantage, by avoiding wasteful duplication and achieving those economies of scale which always haunt ministerial thinking but which
higher institutions of learning mysteriously find it so difficult to achieve
by themselves. No-one doubts the sincerity of these motives, but there
may also have been another one less easy to proclaim from the roof-
tops. It has been suggested – and the suggestion persists despite official
denials – that to make TCD and UCD one flesh would be to circumvent
the ecclesiastical ban against the former. If this were indeed an object
of policy it would be open to the criticism that to disrupt the entire
structure of two important institutions with the aim (admittedly, among
other aims) of finding a devious way round a prohibition which ought
to be fought in the open, would be to betray a curious sense of values.
Since the ban was removed in 1970 by the Catholic hierarchy, the question as to whether or not it influenced the government initiative is less
important than the fact that as the official plan for a merger subsequently grew and changed, the rude surgery whereby it was proposed
to 'distribute' subjects arbitrarily between the two Colleges has not only
run into administrative difficulties but has aroused intense academic hostility. The situation remains fluid and all prognostications are hazardous. It begins to seem, however, as if there may be growing support for
the notion that Dublin should be allowed to keep two separate universities but that co-operation between them, and avoidance of duplication, should be achieved through the Higher Education Authority
which the Commission recommended and which was in fact brought
into being in September 1968. It may be that here lies the germ of progress for the future.

It will be obvious that with so much in ferment at every level in the
country's educational system, no easy generalisations are possible. Indeed, with the action still developing, any kind of summing up is quite
out of the question. But it may be possible to make two points in conclusion. One is that whatever the issue of the various controversies now
at boiling point, there can be no going back to the old stagnation. For
good or ill, Irish education finds itself at last in the mid-twentieth

* He made his announcement on 18 April 1967 when the Commission
on Higher Education had just issued a summary of its report and recommendations; the Commission's main report appeared later that year. The
Minister's statement and the immediate academic reactions to it can be
followed in *Studies* (Summer, 1967) which devoted virtually the whole
issue to the university question.

century world. Yet – and here is the second point that needs to be made – the fact that this happened because an economic expansion has enabled it to happen, has occurred, one might say, largely in response to the needs created by that expansion, brings its own dangers. In other countries where rapid educational advance has been carried out under government initiative, it has not been uncommon for a conflict to develop between those who champion what they conceive to be the values of a liberal education – the freedom to question, to teach, to learn, and to engage in independent research without pressure from external forces – and those who see in the whole machinery of school and university a means of fulfilling specific objectives dictated by the state or other agencies to supply the needs, real or supposed, of the community. That a country's educational system has a resopnsibility to meet the reasonable demands of society few would nowadays dispute, but that this responsibility should be balanced by the kind of freedom under which alone universities have been able to flourish in the past, is surely no less essential. To reconcile freedom and responsibility has always been the classic dilemma and it does not get any easier. In Ireland now, politicians, administrators, managers of all kinds, speak with clamant and insistent voices, but perhaps it is not altogether idle to suppose that the words uttered by John Newman in Dublin in the summer of 1852 may still waken a sympathetic echo. Anticipating the demands of those who make 'utility' their touchstone in judging a university training and who ask 'what is the real worth in the market of the article called "a liberal education" on the supposition that it does not teach us definitely how to advance our manufactures, or to improve our lands, or to better our civil economy', his reply is still not without contemporary relevance:

This process of training by which the intellect, instead of being formed or sacrificed to some particular or accidental purpose, some specific trade or profession, or study or science, is disciplined for its own sake, for the perception of its own proper object, and for its own highest culture, is called liberal education; and though there is no one in whom it is carried as far as is conceivable . . . yet there is scarcely anyone but may gain an idea of what real training is, and at least look towards it, and make its true scope and result, not something else, his standard of excellence. . . . And to set forth the right standard, and to train according to it, and to help forward all students towards it according to their various capacities, this I conceive to be the business of a university.[35]

(iii) WELFARE

It is a natural though melancholy consequence of the way an independent Ireland came into being that its history should have been written primarily in terms of political and ideological strife with, latterly, some attention being directed also to the economic factors which are inextricably bound up with that strife. But if the inquirer turns away from the high drama of this familiar and overlit stage, and seeks to find how far revolutions, wars and changes of government have benefited the ordinary citizen in his daily life, the answer is often difficult to elicit. Recently, however, partly as the result of work done in the universities, partly because of the emergence of new centres of research – most notably the Economic and Social Research Institute and the Institute of Public Administration – it has begun to be possible to fill some of the gaps, even though the material for a definitive study is still not as detailed or as plentiful as could be wished. What follows here is an attempt, necessarily brief, to use some of the material these bodies have provided in order to illustrate how, during nearly fifty years of self-government, the twenty-six counties have been drawn gradually but inexorably into the twentieth century world of social welfare. Three main themes have been selected for treatment – health, social insurance and social assistance – but linked with these will be a fourth, the steady adaptation of the structure of Irish local government to meet all sorts of requirements its British originators had never contemplated.

In nothing was this administrative revolution so apparent as in the domain of health and public assistance. We saw earlier that legislation of 1923–5 had swept away some of the more archaic and less efficient machinery – the boards of guardians and the rural district councils – and had vested their functions in the county councils, or more strictly in the boards of health and assistance which were in effect sub-committees of those councils; and since the councils retained the control of the mental health service, the tuberculosis service and the school medical service – all initiated before the transfer of power – it is obvious that the process of concentration of power was already well advanced.* Yet there still remained considerable differentiation of actual

* For the administrative changes wrought by the Local Government Act of 1925, see above pp. 482-4. It should be added here that the sanitary and preventive health services operated by the councils through their new boards applied only to the countryside; the town authorities remained responsible for these services in their areas. The tuberculosis service dated from the Tuberculosis Prevention (Ireland) Act of 1908 which gave power to county councils and county borough corporations to provide sanatoria and clinics for the treatment of this disease, at that time regarded as perhaps the deadliest of all diseases prevalent in Ireland. Shortage of money combined with apathy to prevent anything like an adequate programme of building until, as we saw earlier (p. 572), Dr Noel Browne transformed the situation almost overnight. The medical inspection and treatment of children attending national schools had been provided for by the Public Health (Medical Treatment of Children (Ireland) Act of 1919) legislation of the British parliament passed, by one of those familiar ironies of Irish history, at the very moment when the King's writ was ceasing to run over a large part of the country. The basis for,

executive responsibility. Thus, while the Local Government Act of 1925 provided for the appointment of county medical officers who would be responsible not only for the tuberculosis and school medical services, but also for the various preventive services in both town and country, these new officials were excluded alike from the dispensaries, the general hospitals, and the treatment of mental diseases.[36]

Clearly, there was still a good deal to be done by way of rationalisation. At the higher administrative level this was carried further during the years of the Second World War when the emergence of the county managers led to further unified control, signalised by the disappearance of the boards of health and assistance and the transfer of their functions to the managers.* But the consolidation of the services themselves had to wait until after 'the emergency' was over. By then the climate of opinion in the country had greatly changed. There was mounting dissatisfaction with the existing services, partly because, as we shall see in a moment, they had been demonstrably inadequate ever since independence and in some of their most important aspects were still associated in the popular mind with the hated Poor Law; partly because the middle classes, driven by inflationary pressures to use such facilities as were provided, were now learning for the first time what the poor had to put up with and were becoming correspondingly vociferous in their criticisms; but most of all, no doubt, because the welfare state then being established in Britain cast a long shadow across the Irish Sea. Out of the ferment of discussion – official, medical, even episcopal† – there came a major reorganisation of the whole health administration. The war was scarcely over when the Ministers and Secretaries (Amendment) Act of 1946 at last separated Health from Local Government and brought virtually the whole array of services under the control of one responsible Minister. The new Department, which actually began to function in 1947, was charged with the prevention and cure of disease, and with the treatment and care of the mentally ill or the physically handicapped; with the training and registration of personnel and the control over the appointment of the appropriate local officers; with the initiation and direction of research; with the enforcement of pure food regulations and control of proprietary medical and toilet preparations; with the registration of births, deaths and marriages and also with the collection, preparation and dissemination of

---

a somewhat rudimentary Maternity and Child Welfare Service, to be developed both by local authorities and voluntary agencies, was also established by a British Act of Parliament (Notification of Births (Extension) Act, 1915) at a time when most Irishmen had other things on their minds.

* For the county managers, see above, p. 484.

† The most striking contribution to the debate was made by the then Bishop of Clonfert, Dr Dignan, who proposed a thoroughly comprehensive scheme of social security in 1944 – much too comprehensive, it was soon made plain, for the official mind to digest or the official purse to afford.

health statistics of all kinds.[37]

Side by side with this growth in the power of the central authority marched, almost inevitably, a simplification of local health administration. The Health Act of 1947 concentrated an increasing amount of responsibility into the hands of the county Councils – in effect into those of the county managers – and by taking away from the urban districts (other than the county boroughs) their supervision of preventive services, succeeded in reducing the number of authorities charged with this function from about ninety to thirty-one, composed of the twenty-seven county councils and the four county boroughs of Cork, Dublin, Limerick, and Waterford.* The ancient distinction between 'health' and 'public assistance' authorities remained for a little longer, but it too was swept away when the Health Act of 1953 transferred all services remotely connected with medical care, cure or prevention to the health authorities. The most important effect of this, though it appeared on the surface to be little more than a change of nomenclature, was that the general hospitals previously under the public assistance authorities were placed firmly under the health authorities, thus at last removing from those institutions the stigma of the Poor Law which had been attached to them for over a hundred years. In more general terms, the end result of these various legislative reforms was that the county councils as health authorities thenceforward administered all the health services of the country (Dublin, Cork, Limerick and Waterford being, as we have seen, special cases), except for mental health; this in most instances was the responsibility of joint boards on which neighbouring counties were represented.

It is time now to turn from the machinery to the product and to ask what sort of health service actually emerged from all this juggling of administrative agencies. No single generalisation is possible, except perhaps to stress the importance of the Second World War as a watershed. Up to 1939, indeed even up to 1945, the provision of health services for people who could not afford to pay for private treatment changed little, either in scope or in character, from what it had been in the last years of British rule. It was scanty, old-fashioned and frequently humiliating to those whose poverty left them with no other alternative. It is true that the county medical officers were able to make considerable if unspectacular progress in the curbing of outbreaks of infectious diseases, and in prophylactic measures of which diphtheria immunisation was probably the most important. But in the day to day care of the sick poor, the resources of the local authorities remained very much what they had been – dispensaries and general hospitals, both frequently old, uncomfortable and inadequate, and both administered on the basis of a stringent means test. Things could hardly have been otherwise so long as the services had to be paid for mainly

* The four county boroughs were subsequently fused with the counties of the same name for health purposes giving a total of twenty-seven health authorities.

out of local rates, and we need scarcely look further than the total cost of local authority health services in 1937–8 – amounting only to £2·75 million – to find the most fundamental explanation for the meagreness of what they had to offer. Even ten years later, when expenditure had about doubled to reach £5·7 million (due mainly to inflation) the local authorities were still supplying over eighty per cent of the cost of their services, while the state contribution as recently as 1947–8 was no more than £830,000.

Thereafter the picture changed swiftly and radically. Not only was the burden of expenditure adjusted so that it came to be shared in roughly equal proportions by state and local authorities, but the actual amount of that expenditure climbed steeply. In a single decade it mounted from the £5·7 million of 1947–8 already mentioned (the year in which the local authorities met eighty per cent of the cost) to £16·4 million in 1958–9. Admittedly, this seemingly striking advance occurred – like the smaller one during the Second World War – at a time of rapid inflation; if this is taken into account and the expenditure of 1958–9 restated in 1947–8 terms (the Consumer Price Index in the meantime having risen from 100 to 147) the true figure would be about twelve million pounds.* Even so, this represents a doubling of the outlay corresponding, as we shall see in a moment, to a very real improvement in the services themselves, a fact reflected in the percentage of the country's Gross National Product that was devoted to current public expenditure on the country's health services. This rose from 1·72 in 1947 to 2·74 in 1958, an increase which, remarkable as it is, would without question be even more remarkable if private and capital expenditure were also to be taken into account.[38]

Private expenditure is for obvious reasons impossible to estimate with any accuracy, but capital costs are more easily traced. These – arising principally from the building of new hospitals – have for much of the past forty years been met in the first instance by the brilliantly successful expedient of the Hospital Sweepstakes. Begun in 1930 as a tentative experiment, they were put on a more permanent footing by the Public Hospitals Act of 1933. This set up a statutory body, the Hospitals Trust Board, to administer moneys raised by sweepstakes on the principal horse-races of each year. The money realised by the sweepstakes was lodged in a hospital fund from which the responsible Minister, advised by another body, the Hospitals Commission, was empowered to make grants, not only to the state institutions, but to the voluntary hospitals as well, nearly all of which had deficits and nearly all of which (the Adelaide Hospital was for long a notable exception on grounds of principle) were ready and eager to receive assistance. Up to 1958 the total amount accruing to the fund from the sweepstakes was

* A recent estimate of expenditure suggests that in 1963-4 it was running at £22.5 million (in current, not 1947 values) and that this represented 2.7 per cent of the GNP (P.R. Kaim-Caudle, *Social Policy in the Irish Republic* (London, 1967), p. 29).

£44·5 million. Of this, £11 million was paid out in stamp duty, leaving £33·5 million for health purposes. The voluntary hospitals absorbed nearly a third of this amount between 1933 and 1958, but there still remained some £23 million for capital expenditure. Up to the Second World War advances for this purpose were distinctly meagre, amounting only to £1·8 million, in addition to £3 million handed over before the fund had been established. Between 1934 and 1948 a further £1·6 million was made available, but at that point the situation was transformed, as we saw earlier, by Dr Browne's onslaught on the problem of tuberculosis, and between 1948 and 1958 nearly £24 million was expended on the building programme, in addition to another £3·6 million deriving from the local authorities themselves or from other sources. So great was the outflow, indeed, that for the latter part of that period (1953-7) the state actually had to supplement the fund by nearly £7 million more. To sum up, therefore, between 1948 and 1958, spending on the construction or reconstruction of hospitals amounted to £27·4 million, of which £17 million came from the sweepstakes, £6·8 million from the state subvention and £3·6 million from the local authorities. Of this total, tuberculosis hospitals accounted for £9·3 million, and maternity and children's hospitals absorbed £2·5 million, this last figure being just short of the £2·6 million spent on mental hospitals and homes.[39]

If we now turn to ask what sort of benefits did all this expenditure confer upon the citizen we shall find the key to the answer in what are nowadays called the General Medical Services, but which are in reality the modern version of the old dispensary system. The persons entitled to use these services were defined in the Health Act of 1953 as those 'unable to provide by their own industry or other lawful means the medical or surgical appliances necessary for themselves and for their dependants'. To become eligible every applicant had to be considered individually in relation to his means or lack of means. If he satisfied the means test, his name was then placed on the General Medical Register and he was issued with a blue card, annually renewable. On presentation of this card he was then entitled to the services of the District Medical Officer (the equivalent of the old dispensary doctor) and to medicines and appliances free of charge. It is a striking commentary on the standard of living in the country that in 1958 some 28·5 per cent of the population was recorded as being eligible for this free attention.[40] The remainder of the population had to pay for any general services it made use of, but a very large proportion – between eighty and ninety per cent of the whole – was entitled to use at low cost the Hospital and Specialist Services provided under the 1953 Health Act. This not only included the lower income group already on the register as being in possession of a blue card, but also applied to anyone (and his dependants) who was employed on manual labour and insured under the Social Welfare Acts, and to other employed and insured persons (with their dependants) who were paid less than £1,200 a year (originally £800 but changed in 1965). In addition, the services were open to all whose family income was less than £1,200 a year and their dependants; to agricultural workers whose holdings did not exceed £50 valuation and their dependants – over eighty per cent of all farming families; to children attending the national schools who received hospital treatment for ailments discovered at school medical examinations; and to anyone else who could not without undue hardship provide such services from his own resources.

The benefits thus available to these large classes of the population were considerable – considerable, at least in relation to the Irish past if not in relation to what the contemporary world outside had to offer. For those on the General Register all specialist and hospital treatment was free of charge. All others treated under the Health Act paid very small amounts per day for hospital care and for specialist consultation, fixed initially at ten shillings a day for the former and 2/6 per consultation for the latter. Apart from these basic services the Act provided for a number of other facilities, though their availability depended very much on the economic status of the patient. In the so-called 'higher income group' (over £1,200 a year) which in 1959 was about fifteen per cent of the population, the only free services were those relating to infectious diseases, child welfare clinics, and health examination in the national schools or medical treatment arising therefrom; since many of these families did not use either national schools or welfare clinics they were to all intents and purposes outside the system.[41] The 'middle income group' – that is the group above those who were on the General Register and accounting for fifty-five per cent of the population – could use not only the General Hospital and Specialist Services, but also the services relating to Maternity and Infant Care and those concerned with mental illness. For the lower income-group – consisting of all those who were on the General Register – there were, free and in addition to the facilities already mentioned, dental and eye and ear services, free milk, maternity cash grants, disablement allowances and access to county homes in case of dire need and destitution.

It would be naïve to suppose that because these various kinds of assistance have become available on a larger scale than before that all is for the best in the best of all possible worlds. Even in far more affluent countries with far longer traditions of welfare, islands of hardship and neglect are constantly being discovered, and it was not to be expected that Ireland could wipe out overnight the effects of generations of parsimony and indifference. An example – probably the most extreme example and certainly the one which is attracting most attention today – is the treatment of mental illness. To provide such treatment for those classes of the population that were eligible for it – i.e. those who were also eligible for the Hospital and Specialist Services – a series of acts of the Oireachtas had laid upon the mental health authorities the obligation to supply proper and sufficient accommodation for patients in need of it, whether in a district mental hospital, a county home, or a variety of other institutions. Elaborate regulations surrounded the committal of any individual to these centres and the Inspector of Mental Hospitals was expected to ensure that improper detentions did not occur. No doubt these duties were faithfully carried out, but illicit detention did not exhaust the ills to which the system was prone and in recent years there has been a mounting volume of criticism against the way in which the mentally ill (and indeed the aged also) are cared for. If there have been deficiencies, there have been many well-identified causes for these deficiencies. Not the least of these has been the rise in the number of the mentally ill – more accurately, perhaps, in the number of those who are diagnosed nowadays as mentally ill. At the end of 1957 there were in the Republic nearly 22,000 people officially classed as being in that category, of whom almost 20,000 were in the mental health authorities' institutions. A decade later a government report indicated that mental illness might be more prevalent in Ireland than in any other country and that the rate of beds provided for the mentally ill 'appears to be the highest in the world'. At any one time, it was reckoned, one in every seventy people in the country over the age of twenty-four was in a mental hospital. When to these figures is added another estimated 24,000 mentally handicapped of whom only a fraction ever received institutional treatment, and to these again the 10,000 old people in county homes many of whom suffered from some degree of mental disability, it is clear that there exists a problem whose surface has barely been scratched.[42] Many things have combined to make it a complex and peculiarly intractable problem – the large number of elderly people in the population, the low marriage rate, the burden on some women of bringing up large families in adverse conditions, alcoholism, inbreeding in the remoter parts of the country, the pressures of rural isolation, and, above all perhaps, the selective effects of the emigration which for many years has tended to take the young and vigorous and to leave behind those less well fitted to make their way in the world. But whatever the hierarchy of causes, the facts of the situation have become so starkly self-evident that advance in this sector is now widely recognised to be among the most urgent priorities in any future reform of the health services.

That such reform is already overdue – not just in mental treatment, but over a wide front – was a major contention of the principal opposition parties at the general election of 1965. Both the Fine Gael and Labour parties criticised the means test and the indignities to which it still often exposed the poorer sections of the population, and Fine Gael in particular denounced the system as administratively cumbersome and of varying effectiveness in different parts of the country. Moreover, the fact that the existing structure made no provision for free services for the bulk of the population led the two parties to advocate a comprehensive service based on a free choice of family doctor, embracing hospital and specialist services, and financed in large measure by compulsory social insurance contributions. The principal difference between the programmes was that whereas Labour came out in favour of a universal service covering everyone, the Fine Gael proposals would have extended the free services to eighty-five per cent of the people, while at the same time abolishing the hated means test for all sections of that eighty-five per cent.[43]

Against this philosophy of a greatly expanded scheme of welfare there has been ranged the opposition of a government still, in this sphere at least, apparently wedded to a tradition of laissez-faire, backed by a medical profession which, as in many other parts of the world, sees in the means test an essential instrument for the preservation of private practice and a differential fee-structure, and which also, to put the argument on a broader basis, resents the diminution of the doctor's independence which it feels would result from increased intervention by the state. Nevertheless, the tide appears to be flowing irresistibly in the direction of 'socialised' medicine and a government White Paper, issued in 1966 as a basis for further discussion, envisaged a considerable expansion of the services and a certain degree of liberalisation in the way in which they were administered. But even these proposals did not include the abolition of the means test and they made it plain that a comprehensive and free service for the middle and higher income groups was not immediately in prospect. It was hardly likely, therefore, that they would satisfy the protagonists of reform and, in fact, the debate continues. At the time of writing (1972) there are indications that the pace of change has once more begun to quicken. A new Health Act, passed in 1970, has led to substantial reorganisation of the hospital services, a compulsory health contribution scheme was introduced in 1971 for the middle income group, and in the general medical services a choice of doctor began to be introduced during 1972.

It would, of course, be unreal to assess this debate simply in terms of the health services alone. Other manifestations of the welfare state have also to be taken into account and especially those relating to what is broadly, and sometimes loosely, described as social security.* In the Irish context three separate kinds of benefit are in question – family allowances, social insurance and social assistance. The first of these may be described as 'public service welfare' granted indiscriminately irrespective of contributions of need – and in Ireland it is a type of welfare

* Some definitions of social security include expenditure by the state on education, housing and health, as well as cash payments to individuals for social purposes, but for the purpose of the present discussion I have followed the definition adopted in the International Labour Office paper 'The Cost of Social Security, 1949-57', cited by R. P. Kaim-Caudle in 'Social Security in Ireland and Western Europe', Economic Research Institute, Paper No. 20 (Dublin, June 1964), pp. 9-10. This identifies as social security services those services 'the object of which is (a) to grant curative or preventive medical care or (b) to maintain income in case of involuntary loss of earnings or of an important part of earnings or (c) to grant supplementary incomes to persons having family responsibilities'.

666

represented only by children's allowances. Introduced as far back as 1944, these were then payable for third and subsequent children in a family. In 1952 they were extended to second children and in 1963 to first children – the allowances being paid out of general taxation and to all parents irrespective of their employment status, without a means test. In 1969–70 the annual payment was £6 for the first child, £9 for the second and £16 for each subsequent child. In addition to these universal allowances there were also certain other, roughly analogous, payments on a selective basis – for example, maternity grants and allowances linked to social insurance, supplemental family allowances paid to certain state employees (school teachers, members of the Defence Forces and some civil servants), as well as remissions of income tax where applicable.*

If children's allowances were a creation of the comparatively recent past, the same cannot be said of either social insurance or of social assistance, both of which were inherited in a rudimentary form from

* Any overall assessment of state benefits to the family would of course have to include the medical and educational facilities discussed earlier in this book. It would also have to take account of subsidised housing. In Ireland this dated from the late nineteenth century, local authorities having provided cottages for agricultural labourers since 1883 and town dwellings since 1890. Between those dates and the early 1960s the local authorities had built about 180,000 houses, roughly a quarter of all the dwellings in the state. In this enterprise they were stimulated from time to time by contributions from central funds, amounting latterly to about two-thirds of the loan charges incurred by the local authorities up to a certain price limit per house or apartment. So large have the subsidies been, in fact, that it is arguable that many rents have been fixed, or held, so low as to be hopelessly uneconomic. The rate of building in recent years has not been rapid, certainly not rapid enough to replace the 50,000 local authority houses – outside Cork and Dublin – which as long ago as 1960 were described as unfit for human habitation. If the two big cities were included this situation would be revealed as being even worse than appears on the surface; indeed, it is now so bad that any perceptible increase in population would precipitate a crisis. To avoid such a crisis 12,000 – 14,000 houses a year needed to be built between 1960 and 1970 – twice the rate actually attained in 1964, but still one of the lowest in Europe (R. P. Kaim-Caudle, *Social Policy in the Irish Republic*, chap. vii). A more recent official estimate reckons that the number of houses needed for the period 1966 to 1971 was 9,000 a year, but that from then on the rate would rise (partly because of expanding demand, partly because of obsolescence of existing houses) until in the mid-seventies 15,000 to 17,000 houses would be needed each year. Very considerable expansion has already taken place and capital expenditure on housing rose from £65 million in 1970-71 to about £87 million in 1971-2. In the latter year a record total of 15,500 were completed, suggesting that the target for the mid-seventies might be achieved ahead of schedule; it is noteworthy that of 15,500 houses built in 1971-2 private enterprise accounted for about two-thirds (*Housing in the Seventies*, 1969 (Prl. 658), p. 9; *Review of 1971 and Outlook for 1972*, p. 73).

the old regime. These derived in their original, narrow sense, from the acts of parliament which had marked Britain's own first hesitant steps along the road to the welfare state. The first of these, the Old Age Pensions Act of 1908, had provided non-contributory pensions for old people over seventy at the initial rate of five shillings, or twenty-five new pence, a week (raised in 1919 to ten shillings, or fifty new pence) subject to a severe means test and certain other restrictions; in 1920 this legislation was supplemented by an equivalent pension to every blind person of not less than fifty years of age who was incapacitated for any work for which eyesight was essential. The second part of the inheritance from Britain, the National Insurance Act of 1911, instituted a compulsory insurance scheme whereby virtually all manual workers and non-manual workers earning less than £160 a year (£250 after 1919) were to be insured by contributions from the state, the employers and the workers themselves, to a scheme which was intended to provide sickness benefit for those eligible at the rate of 10 shillings (50 p.) a week for a man and 7/6 (37.5 p.) for a woman (15 shillings (75 p.) and 12 shillings (60 p.) respectively after 1920); full benefit was to be paid for the first half-year, reduced benefit thereafter without limitation of time.* This same legislation also provided a minimal scheme of unemployment insurance, but this was radically amended by the Unemployment Insurance Act of 1920. That Act applied unemployment insurance to almost all industries except agriculture, covering manual workers and also non-manual workers earning less than £250 a year. Unemployed people who were able and willing to work but could find no one to use their labour were to receive fifteen shillings (75 p.) a week for a man and twelve shillings (60 p.) a week for a woman, up to a period of fifteen, later twenty-six, weeks; after 1921, originally as a temporary measure, these amounts were supplemented for married men by five shillings (25 p.) a week for a wife and one shilling (5 p.) a week for each child. Even by the standards of the time these payments were meagre enough and the expectation seems to have been that they would be supplemented – as in many cases, of course, they were – by savings, charity or other kinds of assistance.

Such, then, were the foundations on which an Irish social insurance system was to be built. At first, admittedly, the native government showed little inclination to do more than keep the existing system in being. Indeed, in 1924 the old age pension was actually cut for some categories by a shilling (5 p.) a week and not restored until 1928. It was only after Fianna Fáil came to power in 1932 that a slightly more humane approach began to be apparent with the reduction of the age for blind pensions to thirty and the decision to assess applications for old age pensions without reference to the means possessed by other members of the family. Thereafter, there were frequent changes in the

* This legislation also included a rudimentary scheme for the provision of medical care for employees, but largely because of the opposition of the medical profession, Ireland was excluded from that section of the Act.

amount of both blind and old-age pensions in a vain attempt to keep pace with the rising cost of living, while the Social Welfare Act of 1948 further reduced the age-qualification for blind pensions to twenty-one and eased the conditions under which such pensions would be granted. Nevertheless, despite the passing of no less than nine further Social Welfare Acts between 1951 and 1963, the age at which old people could qualify for a pension remained at seventy and the means test still limited the applicant to an independent income of not more than about £2 15s. od. (£2.75 p.) a week; moreover, the amount paid out was on a graduated basis, the maximum for a pensioner whose means did not exceed roughly a pound a week being 35 shillings (£1.75 p.) a week in 1964, falling to as little as 5 shillings (25 p.) a week where his own means amounted to approximately £2 15s. od. (£2.75 p.) a week. Even with such stringent and not over-generous provisions, the annual cost to the state of these non-contributory pensions amounted to between £10 and £11 million between 1959 and 1964. Another way of putting this, and of emphasising the critical age-structure of the population, is to point out that at that time out of every 1,000 persons in the total population thirty-nine (or forty-one if the blind are included) were in receipt of old-age or equivalent pensions.[45]

In the broader area of contributory insurance there has been, admittedly, more experimentation and a greater readiness to extend the range of benefits available. Thus, before the Second World War, marriage benefits and widows' and orphans' pensions had been added to the existing payments, while during the war itself – apart from the introduction of the children's allowances already mentioned – an interesting innovation, 'wet-time insurance', was adopted in order to protect manual workers in certain trades against loss of wages due to bad weather. But in this sphere, as in so many others, it was the ferment of ideas during and after 'the emergency' that produced the most important changes. As a result of the governmental reconstructions of 1947 a separate Deparment of Social Welfare was created which immediately set about the task of unifying the various kinds of social benefit that had evolved almost haphazardly in the previous quarter-century. As a result, the Social Welfare Act of 1952 (Fianna Fáil's substitute for the ill-fated inter-party scheme aborted by the 'mother and child' crisis) brought together into a single unified conception national health insurance, unemployment insurance and the widows' and orphans' schemes. The principal provisions of this comprehensive scheme were: equal benefits for men and women; identical benefits for unemployment, sickness and widowhood; increases of all benefits in respect of dependants; a new disability benefit without time limit in place of the old restricted provisions governing sickness and disablement. It was particularly significant that it extended unemployment insurance to employees in agriculture (at a lower rate of contribution) and that it substituted new conditions under which the duration of the benefit was not limited to the number of contributions paid.

In short, from 1952 onwards the state was committed to operating a compulsory insurance system of which it paid approximately two-fifths of the cost and to which employers and employees contributed weekly at flat rates, with benefits, also at flat rates, covering unemployment, disability, marriage, maternity, widows' pensions, orphans' allowances, and various kinds of treatment, mainly dental and optical. As originally envisaged the scheme had made no provision for contributory old age pensions, but this omission was rectified in 1961 when legislation provided that old people over seventy might qualify for contributory pension of £3 a week for a single person and £5 7s. 6d. (£5.37½) for a married couple as from 1 January 1966.[46]

The level of social insurance, sickness and unemployment benefit at that date was to be 52/6 (£2.62½) a week per person, 92/6 (£4.62½) for a married couple, plus 13 shillings (65p.) a week each for two children and 8 shillings (40p.) for subsequent children. This was certainly a considerable advance on the conditions obtaining before the Second World War, but it was less than some reformers had hoped for and less in every respect than the comparable benefits in Northern Ireland.[47] Or, to take another example, in the republic in the early 1960s, a married man with three children who was dependent on social insurance benefits might have expected to receive approximately forty per cent of the earnings of a male industrial worker in the transportable goods industries, a proportion which was markedly lower than that prevailing even in the poorer countries of the European Economic Community. Comparisons with Britain are perhaps more relevant, but even they redound to the disadvantage of the republic. At face-value, the benefits available in the early 'sixties were at about two-thirds the level of those available in the United Kingdom, but in reality, since Irish prices were no lower than British ones, and possibly even higher, the actual benefits accruing were almost certainly less than two-thirds.[48] Moreover, it has to be remembered that large categories of the Irish population were excluded, partially or wholly, from the operation of the scheme. Some of these – for example, female domestic servants, fishermen or out-workers – were excluded from unemployment benefit; others – such as civil servants, teachers, local government officials, officers in the Defence Force and employees of statutory transport undertakings – were insured for widows' and orphans' pensions only. In addition, persons whose employment was non-manual and at a rate of salary exceeding £800 (originally £600) a year, or whose work was family employment, were not covered at all by compulsory insurance; subsequent legislation periodically raised the remuneration limit for compulsory social insurance until in 1971 it stood at £1,600 for a non-manual worker.[49]

From time to time efforts have been made to win government sanction for much more wide-reaching suggestions. One of the most famous of these, the scheme put forward by Dr Dignan as long ago as 1944, advocated that all employed persons should be compulsorily and comprehensively insured and that all who did not come within this category should have the right to become voluntary contributors. Somewhat on the same lines, but going in certain respects even further, the White Paper of 1949 had proposed that social insurance should be extended to every person over sixteen who worked for an employer, that there should be a retirement pension for men at sixty-five and for women at sixty, and that there should be a death benefit. All these schemes, and even one put forward by the Labour party in 1965 for graduated social insurance contributions, were resisted by the party (Fianna Fáil) then in power. Partly, no doubt, this was on grounds of financial caution, but partly also this resistance may have reflected two deep-rooted characteristics of Irish society. One is the tradition whereby the unfortunate have been able to call on the resources of various kinds of private or institutional charity; the modern view that such transactions are humiliating for the recipient and a source of spiritual pride in the donor seems not to have penetrated very far as yet in Ireland. If this is so, perhaps it is because of the second characteristic, one which Dr Dignan warned against – the Irish dislike of regimentation and the feeling, still strongly represented inside and outside official circles, that the individual ought, in some way not always clearly specified, to take arms himself against his own particular sea of troubles.

But suppose there were individuals and families, as there always are, who, if no lifebelt was thrown to them, would infallibly go under in their own seas of troubles? For them contributory insurance schemes were not, and could not be, the answer. To meet this problem, and to deal with the different kinds of hardship by which these unfortunates were threatened, the state assumed the burden of assistance – to such a degree, that in the mid-1960s the amount paid out in this way was over one third of expenditure on all social security cash payments.[50] Most of this went on non-contributory pensions for old people over seventy, for widows, for orphans and for blind persons, but some went also on unemployment assistance, home assistance, disability allowances and certain payments for medical treatment. A detailed analysis of a single year, 1962, indicated that of a total of about £13·5 million spent in these various kinds of relief £8·5 million went to old people and their dependants, nearly £2 million to widows and their families and about £500,000 to the blind. Unemployment assistance and health allowances each accounted for about £1 million. A more recent estimate suggests that the total amount spent on these services may have risen to about £90 million.[51] A great part of the explanation both of the extent of this burden and of its distribution is to be found, yet again, in the structure of Irish society. At the time of the 1961 Census some two-fifths of gainfully employed men were self-employed – many of them small farmers. These stood outside the contributory insurance schemes and might have found it hard enough to sustain their contributions even if they had been included. Such people were of course entitled, subject to the usual test, to old age pensions when they reached seventy, but before that their main resource equally subject to the means test, was unemployment assistance. That this was a problem with roots deep in the countryside is suggested by the fact that as recently as 1965 the five counties of Connacht and the three Ulster counties in the republic, which together accounted for twenty-two per cent of the population, supplied no less than sixty per cent of the persons receiving unemployment assistance.[52] Even though the rates actually paid out, not just for unemployment assistance but for other kinds as well, have tended to rise steadily in recent years, they have remained low in relation to the level of prices, low in relation to earnings and low also in relation to the comparable benefits offered in Northern Ireland. In 1966, for example, old age pensions were 47/6 (£2.37½) a week in the republic compared with 76 shillings (£3.80) in Northern Ireland (where the pensionable age was sixty-five for men and sixty for women); for widows the comparable figures were 46 shillings (£2.30) in the republic, 76 shillings (£3.80) in the north; for unemployment, 34 shillings (£1.70) in the republic and 76 shillings (£3.80) in the north.[53]

But not only was assistance in the south less generous than in the north, it was available to fewer categories of people. In the republic, deserted wives and families, and mothers of illegitimate children, did not qualify. Neither did men suffering from short or long term illness, nor persons permanently handicapped by mental or physical disabilities. This last group were, indeed, allowed meagre grants of not more than two pounds a week irrespective of the number of dependants and in 1966 some 17,000 were receiving such aid, together with a further 2,000 tuberculosis patients who got similar payments. But all other necessitous persons had still in effect to rely upon poor relief – or home assistance as it has come to be called. This, which was paid for out of local rates, was provided generally by the county councils or in the larger centres of population by the health authorities. Sometimes these grants were used to supplement payments from social insurance benefits, or other forms of assistance, but often enough they represented all that the recipient could count on receiving from any source except charity. There was no national scale according to which this dole was meted out, but in the most extreme cases these poor people had to be given institutional aid, either in county homes or, in the case of children, by boarding-out with families or by residence in approved schools. Within the homes themselves, which have attracted much adverse comment, some of it official, a commission of inquiry found in 1951 an intermingling of sick, aged, blind, deaf, mentally defective, unmarried mothers and casual vagrants reminiscent of the eighteenth century. The aim of subsequent policy has been to house only the sick and aged in these homes, but ten years after the commission's report had appeared little progress had been made and the sum of human flotsam washed up on those bleak shores had not significantly diminished.[54]

One of the most striking aspects of the slow and uneven progress towards a greater degree of social security for the underprivileged which we have just been discussing was the extent to which that progress, such as it was, was made without the strong and sustained pressures of a vigorous labour movement. This is not to say that individual labour leaders were not in favour of welfare, nor that the Labour party and the trade unions were not committed to fight for better conditions for the workers. Of course they were in favour of welfare, and of course they fought for better conditions. Nevertheless, the fact remains that their influence on the course of events, their ability to shape the development of Irish society in any fashion that would have been remotely acceptable to, say, James Connolly, seemed almost in inverse ratio to the vehemence of their protestations.

For this yawning gap between what the Labour movement ostensibly stood for and what it actually achieved there are many explanations. Some of these we glanced at earlier when tracing the political ineffectiveness of Labour between the two world wars.* But although the reasons there suggested – the poisoning of the national life by the Civil War, the continuing predominance of political over social issues, the unwillingness of working-class leaders to fall foul of the Church by openly espousing socialist doctrines, the sheer difficulty of winning support in a country where rural and small-town conservatism easily outweighed urban radicalism – all doubtless contributed to the feebleness of the workers' attempts to form a large and efficient pressure-group, other factors, which relate more directly to the industrial side of the movement, have also to be taken into account. If, that is to say, we wish to understand the partial paralysis of organised Labour for much of the period since 1922, we shall have to reckon with the infirmities of the trade unions as well as with those of the political party.

On a superficial view, but on a superficial view only, the Irish trade union movement was well placed in 1922 to play an important role on both sides of the border. Indeed, for it the border could scarcely be said to have existed, since unions in north and south continued for the most part to be linked with the Irish Trades Union Congress formed nearly thirty years before. The total membership affiliated to the ITUC in that year of the great divide was not far short of 200,000.[55] Many of these members belonged to small craft unions which were still, as they had been since their inception, branches of larger organisations with their headquarters in Britain. But the dominant feature of the Irish movement, giving it an appearance of strength and unity that time was to prove deceptive, was the central position occupied by the Irish

* See above, pp. 524-5.

Transport and General Workers' Union. This, as we saw earlier, though badly battered in the fight with the employers in 1913, had survived not only that ordeal, but also the departure to America of its General Secretary, Jim Larkin, the following year. Although Larkin retained his title during the eight and a half years he was away, the very length of his absence and the fact that during it he became involved in American affairs to the virtual exclusion of everything else, meant that the ITGWU fell into other hands. It fell, in fact, largely into the capable hands of its President, Thomas Foran, and its General Treasurer, William O'Brien. Within a few years they had completely transformed the situation, and when Larkin returned at the end of April 1923 he found his union financially solvent and approximately 100,000 strong in numbers.

The importance of this development cannot be overstated. From it there sprang almost at once a deep division within the ranks of Labour which was to last for nearly forty years and to damage severely its industrial effectiveness. The root of the trouble was that Larkin had come back apparently believing that he had only to take up the threads where he had dropped them in 1914, whereas the new leaders, not unnaturally, regarded the revivified ITGWU as their own creation and, being ambitious as well as efficient men, were reluctant to share the power they had gathered into their own grasp. Even before Larkin's return there had been friction between these *apparatchiks* and an opposition composed mainly of former intimates of 'Big Jim' who still persisted in regarding him as the ultimate court of appeal. They were no match, however, for the union's officers who, just at the very moment that Larkin reappeared in Dublin, succeeded in revising the rules in such a manner as to give increased power to the Executive Committee on which they had an assured majority.

The primary responsibility for carrying through this *coup de main* rested with William O'Brien – a man of great ability, but also dour, suspicious, unyielding and, once involved in a quarrel, capable of carrying it on with extreme tenacity for a lifetime if need be.[56] The contrast between this superb, coldly-efficient organiser and the flamboyant and impulsive Larkin could not have been more extreme, and historians ever since have seen in it a main reason for the quarrel that now broke out. Although it is not the whole explanation of what followed, there is no doubt whatever that a formidable clash of personalities occurred within weeks, almost days, of Larkin's return. The details of the quarrel need not concern us here – they revolved round the control of the union, even the physical control of its premises – but the results were of the utmost significance. Larkin was expelled from the union he had himself originally created (the formal breach occurred in March 1924, but it had been preceded by months of recrimination) and while the former leader was absent in Russia, throwing himself with characteristic zest into the affairs of international communism, his brother, Peter Larkin, in June 1924 formed a break-away organisation, the Workers' Union of Ireland. But this, though it initially succeeded in attracting into its rank about two-thirds of the Dublin membership of the ITGWU (roughly 16,000 men), made little headway in the rest of the country, only twenty out of some 300 branches transferring their allegiance.[57]

The split could scarcely have come at a worse time. The year 1923, which saw the quarrel become virtually irreconcilable, was not only the time chosen by the employers to carry out extensive wage-cuts during a period of economic depression, but it was also the year of a general election at which the Labour party had hoped to establish its image as a large and coherent opposition party. To that end it put up fifty-three candidates, only to find when all was over that its representation in the Dáil had actually fallen from seventeen to fourteen. No doubt this eclipse was partially to be explained by lack of funds, and of political organisation and experience, as well as by the continued preoccupation of the electors with the aftermath of the Civil War, but it is not unreasonable to suppose that the Labour showing at the polls was also directly affected by the uninhibited rancour with which it was washing its dirty linen in public. A movement that could not even govern itself scarcely inspired confidence as to its capacity to govern the country.

Yet, if the Larkin-O'Brien split did undeniably contribute to the eclipse of Labour at a crucial moment in Irish history, it is not enough to explain that split solely in terms of an ugly dispute between two totally incompatible individuals. The fact is that Larkin and O'Brien represented fundamentally different conceptions of what the role of the Irish trade union movement should be. The predominance of Larkin and Connolly in union affairs before the First World War has sometimes led observers to take an exaggerated view of the extent to which that movement was as extreme as its leaders. It is, in reality, very doubtful if their Marxism was shared by more than a small minority of the rank-and-file. Most Irish working-men remained as before – undeviatingly Catholic in their personal beliefs and incorrigibly opportunist in their economic demands. Indeed, the 'Trade Union Congress and Labour Party' which had come into being in 1912 shared, as a modern commentator has pointed out, 'neither Connolly's Marxism nor his militant and explicit nationalist republicanism'.[58] And although the Citizen Army of 1913 might be claimed as the spearhead of that militancy it was, as we saw earlier, always a very small body and not in any true sense the striking-force of a large and committed trade union movement. For most trade unionists after 1916 – and this holds good especially for the ITGWU as it was refashioned by Foran and O'Brien – the safeguarding of their wages and the improvement of their working-conditions continued to be their primary concern.

We are confronted here, of course, with a phenomenon by no means peculiar to Ireland. What was being fought out in the Irish labour movement during those confused and angry months of 1923 and 1924 was the battle that had been fought in many countries, and even in the Second International itself, before 1914 – the battle between revolution and reformism. For Larkin a trade union was still an instrument to be used for an end far greater than the short-term advantage of its members – the overturning of capitalism and the creation of a totally new kind of society.* For O'Brien, on the other hand, a trade union remained what it had habitually been, a bargaining mechanism whereby the workers could achieve material betterment within the existing framework of state and economy.

The real significance, then, of the dispute which racked the Labour movement in those years, and which left O'Brien dominant in the ITGWU, was that it marked a decisive turn to the right. This had two important consequences – one doctrinal, the other practical. In doctrinal terms the turn to the right meant that despite annual lip-service to the memory of Connolly, which year by year came to seem more and more unreal, there would not in the foreseeable future be a place in the movement for anything that could be recognised as a full socialist programme, with the result that men of the more extreme left were increasingly deflected into splinter-groups or even into organisations, like the IRA for example, which were dedicated to political objectives that might or might not be compatible with social radicalism.†

The practical consequence of the turn to the right was that the labour movement as a whole failed to offer a credible alternative to the middle-class, conservative regime inaugurated by Mr Cosgrave and his colleagues. And although it is true that the chief burden of opposition in the Dáil during the 'twenties did fall upon the Labour group – a burden carried conscientiously if not always very effectively – the return of Mr de Valera and his followers to constitutional politics in 1927, not merely deprived Labour of a good part of its role, but also brought back into the foreground all those political issues arising out of the Treaty and the Commonwealth connection which succeeded only too well after 1932 in deafening the ears of the electorate to social and economic abuses that clamoured in vain for redress.

It has to be admitted, however, that external circumstances, quite apart from internal divisions, militated against any strong labour pressure for reform. The power of trade unions to protect their members, let alone secure large improvements, is notoriously weak in times of economic stringency and the Irish unions, still deeply divided by the Larkin-O'Brien dispute, were in no position to resist the onset of depression in and after 1929. Moreover, although north and south were

* Larkin's espousal of communism (albeit of a very individual brand) in America and after his return home can only have added to his difficulties in a country where even 'liberalism' was sometimes used as a term of abuse.

† It was a process that could cut both ways. As we saw earlier, the IRA itself was socially as well as politically to the left in the inter-war years, and shows signs of being so again at the present time.

both affected by the depression, and though the bulk of unions on either side of the border were still affiliated to the same Congress, the very fact of political separation brought with it different preoccupations which impeded concerted action on economic problems that were often at bottom very similar. The northern unions, which might reasonably have been expected to provide a secure industrial base for the promotion of an all-Ireland movement, were if anything in even greater disarray than their southern counterparts, since the collapse of the General Strike in 1926 had left them with a legacy of depleted membership and, as a result of the Trade Disputes and Trade Union Act of 1927, diminished freedom of action.*

Disunity and depression together cast a gloom over the whole movement which expressed itself in a steady decline of numbers and resources. By 1929 affiliated membership of Congress for the whole country had dropped to under 100,000 while members' contributions had fallen from £184,000 in 1923 to £78,000 in 1929.[59] Nor was there much sign of recovery in the years that followed. The formal connection between the political party and the union movement was severed in 1930, but the ostensible purpose of this manoeuvre, which was to allow the party to develop its organisation in the constituencies, did not in fact lead to any marked extension of Labour support in the countryside. The party remained predominantly rural – only within the past few years has it seemed that expanding industrialism may enable it to broaden its industrial base – and although it might have been expected to appeal strongly to the rural and small-town proletariat which undoubtedly existed, it found difficulty in competing either with the extremism of the IRA or the reformism of Fianna Fáil. Once the latter achieved power its attractiveness to the working-class voter increased – at least in the earlier years of Mr de Valera's long tenure of office – and there is good reason to believe, in the words of a recent writer, that 'Labour's failure to win any real measure of popular support was due to the fact that it was forced to compete, on very unequal terms, for the same votes as Fianna Fáil.'[60] Individual unions – especially the ITGWU – did certainly maintain close ties with the Labour representatives in the Dáil, but, because of the relatively small numbers of the industrial working-class, this did not in itself guarantee any growth of political effectiveness. On the contrary, Labour's share of seats after the general election of 1932 sank to seven (improving slightly to eight at the election of the following year), and although the even balance of the other parties made Mr de Valera dependent for a time on Labour support, this was not a situation that was likely to endure indefinitely. True, as we saw earlier, the Labour party under its new leader, William Norton, a shrewd and able bargainer, did its best to push Fianna Fáil to the left, or rather to compel it to honour its election promises of social reform, but although in the early 'thirties these efforts had some moderate success, they were constantly frus-

* See Part IV B, chap. 5.

trated by the intrusion of other issues, and especially of course by the dispute with Britain.

In the years immediately before the Second World War, however, the situation seemed at last to be improving. The new industries established behind tariff barriers had given some additional employment and trade union numbers in the twenty-six counties responded to this stimulus, rising by 1939 to about 150,000.[61] But at this point the war called an abrupt halt to progress. Not only was industry crippled by shortages of fuel, raw materials and equipment – with obvious repercussions on the level of employment – but since the shortages themselves drove prices steadily upwards, wages and social benefits alike were quite unable to keep pace with the resulting inflation. There was in all this the material for an explosion of working-class discontent of which, it might be assumed, the labour movement would be the obvious spokesman. The discontent and unrest were certainly there, but events were soon to show how powerless either the political party or the trade unions were to exploit them.

Two developments in 1941 demonstrated this with painful clarity. First of all, in May the government introduced a Wages Standstill Order which in effect prevented any union from striking for higher wages by removing the legal protection for strike action afforded by previous legislation. Although a partial concession was made the following year – relating only, however, to increases in the cost of living from 1942 onwards – the Wages Standstill Order remained substantially intact until September 1946. How effective it was in depressing the standard of living may be judged from the fact that whereas the cost of living index had risen by about two-thirds between 1939 and 1946, the average weekly wage in industry went up by no more than one-third during the same period.

No less direct an interference with the bargaining power of the workers was the second development of that year – the passing of a Trade Union Act designed to achieve two objects. First, it laid down that while only government licensed trade unions could carry on collective bargaining, to obtain a licence it was first necessary for a union to lodge a substantial sum of money with the High Court. This, though bearing heavily on very small unions, was at least defensible as a safeguard against wild-cat or unofficial strikes. But the second feature of the Act was more ominous. With the intention of avoiding inter-union disputes, it was proposed to set up a tribunal which should have the power of determining that one union alone should be entitled to organise a particular class of workers if that union could show that it already had the allegiance of a majority of the workers in the class in question. Additionally – though this was later ruled as unconstitutional by the Supreme Court – it was intended that only an Irish-based union should be given sole negotiating rights by the tribunal.

This far-reaching proposal evoked very different reactions within the Irish Labour movement. The biggest union, the ITGWU, recognised the need for rationalisation – naturally, since it stood to gain from the disappearance of what William O'Brien called with remarkable frankness 'the superfluous unions which we all want to see eliminated – or, to use an expression in fashion in some quarters "liquidated".'[62] Many others, however, combined to form a Council of Action to oppose the measure and in the campaign which followed James Larkin once more regained something of his old authority. His Workers' Union of Ireland was still excluded from the Irish TUC – O'Brien's influence had seen to that from the beginning – but he himself had sufficient following in the capital to have sat for a while on the City Council and even to have represented northeast Dublin briefly in the Dáil just before the war.* In 1941, spurred on by the belief that the workers must make a united stand against the Trade Union Act, he applied to join the Labour party and he and his son James were admitted in December. The next year he was elected as an official Labour candidate to the City Council and followed this by recapturing northeast Dublin at the general election of 1943. But in doing so he precipitated a fresh quarrel with O'Brien and the ITGWU. Worsted in his attempt to prevent Larkin from receiving official backing for his candidature, O'Brien then led his union into the very serious step of withdrawing their affiliation from the Labour party which thus found itself deprived not only of valuable financial support, but also of some of its parliamentary representatives, five out of eight of whom (as members of the ITGWU) broke away from the main body to form their own group, the National Labour Party. Not surprisingly, the Labour vote, which in 1943 had topped 200,000 for the first time (and in doing so had captured seventeen seats) fell sharply when Mr de Valera called another election the following year; indeed, the Labour performance in 1944 was so lack-lustre that the party might almost be said to have abstained from participating. Only after both sections had agreed to join the inter-party government in 1948 was the way opened for the reconciliation which took place two years later.

It proved, unhappily, less easy to heal the deep wounds in the trade union movement. These, indeed, were if anything aggravated by the course of events in the latter part of the war. As we have seen, the Irish TUC, since its first small beginnings in 1894, had catered for the whole country and for all kinds of unions regardless of whether these were based in either part of Ireland or in England. In practice the Irish-based unions had operated mainly in the south, while the British-based unions were strongest in the north. But over the years the feeling had grown, especially among the Irish-based unions – and among these, especially inside the ITGWU – that Irish workers ought to be organised in Irish unions, a xenophobic view to which the wartime Irish government was not unsympathetic. It was indicative of the prevailing mood that when in 1943 the Irish TUC was invited by the British TUC to attend a world conference of trade unionists to be held in

* Elected in 1937 he lost his seat at the general election the following year.

London in 1945, the National Executive of the Irish Congress, though sharply divided on the matter, should in the end have declined the invitation on the ground, which at this distance seems a shade metaphysical, that acceptance would involve a breach of Irish neutrality. The following year, at the annual meeting of the Irish TUC, the British-based unions launched their counter-attack and succeeded in passing a resolution reversing the previous decision, thus enabling representatives to attend the conference, which they duly did in February 1945. This action provoked – more accurately, perhaps, brought to a head – yet one more dispute within the movement in which the Transport and General Workers Union was intimately involved. Shortly after the London conference was held, the ITGWU, together with a number of other Irish based unions, withdrew from Congress and established their own organisation, the Congress of Irish Trade Unions, dedicated to the principle that Irish workers must free themselves from the domination of British-based unions.[63]

For the next fifteen years this division within the ranks of the Irish movement continued. At the time of the split the ITUC had an affiliation of about 145,000 members; those belonged to both British and Irish-based unions, among the latter being Larkin's Workers' Union which, true to form, entered at one door as O'Brien's ITGWU left by another. The Congress of Irish Unions was, and remained, smaller, having at the outset an affiliation of about 77,500.[64] But both organisations stood to gain from the rise in trade union membership which came with increasing industrial activity, north and south, after the war. In 1958, for example, the ITUC had a quarter of a million members in sixty-four unions, while the Congress of Irish Unions had 188,000 in twenty-one unions.[65] By then, however, the long dispute was drawing to a close, partly because, of the two ancient protagonists, Larkin was dead and O'Brien had retired, but also perhaps because the idea of the solidarity of labour, which had been at the root of the original TUC conception, had come again to appear more attractive and more feasible at a time when the emphasis in both parts of the divided island seemed to be directed more towards stimulating economic growth than towards reopening political animosities. At any rate, after long and arduous negotiation, the two organisations reunited in 1959 to form the Irish Congress of Trade Unions, membership of which was open to unions with headquarters in any part of Ireland, and to unions based outside Ireland provided the latter safeguarded the autonomy of their Irish members.

But not only were the unions larger in numbers and more united in purpose than they had been for a long time, they were also moving steadily towards a better bargaining position. In the south this had been foreshadowed as far back as 1946 when the Industrial Relations Act of that year had established an independent tribunal, the Labour Court, on which employers and employees had equal representation. True, the recommendations of the Court as to the settlement of industrial disputes were not mandatory, but as its first chairman observed, it 'helps to create a kind of voluntary law or common rule' by a process of inquiry or conciliation.[66] It could not prevent strike action, nor was it designed to do so, but it did markedly reduce tension and it did succeed in gaining acceptance for a large proportion – possibly as high as four-fifths – of its suggestions.[67] Moreover, apart from its action in specific cases, the Labour Court was instrumental in negotiating the first National Wage Agreement in 1948, a precedent that was to be followed later on numerous occasions and which undoubtedly helped to reduce the amount of direct industrial action taken by workers in support of their claims, though not, of course, to eliminate it entirely.

In the north, the development of bargaining power took a rather different direction, being directed mainly towards the removal of two deeply-felt grievances. One of these was the reluctance of the Northern Ireland government to follow the lead of Westminster in repealing the Trade Disputes Act of 1927. It was not in fact until 1959, thirteen years after the decisive step had been taken in Britain, that the Act, with its vexatious restraints upon union activity, at last disappeared in the six counties.* But it was not for another four years after that the second grievance was remedied. When the Irish movement had split in 1945, the affairs of the northern unions which had remained affiliated to the ITUC were entrusted to a 'Northern Committee' of trade unionists elected each year by their fellow-members of the ITUC unions in Northern Ireland. The official, governmental line in the north (though not in practice followed with equal rigidity by all departments) was that this Committee, being subordinate to a Congress which had its headquarters outside the state, could not be formally recognised. In 1964, however, the Irish Congress of Trade Unions amended its constitution so as to make it clear that the Northern Committee did enjoy real autonomy, whereupon the Northern Ireland government took steps to establish an Economic Council on which. the unions were represented.[68]

There remained, however, and must still remain, an unanswered question about the future growth of trade unionism in Northern Ireland – the fundamental question of whether or not union solidarity is a strong enough force to overcome religio-political sectarianism. As recently as 1962 two perceptive and sympathetic observers of the Ulster scene concluded that it was. Citing the action of northern trade unionists in condemning discrimination of all kinds, they commented that it 'seems reasonable therefore, to regard the signs of religious difference within the trade union movement as secondary, the natural result of other divisions in the province, and to consider the movement as being an important uniting influence'.[69] Who now could echo the confidence

* Among other things, the Act had placed difficulties in the way of sympathetic strikes, had declared certain forms of industrial action illegal as 'intimidation', and had introduced a 'contracting-in' system for the payment of the political levy to the Labour party.

of that assertion?*

(v) RECONCILING PAST AND PRESENT

In all that has been said in the preceding sections about policy even the non-Irish reader will have found a good deal that is familiar. Irish governments in the last few decades – their preoccupation with the language revival apart – have shared the general concern of governments in most parts of the world to open to their citizens the possibility of a decent existence and to save them from the worst abysses of poverty by hanging beneath them a safety-net of social security. But although the 'minimum standard' which society nowadays takes for granted may not in Ireland be very imposing, at least compared with that of the European Community to which she aspires, the same impatience with welfare, the same distrust of bureaucracy, the same instinctive urge for the individual to assert himself against the impersonal complexities of the modern world, that have become so characteristic of the age in so many places, have begun to manifest themselves in the republic also.

Yet, while the problem of reconciling private liberty with the demands of society may be a universal one, the form it takes in a particular country will obviously depend upon the situation in that country at any given time. In Ireland it is clear that past history and present circumstances both play an important part in generating the tensions that are now so conspicuous. It would be easy, but extremely misleading, to say that these tensions result from the interplay between an old, deep-seated conservatism and a new liberalism still seeking a direction and a goal. It would be misleading to say this because although there are senses in which it is certainly true that Irish society has been profoundly conservative ever since independence, to confuse this conservatism with simple reaction would be to misunderstand the whole drift of history in the last fifty years. On the contrary, it was of the highest importance to the men who took power in 1922, and no less so to the men who replaced them in 1932, that the part of Ireland over which they ruled should be seen to be a successful experiment in building a modern state. This was necessary, not only to establish the regime in the eyes of the outside world as eligible to be admitted to the

* It is fair to add that since this was written evidence has come to light of the constructive and moderating influence exercised by the northern trade unionists in Belfast during the disturbances of August 1969; since northern trade unionists numbered 215,000 out of a total membership for all Ireland of more than half a million, their role clearly was, and could be again, important. See *Irish Times*, 29, 30 and 31 Dec. 1969. It should be noted also that the labour movements in both parts of the island have a common meeting-place in the National Council of Labour proposed by the Irish Labour Party Conference of 1966.

comity of nations, but also as a standing demonstration to the minority inside the twenty-six counties, and to those who were watching critically from across the border, that revolution would not be the prelude to sectarian tyranny – in short that Home Rule would not mean Rome Rule. Nor, despite certain manifestations of clerical influence mentioned earlier in this book – notably the Browne affair and the ecclesiastical ban on Trinity – has Home Rule in fact meant Rome Rule.* The new creation, through all its constitutional mutations from Free State to Republic, has remained a parliamentary democracy of a classically simple kind, in which freedom of speech, of worship and of political association have in all essentials been preserved intact. True, the state, like most other states, has from time to time taken special powers against those who would destroy it, but one has only to point to the way in which the path was made clear for Mr de Valera to return to constitutional politics in 1927, to the secure – not to say privileged – position of southern Protestants, and to the fact that twice in a decade the electorate has resisted proposals for the abolition of proportional representation, to realise something of the stability and maturity which have come with the years.

However, even if all this be conceded, certain dark shadows fall across the scene and will not easily fade. No one can study the history of Irish politics in the last forty years, no one can read what Irish writers have written about their country's condition (especially the numerous and recurrent variations on the theme of alienation), no one can look at the evolution of Irish society, without becoming aware of an undercurrent of frustration and cynicism thrusting its way steadily to the surface. For this there would appear to be four principal explanations – the feeling, until recently almost inarticulate, that much that has happened since 1916 has in some sense been a betrayal of the rebellion; the deep, perhaps permanent, wounds left by the Civil War; the traumatic effects of the realisation that political independence of England did not mean the end of English influence in Ireland; and finally, the internal stresses that have resulted from the exposure of a deeply Catholic country to a modern world itself changing with unparalleled

* Apart from the instances mentioned in the text, the principal grievances of Protestants relate chiefly to the exclusion of divorce from the law of the land, the prohibition against birth control (which, however, can be surmounted without much difficulty), and the operation of the Ne Temere decree, which entails that the children of a mixed marriage should be brought up as Catholics. Protestant opinion was particularly alarmed by the Tilson case, when the Supreme Court ruled in 1951 that a promise to do this given in writing by a Protestant husband was enforceable in law despite his subsequent wish to revoke the promise. Such instances are exceptional, however, and I have tried elsewhere to do justice to the generally favourable position of Protestants in the community (see my essay, 'The Minority in the 26 Counties', in F. MacManus (ed.), *The Years of the Great Test*, 1926-39, pp. 92-103). For the more generalised influence of the Church on Irish society at large, see below, pp. 688-90.

speed and completeness. Each of these important elements in the present mood of restlessness needs some further consideration.

We may start with the obvious proposition that the spick-and-span republic of 1970 is not the republic of 1916. It remains only a part of what the dead men died for. Not just a geographical part, but even within its own truncated frontiers something less than the society which Connolly and Pearse had sought to bring to birth. Not united, not Gaelic, not 'cherishing all the children of the nation equally', not even a republic at all until the hurried *accouchement* of 1948, it is not really surprising if it has seemed to a disenchanted generation a crude parody of everything they have been taught to believe.

But linked with this – and a second element in the climate of disillusionment – is the way in which the state actually came into being. That revolutions devour their children is a trite enough observation, but it is necessary to insist that when they devour them as a result of civil war the consequences are more than usually dire and far-reaching. Time and again in these pages we have had occasion to trace the distorting effects of that central and crucial disaster upon subsequent events and policies in Ireland. Only two points need to be made here by way of recapitulation. The first is that from 1922 to the present the real has been haunted by the ideal – or, to put it another way, that sober calculation has been at endless war with irrepressible fantasy. In practical terms, this has meant that on the one hand the gun has always been liable to re-enter politics and, on the other, that those in power at any given moment have been led by the inexorable logic of their situation to use force against those who claimed that their sole allegiance was to that indivisible republic to which all had at one time subscribed – hence the Civil War reprisals, hence the special powers taken first by Cosgrave's government and then by de Valera's, hence the Curragh detention-camp and the long running fight between the IRA and the police, hence also (to some extent) the recent fissures within Fianna Fáil. That governments so placed could not have done other than they did most Irishmen would probably agree – at least, they have been slow to overthrow governments that acted thus – yet the compulsion to behave in this way has been precisely the tragedy of those governments. Caught in the collision between the unattainable absolute and the realisable compromise, they have opted for the latter and, given that their aim has been to create an orderly society, they could have made no other choice. But still 'those dead men are loitering there to stir the boiling pot'.

The second point that needs to be made about the regime that emerged from the Civil War is the superficially obvious one that it was a regime wedded to the economic ideas of Griffith rather than to those of Connolly. The programme of intensive industrial development behind a tariff wall, which Griffith had laid down in those early, idyllic years of the new century when the most doctrinaire theories could be formulated in the blissful certainty that they would not be put to the rest in the foreseeable future, became in the course of time the foundation of a policy which, it is scarcely too much to say, has influenced, where it has not dictated, the evolution of the entire economy. But because it was at bottom a business policy and not a social policy, it conflicted from the very beginning with those ringing declarations of the Proclamation of Independence and of the First Dáil which promised a new world for the poor and downtrodden. It was, however, the function of the Civil War to make that new world safe, not for Wolfe Tone's men of no property, but rather for business, for the shopocracy, and for the farmer-owners of the rising generations. From that single fact a long, sad history of disillusionment was to follow.

We saw earlier, of course, that to think of economic policy as if it were something consciously framed in Dublin and carried out by Irishmen under laboratory conditions and free of all extraneous influences, was always an illusion. It was an illusion for the sufficient reason that in the years after 1922, as for many centuries before that date, what men made or grew or bought or sold in Ireland depended in the last resort upon the state of the larger economy of the British Isles, to which the country continued to belong regardless of treaties signed in London or of lines drawn upon the map. The lesson of interdependence has been etched deeply into the national consciousness by a continuing process in which, at different times and in different ways, emigration, economic war, trade agreements and currency crises have all played their part. And although one of the attractions to many people of entry into the Common Market is precisely that it may diminish the closeness of the connection with Britain, ordinary commonsense suggests that what will in fact happen will be the replacement of one form of interdependence by another.

But while this kind of interdependence is tolerable, because unavoidable, there exists simultaneously a different kind of interdependence which has seemed to some people not unavoidable and therefore intolerable. It is the interdependence that comes from sharing a common language – English – with a powerful neighbour, and from being exposed to all sorts of contacts and pressures which a small country is ill-equipped to resist.* There is at stake here – and it is the third element in the contemporary unease – not merely the problem of how to preserve and revive the Irish language, but the much larger question of how, if at all, to maintain intact the values that are felt both to be characteristic of a separate Irish culture and essential to its continued existence. The fact that these values have proved notoriously difficult to define and, when defined, have often proved to be strangely

* To speak of the common language as English is perhaps an over-simplification, since the pressures have come from across the Atlantic as well as from across the Irish Sea. But it remains true that the constant traffic between England and Ireland, the intermingling of peoples and the influence of the mass media based on Britain have all combined to make the threat seem in Irish eyes a distinctively English threat.

at odds with contemporary reality, is perhaps less important for the historian than the fact that many people have been content to sum them up as Catholic and Gaelic. What do these large and vague terms mean in the Irish context? They mean simply that there has existed, and still exists, a substantial body of opinion which holds that Irish society should be governed by Catholic principles of morality and also that it should strive to preserve whatever of speech, or music, or literature, or customs and pastimes, still links the present to an antiquity passionately invoked, if imperfectly comprehended.

The attempt to keep these values inviolate has produced over the years a vast amount of honest (if misdirected) effort, a good deal of more or less conscious hypocrisy, and one specific experiment which has possibly done more to damage the reputation of Ireland abroad than anything that has happened outside Londonderry or West Belfast. This has been the attempt by censorship to preserve the Irish public from noxious and corrupting influences from elsewhere. In 1926 the Cosgrave administration set up a committee of investigation into 'evil literature' with a view to excluding from the country the steady stream of English newspapers and magazines which trafficked chiefly in the more lurid aspects of sex.* But when, three years later, the Censorship of Publications Act was passed, it went much further than striking at the gutter press and at salacious paperbacks. Not only did the Act contain a section designed to banish from Ireland any publication advocating birth control, but it also set up a Censorship Board with the responsibility of recommending to the Ministers of Justice the banning of books which they considered to be indecent or obscene. The censorship thus imposed was, it must be emphasised, motivated neither by political nor religious intolerance. It was, indeed, reinforced by the argument that neither art nor literature had any rights against God and the censorship at its inception and afterwards certainly had strong clerical approval. Equally, many politicians supported it at the time and would, presumably, support it at the present day. But churchmen and politicians did not welcome it because it protected specific creeds or parties. Their attitude may rather be seen as an extreme example of the maxim that the worst is sometimes the corruption of the best. For them the censorship in its pristine form was at least in part an attempt to translate into reality the puritanism that often goes with revolution – to establish, so far as laws could establish it, that the new Ireland should shine like a good deed in a naughty world. But it is essential to an understanding of modern Ireland (north and south) to realise that

* In the early days of the Free State the old British machinery of police seizure of obscene articles and subsequent trial of the offender before a magistrate's court was all that was available to the government, but these prosecutions could not touch the publisher, who was usually outside Irish jurisdiction. See M. Adams, *Censorship: the Irish Experience* (Dublin, 1968), pp. 14-15. This book is much the most complete account of the Irish censorship in operation.

this puritanism – especially in regard to obscenity and pornography – is an important element in the Irish character and more enduring than the products of more permissive societies elsewhere can easily grasp. There is, in fact, a case for arguing that, at least at the outset, the policy of the government reflected rather than distorted the idealism of the people.

Of course in practice it did not work out like that for long. The Censorship Board, composed of five people (intended originally to consist of a representative of the Catholic Church, a lawyer, a medical man and one representative from each of the two universities), was set up in 1930 and went to work with a will. Before long it had begun to make not only itself, but the whole country, ridiculous as its probing finger moved on from the pornography which had set the whole strange mechanism in motion to the works of eminent contemporary authors, and even to those of other authors long since dead. Nevertheless, despite the outraged protests of Irish intellectuals – and scarcely any Irish writer of note in the last fifty years has escaped condemnation – the principle of censorship was written into the Constitution of 1937 and the Censorship Act itself amended in 1946.* Ostensibly a relaxation of the system in the sense that it provided for appeal machinery (though too cumbersome and expensive to be very helpful), the amended law formally empowered the Board itself to ban books – which, in effect, it had been doing from the outset – and also gave authority to the customs officials to seize any literature which in their opinion ought to be brought to the Board's attention.† In practice, the way the censorship had functioned has been that anyone who considers a book in any way objectionable can send it, with the offending passage clearly indicated, to the Censorship Board. If the complaint is accepted as serious by the secretary, the book is then circulated to the five members of the Board who meet once a fortnight to discuss the books they have been sent. If three out of five favour a ban and there is no more than one dissentient, the book is then automatically banned. Since in the mid-sixties the censors were receiving about 500 books a year it does not seem as if the attention individual books received could have been very great. Nevertheless, between January 1960 and January 1965 – and this was a period of relative relaxation compared with the 1950s – some 1,900 books were banned, an average of about thirty a month.[70] Since then there has been a marked reduction and in 1967 it was decided to 'release' from banning many books previously condemned, and to

* Mention should be made here of the courageous fight against the censorship led by the distinguished Irish writer, Mr Sean O'Faolain, especially when he was editor of *The Bell* magazine. He fought this battle mainly in the 1940s but it is plain from the recently revised edition (1969) of his famous book, *The Irish*, that his attitude has not changed; see pp. 161-2.

† For the official role of the Customs officials, see Adams, op. cit., pp. 171-6.

amend the law so that newly banned books could not be prohibited for more than twelve years, though they could of course be banned again thereafter.

The cynic may say, perhaps, that one reason why book censorship has lasted so long is because so few people in Ireland read or buy books. If the mass of the population was to be protected against indecency and obscenity, then foreign periodicals and films were arguably a more important target. Periodicals were dealt with (and ruthlessly) by the ordinary machinery, but films required special treatment. In fact, they have had it from as far back as 1925 when a Film Censor was first appointed. This was a paid government appointment (unlike the literary censors who were part-time and unpaid) and it carried with it very considerable power, since no film could be shown in the country without a certificate from the Censor. There developed, indeed, a hierarchy of certificates, as elsewhere, but the much cruder method of simply cutting out passages deemed to be objectionable has always been extensively used. Aimed ostensibly at preventing what has been called 'Californication', the censorship has not in practice been restricted to the cruder fantasies of Hollywood, but has also been used, often with devastating effect, upon some of the masterpieces of the modern cinema. Here too, however, there has latterly been a shift towards a more liberal policy, with the appointment in 1964 of a Film Appeal Board which has undoubtedly introduced an element of discrimination into a process that was frequently ludicrous and always vexatious.

The attempt to maintain 'values' against corrupting influences from outside which lies at the very heart and core of the censorship is in essence the attempt to maintain Christian – more specifically Catholic – values, and it leads us straight to the fourth strand in the current restlessness – the tensions inevitably experienced by a long-sheltered Catholic community abruptly confronted with the need to come to terms with a largely pagan world. From what has already been said earlier in this book it will be apparent that no easy generalisations are possible about the influence of the Church upon Irish society. Even in the nineteenth century, as we saw, although the bishops were frequently a conservative force in politics, this was not invariably the case, and even when it was the case – as, for example, in the Fenian period – there were still to be found parochial clergy who were prepared to disregard episcopal thunders and minister to men whom their superiors had excommunicated. Much the same was true of the troubled years from 1916 onwards, and although the Church was uncompromising in its denunciation of republicans who refused to accept the Treaty, at the parish level some of the old flexibility still remained.

Just because the Church was not in reality so monolithic as it seemed on the surface, it was relatively easy for Irishmen to display that curious dualism so often seen in Catholic countries – combining devotion to their faith with frequently outspoken anti-clericalism. The devotion is real enough, though it would perhaps be excessively naïve to judge it by external manifestations, frequent and striking as these may be. Thus, the fact that of a population which is ninety-five per cent Catholic, something like ninety per cent go to Mass on Sunday, though a remarkable phenomenon, might on investigation turn out to be as much a sociological as a religious one; the high ranking of the Cardinal (directly after the President) in the Irish order of precedence does not exempt the bishops, individually or collectively, from frequent and searching criticism; and the insertion of a clause in the Constitution (Article 44), recognising the 'special position' of the Church as 'guardian of the Faith professed by the great majority of the citizens', has not in practice affected the broad toleration to which the state is committed, and in any event is unlikely to survive much longer.* The convincing proofs of Irish devotion lie less in these outward evidences than in the underlying reality of a simple faith early inculcated but tenaciously retained, and in the special position which the parish priest still holds in his community. The peculiar authority, and often affection, the priest enjoys, derives of course partly from the nature of his office, but also from his historical role. Given the penal discrimination against Irish Catholicism in the eighteenth century, and the absence of a Catholic ruling class for most, if not all, of the nineteenth century, the priest found himself in the position where he and he alone supplied the necessary local leadership, not just in matters of religion, but in all sorts of other matters as well, a leadership which, as we have seen, gained added force once the national school system had planted him, as the school manager, at the very heart of the country's educational network. His influence, then, was paramount, but although in political questions it might in certain circumstances take a radical form, in questions of faith and morals it was, with very few exceptions, conservative. Conservative, not just because the priest was the humble instrument of an international Church dedicated to the preservation of standards and attitudes which the world at large was prepared to ignore, but also because his own training in the seminary, and the fact that full control of a parish might often not come to him until he was near sixty, combined to make him, as an individual, resistant to change.

Yet change there has been and change there is likely to be in the future. Whether elderly bishops were prepared to recognise it or not, a new era began with the short but revolutionary reign of Pope John XXIII and with the deliberations of the Second Vatican Council. The discussion of ideas previously stifled, the questioning of authority hither-

* Note that although the clergy in Ireland are numerous, the ratio of priests to population is not quite so high as is sometimes supposed. In 1958 there were 3,833 secular clergy and 1,776 regular clergy, giving a ratio of 585 Catholics to one priest (secular and regular). A further calculation of 1965 suggested a ratio of one priest (secular and regular) to 553 Catholic laity, as compared with a world ratio of 1 : 1,270; the English ratio, however, was 1 : 500. See K. Connell, *Irish Peasant Society*, pp. 160-1; T. Gray (citing D. A. Thornley), *The Irish Answer*, pp. 280-1.

to taken for granted, the reconsideration of questions, like the celibacy of the clergy or the Church's attitude to birth control, have sent shock-wave after shock-wave through Catholicism all over the world. If Ireland has been rather more insulated against these shock-waves than many other countries, this is no doubt due mainly to the deep-seated conservatism already mentioned. It may also, however, have been due to the presence within the hierarchy of strong personalities disinclined for change. Of these the most eminent was certainly the Archbishop of Dublin, Dr John Charles McQuaid, a devoted ecclesiastic who over many years worked to better the conditions of the poor in his diocese, but at the same time sought so to shelter them from the winds blowing from without that, returning from the Vatican Council, he was able to tell them that they need not heed the talk of changes to come. 'Allow me to reassure you. No change will worry the tranquillity of your Christian lives.'[71]

Even so, although this tranquillity may to a considerable extent still be unimpaired, initiatives which have already been taken suggest that no archbishop, however authoritative or authoritarian, can long arrest the movement towards change, and indeed Dr McQuaid himself has not been immune to the process. At the beginning of 1972 he resigned the see to which he had been appointed in 1940 at the age of forty-five. It is too soon yet to say what the effects of this epochal event may be, but already there are indications that his successor, Dr Dermot Ryan, a distinguished Jesuit scholar who was long a professor at University College, Dublin, has begun to establish a reputation for greater humanity and accessibility. Change can be traced in many different directions – in the co-operative venture of Father James McDyer at Glencolumcille, an effort by one man to restore life and soul to a dwindling community in a remote part of Donegal; in the growing interest of the Church in sociology, evidenced among other things by the influential periodical, *Christus Rex*;* in the ferment of ideas inside the seminaries, and especially in Maynooth itself, where a new periodical, *The Furrow*, has become an important channel for communicating to Irish readers the trend of ideas and events outside Ireland; in the recent adoption of the vernacular for the service of the Mass and the new emphasis on liturgical reform; in an increasing discussion of ecumenism and an increasing preoccupation with the mission of the Church in a secular world. The results that flow from all this debate and reappraisal may not as yet appear very impressive – it would be premature to expect that they would be – and the forces that favour the maintenance of the status quo are by no means routed. Indeed, it may even be that *Humanae Vitae* has given them a new lease of life, and not only on the central issue of resisting birth control. Nevertheless, the evidence ad-

* It is proper to add that this interest was shared by Archbishop McQuaid himself who founded not only the Dublin Institute of Catholic Sociology, but also the Catholic Social Service Conference and the Catholic Social Welfare Bureau.

duced by Catholic writers themselves that there can be no return to the old quiescence is, to an outsider, cumulatively convincing.[72]

There can be no return because no man is an island and no island is – any longer – an entity. The twentieth century cannot be kept out of Ireland because it is already and inexpugnably there through the simple fact of physical and cultural permeation. Latterly, this has taken two specific forms whose ultimate importance has hardly yet begun to be understood. The first of these derives from the much greater direct contact Irish men and women now have, not merely with their English neighbours, but with people from other countries as well. To the traditional intermingling that emigration has always brought in its train has been added both the visible presence of foreign firms employing Irish labour in Ireland, and the even more potent influence of tourism. This last has cut two ways. On the one hand, the Irish themselves now travel abroad for their holidays much more than previously, and on the other hand their own country has become a highly attractive magnet to visitors from other lands. The Irish tourist industry, at least on an economically significant scale, is very much a creation of Bord Fáilte, the organisation set up in 1957 as a state-sponsored body with the function of co-ordinating the work of the various tourist interests in the country. It has itself undertaken numerous initiatives, chiefly in the improvement and extension of hotel accommodation and in mounting an exceedingly effective campaign of advertising. The results are writ large in the trade returns, which indicate that the gross receipts from tourism rose from about forty-six million pounds in 1962 to eighty million pounds in 1967, with every expectation – until the northern crisis intervened – that they would rise still higher in time to come.[73]

But while this kind of contact with visitors has no doubt had a liberating effect, there is another kind of contact – ethereal rather than corporal – which has beyond question made an even more dramatic impact upon popular attitudes. This is, of course, television. Ireland had developed its own wireless service – Radio Eireann – as early as 1925, in effect as a branch of the civil service under the control of the Department of Posts and Telegraphs. It derived its revenue mainly from licence fees and from sponsored programmes, but despite this slender foundation soon became something of a national institution, attracting a number of very able men into its service. In the post-war years, however, it fell inevitably under the shadow of its natural competitor, television. When in 1960 the government decided to provide the new medium in Ireland, it created a state-sponsored body to administer both kinds of broadcasting. A special authority was set up to launch the new service, which was to be financed mainly on the basis of licence fees and receipts from commercial advertising. Telefís Eireann went on the air for the first time on New Year's Eve, 1962, and was, predictably, assailed from all points of the compass before it was very much older. It was said to devote too little time – or too much – to the Irish language; it was either dominated by the Church or did not spend enough time on religion; it was too parochial, but it also relied too heavily on American material; it was either under the thumb of the government, or else it was dangerously outspoken. Nevertheless, despite these and many other accusations, it matured remarkably quickly, breaking through taboos of all kinds to discuss before a startled public such issues as birth control, drugs, premarital relations, pornography, and the place of the Church in the modern world. By the mid-1960s it was reckoned that about 348,000 out of 680,000 homes in the country had television sets; the total impact of television, however, has to be measured not just by this figure but by the estimated number of homes – 137,000 – which were able to receive the BBC and Independent Television programmes as well.* The fact that such a considerable proportion of Irish families could see on their hearthrugs all the manifestations of the permissive society which British television relays with such unflagging zeal, not only made nonsense of the censorship of books and films, but threw many stones, or rather bombshells, into the quiet waters of Irish domesticity.

These diverse pressures, combined with the economic and social changes described earlier, have wrought such a transformation that the traveller returning after ten, or even five, years' absence finds himself almost a Rip Van Winkle in this pushing and restless society. The mood that now possesses the country is one of impatience and of criticism, but also one of excitement, which seems indeed to have been checked by a sense of horrified impotence in the face of events in the north, but which may before long be rekindled by the challenge of entry into Europe. It is, naturally, a mood that is expressed with least inhibition by the young and among them it has taken forms familiar elsewhere, including a measure of student unrest, a revival of interest in politics and a growing preoccupation with social justice.† But also, and in the long run, this may prove to be of crucial importance, the new generation is to be distinguished from its predecessors by its changed attitude to the past. It is not the case, as some have said, that young people in Ireland have become indifferent to, or ignorant of, their history. On the contrary, there has never been a time when the past was more accessible to them, by reason of the quiet revolution which has taken history out of the realm of myth and passion and into that of reason and ascertainable fact. The first steps in this revolution

* A survey made in 1967 showed that 77 per cent of households in Dublin City and County owned television sets; for the rest of Leinster the percentage was 55. Munster registered 54 per cent, but in Connacht and the three Ulster counties only 31 per cent of households owned sets. In all regions the proportion of urban owners was, predictably, much higher than that of rural owners. For a valuable account of the impact of television on the electorate, see B. Chubb, *The Government and Politics of Ireland*, pp. 134-44.

† Student unrest in the Republic, it should be said, has hitherto been more pragmatic than ideological, concerned essentially with real grievances about accommodation, library facilities, contact with teachers, and the like.

were taken just over thirty years ago by two scholars, T. W. Moody and R. Dudley Edwards, when, with the encouragement in his old age of no less a figure than Eoin MacNeill, they founded the journal, *Irish Historical Studies*, which at once became, and has since remained, the vehicle for accurate, informed and judicious historical research, not just in the twenty-six counties but in the whole of Ireland. This venture has been followed by others in which the same two pioneers, with the aid of such colleagues as D. B. Quin, J. C. Beckett, T. Desmond Williams and F. X. Martin, have repeatedly taken a leading part, and of which the cumulative effect has been to change the historical outlook of a whole generation.*

It is true, of course, that the new Irish historiography has scarcely yet graduated from fundamental research to synthesis, and that therefore its ability to penetrate into the schools has so far been limited. But it is not too much to claim for it that it has had a very direct effect upon the ideas of an intellectual elite both inside and outside the universities. And since it is this elite which is making its way into politics and into the public service, the fact that its attitude towards the past should have become less romantic, less distorted by prejudice and by patriotic over-simplification, than that of its predecessors may yet prove to be one of the great formative influences upon the future. Some change of attitude there would have been in any event because of the mere passage of time, but the historiographical revolution has helped to ensure that it would be a change in the direction of understanding, not indifference. In this there is a germ of liberation, for to understand the past fully is to cease to live in it, and to cease to live in it is to take the earliest steps towards shaping what is to come from the materials of the present. For the first time in fifty years it is legitimate to believe that those steps are at last being taken.

* Among these ventures may be numbered two series of historical monographs; the establishment of the Thomas Davis lectures broadcast every winter on a wide variety of historical themes extending even to events so near in time as 1951; the launching of a television series of lectures which, when published as *The Course of Irish History*, at once established itself as the balanced yet readable general work the country had been lacking since Edmund Curtis had produced his *History of Ireland* thirty years earlier; and, now in prospect, a multi-volume *New History of Ireland* which will bring together the work of a whole generation of historians who, like the present writer, have had the great good fortune to be trained in this famous school. It would be invidious to name names here, but in the preface will be found listed those among them who, either by their research or their personal assistance, helped in the preparation of this book.

I am not saying that they did not do right in starting their government, they were compelled to do it because they had yelled about 'No Home Rule' for a generation and then they were compelled to take a form of Home Rule that the Devil himself could never have imagined.

Rev. J. B. Armour, cited in W. S. Armour, *Armour of Ballymoney*, p. 332

B. NORTHERN IRELAND UNDER HOME RULE

1. Growing-pains of Devolution

The history of Northern Ireland has been dominated by three principal problems which have changed extraordinarily little throughout the entire period of its existence. These are, first, the problem of the triangular relationship with the rest of the United Kingdom and the rest of Ireland; second, the problem of the deep and continuing internal division of the population between, in the main, Unionists and Protestants on the one hand, and Nationalists and Catholics on the other; finally, the problem not only of developing a viable economy in such a small area, but of securing for the people public services and standards of welfare comparable with those in Britain. It would be difficult to determine any order of importance for these problems; indeed, they were all interconnected in one way or another, since each was powerfully influenced by the form of government which the six counties found themselves saddled with in and after 1920. The logical starting point, therefore, for any survey of the province in the early years of partition is to examine the curious experiment in devolution which started it on its course and remained virtually intact until the crisis began in 1968.

The constitutional basis of the experiment is to be found in the Government of Ireland Act of 1920. Originally, as we saw earlier, that Act had been intended to confer Home Rule upon the whole of Ireland. It had recognised, of course, that the deep divisions between north and south could not be ignored and it had provided for separate parliaments and separate executives in the six counties and in the twenty-six counties. But at the same time it had envisaged a single Lord Lieutenant to represent the King in both areas and it had proposed a Council of Ireland consisting of twenty representatives from each parliament through which, it was fondly hoped, better relations between the sundered portions of the country would be established, leading in the end to the peaceful evolution of a single parliament for all Ireland.

This conception has never yet emerged from the realms of fantasy.*

* We may not have heard the last of it, however. At the time of writing

695

The course of events in the south between 1920 and 1922 made it plain that the kind of Home Rule embodied in the Government of Ireland Act would meet with no acceptance there and that the Act, if it was to work at all, would be worked only within the area of the six counties, though even this area was a subject of argument and uncertainty until the collapse in 1925 of the Boundary Commission appointed to adjust the division of territory between north and south. In December of that year it was agreed 'in a spirit of neighbourly comradeship' that the extent of Northern Ireland should continue to be the six counties designated in the Government of Ireland Act – that is, Antrim, Armagh, Down, Fermanagh, Londonderry and Tyrone.

Long before then, however, Northern Ireland had begun to function as a separate entity, accepting that status reluctantly and as a sacrifice, but accepting it because that was the only way in which Ulster Unionists could be sure of staying within the United Kingdom until, of their own volition, they joined the rest of Ireland.[1] It followed, therefore, that since they had no real wish for self-government, the actual form of that self-government reflected, not the striving for autonomy usual in a newly-emerging state, but rather a deep-seated desire to disturb the close relationship with Britain as little as possible. Their leader, and Northern Ireland's first Prime Minister, Sir James Craig, summed up this attitude best in a letter to Lloyd George in 1921 : 'As a final settlement and supreme sacrifice in the interests of peace the Government of Ireland Act was accepted by Northern Ireland, although not asked for by her representatives.'[2]

The basis of Northern Ireland's limited self-government is a parliament consisting of the Sovereign, the Senate and the House of Commons. The Sovereign is represented by the Governor (until 1922 by the Lord Lieutenant) who summons, prorogues and dissolves parliament in the Queen's name and gives the royal assent to bills. Although technically the Governor must comply with any instructions issued by the Crown (i.e. Whitehall) in respect of any bill, and must, if so directed, reserve the royal assent, this has only been done once – in 1922 – when it provoked a very sharp reaction in the Northern Ireland parliament. Normally, his functions are mainly ceremonial, though the first Governor, the Duke of Abercorn, probably exerted considerable indirect influence upon ministers partly because he was personally respected, and partly because, as the head of a great Ulster family, he had an intimate knowledge of the province. Of the two Houses, the Senate, as usual in modern bicameral legislatures, is much the less important. It is composed of only twenty-six members. Of these, two – the Lord Mayor of Belfast and the Mayor of Londonderry – are members *ex officio*, the remainder being elected by the House of Commons by proportional representation. Senators hold office for eight years, half re-

---

it still figures occasionally among the mechanisms by which men of good will hope to foster better relations between the two parts of the country.

tiring, every four years, and although their power of amending legislation (except, of course, financial legislation) could theoretically lead to a conflict between the two Houses and thence to a joint sitting as laid down in the Government of Ireland Act, that has never happened. This is scarcely surprising. Since all but two of the Senators are elected by the House of Commons, for them not to echo the opinions of that House would be as much against nature as for a ventriloquist to be contradicted by his dummy.

The House of Commons itself consists of fifty-two members, elected for five years, forty-eight of whom represent territorial constituencies and (until 1969) four the Queen's University, Belfast. The latter were elected by proportional representation, but this method, which applied initially to all constituencies, was replaced in 1929 by a system of simple majorities in single-member constituencies for elections outside the university. The franchise, though based on universal suffrage and broadly similar to that in Britain, had two peculiarities. One was that an elector had to have been born in Northern Ireland or resident in the United Kingdom for seven years. The other was that plural voting was retained, though an elector could only vote once in one constituency. The territorial constituencies underwent no general adjustment of their boundaries between 1929 and 1969, though four new ones replaced the university seats in the latter year. In addition, Northern Ireland sends twelve members to the British House of Commons, the majority of whom over the years have been in effect members of the British Conservative and Unionist party.*

The executive power technically vested in the Sovereign, and on her behalf by the Governor, was in fact exercised by the Executive Committee, commonly called the Cabinet, which normally consisted of nine members – the Prime Minister, a Minister in the Senate, and Ministers responsible respectively for Finance, Home Affairs, Health and Social Services, Education, Agriculture, Commerce and Development. In 1969 a Ministry of Community Relations was added in circumstances later to be described. These ministries have tended over the years to bring within their own control an increasing range of activities which elsewhere in the United Kingdom were still, partially at least, under the control of the local authorities – thus police, fire service, electricity, housing, health and public transport have all been heavily centralised. Local government itself had changed little in structure from that established for all of Ireland by the Act of 1898. Northern Ireland still had, up to 1969, two county boroughs (Belfast and Londonderry), six administrative counties (i.e. the six designated in the Government of Ireland Act), ten boroughs, twenty-four urban districts and thirty-one rural districts. Each of these bodies had an elected council with functions,

* Initially, a university seat was included in the Ulster representation at Westminster, but this was abolished in 1948. Note that the above description of the Stormont parliament applies only to the period before the imposition of direct rule in 1972.

composition and sources of revenue broadly similar to the English pattern, but the most significant departure from that pattern lay in the fact that the local government franchise was largely restricted to ratepayers and weighted in favour of property. As a result of this it has turned out that perhaps as many as a quarter of those who were on the parliamentary register had no vote in local elections. We shall have to return to this subject – one of the most explosive in Northern Ireland politics – when we come to deal with the theme of discrimination in northern society.*

The legal system, as one would expect, is similar in its essentials to that of England, since it has changed little in the years after 1920. There is a Supreme Court (as there was in Dublin in the days before partition), there are county courts (as there had been in Ireland for many generations) and there are magisterial courts. The latter were created for all Ireland in the nineteenth century because, with a landed class that tended to be absentee, the English system of justices of the peace had proved ineffective. Consequently resident salaried magistrates were appointed – the 'Irish RMs' described in a previous chapter.† This practice was taken over by Northern Ireland, or rather, taken further, since an act of the local parliament in 1935 discontinued the old method whereby lay justices sat with the resident magistrates and put the latter in sole control of summary jurisdiction.

But to this pattern of an old-established legal system based on a long-accepted English model there is one outstanding exception, the Civil Authorities (Special Powers) Act. In assessing the institutions and practices of government in Northern Ireland it is never possible to move very far from the tumultuous origins of the state. The Government of Ireland Act came into operation in May 1921 and both then and for many months afterwards there was much violence and disorder inside the six counties and along their borders – and this at a time when control of the police was still vested in the British government.‡ In the face of this, and of a campaign of what amounted almost to civil disobedience by many Nationalists, the newly-fledged government in 1922 passed rapidly through the Northern Ireland parliament a bill which, as one member remarked, really only needed to have one clause : 'The Home Secretary shall have powers to do what he likes, or else let somebody else do what he likes for him.' What the Act, when passed, did was to give the Minister power 'to take all such steps and issue all such orders as may be necessary for preserving the peace' according to the regulations laid down, regulations which he could add to from time to time. Originally intended as an annual Act, and as such renewed from year to year from 1922 to 1928, in 1928 it was renewed for five years

* There is a useful account of the evolution of local government in M. Wallace, *Northern Ireland: 50 Years of Self-Government* (Newton Abbott, 1971), pp. 44-56; for recent developments, see below, chap. 6.

† See above, part I, chap. 3.

‡ For this situation, see Part II, chap. 6.

and in 1933 was made permanent. The regulations to which the Act opened the way certainly covered a wide field. There could, if and when required, be regulations imposing a curfew and against the possession of firearms and explosives; there could be others against unlawful drilling and illegal uniforms, or against membership of illegal organisations; there could even be regulations empowering the arrest and detention of persons suspected of having acted or being about to act in a manner prejudicial to peace and order, or regulations enabling the authorities to exclude a person from entering Northern Ireland or confining him to a specific area of the province. And not only this – these regulations were reinforced by the Public Order Act of 1951 imposing controls on disorderly meetings and processions, and by the Flags and Emblems Act of 1954 giving the police powers to seize provocative emblems. In 1970, following the disturbances to be described later, a Public Order (Amendment) Act was passed in the teeth of bitter opposition at Stormont, with the dual object of giving better protection to lawful processions and of enabling the government to deal more effectively with counter-demonstrations.[3]

It has to be said in fairness that while the mainspring of all these special regulations – the so-called Special Powers Act itself – is permanent, the regulations are not, and many of them from time to time have been revoked. Nevertheless, two comments need to be made. One is that so long as the internal tensions within Northern Ireland persist, the government is unlikely to abandon the measures it originally took as necessary to its survival and which, to the extent that its survival is still in question, it may need to revive again at any moment. And the other comment is that an unfortunate consequence of the semi-anarchical circumstances in which the Special Powers Act emerged was that, lacking at first full control of the Royal Ulster Constabulary (replacing the Royal Irish Constabulary), the government took steps to strengthen its position by relying upon a special constabulary created in 1920. It is true that from 1925 this ceased to be a full-time force, but one class, the 'B specials', was retained on a part time basis subject to full-time duty if the need arose.* It has also to be remembered in this context that when control over the Royal Ulster Constabulary did pass to Northern Ireland that force continued to carry arms, as the old Royal Irish Constabulary had done in the days of the Union. Few outward features of life in Northern Ireland have attracted so much adverse comment as the presence in the streets of armed police, and even though critics are often ignorant of the historical reasons for the existence of such a force, the simple fact that it did exist was a perpetual irritant.

It would, however, be unjust to lay too much emphasis upon the special powers that the Northern Ireland government has from time to time made use of. What is most likely to strike the dispassionate ob-

* For the circumstances leading to the decision to disband them in 1969, see below, chap. 5.

server is not the magnitude of the government's powers but rather the curious gaps in its armoury. Unlike, say, the dominion parliaments, or the imperial parliament itself at Westminster, it is in general unable to make laws having extra-territorial effect – its basic function is to legislate on matters relating only to Northern Ireland. But it is far from having a monopoly of these. The Government of Ireland Act set out a list of 'excepted' matters over which the Northern Ireland parliament had no powers of legislation. These were matters concerning the Crown, peace and war, the armed forces, treaties with foreign states, dignities and titles, treason, naturalisation, domicile, trade with any place outside Northern Ireland, cables and wireless, air navigation, lighthouses, coinage and negotiable instruments, weights and measures, trade marks, copyright and patents.

This is a formidable list, but it can be justified on the ground of the need for uniformity within that United Kingdom of which the majority in Northern Ireland so passionately claimed to be a part. But that is not the end of the story. There were three further kinds of limitation on the powers of the Northern Ireland parliament – one negative, the others positive. Negatively, there was a prohibition of laws aimed at religious discrimination, and there was a prohibition against the state taking property without compensation. More positively, there were, in addition to the 'excepted' matters already mentioned, certain other 'reserved' matters on which also the Northern Ireland parliament had not power to legislate. These included the Supreme Court, the postal service, the imposition and collection of customs duties, excise duties on articles manufactured or produced, income tax and surtax, purchase tax and any tax on profits. Further, and as a kind of blanket proviso, the Government of Ireland Act had laid it down that the supreme authority of the United Kingdom parliament at Westminster remained undiminished, that the local parliament could not repeal or alter either the constituent Act (the Government of Ireland Act) or any United Kingdom statute passed after 3 May 1921 and extending to Northern Ireland, and that Northern Ireland statutes would themselves be void to the extent that they were repugnant to the United Kingdom statutes passed after 3 May 1921 and extending to Northern Ireland.[4]

Clearly we have here a complicated situation, arising from the fact that the government of this small area was deliberately divided between two different parliaments and two different administrations. Perhaps it would be more correct to say that it was divided between the Northern Ireland government and legislature on the one hand and Whitehall on the other. Although in theory the shadow of Westminster legislation loomed over Northern Ireland from the beginning, in practice the mother parliament has devoted very little time to the affairs of the six counties – in one period of just over a year in 1934-5 the time spent was one hour and fifty minutes, and that seems, until very recently, to have been about the average.[5] The real crux of relations between the authorities in Belfast and the authorities in London has been the question of services – which services shall be administered by which authority and how the cost of these services shall be met. Since, as we have already seen, most kinds of major taxation were among the matters 'reserved' to the parliament at Westminster, it follows that those which were transferred to the Northern Ireland government were few and unimportant – they consisted, in the main, of motor-vehicle and stamp duties, death duties and a few minor excise duties. Altogether, these produced about one-tenth of the revenue raised in the province. Most of the rest came from the 'reserved' taxes, the chief of these being customs duties, the greater part of the excise duties, and taxes on incomes – all of them, of course, being imposed and collected at uniform rates throughout the United Kingdom. The amount of this revenue to be handed over to Northern Ireland was calculated by the Joint Exchequer Board, consisting of a chairman appointed by the Crown and one member each from the Treasury and the Ministry of Finance in Belfast. From Northern Ireland's share of this revenue were, however, deducted, first, the cost of the reserved services (for example the Supreme Court), and second, the contribution to be made by the six counties to the imperial services – such as defence or diplomatic and consular representation – from which Northern Ireland benefited in the same way as other parts of the United Kingdom. The logic of this 'imperial contribution' seemed impeccable – that to the extent that Northern Ireland gained from being an integral part of the empire, so she should be prepared to pay a proportionate amount to the expense of running that empire – but almost from the beginning it was a source of passionate, though frequently ill-conceived, argument. Even more productive of possible friction was the strange arrangement whereby the Northern Ireland government, though charged with the responsibility of administering the wide area of services assigned to it, was utterly unable to control, or even to anticipate in advance, what money (other than the share represented by the transferred taxes) would be available for this purpose. Not only had the imperial contribution to be met each year, and the full cost of the reserved services, but since the actual rate at which taxes would be collected in Northern Ireland was fixed at Westminster, the local Minister for Finance was faced with a revenue that would expand or contract entirely without regard to whatever policies he might be planning to pursue. It was true that the Government of Ireland Act empowered the local parliament to grant relief from income tax, but this was of little real help since this relief could be met only from the six counties' own resources and not at the expense of the United Kingdom.

It was not long before this complex plan began to show itself to be unworkable. Under the Government of Ireland Act the imperial contribution was initially fixed at £7·9 million and the cost of reserved services at £2·2 million. Since the estimated reserved revenue for the province was £14·7 million and the estimated transferred revenue was £1·8 million, this meant that what would be left to Northern Ireland would in fact be £6·4 million. Out of this sum all the domestic services would have to be financed. To the new government, anxious to sweep away the consequences of many years of neglect and to develop schemes of housing, public health and education, this was a very narrow margin within which to have to operate. Too narrow, as it turned out. It was quite true that at the moment when Northern Ireland was being created revenue was buoyant – the total was £16·5 million and expenditure on services (i.e. excluding the imperial contribution) was only £6·3 million. But by 1923, the first full financial year, revenue was down to £13·8 million and from this was deducted an imperial contribution of £6·7 million and payments for reserved services of £1·9 million, leaving little more than £5 million for the province's own expenditure. Thus by 1923, even with an imperial contribution that had not reached the amount originally fixed, the Northern Ireland government was already in difficulties. Indeed, had the full amount of the imperial contribution been insisted upon, either then or in the immediately succeeding years, Northern Ireland would straightway have begun to run at a deficit. What had been left out of account was the way in which the economic circumstances of the whole of the United Kingdom had altered in the years after the war. The six counties suffered their share of the industrial depression of the early twenties – as we shall see presently, unemployment in north-east Ulster was exceptionally high – while at the same time they had to accept the consequences of tax cuts introduced in Britain in 1924.

It is not surprising that this situation resulted in what the Northern Ireland Minister of Finance described as 'long and irritating controversies with the Treasury', which ceased only when an arbitration committee under Lord Colwyn was appointed in 1923 to consider whether any alteration in the imperial contribution was needed. After two years of arduous negotiation, this committee produced an acceptable formula which was partly obtained by standing the Government of Ireland Act on its head. It was recognised that to make the imperial contribution a first charge on the revenue of the province was no longer feasible. Therefore logic dictated that the imperial contribution must be the residue left over *after* domestic expenditure had been met. But what was to prevent an ingenious Minister of Finance in Belfast ensuring that there never was any residue of this kind? Even in 1924, the then Minister of Finance had delivered himself of the, from the British point of view, slightly sinister remark that 'in all matters of social welfare we should be entitled to the same benefits as in Great Britain . . . local autonomy did not necessarily imply any lower social status.'[6]

But did it not? The Colwyn committee was not so sure. True, it accepted the argument that as taxation fell with equal severity upon the Ulsterman as upon the Englishman, Scotsman or Welshman, so, from 1924 onwards, expenditure per head of the population should increase at the same rate as in Britain. But, while this seemed to concede parity of a kind, it was in fact qualified by the way in which the committee defined the *necessary* domestic expenditure of Northern Ireland. That key word 'necessary' was hedged round by three qualifications. First, it must not be taken as allowing Northern Ireland a higher average standard of service than existed in Britain. Second, because the social structure of Northern Ireland was different from that of Britain, expenditure on services was to have regard to 'any lower general level of prices, of wages, or of standards of comfort or general amenity which may exist in Northern Ireland as compared with Great Britain'. Finally, and almost too obvious to be stressed, Northern Ireland would not be allowed to spend money on services which did not exist in Britain.[7] In short, Northern Ireland's permissible expenditure would be limited in two ways – by the fact that spending per head must keep pace with the rate set by Britain, and by the fact, given her social and economic *disparity*, she ought not to expect to be able to finance services of the same scale and scope as those across the water.

There can be little doubt that this arrangement represented clear gain for Northern Ireland, since it ensured that if revenue continued to fall, then so would the imperial contribution to the extent that it might even disappear altogether. Moreover, although the Colwyn committee might frown on the Ulsterman's ambition to have the same social services as his fellow-citizens in Britain, he had no intention of abandoning that ambition. Provided he did not seek to exploit his British connection, either by keeping his own transferred taxes below the levels obtaining in the rest of the United Kingdom, or by pushing his expenditure above that prevailing elsewhere, he could easily convince himself that parity in taxation meant parity in the public services.

But although this may have been the activating principle in Belfast it proved very difficult to put into practice, especially during the depression years of the 1930s, as revenue continued to fall and expenditure continued (with a vengeance) to rise. And even though one consequence of this was that by 1933 the imperial contribution had dwindled almost to vanishing point, the Northern Ireland Minister of Finance was still desperately hard put to it to balance his budget. He was in difficulties, ironically enough, precisely because the increased expenditure on these basic services was necessitated by the principle of parity, and parity was fast becoming a test of the viability of the whole devolutionary experiment. Northern Ireland had to offer its citizens not less than what they would achieve elsewhere in the United Kingdom or it would stand condemned in the eyes of its numerous and implacable critics.

It was unemployment that provided the most extreme test of the principle of parity. Northern Ireland had an insurance scheme identical with that of Britain, the Unemployment Fund being financed by contributions from employers, employees and the state. The trouble was that the amount of unemployment was proportionately much greater in northeast Ulster than in most (though not all) parts of Britain. By 1925 almost a quarter of the insured population in the six counties was out of work and the *deficit* in the Unemployment Fund was £3·6 million. The

Northern Ireland government was caught in a terrible dilemma. On the one hand, it could not hope to exert more than a marginal influence on economic policies which were determined in London for the United Kingdom as a whole. On the other hand, it could not increase its contribution to the Unemployment Fund, partly because the Colwyn formula bound it to observe the same rate as prevailed in Britain, but also because, if it had had liberty to enlarge its contribution, this would only have been liberty to plunge deeper into debt. The orthodox remedies would have been either to increase employers' and workers' contributions, or to cut benefits, or both. But any of these remedies would have been political suicide, since they would at once have been taken to mean that Northern Ireland was no longer able to carry on as a separate entity.

The only course that remained was to plead in London that because Northern Ireland was, after all, not just a separate entity, but also an integral part of the United Kingdom, she deserved to be helped. Up to a point this plea was successful. By the Unemployment Insurance Agreement of 1926 it was settled that the Unemployment Funds of the two parts of the United Kingdom might be kept in a state of parity on the basis of insured populations by making grants to the poorer fund. Ostensibly reciprocal, the Agreement in fact resulted in grants being made by the United Kingdom to Northern Ireland, though this was – it was hoped – to be kept within bounds by the proviso that if in any year the Northern Ireland government paid out more per head of the *total* population than did the British government, then Britain would only meet three-quarters of this excess expenditure.

Even with this limitation it seemed for a time as if the arrangement might work. In 1926–7 the British government paid over to the Northern Ireland government nearly £900,000 in 'equalisation' grants and though in succeeding years the figure never approached that level, it remained substantial up to 1931. But then in 1932 it suddenly ceased altogether. The explanation was simple – though devastating in its effect. Because equalisation payments were made on the basis of total population, and because after 1929 unemployment in Britain was so heavy, she was actually making a heavier payment per head than Northern Ireland was. Consequently no more grants were made and for the next three years Northern Ireland had to try to keep her Unemployment Fund in parity with that of Britain from current revenue alone. It was an impossible task and between 1932 and 1935 the Minister for Finance balanced his budget – if balanced is the right word – by a series of expedients that, had he been there to see them, might have served to convert even Gladstone himself from Home Rule. Indeed, so far from receiving assistance from a hard-pressed Treasury in London, Northern Ireland was required to take two further steps – to revalue the province so as to produce a larger yield in taxes, and to impose an education rate – which were, indeed, long overdue, but which could hardly have come at a worse time.

However, virtue, even if enforced, proved its own reward. In 1936 the Unemployment Insurance Agreement was amended so that equalisation payments should thenceforth be calculated on the basis not of total, but of insured, populations. Since the proportion of the population in Ulster in insurable employment was much smaller than in Britain, the former's *per capita* payments were inflated. It followed, therefore, that manna not only again began to fall from Whitehall, but that it did so more abundantly. And there was even better to come. In May 1938 the Minister of Finance extracted from the British Chancellor of the Exchequer a promise that in the event of a deficit in the Northern Ireland budget money should be found to make it good, *provided* that the deficit was not the result of a standard of social expenditure higher than, or of a standard of taxation lower than, that of Britain. Whether or not it was a coincidence that this announcement was made only a matter of days after Britain had agreed to the return of the treaty ports to the Irish Free State it is impossible to say, but that decision had at one stroke enormously increased the importance of northeast Ulster to British naval strategy. Northern Ireland was no longer just an embarrassingly demanding poor relation, she had become a vital link in the defences of the United Kingdom.

The internal consequences for the province of this change of status, as it might almost be described, will be discussed later.* Here it is sufficient to draw three conclusions from these intricate but crucial transactions of the inter-war years. First, it is evident that the financial provisions of the Government of Ireland Act, even though amended in the ways that we have seen, condemned Northern Ireland to much uncertainty and difficulty in her day-to-day administration. It is true that in the key areas of pensions and unemployment insurance the great objective of parity was achieved, but it was achieved at a price. And this leads us to the second conclusion – that so much effort and so much money went into the frantic race to keep up with Britain in the scale of social benefits paid out, that there were no resources left to put through those essential long-term reforms that ministers had set their hearts on in the first flush of enthusiasm. So in 1939, as in 1922, the province was still plagued by ill-health, poor housing, bad roads, and inadequate schools.

To say all this is to point to the final inescapable conclusion – that whatever hope Ulstermen might have had of turning the unwanted gift of self-government to constructive ends through developing the powers of their own legislature, it was thwarted by the bitter experience of life as part of the United Kingdom in the depression years. A recent verdict on the achievement of Lord Craigavon (as Sir James Craig had become in 1927) sums up that experience harshly but not unfairly : 'On the ramshackle foundations of the Act of 1920 he and his colleagues had built, not a half-way house, but a lean-to whose stability depended on ties that bound it to Britain.'[8]

* See chap. 5 below.

2. The Depression Years

In economics, as in politics, the aim of Northern Ireland in the inter-war years might be summed up by the single word – survival. Yet the very nature of devolution complicated the task of economic adjustment. In one sense, of course, it was true that the continuance of close political ties with Britain only reflected the economic realities of the situation. Even in the nineteenth century northeast Ulster had been much more closely integrated with the economy of the rest of the United Kingdom than with the economy of the rest of Ireland. That integration was bound to continue, perhaps even to grow, given the fact that from 1921 onwards the six counties remained part of a free trade area in which men, capital and goods could move easily to and fro, which shared the same monetary and financial system, and which, without significant differentiation, participated in the same economic institutions and social services.

However, although Northern Ireland seemed inescapably a part of the British economy, it was, like some of the distressed areas across the water, a part which, being highly specialised, had its own particular problems that required local knowledge if they were to be successfully dealt with. And this was where the political settlement created a difficulty. Because, although the Government of Ireland Act did entrust considerable powers of economic regulation to the region, those powers had to be exercised within a broader framework of policy that was laid down at Westminster for the United Kingdom as a whole and over which Belfast had little enough influence. Thus, devolution in effect restricted Northern Ireland not only, as we have seen already, in matters of taxation, but in the power to achieve any measure of real economic independence. It could not set up its own tariffs, or interfere in other ways with external trade, it could not have a separate fiscal policy, and it had to accept whatever monetary policy happened to be in vogue in London. Any survey of the economy of the province, therefore, has to strike a balance of profit and loss between the effects of integration on the one hand and of decentralisation on the other.

An orphan of the political storm, almost, one might say, a *faute de mieux* creation, the six counties hardly seemed a rational, let alone an ideal, economic unit. Even its borders seemed to militate against it. On the landward side, a straggling frontier which owed more to religious than to economic geography, and cut off one of its two large towns, Londonderry, from its natural hinterland; to the east, the inhospitable sea, adding to the cost of its imports and subtracting from the value of its exports. Within these boundaries was a small and fairly thinly populated area. The province consisted of 5,238 square miles – about one-sixth of the land area of all Ireland – supporting a population which, though it fell in the later nineteenth century like that of other parts of Ireland, had tended to increase from the turn of the century onwards. In 1911 it was 1¼ million. When the next census was taken in 1926 it had increased by 7,000 and in 1937 it had gone up to 1,280,000. Emigration had taken its toll in the earlier years, here as elsewhere in the country, but during the inter-war years it had slowed down. Between 1926 and 1937, for example, the net loss seems only to have been about 20,000 altogether, although this is difficult to measure precisely as there is evidence of a considerable mobile element in the population which moved, and still moves, to and fro between Northern Ireland and Great Britain according to the state of the labour market.[1]

The most striking feature of this population was its distribution. By 1937 about sixty-three per cent of the whole population lived either in Belfast or in towns and villages within a thirty mile radius of the city.[2] It was this which gave the demographic structure of Northern Ireland its curiously lopsided appearance and, as we shall see, it was this which made the problem of industrial employment so crucial to the welfare of the province as a whole.

The growth of the Belfast conurbation was no doubt at the expense of the countryside and even though it sometimes happened that in years of acute industrial depression the flow of migrant labour would be from the urban to the rural areas, on balance it was the farm-worker who was attracted to the town rather than the other way about; between 1926 and 1937, it has been calculated, the net outflow from agriculture was about 5,000, and this would probably have been considerably larger but for a transfer of nearly 4,000 in the other direction in 1931–2.[3] Nevertheless, the extent of this agrarian depopulation should not be exaggerated. Both in appearance and in economic reality the northeast remained strongly agricultural. In 1926 farming accounted for about a quarter of all occupied persons and this proportion was to remain remarkably stable over the years – as late as 1945 the percentage was almost exactly the same, the actual number then employed being the equivalent of about 140,000 full-time workers.[4]

Agriculture was thus, in terms of the amount of labour employed, the largest single industry in Northern Ireland, but, paradoxically, it was also an industry which was organised on a very small scale. The typical unit was the family farm making little use, and that generally on a seasonal basis, of outside agricultural labour. The tendency towards consolidation of holdings which we have noticed elsewhere in Ireland, was evident in the six counties also, though up to the time of the 1937 census, and indeed beyond it, the emphasis was still overwhelmingly on farms of between one and thirty acres which – in that year – accounted for nearly 60 per cent of the total. Farms of over one hundred acres were relatively few and totalled only 4.1 per cent of all holdings, compared with nearly 9 per cent in the Irish Free State.[5]

As might be expected from such a structure – though influenced also, it must be said, by soil and climate – there was little attempt between the wars to grow wheat on any extended scale and crops in general were much less important than livestock. It was characteristic of this intensive, small-scale farming that while livestock of all kinds figured largely, the trend was somewhat away from cattle (declining from 173,000 in 1930–1 to 156,000 in 1938–9) and towards sheep, pigs and poultry. Sheep went up in the same period from 261,000 to 397,000, pigs from 250,000 to 844,000 and poultry from almost 5½ million to almost 6¼ million. To a limited extent this emphasis may have been influenced by subsidies (which went mainly to beef producers) but it is more likely that the real salvation of agriculture in the six counties during the 1930s was that it continued to enjoy access to the British market.[6]

The pattern of production which these figures reflect, while no doubt dictated by the environment and the market, was sedulously fostered by the government through an agricultural policy which might almost have been said to march step by step with that of the Irish Free State in the first decade of its existence. Thus in the north, as in the south, the process of land purchase was rounded out by further legislation (in the case of Northern Ireland by an act of the imperial parliament in 1925) applying the principle of compulsion and creating in the course of time 40,000 more farmer-owners; it is perhaps worth adding, in view of Mr de Valera's policy after 1932, that when Northern Ireland was set up it was conceded that the land annuities worth about £658,000 in the mid-thirties, arising out of agreements to purchase *before* 1920, should be transferred to the new government as a 'free gift'.[7] Apart from this legislation, reinforcing, if reinforcement were needed, the dominance of the small family farm, the local parliament passed its own measures designed primarily to improve agricultural education and to increase the value of the product. Into the former category fell the creation of a Faculty of Agriculture in the Queen's University, Belfast, which had from the beginning a strong bias towards research and, at a humbler level, the provision of winter classes throughout the province and the establishment of residential schools in selected places. Side by side with these projects went a series of enactments between 1924 and 1933, prescribing minimum standards of quality and packing to be observed by exporters of eggs, fruit, meat and dairy products at the same time, and again reminiscent of the Free State, the Livestock Breeding Act of 1922 required the registration of all bulls and thus enabled the Ministry of Agriculture to supervise the transition to a better quality of cattle. In the realm of marketing, also, the government was ready to intervene: the Agricultural Marketing Acts of 1931 and 1933 set up marketing boards, composed of representatives of producers and of the Ministry of Agriculture, which had power not only to compel registered producers to sell direct to the Board, or through its agency, but also to fix prices and determine the conditions of sale.

These various measures, combined with the native shrewdness and industry of the Ulster farmer, helped to produce an increase in the gross agricultural output of Northern Ireland from about £11 million in 1926 to an average of £16·4 million for the years 1936–7 to 1938–9 inclusive. Although modest in scope, this increase, it has to be remembered, was made at a time of worldwide depression and is evidence of perhaps greater vitality than the bare figures would suggest.[8]

Yet, although the state of Ulster agriculture would doubtless have been worse if there had been no governmental initiatives of this kind, that is not to say that all was well during the inter-war years. On the contrary, small farmers in the six counties were much like small farmers elsewhere. They lived a hand-to-mouth existence with little or no capital to spare for improving their buildings, or buying fertilizers and machinery. Even as late as 1947, an inquiry revealed that in many parts of the province, farmers and labourers were working with implements little different from those used a hundred years earlier.[9] Moreover, the wages of agricultural labourers before the war were substantially lower than those of their British counterparts (22/3 a week in 1936 on average, compared with 32/6 in England and Wales) while the working week was longer.[10] No doubt this was an important factor in the drift from the land even before the Second World War, just as the prominence of agriculture itself in the whole economy had the effect of depressing income in total and per head.[11]

But agriculture, significant though it might be, was not what made the province unique in Ireland. In the first half of the twentieth century, as in the second half of the nineteenth, its economic welfare was inextricably bound up with the fate of its industries. Even before 1914 these industries had begun to reveal serious deficiencies, some at least of which seemed beyond the power of man to remove. Thus it was a geological, and not a human fault, for example, that the northeast, like the rest of Ireland, lacked mineral resources, especially coal, and that fuel, iron and steel had to be imported from the mainland. This had a doubly damaging effect. On the one hand, the cost of bringing the fuel to the industrialist added to the cost of the product. And on the other hand, precisely because the supply and cost of fuel was a critical factor, industry tended to be concentrated into a few highly specialised lines. This tendency in its turn was reinforced both by the smallness of the domestic market and by the consequent necessity of exporting overseas a large part of what was manufactured in the province.

We find, therefore, that in the first half of the twentieth century specialisation continued in much the same direction as before, with two main groups of industries absorbing between them about fifty per cent of the labour force. One of these was textiles – where linen was still predominant, though increasingly under strain – and the other was shipbuilding, engineering, vehicle building and repairing. These two groups were complementary rather than competitive, for whereas the first employed mainly women, the second relied almost entirely upon male workers. Unhappily, both groups proved to be extremely vulnerable in the situation that developed after 1918. Being so heavily dependent upon their ability to export, they suffered naturally from every deterioration of trading conditions. Thus they were hit by the postwar slump which set in about 1921 and in the first full year of the new Ministry of Labour's administration eighteen per cent of insured workers were unemployed. Next, they were put at a heavy disadvantage by the return to the gold standard in 1925 and the consequent overvaluation of sterling, with the result that both in that year and in 1926 about a quarter of the insured labour force was out of work. Things improved somewhat during what came to be regarded as the 'boom years' of 1927–9, but as the level of unemployment continued to average about fifteen per cent it will be seen that the definition of a boom is rather elastic. Even this improvement was speedily halted by the world depression and by 1932 the percentage of unemployed was over twenty-seven. Throughout the decade 1930–9 it never fell below twenty per cent and averaged about twenty-five per cent. In 1938, indeed, nearly 85,000, or 28·3 per cent of the insured population, had no jobs.[12]

Within individual industries there were, of course, different problems, but most of them had this in common – that not only were they export industries adrift in an increasingly protectionist world, but they were also industries for whose products there was likely to be a diminishing demand even in reasonably prosperous times. Linen was perhaps a supreme example of this, losing ground, as it did, first to cotton, then to man-made fibres. And the decline in linen affected also the highly specialised engineering industry which had developed great expertise in the manufacture of textile machinery, not only for the mills and factories of the Lagan valley, but for buyers overseas. The shipping industry, and with it the closely associated rope-making industry, was likewise faced with a shrinking market. As world trade dwindled, so the need for ships to carry goods or passengers also declined, until in the Belfast shipyards employment shrank from about 20,000 in 1924 to scarcely more than 2,000 in 1933. In that grim year Harland and Wolff launched no ships at all, the first time a year had passed without a launching from their slipways for over a century. And when in 1934 the other large firm, Workman and Clark, went out of business, the industry seemed to be within sight of the end.[13]

Was it not possible to arrest this decay, if necessary by government action? To a generation well accustomed to the intervention of the state in all sorts of economic matters the urgent need of some kind of official initiative will seem self-evident. It was not so self-evident in the 1930s, partly because the Keynesian revolution in economic thinking had not yet taken its effect in government circles, and partly because, in the absence of any commitment to the idea of deficit finance, ministers and parliaments were mesmerised by what seemed the inescapable duty of facing a wholly unorthodox situation by the orthodox methods of unemployment assistance and relief. It is, however, only fair to add that the Northern Ireland government did seek legislation empowering it to assist, financially or by other means, firms wishing to start new enterprises or to extend existing businesses. These powers were embodied in the Loan Guarantee Acts passed between 1922 and 1938, and in the New Industries (Development) Acts of 1932 and 1937. The Loan Guarantees were of only very limited scope and were aimed mainly at the rescue of the shipping industry. Up to the time when the Acts ceased to operate (1940) a total of £22½ million had been advanced to firms in need of support and by 1950 nearly all of this had been repaid. The New Industries (Development) Acts, on the other hand, were more directly designed to attract new business to the area, since they contained a proviso that the government could make grants to undertakings established in order to produce goods not available in Northern Ireland – the grants being equivalent to about twenty years' rent of premises and supplemented sometimes by exemption from rates. The 1937 Act went even further by making interest-free loans available for building or adapting factories or works. But it cannot be said that the response was overwhelming. There was certainly some evidence of differentiation in the engineering industry – a switch, in some cases, from textile machinery to heating equipment, industrial fans, electric motors and so on – while the establishment of an aircraft factory by Short and Harland in Belfast in 1937 was a new portent. However, the total number of firms taking advantage of the new facilities was only fifty-four, and even by 1955 they were providing employment for not much more than 6,000 workers.[14]

This bleak picture of the situation in Belfast is to some extent offset by the growth in the so-called 'service industries' – in the distributive trades, the professions, education and administration. Because, despite unemployment, the city continued to grow in population, the need for such services increased, as indeed it did also, though to a lesser degree, throughout the province. In the whole of Northern Ireland the number of insured workers in the service industries in 1926 was 70,000 and by 1939 this had grown to 102,000. Even here, however, there were 20,000 out of work in the latter year.[15] It is, in short, impossible to escape for long from the overwhelming problem of economic life in the six provinces between the wars – the persistence at all times and in every sector of massive unemployment.

The government response to this challenge was scarcely impressive. True, within the framework of devolution and of the financial orthodoxies of the time, there may not have seemed to be over-much room for manoeuvre, although it is hard to resist the impression that some of the inadequacies of these years may also have been due to lethargy, or even complacency, especially among local authorities. Housing is a case in point. Even though the first census (in 1926) showed that eighteen per cent of the population lived at a density of more than two persons to a room, no housing survey was undertaken until the middle of the war, when it was found that 100,000 new dwellings were urgently needed. Yet between 1919 and 1936 the *total* of all types of dwellings built in Northern Ireland was only 50,000 and of these the vast majority were built by private enterprise. Lack of money, no doubt, is part of the explanation but not all, since at least for rural housing, generous exchequer assistance was available in the early years of the state. Even so, by 1939 less than 4,000 labourers' cottages were built by local authorities under legislation passed by the Northern Ireland government and of these Antrim, Down and Londonderry accounted for most. Not a single cottage was built in Fermanagh by a rural district council in the whole of that time. Such cottages as were built elsewhere were for the most part of a very low standard, frequently lacking gas or electricity or reasonable sanitation; on the eve of the war eighty-seven per cent of rural dwellings had no running water.[16]

Nor were conditions any better in the towns – if possible, they were worse. Under the various Northern Ireland Housing Acts passed in the inter-war period a total of 34,312 houses was built in Ulster towns and of this total the local authorities provided precisely 2,166. It was not all, of course, the fault of the local authorities. Many of them were too small to conduct such operations and they were not helped by the fever chart of government subsidies which shot up and down with bewildering rapidity, vanishing altogether in 1937. The result was that although the bad times drove down the rents of houses that were built, even these houses were beyond the reach of the very poor, who still often lived in dwellings officially regarded as uninhabitable, but which could not be destroyed because there was no money (and indeed no coherent plan) for slum-clearance and nowhere for the occupants to go if their tenements were pulled down.[17]

The imprint of the grim years of depression was felt in other spheres also. Public health, for instance, which should have been a matter of the highest urgency, was seriously neglected throughout this period. Ministers who would have liked to have cut a path through the administrative jungle inherited from Dublin Castle were inhibited from doing so time and time again by lack of finance. Thus, although at the outset of the new regime Northern Ireland actually had the worst death rate in the British Isles (in the years 1922–4 it averaged 15.5 per 1,000 of the population) its position on the eve of the war had scarcely improved at all. The death-rate was then 14.4 per 1,000 and it was a poor consolation to know that although Northern Ireland was still at the bottom of the list, it now shared that place with the Irish Free State. The contributory factors to this sorry situation were many – they included a serious scarcity of hospitals; grossly inadequate pay for dispensary doctors, and for nurses and midwives; sanitary conditions throughout the province of an almost medieval primitiveness; little effective check on the purity of food and milk; above all, perhaps, no serious effort to deal with the ravages of tuberculosis, which in 1938 reached such an appalling degree of intensity that it carried off forty-six per cent of all those who had died between the ages of fifteen and twenty-five, and thirty-eight per cent of those between twenty-five and thirty-five. This fearsome wastage of young life was further compounded by extremely high rates of both maternal and infant mortality. *More* mothers died in childbirth at the end of the inter-war period than they did at the beginning (5.5 per 1,000 births in 1936–8 compared with 4.7 in 1922–4), and although the number of infants dying did decrease slightly (from seventy-nine per 1,000 in the earlier years to seventy-six in the later), the Northern Ireland rate was considerably above that prevailing in the twenty-six counties. No doubt the concentration of population in Belfast had a good deal to do with this, but a committee reporting on the problem in 1939 commented that 'for the whole of the population above the status of pauper, midwifery provision in the broader sense is a private matter'. Paupers, however, were not so privileged as this might seem to indicate, for despite the sweated labour of over-worked midwives, perhaps a quarter of all children dying under the age of one year in 1937–8 died in a workhouse.[18]

The shadow of the workhouse, indeed, hung over all categories of the very poor, for although in practice outdoor relief had been becoming steadily more usual over the whole of Ireland in the second half of the nineteenth century, the Irish poor law still placed institutional relief at the centre of the system. Increasingly, however, 'the house' had become the refuge not of the able-bodied poor, but of the sick, the aged, infirm, and insane, as well as of illegitimate children and their mothers. The new brooms at Stormont had hoped to abolish this ancient system with its apparatus of unions and boards of guardians, but they were hamstrung by lack of resources and until after the Second World War the poor of the six counties continued to depend either on the shelter of the workhouse or on a meagre pittance of relief if they managed to stay outside. It is true, of course, that Northern Ireland followed the United Kingdom's lead in extending the scope of unemployment insurance and in introducing unemployment assistance in 1934 (not fully operative until 1937) for those who had no right to insurance benefit. But these innovations did not exempt the local authorities from having to shoulder the main part of the burden of poor relief which, at a time of heavy unemployment, could reach astronomical proportions. In Belfast alone expenditure under this head rose from £98,265 in 1923–4 to over £330,000 in 1933–4, by which time it was absorbing more than a third of all the revenue from the rates.

Vast though such expenditure seemed to contemporaries, it trickled through to the individual recipients as the bitter dregs of official charity grudgingly conceded after a searching means test. In some country districts it was apparently deemed possible to support life on as little as 2/6 a week for a single person, and in Belfast in 1932 a married man with one child could expect only 12 shillings a week. It is hardly surprising that that very year saw a remarkable demonstration in the city's streets in which both Protestant and Catholic workers joined together – hunger and degradation obscuring for a brief moment the deeply etched lines of religious and political division.[19] Nor was it surprising that the children of the Belfast unemployed in the 'thirties were reported to be two or three inches shorter and ten pounds lighter than their middle-class contemporaries, or that a survey of working-class conditions in the city in 1938–9 showed that thirty-six per cent of those investigated were living in absolute poverty – unable to buy enough food, clothing or fuel to maintain health and working capacity.[20] It was the final ironic comment on the Prime Minister's clarion call of 23 June 1921, the very day after the formal opening of the new parliament: 'We have nothing in our view except the welfare of the people. Our duty and our privilege are from now onwards to have our parliament probe to the bottom those problems that have retarded progress in the past, to do everything that lies in our power to help forward developments in the town and country. . . .'[21]

3. The Politics of Siege

The defence of Derry against the investing forces of James II ranks with the battle of the Boyne in the mythology of Ulster Protestantism. Indeed, even more than the Boyne, Derry is an exact and enduring symbol of the siege mentality – outwardly aggressive, but masking a deep sense of insecurity – which has distinguished the northern Protestant for most of his history. Admittedly, the Act of Union with Britain, by binding the two islands closer together politically and economically, ended the isolation which lay at the root of Protestant anxiety, and also helped to make possible the remarkable industrial expansion of the northeast in the latter part of the nineteenth century. But when that Union began to be threatened and was eventually broken then the old fears came flooding back and the siege mentality reasserted itself. For the first twenty years of Northern Ireland's existence this mentality dominated the politics of the six counties. Indeed, even the very acceptance of the fact that 'Ulster' was to consist of six counties, rather than of the traditional nine, reflected the siege mentality, indicating as it did that, given the heavy preponderance of Unionists over Nationalists in the area marked out for Home Rule, the Unionist leaders had finally accepted that six would be easier to control than nine.

'What we have now we hold', Sir James Craig had said in 1922, when refusing to co-operate with the Boundary Commission, and in this single phrase he summed up the central creed of Ulster Unionism, which ever since has been dedicated to the proposition that the status of Northern Ireland as a self-governing entity within the United Kingdom must at all costs be preserved. And since he himself remained in power uninterruptedly until his death in 1940, it followed that continuity, both of leadership and of belief, was preserved intact for the first crucial generation of the experiment in devolution. A man of undoubted courage and ability, though of limited intellectual horizons, he had begun to make a name for himself before the First World War as one of the more intransigent Ulster Unionists in the British House of Commons. At that time somewhat overshadowed by Carson, he differed from his leader in two important respects. One was in the matter of temperament. Carson, though dogged by ill-health and a prey to hypochondria, was intensely dramatic, almost flamboyant, in his approach to politics, bringing to his role not only the forensic skill of a great advocate, but also a genuine, if sometimes theatrical, passion. Craig on the other hand, as befitted a northern Presbyterian who was also the son of a wealthy distiller, was more cautious, more dour, but also – and in the long run – more tenacious.

The other difference between them went much deeper. Carson, though he had led *Ulster* Unionism brilliantly, was at heart an *Irish* Unionist, and for him – just as much as for any Nationalist, though, of course, for quite opposite reasons – partition was a tragedy. It was a tragedy because it left the southern Unionists, to whom he belonged and whom he understood so well, isolated in what seemed in 1921 circumstances of deadly danger. It is legitimate to doubt whether Craig's heart was wrung to any overwhelming degree by the loss of his colleagues in the south. He was an Ulsterman through and through, and once it became apparent that the Union, and with it the unity of Ireland, was doomed, his business was to do the best he could for his own people.

At first it hardly seemed that that best could be good enough. Not only did the actual area of the six counties remain in doubt until the collapse of the Boundary Commission in 1925, but at the very moment the new government was set up in the north its physical existence was threatened by violence from the IRA along its borders as well as by the internal religio-political frictions between Protestant Unionists on the one hand and Catholic Nationalists on the other.* So bad did the situation become that in 1922 no fewer than 232 people were killed in the north and nearly 1,000 were wounded, while more than three million pounds' worth of property was destroyed.[1]

The danger from without was overcome, partly with the help of the British army, partly by the use of emergency powers and the creation of the special constabulary, and most of all, perhaps, because the outbreak of the Civil War in the south relieved the pressure on the north. But the internal division within the province remained, heavy with menace and apparently insoluble. Put in its starkest terms, it was the division between those who were committed to upholding the new state and those who regarded it as an intolerable tyranny to be torn down as soon as possible. The polarisation of politics around this single issue, which derived additional bitterness from the inescapable fact that it was a religious as well as a constitutional issue, condemned public life to what, on the face of it, seemed perpetual paralysis.

This superficial impression is misleading. Tension, not stasis, has been the normal condition of politics in Northern Ireland. But it is true that the tension, at any rate between the wars, arose mainly out of the constitutional question and that, by comparison, important aspects of the economic or social well-being of the community tended either to be neglected altogether or to be treated within the framework of the abiding political and religious rivalries of majority and minority. For that generation there could be no real work of reconciliation – all at-

* The identification of a particular creed with a particular political attitude is not absolute. There have of course been exceptions on both sides, but most commentators agree that, unhappily, a man's politics in Northern Ireland can generally be deduced from his religion.

titudes had to be related to the central problem of whether or not the state was to continue in being.

For the Unionist majority, therefore, politics reduced itself to two main preoccupations: first, to develop the concept of devolution (as we have already seen them developing it) in such a way as to make the British connection more indissoluble, while at the same time making it financially more beneficial to the six counties; and secondly, to maintain the status quo at home. That status quo may in fact have been safer than they believed, or affected to believe. Later we shall examine some of the internal weaknesses in the Nationalist position, but first it is necessary to insist upon the strength of the Unionists. If, as is unfortunately to a large extent the case, religious persuasion is an index of political affiliation, then census of population will help us towards at least an approximate estimate of the relative proportions of the two opposing groups. During the inter-war period (and the pattern did not alter greatly after 1945), Catholics amounted to about a third of the population. To be more precise, in 1926, the first census of the new regime showed the Catholic proportion to be 33·5 per cent. Presbyterians came next with 31·3 per cent, followed by the Church of Ireland with 27 per cent. The remainder consisted of Methodists (3·9 per cent) and others (4·3 per cent).[2]

How, it may be asked, were these groupings reflected in the results of general elections? In 1921 the Unionist party gained forty seats, the Nationalists six and the Republicans six. In 1925 the comparable figures were Unionists thirty-seven (but including four Independents of various kinds), Nationalists ten, Labour three and Republicans two. Subsequent elections continued to produce broadly similar results, the dominant parties being the Unionists and, to a markedly lesser degree, the Nationalists. The cry has repeatedly been raised that the boundaries of constituencies were drawn in such a way as to discriminate against Nationalists. If this were true on the massive scale that is sometimes alleged one would expect to see that constituencies held by Nationalists had larger populations than those held by Unionists; in fact they tended on the average to have smaller populations. Alternatively, one would expect to see small Unionist majorities in some areas, with large Nationalist majorities in adjoining areas. Something of this kind has happened in Fermanagh and in Londonderry, though in the former case geography may have had as much to do with the result as conscious manipulation. The subject has long been, and still is, extremely controversial, but the charge of extensive gerrymandering for elections to the Northern Ireland parliament is difficult to prove conclusively. Perhaps the fairest comment is that made in a recent and admirably detached survey: 'Our inquiries do not, however, support the view that "gerrymandering" has any large influence on parliamentary (as opposed to local) elections.'[3] Local elections are, indeed, a very different matter and will be considered later in the broad context of discrimination in general.* But so far as elections to the parliament at Stormont are concerned, the fact seems to be that, as one would expect, the election results follow very closely the geographical distribution of the different religious groupings; but since Nationalist support is drawn mainly from the rural areas it is more widely dispersed and therefore often unable to bring its weight to bear very effectively. It is, however, true that Unionists have had two built-in advantages – three out of the four university seats went regularly to swell their strength, and the plural vote for business premises also worked in their favour. On the other hand it is surely significant that in the election for seats in the imperial parliament at Westminster, for which the constituencies were drawn up by independent Boundary Commissions, the usual pattern has been for Unionists to win from eight to ten out of twelve seats.

It seems then that Unionist fears of being out-voted were from the beginning ill-founded. This, however, did not prevent them from making assurance doubly sure. The abolition of proportional representation for local elections as early as 1922 was bitterly criticised on this ground, and though other forms of discrimination (for example, qualifications regarding property and residence) may have been just as damaging, there can be little doubt that when proportional representation was withdrawn from parliamentary elections also in 1929, the motivation was directly political. The immediately preceding years had seen the return to Stormont of a sprinkling of Independent Unionists claiming to represent either specific interests – ratepayers, for instance, or temperance enthusiasts – or else a more generalised desire to move the government forward along the path of social and economic reform. Lord Craigavon had no doubts at all about the possible effects of such deviationism. Proportional representation, he made it clear, 'submerges and clouds the issue. At election times, the people do not really understand what danger may result if they make a mistake when it comes to third, fourth, fifth or sixth preferences. By an actual mistake they might wake up to find Northern Ireland in the perilous position of being submerged in a Dublin parliament.'[4] In practice, however, it seems to have been the peripheral parties that suffered most and the two elections that followed the abolition of proportional representation reproduced the old pattern in all essentials. In 1929 Unionists, including Independents, had forty-one seats, Nationalists ten, and Labour and Republicans one each. In 1933, the grouping was little different – Unionists of various shades won thirty-nine seats, Nationalists nine, Labour and Republicans two each.[5]

From this electoral pattern two consequences followed – each with an important bearing on the character of northern politics. One was that the opposition throughout this period was painfully weak. Indeed, in the technical sense of the term, there was no *official opposition*, since the Nationalists refused to play that role and did not even take their seats at all until 1925. This led directly to the second consequence im-

* See chap. 5 below.

posed by the electoral pattern – that because there was no possibility of government alternating between rival parties, the Unionist bloc remained virtually unchanged year after year. Even the intermittent (though persistent) eruptions of Independent Unionists failed to fracture this monolithic structure, which was characterised not only by the regular return of a large number of Unionists without a contest, but also by the fact that many of the same people sat for long periods without replacement. Of the fifty-two members sitting in 1927, fifty-four per cent were still members in 1936, and forty per cent of *them* had sat in the Northern Ireland parliament since 1921.[6] The same tendency was repeated within the government itself. Not only did Lord Craigavon die in office (in November 1940), but no fewer than four of his six cabinet colleagues had held government posts continuously from 1921 onwards.[7] It is true that this state of affairs was eventually to produce a demand for change, and even something approaching a palace revolution, but the fact remains that in the innermost citadel of Unionist power there has been unbroken continuity since the foundation of the state.

Yet although this points towards an old, stale oligarchy, it would be wrong to underestimate the extent to which official Unionism appealed to a wide variety of classes and interests. Admittedly, the representation of the party in the Northern Ireland House of Commons was mainly confined to industrialists, lawyers and other professional men, with a handful of the landed gentry. But outside Stormont its roots went much deeper. The essence of its strength, as has been well said, was that it was 'a party of the Protestant people'. As such it had to contain not only the old, and by no means dormant, radicalism of the Presbyterians, but also the Anglican conservatism of the landed gentry, while taking account at the same time of the needs and prejudices of a largely urban working class which, in the dockyards or on the factory floors, was deeply sensitive to economic as well as religious rivalries with its Catholic counterpart.[8]

In the more distant past there had been deep divisions between the non-conforming churches and the Anglicans. These, however, had tended to disappear during the nineteenth century. On the one hand, the disestablishment of the Church of Ireland and the land legislation enabling farmers to buy out their landlords had together undermined the position of the traditional leaders of society. On the other hand, the growth of industrialism and the obvious benefits accruing from membership of the British free trade system had helped to convince both manufacturers and workers that the Union was essential to their well-being. This is not to deny that social divisions remained in the six counties – they did and do. But it is indisputable that the things which divided Protestants from each other had come to be much less important than the things which united them against Catholics.

One of the things uniting them most was undoubtedly the Loyal Orange Order. We have seen already how during the Home Rule crisis it served as a focus of political and religious sentiment. It continued to fulfil that function after 1921 and although it may be true that among the middle-class some of its rituals began to be regarded as archaic, if not laughable, its influence should not be under-estimated. Even now, for a Protestant to seek a career in politics without joining the Order would be foolhardy and almost certainly futile.* No details of membership are published, but it has been estimated that two-thirds or more of the adult male population may belong to it.[9] For them it has traditionally fulfilled two essential functions. First, with its marches, its sashes and banners, its bands (and above all those thudding, evocative drums), it has provided the Ulster Unionist with much of the colour and drama of his creed. Each year the twelfth of July is a gigantic exercise in catharsis which serves to give a kind of identity to what otherwise would be a variegated and much fragmented Protestantism. The Order's other function is, if anything, even more important. It serves as a link between different sections of society – small farmers, aristocratic landlords, linen magnates, shipyard workers – all can enter it on the same basis of equality. As a social emollient, therefore, no less than as a stimulus to patriotic emotions, the Orange Order has been essential to the structure of Unionism.

The very fact that it spread its net so wide may help to explain one feature of politics in the six counties which is apt to puzzle the outside observer – the absence of any strongly developed Labour party. Such development as there has been belongs mainly to the years after 1945, and although two or three seats at Stormont were won from time to time in the inter-war period by Labour candidates, there was little indication of anything resembling a modern Labour party emerging at that time. There were, of course, other reasons for this besides the attractions of the Orange Order. One was the fact that although there was a trade union movement in Northern Ireland it lacked any real centre of authority. Northern trade unionists were either affiliated to British unions with headquarters across the Irish Sea, or else they hankered after affiliation with southern Irish unions with headquarters across the border.† In the first case they could exercise little influence upon policy, and in the second case they were baulked by the refusal of the Northern Ireland government to recognise either the Irish Congress of Trade Unions or its Northern Ireland Committee.[10] In any event, the numbers involved were very small. In 1935 only twenty-six per cent of the total of insured workers (excluding agriculture) belonged to a trade union, which, in numerical terms, would give a membership of about 72,000, in that year.[11]

* There were indications in the late 1960s that membership of the Order was ceasing to be a *sine qua non* for a political career in the Unionist party. On the other hand, the Orange lodges are heavily represented on the Ulster Unionist Council and, perhaps more important, also play a part on its standing and executive committees.

† See above, Part IV A, chap. 5, section iv.

720

Apart from this, it cannot be too heavily stressed that while individual Ulster labour leaders might claim an apostolic descent from James Connolly, the rank and file were generally either too absorbed in the main constitutional and religious issues, or too cowed by unemployment, to be ready to absorb socialist doctrines of the inevitable class war. It was unlikely, indeed, that class conflict would be very clearly defined in a community such as that of the six counties, where nearly half the population lived on the land, where the size of the average business was small and where the possibility of self-employment was greater than in many other industrial regions. Amongst the workers, therefore, as elsewhere in northern society, the line of fracture was not economic, it was based on religion and on the great debate over the legality of the government. Northeast Ulster, stubbornly resistant to most kinds of schematic analysis, did not readily fall into any of the more conventional Marxist categories. Perhaps it was symptomatic of this obstinate illogicality that not long before he succeeded Lord Craigavon as Prime Minister, Mr J. M. Andrews was in the same year Minister of Labour, Chairman of the Belfast Chamber of Commerce and President of the Unionist Labour organisation.

We are driven back then, as in Northern Ireland one is always driven back, to the fundamental divisions – Catholic versus Protestant, Nationalist versus Unionist. As we have seen, it was the threat from the large Catholic-Nationalist minority that caused the majority most anxiety and it was this threat that was used with monotonous regularity by the Unionist leaders to maintain conformity and discipline within their own ranks. Yet how far were these fears really justified? How great a threat to the status quo did the minority actually constitute? In the sense that they repudiated the whole concept of a separate parliament in the six counties and looked longingly southward towards reintegration with the rest of Ireland they were, of course, to use a term that belongs to the 'thirties rather than the 'twenties, a permanent fifth column. But their immediate reaction to the setting-up of the new regime was one of stunned disbelief, mingled with acute fear for their own future safety. Their instinct was to hold themselves absolutely apart. Thus, not only did their elected representatives refuse to take their seats, but Catholics refused to sit on the Lynn committee to examine the whole structure of education, Catholic school managers refused to accept grants and some school-teachers even – for a while – declined their salaries.

These gestures reflected an attitude of mind which was natural enough in 1921, but which the passage of time was soon to make irrelevant. In 1921 it was possible to believe, as many of the minority evidently did believe, that the regime would not last, that the government would be brought down, either by pressure from outside or by non-cooperation from within – even, in the last resort, that the Boundary Commission would put paid to the whole sorry farce. But when none of these things happened some urgent rethinking became necessary. If the new government were once to establish itself, then it would be certain to take decisions directly affecting the welfare of Catholic families. Could Nationalists continue to stand on one side and let these decisions be taken without seeking to influence them?

This was not a hypothetical question. Almost at once a major issue arose which revealed with cruel clarity the nature of the Nationalist dilemma. In 1923, after receiving the report of the Lynn committee, the Northern Ireland parliament passed an Education Act, designed to remodel the primary – or public elementary – school system. There were to be three types of school in the future – schools wholly maintained or 'provided' by the local authorities, including any former private or denominational schools that were transferred to 'wholly maintained' status; voluntary schools under 'four and two committees'; and other voluntary schools. The 'four and two committees' consisted of four representatives of the body providing the school (usually a church) and two representatives of the school authority. Such schools would qualify for grants in payment of teachers' salaries, for help with maintenance and even, in certain circumstances, for capital grants. The pure voluntary schools, on the other hand, would qualify only for the payment of teachers' salaries and of half the cost of heating, cleaning and lighting. But the Act went much further than that. It stipulated that every public school should be open to children of all denominations and that religious instruction should not be given within the hours of compulsory attendance. In those schools that were wholly financed by public money the local education authorities were forbidden to require teachers to belong to any particular church or to provide religious instruction – though the local authorities could provide for any religious teaching outside the hours of compulsory attendance to which parents did not object.

Education, then, was to be essentially secular. The laudable intention behind the Act was no doubt to try to break down sectarian barriers by providing mixed schools in which Catholic and Protestant children could mingle without affront to their separate religions. But religious education was something about which many people of many different persuasions felt passionately. The Catholic bishops condemned the Act and very few Catholic clergy allowed their schools to pass under the control of the 'four and two committees'. Protestants, too, were deeply displeased and in 1925 they secured an Amending Act which was negotiated by the Prime Minister over the head of his Minister of Education. This Act restored Bible teaching to schools under the control of local education authorities, who were now allowed to require teachers in provided and transferred schools to give such instruction as part of the ordinary school course. Even this concession, however, was soon felt to be inadequate. Simple Bible teaching was all very well, but the highly self-conscious and articulate denominations of Northern Ireland began to ask why they should not prescribe more exactly what religious teaching was to be given to their children, and why they should not have a greater say in the appointment of teachers. They had only to press hard enough for the government to yield, and a further Amending Act in 1930 conceded in effect what they demanded. In addition, it was laid down that in all provided and transferred schools it was the duty of the education authority to provide Bible instruction if the parents of not less than ten children asked for it. Thus, in the Prime Minister's words, were the schools made 'safe for Protestant children'.

This in itself was hardly likely to recommend them to Catholics. Bible teaching was not what they wanted. They wanted quite simply the Catholic teaching of Catholic children in Catholic schools under their own managers. And they viewed with intense distrust a system which, given the way in which local elections were, in their eyes, rigged, might put their children at the mercy of education authorities in which Protestants had a majority. The issue was too explosive to be allowed to rest in this unsatisfactory state and in the end a compromise of a kind was reached. The government refused to accept the Catholic suggestion that in the four and two committees Catholics should be allowed to control religious teaching and the selection of the teachers responsible for it. But, since it was realised that the effect of this refusal would be that Catholics would continue to boycott the four and two arrangement, it was agreed instead that the government would pay half the cost of building or reconstructing voluntary schools and would lend the other half, irrespective of whether the schools had a four and two committee or not. So, from 1930 onwards, in the provided and transferred schools (overwhelmingly Protestant) Bible instruction carried out by teachers approved by the denominations was the normal practice, while in the voluntary schools (overwhelmingly Catholic) distinctive religious education was assured, but the state assumed a share of the responsibility for their cost.[12]

It has been necessary to treat this episode in some detail, since it brought into the open so many of the points at issue between the minority and the majority. It touched so intimately the lives of the people that the political representatives of nationalism could scarcely hold aloof even when they resented – as Joseph Devlin, the most eminent of them did resent – being caught up in what appeared to be a sectarian quarrel. And in fact, while the controversy was at its height, Devlin had made up his mind to enter the northern parliament. After 1921 he had taken the view that he would not do so until he had seen what the Boundary Commission might propose. When the Commission ended in fiasco, he and another Nationalist MP duly took their seats; others followed gradually and by 1927 he was leading a group of ten in the northern House of Commons. The following year (1928) he took a main part in founding the National League which, while aiming at the unity of Ireland, was more conciliatory than Nationalists had previously been towards the existing regime. Devlin himself, indeed, declared that there was no conspiracy to force northerners into a Dublin parliament and he and his colleagues tried hard to work constructively for social amelioration; it is doubtful, however, whether he ever fully realised how far Northern Ireland was restricted by the finances of devolution and the last years of his public life were a sad anti-climax to the notable reputation he had won at Westminster in the generation before 1918.

He, and others like him, laboured under a double difficulty, which curiously repeated in microcosm the difficulty of the old Irish parliamentary party during the later stages of its career in the British House of Commons. The constitutional Nationalists who sat in Belfast, like the constitutional Nationalists who had sat in London, were in the assembly but not of it. They were there only for the purpose of breaking the system that had brought them there. Being a minority, they could never hope to be other than an opposition. But they could not become an *official* opposition since, by definition, they could not form a government. Their participation in local parliamentary politics was always bedevilled by this dilemma and it is not surprising that, so far from forming an official opposition, they pursued a wavering course even towards actual participation in the proceedings of the Northern Ireland House of Commons, and were still apt to withdraw from time to time under the pressure of other forces.

The chief of these forces was republicanism. And this was where Devlin encountered his second difficulty. He and his colleagues were competing, just as the old parliamentary party had had to do, against a more extreme form of nationalism. The old party had been wiped out in 1918 by the victory of Sinn Féin, identified at that time with the triumph of the republican ideal. From the point of view of constitutional politics, therefore, it was distinctly sinister that in the first Northern Ireland election of 1921 the six Nationalist seats were exactly balanced by six Republican seats. The Republicans, of course, followed the classical Sinn Féin tactic of total abstention, but it was not easy then, and it is not easy now, to be sure how much those six seats were a product of the general upsurge of revolutionary nationalism throughout Ireland, or how much they represented a substantial amount of separatist feeling in the north. It has to be remembered that the Nationalist population in the six counties consisted chiefly of small farmers, shopkeepers, publicans and unskilled labourers, with some reinforcement from the professions, especially law and medicine. Many of these people were self-employed, and in social and political matters were conservatively inclined. Moreover, they were nearly all Catholic and as such amenable to the leadership of bishops and priests, leadership which the Church was not backward in providing. This was the environment Devlin had grown up in, which he understood intimately, and where he enjoyed enormous influence and respect, intensified no doubt by his long-standing connection with the Ancient Order of Hibernians, providing for Catholics, though on a smaller scale, the same kind of rallying-point as the Orange Order did for Protestants. It has to be admitted, however, that this kind of social structure and this kind of organisation had not been enough to halt the growth of Sinn Féin in the rest of Ireland in the decade before 1921 and it was, if anything, less likely that it would do so in the north where the minority, surrounded – as they felt – by the bigoted intolerance of the majority, might well be pushed towards their own extremists by the extremism of their neighbours. There are signs that this was in fact an attitude held by many of the younger people. Certainly, between 1916 and 1921 Sinn Féin made the same sort of headway in the north as it had done elsewhere and Ulster Nationalists contributed their share of the republican leadership.

But this movement towards the left was checked by the course of events after the Treaty. The split in the revolutionary forces in the south, the toughness and resilience of the new regime in the north, the growing suspicion that perhaps Sinn Féin did not really know a great deal about the special problems of northern Nationalism – all this served to diminish the attractions of republicanism. And when the dust had settled after the Civil War in the south, and the Irish Free State stood revealed as a correct, if restive, member of the Commonwealth, the impetus towards violent change slackened. The way was clear, therefore, for Devlin and his friends to take their seats in the northern parliament and to begin that frail and tenuous experiment in co-operation of which we have already spoken.

It was an experiment destined to be shattered when the coming of Fianna Fáil to power in the south in 1932 promised a resumption of more vigorous policies. The release of republican prisoners, the beginnings of the dispute with Britain, the fact that de Valera himself contested and won the northern seat of South Down in the election of 1933 on an 'abstentionist' platform – these were straws in the wind eagerly grasped by the more extreme Nationalists in the north.* But as the Fianna Fáil campaign to loosen the ties binding the Free State to the Commonwealth developed year by year this action called into being an equal and opposite reaction from Northern Ireland Unionism. The more de Valera seemed bent on destroying the imperial connection in the south, the more Craigavon and other Unionists insisted upon it in the north. These years, therefore, saw an intensification of the familiar stresses in the six counties and a renewal of sectarian bitterness of which the Twelfth of July orations of 1933 may serve as a lamentable example. It was on this occasion that Sir Basil Brooke (Minister of Agriculture at the time and later Prime Minister) made his famous declaration that he had not one Catholic in his employment. 'Catholics', he was reported as saying, 'were out to destroy Ulster with all their might and power. They wanted to nullify the Protestant vote and take

* Mr de Valera's electoral success, and that of another abstentionist in West Tyrone, led the government in 1934 to pass an act providing that unless a candidate declared his intention to take his seat if elected his nomination would be refused.

all they could out of Ulster and then see it go to hell.' And it was on this occasion also that J. M. Andrews, the Minister of Labour (and destined to succeed Craigavon as Prime Minister), solemnly declared that after investigating the thirty-one porters employed at the newly opened parliament buildings at Stormont 'I have found that there are thirty Protestants and only one Roman Catholic – there temporarily.'[13]

It would be easy to point to other similar instances of bigotry, and indeed to match them with utterances from the other side, for example Cardinal MacRory's provocative remark, also dating from this decade of bitterness, that the Protestant churches did not form part of the true Church of Christ.[14] It would be easy, but it would be pointless. It is enough to record that in the years between 1932 and the outbreak of the Second World War religious and political frictions, which had never at any time disappeared, were intensified. And it is important to realise that this occurred not only during a period of worsening relations between north and south, but during a period of dire distress when competition for jobs was added to inherited prejudices. It was characteristic of Ulster society that economic pressure should produce not a class war, but a religio-political explosion. There is some evidence, indeed, that one wing of the IRA which had communist sympathies attempted to collaborate with some of the more militant trade unionists, and certain Roman Catholic bishops took this seriously enough to warn their flocks against such manoeuvres. But this alliance, such as it was, sank into insignificance in the face of the bitter, long-drawn-out and bloody riots which disgraced Belfast in the summer of 1935. As a result of this religious war – which was what, in effect, it was – 11 people were killed and nearly 600 injured, while cases of arson amounted to 133 and of malicious damage to 367. Catholics demanded a commission of inquiry, but this was refused. Instead, in 1936, a report issued by a private body, the Council of Civil Liberties, charged the government with using the Special Powers Act in such a fashion as to drive its opponents 'into the way of extremism'. It is true that this report has subsequently been assailed as suspect, on the ground that some members of the Council were allegedly communists or fellow-travellers, but the observer of Northern Ireland in the mid-thirties did not have to stand very far to the left to see how deep were the divisions in the province and how vulnerable was the minority, alike to the unbridled violence of private individuals and to the special powers of the government.[15]

For the majority such considerations were of only secondary importance. To them the safety of the state was the supreme law and in the late 'thirties the safety of the state seemed more than ever at risk. To safeguard the British connection was, as always, the overriding aim of policy, and with the return of the treaty ports to the Irish Free State that connection had come to be even more precious, not just to Northern Ireland, but to the rest of the United Kingdom as well. There were, it is true, flashes of enlightenment and gestures of mutual goodwill. In 1936, for example, two bishops, the Catholic Dr Mageean and the Anglican Dr MacNiece, called upon their flocks to live together in Christian unity. Two years later Major-General Hugh Montgomery founded the Irish Association for Cultural, Economic and Social Relations, to encourage respect for the convictions of others and 'to foster . . . more neighbourly relations between those Irish people who differ from each other in politics and religion'.[16] These, however, were portents for the future; they could do little in the short run to mitigate the harshness with which the two communities confronted each other. And in 1938, Dr Mageean, despite his earlier appeals for tolerance, was driven to denounce the history of the Northern Ireland parliament as 'one long record of partisan and bigoted discrimination'.[17] But this was a vain outburst. As the international horizon darkened and war approached the old siege mentality began to assert itself amongst the majority once more. That mentality was described, simply and concisely, by the *Belfast Newsletter* in the same year, 1938, on the eve of an election which gave Lord Craigavon his customary assured majority :

Lord Craigavon's purpose in this election is to show that Ulster stands precisely where it did in relation to the Free State, or rather that its attachment to Great Britain and the Empire is as strong as ever and that in no circumstances will they give up their place in the United Kingdom.[18]

It was the old philosophy of 'not an inch' restated in language that had altered hardly a syllable in a generation. Upon this beleaguered garrison the Bishop's denunciations would have no effect whatever. It would be a long time yet before the walls of Derry would crumble at the blast of an ecclesiastical, or any other, trumpet.

4. War as a Catalyst

When Lord Craigavon hailed the result of the general election of 1938 as a vindication of the Unionist resolve 'that come what may our position within the United Kingdom and the Empire must remain unchanged', he could not have known that the war which was already looming was going to affect Northern Ireland's position dramatically – not, indeed, by changing it, but by reinforcing it beyond his wildest hopes. His own instinctive reaction when war actually broke out – and in this he spoke for Ulster Unionism in general – was 'to place the whole of our resources at the command of the government in Britain'. 'We are King's men', he said in a famous broadcast, and he and his followers never wavered from that stance. Admittedly, the existence of a large Nationalist minority in the province made it inexpedient to apply conscription, as many Ulstermen would have wished, but, this apart, the involvement of Northern Ireland was as near total as it was possible to be. Ulster men and women served and died all over the world and Ulster men and women served at home, and died in the severe air-raids on Belfast in the spring of 1941. All told, war casualties amongst persons born in the province totalled more than five and a half thousand, of whom nearly 900 were civilians.[1]

But the contribution of this small fragment of the United Kingdom to the Allied cause was far greater than either its casualties or its resources would lead one to expect. With Mr de Valera's resolute adoption of a policy of neutrality for the south, the geographical situation of Northern Ireland in relation to the sea-lanes connecting Britain with North America at once became exceedingly important. This importance was immeasurably heightened after the fall of France in 1940, when German submarines and aircraft were in a position to range far out into the Atlantic in pursuit of Allied shipping. To combat them naval bases were necessary and Belfast, Londonderry and Larne supplied this vital need. From these ports went out many of the escort vessels used in the early stages of the war at sea to bring in the convoys heading for the Mersey and the Clyde by the only avenue left to them – the northwest approaches where Ulster, as Churchill later wrote, 'stood a faithful sentinel'. And even while the war still raged he paid this tribute to Northern Ireland:

> We were alone and had to face single-handed the full fury of the German attack, raining down death and destruction on our cities and, still more deadly, seeking to strangle our life by cutting off the entry to our ports of the ships which brought us food and the weapons we so sorely needed. Only one great channel remained open.

That channel remained open because loyal Ulster gave us the full use of the Northern Irish ports and waters, and thus ensured the free working of the Clyde and the Mersey.[2]

So long as the battle of the Atlantic continued, so long did the Ulster bases remain essential to the Allied cause. But as time went on those bases were put to other uses besides the sheltering of British naval units. As early as March 1941 – nine months *before* Pearl Habour – Londonderry had been selected as a depot for American destroyers should need arise, and when the need did arise the port became a 'US naval operating base' for the American Atlantic fleet within three months of the United States entering the war. Moreover, as the character of the Atlantic battle changed – especially during 1943 – Northern Ireland became almost as important as an aircraft carrier as it had been in the role of naval fortress. Simultaneously, it provided one of the main training-grounds for American forces preparing to invade Axis territory. The first American troops arrived there in January 1942 and large forces were stationed in the six counties for nearly a year before the Normandy invasion.[3]

To the comradeship Northern Ireland could claim with the Allies through her key function as a base of operations could be added also a community of suffering. True, the ordeal of the civilian population was not so prolonged as that endured by the citizens of, say, London or Liverpool. Nevertheless, the four air raids on Belfast in April and May 1941 were a grievous blow and brought home to the inhabitants, not only of the city but of the whole province, the realities of total war. Inadequately provided with air protection, short of anti-aircraft guns and fire-fighting equipment, with a programme of evacuation only sketchily carried out, Belfast was fearfully vulnerable. Two of the raids – on Easter Tuesday (15-16 April) and on 4-5 May – were exceptionally severe. In the first of these attacks large areas of the city were demolished either by direct hits or by fire, over 700 people killed and some 1,500 injured, a third of them seriously. 'No other city in the United Kingdom save London', the official historian has written, 'had lost so many of her citizens in one night's raid. No other city, except possibly Liverpool, ever did.'[4] The defence services, depleted though they were, responded gallantly to the challenge, but it was understandable that the terrible experience of a major air raid should have caused some panic, especially as many had convinced themselves that Northern Ireland was beyond the range of enemy bombers. In consequence, at least a hundred thousand people, it was officially estimated, left the city to try to find homes in the country.

Yet when the second serious raid came three weeks later – this time largly an ordeal by fire – Belfast was again inadequately protected and, although there was less loss of life, there was enormous damage to property, while production at Harland and Wolff's works and other important factories was brought almost to a halt. And since, to quote the official war historian again, 'the degree of shelter protection available to the citizens of Belfast was probably lower than that in any other British city of comparable size and vulnerability', it was not surprising that what he calls 'a powerful surge' developed to get away from the city at all costs.[5] Unhappily, there was all too little accommodation to spare in the surrounding countryside; even more unhappily, many of the refugees were among the poorest of the poor, who had now been blasted or burnt out of slums the authorities had been neglecting for twenty years. They brought with them standards of hygiene and problems of public health that were a revelation to the comfortable bourgeoisie. 'I have been working nineteen years in Belfast', said a leading Presbyterian clergyman of his newly discovered fellow-citizens, 'and I never saw the like of them before. If something is not done now to remedy this rank inequality there will be a revolution after the war.'[6]

This belated recognition of social evils that needed a radical cure was one positive result to flow from the bombing. Another was the spontaneous coming together of Catholic and Protestant in their hour of crisis when death fell on them impartially from the sky.

> More than all else [Professor Blake has written] it was this tragic aspect of the raid which left indelible memories : of the queue at the mortuary in St George's market where men and women tried to identify their missing; and of the public funeral . . . when Protestants and Roman Catholics joined in prayer, and, as the cortege of five covered waggons moved slowly through the scarred city streets paid their last respects to over 150 of the victims.[7]

This softening of ancient asperities was helped also by the fact that even the border, so implacably defended over the years, ceased miraculously to exist when, during each of the heavy raids, fire-brigades hastened northwards from as far away as Dublin to do what they could to help.

Time alone would tell whether these spontaneous gestures of goodwill could be translated into something permanent. What was permanent, and seen even at the time to be permanent, was that the connection with the United Kingdom had been formidably strengthened by the fact that Northern Ireland had made good in blood its pledge to stand by Britain 'come what might'. And even though for the time being politics had been thrust into the background, when they came to the fore again, as they inevitably would, that blood would not be denied. The six counties, by the magnitude and devotion of their war effort, had done more to perpetuate the partition of Ireland than a whole generation of Twelfth of July demonstrations.

But the war had two additional and no less far-reaching consequences. At one and the same time it raised the Ulsterman's standard of living in the present and aroused his expectations for the future. Although the six counties shared with the rest of the United Kingdom in the rationing and other austerities of those years, the immediate economic effects of the war were dramatically beneficial. Almost overnight Northern Ireland was wafted from chronic depression to bustling prosperity.

This prosperity was experienced in many sectors of the economy, but it was most marked, as might be expected, in the shipbuilding and engineering industries. Harland and Wolff, and the associated firm of Short and Harland, were transformed into a veritable arsenal. The shipyards had almost more work than they could cope with, launching more than 150 vessels, totalling over half a million tons, during the war years. In addition, 550 tanks of various kinds were produced between 1939 and 1943, while the war-time output of bombers alone was 1,500.* Such feverish activity (which extended also into other kinds of war production) resulted in a steady flow of manpower into the various industries concerned. This caused various problems of adaptation, and it has even been suggested that if there had been military conscription, the use of civilian labour might have been more efficient. But however this may be, to an area that had known two decades of dire unemployment the creation of so many jobs seemed the beginning of a new era. In shipbuilding, for example, the numbers employed went up from 7·3 thousand in 1938 to 20·6 thousand in 1945. In engineering the increase during the same years was from 14·0 thousand to 26·1 thousand. Most remarkable of all, the aircraft industry, which before the war had been struggling to establish itself, rose from a mere 5·8 thousand in 1938 to 23·5 thousand in 1945.[9]

The contribution of the other main branch of Ulster industry – textiles – was more limited but still considerable. The great Belfast ropeworks, for example, was fully extended by War Office and Admiralty contracts. The shirt-making industry based on Londonderry also woke to new life, producing not only shirts for military use, but battle-dress and denim overalls as well. Production of shirts was about fifteen million a year (double the peacetime figure) and employment rose by twenty-five per cent to a total of nine thousand. It was, however, in the linen industry – which, after all, was and remained the predominant element in the textile group – that the problems of adaptation were most severe. There were problems of supply, of machinery, even problems of marketing. Shortages of flax were to some extent remedied by intensive cultivation on home farms, the acreage under this crop rising from 21,000 in 1939 to 124,000 in 1944. At the same time the most stringent rationing of flax and linen stocks was imposed, and efforts were made to divert highly specialised linen machinery to work on other fabrics. Even so, the industry was in a critical condition by September 1940 with 23,000 operatives out of work and another 20,000 threatened with the loss of their jobs. Gradually, thanks to war contracts, efficient management and experimentation with new fabrics – notably rayon – the linen manufacturers began to surmount the worst of their difficulties and although under-employment persisted, they were able to contribute to the supply not only of uniforms, but of a host of other articles, including wing fabrics, parachutes, flying-suits, sailcloth and various kinds of tenting. There is no disguising the fact, however, that progress was decidedly uneven. The peak year for production came as early as 1940 when 125 million lineal yards of cloth were produced, but nearly two-thirds of this was for civilian use or export. Thereafter, government contracts took the larger share of an output which could go as high as 106 million lineal yards in 1941 or sink as low as 64·5 million in the wartime months of 1945.[10]

Problems of unemployment, though more serious in the linen industry than in most others, persisted at various levels throughout the war. Even during the years of maximum mobilisation of labour, 1942 – 44, there were always some who could not get work, though it is probably true to say that most of these were unskilled workers for whom appropriate jobs could not easily be found. The dates of maximum mobilisation suggest that the deployment of labour was a rather more leisurely process than it might have been. Indeed, so slowly did the pace gather way that in January 1941 the total of unemployed, 68·7 thousand, was 4,000 more than it had been at the outbreak of war. This, admittedly, was due mainly to the crisis in the linen industry, and once the great construction boom began, with the building not only of ships and planes and weapons, but also of aerodromes, barracks, factories and other adjuncts to the war effort, the amount of unemployment dropped very strikingly. For most of the period 1942–4 it fluctuated between 15,000 and 20,000, occasionally falling to around 10,000 in the peak summer months. This was still, of course, a considerable figure in relation to the labour force as a whole – as late as June 1943 one in every twenty insured persons was unemployed in Northern Ireland compared with one in two hundred in Britain – and the situation would have been even worse if there had not been an outflow of some 60,000 persons to work in England, Scotland and Wales during the war. The difference in the speed and thoroughness with which the labour force was mobilised in Britain and in Northern Ireland was no doubt partly due to the specialised character of many of the latter's industries which made them specially vulnerable to war conditions, but a more important factor was that Britain was able to apply industrial conscription, whereas Northern Ireland, though possessing the power to do so, was reluctant to use it in the absence of conscription for the armed forces. Movement out of certain key industries – agriculture or engineering, for instance – was from time to time restricted, but for the most part the government relied on inducement and persuasion rather than coercion.[11]

Almost more than any other industry, agriculture was fully stretched by the war and, although there was no dramatic change in the structure of farming, there was a remarkable improvement in its productivity. This was in part a response to firm leadership by the Northern Ireland government, even more perhaps it was the farmer's natural reaction to the British government's decision to buy the main products of agriculture at uniform prices throughout the United Kingdom, thus removing at a stroke the Ulsterman's long-standing disadvantage of having to accept as his net price the British market price less the cost of transporting his products. The effect of this is to be seen in the steep rise in the value of net as contrasted with gross agricultural output. The value of gross agricultural output in Northern Ireland in 1945 was 122 per cent of the average for the years 1936–7 to 1938–9, which differs little from the comparable British figure of 116 per cent. But whereas in Britain the value of net output (that is gross output less purchases of feeding-stuffs, stores and seeds from abroad) in 1945 was 176 per cent of what it had been in the pre-war years, in Northern Ireland this was 205 per cent.[12]

To the Ulster farmer the system of uniform prices brought two major benefits. First, it reduced the normal uncertainties of farming, since prices were fixed in advance each year. And second, the price structure was so devised as to ensure that in normal circumstances farmers would earn a reasonable profit. However, even these inducements would hardly have sufficed to produce the great expansion in northern farming, had the government not taken steps to guide agriculture along the lines of maximum advantage to the community as a whole. A primary aim, of course, was to increase tillage up to the furthest possible limits, bearing in mind that those limits were fixed not only by the physical area of the six counties, but also by the inevitable shortages of fertilizers, seeds and farm machinery. To bring about this increase the Northern Ireland government, like that of Eire, resorted to compulsory tillage orders, requiring first twenty per cent and later forty-five per cent of all arable land to be put under the plough. By 1943 this process had gone about as far as it could and from then on increased productivity had to be won by raising the yield per acre. In that year the total acreage of tillage was 851,000 – almost double what it had been in 1939.

This great drive towards higher production was not directed primarily towards wheat. Wheat production did indeed increase, rising from 3,000 tons in 1939 to 18,000 in 1941, but falling thereafter until in the last year of the war a diminishing acreage produced only 2,000 tons. Barley and mixed corn also rose, in acreage and in volume, but the most important and sustained growth was in flax, oats and potatoes. We have already seen something of the effort farmers made to meet at least some of the flax needs of the linen industry, but it was in oats and potatoes that they really excelled themselves. Where in 1939 the six counties produced 270,000 tons of oats, two years later they produced 432,000 tons and although this tapered off to 383,000 in 1945, the total remained extraordinarily high. So also with potatoes, where a 1939 production of 864,000 tons was raised to about 1¼ million for each of the years 1941, 1942, and 1943, and was still over a million in 1944 and 1945.

By no means all of this increased production was intended for human consumption. On the contrary, it was an essential part of policy to nurture the livestock and dairying industries which had been the strongest sectors of northern agriculture before the war. The shortage of feeding-stuffs had its effect, of course – chiefly in the sharp decline of sheep and pigs. But the number of cattle in the province was driven steadily upwards from 753,000 in 1939 to 919,000 in 1945, while poultry increased from 10·2 million to 17·5 million during the same period. The raising of these levels of output was no doubt achieved partly at the expense of sheep and pigs, since the precious feeding-stuffs were diverted from them to cattle, but it was made possible also by the massive growth in the tonnage of oats and in the amount of root crops produced. The results of this very considerable achievement were of importance not only for the domestic supplies of Northern Ireland but for the rest of the United Kingdom, whither the surplus was regularly exported under the all-pervading authority of the local Ministry of Agriculture. It was no insignificant matter, for example, that Northern Ireland supplied about one-fifth of all the eggs produced in the United Kingdom during the war, or that Ulster farmers, at last weaned from milk produced mainly for manufacture to the production of liquid milk, were not only able to meet the increased needs of their own province but to send some three million gallons to Britain in the last year of the war.[13]

It was extraordinary, but true, that this prolonged effort did not result in serious deterioration of the soil. Some deterioration there was, no doubt, but although for most crops the yield per acre did decline in the later years of the war, this was in no case catastrophic. That the damage was not worse was primarily due to intelligent planning from the centre. Conservative farmers were given constant advice and assistance with crop rotation; the import of fertilizers, though hard hit in the early stages, never altogether ceased and in fact developed considerably from 1943 onwards, by which time Ulster agriculture had trebled its pre-war consumption of these artificial aids to agriculture. Intensive cultivation also demanded the employment of a large labour force and that this labour force should be supplemented by mechanisation. Both these demands were met in all essentials. Despite enlistments in the forces and the lure of highly paid jobs in industry, the total number of workers on the land (most of them full-time) rose from 154 thousand in 1939 to 184 thousand in 1945. Even more striking was the growth in mechanisation. In 1939 there were, to take the extreme example, only 858 tractors in the whole province; by 1945 this figure had been multiplied nearly nine times to reach a total of 7,240.[14] The contrast in all this with the slow development of agriculture in Eire was very marked. So marked indeed that the historian of wartime Northern Ireland was moved to comment, in a moment of patriotic exuberance, that to go south across the border 'was to be transported in a matter of minutes from the twentieth to the seventeenth century'.[15] This was, perhaps, a little harsh; the southern observer who wrote more sedately that 'while the twenty-six counties repeated the experience of the First World War, Northern Ireland was able to follow a new and more profitable course', was rather nearer the mark [16]

It was scarcely surprising in these conditions of strenuous agricultural and industrial endeavour that the material well-being, not just of the farmer, but of the urban worker as well, was greatly improved during the war. Wages went up sharply and, since there was little enough to spend them on, savings also increased, to the extent that during the war years £152 million was invested, nearly half of which was in small individual savings.[17] Real wages in a situation where there is a shortage of consumer goods are difficult to compute and not entirely reliable, but two significant pointers to the wartime prosperity of Northern Ireland may be mentioned. One was that income per head, which had been less than three-fifths of that in Britain, before the war, rose in Northern Ireland between 1939 and 1945 until it was three-quarters of the British figure.[18] The other pointer is that although the government was necessarily involved in all sorts of additional expenditure, revenue (mainly from taxation) was so buoyant that the amount of the 'imperial contribution' rose to what only a few years earlier would have been regarded as fantastic heights. From a total of three million pounds in 1939–40 it climbed more and more steeply until in each of the last two years of the war it was thirty-six million pounds. Another way of putting this is to say that whereas the total payment for the entire period from 1921 to 1939 had been twenty-nine million pounds, the amount paid over during the six war years came to no less than £131 million.[19]

All this was evidence of a state of affairs very far removed from the dire stringencies which had been the lot of the six counties in the inter-war period. Yet there was another side to the story. Total war brought with it a readiness to look freshly at old institutions, to look critically at old men who had been in power too long. The very fact that Northern Ireland moved onto a war footing more slowly than the rest of the United Kingdom exposed the government to criticism and even Lord Craigavon himself, only two months before his death, had to face a vote of censure. His successor, J. M. Andrews, had been as long in office as his former chief and was no more prepared than he had been to make sweeping changes. Consequently, between 1941 and 1943 the murmurings of complaints grew steadily louder. Two normally safe seats at Stormont were lost – one to an Independent Unionist and the other to Labour – and in addition a Labour candidate captured one of the Westminster seats. Early in 1943 matters came to a crisis. In January the back-benchers revolted, demanding more new faces in the cabinet, and in May Mr Andrews resigned to make room for Sir Basil Brooke (later Lord Brookeborough). There is a certain irony in the fact that Sir Basil was himself destined to hold office as Prime Minister for over twenty years – longer even than Craigavon – but at the time, and in the midst of a great war, he seemed to be the new broom that the situation demanded. He got rid of practically all the older men, replacing them by a new generation which was ready and willing to direct the war effort more vigorously, and, perhaps most important of all, he and his cabinet began to lay plans for the development of Northern Ireland after the war.

Here, indeed, lay the crux of the matter. What *was* to be the future of Northern Ireland after the war? It was this nagging preoccupation with what might be in store that lay behind a good deal of the restlessness which even the Unionist rank-and-file manifested from time to time. And as men's horizons began to widen, as they saw more of the world themselves and acted as hosts to hundreds of thousands of servicemen stationed in the six counties, so the old isolation, and with it the old complacency, began to break down. The shabbiness, the poverty, the lack of adequate schools, houses, hospitals or roads, the ill-health, the squalor of the slums – all these things, which had to be put up with at a time when there seemed no way to do anything about them, became all at once an intolerable affront, to be wiped out as quickly as possible in the new world that men began to look for with growing impatience as the war drew near its close.

Moral indignation and high ideals were, however, equally impotent without money. And money, in the quantity that would be needed, could only be obtained with the help and favour of Britain. True, the case for parity in the social services had been argued over and over again before the war, but could this be maintained in the light of the enormous expansion of welfare envisaged in the Beveridge Report? For Northern Ireland this new trend involved the addition of a second concept to the original and well-worn formula about advancing 'step by step' with Britain. Now, it was argued, the province must not only march 'step by step' in the existing services, but must also be enabled to make up the 'leeway' that separated her from her more prosperous neighbour in a whole range of amenities hitherto either rudimentary or even non-existent in the pre-war years. It was a large claim, but the north would never be in a better position to press it than in the midst of the war which had so triumphantly demonstrated her value to the whole Allied cause. And in 1942 that claim was conceded in principle, when the British Chancellor of the Exchequer assured Mr Andrews that he recognised that in certain spheres Northern Ireland had 'considerable leeway' to make up if she were to attain equality with the United Kingdom as a whole. 'You can confidently rely', he added, 'on the Treasury always considering such a case sympathetically, as indeed the principle of parity requires us to do.'[20]

What this might involve for the future it was impossible to forecast in wartime. But it is evidence of the catalytic effect the war itself was having on Northern Ireland that long before the fighting was over severe and searching scrutinies had begun to be made into the various services that would need overhauling if 'leeway' was to be overcome. Health, housing, education, roads, the reconstruction of Belfast – one after another each was investigated and for each a plan was devised in readiness for the day when it might be possible to translate these dreams into reality. By the spring of 1945 it was clear that that day was close at hand. In May it was announced that the province would enjoy the full range of the social security schemes that would be introduced in Britain and that, where necessary, finance would be available to raise the standard of the social services to the level achieved in other parts of the United Kingdom. For a moment at least it was possible to believe that the past had been left behind for ever.

5. The Politics of Welfare

The past had not gone for ever, of course. On the contrary, politics in Northern Ireland still continued to revolve round the three great issues that had filled all horizons in the inter-war period – the maintenance of the British connection, the fate of the economy, the internal tensions generated by a deeply divided society. Nevertheless, the war had changed the context in which these problems were discussed and the events of the immediate post-war years were to change that context even further.

The most striking illustration of this is the way in which the constitutional position of the six provinces was reinforced not only, as was suggested in the previous section, by the claims the Northern Irish war effort established on British gratitude, but also, ironically enough, by Britain's own reaction to the establishment of the Republic in the twenty-six counties. In the Ireland Act of 1949, regulating the relations between the United Kingdom and the Republic, it was laid down in the most explicit fashion that the existing status of Northern Ireland would be maintained:

> It is hereby declared that Northern Ireland remains part of His Majesty's dominions and of the United Kingdom and it is hereby affirmed that in no event will Northern Ireland or any part thereof cease to be a part of His Majesty's dominions and of the United Kingdom, without the consent of the parliament of Northern Ireland.

This seemed as watertight a pledge as any die-hard Unionist could desire and it was certainly a remarkable concession from a British Labour government, some of whose supporters had long looked with a very cold eye on what they regarded as the reactionary character of Northern Ireland politics. But the pledge was not as absolute as appeared on the surface. The legislative supremacy of the Westminster parliament was left intact and what one statute of that parliament could ordain another statute could repeal. To say this is merely to emphasise what has been from the beginning a constant element in the link between the two areas – which is that the supremacy of the Westminster parliament carried with it the implication that any radical shift of political attitudes in Britain could have direct and drastic effects upon Northern Ireland.

But the strength of the British connection did not rest solely on a legalistic basis. We have seen already how closely intertwined were the finances of Northern Ireland and the rest of the United Kingdom before the war, and that during the war the province received a clear promise of assistance from Britain in bringing its social services up to the standards established in England, Scotland and Wales. The return of Labour to power in 1945 was a traumatic experience for Ulster Unionists, so long and so deeply embedded in the fabric of British conservatism, but they managed to keep their balance and to dispose their forces in a manner that did credit to their heads, if not perhaps entirely to their principles. What happened was that at Westminster the Unionist representatives joined with the Conservative opposition in resisting the socialist legislation which established the welfare state, while at Stormont the Unionist party solemnly resolved to annex as much of this legislation as possible to its own purposes. To be able to do this satisfactorily, however, the Belfast government needed to revise its financial relations with Whitehall. Between 1945 and 1951 that revision was successfully carried out by a series of agreements relating to financial and insurance problems. These had two principal effects. One was to reduce the financial autonomy previously enjoyed by the Northern Ireland government. In the depression years, indeed, that autonomy may often have seemed somewhat unreal already, but after 1945 it was made clear that if the six counties were to receive more money from Britain then there would have to be closer Treasury control. It was decided, therefore, in 1946 that the Northern Ireland budget would be agreed each year between the Treasury and the Ministry of Finance for submission to the Joint Exchequer Board; that Northern Ireland Supplementary Estimates would also be put before the Treasury for information and agreement; and finally, that the Ministry of Finance would consult with the Treasury in advance about any new items of expenditure of over £50,000 in Northern Ireland, other than expenditure incurred on services that were being kept in parity with those in Britain.

The logic behind this arrangement was still the old logic – that parity of services *and* of taxation must be the guiding principle in the financial relations of the two areas. But the other two agreements that were reached in these crucial years were, so to speak, the sugar that coated the pill of increased Treasury supervision. And from them flowed the second consequence of importance to Northern Ireland – that provided parity was maintained, Britain would in effect finance the increased expenditure that the enlarged social services would entail. One of these agreements (actually signed in 1951, but taking effect from 1948) concerned national insurance covering payments for unemployment, sickness, maternity, widowhood, orphanhood, retirement and death. As a result of the agreement the two National Insurance Funds (originally separate) were virtually amalgamated and the principle established that in case of need money could be transferred from one to the other on a basis of reciprocity. Since Northern Ireland was the poorer area with the higher rate of unemployment, the transfer principle worked consistently in her favour. Similarly with the Social Services Agreement (signed in 1949, but again taking effect from 1948). This applied to the four main services of national assistance, family allowance, non-contributory pensions and health. It laid down that if the cost of these four services in Northern Ireland was proportionately higher than in the rest of the United Kingdom, Britain would pay eighty per cent of the cost of the excess. Technically, this too was a reciprocal agreement, but once again the movement of funds was one way only – towards Northern Ireland.

The expansion of the social services which these agreements took for granted inevitably involved the Northern Ireland government in heavy expenditure of its own. It was able to meet this, partly because it was bound by the rules of the game to impose the same heavy taxes as in Britain, and partly because (again by the rules of the game) it was able *pari passu* to reduce the amount of the imperial contribution. That annual contribution which, as we saw, had reached thirty-six million pounds at the end of the war, might, it has been calculated, have reached about sixty million pounds fifteen years later – if the cost of common services had been shared out solely on a basis of relative populations. In fact, of course, this criterion was not used. On the contrary, not only was the imperial contribution allowed to fall (in 1962–3 it was only £7·5 million) but in addition Britain paid over every year large amounts to the National Insurance Fund, large amounts under the Social Services Agreement, and even larger amounts in the form of subsidies, mainly to agriculture. During the three years 1961–3 these payments, with some other minor ones, averaged no less than forty-five million pounds a year, and this did not include special measures to encourage industry in the province, costing the British taxpayer about fifteen million pounds a year, even if some of this fifteen million pounds represented a reduction of the increasingly mythical imperial contribution he might otherwise have received.*

* Since this was written two calculations have been made as to the extent of inter-regional transfers from Britain to Northern Ireland, one for 1967-8 and one for 1971-2. For 1967-8 the direct transfers are reckoned at £51 million and the 'shortfall' of the imperial contribution (i.e. the amount that would have been due *from* Northern Ireland if this contribution had been paid at full rate instead of being left at a nominal £1 million) at £70 million. The total of £121 million thus reached has to be further corrected to take account of an additional £16 million paid by Britain under Reinsurance Agreement and also, on the other side, of an estimated shortfall of £11 million in capital receipts which could have been borrowed by the Northern Ireland government if it had not been restricted by its financial links with Britain. For 1967-8, therefore, the final total would appear to be of the order of £126 million. By 1971-2, however, the direct transfers are calculated at £135 million and the shortfall in the imperial contribution at £85 million, to which should be added payments under the Reinsurance Agreement of £15 million. Together these produce the staggering total of £235 million. It may be objected that the allowance for the shortfall in the imperial contribution is unrealistic, though in a UDI situation this would not necessarily be so, for an independent Northern Ireland government would almost certainly be faced with heavy defence expenditure. Even if it were to form part of an all-Ireland regime its pro rata defence bill would amount to approximately

Despite these contributions, there was so much 'leeway' to be made up in the building of houses, schools and hospitals, and in staffing the health and educational services, that Northern Ireland expenditure was bound to be heavy. A large part of this expenditure was met out of the proceeds of taxation. The 'transferred' taxes which Northern Ireland herself could impose were, as always, relatively insignificant. In the last decade before the war they had averaged only £1·7 million a year and in the first decade after the war they averaged £4·2 million. But in the same two periods the yields from the major 'reserved' taxes went up from £7·8 million a year to £52·4 million. And this figure continued to rise dramatically – by 1963 it had been more than doubled to reach nearly £109 million, which was not far from the amount spent in 1962–3 on transferred services, the chief of these being education, health and development. With remarkable ingenuity, the Northern Ireland government managed not only to meet a large part of the running cost of these services, but also to undertake very considerable capital expenditure, especially in the building of houses. It was this achievement, combined with the effect of the special agreements already mentioned, that provided the main justification for the decline of the imperial contribution, which by the early 'sixties stood at what must be reckoned in modern terms a purely nominal figure. 'Lord Craigavon's prophecy', it has been well said, 'to the effect that in the long run a contribution would be paid to, and not by, Northern Ireland has been borne out in full measure.'[1]

The consequence of this transformation can be summed up in a single sentence. Within a decade Northern Ireland passed from the status of an exceptionally backward area to full membership of the welfare state. The picture was not without its dark shadows, as we shall see, but it is necessary to insist on the extent of the improvement, since this improvement opened a wide gap between the social services in the two parts of Ireland and in doing so did more to reinforce the partition of the country than perhaps any other single factor. If the figures recently cited are correct – and comparisons between different systems are apt to be misleading – then the contrast between north and south has become formidable. A few examples of this trend must suffice. Thus in education, Northern Ireland, with a population less than half of that of the Republic, had 95,000 children in secondary schools in 1964 compared with 85,000 in the south, while expenditure on university education in 1963 was 17 shillings (85p.) per head in the Republic and 48/9d (2.44) in the six counties. And as recently as 1969 unemployment benefit for a single man was £3.25 per week in the

£11 million. On this (probably over-generous) basis the total to be found if British resources were cut off and if existing standards were to be maintained would still be in the neighbourhood of £160 million. For these calculations, see J. Simpson, 'Regional analysis: the Northern Ireland experience', in *Economic and Social Review*, vol. 2, No. 4 (July, 1971) and G. FitzGerald, *Towards a New Ireland*, pp. 54-7, 180-7.

Republic as against £4.50 in Northern Ireland. An unemployed man with two children drew £7.42½ per week in the south as compared with £9.20 in the north. Similarly, a widow's weekly pension in the Republic is £3.25; in Northern Ireland it was £4.50. In the south again children's allowance and maternity benefits were considerably lower, while between the health services the differences were so great that little comparison was possible.[2] Even if it be conceded that much of this contrast reflected higher taxation in the north than in the south, and that in any event Northern Ireland could not have afforded her benefits without the massive financial contribution from Britain, the fact remains that the differential exists and that until the Republic is able to overcome it, the hard-headed northerner is unlikely to see much inducement to abolish the border.

Attempts have been made from time to time to estimate how much it would cost the Republic to bring its social services into line with those of Northern Ireland and thus to remove, or lessen, one of the chief disincentives to reunion. Calculations cannot be absolutely exact because in certain respects the two systems are not comparable, but a recent and detailed analysis by the principal opposition spokesman for Finance in the Dáil, Dr FitzGerald, suggests that if northern eligibility provisions and benefit rates were to have been applied in the Republic in the year 1969/70, the existing expenditure of almost £143 million would have had to be increased by about a further £150 million, in other words by *one hundred and five per cent*. The same authority calculates that if, in addition to raising its own standards by this amount, the Republic had also to shoulder the cost of the inter-regional transfers from Britain to Northern Ireland – when mentioned earlier (p. 740n above) these were reckoned at upwards of £130 million – the effect would be to raise the level of taxation by nearly sixty per cent. This would, in practice, be an impossible burden and would in itself seem to suggest that until the Republic can increase its rate of economic growth sufficiently to narrow the gap between the two regions, any conceivable scheme of reunification would have to be underpinned for perhaps a generation by outside assistance – either from Britain, or from the European Economic Community, or both – if it were to have any prospect of being financially viable.[3]

It would be fairer perhaps to compare, not the Northern Ireland and the Republic of the 'sixties, but rather the Northern Ireland of the 'sixties with the Northern Ireland of the pre-war generation. The change is certainly very remarkable, whether one looks at the remodelling of the educational system, the creation of the Health Service, or the great expansion in state-subsidised housing. In the area of schooling alone, the seventeen years after the new Education Act of 1947 was passed showed an increase in pupils in grant-aided schools from 213,211 to 295,855, an increase paralleled in the building and extension of many new schools, especially at the secondary level which had been so much neglected before 1939. The structure of education followed the changes already brought about in England – primary education ending at the age of eleven plus, and all children thereafter receiving secondary education until the age of fifteen in grammar schools, secondary intermediate schools or technical intermediate schools. In addition, such generous provision was made for grants enabling students to go to the university that it might be said without too much exaggeration that the door to higher education was open to any child of sufficient ability to qualify for admission, regardless of what his social or economic background might be. Against this progress has to be set the fact that the Northern Ireland government's aim of overcoming denominational separation was not fulfilled. The voluntary schools – the great majority Catholic – remained obstinately under their own, mainly clerical, management and even won a great victory when they succeeded in extracting from the government the concession that the grants which they received under the Act of 1930 for fifty per cent of running costs, new building and reconstruction would be raised to sixty-five per cent. It was, however, symptomatic of how deep-rooted sectarian sentiment continued to be in the province that the courageous Minister who carried through this amendment with the interests of the children at heart was bitterly assailed by Nationalists for not offering grants of a hundred per cent, and by Unionists for yielding as much to the Catholics as he had done; eventually, in 1949, unable to make headway against persistent opposition from within his own party and from the Orange Order, he resigned.*

Just as education benefited from what was happening in Britain, so also the rapid development of the Health Service across the water had its repercussions in Northern Ireland. The old dispensary system went by the board, as did the other survivals of the poor law, and in 1944 a new Ministry of Health and Local Government was created. Within three years of the end of the war the north had its own General Health Services Board, its Hospitals Authority and – an innovation peculiar to Northern Ireland – its own Tuberculosis Authority. Thus the principle of parity was again demonstrated in action and, with very little ad-

* Education continued – and still continues – to be a source of controversy. Thus, the Education Act of 1968, while increasing building grants to voluntary schools from sixty-five to eighty per cent of the total, linked this with the proviso that such schools must become 'maintained' schools and as such come under the management of 'four and two' committees, i.e. committees on which the managers and the education authority should be respectively represented in those proportions. It was only after prolonged negotiation and the working out of the most elaborate rules for the constitution and conduct of such committees that the Catholic Church agreed, with reservations, to give the new system a fair trial. It is not surprising that liberal voices – including that of Captain O'Neill as he then was – should from time to time have been raised in criticism of segregated education. But such criticism, however muted, has always rebounded from the iron front presented by the Catholic bishops and, to a lesser extent, by other religious leaders as well.

743

ditional cost to themselves, Ulstermen were able to enjoy a comprehensive medical service on all fours with that of Britain. No doubt other factors – better medical knowledge, better housing and food, less unemployment – would have led to an improvement in the health of the community anyway, but the change would hardly have been so dramatic had the state not intervened to the extent it did. The end result was a striking decline in mortality (amongst mothers and infants, as well as in the population at large), a successful onslaught on tuberculosis, a remarkable advance in dealing with mental health, an extensive programme of water and sewerage schemes, and a spate of hospital building which, it was estimated, would have cost £66·5 million by the time it was completed in the early 'seventies.[4]

In all these aspects of social improvement Northern Ireland was being drawn into the contemporary pattern of increasing state intervention. Even before the war, indeed, this had begun to happen, when the road transport board had taken over large sections of road services formerly in private hands. After 1945 the pace was much accelerated and the scope greatly widened. This was true not only of transport – in 1948 the Ulster Transport Authority was formed to bring rail as well as road transport under public control – but also in a sphere where formerly the central and local authorities had been conspicuously inadequate. Long before the bombs had done their worst, Ulster housing had been sadly dilapidated. The housing survey carried out in 1943 showed that most of the houses in the entire province would have had to be condemned if the best modern criteria were to be strictly applied; and even if they were not, as nobody seriously suggested they could be, the minimum required in the immediate future would be 100,000 – twice that number if any real progress was to be made with slum clearance. The response to this challenge was at first sluggish, but within a few years the pace began to quicken.* This was partly due to an exceptionally generous policy of state subsidies for house-building in both the private and the public sectors, and partly due to the creation in 1945 of a special government agency, the Northern Ireland Housing Trust, which had the duty of providing and managing houses built at the Exchequer's expense. Admittedly, it took nearly twenty years before the 'immediate' target of 100,000 houses was reached – slightly over 112,000 had been built by 1963. But this progress, even though sedate enough in relation to the needs of the community, would probably have been much slower but for the initiative taken by local and central authorities. Thus of the total number built by 1963, local authorities provided about a third and the Housing Trust about a quarter. Private builders accounted for just over 40,000 new houses and all but about 5,000 of these had the benefit of a government subsidy.[5]

This growing activity by a seemingly benevolent state, impinging upon so many aspects of the lives of its citizens, has however to be seen against the background of a community where many old problems –

* For the darker side of the housing policy, see the next chapter.

744

economic, political and religious – still remained unsolved. It is, of course, true that the economic outlook was by no means as grim as it had been before the war and that this very fact at least helped to remove one complicating factor from the political and religious rivalries that continued to obsess so many Ulstermen. But the economic performance of the six counties, though improved, was so far from being completely satisfactory that any serious trade recession would be only too likely to bring back the competition for jobs and thus, with the help of all the other frictions, to recreate, especially in Belfast, the pre-war paradox of a society that contrived to be both inert and explosive.

In most sectors of the economy some at least of the impetus gained during the war was carried over into the peace. The modernisation of agriculture, in particular, continued to yield results in the shape of steadily expanding production of which a large share went, as before, to Britain. The privileged position the Ulster farmer enjoyed as the recipient of British agricultural bounties, and with access to the British market on terms not quite so favourable as in war-time, but still more than adequate, allowed him to benefit from steadily rising prices, especially of the livestock on which he most relied.[6] Indeed, it could be said that the war, while providing him with an assured market, had in a sense distorted his agriculture because of the insistence upon tillage beyond what in other circumstances would have been an economically acceptable limit. Once the need to produce crops was over, land reverted fast to its more normal uses and this in its turn was soon reflected in output. The volume of net agricultural output in 1946 was actually only five per cent greater than in 1937; in 1951 it was seventeen per cent higher than it had been in 1946. In terms of 1948–9 prices, the money value of net agricultural output reached its wartime peak in 1940–1 with a total of £43·7 million. In 1946–7 the comparable figure was £41 million. But by 1951–2 it had gone up to £46·8 million. Gross output in 1964–5 was estimated at just under £117 million. An estimate for the previous year, 1963–4, suggested that in comparative terms (1924–5=base 100) gross agricultural output for cattle stood at 188, for pigs at 1,142, for milk at 156, but for crops and garden produce at 95.[7] It was not surprising, in this context, that exports of certain key commodities should have risen very sharply. Thus, whereas in 1940 66,000 cattle were sent out of Northern Ireland, in 1952 the total was 90,000, rising to 216,000 in 1965. In 1940, 92,000 tons of potatoes were exported; by 1952 this had become 211,000 tons, though by 1965 that figure had declined to 116,000. And between 1940 and 1952 the outflow of fresh milk climbed from 9,000 cwt to 684,000 and of processed milk from 45,000 cwt to 674,000; in 1965 the combined amount of milk products was 1½ million cwt.[8]

This, certainly, was a remarkable transformation, but northern agriculture had always been a sturdy plant, needing only adequate opportunity to grow and flourish. Northern industry, however, was another matter. The hectic conditions of the war years could not be expected to continue. And indeed the old spectre of unemployment, not by any means exorcised between 1939 and 1945, soon again began to haunt the mills and dockyards. During the two decades after the war it fluctuated between five and ten per cent, and was consistently well above the overall British figure. This was bad, but it might have been much worse had the government not taken vigorous action to prevent it. That action was mainly embodied in a series of acts of parliament designed to attract new industry to the province by offering various inducements. This legislation took several forms. First in point of time was the series of Industries Development Acts passed between 1945 and 1953 and designed to give financial assistance to firms starting new industries or extending old ones; grants or loans could be made especially for the purchase of new plant, machinery and buildings. Next came the Capital Grants to Industry Acts (1954-62) providing government grants of a proportion (usually a third) of the expenses incurred by firms in new buildings or new installations. This was followed by the Aid to Industry Acts (1961-4) by which the government undertook to pay further grants to industry to help with the cost of fuel (always a hampering factor where northern industry is concerned) and, finally, by the Industrial Advice and Enterprise Acts of 1964 and 1967 providing yet more money for replacement of obsolete plant and buildings as well as special payments to firms employing consultants with a view to improving their efficiency.* Left-wing critics, who see in the economic plight of Northern Ireland an inevitable outcome of 'monopoly capitalism', contend that the influx of foreign capital is at best a temporary palliative, not a permanent cure. Not only, they argue, is new industry labour intensive and therefore incapable of taking up the slack left by the old declining staple industries, but its economic surplus is exported and it will in any event move out again if and when government aid begins to dry up. On the other side it is worth pointing out that although fly-by-night firms may indeed be tempted to take what quick pickings they can get, the whole policy of introducing new business is too recent for the long-term results to be assessed. In the short term, it is hard to see how Northern Ireland could otherwise have found the new industrial concerns (over 160 of them) and the 55,000 new jobs

* Other inducements included a generous de-rating policy and a large coal subsidy; for full details, see *Report of the Joint Working Party on the Economy of Northern Ireland* (Cmd. 1835), 1962, Appendix ix, pp. 75-7. Another Industrial Development Act in 1966 increased the government grants to industry and this was further augmented for a three-year period following the disturbances of 1969. In addition, key industries, notably shipbuilding and aircraft, have received individual treatment, for instance the £3½ million lent to Harland and Wolff under special legislation of 1966, the £8 million lent towards the construction of a new shipbuilding dock in 1970 and the grants and loans, totalling some £16 million, to the aircraft industry between 1963 and 1969. The assistance given to these heavy industries has generally been shared by the British and Northern Ireland governments.

which, it is estimated, had been created by the mid-1960s.[9] Furthermore, the post-war development was not intended to be a mere flash in the pan. The *Report of the Joint Working Party* (the Hall Report cited in the footnote on the previous page set out starkly enough the problems with which the government and the province were confronted in their quest for further expansion. Yet the response to this challenge was anything but defeatist. The immediate sequel to the Hall Report was the scheme propounded by Sir Robert Matthew. His main proposal, embodied in the *Belfast Regional Survey and Plan* (1963), was to 'demagnetize' Belfast as the centre of the region and to link Portadown and Lurgan in a new city, subsequently called Craigavon. It is true that both the name of the city and its situation – it was of little relevance to the underdeveloped west of the province – aroused Nationalist criticism, but in other ways the conception was imaginative and, above all, it portended further growth. This also was the theme of another document, 'Economic Development in Northern Ireland', drawn up by Professor T. H. Wilson and published in 1965. This set targets for housebuilding and for employment which called for the construction of 12,000 new houses a year by 1970 and for 30,000 new jobs to be created in manufacturing, 5,000 in the building industry and a further 30,000 in the service industries.[10]

This sounded impressive, and to a certain extent it was impressive, but it was not in itself enough to banish unemployment. True, the target in housing (both for actual houses and for jobs) was reached in 1968, but it was not reached in the service industries and the very real achievement in manufacturing was to a considerable extent off-set by the contraction and closure of existing firms. The growth rate, particularly in male employment, was not unimpressive. But the pious hope expressed in the *Northern Ireland Development Programme* for 1970-5, that 'if Northern Ireland can maintain these faster growth rates in the years ahead, and if major adjustments such as the decline in shipbuilding employment are no longer required on the same scale, then faster employment growth will be possible in the future', was already being jeopardised by events. The consultants who drew up the *Development Programme* themselves pointed out that in mid-1969 unemployment stood at 6·8 per cent compared with 2·2 per cent for the United Kingdom as a whole, and that output per head of the working population was then running at about three-quarters of the national average. They recognised even then the danger that the province would be caught 'in a vicious circle of political instability and industrial decline'. The forecast of 40,000 new jobs to be provided between 1970 and 1975, at first regarded as the minimum desirable now, in their view, 'has . . . the appearance of presenting a formidable task'.[11] By no means all of the trouble was due to a political disturbance, of course. Despite all the efforts of the government – and further steps were and are being taken to implement the *Development Programme* – Northern Ireland cannot escape its economic heritage overnight. A good part of the explanation for the sluggishness of the economy to respond rapidly to all these well-intentioned initiatives is to be found in the fact that many of the new enterprises are light industries or else variants of the textile industry – either consumer-goods such as processed foods and electrical equipment, or the manufacture of man-made fibres such as Acrilan, Terylene or Ulstrom. What this means in effect is that new industries can prosper if they can minimise the traditional defects of the economic structure of the region. But for the industries which, so to speak, have been bred in the bone in the six counties, those traditional defects still remain – the difficulty of maintaining themselves in a world which no longer needed so much of their products (this applied to both linen and shipbuilding), the absence of minerals and fuel, the smallness of the domestic market, the cost of reaching the all-important export market, the difficulty of finding work for men rather than for women, and the lack of capital at home. While the bringing in of new industries no doubt helped to solve some of these problems in this sector or in that, it could not give rapid relief to those who still depended on the old, specialised, highly vulnerable industries. There, the outlook remained gloomy and because this was so there still remained the possibility – latent but nevertheless real – that competition for jobs could once again aggravate an already tense situation as it had done in the thirties.*

How far was this tense situation reflected in the political life of the province? The answer depends upon how deep one digs. On the surface, what mostly strikes the observer is the apparent immobility of politics and society in Northern Ireland during the first forty-five years of its existence. The same party was still in power that was in power at the beginning of the state and although the men may have changed within the last few years the policies – at least until very recently – were much as they had always been. It is not the purpose of this survey to carry the history of Northern Ireland in any detail beyond the early 1960s and at that time, certainly, with Sir Basil Brooke still in the saddle, continuity with the past of Ulster Unionism seemed almost unbroken. Even the population the politicians were there to represent, though growing slightly, was not very different from what it had been before the war. From a total of 1,256,561 in 1926 it had moved only to 1,425,042 in 1961. The number of members representing that population in the Northern Ireland House of Commons remained at fifty-two (or fifty-one if we exclude the Speaker) and the Unionist dominance in that House was still much the same as ever. In the years before the war the various opposition parties could seldom hope to win more than ten or a dozen seats; in 1958 the total 'anti-partition' representation was ten,

* The overall unemployment level has stayed obstinately high. Since 1951 the average has never remained below 30,000 for a full year; in the mid-1960s it hovered about the six per cent mark in an insured population of roughly half a million (*Report of the Joint Working-Party*, pp. 18-9; *Ulster Yearbook*, 1966-68, pp. 188-9).

in 1962 it was twelve, and in 1965 eleven. Political parties, as we have seen, tended to follow very closely the lines of religious affiliation and here, too, there had been no very marked shift in the distribution of the population. In 1926 Catholics had accounted for 33·5 per cent, in 1961 they accounted for roughly 35 per cent. The remainder were almost entirely Protestant of one denomination or another. Presbyterians remained the largest of the Protestant groups – 29 per cent in 1961, against 31·3 per cent in 1926. The Church of Ireland share also fell slightly, from 27 to 24·2 per cent; among other denominations Methodists remained the most numerous, though small in relation to the three major gaps.*

Given this kind of stability, it was not to be expected that the Northern Ireland parliament would be the scene of any very exciting new development. In fact, it remained much what it had always been – a chamber where ministers explained their policies to the faithful (who, however, could be critical), and endured with equanimity protests from the minority which both protesters and protested against knew to be chiefly for the record and without much likelihood of influencing the course of government action. In short, those who might in ordinary circumstances have done most to challenge the existing scheme of things and even in time produce alternative governments – either the Nationalists or the Labour representatives – were debarred from doing so by the operation of the same factor that had deprived them of their usefulness before the war – the overwhelming importance of the constitutional issue and the seemingly inescapable need to discuss everything else in the light of that issue.

Both these potential centres of opposition had, therefore, very dispiriting records in the years after 1945. It might have been expected, in view of the industrial revival during the war and of the attempts to develop industry after it was over that a strong Labour party would emerge as the principal alternative to Unionism. It is true that the membership of the trade union movement did increase very considerably. By the early 'sixties there were about 200,000 trade unionists, about ninety per cent of whom belonged to unions which had their headquarters in Britain. Since some of these unions also had members in the Republic there was here, one would have thought, a nucleus around which might have developed that working-class solidarity which James Connolly had striven for in the past and which, correctly, he had anticipated would be one of the first casualties of partition. But such solidarity proved hard to achieve. This was partly, as we saw earlier, because of divisions within the Irish movement as a whole, but partly also because the stature of the northern unions was diminished by the reluctance of the Northern Ireland government either to repeal the obnoxious Trade Union Act of 1927, or to recognise the Northern Committee of the Irish Congress of Trade Unions. With the advent to power of Captain O'Neill, these obstacles were at

* Religious groupings are listed in *Ulster Yearbook*, 1966-68, pp. 8-10.

last removed and the way was cleared for somewhat easier relations between organised labour and the authorities.*

Nevertheless, this improved status of the trade unions was not reflected in the improved status of Labour as a political force. On the contrary, the electoral showing of Labour candidates for the local parliament continued to be extremely poor. The reason for this was essentially the same as the reason for their poor showing before the war. In a society where the fundamental cleavage was religious and political, the concept of a workers' party dedicated to the overthrow of capitalism still seemed to many workingmen to be peripheral, even irrelevant.† Consequently, after the war as before it, Labour candidates were apt to come forward with qualifying epithets – 'Commonwealth' Labour, 'Republican' Labour, 'Eire' Labour and so on – which pointed firmly to their attitude towards partition, the presumption being that this was what really interested the electors. In an effort to counteract this fissiparous tendency the Northern Ireland Labour party took two important steps in 1949. On the one hand, it made it clear that it wished to be a party on the lines of the British Labour party and to be associated with that party. And on the other hand, it put all its eggs in the basket of constitutionalism. Following the declaration of the Republic in the south (April 1949), a Labour conference in the six counties passed the following resolution: 'That the Northern Ireland Labour party believes that the best interests of Northern Ireland lie in maintaining the constitutional links with the United Kingdom.' But the chill wind that blew across northern politics in that bleak year was unkind to the delicate plant of Labour orthodoxy. In the general election which was Stormont's immediate reaction to Mr Costello's Republic, all nine Labour candidates were defeated. They did no better in 1953, but in 1958 and 1962 managed to secure four seats, though even these were likely to remain precarious so long as the central preoccupation of northern politics continued to be with issues that had little to do with the role of Labour in modern society. The fact that other 'unofficial' Labour candidates, with prefixes of various kinds, managed to win two or three seats in those same elections does not affect the generalisation – on the contrary, the very paucity of their representation reinforces it.

* For the all-Ireland context of these developments, see Part IV A, chap. 5, section iv.

† This is confirmed by the researches of Professor Richard Rose during the late 'sixties. Of the trade unionists, he writes: 'The absence of a strong relationship between union membership and political outlooks is surprising and significant. It is surprising because of the extent to which union membership is strongly associated with political attitudes elsewhere. It is significant because the failure of unions to encourage a more secular approach to politics is not a function of weak union organisation, but in spite of the well-established position of unions in Northern Ireland'. And he adds: 'Religion more than economics determines who the enemies of the workers are thought to be'. (Governing Without Consensus (London, 1971), pp. 261, 284.)

If, then, Labour suffered because in the last resort it was crowded out by the all-devouring issue of partition, did this not mean that the Nationalist party, which by definition was totally concerned with that issue, had a golden opportunity to assume the main role in opposition? In a sense it did assume that role, since it was the second largest party in the Northern Ireland parliament, but it was still inhibited from becoming an *official* opposition because this would imply more recognition of the existing regime than it was prepared to concede.* The very fact that it was bound by its history and situation to remain obsessed by the border had several consequences which seriously affected its ability to win more votes and move nearer to power. One was that, so long as the constitutional issue remained in effect the only issue, its policy on other matters appeared to be unconstructive, or even non-existent. Nationalists were certainly prompt to expose and to denounce instances of what seemed to them unfair discrimination against their fellow citizens and co-religionists, but this, though a necessary function, was also a negative one. Again, it has to be remembered also that although there have always been important Nationalist enclaves in Belfast, Londonderry, and other towns (Newry, indeed, being predominantly Nationalist), the main electoral support for the party has come from the rural areas where the opinion they had to represent is the opinion of mainly conservative farmers and shopkeepers. When to that is added the further fact that Nationalist members at Stormont were the spokesmen for the Catholic Church on such matters as education, health and the social services, it will be seen that the opportunities open to them for taking a radical line were severely limited. The epithet derisively applied to them by some workingmen – 'Green Tories' – indicates sufficiently where their sympathies were believed to lie.

Unfortunately these have not been the only weaknesses in their position. They have inherited from their predecessors of the 1920s that nervous paralysis which comes from awareness of another and more extreme form of nationalism at their elbow with which at any time they might expect to be in competition. This has led them at times into irresolution and inconsistency. Lacking the will or the wish to join the Republicans, they have also lacked the nerve to fight them tooth and nail. Accordingly, under stress, they have tended to compromise. The most striking political example of this was the tacit agreement in the late 'fifties to leave electioneering for the Westminster seats to Sinn Féin, while the constitutional Nationalists concentrated on the elections to the local parliament at Stormont.

But to sup with Sinn Féin needed a longer spoon than the constitutional Nationalists possessed. For militant republicanism had more than one weapon in its armoury. To mark one's disapproval of the

* It became the official opposition in 1965, but subsequently (autumn 1968) withdrew again in protest against police action in breaking up the Civil Rights demonstration in Londonderry.

British connection by winning seats in the Westminster parliament one never meant to occupy was too negative to appeal for long to the more hot-headed young men in the movement. When the military wing of that movement – the Irish Republican Army – was reorganised in the mid-fifties it soon became clear that the use of force to overthrow 'British rule in occupied Ireland' had by no means been abandoned. The campaign of violence which then developed was confused and largely ineffective – chiefly because of the tendency of the extremists to split into splinter groups owing little or no obedience to the Army Council of the IRA. Nevertheless, the campaign, whether 'official' or 'unofficial', produced some very ugly incidents along the border, where several policemen were killed in circumstances that deeply shocked public opinion – one constable, for example, being riddled with bullets as he was returning from a visit to his fiancée, and a sergeant being blown to pieces by a booby-trap in a deserted farm-house. Altogether, the 'offensive' waged by the IRA and other groups cost nineteen lives between 1956 and 1961, caused considerable material damage, and led to heavy expenditure in north and south on increased security precautions. Indeed, the governments of Northern Ireland and of the Republic both reacted with similar firmness to the threat posed by these new outbreaks. There appears to have been considerable exchange of information between their police forces and, although there were no extradition arrangements between the two parts of Ireland, each government used its powers to intern the members of these 'illegal organisations'. In Northern Ireland, the peak period of attack was between 1957 and 1959, and in those years an average of 150 IRA members or sympathisers were detained in the six counties under the special regulations. It was, however, impressive evidence of the then stability and strength of the Stormont government that not only was it able to restrain its own partisans from massive reprisals (a very real danger in the light of previous history) but it also felt able to release all the internees in 1961 – a year before the campaign was called off by the Army Council of the IRA.[12]

Although both governments had behaved responsibly and with restraint during the episode there can be little doubt that among ordinary men and women in the north this recrudescence of violence simply tended to reinforce traditional attitudes. Unionists, certainly, were much inflamed not simply by the violence, but by the fact that in some quarters in the south its perpetrators were apparently regarded as heroes in the Fenian tradition. For constitutional and conservative-minded Nationalists this hardening of tempers could only spell further damage. Many of them, anyway, were totally alienated by a campaign which was at variance with everything constitutional Nationalism stood for and which, moreover, had repeatedly been condemned by the leaders of their Church. It was not surprising, therefore, that in 1959-60, when the threat from the IRA was still very much of a reality, more moderate Nationalists began to draw together into a new organisation,

National Unity, pledged to work for the unification of the island by the consent of the people of Northern Ireland. A few years later this was transformed into the Nationalist Political Front, to bring together all those Nationalists who were repelled by violence and were at the same time impatient with the lack of progress of the older generation of parliamentarians.

To look back at such developments across the chasm which now separates Northern Ireland from even its recent past is to peer dimly into a world so different from the present as to be almost incomprehensible. With hindsight we can see – contemporaries themselves, indeed, can never really have forgotten it – that political, like religious, ecumenism is at best a struggling plant where the soil remains so bleakly inhospitable. What most affects the man in the street, after all, is what happens in his own locality or in his own personal experience. It is at this level that the burden of discrimination makes itself felt most heavily and it has usually been at this level that the most grating frictions have occurred. What constitutes discrimination is, of course, a vexed question. No doubt much that seems to the minority to be diabolically deliberate discrimination may in reality be the results of the geographical and economic configuration of the country. The fact that Catholics, for example, are thickest on the ground in the south and west of the province is a partial consequence of the Plantation of three hundred years ago, just as the industrialisation of the east is the product of the technological revolution of a hundred years ago. But to argue that because the east figures largely in the development plans of the government and the west does not, this is part of a general scheme of discrimination, is to fall into the all-too common error of oversimplification by foreshortening history.

Nevertheless, if some of the economic and social discrimination against Catholics can be explained away as the historical consequence of their having been for many years a poor and exploited section of the population this is no argument either for condoning or for continuing the exploitation. Nor is it any justification for the other kinds of discrimination that have arisen directly from the siege mentality of the majority – from their fierce determination, that is, to maintain their Protestant and Unionist faith and institutions against all comers. These have generally been seen by the minority as a deliberate attempt to 'hold the pass', so to speak, against Catholic infiltration. Many and various have been the allegations made in support of this contention – ranging from the siting of the projected new town (to be called, provocatively enough, Craigavon) and the placing of the new university in Coleraine in preference to Londonderry, to the general and never-ending complaint about a religious test being applied in a wide variety of employments. Such a test certainly is applied (it may not be unknown in Catholic areas, either, but since Protestants dominate most councils their actions are more conspicuous) and no doubt the intention is often to preserve the status quo intact. It is, however, only fair to add two comments. One is that many of the better-paid and more senior posts, for example in the civil service, require a standard of education to which relatively few Catholics have in the past been able to aspire. There is a vicious circle here. They have not been able to aspire because so many are in the poorer-paid occupations. Because they are in the poorer-paid occupations they have to leave school as early as possible. Because they leave school as early as possible they cannot aspire to the quality of education which would admit them to the more prestigious jobs. No doubt over the years more Catholic children have been benefiting from a longer and better education, but it is significant that in the early 'sixties the proportion attending the Queen's University was still only twenty-two per cent of the total student population in the university.[18]

The second comment to be made is this. Each side has its own reasons for regarding certain kinds of employment as unsuitable. Many Nationalists have been reluctant to enter the service of a state whose legality they refuse to recognise. This has, of course, been pre-eminently true of the Royal Ulster Constabulary, where, despite efforts from the earliest days to make the force non-political and inter-denominational, in 1961 only twelve per cent of the police were Catholic, as against thirty-seven per cent Church of Ireland and forty per cent Presbyterians.* These proportions, however, suggest another consideration of wider relevance – which is that if Catholics themselves would regard acceptance of certain kinds of employment as a betrayal of their principles, some Protestants would hesitate to employ them anyway lest they should prove untrustworthy or even engage in what, from a Unionist viewpoint, might be regarded as treasonable activities. This, incidentally, is an argument that has been used not only about employment, but also to justify the exclusion of Catholics from their due share in local government.

Much of all this, however objectionable, can be seen as a natural outcome of the unhappy but inescapable fact that over many generations (this is true in the south as well as in the north) the different religious denominations have tended to keep very much to themselves. We have seen how this has affected the pattern of education; it has affected similarly not only the pattern of employment but even the use of leisure and the social groupings in which people live. There are exceptions to this, of course. The trade unions have to a considerable extent, though not entirely, cut across the frontiers of religion and politics; the professions, notably the law, have enabled considerable mixing to take place; most of all, perhaps, the Queen's University has played a conspicuously successful part in breaking down among its students barriers which their home environment had often enough raised against common understanding.

But such shafts of light are rare enough in a situation which has

* The part-time B Specials were, for obvious historical reasons, exclusively Protestant.

been gloomy ever since the foundation of the state and in the last few years has become steadily gloomier. Over the years, the key to advance has generally been seen not so much in some magical formula for apportioning jobs in an equitable fashion between the various denominations, but in applying democratic concepts to local government, which impinges so directly and in so many ways upon the lives of men, women and children. Naturally, therefore, since the effective working of the social services depends in such large measure upon fair and efficient administration by the local councils, the battle for representation on them has grown steadily more bitter in the last twenty years.

The most frequent accusation levelled against the Unionist majority has been that they have retained control of the local councils in certain areas by shameless gerrymandering – that is, by so drawing the boundaries of the various districts and wards that even where Nationalists have been in a majority, that majority has not been reflected in the composition of the councils. This is still the subject of the most acute and violent controversy and the historian can do little more at this point in time than illustrate the nature of the controversy by referring to what is generally regarded as a crucial instance.

The *locus classicus* of this dispute about local representation is the city of Londonderry, where the issues involved were not only religious, political and economic, but also social, since, as seems to be clear beyond all reasonable doubt, a deliberate policy had there been followed of manipulating council housing policy so that Catholic voting power would not increase to such an extent as to endanger the Unionist supremacy on the city council. In general, in Londonderry as in other local government areas, the vote was given to 'resident occupiers' and to 'general occupiers'. The first category consisted of persons residing in dwelling-houses as owners or tenants. In such cases the resident occupier's wife could also vote, but others living under the same roof would normally be excluded, even if they were of voting age.* To vote as a 'general occupier' a person had to be the occupier of land or premises (other than a dwelling-house) of annual valuation of not less than ten pounds; no more than two joint-occupiers could qualify for the franchise unless they were engaged in business as partners. Limited companies were entitled to appoint one nominee for every ten pounds' valuation of their premises up to a maximum of six nominees. This system, weighted in favour of property as it obviously was, has been defended on the grounds that since the essential function of a local council is to fix and to spend rates then those who are to pay the piper should choose the tune, but the 'business vote' always attracted great hostility

* Legislation of 1946, 1948 and 1962 did, however, extend the definitions of 'resident occupier' to include certain other categories of persons, including married couples who, living in part of a dwelling-house let to them furnished or unfurnished, had qualified hitherto as parliamentary electors but not as local government electors. See *Ulster Yearbook, 1966-68*, pp. 37-8.

and, like so much else in the province, has disappeared in the turmoil of the last four years.*

Over the province as a whole these regulations resulted in a striking difference between the number of electors for the parliament at Stormont and for the local councils; according to the register of February 1964 there were 911,940 of the former, but only 658,778 of the latter.† In Londonderry itself the system worked as follows. The city was divided into three wards, containing in all a population which in 1961 amounted to 53,762. In that year (the last, incidentally, when religious affiliation was listed), there were 36,073 Catholics and 17,689 others; roughly half the Catholics and forty per cent of the others were under the voting age of 21. By 1967, the last year for which reliable figures are available at the time of writing, the number of Catholics entitled to vote was 14,429 and the number of others similarly qualified was 8,781. The fact the Catholic majority among voters was so small in relation to their overall majority of the population reflected of course their economically inferior status, but it was also directly related to their lack of houses since, as we have just seen, to be a resident occupier was one of the principal qualifications for the franchise. But this Catholic majority, such as it was, did not produce a majority in the city council, where the normal division of parties had long been twelve Unionists against eight non-Unionists. This result was achieved by the curious fashion in which the population was grouped within the three wards. In 1967 the North Ward, with 2,530 Catholic voters and 3,946 others, returned eight Unionists. The Waterside Ward had just over 5,500 voters divided between 1,852 Catholics and 3,697 Unionists – it returned four Unionists. The South Ward, with slightly more than 11,000 voters, of whom 10,000 were Catholics, accounted for the entire non-Unionist representation of eight seats.[14]

Thus, by a heavy concentration of Catholics into one ward, was the Unionist majority obtained, even though over sixty per cent of the adult population was Catholic. To some extent, it is fair to say, a concentration of Catholic Nationalists into one area, and of Protestant Unionists into others, might have happened anyway, since that is part and parcel of the segregation of the two communities to be found all over the province, but the fact remains that the particular form this segregation took in Londonderry city resulted in a pattern of Unionist control which was too consistent too long to be anything other than deliberately contrived.

The crux of this unhappy situation was the housing problem – both because houses meant votes and because lack of houses meant miserably cramped conditions for those who felt they were being dis-

* This was written shortly before the reforms of November 1968 announced its impending abolition.

† More recent figures (for 1967) give the Stormont electorate in that year as 933,724, the Westminster electorate as 909,841, and the local government electorate as 694,483.

criminated against on religious and political grounds. Much play, it is true, has been made with the argument that in the twenty years after the war Catholics have received more than twice the number of houses allotted to Protestants. But against this have to be set three other considerations – that the Catholic population was larger, that the Catholic need was greater, and that many of the houses, those built by the Housing Trust for example, represented replacements of houses condemned or demolished. Moreover, so long as political considerations were deemed to require the containment of Catholics mainly within the South Ward, then the sheer physical facts of the situation were bound sooner or later to confront the Unionist-dominated council with a terrifying dilemma. Eventually it would be impossible to put any more houses in the Catholic ward. Would Catholics then be allowed to spill over into the other wards with all that that implied or would there be some other, more explosive outcome? The whole world now knows the answer to that question even if it remains as much in the dark as ever about the ultimate solution to the problems of discrimination and segregation of which Londonderry has become, in a sense, the symbol.*

Londonderry may be a symbol, and no doubt it is an extreme case, but it is by no means unique. The manipulation of local government boundaries, it now seems abundantly plain, had created in other centres also large pockets of under-represented and deeply resentful Catholics.[15] This in turn produced a dangerous situation which could at any time be precipitated into crisis by an increase in the number of Catholics above the opportunities of employment or housing available to them. Until the early 1960s, it has been suggested, the safety-valve of emigration operated to reduce the tension to some extent, since in the six counties between 1937 and 1961 Catholics, who were consistently about a third of the population, accounted for fifty-five to fifty-eight per cent of all Ulstermen leaving the province.[16] Apart from the fact that the vicissitudes of the British economy render this a safety-valve of dubious value, the very fact that it was Catholics who had, proportionately, to make most use of it, in itself constituted a grievance, reinforcing both their sense of an imposed inferiority and the bitter resentment which that sense of inferiority evoked.

The problem of Northern Ireland has been complicated by the rise of the welfare state, but it is at heart the old problem. When most people were poor and the whole province was backward inequalities seemed less blatant. But now, when spending is so much greater, and the expectations of the people have risen so much higher, it is inevitable that the local councils should be seen to be important centres of influence and power. In a small area such as Northern Ireland the politics of welfare are necessarily and properly local politics. But the tragedy of the six counties is that it has not been possible to disentangle

* The answer, and the problem to which it in turn gave rise, are discussed in the next chapter.

the politics of welfare from the politics of siege. The work of local councils, valuable and constructive as it often is, cannot simply be judged, as it might be elsewhere, from the way these bodies deal with drainage, health, education or the social services. Always overshadowing these preoccupations is the larger question – is local government to remain in the hands of those who uphold the political settlement as it is now or of those who wish to destroy it? Is it, to put the matter more brutally, designed to intensify the existing segregation or to alleviate it? Up to the mid-sixties, certainly, the aim of policy seemed to go no further than the maintenance of the status quo. But there was always the possibility that, as so often before, any action to change the status quo in a sense favourable even to moderate Catholic or Nationalist aspirations would call into being an ardent Protestant and Unionist reaction.

Already, by the mid-sixties, there were signs that exactly this might be about to happen. Ironically, it was the accession to power in 1963 of a Prime Minister, Captain Terence O'Neill, who appeared to turn his face firmly against sectarian bigotry, that may eventually be seen as the catalyst that set sectarian bigotry in motion once more. Born in 1914, of an ancient, landed family, educated at Eton, and Anglican by religion, Captain O'Neill set himself not only to divert domestic energies away from internecine quarrels and towards constructive policies, but also to cultivate more amicable relations with the south, a new departure dramatised, as we have seen, by his exchange of visits with Mr Sean Lemass in 1965. This change of style in government did not mean that Captain O'Neill had ceased to be a Unionist, and it emphatically did not imply any weakening of official determination to maintain the sanctity and integrity of the border, but precisely because his regime had broken – or, more accurately, was believed to have broken – so radically with tradition, it brought out again into the open all the deeply-felt fears and antagonisms of old-style Unionism. Of this Unionism, which still remained extremely strong in the constituencies, representatives were to be found even in Captain O'Neill's own cabinet and, as we shall see, they were eventually to topple him from power. Yet, although Captain O'Neill was clearly pursuing a course which was likely to alienate many Unionists it seemed for his first five years of office that he was strong enough to withstand reactionary pressures. Indeed, if there was a threat to his position in those relatively untroubled years, it appeared to come less from the politicians than from embattled Protestantism in the formidable shape of the Reverend Ian Paisley, the dominating figure, one might say the Alpha and Omega, of the militant Free Presbyterian Church. Mr Paisley, still in his early forties, but with a decade of strenuous activity behind him, is a very large man with a very loud voice which has been raised at all times and seasons to warn his fellow-citizens against the perils of Popery and the dangers of tampering with entrenched Protestant and Unionist positions. His protests against 'Romanism' had begun to take on a political tinge in the (Westminster) general election of 1964 when he organised demonstrations against a Republican candidate in Belfast, but it was in 1966 that his Protestantism and his Unionism really combined to make him a powerful, if somewhat unpredictable, figure. His own emphasis was then – as it probably still is, at bottom – primarily upon the threat to the Protestant position poised by the fast-growing ecumenical movement, but the very year in which he chose to launch his anti-ecumenical thunders was also the year in which Unionist sensibilities were ruffled by the celebrations attending the fiftieth anniversary of the 1916 Rising. Mr Paisley's activities that summer earned him a prison sentence and also laid the foundation for the fierce hostility between himself and Captain O'Neill which, before long, was to have dire consequences for the latter. Nevertheless, although a preacher and orator of undeniable power and magnetism, and later to be the driving-force behind the extreme right-wing Ulster Constitution Defence Committee and its Ulster Protestant Volunteers, Mr Paisley, in the middle 1960s, might still perhaps have been dismissed as *vox et praeterea nihil*. Whether the future belonged to his brand of Unionism or to Captain O'Neill's was then impossible to predict, though onlookers who did not know the north too well would probably have been disposed to plump for the Prime Minister. But all guesses and calculations as to how the delicate balance of power within the Unionist party might turn were soon to seem crudely inadequate when in 1968 the long-stifled resentment of the deprived sections of the population began to force its way inexorably to the surface. For upholders of the status quo, whether moderate or extreme, time was beginning to run out.

6. The Continuing Crisis

It is extraordinary to reflect in 1972 that as recently as six years ago the state of Northern Ireland appeared even to well-informed observers to be quiescent and the omens for a brighter and more harmonious future decidedly propitious. The advent to power of Captain Terence O'Neill as a more 'liberal' Unionist than any of his predecessors, the *rapprochement* between north and south, the initially favourable effect of development policies on the northern economy, the decision of the Nationalist party to accept the role of official Opposition at Stormont – all these pointed, or seemed to point, to the success of the Prime Minister's avowed intention to build bridges between the rival communities and, by emphasising the need for the common pursuit of prosperity, to obtain Catholic as well as Protestant support for his programme.[1]

Yet, despite these hopeful signs, very little hindsight is needed to see that the anticipated golden age was largely the product of wishful thinking. No-one acquainted with the history of the province could rationally have supposed that the memory of centuries of conflict and tension could be forgotten overnight or that the realities of discrimination and alienation could be dispelled by a wave of Captain O'Neill's wand. But even if we were to think the unthinkable and leave Ulster history for the moment out of Ulster politics, it would still be clear that Captain O'Neill's initiative was threatened at the very moment he made it by both external and internal factors over neither of which did he have much, if any, control. The most important external factors were the rise of religious ecumenism in the outside world and the revival of interest in republicanism in nationalist Ireland following the fiftieth anniversary of the 1916 Rising. The first of these aroused the anger and apprehension of the extremer Protestant elements in Northern Ireland and, as we have seen, the Reverend Ian Paisley first achieved extensive notoriety by his attacks upon what he conceived to be the 'Romeward' tendencies of the Presbyterian Church. Although these may not have been very apparent to less prejudiced observers, there was enough Protestant fundamentalism in the province for this accusation to carry with it an element of political danger for a prime minister who was deliberately seeking to cultivate better relations with Catholics. And few antagonisms in the next few years were to be so bitter or so personal as those which developed between Captain O'Neill and Mr Paisley.

The republican revival in the south was, in 1966, perhaps a less obvious fact than ecumenism, but its importance for the future was to be far greater. Although the Easter celebrations produced the usual surplus of frothy rhetoric they also provoked a reassessment of the Rising which the rhetoricians themselves had been shirking for most of the previous fifty years. From this reassessment flowed three consequences, each of them directly relevant to both parts of the island. One was a tendency to contrast the ideals of 1916 with the realities of partition and thus to reawaken, especially in the young, an interest in, even a sympathy with, the IRA, which still continued to claim continuity of tradition with the men who had made the Easter rebellion. A second consequence was that increased attention was paid to James Connolly, with the inevitable corollary that the abortive social programme of the original revolution came to be critically contrasted with the existing condition of affairs in both north and south. Finally, the 1916 anniversary convinced staunch Ulster Unionists, if they needed any convincing, that the leopard had not changed his spots and that inside every nationalist there was a ravening republican waiting to get out.

By any reckoning this was an absurd over-simplification which took no account of the changes wrought on either side of the border by fifty years of partition. But it was especially an over-simplification when applied to the Catholic third of the population of Northern Ireland. No doubt that population did contain a militantly republican minority, and no doubt also a larger number were capable of an emotional response to the songs and symbols of extreme nationalism, but it is worth remarking that a survey carried out as recently as 1968 indicates that while about two-thirds of the Catholics questioned were in favour of abolishing the border, few of them regarded the issue as one of immediate importance.[2] More to the point, perhaps, is the evidence of the IRA itself which, when it called off its previous campaign in 1962, publicly admitted that lack of Catholic support in Northern Ireland was 'foremost' among the reasons for this defeat.[3]

In 1966, however, these external factors menaced Captain O'Neill's peace of mind less than the internal pressures which were already building up against him. These came both from within his own party and from outside it. His emergence as Prime Minister in 1963 (prime ministers in Northern Ireland were not at that time elected by their colleagues) had been a source of some uneasiness to the right-wing members of his party and as his policies unfolded in the succeeding years this uneasiness increased. It was accentuated when, following Mr Paisley's religious demonstrations, that forceful cleric was jailed for three months, and when the government showed a mounting disposition to deal harshly with Protestant gunmen who had begun to attack and kill Catholics in Belfast. The secret or semi-secret Protestant extremist organisation, the Ulster Volunteer Force, was declared illegal under the Special Powers Act in June 1966 and it was not, perhaps, entirely coincidental that O'Neill's first leadership crisis occurred that autumn when he faced and overcame what he himself described as a 'conspiracy' against him. The vote of confidence he then received was substantial, but more significant was the fact that the Unionist back-benchers set up a '66 Committee' to scrutinise more closely the actions of their leader. It was believed at the time that three ministers, Mr Brian Faulkner (then Minister of Commerce), Mr Harry West (Minister of Agriculture) and Mr William Morgan (Minister of Health and Social Services) would even then have welcomed a change of leadership.[4]

Seemingly unperturbed by these criticisms Captain O'Neill continued to shape his course towards reform – outlining a programme whereby the business vote in Stormont elections would be abolished, the four Queen's University seats would be suppressed and redistributed, and a boundary commission would re-draw the constituencies, first in Belfast and then for the province as a whole. These however, did not touch the roots of Catholic resentment of discrimination and there were indications that even to moderate nationalists Captain O'Neill's liberal protestations were beginning to ring rather hollow, partly because it was dubious whether he would survive the impending conflict with his own right wing, and still more because his reforms were projected within a framework of uncompromising Unionism which did not hold out to Catholics much, if any, hope of real participation in government. Moreover, even though it could be demonstrated that genuine economic progress was being made in the mid-sixties, this did not lead to a significant reduction in the rate of unemployment and competition between Catholics and Protestants for jobs as well as for houses remained acute.

Historically, it was the competition for houses which provided the spark that was to set the whole province alight. As far back as 1963, Mrs Patricia McCluskey, wife of a doctor in the town of Dungannon, was provoked by the failure of the Protestant-dominated council to provide adequate accommodation for Catholics into establishing a Homeless Citizens League which, by adroit publicity and direct action in the form of 'squatting', secured its desired objective. Recognising this as merely a local manifestation of a much wider problem, Mrs McCluskey and her husband went on to found the Campaign for Social Justice in January 1964 to collect and publicise information about cases of discrimination in Northern Ireland. This body, though itself non-political in origin and intention, speedily established contacts with critics of the Unionist regime inside and outside Ulster. In 1965 it affiliated with the National Conference of Civil Liberties in London and it may be regarded as the forerunner of the Northern Ireland Civil Rights Association which was formed two years later. It was not, however, until the summer of 1968 that the latter organisation found its opportunity and its role. Once again, the flash-point was housing. A Nationalist MP for county Tyrone, Austin Currie, failed to secure a council house in the village of Caledon for a Catholic family because the local council intended to let it to an unmarried nineteen-year-old Protestant girl who happened to be the secretary of a Unionist politician. Mr Currie responded by organising a 'squat in' at the house and followed this up by a Civil Rights march at the neighbouring town of

Dungannon. The march received wide coverage from the mass media, it was attended by leading non-Unionist politicians and it was peaceful and well-conducted. Its real importance, however, had little to do with the rectification of the housing situation in Caledon, or even in Tyrone. The Dungannon march was both a symbol and a portent. It was a symbol because it demonstrated that opponents of the regime could combine against it, however diverse their own backgrounds and interests. It was a portent because its success was eagerly watched elsewhere and nowhere more than in the city of Londonderry where the Civil Rights Association planned to widen their protest on a much larger scale and in a much more explosive situation.

Their attempt to do so on 5 October 1968 has already passed into history. That public marches and parades should lead to violence was nothing new in the experience of that bitterly divided city, but two factors ensured that the Civil Rights demonstration, though intended to be peaceful, would in reality be highly dangerous. One was the growing interest in the Civil Rights movement of various left-wing bodies for whom a confrontation with the police in full view of the television cameras would be the kind of publicity on which they throve. And the other was the intervention of the Minister for Home Affairs, Mr William Craig, who, two days before the march was due to take place, had prohibited it from following part of its advertised route. Almost inevitably confusion resulted and a section of the march collided with the police who, in their turn, used excessive and indiscriminate violence.[5]

The immediate and predictable outcome of the affair was an intensification of protest and a growth of organisation among both moderates and extremists. In Londonderry itself a number of the groups involved in the demonstration of 5 October met four days later in that city and elected the Derry Citizens Action Committee, pledged to non-violent pursuit of the same kind of aims as those enunciated by the Civil Rights Association. It soon became an effective exponent of Civil Rights ideas and its spokesmen, Mr John Hume and Mr Ivan Cooper, emerged as among the most capable, articulate and responsible of the leaders.[6] The same day which saw the formation of the Derry Citizens Action Committee saw also the creation in the Queen's University of a new and potentially more extreme protest group. This, which became known a little later as the People's Democracy, contained from the outset a number of Young Socialists and others whose politics inclined, in varying degrees, to the left. Miss Bernadette Devlin was one of the students prominent in the earliest days of this organisation, but control soon passed to former members of the university, when Mr Michael Farrell and Mr Eamonn McCann became the effective leaders.[7] Their aims, while embracing the anti-discriminatory ideas of the Civil Rights Association, in fact went far beyond the redress of immediate grievances, envisaging as they did the eventual creation of a 'workers' and small farmers' republic' for the whole of Ireland.[8] Although it too professed non-violence, the People's Democracy was not averse to confrontations with the police and in the course of time developed the techniques of 'defensive' violence with considerable expertise.

During the two months after the Londonderry demonstration intermittent protest marching continued there and in Belfast, carried out by the Civil Rights Association and the People's Democracy on the one hand, and by the militant Protestant followers of Mr Paisley and one of his associates, Major R. Bunting, on the other. In an effort to end what was rapidly becoming an intolerable situation the Northern Ireland government, after consultation with the British government, announced a series of reforms. These included promises to ensure that housing authorities 'placed need in the forefront in the allocation of houses' and made their future allocations on the basis of published and 'readily-understood' schemes; to appoint a Parliamentary Commissioner (or 'Ombudsman') to investigate citizens' grievances; to press on with the appointment of a Development Commission for the city of Londonderry; to reform local government comprehensively within three years; and finally, to withdraw their special powers as soon as they considered that this could be done without hazard.

Such concessions represented a very considerable advance on anything that had previously been offered, but because some of them were intended to be spread over a period of years, and particularly because the local government proposals did not include the immediate grant of 'one man, one vote', the tension in the province remained unabated. Indeed, it was further accentuated by an exceedingly ugly incident at Armagh on 30 November when a Civil Rights march in that city was rendered impossible through the virtual occupation of the centre of the town by followers of Mr Paisley. A momentary lull followed after Captain O'Neill had made a moving television appeal for support and had followed this up with the dismissal of his Minister for Home Affairs, Mr Craig, whose handling of the demonstrations was shortly to be severely criticised by the Cameron Commission and whose relations with his prime minister on the broad issue of the future of the province were distinctly cool. The Civil Rights Association responded to Captain O'Neill's appeal by a month's moratorium on demonstrations. But the People's Democracy, which at this point seemed to be steadily diverging from the Civil Rights movement, persisted with its provocative scheme for a march from Belfast to Londonderry, which duly took place between 1 and 4 January 1969. The marchers were seriously harassed during their journey, especially by a savage attack from militant Protestants at Burntollet, and their appearance in Londonderry itself was the signal for a further clash with the police.

More violence followed at Newry a few days later and it was against this sombre background that Captain O'Neill announced that a general election would be held on 24 February. His intention presumably was to establish such an ascendancy within his own party as to be able to carry through the November reforms with the minimum of delay. But his plan miscarried and the election was notable for the appearance in the field of a number of Unionist candidates openly hostile to the Prime Minister. These divisions did not of course disturb the usual overall Unionist majority, but they did open the door for the election of a number of Independents (including Mr Hume and Mr Cooper) and, even more ominously, they left Captain O'Neill in a fatally exposed position. Nevertheless, despite the fact that his control over his own party was growing weaker almost day by day, he attempted as before to combine firmness with moderation. Thus the month of March saw the imprisonment of Mr Paisley and Major Bunting for their part in the Armagh disturbances of the previous November, and the month of April brought the key decision to concede the Civil Rights demand of 'one man, one vote' at local elections, while at the same time postponing the elections due in 1970 until the new register could come into full operation.[9]

Unhappily for Captain O'Neill this concession came too late. It was, in fact, a classical example of the inadequacy of reform conceded under duress. Had it come earlier it might have obviated crisis, but to those whom it was designed to placate, it clearly had come only as a result of crisis. And so the situation continued, almost of its own momentum, to deteriorate – on the one hand, sporadic outbursts of violence, on the other hand growing dismay among Unionists at the speed and completeness with which their 'heritage' was being dismantled. It was this latter factor which was immediately decisive for Captain O'Neill's career. The party vote of 23 April in favour of universal adult suffrage for local elections was only twenty-eight in favour to twenty-one against and for the Prime Minister this was virtually the signal to go. On 28 April he finally relinquished office.

His successor was Major J. D. Chichester-Clark, a distant cousin of O'Neill's and, like him, sprung from an ancient Ulster landed family. But there the resemblance ended. O'Neill, though he had incurred the bitter enmity of his own right-wing both by his aloof style of government and by his reform initiatives, had at least left the Unionist party in no doubt that he intended to be a governing Prime Minister so long as he could outface and outmanoeuvre his critics. But Major Chichester-Clark, apart from his habitual air of shambling bewilderment, as of an amateur fallen among professionals, never had the remotest chance of dominating his party. He was in fact elected as leader and Prime Minister by a solitary vote, seventeen to sixteen. And time was to show that this margin was to be more significant as indicating the strength of the support for the runner-up than as evidence of the party's confidence in its new head. The runner-up was Mr Brian Faulkner and his emergence so near the top of the greasy pole was a portent in several different ways. First, he represented a different social order from that typified by the Brookes, the O'Neills and the Chichester-Clarks. The son of a shirt manufacturer and himself a business-man of no mean capacity, his growing importance in Ulster politics reflected the impatience of the commercial middle-class with half a century of semi-oligarchical rule by the landed gentry. Second, although his ability in a Stormont which was never over-stocked with that commodity ensured him a rapid advance in the party hierarchy, his differences with Captain O'Neill had been both widely-publicised and almost unbridgeable even before the Civil Rights agitation had begun to shake Unionism to its foundations.[10] He had been absent in America – and noncommittal in his comments – when O'Neill had been fighting for his political life in 1966; and in 1967, when the Prime Minister had dismissed Mr Harry West, his Minister for Agriculture, for failing to live up to the code of conduct he expected his cabinet to observe whenever a possible conflict arose between private interests and public duties, it was observable that Mr Faulkner had declared the dismissed Minister to be 'absolutely blameless'. Moreover, it was Mr Faulkner's resignation in January 1969 in protest against Captain O'Neill's insistence on setting up the Cameron Commission that had helped to push the Prime Minister into the election which, as we have seen, decisively registered his impotence.* But this past history of conflict between Mr Faulkner and Captain O'Neill itself indicates a final reason why the former's challenge to O'Neill's successor should have been so significant. It is difficult to avoid the conclusion that Mr Faulkner came so near to defeating Major Chichester-Clark because he was thought to be – and at that time was, whatever flexibility he may later have revealed – to be the man whom the right-wing of the party instinctively felt would do what had to be done to maintain the Unionist stranglehold on power.

This, however, could hardly be said with equal confidence of Major Chichester-Clark. Taking up O'Neill's commitment to reform, he did his best to prepare the way for peaceful change by declaring an amnesty soon after he became Prime Minister. But in fact the tension in the province was already too great for olive-branches of this kind to have any hope of success. Perhaps, if the government had felt able to ban the Protestant marches customary in July and August, some degree of relaxation might have been achieved, though even this is doubtful. As things were, however, the marches assumed in Protestant eyes even greater significance than usual, since they represented a reaffirmation of the Unionist ascendancy which had been threatened or 'betrayed' by Captain O'Neill's policies of the previous twelve months. Predictably, there were serious riots in various parts of the province on 12 and 13 July, but these paled into insignificance beside the naked and unbridled

* Yet, such were the complexities of Ulster politics even in that relatively uncomplicated phase, it has also to be recorded that Major Chichester-Clark himself had resigned from Captain O'Neill's administration on 23 April 1969, the last straw which preceded the Prime Minister's own departure. There remained, however, one further irony. The issue on which Major Chichester-Clark resigned was O'Neill's promise to institute 'one man, one vote' in local elections, the very policy which the Major had himself to accept after he became Prime Minister.

sectarian warfare that broke out in Londonderry during the Apprentice Boys' march on 12 August and spread soon afterwards to Belfast. Naturally the police – the Royal Ulster Constabulary – were heavily involved, but it soon became apparent that they were neither numerous nor strong enough either to hold the combatants apart or to reimpose peace and order in Londonderry and Belfast. In the former city, indeed, they were unable even to enter the Catholic stronghold of the Bogside and part of that district – known to its defenders as 'Free Derry' – was to continue for another three years to be what later became known as a 'no-go' area, that is an area into which the police, and subsequently the army, could not enter without grave risk of provoking large-scale hostilities and which, consequently, they tended to leave severely alone.

The riots of July and August caused, directly or indirectly, the deaths of ten people, eight Catholics and two Protestants. But in addition to that tragic outcome, and over above the numerous cases of bodily injury and the damage to property amounting to several million pounds, the eruption of those months had other far-reaching consequences. The inadequacy of the police, and the fact that their actions finally confirmed the Catholic population in their already ingrained distrust of the force, led to the intervention of the British Army. Without that intervention it is very possible that a sectarian civil war might have developed in Belfast, or even in the province as a whole, and in the light of what was to come it is important to be clear that to the Catholic minority the soldiers were regarded at the time as all that stood between them and a merciless pogrom. But the Army could not be committed without the British government being led to concern themselves directly with what was happening in this remote and incomprehensible province which was nevertheless a part of the United Kingdom.

The responsibility for translating this concern into action was entrusted to the Home Secretary, Mr James Callaghan. After the ground had been prepared by a joint communiqué issued by the two governments on 19 August – the Downing Street Declaration – disclaiming any intention to alter Northern Ireland's constitutional status but stressing the need to maintain the momentum of internal reform, Mr Callaghan visited the province later that month and elicited from Major Chichester-Clark and his colleagues the promise that further rapid progress would be made in a programme designed to achieve equality of opportunity in employment and in housing; to prevent religious discrimination and incitement to religious hatred; to develop the Northern Ireland economy; to foster better community relations; and to examine the role and function of the police.[11]

These initiatives did not in themselves constitute a solution of the Ulster problem but they did at least offer a breathing-space in which the effectiveness of the promises made in August might be assessed. This, however, did not mean that the Catholics were ready to abandon the barricades they had built for their protection in Belfast and Londonderry, nor did it mean that the Protestant majority had relaxed its suspicions that it had been, or was about to be, sold down the river. Each side regarded the breathing-space as no more than a truce, and an imperfect truce at that broken almost from day to day by sporadic outbursts of violence. The government's attempt to walk a tight-rope between the two angry communities was made first difficult and then almost impossible by the publication of the Cameron Report in September and of the Hunt Report on the police in October. The Cameron Report, with its direct criticism of Unionist attitudes and policies, was a bitter enough pill to swallow, but it was as nothing compared with the Hunt Report, which recommended unequivocally the disbandment of the 'B' specials and the disarming and reorganisation of the main body of the RUC.[12] The Northern Ireland government, under pressure from London, had little option but to accept the report in its essentials. But when these became known the Protestant Shankill Road erupted in a riot of which the first victim, by a cruel irony, was an RUC constable shot by a mob protesting against the disarming of the force of which he was a member. Once more the Army had to intervene, killing two Protestants, wounding many more, and using, it has been alleged, a degree of force considerably in excess of that which the RUC had been accustomed to employ in like circumstances.[13]

On the short-term view it was still, by the end of 1969, possible to hope that the military intervention, however brutal, had achieved its primary purpose of keeping the peace. Unfortunately, however, this achievement, such as it was, was not matched by any corresponding political advance. People's expectations – hopeful on the one side, dire on the other – had been aroused, but there was no clear way either to gratify or to allay them. Reforms had indeed been agreed – and at the Ministry of Development Mr Faulkner was deploying his administrative talent in implementing some of them as quickly as possible – but of their very nature their impact upon Ulster society was bound to be gradual. Nevertheless, a large part of the tension which persisted in Northern Ireland during the winter of 1969–70 sprang from the Catholic frustration that the changes did not occur overnight and the Protestant fear that they might.

Something else, however, had begun to happen behind the scenes which before long was to make all talk of phased reforms largely irrelevant. We are still too near the events of these last few years to achieve a proper perspective, but it may confidently be predicted that future historians of the Ulster crisis will recognise as one of the crucial turning-points in the drama the moment when the IRA began to emerge from the shadows. This, despite the deeply ingrained tendency of many Unionists to attribute the worsening situation to the Machiavellian tactics of the Republicans, came at a much later stage in the crisis than might have been expected. Even during the disturbances of August 1969, although the Tribunal of Inquiry appointed to investigate that episode found traces of IRA activity, the verdict then and since has been that the organisation was taken by surprise and did less for the Catholics than the latter thought they had a right to expect.* This relative inactivity (such activity as there was before the August débâcle may indeed have been devoted to staving off rather than provoking sectarian clashes) reflected the deep internal stresses which by the middle 'sixties had reduced the IRA to a condition of paralysis. The whole militant movement had been disrupted by the failure of the 1956-62 campaign and especially by the double traumatic experience of its members having been interned by both Irish governments and rejected by northern Catholics. When it began painfully to regroup the new leaders – Cathal Goulding (Chief of Staff) and Tomás Mac Giolla (President of Sinn Féin, the 'political wing' of the IRA) – sought to turn the movement towards a less physical approach to the problem of Irish unity. The emphasis was increasingly on economic analysis along Marxist lines (provided partly, it would appear, by a Dublin intellectual, Dr Roy Johnston who later resigned, seemingly in protest against violence) with the implication that the masses should be educated to see that their common interest was to forget their sectarian rivalries and combine to end the colonial relationship which still bound Northern Ireland to Britain.

Not unnaturally this more sophisticated trend held little appeal for the traditionalists of the northern IRA. They were, after all, traditionalists precisely because they recognised the ever-present danger of a Protestant pogrom against the Catholic minority and because they regarded it as their function both to protect that minority in the short term and to rescue it permanently by achieving the thirty-two county republic which was, or had been, the *raison d'être* of the IRA throughout its history. There was in fact nothing new about an internal conflict between the ideologues and the traditionalists – a similar conflict had developed in the 'thirties – but it was given a sharper edge by the recrudescence of crisis in the north. The details of how the northern wing now began to diverge from their leaders in the south may never be known in their entirety, but enough has emerged to indicate that as early as February 1969 – that is to say, little more than a month after the Protestant attack upon the People's Democracy march at Burntollet – the Derry section of the IRA was approached by an emissary from the south, allegedly with Fianna Fáil contacts, promising them financial aid if they organised themselves for self-defence. By self-defence was meant the creation of a northern command quite separate from the headquarters of the IRA based, as always, on Dublin. Four months later the offer was repeated but, although it was then neither accepted nor rejected, it gave rise to fierce argument within the IRA. The northern leaders were naturally apprehensive about the continued

* This was the finding of the Scarman Tribunal itself. See *Violence and Civil Disturbances in Northern Ireland in 1969: Report of Tribunal of Inquiry* (Cmd. 566), Apr. 1972, vol. i, pp. 11-12. The opinion of some of the local inhabitants can be gathered from the graffiti on the walls of Derry and Belfast, 'IRA. I Ran Away'.

isolation of the Catholic community and, lacking guns or money, were in no position to defend them. Moreover, they were distrustful of the new ideology and particularly critical of the way in which IRA support had been thrown behind Miss Bernadette Devlin to secure her election to Westminster as member for Mid-Ulster in April 1969. This seemed to traditionalists not merely an unwarrantable recognition of an alien institution, but also irrelevant to the serious business in hand.

It seemed more than ever irrelevant in the aftermath of the violence of July and August when the impotence of the IRA had been made pitilessly clear. This in itself would probably have precipitated the final split in the movement, but when the break eventually came it may have had something to do with the internal stresses in Mr Lynch's government in the Republic as well as with the organisation's own internal stresses. It was Mr Lynch's misfortune that his cabinet contained a strong representation of 'northerners', of whom the chief were Mr Charles Haughey (Minister of Finance), Mr Neil Blaney (Minister of Agriculture) and Mr Kevin Boland (Minister of Local Government). When the street-battles began in Belfast and Londonderry this group pressed for strong action – apparently for actual armed intervention – but although Mr Lynch was able to prevent the disintegration of his government on this issue and also to avoid any formal involvement in the crisis, the solution he actually adopted, the creation of a Northern Sub-Committee of the cabinet, was potentially a dangerous one for a leader who wished to keep his options open, since the Sub-Committee was dominated from the outset by Messers Haughey and Blaney.*

Meanwhile, in the north the local IRA leaders were still desperate for arms and still contemplating a breach with the rest of the organisation. Early in September 1969, after a conclave held at Moville in county Donegal, they decided in principle to accept the offer of financial aid from the south, now for the third time made to them on the familiar condition that they should set up their own command. They appear to have been led to believe that the offer came not only from businessmen but also from politicians – an assumption that raises all sorts of questions to which no clear answers have emerged at the time of writing. How 'official' was the approach from the south? Were ministers implicated, and if so, which? How much did Mr Lynch know at

* Mr Lynch's public stance, as enunciated in his speech of 12 August 1969, was that his government could no longer stand by (or 'idly by' in some versions) and see innocent people injured 'or perhaps worse'. The use of British troops in the north was not acceptable 'certainly not in the long term'. He announced the establishment of Irish Army field hospitals along the border and called for the dispatch of a United Nations peace-keeping force to Northern Ireland. He also added this pregnant sentence: 'Recognising, however, that the re-unification of the national territory can provide the only permanent solution of the problem, it is our intention to request the British Government to enter into early negotiations with the Irish Government to review the present constitutional position of the Six Counties of Northern Ireland.'

the time of what was going on? And if these negotiations had a political motivation, was this no more than a simple desire to help, or was it rather a Machiavellian scheme to allow the IRA in the north to bear the brunt of the fighting, to split the organisation in two and thus ease the task of government in the south?

Set out thus starkly the questions seem to raise so many embarrassing issues that it is not in the least surprising that no-one has yet been able to give a satisfactory reply to any of them. But one or two details have since emerged which throw a wavering light on an admittedly confused and murky scene. It is known, for example, that an officer of the Irish Army, Captain James Kelly, was, in the course of duty, in regular contact with the northern IRA leaders before and after the 1969 disturbances and that he kept his superiors informed of their needs and their attitudes. It is also known – in fact a matter of public record – that the government set aside £100,000 for the relief of suffering and distress in the north. It would appear, further, that a training scheme for northern Catholics was to be instituted under cover of their being sworn into the Local Defence Force (the Irish equivalent of the Territorial Army). That particular scheme, it would appear, had been launched without Mr Lynch's knowledge and, on learning of it, he halted it at once. The destination and function of the money voted for relief is, however, a more obscure subject and up to the time of writing it is impossible to be sure how much reached the northern Catholics by various routes and how precisely they spent whatever did succeed in reaching them.*

More important than such speculations is the fact – and it at least does seem to be a fact – that the northern IRA leaders were convinced that the south was on their side and that help of one kind or another was

* The Dublin Arms Trials of September and October 1970 (see p. 587 above) threw only a few fugitive gleams of light on these obscure matters. In December 1970 the Dáil ordered that the Committee of Public Accounts should examine the Grant-in-Aid for Northern Ireland Relief (which the Dáil had accepted without debate in the supplementary estimates of March 1970) but it was not until August 1972 that the Committee of Public Accounts was in a position to report. Its investigation had been severely hampered by the absence of certain key documents and by the refusal of various witnesses to co-operate; legal action to compel the appearance of certain individuals was ruled unconstitutional by the Supreme Court. Nevertheless, the Committee found that of £110,000 intended to be spent on Northern Ireland Relief (consisting of the Dáil grant of £100,000 together with additional payments from elsewhere), just under £30,000 could be identified as having been so spent. A further sum of almost £35,000 was possibly spent in Belfast on undetermined purposes, but there still remained £41,000 which was *not* spent on relief. Another way of putting this is that a total of just over £76,500 was unaccounted for, though it appeared that there had been withdrawn from this part of the fund an amount totalling £32,000 which was used for the arms purchases that precipitated the 1970 trials. For text of the Committee's report, see *Irish Times*, 23 Aug. 1972.

771

about to reach them. Conscious of sympathy, expectant of aid, their desire to form a separate command could no longer be withstood, though the actual break did not come until an IRA conference in Dublin during November 1969 delivered the final insult by agreeing to recognise *de facto* the two Irish governments and the Westminster parliament. It was significant that this conference was boycotted by the Belfast dissidents; even more significant for the future was that one of the leading Dublin officers, John Stephenson – or Sean Mac Stiofáin as he preferred to be called – walked out of the conference with some of his colleagues announcing the establishment of the 'Provisional Army Council', dedicated to the traditional fight for the traditional goal of the thirty-two county Republic. When, shortly afterwards, the political wing of the movement, Sinn Féin, also split in two – with Rory O'Brady as head of the 'Provisional Sinn Féin' – the fissure in the movement was now complete. North and south, 'Officials' and 'Provisionals' faced each other in an uneasy hostility which sometimes seemed hardly less than that with which both regarded their hereditary foes, the Unionists.[14]

These complicated transactions partly explain the relative calm of Northern Ireland during the winter of 1969-70. But it was an illusory calm which was soon to be broken when the dreaded 'marching season' began again. Punctually, as if on cue, Easter provided the first premonitions of what was to come. Sporadic scuffles between Protestants and Catholics found the soldiers, as in 1969, interposed between the rival mobs. But this time there was a difference. The stones and bottles began to come from the Catholic side – the Catholics were resentful of the Army's show of force *inside* a Catholic area – and the military retorted with CS gas. This did not provoke an IRA intervention – the Provisionals were still only a handful at that stage, but it has its own historical significance in that it registered the first clash between the Catholics and the Army they had welcomed with open arms the year before. From the distrust implanted on this occasion the Provisionals were to reap a formidable harvest in the future.

April, as so often, was merely a dress-rehearsal for the summer. Just conceivably, trouble might have been avoided if the traditional Orange parades had been banned. But this presupposes that the Orangemen would have obeyed the ban which was by no means certain. It also presupposes that it would have been politically possible for Major Chichester-Clark to impose the ban and to remain Prime Minister; this was, if anything, still more doubtful. By an unfortunate coincidence pressure which might have been applied from London in favour of defusing the situation was not forthcoming for the simple but sufficient reason that the transfer of power from Labour to Conservatives left the latter with no time to get their bearings. So, when the usual provocative marches produced the usual response and the shooting began in east and west Belfast, the Army was hopelessly overstretched and quite unable to prevent the serious riots which then developed. But worse was to come. Following a successful search for arms in the Falls Road area on July 3 the troops were stoned by indignant Catholics and only extricated themselves with difficulty. Later that evening they went in again in an attempt to bring the district under control and came under fire from the IRA. They returned the fire, and used CS gas; to prevent large-scale bloodshed the Army Commander, General Freeland, imposed a thirty-five hour curfew. During that curfew a house-to-house search for arms was carried out. Some were found, but the political price paid for them was enormous. The inhabitants of the Falls Road saw the troops as invaders and no longer as protectors.* They drew their own conclusions and IRA recruiting, particularly into the Provisionals, went up so fast that their strength increased from about a hundred in the early summer to nearly 800 by the end of the year.[15]

It was hardly surprising, therefore, that friction should have persisted or that a fresh outburst of rioting should soon have occurred. What *was* new, and ominous, was that it should have begun in the New Year of 1971, outside the usual 'season'. On the Catholic side this was evidence both of increasing hostility towards the Army and of a more generalised frustration. But to Unionists it betokened gross ingratitude for the reforms already passed and this in turn strengthened the determination of the right wing – always buoyant and vocal in the rare intervals of calm – that there should be no more pandering to the minority. It was understandable that each side should feel a sense of grievance. The Unionists could point to a whole series of enactments and while these had, as it seemed to them, dismantled a large part of their ascendancy, the violence in the streets showed no sign of ceasing It was certainly true that since the resignation of Captain O'Neill much indeed had changed. The police had been disarmed and civilianised (though they had not been able to resume patrolling in the Catholic ghettoes); an Ombudsman had been established to investigate grievances against the central government and a similar official appointed to do the same in local affairs; electoral changes had brought the franchise at last into line with that of Britain; a points system related to need had been adopted for the allocation of houses (a Housing Executive Act to carry this policy still further became law at the end of February); a Ministry of Community Relations had been created and a Community Relations Commission set in motion. On the other hand, these changes

* This disenchantment was undoubtedly hastened by the Criminal Justice (Temporary Provisions) Act which the Northern Ireland government rushed through Stormont at the end of June 1970. This made mandatory a sentence of six months' imprisonment for anyone convicted of 'riotous behaviour', 'disorderly behaviour', or 'behaviour likely to cause a breach of the peace'. Upon the Army fell the brunt of the arrests to be made under the act and since these were very numerous during the six months before the Act was partially repealed in December, this further worsened the relations of the troops with the civilian population and especially the Catholics, by whom the new measure came to be regarded as almost as objectionable as the Special Powers Act itself.

took time to implement and there were other areas where there had been little or no movement – for example, in the appointment of a public prosecutor distinct from the police, the introduction of anti-discrimination clauses into government contracts and, of course, the notorious Special Powers Act itself. Consequently, the Catholic community, impatient at the lack of visible progress and deeply confused about the direction in which it ought to be going, inclined more and more to the view that reforms handed down from on high in response to the threat or the actuality of violence were in themselves an insufficient substitute for the recognition they sought of their right to play their part as full and equal citizens in the life of the province.*

But as the disturbances continued Unionist thoughts ran not unnaturally upon the suppression of violence rather than upon the extension of concessions. The Prime Minister appealed repeatedly to London for more troops and firmer action from those already on the ground. For a time he got neither and there are indications that early in 1971 the Army and the Provisionals were precariously co-operating in an effort to keep the ghetto mobs under control.[16] But this could scarcely be expected to last – for the Provisionals, who were bound by their history to regard the British as an army of occupation, it can never have been more than a temporary, tactical expedient – and, in fact, at the beginning of Februry, an Army search in a Catholic area brought on renewed fighting which resulted in the death of the first soldier since the troops had intervened the previous August. Thereafter the situation worsened rapidly, reaching a pitch of horror then unprecedented (but later often to be equalled, if not surpassed) in the cold-blooded murder of three Scottish soldiers on the outskirts of Belfast. Major Chichester-Clark flew to London to seek further reinforcements. He got some, but by no means all he reckoned he needed. Worse, he failed to convince the British government of the urgency of the situation and on 20 March, to underline that urgency, he resigned.

His logical, almost inevitable, successor was Mr Faulkner who, despite his earlier criticisms of the reformist tendencies of Captain O'Neill, had himself been actively concerned in implementing the reforms introduced by the Chichester-Clark régime. At first it seemed as if he would continue on this course and in June he offered not only to create three new committees at Stormont, to consider and advise on government policy in regard to the social services, industrial development and environmental matters, but also to entrust the chairmanship of at least two of these committees to opposition MPs.[17] It is true that

* Later in 1971 the government published details of its performance, *A Record of Constructive Change* (Cmd. 558), August 1971. It is however symptomatic of the general deterioration in the situation by then that some of the most pungent criticism of that document should have come not from IRA militants but from Catholic moderates in a pamphlet, *Commentary upon the White Paper entitled A Record of Constructive Change*, Sept. 1971. It should be noted, however, that this publication followed hard on the heels of internment.

the committees were to be devoid of executive or legislative powers, and also that they would have permanent Unionist majorities, since membership was to be proportional to existing party strength at Stormont, but this should not detract from the importance of the gesture, particularly since it was made at a time when all the indications were that the Provisionals had abandoned the tactic of gun-battles with the Army in favour of a massive campaign of bombing which, producing as it did 37 explosions in April, 47 in May and 50 in June was calculated to exacerbate Unionist opinion still further.

The first impulse of the leading opposition party was, if not to grasp the olive-branch, at least to examine it closely and not unsympathetically. This in itself was a major development since that party, the Social and Democratic Labour Party, represented most sections of what might reasonably be called moderate and Catholic opinion. It had only been formed the previous August and it brought together six members of the Northern Ireland House of Commons and one Senator. Its leader was Mr Gerry Fitt (Republican Labour) who sat at Westminster as well as at Stormont, and the remaining five Stormont MPs included John Hume and Ivan Cooper (Independents), Austin Currie (Nationalist), Patrick O'Hanlon (Independent Nationalist) and Paddy Devlin (Northern Ireland Labour Party). The policies of the new party were stated at the outset to be based on 'radical left of centre principles' and its first public statement certainly laid much emphasis on the redistribution of wealth. But in the circumstances of the time it was inevitable that the question most people asked was where it stood on the fundamental question of the future of Northern Ireland. It expressed itself as avowedly non-sectarian, but since at the time it announced its intention 'to promote co-operation, friendship and understanding between north and south with a view to the eventual reunification of Ireland through the consent of the majority of the people in the North and in the South', its chances of making any immediate appeal to northern Protestants did not seem bright [18]

Although it was difficult at first to determine whether the new party was a vehicle for reform or merely a tessellated pavement without cement, it embraced such a diversity of talent and outlook (as well as of temperament) that it was clearly a great potential source of constructive effort. It was therefore a major tragedy that within days of Mr Faulkner's initiative in June 1971, the cautiously approving reception the SDLP gave to the committee scheme should have vanished in the face of further catastrophe on the streets. This time it was in Londonderry where the Army had been under strain for many weeks and where eventually, as was almost bound to happen, two men were shot dead whom the Army judged to be gunmen but whom local opinion passionately insisted were harmless civilians. A hurriedly assembled meeting of such of the SDLP as were available was summoned by Mr Hume – in the absence of the party leader, Mr Fitt – and this meeting approved an ultimatum to the British government, demanding an independent inquiry into the two deaths within a matter of days, 'failing which the SDLP would leave Stormont and set up an alternative parliament.' The British government, not unnaturally, refused to accept this ultimatum and though it appears that Mr Fitt risked the wrath of his more impulsive colleagues by seeking some compromise solution in London this proved impossible and on 16 July he had no option but to announce his party's withdrawal from Stormont the previous day.[19]

This decision by the SDLP marked a further serious deterioration in the general situation. At one stroke Stormont was deprived of the steadying influence of a constitutional opposition and that constitutional opposition itself, in its anxiety not to be outbid from the left, had ended by creating a vacuum that was soon to be filled by what was to all intents and purposes a large-scale conflict between the Army and the Provisionals. Incidents, and deaths multiplied so rapidly that the government, apparently believing a major assault to be imminent, resolved at last to use the weapon which right-wing Unionists had long insisted should be brought into play. In the early hours of 9 August the machinery of internment was set in motion and by the evening of that day nearly 350 people had been arrested and lodged in three detention centres. The operation, however, appears to have been mishandled. The key figures among the Provisionals escaped arrest and the months after the crucial decision to intern had been taken witnessed a crescendo of violence. In the seven months before internment ten soldiers were killed, two policemen and fifteen civilians. In the four months after internment, thirty-two soldiers were killed, nine policemen, ninety-eight civilians, and five members of the Ulster Defence Regiment which had been formed to take over some of the duties of the defunct 'B' specials.[20]

Against this horrendous background has to be placed a political fact of the first magnitude – the total alienation of the Catholic community (or a very large part of it) from the regime. The very fact that internment appeared to operate almost entirely, if not wholly, against Catholics (up to December 1,576 arrests had been made though nearly 1000 of these were released by the end of the year) would in itself have created a wave of indignation. But when to the facts about internment were added rumours, and later well-authenticated stories, about the ill-treatment of the internees when undergoing interrogation by the Army, the fury of the Catholic minority knew no limits, with the natural result that moderates were increasingly driven into the arms of the IRA.* The government, on the other hand, seemed to have miscal-

* The persistent critical reports of Army methods during the arrest and detention of internees led the British government on 31 August to appoint a committee of inquiry headed by Sir Edmund Compton, the Ombudsman for Britain and for Northern Ireland. Despite the fact that it operated under such severe difficulties that its report was in various ways unsatisfactory the committee did adduce sufficient evidence of ill-treatment under 'deep interrogation' as to cause the government to order the methods used by the Army to be modified forthwith. These criticisms,

culated, perhaps because Mr Faulkner put too much reliance on the false analogy of previous experience. Internment could not work in 1971 as it had worked a dozen years earlier, partly because there was no corresponding will in the south to proceed simultaneously against the IRA, partly because the new IRA were urban guerrillas fighting in streets where they had overwhelming advantage of local knowledge, and most of all because the Catholic population, previously inert, had in the past two years been wrought to such a high pitch of anger and frustration that for the time being at least it was willing to provide the safe cover which the guerrillas needed. Not until nearly a year after internment did ground support for the IRA begin to waver in face of the ferocity and indiscriminateness of the Provisionals' bombing campaign, but even then Catholic opinion remained, and remains, extremely volatile, liable to desert the middle ground at the slightest indication of military toughness or Protestant backlash.

As the months passed without any sign of a way out of the vicious circle of outrage and arrest the province moved steadily closer to anarchy. Whatever faint hope there may once have been of bridging the gulf between the two communities vanished in the angry aftermath of internment. Catholics boycotted not only Stormont but also local councils and other bodies. The dissident MPs set up their own assembly at Dungiven which, though apparently not much more than a talking-shop, awakened uneasy echoes of the establishment of Dáil Eireann in 1919. Ordinary citizens, perhaps 20,000 of them, participated in a campaign of disobedience by withholding their rents and rates. Against this evidence of massive estrangement Unionists could only point indignantly to the reforms already conceded and demand, still more indignantly, that law and order be restored. But while the Army battled with the IRA on the streets Mr Faulkner moved cautiously towards a further instalment of change. In October he published proposals for proportional representation and for a larger House of Commons and Senate at Stormont. He also appointed to a cabinet post Dr Gerard Newe, the first Catholic to hold such a post in the fifty year history of the state. But the effect of both these gestures was somewhat blunted by the fact that, in putting forward his suggestions, Mr Faulkner made it absolutely clear that his administration was still committed to the maintenance of Northern Ireland as an integral part of the United Kingdom and also that it regarded as 'fundamentally unrealistic' the idea of a 'mixed' government of Catholics and Protestants which was being much touted at that time.[21]

however, should be seen in the context of the claim repeatedly made by the British authorities that the Army's discipline and morale remained high and that, considering the provocation under which it was operating, its restraint was most of the time remarkable. The crucial objection to its actions ought, one feels, to be based on the fact that it was constantly being used for duties for which it was not really fitted.

Although these initiatives were a world away from the Unionist stance of only three years previously they were already outmoded at the moment when Mr Faulkner made them. He was in fact imprisoned in a dilemma from which there seemed no possible escape. On the one hand, partial concessions were regarded as irrelevant by extremists who wanted only the end of Stormont and the reunification of Ireland and, although his new proposals might at one time have appealed to moderate Catholics, it was doubtful if this was any longer the case, while the possibility of discussing the matter with their representatives, the SDLP, was inhibited by the latter's unbending insistence that internment must be ended before they could come to any conference-table. On the other hand, Mr Faulkner could not but be aware of a rising tide of Unionist bitterness and resentment. This made the abolition of internment unthinkable – though there is no evidence to indicate that Mr Faulkner was thinking of it – and it also put a large question-mark opposite the future of any Prime Minister who jeopardised the Unionist position by going further along the road of reform. This, indeed, was the real core of the dilemma. Given that the state had been built around the concept of Protestant ascendancy, to dismantle that ascendancy piece-meal, however severe the pressure to do so, was to weaken the credibility of the whole regime and to weaken it, not merely in the eyes of its declared enemies, but in those of its supposed friends – the Conservative government in Britain – who in the last resort carried the responsibility for propping it up.

There were in fact indications, as well as many rumours, that in both main British parties the belief was growing that Stormont was becoming too costly a luxury. For the Opposition, Mr Wilson, in September and again in November, made detailed proposals for modifying the structure of Northern Ireland government very substantially, and there were persistent stories – one of which was given currency by Mr Paisley, and another of which emanated from a highly responsible journalist, Mr James Downey, London editor of the *Irish Times* – that direct rule was on the way. The British government hesitated, however, perhaps because the nettle was so difficult to grasp, probably also because of the pressure of other events. But while they hesitated the situation in Northern Ireland deteriorated still further. On January 30, despite an official prohibition, a Civil Rights march took place in Londonderry. The authorities decided not only to contain it within the Bogside but also to combine this with one of the 'snatching', or arresting operations they mounted from time to time. The troops employed were from the Parachute Regiment and when, on going in among the crowd they came under fire – or believed they came under fire – they retaliated, with the result that thirteen civilians were shot dead and others wounded. An inquiry under Lord Widgery was at once set up. His tribunal was faced with the usual difficulty of obtaining reliable evidence and his report, like other investigations into earlier disasters, was predictably written off by the opponents of the regime as just one more exercise in whitewashing. He found that the troops had in fact been fired on *before* they fired back, but he also found – and it was on this that the Catholic community naturally fastened – that 'none of the deceased or wounded is proved to have been shot whilst handling a firearm or bomb' though there was a strong suspicion that some of them had been so engaged in the course of the afternoon.[22]

This deplorable affair was at once recognised on all sides to be a major catastrophe and many consequences, direct or indirect, were to flow from it. One of the most direct was the burning of the British Embassy in Dublin on 2 February in the presence of a huge crowd which, though probably manipulated by the IRA, was animated by a hatred and revulsion which to some observers recalled the mood which had spread through Dublin in the aftermath of the executions of 1916. This passion subsided rather sooner than might have been expected but it contributed to a marked worsening of Anglo-Irish relations at a critical moment. In Northern Ireland itself 'Bloody Sunday', as it was almost immediately called, had the predictable effect of polarising the conflict still further. Although another Civil Rights march in Newry the following Sunday passed off peacefully, the tempo of violence increased. This in turn stimulated the Protestants into activity and led directly to the formation of the Vanguard movement in February 1972. This, which had been foreshadowed since the previous autumn, was intended as a kind of 'umbrella' under which might shelter a variety of militant Unionist organisations.* It was pledged to maintain the constitution, but it was widely believed that, if pushed to the brink, it would not stop short of unilateral independence. Led by Mr William Craig, its real strength lay in the support it received from Protestant workers, whose organisation, the Loyalist Association of Workers, had it in its power to disrupt the entire life of the province if it so chose.[23]

Although the extremism of Vanguard was no doubt the obverse of the extremism of the IRA, it owed something also to a well-founded suspicion that Mr Faulkner was running out of time. Indeed, he was also running out of support. The previous autumn Mr Paisley and Mr Desmond Boal had formed their own Democratic Unionist party and soon constituted themselves an effective opposition party. And in February 1972 a former minister, Mr Phelim O'Neill, left the Unionist party and, with two other MPs, joined the moderate, non-sectarian Alliance Party which, though formed as far back as 1970, had hitherto lacked representation in Stormont. All these signs and portents, together with the manifest inability of the Northern Ireland government to restore peace to the province, led inexorably to the decision announced by Mr Heath on 24 March to suspend Stormont and to institute direct rule from Westminster. True, this decision was accompanied by

* Subsequently, the role of 'umbrella' was taken over by the Ulster Loyalist Council, on which were represented all the leading militant organisations, including what is probably the most effective striking force of all, the Ulster Defence Association, allegedly 50,000 strong.

the promise of periodic plebiscites on the border issue and by a pledge to 'phase out' internment, but nothing could disguise the brute fact that the British government had at last recognised the necessity of itself taking responsibility for law and order and in doing so had drawn the further conclusion that to 'suspend' Stormont for a year would give the best opportunity for a new initiative towards a permanent settlement. Responsibility was therefore entrusted to a member of the British government and Mr William Whitelaw, as Secretary of State for Northern Ireland, stepped into the vacuum left by the ending of the fifty years' experiment in devolution.

It is at that point that this brief survey must cease, for the situation created by direct rule is still evolving and remains so unstable that no assessment of its effects can yet be attempted. It is sufficient to point out that direct rule itself cannot be – nor was it intended to be – a solution. Its purpose was to secure a breathing-space so that a fresh approach to a solution might be made. But this has always depended upon the British government's ability to contain and suppress violence – Protestant no less than Catholic – and to bring the conflicting parties to the conference-table. The first attempt to achieve the latter aim – the Darlington Conference of September 1972 – was little more than a travesty since it was boycotted both by the SDLP and by Mr Paisley's Democratic Unionist party. And although on all sides Mr Whitelaw's next step, the issuing of a 'Green Paper' surveying the possible forms a new regional administration might take, is awaited with painful expectancy, the very fact that two of his most cherished expedients – the holding of local government elections under the reformed franchise and of a referendum on the border issue – are, at the time of writing, shrouded in uncertainty, indicates the extreme difficulty he is encountering in undertaking any constructive policy whatever. Meanwhile violence has continued unabated and by the autumn of 1972 the total of deaths in Northern Ireland resulting from the troubles has passed the appalling figure of 600. The continuing hostility between the troops and the Provisionals has begun to be matched by a corresponding hostility between the troops and the striking-force of Protestant militancy, the Ulster Defence Association, and it is hardly surprising that in Britain there should have begun to emerge a movement of opinion in favour of withdrawing the Army whatever the cost might be. So the historian can only draw his bleak tale to a close by recording that the fate of the province is still, as it has been for so long, poised on a knife-edge between a slow climb back to some form of ordered existence, or a swift plunge into unimaginable anarchy and civil war.

Notes

Part I

1. CHANGING THE QUESTION? (pp. 15-33)

1 R. Dudley Edwards and T. Desmond Williams (ed.), *The Great Famine* (Dublin, 1956), p. 1.
2 Arnold Schrier, *Ireland and the American Emigration, 1850-1900* (Minneapolis, 1958), especially chap. i and appendix table 4.
3 See the admirable study by D. W. Harkness, *The Restless Dominion* (London, 1968) which deals mainly with the decade after the Treaty. For Ireland as a factor in Anglo-American relations, see A. J. Ward, *Ireland and Anglo-American Relations, 1899-1921* (London, 1969).
4 For the size of the various denominations see *Census of Ireland, 1911*, General Report, pp. xlvi-vii.
5 J. C. Beckett, *The Making of Modern Ireland* (London, 1966), p. 285.
6 E. Larkin, 'Economic Growth, Capital Investment and the Roman Catholic Church in Nineteenth Century Ireland', in *American Historical Review* (Apr. 1967), lxxii, pp. 856-8.
7 Ibid., pp. 864-5.
8 Cited in E. R. Norman, *The Catholic Church and Ireland in the Age of Rebellion* (London, 1965), pp. 18-19.
9 On this general theme, see J. H. Whyte, 'Revolution and Religion', in F. X. Martin (ed.), *Leaders and Men of the Easter Rising: Dublin, 1916* (London, 1967), pp. 215-26; also R. McHugh, 'The Catholic Church and the Rising', in O. Dudley Edwards and F. Pyle (ed.), *1916: The Easter Rising* (London, 1968), pp. 196-201. Dr Whyte estimates that whereas one bishop, Dr O'Dwyer of Limerick, in effect condoned the Rising, seven published emphatic condemnations and one a somewhat equivocal condemnation. No less than twenty-three, however, remained silent.
10 *Census of Ireland, 1911*, pp. xlvii-viii; M. O'Riordan, *Catholicity and Progress in Ireland* (Dublin, 1906), pp. 315-16.
11 For these developments see J. C. Beckett, 'Ulster Protestantism', in T. W. Moody and J. C. Beckett (ed.), *Ulster Since 1800: A Social Survey*, pp. 159-69.

2. THE ECONOMIC ENVIRONMENT (pp. 34-70)

1 For a recent discussion of these developments see R. D. Crotty, *Irish Agricultural Production: Its Volume and Structure* (Cork, 1966), chap. i. For Irish agricultural exports in the eighteenth century see Tables 2 and 3 on pp. 19-20 of his book.
2 See especially, R. N. Salaman, *The History and Social Influence of the Potato* (Cambridge, 1949) and K. H. Connell, *The Population of Ireland,*

1750-1845 (Oxford, 1950). For a criticism of Professor Connell's seminal work, see M. Drake, 'Marriage and Population Growth in Ireland', in *Economic History Review*, second series (1963), xvi, 301-13.

3 R. D. Crotty, *Irish Agricultural Production*, Appendix Note II, pp. 294-307, examines pre-Famine rents in detail, and suggests that landlords' rents may have quadrupled between 1760 and 1815. For the function of the potato in eighteenth century Ireland, see M. Drake, 'The Irish Demographic Crisis of 1740-41', in T. W. Moody (ed.), *Historical Studies* (London, 1968), vi, 101-24.

4 K. H. Connell, *The Population of Ireland*, especially chap. iii, but Professor Connell's views have been to some extent modified since he wrote his book.

5 R. D. Crotty, op. cit., p. 32.

6 Ibid., p. 35.

7 Ibid., pp. 38-9. See also M. Drake, op. cit., pp. 312-13.

8 R. D. Crotty, op. cit., p. 39; also K. H. Connell, *The Population of Ireland*, pp. 27-9. See also the criticisms of Joseph Lee, reviewing Mr Crotty's book in *Agricultural History Review* (1969), xvii, part 1, pp. 64-76.

9 R. N. Salaman, *The History and Social Influence of the Potato*, pp. 603-8.

10 R. D. Crotty, op. cit., and sources quoted, p. 40.

11 E. R. R. Green, 'Agriculture', in R. Dudley Edwards and T. Desmond Williams, *The Great Famine* (Dublin, 1956), p. 99; K. H. Connell, 'The Colonization of Waste Land in Ireland, 1780-1845', in *Econ. Hist Rev.*, 2nd series (1950), iii, 44-7; J. Lee, 'Irish Agriculture', in *Agricultural History Review* (1969), xvii, part 1, pp. 64-76.

12 For analyses (sometimes differing in detail) of the division of holdings see K. H. Connell, 'Marriage in Ireland after the Famine: the Diffusion of the Match', in *JSSISI*, xix (1955-6), 82-103; E. R. R. Green, op. cit., p. 89; T. W. Freeman, *Pre-Famine Ireland* (London, 1957), pp. 54-8.

13 L. M. Cullen, *An Economic History of Ireland since 1660* (London, 1972), pp. 114-15.

14 *Return of Evictions Known to the Constabulary in Each Year from 1849 to 1880*, P.P. (1881), lxxvii, 725. For the administrative problems presented by the Famine, see T. P. O'Neill, 'The Administration of Relief', in Edwards and Williams (ed.), *The Great Famine*, pp. 207-59.

15 Cited by O. MacDonagh, 'Emigration During the Famine', in Edwards and Williams, op. cit., p. 321.

16 Ibid., pp. 324-9.

17 S. H. Cousens, 'Emigration and Demographic Change in Ireland, 1851-61', in *Economic History Review*, 2nd series (1961-2), xiv, 275-88.

18 *Report of the commission on emigration and other population problems, 1948-54* (Dublin, 1954), Pr. 2541. See especially chap. vii.

19 Ibid., p. 63.

20 Ibid., pp. 73-8.

21 K. H. Connell, 'Catholicism and Marriage in the Century after the Famine', in *Irish Peasant Society* (London, 1968), p. 113.

22 *Report of Emigration Commission*, chap. v.

23 Ibid., chap. vi. As late as the 1940s the figure for the twenty-six counties was sixty-six per thousand.

24 Ibid., pp 9-13.

25 R. D. Crotty, *Irish Agricultural Production*, pp. 351, 353; P. M. A. Bourke, 'The Agricultural Statistics of the 1841 Census of Ireland: A Critical

Review', in *Econ. Hist. Rev.*, 2nd series (1965), xviii, 376-91.

26 L. M. Cullen, *An Economic History of Ireland since 1660*, pp. 138-40, 150-51; B. Solow, *The Land Question and the Irish Economy, 1870-1903* (Cambridge, Mass., and London, 1972), pp. 72-4.

27 The price statistics in this and the succeeding paragraph are based on Thomas Barrington, 'A Review of Irish Agricultural Prices', in *JSSISI* (1926-7), xv, 249-80.

28 For the export trade, see J. O'Donovan, *The Economic History of Livestock In Ireland* (Dublin and London, 1940), chap. xi; Crotty, op. cit., p. 72.

29 See T. Grimshaw, 'A Statistical Survey of Ireland from 1840 to 1888', in *JSSISI* (1889), ix, 321-61; W. P. Coyne (ed.), *Ireland: Industrial and Agricultural* (Dublin, 1901), pp. 191-2; P. M. A. Bourke, op. cit.

30 The point has been developed by K. H. Connell in three articles – 'Marriage in Ireland after the Famine: The Diffusion of the Match', in *JSSISI* (1955-6), xix, 82-103; 'Peasant Marriage in Ireland after the Great Famine', in *Past and Present* (1957), pp. 76-91; 'Peasant Marriage in Ireland: Its Structure and Development Since the Famine', in *Econ. Hist. Rev.* (1961-2), 2nd series, xiv, 502-23.

31 W. P. Coyne (ed.), *Ireland Industrial and Agricultural*, pp. 60-1; *Census of Ireland for the Year 1911: General Report*, H.C. (Cd. 5691), 1911, pp. 10, 15.

32 R. E. Matheson, 'The Housing of the People of Ireland, during 1841-1901', in *JSSISI* (1904), xi, 196-213; N. J. Synnott, 'Housing of the Rural Population in Ireland,' in *JSSISI* (1904), ix, 215-301.

33 For the two economies, see especially, P. Lynch and J. Vaizey, *Guinness's Brewery in the Irish Economy, 1759-1876* (Cambridge, 1960), chap. i; also E. Larkin, 'Economic Growth, Capital Investment and the Roman Catholic Church in Ireland', in *American Historical Review* (April, 1967), lxxii, 852-84.

34 The stages by which currency assimilation was achieved are well set out in the introduction to F. W. Fetter, *The Irish Pound, 1797-1826* (London, 1955).

35 W. P. Coyne (ed.), *Ireland: Industrial and Agricultural*, pp. 72-83; E. J. Riordan, *Modern Irish Trade and Industry*, chap. xiii; F. G. Hall, *History of the Bank of Ireland* (Dublin and Oxford, 1949), pp. 172-86; K. Milne, *A History of the Royal Bank of Ireland* (Dublin, 1964), chaps. iii and iv.

36 Cited by E. R. R. Green, 'Early Industrial Belfast', in J. C. Beckett and R. E. Glasscock (ed.), *Belfast* (London, 1967), p. 85. For these developments see also the same author's articles 'The Beginnings of Industrial Revolution', and 'Business Organization and the Business Class', T. W. Moody (ed.), *Ulster Since 1800*, vols i and ii (London, 1954 and 1957). The growth of the city of Belfast is best followed in E. Jones, *A Social Geography of Belfast*, part ii (London, 1960).

37 W. E. Coe, *The Engineering Industry of the North of Ireland* (Newton Abbot 1969), chap. v.

38 E. J. Riordan, *Modern Irish Trade and Industry*, p. 111. See also D. L. Armstrong, 'Social and Economic Conditions in the Belfast Linen Industry, 1850-1900', in *IHS* (1950-51), vii, 235-69.

39 *Final Report of the First Census of Production of the United Kingdom* (1907), P.P. [Cd. 6320] 1912, pp. 352-7. The figures given in E. Riordan, op. cit., pp. 112-13 are in some instances wrongly transcribed.

40 E. J. Riordan, op. cit., pp. 122-3, L. M. Cullen, op. cit., p. 160.
41 *Census of Production* (1907), p. 346.
42 E. J. Riordan, op. cit., p. 126; *Census of Production* (1907), p. 346.
43 For the history of shipbuilding in Belfast, see C. H. Oldham, 'The History of Belfast Shipbuilding', in *JSSISI*, xii, 417-43; E. J. Riordan, *Modern Irish Trade and Industry*, pp. 227-36; E. Jones, *A Social Geography of Belfast*, pp. 46-50; J. C. Beckett and R. E. Glasscock (ed.), *Belfast*, chaps. vii-x. Most modern accounts of the genesis of nineteenth century shipbuilding lean heavily on the unpublished doctoral thesis of a former managing director of Harland and Wolff, D. Rebbeck, 'The History of Iron Shipbuilding on the Queen's Island up to July, 1874', completed 1950.
44 *Census of Production* (1907), p. 19.
45 E. J. Riordan, op. cit., pp. 92-4.
46 P. Lynch and J. Vaizey, *Guinness's Brewery in the Irish Economy, 1759-1876*, p. 260; E. J. Riordan, op. cit., pp. 156-7.
47 *Census of Production* (1907), p. 524.
48 Ibid., pp. 527-8; E. J. Riordan, op. cit., pp. 160-4.
49 Scattered evidence of wage-rates is to be found in E. J. Riordan, *Modern Irish Trade and Industry*, pp. 46-7; J. W. Boyle, 'Industrial Conditions in the Twentieth Century', in T. W. Moody and J. C. Beckett (ed.), *Ulster Since 1800* (second series), pp. 130-1; D. L. Armstrong, 'Social and Economic Conditions in the Belfast Linen Industry, 1850-1960', in *IHS* (Sept. 1951), vii, 263-7; P. Lynch and John Vaizey, *Guinness's Brewery in the Irish Economy, 1759-1876*, p. 146; E. Larkin, *James Larkin, 1876-1947*, pp. 45-6; L. M. Cullen, *Life in Ireland*, pp. 167-8; W. E. Coe, *The Engineering Industry of the North of Ireland*, pp. 177-8.
50 *Census of Production* (1907), p. 19.
51 A. W. Semmels, 'The External Commerce of Ireland', in *JSSISI* (1909), xii, 193-218. Slightly different figures (but pointing towards the same conclusion) are given in E. J. Riordan, op. cit., p. 228.
52 C. H. Oldham, 'Economics of Industrial Revival in Ireland', in *JSSISI* (1909), xii, 175-89. See also his two articles, 'Changes in Irish Exports During Twelve Years', and 'Changes in Irish Exports', both in *JSSISI* (1919), xiii, 541-53 and 629-37.

3. GOVERNMENT AND SOCIETY (pp. 71-103)

1 Cited in R. B. McDowell, *The Irish Administration* (London, 1964), p. 51.
2 For an excellent outline of the Irish departmental system see R. B. McDowell, op. cit., chap. i.
3 Ibid., p. 28. The official was Sir Algernon West Ridgeway, but at the time of his comment, 1889, the Irish government generally had been under several years of heavy strain.
4 The phrase was first used by W. L. Burn about the British readiness to uproot accepted notions of property when legislating about Irish land, but it has a much wider application. See his article, 'Free Trade in Land: An Aspect of the Irish Question', in *Transactions of the Royal Historical Society*, 4th Series, vol. xxxi. For the development of this idea in depth, see also O. MacDonagh, *Ireland*, chap. ii.

5 R. B. McDowell, op. cit., pp. 114-16; V. T. H. Delany, *The Administration of Justice in Ireland* (Dublin, 1965), p. 31.

6 R. B. McDowell, op. cit., pp. 135-45; see also R. Hawkins, 'Dublin Castle and the Royal Irish Constabulary, 1916-1922', in T. Desmond Williams (ed.), *The Irish Struggle, 1916-1926* (London, 1966), pp. 167-81.

7 R. B. McDowell, op. cit., chap. vi; see also B. Hensey, 'The *Health Services of Ireland* (Dublin, 1959), chap. i.

8 O. MacDonagh, *Ireland*, p. 27.

9 T. W. Grimshaw, 'A Statistical Survey of Ireland from 1840 to 1888', in *JSSISI* (1889), iv, 321-61.

10 *Census of Ireland, 1911*, p. lxiv.

11 For the working of the Local Government Board, see McDowell, op. cit., chap. vi.

12 Ibid., pp. 203-14.

13 G. Balfour, *The Educational Systems of England and Wales* (London, 1898), pp. 82-3; D. H. Akenson, *The Irish Education Experiment* (London, 1970), chaps. i and ii.

14 For these developments, see N. Atkinson, *Irish Education* (Dublin, 1969), chap. 5; also J. Murphy, 'Primary Education', in P. J. Corish (ed.), *A History of Irish Catholicism* (Dublin, 1971), vol. 5, fascicule vi, *Catholic Education*, pp. 5-47.

15 T. J. McElligott, *Education in Ireland* (Dublin, 1966), pp. 4-5.

16 G. Balfour, op. cit., pp. 91-2; R. B. McDowell, *The Irish Administration*, pp. 244-5.

17 T. J. McElligott, op. cit., p. 6.

18 Ibid., p. 7.

19 G. Balfour, op. cit., pp. 115-16; R. B. McDowell, op. cit., pp. 252-3; T. J. McElligott, op. cit., pp. 100-2.

20 G. Balfour, op. cit., pp. 112-13; *Census of Ireland, 1911*, pp. 84-5; T. J. McElligott, op. cit., pp. 13, 15-16.

21 P. H. Pearse, 'The Murder Machine', in *Political Writings and Speeches* (Dublin, n.d.), pp. 39-40.

22 G. Balfour, op. cit., p. 203.

23 Ibid., p. 204.

24 W. B. Kelly, *Intermediate and University Education in Ireland* (London and Dublin, 1872), *passim*; M. O'Riordan, *Catholicity and Progress in Ireland* (London, 1906), pp. 460-1.

25 *Census of Ireland, 1911*, p. 256, Table 133.

26 T. J. McElligott, *Education in Ireland*, p. 62.

27 For a very fair and thorough account of the development of the intermediate system, see S. V. O'Sulleabhain, 'Secondary Education', in P. J. Corish (ed.), op. cit., pp. 53-81.

28 For the history of the Catholic University, see *A Page of Irish History*, by the Jesuit Fathers (Dublin, 1930); F. McGrath, *Newman's University: Idea and Reality* (Dublin, 1951); M. Tierney (ed.), *Struggle with Fortune: A Miscellany for the Centenary of the Catholic University of Ireland, 1854-1954* (Dublin, n.d.); K. Sullivan, *Joyce among the Jesuits* (New York and London, 1957).

29 T. J. McElligott, *Education in Ireland*, p. 138.

30 These developments are well treated in F. McGrath, 'The University Question', in P. J. Corish (ed.), op. cit., pp. 84-142.

31 Ibid., p. 139.

32 *Census of Ireland, 1911*, p. liii; T. J. McElligott, op. cit., p. 140. The Census gives the figures for 1901 and 1911, but those for the latter year, which are nearly a thousand *lower*, are completely unreliable because of the failure of both Trinity College and University College, Dublin, to make any return.

33 T. W. Moody, 'The Irish University Question of the Nineteenth Century', in *History* (1958), xlii, 90-109. See also the detailed investigation of the whole subject in T. W. Moody and J. C. Beckett, *Queen's Belfast, 1845-1949: The History of a University* (London, 1959), 2 vols.

34 L. Paul-Dubois, *Contemporary Ireland* (Translated by T. M. Kettle, Dublin, 1908), p. 335.

35 For their numbers in Dublin, see E. Larkin, *James Larkin* (London, 1965), pp. 43-4.

4. VARIATIONS ON THE THEME OF NATIONALITY (pp. 104-38)

1 For this aspect of his career, see Angus Macintyre, *The Liberator* (London, 1965), *passim*.

2 The best recent account of Thomas Davis and of his relations with his friends is in T. W. Moody, 'Thomas Davis and the Irish Nation', in *Hermathena* (Dublin, 1966), ciii, 5-31. See also the valuable bibliography appended to this article.

3 These phrases are taken from the prospectus Davis himself wrote for the new paper; it is reprinted in *Thomas Davis: Essays and Poems, with a Centenary Memoir* (Dublin, 1945), p. 13.

4 For the extraordinary activity of the immediate post-Clontarf years, see R. Kee, *The Green Flag* (London, 1972), pp. 232-41.

5 For a summary of the problem see T. W. Moody, 'The Irish University Question of the Nineteenth Century', in *History*, xliii, 90-109. The matter is authoritatively discussed in a wider context by T. W. Moody and J. C. Beckett, *Queen's Belfast, 1845-1909: The History of a University* (London, 1959), i, 1-103.

6 L. Fogerty (ed.), *James Fintan Lalor: Patriot and Political Essayist, 1807-1849* (Dublin and London, 1918), p. 10.

7 Ibid., p. 21.

8 K. B. Nowlan, *The Politics of Repeal*, chap. viii.

9 Ibid., chap. x.

10 O. Dudley Edwards, 'Ireland', in O. Dudley Edwards, Gwynfor Evans, Joan Rhys, and Hugh MacDiarmid, *Celtic Nationalism* (London, 1968), p. 142.

11 P. H. Pearse, *Political Writings and Speeches* (Dublin, n.d.), 'The Sovereign People', p. 369.

12 L. Fogerty, op. cit., pp. 60-1.

13 O. Dudley Edwards, op. cit., p. 141.

14 *Return . . . of Cases of Evictions which have Come to the Knowledge of the Constabulary in Each of the Years from 1849 to 1880*, H.C. (1881) (185), lxxvii.

15 J. H. Whyte, *The Independent Irish Party, 1850-9* (London, 1958), pp. 5-6.

16 Ibid., pp. 7-8; see also B. Kennedy (ed.), 'Sharman Crawford on Ulster Tenant Right, 1846', in *IHS* (Mar. 1963), viii, 246-53.

17 C. Gavan Duffy, *The League of North and South* (London, 1886). Like all of Gavan Duffy's works, this history tends to exaggerate the importance of the part played by Gavan Duffy.

18 M. G. Moore, *An Irish Gentleman – George Henry Moore* (London, 1913).

19 J. H. Whyte, 'Political Problems, 1850-1860', in P. J. Corish (ed.), *A History of Irish Catholicism* (Dublin, 1967), vol. iii, fascicule 2, p. 23. See also the same author's *The Independent Irish Party*, chap. ix.

20 J. H. Whyte, *The Tenant League and Irish Politics in the Eighteen-Fifties* (Dundalk, 1966), p. 22.

21 For a reconstruction of his early career, see D. Ryan, *The Fenian Chief* (Dublin, 1967), chap. i.

22 See Michael Doheny, *The Felon's Track* (Dublin, 1914 ed., reprinted 1951).

23 For Luby's career see D. Ryan, 'James Stephens and Thomas Clarke Luby', in T. W. Moody (ed.), *The Fenian Movement* (Cork, 1968), pp. 49-61.

24 E. R. R. Green, 'The Beginnings of Fenianism', in T. W. Moody, op. cit., pp. 17-18; also D. Ryan, *The Fenian Chief*, chap. xiv. For the other side of the question see A. M. Sullivan's own account in *New Ireland* (London, 1877), chap. xvii. This work went through many editions and became almost the political testament of the new generation of constitutional nationalists.

25 E. R. R. Green, 'Charles Joseph Kickham and John O'Leary', in T. W. Moody, op. cit., pp. 77-88. See also the recent biography, *John O'Leary*, by Marcus Bourke (Tralee, 1968). The influence of O'Leary upon Yeats is manifest in the latter's *Autobiographies* (see especially pp. 209-13) and in much of the poetry he wrote between 1900 and 1913. O'Leary's own *Recollections of Fenians and Fenianism* (London, 1896) is a rambling and sadly disappointing mélange of frequently inaccurate recollections.

26 P. J. Corish, 'Political Problems, 1860-1878', in *A History of Irish Catholicism*, vol. v, fascicule iii, p. 7.

27 *Freeman's Journal*, 10 March 1867.

28 *Irish People*, 9 Apr. 1864. For the context of this article, see Donal Macartney, 'The Church and Fenianism', in *University Review* (Dublin, 1967), iv, 203-15. For more detailed investigation of the problem, see E. R. Norman, *The Catholic Church and Ireland in the Age of Rebellion, 1859-1873* (London, 1965), especially chap. iii; also P. J. Corish, op. cit.

29 See, for example, the kind of changes envisaged in the *Irish People*, 7 May 1864.

30 D. Macartney, op. cit., p. 208.

31 Ibid., p. 215.

32 The most interesting study of his career remains that by Desmond Ryan, *The Phoenix Flame* (London, 1937). Devoy's own *Recollections of an Irish Rebel* (New York, 1929), are, like the memoirs of most other Fenians, unreliable and much given to special pleading. These faults can, however, be corrected to some extent from his published correspondence; see D. Ryan and W. O'Brien (ed.), *Devoy's Post Bag, 1871-1928*, 2 vols. (Dublin, 1948 and 1953).

Part II

1. GENESIS OF HOME RULE (pp. 141-59)

1 For the context of this speech, see R. Blake, *Disraeli* (London, 1966), pp. 178-9.

2 J. L. Hammond, *Gladstone and the Irish Nation* (London, new impr. 1964), p. 51.

3 Ibid., p. 80.

4 E. R. Norman, *The Catholic Church and Irish Politics in the Eighteen-Sixties* (Dundalk, 1965), pp. 16-17. For an admirable but detailed treatment of the same theme see E. R. Norman, *The Catholic Church and Ireland in the Age of Rebellion, 1859-1873* (London, 1965), chap. vii.

5 E. R. Norman, *The Catholic Church and Ireland in the Age of Rebellion*, chap. viii; J. C. Beckett, 'Gladstone, Queen Victoria and the Disestablishment of the Irish Church, 1868-9', in *IHS*, xiii (Mar. 1962); J. C. Beckett, *The Making of Modern Ireland, 1603-1922* pp. 367-9; P. J. Corish, *A History of Irish Catholicism: Political Problems, 1860-78* (Dublin, 1967), vol. v, fascicule 3, pp. 23-36; P. M. H. Bell, *Disestablishment in Ireland and Wales* (London, 1967); H. Shearman, *How the Church of Ireland was Disestablished* (Dublin, 1970), a distillation of his important doctoral thesis (Trinity College, Dublin), 'The Economic Results of the Disestablishment of the Irish Church'; M. Hurley (ed.), *Irish Anglicanism, 1869-1969* (Dublin, 1970); D. H. Akenson, *The Church of Ireland: Ecclesiastical Reform and Revolution, 1800-1885* (New Haven and London, 1971).

6 H. Shearman, 'State-Aided Land Purchase under the Disestablishment Act of 1869', in *IHS*, iv (Mar. 1944), 58-80.

7 E. R. Norman, *The Catholic Church and Ireland in the Age of Rebellion*, p. 382.

8 The comparable Conservative figures were thirty-six from the landed interest, one from the professions and three from commerce. Neither party possessed a tenant-farmer representative. For details, see D. Thornley, *Isaac Butt and Home Rule* (London, 1964), chap. vi.

9 See the list in A. M. Sullivan, *New Ireland* (London, 16th ed., n.d.), pp. 339-41; it is somewhat amended in Thornley, op. cit., pp. 92-3.

10 For the growth of the movement, see L. J. McCaffrey, 'Irish Federalism in the 1870s: A Study in Conservative Nationalism', in *Transactions of the American Philosophical Society* (Philadelphia, 1962), new series, vol. lii, pp. 10-12 (cited hereafter as 'Irish Federalism').

11 D. Thornley, *Isaac Butt and Home Rule*, pp. 90-1.

12 Butt's own exposition of his ideas is still the best. See his pamphlet, of which the full title is: *Home Government for Ireland, Irish Federalism: Its Meaning, Its Objects and Its Hopes* (Dublin, 1870).

13 P. J. Corish, 'Political Problems, 1860-1878', pp. 55-7.

14 D. Thornley, *Isaac Butt and Home Rule*, p. 167.

15 Ibid., chap. v, for the political affiliations of the newly returned members. See also L. J. McCaffrey, 'Home Rule and the General Election of 1874', in *IHS* (Sept. 1954), ix, 190-212, and the same author's 'Irish Federalism

in the 1870s', pp. 16-21. Professor McCaffrey differs from Professor Thornley in allotting twelve seats to the Liberals instead of ten, and thirty-two to the Conservatives instead of thirty-three. In fact, the number of *individuals* elected in 1874 was 102; two boroughs (Cashel and Sligo) had been disfranchised and one member, Philip Callan, held two seats.

16 D. Thornley, *Isaac Butt and Home Rule*, chap. vi.

17 Ibid., p. 213.

18 For Parnell's early career see R. B. O'Brien, *The Life of Charles Stewart Parnell* (London, 3rd ed., 1899), i, chaps. ii and iii; also F. S. L. Lyons, *Parnell* (Dundalk, 1963), pp. 3-5. There is an interesting 'revisionist' essay by Michael Hurst, *Parnell and Irish Nationalism* (London, 1968), chaps. ii and iii.

2. LAND AND POLITICS (pp. 160-77)

1 Cited in T. N. Brown, *Irish-American Nationalism* (Philadelphia and New York, 1966), p. 24. Professor Brown's admirable study is essential to an understanding of the Irish-American contribution to the Irish cause and indeed lifts the whole discussion of this question onto a new plane.

2 For the 'New Departure', see T. W. Moody, 'The New Departure in Irish Politics, 1878-9', in *Essays in British and Irish History in Honour of James Eadie Todd*, ed. H. A. Cronne, T. W. Moody and D. B. Quinn (London, 1949). See also T. N. Brown, *Irish-American Nationalism*, chap v. and T. W. Moody's review of that book in *IHS*, xv, no. 60 (Sept. 1967).

3 R. B. O'Brien, *Parnell*, i, 177.

4 *Return of Evictions Known to the Constabulary in Each Year, 1849 to 1880*, P.P. (1881), vol. lxxvii, p. 725. The total number of families evicted in 1879 was 1,238, involving 6,239 persons; but of these, 140 families (663 persons) were subsequently reinstated.

5 *Preliminary Report on the Returns of Agricultural Produce in Ireland*, P.P. (1880) [c. 2495], table v, p. 899; N. D. Palmer, *The Irish Land League Crisis* (New Haven and London, 1940), p. 64.

6 F. S. L., Lyons, 'The Economic Ideas of Parnell', in M. Roberts (ed.), *Historical Studies*, ii (London, 1959), p. 64.

7 R. B. O'Brien, *Parnell*, i, 240.

8 *Nation*, 11 Oct. 1879.

9 R. B. O'Brien, *Parnell*, i, 247, *n* 1; J. L. Hammond, *Gladstone and the Irish Nation*, p. 155.

10 J. L. Hammond, op. cit., pp. 196-7.

11 C. Cruise O'Brien, *Parnell and His Party* (London, 1957), chap. i. The most striking 'militarists' were Lysaght Finigan (Foreign Legion), J. J. O'Kelly (war correspondent and duellist), and The O'Gorman Mahon, who had been not only a duellist and soldier of fortune, but an admiral in one country and a general in another. It is fair to set against this the fact that the party also contained one well-known novelist (Justin McCarthy) and several prosperous business men.

12 J. L. Hammond, *Gladstone and the Irish Nation*, pp. 192-3. See F. S. L. Lyons, *John Dillon*, pp. 37-40 for the leading part taken by Dillon in the agitation at this time. His speech at Kildare in August was one of the most extreme he ever made and led to an angry scene in parlia-

ment. In that speech he urged the farmers to bring pressure on their neighbours to join the League, hinted at a policy of a general strike against the payment of rent, and talked darkly about the possibility of seeing 'that every man had a right to have a rifle if he liked'. This went a good deal further than either Parnell or Davitt would have deemed politic and indicated that this new and passionate recruit to the cause might be difficult to control.

13 B. Solow, *The Land Question and the Irish Economy, 1870-1903*, p. 155. See chap. 6 of this book for a penetrating criticism of the presuppositions and the actual terms of the Land Act of 1881.

14 *Freeman's Journal*, 8 and 10 Oct. 1881.

15 K. O'Shea, *Charles Stewart Parnell: His Love Story and Political Life* (London, 1914), i, 207.

16 For a consideration of the forces affecting the fate of the land agitation at this time, see C. Cruise O'Brien, *Parnell and His Party*, pp. 65-72; M. Hurst, *Parnell and Irish Nationalism*, chap. iv; F. S. L. Lyons, *John Dillon*, chap. ii.

17 J. L. Hammond, *Gladstone and the Irish Nation*, pp. 266-7; more extended details are in R. B. O'Brien, *Parnell*, i, 329-30.

18 For the question of Parnell's supposed swing towards constitutionalism, see C. Cruise O'Brien, op. cit., pp. 72-9; F. S. L. Lyons, *Parnell* (Dundalk, 1963), pp. 12-13; M. Hurst, *Parnell and Irish Nationalism*, pp. 73-8.

3. PARNELL: ZENITH AND NADIR (pp. 178-201)

1 For the working of the League and the general question of finance see C. Cruise O'Brien, *Parnell and His Party*, chap. iv. The surplus of the Land League funds – estimated variously at between £30,000 and £40,000 – were not handed over to the Land League, but lodged in Paris under the control of Parnell and two of his colleagues. This 'Paris fund' was later to be the subject of angry dispute between them.

2 Ibid., p. 152.

3 C. H. D. Howard (ed.), 'Documents Relating to the Irish "Central Board" Scheme, 1884-5', in *IHS* (March, 1953), vii, 237-63; C. H. D. Howard, 'Joseph Chamberlain, Parnell and the Irish "Central Board" Scheme, 1884-5', in *IHS* (Sept. 1953), viii, 324-61. As to the fall of the Liberal government, contemporaries were hard put to it to decide whether ministers were more relieved, or their opponents more delighted, at the result.

4 The Churchill-Parnell meeting is described in L. P. Curtis, *Coercion and Conciliation in Ireland, 1880-1892* (Princeton, 1963), p. 36.

5 S. J. Lynch, 'Land Purchase in Ireland', in *JSSISI*, xiii, 1-16; B. Solow, op. cit., pp. 188-9, 193.

6 The electoral situation is discussed in C. Cruise O'Brien, op. cit., pp. 105-118. See also C. H. D. Howard, 'The Parnell Manifesto of 21 November 1885 and the Schools Question', in *EHR* (Jan. 1947), lxii, and the criticisms of that article in V. A. McClelland, *Cardinal Manning, His Public Life and Influence, 1865-92* (London, 1962), pp. 83-5, 187-9, and in Michael Hurst, *Parnell and Irish Nationalism*, pp. 104-7.

7 E. Strauss, *Irish Nationalism and British Democracy* (London, 1951), pp.

168-80; C. Cruise O'Brien, op. cit., pp. 109-14; F. S. L. Lyons, 'The Economic Ideas of Parnell', in *Historical Studies*, ii, 70-2.

8 J. L. Garvin, *Joseph Chamberlain* (London, 1932), ii, 12.

9 D. C. Savage, 'The Origins of the Ulster Unionist Party, 1885-6', in *IHS* (March 1961), xii, 185-208.

10 R. B. O'Brien, *Parnell*, ii, 38-9.

11 L. P. Curtis, *Anglo-Saxons and Celts* (New York, 1968), p. 100.

12 Professor Curtis discusses the general problem of anti-Irish feeling in his interesting and original essay; for its particular bearing on the Home Rule debate see chap. viii.

13 *United Ireland*, 23 Oct. 1886.

14 I have described the working of the Plan of Campaign in detail in *John Dillon*, chap. iv.

15 For the syndicate, see L. P. Curtis, *Coercion and Conciliation in Ireland*, pp. 248-52.

16 Cited in F. S. L. Lyons, op. cit., pp. 94, 97.

17 The best account of the special commission is in J. L. Hammond, *Gladstone and the Irish Nation*, chap. xxix.

18 F. S. L. Lyons, op. cit., pp. 106-7.

19 C. Cruise O'Brien, *Parnell and His Party*, pp. 233-4.

20 M. Hurst, *Parnell and Irish Nationalism*, p. 96. For the background to Parnell's more extreme speeches, see F. S. L. Lyons, *The Fall of Parnell* (London, 1960), chap. vi.

4. CONSTRUCTIVE UNIONISM (pp. 202-23)

1 I have tried to indicate the issues involved in two books: *The Irish Parliamentary Party* (London, 1951), chaps. i and v; *John Dillon*, chap. vi.

2 L. P. Curtis, *Coercion and Conciliation in Ireland*, p. 344.

3 S. J. Lynch, 'Land Purchase in Ireland', *JSSISI*, xiii, 1-16; L. P. Curtis, op. cit., pp. 350-55; B. Solow (op. cit., p. 193) gives a figure of 35,000 which includes some additional sales under variants of the acts.

4 The history of the Board has been written – largely from the inside – by W. L. Micks, *An Account . . . of the Congested Districts Board for Ireland from 1891 to 1923* (London, 1925).

5 For Plunkett's career, see Margaret Digby, *Horace Plunkett* (Oxford, 1949); also J. J. Byrne, 'AE and Sir Horace Plunkett', in C. Cruise O'Brien (ed.), *The Shaping of Modern Ireland* (London, 1960), pp. 152-63.

.6 Sir H. Plunkett, *Ireland in the New Century* (London, 1904), p. 82.

7 Ibid., p. 68.

8 Ibid., pp. 80-1.

9 Ibid., chap. iv.

10 J. G. Knapp, *An Appraisement of Agricultural Co-operation in Ireland* (Dublin, 1964, Pr. 7464), pp. 9-50.

11 R. B. McDowell, *The Irish Administration, 1801-1914*, pp. 224-9.

12 R. D. Crotty, *Irish Agricultural Production: Its Volume and Structure* (Cork, 1966), pp. 117-19.

13 Margaret Digby, *Horace Plunkett*, chaps. v and vii; J. G. Knapp, *An Appraisement of Agricultural Co-operation in Ireland*, pp. 25-38.

14 J. J. Byrne, op. cit., p. 162.

15 William O'Brien, *An Olive Branch in Ireland* (London, 1910), chaps. vi. viii and ix; the report is printed in an appendix, pp. 475-9.

16 For details of these two Acts see F. S. L. Lyons, *John Dillon*, pp. 229-35, 307-8; under the Wyndham Act alone some 200,000 tenants purchased their holdings (B. Solow, op. cit., p. 193).

17 Earl of Dunraven, *Past Times and Pastimes* (London, 1922), ii, 25.

18 The politics of the devolution crisis are sketched in F. S. L. Lyons, 'The Irish Unionist Party and the Devolution Crisis of 1904-5', in *IHS* (Mar. 1948), vi, 1-21.

19 *National Review*, Oct. 1904, p. 368.

5. THE BATTLE OF TWO CIVILISATIONS (pp. 224-46)

1 There is an excellent sketch of the growth of these Irish studies in W.I. Thompson, *The Imagination of an Insurrection* (New York, 1967), chap. i.

2 For Cusack's career see David Greene, 'Michael Cusack and the Rise of the G.A.A.', in C. Cruise O'Brien (ed.), *The Shaping of Modern Ireland*, pp. 74-84.

3 T. F. O'Sullivan, *The Story of the G.A.A.* (Dublin, 1916), pp. 9-10.

4 The two Literary Societies are described in Ernest Boyd, *Ireland's Literary Rennaissance* (Dublin, 1916; new ed., 1968), pp. 84-93.

5 Douglas Hyde, 'The Necessity for De-Anglicising Ireland', in *The Revival of Irish Literature* (London, 1894), p. 119.

6. Ibid., p. 160.

7 William Rooney, *Prose Writings* (Dublin, 1909), pp. 244, 250. For the history of the language revival, see especially B. O. Cuiv, 'The Gaelic Cultural Movements and the New Nationalism', in K. Nowlan (ed.), *The Making of 1916*, pp. 1-27.

8 Ibid., pp. 230, 231-2.

9 *Leader*, 1 Sept. 1900.

10 D. P. Moran, *The Philosophy of Irish Ireland* (Dublin, 1905), p. 34. The essays in this book were all written between 1893 and the first appearance of the *Leader* in Sept. 1900.

11 Ibid., pp. 40, 43.

12 D. Macartney, 'Hyde, D. P. Moran and Irish Ireland', in F. X. Martin (ed.), *Leaders and Men of the Easter Rising*, p. 49.

13 D. P. Moran, *The Philosophy of Irish Ireland*, p. 37.

14 Ibid., p. 96.

15 M. Digby, *Horace Plunkett*, p. 152.

16 For these preoccupations, see Ernest Boyd, *Ireland's Literary Renaissance*, pp. 213-15; John Eglinton, *A Memoir of AE* (London, 1937), pp. 11-12; J. M. Hone, *W. B. Yeats, 1865-1939* (London, second ed., 1962), chaps iii and v; A. N. Jeffares, *W. B. Yeats, Man and Poet* (London, 1949), chaps. iii, iv and v; Richard Ellman, *Yeats, the Man and the Masks* (revised ed., London, 1960), chaps. iv to vii; H. Howarth, *The Irish Writers, 1880-1940* (London, 1958), *passim*.

17 See especially, H. Howarth, op. cit., chaps. i and v; also R. J. Loftus, *Nationalism in Modern Anglo-Irish Poetry* (Madison and Milwaukee, 1964), chaps. 3, 4 and 5.

18 AE, 'The Dramatic Treatment of Heroic Literature', in *United Irishman*, 3 May 1902.

19 Yeats's own later account of this clash is illuminating. See especially *Autobiographies* (London, 1955), pp. 224-8.

20 D. P. Moran, *The Philosophy of Irish Ireland*, p. 22.

21 John Eglinton, 'The Island of Saints', in *United Irishman*, 8 Feb. 1902.

22 *United Irishman*, 22 Feb. 1902.

23 John Eglinton, 'A Word for Anglo-Irish Literature', in *United Irishman*, 22 Mar. 1902.

24 *United Irishman*, 31 Mar. 1902.

25 *The Leader*, 11 Jan. 1902.

26 A. N. Jeffares, *W. B. Yeats: Man and Poet*, pp. 137-8.

27 For Synge's career, see David H. Greene and Edward M. Stephens, *J. M. Synge, 1871-1909* (New York, paperback ed. 1961); also R. Skelton, *The Writings of J. M. Synge* (London, 1971).

28 *United Irishman*, 10, 17 and 31 Oct. 1903.

29 Ibid., 24 Oct. 1903; F. S. L. Lyons, 'James Joyce's Dublin', in *Twentieth Century Studies* (1970).

30 C. Cruise O'Brien, 'Passion and Cunning', in A. N. Jeffares and K. G. W. Cross (ed.), *In Excited Reverie* (London, 1965), pp. 212-16.

31 *Samhain*, Oct. 1901.

32 W. B. Yeats, 'The Cutting of an Agate' (written in 1907), in *Essays and Introductions* (London, 1961), p. 259.

33 *United Irishman*, 10 Oct. 1903; *Samhain*, 1903.

34 *United Irishman*, 17 Oct. 1903.

35 Ibid., 24 Oct. 1903.

6. THE RISE OF SINN FEIN (pp. 247-59)

1 William Rooney, *Prose Writings* (Dublin, 1909), pp. 73-5.

2 R. M. Henry, *The Evolution of Sinn Féin* (Dublin, 1920), p. 63.

3 P. S. O'Hegarty, *A History of Ireland Under the Union* (London, 1952), p. 639.

4 Ibid., p. 640; but drink was discouraged, says O'Hegarty, 'because it ruined the character'.

5 *United Irishman*, 1 Nov. 1902.

6 Arthur Griffith, *The Resurrection of Hungary*, first preface to the third (Dublin, 1918) edition.

7 *United Irishman*, 23 July 1904.

8 Cited in Griffith's pamphlet, 'The Sinn Féin Policy', and reprinted in 1918 with *The Resurrection of Hungary*. See especially p. 143. Griffith was also to some extent influenced by the American protectionist, Henry Carey, but List's work, which he read in translation, was much the most important formative element in his economic policy.

9 Ibid., p. 144.

10 P. S. O'Hegarty, *A History of Ireland Under the Union*, p. 643.

11 Ibid., p. 652. These words he actually spoke to P. S. O'Hegarty. The discussions behind the scenes which eventually produced the ambivalent constitution are described on pp. 651-3.

12 D. Macartney, 'The Sinn Féin Movement', in K. B. Nowlan (ed.), *The Making of 1916* (Dublin, 1969), p. 38.

13 Ibid., p. 39.

14 R. M. Henry, *The Evolution of Sinn Féin*, p. 87.

1 The standard biography is D. R. Gwynn, *The Life of John Redmond* (London, 1932). See also the illuminating essay by N. S. Mansergh, 'John Redmond', in C. Cruise O'Brien (ed.), *The Shaping of Modern Ireland*, pp. 38-49.

2 The circumstances and aftermath of reunion are described in F. S. L. Lyons, *The Irish Parliamentary Party*, chap. iii and the same author's *John Dillon*, chaps. vii and viii. For the Hibernians see J. J. Bergin, 'History of the Ancient Order of Hibernians' (Dublin, 1910).

3 H. W. McCready, 'Home Rule and the Liberal Party', in *IHS*, xiii (Sept. 1963), 316-48.

4 F. S. L. Lyons, *John Dillon*, pp. 292-8; A. C. Hepburn, 'The Irish Council Bill and the fall of Sir Antony MacDonnell in 1906-7', in *IHS*, xvii (Sept. 1971).

5 F. S. L. Lyons, op. cit., pp. 308-11.

6 J. R. Fanning, 'The Unionist Party and Ireland, 1906-10', in *IHS*, xv (Sept. 1966), 147-71. For another attempt to popularise the idea of federalism as a solution of the Irish question, see A. J. Ward, 'Frewen's Anglo-American Campaign for Federalism, 1910-21', in *IHS*, xv (Mar. 1967), 256-75.

8. LABOUR IN FERMENT (pp. 270-86)

1 J. D. Clarkson, *Labour and Nationalism in Ireland* (New York, 1925), p. 167.

2 Ibid., p. 183.

3 Ibid., chap. vii.

4 For Connolly's early life, see D. Ryan, *James Connolly* (Dublin and London, 1924); see also Ryan's essay – the last he ever wrote on this subject – in J. W. Boyle (ed.), *Leaders and Workers* (Cork, n.d.), pp. 67-75.

5 Cited in C. D. Greaves, *The Life and Times of James Connolly* (London, 1961), pp. 60-2.

6 J. D. Clarkson, op. cit., p. 252.

7 For his career see the essay 'William Walker' by J. W. Boyle in *Leaders and Workers*, pp. 57-65. Walker was not, as has sometimes been stated, the first labour candidate to contest an election. In 1885 Alexander Bowman contested North Belfast and was soundly beaten; he stood ostensibly as a Liberal, but was closer to what in England would have been called a 'Lib-Lab' candidate. Dr Boyle has dealt with Walker's career in greater detail in chap. viii of his unpublished doctoral thesis. 'The Rise of the Irish Labour Movement'.

8 E. Larkin, *James Larkin* (London, 1965), pp. 25-40.

9 Ibid., pp. 41-8.

10 *Sinn Féin*, 9 Sept. 1911; see also the articles on the Cork dispute in the same paper, 3 and 24 July 1909.

11 Cited in C. D. Greaves, op. cit., pp. 176-7.

12 James Connolly, *Labour in Irish History* (original ed., 1910, revised ed.,

Dublin, n.d.), pp. 167-8.
13 C. D. Greaves, op. cit., p. 203.
14 J. D. Clarkson, *Labour and Nationalism in Ireland*, pp. 292, 295-7.
15 E. Larkin, *James Larkin*, pp. 108-9. Contemporary estimates, friendly and unfriendly alike, went nearly as high as 25,000 but these were exaggerated.
16 For his two verdicts, see *Forward*, 7 Feb. 1914 and *Irish Worker*, 28 Nov. 1914. The best account of this whole episode is in E. Larkin, *James Larkin*, chaps. vi and viii.
17 J. W. Boyle, 'Connolly, the Citizen Army and the Rising', in K. Nowlan (ed.), *The Making of 1916*, pp. 53-7.
18 A considerable literature has grown up around the Countess. The most valuable studies are: S. O'Faoláin, *Constance Markievicz* (London, 1938; new paperback edition, 1967); E. Coxhead, *Daughters of Erin* (London, 1965); Anne Marreco, *The Rebel Countess* (London, 1967); Jacqueline Van Voris, *Constance de Markievicz in the Service of Ireland* (Massachusetts, 1967).

9. ULSTER BLOCKS THE WAY (pp. 287-311)

1 For its previous history, see H. Senior, *Orangeism in Ireland and Britain, 1795-1836* (London, 1966).
2 The organisation of Irish and Ulster Unionism is the subject of two recent studies: D. C. Savage, 'The Origins of the Ulster Unionist Party, 1885-6', in *IHS*, xii (Mar. 1961), 185-208; and P. J. Buckland, 'The Southern Irish Unionists and British Politics, 1906-14', in *IHS*, xv (Mar. 1967), 228-55.
3 R. Lucas, *Colonel Saunderson, MP: A Memoir* (London, 1908), *passim*.
4 Cited in D. C. Savage, op. cit., p. 196.
5 *Belfast Newsletter*, 22 and 23 Feb. 1886 for Churchill's visit.
6 The quotation is from 'Belfast' by Louis MacNeice in his *Collected Poems, 1925-1948* (London, 1949), p. 73.
7 For this incident, see R. Lucas, *Colonel Saunderson*, pp. 318-23.
8 For these developments, see F. S. L. Lyons, *The Irish Parliamentary Party*, pp. 134-6; also J. W. Boyle, 'Belfast and the Origins of Northern Ireland', in J. C. Beckett and R. E. Glasscock (ed.), *Belfast: The Origin and Growth of an Industrial City* (London, 1967), pp. 133-7. The origins of the Independent Orange Institution are explored in E. Larkin, *James Larkin, 1876-1947*, appendix D; see also J. W. Boyle, 'The Belfast Protestant Association and the Independent Orange Order', in *IHS*, xiii (Sept. 1962), pp. 117-52.
9 P. J. Buckland, 'The Southern Irish Unionists and British Politics, 1906-14', in *IHS*, xv, 228-55.
10 H. M. Hyde, *Carson* (London, 1953), p. 291. For the background to the meeting, see also A. T. Q. Stewart, 'Craig and the Ulster Volunteer Force', in F. X. Martin (ed.), *Leaders and Men of the Easter Rising: Dublin, 1916*, pp. 701-1, and the same author's *The Ulster Crisis* (London, 1967), pp. 47-8.
11 R. Blake, *The Unknown Prime Minister* (London, 1955), p. 129.
12 The arguments can be followed through many pages of Hansard, in H.C. Debates, 5th series, vol. 46. See also the introduction to, and

appendix I of, R. J. Lawrence, *The Government of Northern Ireland* (London, 1965).

13 R. Blake, *The Unknown Prime Minister*, p. 130.

14 R. Jenkins, *Asquith* (London, 1964), p. 279.

15 For these exchanges, see F. S. L. Lyons, *John Dillon*, pp. 332-4.

16 The Ulster gun-running is briefly described by A. T. Q. Stewart, 'Craig and the Ulster Volunteer Force', in *Leaders and Men of the Easter Rising*, pp. 74-6, and at more length in the same author's *The Ulster Crisis*, chaps viii to x, and xiv to xvi. See also Crawford's own account, *Guns for Ulster* (Belfast, 1947).

Part III

1. PHOENIX RESURGENT (pp. 315-28)

1 See the amended Constitution, Article 3, in Bulmer Hobson, *Ireland Yesterday and To-morrow* (Tralee, 1968), p. 103.

2 Ibid., p. 28.

3 F. X. Martin, 'McCullough, Hobson and Republican Ulster', in F. X. Martin (ed.), *Leaders and Men of the Easter Rising: Dublin 1916* (London, 1967), p. 98.

4 Bulmer Hobson's recollections (1947), in F. X. Martin (ed.), *The Irish Volunteers, 1913-1915*, pp. 19-20.

5 B. Hobson, *Ireland Yesterday and To-morrow*, p. 104.

6 For these incidents see D. Ryan and William O'Brien, *Devoy's Post Bag* (Dublin, 1953), ii, 401, 570.

7 B. Hobson, *Ireland Yesterday and To-morrow*, pp. 38-9. The nominal editor was Patrick MacCartan, who, after leaving school, had gone to America. There he joined Clan na Gael and on his return to Ireland was transferred to the IRB. He then began to study medicine (qualifying in 1910) but combined this with extensive work for Sinn Féin. He was co-opted to the Supreme Council in 1914-15.

8 B. Hobson, op. cit., p. 36; see also S. Cronin, 'The Fenian Tradition', in *Irish Times*, 9 Apr., 1969.

9 Ibid., p. 43.

10. For details of The O'Rahilly's early career, see Marcus Bourke, *The O'Rahilly* (Tralee, 1967), chaps. 3 and 4; for the writing of 'The North Began', see MacNeill's own account, dictated in 1932 and published in F. X. Martin (ed.), *The Irish Volunteer, 1913-1915*, pp. 71-2.

11 *An Claidheamh Soluis*, 1 Nov. 1913.

12 Events moved so rapidly in November 1913 that even the principals most heavily involved have differences of recollection. Thus Hobson states that he asked The O'Rahilly to see MacNeill, whereas MacNeill conveys the impression that The O'Rahilly was accompanied by Hobson. The O'Rahilly's biographer accepts Hobson's version, but it is possible of course that several interviews took place within the same few days and that in retrospect it became impossible to tell who was present at which. See F. X. Martin (ed.), *The Irish Volunteers, 1913-15* (Dublin,

1963), pp. 24-5, 71-2; also M. Bourke, *The O'Rahilly*, p. 71.

13 For the membership see F. X. Martin (ed.), *The Irish Volunteers*, pp. 95-6. Originally, twelve names were selected: Eoin MacNeill, Bulmer Hobson, The O'Rahilly, P. H. Pearse, Sean MacDermott, W. J. Ryan, Eamonn Ceannt, Sean Fitzgibbon, J. A. Deakin, Piaras Béaslaí, Joseph Campbell, D. P. Moran. Of these Moran declined and Hobson, as already stated, absented himself: Deakin, Campbell and Ryan withdrew after the first meeting.

14 Ibid., pp. 98-101.

15 D. Ryan and W. O'Brien (ed.), *Devoy's Post Bag*, ii, 426.

16 See R. B. McDowell, *Alice Stopford Green: A Passionate Historian* (Dublin, 1967).

17 It is reprinted in B. Hobson, *Ireland Yesterday and To-morrow*, pp. 99-102.

18 Casement's career has produced an enormous, and frequently controversial, literature. The following works are useful guides to the career and the controversies: C. E. Curry, *The Casement Diaries and the Findlay Affair* (Munich, 1922); D. R. Gwynn, *The Life and Death of Roger Casement* (London, 1931); G. de C. Parmiter, *Roger Casement* (London, 1936); W. Moloney, *The Forged Casement Diaries* (Dublin, 1936); R. Monteith, *Casement's Last Adventure* (Dublin, 1953); H. O. Mackey, *The Life and Times of Roger Casement* (Dublin, 1954); R. MacColl, *Roger Casement* (London, 1956); Alfred Noyes, *The Accusing Ghost: Or Justice for Casement* (London, 1957). In 1959 there appeared *The Black Diaries*, edited by P. Singleton-Gates and Maurice Girodias and published originally in Paris by the Olympia Press. The editorship of this volume leaves something to be desired and some mysteries remain unsolved, but the book contains what are described as 'faithful reproductions' of the typewritten copies of Casement's alleged diaries for 1903 and 1910 made in Scotland Yard at the time of his trial in August 1916. Recently the British government has made the diaries available for inspection by *bona fide* scholars, but a definitive judgment as to their authenticity has not yet emerged.

19 The personalities and the plotting in this extraordinary incident are admirably brought to life in F. X. Martin (ed.), *The Howth Gun-Running, 1914* (Dublin, 1964). See also, for Mrs Green's anxieties lest MacNeill be exploited by extremists, R. B. McDowell, *Alice Stopford Green: A Passionate Historian*, pp. 100-1.

20 F. X. Martin (ed.), *The Irish Volunteers*, p. 47.

21 For this crisis, see D. R. Gwynn, *The Life of John Redmond*, pp. 307-22; F. X. Martin, *The Irish Volunteers*, pp. 43-53, 141-4; B. Hobson, *Ireland Yesterday and To-morrow*, pp. 48-56; F. S. L. Lyons, *John Dillon*, pp. 350-2.

22 The effect of the Howth gun-running on recruiting was frequently commented on by the police. See B. MacGiolla Choille (ed.), *Intelligence Notes, 1913-16* (Dublin, 1966), pp. 81, 83, 85.

2. THE ROAD TO REVOLUTION (pp. 329-58)

1 For these events see D. R. Gwynn, *Life of John Redmond*, pp. 384-92, and F. X. Martin (ed.), *The Irish Volunteers*, pp. 144-55.

2 F. X. Martin (ed.), *The Irish Volunteers*, pp. 194-5.

3 F. X. Martin (ed.), 'Eoin MacNeill on the 1916 Rising', in *IHS* (March 1961), xii, 228. For a penetrating analysis of the recent literature on the rising and its antecedents, see F. X. Martin, '1916 – Myth, Fact, and Mystery', in *Studia Hibernica* (Dublin, 1967), no. 7, pp. 7-24. See also the same author's further study of the same subject, 'The 1916 Rising – Coup d'Etat or a "Bloody Protest"?' in *Studia Hibernica* (1968), no. 8, 106-37 and the two excellent essays by Maureen Wall in K. B. Nowlan (ed.), *The Making of 1916* (Dublin, 1969), pp. 157-97; they are entitled 'The Background to the Rising from 1914 Until the Issue of the Countermanding Order on Easter Saturday, 1916', and 'The Plans and the Countermand'.

4 M. Bourke, *The O'Rahilly*, p. 94. For Plunkett's background see the essay by his godson, Donagh MacDonagh, 'Plunkett and MacDonagh', in F. X. Martin (ed.), *Leaders and Men of the Easter Rising*, pp. 165-76.

5 For MacDonagh see Donagh MacDonagh (his son) 'Plunkett and MacDonagh' in *Leaders and Men of the Easter Rising*, pp. 165-76, also Michael Hayes, 'Thomas MacDonagh and the Rising', in F. X. Martin (ed.), *1916 and University College, Dublin* (Dublin, 1966), pp. 35-49.

6 Pearse has not, on the whole, been fortunate in his biographers. For long the 'standard' life of him was a somewhat cloying book, *Patrick N. Pearse* by L. N. Leroux (Dublin, 1932); more recently there has been a slender volume by H. McCay, *Padraic Pearse* (Cork, 1966), which does not add a great deal to our knowledge. There are two interesting articles by D. A. Thornley, 'Patrick Pearse – the evolution of a republican', in F. X. Martin (ed.), *Leaders and Men of the Easter Rising: Dublin 1916* (London, 1967), pp. 151-63, and 'Patrick Pearse and the Pearse Family' in *Studies* (Nos. 239-40, autumn-winter, 1971) xl, 332-46. See also the important revisionist essay by Father F. Shaw, S.J., 'The Canon of Irish History – a Challenge', in *Studies* (no. 242, summer, 1972) xli, 115-53, and my comment upon it in *Irish Times*, 11 Sept. 1972.

7 D. Macardle, *The Irish Republic* (American ed., New York, 1965), pp. 81-2.

8 P. H. Pearse, *Political Writings and Speeches*, pp. 58-9.

9 Ibid., pp. 176-7, 179, 185, 194-5.

10 Two recent investigations of this subject are especially to be noted – R. J. Loftus, *Nationalism in Modern Anglo-Irish Poetry* (Madison and Milwaukee, 1964), chap. vi, and W. I. Thompson, *The Imagination of an Insurrection: Dublin, Easter 1916* (New York, 1967), pp. 113-39.

11 P.H. Pearse, *Political Writings and Speeches*, p. 226, from 'Ghosts', written late in 1915.

12 T. MacDonagh, *Poetical Works: Lyrical Poems* (Dublin, 1916), p. 48. This particular poem was written in 1912.

13 Joseph Plunkett, *Poems* (Dublin, 1916), pp. 59-60.

14 P. H. Pearse, *Political Writings and Speeches*, pp. 91-9.

15 W. I. Thompson, *The Imagination of an Insurrection*, p. 77.

16 P. H. Pearse, *Political Writings and Speeches*, pp. 133-7.

17 Ibid., pp. 215-18.

18 P. H. Pearse, *Plays, Stories, Poems* (Dublin, 1924), pp. 324-5.

19 Ibid., p. 333. The prison poem to his mother is printed for the first time by Leon O Broin, *Dublin Castle and the 1916 Rising* (Dublin, 1966), p.

137. It ends thus:

> I would have brought royal gifts, and
> > I have brought you
> Sorrow and tears: and yet, it may be
> That I have brought you something else beside –
> A splendid thing which shall not pass away.
> When men speak of me, in praise or dispraise,
> You will not heed, but treasure your own memory
> Of your first son.

20 P. H. Pearse, *Plays, Stories and Poems*, p. 44.

21 Ibid., pp. 335-6.

22 For these events see S. T. O'Kelly in *An Phoblacht* 30 Apr. 1926; W. O'Brien, introduction to James Connolly, *Labour and Easter Week* (Dublin, 1949); D. Lynch, *The I.R.B. and the 1916 Insurrection* (Cork, 1957); F. X. Martin (ed.), 'Eoin MacNeill on the 1916 Rising', in *IHS* (Mar. 1961), no. 47, xii, 226-71.

23 For Casement in Germany, see D. Ryan, *The Rising* (Dublin, 3rd ed., 1957), chaps. ii and iii; also R. MacColl, *Roger Casement*, chap. viii. A sympathetic view of his mission is given in Roger McHugh, 'Casement and German Help', in F. X. Martin (ed.), *Leaders and Men of the Easter Rising*, pp. 177-87.

24 F. X. Martin (ed.), 'Eoin MacNeill on the Rising', p. 243, *n.* 15.

25 For the Volunteer strategy see Bulmer Hobson, *Ireland To-day and To-morrow*, pp. 69-71; see also M. Bourke, *The O'Rahilly*, pp. 87-8.

26 M. Bourke, op. cit., pp. 94-5.

27 D. Lynch, *The I.R.B. and the 1916 Insurrection*, passim; F. X. Martin (ed.), 'Eoin MacNeill on the Rising' – see especially the informative notes to MacNeill's two memoranda.

28 Cited by William O'Brien, introduction to James Connolly, *Labour and Easter Week* (ed. D. Ryan), pp. 1-2.

29 *Worker's Republic*, 18 Dec. 1915.

30 *Worker's Republic*, 15 Jan. 1916.

31 This passage is cited in Pearse's pamphlet. The whole article can be read in L. Fogarty (ed.), *James Fintan Lalor: Patriot and Political Essayist* (Dublin, 1918), pp. 52-66.

32 P. H. Pearse, 'The Sovereign People', in *Political Writings and Speeches*, especially pp. 335-40.

33 *Worker's Republic*, 30 Oct. 1915.

34 F. X. Martin (ed.), 'Eoin MacNeill on the 1914 Rising', *IHS*, xii, 246, 'Memorandum II'. Professor Martin would place this interview as taking place about 16 Jan. 1916.

35 Ibid., p. 253, *n.* 6, drawing especially upon the new evidence supplied by P. Béaslaí in *Irish Independent*, 29-31 May 1957 and in C. O'Shannon (ed.) *Fifty Years of Liberty Hall* (Dublin, 1959).

36 F. X. Martin (ed.), 'Eoin MacNeill on the 1916 Rising', p. 247 and *n.* 14 and 15. For the network radiating outwards from Dublin see D. Ryan, *The Rising*, pp. 78-89. There is interesting confirmation of IRB activity in the Volunteers in D. FitzGerald, *Memoirs* (London, 1968), chaps. iv and v.

37 F. X. Martin (ed.), 'Eoin MacNeill on the 1916 Rising', p. 246 and p. 254, *n.* 11.

38 Ibid., pp. 246-7 and pp. 254-5, n. 12 and 13.

39 Ibid., p. 242, n. 8; p. 243, n. 15; pp. 243-4, n. 16. Police estimates for mid-April 1916 give the number of Volunteers loyal to Redmond as about 105,000 and those adhering to MacNeill as 15,000. The Citizen Army is given as 100, but this seems a notional figure which had remained unchanged since the previous August (B. MacGiolla Choille (ed.), *Intelligence Notes, 1913-16*, p. 176). The most recent estimates of Citizen Army men (and women) participating in the rising are about 210 (D. Nevin, 'The Irish Citizen Army', in O. Dudley Edwards and F. Pyle (ed.), *1916: The Easter Rising* (London, 1968), p. 130), or 218 (F. X. Martin '1916 – Myth, Fact and Mystery', in *Studia Hibernica* (1967), no. 7, p. 19).

40 For the arms landing D. Ryan, *The Rising* is still indispensable, especially chap. vii. See also the two essays in F. X. Martin (ed.), *Leaders and Men of the Easter Rising* and the bibliographies attached thereto: (1) R. McHugh, 'Casement and German Help', and (2) F. O'Donoghue, 'Ceannt, Devoy, O'Rahilly and the Military Plan'.

41 F. O'Donoghue, op. cit.

42 F. X. Martin (ed.), 'Eoin MacNeill on the 1916 Rising', p. 247 and pp. 255-6, n. 18. The reference here is to MacNeill's Memorandum II which was written in the latter half of 1917. Thanks to Professor Martin's careful scholarship it is now possible to check the statements in this document against many other sources.

43 For the 'Castle Document', see D. Ryan, op. cit., chap. vi; also F. X. Martin, op. cit., pp. 247-8 and pp. 257-8, n. 23-6.

44 Bulmer Hobson's statement of 1 May 1916 in F. X. Martin, op. cit., p. 261; also B. Hobson, *Ireland Yesterday To-morrow*, pp. 76-7. It appears to be a by-product of this meeting on Friday morning that Sean MacDermott, who reached MacNeill's house ahead of the others, subsequently spread abroad the quite unfounded rumour that MacNeill had resigned as Chief of Staff. In the same way, earlier that week, he had told Tom Clarke, among others, that MacNeill knew of the plan for an Easter Sunday rising and had agreed to it. Both of these statements were untrue and were used deliberately as *ruses de guerre* – in the former instance to eliminate MacNeill from the situation and in the latter case to quieten the misgivings of those who took their cue from him.

45 F. X. Martin, op. cit., 'Memorandum II', p. 249. In a note written earlier than this Memorandum (in fact on 9 May 1916) MacNeill commented that he had tried to dissuade both his visitors from going on with the hopeless venture, 'They were a bit shaken but not convinced.' For Pearse's movements on the night of Good Friday see D. Ryan, *The Rising*, p. 94.

46 Ibid., pp. 249-50, pp. 264-5, n. 45-7. Casement had tried to get a message to MacNeill from Kerry and John Devoy later believed that it was this, together with the sinking of the *Aud*, which impelled him to call off the rising. It is doubtful if MacNeill ever received this message and possible that it got as far as Connolly who did not forward it (ibid., p. 264, n. 43).

47 Ibid., pp. 265-6, n. 48.

48 F. X. Martin, 'Eoin MacNeill and the Easter Rising: Preparation', in F. X. Martin (ed.), *1916 and University College, Dublin*, pp. 30-1.

49 F. X. Martin (ed.), 'Eoin MacNeill on the 1916 Rising', p. 268, n. 53.

3. THE RISING (pp. 359-80)

1 F. X. Martin (ed.), 'Eoin MacNeill on the 1916 Rising', in *IHS* (Mar. 1961), xii, 240.

2 B. MacGiolla Choille (ed.), *Intelligence Notes, 1913-16*, pp. 201, 202, 205, 209, 211. The information to be gathered from these police reports needs to be used with the caution indicated by the editor in his admirable introduction. It has to be remembered especially that the *Intelligence Notes* are only a précis of general reports which themselves were compiled from a multitude of local reports, and also that the police, though knowledgeable, did not know everything and were often, indeed, much isolated from the communities among which they lived. Nevertheless, the cumulative evidence of agricultural prosperity is very strong.

3 C. H. Oldham, 'Changes in Irish Exports', in *JSSISI* (Feb. 1919), xiii, 629-37, especially the tables in pp. 631 and 637.

4 E. Holt, *Protest in Arms* (London, 1960), p. 68.

5 L. O Broin, *Dublin Castle and the 1916 Rising*, p. 73. The government apparently hoped to reduce tension by deporting two of the most ubiquitous agitators – Ernest Blythe and Liam Mellows. These two 'Banishees' (to use the irrepressible Birrell's term for them) were seized on 25 March and sent to England shortly afterwards. Mr O Broin surveys the tangled problem of the intelligence reports in chap. x and xv of his excellent book.

6 Ibid., p. 85.

7 James Connolly, *Labour and Easter Week* (ed. D. Ryan, Dublin, 1949), p. 21; the most complete summary of the numbers involved on the insurgents' side is in D. Lynch, *The I.R.B. and the 1916 Resurrection*, edited by F. O'Donoghue (Cork, 1957), pp. 105, 143-4.

8 W. B. Yeats. 'The O'Rahilly', in *Collected Poems* (London, 2nd ed., 1950), p. 354. Desmond FitzGerald, one of his closest friends, wrote this about him long afterwards: 'He had shown his readiness to give his life for Ireland as anyone who knew him as I did knew he would do. But the joy of that sacrifice had been marred by the knowledge that those with whom he worked and with whom he shared his hopes thought that a consideration of his personal safety would influence his decision. I felt that he was the most tragic figure in that tragic gathering of men. He was devoted to his wife and family with a rare devotion, but he had decided to leave them to serve Ireland even when the call to service came from men who were revealed as not having realised how ready he was to give all for his country.' (*Memoirs of Desmond FitzGerald, 1913-1916* (London, 1968), p. 155).

9 *Irish Times*, 7 and 15 Apr. 1966; *Memoirs of Desmond FitzGerald*, pp. 140-1.

10 The best of the accounts by contemporaries, though written long after the event, is Desmond Ryan, *The Rising* (Dublin, 3rd ed., 1957). Of recent narratives by outsiders the best are E. Holt, *Protest in Arms*, chaps. viii and ix; M. Caulfield, *The Easter Rebellion* (London, 1965) and C. Younger, *Ireland's Civil War* (London, 1968), chap. ii. For a critical survey of the recent literature, see F. X. Martin, '1916, Myth, Fact and

Mystery', in *Studia Hibernica* (Dublin, 1967), no. 7. An indispensable contemporary source remains the *Royal Commission on the Rebellion in Ireland: Minutes of Evidence and Appendix of Documents* (London, 1916).

11 For Sheehy-Skeffington, see the narrative by his son Owen, in O. Dudley Edwards and F. Pyle, *1916: The Easter Rising*, pp. 135-48. Sheehy-Skeffington's views on the Volunteers and the dangers of militarism are in his 'Open Letter to Thomas MacDonagh', printed in the same volume, pp. 149-52.

12 B. MacGiolla Choille (ed.), *Intelligence Notes, 1913-16*, pp. 240-1. One estimate (E. Holt, *Protest in Arms*, p. 117), places the damage at 2.5 million pounds.

13 Ibid., p. 238.

14 Ibid., pp. 238-9.

15 For an interesting survey of press reactions, see the two appendices in F. Pyle and O. Dudley Edwards (ed.), *1916: The Easter Rising*, pp. 241-71. Of the other three daily newspapers published in the capital, the *Irish Times* and the *Daily Express*, being Unionist, were predictable in their attitude to the rising, though this did not prevent the *Irish Times* from producing a highly professional *Sinn Féin Rebellion Handbook*, which is still a source of valuable material. The *Freeman's Journal*, the organ of the parliamentary party, was handicapped by the destruction of its premises but when it did begin to appear again, on 5 May, it was of course hostile to the rising. It was, however, closely under the eye of John Dillon and reflected his view that what the situation now needed was leniency not severity.

16 The speech is in Hansard, H.C. Debates, 5th series, vol. 82, cols. 935-51. It has lately been reprinted in F. Pyle and O. Dudley Edwards (ed.), *1916: The Easter Rising*, pp. 62-78. For the background see my essay, 'Dillon, Redmond and the Irish Home Rulers', in F. X. Martin (ed.), *Leaders and Men of the Easter Rising*, pp. 29-41; also the more extended treatment in chap. xiii of my biography of John Dillon.

17 B. MacGiolla Choille (ed.), *Intelligence Notes, 1913-16*, pp. 199-220 *passim*.

18 For a detailed examination of this crisis, see my *John Dillon*, pp. 387-403.

4. SINN FEIN TRANSFORMED (pp. 381-99)

1 S. O Luing, 'Arthur Griffith and Sinn Féin', in F. X. Martin (ed.), *Leaders and Men of the Easter Rising*, pp. 62-3.

2 F. S. L. Lyons, *John Dillon*, p. 391.

3 Ibid., p. 395.

4 Ibid., pp. 410-11.

5 D. Macardle, *The Irish Republic* (American ed., New York, 1965), pp. 223-4.

6 Ibid., p. 222. For the American background see Charles A. Tansill, *America and the Fight for Irish Freedom, 1866-1922* (New York, 1957), especially chaps. vii and viii. This is a highly controversial work which needs to be used with caution. It should be supplemented by Owen Dudley Edwards's essay 'American Aspects of the Rising', in F. Pyle and O. Dudley Edwards, *1916: The Easter Rising*, and by Alan J. Ward, 'America and the Irish Problem', in *IHS* (March, 1968), xvi, 64-90;

see also Dr Ward's book, *Ireland and Anglo-American Relations, 1899-1921* (London, 1969), chap. vi.

7 P. Béaslaí, *Michael Collins and the Making of a New Ireland* (London, 1926), i, 166.

8 D. Ryan, *Remembering Sion* (London, 1934), pp. 229-38 still remains the best description. For his early career, see P. Béaslaí, op. cit., i, chaps. v to x; also R. Taylor, *Michael Collins* (London, paperback edition, 1961), chaps. i to vi, and *Memoirs of Desmond FitzGerald*, p. 144.

9 The cabinet dilemma is well described, on the basis of recently available documents, by C. Younger, *Ireland's Civil War* (London, 1968), chaps. iii and iv.

10 D. Macardle, *The Irish Republic*, p. 251.

11 Ibid., pp. 249-52.

12 F. S. L. Lyons, *John Dillon*, p. 435.

13 Ibid., pp. 437-40 for the election and its significance.

14 P. S. O'Hegarty, *A History of Ireland Under the Union* (London, 1952), pp. 721-2.

15 D. Macardle, *The Irish Republic*, pp. 253-5. For the meagre evidence made public see 'Minutes of Meeting of War Cabinet, 23 May 1918' (PRO, War Cabinet Papers, Cab. 23/6, 416 and appendix). The background material, which for obvious reasons could not be published at the time is in PRO, Cabinet Paper CP 2392 of 31 Dec. 1920 and is summarised in C. Younger, *Ireland's Civil War*, pp. 65-6.

16 R. Taylor, *Michael Collins*, p. 71 and note.

17 F. S. L. Lyons, op. cit., p. 441.

18 P. Béaslaí, *Michael Collins and the Making of a New Ireland*, i, chap. x; R. Taylor, op. cit., pp. 71-2; E. Holt, *Protest in Arms*, pp. 163-5.

19 P. Béaslaí, op. cit., pp. 208-9, 211-12.

20 The censored and uncensored versions of the manifesto are in Macardle, op. cit., pp. 919-22.

21 B. Farrell, *The Founding of Dáil Eireann* (Dublin and London, 1971), chaps. 3 and 4.

22 J. L. McCracken, *Representative Government in Ireland* (London, 1958), pp. 20-1; F. S. L. Lyons, op. cit., pp. 451-3.

5. THE STRUGGLE FOR INDEPENDENCE (pp. 400-38)

1 For the attendance see the roll-call, in *Dáil Eireann: Minutes of Proceedings*, 21 Jan. 1919, pp. 10-12; also J. L. McCracken, *Representative Government in Ireland*, p. 22. The figure of thirty-six imprisoned members given in D. Macardle, *The Irish Republic*, p. 272 is incorrect, perhaps because two members elected for two constituencies each have been counted twice.

2 For the English version, see Macardle, op. cit., pp. 923-4.

3 The Declaration appears in Irish, French and English in *Dáil Eireann: Minutes of Proceedings*, pp. 14-16.

4 Ibid., pp. 17-20.

5 Ibid., pp. 21-3.

6 P. S. O'Hegarty, *A History of Ireland Under the Union*, p. 727. O'Hegarty was at this time a member of the IRB and stood very close to Michael Collins.

7 B. Farrell, *The Founding of Dáil Eireann*, p. 54; see also M. Comerford, *The First Dáil* (Dublin, 1971).

8 Ibid. See also Patrick Lynch, 'The Social Revolution that Never Was', in T. Desmond Williams (ed.), *The Irish Struggle, 1916-1926*, pp. 41-54. Collins though officially recorded as present at the inaugural meeting of the Dáil, was in fact absent on a secret mission which will be described presently. The most convincing summary of the argument is in B. Farrell, op. cit., pp. 56-61.

9 For a corrosive statement of the disillusionment of a subsequent generation at this and other failures to live up to the ideals of 1916, see Conor Cruise O'Brien, 'The Embers of Easter', in O. Dudley Edwards and F. Pyle (ed.), *1916: The Easter Rising*, pp. 225-40.

10 For Irish-American opinion and the presentation of the Irish case see the account, hostile to Devoy and Cohalan, by the then Irish envoy to the USA, Dr Patrick McCartan, *With de Valera to America* (Dublin, 1932). This hostility is repaid with interest (and combined with a bitter attack on Wilson) by Charles C. Transill, *America and the Fight for Irish Freedom*, chaps. viii, ix and x. There is a more recent and more balanced account by Alan J. Ward, 'America and the Irish Problem, 1899-1921', in *IHS* xvi, 83-6.

11 J. L. McCracken, *Representative Government in Ireland*, pp. 29-34.

12 Ibid., pp. 23-4.

13 R. Taylor, *Michael Collins*, Appendix C., pp. 245-6. The figure of £379,000, which is sometimes given, appears to be an overestimate.

14 D. Macardle, *The Irish Republic*, p. 981.

15 *Dáil Eireann: Minutes of Proceedings, 1919-1921*, pp. 178-80; *The Constructive Work of Dáil Eireann, No. 1: The National Police and Courts of Justice* (Dublin, 1921). See also the comments of V. T. H. Delany, *The Administration of Justice in Ireland* (Dublin, 2nd ed., 1965), pp. 38-9.

16 *Dáil Eireann: Minutes of Proceedings* (10 Apr. 1919), pp. 67-9.

17 For the decline of the RIC see the scholarly article by Richard Hawkins, 'Dublin Castle and the Royal Irish Constabulary, 1916-1922', in T. Desmond Williams (ed.), *The Irish Struggle*, pp. 167-81. For a more indulgent view of the force, see G. C. Duggan, 'The Royal Irish Constabulary', in O. Dudley Edwards and F. Pyle (ed.), *1916: The Easter Rising*, pp. 91-9.

18 *Dáil Eireann: Minutes of Proceedings* (10 Apr. 1919), p. 47.

19 Ibid. (20 Aug. 1919), pp. 151-3.

20 P. Béaslaí, *Michael Collins and the Making of Modern Ireland*, i, 377-8.

21 B. Taylor, *Michael Collins*, p. 12.

22 K. B. Nowlan, 'Dáil Eireann and the Army: Unity and Division', in T. Desmond Williams (ed.), *The Irish Struggle*, pp. 67-77. This is a very fair and perceptive survey of an extremely complex problem.

23 There is already a large literature on the Anglo-Irish war. A helpful summary of the earlier work on the subject – and the struggle itself – is to be found in C. L. Mowat, *Britain Between the Wars, 1918-1940* (London, 1955), chap. i, sections 15 and 16 and chap. ii, sections 1-8; see especially the *Note on Authorities on the Irish War* at the foot of p. 72. Two recent accounts contain in their bibliographies further guidance to the main printed sources. These are E. Holt, *Protest in Arms*, chap. xxv, and C. Younger, *Ireland's Civil War*, passim. Much work, however, remains to be done on the whole subject and this will not be possible

until the Irish archives – especially those of the Bureau of Military History – are made available to students.

24 *Constabulary Gazette*, 6 Sept. 1919, p. 90.
25 For English reactions see C. L. Mowat, 'The Irish Question in British Politics, 1916-1922', in T. Desmond Williams (ed.), *The Irish Struggle*, pp. 141-52. Since the first edition of this book appeared the whole subject of British opinion about Ireland in these critical years has been thoroughly investigated in D. G. Boyce, *Englishmen and Irish Troubles* (London, 1972).
26 It is fair to say that Crozier had a reputation for unreliability among some who knew him well; all the same, his resignation was decidedly inconvenient for the government (D. G. Boyce, op. cit., pp. 96-7.).
27 See the figures quoted in C. L. Mowat, *Britain Between the Wars*; also R. Hawkins, 'Dublin Castle and the Royal Irish Constabulary', in T. Desmond Williams (ed.), *The Irish Struggle*, pp. 178-9 and notes; G. C. Duggan, 'The Royal Irish Constabulary', in O. Dudley Edwards and F. Pyle (ed.), *1916: The Easter Rising*, pp. 96-9; E. Holt, *Protest in Arms*, p. 252, accepts Collins's figure of 3,000 but suggests that the total strength of the IRA was 112,000. It had indeed stood at or about this figure in the closing months of 1918, but it was a largely nominal figure thereafter, partly because of resignations and partly because of the sheer inertia in some areas of which Collins violently and repeatedly complained.
28 C. L. Mowat, *Britain Between the Wars*, p. 69; E. Holt, op. cit., p. 210.
29 C. Younger, *Ireland's Civil War*, pp. 116-17.
30 The best description of these events is James Gleeson, *Bloody Sunday* (London, 1962).
31 C. Younger, op. cit., p. 119.
32 Macardle, op. cit., p. 368; K. O'Doherty, *Assignment – America* (New York, 1957), pp. 132-4.
33 For the American visit, apart from the works by Macardle and O'Doherty already cited, see also D. R. Gwynn, *Eamon de Valera* (London, 1933) and Charles C. Tansell, *America and the Fight for Irish Freedom*. Details of finance are in Alan J. Ward, 'America and the Irish Problem, 1899-1921', in *IHS*, xvi, 88-9.
34 *Dáil Eireann: Minutes of Proceedings*, 25 Jan. 1921, pp. 240-1.
35 These preliminaries are clearly set out by T. P. O'Neill in his introduction to Frank Gallagher, *The Anglo-Irish Treaty* (London, 1965). For the British attitude at this crucial stage in the Anglo-Irish war, see D. G. Boyce, op. cit., chap. 4.
36 *Dáil Eireann: Minutes of Proceedings*, 25 Jan. 1921, pp. 240-1.
37 J. L. McCracken, *Representative Government in Ireland*, pp. 30-4.
38 For the speech, see Harold Nicolson, *King George V* (London, 1952), chap. xxi.
39 A. J. P. Taylor, *English History, 1914-1945* (Oxford, 1965), p. 157.
40 L. S. Amery, *My Political Life* (London, 1954), ii, 230. It has been also suggested that one of the guerrilla leaders in the south, Liam Lynch, had told Collins a month earlier that the war would have to end soon because of the shortage of arms, but this has been emphatically denied by other IRA officers (E. Holt, *Protest in Arms*, p. 255). Collins himself, on the other hand, was under no illusions. 'Once a truce is agreed and we come out into the open, it is extermination for us if the truce should fail . . . we shall be, in the event of a truce, like rabbits coming out

from their holes . . . (R. Taylor, *Michael Collins*, p. 110).

41 Lord Beaverbrook, *The Decline and Fall of Lloyd George* (London, 1963), p. 84.

42 These developments are chronicled in *Dáil Eireann: Official Report*, 16, 17 and 26 Aug. 1921, pp. 1-87.

43 D. Macardle, *The Irish Republic*, p. 491.

44 *Dáil Eireann: Official Report*, 16 Aug. 1921, pp. 7-8.

45 Ibid., 17 Aug. 1921, p. 15.

46 The correspondence is printed at length in Macardle, op. cit., chaps. xlix-lii.

47 F. Pakenham, *Peace by Ordeal*, pp. 177-9 for the session of October 24; also T. Jones, *Whitehall Diary, vol. iii, Ireland, 1918-1925*, ed. K. Middlemass (London, 1972), pp. 141-4.

48 Thomas Jones, *Whitehall Diary*, iii, 155-6.

49 For these discussions, and the notes made of them at the time, see R. Taylor, *Michael Collins*, pp. 144-6.

50 M. Forester, *Michael Collins: The Lost Leader* (London, 1971), pp. 248-50.

51 These crucial exchanges are set out in F. Pakenham, *Peace by Ordeal*, pp. 206-302 and in R. Taylor, *Michael Collins*, Appendix D, pp. 247-52.

6. THE GREAT DIVIDE (pp. 439-68)

1 Michael Collins writing to a friend on 6 Dec. 1921, cited in R. Taylor, *Michael Collins*, p. 152.

2 For these exchanges see D. Macardle, *The Irish Republic*, p. 596; also Earl of Longford and T. P. O'Neill, *Eamon de Valera* (London, 1970), pp. 166-70.

3 *Private Sessions of Second Dáil* (Dublin, n.d. [1972]), pp. 141-218.

4 *Official Report: Debate on the Treaty between Great Britain and Ireland Signed in London on 6 December 1921* (Dublin, n.d., hereafter cited as *Treaty Debates*), 19 Dec. 1921, pp. 20-3.

4 Ibid., pp. 24-7.

6 Ibid., pp. 27-8.

7 See above, p. 437.

8 P. S. O'Hegarty, *Ireland Since the Union*, p. 754.

9 *Treaty Debates*, pp. 36-42.

10 Ibid., pp. 42-8. See also T. de V. White, *Kevin O'Higgins* (Tralee, paperback edition, 1966), chap. vi.

11 Both versions are printed in *Private Sessions of Second Dáil*, pp. 317-24. The clauses omitted from the second version all dealt with Northern Ireland and in effect accepted the Treaty position on that subject.

12 *Treaty Debates*, 6 Jan. 1922, p. 274.

13 For examples of joint meetings see Ernest Blythe, 'Birth Pangs of a Nation', *Irish Times*, 19 and 20 Nov. 1968. This article a (review of Calton Younger's *Ireland's Civil War*) is a striking example of how even the most meticulous and recent research can still be supplemented by the recollections of men still living.

14 For this see R. Taylor, *Michael Collins*, pp. 174-5.

15 S. O Luing, *Art O Griofa* (Dublin, 1963), p. 395, based on information supplied by Ernest Blythe. Mr Blythe has confirmed this interpretation in 'Birth Pangs of a Nation', *Irish Times*, 19 Nov. 1968.

16 See *Irish Independent*, 17, 18 and 20 March 1922, for speeches at Dungarvan, Carrick-on-Suir, Thurles and Killarney.

17 The question of nomenclature presents a problem. Each side was reluctant to abandon the title, Irish Republican Army, though in practice this came in time to be identified more with the anti-Treaty forces. For the purposes of this study the pro-Treaty men will be called 'government forces' and their opponents anti-Treaty forces or 'Irregulars'. The origin of the latter term has been the subject of some dispute but it may first have been coined by Piaras Béaslái.

18 For this interesting memorandum, see C. Younger, *Ireland's Civil War*, pp. 256-8.

19 P. Béaslái, *Michael Collins and the Making of a New Ireland*, ii, 385-90.

20 Ibid., ii, 393-4.

21 Ernest Blythe, 'Birth Pangs of a Nation', *Irish Times*, 19 Nov. 1968. For Collins's own defence see his *The Path to Freedom* (Dublin, 1922), pp. 15-17. This follows the line already indicated – that the pact was 'a last effort on our part to avoid strife'. Blythe's recollections are also in S. O Luing, *Art O Griofa*, p. 396.

22 Cited in C. Younger, op. cit., pp. 285-6.

22 D. Macardle, *The Irish Republic*, p. 982, gives figures slightly more favourable to the republican side, but the difference amounts only to the transfer of one Independent to the republican total. The guerrilla leader, Dan Breen, appeared on both panels, but belongs more properly to the anti-Treaty side.

24 Ernest Blythe, 'Birth Pangs of a Nation', *Irish Times*, 19 Nov. 1968.

25 The evidence, which no historian could regard as completely conclusive, is gathered together in R. Taylor, *Assassination* (London, 1961). See especially chaps. iv and ix and the documents printed on pp. 207-19. It should be noted also, as Mr Taylor demonstrates, that Collins concerned himself closely with abortive plans for the rescue of Dunne and O'Sullivan. This in itself does not of course prove complicity; he would have done as much for any IRA men under sentence of death.

26 E. Neeson, *The Civil War in Ireland, 1922-1923* (Cork, revised paperback ed., 1969), p. 152.

27 For the circumstances surrounding the death of Collins – some of them strange enough to have led to the wildest rumours – see P. Béaslái, *Michael Collins and the Making of a New Ireland*, ii, 418-42; R. Taylor, *Michael Collins*, pp. 197-211, 270-3; C. Younger, *Ireland's Civil War*, chap. xx; E. Neeson, *The Life and Death of Michael Collins* (Cork, 1968), pp. 98-142; M. Forester, *Michael Collins: the Lost Leader*, chap. 20.

29 For the policy of reprisals, see especially T. de V. White, *Kevin O'Higgins*, chap. viii and the articles already cited by Ernest Blythe in *Irish Times*, 19 and 20 Nov. 1968. The prison atmosphere at the time of the executions has been powerfully caught in Peadar O'Donnell, *The Gates Flew Open* (London, 1932; paperback ed., Cork, 1965).

28 Earl of Longford and T. P. O'Neill, *Eamon de Valera*, chap. 18. The phrase is taken from a letter de Valera wrote to a friend and colleague, P. J. Ruttledge, on 11 April 1923.

I. BUILDING THE NEW STATE (pp. 471-510)

1 N. S. Mansergh, *The Irish Free State: Its Government and Politics* (London, 1934), p. 45. In practice, as Professor Mansergh points out (pp. 47-8), there were several instances in which the provisions of the Treaty conflicted with those of the Constitution.

2 L. Kohn, *The Constitution of the Irish Free State* (London, 1932), p. 172.

3 Articles 10 and 11 of the Constitution.

4 Article 8.

5 For this episode, see D. O'Sullivan, *The Irish Free State and its Senate* (London, 1940), pp. 75-82.

6 F. S. L. Lyons, 'The Minority Problem in the Twenty-six Counties', in F. J. Macmanus (ed.), *The Years of the Great Test, 1926-39* (Cork, 1967), pp. 92-103. Dr O'Sullivan, it is fair to add, has attached greater importance to the work of the Senate in its early years, particularly the contribution made by Lord Glenavy and Senator J. G. Douglas in upholding the Senate's position in relation to the Dáil – see especially *The Irish Free State and its Senate*, chaps. vi, viii and ix.

7 Articles 28 and 53.

8 Cited in B. Chubb, *The Government: An Introduction to the Cabinet System* (Dublin, 1968), p. 29. Professor Chubb's pamphlet is an admirable brief exposition of the evolution of the cabinet system in Ireland.

9 The status and powers of ministers are defined in Articles 51 and 59 of the Constitution; see also L. Kohn, op. cit., pp. 271-83, and N. S. Mansergh, op. cit., chap. ix.

10 Mansergh, op. cit., pp. 137-8; for the opposite view, that it was the post-1918 fashion which chiefly influenced the framers of the Free State Constitution, see Kohn, op. cit., p. 238.

11 Article 50 deals with constitutional amendments.

12 Article 47.

13 Kohn, op. cit., pp. 244-5.

14 B. Chubb, *The Government: An Introduction to the Cabinet System in Ireland*, p. 29.

15 *Final Report of the Commission of Inquiry into the Civil Service* (1932-5), cited in B. Chubb (ed.), *A Source Book of Irish Government* (Dublin, 1964), p. 117.

16 Ibid., p. 118. In 1965 the total was just short of 32,000 (S. Finlay, *The Civil Service* (Dublin, 1966), p. 12).

17 In place of the Justice of the Peace, a new office, that of Peace Commissioner, was created for the performance of the non-judicial functions of the former JPs.

18 Article 66.

19 For the legal and judicial reforms see L. Kohn, *The Constitution of the Irish Free State*, pp. 336-63; N. S. Mansergh, *The Irish Free State: Its Government and Policies*, chap. xvii; V. T. H. Delany, *The Administration*

of *Justice in Ireland* (Dublin, 2nd revised ed., 1965), chaps. v and ix; B. Chubb (ed.), *A Source Book of Irish Government*, chap. xi.

20. B. Chubb (ed.), *A Source Book of Irish Government*, p. 261.

21 For local government in general, see N. S. Mansergh, op. cit., chap. xiii; also J. Collins (2nd ed. by D. Roche, Dublin, 1963), *Local Government*. There is a brief description in J. O'Donnell, *How Ireland Is Governed* (Dublin, 1965), chap. ix. For the principal provisions of the County Management Act of 1940 which made provision for every county to have or share a manager, see B. Chubb (ed.), *A Source Book of Irish Government*, pp. 282-7. It should perhaps be mentioned here that the trend towards centralisation, and perhaps also purification, of local government was reinforced by the establishment of the Local Appointments Commission in 1926 and by the development of bulk purchasing arrangements.

22 For his career see the sympathetic but penetrating biography by T. de V. White, *Kevin O'Higgins* (paperback ed., Dublin, 1966).

23 D. O'Sullivan, *The Irish Free State and its Senate*, pp. 138-41.

24 T. de V. White, *Kevin O'Higgins*, chap. x; T. P. Coogan, *Ireland Since the Rising*, pp. 56-60, supplies some new facts. It is proper to add that General Mulcahy remained entirely loyal to Mr Cosgrave and in fact re-entered the government in 1927. Mr McGrath attempted, with some other dissident members of Cumann na nGaedheal to form a new party, the National Party, and they resigned in a body from the Dáil. However, on offering themselves for re-election they were heavily defeated, the only mandate their party received from the electorate being, it has been said, 'a mandate to efface itself' (O'Sullivan, op. cit., p. 142). Mr McGrath, who was a man of great wealth and strong personality, became in 1930 the chief organiser of the Irish Hospitals Sweepstake and was largely responsible for its phenomenal success over the next thirty years.

25 It appears, however, that Mr Fisher did write quite freely to the wife of an Ulster Unionist MP about the progress of the Commission (St J. Ervine, *Craigavon: Ulsterman*, pp. 498-500). MacNeill, on the other hand, carried his scrupulous reticence so far as to keep his own cabinet colleagues completely in the dark; for his resignation speech see *Dáil Debates*, xii, 796-804.

26 T. de V. White, *Kevin O'Higgins*, p. 210.

27 The history of the Boundary Commission can be followed in T. de V. White, op. cit., chap. xii; D. O'Sullivan. *The Irish Free State and its Senate*, chap. xi; D. R. Gwynn, *The History of Partition, 1912-1925* (Dublin, (1950), chaps. vii-ix; Maureen Wall, 'Partition: The Ulster Question (1916-1926)', in T. D. Williams (ed.) *The Irish Struggle*, pp. 79-93.

28 For an account of the evolution of Sinn Féin, see P. Pyne, 'The third Sinn Féin party, 1923-26', in *Economic and Social Review*, vol. 1, Nos. 2 and 3 (1969-70).

29 For the budgetary problems of the government at this time, see D. R. Gwynn, *The Irish Free State, 1922-27*, (London, 1928), chap. xvii.

30 *Irish Independent*, 24 June 1927, cited in D. O'Sullivan, op. cit., p. 194.

31 T. de V. White, *Kevin O'Higgins*, pp. 240-2.

32 Statement to the press on behalf of the Fianna Fáil party, *Irish Times*, 11 Aug. 1927.

33 *Dáil Debates*, xii, 1101-2. For a slightly different wording based on Mr

de Valera's own written record, see Earl of Longford and T. P. O'Neill, *Eamon de Valera*, p. 256. On entering the Dáil Fianna Fáil promptly combined with Labour to obtain the necessary signatures for a 90-day suspension of the Electoral Amendment Bill to enable it to be submitted to a referendum. This should have been followed up by a petition signed by not less than one-twentieth of the voters, but this did not materialise and on 9 November 1927 the Bill became law. It had, however, been rendered virtually obsolete from the moment Fianna Fáil had taken its decision.

34 O'Sullivan, op. cit., pp. 219-20; T. P. Coogan, *Ireland Since the Rising*, pp. 65-6.

35 D. Nevin in *The Years of the Great Test*, pp. 56-7.

36 Cited in O'Sullivan, op. cit., p. 224.

37 For the speech at length see *Dáil Debates*, xxviii, 1398-1405.

38 E. Larkin, *James Larkin*, p. 288; T. P. Coogan, op. cit., pp. 256-9.

39 D. O'Sullivan, op. cit., pp. 255-65.

40 F. S. L. Lyons, 'The Minority Problem in the Twenty-six Counties', in F. MacManus (ed.), *The Years of the Great Test*, p. 102.

41 Cited by N. Mansergh, 'Ireland and the British Commonwealth of Nations', in T. Desmond Williams (ed.), *The Irish Struggle, 1916-1926*, p. 136; see also T. de V. White, *Kevin O'Higgins*, pp. 71-4.

42 Mansergh, op. cit., p. 135.

43 N. Mansergh, *Survey of British Commonwealth Affairs: Problems of External Policy, 1931-39* (London, 1952), pp. 10-11; the memorandum was originally published in C. M. van der Heever, *General J. B. M. Hertzog* (Johannesburg, 1946), p. 232

44 W. K. Hancock, *Survey of British Commonwealth Affairs, 1918-1939* (London, 1937), i, 147.

45 Ibid., i, 146.

46 Other examples of the same tendency were the appointment of diplomatic and consular representatives by the Irish Free State in various parts of the world and also the insistence of the Free State government on using its own Seal rather than the Great Seal of the Realm.

47 L. Kohn, *The Constitution of the Irish Free State*, pp. 71-2. The position was, however, more complex than this forthright statement would lead one to believe. For an indication of its ramifications see N. Mansergh, *The Irish Free State*, chaps. ii, iii and xv; also W. K. Hancock, op. cit., chap. iii, sections 1, 3 and 4.

48 In effect this became the situation in Ireland from the moment the first Governor-General (the indestructible T. M. Healy) was appointed. Not only did the Constitution succeed in eliminating the discretionary authority of the holder of the office, but the Free State government persistently maintained, long before this view was accepted by the Imperial Conference of 1930, that a Governor-General should not merely be acceptable to the government concerned but should only be appointed on the advice of that government. From 1930 onwards the dominions in general secured direct access to the King for this purpose (Mansergh, *The Irish Free State*, pp. 147-52).

49 *Report of the Inter-Imperial Relations Committee* (Cmd. 2768), p. 14.

50 T. de V. White, *Kevin O'Higgins*, pp. 222-3.

51 N. Mansergh, *Survey of British Commonwealth Affairs*, pp. 14-15.

52 T. de V. White, *Kevin O'Higgins*, p. 223.

53 D. W. Harkness, *The Restless Dominion* (London, 1969), chap. vi.
54 See generally K. C. Wheare, *The Statute of Westminster and Dominion Status* (London, 4th ed. 1949).
55 D. O'Sullivan, *The Irish Free State and its Senate*, pp. 253-4. It does not seem that Churchill had the best legal authorities on his side (Hancock, op. cit., i, 330-1).

2. THE ASCENDANCY OF DE VALERA (pp. 511-58)

1 For these exchanges, see W. K. Hancock, *Survey of British Commonwealth Affairs*, i, 320-50.
2 D. O'Sullivan, *The Irish Free State and its Senate*, pp. 291-4.
3 For the history of the right of appeal to the Judicial Committee of the Privy Council, see N. Mansergh, *The Irish Free State*, pp. 320-7; J. G. Latham, 'The Law and the Commonwealth', in Hancock, op. cit., i, 546-60. The irritation felt by O'Higgins and others on this subject is well described in D. W. Harkness, *The Restless Dominion* (London, 1969), chap. vi, and (in relation to the Imperial Conference of 1930), pp. 204-7.
4 Lord Hailsham in the House of Lords (25 July 1934), cited in Hancock, op. cit., i, 372.
5 *Moore and others* v. *Attorney-General for the Irish Free State*, 1935 A.C. 434, 51, T.L.R.
6 Hancock, op. cit., i, 373, citing the Attorney-General, Sir Thomas Inskip.
7 Ibid., i, 378-9.
8 They were entitled the Constitution (Amendment No. 27) Act and the Executive Authority (External Relations) Act respectively.
9 N. Mansergh, 'Ireland: External Relations 1926-1939, in *The Years of The Great Test*, p. 134.
10 N. Mansergh, 'Ireland and the British Commonwealth of Nations', in T. Desmond Williams (ed.), *The Irish Struggle, 1916-1926*, p. 139.
11 *Bunreacht na h Eireann*, Article 29, sections 2 and 5.
12 Hancock, op. cit., i, 327.
13 Cited in N. Mansergh, *Survey of British Commonwealth Affairs*, p. 305.
14 For this incident see T. Desmond Williams, 'De Valera in Power', in F. MacManus (ed.), *The Years of the Great Test*, pp. 30-1.
15 J. L. McCracken, *Representative Government in Ireland* (London, 1958), pp. 114-16. Professor McCracken has assembled evidence to show that once Fianna Fáil had consolidated its position, the lines of social cleavage between the two main parties tended to become blurred, though in his view Fine Gael (the later name of the Cosgrove party) 'is still in the main, the party of wealth, property and position'. See also B. Chubb, *The Government and Politics of Ireland* (London and Stanford, Cal., 1970), chap. 3; also M. Manning, *Irish Political Parties* (Dublin and London, 1972), chaps. 2 and 3.
16 D. Nevin, 'Labour and the Political Revolution', in F. MacManus (ed.) *The Years of the Great Test*, pp. 55-68. Mr Nevin, who is a Research Officer of the Irish Congress of Trade Unions, makes the point (p. 67) that even in Dublin, where trade unionists were heavily concentrated, the Labour party had negligible support. 'Loyalties born of the Civil War divisions', he writes, 'proved stronger than any class consciousness or any disposition to follow the political promptings of the trade union movement.'

17 *Irish Press*, 21 Jan. 1933.
18 While these figures indicate the extent to which Fianna Fáil had improved its position in the Dáil, the first preference votes showed that Mr de Valera's party had won less than the other parties put together – 689,043 against 697,326.
19 Quoted by D. Thornley, 'The Blueshirts' in *The Years of the Great Test*, pp. 45, 49.
20 Statements on the National Guard by General O'Duffy, cited in M. Manning, *The Blueshirts* (Dublin and London, 1971), chap. 3.
21 D. O'Sullivan, *The Irish Free State and its Senate*, pp. 407-8.
22 For a first-hand account of some of these incidents, see S. O'Callaghan, *The Easter Lily* (London, revised ed., 1966), chap. xi; he maintains that the Blueshirts retaliated in kind, whereas Dr O'Sullivan (op. cit., chap. xix) emphasises their restraint under provocation; being less well-armed than their opponents they probably were more restrained, but it would be strange if sometimes their reactions had not been violent.
23 Cited in O'Sullivan, op. cit., p. 404.
24 M. C. Bromage, *De Valera and the March of a Nation* (London, paperback ed., 1967), pp. 129-30.
25 For these events, see D. O'Sullivan, op. cit., chap. xxv.
26 See T. P. Coogan, *The I.R.A.* (London, 1970), chaps. v to vii; also S. O'Callaghan, *The Easter Lily* (revised, paperback ed., London, 1967), chaps. xiii, xiv; and L. B. Bell, 'Ireland and the Spanish Civil War, 1936-1939, in *Studia Hibernica*, No. 9 (1969), pp. 137-63.
27 M. MacSwiney, *The Republic of Ireland* (Cork n.d.), p. 34.
28 B. Chubb, *The Constitution of Ireland* (Dublin, 1966), p. 25.
29 For cabinet government see B. Chubb, *The Government: An Introduction to the Cabinet System in Ireland* (Dublin, 2nd ed., 1968), chap. vii.
30 Under the Electoral Act of 1923 there were only ten constituencies with less than five members out of a total of twenty-eight.
31 Cited in O'Sullivan, op. cit., p. 234.
32 Ibid., pp. 489-90. This involved special legislation – the Executive Powers (Consequential Provisions) Act.
33 N. Mansergh, *Survey of British Commonwealth Affairs*, p. 297.
34 *Bunreacht na h Eireann*, preamble.
35 *Dáil Debates*, 14 June 1937, col. 430.
36 Article 12.
37 *Dáil Debates*, 11 May 1937, col. 51.
38 Article 26. Article 24, which provided for abridging the time allowed to the Senate for consideration of Bills judged by the government to be urgently and immediately necessary for the preservation of peace or in case of emergency, could only be brought into operation by resolution of the Dáil or 'if the President, after consultation with the Council of State, concurs'. Moreover, if dispute arose between the two Houses as to whether a given Bill was or was not a Money Bill (the Dáil of course had primary responsibility for, and control of, Money Bills) then the Senate, by Article 22, could request the President to refer the disputed Bill to a Committee of Privileges. The President, however, after consultation with the Council of State, had the power to decide whether to accede or not to accede to this request.
39 Article 27.
40 Article 13.

41 Article 13 (2) and 28 (10).

42 Articles 31 and 32.

43 Article 28 (10).

44 For his powers see Article 28; also B. Chubb (ed.), *A Source-book of Irish Government*, pp. 100-1.

45 B. Chubb, *The Government: An Introduction to the Cabinet System in Ireland*, p. 37.

46 *Dáil Debates*, vol. lxvii, col. 56.

47 Article 18 (7.1).

48 For stringent criticism, see B. Chubb, 'Vocational Represenation and the Irish Senate', in *Political Studies* (1954), ii, 97-111.

49 V. T. H. Delany, 'The Constitution of Ireland: Its Origins and Development' in *University of Toronto Law Journal* (1957), xii, 1-26.

50 Article 23 (1) (ii); Article 24 (1).

51 Article 16 (2).

52 J. C. Smyth, *The Houses of the Oireachtas* (Dublin, 1964), p. 9. For the delimitation of powers between the two houses, see chaps. vi to ix of Mr Smyth's pamphlet; also J. L. McCracken, *Representative Government in Ireland*, especially chaps. x to xii.

53 J. C. Smyth, op. cit., chap. ix.

54 Ibid., p. 50, referring to the period, 1958-62.

55 B. Chubb, *The Government and Politics of Ireland*, p. 195.

56 Article 50 (1).

57 See V. T. H. Delany, op. cit., pp. 13-14. As Professor Chubb has pointed out, there resulted from the fact that Article 58 was one of the 'transitory provisions' of the Constitution doomed to disappear after a certain lapse of time, the curious situation that the whole court system depended on an Article which was not to be found in copies of the Constitution printed between 1941 and 1961. In the latter year this anomaly was rectified by the enactment of the Courts (Establishment and Constitution) Act (B. Chubb, *The Constitution of Ireland*, pp. 30-1.).

58 V. T. H. Delany, op. cit., pp. 21-2.

59 The best analysis is in J. M. Kelly, *Fundamental Rights in the Irish Law and Constitution* (Dublin 1961). But see also B. Chubb, *The Constitution of Ireland*, chap. vii; D. Barrington, 'The Irish Constitution', in *Irish Monthly* (1952-3), vols. lxxxi and lxxxii; D. Costello, 'The Natural Law and the Constitution', in *Studies* (1956), xlv, 403-14; V. T. H. Delany, 'Fundamental Rights in the Constitution of Ireland', in *University of Malaya Law Review* (1960), ii, 17-18; V. Grogan, 'The Constitution and the Natural Law', in *Christus Rex* (Dublin, 1954), viii, 201-18.

60 See D. Barrington, 'The Irish Constitution', in *Irish Monthly*, vol. 80, pp. 133-4, 226-30, 268-72; J. M. Kelly, *Fundamental Rights*, especially pp. 25-30.

61 J. M. Kelly, op. cit., p. 33 and V. Grogan, 'Towards the New Constitution', in F. MacManus (ed.) *The Years of the Great Test*, pp. 170-1.

62 Articles 41 (2) (i and ii).

63 B. Chubb, *The Constitution of Ireland*, pp. 35-6.

64 N. Mansergh, *Survey of Commonwealth Affairs*, p. 302.

65 D. W. Harkness, *The Restless Dominion*, pp. 74-7.

66 Ibid., pp. 174-6.

67 T. de V. White, *Kevin O'Higgins*, p. 193.

68 *Peace and War: Speeches by Mr de Valera on International Affairs*, (Dublin, 1944), p. 10.
69 M. J. MacManus, *Eamon de Valera* (Dublin, 1944), p. 324.
70 *Peace and War*, pp. 45-6, 47-8.
71 Ibid., p. 50.
72 N. Mansergh, *Survey of Commonwealth Affairs*, p. 325.
73 *Peace and War*, p. 59.
74 Ibid., p. 62.
75 N. Mansergh, op. cit., p. 329.
76 *Peace and War*, p. 76.
77 Cited in Mansergh, op. cit., p. 332.
78 T. P. Coogan, *Ireland Since the Rising*, pp. 119-20.
79 J. W. Blake, *Northern Ireland in the Second World War* (Belfast, 1956), pp. 154-7; G. A. Hayes-McCoy, 'Irish Defence Policy, 1938-51, in K. B Nowlan and T. Desmond Williams (ed.), *Ireland in the War Years and After* (London, 1969), pp. 39-51.
80 T. P. Coogan, op. cit., p. 119 n.
81 S. O'Callaghan, *The Easter Lily*, p. 168. During 1939 a German intelligence agent, Oskar Pfaus visited Ireland and J. O'Donovan, an IRA explosives expert, visited Germany.
82 Ibid., p. 173. There is an excellent account of the whole subject in E. Stephan, *Spies in Ireland* (London, 1963).
83 T. P. Coogan, op. cit., p. 274 n.
84 Part of the difficulty was to keep rolling-stock in repair. When the situation was reviewed after the war, it was found that the average age of the steam locomotives then in use was fifty-one years and that of passenger-coaches forty-eight years. (*Report of Committee of Inquiry into Internal Transport*, 1957 (Dublin), Pr. 4091, pp. 11-17.)

3. NEW BEGINNINGS (pp. 559-98)

1 Dr Browne's early career is sympathetically sketched in T. P. Coogan, *Ireland Since the Rising*, pp. 101-2; see also M. McInerney, 'Noel Browne: Church and State', in *University Review*, vol. v, no. 2 (Summer, 1968).
2 For General Mulcahy's part in these negotiations, see the remarks of Mr Costello in an interview with Michael McInerney, 'Mr John A. Costello Remembers', part 4, *Irish Times*, 7 Sept. 1967.
3 *Dáil Debates*, vol. 107, cols. 86-7.
4 J. A. Costello to F. S. L. Lyons, 6 Jan. 1967. This letter followed an interview Mr Costello was kind enough to give me on 2 Jan. 1967, at which we discussed this and other matters at considerable length.
5 Mr Costello made this point most emphatically to me in the interview mentioned in the previous footnote. See also his speech of 24 Nov. 1948 in *Dáil Debates*, vol. 113, cols. 347-87.
6 *Dáil Debates*, 20 July 1948, cited in *Irish Times*, 10 July, 1962.
7 *Dáil Debates*, 6 Aug. 1948, cited in *Irish Times*, 10 July, 1962.
8 J. A. Costello, *Ireland in International Affairs* (Dublin, n.d.), p. 27.
9 J. A. Costello to F. S. L. Lyons, 6 Jan. 1967.
10 *Sunday Independent*, 5 Sept. 1948.
11 *Sunday Independent*, 15 July, 1962; see also *Sunday Independent*, 1 Nov. 1970.

12 J. A. Costello to F. S. L. Lyons, 6 Jan. 1967.
13 On this point, see Nicholas Mansergh, 'Irish Foreign Policy, 1945-1951', in K. B. Nowlan and T. D. Williams (ed.), *Ireland in the War Years and After*, 1938-51 (Dublin and London, 1969), p. 140.
14 *Dáil Debates*, vol. 113, cols. 347-87.
15 Cited by C. Cruise O'Brien, 'The Embers of Easter', in O. Dudley Edwards and F. Pyle (ed.), *1916: The Easter Rising*, p. 230.
16 Nicholas Mansergh, op. cit., pp. 142-3.
17 Nicholas Mansergh, *Survey of British Commonwealth Affairs: Problems of Imperial Policy*, 1931-39 (London, 1952), p. 272.
18 Patrick Pearse, 'The Spiritual Nation', in *The Complete Works of P. H. Pearse: Political Writings and Speeches*, p. 299.
19 'Mr John A. Costello Remembers', in *Irish Times*, 7 Sept. 1967.
20 P. Lynch, 'The Irish Economy in the Post-war Era', in K. B. Nowlan and T. Desmond Williams (ed.), *Ireland in the War Years and After*, p. 198. Mr Dillon's energy overflowed in many other directions also, including a new drive to promote agricultural education at the parish level and an imaginative attempt to co-operate with the Northern Ireland government in the development of the Foyle fisheries which lay on both sides of the border.
21 *Report of the Commission on Emigration and Other Problems* (Dublin, 1954), Pr. 2541, chap. vi.
22 T. Gray, *Ireland's Answer* (London, 1966), p. 330.
23 *Report of the Commission on Emigration*, chap. vi; B. Hensey, *The Health Services of Ireland* (Dublin, 1959), pp. 105, 134.
24 P. Lynch, op. cit., p. 187.
25 Ibid., p. 194.
26 *Bunreacht na h Eireann*, Article 41. See also pp. 539-41 above.
27 The essential documents are printed in *Irish Times*, 12 Apr. 1951; see also the *Dáil Debates* for the whole of that month. This, and much more relevant information, is brought together in J. H. Whyte, *Church and State in Modern Ireland*, 1923-1970 (Dublin and London, 1971), chap. 7.
28 J. H. Whyte, op. cit., chap. 9.
29 'Mr John A. Costello Remembers', in *Irish Times*, 7 Sept. 1967.
30 See the valuable articles by T. Desmond Williams in the *Leader* 31 Jan. to 25 Apr. 1953 and in the *Irish Press*, 27 June to 17 July, 1953. There is a more extended analysis in V. P. Hogan, *The Neutrality of Ireland in World War II* (Michigan, 1953).
31 A contemporary description of his activities by the *Leader*, cited by C. Cruise O'Brien, 'Ireland in International Affairs', in O. Dudley Edwards (ed.), *Conor Cruise O'Brien Introduces Ireland*, p. 123.
32 *Dáil Debates*, vol. cxiv, cols 323-6.
33 Nicholas Mansergh, 'Irish Foreign Policy, 1945-1951', in K. B. Nowlan and T. Desmond Williams (ed.), *Ireland in the War Years and After*, 1938-1951, p. 137.
37 *Dáil Debates*, vol. clix, cols 127-226. For a critical analysis of the 'Three Principles', see C. Cruise O'Brien, 'Ireland in International Affairs', pp. 127-34. This essay, though written some years after the events it describes, deserves to be regarded as in some sense a primary source.
35 *Ireland at the United Nations: Speeches by Mr Frank Aiken* (Dublin,

1960), pp. 3-5.

36 C. Cruise O'Brien, *To Katanga and Back* (London, 1962), chap. i.

37 *Ireland at the United Nations: Speeches by Mr Frank Aiken* (Dublin, 1959), pp. 29 et. seq.

38 Tony Gray, *The Irish Answer* (London, 1966), p. 366.

4. THE QUEST FOR PROSPERITY (pp. 599-634)

1 Cited by James Meenan, 'From Free Trade to Self-Sufficiency', in F. MacManus (ed.), *The Years of the Great Test* (Cork, 1967), p. 70.

2 For the effects of the tariff upon industry, see George O'Brien, 'Industries', in *Sáorstat Eireann: Official Handbook* (Dublin, 1932), chap. xv; also *Report of the Commission of Inquiry into Banking, Currency and Credit*, 1938 (P. no. 2628), pp. 58-64; and J. Meenan, *The Irish Economy Since 1922* (Liverpool, 1970), p. 132.

3 *Report of the Banking, Currency and Credit Commission*, pp. 25, 58-68; *Reports of the Commission on Emigration and other Population Problems, 1948-1954* (Pr. 2541), p. 31.

4 R. D. Crotty, *Irish Agricultural Production: Its Volume and Structure* (Cork, 1966), Appendix II, p. 353.

5 Derived from *Reports of Emigration Commission*, Table 23, p. 38.

6 Ibid., p. 43; T. K. Whitaker, *Economic Development*, p. 55.

7 *Reports of Emigration Commission*, pp. 34-5; J. Meenan, op. cit., p. 41, has slightly different figures.

8 *Reports of Emigration Commission*, p. 42. The nineteenth century calculations were made by H. Stäehle, 'Statistical Notes on the Economic History of Irish Agriculture, 1847-1913', in *Journal of the Statistical and Social Inquiry Society of Ireland* (May, 1951), xviii, 444-71.

9 Derived from *Report of Commission on Banking and Credit*, pp. 37-8, 107, 109-10.

11 Crotty, *Irish Agricultural Production*, p. 90. For a detailed analysis of the economic effects of owner-occupancy upon Irish agriculture, see chap. iv of that book. Two other aspects of farming that suggest reluctance to invest are machinery and fertilizers. Up to 1929, at least, the evidence points to an overwhelming reliance upon draught animals on farms; in that year 436,000 horses and 202,000 mules, jennets and asses were in use. Thirty-five years later these had declined to 190,000 and 82,000 respectively, the change being mainly due to the introduction of 40,000 tractors (Crotty, op. cit., p. 161). As for fertilizers, though they had been used in one form or another from the mid-nineteenth century, the amount spent on them was certainly inadequate, especially in the vital areas of pasture. Even as late as 1948 a foreign observer commented that 'in any attempt to estimate the fertilizer requirements of Irish grasslands one is dumbfounded by the magnitude of the problem' (T. K. Whitaker, *Economic Development*, p. 65).

12 Crotty, op. cit., p. 91.

13 K. H. Connell, 'Peasant-Marriage in Ireland: Its Structure and Development Since the Famine', in *Econ. Hist. Rev.*, 2nd series (1961-2), xiv, 503-23; also Crotty, op. cit., pp. 91-2, who makes the point that since the farm itself would descend to only one child, there was an element

of equity in using the dowry of benefit others if possible. The same argument would apply to any means taken to improve living standards, whether through more varied diet, the purchase of a car, or a wireless-set. Such improvement would be shared among the whole family.

14 *Reports of the Emigration Commission*, pp. 84-5; Crotty, op. cit., pp. 104-5.

15 *Report of Banking, Currency and Credit Commission*, p. 14.

16 *Sáorstát Eireann: Official Handbook*, p. 95; Crotty, op. cit., p. 113.

17 T. K. Whitaker, Economic Development, chap. xii; *Sáorstát Eireann: Official Handbook*, pp. 119-27; Crotty, op. cit., p. 120. A more favourable view of the Department of Agriculture's record is given by one of its late officials, D. Hoctor, *The Department: a History of the Department of Agriculture* (Dublin, 1971), especially chaps. 5 and 6.

18 The working of the Agricultural Credit Corporation in its early years is detailed in *Report of the Commission on Banking, Currency and Credit*, pp. 251-63.

19 Ibid., p. 35.

20 Ibid., pp. 62-4, 109-110. It appears that industrial wages in a number of trades in Dublin held up exceptionally well; between 1929 and 1936 they may have even have been better maintained than comparable wages in London.

21 Ibid., p. 640; *Reports of the Emigration Commission*, pp. 33-4.

22 *Reports of the Emigration Commission*, p. 10, Table 3 and p. 20, Table 11; see also *Census of Population, 1961* and D. O'Mahony, *The Irish Economy* (Cork, 2nd ed., 1967), p. 4.

23 Cited by James Meenan, 'From Free Trade to Self-Sufficiency', in F. MacManus (ed.), *The Years of the Great Test* (Cork, 1967), p. 74.

24 For this account I have drawn upon a summary of the dispute made for the use of the British cabinet in July 1935 by the Dominions Secretary, Malcolm MacDonald, and also upon Mr MacDonald's memorandum, 'Relations with the Irish Free State', drafted for the cabinet in May 1936 (PRO 1517, Cabinet Papers 24/262). I am indebted to Dr D. Harkness for drawing my attention to these documents. For the general history of the dispute, see the admirable analysis by W. K. Hancock, *Survey of British Commonwealth Affairs, 1918-1939* (London, 1937), vol. 1, chap. vi; also *Report of the Banking, Currency and Credit Commission*, pp. 89-91, and N. Mansergh, *Survey of British Commonwealth Affairs* (London, 1952), pp. 307-12.

25 Hancock, *Survey of Commonwealth Affairs*, i, 356.

26 *Report of Banking, Currency and Credit Commission*, pp. 91-2; see especially the graph of price movements on p. 91.

27 Ibid., p. 89.

28 Ibid., p. 84. A more tentative estimate by Hancock (*Survey of Commonwealth Affairs*, i, 358) reckoned that the Free State's excess of external assets over debits sank from £88 million to £74 million during the same period.

29 Hancock, op. cit., pp. 364, 367 n. 2; Mansergh, op. cit., p. 308.

30 *Report of the Banking, Currency and Credit Commission*, p. 53.

31 The agreements are printed in N. Mansergh (ed.), *Documents and Speeches on British Commonwealth Affairs, 1931-1952* (London, 1953), pp. 367-76.

32 Crotty, *Irish Agricultural Production*, p. 134.

33 Hancock, *Survey of Commonwealth Affairs*, i, 359. It has been estimated that in 1937 Ireland stood fourth in a list of the relative tariff levels in twenty countries. Only Spain, Turkey, Germany and Brazil had higher tariffs (W. J. L. Ryan, 'Measurement of Tariff Levels for Ireland', *JSSISI* (1948-9), xviii, 130).

34 For details of these credit operations, see *Report of the Banking, Currency and Credit Commission*, pp. 56, 267-80. In a different direction, the government also sought to develop industry by making it more attractive to those who worked in it. Thus the Conditions of Employment Act (1936) sought to fix maximum working hours per week and also provided for holidays with pay for certain categories of employee. In the same way, the Control of Prices Act (1957) attempted, though with questionable success, to mitigate for the consumer some of the more unpleasant effects of tariffs on home prices.

35 Ibid., 319-20, 350-52.

36 *Sáorstát Eireann: Official Handbook*, pp. 157-62; also the unpublished thesis by Miss U. Munikanon, 'The Use of State-Sponsored Bodies in the Exploitation of the Natural Resources in Ireland', pp. 61-8, 105-30.

37 Garret FitzGerald, *State-Sponsored Bodies* (Dublin, second ed., 1963), p. 5.

38 Ibid., p. 7.

39 Ibid., pp. 2-3.

40 *Report of the Banking, Currency and Credit Commission*, pp. 58-60; Crotty, *Irish Agricultural Production*, pp. 135-6, citing the *Statistical Abstracts* (1935), p. 70 and (1940), p. 83; J. Meenan, op. cit., p. 57.

41 *Report of the Banking, Currency and Credit Commission*, pp. 66-7; Crotty, op. cit., p. 137.

42 Crotty, op. cit., p. 137.

43 *Report of the Banking, Currency and Credit Commission*, pp. 109-10.

44 Crotty, op. cit., pp. 137-8.

45 Ibid., pp. 141-2; Hancock, op. cit., pp. 360-1; J. Meenan, 'From Free Trade to Self-Sufficiency', in *The Years of the Great Test*, p. 78, where by a misprint the wheat acreage for 1931 appears as 2,000.

46 Crotty, *Irish Agricultural Production*, pp. 141-55.

47 Ibid., p. 156. The chief barrier against a major increase in cattle exports was that, given the extensive methods of cattle production used in Ireland, it could only be achieved by a contradiction of the area devoted to other forms of agriculture – in short by upsetting the equilibrium which had established itself in Irish farming over many years. In war conditions, with renewed emphasis on tillage, this barrier to increased cattle production was of course still further heightened. For the achievement of equilibrium, or 'stability' in Irish farming, see Crotty, chap. iv.

48 Ibid., pp. 131, 156.

49 John Healy, *The Death of an Irish Town* (Cork, 1968), p. 17.

50 *Reports of the Emigration Commission*, p. 115; also the summary in D. O'Mahony, *The Irish Economy*, p. 4.

51 Crotty, op. cit., pp. 158-9.

52 *Reports of the Emigration Commission*, pp. 38-9; Crotty, op. cit., p. 353.

53 *Reports of the Emigration Commission*, p. 42.

54 T. K. *Whitaker, Economic Development*, p. 15; J. Meenan, *The Irish Economy Since 1922*, p. 84. P. Lynch, in *Ireland in the War Years and After* (ed. K. B. Nowlan and T. Desmond Williams), p. 196, reckoned gross Irish sterling assets at 'around £430 million'; for the figure in the text, see Crotty, op. cit., p. 166.

55 Whitaker, op. cit., pp. 10-20; Crotty, op. cit., pp. 163-4.

56 *Census of Population, 1961* (Pr. 6991), vol. i, Table 1; Crotty, op. cit., pp. 165-6.

57 Crotty, op. cit., p. 160.

58 *Reports of the Emigration Commission*, pp. 41-2; Crotty, op. cit., p. 160. The estimates relating to the nineteenth and early twentieth centuries are by H. Stäehle, 'Statistical Notes on the Economic History of Irish Agriculture, 1847-1913', in *JSSISI* (May, 1951), xviii, 444-71.

59 Whitaker, *Economic Development*, pp. 101-3; Crotty, op. cit., pp. 167-78.

60 Crotty, op. cit., pp. 187-8.

61 Ibid., p. 187. The involved technical argument underlying this assertion will be found in chap. vii of Mr Crotty's book.

62 *Programme for Economic Expansion* (Pr. 4796), especially pp. 26-7, 35-45.

63 D. O'Mahony, *The Irish Economy*, pp. 4. 182-3; O. MacDonagh, *Ireland* (New Jersey), (1968), p. 133; J. Meenan, *The Irish Economy Since 1922*, p. 206.

64 Crotty, *Irish Agricultural Production*, chap. viii; see also G. FitzGerald, *Planning in Ireland* (London and Dublin, 1968), p. 45.

65 See the summary of objectives in *Second Programme for Economic Expansion*, Part I (Pr. 7239), p. 17 and also the estimate of future exports on p. 57. The figures for industrial and agricultural growth for the period 1964-70 are taken from the revised tables in *Second Programme for Economic Expansion*, Part II (Pr. 7670), Appendix I, p. 298. See also the criticisms by G. FitzGerald, *Planning in Ireland*, chap. 8.

66 See *Second Programme for Economic Expansion: Review of Progress, 1964-7* (Pr. 9949), especially the first three chapters.

67 *Review of 1971 and Outlook for 1972* (1972) (Pr. 2357), Table 7, p. 86.

68 Ibid., pp. 27, 33.

5. PROBLEMS OF SOCIAL POLICY (pp. 635-93)

1 P. H. Pearse, 'O'Donovan Rossa: Graveside Oration', in *Collected Works: Political Writings and Speeches*, p. 135.

2 *Census of Population of Ireland, 1961*, vol. ix, Table 2; *An Coimisiun um Atribheochan na Gaelige* (Commission on the restoration of the Irish language), Summary, in English, of Final Report, July 1963 (Pr. 7256), p. 10.

3 B. O Cuiv, 'Education and Language', in T. Desmond Williams (ed.), *The Irish Struggle, 1916-1926*, pp. 160-1.

4 Ibid., pp. 162-3.

5 Ibid., p. 163. As Professor O Cuiv points out this programme was even more ambitious than the Gaelic League proposals of 1920.

6 T. J. McElligott, *Education in Ireland*, pp. 30-1.

7 Ibid., p. 19.

8 *Commission on the Restoration of the Irish Language*, Final Report (English summary), pp. 11-12; T. P. Coogan, *Ireland Since the Rising*, p. 194.

9 *Commission on the Restoration of the Irish Language*, Final Report, pp. 11-12; T. J. McElligott, op. cit., pp. 34-5. The high-water mark for primary schools teaching through Irish was about 1939, when the number was 704. Thereafter it fell steeply and by 1951 had dropped to 523; the figure for 1960-1 therefore represents an accentuation of a long-continuing trend.

10 *Athbeochan na Gaelige* (government white paper on the restoration of the Irish Language), 1965 (Pr. 8061), p. 56; T. J. McElligott, op. cit., pp. 33-4.

11 *Athbeochan na Gaelige*, Appendix, pp. 172-81. But note on the other side the criticism that of moneys made available for capital investment in the Republic (4½ million by March 1961), the Gaeltacht received only £33,000.

12 *Comhairle na Gaelige, Local Government and Development Institutions for the Gaeltacht* (Dublin, 1971); *Review of 1971 and Outlook for 1972*, p. 58-9.

13 Desmond Fennell, 'Language Revival: Is It Already a Lost Cause?', in *Irish Times* (supplement), 27 Jan. 1969. The distinguished folklorist, Kevin Danaher, put the number as low as 50,000 in 1969. See his article 'The Gaeltacht' in B. O Cuiv (ed.), *A View of the Irish Language* (Dublin, 1969), especially pp. 118-19.

14 *Commission on the Restoration of the Irish Language*. Final Report, p. 38.

15 For a brief survey of these new developments, see T. P. Coogan, *Ireland Since the Rising*, pp. 198-205.

16 B. O Cuiv, *Irish Dialects and Irish-Speaking Districts* (Dublin, 1951), pp. 31-2.

17 *Census of Population of Ireland*, 1961, vol. ix, Tables 1 and 2.

18 For the contemporary situation, see Tony Gray, *The Irish Answer*, chap. x; T. P. Coogan, op. cit., chap. ix; Donald S. Connery (London, 1968), pp. 154-9; Máire Cruise O'Brien, 'The Two Languages', in O. Dudley Edwards (ed.), *Conor Cruise O'Brien Introduces Ireland*, pp. 43-60; Desmond Fennell, article already cited in *Irish Times* supplement, 27 Jan. 1969.

19 *Investment in Education: Report of the Survey Team Appointed by the Minister for Education in October, 1962* (Pr. 8311), pp. 6-7, 246-7. The figures are as at 1 Feb. 1964.

20 Ibid., pp. 88, 91-2; T. J. McElligott, *Education in Ireland*, pp. 24-5, 153-4.

21 T. J. McElligott, op. cit., pp. 24-9.

22 Ibid., pp. 20-1.

23 *Investment in Education*, p. 226, Table 9.2.

24 T. J. McElligott, op. cit., pp. 38, 50; see also *Investment in Education*, p. 247, for slightly more recent, and slightly more favourable, figures.

25 *Council of Education Report*, 1960, p. 64.

26 *Investment in Education*, pp. 10-11.

27 Ibid., chap. iii, Table 1.1 on p. 4, and pp. 11-15; T. J. McElligott, op. cit., chap. iii.

28 *Investment in Education*, pp. 276-80.

29 T. J. McElligott, *Education in Ireland*, pp. 68-9, 76-82, 96-7. Spanish,

Italian and German are exempt from this generalisation, but they are taken by only a tiny handful of students.

30 These are the calculations of Dr Valentine Rice, Professor of Education in the University of Dublin. See his article, 'Education in Ireland', in O. Dudley Edwards (ed.), *Conor Cruise O'Brien Introduces Ireland*, pp. 170-8. The fate of the different categories of school-leavers is minutely examined in *Investment in Education*, pp. 111-47.

31 V. Rice, op. cit., p. 173. The situation regarding university entrants is also analysed in depth in *Commission on Higher Education, 1960-67 Report*, 11, p. 760-4.

32 See on this, *Investment in Education*, pp. 148-76; *Commission on Higher Education, Report*, 11, pp. 725-8 and 760-4.

33 For criticisms of the various new proposals, see N. Atkinson, *Irish Education*, chap. 7, and G. FitzGerald, *Towards a New Ireland* (London, 1972), pp. 49-50.

34 *Commission on Higher Education, Report*, 11, pp. 855-60 ('Conclusion'); for university statistics, see also T. J. McElligott, op. cit., chap. iv.

35 J. H. Newman, *The Idea of a University* (Image Books Edition, New York, 1959), pp. 171-2.

36 For these developments see B. Hensey, *The Health Services of Ireland* (Dublin, 1959), chap. i; also *The Child Health Services: Report of a Study Group appointed by the Minister for Health, 1967* (Pr. 171), chaps. 1 and 2.

37 B. Hensey, op. cit., p. 17.

38 Ibid., pp. 44-7.

39 Ibid., pp. 49-50.

40 Ibid., pp. 60-1; R. P. Kaim-Caudle, *Social Policy in the Irish Republic*, pp. 26-7, reckons the average percentage receiving free medical treatment at the time of his study (1967) to have been thirty.

41 B. Hensey, op. cit., p. 24.

42 See especially the informative articles, 'Mental Illness', by Michael Viney, originally printed in the *Irish Times*, 1963, and later published separately (Dublin, 1964); also the brief account in Donald Connery, *The Irish*, pp. 146-8; and *Report of Commission of Inquiry on Mental Illness, 1966* (Pr. 9181), passim. It should be added that a subsequent inquiry found that the provision of beds for psychiatric patients was 'generally considered excessive' and explained this mainly in terms of the necessity for providing for senile patients with nowhere else to go (*Report of the Consultative Council on the Health Services, 1968* (Pr. 154), p. 72). The numbers in health board psychiatric hospitals have recently declined quite sharply, from just over 19,000 at the end of 1960 to just under 15,000 at the end of 1971 (*Review of 1971 and Outlook for 1972*, pp. 70-2).

43 R. P. Kaim-Caudle, *Social Policy in the Irish Republic*, pp. 29-35.

45 D. Farley, *Social Insurance and Social Assistance in Ireland* (Dublin, 1964), passim and Appendix II. By 1966 the top-rate for old-age pensions had risen from 35 shillings (£1.75) to 47/6 (£2.37½).

46 Ibid., chap. xi.

47 See the revealing table of comparisons in R. P. Kaim-Caudle, *Social Policy in the Irish Republic*, pp. 114-15.

48 Ibid., pp. 47-8; see also the elaborate tables in the same author's paper, 'Social Security in Ireland and in Western Europe', Economic and Social

Research Institute (Dublin, 1964), p. 15.

49 For the various categories, see D. Farley, op. cit., pp. 84-7; *Review of 1971 and Outlook for 1972*, p. 76.

50 R. P. Kaim-Caudle, *Social Policy in the Irish Republic*, p. 61.

51 R. P. Kaim-Caudle, 'Social Security in Ireland and in Western Europe', p. 17; G. FitzGerald, *Towards a New Ireland*, p. 186.

52 R. P. Kaim-Caudle, *Social Policy in the Irish Republic*, p. 64.

53 Ibid., pp. 114-15.

54 D. Farley, op. cit., pp. 5-7; B. Hensey, *The Health Services of Ireland*, chap. ix.

55 The exact figure appears to have been 189,000. See R. Roberts, 'Trade Union Organisation in Ireland', *JSSISI* (1958-9), xx, part ii, pp. 93-111.

56 For a recent assessment, see Arthur Mitchell, 'William O'Brien, 1881-1968, and the Irish Labour movement', in *Studies* (Nos. 239-40, autumn-winter, 1971), pp. 311-31. O'Brien's memoirs, *Forth the Banners Go*, were edited by E. McLysaght (Dublin, 1969).

57 E. Larkin, *James Larkin*, p. 262.

58 David Thornley, 'The Development of the Irish Labour Movement', in *Christus Rex* (1964), xviii, 16.

59 R. Roberts, op. cit., reckons affiliated membership at 92,000 in 1929; Professor Larkin, whose estimate of contributions I follow in the text, places membership even lower – at 85,000 by 1929 (*James Larkin*, p. 286 *n*).

60 M. Manning, *Irish Political Parties*, p. 71.

61 D. Nevin, 'Industry and Labour', in K. B. Nowlan and T. Desmond Williams (ed.), *Ireland in the War Years and After*, p. 95; for the difficulties of obtaining accurate figures see D. O'Mahony, 'Industrial Relations in Ireland: the Background', Economic and Social Research Institute Paper, no. 19 (May 1964).

62 Cited in D. Nevin, op. cit., p. 98.

63 Ibid., pp. 98-104.

64 R. Roberts, op. cit., p. 95.

65 Ibid., p. 95. The total number of trade unionists in the Republic in 1958 was estimated at 291,000 (D. O'Mahony, op. cit., p. 9).

66 R. P. Mortished, 'The Industrial Relations Act, 1946', in *Public Administration in Ireland*, iii.

67 See the estimate in D. O'Mahony, *The Irish Economy*, p. 70; see also the table in the same author's article, 'Industrial Relations in Ireland: the Background', p. 9.

68 D. W. Bleakley, 'The Northern Ireland Trade Union Movement', in *JSSISI* (1953-4), xix, 159-69; R. J. Lawrence, *The Government of Northern Ireland* (Oxford, 1965), p. 30.

69 D. P. Barritt and C. F. Carter, *The Northern Ireland Problem* (London, 1962), p. 142.

70 Tony Gray, *The Irish Answer*, p. 235; P. Blanshard, *The Irish and Catholic Power* (London, 1954), pp. 89-90.

71 Cited in D. Connery, *The Irish*, p. 138. See also the illuminating essay, 'Dublin's Archbishop', in D. Fennell (ed.), *The Changing Face of Catholic Ireland* (London, 1968), pp. 109-20.

72 The best evidence for the continued vitality of the reform movement is in the periodicals – chiefly *Christus Rex*, *The Furrow* and the Jesuit quarterly, *Studies*. See also the penetrating essay by S. Mac-

Reamoinn, 'The Religious Position', in O. Dudley Edwards (ed.), *Conor Cruise O'Brien Introduces Ireland*, pp. 61-70. For more pessimistic appraisals, see Sean O'Faoláin, *The Irish* (revised ed., London, 1969), and a very angry but curiously appealing book by Michael Sheehy, *Is Ireland Dying?* (London, 1968).

73 *Second Programme for Economic Expansion*, Part I (P. 7239), 1963, pp. 43-4; D. Connery, *The Irish*, p. 39.

Part IV, B

I. GROWING PAINS OF DEVOLUTION (pp. 695-705)

1 See especially the speech of Charles Curtis Craig, brother of Sir James Craig on 29 March 1920 in Hansard, H.C. debates, 5th series, vol. cxxvii, cols 189-90.

2 *Correspondence between His Majesty's Government and the Prime Minister of Northern Ireland Relating to the Proposals for an Irish Settlement* (Cmd. 1561), 1921.

3 The best brief account of the Special Powers Act is by F. H. Newark, 'The Law and the Constitution', in Thomas Wilson (ed.), *Ulster Under Home Rule* (London, 1955), pp. 46-51.

4 R. J. Lawrence, *The Government of Northern Ireland: Public Finance and Public Services, 1921-1964* (Oxford, 1965).

5 N. Mansergh, *The Government of Northern Ireland* (London, 1936), pp. 166-7.

6 Cited in R. J. Lawrence, op. cit., p. 45; for the figures cited in the text, see pp. 41-3 of his book.

7 *Final Report of the Northern Ireland Special Arbitration Committee* (Cmd. 2073), 1925.

8 R. J. Lawrence, *The Government of Northern Ireland*, p. 61. Chapter iii of his book is an excellent guide to the financial intricacies of devolution. See also N. Mansergh, *The Government of Northern Ireland*, chap. x and T. Wilson (ed.), *Ulster Under Home Rule*, chap. vi.

2. THE DEPRESSION YEARS (pp. 706-14)

1 K. S. Isles and N. Cuthbert, 'Ulster's Economic Structure', in T. Wilson (ed.), *Ulster Under Home Rule*, pp. 96-7. See also *Report of Emigration Commission*, p. 3, for the earlier figures of the population of the six counties; the same Report suggests an annual average emigration of about 5,000 for 1926-37, which would give a total nearer 50,000.

2 L. O Nualláin, 'A Comparison of the Economic Position and Trend in Eire and Northern Ireland', in *JSSISI* (1942-7), xvii, pp. 504-40.

3 K. S. Isles and N. Cuthbert, *An Economic Survey of Northern Ireland* (Belfast, 1957), pp. 58, 515-16.

4 K. S. Isles, 'Northern Ireland: An Economic Survey', in T. W. Moody (ed.), *Ulster Since 1800* (London, 1954), p. 113; Isles and Cuthbert, *An Economic Survey of Northern Ireland*, p. 53.

5 L. O Nualláin, op. cit; even in 1945 eighty per cent of Northern Ireland farms did not exceed fifty acres (Isles and Cuthbert, *An Economic Survey of Northern Ireland*, p. 55).

6 K. S. Isles and N. Cuthbert, 'Economic Policy', in T. Wilson (ed.), *Ulster Under Home Rule*, p. 143. See also L. P. F. Smith, 'Recent Developments in Northern Irish Agriculture', in *JSSISI* (1947-52), xviii, pp. 143-60.

7 N. Mansergh, *The Government of Northern Ireland*, pp. 202-3. Annuities dating from the post-1920 period were also collected by the local government, but were set off by an equivalent deduction from the province's share of the reserved taxes; see also F. S. L. Lyons, 'The Twentieth Century', in T. W. Moody (ed.), *Ulster Since 1800*, II (London, 1957), p. 55.

8 Isles and Cuthbert, in *Ulster Under Home Rule*, pp. 138-40; L. P. F. Smith, op. cit., emphasises the element of compulsion in the pre-war marketing legislation of Northern Ireland. For figures of output see the articles by L. O Nualláin and L. P. F. Smith already cited; also Table ix (XVI) in Isles and Cuthbert, *An Economic Survey of Northern Ireland*, p. 291. The latter authorities reckon that the index number of the value of agricultural produce in the pre-war years (1936-7 to 1938-9) was forty-one compared with one hundred for 1945-6. Calculating pre-war *net* output at 1945-6 prices, they estimate the value to have been £31.3 million.

9 *Report of the Agricultural Enquiry Committee* (N.I., Cmd. 249, 1947), p. 212.

10 Isles and Cuthbert, *An Economic Survey of Northern Ireland*, (p. 227).

11 Ibid., p. 13.

12 K. S. Isles in *Ulster Under Home Rule*, pp. 116-17; see also the annual percentages and numbers of unemployment in Isles and Cuthbert, *An Economic Survey of Northern Ireland*, pp. 566, 577.

13 W. Black, 'Industrial Change in the Twentieth Century', in J. C. Beckett and R. E. Glasscock (ed.), *Belfast: The Origin and Growth of an Industrial City*, pp. 161-2.

14 Isles and Cuthbert in *Ulster Under Home Rule*, pp. 144-5.

15 Isles and Cuthbert, *An Economic Survey of Northern Ireland*, Table 28, pp. 606-7. Dr Black, in his essay on industrial change in Belfast in the twentieth century, gives the figures for service industries in Belfast alone as rising from 80,000 in 1926 to 100,000 in 1937. Sources are not given, but the dates suggest he is using the broader categories of the censuses of population; it is very possible that the whole total is greater than the number of insured people in the industries. For his estimate see J. C. Beckett and R. E. Glasscock (ed.), *Belfast: The Origin and Growth of an Industrial City*, pp. 163-4.

16 R. J. Lawrence, *The Government of Northern Ireland*, pp. 147-9.

17 Ibid., pp. 149-51. Figures in the text refer to 1924-39; in 1919-23, local authorities built 1,657 out of 2,155.

18 Ibid., chap. vii for a brief penetrating account of the state of public health in the province.

19 The rate of relief was doubled as a result.

20 R. J. Lawrence, op. cit., chap. ix, for the poor law in the six counties. See also J. W. Boyle, 'Industrial Conditions in the Twentieth Century', in

Ulster Since 1800, II, p. 133; J. J. Campbell, 'Between the Wars', in Belfast: The Origin and Growth of an Industrial City, pp. 150-1.
21 R. J. Lawrence, op. cit., p. 38.

3. THE POLITICS OF SIEGE (pp. 715-27)

1 J. L. McCracken, 'Northern Ireland, 1921-66', in T. W. Moody and F. X. Martin (ed.), The Course of Irish History (Cork, 1967), p. 315.
2 N. S. Mansergh, The Government of Northern Ireland, p. 230.
3 D. P. Barritt and C. F. Carter, The Northern Ireland Problem (London, 1962), p. 42.
4 St J. Ervine, Craigavon: Ulsterman, p. 516.
5 The whole subject has been exhaustively documented in a hitherto unpublished doctoral thesis (Queen's University, Belfast) by S. Elliott, 'The Electoral System in Northern Ireland since 1920'.
6 J. L. McCracken, 'The Political Scene in Northern Ireland, 1926-37', in F. MacManus (ed.), The Years of the Great Test, 1926-39, p. 155.
7 R. J. Lawrence, The Government of Northern Ireland, p. 65 and n. 1.
8 D. P. Barritt and C. F. Carter, The Northern Ireland Problem, p. 43.
9 J. M. Mogey, 'Ulster's Six Counties', in T. Wilson (ed.), Ulster Under Home Rule, p. 9.
10 R. J. Lawrence, op. cit., p. 30.
11 K. S. Isles and N. Cuthbert, An Economic Survey of Northern Ireland, pp. 211, 571.
12 The educational controversy can best be followed in D. P. Barritt and C. F. Carter, The Northern Ireland Problem, chap. v, and R. J. Lawrence, The Government of Northern Ireland, chap. vi. See also D. Kennedy, 'Catholics in Northern Ireland, 1926-39', in F. MacManus (ed.), The Years of the Great Test, pp. 140-2; and M. Wallace, Northern Ireland: 50 years of Self-Government (Newton Abbott, 1971), pp. 102-7.
13 Belfast Newsletter, 13 July 1933. Lord Craigavon himself declared the following year: 'We are a Protestant parliament and a Protestant state . . .' (cited by J. J. Campbell in 'Between the Wars', in J. C. Beckett and R. E. Glasscock (ed.), Belfast: The Origin and Growth of an Industrial City, p. 152).
14 D. Kennedy, op. cit., p. 143.
15 Ibid., pp. 146-7; but see the criticisms by F. Newark in T. Wilson (ed.), Ulster Under Home Rule, pp. 48-9 and note.
16 J. J. Campbell, op. cit., pp. 155-6.
17 D. Kennedy, op. cit., p. 146.
18 Cited in D. P. Barritt and C. F. Carter, The Northern Ireland Problem, p. 45.

4. WAR AS A CATALYST (pp. 728-37)

1 For the statistics, which are strangely incomplete, see J. W. Blake, Northern Ireland in the Second World War (Belfast, 1956), pp. 534-5.
2 A tribute to J. M. Andrews read out in the Northern Ireland House of Commons (cited by R. J. Lawrence, The Government of Northern Ireland, p. 64).

3 See Cyril Falls, 'Northern Ireland and the Defence of the British Isles', in *Ulster Under Home Rule*, chap. iv; also J. W. Blake, *Northern Ireland in the Second World War*, chaps. vii, viii and ix.

4 J. W. Blake, op. cit., pp. 232-3.

5 Ibid., pp. 238-9.

6 Cited in Lawrence, op. cit., p. 67.

7 J. W. Blake, op. cit., pp. 233-4.

8 For shipping figures see Blake, op. cit., Appendix II; aircraft production is dealt with in chap. ix of the same work and more briefly by Cyril Falls in *Ulster Under Home Rule*, pp. 87-8.

9 J. W. Blake, op. cit., p. 395.

10 Ibid., pp. 383-94.

11 Ibid., pp. 418-26.

12 K. S. Isles and N. Cuthbert, 'Economic Policy', in *Ulster Under Home Rule*, p. 141; see also the table on p. 291 of the authors' *An Economic Survey of Northern Ireland*.

13 J. W. Blake, op. cit., pp. 555-6, 413-18.

14 Ibid., p. 558.

15 Ibid., p. 410.

16 L. P. F. Smith, 'Recent Developments in Northern Irish Agriculture', in *JSSISI* (1947-52), xviii, p. 149.

17 J. W. Blake, op. cit., p. 432.

18 K. S. Isles, 'Economic Survey' in *Ulster Since 1800*, p. 118. According to the calculations of Isles and Cuthbert the money wage index for Northern Ireland showed a rise of one hundred per cent between 1939 and 1948 compared with seventy-five per cent in Britain (*Ulster Under Home Rule*, p. 107).

19 J. W. Blake, op. cit., p. 434.

20 R. J. Lawrence, *The Government of Northern Ireland*, p. 70. This assurance was not made public until 1945, but a similar statement was read out in the Northern Ireland House of Commons in November 1943.

5. THE POLITICS OF WELFARE (pp. 738-59)

1 R. J. Lawrence, *The Government of Northern Ireland*, p. 88. Most of what has been said above is based on the extremely illuminating account of these matters in chap. v of Dr Lawrence's book.

2 *Financial Times*, 29 Aug. 1969, cited in P. Riddell, *Fire over Ulster* (London, 1970), pp. 185-6.

3 G. FitzGerald, *Towards a New Ireland*, pp. 161-66, 181-7.

4 R. J. Lawrence, op. cit., chap. vii. Even this, however, could not be carried through without controversy, for the leading Catholic hospital, the Mater, found itself, as a voluntary hospital outside the Health Service, ineligible for certain State grants. The resulting argument has continued in one form or another almost to the present day. (M. Wallace, *Northern Ireland*, pp. 112-16.)

5 Ibid., chap. viii; for the early beginnings of the Housing Trust see *Ulster Year Book*, 1950, pp. 233-4. Up to the early fifties, it has been suggested, the Northern Ireland government tended to stint somewhat on its domestic expenditure because of its obsession with the imperial contribution, but this could hardly be said to hold true of

the sixties (see K. S. Isles and N. Cuthbert in *Ulster Under Home Rule*, pp. 163-4). By September 1968 the total of new houses built since 1944 stood at 161,518 (*Disturbances in Ireland: Report of the Commission Appointed by the Governor of Northern Ireland*, Sept. 1969 (Cmd. 532), pp. 56-8), hereafter cited as *Cameron Commission: Report*).

6 Purchases by the British Ministry of Food at uniform prices were gradually modified after the war, but Northern Ireland farmers received, apart from the general subsidies, a special payment to offset their old bugbear, the transport differential.

7 K. S. Isles and N. Cuthbert, *An Economic Survey of Northern Ireland*, pp. 295, 297; also *Economic Development in Northern Ireland* (Cmd. 479), 1964 (reprinted 1967), p. 120; *Ulster Year Book, 1966-68*, p. 153.

8 K. S. Isles and N. Cuthbert, 'Economic Policy', in T. Wilson (ed.), *Ulster Under Home Rule*, p. 143.

9 T. P. Coogan, *Ireland Since the Rising*, pp. 294-5.

10 The relevant documents are *Belfast Regional Survey and Plan: Recommendations and Conclusions* (Cmd. 465), 1963; and *Economic Development in Northern Ireland* (Cmd. 479), 1965. For a convenient summary of the problem, see M. Wallace, *Northern Ireland*, chap. 5.

11 *Northern Ireland Development Programme, 1970-75*.

12 For the armed raids on Northern Ireland, see T. P. Coogan, *The I.R.A.*, chap. xiv; also D. P. Barritt and C. F. Carter, *The Northern Ireland Problem*, pp. 129-37; and J. Bowyer Bell, *The Secret Army* (London, 1970).

13 For economic discrimination see especially Barritt and Carter, op. cit., chap. vi, and for Catholics in higher education, chap. v of the same work. A survey of the Northern Ireland school population for 1963-4 (T. P. Coogan, op. cit., p. 301) suggests that the number of Catholics going to a university was 1,006 compared with 3,765 Protestants. This would give a Catholic proportion of about twenty-seven per cent. Most of these, no doubt, would have gone to Queen's University, but some may have gone to universities in the south.

14 The Londonderry situation is described in Coogan, op. cit., pp. 382-5 and in Barritt and Carter, op. cit., pp. 120-4; see also *Cameron Commission: Report*, pp. 57-9.

15 *Cameron Commission: Report*, p. 57.

16 Barritt and Carter, op. cit., pp. 120-4.

6. THE CONTINUING CRISIS (pp. 760-80)

1 See especially the 'key-note' speech he delivered at Pottinger in November 1962 when Minister of Finance. It is printed in T. O'Neill, *Ulster at the Crossroads* (London, 1969), pp. 32-40.

2 R. Rose, *Governing Without Consensus* (London, 1971), p. 213. Of the Catholics questioned only 14 per cent favoured union with the rest of Ireland, but it is probable that most of the other abolitionists who were vague about what they would put in the place of the border favoured reunification. To this it is perhaps worth adding that in March 1972 (on the very eve of direct rule) a *Sunday Telegraph* survey indicated that 82 per cent of Catholics asked and 66 per cent of Protestants asked were prepared to accept proposals which guaranteed Northern Ireland's existing link with Britain but also deliberately kept open the

possibility of future Irish reunification (*Sunday Telegraph*, 19 Mar. 1972).

3 Statement of Rory Brady; cited in *Sunday Times* 'Insight', *Ulster* (London, 1972, hereafter cited as *Sunday Times* 'Insight', *Ulster*), p. 21.

4 For the background to these events, see M. Wallace, *Drums and Guns: Revolution in Ulster* (London, 1970), pp. 89-98.

5 See chap. 4 of *Disturbances in Northern Ireland: Report of the Commission Appointed by the Governor of Northern Ireland* (Cmd. 532), Sept. 1969 (hereafter cited as *Cameron Commission: Report*. This careful inquiry, though criticised by some of those who were criticised in it, still remains the most reliable account of the events between October 1968 and April 1969.

6 Ibid., p. 84-6.

7 Miss Devlin's autobiography, *The Price of My Soul* (London, 1969), is essential reading for this phase of the developing crisis.

8 *Cameron Commission: Report*, pp. 80-4 and p. 123, Appendix xii.

9 For these and other attempts to implement the reform programme, see *A Commentary by the Government of Northern Ireland to Accompany the Cameron Report* (Cmd. 534), Sept. 1969, especially pp. 6-11. For the leisurely history of the official proposals for local government reform before the disturbances, see *The Reshaping of Local Government: Statement of Aims* (Cmd. 517), Sept. 1967. The accelerated pace of change can be judged by comparing this with a second White Paper, *The Reshaping of Local Government Further Proposals* (Cmd. 530), July 1969. It should be noted, to avoid confusion, that the decision to adopt one man, one vote was initially a decision of the Unionist party; it was only announced as government policy the following month, May 1969, i.e. *after* Captain O'Neill had fallen from power.

10 Some of the key exchanges between the two men are given in A. Boyd, *Brian Faulkner* (Tralee, paperback ed., 1972), chap. 7. This is an embittered and polemical book, but the author has a keen, journalistic instinct for the relevant facts.

11 *A Commentary by the Government of Northern Ireland to Accompany the Cameron Report* (Cmd. 534), Sept. 1969.

12 *Report of the Advisory Committee on Police in Northern Ireland* (Cmd. 535), Oct. 1969.

13 See the evidence collected in *Sunday Times* 'Insight', *Ulster*, pp. 164-8.

14 For this account I have drawn heavily upon the only detailed analysis which has yet appeared, *Sunday Times* 'Insight', *Ulster*, chaps. 1, 5 and 11.

15 For these events, see *Sunday Times* 'Insight', *Ulster*, chap. 12; also C. Cruise O'Brien, *States of Ireland* (London, 1972), chap. 10, which includes his diary of the events of that summer.

16 *Sunday Times* 'Insight', *Ulster*, pp. 238-42.

17. The offer was to be repeated later in the year in the context of further possible change. See *The Future Development of the Parliament and Government of Northern Ireland* (Cmd. 560), Oct. 1971.

18 For the press conference at which the new party was launched in Belfast, see *Irish Times*, 22 Aug. 1970.

19 *Sunday Times* 'Insight', *Ulster*, pp. 256-9. For the apologia which this incident evoked from the S.D.L.P., see H. Kelly, *Hhow Stormont Fell*, pp. 51-55.

20 A. Boyd, *Brian Faulkner*, p. 92, citing figures published by the National

Council of Civil Liberties. Another estimate, somewhat less and for a shorter period, but still bad enough, is given in *Sunday Times* 'Insight', *Ulster*, p. 269.

21 *The Future Development of the Parliament and Government of Northern Ireland* (Cmd. 560), Oct. 1971.

22 *Report of the Tribunal Appointed to Inquire into the Events on Sunday, 30th January 1972, which Led to Loss of Life in Connection with the Procession in Londonderry on that day* (H.L. 101, H.C. 220), April 1972, p. 38.

23 *The Times*, 13 Mar. 1972, interview with Mr William Hull, leader of the Loyalist Association of Workers.

Select Bibliography

An exhaustive bibliography of Ireland in the last hundred and twenty years would require a volume to itself. What follows is an attempt to provide some guidance to the existing sources, and especially to the very recent publications, for the reader who wishes to penetrate further into the subject. I have not attempted to list unpublished material, but I have included the more important newspapers and periodicals, as well as a selection from the relevant official publications. The sections devoted to secondary works are not intended to give total coverage, though they do contain the titles of the principal books and articles used in the preparation of this history; certain items with an unusually wide range of reference have been repeated in more than one section where appropriate. Many studies primarily relating to Great Britain also have a bearing on Irish affairs, but these have generally been omitted, except where a particularly close connection exists.

All books cited in the bibliography may be assumed to have been published in London, unless otherwise stated. Paperback editions are indicated by an asterisk. The abbreviations used are the same as those listed at the beginning of the book.

I. GENERAL HISTORIES

* Beckett, J. C., *A Short History of Ireland*, 3rd ed., 1966.
* Beckett, J. C., *The Making of Modern Ireland, 1603-1923*, 1966; paperback edition, 1969.
* Curtis, E., *A History of Ireland*, 6th ed., 1950; paperback ed., 1961.
  Dudley Edwards, R., *A New History of Ireland*, Dublin, 1972.
* Inglis, B., *The Story of Ireland*, 1956; paperback ed., 1965.
  McCaffrey, L. J., *The Irish Question, 1800-1922*, Kentucky, 1968.
* MacDonagh, O., *Ireland*, Englewood Cliffs, New Jersey, 1968.
* Moody, T. W., and Martin, F. X. (ed.), *The Course of Irish History*, Cork, 1967.
  Norman, E. R., *A History of Modern Ireland*, 1972.
  O'Brien, Máire and Conor Cruise, *A Concise History of Ireland*, 1972.
  White, T. de V., *Ireland*, 1968.

2. BIBLIOGRAPHIES

Carty, J., *Bibliography of Irish History, 1870-1911*, Dublin, 1940.
Carty, J., *Bibliography of Irish History, 1911-21*, Dublin, 1936.
Eager, A. R., *A Guide to Irish Bibliographical Material*, 1964.
Hayes, R. J. (ed.), *Manuscript Sources for the History of Irish Civilisation*, 11 vols., Boston (Mass.), 1966.

Johnston, Edith M., *Irish History: a Select Bibliography*, revised ed., 1972.
Moody, T. W. (ed.), *Irish Historiography, 1936-70*, Dublin, 1971.
Writings on Irish history, 1936-   . A bibliography of current publications, published annually in *Irish Historical Studies* since 1938.

3. OFFICIAL PUBLICATIONS

Belfast Regional Survey and Plan: Recommendations and Conclusions
(Cmd. 451), Belfast, 1965.
Bunreacht na h Eireann (Constitution of Ireland), Dublin, 1937.
Census of Population (Ireland), especially 1841, 1851, 1901 and 1911.
Census of Population (Irish Free State and Republic), 1926, 1936, 1946, 1951,
1956, 1961, 1966.
Census of Population (Northern Ireland), 1926, 1937, 1951, 1961, 1966.
*Child Health Services: Report of a Study Group appointed by the Minister
for the Gaeltacht*, Dublin, 1971.
*Comhairle na Gaelige, Local Government and Development Institutions
for Health*, 1967 (Pr. 171).
Commission on Higher Education, 1960-67: I Presentation and summary
of report [Pr. 9326], Dublin, 1967; II Report, 2 vols. [Pr. 9588], Dublin,
1967.
*Commission on the Restoration of the Irish Language: Summary, in
English, of the Final Report* [Pr. 7256], Dublin, 1963. Also : *The Restoration of the Irish Language: Government White Paper* [Pr. 8061], Dublin,
1965.
Constitution of the Irish Free State, Dublin, 1922.
*Dáil Eireann. Minutes of Proceedings of the First Parliament of the
Republic of Ireland, 1919-21: Official Record*, Dublin, 1921.
*Dáil Eireann. Official Report: Debate on the Treaty Between Great Britain
and Ireland Signed in London on 6 December 1921*, Dublin, 1922.
*Dáil Eireann. Official Report for the Periods 16-26 August 1921 and 28
February to 8 June 1922*, Dublin, 1922.
Dáil Eireann. Parliamentary Debates: Official Report, Dublin, 1922-   .
*Disturbances in Northern Ireland: Report of the [Cameron] Commission
Appointed by the Governor of Northern Ireland* [Cmd. 532], Belfast,
1969. Also : *A Commentary by the Government of Northern Ireland to
Accompany the Cameron Report* [Cmd. 534), Belfast, 1969.
Economic Development, Dublin, 1958.
Economic Development in Northern Ireland [Cmd. 479], Belfast, reprinted 1967.
*Investment in Education: Report of the Survey Team Appointed by the
Minister for Education in October, 1962* [Pr. 8311], Dublin, 1967.
Northern Ireland Development Programme, 1970-75. Belfast, 1970.
Northern Ireland Development Programme, 1970-75: Government Statement
(Cmd. 547), Belfast, 1970.
Private Sessions of Second Dáil, Dublin, n.d. [1972].
Regional Studies in Ireland (the Buchanan Report, Dublin, 1968).
Report of the Consultative Committee on the Health Services, 1968.
(Pr. 154), Dublin, 1969.
Report of the Advisory Committee on Police in Northern Ireland [Cmd.
535], Belfast, 1969.

Report of the Commission of Inquiry into Banking, Currency and Credit [P. No. 2628], Dublin, 1938.

Reports of the Commission on Emigration and Other Population Problems, 1948-1954 [Pr. 2541], Dublin, 1956.

Report of the Council of Education: the Curriculum of the Secondary School [Pr. 5996] Dublin, 1960-1961.

Report of the Boundary Commission, 1925, with introduction by G. J. Hand, Shannon, Ireland, 1969.

Report of the Enquiry into Allegations against the Security Forces of Physical Brutality in Northern Ireland, arising out of events on the 9th August, 1971 (Cmd. 4823), 1971.

Report of the Joint Working Party on the Economy of Northern Ireland [Cmd. 1835], 1962.

Report of the Royal Commission on the Rebellion in Ireland [Cmd. 8279], H.C. 1916, xi, 171.

Report of the Select Committee on Industries (Ireland), H.C., 1884-5, ix.

Report of the Tribunal appointed to inquire into the events on Sunday, 30th January, 1972, which led to loss of life in connection with the procession in Londonderry on that day, 1972.

Return of Evictions Known to the Constabulary in Each Year, 1849 to 1880, H.C. 1888, lxxvii, 725.

Reshaping of Local Government: Further Proposals (Cmd. 530), Belfast, 1969.

Review of 1971 and Outlook for 1972 (Pr. 2357), Dublin, 1972.

Sáorstát Eireann: Official Handbook, Dublin, 1932.

Seanad Eireann. Parliamentary Debates: Official Report. Dublin, 1922-

Second Programme for Economic Expansion, Parts I and II (Pr. 7239 and Pr. 7670), Dublin, 1963-4. Also: Progress report for 1964 [Pr. 8244]; Progress report for 1965 [Pr. 8703]; Review of Progress, 1964-7 [Pr. 9949].

The Reshaping of Local Government: Further Proposals [Cmd. 530], Belfast, 1969.

Ulster Year Book, 1966-1968, Belfast, 1967.

Violence and Civil Disturbances in Northern Ireland in 1969 (Cmd. 566), Belfast, 1972.

4. BIOGRAPHICAL AND OTHER WORKS OF REFERENCE

Crone, J. S., A Concise Dictionary of Irish Biography, Dublin, 2nd ed., 1937.

Dictionary of American Biography, New York, 1928-37.

Dictionary of National Biography, 1908-9. Later volumes, of which the most recent appeared in 1960, bring the dictionary as far as 1950.

Dod's Parliamentary Companion, 1852.

Thom's Irish Almanac and Official Directory, Dublin, 1844- .

Who's Who, 1870-.

Who Was Who (1897-1916), 1920.

Who Was Who (1916-1928), 1929.

5. NEWSPAPERS AND PERIODICALS

An Claideamh Soluis.
Annual Register.
Belfast Newsletter.
Belfast Telegraph.
Cork Examiner.
Freeman's Journal.
Irish Independent.
Irish Press.
Irish Times.
Irish Worker.
Leader.
Nation.
Round Table.
Sinn Féin.
Times.
United Ireland.
United Irishman.
Worker's Republic.

6. POLITICAL DEVELOPMENTS TO 1922

Béaslaí, P., *Michael Collins and the Making of a New Ireland*, 2 vols., Dublin, 1926.

Beaverbrook, Lord, *The Decline and Fall of Lloyd George*, 1963.

* Bennett, R., *The Black and Tans*, 1959; paperback ed., 1961.

* Blake, R., *Disraeli*, 1965; paperback ed., 1969.

Blythe, E., 'Birth Pangs of a Nation', *Irish Times*, 19 and 20 Nov. 1968.

Bourke, M., *John O'Leary*, Tralee, 1967.

* Bourke, M., *The O'Rahilly*, Tralee, 1967.

Boyce, D. G., *Englishmen and Irish Troubles*, 1972.

* Boyd, A., *Holy War in Belfast*, Tralee, 1969.

Boyle, J. W. 'The Belfast Protestant Association and the Independent Orange Order', in *IHS.*, xiii (Sept., 1962).

Boyle, J. W., (ed.), *Leaders and Workers*, Cork, n.d.

Boyle, J. W., 'Belfast and the Origins of Northern Ireland', in Beckett, J. C., and Glasscock, R. E. (ed.), *Belfast: The Origin and Growth of an Industrial City*, 1967.

Boyle, J. W., 'Connolly, the Citizens Army and the Rising', in Nowlan, K. B. (ed.), *The Making of 1916*, Dublin, 1969.

Brennan, R., *Allegiance*, Dublin, 1950.

* Bromage, M. C., *De Valera and the March of a Nation*, 1956; paperback ed., 1967.

Brown, T. N., *Irish-American Nationalism*, Philadelphia and New York, 1966.

Buckland, P. J., 'The Southern Irish Unionists and British Politics', in *IHS*, xii (Mar. 1961).

Buckland, P. J., *Irish Unionism*, 1: *The Anglo-Irish and the New Ireland, 1885-1922* (Dublin and London, 1972).

Butt, I., *Home Government for Ireland*, Dublin, 1870.

Byrne, J. J., 'AE and Sir Horace Plunkett', in C. Cruise O'Brien (ed.), *The Shaping of Modern Ireland*, 1960.

* Caulfield, M., *The Easter Rebellion*, 1964; paperback ed., 1965.

Chavasse, M., *Terence MacSwiney*, Dublin and London, 1961.

Clarkson, J. D., *Labour and Nationalism in Ireland*, New York, 1925.

* Collins, M., *The Path to Freedom*, Dublin, 1922: paperback ed., Cork, 1968.

Colum, P., *Arthur Griffith*, Dublin, 1959.

* Comerford, M., *The First Dáil*, Dublin, 1971.

Connolly, J., *Socialism and Nationalism*. Introduction and notes by D. Ryan, Dublin, 1948.

Connolly, J., *Labour and Easter Week*. Introduction by William O'Brien, Dublin, 1949.

Connolly, J., *The Worker's Republic*. Introduction by W. McMullen, Dublin, 1951.

Corfe, T., *The Phoenix Park Murders*, 1968.

Coxhead, E., *Daughters of Erin*, 1965.

Curry, C. E., *The Casement Diaries and the Findlay Affair*, Munich, 1922.

Curtis, L. P., *Coercion and Conciliation in Ireland, 1880-92*, Princeton and London, 1963.

Curtis, L. P., *Anglo-Saxons and Celts*, New York, 1967.

Davis, Thomas, *Essays and Poems*, with a centenary memoir, Dublin, 1945.

Davitt, M., *The Fall of Feudalism in Ireland*, London and New York, 1904.

Devoy, John, *Recollections of an Irish Rebel*, New York, 1929.

Digby, M., *Horace Plunkett: An Anglo-American Irishman*, Oxford, 1949.

Dudley Edwards, O., and Pyle, F. (ed.), *1916: The Easter Rising*, 1968.

Dudley Edwards, O., 'Ireland', in Dudley Edwards, O., Evans, G., Rhys, J., and MacDiarmid, H., *Celtic Nationalism*, 1968.

Dudley Edwards, O. (ed.), *Conor Cruise O'Brien Introduces Ireland*, 1969.

Dudley Edwards, R., and Williams, T. Desmond (ed.), *The Great Famine*, Dublin, 1956.

Duggan, G. C., 'The Royal Irish Constabulary', in Dudley Edwards, O., and Pyle, F. (ed.), *1916: The Easter Rising*, pp. 91-9.

Ervine, St J., *Craigavon*, 1949.

Fanning, J. R., 'The Unionist Party and Ireland, 1906-10', in *IHS*, xv (Sept. 1966).

* Farrell, B., *The Founding of Dáil Eireann*, Dublin and London, 1971.

Fergusson, Sir J., *The Curragh Incident*, 1963.

FitzGerald, D., *Memoirs*, 1969.

Fogarty, L., *James Fintan Lalor: Patriot and Political Essayist, 1807-49*, Dublin and London, 1918.

Forester, M., *Michael Collins: The Lost Leader*, 1971.

Gallagher, F., *The Anglo-Irish Treaty*, 1965.

Gavan Duffy, Sir Charles, *The Legend of North and South*, 1886.

* Gleeson, J. *Bloody Sunday*, 1962; paperback ed., 1963.

Greaves, C. D., *The Life and Times of James Connolly*, 1961.

Greaves, C. D., *Liam Mellows and the Irish Revolution*, 1971.

Green, E. R. R., 'The Beginnings of Fenianism', and 'Charles Joseph Kickham and John O'Leary', both in Moody, T. W. (ed.), *The Fenian Movement*, Cork, 1968.

Greene, D., 'Michael Cusack and the Rise of the GAA', in O'Brien, Cruise, C. (ed.), *The Shaping of Modern Ireland*, 1960.

Griffith, Arthur, *The Resurrection of Hungary*, 3rd ed., Dublin, 1918.

Gwynn, D. R., *The Irish Free State, 1922-27*, 1928.

Gwynn, D. R., *The Life and Death of Roger Casement*, 1931.

Gwynn, D. R., *The Life of John Redmond*, 1932.

Gwynn, D. R., *Eamon de Valera*, 1933.

Gwynn, D. R., *The History of Partition, 1912-25*, 1950.

Hamer, D. A., *John Morley: Liberal Intellectual in Politics*, London, 1968.

Hamer, D. A., 'The Irish Question and Liberal Politics, 1886-1894', in *The Historical Journal*, xii, 3, (1969).

Hammond, J. L., *Gladstone and the Irish Nation*, 1938; new impression, 1964.

Harrison, H., *Parnell Vindicated*, 1931.

Hawkins, R., 'Dublin Castle and the Royal Irish Constabulary, 1916-1922', in Williams, T. Desmond, *The Irish Struggle, 1916-1926*, 1966.

Hayes-McCoy, G. A., 'A Military History of the 1916 Rising', in Nowlan, K. B. (ed.), *The Making of 1916*, Dublin 1969.

Henry, R. M., *The Evolution of Sinn Féin*, Dublin, 1920.

Hepburn, A. C., 'The Ancient Order of Hibernians in Irish Politics, 1905-14', in *Cithara*, x, No. 2 (St Bonaventure University, May 1971).

Hepburn, A. C., 'The Irish Council Bill and the fall of Sir Anthony MacDonnell in 1906-7', in *IHS*, xvii (Sept. 1971).

Hobson, B., *Ireland To-day and To-morrow*, Tralee, 1968.

Holt, E., *Portrait in Arms: The Irish Troubles, 1916-23*, 1960.

Horgan, J. J., *Parnell to Pearse*, Dublin, 1948.

Howard, C. H. D., 'The Parnell Manifesto of 21 November, 1885 and the Schools Question', in *EHR*, lxii (Jan. 1947).

Howard, C. H. D., (ed.), 'Joseph Chamberlain, W. H. O'Shea, and Parnell, 1884, 1891-2', in *IHS*, xiii (Mar. 1962).

Hurst, M., *Parnell and Irish Nationalism*, 1968.

Hyde, H. M., *Carson*, 1953.

Jenkins, R., *Asquith*, 1964.

Jones, T., *Whitehall Diary*, vol. iii, *Ireland, 1918-1925*, edited by K. Middlemass, 1971.

Kee, R., *The Green Flag*, 1972.

Laffan, M., 'The unification of Sinn Féin in 1917', in *IHS*, xvii (Mar. 1971).

Larkin, E., 'The Roman Catholic Hierarchy and the Fall of Parnell', in *Victorian Studies*, iv (June 1961).

Larkin, E., *James Larkin, Irish Labour Leader, 1876-1947*, 1965.

Larkin, E., 'Launching the Counter-attack: Part ii of the Roman Catholic Hierarchy and the Destruction of Parnell', in *Review of Politics*, xxviii (July 1966).

Le Roux, L. N., *Patrick H. Pearse*, trans. D. Ryan, Dublin, 1932.

Longford, Earl of, and O'Neill, T. P., *Eamon de Valera*, 1970.

Lucas, R., *Colonel Saunderson, M.P.: A Memoir*, 1908.

Lynch, D., *The IRB and the 1916 Rising*, ed. F. O'Donoghue, Cork, 1957.

Lyons, F. S. L., 'The Irish Unionist Party and the Devolution Crisis of 1904-5', in *IHS*, vi (Mar. 1948).

Lyons, F. S. L., *The Irish Parliamentary Party, 1890-1910*, 1951.

Lyons, F. S. L., *The Fall of Parnell, 1890-91*, 1960.

Lyons, F. S. L., *Parnell*, Dundalk (for Dublin Historical Association), 1963.

Lyons, F. S. L., 'The Passing of the Irish Parliamentary Party, 1916-18', in Williams, T. Desmond (ed.), *The Irish Struggle, 1916-1926*, 1966.

Lyons, F. S. L., 'Dillon, Redmond and the Irish Home Rulers', in Martin, F. X. (ed.), *Leaders and Men of the Easter Rising: Dublin 1916*, 1967.

Lyons, F. S. L., *John Dillon: A Biography*, 1968.

Lyons, F. S. L., 'Decline and Fall of the Nationalist Party', in Dudley Edwards, O., and Pyle, F., *1916: The Easter Rising*, 1968.

Lyons, F. S. L., 'The Two Faces of Home Rule', in Nowlan, K. B. (ed.), *The Making of 1916*, Dublin, 1969.

* Macardle, D., *The Irish Republic*, 1937; American edition, New York, 1965; paperback ed., 1968.

Macardle, D., 'Hyde, D. P. Moran and Irish Ireland', in Martin, F. X. (ed.), *Leaders and Men of the Easter Rising: Dublin, 1916*, 1967.

Macartney, D., 'The Church and Fenianism', in *University Review*, iv (Winter, 1967).

Macartney, D., 'Gaelic Ideological Origins of 1916', in Dudley Edwards, O., and Pyle, F., (ed.), *1916: The Easter Rising*, 1968.

Macartney, D., 'The Sinn Féin Movement', in Nowlan, K. B. (ed.), *The Making of 1916*, Dublin, 1969.

McCaffrey, L. J., 'Home Rule and the General Election of 1874', in *IHS*, ix (Sept. 1954).

McCaffrey, L. J., 'Irish Federalism in the 1870s: A Study in Conservative Nationalism', in *Transactions of the American Philosophical Society* (Philadelphia, 1962).

McCaffrey, L. A., *Daniel O'Connell and the Repeal Year*, Kentucky, 1966.

McClelland, V. A., *Cardinal Manning, His Public Life and Influence, 1865-92*, 1962.

McColl, R., *Roger Casement*, 1956.

McCready, H. W., 'Home Rule and the Liberal Party, 1890-1910', in *IHS* xiii (Sept. 1963).

MacDonagh, D., 'Plunkett and MacDonagh', in Martin, F. X. (ed.), *Leaders and Men of the Easter Rising: Dublin, 1916*, 1967.

McDowell, R. B., 'Edward Carson', in Cruise O'Brien, C. (ed.), *The Shaping of Modern Ireland*, 1960.

McDowell, R. B., *Alice Stopford Greene: A Passionate Historian*, Dublin, 1967.

McDowell, R. B., *The Irish Convention, 1917-18*, 1970.

Mac Giolla Choille, B. (ed.), *Intelligence Notes, 1913-16*, Dublin, 1966.

McHugh, R., 'Casement and German Help', in Martin, F. X. (ed.), *Leaders and Men of the Easter Rising: Dublin, 1916*, 1967.

McHugh, R., 'The Catholic Church and the Rising', in Dudley Edwards, O., and Pyle, F. (ed.), *1916: The Easter Rising*, 1968.

Mackey, H. O., *The Life and Times of Roger Casement*, Dublin, 1954.

Macintyre, A., *The Liberator: Daniel O'Connell and the Irish Party, 1830-1847*, 1965.

Mansergh, N. S., *The Irish Question, 1840-1921*, 1965, first published as *Ireland in the Age of Reform and Revolution*, 1940.

Mansergh, N. S., 'Ireland and the British Commonwealth of Nations: The Dominion Settlement', in Williams, T. Desmond, *The Irish Struggle, 1916-1926*, 1966.

Mansergh, N. S., 'John Redmond', in Cruise O'Brien, C. (ed.), *The Shaping of Modern Ireland*, 1960.

Marreco, A., *The Rebel Countess*, 1967.

Martin, F. X. (ed.), 'Eoin MacNeill on the 1916 Rising', in *IHS*, xii (Mar. 1961).

* Martin, F. X. (ed.), *The Irish Volunteers, 1913-1915*, Dublin, 1963.

Martin, F. X. (ed.), *The Howth Gun-running, 1914*, Dublin, 1964.

Martin, F. X. (ed.), *1916 and University College, Dublin*, Dublin, 1966.

Martin, F. X., 'The Origins of the Irish Rising of 1916', in Williams, T. Desmond (ed.), *The Irish Struggle, 1916-1926*, 1966.

Martin, F. X. (ed.), *Leaders and Men of the Easter Rising: Dublin 1916*, 1967.

Martin, F. X., '1916 – Myth, Fact and Mystery', in *Studia Hibernica* (Dublin, 1967).

Martin, F. X., 'The 1916 Rising – A *Coup d'Etat* or a "Bloody Protest"?' in *Studia Hibernica* (Dublin, 1968).

Moloney, W., *The Forged Casement Diaries*, Dublin, 1936.

Monteith, R., *Casement's Last Adventure*, Dublin, 1953.

Moody, T. W., 'The New Departure in Irish Politics', 1878-79', in Cronne, H. A., Moody, T. W., and Quinn, D. B. (ed.), *Essays in Honour of James Eadie Todd*, 1949.

* Moody, T. W., and Beckett, J. C. (ed.), *Ulster Since 1800*. 2 series. (1) A political and economic survey, 1955; (2) A social survey, 1957.

Moody, T. W., 'Parnell and the Galway Election of 1886', in *IHS*, ix (March 1955).

Moody, T. W., 'Thomas Davis and the Irish Nation', in *Hermathena*, cii (1966).

* Moody, T. W. (ed.), *The Fenian Movement*, Cork, 1968.

Mowat, C. L., *Britain Between the Wars, 1918-1940*, 1955.

Mowat, C. L., 'The Irish Question in British Politics, 1916-1922', in Williams, T. Desmond, *The Irish Struggle, 1916-1926*, 1966.

* Neeson, E., *The Civil War in Ireland, 1922-1923*, Cork, 1967; paperback ed., Cork, 1969.

Neeson, E., *The Life and Death of Michael Collins*, Cork, 1968.

Nevin, D., 'The Irish Citizen Army', in Dudley Edwards, O., and Pyle, F., *1916: The Easter Rising*, 1968.

Nicolson, Sir Harold, *King George V*, 1952.

Nowlan, K. B., *The Politics of Repeal, 1841-50*, 1965.

Nowlan, K. B., 'Dáil Eireann and the Army: Unity and Division, 1919-1921', in Williams, T. Desmond, *The Irish Struggle, 1916-1926*, 1966.

Nowlan, K. B., 'Tom Clarke, MacDermott and the IRB', in Martin, F. X., *Leaders and Men of the Rising: Dublin 1916*, 1967.

Nowlan, K. B. (ed.), *The Making of 1916*, Dublin, 1969.

* O'Brien, C. Cruise (ed.), *The Shaping of Modern Ireland*, 1960; paperback ed., 1970.

O'Brien, C. Cruise, *Parnell and His Party, 1880-90*, Oxford, 1957; corrected impression, 1964.

O'Brien, C. Cruise, 'The Embers of Easter', in Dudley Edwards, O., and Pyle, F., *1916: The Easter Rising*, 1968.

O'Brien, R. B., *The Life of Charles Stewart Parnell, 1846-1891*, 2 vols., 1898.

O'Brien, W., *An Olive Branch in Ireland*, 1910.

O'Brien, W. and Ryan, D. (ed.), *Devoy's Post Bag*, 2 vols., Dublin, 1948 and 1953.

O Broin, L., *Dublin Castle and the 1916 Rising*, Dublin, 1966.

O Broin, L., *Charles Gavan Duffy*, Dublin, 1967.

O Broin, L., *The Chief Secretary: Augustine Birrell in Ireland*, 1969.

O Broin, L., *Fenian Fever*, 1971.

* O'Connor, F., *The Big Fellow*, Dublin, revised ed., 1965; paperback ed., 1969.

O'Doherty, K., *Assignment – America*, New York, 1957.

* O'Donnell, P., *The Gates Flew Open*, 1932; paperback ed., Cork, 1965.

O'Donoghue, F., *No Other Law*, 1954.

O'Donaghue, F., *Tomás Mac Curtain*, 1958.

O'Donoghue, F., 'Plans for the 1916 Rising', in *University Review*, iii (1962).

O'Donoghue, F., 'Ceannt, Devoy, O'Rahilly and the Military Plan', in Martin, F. X., *Leaders and Men: Dublin 1916*, 1967.

O'Faoláin, S., *Constance Marciewicz*, 1934; paperback ed., 1968.

O'Farrell, P., *Ireland's English Question*, 1971.

O'Hegarty, P. S., *The Victory of Sinn Féin*, Dublin, 1924.

O'Hegarty, P. S., *A History of Ireland Under the Union, 1801-1922*, 1952.

O'Leary, John, *Recollections of Fenians and Fenianism*, 2 vols., 1896.

O Luing, S., *Art O Griofa*, Dublin, 1953.

O Luing, S., 'Arthur Griffith and Sinn Féin', in Martin, F. X., *Leaders and Men: Dublin, 1916*, 1967.

* O'Malley, E., *Army Without Banners*, 1936 (as *On Another Man's Wound*); in paperback under present title, 1967.

O'Shannon, C. (ed.), *Fifty Years of Liberty Hall*, Dublin, 1959.

O'Shea, K., *Charles Stewart Parnell: His Love-story and Political Life*, 2 vols. (1st ed.)., 1914.

* O Tuathaigh, G., *Ireland Before the Famine, 1798-1848*, Dublin and London, 1972.

Pakenham, F. (Lord Longford), *Peace by Ordeal*, 1935.

Pakenham, F., 'The Treaty Negotiations', in Williams, T. Desmond, *The Irish Struggle, 1916-1926*, 1966.

Palmer, N. D., *The Irish Land League Crisis*, New Haven, 1940.

Parmiter, G. de C., *Roger Casement*, 1936.

Paul-Dubois, L., *Contemporary Ireland*. Translated by T. M. Kettle, 1908.

Pearse, P. H., *Political Writings and Speeches*, Dublin, 1922.

Phillips, W. A., *The Revolution in Ireland, 1906-1923*, 2nd ed., 1926.

Plunkett, Sir Horace, *Ireland in the New Century*, 1904.

Ryan, A. P., *Mutiny at the Curragh*, 1956.

Ryan, D., *The Phoenix Flame: A Study of Fenianism and John Devoy*, 1937.

Ryan, D., *The Rising: The Complete Story of Easter Week*, Dublin, 3rd ed., 1957.

Ryan, D., 'Sinn Féin Policy and Practice', in Williams, T. Desmond, *The Irish Struggle, 1916-1926*, 1966.

Ryan, D., *The Fenian Chief*, Dublin, 1967.

* Ryan, D., 'James Stephens and Thomas Clark Luby', and 'John O'Mahony', in Moody, T. W. (ed.), *The Fenian Movement*, 1968.

Savage, D. C., 'The Origins of the Ulster Unionist Party, 1885-6', in *IHS*, xii (Mar. 1961).

Senior, H., *Orangeism in Ireland and Great Britain, 1795-1836*, 1966.

Shaw, F., 'The Canon of Irish History – a Challenge', in *Studies*, xli (summer 1972).

Sheehy-Skeffington, F., *Michael Davitt: Revolutionary, Agitator and Labour*

Leader, 1908; reprinted 1967.

Sheehy-Skeffington, O. S., 'Francis Sheehy-Skeffington', in Dudley Edwards, O., and Pyle, F. (ed.), *1916: The Dublin Rising*, 1968.

Singleton-Gates, P., and Girodias, M. (ed.), *The Black Diaries*, Paris, 1959.

Snoddy, O., *Comhghuai Uitne na Reabhtoide, 1913-1916* (Dublin, 1966).

Snoddy, O., 'The Midland Volunteer Force, 1913', in *Journal of the Old Athlone Society* (1968).

Steele, E. D., 'Ireland and the Empire in the 1860s: Imperial precedents for Gladstone's first Irish Land Act', in *The Historical Journal*, xi, 1 (1968).

Steele, E. D., 'J. S. Mill and the Irish Question: The Principles of Political Economy, 1848-1865', in *The Historical Journal*, xiii, 2 (1970).

Steele, E. D., 'J. S. Mill and the Irish Question: Reform and the Integrity of the Empire, 1865-1870', in *The Historical Journal*, xiii, 3 (1970).

Steele, E. D., 'Gladstone and Ireland' in *Irish Historical Studies*, xviii (Mar. 1970).

Stewart, A. T. Q., *The Ulster Crisis*, 1967.

Stewart, A. T. Q., 'Craig and the Ulster Volunteer Force', in Martin, F. X. (ed.), *Leaders and Men of the Easter Rising: 1916*, 1967.

Strauss, E., *Irish Nationalism and British Democracy*, 1957.

Sullivan, A. M., *New Ireland*, 2 vols., 1877.

Tansill, C. C., *America and the Fight for Irish Freedom, 1886-1922*, New York, 1957.

* Taylor, R., *Michael Collins*, 1958; paperback ed., 1961.

Taylor, R., *Assassination*, 1961.

Thornley, D. A., *Isaac Butt and Home Rule*, 1964.

Thornley, D. A., 'Patrick Pearse – The Evolution of a Republican', in Martin, F. X. (ed.), *Leaders and Men of the Easter Rising: Dublin, 1916*, 1967.

Thornley, D. A., 'Patrick Pearse and the Pearse Family', in *Studies*, xl (autumn-winter, 1971).

Travers, C. J., 'Seán Mac Diarmada, 1883-1916', in *Breifne* (1966).

Van Voris, J., *Constance de Markiewicz in the Service of Ireland*, Amherst (Mass.), 1967.

Wall, M., 'Partition: The Ulster Question, 1916-1926', in Williams, T. Desmond (ed.), *The Irish Struggle, 1916-1926*, 1966.

Wall, M., 'The Background to the Rising, from 1914 until the Issue of the Countermanding Order on Easter Saturday 1916', and 'The Plans and the Countermand: The Country and Dublin', in Nowlan, K. B. (ed.), *The Making of 1916*, Dublin, 1969.

Ward, A. J., 'Frewen's Anglo-American Campaign for Federalism, 1920-21', in *IHS*, xv (Mar. 1967).

Ward, A. J., 'America and the Irish Problem, 1899-1921', in *IHS*, xvi (Mar. 1968).

Ward, A. J., *Ireland and Anglo-American Relations, 1899-1921*, 1969.

White, T. de V., *The Road of Excess*, Dublin, Dublin [1946].

White, T. de V., 'Arthur Griffith', in O'Brien, C. Cruise (ed.), *The Shaping of Modern Ireland*, 1960.

White, T. de V., 'Mahaffy, the Anglo-Irish Ascendancy and the Vice-Regal Lodge', in Martin, F. X. (ed.), *Leaders and Men of the Easter Rising: Dublin, 1916*, 1967.

White, T. de V., *Kevin O'Higgins*, 1948; paperback ed., Tralee, 1967.

Whyte, J. H., *The Independent Irish Party, 1850-59*, Oxford, 1958.

Whyte, J. H., *The Tenant League and Irish Politics in the Eighteen-Fifties*, Dundalk, 1966.

Whyte, J. H., 'Political Problems, 1850-1860', in Corish, P. J. (ed.), *A History of Irish Catholicism*, Dublin, 1967.

Whyte, J. H., 'Revolution and Religion', in Martin, F. X., *Leaders and Men of the Easter Rising: Dublin 1916*, 1967.

* Younger, C., *Ireland's Civil War*, 1968; paperback ed., 1970.

7. POLITICAL DEVELOPMENTS SINCE 1922

A. From Free State to Republic

Aiken, F., *Speeches at the United Nations*, Dublin, 1958 to 1963.

* Bell, J. Bowyer, *The Secret Army*, 1970.

* Bromage, M. C., *De Valera and the March of a Nation*, 1956; paperback ed., 1967.

* Cohen, A., *The Irish Political Elite*, Dublin and London, 1972.

Coogan, T. P., *The I.R.A.*, 1970.

Coogan, T. P., *Ireland Since the Rising*, 1966.

Costello, J. A., *Ireland in International Affairs*, Dublin, n.d.

Dudley Edwards, O. (ed.), *Conor Cruise O'Brien Introduces Ireland*, 1969.

* Farrell, B., *Chairman or Chief?*, Dublin and London, 1972.

FitzGerald, G., *Towards a New Ireland*, 1972.

Gray, T., *Ireland's Answer*, 1966.

Gwynn, D. R., *The Irish Free State, 1922-7*, 1928.

Gwynn, D. R., *The History of Partition, 1912-1925*, Dublin, 1950.

Hancock, W. K., *Survey of British Commonwealth Affairs*, vol. i, Problems of Nationality, 1918-1936, London, 1937.

Harkness, D. W., *The Restless Dominion*, 1969.

Harrison, H., *Ireland and the British Empire*, 1937.

Harrison, H., *The Neutrality of Ireland*, 1941.

Hayes-McCoy, G. A., 'Irish Defence Policy, 1938-51', in Nowlan, K. B., and Williams, T. Desmond (ed.), *Ireland in the War Years and After, 1939-51*, 1969.

Hogan, V. P., *The Neutrality of Ireland in World War II*, Michigan, 1953.

Larkin, E., *James Larkin, Irish Labour Leader, 1876-1947*, 1965.

Longford, Earl of, and O'Neill, T. P., *Eamon de Valera*, 1970.

* Lyons, F. S. L., 'The Minority Problem in the 26 Counties', in MacManus, F. (ed.), *The Years of the Great Test, 1926-39*, Cork, 1967.

Lyons, F. S. L., 'The Years of Readjustment, 1945-51', in Nowlan, K. B., and Williams, T. Desmond (ed.), *Ireland in the War Years and After, 1939-51*, 1969.

McCracken, J. L., *Representative Government in Ireland, 1919-48*, 1958.

McInerney, M., 'Mr John A. Costello Remembers', part 4, in *Irish Times*, 7 Sept. 1967.

McInerney, M., 'Noel Browne: Church and State', in *University Review*, v (Summer, 1968).

* MacManus, F. (ed.), *The Years of the Great Test, 1926-39*, Cork, 1967.

Manning, M., *The Blueshirts*, Dublin and London, 1970.

* Manning, M., *Irish Political Parties*, Dublin and London, 1972.

Mansergh, N. S., *The Irish Free State: Its Government and Politics*, 1934.

Mansergh, N. S., *Survey of British Commonwealth Affairs: Problems of Imperial Policy, 1931-39*, 1952.

Mansergh, N. S. (ed.), *Documents and Speeches on British Commonwealth Affairs, 1931-52*, 1953.

Mansergh, N. S., 'Ireland and the British Commonwealth of Nations', in Williams, T. Desmond (ed.), *The Irish Struggle, 1916-1926*, 1966.

Mansergh, N. S., 'Ireland: External Relations 1926-1939', in MacManus, F. (ed.), *The Years of the Great Test, 1926-39*, Cork, 1967

Mansergh, N. S., 'Irish Foreign Policy, 1945-51', in Nowlan, K. B., and Williams, T. Desmond (ed.), *Ireland in the War Years and After, 1939-51*, 1969.

Mitchell, A., 'William O'Brien, 1881-1968, and the Irish Labour movement', in *Studies*, xl (autumn-winter, 1971).

Moss, W., *Political Parties in the Irish Free State*, Harvard, 1933.

Murphy, J. A., 'The Irish Party System, 1938-51', in Nowlan, K. B., and Williams, T. Desmond (ed.), *Ireland in the War Years and After, 1939-51*, 1969.

Nevin, D., 'Labour and the Political Revolution', in MacManus, F. (ed.), *The Years of the Great Test, 1926-39*, Cork, 1967.

Nowlan, K. B., 'President Cosgrave's Last Administration', in MacManus, F. (ed.), *The Years of the Great Test, 1926-39*, Cork, 1967.

* O'Brien, C. Cruise, *To Katanga and Back*, 1962; paperback ed., 1965.

O'Brien, C. Cruise, 'Ireland in International Affairs', in Dudley Edwards, O. (ed.), *Conor Cruise O'Brien Introduces Ireland*, 1969.

O'Brien, C. Cruise, *States of Ireland*, 1972.

O'Brien, William, *Forth the Banners Go*, edited by E. McLysaght, Dublin, 1969.

* O'Callaghan, S., *The Easter Lily*, 1956; paperback ed., 1967.

O'Sullivan, D., *The Irish Free State and its Senate*, 1940.

Pyne, P., 'The third Sinn Féin party, 1923-26', in *Economic and Social Review*, i (1969-70).

Shearman, H., *Anglo-Irish Relations*, 1948.

Stephan, E., *Spies in Ireland*, 1963.

Thornley, D., 'The Blueshirts', in MacManus, F. (ed.), *The Years of the Great Test, 1926-39*, Cork, 1967.

Viney, M., and Dudley Edwards, O., 'Parties and Power', in Dudley Edwards, O. (ed.), *Conor Cruise O'Brien Introduces Ireland*, 1969.

Wheare, K. C., *The Statute of Westminster*, 4th ed., 1949.

* White, T. de V., *Kevin O'Higgins*, 1948; paperback ed., 1967.

Williams, T. Desmond, 'De Valera in Power', in MacManus, F. (ed.), *The Years of the Great Test, 1926-39*, Cork, 1967.

Williams, T. Desmond (ed.), *The Irish Struggle, 1916-1926*, 1966.

B. Northern Ireland Under Home Rule

Armour, W. S., *Armour of Ballymoney*, 1934.

Barritt, D. P., and Carter, C. F., *The Northern Ireland Problem*, 1962.

Beckett, J. C., and Glasscock, R. E. (ed.), *Belfast: The Origin and Growth of*

An Industrial City, 1967.

Blake, J. W., Northern Ireland in the Second World War, Belfast, 1956.

* Boyd, A., Holy War in Belfast, Tralee, 1969.

* Boyd, A., Brian Faulkner and the Crisis of Ulster Unionism, Tralee, 1972.

* de Paor, L., Divided Ulster, 1970.

* Devlin, B., The Price of My Soul, 1969; paperback ed., 1969.

Dudley Edwards, O., The Sins of our Fathers, Dublin and London, 1970.

* Egan, B., and McCormack, V., Burntollet, 1969.

Elliot, R. S. P., and Hickie, J., Ulster: a Case Study in Conflict, 1971.

Ervine, St J., Craigavon: Ulsterman, 1949.

Falls, C., 'Northern Ireland and the Defence of the British Isles', in Wilson, T. (ed.), Ulster Under Home Rule, 1955.

Gwynn, D. R., The History of Partition, 1912-1925, Dublin, 1950.

Hastings, M., Ulster 1969, 1970.

* Heslinga, M. W., The Irish Border as a Cultural Divide, Assen, Neths., 1971.

Hyde, H. M., Carson, 1953.

* Kelly, H., How Stormont Fell, Dublin and London, 1972.

* Kennedy, D., 'Catholics in Northern Ireland, 1926-39', in MacManus, F. (ed.), The Years of the Great Test, 1926-39, Cork, 1967.

Kennedy, D., 'Ulster During the War and After', in Nowlan, K. B., and Williams, T. Desmond, Ireland in the War Years and After, 1939-51, 1969.

Lawrence, R. J., The Government of Northern Ireland: Public Finance and Public Services, 1921-1964, Oxford, 1965.

* Lyons, F. S. L., 'The Twentieth Century', in Moody, T. W., and Beckett, J. C. (ed.), Ulster Since 1800, second series, 1957.

* McCracken, J. L., 'Northern Ireland, 1921-66', in Moody, T. W., and Martin, F. X. (ed.), The Course of Irish History, Cork, 1967.

* McCracken, J. L., 'The Political Scene in Northern Ireland, 1926-57', in MacManus, F. (ed.), The Years of the Great Test, 1926-39, Cork, 1967.

McDowell, R. B., The Irish Convention, 1917-18, 1970.

Mansergh, N. S., The Government of Northern Ireland, 1936.

Mogey, J. M., 'Ulster's Six Counties', in Wilson, T. (ed.), Ulster Under Home Rule, 1955.

* Moody, T. W., and Beckett, J. C. (ed.), Ulster Since 1800, 2 series; (1) a political and economic survey, 1955; (2) a social survey, 1957.

Newark, F. H., 'The Law and the Constitution', in Wilson, T. (ed.), Ulster Under Home Rule, 1955.

O'Neill, T., Ulster at the Crossroads, 1969.

Riddell, P., Fire Over Ulster, 1970.

Rose, R., Governing Without Consensus, 1971.

Rose, R., 'Ulster Politics: a Select Bibliography of Political Discord', in Political Studies, xx (June 1972).

Shearman, H., Not an Inch: A Study of Northern Ireland and Lord Craigavon, 1942.

* Sunday Times 'Insight Team', Ulster, 1972.

* Target, G. W., Unholy Smoke, 1969.

* The Ulster Debate: Report of a Study Group of the Institute for the Study of Conflict: papers by J. C. Beckett, Sir F. Catherwood, Lord Chalfont, G. FitzGerald, F. S. L. Lyons, R. Moss, 1972.

Wall, M., 'Partition: The Ulster Question, 1916-1926', in Williams, T. Desmond (ed.), The Irish Struggle, 1916-1926, 1966.

Wallace, M., *Drums and Guns: Revolution in Ulster*, 1970.
Wallace, M., *Northern Ireland: 50 Years of Self Government*, Newton Abbott, 1971.

8. GOVERNMENT AND LAW

Akenson, D. H., *The Irish Education Experiment: The National System of Education in the Nineteenth Century*, 1969.

Auchmuty, J. J., *Sir Thomas Wyse, 1791-1862: The Life and Career of an Educator and Diplomat*, 1939.

Auchmuty, J. J., *Irish Education, A Historical Survey*, 1937.

Balfour, G., *The Educational Systems of Great Britain and Ireland*, 1898.

Barrington, D., 'The Irish Constitution' in *Irish Monthly*, vols. 80, 81 and 82 (1951-3).

Barritt, D. P., and Carter, C. F., *The Northern Ireland Problem*, 1962.

Bunreacht na h Eireann: Constitution of Ireland, Dublin, 1937.

Chubb, F. B., 'Vocational Representation and the Irish Senate', in *Political Studies*, ii (1954).

Chubb, B. (ed.), *A Source Book of Irish Government*, Dublin, 1964.

Chubb, B., *The Constitution of Ireland*, 1966.

Chubb, B., *The Government: An Introduction to the Cabinet System in Ireland*, 2nd (revised) ed., Dublin, 1968.

Chubb, B., *The Government and Politics of Ireland*, Stanford and London, 1970.

Collins, J., *Local Government*, 2nd ed. by Roche, D., Dublin, 1963.

Costello, D., 'The Natural Law and the Constitution', in *Studies*, lv (1956).

Delany, V. T. H., 'The Constitution of Ireland, its origins and development', in *University of Toronto Law Journal*, xii (1957).

Delany, V. T. H., 'Fundamental Liberties in the Constitution of Ireland,' in *University of Malaya Law Review*, ii (1960).

Delany, V. T. H., *Christopher Palles*, Dublin, 1960.

Delany, V. T. H., *The Administration of Justice in Ireland*, 2nd ed., revised by Grogan, V., Dublin, 1965.

Digby, M., *Horace Plunkett: An Anglo-American Irishman*, Oxford, 1949.

Farley, J., *Social Insurance and Social Assistance in Ireland*, Dublin, 1964.

Farrell, B., 'Dáil Deputies: the "1969 Generation"', in *Economic and Social Review*, ii, No. 3 (1971).

Finlay, I., *The Civil Service*, Dublin, 1966.

FitzGerald, G., *State-Sponsored Bodies*, 2nd (revised) ed., Dublin, 1963.

FitzGerald, G., *Planning in Ireland*, Dublin and London, 1968.

Garvin, T., 'Continuity and Change in Irish Electoral Politics, 1923-1969', in *Economic and Social Review*, iii, No. 3 (1972).

Grogan, V., 'The Constitution and the Natural Law', in *Christus Rex*, viii (1954).

Grogan, V., 'Towards the New Constitution', in MacManus, F. (ed.), *The Years of the Great Test*, 1926-39, Cork, 1967.

Hensey, B., *The Health Services of Ireland*, Dublin, 1959.

Hoctor, D., *The Department: a History of the Department of Agriculture*, Dublin, 1971.

Hughes, J. L. J., 'The Chief Secretaries in Ireland', in *IHS*, viii (1952-3).

Kaim-Caudle, R., 'Social Security in Ireland and in Western Europe', Economic and Social Research Institute Paper, No. 20, Dublin, 1964.

Kaim-Caudle, R., *Social Policy in the Irish Republic*, 1967.

Kelly, J. M., *Fundamental Rights in the Irish Law and Constitution*, Dublin, 1961; second edition, Dublin, 1967.

Kelly, W. B., *Intermediate and University Education in Ireland*, London and Dublin, 1872.

Kohn, L., *The Constitution of the Irish Free State*, 1932.

Lawrence, R. J., *The Government of Northern Ireland: Public Finance and Public Services, 1921-1964*, Oxford, 1965.

McCracken, J. L., *Representative Government in Ireland: A Study of Dáil Eireann, 1919-48*, 1958.

McDowell, R. B., 'The Irish Executive in the Nineteenth Century', in *IHS*, ix (Mar. 1955).

McDowell, R. B., *The Irish Administration, 1801-1914*, 1964.

McElligott, T. J., *Education in Ireland*, Dublin, 1966.

McGrath, F., *Newman's University: Idea and Reality*, Dublin, 1951.

Mansergh, N. S., *The Irish Free State: Its Government and Politics*, 1934.

Mansergh, N. S., *The Government of Northern Ireland*, 1936.

Micks, W. L., *An Account of the Congested Districts Board of Ireland, 1891-1923, Dublin*, 1925.

Moody, T. W., 'The Irish University Question of the Nineteenth Century' in *History*, xliii (1958).

Moody, T. W., and Beckett, J. C., *Queen's Belfast, 1845-1949: The History of a University*, 2 vols., 1959.

O'Sullivan, D., *The Irish Free State and its Senate*, 1940.

A Page of Irish History. By the Jesuit Fathers, Dublin, 1930.

Rice, V., 'Education in Ireland', in Dudley Edwards, O. (ed.), *Conor Cruise O'Brien Introduces Ireland*, 1969.

Sáorstát Eireann: Irish Free State Official Handbook, Dublin, 1932.

Smyth, J. C., *The Houses of the Oireachtas*, 2nd (revised) ed., Dublin, 1964.

Sullivan, K., *Joyce Among the Jesuits*, New York and London, 1957.

Tierney, M. (ed.), *Struggle with Fortune: A Miscellany for the Centenary of the Catholic University of Ireland, 1854-1954*, Dublin, n.d.

9. THE ECONOMY

Armstrong, D. L., 'Social and Economic Conditions in the Belfast Linen Industry, 1850-1900', in *IHS*, vii (Sept. 1951), 263-7.

Barrington, T., 'A Review of Irish Agricultural Prices', in *JSSISI*, xv, (1926-7).

Beckett, J. C., and Glasscock, R. E. (ed.), *Belfast: Origin and Growth of An Industrial City*, 1967.

Black, R. D. C., 'The Progress of Industrialization, 1850-1920', in Moody, T. W., and Beckett, J. C. (ed.), *Ulster Since 1800*, first series, 1954.

Black, R. D. C., 'Sir James Pirrie', in O'Brien, C. Cruise (ed.), *The Shaping of Modern Ireland*, 1960.

Black, R. D. C., *Economic Thought and the Irish Question, 1817-1870*, Cambridge, 1960.

Black, W., 'Industrial Change in the Twentieth Century', in Beckett, J. C., and Glasscock, R. E. (ed.), *Belfast: Origin and Growth of an Industrial City*, 1967.

Bleakley, D., 'Industrial Conditions in the Nineteenth Century', in Moody,

T. W., and Beckett, J. C. (ed.), *Ulster Since 1800*, second series, 1957.

Bleakley, D. W., 'The Northern Ireland Trade Union Movement', in *JSSISI*, xix (1953-4).

Bourke, P. M. A., 'The Extent of the Potato Crop in Ireland at the Time of the Famine', in *JSSISI*, xix (1955-6).

Bourke, P. M. A., 'Uncertainties in the Statistics of Farm Size in Ireland, 1841-1851', in *JSSISI*, xx (1959-60).

Bourke, P. M. A., 'The Agricultural Statistics of the 1841 Census of Ireland: A Critical Review', in *Economic History Review*, 2nd series, xviii (1965).

Boyd, A., *The Rise of the Irish Trade Unions, 1729-1970*, Tralee, 1972.

Boyle, J. W., 'Le développement du mouvement ouvrier irlandais de 1800 à 1907', in *Le Mouvement Social*, No. 52 (juillet-sept. 1965).

Boyle, J. W., 'Industrial Conditions in the Twentieth Century', in Moody, T. W., and Beckett, J. C. (ed.), *Ulster Since 1800*, second series, 1957.

Boyle, J. W. (ed.), *Leaders and Workers*, Cork, 1965.

Burn, W. L., 'Free Trade in Land: An Aspect of the Irish Question', in *Transactions of the Royal Historical Society*, 4th series, xxxi (1949).

Campbell, J. J., 'Between the Wars', in Beckett, J. C., and Glasscock, R. E. (ed.), *Belfast: Origin and Growth of an Industrial City*, 1967.

Clarkson, J. D., *Labour and Nationalism in Ireland*, New York, 1925.

Coe, W. E., *The Engineering Industry of the North of Ireland*, 1969.

Connell, K. H., *The Population of Ireland, 1756-1845*, Oxford, 1950.

Connell, K. H., 'Marriage in Ireland after the Famine: The Diffusion of the Match', in *JSSISI*, xix (1955-6).

Connell, K. H., *Irish Peasant Society*, 1968.

Connell, K. H., 'Peasant Marriage in Ireland: Its Structure and Development Since the Famine', in *Econ. Hist. Rev.*, 2nd series, xiv (1961-2).

Connolly, J., *Labour in Ireland*, new edition, with an introduction by O'Shannon, C., Dublin, 1960.

Coyne, W. P. (ed.), *Ireland: Industrial and Agricultural*, 1st ed., Dublin, 1901.

Cousens, S., 'Emigration and Demographic Change in Ireland, 1851-61' in *Econ. Hist. Rev.*, second series, xiv (1961-2).

Crotty, R. D., *Irish Agricultural Production: Its Volume and Structure*, Cork, 1966.

Cullen, L. M., 'Irish History Without the Potato', in *Past and Present*, No. 40 (July, 1968).

Cullen, L. M., *An Economic History of Ireland since 1660*, 1972.

Cullen, L. M. (ed.), *The Formation of the Irish Economy*, Cork, 1969.

Cullen, L. M., *Life in Ireland*, 1968.

Drake, M., 'Marriage and Population Growth in Ireland, in *Econ. Hist. Rev.*, second series, xvi (1963).

Drake, M., 'The Irish Demographic Crisis of 1740-41', in Moody, T. W. (ed.), *Historical Studies*, vi (1968).

Dudley Edwards, R., and Williams, T. Desmond (ed.), *The Great Famine*, Dublin, 1956.

Fetter, F. (ed.), *The Irish Pound, 1797-1826*, 1955.

FitzGerald, G., *State-sponsored Bodies*, 2nd (revised) ed., Dublin, 1963.

FitzGerald, G., *Planning in Ireland*, Dublin and London, 1968.

Freeman, T. W., *Pre-famine Ireland: A Study in Historical Geography*, 1957.

Geary, R. C., 'Irish Economic Development Since the Treaty', in *Studies*, xl (Dec. 1951).

Goldstrom, J. M., 'The Industrialisation of the North-East', in Cullen, L. M. (ed.), *The Formation of the Irish Economy*, Cork, 1969.

Greaves, C. G., *The Life and Times of James Connolly*, 1961.

Green, E. R. R., *The Lagan Valley, 1800-1850*, 1949.

Green, E. R. R., 'Agriculture', in Dudley Edwards, O., and Williams, T. Desmond (ed.), *The Great Famine*, Dublin, 1956.

Green, E. R. R., 'Early Industrial Belfast', in Beckett, J. C., and Glasscock, R. E. (ed.), *Belfast: The Origin and Growth of an Industrial City*, 1967.

Green, E. R. R., 'Industrial Decline in the Nineteenth Century', in Cullen, L. M. (ed.), *The Formation of the Irish Economy*, Cork, 1969.

Grimshaw, T., 'A Statistical Survey of Ireland from 1840 to 1888', in *JSSISI*, ix (1889).

Hancock, W. K., *Survey of British Commonwealth Affairs, 1918-1939*, vol. 1, 1937.

* Healy, J., *The Death of an Irish Town*, 2nd ed., Cork, 1968.

Isles, K. S., 'Northern Ireland: An Economic Survey', in Moody, T. W., and Beckett, J. C. (ed.), *Ulster Since 1800*, first series, 1954.

Isles, K. S., and Cuthbert, N., 'Ulster's Economic Structure', in Wilson, T. (ed.), *Ulster Under Home Rule*, 1955.

Isles, K. S., and Cuthbert, N., *An Economic Survey of Northern Ireland*, Belfast, 1957.

Johnston, J., *Irish Agriculture in Transition*, Dublin, 1951.

Jones, E., *A Social Geography of Belfast*, 1960.

Larkin, E., *James Larkin, Irish Labour Leader, 1876-1947*, 1961.

Larkin, E., 'Economic Growth, Capital Investment and the Roman Catholic Church in Nineteenth Century Ireland', in *American Historical Review*, lxxii (Apr. 1967).

Lawrence, R. J., *The Government of Northern Ireland: Public Finance and Public Services, 1921-1964*, Oxford, 1965.

Lee, J., 'The Construction Costs of Early Irish Railways', in *Business History*, ix (1967).

Lee, J., 'The Provision of Capital for Early Irish Railways', in *IHS*, xvi (Mar. 1968).

Lee, J., 'Capital in the Irish Economy', and 'The Railways in the Irish Economy', both in Cullen, L. M. (ed.), *The Formation of the Irish Economy*, Cork, 1969.

Lee, J., 'Irish Agriculture', review article in *The Agricultural History Review*, xvii, part 1 (1969).

Lynch, P., and Vaizey, J., *Guinness's Brewery in the Irish Economy, 1759-1876*, Cambridge, 1966.

Lynch, P., 'The Social Revolution That Never Was', in Williams, T. Desmond (ed.), *The Irish Struggle. 1916-1926*, 1966.

Lynch, P., *The Irish Economy Since the War, 1946-51'*, in Nowlan, K. B., and Williams, T. Desmond (ed.), *Ireland in the War Years and After, 1939-51*, 1969.

Lynch, P., 'The Economic Scene', in Dudley Edwards, O. (ed.), *Conor Cruise O'Brien Introduces Ireland*, 1969.

Lynch, S. J., 'Land Purchase in Ireland,' in *JSSISI*, xlii (1912).

Lyons, F. S. L., 'The Economic Ideas of Parnell', in Roberts, M. (ed.), *Historical Studies*, ii (1959).

846

MacDonagh, O., 'Emigration During the Famine', in Dudley Edwards, R., and Williams, T. Desmond (ed.), *The Great Famine*, Dublin, 1956.

Matheson, R. E., 'The Housing of the People of Ireland During 1841-1901', in *JSSISI*, xi (1904).

Meenan, J., 'From Free Trade to Self-sufficiency', in MacManus, F. (ed.), *The Years of the Great Test, 1926-39*, Cork, 1967.

Meenan, J., 'The Irish Economy During the War', in Nowlan, K. B., and Williams, T. Desmond (ed.), *Ireland in the War Years and After, 1939-51*, 1969.

Meenan, J., *The Irish Economy since 1922*, Liverpool, 1970.

Milne, K., *A History of the Royal Bank of Ireland*, Dublin, 1964.

Mortished, R. J. P., 'The Industrial Relations Act, 1946', in *Public Administration in Ireland*, iii.

Munikanon, U., *The Use of State-sponsored Bodies in the Exploitation of the Natural Resources of Ireland, Unpublished Thesis*, Dublin, n.d.

Nevin, D., 'Labour and the Political Revolution', in MacManus, F., (ed.), *The Years of the Great Test, 1929-39*, Cork, 1967.

Nevin, D., 'Industry and Labour', in Nowlan, K. B., and Williams, T. Desmond (ed.), *Ireland in the War Years and After, 1939-51*, 1969.

Nevin, E., *Wages in Ireland, 1946-62*. Paper No. 12 of the Economic and Social Research Institute, Dublin, 1963.

Nowlan, K. B., and Williams, T. Desmond (ed.), *Ireland in the War Years and After, 1939-51*, 1969.

O'Brien, G., *Economic History of Ireland from the Union to the Famine*, 1921.

O'Brien, G., 'Industries', in *Sáorstát Eireann: Official Handbook*, Dublin, 1932.

O'Brien, J. A. (ed.), *The Vanishing Irish*, 2nd impression, 1955.

O'Carroll, B. M., and Attwood, E. A., *The Structure of the Food Industry in Ireland*, Economic Research Series, No. 4, An Foras Taluntais (August, 1962).

O'Donovan, J., *The Economic History of Live-stock in Ireland*, Cork, 1940.

Oldham, C. H., 'Economics of Industrial Revival in Ireland', in *JSSISI*, xii (1909).

Oldham, C. H., 'The History of Belfast Shipbuilding', in *JSSISI*, xii (1909).

Oldham, C. H., 'Changes in Irish Exports During Twelve Years', and 'Changes in Irish Exports', both in *JSSISI*, xiii (1919).

O'Mahony, D., *Industrial Relations in Ireland: The Background*, Paper No. 19 of the Economic and Social Research Institute, Dublin, 1963.

O'Mahony, D., *The Irish Economy*, 2nd ed., Cork, 1967.

O Núalláin, L., 'A Comparison of the Economic Position and Trend in Eire and Northern Ireland', in *JSSISI*, xvii (1942-7).

Pomfret, J. E., *The Struggle for Land in Ireland, 1800-1923*, Princeton, 1930.

Rebbeck, D., *The History of Iron Shipbuilding on the Queen's Island up to July, 1874*, unpublished doctoral thesis, Belfast, 1954.

Riordan, E. J., *Modern Irish Trade and Industry*, 1920.

Roberts, R., 'Trade Union Organisation in Ireland', in *JSSISI*, xx (1958-9).

Robinson, H. W., *A History of Accountants in Ireland*, Dublin, 1964.

Ross, M., *Personal Incomes by County, 1965*, Paper No. 49 of the Economic and Social Research Institute, Dublin, 1969.

Ryan, W. J. L., 'Measurement of Tariff Levels for Ireland', in *JSSISI*, xviii (1948-9).

Salaman, R. N., *The History and Social Influence of the Potato*, Cambridge, 1969.

Sáorstát Eireann: Official Handbook of the Irish Free State, Dublin, 1932.

Schrier, A., *Ireland and the American Emigration, 1850-1900*, Minneapolis, 1958.

Semmels, A. W., 'The External Commerce of Ireland', in *JSSISI*, xii (1909).

Shearman, H., 'State-aided Land Purchase Under the Disestablishment Act of 1869', in *IHS*, iv (Mar. 1944).

Smith, L. P. F., 'Recent Developments in Northern Irish Agriculture', in *JSSISI*, xviii (1947-52).

Solow, B., *The Land Question and the Irish Economy, 1870-1903*, Cambridge, Mass., and London, 1972.

Synnott, N. J., 'Housing of the Rural Population in Ireland', in *JSSISI*, ix (1904).

Thornley, D., 'The Development of the Irish Labour Movement', in *Christus Rex*, xviii (1964).

10. RELIGION AND THE CHURCHES

Akenson, D. H., *The Irish Education Experiment*, 1969.

Akenson, D. H., *The Church of Ireland: Ecclesiastical Reform and Revolution, 1800-1885*, New Haven and London, 1971.

Barkley, J. M., *A Short History of the Presbyterian Church in Ireland*, 1959.

Barritt, D. P., and Carter, C. F., *The Northern Ireland Problem*, Oxford, 1962.

Beckett, J. C., 'Ulster Protestantism', in Moody, T. W. and Beckett, J. C. (ed.), *Ulster Since 1800*, second series, 1957.

Beckett, J. C., 'Gladstone, Queen Victoria and the Disestablishment of the Irish Church, 1868-9', in *IHS*, xiii (Mar. 1962).

Bell, P. M. H., *Disestablishment in Ireland and Wales*, 1967.

Blanshard, J., *The Church in Contemporary Ireland*, Dublin, 1963.

Blanshard, P., *The Irish and Catholic Power*, London, 1964.

Connell, K. H., *Irish Peasant Society*, 1968.

Connery, D., *The Irish*, 1968.

Corish, P. (ed.), *A History of Irish Catholicism*, Dublin, 1967.

Corish, P., 'Political Problems, 1860-1878', in *A History of Irish Catholicism*, vol. 5, fascicule 3, Dublin, 1967.

* Corkery, J., 'Ecclesiastical Learning', in Corish, P. J. (ed.), *A History of Irish Catholicism*, vol. v, fascicule 9, Dublin, 1970.

Costello, N., *John McHale, Archbishop of Tuam*, Dublin, 1939.

* Cunningham, T. P., 'Church reorganization', in Corish, P. J. (ed.), *A History of Irish Catholicism*, vol. v, fascicule 7, Dublin, 1970.

Dudley Edwards, R., 'Church and State in Modern Ireland', in Nowlan, K. B., and Williams, T. Desmond (ed.), *Ireland in the War Years and After, 1939-51*, 1969.

Fennell, D., *The Changing Face of Catholic Ireland*, 1968.

Fitzpatrick, J. D., *Edmund Rice, Founder and First Superior General of* the Brothers of the Christian Schools of Ireland, Dublin, 1945.

Hurley, M. (ed.), Irish Anglicanism, 1869-1969. Dublin, 1970.

Johnston, T. J., Robinson, J. L., and Jackson, R. W., A History of the Church of Ireland, Dublin, 1953.

Kennedy, D., 'The Catholic Church', in Moody, T. W., and Beckett, J. C. (ed.), Ulster Since 1800, second series, 1957.

Kennedy, D., 'Catholics in Northern Ireland', in MacManus, F. (ed.), The Years of the Great Test, 1926-39, Cork, 1967.

* Kennedy, T. P., 'Church Building', in Corish, P. J. (ed.), A History of Irish Catholicism, vol. v, fascicule 8, Dublin, 1970.

Larkin, E., 'Church and State in Ireland in the Nineteenth Century', in Church History, xxxi (Sept. 1962).

Larkin, E., 'Economic Growth, Capital Investment and the Roman Catholic Church in Nineteenth Century Ireland', in American Historical Review, lxxii (Apr. 1967).

Latimer, W. T., A History of the Irish Presbyterians, 2nd ed., Belfast, 1902.

McCarthy, M. J. F., Priests and People in Ireland, Dublin, 1902.

Macartney, D., 'The Church and the Fenians', in University Review, iv (Winter, 1967).

McClelland, V. A., Cardinal Manning, His Public Life and Influence, 1865-92, 1962.

McGrath, F., Newman's University: Idea and Reality, 1951.

McHugh, R., 'The Catholic Church and the Rising', in Dudley Edwards, O., and Pyle, F. (ed.), 1916: The Dublin Rising, 1968.

McKevitt, P., 'Epilogue: Modern Ireland', in Corish, P. J. (ed.), A History of Irish Catholicism, vol. v, fascicule 10, Dublin, 1970.

MacRéamoinn, S., 'The Religious Position', in Dudley Edwards, O. (ed.), Conor Cruise O'Brien Introduces Ireland, 1969.

MacSuibhne, P., Paul Cullen and His Contemporaries, vol. iii, Naas, 1965.

Moody, T. W., and Beckett, J. C., Ulster Since 1800: A Social Survey History of a University, 2 vols, 1959.

Norman, E. R., The Catholic Church and Ireland in the Eighteen Sixties, Dundalk, 1965.

Norman, E. R., The Catholic Church and Ireland in the Age of Rebellion, 1859-1873, 1965.

* O'Faoláin, S., The Irish, revised paperback ed., 1969.

O'Riordan, M., Catholicity and Progress in Ireland, Dublin, 1906.

Phillips, W. A. (ed.), History of the Church of Ireland from the Earliest Times to the Present Day, vol. iii, 1933.

Plunkett, Sir H., Ireland in the New Century, 1904.

Seaver, G., John Allen FitzGerald Gregg, Archbishop, Dublin, 1963.

Senior, H., Orangeism in Ireland and Britain, 1795-1836, 1966.

* Shearman, H., How the Church of Ireland was Disestablished, Dublin, 1970.

Sheehy, M., Is Ireland Dying? 1968.

Viney, M., The Five Per Cent, Dublin, 1965.

Walsh, P. J., William J. Walsh, Archbishop of Dublin, Cork and Dublin, 1928.

Whyte, J. H., 'Political Problems, 1850-1860', in Corish, P. J. (ed.), A History of Irish Catholicism, vol. iii, fascicule 2, Dublin, 1967.

Whyte, J. H., '1916 – Revolution and Religion', in Martin, F. X. (ed.), Leaders and Men of the Easter Rising: Dublin 1916, 1967.

Whyte, J. H., *Church and State in Modern Ireland*, 1923-1970, Dublin and London, 1971.

II. SOCIETY AND CULTURE

Adams, M., *Censorship: The Irish Experience*, Dublin, 1968.

Arensberg, C., and Kimball, S. T., *Family and Community in Ireland*, 2nd York, 1937; reprinted, Gloucester, Mass., 1959.

Arensberg, C., and Kimball, S. T., *Family and Community in Ireland*, 2nd ed., Cambridge, Mass., 1968.

Atkinson, N., *Irish Education*, Dublin, 1969.

Beckett, J. C., and Glasscock, R. E. (ed.), *Belfast: The Origin and Growth of an Industrial City*, 1967.

Bell, S. H. (ed.), *The Arts in Ulster*, 1951.

Boyd, E. (ed.), *Standish O'Grady: Selected Essays*, Dublin, 1918.

Boyd, E., *Appreciations and Depreciations*, Dublin, 1918.

Boyd, E., *Ireland's Literary Renaissance*, new and revised ed., 1922; reprinted, Dublin, 1968.

Collis, M., *Somerville and Ross: A Biography*, 1967.

Colum, M., *Life and the Dream*, revised ed., Dublin, 1966.

Connell, K. H., *Irish Peasant Society*, Oxford, 1968.

Connery, D. S., *The Irish*, 1968.

* Corkery, D., *Synge and Anglo-Irish Literature*, paperback ed., Cork, 1966.

Coxhead, E., *Lady Gregory*, 1961.

Craig, M. J., *Dublin*, 1660-1860, Dublin and London, 1952.

Cullen, L. M., *Life in Ireland*, 1968.

Curran, C. P., *James Joyce Remembered*, 1968.

Curtis, L. P., *Anglo-Saxons and Celts*, New York, 1968.

Curtis, L. P., *Apes and Angels*, Washington and London, 1972.

Dillon, M., 'Douglas Hyde', in O'Brien, C. Cruise (ed.), *The Shaping of Modern Ireland*, 1960.

* Donoghue, D., *Yeats*, 1971.

Dudley Edwards, O. (ed.), *Conor Cruise O'Brien Introduces Ireland*, 1969.

Eglinton, J., *Irish Literary Portraits*, 1935.

Eglinton, J., *A Memoir of AE*, 1937.

Elliott, R., *Art and Ireland*, Dublin, n.d.

* Ellis-Fermor, U., *The Irish Dramatic Movement*, 2nd ed., 1954; paperback ed., 1967.

* Ellmann, R., *Yeats: The Man and the Masks*, 1949; paperback ed., 1961.

* Ellmann, R., *The Identity of Yeats*, 1954; paperback ed., 1964.

Ellmann, R., *James Joyce*, New York, 1959.

Ellmann, R., *Ulysses by the Liffey*, 1972.

Evans, E. E., *Irish Heritage*, 1942.

Evans, E. E., *Irish Folkways*, 1957.

Fay, G., *The Abbey Theatre, Cradle of Genius*, 1957.

Freeman, T. W., *Pre-famine Ireland: A Study in Historical Geography*, 1957.

Freeman, T. W., *Ireland: A General and Regional Geography*, 3rd ed., 1965.

* Gogarty, O. St J., *As I was Going Down Sackville Street*, 1937; paperback ed., 1954.

Greene, D., 'Michael Cusack and the Rise of the GAA', in O'Brien, C. Cruise (ed.), *The Shaping of Modern Ireland*, 1960.

* Greene, D. H., and Stephens, E. M., *J. M. Synge, 1871-1909*, New York, 1959; paperback ed., New York, 1961.

Gregory, Lady A. (ed.), *Ideals in Ireland*, 1901.

Gregory, Lady A., *Our Irish Theatre*, 1914.

Gregory, Lady A., *Hugh Lane's Life and Achievement*, 1921.

Gwynn, D. R., *Edward Martyn and the Irish Revival*, 1930.

Harvey, J., *Dublin, A Study in Environment*, 1949.

* Henn, T. R., *The Lonely Tower*, 1950; paperback ed., 1965.

Hone, J. M., *The Life of George Moore*, 1936.

* Hone, J. M., *W. B. Yeats, 1865-1939*, 1942; 2nd ed., 1962; paperback ed., 1965.

Howarth, H., *The Irish Writers: Literature under Parnell's Star*, 1958.

Humphreys, A. J., *New Dubliners: Urbanization and the Irish Family*, 1966.

Hyde, D., 'The Necessity for De-Anglicising Ireland', in Gavan Duffy, Sir G., Sigerson, G., and Hyde, D., *The Revival of Irish Literature*, 1894.

Hyde, D., *A Literary History of Ireland from the Earliest Times to the Present Day*, 1899; new ed., 1968.

Jackson, J. A., *The Irish in Britain*, 1963.

* Jeffares, A. N., *W. B. Yeats: Man and Poet*, 1949; paperback ed., 1962.

Jeffares, A. N., and Cross, K. G. W. (ed.), *In Excited Reverie*, London and New York, 1965.

Jones, E., *A Social Geography of Belfast*, 1960.

* Kaim-Caudle, P., *Social Policy in the Irish Republic*, 1967.

Loftus, R. J., *Nationalism in Modern Anglo-Irish Poetry*, Madison and Milwaukee, 1964.

Lyons, F. S. L., 'George Moore and Edward Martyn,' in *Hermathena*, xcviii (1964).

Macartney, D., 'D. P. Moran and Irish Ireland', in Martin, F. X. (ed.), *Leaders and Men of the Easter Rising: 1916*, 1967.

MacDonagh, T., *Literature in Ireland*, Dublin, 1916.

McElligott, T., *Education in Ireland*, Dublin, 1966.

McGrath, F., *Newman's University*, Dublin, 1951.

* McGrath, F., 'The University Question', in Corish, P. J. (ed.), *A History of Irish Catholicism*, vol. v, fascicule 6, Dublin, 1970.

MacManus, F., Imaginative Literature and the Revolution', in Williams, T. Desmond (ed.), *The Irish Struggle, 1916-1926*, 1966.

* MacManus, F., 'The Literature of the Period', in MacManus, F. (ed.), *The Years of the Great Test, 1926-39*, Cork, 1967.

MacNiece, L., *Collected Poems, 1925-1948*, 1949.

Malone, A. E., *Irish Drama*, 1929; reprinted New York, 1965.

Martin, A., 'Literature and Society, 1938-51', in Nowlan, K. B., and Williams, T. Desmond (ed.), *Ireland in the War Years and After, 1939-51*, 1969.

Meenan, J. (ed.), *Centenary History of the Literary and Historical Society of University College, Dublin, 1855-1955*, Tralee, n.d.

Mogey, J. M., *Rural Life in Northern Ireland*, 1950.

Moody, T. W., and Beckett, J. C., *Queen's University, 1845-1949: The* (second series), 1957.

Moore, G., *Hail and Farewell*, Ebury ed., 1937.

Moran, D. P., *The Philosophy of Irish Ireland*, Dublin, 1905.
* Murphy, I., 'Primary Education', in Corish, P. J. (ed.), *A History of Irish Catholicism*, vol. v, fascicule 6, Dublin, 1970.
O'Brien, C. Cruise, 'Passion and Cunning', in Jeffares, A. N., and Cross, K. G. W. (ed.), *In Excited Reverie*, 1965.
*O'Connor, F., *An Only Child*, 1961; paperback ed., 1965.
* O'Casey, S., *Autobiographies*, 1939-54; combined paperback ed. (2 vols.), 1963.
O Catháin, S., 'Education', in *Studies*, xl (Dec. 1951).
O Catháin, S., 'Education in the New Ireland', in MacManus, F. (ed.) *The Years of the Great Test, 1926-39*, Cork, 1967.
O Cúiv, B., 'Education and Language', in Williams, T. Desmond (ed.), *The Irish Struggle, 1916-1926*, 1966.
O Cúiv, B. (ed.), *A View of the Irish Language*, Dublin, 1969.
O'Driscoll, R. (ed.), *Theatre and Nationalism in 2oth Century Ireland*, 1971.
* O Faoláin, S., *The Irish*, 1948; revised paperback ed., 1969.
O'Farrell, S., 'The Changing Pattern of Irish Life', in *Studies* (Dec. 1951), xl.
O Suilleabháin, S. V., 'Secondary Education', in Corish, P. J. (ed.), *A History of Irish Catholicism*, vol. v, fascicule 6, Dublin, 1970.
O'Sulleahháin, S., *A Handbook of Irish Folklore*, Dublin, 1942.
O'Sullivan, D., *Irish Folk Music and Song*, Dublin, 1952.
O'Sullivan, T. F., *The Story of the GAA*, Dublin, 1916.
Plunkett, Sir H., *Ireland In the New Century*, 1904.
Praeger, R. Lloyd, *The Way That I Went*, Dublin, 1937.
Pritchett, V. S., *Dublin*, 1967.
Robinson, L. (ed.), *Lady Gregory's Journal, 1916-1930*, 1946.
Robinson, L., *Ireland's Abbey Theatre*, 1951.
Skelton, R., *The Writings of J. M. Synge*, 1971.
Stanford, W. B., and McDowell, R. B., *Mahaffy*, 1971.
Strickland, W. G., *A Dictionary of Irish Artists*, Dublin, 1913.
Synge, J. M., *Plays, Poems and Prose*, Everyman ed., 1941.
Thompson, W. I., *The Imagination of an Insurrection: Dublin, Easter 1916*, New York, 1967.
Tierney, M. (ed.), *Struggle with Fortune*, Dublin, n.d. [1954].
Ussher, A., *The Face and Mind of Ireland*, 1949.
Wade, A. (ed.), *Letters of W. B. Yeats*, 1954.
White, T. de V., *The Story of the Royal Dublin Society*, Tralee, 1955.
White, T. de V., *Ireland*, 1968.
White, T. de V., *The Anglo-Irish*, 1972.
Yeats, W. B., *Collected Poems*, 1952.
Yeats, W. B., *Autobiographies*, 1955.
Yeats, W. B., *Essays and Introductions*, 1961.
Zimmermann, G. D., *Songs of Irish Rebellion*, Dublin, 1967.

Index

Burntollet, 764

Butler, Maire, 255-6

Butt, Isaac, his career as a lawyer, 147-8; founds the Home Government Association, 149-50; and development of Home Rule movement, 140-56, 158, 163, 180; and foundation of Home Rule League, 152; Moran's comments on, 232; mentioned, 30, 168, 247, 261; *see also Irish Federalism*

Cadhain, Maírtín O., 643

Cahirciveen, 356

Callaghan, Rt. Hon. James, M.P., 767

Callan, 114

Cameron Commission: Report, 768

Campbell-Bannerman, Sir Henry, 264

Canada, Irish emigration to, 16, 38, 45; Fenian invasions of, 135; Bonar Law's birth in, 301; at Imperial Conference (1926), 508-9; Costello's visit to (1948), 564-9; at Commonwealth Conference (1948), 569; Irish exports to, 573; and United Nations, 593; mentioned, 150, 435, 443-6, 504, 505, 515, 518

Capital Grants to Industry Acts (1954-62) *see* Northern Ireland

Capital Investment Advisory Committee (1955), 583, 628

Carlow, 90, 117, 199, 360

Carnarvon, Earl of, 181-2, 183

Carney, Winifred, 374

Carroll, Dr William, 160-2, 164

Carson, Sir Edward, 97n-8n, 255, 299-310, 327, 329, 378-9, 414, 715-16

Casement, Sir Roger, 323-8, 339-40, 350-5, 364-5, 377, 382, 396, 570

Castle Document, the, 354, 356

Castletownshend, 533

Cathleen ni Houlihan (Yeats), 241

Catholic Church, membership of, 17-18, 19, 23, 143, 688-9, 749; emancipation of (1829), 18-19, 22, 71-2, 104, 107; and education, 19, 21, 31, 81-6, 90-8, 106, 144-5, 152, 266, 654-5, 689, 721-3, 743, 754; and ultra-montanism, 20; attitude of towards Fenian movement, 21, 126-33, 137-8, 688; and Easter Rising, 21, 133; and Home Rule movement, 22, 23, 153, 288-9, 683; and marriage, 52; and Ecclesiastical Titles Act, 116, 118; and Catholic Defence Association, 116, 119; and Tenant League, 116, 117, 119-20, 122; attitude of towards socialism, 127, 129, 525; and disestablishment of Church of Ireland, 143-4, 146; and Home Government Association, 148-50; and Land League, 169; and Irish National League, 179, 182; and 'Plan of Campaign', 190-1; Plunkett's criticisms of, 209; and trade union movement, 283, 673, 675, 726-7; and Home Rule Bill (1912), 309; and I R B, 389; and anti-conscription campaign (1918), 393; and Treaty (1921), 465;

and teachings of Pius XI, 528, 545; status of under Constitution of 1937, 545-8, 577; and contraception, 548, 682n, 686, 690; and League of Nations, 552; opposed to 'the mother and child scheme', 574-8; and Ne Temere decree, 683n; and censorship, 686-8; and influence of priests, 688-90; and Second Vatican Council, 689-90; changes in, 690-1; and development of television, 691-2; mentioned, 100, 263, 282, 686, 713

Catholic Defence Association, 116, 119

Catholic Relief Act (1793), 90

Catholicism, and employment, 27, 74, 102, 289, 293, 725-6, 753-5, 757, 762; in Northern Ireland, 23, 309, 414, 425, 452-3, 455, 460, 695, 716-17, 719-27, 730, 749-80; representation of in Dáil, 405; ratio of priests to population and, 689n

cattle-farming, development of, 19, 26, 37, 40, 49-51, 620-1, 623, 626-7, 631, 708, 733-4; and export market, 40, 48-9, 58, 557, 608, 612-13, 620, 623, 626-7, 745; mentioned, 602-3, 605

Cavan, 165, 292, 394-6

Cavendish, Lord Frederick, 176

Ceannt, Eamonn, 341, 342, 343, 352, 353, 370, 376, 377n

Celtic Literary Societies, 247

Celtic sagas, 234-6

Celtic Society, 225

censorship, and Censorship of Publications Act (1929), 686, 687; and Censorship Board, 686-7; and Constitution of 1937, 687; and Film Censor, 688; and Film Appeal Board, 688; and television, 692

Censorship Board *see* censorship

Censorship of Publications Act (1929) *see* censorship

Census of Ireland (1841), 36, 38n, 39, 41n, 53

Census of Ireland (1861), 18, 23, 143

Census of Ireland (1901), 53, 88n, 97

Census of Ireland (1911), 24, 53, 88, 92, 93, 635, 707

Census of Ireland (1926), 601, 707, 711

Census of Ireland (1937), 707

Census of Ireland (1961), 671

Census of Ireland (1966), 630

Censuses of Industrial Production, 63, 64, 67, 68, 69, 601-2

Chamberlain, Rt. Hon. Sir Austen, M.P., 430, 436-7

Chamberlain, Rt. Hon. Joseph, M.P., 180, 182-6, 195, 205

Chamberlain, Rt. Hon. Neville, M.P., 364, 522, 554, 622

Chichester-Clarke, Major J. D., 765-6, 772, 774

Childers, Erskine, 325, 406, 427, 431, 434, 439, 445-6, 455n, 466

Christensen, Adler, 340

Christian Brothers, schools run by, 82, 84, 89, 92, 331, 384

burnt in (1972), 588, 779; and economic developments, 599, 618, 685; emigration from, 622; teachers' training colleges in, 638; Irish-speakers in, 644-5; welfare in, 661; education in (1971), 654; television in, 692n; IRA headquarters in, 769, 772; arms trials in, 771n

Dublin Hermetic Society, 234

Duffy, Charles Gavan, Sir, 105, 107-10, 113, 115-16, 120, 122, 126, 130, 162, 237, 238

Duffy, Charles Gavan, son of the above, 430, 436-9, 451

Duggan, Eamon, 430, 438, 451

Duke, H. E., 382

Dun Laoghaire, 484

Dundee, 306

Dungannon, 353, 762, 763

Dungannon Clubs, 255, 256, 316, 324

Dungarvan, 533

Dungiven, 777

Dunne, Reginald, 459-60

Dunraven, Earl of, 32, 218, 219n, 220, 222, 233, 246, 264, 474

Dunsany, Baron, 207

Easter Rising (1916), Catholic Church's attitude to, 21, 133; Irish-American support for, 29, 339-40, 350, 395; Pearse's role in, 111, 330, 342, 344-7, 353-8, 570, 635; and influence of Fenianism, 137, 235; Ryan's view of, 239n; Connolly's role in, 275, 280, 339, 342-8, 353-5; preparations for, 329-58; and Proclamation of Independence, 342, 344-5, 368-71, 377, 383-4, 545; events of, 374-83; consequences of, 375-83; de Valera's role in, 384, 389; Collins's role in, 388; Lemass's role in, 584; and republican revival (1966), 759, 760-1; mentioned, 237, 317, 447, 449, 462, 539, 683-4, 779

Ecclesiastical Titles Act (1851), 116, 118

Economic and Social Research Institute, 659

Economic Development (Whitaker Report, 1958), 583, 584, 599, 603, 607, 628, 652

Edgeworthstown, murder of Richard More O'Ferrall in, 533

education, and Catholic Church, 19, 21, 31, 81-6, 90-8, 106, 144-5, 148, 266, 652, 654-5, 689, 721-3, 743, 754; and Protestant Church, 82-6, 90-1, 93-8, 106, 654-5, 722-3; University, 31, 93-8, 106, 144, 152, 229, 266, 645n, 653-8, 741, 742, 753-4; under British administration, 80, 81-98, 655; and National Schools, 82-9, 94, 229, 274, 384, 387, 636, 645-8, 659; and Model Schools, 85-6; and Irish Education Act (1892), 87, 647; and Educational Endowments Act (1885), 91; and Intermediate Education Act (1878), 91; and Intermediate Education Act (1914), 91; and University Education (Ireland) Act

(1879), 96; Pearse's work in, 331-3, 652; in Irish Free State, 546, 635-40, 645-52; and Constitution of 1937, 546; in Republic of Ireland, 639-40, 647-58, 742; and Intermediate Education Act (1921), 647; and Local Authorities (Education Scholarships) Amendment Act (1961), 647; and School Attendance Act (1926), 647-8; and Intermediate Education (Amendment) Act (1924), 649; and Vocational Education Act (1930), 650; in Northern Ireland, 702, 704, 705, 722-3, 736, 741-3, 751, 753-4, 758

Education Act (1892), 647

Education Act (1923) *see* Northern Ireland

Educational Endowments Act (1885) *see* education

Edward VII, King, 254, 268

Edward VIII, King, 517-18

Edwards, Professor R. Dudley, 693

Edwards, O. Dudley, 586n, 591

Egan, John, 533

Egan, Patrick, 158, 161, 176

Eglinton, John, 234, 239-40, 245

Eighty Club, 191

Electoral Amendment Act (1927), 477, 498-9

Electricity Supply Board, 608, 616-19

Eltham, 195

Emancipation Act (1829), 116, 117

Emergency Powers Act (1940), 534-5

emigration, as a result of the Famine, 15-16, 27, 44-5, 114; to America, 16, 38, 44-5, 123; to Canada, 16, 38, 44-5; to Australia, 16, 44-5 to New Zealand, 16; to Britain, 16, 38, 44-5, 123, 164, 622, 624, 685, 679, 707, 732; population decline affected by, 38, 44-7, 99, 609, 622, 707, 757; of agricultural labourers, 54, 101, 603; during Second World War, 557, 603, 622-3, 732; post-war, 573, 625, 630, 632; effects of, 665, 691

Emigration Commission Report, 604

Emmet, Robert, 232, 387n

Emmet Monument Association, 387n

Employers' Federation, 282

Encumbered Estates Act (1849), 26, 47, 114

Ennis, 168

Enniscorthy, 366

Erne, Lord, 168

European Economic Community *see* Common Market

European Recovery Programme, 571

Everard, Colonel Nugent T., 218

Everett, J., 562

evictions, 42, 43, 114-15, 145, 165, 168, 170, 188-90, 266

External Relations Act (1936), 520, 550, 563-7

Famine, 15-16, 19, 25-6, 34, 40-6, 78-9, 104, 107-8

864

MacGiolla, Tomás, 769
McGrath, Joseph, 451, 485, 489, 490, 492
McGuinness, Sean, 532
MacHale, Archbishop John, 84, 130
McInerney, M., 586n
McKee, Richard, 419, 423-4
Mackintyre, Patrick, 373
McLaughlin, Dr T. A., 616
MacManus, F., 683n
MacManus, Terence Bellew, 131
MacNeill, Eoin, and Gaelic League,
227-9, 320, 333; his comments on
Ulster Volunteers, 321, 336; his role in
the Irish Volunteers, 321-3, 325, 327-8,
330, 341, 346-50, 353-8, 361; and
Easter Rising (1916), 347-50, 353-9,
364-5; and first session of Dáil Éireann
(1919), 404; and second session of Dáil
Éireann (1919), 406; and War of Inde-
pendence (1919-21), 424; in Provisional
Government (1922), 451; as Minister
of Education, 485, 491, 646; and Boun-
dary Commission, 491-2; mentioned,
369, 381, 385, 498, 693; see also 'The
North Began'
MacNeill, James, 514, 518
MacNiece, Dr, Anglican Bishop of Down,
727
Macpherson, James, 224n-5n
McQuaid, Dr John Charles, Catholic
Archbishop of Dublin, 690
McQuillan, J., 561
Macready, General Sir Neville, 416-17,
418n, 460-1
MacRory, Cardinal, 726
MacStiofáin, Sean, 772
MacSwiney, Mary, 448, 455n, 467, 535
MacSwiney, Terence, 366, 418, 448
Maffey, Sir John see Rugby, Lord
Magee, Mrs, 95
Magee, W. K., see Eglinton, John
Mageean, Dr, Catholic Bishop, 727
Magennis, Professor William, 493
Magheramorne Manifesto, 296
Mallin, Michael, 367, 376, 377n
Mallow, 104
Manchester, 137, 157, 571
Manchester Guardian, 415
'Manchester Martyrs' see Britain
Mangan, James Clarence, 228n, 239
'Manifesto to the Irish People' (Parnell),
198
Manning, M., 528n
Mansergh, Professor N., 476, 508, 516n
Mansion House Conference (1918), 394
Markievicz, Count Casimir, 285
Markievicz, Countess Constance, 285-6,
317, 366, 367, 375, 376, 406, 428, 455n,
462
Marshall Aid, 589
Martin, Rev. Professor F. X., 342n, 343n,
693
Martyn, Edward, 230, 234, 236, 238, 255,
280
Marxism, 138, 184, 275, 280, 334, 345n,
502, 528, 675, 721, 769; see also
communism

Matthew, Sir Robert, 747
Maxwell, Major-General Sir John, 375,
376, 382
Maynooth Act (1845), 94
Mayo, county, population growth in,
44-5; education in, 88; Davitt's birth in,
162, 165; and Congested Districts
Board, 206; and United Irish League,
216; George Moore's connection with,
236; emigration from, 622; and the
Gaeltacht, 640n; mentioned, 117, 526
Mayo, Earl of, 218, 474
Mazzini, Guiseppe, 120, 224
Meagher, Thomas Francis, 109
Meath, county, 156, 418, 640n
Mechanics' Institutes, 86
Medical Charities Act see Poor Relief
(Ireland) Act
Medical Research Council, 618
Mellows, Liam, 366, 450, 451, 454, 467
'Message to the Free Nations of the
World' (Dáil Éireann), 401
Methodist Church, 18, 547, 717, 749
Meyer, Kuno, 225
Midland Volunteer Force, 321n
Midleton, Lord, 291, 298
Milk Boards, 618
Military Pensions Act (1934), 532
Military Service Bill (1918), 393
Ministers and Secretaries Act (1924), 479,
482
Ministers and Secretaries (Amendment)
Act (1946), 660
Mise Eire, 644
Mitchel, John, 109-11, 113, 124, 126, 239,
248
Mitchelstown 'massacre', 191-2
Model Schools, 85-6
Monaghan, county, 105, 455n
Monteagle, Lord, 210, 325
Monteith, Robert, 340, 352
Montgomery, Major-General Sir Hugh,
727
Moody, Professor T. W., 693
Moore, George, 116, 213n-14n, 234,
236-8, 241, 245
Moore, George Henry, 116, 122, 150
Moore, Maurice, 116, 327
Moore, Thomas, 228, 239
Moore, William, 295n
Moran, D. P., 230-3, 238-41; see also
'Philosophy of Irish Ireland'
Morel, E. D., 324
Morgan, William, 762
Moriarty, Dr David, Catholic Bishop of
Kerry, 130
Morley, Rt. Hon. John (later Viscount),
191, 197, 264
Morning Post, 415, 491
Morrissey, Daniel, 562
Mulcahy, General Richard, 397, 404,
411, 427, 450-1, 453-4, 466, 485, 489,
490, 562, 580, 585
Mullinahone, 128
Munich crisis (1938), 554
Municipal Corporations Act (1840) see
local government

Munster, Protestant population of, 23;
Tenant Protection societies in, 114;
IRB activities in, 114, 317; Irish
Volunteers activities in, 353; in Civil
War (1922), 464-5; television in, 692n
The Murder Machine (Pearse), 89, 652
Murphy, T. J., 562, 571
Murphy, William Martin, 243, 245, 263,
282, 284
Mussolini, Benito, 528, 529
Myles, Sir Thomas, 326

Na Fianna Éireann, 317
Nannetti, J. P., M.P., 275
Nathan, Sir Matthew, 362-7, 377
Nation, launching of, 105; Lalor's con-
tributions to, 108; Mitchel's contribu-
tions to, 109-10; Stephens influenced
by, 123-4; O'Mahony and, 124; Luby
influenced by, 126; opposed to
Phoenix Society, 126; O'Leary in-
fluenced by, 128; and Home Rule
movement, 156; mentioned, 224, 225,
243n, 248
National Association, 143
National Board of Education, 82, 83-6,
88-9
National Brotherhood of Saint Patrick,
131
National Centre Party, 526-7, 530
National Corporative Party, 531
National Council, 255-6
National Defence Fund, 394
National Farmers' and Ratepayers'
League, 526
National Gaelic Congress *see* Comhdháil
Náisiúnta na Gaelige
National Guard, 529-30
National Insurance Act (1911), 668
National Labour Party, 562, 679
National League *see* Northern Ireland
National League Party, 497, 499-500
National Liberal Club, 194
National Library, 213
National Literary Society *see* Irish
National Literary Society
National Museum, 213, 330
National Progressive Democratic Party,
586
National Repeal Association, 104-9, 124,
251
National Review, 415
National Schools *see* education
National System of Protection (List),
253-4
National Union of Dock Labourers *see*
trade union movement
National Volunteers, 330, 349
Nationalist party (Northern Ireland),
Catholic allegiance to, 695, 716, 717,
721; and Special Powers Act, 698;
and Boundary Commission, 715; and
general election (1921), 724; and local
government, 717-18, 755-6; and general
election (1929), 718-19; and general
election (1933), 718; and Education

Acts, 722-3, 743; problems facing, 722-
5, 749, 751-4; composition of, 724,
751; and Second World War, 728
Nationalist Political Front, 752-3
Nationality, 381
'The Necessity for de-Anglicising Ireland'
(Hyde), 228-9
Neeson, E., 462n; *see also The Civil War
in Ireland*
'New Departure', the, 132, 164, 166, 168
New Industries (Development) Act (1932)
see Northern Ireland
New Industries (Development) Act (1937)
see Northern Ireland
New Ireland, 243n
New Ireland Review, 230
New Ireland Society, 332
New Tipperary, 190
New Zealand, Irish emigration to, 16; at
Commonwealth Conference (1948),
569; mentioned, 505, 518
Newe, Dr Gerald, 777
Newman, Cardinal John, 94-6, 144, 658;
see also The Idea of a University
Newport, county Mayo, 418
Newry, 98, 292, 751, 764
North Atlantic Treaty Organisation,
591-2, 598
'The North Began' (MacNeill) *see An
Claidheamh Soluis*
Northern Ireland, and Government of
Ireland Act (1920), 424-5, 492-3, 695-8,
700-2, 705-6; and general election
(1921), 425, 717; and treaty negotiations (1921), 427-8, 432-8; and Treaty
of 1921, 444-5, 490, 506; and Boundary Commission, 452, 490-3, 696,
715-16, 721, 723; IRA attacks on
(1922), 452-3, 454-5; and Civil War,
454-5; and Council of Ireland, 492-3;
Royal Ulster Constabulary in, 480,
699, 754, 767, 768; and Republic of
Ireland Act (1948), 567; and Ireland
Act (1949), 568, 738; IRA arms raids
on (1952), 581; and Labour party,
(1970s), 586; religio–political riots in
(1960s-70s), 587-8, 582n, 766-80; and
O'Neill's meeting with Lemass (1965),
587; and Common Market, 598n;
welfare in, 670, 672, 736-7, 738-44,
757-8; and trade union movement,
676-7, 679-82, 720, 749-50, 754; the
franchise in, 697, 698, 718, 755-7, 762,
764-5, 766n, 773; and Civil Authority
(Special Powers) Act (1922), 698-9,
726, 761, 774; and Public Order Act
(1951), 699; and Flags and Emblems
Act (1954), 699; and B specials, 699,
754n, 768, 777; and Colwyn Committee, 702-4; unemployment in, 702,
703-4, 731-2, 739, 741-2, 746, 747-8,
757, 762; and Unemployment Insurance Agreement (1926), 704-5; and
British naval strategy, 705, 728-9;
economic developments in, 706-14,
730-5, 745-8; emigration from, 707,
732, 757; population distribution in,

871

Recess Committee, 211, 213
Redmond, John, M.P., supported by Parnellites, 202-3, 260; and All-Ireland Committee, 212; and Land Conference (1902), 218, 220, 263; D. P. Moran's comments on, 232; parliamentary talents of, 260-1; personality of, 260-1; and United Irish League, 260-2, 265; and general election (1900), 262; opposed by Healy, 263, 265-7; opposed by O'Brien, 263, 265-7; and Irish Council Bill (1907), 265; and budget crisis (1909), 267-8; and Parliament Act (1911), 269; and Irish Volunteers, 286n, 309, 310, 327-8, 329-30, 341; and Home Rule Bill (1912), 302-4, 306-7, 309-10; and First World War, 310, 329, 361; and Government of Ireland Act (1914), 310-11, 379-80; and National Volunteers, 330, 349; and relationship with Nathan, 362; and Easter Rising (1916), 378-9; opposed by Sinn Féin, 383, 386; and Irish Convention (1917-18), 385; mentioned, 30, 258, 320, 333, 361, 393, 433, 489, 495, 497
Redmond, Captain William, M.P., 499
Removal of Oath Act (1933), 513-14, 527, 536
Renunciation Act (1783), 252
Representative Church Body, 144
Republican of Ireland Act (1948), 567
Republican Congress, 532-3
Restoration of Order in Ireland Act (1920), 417
The Resurrection of Hungary (Griffith), 251-2, 257
Ribbon Societies, 262n
Ribbonism, 129
Rice, Sir Cecil Spring, 325
Rice, Rev. Edmund, 82
Rice, Mary Spring, 325
Rice, Vincent, 500
Richardson, Sir George, 305
The Riddle of the Sands (Childers), 325
Ring, 640n
Ritchie, John, 65
Ritchie, William, 65
roads *see* communications
Roberts, Field Marshal Earl, 305
Robinson, Sir Henry, 73
Robinson, Seumas, 409
Rochdale, 115
Rolleston, T. W., 228, 237
Rome, 119, 120, 129-30, 529
Rooney, William, 229, 238, 248-9
Roosevelt, Franklin D., President, 555
Roscommon, county, 206, 227, 236, 382, 389, 526
Rose, Professor Richard, 450n
Rosebery, Earl of, 264
Rosscarbery, 126
Rosse, Earl of, 91
Royal Free Schools, 90
Royal Irish Academy, 224, 225n
Royal Irish Constabulary, functions of, 75-6, 409; and Easter Rising (1916),

349, 364, 366, 375, 377n; and War of Independence (1919-21), 409-10, 412-13, 415-20; and Black and Tans, 415-20, 452; Auxiliary Division of, 416-20, 452; disbandment of, 452; payment of pensions to, 495, 611; mentioned, 480, 560, 699
Royal Ulster Constabulary *see* Northern Ireland
Rugby, Lord, 554-5, 567n
Russell (A E), 210, 215, 234-7, 245
Russell, George William *see* Russell (A E)
Russell, Lord John, 42
Russell, Sean, 450, 532, 534, 556-7
Russell, T. W., 215, 218, 296-7
Russia, 243 *and see* Soviet Union
Russo-Turkish War (1877), 158
'Ruthless Warfare' (Blythe), 397-8
Ryan, Dr Dermot, 690
Ryan, Desmond, 122n, 239n, 368, 388
Ryan, Frank, 556-7
Ryan, Dr James, 368, 584
Ryan, Dr Mark, 255
Ryan, W. P., 239, 240, 258

Sadleir, John, 117-19, 121
St Helen's, 162
Salisbury, Marquess of, and coercion, 31, 181, 183; and Home Rule, 181-2, 187
Salvidge, Sir Archibald, 434
Sandycove, 324
Saoirse?, 644
Saor Eire, 502, 503, 532, 560
Saunderson, Colonel E. J., M.P., 211, 212, 218, 291, 292, 296, 299
Sayers, Peig, 643
School Attendance Act (1926), 647
School Attendance Bill (1942), 544
Schwabe, G. C., 65
Scotland, in economic competition with Ireland, 61; and educational links with Ireland, 93; Irish emigration to, 123, 732; and Irish Home Rule movement, 150; and Ulster Loyalist Anti-Repeal Union, 292; I R B activities in, 318; mentioned, 65, 702, 739
Second International, 676
Second Economic Programme *see* Second Programme for Economic Expansion
Second Programme for Economic Expansion (1963), 631-3
Second World War, and Irish marriage-rate, 46; outbreak of, 535; and League of Nations, 552-3; emigration during, 603, 622-3; and economic developments, 616-17, 619, 622-5, 628; and education, 655, 656; and welfare, 659-63, 669, 670; and trade union movement, 678; and Northern Ireland, 709, 713, 726, 728-38; mentioned, 479-80, 549
Seely, Colonel J. E. B., 308
Sexton, James, 278
Shamrock, 225
Shannon Free Airport Development Company, 642

875

World War, 555, 591, 728, 729; Sean Russell's activities in, 556n; and European Recovery Programme, 571; and Marshall Aid, 589-90; de Valera's anti-partition campaign in (1948), 591; and NATO, 590-1; and United Nations, 594-6; Brian Faulkner in, 766; mentioned, 28, 194, 441, 581, 598, 692; *see also* American Civil War

United Trades' Association *see* trade union movement

University Bill (1873), 152

University Education (Ireland) Act (1879) *see* education

Valera, Eamon de, and Easter Rising (1916), 376, 384, 385, 391; elected as member for East Clare, 383; and I R B, 389, 391; and Sinn Féin, 390-2; and Irish Volunteers, 392; and Mansion House Conference (1918), 394; and general election (1918), 398; and first session of the Dáil (1919), 401-2; escapes from Lincoln Jail (1919), 405; elected as President of Dáil (1919), 406, 421; and denunciation of R I C, 409, 410, 412; his visit to United States (1919-20), 421-3; and treaty negotiations (1921), 424, 427-34, 436-8, 444; opposes Treaty of 1921, 439-43, 445n, 448-51, 453-4, 456-7; and Cumann na Poblachta, 453, 455; and pact with Collins (1922), 456, 457-8, 459; and Army Document (1922), 457; and Civil War (1922-3), 461, 463-4, 466, 467, 478-9, 485, 488; and Boundary Commission (1925), 494; establishes Fianna Fáil, 495; and general election (June 1927), 497, 510; and Electoral Amendment Act (1927), 498-9; and I R A, 501-2, 523, 531-5, 582; and land annuities, 504, 511, 526, 527, 611-12, 614, 708; and Constitution (Amendment No. 17) Act (1931), 503; and general election (1932), 504, 512, 523-4, 607; and removal of Oath of Allegiance from Constitution, 507-14; and general election (1933), 513-14, 527, 725; and Privy Council Judicial Committee, 516-17; and Irish Nationality and Citizenship Act (1935), 517; and Aliens Act (1935), 517; and Constitution of 1937, 518-22, 536-50; and External Relations Act, 550, 563, 565; and League of Nations, 551-4, 594; and Irish neutrality, 553-8, 590-1, 728; and post-war economic problems, 559-60; and general election (1948), 561, 591; and Republic of Ireland Act, 568; and 'mother and child scheme', 576, 578; and general election (1951), 579; and general election (1954), 580; and general election (1957), 581-2; as President of Irish Republic, 583-4, 585; makes 'anti-partition' speeches abroad, 591-2; and emigration, 609; and economic developments, 611-14; mentioned, 368, 449-50, 676, 677, 683-4

Vane, Major Sir Francis, 373

Vatican Council, 152, 547, 689-90; *see also* Papacy

Victoria, Queen, 157, 250

Vocational Education Act (1930) *see* education

Volunteer Convention, 255

Volunteer Force (1934), 532

Volunteer movement (1782), 232n, 286n, 316, 321

Wales, 150, 208, 326, 388, 702, 709, 732, 739

Wales, Prince of, 155

Walker, William, 276

Walsh, J. J., 485

Walsh, Dr W. J., Catholic Archbishop of Dublin, 20, 197, 354

War of Independence (1919-21), 15, 32, 408-28, 441, 446, 481, 488, 535, 599, 636

Warrenpoint, 66

Waterford, county, co-operative societies in, 210; murder of John Egan in, 533; and the Gaeltacht, 640n; education in, 651; welfare in, 661; mentioned, 82, 230, 464

Webb, Beatrice, 73, 323

West, Harry, 762, 766

Westminster Confession of Faith, 24

Westminster Gazette, 415, 422

Westport, 166, 216, 409

Wexford, county, 173, 360, 366

Whateley, Dr R., Anglican Archbishop of Dublin, 89

Whig party, 42, 113, 116-19, 122, 142, 184

Whitaker, Dr T. K., 583, 599, 628; *see also Economic Development*

Whitaker Report *see Economic Development*

Whitelaw, William, 780

White, Captain, J. R., 285

Whyte, John, 547n, 575n, 578n

Wicklow, county, 157, 236, 241, 261, 325, 326, 329, 529n

Widgery tribunal, 778-9

Wilde, Oscar, 299

Wilde, Sir William, 225

William of Orange, 25, 36

Williams, Professor T. Desmond, 431n, 445n, 462n, 565n-6n, 693

Wilson, Harold, M.P., 778

Wilson, Professor T. H., 747

Wilson, President Woodrow, 385, 403-4, 421, 422-3

Wilson, Sir Henry, 308, 452, 459-60

Wimborne, Lord, 361-2, 363-5, 377, 395

Windisch, Ernst, 225

Wolff, G. W., 65

Wolseley, Field-Marshal Lord, 293

Wood, Mrs B., 195, 196

Woodenbridge, 329

Workers' Republic, 273